Detroit Free Press

The Detroit Almanac

300 years of life in the Motor City

EDITED BY PETER GAVRILOVICH
AND BILL McGRAW

Detroit Free Press

600 W. Fort St.
Detroit, Mich. 48226
www.freep.com

Other recent books by the Free Press:

Joyride	Men at Work
Life Lessons	Portraits of War
Life After Baseball	Motoons
Razor Sharp	Time Frames
Hockey Gods	Hang 10
Fishing Michigan	Heart Smart II Cookbook
State of Glory	Corner to Copa
The Corner	Century of Champions
Yaklennium	Believe!
Stanleytown	Heart Smart Kids Cookbook

 To order any of these titles, please call
800-245-5082 or go to **www.freep.com/bookstore**

To subscribe to the Free Press, call 800-395-3300.

 Detroit 300
Partner Program
member

The Detroit Almanac
ISBN 0-937247-48-0
$24.95

Prologue

Welcome to a fixture of Detroit nearly as popular as Faygo and as permanent as great memories of Tiger Stadium: The Detroit Almanac.

The almanac originally was published in October 2000 as metro Detroiters got ready to mark Detroit's 300th anniversary in July 2001. Since then, there have been five additional printings and 65,000 copies sold, making the almanac one of the most popular and most read books ever about the Motor City.

This new edition includes a 16-page prologue on the beginning of metro Detroit's fourth century.

Much has happened as the 21st Century kicked off. We'll touch on some highlights and introduce you to some of the personalities of the century's first five years. Then you'll find the original 648 pages devoted to the region's first 300 years.

This is also the Free Press' 175th anniversary year — we're Detroit's oldest continuously operating business. So happy anniversary to us and happy reading to you.

– Bill McGraw and Peter Gavrilovich, April 2006
thedetroitalmanac@freepress.com

Before you dive into metro Detroit's first three centuries, here's a quick look at how the region's fourth century has started.

Addison Ave

WELCOME TO DETROIT
AN ALL-STAR CIT

OVER THE TOP: Rasheed Wallace and the Pistons powered their way to back-to-back appearances in the NBA Finals, winning the title in 2004 and losing in Game 7 in 2005. In this 2004 photo, Wallace battles Drew Gooden and the Orlando Magic in a regular-season game.

The turn of the century

Despite our winning spirit, the region is still losing ground

GOOD STUFF: Detroit was barely halfway into the first decade of the 21st Century when it claimed bragging rights for these gems: the Stanley Cup (2002), the NBA championship (2004), golf's Ryder Cup tourney (2004), baseball's All-Star Game (2005) and, of course, Super Bowl XL in 2006.

You could hear well-earned crowing from Melvindale to Ferndale for the splendid way the world received metro Detroit during Super Bowl XL week. A perfect score for the region that week was marred by the shooting death of a late-night reveler and lengthy, chilly waits for shuttle buses ferrying fans to suburban parking lots.

Downtown Detroit slowly but steadily began to rehab decades-old buildings, turning what used to be stores and offices into swank lofts.

And people began returning to the concrete canyons as new entertainment venues opened.

LOUSY STUFF: Detroit and Michigan had deep fiscal chasms, wrought by a steadily shrinking population in the city and an anemic economy in the state.

Autoworkers got pink slips; General Motors quit making the Olds — and watched its cash horde nearly slip away as its share of sales dramatically dipped. Ford was no better off, but Chrysler scored some major hits with models people craved — such as the Chrysler 300 — but those sales began to wane, too.

GOOD STUFF, BUT …
■ Casinos continued to thrive and work began on permanent sites or

DAVID P. GILKEY/Detroit Free Press

CHAMPIONS:
Above: Jerome (the Bus) Bettis, left, and Ben Roethlisberger led the Pittsburgh Steelers to a Super Bowl victory in 2006 at Ford Field.

Left: Chauncey Billups and company celebrate after the Detroit Pistons beat the L.A. Lakers, 100-87, in Game 5 of the NBA Finals to clinch the title in 2004.

JULIAN H. GONZALEZ /Detroit Free Press

JULIAN H. GONZALEZ /Detroit Free Press

The ailing auto industry played a big role in the state's economic troubles. The sight of cars parked on lots was commonplace.

Civil rights icon Rosa Parks died in 2005 at age 92, briefly uniting a metro Detroit still divided by race. Her casket lay in state, right, in the Capitol Rotunda in Washington, D.C.

adjacent hotels. Detroit's three casinos recorded $100-million-a-month in revenue in 2005. Mayor Kwame Kilpatrick said in 2005 that Detroit was in transition from a "manufacturing economy to a casino economy."

...BUT among unknown figures: How many paychecks have been lost at gaming tables? How many personal bankruptcies have been filed because of casino gambling?

▮ New homes sprouted across Detroit's landscape, making the city a leader in such construction in 2005. Subdivisions continued to grow in suburbs like Novi and Macomb

Township. Retailers expanded along burgeoning corridors, such as Ford Road, M-59 and Orchard Lake Road.

...BUT the new housing meant existing homes often took more than a year to sell, and the region found itself with a glut of used houses.

WE SHOULD KNOW BETTER: Despite decades of people urging love and unity, tolerance and diversity, the region continued to be racially polarized and the most segregated large metro area in the United States.

One moment of unity: Thousands gathered to pay their respects to civil rights legend Rosa Parks after she died Oct. 24, 2005, in Detroit at age 92.

Detroit's 300th
Pardon our French,
But Detroit, c'est chic!

For most of 2001, the region celebrated Detroit's founding by the French on July 24, 1701. The city said the celebration in July 2001 alone likely pumped more that $150 million into the regional economy. Thousands of people swarmed downtown and other venues to soak up history and check out Detroit. The celebration included some two dozen tall ships parading up the Detroit River and a Hart Plaza concert headlined by metro Detroit natives comic Tim Allen and singer Stevie Wonder.

These fixtures had more longevity:

▮ The RiverWalk from the RenCen to just west of the Joe.

▮ The arch honoring labor at Hart Plaza.

▮ A park at Campus Martius — which includes an ice rink. The Soldiers and Sailors Monument was moved a few feet southwest.

▮ Tricentennial Park just east of the Ren-Cen.

▮ Statues on either side of the river by Denver artist Ed Dwight depicting Detroit's part in the Underground Railroad.

▮ Two time capsules: A bronze box the size of a filing cabinet drawer and crammed with some 100 letters from civic leaders and a video of 50 leaders speaking to the folks who will open the drawer on July 24, 2101, has been stored in the city treasurer's vault. A larger capsule, in the shape of a treasure chest, was squirreled away at the Historical Museum and stuffed with late 20th-Century and 2001 memorabilia, including a copy of this book. But consider what won't be in the capsules because they came after: an iPod, cell phone camera, Xbox.

But the defining event of Detroit's life in the opening years of the 21st Century struck suddenly weeks after the city celebrated its 300th birthday.

The galvanizing moment
Where were you on 9/11?

Seven weeks after that exhilarating birthday party, metro Detroiters joined other Americans stunned by the attacks of Sept. 11. Detroit was no different from the rest of the country when our sense of normal changed dramatically.

We stood in lines, some of us for hours, to buy American flags. We put flag decals on our cars and taped paper flags to our windows. We wore flag caps and shirts and shorts and painted our faces with stars and stripes. We wanted to do something to strike at the terror that so stunned us and in one immense, elegant, serendipitous response, we did exactly the thing that needed to be done: Out of many, we became one.

Perhaps the first shared questions of the new century became: Where were you when the planes hit the towers, the Pentagon and a rural field in Pennsylvania? Where were you on Sept. 11?

People across metro Detroit raised money and donated supplies and goods from bottled water to teddy bears to help families of 9/11 victims.

One of the biggest morale- and economy-boosting moves came out of Detroit: General Motors' 0% financing program. It brought buyers back to showrooms across the nation, and set off a flurry of similar deals from other automakers. The incentives lasted for months — and, some marketers say, conditioned buyers to wait for the next round of incentives.

We found travel suddenly trying and troubling. Crossing into Canada once consisted of a speedy drive and a quick response to the pro forma question, "Anything to declare?" After 9/11, drivers encountered a tedious wait and lengthy round of questioning by now-suspicious customs agents.

Air travel became a chore with lengthy lines at Metro security. Travelers were taking off their shoes for inspection — to make sure no weapons or explosives were hidden away in a heel. Rules kept families from greeting relatives as they got off the plane. The only way to see the shops and ride the monorail at the McNamara Terminal that opened in early 2002 was to be a ticketed airline passenger.

But Detroit soon found itself under far more scrutiny than other American cities because the region is a magnet for Arab and Muslim immigrants. The 9/11 attackers were from Arab countries and were members of Al Qaeda, a Muslim terror organization. Metro Detroit has one of the largest Arab-American populations in North America and thousands of those are recent immigrants with backgrounds in Islam, an expanding faith in metro Detroit.

Many Muslims and Arab-Americans said they felt monitored by a federal government urgently searching for cells of discontent.

▮ Days after 9/11, a troop of five Arab-American Boy Scouts from Dearborn and their leader were questioned and detained by police because a witness said they were speaking a foreign language and taking pictures of the Mackinac Bridge while on a ferry to Mackinac Island.

▮ A U.S. District Court jury in June 2003 convicted two North African immigrants of conspiring to provide material support and resources to terrorists. Their trial was the first terrorism trial after 9/11 and it drew national attention. But the U.S. Attorney's Office later persuaded the trial judge to drop the terrorism

Which of the following was NOT included in the Detroit time capsules set to be opened on July 24, 2101?

An Apple iPod...

A Sony Xbox...

A BlackBerry...

▮ Answer: None of the above; only the BlackBerry even existed.

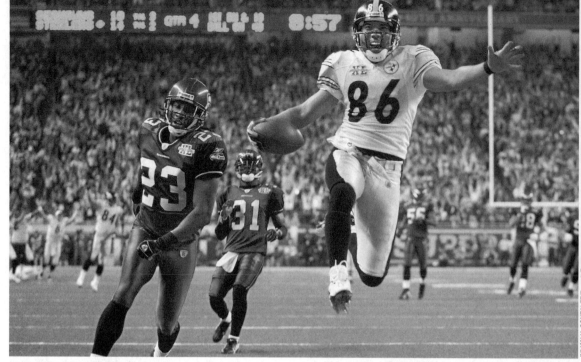

Pittsburgh's Hines Ward leaps into the end zone after catching a touchdown pass during the fourth quarter of Super Bowl XL.

Party town

Some of the hot soirees during XL week:

- ▮ Maxim
- ▮ Playboy
- ▮ SI
- ▮ Penthouse
- ▮ NFL Players
- ▮ Cashmere Luxe
- ▮ The Platinum Party
- ▮ Gospel Fest
- ▮ Shady Records
- ▮ Vivid Club/Jenna Bowl
- ▮ Fight Night at Fisher

charges on the grounds that federal prosecutor Richard Convertino withheld crucial evidence from the defendants. Convertino, who resigned in late 2003, has denied the allegations. An investigation continues.

That super week

Great excitement over a Bus stop

Flawless. Well, OK, almost flawless. Detroit's Super Bowl performance was marvelous. Hundreds of thousands of people swarmed downtown to take part in special events like the NFL Experience and the Motown Winter Blast or to stroll streets looking for celebrities. A study a month after the game said the week of events leading up to Super Bowl XL generated some $274 million for metro Detroit.

The game was OK, too. The Pittsburgh Steelers beat the Seattle Seahawks, 21-10. Steeler running back and Detroit native Jerome (The Bus) Bettis (Mackenzie High School, '89) ended his football career with that game, announcing his retirement amid his team's celebration. He spent much of the two weeks leading to the game talking up his hometown to the national media.

Detroit fell in love with Bettis. Days after the game, Bettis and business partner Dave Bing announced a riverfront condo project just east of the RenCen. If the pair secure the permits and financing needed, construction was expected to begin in the summer of '06.

Jillian Kotlar of Sterling Heights checks out Detroit from the standing-room-only People Mover on her way to the NFL Experience.

Steeler Aaron Smith and daughter watch confetti swirl after Pittsburgh won Super Bowl XL.

FAQs:

▌**How big is Detroit?** Not as big as it used to be. The 2000 U.S. census counted 951,270 Detroiters. By 2005, the census estimated 900,198, which meant Detroit slipped to the nation's 11th largest city. The Southeast Michigan Council of Governments estimated the city's population was 888,975 at the end of 2005. Metro Detroit remained the ninth largest metropolitan area in the country from 2000 to 2005.

▌**Is Oakland County becoming a Democratic stronghold?** It certainly is no longer the safe Republican outpost that it used to be. A significant number of its newer residents appear to be turning away from the far-right conservatives in the Michigan Republican Party on abortion and other cultural issues. Oakland County voted Democratic in the 1996, 2000 and 2004 presidential elections, and County Executive L. Brooks Patterson, once considered a conservative Republican, has moved to the center and battled the archconservatives.

▌**What is the region's fastest-growing community?** Macomb Township in Macomb County. The population of the township, whose southern border is busy M-59, exploded from 22,714 people in 1990 to an estimated 72,406 in early 2006.

▌**What's the Clem?** That's the hip new name for Mt. Clemens. Yes, Mt. Clemens. The seat of Macomb County shook off some of its dust during the early years of the 21st Century and added new clubs, restaurants and bars downtown. The news from the Clem wasn't all good, however. In 2005, the city had to disband its police force because of money problems. Macomb County Sheriff deputies now patrol the Clem.

▌**How big are Detroiters?** Not as big as they used to be, but that's good news. Detroit was named the fattest city in America in 2004 by Men's Fitness magazine, which uses semi-scientific criteria and some marketing hocus-pocus to rate the relative obesity of America's biggest cities each year. By January 2006, the city had fallen to 15th fattest out of 25 cities cited.

KENT PHILLIPS /Detroit Free Press

STEVE WILSON: WXYZ reporter uses muscle.

KWAME KILPATRICK: Detroit mayor has youth going for him.

MIKE COX: State attorney general on hot seat.

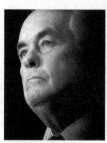

ELLA BULLY-CUMMINGS: First female police chief.

ROGER PENSKE: From race cars to Super Bowl.

RONALD SCHERZ: Graffiti artist unmasked. Below: His Turtle tag.

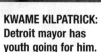

People

Roger Penske: The mastermind of Super Bowl XL.

Steve Wilson: The TV reporter for WXYZ-TV (Channel 7) who likes to get physical.

Ron Gettelfinger: The low-profile UAW veteran took over as union president in 2002, and has been fighting for his members' survival since then.

Mike Cox: Michigan's attorney general held a news conference in 2005 to confess an extramarital affair during a political brawl with attorney Geoffrey Fieger.

William Clay Ford Jr.: Since he orchestrated the firing of Jacques Nasser and added CEO to his chairman title in October 2001, Ford Motor has been mostly in crisis mode. Whether he can save the company his family still controls is a major Detroit drama.

Kwame Kilpatrick: At 31 in 2001, he was Detroit's youngest elected mayor. At 35 in 2005, he almost lost his reelection bid after a stormy four years. But he's back in office, at least until he's 39 in 2009.

Ella Bully-Cummings: Detroit's first female top cop, she was appointed in 2003.

Ben Wallace: Made Pistons' opponents fear the 'fro.

Matt Millen: Becomes more famous with every Lions loss.

Christopher Ilitch: Vanquished his better-known sister Denise Ilitch in 2004 in an internal feud to run the family pizza, sports and entertainment empire.

Robert Porcher: The former Lions star is an investor in some highly touted restaurants, including Seldom Blues in the Renaissance Center and Detroit's Breakfast House & Grill.

Peter Karmanos: The Compuware founder and CEO opened his new downtown headquarters in 2003.

KYM WORTHY:
A pioneering
prosecutor.

PETER KARMANOS:
CEO moved Compu-
ware downtown.

NAIMA MORA:
Cass Tech grad
gets model start.

MARTHA REEVES:
Motown legend takes
seat on council.

KIRK JONES:
Canton man survives
Niagara fall.

Rick Wagoner: The CEO of General Motors Corp. since 2000, his task is simple: Save GM.

Turtle: He's the man who anonymously splashed unique graffiti across Detroit in the early 2000s — images of a green turtle. Real name: Ronald Scherz of Hamtramck.

Martha Reeves: The former Motown star was elected to the Detroit City Council in 2005.

Kym Worthy: Elected Wayne County's first female and first African-American prosecutor in 2004.

Naima Mora: The photogenic Cass Tech alum won the top prize on UPN's "America's Next Top Model" in 2005.

Kirk Jones of Canton downed vodka and Cokes and took the plunge — right over Niagara Falls in 2003, the only person known to have survived the fall from the Canadian Horseshoe Falls without safety equipment.

BOB GUINEY: The Ferndale man parlayed a losing appearance on ABC's "The Bachelorette" into a starring role on "The Bachelor" in 2003.

ROBERT PORCHER:
Former Lion puts
money and time into
restaurants.

MATT MILLEN:
There's a reason he's
not smiling.

BEN WALLACE:
The Piston wears
his 'fro well.

Winky and Wanda, below, cuddle after arriving at their new home in California in 2005. Patti Miles, a Detroit Zoo employee, pats Winky, at right, one of two aging elephants who left the zoo for ethical reasons in 2005.

KATHLEEN GALLIGAN /Detroit Free Press

ERIC SHARP/Detroit Free Press

The mourning dove became a target in 2004.

J. KYLE KEENER/Detroit Free Press

An arrow through the neck couldn't slow this peacock down.

Creatures

▋ **Winky and Wanda:** The elephants became the focus of a nationwide debate when Detroit Zoo officials announced in May 2004 that they wanted to send the pachyderms packing to a more hospitable climate at the Performing Animal Welfare Society's Ark 2000 near Sacramento, Calif. It was the first time a major animal facility chose to give away its elephants solely on ethical grounds.

▋ **Mourning doves:** Michigan's first dove season in 100 years began in fall 2004 in six southern counties. In April, the state Legislature voted to allow the hunting of the songbirds, which had been protected in Michigan for 99 years.

▋ **Beethoven and Cujo:** The two St. Bernards gained notoriety in Macomb County in 2004 after killing a pig, a ewe, two llamas and a quarter-ton steer. The father and son were put down after officials invoked a 1919 livestock protection law.

▋ **Peacock:** A semi-wild male who lives near Wayne State University was shot with a pistol crossbow in 2005, leaving a seven-inch projectile lodged in its neck. A nearby resident pulled out the projectile and the bird survived.

▋ **The steer:** It wound up in a sanctuary in 2003 after fleeing a Detroit slaughterhouse and making a traffic-stopping dash across some of the busiest streets in the city.

▋ **Unnamed wolverine:** The Wolverine State had its first wolverine sighting since the fur-trading days, thanks to a surprise run-in between the petrified creature and a group of Thumb-area hunters in February 2004.

Talini, the first polar bear born at the Detroit Zoo in 15 years, takes swimming lessons from mom Barle in 2005.

The runaway steer kept moving, despite the tranquilizer dart in its side, until he was cornered in a fenced-in lot along Jefferson Avenue.

Jeff Ford of Ubly took this photo of the elusive wolverine in the Thumb (left). Ford, above left, with Jason Rosser of Sandusky, made a cast of the wolverine's right front paw print.

KID ROCK: Stays in the spotlight by mixing it up musically and socially.

AALIYAH: R&B star found greater success after untimely death.

MANDI WRIGHT /Detroit Free Press

EMINEM: The huge rap star, left, won an Oscar, sold millions of records and divorced Kim Mathers, above, in 2001 and then remarried her in 2005. Now he's considering a career behind the scenes.

Culture

Music

Eminem

❚ He won an Oscar in 2002 for "Lose Yourself" and scored major success with "8 Mile," in which he and the city of Detroit starred.

❚ For a couple of years at the turn of the millennium, he was probably the world's biggest music star. He's sold nearly 30 million albums in the United States.

❚ He's great tabloid fodder: The infighting with family, the breakups and reunion with wife Kim, who had her own drug-related court troubles.

❚ In 2005, it was unclear what direction his career was taking, with questions about his possible move away from the Eminem persona, and toward a behind-the-scenes producer role.

Kid Rock

❚ He went from rap to rap-rock, then made an unlikely turn toward country and southern rock.

❚ He has sold well more than 10 million albums.

❚ Unlike the more private Eminem, Kid seems to adore the spotlight, and was a proverbial dating machine, attracting women from Sheryl Crow to Pamela Anderson.

White Stripes

❚ Their popularity was initially fueled by the British press.

❚ The duo of Jack White and Meg White have sold roughly a million copies of the "White Blood Cells" album.

❚ They are critical darlings — their albums "WBC" (2001), "Elephant" (2003) and "Get Behind Me Satan" (2005) all were among the most lauded of their respective years.

❚ Jack White moved to Nashville in 2006.

Others

❚ The return of Detroit's music scene to international prominence went beyond the Big Three. Other artists who had million-plus sellers included Eminem's side group D12, rapper Obie Trice, Kid Rock's pal Uncle Kracker, makeup-wearing Insane Clown Posse, and R&B singer Aaliyah.

❚ Other musicians who gained either significant commercial success or critical acclaim included Kem, the Von Bondies and the Electric Six.

❚ All the news wasn't good. When Aaliyah died in a 2001 plane crash at the age of 22, it generated a huge outpouring of grief — and posthumous record sales — for the former student at the Detroit High School for the Fine and Performing Arts.

❚ In 2006, James Yancey, who recorded under the names Jay Dilla and Jay Dee, died from complications of a rare blood disease at age 32. While not a household name, Yancey was revered among aficionados as among the most important producers in the history of hip-hop, working with artists ranging from D'Angelo to A Tribe Called Quest and his Detroit group Slum Village.

WHITE STRIPES: Jack White and Meg White found great success upending expectations, setting new standards and breaking ground in the indie rock scene.

ROMAIN BLANQUART/Detroit Free Press

Notable local books

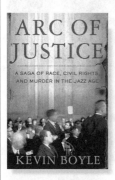

▮ **"Arc of Justice: A Saga of Race, Civil Rights, and Murder in the Jazz Age,"** the story of Ossian Sweet by Detroit-born Kevin Boyle, won the National Book Award in 2004.

▮ **"Made in Detroit: A South of 8 Mile Memoir,"** a memoir of growing up white in a black city by Paul Clemens.

▮ **"Mr. Paradise,"** Elmore Leonard's first Detroit-based book in 24 years came out in 2004.

▮ **"American City: Detroit Architecture 1845-2005,"** a survey of 50 great Detroit buildings published in 2005 by Wayne State University Press.

MAX FISHER: Businessman and philanthropist left a multifaceted legacy upon his death at age 96 in 2005.

ANNE PARSONS: Executive trades ballet world for position with the Detroit Symphony Orchestra in 2004.

The Arts

▮ **Anne Parsons:** The general manager of New York City Ballet became the new executive director of the Detroit Symphony Orchestra in 2004.

▮ **Neeme Jarvi:** His 15-year tenure as music director of the Detroit Symphony Orchestra came to a close in 2005.

▮ **The Max:** The Max M. Fisher Music Center, the $60-million addition to Orchestra Hall, opened in 2003 and includes a grand entry, a smaller stage, dressing rooms, practice rooms and offices.

▮ **Holocaust Memorial Center:** Opened in big new quarters in Farmington Hills in 2004. The center's exterior is designed with cables to evoke the barbed wire around a concentration camp. The exhibit combines video, interactive kiosks and artifacts to depict early Hebrew culture, the rise of Yiddish communities, the effects of anti-Semitism and the resistance of Jews and non-Jews to Nazi brutality.

▮ **Arab American National Museum:** Dedicated to tracing the Arab-American experience from the first Arab slave in 1527 to the great wave of immigration in the early 20th Century to the struggle to overcome negative stereotypes, the museum opened in 2005 on Michigan Avenue in Dearborn.

▮ **Charles H. Wright Museum of African American History:** Received a much-needed infusion of cash in 2004 after an elite group of Detroiters raised about $1 million.

▮ **The Henry Ford:** Took a new name in 2003 that encompasses the renovated Greenfield Village, the Henry Ford Museum, the IMAX Theater, Benson Ford Research Center and Ford Rouge plant tours.

▮ **Detroit Institute of Arts:** In the midst of a three-year, $91-million renovation and expansion that is scheduled to be completed at the end of 2007, both wings of the museum have been closed, forcing the DIA to consolidate its exhibition space into its original 1927 building designed by French architect Paul Cret.

NEEME JARVI: Beloved DSO music director steps down in 2005.

< J. KYLE KEENER /Detroit Free Press

ROMAIN BLANQUART >
Detroit Free Press

CRUISIN': Travis Harriss, left, and Daniel Giannini kick back to watch the parade of cars on Woodward during the 2005 Dream Cruise. The classic car rally and its fans have jammed Woodward for more than a decade.

Fun

■ **Techno Fest:** Operating under a variety of names and producers and always battling money and ego problems, for six years a Memorial Day festival devoted to celebrating Detroit's homegrown electronic dance music has drawn tens of thousands of fans to Hart Plaza.

■ **Dream Cruise:** In 2005, one of the world's biggest classic car rallies cruised for the 11th time. It generally draws more than 1 million spectators and 40,000 cars to Woodward Avenue each August.

■ **Arts, Beats & Eats:** Held each Labor Day weekend, Pontiac's 8-year-old festival has become a hit — and drew about 1 million patrons in 2005, organizers say.

■ **Detroit International Jazz Festival:** Local jazz-label owner Gretchen Valade donated money, then proposed creating a $10-million nonprofit foundation to produce the festival. After months of negotiations, the Music Hall turned over production, artistic and fund-raising responsibilities, laying the groundwork for an era of financial stability.

SPINNIN': DJ Peanut Butter Wolf, above, spins albums at Movement, the Detroit electronic music festival, in 2004. Egos and name changes have plagued the fest that celebrates a homegrown style of music at Hart Plaza. **CHEERIN':** Fans jam with artist Stacey Pullen, below, at the Movement festival in 2003.

JAZZIN': Donald Harrison, above, hammers down the final note of a song during the Detroit International Jazz Fest in 2000.

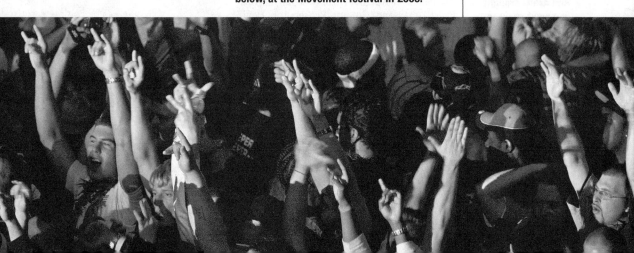

Europe's Paul Casey, left, douses teammate Thomas Levet, far right, with champagne as he holds the pin at the 18th hole after their Ryder Cup victory.

Phil Mickelson is comforted by his wife as his team loses the last match of the opening day of the 35th Ryder Cup, held at Oakland Hills Country Club in 2004.

Sports

■ **Ryder Cup:** The Oakland Hills Country Club in Bloomfield Township hosted the European-American golf showdown in September 2004. The event was a success in every way but one: The Americans were humbled as never before. Their 18 1/2 -9 1/2 loss went down as the worst U.S. performance since the Ryder Cup doubled the total number of points available from 12 to 24 in 1961.

■ **Sports Illustrated's Rick Reilly, on the Ryder Cup at Oakland Hills:** Detroit fans "will be rowdy and loud-y and possibly packing heat. Detroit ain't Boston. Detroit is a lot of guys warming their hands around cop-car fires. ... (Helpful Detroit travel tip: That ain't really a Rolex the dude is selling you for $10, but buy it anyway. Otherwise, he takes your whole wallet.)"

■ **The Brawl:** One of the wildest moments in American sports took place Nov. 19, 2004, at the Palace of Auburn Hills. It began, according to Oakland County Prosecutor David Gorcyca, when a fan threw a plastic cup at Ron Artest of the Indiana Pacers, and Artest ran into the stands. Fights broke out, and tapes of the mayhem played endlessly for days on national TV. Fans and five members of the Pacers received fines, community service, anger management classes and a year of probation, but no jail time. A trial for another fan — John Green, the alleged instigator — was scheduled for spring 2006.

■ **Super Bowl XL:** Pittsburgh won the National Football League championship, but Detroit was also a big winner in Super Bowl XL at Ford Field. The Steelers beat the Seattle Sea-

Indiana Pacers star Ron Artest brought embarrassment to basketball – and to Detroit – in 2004 when he stormed the stands after a fan threw a cup at him. Fights ensued. In the aftermath, fans and Pacer players received fines and other penalties.

European fans celebrate at Oakland Hills after the United States' humiliating defeat.

European team member Sergio Garcia celebrates with teammate Lee Westwood after their team was ensured the win.

hawks, 21-10, and the city reaped reams of positive publicity from the national media for its staging of the greatest show in sports. More than 1 million people participated in the Motown Winter Blast street festival, and late-night TV talk-show host Jimmy Kimmel gave Detroit an extra boost by broadcasting from the Gem Theatre during Super Bowl week.

■ **Pistons:** One of the hottest teams in professional sports won the NBA championship in 2004, beating Los Angeles in five games. The next year was eventful, too: In June 2005, the Pistons kissed their championship run good-bye with a loss to San Antonio in Game 7 of the NBA Finals. In July, they lost their coach, Larry Brown, after Brown's tumultuous year ended with a buyout. They quickly hired Flip Saunders to replace him.

■ **All-Star Game:** The American League won the first All-Star Game at Comerica Park, 7-5, in July 2005. In the Home Run Derby, Philadelphia's Bobby Abreu defeated Tigers

catcher Ivan (Pudge) Rodriguez in the final, 11-5. Abreu hit a record 41 homers during the exhibition.

■ **Wings:** Another one of the hottest teams in sports, the Red Wings defeated the Carolina Hurricanes in five games to win the 2002 Stanley Cup, in what turned out to be the last game in Scotty Bowman's legendary coaching career. Dave Lewis replaced Bowman, but the team fired him in 2005. Mike Babcock replaced Lewis.

■ **Lions:** The hiring of Steve Mariucci in 2003 gave fans a glimmer of hope. But after the Lions went 15-28 under Mariucci, general manager Matt Millen fired him after Thanksgiving 2005. His replacement was Rod Marinelli.

■ **Tigers:** Without publicly citing any reason, the club fired manager Alan Trammell in 2005 after the club's 71-91 finish. Jim Leyland took over the team for spring training 2006.

STEVE MARIUCCI: Mooch, in 2005, is the most recent in a line of Lions coaches to take the fall for the team.

The RenCen gets the All-Star Game treatment in 2005.

ROMAIN BLANQUART/Detroit Free Press

Comerica Park was full of fans and spectacle for the opening ceremony of the Major League Baseball All-Star Game.

AMY SANCETTA/Associated Press

Florida Marlins pitcher Dontrelle Willis greets fans before the start of the Home Run Derby during the All-Star Game.

■ **2006 Olympics:** 11 Olympians with ties to Michigan won medals in Torino, Italy.

Michigan medals

Eleven Olympians with ties to Michigan won medals in Torino. Here's who they are:

ICE DANCING	ICE DANCING	SPEED-SKATING	ICE HOCKEY	SPEED-SKATING	ICE HOCKEY	ICE HOCKEY	ICE HOCKEY	ICE HOCKEY	ICE HOCKEY	ICE HOCKEY
BEN AGOSTO	TANITH BELBIN	SHANI DAVIS	TOMAS HOLMSTROM	ALEX IZYKOWSKI	NIKLAS KRONWALL	ROBERT LANG	NICKLAS LIDSTROM	ANGELA RUGGIERO	MIKAEL SAMUELSSON	HENRIK ZETTERBERG
SILVER	SILVER	GOLD SILVER	GOLD	BRONZE	GOLD	BRONZE	GOLD	BRONZE	GOLD	GOLD
Trained in Canton	Trained in Canton	NMU student	Red Wings forward	Bay City native	Red Wings defenseman	Red Wings forward	Red Wings defenseman	Harper Woods resident	Red Wings forward	Red Wings forward

U.S. automakers' market share keeps shrinking

In 1980, General Motors Corp., Ford Motor Co. and Chrysler Corp. made 75.4% of all the cars and trucks sold in the United States. But their share of the market has fallen steadily since then, to 71.6% in 1990, to 57% in 2005. How low can it go? Industry experts say it could fall to only 53% by 2010.

Time line of trouble

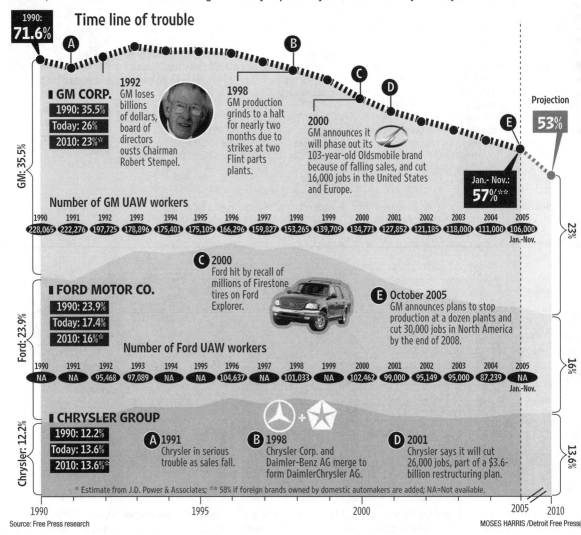

1990: 71.6%

Projection 53%

A GM CORP.
1990: 35.5%
Today: 26%
2010: 23%*

1992
GM loses billions of dollars, board of directors ousts Chairman Robert Stempel.

1998
GM production grinds to a halt for nearly two months due to strikes at two Flint parts plants.

2000
GM announces it will phase out its 103-year-old Oldsmobile brand because of falling sales, and cut 16,000 jobs in the United States and Europe.

Jan.- Nov.: 57%*

GM: 35.5%

Number of GM UAW workers

1990	1991	1992	1993	1994	1995	1996	1997	1998	1999	2000	2001	2002	2003	2004	2005
228,065	222,276	197,725	178,896	175,401	175,105	166,296	159,827	153,265	139,709	134,771	127,852	121,185	118,000	111,000	106,000 Jan.-Nov.

23%

C 2000
Ford hit by recall of millions of Firestone tires on Ford Explorer.

E October 2005
GM announces plans to stop production at a dozen plants and cut 30,000 jobs in North America by the end of 2008.

FORD MOTOR CO.
1990: 23.9%
Today: 17.4%
2010: 16%*

Ford: 23.9%

Number of Ford UAW workers

1990	1991	1992	1993	1994	1995	1996	1997	1998	1999	2000	2001	2002	2003	2004	2005
NA	NA	95,468	97,089	NA	NA	104,637	NA	101,033	NA	102,462	99,000	95,149	95,000	87,239	NA Jan.-Nov.

16%

CHRYSLER GROUP
1990: 12.2%
Today: 13.6%
2010: 13.6%*

Chrysler: 12.2%

A 1991
Chrysler in serious trouble as sales fall.

B 1998
Chrysler Corp. and Daimler-Benz AG merge to form DaimlerChrysler AG.

D 2001
Chrysler says it will cut 26,000 jobs, part of a $3.6-billion restructuring plan.

13.6%

* Estimate from J.D. Power & Associates; ** 58% if foreign brands owned by domestic automakers are added; NA=Not available.

1990   1995   2000   2005   2010

Source: Free Press research

MOSES HARRIS /Detroit Free Press

Cars

The 21st Century has not been kind to Detroit's Big Two automakers. The Auburn Hills-based Chrysler Group, at least, stabilized its position in the marketplace.

The year 2005 was one of the worst for General Motors Corp. and Ford Motor Co. since the Depression. GM lost $10.6 billion. Ford reported earnings of $2 billion for 2005. But that was a 42% drop from 2004 profits and reflected a $1.6-billion loss in North American operations. Both companies announced plant closings and layoffs.

Several auto parts firms filed for bank-ruptcy or appeared on the verge. Delphi Corp., the state's fourth-largest company, flirted with the idea of breaking the weakened UAW, which agreed to reduce health-care benefits for workers and retirees during the middle of the existing contract.

The future?

Scary.

Both GM and Ford announced restructuring plans in 2005, but there was no certainty that either firm would be able to regain market share in the short term. Fortune Magazine, in its February 2006 issue, rattled Detroit's auto community when it said the probability of an eventual bankruptcy for GM is high.

Welcome

DRIVING NORTH ON I-75 TO DETROIT, PUSHING 80.

Past Monroe, the area once called Frenchtown.

Past those Fermi nuke towers and the sprawling Mazda plant, straining to keep pace with the barreling semis hauling who knows what.

Detroit's suburbs begin at the Huron River near Rockwood.

Power lines stretch endlessly, their towers standing in flat lush fields near billboards touting mass-produced homes that start in the low $190,000s.

The radio says rain in Troy. But in Taylor, skies are clear. Traffic heading toward Toledo includes huge carriers hauling Grand Cherokees and scores of cars with Ohio plates heading home from casinos.

By Lincoln Park, overpasses are rusty. The road bobs. A pale gray wall hides houses near the freeway.

Then: **"Detroit City Limit."** The sign is well-worn; somebody's stuck a Hoffa sticker to it. Under the Schaefer-Fort Street sign, a yawning pothole waits to mangle tires. A playground and bungalows on the right, refineries and Ford Rouge on the left. A flame licks from a smokestack.

Then the roadway vaults over the Rouge River.

The road peaks and, stretched across a seemingly endless horizon, Detroit unfolds dramatically in the haze: steel mills, smokestacks, houses, flats, buildings, steeples, skyscrapers, a bridge, a river and the 25-year-old RenCen's still-startling shape.

Detroit is seven counties, 233 communities, nearly 5 million people and 300 years of history, and that's just since the Europeans arrived.

On one block it looks like ground zero of the rust belt, the next, like Jay Gatsby's front lawn.

Burdened by an image of grime and crime, bigger than Madrid, Miami, Saigon and Sydney, beholden to a troubled recent past, metro Detroit is a tough place to figure out.

We've got your groundwork. Maybe not all of it, but much of it — enough to get you well acquainted, well-versed, well on your way to a better feel for the place.

The Detroit Almanac is the most comprehensive reference book ever assembled on the metro area: 648 pages on metro Detroit's greatest music, entertainers, industries, people, landmarks, writers, ships, crooks, losers, leaders, trees, lakes, animals, ethnicities, plutocrats, jocks, clergy, churches ... and much more.

We promise to inform and entertain, debunk myths, break down stereotypes, shed some light.

Our biggest chapter — by far — is on metro Detroit's culture.

Go figure.

It's that kind of a book.

Happy Birthday, Detroit.

– Bill McGraw and Peter Gavrilovich
thedetroitalmanac@freepress.com

> We promise
> to inform
> and entertain,
> debunk myths,
> break down
> stereotypes,
> shed light.

ALAN R. KAMUDA /Detroit Free Press

Thanks

SPECIAL THANKS TO FREE PRESS STAFFERS:
Susan Ager, Amber Arellano, Cecil Angel, Emilia Askari, Tamara Audi, Ruby L. Bailey, Leesa Bainbridge, Brian Ballou, Valarie Basheda, Dawson Bell, Jennifer Bott, Laura Varon Brown, Steve Byrne, Carol Cain, Bob Campbell, Chris Christoff, Ellen Creager, David Crumm, Bernie Czarniecki, Corey Dade, Owen Davis, Jennifer Dixon, Mike Duffy, Ron Dzwonkowski, Julie Edgar, M.L. Elrick, Sally Farhat, Matt Fiorito, Mike Floyd, Daniel G. Fricker, John Gallagher, Joe Grimm, Suzette Hackney, Marty Hair, A.J. Hartley, Matt Helms, Roderick Hicks, James G. Hill, Mei-Ling Hopgood, Carole Leigh Hutton, Sheryl James, Amy Klein, Martin F. Kohn, Ken Kraemer, Jack Kresnak, Bill Laitner, Tina Lam, Terry Lawson, Doron Levin, Tim Marcinkoski, Erin Lee Martin, Jeanne May, Mick McCabe, Brian McCollum, Hugh McDiarmid, Hugh McDiarmid Jr., Robert G. McGruder, Heath J Meriwether, Ann Mieczkowski, Patty Montemurri, Stephen Mounteer, Gene Myers, Dennis Niemiec, Kathy O'Gorman, Mary Owen, Tom Panzenhagen, Dale Parry, Sylvia Rector, Brenda Rios, Dave Robinson, Judy Rose, Becca Rothschild, Jack Saylor, Jim Schaefer, Ben Schmitt, Dan Shine, Kim North Shine, John Smyntek, David R. Squires, Barbara Stanton, Mark Stryker, Joe Swickard, Jeff Taylor, Joel Thurtell, Peggy Walsh-Sarnecki, Niraj Warikoo, Wendy Wendland-Bowyer, Jody Williams, John-John Williams IV, Tracy Van Moorlehem, Laura Wisniewski and Lorene Yue.

THANKS TO: Dan Alpert, Sue Bailey, Jeffery Bass, Mary Lynne Becker, Millard Berry, Curtis Blessing, Julian Bond, Nancy Cain, Dawn Clenney, Avern Cohn, George Costaris, the Rev. Charles A. Craig III, Shabnam Daneshvar, Matt Davis, John Dingell, Brian Dunnigan, Esther Gordy Edwards, Richard Ellena, Reynolds Farley, Lisa Gandelot, Johnette Garner, Cheri Gay, Mark Giannotta, John Gibson, Roman Godzak, Mike Greene, Jenese Harris, Patrick Healy, Thomas Hill, Charles Hyde, Amy Irish, Mike Kolar, John Kerr, Nancy King, Tom Klug, Rick Lancaster, Sarah Lapshan, Matthew Lee, Carl Levin, Nancy Lippert, Debra Lonskey, Richard Maciejewski, Dorothy Mann, Phil Mason, Annette McConnell, James McConnell, John J. McCusker, Kurt Metzger, Lisa Mulcrone, Dorgan Needom, Mike Nevin, Robin Pannecouk, Ross Parker, Sue Piorunek, John Polacsek, Deborah Smith Pollard, David Lee Poremba, Nancy Ross-Flanigan, Neal Rubin, Robert Simanek, Simone Sebastian, Laura Sheehan, Donn Shelton, Suzanne Smith, Sara Snyder, Gayle Spillard, Thomas Sugrue, Bryan Thompson, Jim Triano, E'Lon-Eloni Wilks, Tammy Woobury.

LIBRARIES:
Archdiocese of Detroit Archives
Detroit Free Press
Detroit Historical Museum
Detroit Public Library: Burton Historical Collection, Municipal Reference Library, Main Branch.
Henry Ford Centennial Library, Dearborn
Henry Ford Museum
University of Detroit Mercy Library
University of Michigan: Clements Library, Bentley Historical Library, Harland Hatcher Graduate Library, Labadie Collection of Social Protest Literature.
Wayne State University: Purdy/Kresge Library, Walter P. Reuther Library.

Credits

Editors	Peter Gavrilovich
	Bill McGraw
Contributing Writer	Cassandra Spratling
Photo Editor	Alan R. Kamuda
Chief Copy Editor	Michele Siuda Jacques
Art Director	Steve Dorsey
Assistant Art Directors	Chris Clonts
	Mauricio Gutiérrez
Graphics Director	Rick Nease
Designers	Betty Bazemore
	Kris Belden
	Chris Clonts
	Howard Davy
	Steve Dorsey
	Amy Etmans
	Mauricio Gutiérrez
	Robert Huschka
Special Assistants	Breeze Rusnell
	Angelique Soenarie
Copy Editors	Crystal Davis
	Jeff Juterbock
	Kathleen Knauss
	Meinhart Lagies
	Lisa Manns
	Leah Duncan Maurer
	Emiliana Sandoval
	Shelly Solon
	Sherita Wyche
Free Press Library	Chris Kucharski
	Michelle Lavey
	Barb Loth
	Ruthie Miles
	Chris Schmuckal
	Victoria Turk
Photo Technicians	Rose Ann McKean
	Christine Russell
	Jessica Trevino
	Kathryn Trudeau
Index	Laurie Andriot

Free Press file photo

A REMEMBRANCE

We could not have compiled this almanac without the work of scores of reporters, editors and photographers from this newspaper's 170-year history in Detroit.

The Detroit Almanac

CONT

"I never had
a dull moment
at Detroit."

– **Charles Lindbergh**

ENTS

01 | FAQs

A QUESTION-AND-ANSWER GUIDE TO USING THE ALMANAC. Subjects include the meaning of Detroit in English and French ... Everything you need to know about 8 Mile Road ... Was 1967 a riot or rebellion? ... Surviving an A-bomb in Detroit ... Edmund Fitzgerald: the unknown man behind the legendary ship ... Flogging Detroit's bad guys ... Coleman Young's will ... Henry Ford's grave site ... A pronunciation guide to street tongue-twisters ... The city's toughest cops ... Greeting the new year with guns ... Opening Day with Ernie Harwell. | *Page 16*

02 | History

A NARRATIVE HISTORY OF METRO DETROIT IN SHORT TAKES. From 9,000 BC to the 21st Century; from mastodons to Motown; from Etienne Brule to Jack Kevorkian. Among the hundreds of subjects: the difference between a *voyageur* and a *coureur de bois* ... The first record of a black person in Detroit ... Daniel Boone's forced visit ... The Woodward who named Woodward Avenue ... Gabriel Richard's 1823 Congressional election triumph ... Detroit becomes a boomtown after the opening of the Erie Canal ... Blacks in Detroit celebrate after receiving the right to vote ... The growth of industry in the late 19th Century ... The first skyscraper ... The birth of the auto industry ... Prohibition ... The Depression ... The first local casualty in World War II ... The rising political power of black Detroiters ... Flight to the suburbs ... The renaissance of downtown — 25 years after the RenCen. | *Page 26*

03 | Superlatives

THE BIGGEST, LONGEST, TALLEST, SMALLEST AND MOST PROFITABLE THINGS. **The firsts:** A list of No. 1's ... **Detroit's X files:** Weird, wonderful and wacky tales ranging from a shrine to satan to the Detroit editor who once received a human head in the mail ... **Just passing through:** Famous people with significant links to metro Detroit from Ulysses S. Grant to Malcolm X to Charles Lindbergh to Theodore (The Unabomber) Kaczynski to Jack Kerouac to Harry Houdini ... **Awards, recognition, other big-time kudos:** A list of local recipients of the Medal of Honor, Congressional Gold Medal, Presidential Medal of Freedom, Kennedy Center honors, Rhodes scholarships, Oscars, Pulitzer Prizes, Nobel Prizes, Heisman Trophy. **Also:** Metro Detroiters on the Hollywood Walk of Fame, local Miss Americas and Miss USAs ... **Describing Detroit:** Great quotations about the region from more than three centuries. | *Page 54*

EVERYBODY WHO HAS EVER BEEN ANYBODY IN METRO DETROIT. The real Detroit natives: Brief histories of the Ojibwa, Ottawa, Potawatomi, Huron or Wyandot, and Miami ... Biographical sketches of native leaders Pontiac, Tecumseh, Weyapiersenwah, Michipichy, Le Pesant ... **Immigration:** Facts and summaries of metro Detroit's leading ethnic groups ... **Blacks in Detroit:** A history from the first reference to an "unknown negresse in 1736" to Coleman Young. **Also:** Detroit slave owners; racial registration; the anti-slavery society; the Underground Railroad; legal changes and firsts; prominent members of the community at the end of the 19th Century; the growth in the black population after World War I; black businesses; the Detroit NAACP; the Ossian Sweet case; the demise of Black Bottom; the Rev. Martin Luther King Jr. and the 1963 march on Woodward, including King's "I Have a Dream" speech; the black majority city ... **Achieving women:** Metro Detroit's notable women. | *Page 88*

Nature 05

THE NATURAL WORLD AMID THE SPRAWL. The weather: Facts; historical data; extremes; how to build a backyard ice rink; Sonny Eliot ... Earthquakes ... Schedule of future solar and lunar eclipses ... **Water:** Facts on the Detroit River; Detroit River islands; Lake St. Clair ... **The Boater City:** Commercial vessels on the lakes; cargo; best freighter-watching spots ... **Classic ships of Detroit:** A description of historical vessels from canoes to the Edmund Fitzgerald; historical shipping facts; boat whistles explained ... Lighthouse facts ... **The Great Lakes:** Facts on the five bodies; water levels; Great Lakes time line ... **Oakland County lakes:** Includes ranking of inland lakes in Michigan ... **Household water:** The history of how H_2O gets to faucets ... **Metro Detroit's other rivers:** The Rouge, St. Clair, Clinton and Huron ... Detroit's forgotten streams ... Port of Detroit facts ... **Flora:** the grassy plains of 1701; old fruit trees; flowers; first frost ... **Trees:** Facts; elm disease; Tree of Heaven ... Marty Hair's favorite gardens ... **Animals of Detroit (Real and mythic):** Michigan species in danger; CHIRP! the birds of Detroit; sex and the single Hexagenia limbata; A history of big-cat sightings in suburbia ... **Pets:** Facts and figures on our best friends. | *Page 120*

FIND IT!

➤ The Detroit Almanac from A to Z. **Index**, page 626.

06 | Work & Business

MAKING A LIVING SINCE THE FUR TRADE. Labor force: Statistics on who works where; auto employment; local share of national auto employment ... **Made in Detroit:** List of locally produced products over the years ... **Salaries:** Local earnings vs. national earnings ... **Largest employers:** 1900 and 2000 ... **Detroit jobs:** The work that defined us: fur trapper; iron molder; assembly line worker ... **Art work:** A song and prayer about working on the line ... **The $5 day:** Facts on the Henry Ford's better idea ... **Notable employers:** Famous Detroit workplaces ... **Solidarity:** Unions in Detroit; largest locals; mini-biographies of working-class heroes; Reuther and Hoffa compared; notable labor events ... **On-job violence:** Fatal incidents since 1970 ... **Death on the job:** Summary of noncriminal fatalities, 1999 ... **Taking care of business:** Metro Detroit's 20 biggest publicly owned companies; top private businesses in metro Detroit; 20 oldest companies in metro Detroit; foreign investment in metro Detroit; notable businesspeople; facts on Detroit's casinos; directory of local malls ... **Inventive Detroit:** Famous inventors and their inventions; patents by metro area and county ... **Working in space:** Astronauts with local ties ... **Farms:** Local agriculture facts. | *Page 158*

07 | Wealth

GIVE ME MONEY, THAT'S WHAT I WANT. Richest Detroiters from 1864, 1902 and 2000 ... The rich ARE different: Facts on median income; nuggets about poverty; racial differences in income ... Best-paid executives in Michigan ... **Detroit's first millionaire:** E.B. Ward ... The Dodges ... The Fisher Estate ... How George Davis lost it all ... Yondotega Club ... Debutantes ... Oakland County ... **The Ford family:** Things named after the family; sketches of William Clay Ford Jr., Edsel Ford, William Clay Ford Sr. and Josephine F. Ford; how the family maintains control of the company; the wills of Henry Ford and Henry Ford II; what Henry Ford made besides cars; Ford and anti-Semitism; Ford Motor and Nazi Germany; Henry Ford's homes; when the Fords were nouveau riche. | *Page 194*

Transparation

EVERYTHING YOU NEED TO KNOW ABOUT THE MOTOR CAPITAL. A look to the future of the auto industry; facts on miles driven by local drivers; vehicle numbers; facts and chronology for Ford, General Motors and DaimlerChrysler; auto market share; traffic accident facts; share of U.S. autos made in Michigan; why Detroit became the Motor City; notable auto people; Free Press auto critic Tony Swan's top cars of all time; worst cars of the millennium; sex and the Merry Oldsmobile ... **Flying:** Facts on Metro, Detroit City, Oakland International and Willow Run airports ... **Catching a ride:** Bus systems; railroad mileage; streetcar history ... **Streets:** Mileage; congestion; a driving quiz; freeway origins; townships explained; Woodward Avenue; street namesakes. | *Page 210*

Politics

THREE CENTURIES OF STRANGE BEDFELLOWS. Notable politicians of today: Dennis Archer to L. Brooks Patterson ... **Notable politicians of yesterday:** Lewis Cass to Ken Cockrel ... **Fieger Time:** Geoff's gubernatorial campaign ... **Term limits:** Public officials who went to jail ... **Bosses:** The 107 men who ran Detroit: sketches of the French; British and American city chieftains from Antoine Cadillac to Coleman Young ... **Michigan governors:** A list, with information on metro Detroiters ... **Hail to the chief:** The presidency and metro Detroit ... **Called to the Cabinet:** Presidential advisers from Detroit ... **The Wings (Left and Right) of Detroit:** Political extremes through history. | *Page 246*

Geography

THE REGION, UP CLOSE AND PERSONAL. Choose up sides. Which is the best: East side, west side — or north side? Neal Shine on east side vs. west side ... **The region:** Seven-county demographics; 10 largest U.S. cities ... **Detroit:** Population; nicknames; slogans; a detailed census 1701-2000; notable Detroit neighborhoods; 19th-Century neighborhoods; Detroit's abandonment explained ... **The Border/La Frontière:** Everything you need to know about Windsor; what's different; famous Detroiters who made it big there; famous Canadians who made it big in Detroit; border traffic; information on the bridge and tunnel; what you need to know about customs and crossing the border ... **Beyond 8 Mile:** Why the suburbs flourished; largest cities; detailed information and history on seven counties and most cities in Wayne, Oakland and Macomb; information on main cities in Livingston, Monroe, Washtenaw and St. Clair ... **Michigan:** Facts on the state. | *Page 284*

11 | Culture

METRO DETROIT'S CREATIVE SIDE. Literary Detroit: Notable writers of fiction; famous poets and playwrights; fictional quotes about Detroit; novels set in Detroit; a nonfiction Detroit bibliography ... **Moving pictures:** Firsts; a brief history; Detroit: Hollywood of industrial film; drive-ins; Detroit Film Theatre; Ann Arbor Film Fest; classic theaters; 41 movies set – and sometimes made – in Detroit; names and faces of local film folks ... **Legitimate theater:** A guide to local venues; notable Detroit theater people; Larry DeVine's best Detroit productions ... **Music:** Classical music: brief history; DSO conductors ... Jazz: brief history; jazz all-stars ... Motown: brief history; 40 greatest hits; Motown time line; Motown bibliography ... The blues: brief history; all-stars ... Detroit rock: brief history; all-stars; best-sellers; pop music landmarks; memorable concert dates ... Detroit techno: a summary ... Country/folk: a summary ... R&B/hip-hop: summary ... Gospel: summary; all-stars ... Metro Detroit's musical all-stars ... **Art:** History of the DIA; a DIA mini-tour; Keri Guten Cohen's faves; other art and artists ... **Museums:** A guide to institutions of all types ... **Zoos:** Facts and history ... and the **best libraries.** | *Page 332*

12 | Communications

GETTING THE MESSAGE ACROSS. Talking, Detroit-style: Why our lingo fascinates linguists ... **Please,** *Monsieur* **Postman:** Mail delivery over the years ... **Telegraph:** Facts ... **Telephone:** History; old letter prefixes ... **Extra! A history of newspapers** ... **Airwaves:** Radio facts; Detroit radio landmarks; deejays and their trademark mantras; top 10 songs from various eras; Ernie Harwell's first farewell ... **TV:** A history of local channels; does size matter when it comes to broadcast towers? | *Page 442*

Buildings 13

OUR OFFICES, FORTS AND HOMES. Detroit's masterpieces: The most distinctive structures; in metro Detroit; details on the first skyscraper; the tallest towers today; notable architects ... **Landmarks:** From the silly to the sublime; the statues (and tires and stoves) that make Detroit Detroit ... **Bastion Detroit:** History of the city's forts and Selfridge Field ... **Homes:** A survey of 300 years of housing; notable homes. | *Page 464*

Mayhem 14

THE SAD SIDE OF HISTORY. Crime: *"Slain man in lingerie eaten by dog"* — famous murders; car thefts; Detroit Police history; year-by-year homicide totals; notorious serial killers ... **Self-made men:** Organized crime in Detroit history; mob hits and mobsters ... **Drugs:** Detroiters and their narcotics ... **Poster boys:** Bad guys on the FBI Most Wanted list ... **RIP I:** Cops who have died in the line of duty ... **Motor City is burning:** Famous fires and explosions; history of Devil's Night; Detroit Fire Department history ... **RIP II:** Firefighters who died in the line of duty ... **Aircraft disasters:** Flight 255 was only the biggest of many ... **Mobocracy:** Riots in Detroit history from 1833 to 1984 ... Detroit's worst week: the 1967 riot seen from a variety of angles ... **MAYDAY! Disasters on the waters of Detroit:** Storm sinkings; accidents and explosions; hydroplane deaths; a tale of survival ... **Death in Vietnam:** Soldier deaths from metro Detroit. | *Page 480*

15 | Fun!

THE JOY OF LIVING. Great celebrations: Detroiters greet the arrival of the first train from the east; the 20th Century; Nelson Mandela and much more ... **Metro fun:** Tales of J.L. Hudson's; Opening Day and many more of the places and events Detroiters have loved; top tourist destinations ... **Detroit's amusement parks:** Boblo to Electric Park ... **We are what we eat:** A gourmand's guide to kielbasa, coneys, paczki and other local culinary treats ... **Booze:** Details and history from Michigan's $4.6-billion-a-year industry; famous brewers; famous bars and five drinks concocted in Detroit. | *Page 528*

16 | Sports

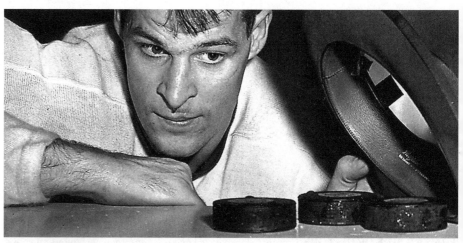

GIMME A 'D'! Boxing: Joe Louis — No. 1 ... Thomas Hearns ... Emanuel Steward ... **Our favorite teams:** 15 great squads from football to bowling ... **Baseball:** Historical facts; firsts; Tigers history; World Series records; all-time Tigers; memorable fan moments at Tiger Stadium; all-time record ... **Hockey:** 10 reasons why Detroit is Hockeytown; Red Wings history; bringing home Stanley; all-time Red Wings; great moments; all-time record ... **Basketball:** Pistons' history; championship seasons; all-time Pistons; all-time record ... **Football:** Lions history; championship seasons; all-time Lions; all-time record ... **Collegiate sports:** University of Michigan basketball: national championships; all-time players; all-time record ... Michigan football: national champs; all-time players; all-time record ... Michigan State basketball: national championships; all-time players; all-time record ... MSU football: national championships; all-time players; all-time record ... **Prep sports:** Best players to come out of metro Detroit; Goodfellow Game all-time record ... **Bowling:** Historical highlights and great players ... **Golf:** Historical highlights and great players ... **Powerboat racing:** History; racer deaths and Gold Cup results. . . **Grand Prix:** All-time winners ... **Stadiums:** Facts on current and past sports venues. | *Page 550*

FIND IT!

➤ The Detroit Almanac from A to Z, page 626.

The Detroit Almanac

01. FAQ

"So who was this John R guy?"

— *Countless newcomers*

FAQs about the Big D

OK, these may not be the most frequently asked questions about Detroit, but they are facts well-informed people should know. There won't be a quiz.

What is Detroit?

Frontier fort. British outpost. Small town. Big town. French town. Irish town. Black town. Motor City. Motown.

The definition keeps changing. In just two generations, Detroit has gone from the symbol of U.S. industrial might to a metaphor for urban decay.

"Detroit is growth," proclaimed the New York Times in 1927, a pinnacle of Detroit's hyper-expansion years.

In 1990, author Ze'ev Chafets described Detroit as a "third-world city" — a predominantly black community, surrounded by mostly white suburbs, with showcase projects, black-fisted symbols, an external enemy (white people), the cult of personality (Coleman Young), and even a quasi-official ideology. Young himself noted how Detroit often serves as a synonym for "blacks," especially outstate.

For decades, observers called Detroit the nation's largest small town, its bungalow-filled streets stretching for miles.

Detroit remains tantamount to the auto industry to the rest of the world, just as Washington stands for the U.S. government.

Then there's the "healthy dose of bad-ass credibility" that, according to the "Underground USA" travel guide, attaches to anything and anyone from Detroit. You got a problem with that?

Detroit is also more than Detroit proper: The roads that carry people back and forth generally keep their names when they cross the borders, and the communities generally keep the character of the town that spawned them:

Working-class suburbs with a slew of those bungalows; elegant suburbs built by auto sales; sprawling communities that rely on the family car to get a loaf of bread. **See Chapters 2, 3, 4....well, just read the whole darn book.**

Visiting Detroit in 1941, you might send grandma this postcard. Tourists are reminded that Detroit is only 3 hours from New York, 10 hours from Miami and 12 hours from Los Angeles by air.

Top left: Lots of hustle and bustle back in '20, eh? Today, Compuware world headquarters is going up on this site.

Left: Also around 1920, see Woodward split the city. The lower left is now Comerica Park.

Where is Detroit?

Depends on whom you ask — and when. The **Midwest**. OK, but Des Moines, Iowa, is in the Midwest. And what do Detroit and Des Moines have in common?

Detroit is on **Eastern** Standard Time.

The National Hockey League places the Red Wings in the **Central** Division of the **Western** Conference, but the National Basketball Association places the Pistons in the Central Division of the **Eastern** Conference. At times, the NCAA has assigned Michigan teams to the **Mideast** Regional tournament. University of Michigan teams are "champions

Sept. 27, 1954: Traffic heads north on Woodward at 8 Mile. You can see the construction equipment on 8 Mile west of Woodward used to remodel the intersection into the underpass and overpass we know today.

of the **West,"** and they play only 35 miles from downtown.

In the 18th Century, Americans considered Detroit to be part of the **Northwest.** If the United States should ever swallow Canada — hey, it could happen — would Detroit be considered **Midsouth**? Geographer Richard Santer has noted the U.S. government categorizes Michigan as an **East North-Central** state. Santer's solution? Detroit is part of the **Great Lakes** region, and always will be.

Geographically speaking, at Cobo Hall downtown, Detroit is 42 degrees, 19 minutes, 55 seconds latitude and 83 degrees, 02 minutes, 88 seconds longitude. Head due east, you'll hit Ortona, Italy; Ts'khinvali, Georgia, in the former Soviet Union; Jingyu, China; Muroran, Japan; Muddy Gap, Wyo., and Rockford, Ill.

And if you fly straight south, you will pass Limon, Costa Rica, and San Cristobal, Cuba, but you will miss South America. Really. **See page 287.**

What does Detroit mean?

In French, Detroit is a masculine noun that means "strait," as in a narrow body of water connecting larger bodies. *Les detroits de Mackinac* would be the Straits of Mackinac, for instance. The French and British considered

the strait to be the water system connecting lakes Huron and Erie: the St. Clair River, Lake St. Clair and the Detroit River **See page 29.**

Did Detroit have any other names?

Not really. Initially, the settlement was called Ft. Pontchartrain after the fortress, but it soon became widely known as Detroit. **See page 29.**

What is 8 Mile Road 8 miles from?

Two answers:
1) Metro Detroit's mile roads are measured from Michigan and Woodward downtown. But they are measured **due north** from that intersection.

That means there's only one point where 8 Mile is 8 miles due north of downtown: East 8 Mile and Bloom Avenue, near Mound Road.
2) On the west side, 8 Mile also is 8 miles north of Ford Road, the important east-west thoroughfare that runs from Wyoming Avenue on the Detroit/Dearborn border to the outskirts of Ann Arbor. Ford Road is essentially Zero Mile Road.

Main streets are found at 1-mile intervals to the north — Warren (1 Mile); Joy (2 Mile); Plymouth (3 Mile); Schoolcraft (4 Mile). No one calls those streets by their numerical designations. But mile roads starting with Fenkell (5 Mile) are at least somewhat known by their numbers — McNichols (6 Mile), 7 Mile and 8 Mile, etc. **See Chapter 8**

What's the big deal about 8 Mile?

More than 150 years before it became one of metro Detroit's best-known streets, it was an important survey line — the so-called baseline that forms the borders for counties and townships across southern Michigan. Eight Mile (or Baseline Road), which extends westward across Lake Michigan, also is the boundary between Illinois and Wisconsin. That line is at 42 degrees, 26 minutes, 30 seconds. **See page 233.**

OK, what about 3 Mile Drive on the east side?

That residential street runs from Lake St. Clair in Grosse Pointe Park to Harper in Detroit — 3 miles.

"Temptations," "Miracles" and "Supremes" I understand. But what is a "Vandella"?

Martha Reeves named her famous Motown group after Van Dyke, the Detroit street, and Della Reese, the Detroit-born singer and actress. **See page 383.**

What is a Comerica?

Corporate identity specialists in New York coined the name in 1982. Into the corporate-renaming machine went Detroit Bank & Trust Co. Out came Comerica, a combination of "cooperation and America." Comerica, of course, became the name of Detroit's ballpark after Comerica Bank bought the naming rights. **See page 181.**

Was Captain Boblo really buried at sea off the Boblo boat in Lake Erie?

Urban legend. The diminutive captain, whose real name was Joe Short, right, dressed in a sea captain's costume and greeted children at the Boblo docks in Detroit from 1953 to 1973. Earlier, he had been a circus clown under the name "Little Joe from Kokomo," and had played roles in movies about the Katzem-

jammer Kids and Mutt and Jeff. He died at 91 in 1974. The Detroit Fire Department Clown Team served as pallbearers. He was cremated, and the remains were placed next to those of his wife in Woodlawn Cemetery. **See page 539.**

How come some folks call the 1967 civil disturbance a riot and others a rebellion?

Depends on your politics. Riot is the more widespread term. People who call it a rebellion argue that black people were rising in anger over the housing, hiring and other conditions of the day. One thing is clear: What happened in July 1967 was not a race riot.

There was virtually no fighting between black and white residents, as happened during Detroit's 1943 riot. The first riot fatality in 1967 was a white man, who was shot looting. **See page 519.**

What would happen if an atomic bomb hit metro Detroit?

If a 5-megaton bomb — that's 5 million tons of TNT — hit at 12 Mile and Dequindre in Warren, a searing, white-hot flash would vaporize all life at ground zero instantaneously.

A red ball of fire would surge outward, along with a 2,000-m.p.h. wind. Everything within 3 miles of the epicenter would be destroyed. Bungalows across Warren would disappear. The siding on homes in Hazel Park would erupt into flames, and the structures on Detroit's northeast side would crumble in the wind.

The blast also would level the northeast corner of Hazel Park, the eastern part of Royal Oak and the southwest corner of Sterling Heights. The General Motors Tech Center?

History. In this 3-mile radius, 70 percent of the people would be killed, and 20 percent would be injured. Within 5 miles of ground zero — most of Royal Oak, Ferndale and Hazel Park — heat waves would start fires and knock steel-frame buildings off their foundations. In seconds, effects of the blast would reach 19 Mile Road on the north and East Davison on the south. Fires would start in Clinton Township, Fraser and parts of Roseville and Eastpointe. Shock waves would move across northeast Detroit. Oak Park, Huntington Woods, Berkley and parts of Birmingham would be rocked. The wind would diminish as it moved downtown, but windows would pop out of the Fisher Building. Ruptured fuel and gas lines would touch off more fires across the

United Press International

WHO WAS EDMUND FITZGERALD?

From 1947 to 1958, Mr. Fitzgerald was the chairman and chief executive officer of the Milwaukee-based Northwestern Mutual Life Insurance Co., which owned the ill-fated ship. When it sank on Nov. 10, 1975, the Fitzgerald was chartered by the Oglebay Norton Co. of Cleveland. The ship, the longest and most capacious to sink in Great Lakes history, was launched from Great Lakes Engineering in River Rouge in 1958. Mr. Fitzgerald's wife, Elizabeth Fitzgerald, christened the ship. It took her three attempts to break the champagne bottle against the hull; sailors consider anything more than one try to be bad luck. **See page 139.**

J. KYLE KEENER/ *Detroit Free Press*

As the funeral procession for Coleman Young moved toward nearby Elmwood Cemetery on Dec. 5, 1997, it passed a car repair shop owned by Larry Meeks, from left, with employees Fernando Gonzalez and William Frank. The sign is atop Meeks' 1948 Plymouth.

region. Survivors from the fires would then have to worry about radioactive fallout from the mushroom cloud.

We are not making this up. During the Cold War, the greatest horror on earth was make-believe visited on Detroit so civil defense officials could plan a worst-case scenario. Of course, that *greatest* never really happened, but lots of other superlatives have been recorded here. **See page 506.**

Did Detroit ever flog criminals?

Yes. Beginning in 1818, a judge in Detroit could order the whipping of "lewd, idle or disorderly persons, stubborn servants, common drunkards and those who neglect their families, with 10 stripes." There was a whipping post at Woodward and Jefferson that was 5 feet high and shaped like the letter T. Offenders were stripped to the waist and whipped. The practice was discontinued in 1830 — the same year the last person was executed in Detroit. **See page 483.**

TONY SPINA/*Detroit Free Press*

Dec. 28, 1973: Young's official inaugural photo. He served as mayor for 20 years.

Did Coleman Young die a multimillionaire?

No. Lots of rumors suggested the late mayor was worth a ton, but probate court records show 79-year-old Young left an estate estimated at $500,000 when he died Nov. 29, 1997, of complications from emphysema. After expenses were paid, the estate was split evenly among Young's two sisters, his son and his longtime female companion. A personal secretary and housekeeper each received six months' salary. **See page 267.**

Who is buried in Ford's tomb?

What tomb? Henry Ford is not buried in a tomb. His resting place is modest and obscure, a grave with a relatively small marker in a church cemetery on Joy Road west of Greenfield, below. Henry Ford II was cremated. **See pages 203 and 611.**

What is buried in Michigan Stadium?

A construction crane. Before the Big House opened in 1927, the site was a big underground lake. That's why three-quarters of the stadium is below ground. During construction, the quicksand-like earth swallowed the crane. **See page 592.**

How come you Detroiters pronounce Freud Street "Frood"? Uncouth.

Get a life. It is "Frood." The east side road was named after turn-of-the-century developer Henry Freud, not Sigmund Freud, the famous shrink ("Froyd"). Lest you brood over Freud, here are more mispronounced streets:

	Them	Us
Goethe	*Ger-ta*	*GO-Thee*
Charlevoix	*Shar-luh-vwa*	*SHAR-la-voy*
Cadieux	*Cahd-yuh*	*Cadg-joo*
Lahser	*Lazh-ur*	*Lash-err*
Livernois	*Lee-vair-nwah*	*Liver-noise*

See page 445.

How come Boston Coolers are a Detroit drink?

Detroit was the birthplace of Vernors. A cooler is two scoops of Sanders vanilla ice cream in a glass of amber, bubbly Vernors. It's uncertain why they named it after Boston. **See page 543.**

A construction crane's final resting place is under Michigan Stadium.

Free Press file photo

The most influential business leader in Detroit in the 20th Century, Henry Ford is buried in a church cemetery on Joy Road, west of Greenfield. An iron fence surrounds his grave.

© Detroit Institute of Arts

Above: The south wall of the Rivera murals at the Detroit Institute of Arts.

Right: Before patrons traipsed through the museum on Woodward, they toured the art museum on East Jefferson near Hastings, which was demolished decades ago.

Burton Historical Collection

What is the Detroit's greatest claim to fame in the art world?

Diego Rivera's murals at the Detroit Institute of Arts? Or Tyree Guyton's street art?

How about Dan Robbins?

In 1951, Detroiter Robbins invented Paint-by-Numbers, arguably the 20th Century's most popular art form. At its peak in the mid-1950s, there were more than 50,000 sold every day. **See page 421.**

The Big Four?

If you were into autos, Ford, General Motors, Chrysler and American Motors were the Big Four in the postwar era when a quartet of American companies ruled the auto world.

If you grew up in Detroit from the 1950s to the 1970s, the big black police car with four officers that cruised precincts, looking for trouble, was the Big Four. A uniformed officer drove, and three plainclothes cops rounded out the quartet. Officially, the Big Four searched for major felons. Unofficially, the team of officers messed with whomever needed messing with.
See page 483.

Where is Detroit's Tree of Heaven?

It's not one tree. It's a plague. The smelling, pervasive plant can be found throughout southeast Michigan and especially in older Detroit neighborhoods, growing wherever enough dirt can be found to support a seed. It's one of many tree varieties in Detroit, of course. **See page 151.**

The Detroit practice of shooting guns at midnight on New Year's Eve is an indication that something is wrong with modern society, right?

Well, it might indicate dysfunction, but it has nothing to do with the modern age. Detroiters fired weapons into the air to greet the 20th Century, which they celebrated Jan 1, 1901. **See page 531.**

What is the Bible passage that Tigers broadcaster Ernie Harwell reads before the first game of spring training?

It's from the Song of Solomon:

"Lo, the winter is past ... The rain is over and gone ... The ... flowers appear on the earth ... The time of the singing of birds is come ... And the voice of the turtle is heard in our land ..."

See pages 455 and 458.

To many, Ernie Harwell is synonymous with Tigers baseball. The announcer can remember Opening Days going back to 1960, when he started his career with the Tigers.

Free Press file photo

The Detroit Almanac

02.HIS

"History is more or less bunk. The only history that is worth a tinker's dam is the history we make today."

— **Henry Ford**, *Chicago Tribune, May 25, 1916*

TORY

The Saga of Detroit

An 11,000-year chronicle

9,000 BC — The ice age ends and the Great Lakes region becomes habitable. Mastodons and caribou graze in the region. Humans migrating from the west settle shorelines. During several thousand years, humans develop clans and villages. They bury their dead in mounds and make tools, weapons and jewelry from copper and stone. A settlement from 9,000 BC has been found near what's now Flint. And just east of the mouth of the Rouge River, there are remains of a massive burial mound built centuries ago.

1500 AD — Most humans in Michigan are nomadic, spending warmer months along lake shorelines and winter months inland, near the mouths of rivers. Encampments among evergreens towering to 200 feet provide shelter during winter. By the 1530s, the French have built settlements along the St. Lawrence River.

1600 — The French are firmly established in eastern Canada and planning to explore the upper Great Lakes in search of furs and a route to Asia. They become the first Europeans on record to explore today's Michigan. Anthropologists estimate that about 100,000 native people live throughout Northern Michigan and the shoreline of Georgian Bay. The beaver population then — about 10 million.

1618 — Etienne Brule paddles up the St. Marys River, portages the rapids and becomes the first European to see Lake Superior. He follows the southern coast to present-day Duluth, Minn.

Getting it strait

Detroit comes in focus

Who from Europe first saw the site of Detroit? It may have been Brule, but there's no account that he ventured so far south. Iroquois control the region of southern Michigan and much of the area surrounding lakes Erie and Ontario, and the French and Iroquois aren't on good terms. Thus French explorers travel the Ottawa River and portage several streams to Ontario's Lake Nipissing, then take the French River to Georgian Bay in northern Lake Huron. From there, they go on to the Upper Peninsula or pass through the Straits of Mackinac to Lake Michigan.

There are regular, temporary Indian encampments along the Detroit River near the mouth of the Rouge River and by Parent Creek, a stream that once met the river about 400 feet west of today's Belle Isle Bridge. The Indians have several names for the strait:

WAWEATUNONG — It means crooked way.

TSYCHASARONDIA — It refers to the bend in the river at today's Ambassador Bridge.

KARONTAEN — The coast of the straits.

After settlement, some Indians call the area **YONDOTIGA**, which means Great Village.

1669 — Adrien Joliet leaves the St. Marys River area with an

A depiction of Cadillac's landing from a 19th-Century Harper's magazine. Chances are he was more casually attired.

ZUT ALORS! HARDY FRENCH OPEN MICHIGAN FOR EUROPE

There were three types of explorers from France:

➤ **VOYAGEURS:** The men who steered the boats and canoes through unchartered waters.

➤ **COUREURS DE BOIS:** The inland explorers who looked for furs, then searched for the best deal for their pelts. They were hardy men who spent Michigan winters in the wild.

➤ **CLERGY:** The priests who were anxious to convert North America's natives. The three orders most common to the region were the Jesuits, Sulpicians and Recollects.

FIND OUT MORE

➤ Great Lakes history, page 142.

➤ American Indians, page 91.

Iroquois man recently freed by Huron captors. The man promises to show Joliet a faster water route to the St. Lawrence River. Joliet was the brother of Louis Joliet, traveling companion of much-honored Jesuit, Father Jacques Marquette, founder of St. Ignace and explorer of the Mississippi River and the Lake Michigan coast.

Adrien Joliet and his canoe companion paddle south past what will be Detroit in early September. They may stop, perhaps on a river island, to camp overnight.

April 1670 — French priests Father Rene de Brehan de Galinee and Father Francois Dollier de Casson, after a chance meeting several months earlier with Joliet, retrace Joliet's route to reach the Sault. Somewhere along the Detroit River, possibly near the mouth of the Rouge River, the priests see a monument on shore. They determine that it's an idol erected by Indians as a charm to assure safe passage on Lake Erie. The priests smash the rock, scoop up the refuse and dump the remains into the river. They continue to the Sault.

Aug. 10, 1679 — The first sailing vessel passes what will be Detroit en route to the upper Great Lakes. It is the Griffon, built by explorer Robert La Salle, who is anxious to find a route to Asia. On board with La Salle is Recollect Father Louis Hennepin. He writes:

"The banks of the strait are vast meadows . . . with some hills covered with vineyards, trees bearing good fruit, groves and forests . . . The country is stocked with stags, wild goats and bears . . .

"Those who shall be so happy as to inhabit that noble country cannot but remember with gratitude those who have discovered the way."

After the Griffon enters the shallow lake north of the strait, Hennepin names it St. Clair, for the saint whose feast day is Aug. 11. (A Hennepin aside: He was in a small band of explorers who became the first Europeans to see Niagara Falls.)

The Griffon reaches St. Ignace and then the western shore of Lake Michigan near Green Bay, where La Salle leaves the ship and with a complement of men rows south along the Lake Michigan shore. He instructs the Griffon's crew to return to the eastern shore of Lake Erie, drop off its furs and set sail for the southern end of Lake Michigan. But the Griffon disappears, likely blown into rocks during an autumn gale in northern Lake Huron.

April 1680 — La Salle and his party cross

The Griffon: The first sailing vessel met a stormy end.

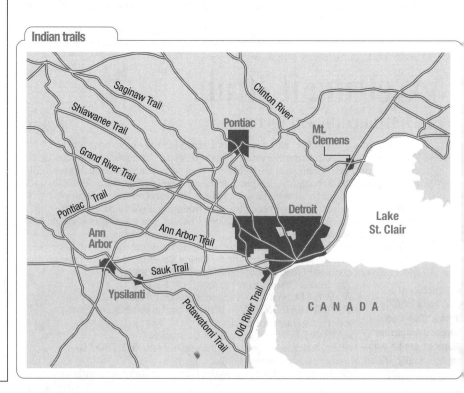

Indian trails

Saginaw Trail

Shiawanee Trail

Clinton River

Grand River Trail

Pontiac Trail

Pontiac

Mt. Clemens

Ann Arbor Trail

Ann Arbor

Detroit

Lake St. Clair

Sauk Trail

Ypsilanti

Potawatomi Trail

Old River Trail

CANADA

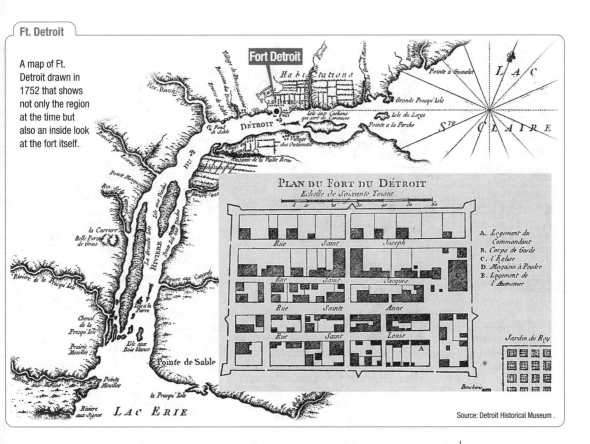

Ft. Detroit

A map of Ft. Detroit drawn in 1752 that shows not only the region at the time but also an inside look at the fort itself.

Fort Detroit

PLAN DU FORT DU DÉTROIT
Echelle de Soixante Toises

A. Logement du Commandant
B. Corps de Garde
C. L'Église
D. Magasin à Poudre
E. Logement de l'Aumonier

Source: Detroit Historical Museum.

lower Michigan on foot, becoming the first Europeans on record to traverse the peninsula, reaching the Huron River likely near what would become Dexter, then paddling with the current, then continuing on foot along the route of the Rouge River until they reach the strait.

May 21, 1696 — King Louis XIV orders France's western Great Lakes outposts destroyed, the soldiers and all trade transactions sent to Montreal. The fort at St. Ignace, two near today's St. Joseph and one near today's Port Huron are affected. He also orders the governor in New France, the French designation for what would become Canada, to negotiate a peace with the Iroquois. France wants to centralize the fur trade — and cut back on the pelts since the country is now awash in beaver. The king's order is not good news for commanders and explorers of New France. It is widely ignored.

1698 — Antoine Laumet de la Mothe Cadillac, a savvy businessman and trader and former French commander at Ft. de Baude at St. Ignace, journeys to Paris to petition Louis XIV to rethink western exploration and allow him to establish an outpost along the entrance to the western Great Lakes. He suggests a fort on *le detroit* — the strait — a stretch of water about 80 miles long linking Lake Erie and

Antoine de la Mothe Cadillac

Lake Huron. The French considered the waterway that is today's Detroit River, Lake St. Clair and the St. Clair River, *le detroit*. Cadillac impresses the king's chief counselor, Count Pontchartrain, with his argument that if France does not secure the region, the English will. Cadillac gets the OK and 1,500 livres to build a fort — about $12,000 in today's dollars. Remember: The trees were free.

June 5, 1701 — Cadillac, 43, leaves La Chine, a settlement on the northern shore of the St. Lawrence just below Montreal. He is in command of 25 long canoes, 100 Frenchmen and about 100 natives. His 9-year-old son, Antoine, is with him. Cadillac's destination: *le detroit*. The party rows 12 miles west to the mouth of the Ottawa River and then rows upstream some 180 miles until the company has to make about 30 difficult portages to reach Lake Nipissing. They row across the lake and out the French River nearly 100 miles to reach Georgian Bay in northern Lake Huron. They follow the eastern shore of the

Cadillac suggested a fort on **le detroit** — the strait — a stretch of water about 80 miles long linking Lake Erie and Lake Huron.

Burton Historical Collection

The first Ste. Anne's church was a small building that stood about two years before being destroyed by fire.

The feast day of St. Anne, who in Christian tradition was the mother of Mary, is held on July 26, 1701.

FIND OUT MORE

➤ Antoine Cadillac, pages 60, 83, 257.

➤ List of French commanders, page 257.

lake to the beginning of *le detroit,* near today's Port Huron, some 250 miles from the French River. The swift current of the St. Clair River quickly carries them 30 miles to the top of Lake St. Clair, an area known today as the St. Clair Flats. They may spend the night on the shore of what is now Harsens Island.

July 23, 1701 — Cadillac rows across Lake St. Clair. His company passes Windmill Point and Peche Isle — and maybe splits as it rows past Belle Isle. Stopping on the island might be foreboding: The sight of swarms of mosquitoes and the occasional threatening rattle of massasauga rattlesnakes may convince them to keep rowing — past the site of Detroit, the mouth of the Rouge River, to present-day Grosse Ile, where the company camps.

July 24, 1701 — Cadillac and company row upstream, beyond the bend in the river to a spot where a bluff on the northern shore gives them unobstructed views downriver and up.

The company pulls its canoes onto the sandy shore. Tall conifers, maple and oak and wild pear trees abound. They start cutting them down for a fort.

July 26, 1701 — The feast day of St. Anne, in Christian tradition the mother of Mary. Cadillac and crew begin building a church, to be named Ste. Anne's. In about a month, the church is finished, about 25 feet by 35 feet. The door has a lock, the windows have no glass. The structure is torched by Indians in 1703.

Feb. 2, 1704 — First baptism — Marie Therese Cadillac — named for her mother. She is born about nine months to the day that Marie Therese Cadillac arrives in Detroit from Montreal.

June 6, 1706 — The first major row between the French and nearby Indians happens while Cadillac is out of town and the temporary commander's dog bites an Ottawa. The Ottawa beats the dog. The commander beats the Ottawa to death. Ottawas attack a group of Miami Indians — who had good relations with the French — in retaliation, killing five. Soldiers at the fort fire on several Ottawas, killing them. Meanwhile, the Ottawas capture Ste. Anne's priest, Father Nicolas de L'Halle. An Ottawa chief releases the priest, but another Ottawa shoots and kills de L'Halle moments before he is to enter the fort. Soldiers then fire on Ottawas, killing 30.

1710 — Cadillac becomes governor of Louisiana.

May 5, 1710 — Baptiste Turpin and Margaret Fafard marry at Ste. Anne's. Fafard likely was related to Jean and Francois Fafard, brothers who landed with Cadillac and served as interpreters between the French and various local groups. Fire destroyed some of Ste. Anne's records in 1703, so it's possible that a marriage occurred during the first two years of the settlement. There is no record of Indian marriages.

Ribbon farms

The extent of white settlement during Detroit's first 100 years. The French ribbon farms, in narrow strips that ran from the river back 1 or 2 miles, gave every family a bit of waterfront.

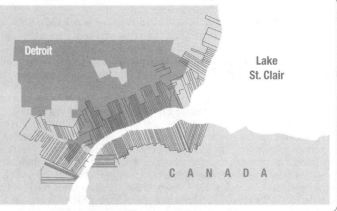

Detroit

Lake St. Clair

CANADA

May 13, 1712 — More than 1,000 Fox Indians journey from southwestern Michigan to Ft. Pontchartrain, saying they were accepting an earlier invitation to settle the region by the now-gone Cadillac. But the Fox plan to attack the fort. Their campsite is near the present-day Penobscot Building, north of the stockade. French commander Jacques-Charles Renaud Dubuisson, with help from Huron and Ottawa Indians, including Chief Saginaw, battle the Fox for the next several days. Soon the Fox flee northeast of the fort, to an area along today's Windmill Pointe Drive in Grosse Pointe Park. French and Indian forces catch the Fox and kill hundreds in a battle on **May 20, 1712**.

1718 — The fort's perimeter is rebuilt; the French next expand the fort in 1749 and again in 1754.

June 6, 1721 — The Rev. Peter Charlevoix visits and says the place looks deserted and abandoned because of government neglect.

Oct. 18, 1730 — Cadillac dies in France.

October, 1736 — The earliest record of a black person in Detroit: the burial notation of an unnamed black woman in Ste. Anne's records.

1751 — The settlement is 50 years old. The fort's name is changed to Ft. Detroit. There are 483 people in the village, 33 of whom are slaves. There are 471 cows — nearly one cow a person — and 160 horses. Settlers on both sides of the fort farm along narrow but deep strips of land called ribbon farms. The concept allows farmers access to water along the river. The farmers will be remembered because their names coincide with streets along their property boundaries: St. Aubin, Beaubien, Chene . . .

Nov. 29, 1760 — The French and Indians are vanquished by the English in the 7-year French and Indian War. The outpost at Detroit is among the spoils. French settlers seem indifferent to English occupation. Indians are wary, especially when they discover the English exchange for pelts is not as lucrative as the French. The English also expand the fort.

Feb 10, 1763 — Treaty of Paris is signed between France and England, which takes control of nearly all of Canada after 230 years of French rule.

May 1763 — Ottawa Chief Pontiac, 43, plots a surprise attack on Ft. Detroit. He fought the English during the French and Indian War and hates them. He convinces other Indian leaders that now is the time to strike at Detroit, that France will send troops to help, that the land belongs to the Indians, not the English and that the English are cheap in their trade dealings.

May 7, 1763 — Pontiac's plan is to peacefully enter the fort, greet commander Maj. Henry Gladwin, display a belt — and signal the attack by a turn of the extended belt. But Gladwin has been tipped off. The daughter of a French settler who overhears her father speak of the plot warns her beau, an English merchant inside the fort.

When Pontiac enters, he finds Gladwin and the fort's troops surrounding the parade field fully armed. Pontiac doesn't signal the attack.

Many legends cloud Detroit history, like the one in this 19th-Century painting of a young Indian woman tipping Detroit commander Maj. Henry Gladwin to Pontiac's plans. It didn't happen that way.

FIND OUT MORE

➤ List of British commanders, page 258.

➤ Bios of Pontiac and other Indian leaders, page 92.

Free Press files

Artist Frederic Remington depicts Pontiac's plot to hatch a surprise attack May 7, 1763, on Ft. Detroit. When Pontiac and his men enter the fort, they are surrounded by heavily armed troops.

Within days, Pontiac orders attacks on English settlers. He takes hostages and for several weeks lays siege to the fort. Pontiac's forces greatly outnumber Gladwin's 170 troops. But in July, reinforcements arrive.

July 31, 1763 — Nearly 250 troops march North from the fort to confront Pontiac's forces. But this time, it is Pontiac who gets advance word. Hundreds of Indians watch quietly as the English march along the river road. When the column begins crossing a small bridge at Parent Creek, which meets the river near present-day Mt. Elliott, Indians ahead of them begin firing. The Indians now behind the column move forward to complete the ambush. About 1 in 5 troops are killed or wounded; the remainder fight back to the fort. The siege continues.

October 1763 — As suddenly as the siege begins, after 153 days, Pontiac ends it. His soldiers are anxious to return to their families and to prepare for winter. Pontiac sends word to Gladwin in the hope that English commander will be a sport and forget the whole incident. On **Aug. 17, 1765**, Pontiac signs a formal peace with the English.

Chief Pontiac (1720-1769)

Chief Pontiac

The son of an Ottawa chief, born either at the Straits of Mackinac or along the Maumee River in northern Ohio, Pontiac arguably is the greatest Great Lakes Indian leader of the 18th Century and the only one to mount a nearly successful rout of the English from the region. His plan to capture Detroit fails, but his men capture nearly all the other English forts and outposts in the region, including the key fort at Michili-

mackinac. After his reluctant peace with the English, Pontiac becomes a wanderer, unable to raise an army to renew the battle. Just outside St. Louis, Mo., in 1769, an Indian from a rival nation fatally stabs a drunken Pontiac in the back. In **1859**, the City of Pontiac is incorporated in Oakland County.

1775 — As England's seaboard colonies continue to stir with talk of revolution, the government in Canada declares martial law applying to western outposts including Detroit. In November, Henry Hamilton arrives in Detroit as lieutenant governor, a civilian position that gives him authority over the post commander. Hamilton soon appoints Philippe Dejean as justice of the peace.

Dejean overreaches his authority — and Hamilton's — when he orders in **December 1775** a man executed on a murder charge and in **March 1776**, a man and a woman hanged for robbing a local merchant of $6. That order is particularly galling to Detroiters. When nobody can be found to perform the hanging, Dejean offers the woman, Ann (Nancy) Wiley, a pardon and her freedom if she will carry out the execution of accomplice John Contencineau. Wiley, a slave, accepts and executes Contencineau.

Several Detroiters warn provincial authorities in Montreal about Hamilton and Dejean. In **September 1778**, a grand jury indicts the pair on murder charges because neither had authority to issue a death penalty. An arrest warrant is issued a month later. Meanwhile, Hamilton, expecting arrest, leads a troop of Indians and Detroit garrison soldiers against rebels in Indiana. They take one fort, but soon Revolutionary leader Col. George Rogers Clark, retakes the post and Hamilton becomes a POW of the rebels. Dejean, meanwhile, leaves Detroit to join Hamilton and is captured by Clark's men en route.

Both are sent to jail in Virginia. When news of the capture reaches Detroit, there is great joy — even if the capture was at the hands of the rebels. Just after their capture, the English governor in Canada on **April 16, 1779,** reviews the indictment and decides to drop the charges. Dejean and Hamilton were only looking after English interests in Detroit, he reasons.

Fall 1778 — Garrison commander Capt. Richard Lernoult fears an attack by U.S. commanders Col. George Rogers Clark and Col. Daniel Brodhead. He builds a new fort on a hill north of the stockade at a site centered roughly at Fort and Shelby. It is from this position in 1712 that the Fox Indians attacked the old fort. The new installation is called Ft. Lernoult.

In **1779,** George Washington contemplates an attack on Detroit, but the American rebels ultimately avoid an assault on Ft. Lernoult, with Clark at one point sending a message to adversary Lernoult that he is glad to hear of the new fort because "it will save the Americans some expenses in building."

April 5, 1778 — Daniel Boone is brought to Detroit as a prisoner of the Shawnee Indians. He stays 10 days, then is released.

Chicago, Chicago . . .

Hello, Detroit!

About a year after Dan'l heads to Kentucky, Jean Baptiste Pointe du Sable becomes a captive of the British in Detroit, suspected of spying for the Americans. Though a prisoner, he is treated well, most likely because he's well-educated and has a business acumen. Du Sable is black. He eventually returns to wilderness on the southern shore of Lake Michigan and founds the city of Chicago.

July 22, 1782 — A group of Protestant missionaries called Moravians start a settlement along the Clinton River near today's Moravian Hills Country Club. It will be the first European settlement in what is now Macomb County. The Moravians named it New Gnadenhutten, a name that won't stick. After building about 25 dwellings, the Moravians leave in 1786. One of their lasting projects: the first road from roughly Mt. Clemens to Detroit, today's Moravian Drive .

Nov. 8, 1782 — Negotiators in Paris write a treaty that will formally end the Revolutionary War and set the northern boundary of the United States. Canada will lie north of the 45th parallel from the headwaters of the Mississippi east to the south shore of Lake Nipissing, then southwest in a line to the beginning of the St. Lawrence River, then downriver to the 45th parallel and east to the Atlantic. The plan very nearly survives. And if it had: Da Yoopers would be a Canadian band. Alpena

would be a border crossing. And the Maple Leafs would be an American team. Heck, Toronto might even be in Michigan.

July 4, 1783 — American Maj. Ephraim Douglass arrives at Detroit, is greeted cordially by Col. Arent Schuyler De Peyster, the English commander. Douglass wants to speak with a gathering of Indian leaders July 6, to let them know that the new country includes Detroit and Michigan. De Peyster won't allow Douglass to meet the Indians and on July 7, cordially asks Douglass to leave.

The English will control Detroit for 13 more years, charging over that time that they will not abandon their western Great Lakes outposts because of U.S. violations of the treaty. But mostly the English want to continue to reap the proceeds of the lucrative fur trade. Indians are told by the English that the Americans are hostile.

Dec. 26, 1791 — Detroit becomes part of Kent County in Upper Canada.

June 24, 1793 — Jacob Young becomes the first black person to own land in Detroit, a parcel he buys from Joseph Bourdeaux.

Aug. 20, 1794 — American Gen. Anthony Wayne defeats English and Indian force in northern Ohio at the battle of the Fallen Timbers — so named because a tornado days earlier had uprooted many trees. Wayne lays waste to several neighboring Indian villages. For weeks afterwards, the English fear American troops will move north to attack Detroit. But Wayne regroups his troops and the various Indian nations meet the following summer and make peace with the Americans on **Aug. 3, 1795.** At almost the same time, the English sign a treaty surrendering Detroit and other northwestern outposts to the United States.

July 11, 1796 — Sixty-five U.S. troops take control of Detroit. Army Capt. Moses Porter raises the American flag. Detroit is now part of the United States. On July 13, Col. John Hamtramck, first commander of troops in Detroit, arrives. Hamtramck, 38, is 5-foot-5, has a temper and is big on discipline.

John Francis Hamtramck (1758-1803) — Most reburied Detroiter?

The city's first American commander may be the most reburied Detroiter. He died in 1803, was buried in Ste. Anne's graveyard, but his grave was moved to a new graveyard after fire destroyed the city in 1805. It was moved again before a third move in 1866 to a plot in Mt. Elliott Cemetery. The fourth burial was in 1962 in Hamtramck, the city named for him.

July 15, 1796 — Wayne County is established, named for Gen. Anthony Wayne.

Northwest Territory (1787)

On July 11, 1796, 65 U.S. troops take control of Detroit. Army Capt. Moses Porter raises the American flag. Detroit is now part of the United States.

FIND OUT MORE

➤ "The Americans arrive," page 260.

On June 11, 1805, fire destroys Detroit except for a stone building and Ft. Lernoult. Father Gabriel Richard pens in Latin: **Speramus meliora; resurget cineribus** (We hope for better days; it shall rise from its ashes). The city's motto endures today.

FIND OUT MORE

➤ Map of Woodward plan, page 331.

➤ Woodward Avenue, page 236.

➤ Wayne County today, page 312.

➤ William Hull, page 83.

➤ Major fires, page 506.

June 3, 1798 — The Rev. Gabriel Richard, 30, arrives to be assistant pastor at Ste. Anne's. For 34 years, Richard will be a major force in the shaping of Detroit.

July 24, 1801 — Detroit is 100 years old. Few notice.

Jan. 11, 1805 — The Michigan Territory is established with Detroit as its capital. Territorial leaders decide to hold four lotteries to raise $20,000 for civic improvements and to teach reading. But the lotteries are scuttled before the first drawing when no agreement is reached on how to divvy the proceeds.

June 11, 1805 — Fire destroys Detroit except for a stone building and Ft. Lernoult. No lives are lost. Father Gabriel Richard pens in Latin: *Speramus meliora; resurget cineribus.* That is: We hope for better days; it shall rise from its ashes. The city's motto endures today.

Woodward Plan
Judge angles for the future

The stars in the heavens and the streets of the nation's new capital inspire Augustus B. Woodward to map Detroit's wide avenues into their wagon-wheel design.

The chief of the Michigan Territory's first three judges, Woodward arrives in Detroit soon after the fire of 1805.

Within months, he persuades citizens that he could create the best plan for the future, which he bases on the layout of Washington, D.C. (modeled, in turn, after Paris). There are stories that Woodward also spends a month contemplating stars and planets, using their orbits as his guide.

Woodward sees wide boulevards as a central feature of the city, and he names the main thoroughfare for himself. The self-centered eccentric insists, however, that it wasn't vanity but direction that inspires the moniker. "I called it Wood-ward, meaning toward the woods," he says. Uh-huh.

Woodward's plan is based on joining equilateral triangles at spoked "circuses." Homestead lots line the triangles — which are also subdivided into right angles. There are open spaces for education and other purposes. The bisected curves and angles can prove confusing to this day, but some historians contend the only chaos that was created came from those who deviated from Woodward's plan.

Before he can see his vision through, Woodward loses his judgeship when a smear campaign convinces President James Monroe not to renominate him in 1823. Once Monroe learns that political enemies offended by Woodward's power and bullheadedness concocted the stories, the president appoints Woodward to the bench in Florida, where he

Wayne County's evolution

1796 | 1800 (May 7) | 1800 (July 10)

1802 | 1803 | 1805

1815 | 1816 | 1817

1818 | 1822 | 1826

died in 1827.

November 1807 — The United States signs a treaty with several American Indian nations at what is now Brownstown Township, a hamlet on the Detroit River. The Indians cede roughly the southeastern quarter of lower Michigan for about $10,000. Secretary of War Henry Dearborn warned negotiator William Hull, the commander of troops in Detroit, not to budge beyond 2 cents an acre. He doesn't.

The United States fears most Great Lakes area Indians because it suspects they are in cahoots with the British. Many are. But Hull is a skilled negotiator and genuinely wants to befriend the Indians.

He promises to supply a blacksmith to the Indians for 10 years to meet their horseshoe and weapon needs and continues to support a school run by Father Gabriel Richard to teach English to them. Among the naysayers: Chief Tecumseh and his brother, the Prophet, so named because he claimed to be in touch with "the Master of Life." Both warn Indians to stay clear of Americans.

1809 — Father Gabriel Richard imports

the first printing press to Detroit. He publishes one edition of a newspaper. But while the newspaper fizzles, Richard continues to crank out pamphlets. One urges the United States to open trade with China.

War of 1812

Detroit surrenders to a British force that bluffs its way to victory. Weeks after the United States declared war on Britain, Detroit commander William Hull leads a force across the river to attack the British at Ft. Malden south of Windsor. But he suddenly returns without engaging the enemy when he hears a supply line near Monroe has been breached.

The British plan a ruse, stirring up false rumors about troop strength. The British commander, who had about 5,000 Indians on his side, also sends Hull a missive that if Detroit falls in battle, the Indians would probably slaughter the inhabitants. Hull chooses caution and surrenders without a shot on Aug. 13, 1812. The British occupy Detroit for more than a year, but leave the city after numerous defeats in the region.

Hull is hauled before a court-martial and found derelict of duty, but is spared a firing squad because of his distinguished service during the Revolutionary War.

Hull's Detroit surrender becomes his legacy of shame, although historians later write that Hull was correct in choosing to avoid a possible Indian massacre.

Winter 1815 — A grateful nation wants to reward War of 1812 veterans by parceling out 2 million acres of land. Government surveyor Edward Tiffin and crew check out land north of today's 8 Mile Road to see if it's a fitting gift.

Tiffin says no way. It's marshy, probably buggy and not suitable for crops or much anything else. In criticizing what would someday become Oakland County, Tiffin's report for years is cited by Easterners as good enough reason to avoid Michigan.

1816 — Workers begin a road linking Detroit to the settlement at Pontiac, forerunner of Woodward Avenue.

June 30, 1816 — The Rev. John Monteith, 27, newly graduated from Princeton University, gives his first sermon in Detroit. A Presbyterian, Monteith spends five years in Detroit before moving to New York. But his time here is active:

Aug. 26, 1817 — The Rev. Monteith, Father Richard and Judge Woodward establish a college that eventually is named the University of Michigan — which is why U-M's main number is 734-764-**1817**. The university opens on Bates between Larned and Congress. Monteith is president and professor of six courses; Richard is vice president and also teaches six courses. Woodward is also a professor. Monteith and Richard forgo the mistrust and quiet hostility that exists between Christian denominations and work together well.

Dec. 29, 1817 — The Moral and Human Society becomes Detroit's first charitable organization.

March 31, 1818 — Protestants open a church, their first in Michigan. It is near today's River Rouge. Protestants have been holding services in Detroit since the 1760s when England ran the city, but the services are in public buildings or homes. The first Protestant church in Detroit opens on Woodward north of Larned on Feb. 27, 1820.

July 6, 1818 — The first public auction of land in Michigan is held in Detroit. Average price: $4 an acre.

Oct. 29, 1818 — John Hersey buys land on Paint Creek in what is now Oakland County and builds a sawmill, thus becoming first official land holder in the county.

Jan 12, 1819 — Territorial governor Lewis Cass sets the boundaries for Oakland County, at twice its current size. On **March 28, 1820**, Cass makes Pontiac the county seat and three months later divides the county into Oakland

Burton Historical Collection

The British capture Detroit during the War of 1812. Commander William Hull is vilified for decades because he surrenders with city with nary a shot fired.

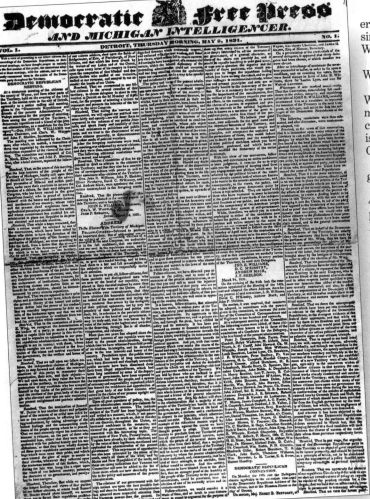

Drum roll, please. The very first edition of the Free Press appears May 5, 1831.

FIND OUT MORE

➤ Free Press history, page 450.

➤ Detroit's other rivers, page 145.

Election of '23

Priest's path crosses John R

Businessman John R. Williams wants to represent Michigan in Congress. The field in 1823 narrows to Williams, businessman John Biddle and Wayne County Sheriff Austin Wing.

Williams, a Catholic and nephew of the town's richest man, Joseph Campau, consid-

Township and Bloomfield Township. The 1820 census records 59 families in the county. On **April 27, 1827**, the county is reorganized into five townships: Farmington, Troy, Oakland, Bloomfield and Pontiac.

ers himself a foregone conclusion, especially since he'll sew up the heavily Catholic vote in Wayne and Monroe counties.

Lo, Father Gabriel Richard decides to run. Williams goes ballistic.

Richard lets parishioners pillory Williams and other opponents. But four months before the Sept. 3 election, Williams charges that Richard, a native of France, isn't a U.S. citizen and therefore can't run for Congress.

The priest petitions for citizenship and is granted the status June 28.

Richard wins with 444 votes to Biddle's 421, Wing's 335 and Williams' 51. Nobody in protestant-heavy Oakland County votes for Richard.

An angry Williams and Campau leave the Catholic Church.

Today, Campau's Catholic relatives are buried in Mt. Elliott, the oldest Catholic cemetery in Detroit. Campau — and Williams — are buried across the fence in Elmwood Cemetery, the Protestant graveyard.

In **1825**, Richard loses re-election by four votes to Wing.

Sept. 6, 1824 — John R. Williams becomes Detroit's first elected mayor, tallying 102 votes to his opponents' collective 11. The first elected council — they're called aldermen — consists of Shubael Conant, Orville Cook, Peter Desnoyers, Melvin Dorr and David McKinstry. At the council's first meeting, **Sept. 21, 1824**, members vote to buy four brass candlesticks, two snuffers, 10 pounds of sperm candles and a box to store the stuff to provide light for the meetings.

October 1825 — The Erie Canal, a 363-mile waterway across New York from Albany to Lake Erie at Buffalo is completed. Thousands of Easterners soon use the waterway as a rapid route west, cutting expenses by nearly 80 percent. The canal is to Detroit in the 19th Century what the automobile industry will be in the 20th: the entity that spurs rapid growth for the city and region.

1826 — Downtown Detroit as we know it today begins to take shape. Ft. Shelby is demolished. The streets that define downtown west of Woodward are constructed over several years.

1827 — The Savoyard River is altered. It once ran west from about the site of today's 1300 Lafayette apartment building in Lafayette Park to near Third and Congress where it headed south to the Detroit River. But by 1827, the Savoyard is becoming a sewer. Locals say that's a shame since its 8-foot depth near Woodward and Congress made for good fishing. It's filled in and becomes an underground sewerage line in **1836**.

1829 — Work begins on a road from Detroit to Chicago. No orange barrels are posted. The road is finished in 1836, but it's no travelers' treat — little more than logs covered by dirt. If a coach had fast horses and dry weather, it might make the 300-mile trip in six days.

May 5, 1831 — The Michigan Intelligencer and Democratic Free Press, later named the Detroit Free Press, starts publishing. The Free Press is the oldest continually operated business in Detroit.

March 8, 1833 — The Catholic Church establishes a diocese with Detroit as its center. The diocese includes today's Michigan, Wisconsin, Minnesota and parts of the Dakotas. It's first bishop is Frederic Rese. In **1837**, the diocese shrinks to the size of the newly named state of Michigan.

Nov. 18, 1835 — The first Detroit City Hall opens. The building is 50 feet by 100 feet, and fits roughly in today's eastbound lane of Cadillac Square near the Soldiers and Sailors Monument. The first floor is a meat market. Some city offices are on the second floor, and the city council meets on the top floor in chambers often used for church services, theater productions and other meetings.

On **July 4, 1871**, a new city hall is dedicated on Woodward between Michigan Avenue and Fort Street. Kennedy Square is there today. That site had been a train terminal. The building is demolished in **1961** and city offices are moved to the then just-completed City-County Building.

1836 — Detroit is a boomtown. Lewis Cass has already subdivided much of his farmland on the western edge of the city. Land-hungry Easterners are paying $1,000 an acre for land about one mile north of the river up Woodward — near the site of today's Comerica Park.

The riverfront cove where baptisms are held in summer and ice-skaters play in winter is filled in. The work is the first alteration to the shoreline. The cove existed inland and would today swallow Cobo Area and the Veterans Memorial Building.

March 5, 1836 — Thirteen people who were escaped or freed slaves petition the legislature for a church, leading to the formation in **1839** of Second Baptist Church — the first black church in Detroit.

April 3, 1837 — Detroit is no longer a boomtown. Land speculation leads to increased building and demand for carpenters, who pulled in good money. But a depression sets in and wages are cut while hours are extended. Carpenters strike, demanding $2 for a 10-hour day. Shoemakers — in a union called the Detroit Cordwainers Association — strike in 1838, demanding more money.

1838 — Some 300 refugees from Canada come to Detroit to plan the overthrow of the Canadian government. Numerous Detroiters sympathize with the rebels, called Patriots, leading the U.S. government to order troops to the city to enforce neutrality laws.

But Patriots raid local arsenals, confiscate a steamer and set out in early January to invade Canada. They fail, their leaders are arrested, the steamer is confiscated and several Patriots are killed by British and Canadian troops in skirmishes on several islands near the mouth of the Detroit River.

Patriots try again in December, crossing the Detroit River and attacking a garrison in Windsor while soldiers slept. Several Canadians were burned to death, other soldiers were shot dead fleeing their barracks. But the Canadians overwhelmed the Patriots, summarily executing four.

July 20, 1838 — Investors begin to dig a canal across Michigan, linking water traffic on Lake St. Clair with Lake Michigan. Pickaxes and shovels are used to start a 216-mile project that begins near the Clinton River and Moravian Road in Macomb County. When finished, the plan is to include the Kalamazoo and Grand rivers and then Lake Michigan. Alas, rail transportation makes a canal a relic. The project is halted in **1843** after it plods only as far as Rochester.

1841 — A school for black children opens in the basement of Second Baptist Church. There are 88 students.

March 15, 1842 — The Detroit Board of Education is organized.

1843 — Detroit & Pontiac RR completes track. Before the railroad, a journey from Detroit to Pontiac took 10 hours on horseback. That time is cut in half, but the train excursion is often frustrating because conductors stop frequently to shoot the breeze with farmers.

June 9, 1845 — St. Vincent's, formed by four Catholic nuns of the Sisters of Charity, becomes the region's first hospital. It's built on the southwest corner of Randolph and Larned. A parking lot for city council members is there today. First patient: an indigent, Robert Bridgeman. The hospital moves to Clinton Street in **1850** and is renamed St. Mary's and later Detroit Memorial Hospital.

FIND OUT MORE

➤ Gabriel Richard, page 603.

➤ The Border, page 296.

Frederic Rese is named the first Catholic bishop of the Detroit diocese in 1833.

Free Press file photo

Detroiters gather on Griswold near Larned in late spring 1861 for news about the Civil War. That's the old state capitol in the upper right. By the time of the Civil War, it is the city's high school.

1848 — Lewis Cass runs as a Democrat for president but loses to Zachary Taylor.

Sept. 22, 1850 — There are about 50 Jews in Detroit, half from Germany and most of the rest from venues in the United States. Among them are Issac and Sarah Cozens and their five children. In time for the high holy days, the Cozens gather 12 other German Jews and form an Orthodox congregation that on **April 21, 1851**, was formally named Beth El. They meet in a private home.

1851 — One hundred and fifty years after its founding, Detroit is a city of about 26,000 people. There are about 600 brick buildings and 4,000 wood buildings in the city — 286 of those buildings are selling groceries, provisions or liquor.

March 12, 1859 — Abolitionist

John Brown

John Brown arrives in Detroit with 14 people who escaped slavery in Missouri. Brown meets Frederick Douglass — and later hatches his ill-fated plan to attack Harpers Ferry, W.Va. Brown will be captured there and hanged for treason.

April, 1859 — The first national billiards championship is held in Detroit. Winner Michael Phelan of New York takes home $15,000.

Jan. 16, 1860 — Detroit's only high school allows girls to enroll. Student body: 85 pupils.

March 12, 1861 — The Detroit Police Department is formed. But the first uniformed street patrol takes place **May 15, 1865**. Presumably, the Civil War delayed deployment of police.

May 13, 1861 — Michigan's first

Burton Historical Collection

Troops of Michigan's 2nd Regiment drill at Ft. Wayne in June 1861.

Burton Historical Collection

On April 25, 1865, Detroiters gather at Campus Martius for a memorial service for the assassinated President Abraham Lincoln.

FIND OUT MORE

➤ Lewis Cass, pages 251, 275.

➤ Black Detroit, page 103.

➤ Detroit Police, page 484.

➤ Oakland County today, page 302.

troops enlisted to fight in the Civil War arrive in Washington. "Thank God for Michigan," President Abraham Lincoln tells them.

Dec. 30, 1861 — A speed limit is set for city streets: 6 m.p.h.

Jan. 6, 1863 — The Emancipation Proclamation is celebrated at Second Baptist Church.

Feb. 3, 1863 — Negro Regiment Law is passed allowing blacks to serve in the Union Army. The First Michigan Colored Infantry Regiment is formed in Detroit. It's called the Corps d'Afrique by the Free Press. The regiment's 1,446 officers and men see battle in South Carolina, Georgia and Florida.

May 4, 1863 — Harper Hospital opens as a military hospital.

Dec. 28, 1863 — Oakland County's manpower contribution to the Civil War trails the rest of Michigan, so residents in Troy Town-

ship vote overwhelmingly for a tax to raise enough cash to offer $100 bonuses to volunteers.

When the war began, abolitionist Gov. Moses Wisner, a Pontiac resident, resigned to lead a troop of Michigan infantry. His barn was torched, some say by locals upset with the war's sentiment of freeing blacks. Wisner, 47, dies of typhoid in Kentucky in 1863.

May 10, 1865 — Lt. Julian Dickinson of Detroit and men of Michigan's 4th Cavalry capture Confederate President Jefferson Davis near Irwinsville, Ga.

1870 — Eighty-eight percent of Oakland County's population — some 35,000 people — live on farms.

April 7, 1870 — The 15th Amendment is ratified by the Michigan legislature prohibiting any state from denying the right to vote to anyone (except women). Many Detroit blacks, and a number of whites, celebrate the ratification. A cannon fired at 10 a.m., kicks off a parade. The crowd also attends a rally

William Lambert

at the Opera House. The show ends with a song by Detroiter William Lambert, "The Martyr's Triumph..."

J.L. Hudson's first store on Campus Martius in the late 1880s.

A HUDSON GENEOLOGY

J.L. Hudson was a bachelor. When he died in 1912, control of the company passed to nephews whom he had been grooming. They were Oscar, Richard, Joseph L. and James Webber, the sons of J.L.'s sister. As the Webber brothers grew older in the 1950s, they groomed J.L. (Joe) Hudson Jr., the current community leader. Joe Hudson's grandfather was J.L. Hudson's brother. That makes the original J.L. Hudson the great uncle of Joe Hudson. Joe Hudson's father was J.L. Hudson II.

Due to an early 20th Century marriage, Joe Hudson is also the second cousin of Lions' owner William Clay Ford Sr.

FIND OUT MORE

"Freedom reigns today!
The ballot box has come;
Now let us all prepare to vote
With the party that makes us free . . . Hallelujah."

Blacks vote for the first time on Nov. 8, 1870, and are called to jury duty for the first time, too.

Nov. 29, 1870 — Human rights champion Susan B. Anthony speaks to the Northwestern Women's Suffrage Association in Detroit, praising the city for its ties to the Underground Railroad. She reminds Detroiters that poverty among emancipated people means "every year, 400,000 children are born in the condition of slaves."

Susan B. Anthony

April 1871 — Detroiter Nanette Gardner becomes the first woman in Michigan to vote. She earlier petitioned the city's Board of Representatives that she must vote because there was no one to look after her interests. The board voted 12-6 to let her vote. Forty-nine years later, all U.S. women were given the right to vote.

Sept. 3, 1877 — Jesuits open Detroit College in a house on the south side of Jefferson downtown. In **1911**, it's renamed the University of Detroit. In 1990, it merges with Mercy College to become Detroit Mercy.

July 4, 1877 — Cornerstone is installed at St. Antoine and Congress for Congregation Shaarey Zedek. It will be the first Jewish synagogue building erected in Detroit. The city's Jewish community is spread through much of the near east side and just north of Grand Circus Park.

April 8, 1879 — City agrees to buy Belle Isle for $200,000 from its owners, various members of the Campau family. The island is the first major city park in Detroit. In 1884, construction of a grand boulevard begins to run from Belle Isle to West Jefferson, 11.3 miles around the city proper.

1880 — As the city and region prosper, Detroit becomes a diverse economic center. The leading industry: cigars.

April 2, 1881 — Retailer J.L. Hudson, 35, opens his first store downtown, a haberdashery, on Campus Martius. On **Sept. 17, 1891,** he opens a department store at Gratiot and Farmer.

1885-87 — For 18 months, going to mass at St. Albertus Catholic Church seemed anything but serene. One person was killed and many injured in fights with police during that period after Bishop Caspar Borgess removed the charismatic and controversial priest, the Rev. Dominic Kolasinski. In one of the first standoffs, a mob of parishioners grabbed the new priest and threw him out of the church. Police finally had to stand guard so the priest could celebrate mass while parishioners were "leaning over the communion rail, yelling and brandishing fists," a newspaper reported.

Kolasinski returned to Detroit in 1888 and took dozens of St. Albertus parishioners with him when he founded Sweetest Heart of Mary, in defiance of the hierarchy. In response, Bishop John Foley sponsored a third Polish Catholic church, St. Josaphat.

If anything, the controversy certainly speaks of the densely populated and steadily growing Polish community in the late 19th Century. All three churches have East Canfield as a common link. St. Albertus, at Chene and East Canfield, is a tad over half a mile east of St. Josaphat on Canfield at the Chrysler Freeway. Sweetest Heart of Mary is on Russell at Canfield and is the largest Catholic Church in Detroit, with capacity for 2,500.

On any Sunday in, say, 1923, each church held several masses, each mass well attended.

1887 — The Salvation Army opens a headquarters at Cadillac Square. The members aren't well received, usually laughed at by Detroiters unaccustomed to the demonstrative proselytizing of the Salvationists. Detroit City Council passes a order that "no man may make a speech or blow a horn or beat a drum within a half-mile of City Hall." The Army is their target. Lt. Col. Blanche Cox gets tossed into the Detroit House of Correction 12 times for breaking the law by preaching in Cadillac Square.

Sept. 1, 1888 — Detroit Museum of Art, forerunner of the Detroit Institute of Arts, opens at Jefferson and Hastings.

Feb. 3, 1889 — The Hammond Building is completed. At 10 stories, it is the city's first skyscraper. And, yes, it is a big deal. People come from miles just to gaze from the lofty

height that rose at the southeast corner of Griswold and Fort. The building was demolished in 1956.

June 6, 1894 — D-Day. Mayor Hazen S. Pingree declares war on the economic depression that struck the nation in 1893 and by now has put one of three Detroit workers on relief rolls. He announces a plan to allow citizens to plant potatoes on city land, and urges a fund drive in the community to buy seed. Pingree later auctions his prize horse, Josie Wilkes, for $387 — about $1,000 *less* than the animal's worth — to raise money for seed. Pingree's assault on poverty and hunger amid the financial downturn is a success. On 430 acres of land scattered about the city, 945 families produce $14,000 worth of food.

March 6, 1896 — Charles B. King drives first auto in Detroit.

March 20, 1897 — The Michigan Supreme Court rules that Pingree can't serve as both mayor and governor, a post he recently won at the polls. So Pingree quits the mayor's job.

1900 — There is much talk about the progress Ransom Olds, Henry Ford and others are making with the horseless carriage. Soon, what's shared between friends and chatted about over fences becomes a roar across the region.

Not that the automobile is *that* new. Major American and European cities in the 1890s are getting used to cars. But Detroit . . .

Consider: The automobile show in Chicago in 1900 displays only one car from Detroit — an Oldsmobile. An auto show that same year in New York has zilch from Detroit. Hundreds of small automobile companies are scattered in cities in the Midwest and New Eng-

land by 1905. Yet, they would diminish, and Detroit would prevail. Between 1900 and 1920, 245 automobile companies would start up in Michigan — 125 of them in Detroit.

July 24, 1901 — Pageants and a huge parade south on Woodward herald Detroit's Bicentennial. The city of nearly 300,000 boasts of its French and English heritage while absorbing increasing numbers of immigrants from eastern and southern Europe and the Near East. But revelers along Woodward that day had no clue of the awesome changes soon to hit their fair, provincial city. The community with a diverse economy, stable neighborhoods, many green spaces, a progressive political culture and a first-class opera house was about to become the Motor City.

May 5, 1903 — Booker T. Washington tells an enthusiastic audience at the Light Guard Armory: "Any race that yields to the temptation of hating another race because of its color weakens and narrows itself. Wherever I can I propose to teach my people to take high ground, to teach them if others would be little, we must be great, if others must be mean, we must be good, if others should try to push us down, we must show a broader spirit and help push them up."

His solution for racial harmony:

"One farm bought, one house built, one home sweetly and intelligently kept . . . one school or church maintained, one factory running successfully . . . one patient cured by a Negro doctor, one sermon well-preached, one life cleanly lived, these will tell more in our favor than all the abstract eloquence that can be summoned to bleed our cause."

The old City Hall, as shown in 1910, was demolished in 1961. Today it's the site of Kennedy Square. Detroit's first skyscraper, the Hammond Building, is to the left at Fort and Griswold.

> "Any race that yields to the temptation of hating another race because of its color weakens and narrows itself..."
>
> — **Booker T. Washington** in 1903

Burton Historical Collection

Above: A bustling Detroit in 1927 is shown looking west on Michigan Avenue at Cass.

Right: Detroit police in one of the department's first patrol cars in 1908. The coppers: driver Patrolman William Schrimer, Patrolman William Savory in the rear and Detective Dave Thomas.

FIND OUT MORE

➤ Henry Ford, pages 165, 203, 347, 610.

➤ Classic cars, page 223.

Burton Historical Collection

June 16, 1903 — Henry Ford forms the Ford Motor Co. On **Oct. 1, 1908**, the Model T goes on the market.

June 1, 1910 — Horace and John Dodge break ground on a car parts factory in Hamtramck. By the time Dodge Main is deemed obsolete and closed in **1980**, it will have grown to 33 buildings and 5 million square feet, employing 40,000 workers a day at its height in the 1940s. Dodge Main remakes Hamtramck, too, from a sleepy town to a city of nearly 50,000 by 1920, most of its population recent immigrants from Poland. So Polish is the city that the workday language in Dodge Main during World War II is Polish.

Jan. 5, 1914 — Henry Ford announces he'll pay workers $5 a day, nearly doubling the best daily rate for skilled workers.

Jan. 21, 1915 — Some downtown merchants and professionals form a benevolent club and plan to call themselves the Benevolent Order Brothers. That moniker is rejected when one member says recruiting would be tough. "Who'd want to belong to an organization called BOB?" The name selected instead: Kiwanis, for an American-Indian phrase that means "we get together." The club becomes the first Kiwanis Club in the world. Today there are more than 8,500 globally. No. 1 still meets, twice monthly, at the Detroit Athletic Club. Membership: 43.

Oct 13, 1916 — General Motors is incorporated. By **1921**, the automaker builds what is then the world's largest office building on Grand Boulevard.

April 30, 1918 — The state goes dry. Days earlier, about 1,250 bars operate in Detroit. Police are antsy as the Prohibition dictum takes effect. But there are no riots, just a ton of last-minute drinking. For many months, Detroit seems to be coping well without liquor. But soon, by the tally of police and newspapers, illegal drinking joints climb into the thousands — 16,000 to 25,000 by one estimate in 1928. And the import (from Canada) and export of illegal hooch becomes the city's second-largest industry after cars.

Oct. 1, 1918 — Schools, theaters and other public buildings close for one month because of flu. Influenza is a major cause of death in the early 20th Century.

1919 — The Founders Society at the Detroit Institute of Arts is established. First gift: "Girl With Kitten" by William Juen.

Oct. 22, 1919 — Orchestra Hall opens to choruses of huzzahs and a 5-minute standing O. The first piece played in the new hall: "The Star-Spangled Banner."

1920 — Eighty percent of Oakland County is farmland.

Nov. 6, 1923 — The Ku Klux Klan burns a cross at Detroit City Hall.

Sept. 9, 1925 — A crowd of people, some hurling rocks, protests African-American Dr. Ossian Sweet moving into a mostly white neighborhood on the city's east side. When shots are fired from inside the house killing a spectator, police arrest Sweet and several others. All are acquitted in Judge Frank Murphy's courtroom with famed lawyer Clarence Darrow as defense attorney.

Image problem?

What image problem?

"There are no tenements in Detroit. Wages are high, hours of labor are short. The schools are a boast of American education."
— World's Work Magazine, 1927.

In the Roaring '20s, Detroit becomes America's showcase city. The auto industry rules — and the money flows almost unabated. New construction, modern schools and modern approaches to city life left the national news media spellbound.

Olympia Stadium, the Detroit Institute of Arts, and the University of Detroit campus at McNichols and Livernois all opened in 1927. Within a year, the Detroit Zoo, the Penobscot Building and Fisher Building opened, too.

But all was not great.

"The city has its areas of bad housing," the New York Times wrote in 1927. "It has not provided adequately for its colored population of more than 83,000 — almost 90 percent of which have come here since" World War I.

And growing like a social cancer during those good times: corruption in city government, the influence of the Ku Klux Klan and unrest among workers in the auto plants.

Feb. 24, 1928 — Detroit makes marijuana possession illegal.

June 10, 1929 — Eighty-five percent of illegal booze enters the United States along the Detroit River, federal agents say, as they push for more help policing the border.

Oct. 21, 1929 — The Henry Ford Museum

Free Press file photo

Eastern Market in 1932. It is just as busy today.

& Greenfield Village are opened; President Herbert Hoover attends the dedication.

November 1929 — Despite the gyrations on Wall Street the previous month, the region feels financially secure. Brokerage firms buy full-page newspaper ads to assure Detroit clients the markets are stable. Detroit's workers are the most productive in the country — producing $9,500 of goods annually, nearly $1,000 more than second-place St. Louis. And the city can boast of several new housing developments — on top of a banner decade of home building.

These exciting days would end with the Great Depression. As auto production plummeted, so did the average yearly wage of an auto worker, from about $1,600 in 1929 to about $1,000 in 1933. At the Ford Rouge plant, workers making 92 cents an hour in 1929 were collecting 59 cents an hour in 1933.

Detroit's Department of Public Relief listed about 156,000 people on its rolls in late 1929. By mid-1930, the number had skyrocketed: 728,000 — nearly half the population.

On **Nov. 1, 1929**, two priests of the Capuchin order, Solanus Casey and Herman Buss, open a soup kitchen at the St. Bonaventure Monastery on Mt. Elliott. It would be temporary, they figure. It has never closed.

Nov. 15, 1929 — The Ambassador Bridge

FIND OUT MORE

➤ Famous factories, page 164.

➤ Prohibition, page 495.

➤ Whiskey and beer, page 545.

➤ Solanus Casey, page 604.

FIND OUT MORE

➤ Frank Murphy, pages 45, 109, 264.

➤ Ford Hunger March, page 176.

➤ Unions, page 170.

Free Press file photo

The soup kitchen at St. Bonaventure Monastery on Mt. Elliott in 1938.

Burton Historical Collection

Cable is strung for the Ambassador Bridge. The bridge, shown facing Windsor, opened in 1929.

opens to traffic. For nearly two years the suspension bridge — 1,850 feet between towers — is the longest in the world, until the George Washington Bridge opens in New York (3,500 feet) in 1931. The nearly mile-long Detroit-Windsor Tunnel opens **Nov 3, 1930**.

April 5, 1930 — City Airport opens at Gratiot and Conner.

July 22, 1930 — Mayor Charles Bowles is recalled, the first big-city mayor broomed from office in the United States. His term lasts just over seven months. He's broomed for various levels of incompetence, mostly for his failure as a law and order candidate to bring law and order to a gang-riddled city. His solution: let the criminals kill each other in gang warfare.

March 7, 1932 — Some 3,000 workers march on Ford's Dearborn plant demanding jobs. Rioting erupts; five workers are killed.

July 25, 1932 — Diego Rivera, the leftist artist from Mexico, begins his now-famous murals at the Detroit Institute of Arts.

April 3, 1933 — Michigan, the first state to vote for Prohibition, becomes the first state to ratify the 18th Amendment to the Constitution, repealing Prohibition.

Aug. 26, 1935 — The United Auto Workers is organized.

May 22, 1937 — UAW organizers, including Walter Reuther, are attacked and beaten by Ford Motor Co. security men at the Miller Road overpass that carries workers into the massive Ford Rouge plant in Dearborn. The bloodied union workers become symbols for workers now more determined than ever to bring a union to Ford.

June 22, 1938 — In a punch heard 'round the world, Detroiter Joe Louis knocks out Max Schmeling in the first round of their title fight. Schmeling, a German, is the Nazi government's symbol of Aryan superiority, a shoe-in to defeat the African-American Louis. With Louis' knockout, Detroit erupts in celebration.

Nov. 19, 1938 — More than 5,000 Detroiters gather at the Naval Armory for a prayer service and to protest Nazi treatment of Jews. "You just can't remain silent in the face of evil," Gov. Frank Murphy tells the crowd. The crowd votes on a resolution that the United States help resettle Germany's Jews and place an embargo on goods made in Germany.

Sept. 6, 1940 — Michigan Supreme Court rules that women and men doing the same work should receive equal pay.

April 11, 1941 — Ford recognizes the United Auto Workers as the bargaining agent for its workers and signs a contract.

World War II:
Detroit as the Arsenal of Democracy

Tanks, trucks, shells, planes — a multitude of weaponry is manufactured as factories operate around the clock.

As the region's younger men enter military service, thousands of women enter the blue-collar and skilled trades to weld, rivet and wrench. Again, the need for workers draws thousands of people to the city, predominately blacks from the South.

But the region's failure to be all-inclusive leads to racial polarization that plagues southeastern Michigan today.

The war years in Detroit:

Dec. 12, 1941 — At 4 a.m., a telegram is delivered to the Marsh family in Grosse Pointe. It says Navy Ensign Ben Marsh Jr., 25, was killed in action aboard the battleship USS Arizona at Pearl Harbor, Hawaii. Marsh becomes the Detroit area's first reported casualty of World War II.

Feb. 9, 1942 — Automobile assembly lines switch to total war production.

Feb. 28, 1942 — Scores of people are injured in race rioting near the Sojourner Truth public housing project, on Nevada east of Ryan. Neighboring whites don't accept the pocket of blacks in their midst.

April 20, 1942 — German immigrant Max Stephan is arrested for treason for helping an escaped Luftwaffe POW. Stephan, owner of a restaurant at East Jefferson and Grand Boulevard, escorts the POW, Hans Peter Krug through Detroit's German community after Krug reaches the city following an escape from a compound near Toronto. Stephan puts Krug on a bus for Chicago and is arrested the following day. Krug is later recaptured in San Antonio. Stephan is found guilty and sentenced to death; President Franklin D. Roosevelt commutes the penalty to life in prison, where Stephan dies of cancer in 1952. Krug was repatriated after the war.

Stephan's trial at federal court in Detroit is a spectacle with Krug, 22, brought to testify in his German uniform, a air of smugness and defiance on his face.

More than 50 years later, Krug writes a Free Press reporter that he remembered Stephan as a hapless man, but Detroit as an interesting city.

May 15, 1942 — Ford's B24 bomber plant at Willow Run begins operation. The plant, like hundreds of war factories across the country, will employ many women in manufacturing jobs. About 3 of every 4 working women are older than 35, and more than half are married and mothers.

July 25, 1942 — FBI and local police raid 120 homes in the Detroit area belonging to German and Italian immigrants. The next day, 60 more homes are raided. Only one person is arrested, but the FBI confiscates aerial photographs, Nazi flags and literature, 181 cameras, 106 shortwave radios, 73 firearms and hundreds of rounds of ammunition.

Aug. 7, 1942 — Life Magazine writes that labor unrest in Detroit has caused "a morale perhaps the worst in the U.S. ... Detroit can either blow up Hitler or it can blow up the U.S."

April 17, 1943 — Civil rights leader Bayard Rustin and 75 Detroiters visit several restaurants and public places to check on discrimination. Race relations are tense as thousands of Southern whites and blacks stream into the city for war jobs. There is not enough housing, and Detroit officials refuse to integrate public housing.

June 3, 1943 — White workers in Detroit strike for three days at Packard Motor war plants because three blacks are hired to work next to them. Thurgood Marshall, the attorney for the National Association for the Advancement of Colored People, who visits Detroit, charges that the Ku Klux Klan and Nazi agents are promoting race hatred.

June 20, 1943 — Nearly three days of race rioting begin. When it ends, 34 people are dead. On **June 21**, Gov. Harry Kelly orders martial law in Detroit. The Army moves in by 10 p.m. In the end, local black leaders will

Free Press file photo

Joyous Ford Rouge workers celebrate the end of World War II after Japan surrenders Aug. 14, 1945.

FIND OUT MORE

➤ Joe Louis, page 553.

➤ Riots, page 515.

➤ Willow Run bomber plant, page 170.

➤ Medal of Honor winners, page 75.

➤ Diego Rivera, page 422.

Free Press file photo

Downtown shoppers hold a Free Press proclaiming the end of World War II. The war years in Detroit brought fame to the city as the Arsenal of Democracy — and shame, too, in the race rioting of 1943.

FIND OUT MORE

➤ Eddie Slovik, page 83.

➤ Walter Reuther, pages 49, 173.

➤ Detroit census, page 289.

➤ Jerry Cavanagh, pages 111, 253, 265.

➤ Malcolm X, page 70.

charge that Detroit police treated blacks brutally during the melee. Army Brig. Gen. William Guther, in charge of troops in Detroit to quell the riot, concurs:

Detroit's nearly all-white force of 3,400 officers had "been very harsh and brutal. They have treated the Negroes terribly," he later reports. "They have gone altogether too far."

Aug. 24, 1943 — FBI agents arrest six people in Detroit as Nazi spies. All but one are convicted and sentenced to prison terms.

Oct. 2, 1943 — White America has denied blacks a productive role in the war, Howard University President Dr. Mordecai Johnson says in a speech to 3,000 Detroiters.

Jan. 1, 1944 — Detroit leads the nation in war production during 1943, landing $14 billion worth of contracts, about 10 percent of U.S. war spending. About 610,000 people work in Detroit area factories producing war material.

Thanks in part to plentiful jobs, Detroit's tri-county population swells to about 2.7 million, up 300,000 from 1940.

Jan. 30, 1944 — Three million Jews have been murdered in Nazi death camps, U.S. Supreme Court Justice Frank Murphy tells the country. Roosevelt appoints Murphy, former Detroit mayor and Michigan governor, head of the National Committee Against Nazi Persecution and Extermination of the Jews.

Feb. 28, 1944 — Willow Run workers reach Henry Ford's goal of producing a bomber an hour. Ford will make more B24 bombers in the first three months of 1944 than it had the two previous years.

March 27, 1944 — Detroit area police often battle teen gangs wearing floppy, baggy clothing called zoot suits. In Warren, police charge zoot-suited gang members with the murder of a war plant worker outside a bar on Van Dyke. Police say some gangs have 100 members.

March 30, 1944 — Detroit police blast lax regulations that allow trailer parks to flourish in the suburbs. The parks, police say, often are havens for missing girls; nearly 3,100 girls age 17 and under are reported missing in Detroit in 1943. Many are dubbed Victory Girls and Khaki Whackies. Police say the girls seek servicemen to sleep with, viewing their trysts as patriotic service.

June 13, 1944 — In Detroit, 10,000 housing units for black workers are needed, and Mayor Edward Jeffries urges suburbs to build them. About 20,000 blacks work in Detroit's suburbs. He doesn't address integration, which he opposes.

Meanwhile, a national Realtors association report urges the nation's banks to make mortgage money available to blacks, saying "The Negro is a good economic risk."

June 15, 1944 — The special committee Jeffries appointed to study Detroit's race problems after the 1943 riot makes recommendations: more parks, better rush-hour supervision on city streetcars and buses and education programs about black people's contributions to American life.

Jan. 31, 1945 — Detroiter Pvt. Eddie Slovik, convicted of desertion by an Army court, is tied to a stake in a French courtyard and executed. Hit by 11 bullets, the 24-year-old dies 3 minutes later, the only U.S. serviceman executed for desertion during World War II.

July 22, 1945 — Detroit's Interracial Committee issues a report saying available housing for blacks is tight, and public transportation is overcrowded. Also, it says Detroit's image is suffering because of rumors that blacks entering the city in droves are planning riots and are prompting hordes of whites to leave. The report suggests that community organizations be formed to improve race relations.

Aug. 15, 1945 — V-J Day, Victory in Japan. America celebrates. In Detroit, two boys are killed and 53 people injured during victory celebrations.

Sept. 2, 1945 — Formal surrender by Japan ends World War II. Detroit's popular son, U.S. Supreme Court Justice Frank Murphy speaks from City Hall to a crowd of 5,000. America's triumph will ring hollow if racial hatred continues, he says.

"Unless we cleanse our hearts of hate — racial and religious — this war will only be half-won. We still have to stand guard against those in our midst who have been nurtured on the myths of the superior and inferior races and who practice discrimination against fellow Americans because of the color of their skin."

Postwar Detroit

April 7, 1947 — Henry Ford, 83, dies in a candlelit room at his Fair Lane mansion in Dearborn.

April 20, 1948 — An unknown gunman fires a 12-gauge shotgun through the kitchen window of Walter Reuther's northwest Detroit home, critically wounding the UAW president in an assassination attempt.

May 3, 1948 — The U.S. Supreme Court rules racial covenants in housing are unconstitutional. The case comes from Detroit.

The unanimous decision rules courts cannot enforce real-estate covenants that bar blacks from all-white neighborhoods. The case involved, in part, a black couple from Detroit whose white neighbors filed a lawsuit against them because the property deed at 4626 Seebaldt carried a whites-only clause. Orsel and Minnie McGhee lose in state court. Thurgood Marshall, later to be a U.S. Supreme Court justice, argues the case before the Supreme Court. A headline on a related story in the Free Press the next day attempts to calm the fears of white readers. It says: "Migration of Minorities within Detroit Doubted."

Dec. 30, 1949 — Mary V. Beck becomes the first female member of the Detroit City Council.

March 22, 1954 — Northland opens, the first regional shopping center. Eastland, in Harper Woods, which opened in 1957, was actually scheduled to be the first regional shopping center. While Northland is **Mary Beck** expected to serve rapidly growing Oakland County, few then foresee it and other centers challenging Hudson's downtown behemoth. But demographers correctly forecast growth would occur more rapidly northwest of Detroit.

April 18, 1955 — OUCH! Thousands of Detroit area first- and second-graders get polio shots. The Salk vaccine is first distributed nationwide to combat infantile paralysis.

April 7, 1956 — Streetcar service ends in Detroit. The city sells its 184 streetcars to Mexico City for about $1 million.

Nov. 5, 1957 — William Patrick is the first African-American elected to the City Council in the 20th Century.

March 25, 1958 — Leon Wallace, the first African American appointed to a Detroit city commission, is named director-secretary of the Loyalty Investigating Committee.

Jan. 28, 1959 — Detroit police integrate patrol cars.

May 27, 1960 — The census reports Detroit's population dips 9 percent to about 1.6 million. But regional planners say the loss is temporary. "The gloss of the suburbs will wear off," says planning commission member Charles Roemer.

Nov. 7, 1961 — In a major political upset, Jerome Cavanagh, a 33-year-old attorney, defeats Louis Miriani for mayor.

June 23, 1963 — Led by Dr. Martin Luther King Jr., 125,000 people march down Woodward for racial equality.

1965 — Dr. Charles Wright, an obstetrician/gynecologist, opens part of his West Grand Boulevard office as the International Afro-American Museum, containing items from Nigeria and Ghana and some inventions of Elijah McCoy.

July 23, 1967 — Detroit police raid a blind pig on 12th Street and arrest patrons, but are met by a hostile crowd in the early morning hours. Soon a significant section of the near west side is engulfed in rioting. When it ends nearly a week later, 43 are dead.

November 1967 — Unions strike the Free Press and Detroit News — a strike that shuts both papers for nine months. Readers thus don't find local coverage of historical events from the assassinations of Dr. Martin Luther King Jr. and Robert F. Kennedy to much of the

Free Press file photo

Detroit in 1953, at its population pinnacle: about 2 million. This view is from the southwest corner of Fort and Woodward. Nearly all you see is gone.

In 1960, the census reports Detroit's population dips 9 percent to about 1.6 million. "The gloss of the suburbs will wear off," says a regional planning commissioner.

The wreckage of the plane crash in which Walter and Mae Reuther were killed in 1970.

JOHN COLLIER/Detroit Free Press

Detroit Tigers' storied championship year.

March 18, 1968 — Focus: HOPE is founded and adopts this mission statement:

Recognizing the dignity and beauty of every person, we pledge intelligent and practical action to overcome racism, poverty and injustice. And to build a metropolitan community where all people may live in freedom, harmony, trust and affection.

Black and white, yellow, brown and red from Detroit and its suburbs of every economic status, national origin and religious persuasion, we join in this covenant.

Oct. 7, 1968 — Jose Feliciano sings the national anthem for the start of Game 5 of the World Series at Tiger Stadium. His version is bluesy, a far cry from the tradition anthem so many are used to. And the complaints come rolling in. By 2000 standards, Feliciano's rendition is mild — much more a reflection of the tense times between generations during the late 1960s.

Recalled Feliciano years after his performance: "Everybody wants to rush through the anthem and get to the game. I thought people weren't as proud of our national anthem as I was. It was my way of really doing something for America in the sense that America has done a lot for me. I never knew that my patriotism was going to be misconstrued."

March 39, 1969 — Two Detroit Police officers approach a lone gunman on Linwood, who opens fire, killing Officer Michael Czapski, 22, and wounding Officer Richard Worobec, 28.

Within 10 minutes, police storm a meeting of a nearby black separatist group inside New Bethel Church on Linwood. All inside — 140 people — are arrested without regard to their rights.

The legal drama that evolved from the tragedy had a far-reaching impact on Detroit's police department and politics.

Recorder's Court Judge George Crockett Jr. releases many of the people arrested. One person is charged in Czapski's slaying, two with wounding Worobec. All are acquitted.

May 9, 1970 — Walter and Mae Reuther die in a plane crash in northern Michigan.

Aug. 30, 1971 — Extremists bomb 10 Pontiac school buses, a reaction to court-ordered cross-district busing of students to achieve racial integration of public schools.

Nov. 24, 1971 — Henry Ford II announces a consortium of 50 area companies will build a $340-million center downtown on the shore of the Detroit River. After a contest, the projected is named the Renaissance Center. The centerpiece: a 73-story hotel, the tallest hotel in the world when opened in **March 1977**. More than 20 years after the complex opens, General Motors buys it for about $75 million and moves its world headquarters to the Ren-Cen, pledging to spend more than $500 million in renovations.

April 1, 1972 — University of Michigan students and wanna-bes smoke marijuana joints to promote marijuana use — the first April Fools' Day Hash Bash. Two years later, Ann Arbor voters approved a charter amendment making marijuana possession a civil infraction punishable by a $5 fine. In 1990, voters increased the penalty to $25 for a first offense, $50 for a second offense and $100 for subsequent offenses.

Feb. 22, 1973 — Hermus Millsaps of Taylor is the first Michigan Lottery $1-million winner ($50,000 a year for 20 years). His salary at the time: About $160 a week.

January 1974 — Coleman Alexander Young is sworn in as mayor of Detroit, the first African American to be elected to the post.

Detroit at the nation's 200th

1976 — It's an arbitrary call, but metro Detroit hits bottom in 1976 — and stays running in place for several years. It is not the best of times:

➤ The Housing and Urban Development scandal of the early 1970s results in thousands of government-owned vacant and abandoned properties in Detroit after unscrupulous brokers approved mortgages for hundreds of people without the means to make payments. HUD then shells out hundreds of millions to mortgage holders during foreclosures.

➤ Street gangs such as the Coneyonlies, the BKs and the Earl Flynns terrorize Detroiters during a summer of police layoffs and a well-publicized federal probe of high-ranking department officials.

➤ Inflation eats into paychecks from Flat Rock to Ferndale to Fraser; the unemployment rate hovers around 10 percent for the region.

➤ The U.S. auto industry sinks as more fuel-efficient cars from foreign manufacturers flood the market, creating layoffs as sales slump in the metro area. When the nation gets a cold, we are reminded, Detroit gets pneumonia.

➤ Cocaine increasingly becomes the drug of choice, leading to more ruin for addicts and their families.

➤ Racial politics flourish. In Detroit, the leadership of Coleman Young more and more rankles suburban whites. Coupled with economic hardship, resentment about race helps

A woman protests cross-district busing in 1970. The antipathy toward the plan leads to extremists bombing 10 empty buses in Pontiac in 1971.

TONY SPINA/Detroit Free Press

Focus: HOPE leaders Eleanor Josaitis and the Rev. William Cunningham lead the group's annual walk for justice in 1989. Josaitis today is executive director of the civil rights agency. Cunningham died in 1997.

fuel the rise of Reagan Democrats and turns Macomb County into a political laboratory for the nation.

➤ The Lions, Tigers, Pistons and Wings? Awful.

July 1980 — Republicans hold their national convention at Joe Louis Arena, the delegates welcomed by Democratic National Committeeman and Detroit Mayor Coleman Young. Ronald Reagan wins the presidential nomination. After Reagan is elected, Young weighs in with his now-famous description of the new president: "Old Pruneface."

Jan. 17, 1983 — Hudson's closes its 25-story downtown store. The fabled store, where generations of Detroiters first petitioned Santa Claus and two basement levels drew bargain shoppers, had been losing sales to suburban shopping centers. In 1953, downtown Hudson's logged $153 million in sales. By 1982, sales dropped to $45 million. The building sat empty after several plans to recycle the edifice failed. On Oct. 24, 1998, 2,728 pounds of strategically placed explosives brought down the building in seconds as 50,000 spectators cheered.

Work began in November 1999 on the Compuware world headquarters in Campus Martius, including a 1,050-vehicle garage where Hudson's stood.

October 1984 — The Tigers cap a really cool season and win the World Series in five games over the San Diego Padres. But what

could have been a joyous, civic-building celebration is quickly a national punchline as revelers torch and overturn police cars and TV and newspapers show the scene worldwide.

Aug. 16, 1987 — Northwest Flight 255 crashes after takeoff from Metro Airport, killing 156 people.

Sept. 18, 1987 — Pope John Paul II visits Detroit, his last stop on a U.S. tour. But months of news about his visit and elaborate preparations to control anticipated huge crowds wind up bringing out relatively few spectators.

In Hamtramck, he speaks to about 50,000 people; in downtown Detroit, to about 35,000. A Pontiac Silverdome mass is packed, with 90,000 people.

His 12-hour day includes a hurried motorcade down Jos. Campau where the Popemobile hits 35 m.p.h. Before he was pope, John Paul visited metro Detroit as a cardinal.

Dec. 15, 1989 — I-696 opens, ending freeway construction in metropolitan Detroit that began during World War II when the Davison Expressway opened.

The final stretch, completing the 28.2-mile Walter Reuther Freeway, as 696 is named, links I-75 to Lahser Road in south Oakland County.

June 4, 1990 — Jack Kevorkian, a retired pathologist, assists Janet Adkins in her suicide. It is the first assisted suicide by

Kevorkian in a series of up to 120 that ends in April 1999, when he's sentenced to 10- to 25 years in prison for second-degree murder and drug delivery for the lethal injection of 52-year-old Thomas Youk.

June 28, 1990 — Nelson Mandela visits Detroit. He tours an assembly line in Dearborn and speaks to a filled Tiger Stadium. Detroit area businesses and the general public donate at least $1.1 million to Mandela's South African political party, the African National Congress.

Past 10 years

Prelude to our future

Nancy Kerrigan got whacked on the shin, Tiger Stadium got padlocked and the Wings got Stanley — twice. And metro Detroit got better.

Coming out of a wrenching period of lousy car sales, stagnant construction, steadily increasing crime, racial antipathy and urban decay, the 1990s saw the region begin a healing that continued into the new century.

As the nation's economic health increased, car sales rose and auto makers learned to reinvent themselves as leaner, more cost-conscious companies.

The Big Three shrunk into the Big Two after Germany's Daimler-Benz bought Chrysler, keeping the Chrysler HQ in rapidly developing Auburn Hills.

General Motors stunned the community in 1996 when it bought the RenCen for $73 million and said its white-collar jobs would be located on the riverfront. Property values began a welcome climb in many Detroit neighborhoods and nearby suburbs.

New housing in Detroit — something not seen in substance since the end of World War II — began going up.

Oakland County's status as one of the most wealthy in the United States held firm; Macomb County saw residential developments replace farmland north of M-59.

It was the best period for downtown Detroit in three decades, with new baseball and football stadiums, a world headquarters for Compuware Corp., the Detroit Opera Theatre, new clubs and three casinos.

Still, the region remained one of the most racially polarized in the United States.

FIND OUT MORE

➤ J.L. Hudson's, pages 535, 614.

➤ Jack Kevorkian, page 251.

➤ Geoff Fieger, page 255.

➤ Freeways, page 234.

➤ Nancy and Tonya, page 493.

The region's next generation. These boys are now teenagers; the picture was taken at Focus: HOPE in 1989.

Free Press file photo

The Detroit Almanac

03, SU
LA

"Detroit will resolve into one of the greatest industrial islands on Earth."

— **E.B. Ward**, *19th-Century industrialist and Detroit's first millionaire*

PER–

VES

The Hudson's flag — the world's largest — on its Woodward Avenue store on a Flag Day around 1950.

World-class Detroit

HEY!

Yes, we have the biggest tire, largest stove, longest hockey game . . . all sorts of superlatives in this tome. There's a lot to shout about, including:

A PROFITABLE FACTORY: Ford Motor Co.'s Wayne assembly plant generates $3 billion a year in pretax profit, the most in any industry in the world.

AN INDUSTRIAL COMPLEX: The Ford Rouge complex — 1,100 acres — has been tagged the largest manufacturing complex in the Western world. If one is larger, it hasn't made the claim.

A PROJECT: The Renaissance Center was the largest private construction project in Michigan history: one 73-story, cylindrical hotel surrounded by four, 39-story towers; $337 million in cost; a private investment group of 51 members, said to be the largest group ever assembled in the United States for a real estate development.

A HOCKEY GAME: March 24, 1936. Mud Bruneteau scored at 16:30 of the sixth overtime period, and the Red Wings beat the Montreal Maroons, 1-0 — the longest game in NHL history. Maroons? Forerunners of Les Canadiens.

A MAST: The 125-foot flagpole at now-closed Tiger Stadium was the tallest obstacle in fair territory in a major-league park.

FIREWORKS: The annual Freedom Festival display — about 40 minutes of BOOM! — has been called the largest display in North America.

A DINNER: The biggest sit-down meal is the annual Detroit chapter NAACP dinner, which draws 10,000 guests. The chapter is also the largest in the National Association for the Advancement of Colored People.

A FLAG: It used to belong to Hudson's, but the department store donated the world's biggest flag to the Smithsonian in 1976. When unfurled (annually on Flag Day), it draped 235 feet by 104 feet.

A FESTIVAL: Dearborn's annual Arab-American festival in June is the largest in the world in terms of attendance and participants.

Emily Gail, below, onetime Detroit booster and current Hawaii resident, used to urge folks to "Say nice things about Detroit." In margins on the following pages are things said — naughty and nice.

Metalclad Airship Z M C-2
Built by Aircraft Development Corporation
Division of Detroit Aircraft Corporation

Burton Historical Collection

"Groves and forests are so well disposed that one would think Nature alone could not make, without the help of art, so charming a prospect."

— **The Rev. Louis Hennepin**, 1679, after he sailed up the Detroit River, Lake St. Clair and St. Clair River.

AN ATTIC: The Henry Ford Museum & Greenfield Village in Dearborn is the nation's largest indoor/outdoor museum complex. The museum also has the world's largest inlaid teak floor, at 350,000 square feet.

A MARKET: Eastern Market is the largest open-air wholesale/retail market of its kind in the United States. More than 150 food-related businesses operate in the market at Russell and Gratiot in Detroit.

A MAIL BOAT: Detroit is the only place in the country where ships can mail documents and receive deliveries — all while sailing through. Passing freighters on the Detroit River lower pails to collect their mail from the J.W. Wescott II, the small vessel that provides the service. It docks near the foot of West Grand Boulevard.

FUND-RAISING: The United Way in Detroit is the nation's oldest community fund-raising organization. It was founded in 1948.

A SIDE-WHEELER: The City of Detroit III, the largest side-wheel steamer in the world at 470 feet, paddled between Detroit and Cleveland

The dirigible ZMC2 in a hangar at Detroit Aircraft Corp. It was the first metal airship.

from 1912 to 1950.

A FAIR: The State Fair, held annually in Detroit, is the oldest in the nation. It first opened Sept. 25, 1849, on the west side of Woodward near what now is the Fisher Freeway.

CARS: The largest 1-day vintage car event in the world is the Woodward Dream Cruise in August.

ANNULMENTS: The Catholic Archdiocese of Detroit handles the most marriage annulments of any Catholic community in the world — about 1,000 cases a year.

FEATHER BOWLING: Not only does the Cadieux Cafe on Cadieux in Detroit have the most feather bowling lanes in the United States, it has the only feather bowling lanes in the United States.

PARKING: The parking garage at Metro Airport will be the biggest in world at 11,500 spaces and 10 stories tall. It's to open in 2001.

A TECH CENTER: The largest automotive technical campus is the General Motors Technical Center in Warren. It covers nearly 700 acres and employs about 20,000 workers.

A WATERFALL: The tallest indoor waterfall in the world is at Greektown's International Marketplace. The drop is 114 feet.

FACTORIES: In the 1920s, Detroit had the world's largest motor plant, auto body plant, axle factory, windshield plant, wheel plant, auto light plant, tractor plant, adding machine factory, stove factory, drug and chemical plant, vacuum cleaner plant, paint works, electric iron factory, seed house, cigar factory, sports shoe factory, coin machine factory and insulated wire factory. Detroit's industrial output trailed only that of New York and Chicago, and it surpassed those of Cleveland, Buffalo and Toledo combined.

The firsts

Something, someone, someplace has to be No. 1 on any list. So, forget the seconds, here's a list of the Detroit region's firsts.

Airplanes

OVER DETROIT: July 14, 1910. Pilot Arch Hoxsey took off from a strip at the state fairgrounds.

TRANSATLANTIC JET FLIGHT: On July 20, 1948, 16 Lockheed P80 Shooting Stars flew from Mt. Clemens to Odiham, England. They made four refueling stops on their 4,283-mile flight, which took 10 hours and 40 minutes.

BREAK 200 M.P.H.: Lt. Lester Maitland flew a Curtiss pursuit plane at 216.1 m.p.h. at an air show in 1927 at Selfridge Field.

METAL AIRSHIP: A 149-foot dirigible known as the ZMC2 was made by the Detroit Aircraft Corp. and tested at Grosse Ile on Aug. 19, 1929.

Automobiles

STREET RACE: The Free Press reported on March 17, 1895, that two unidentified motorized vehicles raced up Woodward just before dawn.

VEHICLE: Charles King, 29, took his contraption for a short spin downtown on March 6, 1896. Pedestrians yelled, "Get a horse."

FORD: Henry Ford, 32, drove his first quadri-

cycle on Detroit streets June 4, 1896. It was too large to get out of his Bagley garage, so he had to smash a wider opening in the door.

TRAFFIC FATALITY: George W. Bissell was riding in his horse-drawn carriage on Sept. 2, 1902, when it was hit by an automobile, killing him. It happened at Brooklyn and Lysander, just north of today's Jeffries housing project.

CONCRETE MILE: Woodward between 6 Mile and 7 Mile was the first in the world, paved in 1909 for about $14,000.

STOP SIGNS: Detroit police began using signs at major intersections in 1915. The signs were installed on most Detroit corners in 1923.

CENTER LINE: Wayne County Road Commissioner Edward Hines ordered the first center line in the world in 1911; it was put on River Road near Trenton.

PARKING METERS: First installed in Detroit on Oct. 6, 1948.

DRIVE-IN GAS STATION: It was built at First and

The first stop sign was used in Detroit in 1915.

Free Press file photo

Burton Historical Collection

The Detroit Opera House on Campus Martius in the 19th Century. The Detroit Symphony Orchestra's first concert is held in 1914.

Fort by the Central Oil Co. and opened in 1910.

SIGNAL: A three-way signal (red, yellow, green) first flickered at Michigan and Monroe on Dec. 31, 1918. In 1920, Woodward and Fort was the first intersection to show red, yellow and green in all directions.

DRIVER'S TRAINING: River Rouge and Dearborn Fordson began offering driver's education in 1935.

SAFETY PATROL: Detroit introduced them in 1919. In 1951, 55 women became school crossing guards.

LEFT-TURN LANES: Detroit began using five-lane streets in 1952.

DIVIDED, FOUR-LANE HIGHWAY: In 1942, the Willow Run and Detroit Industrial Expressway (today's I-94) began carrying Detroiters to the bomber factory near Ypsilanti.

SPEED GUNS: Detroit police began using electrical speed timers in 1955.

BREATH TESTS: Detroit police started using a chemical test for intoxication in 1945.

MOBILE HOME: The Hudson Motor Car Co. in 1929. It was designed by aviation pioneer Glenn H. Curtiss.

Controversy

FROM THE GET-GO: Cadillac vs. the Jesuits. Cadillac wanted Detroit to grow rapidly and believed the best way was to have hundreds of Indians live near the settlement. He wanted to attract the Indians by offering booze for their animal pelts. The Jesuits objected. Cadillac's plans ultimately prevailed, but the Jesuits remained hostile toward him. Cadillac wrote in 1703 that there were three ways to be friendly with the Jesuits: "Let them do as they like; second, do everything they wish; third, say nothing about what they do."

IMAGE PROBLEM: In June 1721, the Rev. Peter Charlevoix visited Detroit and reported that the fort looked deserted and abandoned because of government neglect.

SLUMLORD: Joseph Campau built shoddy housing for lease to the poor in the 1820s.

Electricity

FIRST LIGHT: A traveling circus illuminated its tent at an appearance in Detroit in June 1879.

BULBS AGLOW: James McMillan, a wealthy businessman and politician who lived on East Jefferson, had the first house in Detroit with electric lights. They were turned on for the wedding of his daughter, Grace McMillan, to William Jarvis on Nov. 12, 1885.

Entertainment

PLAY'S THE THING: The first theater opened in 1819 at Wayne and Woodbridge streets. The first Fisher Theatre performance was "The Gay Life," which opened Oct. 2, 1961. The Free Press' Louie Cook said it was "A musical story about a great Viennese lover who finally decides to cut out the nonsense and settle down to life with a pleasant, sensible wife." It played 25 performances, then went on to Broadway, where it closed after 114 shows.

SYMPHONY CONCERT: The Detroit Symphony's first was at the Detroit Opera House (now the Kern block) on Feb. 26, 1914; Weston Gales conducted.

MOTOWN HIT: The first Motown 1-million seller: *Give me muh-uh-uh-nee (that's what I want)* — came in January 1960 with "Money" by Barrett Strong.

CIRCUS: The first Shrine Circus in the nation played in Detroit on Feb. 26, 1906.

FIRST PIANO: Sarah Whipple Sibley had one hauled here in the early 1800s.

Industry

LABOR & INDUSTRY: Chances are some of the workers demanded better wages when Cadillac opened the first Detroit industry, a grist mill, soon after founding the city in 1701.

STRIKE: Carpenters went on strike carrying signs: "Work $2 for 10-hour day," on April 3, 1837.

AUTO FACTORY: Ransom E. Olds built the world's first auto plant in 1900 on East Jefferson at Concord near the Belle Isle Bridge. Fire destroyed the building in 1901.

AUTO STRIKE: June 17, 1913: Studebaker plant workers at Clark and West Jefferson walked out over the issues of bimonthly paychecks and the firing of a labor activist.

CORPORATION TO NET $1 BILLION IN ONE YEAR: General Motors recorded net income of $1.19 billion in 1955.

FIRST GUARANTEED WAGE: UAW in 1955 contract negotiations.

SHOPPING CENTER: Folks in California disagree, but it's widely accepted that Northland was

HUGH GRANNUM/Detroit Free Press

Coleman Young is elected Detroit's first black mayor in 1973. He would serve 20 years.

the country's first regional shopping center when it opened March 22, 1954.

SKYSCRAPER: The Hammond Building, 10 stories, completed Feb. 3, 1889, demolished in 1956, was Detroit's first. It stood at the southeast corner of Griswold and Fort. And, yes, it was a big deal. People came from miles just to gaze in four directions from the lofty height.

Mayors

APPOINTED: Solomon Sibley, in 1805, was the city's first mayor — by appointment.

ELECTED: John R. Williams, April 4, 1825. He tallied 102 votes to a collective 11 votes for several opponents.

BLACK: Coleman A. Young, who took office in 1974 and served for 20 years.

RECALLED: On July 22, 1930, Charles Bowles lost his recall election nine months after he was elected mayor. Bowles was widely viewed as corrupt; more than 50 police officials were indicted on various corruption charges shortly after Bowles was kicked out of office.

Radio

FIRST COMMERCIAL: We claim a biggie: WWJ-AM made the first commercial radio broadcast in the United States on Aug. 20, 1920. The program was called "Tonight's Dinner."

BROADCAST NUPTIALS: On June 15, 1920, Mabelle Ebert married John Wichman in a service at First Presbyterian Church in Detroit. Ebert was in the church. Wichman, a sailor, was aboard the USS Birmingham in the Pacific. The ceremony was telephoned to the telegraph office, wired to

"I'll be damned if I'm going to let them collect guns in the city of Detroit while we're surrounded by hostile suburbs and the whole rest of the state who have guns…"

– Mayor
Coleman Young

"I issue an open warning now to all those pushers, to all rip-off artists, to all muggers: it's time to leave Detroit; hit 8 Mile Road!"

– Young, in his first inaugural speech, 1974

a naval facility near Chicago and dispatched by radio to the Birmingham.

ORCHESTRA: The 16-piece Detroit News Orchestra, led by piccolo player Otto Krueger and composed mainly of members of the Detroit Symphony Orchestra, began broadcasting over WWJ on May 28, 1922.

BLACK DEEJAY: Jack Surrell of WXYZ-AM in 1952.

The Telephone

PHONE COMPANY: The Telephone and Telegraph Co. began service in October 1877, the nation's first Bell firm.

TELEPHONE: On Sept. 21, 1877, workers strung a telephone wire between Frederick Stearns' Woodward Avenue drugstore and his labora-tory on Fifth Street, about a half-mile away. The store invited passersby to come in and "throw your voice," but people were skeptical; they assumed the person on the other end was actually upstairs.

LONG-DISTANCE: The first line was strung in 1879 among Grosse Pointe, Detroit and Wyandotte.

PHONE BOOK: Published Sept. 15, 1878. Listings included the Free Press, Parke, Davis & Co. and Calvert Lithographing Co.

TRANSATLANTIC NUPTIALS: On Dec. 2, 1933, Detroit Judge John Watts officiated at the wedding of Bertil Clason and Sigrid Carlson. Clason was in Detroit, Carlson in Stockholm, Sweden. The ceremony was relayed from Detroit to New York, then to Maine, London and Stockholm.

SOURCES: FREE PRESS AND MICHIGAN HISTORY MAGAZINE

"The people here are generally poor wretches, and consist of three or four hundred French families, a lazy idle people, depending chiefly on the savages for their subsistence."

— George Croghan, 1765

Detroit's X-Files

True stories from the Motor City. None of the names have been changed.

HIS SATANIC MAJESTY: For decades Detroiters have erected religious shrines in their yards, especially to the Virgin Mary. In 1905, a Detroiter attracted international attention by erecting a shrine to the devil on his front lawn. "He is my friend," said stonecutter Herman Menz of Satan. Menz's shrine, on Stanton near McGraw, was a self-carved gargoyle set atop a stone altar. It carried the Latin inscription: "Man is not created, but developed; God did not make man, but man made the gods." Detroit police had to guard the shrine from stone-throwing protesters.

"TURN ME ON, DEAD MAN:" On Oct. 12, 1969, WKNR-FM deejay Russ Gibb was called by a listener wondering about Beatle Paul McCartney's death. A story circulating through college grapevines said McCartney was dead and a cosmetically altered look-alike had replaced him. Within hours, Uncle Russ — as the deejay was known in his hippie days — had received international acclaim for breaking the story of Paul's hushed-up demise.

It made for great radio. Listeners suggested how to detect supposed clues on Beatles albums and Gibb played the White Album and Sgt. Pepper's Lonely Hearts Club Band album forward and reverse to reveal the hidden messages. Gibb, then the impresario of the Grande Ballroom — Detroit's counterculture headquarters — continues to be an innovative media teacher at Dearborn High.

The clues:

➤ "Revolution No. 9" played backward suggested a line: "Turn me on, dead man."

➤ In "Strawberry Fields Forever," the words, "I buried Paul."

➤ In "I Am the Walrus," the words, "Is he dead . . . bury my body . . ."

Uncle Russ Gibb in the 1960s with his gear glasses.

➤ The Sgt. Pepper's Lonely Hearts Club Band album cover depicted McCartney's funeral, with the Beatles surrounding his freshly dug grave.

➤ The Abbey Road album cover was actually a funeral procession; the four Beatles were walking across the street, and McCartney — or his likeness — wore no shoes, symbolizing that he was a corpse. George Harrison, in work clothes, was said to be the grave digger. Ringo Starr, wearing black formal wear, was the undertaker. John Lennon, in a white suit, was said to represent Christ. The license plate on the Volkswagen reads "28 IF," implying that that would be McCartney's age — if he were alive. McCartney was 27 at the time.

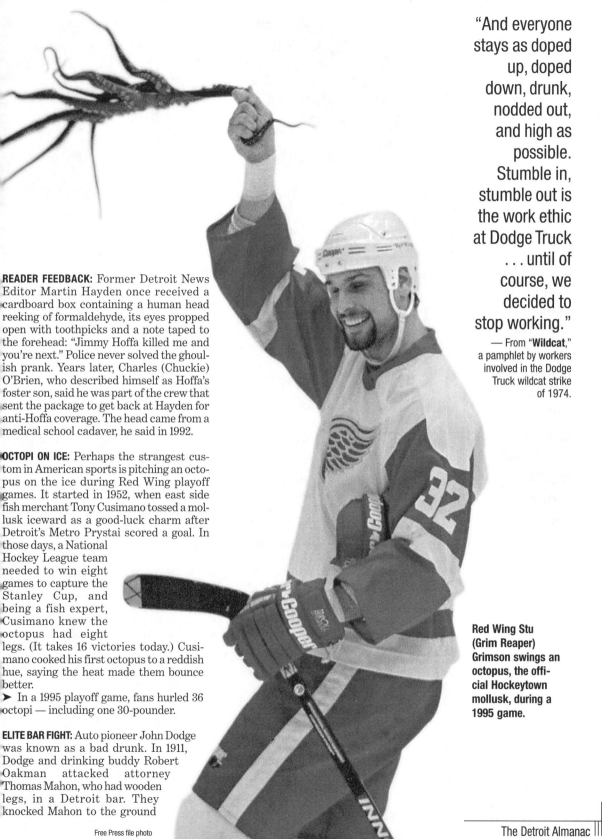

"And everyone stays as doped up, doped down, drunk, nodded out, and high as possible. Stumble in, stumble out is the work ethic at Dodge Truck . . . until of course, we decided to stop working."

— From "**Wildcat**," a pamphlet by workers involved in the Dodge Truck wildcat strike of 1974.

READER FEEDBACK: Former Detroit News Editor Martin Hayden once received a cardboard box containing a human head reeking of formaldehyde, its eyes propped open with toothpicks and a note taped to the forehead: "Jimmy Hoffa killed me and you're next." Police never solved the ghoulish prank. Years later, Charles (Chuckie) O'Brien, who described himself as Hoffa's foster son, said he was part of the crew that sent the package to get back at Hayden for anti-Hoffa coverage. The head came from a medical school cadaver, he said in 1992.

OCTOPI ON ICE: Perhaps the strangest custom in American sports is pitching an octopus on the ice during Red Wing playoff games. It started in 1952, when east side fish merchant Tony Cusimano tossed a mollusk iceward as a good-luck charm after Detroit's Metro Prystai scored a goal. In those days, a National Hockey League team needed to win eight games to capture the Stanley Cup, and being a fish expert, Cusimano knew the octopus had eight legs. (It takes 16 victories today.) Cusimano cooked his first octopus to a reddish hue, saying the heat made them bounce better.

➤ In a 1995 playoff game, fans hurled 36 octopi — including one 30-pounder.

ELITE BAR FIGHT: Auto pioneer John Dodge was known as a bad drunk. In 1911, Dodge and drinking buddy Robert Oakman attacked attorney Thomas Mahon, who had wooden legs, in a Detroit bar. They knocked Mahon to the ground

Red Wing Stu (Grim Reaper) Grimson swings an octopus, the official Hockeytown mollusk, during a 1995 game.

Free Press file photo

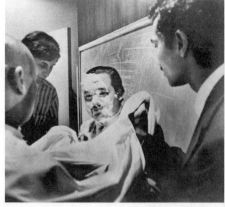

Photos by JOHN COLLIER/Detroit Free Press

Guru Maharaj Ji, left, went to a Detroit City Council meeting for an award. He also received a shaving cream pie in the face, above.

> "Its situation appears to me to be charming... There is nothing milder than the climate, which scarcely counts two months of winter."
>
> – **Francois Clairimbault D'Aigremont**, traveler, 1710

and kicked him repeatedly. Mahon recovered, and received a large cash settlement after Dodge sobered up.

THE BELLE ISLE SKULKER: During the spring and summer of 1970, police were baffled by a man who would strip to his underwear (boxers) on the Detroit side of the Belle Isle Bridge, run out four or five spans, and perform a swan dive into the water. Then he would swim to shore, dress and disappear. The dives were dangerous because of the height, the current and the underwater pilings and other debris near the bridge. Cops called him the Belle Isle Skulker. He pulled the stunt several times before cops finally nabbed him. He received psychiatric care.

PIG'S HEAD ON A PLATTER: On June 13, 1975, the Wayne State University Board of Governors was considering a tuition hike and the possible phasing out of WSU's experimental Monteith College. Members of two far-left organizations, the Workers Revenge Party and the Eat the Rich Gang, walked into the open meeting and presented the board with the large head of a dead pig on a platter. The groups said the act symbolized the governors' "pig-like actions."

NO WAY TO TREAT A GURU: Guru Maharaj Ji — a self-proclaimed child deity who was traveling the country with his mother in 1973 recruiting young people — appeared at a Detroit City Council meeting to receive an award. Pat Halley, a member of the staff of the Fifth Estate alternative newspaper, threw a shaving-cream pie in the guru's face and afterward told reporters the pie was a protest against the guru and "2,500 years of illegitimate spiritual authority." Days later, the guru's followers beat Halley with a hammer, fracturing his skull. He lived, and is an author and cab driver today.

A DRUID IN THE 'HOOD: In the mid-1980s, a Detroit man fought the city over ordinance violations by arguing that he was a Druid — the scholarly class of ancient Celts that had died out 15 centuries earlier. The ancient Druids worshiped trees, and Robert Riley said he believed his religion forced him to let the vegetation grow wildly on his property in the historic Boston-Edison neighborhood. Druid or no Druid, neighbors and the city agreed: The overgrowth had to go. Residents also didn't like Riley parking his big cars in the driveway. He called the autos "Cadillac station wagons." Most people know them as funeral hearses.

GRIP AND GRIN: Opening day at the Detroit Zoo in 1928 provided visitors with a bizarre spectacle. Acting Detroit Mayor John Nagel arrived in front of a moated bear exhibit at exactly the same time a zookeeper arrived with a basket of bread for the bears. Morris, the largest male bear, leaped the moat in a single bound, coming face to face with the mayor. Unflappable, Nagel extended an arm as if to shake hands with the bear. Keepers quickly drove the bruin back into the exhibit.

SPEECH THERAPY: In the early 20th Century, Detroit had the nation's largest school for people who stuttered. The Lewis Phono-Metric Institute, at 71-77 Adelaide St., promised a scientific approach to speech defects and "hardwood floors in every room."

MAY I CUT IN?: A dance called the freaky deaky made headlines around the world in the late 1970s when the sexually explicit steps touched off several shooting incidents in Detroit. Problems arose because guys didn't like their girls doing the freaky with other guys. British tabloids heard about the shootings and wrote stories with headlines such as: "Dance of death sweeps U.S." Metro Detroit detective-fiction star Elmore Leonard titled a 1988 book after the dance.

FIREFIGHTERS WALK OUT: Upset that the city refused to let them haul their rigs along Detroit's wooden sidewalks, volunteer firefighters went on strike in April 1855. They paraded with their helmets on backward, got drunk, and threatened to beat up members of the City Council. The council responded by hiring replacement volunteers.

HOCKEY NIGHT IN CANADA: In April 1969, someone took a hacksaw and severed a guy wire attached to the top of the 655-foot broadcast tower next to CKLW television and radio in Windsor. The sabotage caused the tower to list about 15 degrees and sparked the evacuation of station employees and 200 nearby families. A letter to the station had threatened to do damage to the tower if Channel 9 failed to carry every National Hockey League playoff game that spring.

A HUMAN SACRIFICE: In November 1932, an unskilled Detroit laborer was arrested for a ritualistic killing during a religious service.

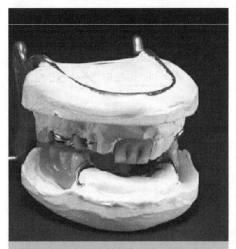

HIGH-PRICED CHOPPERS: Karen Shemonsky of Clarks Summit, Pa., paid $7,475 in an auction for Ty Cobb's dentures in September 1999.

The suspect, 44-year-old Robert Harris, was a follower of Wallace Fard, the door-to-door peddler who was a founder of the Nation of Islam. Harris, whose religious name was Robert Karriem, ordered an initiate, James Smith, to lay on an altar. After asking Smith whether he would sacrifice his life for Islam, Harris then stabbed Smith 13 times and beat him with a steel rod. Smith died as his blood poured onto a white sheet covering the altar. Police arrested Fard and Harris; several hundred of Fard's followers staged protests. Harris eventually pleaded guilty to first-degree murder, explaining he did it because it was "crucifixion time." A judge committed him to the Ionia State Hospital for the criminally insane. Fard was not charged but police ordered him to leave Detroit.

STREAKING, 19TH-CENTURY STYLE: Merchant Robert McNiff had the habit of bartering his clothes for rum and then running naked through the streets of Detroit in the 1820s.

STREAKING, 1970S-STYLE: On Opening Day at Tiger Stadium in 1974, the temperature was 38 degrees, not counting windchill, but dozens of young men cavorted naked in the upper deck. These bleacher streakers ran down the aisles, slid down the railings (sidesaddle) and swung to and fro while hanging from the bottom of the scoreboard.

DOG CHASES HIPPO: Sailing on a boat up the Detroit River toward the city, a circus hippopotamus burst out of his cage on June 22, 1863, and jumped into the water. Chasing the beast were Ali, his Egyptian keeper who rowed a small boat, and a large black dog who slept in the hippo's cage. Eventually the keep-

FOREIGN AFFAIRS: A city of Detroit official who dragged a police officer alongside her car during a Grand Prix incident in 1984 said police could not arrest her because she had "diplomatic immunity." The official was Annivory Calvert, then 29, executive administrator of the Department of Public Works. While it was not widely known at the time, Calvert had dated Mayor Coleman Young and was the mother of his son.

"The stores and shops of the town are well furnished and you may buy fine cloth, linens . . . and every article of wearing apparel as good in their kind, and on nearly as reasonable terms, as . . . in New York or Philadelphia."

– **Isaac Weld,** an Irish traveler, about 1795

> "The town itself is a crowded mass of frame or wooden buildings, generally from one to two and a half stories high, many of them well furnished, and inhabited by people of almost all nations . . . The streets are so narrow as scarcely to admit carriages to pass each other."
>
> – **Gen. Anthony Wayne**, 1796

er and dog managed to chase the hippo onto shore, where it was subdued and transported to Detroit by land.

A MOST UNUSUAL LOOTER: In 1962, police arrested a skin diver for stealing from the Montrose, a British ship that had sunk under the Ambassador Bridge following a collision. The looter, a Detroit police cadet, was caught as he removed the ship's log and flag.

THE BEATLES VS. DETROIT: SOBS — Stamp out the Beatles Society — was a gimmick organization launched in 1963 at the University of Detroit by PR genius Bill Rabe. He wanted to link the university's name with raging Beatlemania. Rabe signed up a naive student, Peter Murphy, to be SOBS president. One of the first questions asked when the Beatles arrived in New York on Feb. 7, 1964, concerned SOBS' supposed campaign. "We're going to start a campaign to stamp out Detroit," a Beatle responded, and suddenly Murphy was public enemy No. 1. Beatles' fans across America demonized SOBS and Murphy, but the Fab Four played Detroit without incident.

DETROIT VS. DISCO: Fifteen years after the move to stamp out the Beatles, Detroit became an incubator of a movement to stamp out disco music. Deejay Steve Dahl was one of the leaders. "Disco music is a disease," he said. After Dahl left Detroit for Chicago, he masterminded Disco Demolition Night, a stunt at Comiskey Park during a doubleheader between the White Sox and Tigers that turned into a famous riot.

LAST CALL OF NATURE: Intermezzo, the snazzy downtown restaurant, filed a lawsuit in 1999 against Detroit-born basketball star Derrick Coleman, saying Coleman urinated in the eatery. In fact, management charged, Coleman did it in the dining room, in plain view of several customers and staff. Coleman also was charged with misdemeanor disorderly conduct and obscene conduct in a public place. Coleman denied he had urinated, saying he simply was wiping a spilled drink from his pants.

SECURITY BEARS: The great Detroit hydroplane racer Gar Wood roared down the river with two of his children's teddy bears in his boat in the '20s.

A WHALE OF AN ARTIST: Lamphere High School in Madison Heights is the home of the first public mural by Wyland, the one-named muralist known nationally for painting stories-tall whales on skyscrapers and stadiums. Wyland, who grew up in Madison Heights and graduated from Lamphere, painted a ram in his school's lobby. In recent years he was invited to paint a larger, wall-size whale mural above the school's swimming pool. In 1997, Wyland turned the sprawling east wall of the David Broderick Tower into an 11,000-square-foot monument to the endangered humpback whale. His first name is Robert.

DAREDEVILS: On July 4, 1983, two men climbed the 73-story Renaissance Center — from the outside. Ron Broyles, 29, of Los Angeles and Kenn Rick, 32, of Lake Orion used suction cups on their hands and legs. Police arrested them on charges of trespassing. In 1981, Rick parachuted from the Ambassador Bridge. In a 1916 stunt promoted by the Detroit News, Harry (Human Fly) Gardiner climbed the 14-story Majestic Building as 150,000 people watched. The Majestic, at Woodward and Michigan, was then Detroit's tallest building.

IT'S LONG GONE: During the final weeks of Tiger Stadium, club and city officials warned fans about stealing from the city-owned building. Fans were on their best behavior and took little. But the biggest theft appeared to have been an inside job. It occurred in owner Mike Ilitch's locked office. An unknown thief took autographed photographs of the DiMaggio brothers and Ty Cobb valued at $2,000.

LIGHT AND GET AWAY: This is why Michiganders have to travel out of state to buy fireworks: Through 1926, it was legal for residents to shoot off powerful fireworks in Detroit, and the results were predictable: numerous deaths and injuries. As the Fourth of July holiday rolled around, city officials would prepare for the annual public health emergency by establishing neighborhood first-aid stations. Over the holiday weekend in 1926, fireworks killed seven children and injured nearly 50. In one incident at Kennedy School on the west side, a rocket fired into a crowd of 100 people, burning several children. Within weeks, then Common Council passed laws banning such fireworks, and the Legislature soon followed with a statewide ban.

CHANGE AT THE ENGINE HOUSE: Detroit began phasing out the traditional brass poles in its engine houses in 1946. Sliding down the poles, too many firefighters were breaking bones in their legs and feet. They did away with the traditional fire dogs in the 1970s. The reason: Too much liability.

FASHION PLATE: In the 1990s, the Notorious B.I.G. immortalized the downtown Detroit clothing store City Slickers as the place to buy "stink pink gators" — pink alligator shoes.

HOCKEYTOWN POLICE BLOTTER: In September 1999, John Fields, an amateur hockey player

> "A barbarous people, depending for subsistence upon the scanty and precarious supplies furnished by the chase, cannot live in contact with a civilized community."
>
> **– Lewis Cass**,
> on the Indians

JOHN COLLIER/Detroit Free Press

Firefighter Sandy Kupper slides down one of the Detroit Fire Department's last poles in 1977.

from St. Clair Shores, pleaded guilty to possession of a bludgeon after an opponent suffered gashes in his face that required close to 200 stitches after a confrontation with Fields. The bludgeon was Fields' prosthetic left arm that is fitted with a hook.

FORMER TIGER KIRK GIBSON: In 1998, Gibson was suspended from his amateur hockey league after he swung his stick like a bat and whacked an opposing player across his back. The blow broke Gibson's stick and left his opponent, Mike Albrecht, with a bruised and sore body. Gibson, known for his World Series home runs, has a personality that is either temperamental or competitive, depending on your point of view. But he's no Gordie Howe. "He's not that good," Albrecht said. "Everyone tries to stay away from him. There are run-ins every time we play."

THE MORE THINGS CHANGE . . . : Detroiters celebrated the turn of the century in 1901 by shooting guns into the air.

DETROIT'S FIRST LOVE-IN TURNS TO HATE: On April 30, 1967 — three months before the start of San Francisco's summer of love — 5,000 Detroiters gathered on Belle Isle for an afternoon of peace, love and marijuana. As people were leaving the island, a policeman issued a ticket to a motorcyclist, and a large melee broke out, with young people pelting cops with sticks, rocks, curses, bottles and bricks. Cops and young people rumbled again later at the entrance to the Belle Isle Bridge.

TEAM-BUILDING EXERCISE: The University of Michigan crew team started an event in 1986 that soon became a rite of spring known as the Naked Mile. Runners doffed their clothes and streaked through Ann Arbor. By the late 1990s, the Mile had attracted international attention, traffic problems and videos of naked people on the Internet.

A BUSY DOCKET: Among the cases heard by the court in Detroit in 1836 were five charges of "encouraging dueling" and one case of "trespass on Indian land."

SOMETHING SMELLS: The biggest complaint in Detroit court in the 1790s: Animal carcasses in every corner of town.

"Nature has destined the city of Detroit to be a great interior emporium, equal, if not superior, to any other on the surface of the terraqueous globe."

– **Judge Augustus Woodward**, 1818

Just passing through

Detroit has been a place where lots of people spend some of their life, moving on to greater fame — or fading from the picture. These folks spent time in the area and went on to greater fame:

ULYSSES S. GRANT: An Army lieutenant, Grant lived in Detroit more than a decade before the Civil War that would propel him to general and later, to president. Grant came to Detroit in 1849 and commanded a company of troops. He boarded in the National Hotel, then moved to a house on East Fort and in 1850, to the northeast corner of Russell and Jefferson. He left in June 1851.

Grant raced horses on West Jefferson and cohosted weekly military balls in the Michigan Exchange Hotel. In 1851, Grant, perhaps in his cups, slipped on the sidewalk in front of Zachariah Chandler's home on East Jefferson. He sued Chandler, a future mayor, abolitionist and U.S. senator, for refusing to pay for medical treatment. A jury awarded Grant 5 cents.

The May 25, 1850, Free Press carried this ad for Grant's home: "For sale, rent or exchange — a two-story dwelling-house on Fort Street, between Rivard and Russell streets, now occupied by Lieutenant Grant of the U.S.A."

THOMAS ALVA EDISON: Moving from his Ohio birthplace in 1854, the 7-year-old Edison caught the steamer Ruby in Detroit and sailed to Port Huron with his parents. Edison, a sickly child known as Al, lived in a big house at today's Thomas and Erie streets. He briefly attended the Family School for Boys and Girls, where a teacher described the child who would become one of the world's greatest inventors as "addled."

Edison dropped out but became a voracious reader. His first laboratory was in the family cellar, as archaeologists from Oakland University confirmed in a 1976 dig at the site. Later, Edison worked as a "news butch" on the Grand Trunk railroad between Port Huron and Detroit, selling candy and newspapers to passengers. During his daily layovers in Detroit, Edison frequented a private library, where he discovered Isaac Newton's *Principa Mathematica*.

Edison also spent time at the Free Press, where he picked up discarded type and ink that helped him launch his unique onboard newspaper, the weekly Grand Trunk Herald, which he printed in the baggage car on a flatbed press.

At 15, Edison, now preferring to be called

Tom, enjoyed hanging out at the Mt. Clemens station, where he became interested in telegraphy and saved a toddler crossing the tracks from a moving train. Edison became a telegraph operator, working in Port Huron, Lenawee County and Ft. Wayne, Ind., before drifting toward Boston. In 1896, after Edison had become world-famous, he met Henry Ford, then a promising mechanic who worked at Detroit Edison.

Nearly two decades later, when Ford had arrived as an international celebrity, the two became business partners and friends. In 1912, Ford lent Edison more than $1 million to design an electrical system for the Model T, which Edison never achieved. The two, though, later traveled together, and Ford bought a vacation home in Ft. Myers, Fla., next to Edison's home. On Oct. 21, 1929, the 50th anniversary of Edison's incandescent lamp, Ford, Edison, President Herbert Hoover and others opened Greenfield Village, which includes the Edison Institute and a replica of Edison's Menlo Park, N.J., laboratory.

JOHN DEWEY: One of America's preeminent philosophers and educators spent a decade of his early academic career teaching at the University of Michigan. Dewey left Ann Arbor for the University of Chicago, where he became nationally famous as one of the founders of the so-called Chicago school of philosophy.

HENRY BILLINGS BROWN: The respected Detroit lawyer is best known — and often reviled — as the U.S. Supreme Court justice who wrote the majority opinion in the infamous 1896 Plessy vs. Ferguson decision, upholding "separate but equal" racial segregation in railway cars. That 7-1 decision, one of the most controversial in court history, established a constitutional basis for Jim Crow laws until the 1950s.

Brown was born into a wealthy family March 2, 1836, in South Lee, Mass. After taking classes at Harvard and Yale law schools, he moved to Detroit in 1859, where he served a legal apprenticeship in the law firm of Walker & Russell. He was a deputy U.S. marshal and a part-time assistant U.S. attorney, and he became an expert in admiralty law, which was the focus of his private practice.

Good friends Henry Ford, left, Thomas Edison and Harvey Firestone in 1930. In 1947, Ford's grandson, William Clay Ford, married Firestone's granddaughter, Martha Firestone.

"It is true that we have two commodious and excellent hotels and a host of others good enough in their way but it is a subject of public notoriety that hundreds of passengers were compelled last season to remain overnight on board the steamboats, or leave the city, for want of lodging . . ."

— **Free Press**, March 23, 1836

In 1875, President Ulysses S. Grant appointed him federal judge for Michigan's Eastern District, where he earned a reputation as a careful listener and good arbiter. In 1890, President Benjamin Harrison appointed him to the Supreme Court, whose chief justice was Melville Fuller. Experts rate Fuller's tenure as one of the worst in court history, especially its "utter indifference to racial injustice," wrote Edward Wise. Brown, a moderate, was not considered a major figure on the court.

Brown died in New York on Sept. 4, 1913, and is buried in Elmwood Cemetery.

MALCOLM X: One of the most famous black Americans was living in Detroit when he became Malcolm X. Born Malcolm Little in Omaha, Neb., Malcolm X grew up in Lansing and moved to Harlem, N.Y., in his late teens. During his hustler days, Malcolm became known as Detroit Red because of his reddish hair and because he told people he was from Detroit, since he figured most New Yorkers would not know of Lansing.

After serving a prison term, Malcolm moved to Detroit in 1952 to live with an older brother and start a new life. He'd begun converting to the Nation of Islam while in prison, at the encouragement of siblings who had already joined.

After moving to Detroit, he became even more convinced of the Nation's power to release black America from the shackles of ignorance and racism. He changed his name to El-Hajj Malik El-Shabazz (though he became known as Malcolm X) and assigned himself the job of recruiting new members to the Nation of Islam, which in 1931 had opened its first temple in Detroit.

While in Detroit, Malcolm X had various jobs, including furniture salesman, cleaning man at the Gar Wood Factory and assembly line worker for Ford Motor Co. In the early to mid-'50s, he left Ford to work full time as a recruiter and minister for the Nation, helping to start temples in such cities as Boston and Philadelphia and New York.

In 1958, he married a Detroiter, Betty Sanders. He and Betty Shabazz had six daughters.

On Nov. 10, 1963, Malcolm gave his "Message to the Grass Roots" speech in Detroit at the Northern Negro Grass Roots Leadership Conference, partly organized by the Shrine of the Black Madonna founder Albert Cleage, at King Solomon Baptist Church. The speech drew a distinction between his vision of black liberation and the nonviolent vision of Dr. Martin Luther King Jr.

On Feb. 14, 1965, the day his home in the East Elmhurst section of Queens in New York City was firebombed, Malcolm delivered one of his

Photo by Gordon Parks

EXCERPT FROM MALCOLM X'S "MESSAGE FROM THE GRASS ROOTS."

"So I cite these various revolutions, brothers and sisters, to show you that you don't have a peaceful revolution. You don't have a turn-the-other-cheek revolution. There's no such thing as a nonviolent revolution. The only kind of revolution that is nonviolent is the Negro revolution. The only revolution in which the goal is loving your neighbor is the Negro revolution. It's the only revolution in which the goal is a desegregated lunch counter, a desegregated theater, a desegregated park, and a desegregated public toilet; you can sit down next to the white folks — on the toilet.

"That's no revolution. Revolution is based on land. Land is the basis of all independence. Land is the basis of freedom, justice and equality. . . . Revolution is bloody, revolution is hostile, revolution overturns and destroys everything that gets in its way. And you, sitting around here like a knot on the wall, saying, 'I'm going to love these folks no matter how much they hate me.' No, you need a revolution. Whoever heard of a revolution where they lock arms, as Rev. Cleage was pointing out beautifully, singing 'We shall overcome?' You don't do that in a revolution. You don't do any singing, you're too busy swinging. It's based on land. A revolutionary wants land so he can set up his own nation, an independent nation. These Negroes aren't asking for any nation — they're trying to crawl back to the plantation."

last major speeches, to a mostly black audience at Ford Auditorium in Detroit.

"I only say that we Negroes should defend ourselves against the violence of others," he declared.

Seven days later, gunmen assassinated him in New York. He was 39.

JIMMY DOOLITTLE: One of the first heroes of World War II spent several months in Detroit before the war broke out. Doolittle was already a famous aviator when he led a bombing raid on Tokyo four months after Pearl Harbor. The raid was a huge boost to morale at a time when the war was not going well. In November 1940, then-Major Doolittle was assigned to Detroit, where he consulted with automakers as they converted plants to aircraft production. He transferred to Washington shortly after the war began.

CHARLES LINDBERGH: The first man to fly the Atlantic spent much time in Detroit. Lindbergh's mother, Evangeline, was descended from two Detroit families, the Lodges and the Lands.

Her uncle was John C. Lodge, the mayor and city councilman who is the namesake of the Detroit freeway. Evangeline's father, Dr. Charles Henry Land, was a Detroit dentist and inventor known as the "Father of Porcelain Dentistry."

Evangeline was living in Minnesota with Lindbergh's father in 1902 when she traveled to Detroit so her uncle, Dr. Edwin Lodge, could deliver Charles in the now-demolished family home at 1120 W. Forest. As a youth, Lindbergh spent weeks each year at his Grandfather Land's next home (also now demolished) on West Elizabeth between Park and Clifford, where he played with Land's tools and grew to appreciate the scientific methods that he applied in his adult life.

Evangeline Lindbergh moved to Detroit in 1922 and began teaching at Cass Tech. During World War II, Charles Lindbergh worked for Henry Ford as an aviation specialist at the Willow Run bomber plant and lived in Bloomfield Hills.

THEODORE KACZYNSKI: The Unabomber, now serving a life sentence in federal prison, earned a master's degree and doctorate in mathematics at the University of Michigan in the mid-1960s. His thesis, "Boundary Functions," was basically the solution to a pure mathematical problem that other mathematicians had been unable to solve.

Later, from his shack in the Montana woods, Kaczynski warned that complex, abusive technology will destroy humanity. Then he used his own technological know-how to build 16 mail bombs that killed three people and

Theodore Kaczynski, also known as the Unabomber.

maimed 23 others.

One bomb was sent to his alma mater. On Nov. 15, 1985, Nicklaus Suino was a research assistant at U-M, opening mail for psychology professor James McConnell at McConnell's home in Scio Township. He picked up a package the size of a phone book, wrapped in brown paper, addressed to McConnell and mailed from Utah.

It held a pipe bomb filled with split-shot lead fishing sinkers, and a mousetrap-like pressure trigger that was kept closed by two manuscript covers. When Suino cut the tape holding the covers together, the bomb went off, blowing a large hole in a kitchen countertop. The force of the blast went downward, away from Suino, who spent a day in the hospital with shrapnel wounds and powder burns on his chest and arms.

In late 1999, U-M announced that Kaczynski's papers would be housed in the university's Labadie Collection of radical writings.

PATTI SMITH: Smith's edgy proto-punk entrenched itself in the rock canon, transforming Smith from underground poet to influential rock icon in the 1970s. She then married Detroit guitarist Fred (Sonic) Smith, became a St. Clair Shores homemaker, and made only nominal nods to music, including 1988's ill-received "Dream of Life." After the 1994 death from heart failure of Fred Smith, formerly of the MC5, Patti Smith began recording again and taking on a more public persona.

JONI MITCHELL: The well-known singer was born in Canada but lived in Detroit after she married local folk singer Chuck Mitchell in 1965. Joni Mitchell performed at the Raven Gallery folk club. In 1968, she joined hands with other singers, including Linda Ronstadt and Bob Seger, plus the Rev. Bill Cunningham of Focus: HOPE, to sing "We Shall Overcome." The Mitchells broke up, and Joni headed to New York, and fame.

BARBRA STREISAND: She was ambitious and talented, with a voice that wowed audiences. She was also temperamental, erratic and a fashion *shlump*. She was also 18. That was Barbra Streisand in Detroit in 1961, the year she played three stints as the Caucus Club's headline singer. They were her first standing gigs out of New York, a chance for the aspiring entertainer to cut her performing teeth before

"Detroit will resolve into one of the greatest industrial islands on Earth. With immense supplies of iron and copper to the north, coal to the south, the Detroit River in front and canals on either end, the city cannot miss."

– **E.B. Ward**, early Detroit industrialist, Civil War era

Eddie Rickenbacker, America's Ace of Aces, heads for his honeymoon in Europe with his wife, Adeline Durant.

an out-of-town audience.

Those who greeted her on Feb. 20, 1961, remember that she wore thrift-shop clothing and carried a stack of dog-eared sheet music. When someone offered to buy her a drink, she'd say, "No, but you can buy me a meal." Streisand lied about her age and told people she was born in Turkey; it was actually Brooklyn, N.Y. She also claimed to have taken belly-dancing lessons. While in Detroit, Streisand used to hitchhike up Woodward to visit the Detroit Institute of Arts. During her second engagement here, she appeared on "The Tonight Show." She also did a radio commercial for Detroit's old Edgewater Park.

EDDIE RICKENBACKER: The famous race car driver became a national hero during World War I when, as a pilot, he shot down 26 German fighters. With considerable financial backing, Rickenbacker came to Detroit and started the Rickenbacker Motor Co., which sold the speedy Rickenbacker Six. Its ads proclaimed: "If you are an exception — if you are super-

critical — then drive this Rickenbacker Six yourself. It will be a revelation to you. You will find it is an exception to all the rules." The firm went out of business in 1927.

JACK KEROUAC: The king of America's Beat Generation writers passed through Grosse Pointe several times after he married a Grosse Pointer in 1944. Kerouac wrote that Edith Francis (Frankie) Parker, his first wife, had "almost a buck-tooth grin, that eagering grin and laugh and eagerness entire that makes the eyes slit but at the same time makes the cheeks fuller and endows the lady with the promise that she will look good all her life."

After their New York wedding, the couple moved in for two months with Parker's mother in her flat at 1407 Somerset in Grosse Pointe Park. Upon entering Grosse Pointe for the first time, Kerouac rolled down the car window and shouted at the stately mansions: "You're nothing but a bunch of old funeral parlors. A bunch of damn, lousy funeral parlors, filled with dead people."

Family members said Kerouac spent hours sitting on the toilet reading Shakespeare and the Bible.

Kerouac worked at the nearby Fruehauf Corp. plant and hung out at the library and the Rustic Cabins bar on Kercheval. The marriage was brief, but Kerouac made other visits to the Pointes. On one trip, he and sidekick Neal Cassady partied at the homes of some wealthy Pointers and took a midnight ride in a car on the Country Club of Detroit's golf course.

Kerouac's usual appearance — 5-o'clock shadow, leather jacket, lumberjack boots — stood out. The police stopped and frisked him on one occasion.

"There is no tragedy in Grosse Pointe," Kerouac later wrote.

Parker died in Grosse Pointe in 1993. Kerouac died in 1969.

THE FLYING WALLENDAS: Their high-wire act has been thrilling circus crowds for 70 years. But they may best be remembered in Detroit for the deadly fall at the State Fair Coliseum on Jan. 30, 1962.

The family was performing its Great Pyramid — the seven-person, three-tier tightrope stunt — when a member lost his footing. The pyramid toppled as 7,000 spectators at the Shrine Circus watched. There was no safety net.

Family patriarch Karl Wallenda didn't use nets because they gave performers a sense of security that could cause a lapse in concentration. Wearing white satin with green spangles, the troupe was moving in formation when Dieter Schepp, Wallenda's nephew, reportedly lost his footing on the bottom pyramid tier.

Free Press file photos

Schepp and Richard Faughnan, Karl Wallenda's son-in-law, fell 70 feet to the circus floor and were killed. Mario Wallenda, Karl's son, also fell to the sawdust- and straw-covered floor and was paralyzed. Gunther, Karl and Herman Wallenda grabbed the wire and Karl snared Jana Schepp — Dieter's sister who had been sitting in a chair at the top of the pyramid — as she fell.

Karl Wallenda held on to Schepp until people on the ground could find a net. The "Washington Post March" was playing as they fell.

After emergency crews left, the show went on. In 1998, sixth- and seventh-generation Wallendas re-created the Great Pyramid for the first time in Detroit, and for only the third time since 1962. Karl Wallenda died in 1978 from a 120-foot fall from a high wire in Puerto Rico.

The pyramid: The Wallendas perform their famous stunt. Jana Schepp is in the chair. Lead man is Dieter Schepp, followed by Mario Wallenda (standing on the pole), Richard Faughnan, Gunther Wallenda, Karl Wallenda (standing on pole) and Herman Wallenda.
Left: The fall.

"There are no tenements in Detroit. Wages are high, hours of labor are short … The schools are a boast of American education … Above all else, Detroit is a freeman's town. It has no political boss, no political machine."

– **World's Work Magazine**, 1926

NBC

Harry Houdini's final performance was in Detroit, where he died.

JOSEPH BRODSKY: The Nobel Prize-winning poet was a well-known Russian exile who became poet laureate of the United States. From 1972 to 1981, he served as poet-in-residence at the University of Michigan. In addition to poetry, he wrote plays, essays and criticism. In 1988, Brodsky delivered the U-M winter commencement address. As a Soviet prisoner, he had hauled manure across the tundra of northern Russia. But he told the 2,000 U-M graduates never to assume the role of victim: "No matter how abominable your condition may be, try not to blame anything or anyone — history, the state, superiors, race, parents, the phase of the moon, childhood toilet training."

ROBERT WILLIAMS: A significant figure in the civil rights movement, if not a household name, Williams lived in the Detroit area on three different occasions. He worked in a Cadillac plant, was caught in a harrowing situation during the 1943 riot, and spent the last 25 years of his life in the tranquil western Michigan town of Baldwin. He died in 1996, and civil rights pioneer Rosa Parks spoke at his funeral. Malcolm X said: "Robert Williams was just a couple of years ahead of his time." As the president of the National Association for the Advancement of Colored People chapter in a small North Carolina town, Williams played a major — and controversial — role in fighting Jim Crow laws in the late 1950s. He

was an early proponent of Black Power, declaring that southern blacks should "meet violence with violence." He wrote a book, "Negroes with Guns." He backed up that message by arming himself and numerous followers with everything from dynamite to machine guns in the face of violent attacks by Ku Klux Klan terrorists. The NAACP hierarchy, Dr. Martin Luther King Jr. and J. Edgar Hoover's FBI attacked Williams for his stance, but Williams found plenty of support, from black radicals in Harlem to Chinese leader Mao Tse-tung, whose country welcomed Williams when he was forced into a long exile because of a trumped-up kidnapping charge in 1961. His years abroad also included a stay in Cuba, from where he broadcast "Radio Free Dixie" to much of the south.

HARRY HOUDINI: He escaped from chains, manacles and straitjackets. But he could not beat death. The great magician died in Detroit on Halloween 1926.

Over the years, Detroiters had watched Houdini break free from handcuffs as he hung by his feet in Grand Circus Park and escape from a sealed trunk at the bottom of the Detroit River.

In what turned out to his last appearance, Houdini collapsed at Detroit's Garrick Theater after his opening-night show. The crowd didn't know it, but Houdini was suffering from being punched in the stomach by a fan three days earlier in Montreal in a test of the magician's strength. After his collapse, Houdini was taken to Grace Hospital, where doctors removed his ruptured appendix. But poison had seeped into his bloodstream and he died three days later, at 1:26 p.m. on Oct. 31. His brother, Theo, and wife, Bess, were at his bedside. Houdini's last words: "Rosabelle, believe," a reference to a song he and his wife enjoyed.

Houdini had devoted the latter years of his life to investigating paranormal activities, especially spiritualists who claimed they could communicate with the dead. While he was skeptical of such claims, stories circulated after his death that Houdini would contact his wife from the grave. Bess Houdini kept a lamp lit near Houdini's portrait in her living room for a decade, but he never returned. For years, people in Detroit and elsewhere have tried to contact Houdini in Halloween seances, with similar results.

SOURCES: "THOUGHT AND ACTION: JOHN DEWEY AT THE UNIVERSITY OF MICHIGAN," BY BRIAN A. WILLIAMS, BENTLEY HISTORICAL LIBRARY; "THE COURT LEGACY," NEWSLETTER OF THE HISTORICAL SOCIETY FOR THE U.S. DISTRICT COURT OF EASTERN MICHIGAN; THE OXFORD COMPANION TO THE SUPREME COURT OF THE UNITED STATES; "LINDBERGH," BY A. SCOTT BERG; "IMAGES OF AMERICA: DETROIT, 1900-1930," RICHARD BAK; "MEMORY BABE: A CRITICAL BIOGRAPHY OF JACK KEROUAC," BY GERALD NICOSIA; "KEROUAC: A BIOGRAPHY," BY ANN CHARTERS; "RADIO FREE DIXIE: ROBERT F. WILLIAMS AND THE ROOTS OF BLACK POWER," BY TIMOTHY B. TYSON.

Top-notch

Awards, recognition, other big-time kudos

Medal of Honor

The Medal of Honor is the highest award for heroism in combat presented to a member of the U.S. armed services. The medal dates to the Civil War. In 1942, the Medal of Honor Society was created to commemorate recipients. In total, 3,429 medals have been awarded to 3,410 recipients, 19 of whom have received the medal twice. Of the recipients, 155 are living.

Here's a list of Detroit-area people who have received the medal and some of their stories:

Vietnam

DWIGHT H. JOHNSON, DETROIT

Army Specialist Fifth Class Johnson was on duty near Dak To, Vietnam, on Jan. 15, 1968.

Johnson's platoon battled a force of about 1,000 North Vietnamese soldiers. Johnson was a tank driver; when his tank became immobile, Johnson grabbed any weapon he could find. He eventually killed about 20 North Vietnamese.

Despite intense gunfire, Johnson climbed into his platoon sergeant's tank, extricated a wounded crew member and carried him to safety at an armored personnel carrier.

Johnson was the first Michigan soldier and the first black soldier to be awarded the Medal of Honor in Vietnam.

Back in Detroit and out of the service in April 1971, Johnson pulled a pistol in a northwest side party store. The owner, also armed, fired five bullets into Johnson, who died at age 24.

Relatives said Johnson had had a hard time dealing with receiving the medal and coming home after many of his buddies had died in Vietnam. Said his mother:

Associated Press

A Medal of Honor rests on a memorial to Korean veterans in a Michigan cemetery.

Free Press file photo

Robert Simanek of Farmington Hills received a Medal of Honor for his bravery in the Korean War.

"Sometimes I wonder if (Dwight) tired of this life and needed someone else to pull the trigger." Johnson's story was depicted in a 1986 play titled "Medal of Honor Rag," which also was performed on TV.

DEWAYNE T. WILLIAMS, ST. CLAIR COUNTY

Marine Corps Pvt. 1st Class Williams was honored for heroism in Quang Nam Province, Vietnam, on Sept. 18, 1968, his 19th birthday. His award was posthumous.

ROBERT LESLIE POXON, DETROIT

Army 1st Lt. Poxon, 22, was honored for heroism in Tay Ninh Province, Vietnam, on June 2, 1969. Posthumous.

WILLIAM MAUD BRYANT, DETROIT

Army Sgt. 1st Class Bryant, 36, Special Forces, was honored for action in Long Khanh Province, Vietnam, March 24, 1969. Posthumous.

Korea

ROBERT E. SIMANEK, DETROIT

Marine Corps Pvt. 1st Class Simanek was on duty in Korea, Aug. 17, 1952.

Simanek of Farmington Hills is the Detroit area's only living Medal of Honor recipient. His unit was ambushed that Aug. 17 and suffering heavy casualties as enemy forces poured on mortar and small-arms fire.

Simanek and remaining members of his patrol sought cover in a trench when a grenade was hurled at them. Simanek, then 22, threw himself on the grenade, absorbing the shattering explosion with his body and shielding his fellow marines from serious injury or death.

Simanek spent months in recovery at a hospital. He received the medal from President Dwight D. Eisenhower.

DONALD R. MOYER, PONTIAC

Army Sgt. 1st Class Moyer, 21, was honored for heroism near Seoul, South Korea, on May 20, 1951. Posthumous.

World War II

CHARLES LEROY THOMAS, DETROIT

Army 1st Lt. Thomas was honored for heroism near Climbach, France, on Dec. 14, 1944.

Thomas was leading a task force storming the town when his vehicle was knocked out by Nazi fire. Wounded, he helped the crew out of the vehicle and was again wounded in the chest, legs and arm. However, Thomas continued to direct placement of two antitank guns, which returned fire. He briefed other soldiers before allowing himself to be evacuated. He was awarded the Distinguished Service Cross for heroism and was the first African American to receive that honor. The medal is a rung under the Medal of Honor.

In civilian life, Thomas was a Cass Technical High School graduate who attended Wayne State University, studying engineering and architecture. He designed his Detroit house on Glendale, flew airplanes, and enjoyed skiing and golf. Thomas worked briefly at Ford Motor Co.'s Rouge plant before the war.

When Thomas recovered from his wounds and returned to Detroit, he was hailed as a hero. Banquets were held. A radio program dramatized his heroics. His likeness and story were featured in True Comics. He then worked for General Motors and later the IRS. He died in 1980 at age 59.

Charles Thomas was the first black man to receive the Distinguished Service Cross.

In 1997, President Bill Clinton presented the Medal of Honor to his family. He was one of seven black soldiers recognized belatedly for their valor.

WALTER C. WETZEL, ROSEVILLE

Army Pvt. 1st Class Wetzel was honored for heroism at Birken, Germany, on April 3, 1945.

Wetzel was guarding his platoon's command post when he noticed that German forces were about to attack. He alerted his colleagues, then began defending the post against heavy automatic-weapons fire. Two German grenades landed in the room Wetzel and others were in. Shouting a warning, Wetzel threw himself on the grenades and absorbed their blast, which killed him. His comrades lived and defended the post.

WILLIAM H. THOMAS, YPSILANTI

Army Pvt. 1st Class Thomas was honored for heroism at Zambales Mountains, Luzon, the Philippines, on April 22, 1945. Posthumous.

THOMAS W. WIGLE, DETROIT

Army 2nd Lt. Wigle was honored for heroism at Monte Frassino, Italy, on Sept. 14, 1944. Posthumous.

RAYMOND ZUSSMAN, HAMTRAMCK

Army 2nd Lt. Zussman was honored for

"Detroit is Eldorado, 1927 model. It is staccato American. It is shockingly dynamic."

— Howard W. Willard, Women's Home Companion, 1927

"Nonwithstanding so large an industrial population, Detroit may fairly be described as a slumless city."

— National Geographic, 1928

heroism at Noroy le Bourg, France, on Sept. 12, 1944.

Commanding two tanks, Zussman, 27, was approaching enemy positions when his lead tank bogged down. He grabbed his carbine and moved forward alone on foot to spot German targets, then hustled back to the tanks to direct fire. One of his several forward forays led to 18 enemy soldiers being killed and 92 captured. Nine days later, he was killed in action.

Zussman was the only Jewish soldier to receive the Medal of Honor during World War II. He was born in Hamtramck, moved to Detroit's west side as a child, graduated from Central High and attended classes at Wayne State University. He was a shipping clerk at Sam's Cut Rate when he entered the Army.

His heroism has not been forgotten. A Detroit park on Davison near Dexter is named for him. And in Hamtramck, where he was born near his father's shoe store on Jos. Campau, the park in front of City Hall is named for him.

Nathan Zussman, when told in 1945 that his son would be awarded the medal, responded: "What good is a medal to me? I'd rather have my boy back. He was a good boy."

Dominican campaign

JOSEPH ANTHONY GLOWIN, DETROIT

Marine Corps Cpl. Glowin was honored for heroism at Guayacanas, Dominican Republic, in July 1916.

Glowin was attached to a company of Marines, one of two sent to the Dominican Republic in 1916 to protect U.S. and Haitian interests after revolution broke out. Near Guayacanas on July 3, Glowin and other marines came under fire from rebels and bandits. Glowin was wounded twice but continued to direct the battle for four hours until the marines were victorious.

Glowin joined the Detroit Police Department in 1923 and spent much of his career as a patrolman in the old Conner Station. He kept mum about his heroics.

When a police boss in 1936 heard about Glowin, the officer was feted as the only member of the police department ever awarded a Medal of Honor. Glowin died in 1952. He was 58.

Philippines

JAMES MCCONNELL, DETROIT

Army Pvt. McConnell was honored for heroism at Vigan, Luzon, in the Philippines on Dec. 4, 1899.

U.S. troops were sent to put down an insurrection launched by rebels on Feb. 4, 1899, nearly two months after the Spanish-American War ended with Spain ceding the islands to the

Associated Press

United States. The insurrection ended in 1902.

McConnell fought rebels for several hours while prone between two dead comrades.

CHARLES CAWETZKA, DETROIT

Army Pvt. Cawetzka was honored for heroism at Sariaya, Luzon, the Philippines, on Aug. 23, 1900.

Indian Wars

JOHN HARRINGTON, DETROIT

Army Pvt. Harrington was honored for heroism at Wichita River, Texas, on Sept. 12, 1874.

Harrington was carrying dispatches when he was attacked by 125 Indians, whom he and comrades fought throughout the day. He was wounded in the hip and unable to walk, but continued to fight, defending another wounded soldier.

"Detroit is a new city. Here the utmost in technology, or applied science, has been put magnificently to work . . . Life in Detroit is empty as a dried gourd for the creatures of the assembly line. Empty and insecure. One feels that about Detroit. It is a city of strangers; two-thirds of the residents came here after 1914."

– **Forrest Davis**, New Republic, June 17, 1936

WILBER E. WILDER, DETROIT

Army 1st Lt. Wilder was honored for heroism at Horseshoe Canyon, N.M., on April 23, 1882.

DAVID HOLLAND, DEARBORN

Army Cpl. Holland was honored for heroism in several actions at Cedar Creek, Mont., from October 1876 to Jan. 8, 1877.

WILLIAM DOUGHERTY, DETROIT

Army blacksmith Dougherty was honored for heroism in several actions in Arizona from August to October 1868.

WILLIAM LEONARD, YPSILANTI

Army Pvt. Leonard was honored for heroism at Muddy Creek, Mont., on May 7, 1877.

Civil War

THOMAS W. CUSTER, MONROE

Army 2nd Lt. Custer of the 6th Michigan Cavalry was the only soldier from Michigan to receive two Medals of Honor. Only 19 people in U.S. history have received two citations.

His first honor for heroism was at Namozine Church, Va., on May 10, 1863. The second was at Sailor Creek, Va., in April 1865, when he was wounded while jumping his horse over an enemy line and capturing two stands of colors. The horse died.

CORNELIUS CRONIN, DETROIT

Navy Chief Quartermaster Cronin was honored for heroism at Mobile Bay on Aug. 5, 1864.

Cool and vigilant at his station on board the USS Richmond, Cronin watched for signals and skillfully steered his ship through heavy Confederate fire as it trained guns at Ft. Morgan.

Cronin also participated in actions at Ft. Jackson and Ft. St. Philip, at the surrender of New Orleans, and on the attacks of the batteries below Vicksburg.

FREDERICK ALBER, MANCHESTER

Army Pvt. Alber, 26, with the 17th Michigan Infantry, was honored for heroism at Spotsylvania, Va., on May 12, 1864.

JAMES I. CHRISTIANCY, MONROE

Army 1st Lt. Christiancy, with the 9th Michigan Cavalry, was honored for heroism at Hawes Shops, Va., on May 28, 1864.

BYRON M. CUTCHEON, YPSILANTI

Army Maj. Cutcheon, 27, of the 20th Michigan Infantry, was honored for heroism at Horseshoe Bend, Ky., on May 10, 1863.

ROBERT F. DODD, HAMTRAMCK

Army Pvt. Dodd, 22, with the 27th Michigan Infantry, was honored for heroism at Petersburg, Va., on July 30, 1864.

JOHN A. FALCONER, MANCHESTER

Army Cpl. Falconer, 19, with the 17th, was honored for heroism at Ft. Sanders, Knoxville, Tenn., on Nov. 20, 1863.

CHARLES S. FALL, HAMBURG

Army Sgt. Fall, 22, with the 26th Michigan Infantry, was honored for heroism at Spotsylvania Courthouse, Va., on May 12, 1864.

EDWARD HILL, DETROIT

Army Capt. Hill, with the 16th Michigan Infantry, was honored for heroism at Cold Harbor, Va., on June 1, 1864.

PATRICK IRWIN, ANN ARBOR

Army 1st Sgt. Irwin, 25, with the 14th Michigan Infantry, was honored for heroism at Jonesboro, Ga., on Sept. 1, 1864.

JOSEPH S. KEEN, DETROIT

Army Sgt. Keen, 21, with the 13th Michigan Infantry, was honored for heroism near Chattahoochee River, Ga., on Oct. 1, 1864.

ANDREW J. KELLEY, YPSILANTI

Army Pvt. Kelley, 18, with the 17th, was honored for heroism at Knoxville, Tenn., on Nov. 20, 1863.

DANIEL MCFALL, YPSILANTI

Army Sgt. McFall, 28, with the 17th, was honored for heroism at Spotsylvania, Va., on May 12, 1864.

JOHN W. MENTER, DETROIT

Army Sgt. Menter, with the 5th Michigan Infantry, was honored for heroism at Sailors Creek, Va., on April 6, 1865.

CONRAD NOLL, ANN ARBOR

Army Sgt. Noll, with the 20th Michigan Infantry, was honored for heroism at Spotsylvania, Va., on May 12, 1864.

GEORGE E. RANNEY, DETROIT

Army surgeon Ranney, 24, with the 2nd Michigan Cavalry, was honored for heroism at Resaca, Ga., May 14, 1864.

CHARLES F. SANCRAINTE, MONROE

Army Pvt. Sancrainte, 24, with the 15th Michigan Infantry, was honored for heroism at Atlanta on July 22, 1864.

IRWIN SHEPARD, CHELSEA

Army Cpl. Shepard, with the 17th, was honored for heroism at Knoxville, Tenn., on Nov. 20, 1863.

> "You can see here, as it is impossible to do in a more varied and complex city, the whole structure of an industrial society."
>
> – Edmund Wilson, "The American Earthquake," 1930s

ORLANDO B. WILLCOX, DETROIT

Army Col. Willcox, with the 1st Michigan Infantry, was honored for heroism at Bull Run, Va., on July 21, 1861.

Congressional Gold Medal

The highest honor the U.S. government awards an individual.

MAJ. GEN. ANTHONY WAYNE

Wayne County's namesake, who lived in Detroit for several months in 1796, was cited for leadership in 1779.

MAJ. GEN. ALEXANDER MACOMB

Macomb County's namesake was cited in 1814 for "gallantry and good conduct" in combat against the British at Plattsburgh, N.Y., during the War of 1812.

COL. GEORGE CROGHAN

A military commander of Detroit in the early 19th Century, Croghan was cited in 1835 for his defense of Ft. Stephenson in Ohio during the War of 1812.

JOE LOUIS

The heavyweight champ from Detroit was cited in 1982 for bolstering "the spirit of the American people" during World War II.

DANNY THOMAS

The Detroit-raised actor and children's hospital founder was honored in 1983 for his humanitarian efforts.

ROSA PARKS

Rosa Parks was cited in 1999 for her leadership in civil rights.

Presidential Medal of Freedom

The nation's highest civilian award, established by President John F. Kennedy in 1963 to recognize civilian contributions to the country.

RALPH BUNCHE, statesman, 1963.

HENRY FORD II, auto chieftain, 1969.

WALTER REUTHER, labor leader (posthumously), 1995.

ROSA PARKS, civil rights icon, 1996.

MILDRED JEFFREY, labor activist, 2000.

Kennedy Center Honors

The John F. Kennedy for the Performing Arts in Washington, D.C., honors artists annually for contributions to the cultural life of the nation. Detroit-area honorees:

STEVIE WONDER, singer, 1999.

ARETHA FRANKLIN, singer, 1994.

ARTHUR MILLER, playwright, University of Michigan graduate, 1984.

Rhodes Scholars

Each year, 32 college students are chosen to study at the University of Oxford in England for two years. The scholarship is named for Cecil Rhodes (1853-1902), British financier and explorer. It's considered the most prestigious available to Americans. You need great grades, some athletic skills and leadership qualities to qualify. Here are recent area students who made the grade:

2000: ILYANA KUZIEMKO of Sterling Heights, a senior studying economics at Harvard University, has a passion for economics, mathematics and sports. She is a marathon runner and has published articles on economics and public policy. A 1996 graduate of Detroit Country Day School, Kuziemko planned to get a master's degree in mathematics for industry at Oxford.

1998: FIONA ROSE of Ann Arbor earned a bachelor of arts degree at the University of Michigan in classical archaeology. A graduate of Ann Arbor's Community High School, she studied for a master's degree in classical archaeology at Oxford.

1997: ANNETTE SALMEEN of Ann Arbor, an honors student in chemistry and a national champion in swimming during her four years at the University of California at Los Angeles, graduat-

"Paris dictates a season's silhouette, but Detroit manufactures a pattern of life, bolder than Moscow in transforming human habits and communizing the output of the machine."

– Anne O'Hare McCormick, New York Times, 1934

> "In the June riots of this year, the Detroit police ran true to form. The trouble reached riot proportions because the Detroit police once again enforced the law under an unequal hand. They used 'persuasion' rather than firm action with white rioters while against Negroes they used the ultimate in force: nightsticks, revolvers, riot guns, submachine guns and deer guns."
>
> – NACCP officials **Walter White and Thurgood Marshall**, "What Caused the Detroit Riots," 1943

ed from Ann Arbor Huron High School in 1992. She won her scholarship months after winning a gold medal in the 800-meter freestyle relay in the Atlanta Olympic Games in 1996.

1997: STEPHANIE PALMER of Walled Lake, a chemical physics major at Michigan State University, was a 1993 Walled Lake Western High School graduate.

1996: DAYNE WALLING of Flint got his bachelor's degree from Michigan State University in social relations and has been active in community work in his hometown.

1994: LEAH NIEDERSTADT of Harbor Springs was a University of Michigan student and rugby player who majored in political science and African-American and African Studies. Her special interest was the mythology of Eastern Africa, particularly Ethiopia, and how that affects the political process.

1993: TAYLOR FRAVEL grew up in Ann Arbor and was living in Pointe aux Barques. A senior at Middlebury College in Vermont, Fravel was a history major with a concentration in Chinese languages.

1991: JASON ZIMBA of Dearborn Heights, a graduate of Crestwood High School, was a mathematics and astrophysics major at Williams College in Massachusetts.

Oscars

For achievement in the motion-picture industry:

KURT LUEDTKE: The Birmingham resident has won two of the nation's best-known awards. In 1986, Luedtke won an Academy Award for Best Screenplay Adaptation for his work on "Out of Africa," the film version of the books on Africa by Danish author Isak Dinesen. As an editor at the Free Press, Luedtke was one of the leaders of a team of reporters and editors who received the 1968 Pulitzer Prize for coverage of the 1967 Detroit riot. He later became the paper's executive editor before going Hollywood.

Kurt Luedtke has won a Pulitzer Prize along with his Oscar.

PAMELA CONN AND SUE MARX: Detroiters who won the Academy Award for best short film in 1988

for "Young at Heart," a lighthearted real story of the companionship of two octogenarian artists, Louis Gothelf, Marx's father, and the widowed Reva Shwayder.

TED PETOK: The Birmingham commercial-maker won an Academy Award in 1972 for his two-minute and 24-second animated rendition of an old but funny joke — the Crunchbird. The story involves a strange-looking bird with big teeth who attacks on command anything that follows his name, as in, "Crunchbird, the chair." The film's punch line came when a tired husband drags himself home one day to find his wife had bought the bird, and says: "Crunchbird, my ass." Guess what gets attacked? Accepting the award, Petok said: "Crunchbird, my Oscar." Petok also was the mastermind who created the little Uptown Bottle Blower who was always "too pooped to participate" until he guzzled a slug of Faygo's Uptown lemon-lime.

CHRISTINE LAHTI: The Birmingham-bred actress has been in dozens of TV shows and movies. In the 1990s, she played Dr. Kathryn Austin on "Chicago Hope." She won an Academy Award in 1995 for her live action short film "Lieberman in Love."

JOHN NELSON: The Grosse Pointe North and University of Michigan alumnus won the 2000 Oscar for his visual effects work on "Gladiator." Nelson's other credits include "Terminator 2," "City of Angels," "The Cable Guy," and "The Pelican Brief."

Pulitzer Prizes

Detroit Free Press

1932: Douglas Martin, James Pooler, William Richards, John Sloan and Frank Webb for coverage of a massive American Legion parade in Detroit.

1945: Ken McCormick for public service in investigating corruption among legislators in Lansing.

1955: Royce Howes for editorial writing about an unauthorized UAW strike against the Chrysler Corp.

1956: Lee Hills for local reporting on deadline for his coverage of the negotiations between the UAW and Ford and General Motors over a guaranteed annual wage.

1968: Free Press staff for reporting on the 1967 Detroit riot.

1981: Taro Yamasaki for his photography giving a close-up look at life inside the State Prison of Southern Michigan in Jackson.

Metro Detroiters on the Hollywood Walk of Fame

Anita Baker	Berry Gordy	Smokey Robinson	The Supremes
Sonny Bono	Charlton Heston	Diana Ross	The Temptations
Chad Everett	John Lee Hooker	Tom Selleck	Danny Thomas
The Four Tops	Casey Kasem	Bob Seger and	Marlo Thomas
Aretha Franklin	George Peppard	the Silver	Robin Williams
Marvin Gaye	Della Reese	Bullet Band	Stevie Wonder

Motown Records founder Berry Gordy Jr. (in sunglasses) celebrates after being awarded the 2,076th star on the Hollywood Walk of Fame in 1996. Joining Gordy are Stevie Wonder, left, honorary Hollywood Mayor Johnny Grant, Otis Williams of the Temptations (wearing the cap), Diana Ross and Smokey Robinson between Gordy and Ross.

1989: Manny Crisostomo for photography depicting the lives of Southwestern High School students.
1990: David Turnley for photographic coverage of political change in Eastern Europe and the Chinese army attack on students in Beijing.

Detroit News

1942: Milton Brooks for Spot News Photography.
1982: David Ashenfelter and Sydney Freedberg for Meritorious Public Service.
1994: Eric Freedman and Jim Mitzelfeld for Beat Reporting.

Pam Eldred of West Bloomfield was Miss America 1970.

Beauty contests

Miss America

PATRICIA DONNELLY, 1939: A 19-year-old Detroiter, she graduated from Northwestern High School and was working as a model when she was crowned. Her talent included playing bass fiddle while singing "Old Man Mose Is Dead." Now Patricia Harris, she overcame throat cancer in the 1980s and is a grandmother living near Boston. In 1999, she served as grand marshal of the Miss America Parade.

> "It is no accident that Coughlin . . . Lindbergh, the Ford manifestations from on high, and other similar fascistic or plain lunatic organizations have their largest audience here. This is a violent and amorphous town."
>
> – **Cyril Cane**, British acting consul-general in Detroit, 1943

PAM ELDRED, 1970: Eldred, 21, of West Bloomfield performed ballet, charmed judges and won the swimsuit competition. An Immaculata High School graduate who was attending Mercy College, Eldred said: "I don't feel like I'm the most beautiful girl in the United States. I'm just representing the girls of the United States." Women, protesting what they called the sexist nature of the pageant, picketed that year.

KAYE LANI RAE RAFKO, 1988: Rafko, 24, of Monroe bowled over judges by wearing a Tahitian headdress while performing a Polynesian dance. Rafko also won the swimsuit competition. She has worked as a registered nurse caring for dying cancer patients. Today she's a registered nurse pursuing a master's degree at the University of Michigan. She has traveled nationwide addressing nurses, hospice and AIDS groups.

NANCY FLEMING, 1961: Fleming was from Montague in western Michigan.

Miss USA

CAROLE ANNE-MARIE GIST, 1990: Gist, 20, became the first black contestant and the first woman from Michigan to capture the Miss USA crown. Gist, a Detroiter, was a student at Northwood Institute in Midland and a 1987 magna cum laude graduate of Cass Technical High School in Detroit.

KENYA MOORE, 1993: Moore, 22, a Detroiter who lived on Central Avenue with her grandmother, was studying child psychology at Wayne State University when she won the crown. Like Gist, she was a graduate of Detroit's Cass Tech.

She had modeled for magazines and appeared on the cover of Ebony Man's swimsuit issue.

But her latest claim to fame was a leading role in the movie, "Trois," an R-rated thriller about a couple that adds another woman to their bedroom.

Nobel Prize

One Detroit-born diplomat has received the Nobel Prize. Six laureates have connections to U-M.

RALPH BUNCHE, Nobel Peace Prize, 1950: Born in Detroit in 1904, he was a member of Second Baptist Church and hawked newspapers to help support his family.

He became a United Nations mediator and an African affairs expert for the U.S. State Department.

Bunche's crowning achievement was negotiating the peace plan that ended the Six-Day War of 1948. That earned him the Nobel. He died in 1971. Bunche Elementary School on Ellery in Detroit is named for him.

MARTINUS J.G. VELTMAN, Nobel Prize in physics, 1999: U-M professor emeritus Veltman shared the Nobel Prize for physics with a former student for their theoretical work on the structure and motion of subatomic particles. The former student was Dutch scientist Gerardus 't Hooft. Veltman came to U-M in 1981 as the John D. MacArthur professor of physics. He retired in 1997.

SAMUEL CHAO CHUNG TING, Nobel Prize in physics, 1976: An Ann Arbor native who received undergraduate, master's and doctoral degrees at UM, Ting shared with Burton Richter the prize for the discovery of a subatomic particle three times heavier than the proton. The discovery led to revisions in the theory of quarks.

JEROME KARLE, Nobel Prize in chemistry, 1985: Karle received his PhD at U-M. He won the prize for work on the development of direct methods for the determination of crystal structures.

STANLEY COHEN, Nobel Prize in medicine and physiology, 1986: Cohen, who received his PhD at U-M, won for discoveries that are of great importance in understanding the mechanisms that regulate cell and organ growth.

MARSHALL NIRENBERG, Nobel Prize in medicine and physiology, 1968: Nirenberg, who received his PhD at U-M in 1957, won the prize for his development of the procedure for deciphering the genetic code in living cells.

THOMAS H. WELLER, Nobel Prize in medicine and physiology, 1954: Weller received his undergraduate and master's degrees from U-M. He shared the Nobel Prize for discovery of the ability of the polio virus to grow in different tissues.

Heisman Trophy

The Heisman Memorial Trophy is presented each year by the Downtown Athletic Club of New York City to the outstanding football player in the nation, as decided by sportswriters and sportscasters.

1940 — TOM HARMON, University of Michigan

1958 — PETE DAWKINS, Army (from Royal Oak)

1991 — DESMOND HOWARD, U-M

1997 — CHARLES WOODSON, U-M

Free Press file photo

Bad press

Some people and places who – rightly or wrongly – carry lots of baggage:

ANTOINE DE LA MOTHE CADILLAC: The big guy himself. Civic boosters have put him on a pedestal purely because he founded the city. But most historians agree that as a military commander, Monsieur Cadillac was a failure. He failed to develop the settlement he had envisioned at Detroit and he failed to Frenchify the Indians, as he had promised. Seven years after he arrived, an official report on his stewardship in Detroit "was a crushing indictment," wrote historian Yves Zoltvany.

WILLIAM HULL: The guy who surrendered Detroit to the British during the War of 1812 without mussing a hair. Hull was an accomplished lawyer, politician and a celebrated military officer during the Revolutionary War. While commanding the army in Detroit in 1812, Hull invited the Brits in after he recognized that his forces were short of supplies, and he feared a massacre. In 1814, a court-martial convicted him of cowardice and neglect of duty, and he was sentenced to be

shot. But President James Madison commuted his sentence. Hull spent the remainder of his life attempting to redeem his reputation.

PVT. EDWARD D. SLOVIK: An estimated 40,000 U.S. soldiers deserted during World War II; 2,864 were tried by court-martial; 49 were sentenced to death; one was executed — Eddie Slovik of Detroit. His was the first execution of a deserter since the Civil War. During his prewar youth in Detroit, Hamtramck and Dearborn, Slovik was the one in his

Edward Slovik was short on luck.

group who always got caught. Petty theft, breaking and entering, stolen cars. "He was the unluckiest poor kid who ever lived," said his widow, Antoinette. Eddie Slovik cast off his rifle and walked away from the war just as the Battle of the Bulge broke out. He died Jan. 31, 1945, before a 12-man firing squad in the garden of a French castle. During 372 days in the Army, Slovik wrote 376 letters to his wife. After his death, she married his brother.

THE RENAISSANCE CENTER: Backers predicted the $337-million complex would do much to reverse the exodus of business from downtown Detroit. The reality: The joint, with its huge berms and mind-boggling design (by architect John Portman) became a fortress that came to stand for isolation, and it did little to halt the bleeding of downtown. The RenCen encountered constant financial problems; its owners tried to unload it for two years before finally selling it to the General Motors Corp. in 1996

NIGHTMARE IN DEARBORN: A hundred Edsels parade toward Ford Motor Co. headquarters in 1977. They belonged to members of an Edsel club, which was celebrating the 20th anniversary of one of Ford's biggest blunders. Some members yelled at the Ford building: "We're coming back to haunt you."

DETROIT: "Where they stand in line for a glass of beer … where more dames wear slacks than in Hollywood … where it takes the reserves to get a vandal out of a theater, where the sidewalk madonnas get too much opposition from home talent … and where everybody has two sawbucks to run against each other. Detroit, the hottest town in America."

– **Daily Variety**, October 1943

Associated Press

WILLIAM HACKEL: For 24 years, William Hackel was the law in Macomb County. The Macomb County sheriff, above right, was also hailed as a champion of victimized women and children. But in 2000, a jury convicted Hackel, 58, of raping a 25-year-old woman at the Soaring Eagle Casino & Resort in Mt. Pleasant. He was convicted and sentenced to serve three to 15 years in prison.

for the bargain-basement price of $73 million. GM, which is using the RenCen as its world headquarters, is investing $500 million to make the complex more people-friendly.

IVAN BOESKY: Said the Wall Street Journal: "No one on Wall Street ever flew as high or crashed as hard as Ivan F. Boesky." Boesky, the son of a Russian immigrant, grew up in Detroit and attended Mumford High School and Detroit College of Law. He started in business at age 13, illegally driving an ice cream truck through west-side streets. He went on to become one of Wall Street's most aggressive, risky and successful stock traders. In the mid-1980s, Boesky was worth $500 million. But he wound up paying $100 million of that in fines to the Securities and Exchange Commission after being busted for insider trading in 1986.

Ivan Boesky

THE EDSEL: A synonym for "loser." Named after Henry Ford's only child, the Edsel was the moniker of a Ford Motor Co. line that debuted in 1957 after 10 years of market research and months of secrecy and hype. Bing Crosby, Frank Sinatra and Kim Novak hawked the car line, which cost Ford $250 million to produce. There were 18 models, from a two-door compact to a nine-passenger behemoth. The company boldly predicted sales of 250,000 cars the first year. The Edsels listed at $2,800 to $4,200 (windshield washer option: $11.50). The result: The economy took a downturn, and the cars became less affordable. One contemporary critic said the car's vertical front grill resembled "an Oldsmobile sucking a lemon." After two years, Ford axed the entire line. In all, Ford built 110,000 Edsels, some of which live today in car clubs.

WILLIAM HART: Detroit's longest-serving police chief and the first black person to head the department, Hart went to federal prison after being convicted in 1992 of embezzling $2.3 million. Because of ill health and cooperation with federal authorities in a trial of cops accused of drug crimes, he was released early from a 10-year prison sentence. In 1999, he was selling shoes in downtown Detroit.

DENNY MCLAIN: The last major-league pitcher to win more than 30 games, McLain struck out off the mound. The 31-game winner for the 1968 World Champion Tigers went to prison in the mid-1980s after being convicted of bookmaking, extortion, racketeering and cocaine trafficking. Freed in 1987 on procedural grounds, he became a radio host for WXYT-AM (1270), but fell hard again in 1996. A judge gave him eight years in prison for looting the pension fund of a Chesaning meat-packing firm.

JOHN Z. DELOREAN: One of the auto industry's best-known engineers, DeLorean created the first muscle car, the Pontiac Tempest GTO. He quit General Motors in 1973 to build his own car in Northern Ireland. That company collapsed after he was arrested in 1982 in a widely seen sting that was captured on a hidden camera. He was accused of conspiring to sell $24 million in cocaine to salvage his venture. An entrapment defense got him acquitted, but he wrestled with 40 other legal cases. In 1998, the U.S. Supreme Court refused to hear his appeal of a jury award of $4.7 million in legal fees — $8 million with interest — owed to Mayer Morganroth in Southfield. In 2000, he was evicted from his 434-acre estate in New Jersey, his home for nearly 20 years. It sold for $15.25 million at a bankruptcy auction.

DODGE FOUNTAIN: It sputters each summer in Hart Plaza like an overgrown lawn sprinkler, unable to make the beautiful water displays promised by its designer in 1975. Keep the faith, Detroit: The seemingly terminal patient known as Dodge Fountain has been healed, officials with straight faces have declared numerous times. The cursed gizmo has undergone various renovations costing more than $700,000 and is always on the verge of doing its high-tech tricks . . . but it never really works as heralded. When construction began, officials described the $3-million fountain as a computerized wonder that would produce a virtually endless series of displays with its 350 water jets and 350 lights. Designer Isamu Noguchi promised it would be the greatest fountain ever assembled. But the fountain, alas, has become a civic joke. Its biggest accomplishment is to spew water like a leaky fountain.

GABRIEL B. TAIT/Detroit Free Press

A soldier's story

TONI CATO RIGGS: She portrayed herself as a grieving widow, mourning the murder of her husband on the lawless battlefield of Detroit's streets one day after he returned to the United States after surviving the Persian Gulf War. Army Spec. Anthony Riggs had been robbed, the police and media said, shot dead March 18, 1991, in front of his loving wife as they prepared to move belongings to a new apartment in Warren. But the truth quickly surfaced, as wife Toni and her brother, Michael Cato, were charged with murdering Anthony Riggs for $150,000 in life insurance. She beat the first rap when a judge ruled that her brother's confession could not be used against her, and brother Michael went to jail for life. But greed drove Toni Riggs to carelessness, and in 1994, she sought to become a hired drug courier and was busted in a federal drug sting. Agents caught her on hidden videotape bragging and laughing about her role in the murder. She is serving life in prison for first-degree murder.

Toni Cato Riggs listens to testimony in court.

Free Press file photo

PEOPLE MOVER: Detroit's 2.9-mile circular railway encountered trouble from the start. It was $170 million over budget. It was 10 years late in opening. Its ridership estimates were overstated. It was damaged by the implosion of the J. L. Hudson Building in 1998 and was partially closed for more than a year. Don't blame it all on Detroit. Though the city runs it, the PM was the brainchild of the old Southeast Michigan Transportation Authority, which had to be rescued by Mayor Coleman Young after it had messed up the PM's construction.

METRO AIRPORT: Among the gripes: it takes forever to get your baggage, long lines at ticket counters, lack of parking, lousy food, few amenities and crummy service by the airport's chief tenant, Northwest Airlines. There are even questions about the books. In 2000, Lansing lawmakers were scrutinizing the financial practices of the airport's managers, who work for Wayne County Executive Ed McNamara. The airport is undergoing a billion-dollar renovation, including a new midfield terminal and mammoth parking garage. Officials promise improvements. We'll see.

The People Mover has encountered its own problems, but the breakdown on June 16, 2000, was due to a Detroit Public Lighting Department power outage. Above, Detroit Transit Officer Sanford Kelly escorts Cady Hadesman, 5, of Bingham Farms to the Renaissance Center station. Cady's mother, Kathy, follows.

The word on the street

"Let white America know that the name of the game is tit-for-tat, an eye for an eye, a tooth for a tooth, and a life for a life... Motown, if you don't come around, we are going to burn you down!"

– H. Rap Brown, chairman of the Student Non-Violent Coordinating Committee, at the Black Arts Convention in Detroit, held June 29-July 2, 1967, three weeks before the riot. He's now known as Jamil Abdullah Al-Amin.

"Detroit is America's fifth-largest city in size; but in the attempt to cope with the problems that lie behind the present convulsion in America's cities, Detroit may well have been No. 1."

– New York Times, 1967

"Difficult as it may be to believe, Detroit as of 1967 was nationally viewed as a model big city in many respects. The Washington Post editorialized while the riot was under way that the riot was 'the greatest tragedy of all the long succession of Negro ghetto outbursts' because Detroit had become 'the American model of intelligence and courage applied to the governance of a huge industrial city.'"

– Historian Sidney Fine, Henry Russel lecture, University of Michigan, 1985

"Macomb County is the site of the real drama in our political life. This is the site of an historic upheaval that has wrecked the old and promises a new kind of politics."

– Pollster Stanley Greenberg in "Middle Class Dreams," referring to the evolution of Reagan Democrats

"The most conspicuous city-suburb contrast in the United States runs along Detroit's Alter Road. Locals call the street the 'Berlin Wall' or the 'barrier,' or the 'Mason-Dixon Line.' It divides the suburban Grosse Pointe communities, which are among the most genteel towns anywhere, from the east side of Detroit, which is poor and mostly black. The Detroit side is studded with abandoned cars, graffiti-covered schools, and burned-out buildings. Two blocks away, within view, are neatly clipped hedges and immaculate houses – a world of servants and charity balls, two-car garages and expensive clothes. On the one side, says John Kelly, a Democratic state senator whose district awkwardly straddles both neighborhoods, is 'West Beirut;' on the other side, 'Disneyland.'"

– Kenneth Jackson, "Crabgrass Frontier: The Suburbanization of the United States," 1985

A poster distributed in Detroit by the H. Rap Brown Anti-Dope Movement in the early 1970s.

"There's going to be emotion, struggle, successes and failures in dramatic social fashion. But when things happen here, there's no blueprint. It's uncharted territory. The same things happen elsewhere, but it's the large scale that gives things an unusual quality – and energy – here."

– The Rev. William Cunningham, founder of the civil rights group Focus: HOPE, 1991

"Aside from adding a healthy dose of 'bad-ass' credibility to anything and anyone coming from here, Detroit's multifold problems have actually aided the growth of the city's diverse and ever-growing underground. The cost of living is about as low as it gets, and the city is nowhere near as dangerous as it is purported to be. Add to that the fact that there are few legitimate forms of culture left in the city, and you can easily see why Detroit is a virtual paradise for artists, musicians and poets."

— **Spin** (Magazine), "Underground USA," 1997

"A city whose beauty is in its scar tissue, its lines of aging."

— Native Detroiter and West Coast music producer **Don Was** in Egg magazine, 1991

"You wouldn't suspect there was such a thing as a soul if you went to Detroit. Everything is too new, too slick, too bright, too ruthless. Souls don't grow in factories. Souls are killed in factories – even the niggardly ones. Detroit can do in a week for the white man what the South couldn't do in a hundred years to the Negro."

— **Henry Miller**, "The Air Conditioned Nightmare," 1945

"For I believe the spiritual combat to be more desperate in the center of chaos, which is Detroit."

— **Theodore Roethke**, "Straw for the Fire," edited by David Wagoner, 1940s

www.yin-sight.com

"My grandfather worked at Ford for 20 years; he was like a career autoworker. A lot of the kids that came up after this integration, they got used to a better way of living. If you had a job at the plant at this time, you were making bucks. And it wasn't like the white guy standing next to you is getting five or 10 dollars an hour more than you. Everybody was equal. So what happened is you've got this environment with kids coming up somewhat snobby, 'cos, hey, their parents are making money working at Ford or GM or Chrysler, been elevated to a foreman, maybe even to a white-collar job."

— **Juan Atkins**, a pioneer of Detroit techno music, discussing affluence among black youth in "Generation Ecstasy"

"Detroit is a place where work, hard daily work – that privilege, duty and vocation of the human person – is a truly distinctive characteristic of urban life."

— **Pope John Paul II**, during his 1987 visit

Detroit is actually but a channel or river of medium breadth and 25 leagues in length, according to my estimate . . . through which flows and escapes slowly and with sufficiently moderate current, the living and crystal waters of Lake Superior, Michigan and Huron," which are so many seas of sweet water, "into Lake Erie, Lake Ontario, or Frontenac, and which finally, together with the waters of the St. Lawrence, mingle with those of the ocean. Its borders are so many vast prairies, and the freshness of the Beautiful waters keeps the banks always green. The prairies are bordered by long and broad rows of fruit trees which have never felt the careful hand of the vigilant gardener. Here, also, orchards, young and old, soften and bend their branches, under the weight and quantity of their fruit, towards the mother earth, which has produced them.

— **Antoine de la Mothe Cadillac**, founder of Detroit, 1701, in "The History of Detroit and Wayne County and Early Michigan," by Silas Farmer.

The Detroit Almanac

04. PE

"Detroit is infinitely fascinating, almost overwhelming. ... Moving here ... gave me visions and perspectives."

— **Joyce Carol Oates**, *1987*

From natives to nationalities

The original Detroiters

When Cadillac landed in 1701, he invited various native groups to settle around Ft. Pontchartrain and build ties with French fur traders. Cadillac wanted to Europeanize the American Indians so they would side with France. His plan failed.

The Indians became pawns in the epic empire struggles of France, England, and later, the United States. The Europeans greatly altered Indian culture, destroying their independence and ultimately forcing them from their centuries-old homelands. Europeans introduced Indians to alcohol, divided them with various strategies, tricking them to gain beaver pelts.

Indians had lived in southeastern Michigan for thousands of years. Anthropologists say Michigan Indians fished at what is now St. Ignace in summer, then traveled to the Detroit area to hunt during winter. They may have also mined copper in the Upper Peninsula and transported it south where the metal eventually reached Mexico.

Cadillac's plan brought Huron and Ottawa Indians from the Straits of Mackinac, the Potawatomi and Miami from the St. Joseph River region of southwestern Michigan, and the Sauk, Mesquakie and Mascouten from Wisconsin to separate villages near Ft. Pontchartrain. Missisauga and Ojibwa from northern Lake Huron settled on the north side of Lake St. Clair.

Animosities flared among tribes with the concentration of about 6,000 Indians in the area. After 1712, only the Huron and Potawatomi remained close to the fort, with the Ottawa on the opposite shore in Ontario, Canada.

Many Indians were pushed out of Michigan after their leaders signed the Treaty of 1836 ceding to the federal government 75 percent of the land that ultimately became the State of Michigan.

Here are five Indian nations who had (and some continue to have) a significant presence in Michigan:

OJIBWA OR OJIBWAY: Often called Chippewa, they were the first natives seen by Europeans when white men reached the present site of Sault Ste. Marie in the early 17th Century. Ojibway means "to roast till puckered up," and refers to the puckered seam on their moccasins. They were experts in the use of the canoes and depended largely on fish for food.

OTTAWA OR ODAWA: Their tribal name means "traders." The French noticed how the Ottawa usually traveled with their goods — guns, powder, metal kettles, hatchets, knives, cornmeal, sunflower oil, furs, mats, tobacco, and medicinal roots and herbs — and were not inclined to war. The tribe is best known for the pan-Indian, anti-English rebellion led by Pontiac at Detroit, which was a fort and some farms. The Ottawa were, until their monopoly was lost, the most important group of middlemen in the fur trade between other Upper Great Lakes tribes and the French and English. At first allied with the French, many Ottawa started shifting their allegiances and business to English traders when they began losing their trade monopoly on the upper lakes.

Future mayor Albert Cobo (in the saucer hat) poses with his Sunday School teachers and classmates, circa 1900.

Free Press file photo

> Many Indians were pushed out of Michigan after their leaders signed the Treaty of 1836 ceding to the federal government 75 percent of the land that ultimately became the State of Michigan.

Clements Library,
University of Michigan, Ann Arbor

"Moonlight Adventure on the St. Clair River," by artist John Mix Stanley (1814-1872), depicts pioneer children rafting toward an Indian encampment.

INDIAN POPULATION BY COUNTY IN SOUTHEAST MICHIGAN IN 1990

Wayne	7,954
Oakland	3,888
Macomb	2,600
Washtenaw	1,051
St. Clair	743
Livingston	701
Monroe	476

POTAWATOMI: Their tribal name means "people of the place of the fire" and they were sometimes known as the Fire Nation. They may have lived in Michigan's Lower Peninsula before their encounter with the French. In Detroit in the early 1700s, tribal women cultivated corn, beans, peas, squashes and melons. Everyone went on autumn hunts — men, women and children. They wintered in the forest and returned in the spring. In early times, the Potawatomi made their clothing from tanned hides and furs. The men wore moccasins, leggings, breechcloths, garters, leather shirts and sometimes belts. On their heads, they wore feathers and fur turbans. Later, when trade goods were introduced, they used glass beads and did applique work on their clothing. The Potawatomi were allies of the French and played a prominent part in Pontiac's uprising. They also fought the United States until the Treaty of Greenville in 1795.

HURON OR WYANDOT/WYANDOTTE: Wyandot is said to mean "islanders" or "dwellers in a peninsula." They resettled from Michilimackinac to the Detroit area in 1704 under French auspices. In the early 1700s, they raised a large amount of Indian corn, peas, beans and some wheat. They built their huts almost entirely of bark, very lofty and long and arched like arbors. The men hunted summer and winter. They were the most faithful nation to the French. After the Revolutionary War, the Wyandot joined the English and the Great Lakes tribes in opposing the Americans. Although they were under heavy pressure to sell their last land in Ohio and Michigan and to move west of the Mississippi, the Wyandot resisted until 1843. Finally selling their last

lands, they boarded steamboats and traveled west to take possession of a tract where Kansas City, Mo., now stands. By 1872, most had moved to Oklahoma.

MIAMI: The tribal name is said to mean "people who live on the peninsula." In 1703, there was a Miami village at Detroit, while their major settlement was on the St. Joseph River in southwestern Michigan. The Miami were farmers living in permanent settlements, never migrating until forced to move by neighboring tribes or, later, by government edict to make way for white settlers. They were inclined to peace. They did most of their traveling by land.

TODAY: Southeast Michigan is home to many American-Indian groups, including Oneida, Potawatomi, Miami, Ojibwa and Mohawk.

SOURCES: MELISSA PFLUG, ANTHROPOLOGY PROFESSOR AT WAYNE STATE UNIVERSITY; "INDIAN TRIBES OF NORTH AMERICA," BY JOHN R. SWANTON; "THE INDIANS OF MICHIGAN," BY EMERSON F. GREENMAN; "ATLAS OF GREAT LAKES INDIAN HISTORY," EDITED BY HELEN HORNBECK TANNER; "MICHIGAN INDIANS A-Z"; U.S. CENSUS BUREAU.

Native leaders

PONTIAC (1720-1769): Born either at the Straits of Mackinac or along the Maumee River in northern Ohio, Pontiac is arguably the greatest Great Lakes Indian leader of the 18th Century and the only one to mount a nearly successful rout of the English from the region. His plan to capture Detroit failed, but his men captured nearly all the other English forts and outposts in the region, including the key fort at Michilimackinac. He died outside St. Louis, Mo., in 1769, when an Indian from a rival nation stabbed the drunken Pontiac in the back.

TECUMSEH: A Shawnee chief believed to have been born in Ohio about 1768, Tecumseh is perhaps the most famous Indian of the Detroit region, next to Pontiac. Tecumseh was inspired by his influential brother, the Prophet (also known as Tenskwatawa), who said Indians should return to their pre-European ways. Tecumseh seized on the Prophet's teachings and organized Indians to oppose Americans, who were taking their land. Based along the Detroit River in present-day Windsor and Amherstburg, Canada, in Ontario, Tecumseh fought with the British during the War of 1812 and was an ally of British Cmdr. Isaac Brock, who captured Detroit in 1812. "Sagacious and gallant," is how Brock described Tecumseh. In April 1813, Tecumseh stopped an Indian massacre of captured Americans after a battle in Ohio, an act that helped to elevate his stature among whites. Tecumseh died in 1813 during the battle of Moraviantown, Canada, when the Indians remained to fight the advancing Americans after the British had retreated.

WEYAPIERSENWAH: Known as Blue Jacket to the British, this Shawnee chief was born in the middle of the 1700s and died about 1810 near Detroit. He was an ally of the British during the American Revolution. He was chief when Gen. Anthony Wayne defeated the Indians at the decisive Battle of Fallen Timbers in Ohio. He also signed the Treaty of Greenville that gave the Americans much of Ohio.

MICHIPICHY: The French called him *Quarante Sols*. A Huron chief known for his bravery during the Huron-Iroquois wars, Michipichy was one of the chiefs who agreed to bring his people to Detroit after Cadillac founded the fort in 1701. Acting as Cadillac's agent, Michipichy also persuaded other Indi-

PONTIAC

Arguably the greatest Great Lakes Indian leader of the 18th Century and the only one to mount a nearly successful rout of the English from the region.

TECUMSEH

Perhaps the most famous Indian of the Detroit region, next to Pontiac. He fought with the British during the War of 1812 and was an ally of British Cmdr. Isaac Brock, who captured Detroit in 1812.

Burton Historical Collection

Chief Pontiac, the Ottawa leader who almost captured Detroit.

Burton Historical Collection

Chief Tecumseh, the Shawnee leader, in a painting by a contemporary British soldier.

CITIZENSHIP

Between 1900 and 1999, there were 629,176 people in Michigan who became U.S. citizens. Foreign-born people in the metro area, and their percentage of total population:

➤ **Detroit:**
1960 .... 201,713 ..12.1%
1990....... 34,490 ... 3.4%

➤ **Wayne County:**
1960..... 285,051..10.7%
1990 ....102,336 ....4.8%

➤ **Macomb County:**
1960... 32,286 ...... 8.0%
1990... 49,109 ...... 6.8%

➤ **Oakland County:**
1960 ...47,238   .... 6.8%
1990....76,157 ...... 7.0%

an tribes to move to Detroit. One of Michipichy's gifts was an ability to see through the Europeans' trickery; while negotiating with Cadillac, he also dickered with the British in search of a better trading deal. Michipichy and Cadillac had a falling-out in 1703. By 1706, when Indians began fighting among themselves at Detroit, some people charged that Michipichy was one of the troublemakers. He then disappeared from French records.

LE PESANT: His name means "the heavy" or "big guy" in French, and he was also called *L'Ours* (the Bear) because of his formidable physique. Le Pesant was an important Ottawa chief during Detroit's first decade. Cadillac enticed him to move to the region after 1701. By 1706, Le Pesant was at the center of turmoil at Detroit. Le Pesant and other Ottawa killed seven Miami chiefs. The Miami and Huron ran to the fort and the Ottawa accidentally killed a French priest and soldier. Intertribal warfare continued for months, and the French sought Le Pesant, blaming him for the trouble. In 1707, soldiers and several Ottawa chiefs arrested Le Pesant at Michilimackinac and took him to Detroit, where he later escaped, perhaps with Cadillac's complicity. In 1708, according to historian Donald Chaput, Le Pesant was again living at Detroit, and his return touched off an attack on the fort by the Miami, who felt the French should have executed him. About 1712, Le Pesant left Detroit for good and settled on Manatoulin Island in northern Lake Huron.

SOURCE: DICTIONARY OF CANADIAN BIOGRAPHY.

Immigration

The draw: In the 19th Century, Detroit offered room to grow, to start a business, to find haven from famine or turmoil in Europe.

Immigration patterns in Detroit then mirrored national patterns, which favored Europeans. In fact by the late 19th Century, Asians were forbidden to immigrate to the United States.

The early 20th Century saw people flock to build cars or work in auto-related businesses. The burgeoning auto companies even advertised for skilled trades in Europe's major cities.

To many, Detroit never was a permanent destination. Immigrants from several Middle Eastern and Eastern European nations fully expected to work long enough to return to their homelands with a relative fortune.

Men came alone, rooming in houses, working in factories. The story goes that in High-

land Park boarding houses, one man would awake for work in time for another man to take his bed.

The first mosque in North America opened in Highland Park to meet the needs of immigrant Muslims working in the Ford plant. In 1930, 1 in 4 Detroiters was foreign-born.

By 1970, after several easings of the quota system from 1965 to 1970, patterns changed radically.

Thousands of people from countries once under small quotas began to flock to Detroit. Chaldeans from Iraq, Muslims from Lebanon, Koreans, Chinese from Taiwan, Filipinos and Asian Indians, Albanians from Yugoslavia's Kosovo province — all became the region's new immigrants. As change coursed through Eastern Europe, Africa and the Middle East in the 1980s and 1990s, some immigrants arrived from Poland, Nigeria and Yemen. Hundreds of people from Mexico and countries farther south moved here, too, although the impact was not as great as in southern states.

THE FLOOD: More immigrants settled in Detroit between 1900 and 1920 than in any other U.S. city but New York and Chicago.

SOURCE: U.S. IMMIGRATION AND NATURALIZATION SERVICE

Ethnic Detroit

Probably no community in the United States celebrates such a large mix of cultures as does metro Detroit.

From Hmong to Hungarian, Nigerian to Nicaraguan, Iraqi to Italian, there are representatives here who can speak to the customs, remember the old country, and promote understanding of cultures and customs. Churches, mosques and temples, fraternal organizations, clubs, sports organizations and specialty stores give evidence of the diverse character.

Who we are

People responding to the 1990 Census were able to provide two ethnic groups for their ancestry. If they provided more than two, only their first two choices were accepted. What follows is based on those figures for metro Detroit. Some of the larger groups are also profiled.

➤ **AFRICANS:** About 7,000 people are from sub-Saharan Africa with about 1,430 from Nigeria.

➤ **ALBANIANS:** 4,706. Perhaps the most telling number from the 2000 Census in metro Detroit will be the tally of Albanians who have arrived since 1990. That figure is expected to

be near 10,000, but could run higher. For years the Census classified ethnic Albanians from Yugoslavia's Kosovo province as Yugoslavs. But the Albanian Kosovars would sooner be classified as Albanian. A clarification soon after Census figures are released in 2001 could put the Albanian population — from Albania and southern Yugoslavia — at nearly 40,000.

➤ **ARABS:** Experts differ widely on the numbers of Arab-Americans in metro Detroit; estimates range from fewer than 100,000 to nearly 300,000. But nearly all agree that southeast Michigan is home to the largest and most influential Arabic-speaking population in North America.

They are most visible in Dearborn, where there are two neighborhoods now commonly identified as Arab: South Dearborn, around Vernor and Dix, and East Dearborn, especially along Schaefer Road between Michigan and West Warren and West Warren between Greenfield and Wyoming.

There are several national groups that make up the Arab community in Detroit. Here is a breakdown:

IRAQI-CHALDEAN: They began coming to Detroit from northwestern Iraq about 1910, but only a handful lived in the city by 1920, most in an enclave near Belle Isle. Another

Free Press photos by Nolan Wells

community was established before World War II on the city's near west side, south of Highland Park.

By 1968, the community numbered about 3,500. Today, following more than 30 years of heavy immigration and a tradition of large families, the Chaldean population is at least 40,000, with some estimates of up to 80,000. It is spread across southern Oakland County and parts of southwestern Macomb County. A major section is in Detroit's 7 Mile-Woodward

Swearing-in of new citizens, 2000. Top: Jiany Lin, Emily Siu, 3, and Alvin Siu, 9, from China now live in Ann Arbor. Above: Rajinder Singh from India now lives in Warren.

KIRTHMON F. DOZIER/Free Press

The Jaafar family from Iraq has dinner at home in Dearborn in July 2000.

The metro community has the nation's largest population of Iraqi Shiite refugees.

area.

Chaldeans are Roman Catholics. In Iraq, they are about 5 percent of the population. There is a continuing debate within the community over their identification as Arabs. Many Chaldeans speak Arabic and the Chaldean language, a form of Aramaic.

Most Chaldeans are in the grocery business, from supermarkets to convenience stores. They own nearly 2,000 food stores in the Detroit area, about 500 of them in Detroit.

IRAQI MUSLIMS: More than 10,000 Iraqi Shiite Muslims settled in metro Detroit in the 1990s. A number were involved in the failed 1991 revolt in southern Iraq against Saddam Hussein following the Persian Gulf War. The metro community has the nation's largest population of Iraqi Shiite refugees.

LEBANESE: Christians from Lebanon first came to Detroit around 1890 and settled just east of downtown. The community grew and established the first Lebanese Maronite Catholic Church in 1916.

Lebanese Muslim immigration began on a smaller scale around 1910 and was concentrated in Highland Park, where the first mosque was established in 1919. A second wave of immigrants, mostly Lebanese Muslims, settled in east and south Dearborn during the 1970s.

The Lebanese community numbers up to 100,000, including new immigrants.

The early Lebanese immigrants became merchants and grocers, although a large number of men were employed at Ford Motor Co. Today, Lebanese are employed in every major occupation.

PALESTINIANS: A small number of Muslim immigrants, mostly men, arrived as early as 1908, though many of them returned to Palestine. A large number of Christian Palestinians arrived in the early 1920s, just before a restrictive U.S. immigration policy was enacted and as a series of events led to the establishment in 1948 of Israel.

The Palestinians settled in various parts of Detroit's west side. Later waves of immigrants came after Israel became a nation in 1948 and after the 1967 Six-Day War.

More than 25,000 Palestinians live in northwestern Wayne County, southwestern Oakland County and parts of south Dearborn.

SYRIANS: For a long time, nearly all immigrants from the Middle East were classified as Turks by the U.S. government. In 1897, Syrians were classified as such because they came from the province of Greater Syria in the Turkish-ruled Ottoman empire. The region included present-day Lebanon.

Syrians began arriving in Detroit around 1910, many from other U.S. cities. The Syrians settled on Detroit's near east side, and until the mid-1950s were concentrated in an enclave just west of Elmwood Cemetery. There has been little immigration here from present-day Syria.

The first Syrian immigrants were peddlers. Later immigrants worked in factories. Mostly Eastern Orthodox, some Syrians educated by Protestant missionaries joined Protestant denominations here.

YEMENI: The first Yemenis arrived in the early 1900s looking for temporary employment; many returned home. The major immigration of Yemenis came after 1968, mostly men looking for work in order to send money to families back home. They settled in a tightly knit clan in south Dearborn during the late 1970s and early 1980s.

There is a community of Egyptians, mostly Christians, who live throughout the northern suburbs. There are also small numbers of Jordanians and Libyans.

➤ **ARMENIANS:** 12,744.

➤ **ASIANS:** 104,057. Most Asian households are in Troy, Bloomfield Hills, West Bloomfield and Ann Arbor. Other concentrations include Laotian and Hmong families in Detroit, Warren and Pontiac. Pockets of Chinese, Korean and Asian-Indian students live on campus at the University of Michigan in Ann Arbor and near Wayne State University in Detroit. More Vietnamese live in Grand Rapids than in metro Detroit.

CHINESE: Anti-Chinese sentiment in the American West drove many Chinese families east. By 1879, Detroit had six Chinese laundries. The first "Chinatown" in Detroit was at Third and Michigan. In 1941, about 1,200 Chinese Americans lived in Chinatown; that number grew to about 3,600 throughout Detroit by 1963.

History: Homer Gam opened Detroit's first Chinese restaurant, King Ying Lo, at West Lafayette and Woodward about 1905. With construction of the Lodge Freeway in the early 1950s, Chinatown moved about a mile north to Cass and Peterboro. The second Chinatown never completely took hold.

Factoid: Many of the earliest Chinese here were from south China and spoke Cantonese. During the mid-1990s, as Chinese immigration declined, Chinese began arriving from Hong Kong and Taiwan and spoke Mandarin. However, immigrants began arriving again from China in the late 1990s.

FILIPINOS: Michigan has seen two waves of Philippine immigration. In the early 1900s, when the United States controlled the Philippines, the government sent many Filipinos to the University of Michigan to prepare them for teaching and leadership positions at home. From 1967 to 1980, many Filipinos came to the United States to escape the regime of dictator Ferdinand Marcos. About one-quarter of local Filipinos are in health professions.

JAPANESE: Families came to Detroit in large numbers after World War II. Detroit's first Japanese community started in the 1940s at Cass and Canfield near Wayne State University. A second wave came as the auto industry began to consolidate in the 1980s.

ETHNIC BACKGROUNDS IN 2000

Here's a picture of the origin of the region's 4.5 million people. The figures won't balance because some people count more than one ethnic background; others don't list one.

Germans	1.12 million
Black	975,000
Irish	637,000
English	574,000
Polish	554,000
Italian	289,000
Arab	275,000
Canadian	121,000
Dutch	96,000
Latino	95,000

A funeral in Detroit's Chinatown at Third near Michigan Avenue in 1951.

Free Press file photo

Burton Historical Collection

Worshipers at St. Clement Ohridski Orthodox Church surround their priest, the Rev. George Nicoloff, at a service in 1942. The church serves the area's Bulgarian-Macedonian community and is located today in Dearborn.

KOREANS: A small number of Koreans arrived after a truce stopped the fighting in the Korean War in 1953. But a major move of Koreans occurred in the late 1970s. Most Koreans are scattered in Oakland County and have built several churches.

INDOCHINESE: Many Indochinese refugees, including **Vietnamese, Cambodian, Laotian** and **Hmong,** immigrated to the United States during or after the Vietnam War. The Hmong are an ethnic group that originated in China but moved into southeast Asia, especially Laos and Thailand. In 1976, having sided with the United States during the Vietnam War, the Hmong began coming to this country as refugees. The largest Hmong neighborhood is in northeast Detroit.

INDIANS: The largest group of Asian immigrants in metro Detroit in the 1990s were Asian Indian. The earliest immigrants relocated to the United States in the early 1900s from Punjab, a province hit by natural disasters. Educated professionals flocked to the United States after 1965.

Metro Detroiters who claim Asian ancestry: Asians make up less than 2 percent of metro Detroit's population. The breakdown: 25 percent Asian Indian descent, 20 percent Chinese, 16 percent Filipino, 14 percent Korean and 10 percent Japanese. The remainder constitute Hmong/Laotians, Vietnamese and Pakistanis.

➤ **ASSYRIANS:** 13,801.
➤ **AUSTRIAN:** 14,752.
➤ **BULGARIANS:** 1,541.

➤ **BELGIANS:** 39,674. Belgians arrived in 1833 and built their first settlement on the near east side. Immigration grew slowly throughout the 19th Century, but soared with the auto age. The number of Belgian-born Detroiters grew from 3,651 in 1910 to 12,310 in 1940.

Flemish-speaking Belgians, known as Flemings, moved steadily eastward over the decades, founding Our Lady of Sorrows Church on the near east side in 1884 and St. John Berchmans on the far east side in 1923.

Immigration from Belgium has been over for years, and descendants of Belgians are spread out across the east-side suburbs. As late as the 1960s, elderly Belgian Detroiters raised racing pigeons in backyard coops, played cards at the Cadieux Cafe and attended Flemish-language masses at St. Philomena Church on Marseilles near Mack.

The Cadieux Cafe, on Cadieux near Mack, is a popular survivor of an era when there were numerous Belgian saloons in Detroit.

➤ **THE BRITISH ISLES:**

BRITAIN: England (560,000), **Scotland** (200,000), **Wales** (28,000): The British took over Detroit from the French in 1760, and Britannia ruled for the next 36 years. But even for a century after U.S. troops marched into Detroit in 1796, Anglo-Saxon people and sensibilities dominated the growing city (as they dominated the nation). The dominance was noticeable in business. Three examples: J. L. Hudson was the son of a British immigrant; James McMillan, one of the richest and most powerful Detroit businessmen and politicians of the late 19th Century, was born in Ontario, Canada, to Scottish parents. Detroit News founder James Scripps was the son of an English bookbinder.

Like the English, the Scots have been in Detroit since the middle of the 18th Century. The metro area is home to a number of Scottish organizations.

IRISH: 636,831. The Irish settled downtown and on the near east side before the Civil War and then moved to the near west side, leading to the designation Corktown after County Cork in Ireland.

By 1850, the Irish were the region's biggest ethnic group, about a third of the foreign-born population. Like elsewhere in the United States, the draw here was the famine there.

In 1850, 1 in 7 Detroiters had been born in Ireland. By 1880, that figure had declined to 1 in 20. In 1910, it was 1 in 80.

Detroit's Irish did not have the clout of the Irish in Boston, Chicago, San Francisco or New York. They were largely members of the working class in the 19th Century. Irish lawyers, politicians and clergy did become influential for much of Detroit's history, from businessman and politician Lewis Cass in the 1830s to Mayor Jerry Cavanagh in the 1960s. The Irish dominated Detroit's Roman Catholic Church throughout the second half of the 19th Century and into the 20th Century. But by 1948, Detroit's Cardinal Edward Mooney said: "We do not have a single parish where people are distinctively of Irish descent."

Today, many families across metro Detroit — like those across the country — have some Irish genes. Detroit has not had a significant recent immigration of Irish.

It still helps to have a name such as Sullivan and Kelly when running for office. "In Michigan to be successful politically you either got to be Irish or figure out how the Irish do it," said U.S. Sen. Spencer Abraham, who is of Lebanese descent.

Factoid: Detroit in the late 19th Century had a secondary Irish neighborhood on the east side, around now-demolished Our Lady of Help Church on Elmwood and Congress.

SOURCE: "THE IRISH ON THE URBAN FRONTIER," BY JO ELLEN VINYARD.

➤ **CANADIANS:** 120,000, including 90,000 French-Canadians, though many people of Canadian ancestry identify with their European or Asian forebears. Canadians are Detroit's invisible ethnic group because they are so much like Americans that they blend in quickly. They immigrated across the Detroit River as early as the 1840s, and it continued for decades.

No ethnic group had an easier trip to Detroit. Canadians are the only foreign people that were one of Detroit's leading immigrant groups in *both* the 1890s and 1990s. You'd never know it, though. Most English-speaking Canadians, once in the United States, identify themselves as Irish, English, Scottish or Welsh.

Between 1983 and 1992, Canadians made up 6.2 percent of immigrants to southeast Michigan.

➤ **CROATIANS:** 15,338.
➤ **CZECHS:** 14,831.
➤ **DANES:** 15,560.
➤ **DUTCH:** 88,718.
➤ **FRENCH:** 287,959.

➤ **GERMANS:** About 1.12 million metro Detroiters — almost 1 in 4 — proudly claim German ancestry. They began arriving in the 1830s, settling the city's east side. Germans were the dominant ethnic group in Detroit for much of the 19th Century. They were better educated and better skilled than the Irish, the other leading group. By 1880, 28 percent of Detroit homes were headed by German immigrants. According to historian John Bukowczyk, most were from Prussia, but a number hailed from Bavaria, Baden, Saxony, Wurtemberg, Hesse and Mecklenburg. About 7 in 10 were Protestants.

Germans began worshiping in the 1830s in a building at Woodbridge and Bates near the present-day Detroit-Windsor tunnel entrance, and continually moved eastward for the next 70 years. Germans in the 19th Century largely worked in the tobacco and stone/marble works industry, and they also were brewers and saloon keepers and included many skilled workers.

Germans have been in the city for so long that they are largely invisible as an ethnic group beyond a number of German restaurants, bakeries and Oktoberfests. Lutheran churches abound in the city, particularly on the east side. In the 1920s, the concentration of Germans along the East Grand Boulevard corridor was so great that the street was dubbed Sauerkraut Row.

Factoid: The German influence can be seen in the names of some Detroit streets, particularly residential streets on the city's east side: Heidelberg, Schiller, Goethe.

➤ **GREEKS:** Nearly 30,000. The influx was greatest from the 1880s through the early 1900s. And by 1910, Greektown was a distinctive Detroit neighborhood.

Many early 20th-Century immigrants came from the city of Sparta and the surrounding region. Many Greeks became successful entrepreneurs and, before World War II, Detroit had numerous Greek-owned restaurants, markets and other small businesses. Detroit's coney island restaurants are a Greek invention. Two Greek newspapers,

About 1.12 million metro Detroiters – almost 1 in 4 – proudly claim German ancestry. Germans were the dominant ethnic group in Detroit for much of the 19th Century.

They were better educated and better skilled than the Irish, the other leading group.

By 1880, 28 percent of Detroit homes were headed by German immigrants.

Free Press file photo

Greek-Americans in front of the Peloponnesus coffee-house in Greektown in 1968.

Greektown remains essentially Greek after a century of urban change elsewhere.

Athenai and Vima, and the first Greek Orthodox church, Annunciation, were located on Macomb Street.

Greektown remains essentially Greek after a century of urban change elsewhere. The metro area has many Greek churches, clubs, cultural centers and newspapers.

➤ **HUNGARIANS:** About 70,000. They settled southwest of Detroit when that area was known as Delray, first arriving just after 1900 to work in the mills along the Detroit River. By 1930, metro Detroit was the fifth-largest center of Hungarians in the country.

Being a Hungarian in Detroit meant, for much of the 20th Century, living in Delray, the working-class neighborhood that was lively from the sound of Gypsy violins but hazy from nearby smokestacks.

Residents spoke Hungarian in Lehotsky's Bakery, Zolkower's Department Store, the Delray Meat Market and Rozi Neni's Bar; danced at the Verhovay and the Petofi social clubs; ate chicken *paprikash* at Al's Lounge, walnut torte at the Fancy Pastry Shop, and *hurka* (rice sausage) at Szabo's Meat Market. They worked at Solvay Process, Peninsular Stove, International Salt Mine, Revere Copper & Brass and the Ford Rouge plant. A few Hungarians were Jews, some of whom migrated to west-side Jewish districts.

SOURCE: "HUNGARIANS OF DETROIT," BY MALVINA HAUK ABONYI AND JAMES ANDERSON.

➤ **IRANIANS:** 2,000.

➤ **ITALIANS:** Nearly 300,000. The first Italian was Cadillac's second in command, Alfonso de Tonti (Alphonse de Tonty in French). A few Italian families lived in Detroit before the Civil War. Most Italians came between 1880 and 1920 and settled on Detroit's near east side.

Italians settled along Gratiot and near Eastern Market and moved northeast and east over the years to St. Clair Shores, Warren and elsewhere in Macomb County. Smaller groups of Italians also settled along Oakwood Boulevard in southwest Detroit and in Dearborn. The early arrivals were a mixture of skilled tradespeople (especially stonecutters), laborers and merchants, especially grocers.

By the late 1920s, there were six Italian-run banks in Detroit.

➤ **JEWISH:** Nearly 100,000. Jews settled during the mid-19th Century and formed the first synagogue in 1850 when there were 51 Jews in a population of more than 20,000. Most Jews were of German descent. By the early 20th Century, there were 34,000 Jews, most from Russia.

The earliest Jewish immigrants were fur traders and dealers in munitions and spirits who had come to the city by way of Canada and northern Michigan. They were followed by German and Polish Jews who made their living peddling dry goods.

The Jews settled on the near east side and just north of Grand Circus Park, later moving to the west side.

In 2000, a Jewish high school that accepts members of the three principal branches of Judaism opened. The Orthodox community, concentrated in Oak Park and Southfield, continues to thrive. Most metro-area Jews live in Oakland County.

Factoid: Temple Beth El, the first Jewish congregation in Detroit, occupied several places of worship but built its first synagogue on Woodward Avenue and Eliot, site of the Bonstelle Theatre. The synagogue was dedicated in 1903.

SOURCE: "THE JEWS OF DETROIT," BY ROBERT A. ROCKAWAY; UNIVERSITY OF MICHIGAN HISTORY PROFESSOR SIDNEY BOLKOSKY.

➤ **LATVIANS:** 1,761.
➤ **LITHUANIANS:** 22,073.
➤ **MACEDONIANS:** 3,370.
➤ **MALTESE:** 12,347.

➤ **MEXICANS:** There are about 95,000 Latinos in metro Detroit, and the great majority are Mexican. Unlike many groups that began immigrating to Detroit around World War I, Mexicans continue to arrive in signifi-cant numbers.

The Mexican neighborhoods in southwest Detroit were first settled by Latinos in the late 1920s.

Once in Detroit, some Mexicans identified themselves as Spanish because of discrimination. The federal government deported most Mexicans in the country during a Depression-era backlash; about 90 percent of Detroit's Mexican community was sent away. By 1940, there were 1,565 foreign-born Mexicans in Detroit.

Mexicans today live in Dearborn and Downriver suburbs such as Melvindale, Taylor, River Rouge and Allen Park. There is also a Mexican community in Pontiac.

Factoid: An estimated 40,000 of Detroit's Latinos come from the Mexican state of Jalisco, which is renowned for producing tequila, mariachi music and rancheros — Mexican cowboys.

➤ **POLES:** 554,481. They came just after the Civil War and immigrated in huge numbers from 1890 to 1920, settling in two areas: the lower east side and the west side near Livernois and Michigan. By 1920, Poles were Detroit's largest immigrant group, making up nearly 20 percent of the population.

In 1871, Polish Catholics opened St. Albertus,

A bride and her attendants at a Polish wedding in Detroit in 1915.

Burton Historical Collection

By 1885, the Rev. Joseph Dabrowski had opened S.S. Cyril and Methodius Seminary at St. Aubin and East Forest — the first Polish seminary in the United States.

Burton Historical Collection

A girl stands in an alley near her home at Monroe and Riopelle in 1930.

at Canfield and St. Aubin, the first of several magnificent churches on the near east side.

By 1885, the Rev. Joseph Dabrowski had opened S.S. Cyril and Methodius Seminary at St. Aubin and East Forest — the first Polish seminary in the United States.

The Poles spread north and east from the lower east side, filling Macomb County suburbs through the end of the 20th Century.

SOURCE: "POLETOWN: URBAN CHANGE IN INDUSTRIAL DETROIT: THE MAKING OF DETROIT'S EAST SIDE, 1850-1990," BY JOHN BUKOWCZYK.

➤ **PORTUGESE:** 2,190.
➤ **ROMANIANS:** 20,000.

➤ **RUSSIANS:** 57,246. Many Jews here count ancestors as Russian immigrants. In the 1970s and 1980s, about 7,000 Soviet Jews settled in Oakland County. By far the most famous Russian immigrants in Detroit are found on the rink at Joe Louis Arena.

➤ **SCANDINAVIANS: Finland (37,000), Norway (26,000) and Sweden (56,000).**

Finns came to Detroit before World War I, when strikes closed Upper Peninsula mines and Henry Ford started paying $5 a day. A number settled around the Ford plant in Highland Park, and nearly 10,000 lived in metro

Detroit in 1930. Woodrow Wilson, between Webb and 6 Mile, became a Finnish business section with a dozen shops. Finns in the 1930s ran a steam bath on Vernor. Over the years, significant numbers of Swedes and Norwegians also immigrated to southeast Michigan.

➤ **SERBS:** 5,888.
➤ **SLOVACS:** 48,658.
➤ **SWISS:** 9,959.
➤ **TURKS:** 1,017.

➤ **UKRAINIANS:** 33,000. Pittsburgh was the starting point for the first Ukrainians who came to Detroit, in the early 1900s. They had been miners there; they worked in auto factories here. Ukrainians settled on the west side and built a church on Cicotte Street. Later arrivals found homes in Hamtramck, which became Detroit's largest Ukrainian community. In 1930, Ukrainians made up about one-third of the students at Hamtramck High and a majority at Chadsey High on Detroit's west side. Today the community is centered in southern Macomb County near its cultural club on Ryan Road.

➤ **WEST INDIANS:** about 6,000, of which 2,708 are Jamaican.

Blacks in Detroit

History never recorded her name, thus the reference "unknown negresse" in the church records of Ste. Anne's. The notation is from October 1736 and marks her burial. She is the first mention of an African in Detroit. To suggest she was in bondage would not be far-fetched. The French who occupied the village owned slaves; by 1750, a census counted 33 people — African and American Indian — as slaves in a population of 483.

Owning slaves was common in Detroit for much of the city's first 130 years. By 1782, when Detroit was ruled by the British, 79 men and 100 women were slaves.

When U.S. troops entered Detroit in July 1796 to formally claim the area for the new nation, British subjects choosing to stay were permitted by a 1794 treaty to keep their slaves.

Those people included two men named Jupiter and Pompey, whose duties included carrying the sedan that ferried their master about town.

In 1810, there were 120 free blacks and 24 slaves. The "peculiar institution" was officially ended when Michigan became a state in 1837, although records suggest that by 1836, no black person in Detroit was a slave.

Nearly 165 years later, few U.S. metropolitan areas boast the racial diversity of Detroit. However, the level of segregation that continues has caused many to wonder whether people will ever live in a truly integrated society. Sociologists and demographers list the metro Detroit area as the most segregated large community in the United States.

That dubious distinction didn't happen in a generation or two, but during a history that included slavery, discrimination, rioting, hate-mongering and injustice.

Black history in metro Detroit is much tied to the battle to secure freedom and rights. It is also a history of families and faith, of music and manufacturing, of community and caring, and of labor and learning.

In the years from statehood to the 21st Century, Detroit proper has developed from a frontier town to a genteel metropolis, to an industrial dynamo and immigrant magnet, to the largest percentage majority black city in the United States. Four of 5 people in Detroit are black.

Here's a look at what happened along the way:

PROHIBITION: In 1803, a law was passed in Detroit making it a misdemeanor for a tavern owner to sell alcoholic beverages to minors, servants and black people without the permission of their parents or masters.

THE WOODWARD RULING: In 1807, Judge

Seymour Finney's barn at State and Griswold in the mid-1850s, a place where people escaping slavery hid before passage to Canada.

Burton Historical Collection

STOCKHOLDERS
OF THE UNDERGROUND
R. R. COMPANY
Hold on to Your Stock!!

The market has an upward tendency. By the express train which ar-rived this morning at 3 o'clock, fifteen thousand dollars worth of human merchandise, consisting of twenty-nine able-bodied men and women, fresh and sound, from the Carolina and Kentucky plantations, have arrived safe at the depot on the other side, where all our sympathising coloniza-tion friends may have an opportunity of expressing their sympathy by bringing forward donations of ploughs, &c., farming utensils, pick axes and hoes, and not old clothes; as these emigrants all can till the soil. N. B.—Stockholders don't forget, the meeting to-day at 2 o'clock at the ferry on the Canada side. All persons desiring to take stock in this prosperous company, be sure to be on hand.
By Order of the
Detroit, April 19, 1853.   **BOARD OF DIRECTORS.**

Burton Historical Collection

Covert handouts, like the one above from 1853, advertised in code the activities of the Underground Railroad.

This historical tablet marks Second Baptist Church, the first black church in Detroit.

Free Press file photo

Augustus Woodward ruled in Detroit that peo-ple born into slavery prior to 1793 were slaves for life. Those born after July 11, 1796, could be held as slaves until their 25th birthday.

Woodward's ruling cited the Treaty of 1794 allowing British citizens to keep slaves after the United States took possession of Detroit. Woodward was against slavery, but said he could not deny the law.

Soon he ruled on a case involving a black couple who escaped from their white slave-holders in Canada. Woodward ruled there was no legal basis for returning the couple to Cana-da, thus signaling to slaves across the river that they could find freedom in Michigan.

THE SLAVE MASTERS: Historians say most wealthy Detroiters owned one or more slaves. Some of the Detroiters who owned slaves in the later 18th and early 19th centuries:

➤ William Macomb
➤ John Askin (also known as Erskine)
➤ Joseph Campau
➤ John R. Williams

RACIAL REGISTRATION: In 1827, a law was enact-ed requiring blacks and mulattos in Michigan to register in the county clerk's office to prove their status as non-slaves. The law also required blacks coming to Michigan to post a $500 bond. The bond would keep poor blacks out of the ter-ritory, lawmakers suggested.

ANTI-SLAVERY SOCIETY: In 1837, the new State of Michigan had a constitution that banned slavery. Although banned, newspapers includ-ing the Free Press continued to run ads seek-ing the recapture of escaped slaves. On April 26, 1837, the Anti-Slavery Society was found-ed in Detroit by whites who vowed to fight against slavery across America.

BANNED MARRIAGES: In 1838, interracial marriages were banned by law. For the remainder of the century, the law was abol-ished and reinstituted. A 1929 state law declared interracial marriages legal.

SKEWED POINT OF VIEW: William Woodbridge (as in the street) wrote in 1839 during his suc-cessful campaign for governor that blacks should be free but there was no reason that whites should allow them voting rights.

SUFFRAGE CONVENTION: On Oct. 26, 1843, blacks held a two-day Negro Suffrage Con-vention at Second Baptist Church. Twenty-three delegates attended. But it would take seven years until a suffrage proposal was put before voters, who in Wayne County rejected it, 3,320 to 608.

THE UNDERGROUND RAILROAD: From 1830 to 1861, Detroit was a major stop on the Under-ground Railroad, the network of trails leading to freedom for people held as slaves in the South.

The operation was covert. Handbills and newspaper ads written in code announced meetings, asked for help and gave updates on safe arrivals of people fleeing slavery.
Detroiters involved included:
➤ George DeBaptiste, a black business-

man and member of Second Baptist Church in Detroit who bought a ship, the T. Whitney, to take runaways across the Detroit River. DeBaptiste was general manager of the Underground Railroad in Michigan.

➤ Seymour Finney, a white hotel owner who hid escapees in his barn at the northeast corner of State and Griswold. As people escaping slavery hid in Finney's barn, their pursuers often stayed at Finney's Hotel, a few blocks away at Woodward and Gratiot. The barn was later replaced by a Detroit Savings Bank building. A plaque marks where the barn stood.

➤ Second Baptist Church Congregants. The church at Beaubien and Monroe in Detroit helped as many as 5,000 people escape slavery.

An effort to preserve another railroad stop is under way in Walled Lake. A group called Friends of the Foster Farmhouse has worked for more than two years to save the farmhouse, where slaves could eat and rest before getting a wagon ride to the next stop. The farmhouse was going to be demolished in 1997 to make way for commercial development.

The exact number of people who escaped slavery is not known; estimates vary from 40,000 to 100,000. Between 20,000 and 30,000 are said to have traveled through Michigan.

POST-CIVIL WAR: A major black migration north began in the 1840s as people freed from slavery fled the South and its restrictive "black codes," which limited the liberties of freed slaves. In Detroit, most blacks settled on the city's lower east side, in an area near today's Randolph and Monroe streets. As that area expanded, it would become known as Black Bottom. By 1870, the black population was 2,235, less than 3 percent of the city's population. It only grew gradually for the next 40 years.

➤ **1865:** Fannie Richards became Detroit's first black teacher.

➤ **1867:** The School Integration Act went into effect, forbidding segregation of schools by race. But when two black families sent their children to Detroit's Duffield Union School, their admission was denied based on race.

The families and a committee of black citizens went to court. The state Supreme Court in 1870 ruled that segregated schools were illegal. Robert Willis and Cassius Workman became the first black students at Duffield Union School.

However, the ruling wasn't broadly enforced and blacks continued to be denied admission to schools in their districts. When blacks were admitted, they were often segregated *in* the schools.

➤ **1876:** Barber John Wilson becomes the first black person in Michigan elected to public office; he was Wayne County coroner.

➤ **1883:** The first prominent black weekly newspaper, the Plain Dealer, hits the streets. It lasts 11 years.

➤ **1885:** The Michigan Civil Rights Act

Dr. James W. Ames

William H. Anderson

James H. Cole Sr.

Harvey Jackson would become a letter carrier.

The Phillis Wheatley home on Elizabeth Street, 1901.

Rep. William Ferguson (1857-1900) was elected in 1893 to represent a state house district in Detroit.

Burton Historical Collection

Iroquois Club members, Feb. 14, 1910. The civic club met on St. Antoine near Jefferson.

Toussaint Lambert

Benjamin Pelham

prohibited racial discrimination in restaurants, public accommodations of inns, barber shops, transportation, theaters and other recreational facilities. But, in reality, discrimination continued.

From 1885 to 1895, there was a marked rise in complaints of discrimination. Often the complaints involved discrimination at restaurants, including one case in 1888 where someone was refused service. A jury found in favor of Dr. W. H. Haynes, but the judge reversed the jury and said that since the restaurant was a private establishment, it was not bound by the law.

Suits against theaters were more successful and by 1890, the practice of forcing blacks to sit in balconies or less desirable seats was abandoned.

➤ **1897:** The Phillis Wheatley Home for Aged Colored Ladies was founded by a group of black women from socially elite Detroit families.

Prominent people

Near the end of the 19th Century, these were the prominent black families of Detroit, listed by the family head and occupation:

James W. Ames.................................. physician
William H. Anderson.......bookkeeper, author
Robert C. Barnes.................................attorney
John W. Byrd ....messenger
George W. Cheek.............................messenger
H. C. Clarke ....contractor
James H. Cole Sr..........................deliveryman
James H. Cole Jr. ....clerk
Lomax Cook.......................................real estate
William H. Dammond........................engineer

Reuben Davis...steward
William Ellis.......................................contractor
William W. Ferguson ....attorney
George H. Fielder...............................physician
Lulu Gregory ....teacher
Frank C. Jackson ....letter carrier
Harvey C. Jackson.......................letter carrier
Albert H. Johnson ....physician
Peyton H. Johnson ....physician
Wm. E. Johnson ....dentist
William Johnson...............................contractor
Preston S. Jones............................bookkeeper
Mary E. Lambert.....................................author
Toussaint Lambert......................letter carrier
John M. Langston ....barber
John B. Lyle...messenger
Douglass E. Marshall ....messenger
Frank W. May.............................lumber dealer
Charlemagne V. Mirault ....barber
William T. Mumford Jr.................postal clerk
Benjamin B. Pelham..................................clerk
Robert Pelham Jr. ....plasterer
G. S. Purvis..druggist
Fanny Richards.......................................teacher
J. Frank Richards...................................nurse
Walter H. Showers..........deputy county clerk
The Rt. Rev. C. S. Smith.........................clergy
Sylvester Smith......................................dentist
William J. Smith.............wood, coal dealer
D. Augustus Straker............................attorney
William C. Swan...................................attorney
Amanda J. Thomas.....................home owner
Henry F. Thompson ....postal clerk
Leonard C. Thompson ....abstract clerk
David Watson...druggist
Bessie Webb..............................music teacher
Charles Webb.............................stenographer
Robert White ....messenger
Robert J. Willis ....attorney

THE WORKING WORLD: As Detroit celebrated its 200th birthday in 1901, the black population lived mostly on the lower east side, where rent costs were higher than comparable dwellings for whites.

A small, upper- and middle-class group of black people lived in finer brick homes, also on the east side.

Most blacks worked in service occupations. Those who had factory jobs had the worst assignments and many folks with professional degrees couldn't find work in their chosen field.

From 1884 to 1910, barbering was the most common route to middle-class success. By 1900, 15 percent of Detroit's barbers were black. They made a good living shaving white faces and cutting white men's hair at shops they owned or hotels where they leased space. As more white immigrants arrived, black barbers lost their leased spaces to white-operated businesses. By 1910, blacks were cutting only black hair.

The emerging black population

World War I created an industrial boom in the North and a huge demand for factory workers. During the next 40 years, millions of Southern blacks moved north in search of more money and less bigotry.

Blacks were generally consigned to the dirtiest, most dangerous jobs and least appealing housing.

A large, relatively prosperous black working-class formed, concentrated in a few segregated areas of Detroit. The largest neighborhood, called Black Bottom, stood just north and east of downtown. St. Antoine Street became the center of black life as a majority of black businesses located there, including mortuaries, groceries, newspapers and pool halls. By mid-century, Hastings Street would be the major artery through Black Bottom.

An entertainment district sprung up, just north of Black Bottom. Called Paradise Valley, it was full of nightclubs and hotels where top entertainers such as Duke Ellington, Billie Holliday and Cab Calloway performed, along with talented local blues and jazz artists.

Among the hot spots were Sunnie Wilson's Bar, Sportree's Lounge and the 666 Lounge. Every couple of years, by popular vote, the

Burton Historical Collection

The Flame Show Bar in Paradise Valley.

Valley elected its own mayor. Though he had no power, he claimed to have a direct link to City Hall.

Black Bottom was a slum, full of rickety frame houses and outdoor toilets, but it also became the cultural and economic center of black Detroit, a base for successful black entrepreneurs.

Black Bottom became "literally a city within a city," wrote historian David Katzman. "The variety and breadth of life and institutions within the black community could match that of Detroit itself."

When the century began, about 7 of 10 black adults worked in domestic and personal-service occupations, according to historian Thomas Klug. Nearly 33 percent of black men were servants or waiters, and 20 percent were laborers. More than half of black women were servants and waitresses, and 20 percent were laundresses.

The population of blacks skyrocketed in tandem with the white population. In 1910, 5,741 blacks lived in Detroit. By 1920, 40,000; by 1930, 120,000, or about 9 percent of the population of Detroit, which by then counted 1 in 4 residents as foreign-born.

From World War I, hundreds of black-owned businesses sprang up to serve the thousands of Southern blacks who migrated to Detroit. Isolated by segregation, blacks built a wide range of businesses. Segregation gave them a captive market, but also prevented them from seeking out white customers and sharpening their skills against white competitors. Local banks usually wouldn't make loans to black entrepreneurs.

One such businessman was pharmacist Sidney Barthwell, who opened a drugstore and soda fountain in Paradise Valley in 1933 with $500 he borrowed from friends. He soon found success and had to open more drugstores to meet the demand. At its peak, there were nine stores in the Barthwell chain, making it the largest drugstore chain in black America. Barthwell also opened three ice cream parlors.

In 1958, Ozzie Virgil became the first black player for the Detroit Tigers, 11 years after Jackie Robinson broke baseball's color barrier.

The Tigers were the second-to-last team in the major leagues to integrate.

The Boston Red Sox (Pumpsie Green) were the last, in 1959.

Free Press file photo

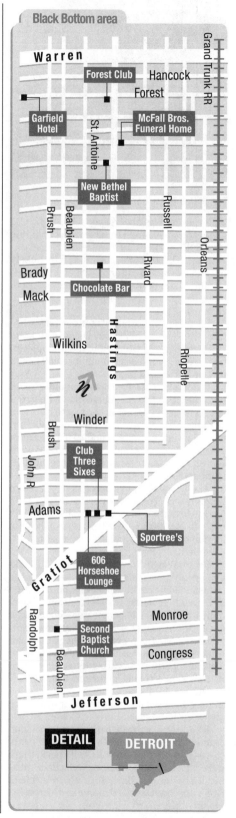

Black Bottom area

Warren

Forest Club Hancock

Forest

Garfield Hotel

McFall Bros. Funeral Home

Grand Trunk RR

St. Antoine

New Bethel Baptist

Russell

Rivard

Orleans

Brush

Beaubien

Brady

Mack

Chocolate Bar

Wilkins

Hastings

Riopelle

Brush

Winder

John R

Club Three Sixes

Adams

Sportree's

Gratiot

606 Horseshoe Lounge

Randolph

Monroe

Second Baptist Church

Beaubien

Congress

Jefferson

DETAIL **DETROIT**

Paradise Valley was the entertainment district within Black Bottom. The neighborhood received its name in the 19th Century from the dark color of its soil.

Ed Davis moved from Louisiana in 1926 and attended Cass Technical High School. In 1936, he landed a sales job at a Chrysler Corp. dealership. Because he was black, Davis wasn't allowed on the showroom floor. He was given a private office upstairs, but blacks soon heard about the black man who sold Chryslers.

In 1939, Davis opened a used-car lot at Vernor and Brush but continued as a new-car broker for black buyers.

Even without a dealership of his own, Davis sold a lot of new cars. To Studebaker Corp. executives, his sales figures meant more than his race. In 1940, they gave him a franchise, making Davis the nation's first black new-car dealer.

Alabama native Edgar Brazelton rode the rails north in 1932. He ended up in Detroit, working as a bootblack.

In 1939, Brazelton got a job driving a mail truck, but found his calling when he sought extra money by selling bouquets of flowers on the street. So he quit his secure job and opened a flower shop in 1941.

Firms like these gave Detroit a nationwide reputation as a haven for black businesses. The city's black-owned institutions could provide virtually anything a person needed, from a shoe shine to oral surgery.

Most of the prominent black businesses founded in Detroit in the 1930s and 1940s are long gone.

DETROIT'S NAACP: To fight against racial oppression and discrimination, the Detroit branch of the National Association for the Advancement of Colored People was formed in 1912 by a group of prominent black leaders, including Father Richard Bagnal, the Rev. Robert L. Bradby Sr., Benjamin Willoughby Lambert and William Osby. Meetings were first held at St. Matthews Episcopal Church on St. Antoine at Elizabeth. Osby was the first president.

The branch is also credited with ending segregation in public housing in 1954 and, in 1966, overturning a city home owners ordinance that allowed home owners to refuse to sell to blacks.

In 1956, the Detroit Medical Society, a group of blacks in the medical profession, joined with the branch to host the first annual Freedom Fund Dinner, one of the group's major fund-raisers.

It funded and won its first major legal battle in 1925: The People of the State of Michigan vs. Sweet.

OSSIAN SWEET — A SHOT HEARD 'ROUND THE WORLD: Whites in Detroit often succeeded in keeping Detroit neighborhoods segregated during the 1920s by using intimidation to keep blacks out.

One incident stands out because it involved a black man who would not be intimidated.

Dr. Ossian Sweet bought an $18,500 home at 2509 Garland, at Charlevoix on Detroit's east side.

A raucous crowd gathered when Sweet moved into the house in September 1925. Some in the crowd of about 300 white people hurled rocks at the house. A shot rang out from the house, striking and killing a man sitting on his porch across the street from Sweet.

Sweet, his brother Henry and nine others were arrested and charged with murder.

The case became a defining moment for the NAACP, which took up Sweet's defense and hired Clarence Darrow to represent the defendants.

The judge was Frank Murphy, a future Detroit mayor, Michigan governor and U.S. Supreme Court justice. Murphy instructed the jury that a house is a man's castle — even if that man is black. After deliberating 46 hours, the all-white jury failed to reach a verdict, and the defendants went free. The prosecutor later acknowledged that the state's case was handicapped because "the colored people involved were so far superior to the white people involved" in the case.

In a second trial, prosecutors tried only Henry Sweet, who had admitted firing a gun. Darrow delivered a seven-hour summation, and another all-white jury acquitted Sweet.

Ossian Sweet committed suicide in 1960.

THE MOVE WEST: Between about 1915 and 1950, blacks began moving to Detroit's west side. Factory wages enabled many to buy homes. The first west-side black neighborhood was bounded by Tireman, Grand River, and Buchanan, Bright and Central streets. Segregation kept west-side blacks from the YMCA at Grand River and West Grand Boulevard, which was within walking distance.

Traveling outside those boundaries often meant harassment from cops and other city residents.

The black community became tightly knit. Churches from the era remain some of the most prominent and influential in Detroit today, including Tabernacle Missionary Baptist Church, which opened on the east side in 1920 and moved to its present location on Beechwood at Milford in 1925, St. Stephens AME Church on Stanford near McGraw opened in 1918,

Free Press file photo

Ed Davis shows a 1968 Plymouth Satellite to a customer in 1967. Davis opened a used-car lot on Vernor in 1939.

U.S. Appeals Court Judge Damon Keith.

Car dealer Nathan Conyers in 1998.

and Hartford Avenue Baptist Church started in 1917 on Hartford at Milford, before moving to its current location on the Lodge Service Drive near 7 Mile. It's now named Hartford Memorial Baptist Church.

The churches were more than centers of worship. They spawned political activism and served as outlets for social and cultural entertainment and expression. While most adults were not college-educated, they made sure their children went beyond high school.

As a result, a black middle-class emerged. Many of their sons and daughters became doctors, lawyers, educators and entrepreneurs.

From that neighborhood and those parents came: Ford Motor Co. Vice President Elliott Hall; U.S. 6th Circuit Court of Appeals Judge Damon Keith; U.S. Rep. John Conyers and his brother, the auto dealer Nathan Conyers; the late Dr. Charles Vincent; former Police Chief Isaiah McKinnon; prominent scholar of African and African-American history and culture Catherine Blackwell; opera singer Florence Cole Talbert, and the city's first black principal, Beulah Cain Brewer.

➤ **1949:** The Cotillion Club formed as a social club for professional blacks who were often excluded from similar white clubs. It soon became a training ground

**A Cotillion Club affair
in the late 1940s.**

Free Press file photo

caused the least disruption to white businesses. Black businesses were expendable.

Former Michigan Secretary of State Richard Austin, who worked as an accountant in Paradise Valley, rejects that theory. "The planners were trying to seek the very best location for the flow of traffic," he once opined.

The demolition of the stores and the nearby housing for the freeway and Lafayette Park continues to be a bitter memory for older black Detroiters. It fueled much of the late Coleman Young's antipathy toward the white gentrification of Detroit.

The early 1960s – By the numbers

28.9: Percent of Detroit population that is black.

35.4: Percent of city workforce that is black; almost 7 of 10 unskilled city jobs were held by blacks.

3.3: Percent of Detroit police officers that are black.

40: Number of black teachers in Detroit schools.

0.9: Percent of those enrolled in construction-apprencticeship programs in Detroit that are black.

16: Percent of workers employed in Detroit-area auto factories that are black.

4.3: Percent of workers employed in Detroit-area shopping centers that are black.

WORKPLACE DISPARITY: In the late 1990s, two-thirds of Detroit's black men between the ages of 25 and 64 were working. Among white men, 87 percent had jobs.

That trend has persisted for decades. Even in the expanding postwar economy of 1950, 84 percent of black men, vs. 92 percent of white men, were employed. Since 1970, when many blue-collar jobs began disappearing, no more than 65 percent of black men have been employed at any point. Blacks in Detroit generally have had unemployment rates 2.5 to 3 times those of whites at all times. Even the prosperous times of the 1990s failed to draw jobless black and white men into the workforce; instead, people with jobs worked more hours.

Black women and white women: Black women in metro Detroit have reached earnings parity with white women.

POPULAR JOBS: These are jobs in which

for young black leaders. Among past presidents: U.S. Rep. Charles Diggs; Judge Damon Keith; U.S. Rep. George Crockett; civic leader William T. Patrick; one of the city's first blacks to work at a daily newspaper, Bill Matney; Dr. Thomas Batchelor, a distinguished physician, and John W. Roxborough II, special assistant in the Eisenhower administration.

➤ **1957:** Continuing harassment led Rosa Parks and her late husband, Raymond Parks, to move from Montgomery, Ala., where she'd sparked the modern-day civil rights movement by refusing to give up her seat on a bus. She came to Detroit at the invitation of her brother, Sylvester, who'd moved to Detroit after World War II. She, her husband and her mother, Leona McCauley, settled in an apartment on Euclid. She worked as a seamstress in a factory and later as an assistant to U.S. Rep. John Conyers from 1965 to 1988. Detroit's 12th Street was renamed Rosa Parks Boulevard in 1975.

➤ **End of Black Bottom:** In the late 1950s, city officials chose to build I-75 (the Chrysler Freeway) over Hastings Street — the main artery of Black Bottom. The route was chosen, many urban experts say, because it

Bettman-UPI

Rosa Parks' earlier refusal to give up her seat on a Montgomery, Ala., bus in 1955 sparked the civil-rights movement.

blacks are most highly represented in metro Detroit.

Men: Nursing aides, security guards, social workers, machine operators, stamping-press operators, welders, janitors, office clerks, police officers and mail carriers.

Women: Postal clerks, practical nurses, orderlies, social workers, assemblers, public administrators, telephone operators, maids, health aides, child-care workers.

BOTTOM JOBS: These are jobs in which blacks are least represented in metro Detroit.

Men: Tool and die makers, construction supervisors, lawyers, carpenters, sales representatives, mechanical engineers, printing press operators, financial managers, engineers, dentists.

Women: Dental assistants, physicians, fam-ily child-care providers, financial managers, computer systems analysts, sales occupations, real estate sales, waitresses, designers.

ELECTION OF 1961: The flexing of black political muscle began with the mayoral election of 1961. Blacks were angry with incumbent Mayor Louis Miriani, who had ordered a crackdown on crime, which his predominantly white police force apparently interpreted as a license to harass innocent black men and women. Blacks organized and got out the vote for a virtually unknown 33-year-old lawyer named Jerome P. Cavanagh, who won what was expected to be an easy win for Miriani. "It was like the awakening of a sleeping giant," former Deputy Mayor Richard Simmons told the Detroit Free Press in 1980. "Blacks began to understand that they could be the pivotal vote in elections."

The civil rights pioneer, in a more recent photo, later moved to Detroit where she lives today.

KING VISITS:

➤ **1956:** Addresses 2,500 people at Ford Auditorium after Montgomery bus boycott.

➤ **1958:** Preaches at St. John Episcopal Church and St. Paul Episcopal Cathedral.

➤ **1961:** Keynote speaker at UAW's 25th anniversary.

➤ **1965:** Attends funeral of civil rights worker Viola Liuzzo.

➤ **1966:** Criticizes violent tactics in speech at Cobo Hall.

➤ **1968:** Speaks at Grosse Pointe South High three weeks before his death.

June 23, 1963: Walter Reuther, left, Benjamin McFall, Commander George Harge, James Del Rio, Dr. Martin Luther King Jr. and the Rev. C.L. Franklin march down Woodward.

Dr. Martin Luther King Jr.

He spoke often in Detroit and, in 1963, led a massive march for civil rights down Woodward. On June 23, more than 125,000 people marched with King.

It became the largest civil rights march in the nation up to that time.

When King arrived in Detroit, Police Commissioner George Edwards met him at his plane and said: "You'll see no dogs and fire hoses here."

➤ I HAVE A DREAM – EARLY VERSION

King delivered his famous speech on Aug. 28, 1963, during the massive civil rights demonstration at the steps of the Lincoln Memorial.

But he delivered a more elaborate version after the Woodward march two months before the Washington rally. Here it is:

I go back to the South not in despair. I go back to the South, not with a feeling that we are caught in a dark dungeon that will never lead to a way out. I go back believing that the new day is coming.

So this afternoon I have a dream.

It is a dream deeply rooted in the American dream.

I have a dream that one day right down in Georgia, in Mississippi, in Alabama, the sons of former slaves and the sons of former slave owners will be able to live together as brothers.

I have a dream this afternoon that one day little white children and little Negro children will be able to join hands as brothers and sisters.

I have a dream this afternoon that one day men will no longer burn down houses and the church of God simply because people want to be free.

I have a dream this afternoon that there will be a day that we will no longer face the atrocities that Emmett Till had to face or Medgar Evers had to face, that all men can live with dignity.

I have a dream this afternoon that my four little children will not come up in the same young days that I came up within, but they will be judged on the basis of the content of their

TONY SPINA/Detroit Free Press

character not the color of their skin.

I have a dream this afternoon that one day right here in Detroit, Negroes will be able to buy a house or rent a house anywhere that their money will carry them, they will be able to get a job.

Yes, I have a dream this afternoon. One day in this land the work of Amos will become real. Justice will roll down like waters and righteousness like a mighty stream.

I have a dream this evening that one day we will recognize the words of Jefferson that all men are created equal. That they are endowed by their creator with certain inalienable rights that among these are life, liberty and the pursuit for happiness.

I have a dream this afternoon. I have a dream that one day every valley shall be exalted. Every hill and mountain shall be made low, the rough places will be made plain, and the crooked places will be made straight and the glory of the Lord shall be revealed and all flesh shall see it together.

I have a dream this afternoon that the brotherhood of man will become a reality in this day, with this faith. I will go out and carve a tunnel of hope through the mountain of despair with this faith. I will go out with you and transform dark yesterdays into bright tomorrows, with this faith we will be able to achieve this new day, when all of God's children, black men and white men, Jews and Gentiles, Protestants and Catholics will be able to join hands and sing with the Negro in the spiritual of old, Free at last! Free at last! Thank God almighty, we are free at last.

1967: A riot erupts in Detroit, largely due to festering anger about police brutality, poverty and economic oppression. The riot accelerated white flight from the city. In the end, 43 people were killed.

DIFFERENCE OF A DECADE: A poll asked this of white Detroiters in 1956 and again in 1969:

"One day a 6-year-old asks her mother if she can bring another girl home to play. The mother knows the other girl is Negro, and that her own daughter has only played with white children before. What should the mother do?"

Three responses were offered:

1. Tell her daughter that she must never play with Negroes.
2. Only play with Negroes at school.
3. Invite the Negro child home.

Response (by percent)	1956	1969
Don't play with blacks	12	2
Play at school only	47	22
Bring the child home	41	76
Depends, don't know and no answer	4	5

SOURCE: DETROIT FREE PRESS, 1969. WRITER, PHILLIP MEYER, WASHINGTON BUREAU.

TONY SPINA/Free Press

THE DESEGREGATION ORDER THAT WASN'T: In 1970, the Detroit NAACP filed suit, charging the city school system with segregation. In 1971, U.S. District Judge Stephen Roth ruled that Detroit schools had been intentionally segregated and ordered cross-district busing. It never happened. The U.S. Supreme Court struck down cross-district busing. A Detroit-only busing plan was ordered in 1975, but by the time the plan was to go into effect in 1976, there were too few whites in the district to effectively integrate. Black children ended up being bused to black schools and federal money was given to Detroit schools to help improve them. But even into this century, the scores of most Detroit students on assessment tests are far below those of their suburban counterparts.

Tony Spina captures King in a moment of contemplation during a news conference. One of the most famous photos of King, it was taken in Grosse Pointe three weeks before his assassination.

The Detroit Almanac ‖ **113**

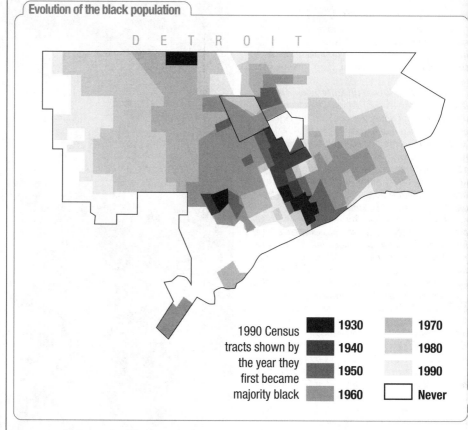

Evolution of the black population

DETROIT

1990 Census tracts shown by the year they first became majority black

1930	1970
1940	1980
1950	1990
1960	Never

Gov. William Milliken and Detroit Mayor Coleman Young at an NAACP dinner in 1981. Although political opposites, the two were good friends.

MARY SCHROEDER/Free Press

COLEMAN ALEXANDER YOUNG (1918-1997): On Jan. 1, 1974, Young became Detroit's first black mayor at a time when the city's population was roughly half white and half black. Some suburbanites said his inaugural call for criminals to "hit 8 Mile" was a goad for lawbreakers to pester the suburbs, but Young was using the local northern boundary of Detroit as a 1970s way of saying get out of town. Young fought difficult battles to further integrate the police and fire departments and to see that blacks received their share of city contracts. In fact, from 1973 to 1974 — his first year in office — contracts to blacks went from $25,000 to $125 million. Among those who benefited from Young's determination to cut blacks a fairer share of the economic pie during his 20-year reign of the city were attorney David Lewis, entrepreneur Don Barden, steel manufacturer and former Piston star Dave Bing and the late auto dealer Porterfield Wilson.

A majority black city

Sometime during the 1970s, Detroit's population became predominantly black. However, not only did the city become more black, so did its suburbs as growing numbers of middle-class blacks moved to nearby suburbs, most notably Southfield and other parts of Oakland County.

The percent of white students in Detroit's public schools was even smaller than the percent of whites in the city. From 1970 to 1980, the white population in the schools plummeted from more than 100,000 to approximately 29,000.

Researchers would come to call Detroit one of America's most segregated cities.

However, blacks also made tremendous political strides during the final decades of the 20th Century.

In addition to the mayor's office, African Americans began leading government departments, serving as elected judges and being appointed to civic committees and boards.

Political and economic empowerment turned the city proper into a magnet for blacks nationwide and scores of families moved to the city and its nearby suburbs.

New leaders emerged as old ones passed on. Black preachers continue to be a source of spiritual and political inspiration. One of the city's most influential groups is the Council of Baptist Pastors of Detroit and Vicinity.

Among the newer voices: the Rev. Wendell Anthony, president of the Detroit chapter of the NAACP, and the late William Beckham Jr., civil rights activist and champion of improved public education.

Additionally, black faces on television, which were rare a couple decades previously, became commonplace as they anchored newscasts on morning and nightly TV news shows.

The city built the largest museum of African-American history in 1997, and later named it for Dr. Charles H. Wright, the man who started the museum in 1965 in the basement of his home office on West Grand Boulevard.

Despite the gains, problems have persisted, particularly with police and racism. City schoolchildren also suffer some of the state's lowest scores on assessment tests, a tragedy at least in part due to continuing economic woes in the city and its schools.

The neighboring City of Dearborn continues to suffer from its racist past when its former mayor, Orville Hubbard, declared that blacks would never live in his city. Blacks have boycotted the Fairlane Town Center in Dearborn because of complaints of unfair treatment and, in 1985, courts declared that a city ordinance barring nonresidents from most city parks — a move that blacks saw as an attempt to keep them out — was ruled unconstitutional. In 2000, thousands of blacks protested the death of a black man, Frederick Finley, who died in a fight with security guards outside Lord & Taylor.

Many blacks are often stopped and harassed by police, particularly while driving through nearby suburbs, a charge that has come to be called DWB — driving while black.

SOURCES: "BLACKS IN DETROIT, 1736 TO 1833: THE SEARCH FOR FREEDOM AND COMMUNITY AND ITS IMPLICATIONS FOR EDUCATORS," BY NORMAN MCRAE (UNIVERSITY OF MICHIGAN DISSERTATION, 1982); FREE PRESS LIBRARY; NAACP DOCUMENTS; "BEFORE THE GHETTO: BLACK DETROIT IN THE 19TH CENTURY," BY DAVID KATZMAN, (UNIVERSITY OF ILLINOIS PRESS, 1973); "LIFE FOR US IS WHAT WE MAKE IT: BUILDING BLACK COMMUNITY IN DETROIT, 1915-1945," BY RICHARD W. THOMAS (INDIANA UNIVERSITY PRESS, 1992); "UNTOLD TALES, UNSUNG HEROES: AN ORAL HISTORY OF DETROIT'S AFRICAN AMERICAN COMMUNITY, 1918-1967," BY ELAINE LATZMAN MOON (WAYNE STATE UNIVERSITY PRESS, 1994); "PARADISE VALLEY DAYS: A PHOTO ALBUM POETRY BOOK: DETROIT'S 1930S TO 1950S," BY THE DETROIT BLACK WRITERS GUILD (PUBLISHED BY THE GUILD WITH A GRANT FROM THE MICHIGAN COUNCIL FOR ARTS AND CULTURAL AFFAIRS, 1998); "REMEMBERING DETROIT'S OLD WESTSIDE: 1920 TO 1950," BY THE WESTSIDERS (WESTSIDERS, DETROIT, 1997).

Achieving women
(Who aren't covered in other chapters)

➤ **Josephine Gomon:** As executive secretary to Detroit Mayor Frank Murphy in the 1930s, Gomon helped organize the original New Deal concept for the city during the Depression — registering unemployed people, mobilizing emergency food programs and arranging housing for homeless people. During World War II she was appointed by Henry Ford as director of female personnel at the Willow Run Bomber Plant. She helped recruit thousands of female defense workers, organized day nurseries for their children and arranged federal financing for workers' housing at Willow Run. Gomon was adviser to Walter Reuther in organizing the UAW, an original member of the national American Civil Liberties Union and a president of the Detroit chapter of the Planned Parenthood League.

➤ **Brownie Wise:** Divorced, middle-aged and working as a secretary at Bendix Aviation Co. in the late 1940s, Wise began throwing "patio parties" to sell Tupperware, the new plastic containers described by its producer as "the nicest thing that could happen to your kitchen." In one week, she sold 56 "wonderbowls." Tupperware founder Earl Tupper turned over his sales operations to Wise in 1951, and she parlayed Tupperware parties into a nationwide network of housewives selling plastic containers out of their living rooms. Lauded as a marketing genius, she graced the cover of Business Week magazine in 1954, a first for a woman. Her papers and memorabilia are in the archives of the National Museum of American History, part of the Smithsonian.

Josephine Gomon at her Ford office during World War II.

Lorraine Beebe in 1969.

Clara B. Arthur around 1910.

Dr. Alexa Canady in 1989.

Fran Harris in 1955.

PEOPLE

➤ **Viola Liuzzo:** On a two-lane blacktop road in Lowdnes County, Ala., on March 25, 1965, Liuzzo was shot to death for the crime of riding in a car with a young black man, who sat beside her. Liuzzo, 39, a white Detroiter and the mother of five, was returning to Selma after the second Selma-to-Montgomery march in Alabama and the triumphant crossing of the Pettus Bridge by civil rights demonstrators. The shot rang out from a car occupied by four Ku Klux Klansmen who had pursued Liuzzo's car through the night at 100 m.p.h. One of the Klansmen, Gary Thomas Rowe, was an FBI informer. The Rev. Martin Luther King Jr. attended her funeral; her death spurred Congress and President Lyndon B. Johnson to pass the Voting Rights Act three months later.

➤ **Patricia Hill Burnett:** The founder of the National Organization for Women's Michigan chapter was named Miss Michigan and was runner-up to Miss America in 1942. Burnett served as president of the World Feminist Commission and NOW International. An Oakland County resident, she's also an internationally recognized painter who made such busy women as Indira Gandhi and Margaret Thatcher sit still for portraits. Her memoir is titled, "True Colors: An Artist's Journey from Beauty Queen to Feminist."

➤ **Elmina Lucke:** She was the founder of Detroit's International Institute and the first woman accepted into Columbia University's doctoral program for International Law and Relations. The International Institute assisted the half-million immigrants who flooded Detroit in the 1920s.

➤ **Lorraine Beebe:** Then representing Dearborn in the state Senate, Beebe drew national headlines when she revealed during a 1969 legislative debate for women's reproductive rights that she had undergone an abortion. She said she underwent the procedure at a doctor's suggestion when she was four months' pregnant and experiencing many health problems. Beebe, a Republican, was defeated in a re-election bid in 1970.

➤ **Clara B. Arthur:** Known as the mother of the playground movement in Detroit, her efforts created a system of 138 playgrounds and 17 swimming pools by 1929. Earlier, as president of the Michigan Equal Suffrage Association, she began the campaign that resulted in a state amendment in 1918 to support giving women the right to vote.

➤ **Sister Theresa Maxis Duchemin:** A Roman Catholic nun, she cofounded the Monroe-based Sisters, Servants of the Immaculate Heart of Mary, one of the dominant religious groups in metro Detroit for the last 150 years. She came to the Monroe area in the mid-1840s with three other sisters from an order of nuns in Baltimore. A Belgian-born Redemptorist priest, Father Louis Gillet recruited the sisters, who then belonged to the Oblates of Providence, an order of black and mixed-race women who wore special bonnets to distinguish themselves from white orders. Priests rarely agreed to say mass for them, but Gillet needed the sisters — especially Sister Theresa, who spoke French, the native tongue of many who had settled in Monroe. The sisters opened the first St. Mary's Academy in a log cabin in 1846 with 40 students.

➤ **Debbie Stabenow:** First woman senator from Michigan. Stabenow built her political career partly by becoming an advocate for families, children and seniors. A Democrat, her first elected office was in 1974 to the Ingham County Board of Commissioners. She later served 12 years in the state House and four years in the state Senate. In 1996, she was elected to Congress from the Eighth District and won her senate seat in 2000. Born in 1950, Stabenow grew up in Clare and graduated from Michigan State University.

Barrier breakers

➤ **Alexa Canady, M.D.:** The chief of neurosurgery at Children's Hospital of Michigan in Detroit; she was the first female African-American neurosurgeon in the United States.

➤ **Fran Harris:** Michigan's first female radio newscaster (WWJ-AM) and the first woman to appear on television in Detroit, in 1946. Harris produced the nation's first courtroom show, "Traffic Court," and was a longtime personality at WWJ-TV, now WDIV-TV. She died in 1998 at age 89.

➤ **Cornelia Kennedy:** The first Michigan woman to serve on a federal bench. She was appointed by President Richard Nixon to the U.S. District Court in Detroit in 1969.

➤ **Lila Neuenfelt:** Michigan's first female circuit court judge. She was seated in Wayne County Circuit Court in Detroit in 1941.

➤ **Marjorie Peeble-Meyers:** The first black woman to graduate from Wayne State's medical school and the first black woman to become an intern and then chief resident at Detroit Receiving Hospital. She graduated from Wayne State's medical school in 1943 and began her internship at what was known as Detroit General Hospital. After completing her residency, she entered what is considered to be the first interracial private practice in Detroit.

➤ **Heather Nabozny:** Detroit Tigers groundskeeper who was the first woman to hold the title of head groundskeeper in baseball's major leagues. The Milford resident got

Judge Cornelia Kennedy in 1977.

Judge Lila Neuenfelt in 1953.

Dr. Marjorie Peeble-Meyers in 1968.

Dr. Clara Raven in 1986.

Judge Jessie P. Slaton in 1958.

the Tigers job in March 1999. Previously, she'd worked for the West Michigan Whitecaps, the Tigers' Class A affiliate.

➤ **Dr. Clara Raven:** The first female doctor to earn the rank of colonel in the U.S. Army, in 1961. A Detroiter, she was among the first women commissioned as physicians in the U.S. Army. She served in field hospitals across Europe during World War II. After the war, she was sent by the Army to study the effects of the atomic bomb in Hiroshima, Japan. Recalled to duty during the Korean War, she served with one of the original MASH units. Raven later became a deputy medical examiner for Wayne County.

➤ **Josephine S. Davis:** First female police officer in Michigan in 1919. A graduate of the University of Michigan and a social worker, Davis' job was to interview women and children detained by the Detroit Police.

➤ **Jessie P. Slaton:** A teacher, Slaton graduated from the University of Detroit Law School in 1951 and became the first female referee in the 43-year history of the Recorder's Court. She died in the crash of Korean Airlines Flight 007, which was shot down by a Russian plane after it strayed over Soviet territory in 1983.

➤ **Dr. Helen Walker McAndrew:** She left her husband and infant son in Ypsilanti so she could study at a New York medical school — the closest one that would accept women — and become Washtenaw County's first female physician. Her advocacy helped open the University of Michigan's Medical School to women in 1870.

➤ **Sarah Van Hoosen Jones:** She was the first woman to earn a doctorate in animal genetics from the University of Wisconsin. Born in Stony Creek near Rochester on a family farm, she raised purebred Holstein cattle for milk and in 1933 was declared a "master farmer" by the trade journal "Michigan Farmer."

➤ **Fannie Richards:** Born in 1840, Richards was the first black teacher in Detroit and the first kindergarten teacher. She became a proponent for education while working against segregation. She was also a

cofounder of the Phyllis Wheatley Home for Aged Colored Ladies.

➤ **Dr. Ethelene Crockett:** Michigan's first black female doctor to specialize in obstetrics and gynecology, she died in 1978.

➤ **Emily Helen Butterfield:** Michigan's first female architect and a Detroiter, Butterfield helped found the Detroit Business Women's Club in 1912. It was the first professional woman's club in the United States.

➤ **Cora Mae Brown:** The first black female state senator in Michigan, she was elected in 1952 from Detroit.

➤ **Dorothy Comstock Riley:** A Detroiter, she was the first woman to serve on the Michigan Court of Appeals (appointed in 1976, elected in 1978). She was overwhelmingly elected in 1984 to the Michigan Supreme Court.

➤ **Emmanuelle Boisvert:** The Detroit Symphony Orchestra violinist was the first woman and youngest person to be named concertmaster for a major U.S. orchestra. In 1988, when Boisvert of Quebec, Canada, was 25, she was chosen concertmaster, the person who heads an orchestra's first violin section. As concertmaster, she led the orchestra in tuning up at the start of each concert and performed all violin solos within orchestral pieces.

➤ **Breann Smith:** First Michigan high school girl to score a touchdown on the varsity level: On Sept. 17, 1999, Smith, 16, a junior defensive end and fullback at Ann Arbor Pioneer, charged into the end zone — and history books — with a three-yard run against Traverse City Central.

➤ **Laura Matson:** The Bloomfield Hills Andover student set a still-standing national high school record in the 1,600-meter run. Matson clocked in at 4:39.4 in the 1,600-meter run in 1985.

➤ **Diane Laffey:** The first Michigan female coach inducted into the National High School Sports Hall of Fame, she is Michigan's all-time leader in victories in girls basketball and softball. A coach and administrator at Harper Woods Regina since 1970, her win-loss record, compiled at old Detroit St. Anthony and Regina, is 468-241 in basketball and 701-236-2 in softball.

Fannie Richards

Dr. Ethelene Crockett in 1971.

Emily Helen Butterfield

Cora Brown in the 1950s.

Judge Dorothy Comstock Riley in 1984.

Laura Matson in 1986.

Sheila Murphy in 1968.

➤ **Carolyn King:** As a 12-year-old Ypsilanti student, King was the first girl to break the gender barrier nationally in Little League baseball. She made history in spring 1973 when she beat out three boys to win a spot on the Ypsilanti Orioles. National Little League officials revoked the Ypsilanti chapter's charter, and the city of Ypsilanti retaliated with a sex-discrimination suit. Ypsilanti Little League prevailed in federal court and received its charter back, and King finished the season.

➤ **Kathy Kozachenko:** In Ann Arbor in 1974, she became the first openly gay candidate elected to a city council seat in the United States.

➤ **Bertha Van Hoosen:** First woman to head a medical division of a coeducational university and a founder of La Leche League. Van Hoosen was born in Stony Creek in 1863 and died in Romeo in 1952. Educated at the University of Michigan and a practicing physician for 64 years, Van Hoosen delivered thousands of babies and became known for making appendectomy incisions of less than an inch. In 1918, Van Hoosen was appointed head of obstetrics at Loyola University Medical School in Chicago, the first woman appointed to such a post. She wrote an autobiography, "Petticoat Surgeon," in 1949.

➤ **Hope Brophy:** A Detroit-area Catholic layperson who in the 1960s began education programs to promote racial understanding among often-balky church members and leaders. Historian John McGreevy called Brophy's efforts "the most impressive" in the nation.

➤ **Helen Thomas:** First woman to head the White House bureau of a major news service. One of nine children of Lebanese immigrants in Detroit, the Wayne State University graduate covered the White House from 1961 to May 2000 for United Press International. President Gerald Ford described her work as "a fine blend of journalism and acupuncture."

➤ **Adrienne Bennett:** America's first African-American master plumber. A single mother in her early 20s, Bennett started out as an apprentice in the mid-1970s in Plumbers Local 98 in Detroit. She passed the state's master plumber test in 1986 and worked for the City of Detroit as a plumbing inspector, later owned a business, and most recently was project manager for Henry Ford Hospital's Detroit addition.

➤ **Sheila Murphy Cockrel:** As a young Detroiter in the 1960s, she helped lead community opposition to brutality by what was then a majority-white police department. She also was in the forefront of the fight against the notorious police undercover decoy squad known as STRESS, which killed 17 black men, and she trained observers to attend Recorder's Court trials to ensure that black people were fairly represented on juries. She later married activist attorney Ken Cockrel and was elected to the Detroit City Council.

Free Press file photo

Emmanuelle Boisvert was the first woman and youngest person to be named concertmaster for a major U.S. orchestra.

RICHARD LEE/Detroit Free Press

Carolyn King of Ypsilanti, in 1973, was the first girl to break the gender barrier in Little League baseball.

Detroiter Helen Thomas covered the White House for United Press International from 1961 until her retirement in 2000. Left: Thomas is hugged by President Bill Clinton.

Thomas chats with President John F. Kennedy.

Big firsts

➤ **Vote to ratify the 19th Amendment, which gave women the right to vote:** Just five days after Congress passed the 19th Amendment, Michigan became the first state to approve ratification, on June 10, 1919. As early as 1867, Michigan women who were taxpayers were permitted to vote in school elections. But state proposals to allow all women to vote were defeated in 1874, and an 1893 law to allow women to vote in municipal elections was declared unconstitutional.

➤ **Daughters of Charity: Four sisters from a Baltimore convent established Detroit's first public hospital in 1845 in a log cabin.** It was called St. Vincent's, later renamed St. Mary's. In 1850, it was the only hospital available to treat victims of a cholera epidemic, which killed 1,000 of Detroit's 40,000 residents. It was the only hospital in the Northwest Territory at the time.

➤ **The Woman's Hospital and Foundling's Home, precursor to Hutzel Hospital.** Established in 1868 by the Ladies Christian Union, it was the first institution of its kind in the nation, governed and staffed exclusively by female doctors and nurses to tend to unwed mothers and their children.

➤ **The nation's first breast milk co-op.** It was founded in Detroit in 1912 at what is now Hutzel Hospital. It proved to be a model program for other hospitals. The bureau acted as a broker between women who produced more human breast milk than they could use and women who couldn't or wouldn't nurse. Women who provided milk were paid 17 cents an ounce. Recipients paid what they could or got it free.

➤ **First state university to open its medical school to women — the University of Michigan.** Women enrolled at U-M's Medical School in 1870.

SOURCES: FREE PRESS; "MICHIGAN WOMEN: FIRSTS AND FOUNDERS," VOLUME I, BY RACHEL BRETT HARLEY AND BETTY MACDOWELL; "MICHIGAN WOMEN: FIRSTS AND FOUNDERS," VOLUME II, FROM THE MICHIGAN WOMEN'S STUDIES ASSOCIATION; "THE BOOK OF WOMEN FIRSTS"; MICHIGAN HISTORICAL CENTER, STATE OF MICHIGAN; "WOMEN'S FIRSTS," EDITED BY CAROLINE ZILBOORG; KELLOGG AFRICAN AMERICAN HEALTH CARE PROJECT; "THE PROMISE OF PLASTIC IN 1950S AMERICA," BY ALISON J. CLARKE; WOMEN'S HEALTHSTYLE MAGAZINE; "THE HISTORY OF HOSPITALS: 150 YEARS OF CARING," BY MARY BYRNE TENNISWOOD, AND MICHIGAN HEALTH & HOSPITAL ASSOCIATION.

The Detroit Almanac

05. NA

"Nature has destined the city of Detroit to be a great interior emporium."

—*Judge* **Augustus Woodward**, *1818*

URE

The Great Outdoors

Weather forecast: Rarely a dull moment

Yeah, yeah, we know: This is Michigan. Don't like the weather? Wait 15 minutes, it'll change. The numbers here are based on records kept since 1870.

Climate

Climate is a sum of the weather over many years. And based on our weather, we can say this about the Detroit region's climate:

➤ **It's temperate:** It has four distinct seasons. To some degree, Michigan's lakes have a moderating influence on the extremes of heat and cold.

➤ **Human activity sets its tone:** Over the last 100 years, southeast Michigan's climate has been influenced by development and growth. Cement, buildings and increased population densities have created a microclimate because developed areas hold more heat.

As the surrounding area has developed, average overnight lows have risen between 1975 and 2000 at Detroit Metropolitan Airport.

➤ **Cycles:** Temperatures tend to run in 20- to 30-year cycles of heat and cold. Four of the coldest winters on record occurred in the 1970s and early '80s. In the late '80s and the '90s, some winters were above normal temperatures.

Warm, warmer, warmest

➤ **Highest temperature:** July 24, 1934, 105 in Detroit.

➤ **Warmest year:** 1998. The average temperature, 53.47. At 51.32, 1999 was the ninth warmest year.

➤ **Nov. 9, 1999:** High, 75 — the warmest temperature so late in the season in Detroit.

➤ **Summer barbecues:** The longest heat wave baked Detroit from July 17-28, 1964, with 12 consecutive days hotter than 90 degrees. The discomfort award, however, goes to the un-air-conditioned summer of 1936, when temperatures boiled over 100 degrees for seven straight days, July 8-14. July 8, 104.4 degrees; 102 on the 9th and 10th; 101 on the 11th; 100 on the 12th; 102 on the 13th; 104 on the 14th. No rain.

Other notables scorchers include 1953, with 11 consecutive days of 90s-plus heat, and the all-time hot summers of 1995 (No. 1, average temperature, 74.5), 1955 (No. 2, 74.43) and 1988 (No. 3, 74.2). Normal is 68.4 degrees.

➤ **Hot March:** March 1945 was the warmest March on record. Seventeen days clocked in above 60 degrees. Nine of those climbed into the 70s and one, March 28, hit 82 degrees.

➤ **Searing summer of '36:** That week of 100-plus degree days was responsible for the deaths of nearly 300 Detroit-

THE AVERAGES

All the weather statistics from 1872 boiled down to an average.

➤ **Rain:** 32.62 inches a year, measured at Detroit Metro Airport.

➤ **Snow:** 41.2 inches.

➤ **Highest average temperature:** 84 degrees, usually from July 16-27.

➤ **Lowest average temperature:** 15 degrees, usually from Jan. 15-Feb. 3.

Free Press file photo, 1970

Frolicking in city hydrant spray has been a Detroit pastime.

Groan! Vehicles sit on I-94 during a snow-induced pileup in January 1999.

WHITE CHRISTMASES

In the 100 years ending in 1999, there have been 46 Christmases with an inch or more of snow on the ground in Detroit.

➤ Christmas 1951 is the fluffiest on record, with 13 inches to play in. The most snow to fall on Christmas day — 6.4 inches — came in 1915.

➤ In 1945, a record 1.16 inches of rain fell and coated every sidewalk and tree limb with ice.

➤ In 1982, tempera tures soared to 64 degrees in Detroit. The following year, frigid wind whipped into Detroit and pulled the Christmas mercury down to -9, and a bitter 50 below with windchill — the coldest holiday on record.

area people. These were days before widespread use of A/C; people sweltered in stuffy, poorly ventilated homes.

Many of the dead drowned seeking relief in the Detroit River or area lakes.

Stores sold out of fans. City offices and private businesses closed or operated with minimal staff. The heat stopped criminals cold: Police reported vast decreases in criminal activity.

Shivering

➤ **Lowest:** Minus 24, on Dec. 22, 1872.

➤ **Brrr, 1875:** The coldest year. Average temperature was 44.08.

➤ **Chilliest summer:** 1915. The average temperature hovered at 66.5 degrees. Normal is 68.4 degrees.

➤ **Blame the volcano:** The summer of 1992 was second coldest at an average 67 degrees, mostly because of the 1991 volcanic eruption of Mt. Pinatubo in the Philippines. That huge event clouded skies with dust, causing temperatures globally to fall. Detroit saw much rain in July 1992. The sun shone only 49 percent of the time, off from the 68-percent average.

Flint notched its coolest and wettest July since record keeping began there in 1942.

➤ **Bitter January:** January 1977 was the coldest January ever recorded in metro Detroit. The monthly average temperature was 10 degrees lower than normal at a bitter 12.8 degrees. The extreme dip bumped the entire winter of 1976-77 into the record books as the third coldest on record. The average temperature was 19.8, or 6 degrees below normal. The award for coldest winter goes to 1903-04, when temperatures averaged a bitter 18.7 degrees.

Snow

➤ **The big kahuna:** On April 6, 1886, 24.5 inches fell in Detroit with some 12-foot drifts — the record one-day snowfall.

➤ **Snowiest month:** February 1908, when 38.4 inches fell.

➤ **Latest flakes:** Snow fell on May 31, 1910, but the biggest unseasonable wallop hit 13 years later. On May 8, 1923, arctic air poured into the region and dropped temperatures 28 degrees in five hours to 34 degrees. Snow started the next morning, and by nightfall May 9, the storm had dumped 6 inches of snow on Detroit, 9 inches in Ann Arbor and a foot in Flint.

➤ **Late flakes:** The balmy fall of 1998 set a record for latest snowfall. Weather watchers at Detroit Metropolitan Airport didn't count the first flake until Dec. 16.

➤ **Ka-plow:** Just weeks later, in early 1999, a snowstorm gridlocked Detroit for a week. That wallop ranked only 15th in the record books, but additional storms made the month the second snowiest January ever with 27.3 inches. The snowiest January was in 1978, when 29.6 inches fell.

➤ **Snowiest season:** Sometimes winter starts slow but ends with a bang. During the winter of 1899-1900, not quite 10 inches of snow had fallen through the end of January 1900. Then a series of snowstorms slammed through Detroit. From Feb. 28-March 6, almost 34 inches of snow fell on Detroit.

The season ended with a total snowfall of 69.1 inches, making it the fourth snowiest winter season in Detroit since 1880.

The snowiest was in 1880-81, when 93.6 inches fell.

Rain

➤ **Wettest year:** 1880, with 47.69 inches of rain. The following year was the second wettest, at 45.44 inches.

➤ **Driest year:** 1963, with 20.49 inches.

➤ **Driest month:** August 1894, 0.16 of an inch. More recent was the near-drought of 1988. Only 0.39 inches of rain fell from late May through the third week of June, and only 0.04 inches fell from late June to mid-July. When the dust cleared, the record books added May 1988 as the third driest May on record (0.87 inches), and June 1988 as the second driest June (0.97 inches).

Storms

Tornadoes have killed 343 people in Michigan since 1882. Since 1950, there have been 129 confirmed twisters in the seven-county metro Detroit region.

➤ **Deadliest twister:** The Flint-Beecher twister of June 8, 1953, was the eighth deadliest in U.S. history, and the last single U.S. tornado to kill more than 100 people. In all, 115 people died and more than 900 suffered injuries when the funnel cloud roared 23 miles from Flushing to Flint to Lapeer around 8:30 p.m. Meteorologists ranked it an F5 on the Fujita scale — the most powerful — with winds of 261 to 318 m.p.h. One woman covered her eyes as her roof collapsed, then came to in a field 100 yards away — still in bed with her purse by her side. The tornado hit the Beecher district of northern Flint hardest, earning its name. Other memorable tornadoes:

➤ **May 25, 1896:** An unclocked funnel cloud killed at least 47 people on its route across Oakland and Lapeer counties.

➤ **May 21, 1953:** Just before the Flint-Beecher storm, an F4 storm with winds of 207-260 m.p.h. leveled south Port Huron, killing two people and destroying 90 homes and 83 buildings.

➤ **May 12, 1956:** An F4 storm hit Genesee County taking out more than 100 homes and five businesses and killing three people.

➤ **May 8, 1964:** In Macomb County, an F4 twister killed 11 people and injured more than 200 as it plowed northeast from Mt. Clemens to Algonac.

➤ **May 2, 1983:** In Macomb County, a smaller F3 storm whipped from Eastpointe to Harsens Island in Lake St. Clair. Winds of 158-206 m.p.h. demolished 25 to 30 homes, an aircraft hangar and a large building.

➤ **The deadly lakes:** A monstrous fall storm rocked the Great Lakes in 1913. Forty ships were believed sunk in the November gale, with at least 235 sailors lost. The worst carnage was on Lake Huron, where eight large freighters went down with all aboard. Howling winds up to 62 m.p.h. and blizzard-like snow squalls pummeled Detroit and Port Huron on Nov. 8-9, while on the lakes, sailors reported battering waves 35 feet high. Before it was over, the freighters John McGean, Isaac M. Scott, Argus, Hydrus, James Carruthers, Wexford, Regina and Charles S. Price sank in central and eastern Lake Huron. A sailor from the Wexford was the first frozen corpse to bob ashore on the Canadian shoreline. Fifty-six bodies eventually washed up on Canadian beaches and one in Port Sanilac. The others were never found.

HURRICANES

Michigan isn't in hurricane country but occasionally feels the impact of those storms.

➤ In 1932, the remnants of a hurricane passed over Detroit. Barometric pressure fell to 29.60 on Sept. 3 and the Detroit area got 2.55 inches of rain.

➤ In June 1968, the area received a total of 2.55 inches of rain in the aftermath of Tropical Storm Candy.

➤ Another storm came following Hurricane Opel in 1995. On Oct. 5, total rainfall was 1.41 inches with wind gusts peaking at 38 m.p.h.

➤ During a strong storm accompanied by a southwest gale on Sept. 25, 1941, part of Belle Isle that was normally under water was exposed as water from the Detroit River was pushed up into Lake St. Clair. The river level fell by 3 feet, leaving many boats marooned in the mud. The wind blew steadily for a while at 56 m.p.h., with gusts reaching 75 m.p.h. The unusual weather followed a tropical storm and hurricane that had moved up from the Gulf of Mexico through the Mississippi Valley and into the Great Lakes region.

Motorists help push a car through flood-waters on I-94 in June 1983.

A full solar eclipse, as viewed in Germany in 1999. We'll get partial ones through 2017.

HEAVENLY OCCURRENCES

Here is a list of heavenly occurrences visible from southeastern Michigan through 2017. The eastern standard times are for mid-eclipse.

➤ Dec. 25, 2000: (12:34 p.m.) partial solar eclipse

➤ Dec. 14, 2001: (3:52 p.m.) partial solar eclipse

➤ May 15, 2003: (11:40 p.m.) total lunar eclipse

➤ Oct. 27, 2004: (11:04 p.m.) total lunar eclipse

➤ Feb. 20, 2008: (10:25 p.m.) total lunar eclipse

➤ Dec. 21, 2010: (3:17 a.m.) total lunar eclipse

➤ April 15, 2014: (3:46 a.m.) total lunar eclipse

➤ Oct. 23, 2014: (5:44 p.m.) partial solar eclipse

➤ Sept. 27, 2015: (10:47 p.m.) total lunar eclipse

➤ Aug. 21, 2017: (2:25 p.m.) partial solar eclipse

SOURCE: CRANBROOK INSTITUTE OF SCIENCE.

The Anomalies

➤ **El Nino's effects:** The United States has experienced 12 El Nino weather patterns since 1950 — one every three to six years. The effect is strongest in the winter in southeast Michigan, but the pattern varies. Eight of the 12 patterns, including 1997-98, brought warmer-than-average temperatures in December and January. On the other hand, the El Nino winter of 1976-77 was among the most frigid.

The El Nino winter of 1997-98 will be remembered for mild, wet weather. Not a single winter day dropped to single-digit temperatures, a phenomenon Detroit hasn't seen since record keeping began. Most notably, February was the second warmest ever, with temperatures above normal every day of the month, and only a trace of snow. The last time we saw anything like it was 1881. In all, the average winter temperature was 33.9 degrees — the fourth warmest on record behind 1881-82 (37 degrees), 1931-32 (35.6) and 1889-90 (35 degrees).

➤ **Winds on the lakes:** Boaters are wisely concerned about the lakes and winds. The National Weather Service posts a small craft advisory when winds are 18 to 33 knots, a gale warning for 34 to 47 knots and a storm warning when winds will reach 48 or more knots.

➤ **Indian summer:** The period in fall after a killing frost or freezing temperatures when the weather turns warm and hazy, often when the wind comes from the south or southwest. It usually occurs in October or November. There can be no Indian summer, one or more than one a year.

Sonny Sez

Sonny Eliot is dean of Detroit weathercasting, a fixture on television and radio here since 1950, when he joined WWJ-TV, now WDIV. The Detroit native was a B-24 pilot in World War II. He was shot down over Germany and spent 18 months as a prisoner of war, boosting the morale of other prisoners by staging original skits. His off-beat weathercasting includes a signature pronunciation of Engadine and mergings or portmanteau words like clear and cold (clold), snow and fog (snog), and fog and drizzle (fizzle). Then there are the similes. A few of Sonny's favorites, special to the Detroit Almanac:

Sonny Eliot spent 18 months as a German POW during WWII.

➤ It's colder than a former wife's hello.
➤ It will be as pleasant as diaper rash.
➤ The storm is as suspicious as a dermatologist with acne.
➤ Driving will be as hazardous as tap dancing in a canoe.

➤ **'This is a storm so bad, it looks like a talent scout for a reform school.'**

Times the earth moved

Michigan never has experienced a killer earthquake, but many moderate tremors have shaken the state.

Minor earthquakes rattled Detroit — or what was to become Detroit — in 1638, 1661, 1664, 1665, 1668, 1672, 1776, 1779, 1795, 1804, 1811, 1812, 1813, 1872, 1875, 1877, 1883, 1884, 1886, 1895, 1905, 1909, 1925, 1928, 1935 (3), 1937 (2), 1943, 1944, 1947, 1980, 1986 and 1998.

The most recent quake hit Sept. 25, 1998, shaking the southern Lower Peninsula and recording the largest magnitude of any temblor in recent decades in the Michigan-Ohio region. It registered a 5.2 on the Richter scale and rattled nerves and knickknacks from Grand Rapids to Detroit to Midland.

No injuries were reported from the temblor, which came at 3:53 p.m. Its epicenter was in northwest Pennsylvania, and it traveled through parts of New York, Ohio and southern Ontario.

The quake shook floors and furniture. A Bloomfield Hills office building was evacuated when occupants smelled gas and feared a break in the line. University of Michigan experts said the earthquake's magnitude far surpassed that of a January 1986 temblor felt in Michigan that registered 5.0 at its epicenter near Cleveland. The intensity of the 1998 tremor diminished by the time it rippled through Michigan, and to Michiganders it probably felt like a quake measuring between 2 and 3.

SOURCES: MUCH OF THIS WEATHER STUFF IS FROM NATIONAL WEATHER SERVICE WEATHER HISTORIAN WILLIAM R. DEEDLER, WHO HAS BEEN TRACKING METRO DETROIT WEATHER SINCE 1973.

Water, water everywhere

And practically all of it drinkable. Detroit's raison d'etre is the strategic place it occupies along the Detroit River, the strait between the lakes.

The Detroit River

➤ **Length:** 32 miles, from Lake St. Clair to Lake Erie. It is an international boundary between the United States and Canada.

➤ **Population:** 5 million people live in the Detroit River watershed.

➤ **Islands:** 21 with 72 miles of shoreline — 33 miles in Canada and 39 miles in United States. The largest island is Grosse Ile, about 10 square miles.

➤ **Flow rate:** 185,000 cubic feet a second.

➤ **Drainage area:** 861 square miles — 213 square miles in Canada and 648 square miles in the United States.

➤ **Water area:** 39 square miles — 16 square miles in Canada, 23 square miles in the United States.

➤ **Speed:** Between .81-2.33 feet per second; on average about 1 mile an hour.

➤ **Depth:** 60 feet at Ambassador Bridge; 27-30 feet in shipping channel.

➤ **Elevation:** 574 feet above sea level at Windmill Point, 573 feet at Ft. Wayne, 572 feet at Gibraltar.

➤ **Cargo:** The river carried 83 million tons of cargo in 1998.

DETROIT RIVER

The river boasts 21 islands with 72 miles of shoreline — 33 miles in Canada and 39 miles in United States. The largest island is Grosse Ile, about 10 square miles.

This map shows 1889 fairgoers where to locate the planned exposition at the Rouge and Detroit rivers.

DOSSIN GREAT LAKES MUSEUM

The first Belle Isle Bridge. It burned down in 1915.

Free Press file photo

Belle Isle looking east in 1999.

MARY SCHROEDER/Detroit Free Press

GROWING PAINS

Belle Isle today is nearly 300 acres larger than it was in 1879. Much of the expansion occurred earlier this century when city ne'er-do-well James Scott willed $500,000 for a fountain that would include his statue in bronze. Scott died in 1910. The city decided to fill and expand the western end of the island to accommodate Scott Fountain. Scott made much of his fortune on the backs of others.

Islands in the strait

Belle Isle

What a gem, eh? Nearly 1,000 acres of getaway from a noisy, stress-filled city. Some stats and things you may not have known about our island:

➤ **Ill named:** The French called it Ile aux Cochons (Hog Island) soon after Detroit was founded. The place was a dandy spot to let your hogs and cattle graze without fear of rustlers, or your beasts wandering off. The hogs ate snakes on the island because hogs like to eat snakes, but the hogs weren't put there to do away with serpents, a myth of Detroit. Before the French, American Indians called it White Swan Island.

➤ **Deadly gains:** In 1762, English Lt. George McDougall cleared a portion of the island, built a house and placed James Fisher and his family on the island as caretakers. In 1763, Ottawa Indians, foiled in their attempt to capture Detroit, went to the island, killed Fisher's wife and two older children and kidnapped the two younger ones. When Fisher returned, the Indians ambushed and killed him.

➤ **Buying power:** George McDougall bought the island from the Indians in 1768 for 194 pounds worth of goods: eight barrels of rum, three rolls of tobacco, 6 pounds of red paint and some trinkets. His descendants sold the island in 1794 to several Macomb brothers who in turn sold it in 1817 to Barnabas Campau for $5,000. Campau was a son of Joseph Campau.

➤ **Duel role:** As often as duels were fought in the late 18th and early 19th Century, many were carried out on Belle Isle. Twelve paces, turn and fire!

➤ **Name change:** On July 4, 1845, a group of Detroiters rowed to the island and declared that henceforth the hideous name of Hog Island would be replaced by Belle Isle. They poured water on the ground to make it official. It is said that Belle is chosen to honor the youngest child of Detroiter Lewis Cass.

➤ **Buying in:** The city paid $200,000 to Campau's descendants for the island in 1879. There were some naysayers, but most of Detroit's population was elated.

➤ **By design:** The island park was designed by Frederick Law Olmstead, the same guy who designed New York's Central Park. Olmstead was paid $7,000 in the 1880s.

➤ **Cold, hard facts:** Diehard Detroiters know the island is home to the statue of James Scott at Scott Fountain and Gen. Williams almost smack dab center, but there is also a bust of Dante Alighieri, the Italian poet; one of German poet and dramatist Friedrich von Schiller and a monument to James J. Brady, founder of the Old Newsboys Goodfellow Fund. There is a monument to temperance, to newsboys, to the Civil War, to the Spanish-American War and one to peace.

James Scott's cold stare.

➤ **Good fit:** So how many people could crowd onto Belle Isle? Everybody in metro Detroit — about 4.7 million people — giving each person about one square yard.

➤ **Nifty flora:** Even in the midst of Detroit,

Free Press file photo

Crowded island canal during a concert, circa 1906.

arboreal discoveries are still being made. In 1998, botanists found massive old pumpkin ash and shumard oak trees on Belle Isle. They were previously not known to grow on the island and are considered highly rare in Michigan.

➤ **Belle Isle Zoo:** Animals: 47 species exhibited; fish (and other creatures) in the aquarium: at least 1,500.

➤ **Trolling the bridge:** The spans: There have been three. The first opened in 1889; cost $295,000 and burned down on April 27, 1915, when embers from a tar wagon set the steel and wood structure on fire. A temporary span served until Nov. 1, 1923, when the current span opened at a cost of $3 million.

It was designed by University of Michigan professors Emil Lorich and Lewis Gram. It is 2,193 feet long and has 19 spans. The bridge was renamed in 1942 to honor Gen. Douglas MacArthur.

➤ **The big din:** Grand Boulevard traffic used to avoid crossing Jefferson via an underpass to the bridge. Authorities plastered DO NOT SOUND HORN signs in the underpass, which, natch, was an invitation to honk. Longtime Detroiters no doubt remember the mandatory underpass BEEP.

➤ **The jams:** Traffic was so bad around the bridge approach that after World War II officials contemplated another bridge and a second deck. The bridge underwent an $11.5-million renovation in the mid-1980s.

➤ **The suicides:** Within 12 years of the new bridge's opening (a period that partially coincided with the Great Depression), 87 people leaped from the bridge to their deaths. Detroit police assigned a "suicide squad" to patrol the bridge. The squad saved 15 people in 1938.

➤ **The barnstormer:** On Aug. 29, 1965, a pilot flew under one of the 34-foot-high arches during intermission of a hydroplane race. The bridge was jammed with racing fans the day Don Pittman, of Sapula, Okla., dusted the water at 160 m.p.h. He had five feet of clearance on either side of his wings.

Bois Blanc

➤ **Size:** 272 acres.

➤ **People:** About 50 families.

➤ **History:** You likely know it as Boblo. It's in Canada and was closed as an amusement park and sold to a private investor in 1994.

Bois Blanc means "white woods" in French, named for the white-barked poplars on the island. In 1898, the Detroit Belle Isle and Windsor Ferry Co. expanded service to Bois Blanc and in 1929 named the place Boblo to keep French-ignorant Americans from fracturing the name. It's Bois Blanc ("bwah blawnh").

Generations of Detroiters have taken the Boblo boats to the amusement park. Two steamers — the Ste. Claire and the Columbia — took 90 minutes each way to make the trip. The park featured more than 30 rides, roller skating and a large marina. Attendance usually reached 1 million a year. But then came the fast-paced '80s and the nearby lure of

THE INFAMY

The 1943 race riot that claimed 34 lives in Detroit got its start on the Belle Isle bridge when a rumor spread that white sailors had thrown a pregnant black woman off the crowded bridge. On Aug. 19, 1995, as dozens of people watched, a 290-pound man beat a woman less than half his size for failing to stop after slightly damaging his car in a traffic accident. Fleeing, 33-year-old Deletha Word jumped from the bridge. Two men leaped into the river to help her, but the frightened Word swam from them and drowned. In 1996, Martell Welch Jr., 20, received a 16- to 40-year sentence for second-degree murder in Word's death.

The bridge to Grosse Ile, the largest island in the Detroit River.

NATURE

GROSSE ILE BRIDGE

A $200,000 toll bridge was completed in 1913, linking the island and its then 2,000 residents to the mainland.

Cedar Point and King's Island. The attraction waned and the park closed.

Owner John Oram is converting the island into a residential-recreational community. The first phase of 52 homes is on the north end; all lots are sold. A condominium development has started and a golf course was scheduled to open in the summer of 2000.

➤ **Getting there:** Year-round car ferry service at Bob-Lo landing in Amherstburg, Ontario. It is a 2-minute ride from mainland to the island. From downtown Windsor, the island is 20 miles south of the Ambassador Bridge on County Road 20 (formerly Highway 18 West).

Calf

➤ **Size:** 11 acres.
➤ **People:** None.
➤ **History:** In the 1800s, farmers from Grosse Ile brought young livestock here to separate them from adults. Thus, the name Calf Island. In 1914, the Marxhausen family bought the island, built a large home and entertained a lot.

The house featured magnificent carvings and antiques. It was destroyed by fire in the 1960s; the foundation is visible. The island was sold for a reported $120,000 in 1974. Louis Miller subsequently sold the island to Slats Three Enterprises of Troy.

➤ **Getting there:** Take the bridge from South Pointe at the south end of Grosse Ile to Swan Lake and a short boat ride from there. Or, go by boat directly from the docks off Trenton or Gibraltar.

Celeron

➤ **Size:** 125 acres.
➤ **People:** None.
➤ **History:** Named after Pierre Joseph Celeron, Sieur de Blainville, the commandant of Detroit from 1742 to 1744 and from 1750 to 1754. The Lowrie family owned it from 1889 to 1966. They built cottages and a boathouse and maintained a small farm.

The Celeron Island Corp. bought the island for a reported $260,000 in 1966 and planned an $8-million complex with 300 homes, a marina, boat club and golf course. But in 1967, Grosse Ile Township won a court battle to stop the development, saying dredging for the project created illegal dumping and filling.

The Department of Natural Resource then bought the island. Today the buildings are gone but the beaches still attract local boaters.

➤ **Getting there:** Celeron is the first island visible from Lake Erie. Take a boat from the Ford Yacht Club at the southwest tip of Grosse Ile.

Fighting (or Turkey)

➤ **Size:** 1,572 acres.
➤ **People:** Two live on the island; three to seven BASF employees work there.
➤ **History:** Known as Great Turkey Island in the 1700s because the wild fowl roamed its prairie. In 1810, the Canadian territory island took the name Fighting from the warlike appearances of Indian entrenchments that had sprouted up. From 1860 to 1880, the island was the site of numerous prizefights. In 1891,

Boblo boats, the Ste. Claire, left, and the Columbia. The 90-minute ride from downtown to the island is now a memory.

a syndicate from Detroit opened a resort featuring a hotel, cottages, boathouses and a beach. It was named Bes-chree-shows-ka, or "Here's Everything." The resort failed. For more than 40 years, the island was a depository for chalk-like material from industries, a practice stopped in 1980. Today, BASF Corp., which bought the island from Wyandotte Chemicals in '69, hosts hunting and fishing guests on the island.

➤ **Getting there:** Take a boat from LaSalle, Canada, south of Windsor, or the Wyandotte Yacht Club. Located 6 miles south of Detroit, the Canadian-U.S. border is between the north end of Grosse Ile and the south end of Fighting Island.

Fox

➤ **Size:** 1.69 acres.
➤ **People:** None.
➤ **History:** In the mid-1970s, at least 50 people gathered nearly every Sunday at a private summer cottage owned by the Gorno family. Vandals and fire destroyed the building. The island is owned by the Bob Brown family of Grosse Ile.

➤ **Getting there:** Located between Powder House Island and Elba Island (part of Grosse Ile). Take a boat from the Grosse Ile Yacht Club on the southeast tip of Grosse Ile.

Grassy

➤ **Size:** 72 acres.
➤ **People:** None.
➤ **History:** Originally two small islands owned by the U.S. Coast Guard, it was diked in 1959 and two years later became part of a National Wildlife Refuge. In the 1970s, dredge material from the Rouge River was dumped among the smaller islands to make it one island. The island is becoming forested with cottonwoods, willows and thick brush. It is owned by the U.S. government.

➤ **Getting there:** By boat, use the Wyandotte Boat Launch on St. John's Street in Wyandotte.

Grosse Ile

➤ **Size:** About 10 square miles, the largest island in the Detroit River.
➤ **People:** about 11,000
➤ **History:** The Potawatomi Indians, who claimed the Detroit River area as their ancestral land, called the island Kitche-minishen, meaning grand or large island. French explorers identified it as la grosse ile because of its grandeur. After the French departed in 1763, the "la" was dropped. Alexander and William Macomb bought the island from the Indians in 1776.

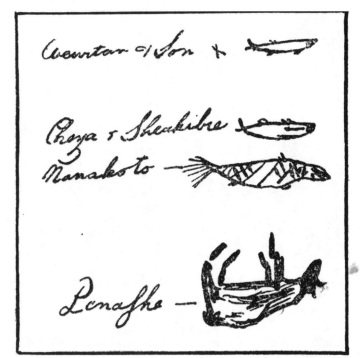

Part of a 1780 agreement regarding Grosse Ile. The symbols represent signatures of American Indian officials.

A $200,000 toll bridge was completed in 1913, linking the island and its then 2,000 residents to the mainland. In 1972, the Grosse Ile Municipal Airport opened.

➤ **Getting there:** From Detroit, take I-75 south to West Road exit and travel east to the Grosse Ile bridge off Jefferson Avenue.

Hickory

➤ **Size:** About 30 acres.
➤ **People:** 240.
➤ **History:** The southernmost island from Grosse Ile, it was a popular camping and picnic site in the late 1800s. Prior to automobiles, it was a summer colony of cottages. It is the home of the Grosse Ile Yacht Club, formed in 1934.

➤ **Getting there:** Take the bridge at the Grosse Ile Yacht Club at the southeast end of Grosse Ile.

Horse

➤ **Size:** About 20 acres.
➤ **People:** About 50 families.
➤ **History:** Part of the city of Gibraltar, it is used as a landmark when entering or leaving the Detroit River or Lake Erie. The original homes on the island were summer cottages built in the 1920s. Now, the cottages are year-round homes and new homes are being developed.

➤ **Getting there:** Accessible by road, take the bridge from the city of Gibraltar off Adams Street.

GROSSE ILE

The Potawatomi Indians, who claimed the Detroit River area as their ancestral land, called the island Kitche-minishen, meaning grand or large island. French explorers identified it as la grosse ile because of its grandeur. After the French departed in 1763, the "la" was dropped. Alexander and William Macomb bought the island from the Indians in 1776.

Free Press file photo

The excursion vessel Tashmoo on a Detroit River voyage.

SUGAR ISLAND

The island became a popular amusement park in the early 1900s until the grounding of the excursion ship Tashmoo in 1936. With about 1,400 passengers aboard, the ship apparently hit a loose rock and made it to the Canadian shore, coming to rest on the shallow bottom. All passengers disembarked safely. The island was abandoned shortly thereafter.

Mamajuda Island Shoal

➤ **Size:** 1.1 acre.

➤ **People:** None.

➤ **History:** Named for an old Indian woman who camped there every year during the fishing season prior to 1807. She died on the island.

Mamajuda really isn't an island, but a shoal covered by water from a few inches to 4 feet deep, and marked by the Mamajuda Light. Government engineers say the shoal has been known by its name since the 1850s.

In 1926, River Rouge Mayor Thomas Bresnahan spearheaded a drive in the Wayne County Board of Supervisors to fill in the shoals between the mouth of the Rouge and Grosse Ile to form a Downriver park. He suggested it be named Hennepin Park, in honor of Father Louis Hennepin, the French missionary and explorer of the Great Lakes and Mississippi River.

The matter resurfaced in 1936 when William Bradley, chairman of the Port of Detroit Authority, suggested that earth and rock taken from a shore channel excavation project be dumped on the shoals to form an 800-acre island.

➤ **Getting there:** A boat ride from the Wyandotte Boat Club on the Detroit River. The island is on the northern tip of Grosse Ile.

Mud

➤ **Size:** 20 acres.

➤ **People:** None.

➤ **History:** In 2001, National Steel Corp., the island owner, donated the piece of land off of Ecorse to the U.S. Fish and Wildlife Service, which added it to the National Wildlife System. The island, a nationally known staging area for such diving ducks as canvasbacks and scaups, forever will be a haven for migratory birds. For years, Ecorse and National Steel fought in court over the island's ownership, and officials dreamed of doing various developments there.

➤ **Getting there:** Privately owned by National Steel, it is best viewed from John Dingell Park in Ecorse, near Jefferson and Southfield roads. For permission to tour the island, contact National Steel at 313-297-2100 anytime.

What might have been: 1966 plans to turn Peche Isle into a ritzy playground.

Free Press file photo

Peche Isle

(Sometimes called Peche Island)
- **Size:** About 90 acres.
- **People:** None.
- **History:** The French called it Ile a la peche. Also known as Peach Island. Peche means both "peach" and "fishing" in French. It formerly housed the private cottage of distiller Hiram Walker, who purchased the property in 1883 and cultivated orchards and gardens while also adding a large house, stables and other buildings. Those structures disappeared over the years, and the island, at the foot of Detroit's Alter Road, reverted to nature and for decades served as a lover's lane for east siders with boats. In 1974, Peche Isle became a park owned by the province of Ontario. The City of Windsor purchased the island in 1999 and committed to maintain it in its natural state. Extensive shoals are off the west, north and east sides of the island.
- **Getting there:** Located off the Canadian shore on the south side of the head of the Detroit River. By boat, launch from the Lake View Marina in Windsor or from any place on the U.S. side.

Powder House

- **Size:** About two-thirds of an acre.
- **People:** None.
- **History:** Sometimes called Dynamite Island, it's located in the Livingstone Channel. According to local folklore, it was the storage spot for the explosives used during construction of the Livingstone Channel shortly after the 1900s. But nautical charts of the area prior to 1900 show that Powder House Island was named before the channel existed.
- **Getting there:** By boat the nearest launch is at Hoover's dockage, at the head of Elba Island off Grosse Ile, or at Elizabeth Park launch.

Stony

- **Size:** 101.43 acres.
- **People:** None.
- **History:** Sacrificed for the Livingstone Channel, it was called Indowaga by the Indians. From 1873 to 1888, trains running between Chicago and Buffalo crossed from Grosse Ile to this island by bridge before being transported by ferry to the Canadian shore. The bridge was removed in 1913. During the construction of the channel from 1907-1912, this island was a beehive of activity featuring a general store, a school and church hall and about 30 houses. Many of the houses were moved to Grosse Ile after the channel was completed.

The island has been for sale for many years. Local investors had hoped to develop upscale homes with a new bridge to Grosse Ile.
- **Getting there:** It's a boat ride from the Grosse Ile Yacht Club.

Lake St. Clair from Harsens Island at the northern end of the lake.

LAKE ST. CLAIR SURFACE AREA

430 square miles — 268 in Canada, 162 in the United States. By Great Lakes standards, that makes it small. Lake Ontario, the smallest Great Lake, has 7,340 square miles. By inland lake standards, it is huge.

LAKE ST. CLAIR GEOLOGY

Roll back the clock 13,000 years and you'd find the last glacial ice in what's now Lake St. Clair. The departure of the ice left behind water that covered much of southern Michigan and drained west. In a geologically speedy change about 12,000 years ago, water began draining east toward Niagara and levels dropped 130 feet as water surged toward the Gulf of St. Lawrence, leaving behind many isolated ponds, small lakes and marshes. The upper lakes were still ice-covered and not supplying water to the lower lakes. But as ice melted in the upper lakes, Lake St. Clair, Lake Erie and Lake Ontario rose. About 5,000 years ago, the water level in Lake St. Clair was about 10 to 13 feet deeper than it is now. Over the next few hundred years, levels fell and have remained in roughly the same range since. Over the last century, water levels have swung about 7 feet.

Sugar

➤ **Size:** 29.42 acres.
➤ **People:** None.
➤ **History:** Indians called it Nassawa. It was named for its sugar maple trees. During the late 1800s, it was a popular destination for boaters. It became a popular amusement park in the early 1900s until the grounding of the excursion ship Tashmoo in 1936. With about 1,400 passengers aboard, the ship apparently hit a loose rock and made it to the Canadian shore, coming to rest on the shallow bottom. All passengers disembarked safely. The island was abandoned shortly thereafter.

In 1944, a group of black Detroit businessmen bought the island, citing bans on blacks in other Detroit-area amusement parks. Facilities were built and boat service began in 1946 but the project failed.

A plan to develop homes, picnic and beach areas was rejected by the federal government in 1960. Fires have destroyed the amusement-park buildings and dance hall. It was purchased in the 1980s by Bill Herschler of Beverly Hills, Mich.

➤ **Getting there:** A boat ride from the Grosse Ile Yacht Club. It is 1,000 feet southeast of Grosse Ile.

Swan

➤ **Size:** About 20 acres.
➤ **People:** About 200.
➤ **History:** Originally, it was known as Snake Island because of its swampy property. A canal was dug in the 1920s to separate the island from Grosse Ile. It was named for the Swan family, early residents of Grosse Ile.

➤ **Getting there:** Take the bridge off South Pointe at the south end of Grosse Ile.

Zug

➤ **Size:** 334 acres.
➤ **People:** 650 National Steel employees.
➤ **History:** The island formerly housed the estate of one of the state's first status seekers: Samuel Zug. In 1836, Zug came to Detroit from Cumberland, Pa., looking to make a fortune. With money earned as a bookkeeper, he bought materials to make fine furniture and opened the Stevenson & Zug Furniture Co. with Detroit financier Marcus Stevenson. Envisioning a luxurious estate on the Detroit River, he bought the marshy island in 1867, but the dampness didn't appeal to Zug and his wife, Ann. After 10 years, they abandoned their home and in 1888 let a company cut a canal through his property to connect the Rouge and Detroit rivers. He sold his island for $300,000 in 1891 to industries for use as a dumping ground. Zug served as Wayne County auditor and died in 1896 at the age of 80, leaving a garbage dump for a memorial. The Detroit Iron Works built two blast furnaces for iron-making on the island in 1901. In 1931, the island became part of Great Lakes Steel, and today Zug Island is owned by National Steel.

➤ **Getting there:** Accessible by bridge off Jefferson Avenue. For permission to tour the island, contact National Steel at 313-297-2100 anytime.

SOURCES: "OUR DOWNRIVER RIVER," BY ROCKNE SMITH; "DETROIT IN PERSPECTIVE, A JOURNAL OF REGIONAL HISTORY," EDITED BY W. SPRAGUE HOLDEN; BASF CORP.; NATIONAL STEEL; GROSSE ILE, BROWNSTOWN TOWNSHIP AND AMHERSTBURG, ONTARIO, ASSESSOR'S OFFICES, AND FREE PRESS RESEARCH.

Lake St. Clair

It's southeast Michigan's blue water special, not quite reaching Great Lakes status on its own, but still a darned good lake and treated for legal purposes as part of the Great Lakes system. Lake experts view it as the wide spot in the strait (the St. Clair and Detroit rivers) connecting Lake Huron and Lake Erie. It's a playground for fishermen, cruisers and partyers, a pathway for freighters from around the world, a nursery for fish and wildlife, home to thousands of people who live along its shoreline and canals and the reason for being for dozens of marinas, restaurants and other businesses that cater to the boating set.

➤ **History:** Named on Aug. 12, 1679, by Rene Robert Cavalier, better known as the Sieur de la Salle. On that day, the young French explorer's schooner, the Griffon, entered the lake and he named it after St. Claire, founder of the order of Franciscan

Burton Historical Collection
Gar Wood (1880-1971) posing at the wheel of Miss America in 1957.

Dossin Great Lakes Museum
Chris-Craft founder Chris Smith; like Gar Wood, he got his start in Algonac.

Free Press file photo

nuns known as "Poor Claires." She was picked because Aug. 12 is her feast day. In 1879 and 1979, celebrations were held in Grosse Pointe commemorating the naming.

➤ **Water volume:** About 1 cubic mile.

➤ **Maximum length:** 26 miles north to south

➤ **Maximum width:** 24 miles east to west

➤ **Shoreline length:** 130 miles of mainland shoreline, 127 miles of island shoreline.

➤ **Length of shipping channel:** 16 miles from the head of the Detroit River to the St. Clair Cutoff Channel at the mouth of the St. Clair River.

➤ **Maximum natural (non-dredged) depth outside shipping channel:** 21 feet.

➤ **Average depth:** 10 feet.

➤ **Flush time:** About seven days on average from the time a molecule of water enters the lake until it exits into the Detroit River.

➤ **Source of water:** 95 percent from Lake Huron via the St. Clair River, 5 percent from the watershed surrounding the lake, including the Clinton, Black, Salt, Ruscom and Thames rivers.

➤ **Number of mayday calls in typical year for U.S. Coast Guard station St. Clair Shores:** 375-400.

➤ **Nicknames:** Lake St. Stupid (a common name among law enforcement officials because of the density of boats — or maybe boaters). In the summer of 2000, with water levels at their lowest point in about 35 years, Lake St. Shallow.

➤ **Water levels:** In 2000, Lake St. Clair depths were at their lowest levels in about 35 years and were not expected to rise much any time soon. The drop was precipitous — a little more than 3 feet in about three years. Lack of rain and snow in the Great Lakes drainage basin is the main reason. More than 95 percent of the lake's water comes from Lake Huron.

Warmer-than-usual weather also has led to more evaporation of water from the lakes. Lake depths also vary by season. Levels are generally lowest in winter and peak in July. The lake reached its modern-day peak in 1986 when levels were nearly 5 feet higher than in 2000.

➤ **Boating:** Picture this. There is no wind, but your boat never stops rocking. It's a non-stop wake-a-thon on the U.S. side of the lower end of Lake St. Clair. At any given time, there are about 2,500 boats on the lake on a hot summer weekend and over the course of the two days, that's about 10,000 boats, according to U.S. Coast Guard Lt. Gerard Williams, commanding officer of the coast guard station in St. Clair Shores. In the 1920s and '30s, hydroplanes that set world speed records were built in Algonac by Christopher Smith and Gar Wood. Today, high-speed offshore boats race through the lake, alongside luxury cruisers, well-equipped fishing boats and fleets of racing sailboats. If you're looking for solitude, head into Ontario waters. The farther you get from the shipping channel the more peaceful it'll get.

➤ **Swimming:** The vast majority of U.S. waterfront on the lake is privately owned. The biggest public beach is at Metro Beach Metropark in Harrison Township. Other beaches are available to city residents only. In recent years, the beaches have had to close occasionally in the summer because of high bacteria levels. Bacterial pollution sources include the droppings of shoreline birds, sewage overflows into rivers and creeks draining into the lake, leaking septic tanks and illegal toilet drain hookups. To swim in the lake's cleanest water, head offshore in a boat. On hot summer weekends, hundreds of boaters gather in the shallow, sandy waters of the St. Clair Flats in places such as Fisher Bay and the Strawberry Bar on the southeast side of

Sharing the waves: Ore boats and sailboats on Lake St. Clair in 1973.

THE BOATER CITY

Before roads, railroads and automobiles, the water that surrounds us was the major means of transportation. From about 1820 to 1920, Detroit was a bustling seaport and one of the most important shipbuilding centers in the United States. The freighters and ore boats and tens of thousands of pleasure craft are the latest in a long line of local vessels that began with the Indians' birchbark canoe. The first European ship on the Great Lakes, Griffon, sailed past the future site of Detroit in 1679. After 1818, the Walk-in-the-Water, a 136-foot steamboat, made regular, 44-hour trips from Buffalo. After the Erie Canal opened in 1825, Detroit became the chief western terminus for travelers, immigrants and others coming from the east.

Burton Historical Collection

The J.T. Wing, last schooner on the Great Lakes, sails the St. Clair River in 1942.

Free Press file photo

The ill-fated Edmund Fitzgerald.

BEST PLACES FOR FREIGHTER WATCHING

➤ Port Huron: Under the Blue Water Bridge.

➤ St. Clair: Along the boardwalk.

➤ Detroit: At the foot of Alter Road, A. Ford Park at the foot of Lakewood, Belle Isle, Hart Plaza and Riverside Park at the foot of West Grand Boulevard.

SOURCES: "SHIPS OF THE GREAT LAKES" AND "GREENWOOD AND DILL'S LAKE BOATS, '99."

Anchor Bay. At the lower end of the lake, boaters head for Ford Cove, off the Edsel and Eleanor Ford Home in Grosse Pointe Shores, the bay between Crescent Sail Yacht Club and Pier Park in Grosse Pointe Farms or many sandy spots along the Canadian shoreline, including an excellent beach off the town of Belle River.

➤ **Water temperature:** The lake is typically ice-covered in winter, though not always safe to walk across because of currents and winds. Because it is shallow, most of the lake warms relatively quickly with temperatures usually peaking in August at around 75 degrees Fahrenheit along the western (Canadian) shoreline. Temperatures are usually 3 to 7 degrees Fahrenheit cooler along the eastern shoreline. Because more than 95 percent of Lake St. Clair's water comes from the cool depths of Lake Huron, the swift-flowing shipping channel stays cooler.

➤ **Fish:** One of the top fishing holes in the nation. It is known internationally for several species, notably muskie and smallmouth bass. Bob Haas, the Michigan Department of Natural Resources' top biologist regarding Lake St. Clair, says it is the best muskie lake in the world and among the five best for smallmouth bass. The most sought-after species is the abundant and tasty yellow perch. Walleye, arguably the tastiest fish in the lake, are also

highly sought after in the spring and early summer along the U.S. shoreline and in deeper water, primarily on the Canadian side, as the water warms. The largest fish on Lake St. Clair is the sturgeon, once caught in large numbers by commercial anglers near the head of the Detroit River. They can grow larger than 6 feet, but few are caught. In the delta known as the St. Clair Flats on the northeast corner of the lake, many anglers pursue northern pike, largemouth bass and panfish such as bluegill.

Ecosystem changes in the lake since the late 1980s followed the invasion of zebra mussels, round goby fish and drought. Mussels, a European native transported to the Great Lakes in the ballast water of an ocean-going ship, eat by filtering tiny organisms that live in the water. They have adapted and prospered to such a degree that the water of Lake St. Clair has become much clearer, which, in turn, allows light to penetrate more deeply, causing more plant growth. Water plants generally are good for fish because they enhance the food chain, providing habitat for small organisms and fish, but in the long term are bad. Zebra mussels clog water-intake systems of power plants, water treatment facilities and boat cooling systems. They cling to the bottoms of boats and are difficult to walk on when they stick to docks and rocks.

On the plus side, gobies eat zebra mussels

and are, in turn, eaten by larger predator fish such as bass, walleye and muskie, but they also pose threats to other bottom-living fishes because they compete for the same food.

➤ **Pollution:** Lake St. Clair got a huge black eye in the early 1970s when authorities banned anglers from keeping any fish because of high levels of mercury contamination traced to discharges from chlor-alkali plants on the St. Clair and Detroit rivers. After the plants were ordered to stop their dumping, the levels of mercury in fish came down as sediment slowly buried the mercury on the lake's bottom.

Since then, pollution concerns have focused mainly on biological contamination — high bacteria levels — that has forced beach closings in the last decade. Major efforts are under way to reduce raw sewage dumped into the lake during storms. Some communities are separating storm and septic sewers, while others are building retention basins to store storm water and avoid sewage overflows.

Meanwhile, Lake St. Clair anglers, like their counterparts who fish virtually anywhere in the state, face concerns about eating fish contaminated with even small amounts of chemicals such as PCBs and mercury. Larger, older, fatty fish generally pose the greatest risk and children and women who intend to have children should exercise the greatest caution. For more information, fishing license dealers should have a pamphlet on the concerns about eating fish.

➤ **Marshes:** The St. Clair Flats, at the northeast corner of the lake, and St. John's Marsh, between Fair Haven and Algonac, represent the largest wetlands on the intensely developed U.S. side of the lake. As such, they are remarkable nurseries for fish, waterfowl, frogs, turtles and other wildlife.

SOURCES: JOHN P. COAKLEY, NATIONAL WATER RESEARCH INSTITUTE, BURLINGTON, ONTARIO; MACOMB MSU EXTENSION; BOB HAAS, FISHERIES BIOLOGIST, MICHIGAN DEPARTMENT OF NATURAL RESOURCES; "LAKE ERIE AND LAKE ST. CLAIR HANDBOOK," WAYNE STATE UNIVERSITY PRESS; U.S. COAST GUARD STATION ST. CLAIR SHORES.

The big ships

There are about 200 Canadian and U.S. commercial vessels on the Great Lakes today, including bulk freight carriers, ferries, tankers and tugs.

➤ **Freighters:** In 1957, 251 ships carried iron ore on the Great Lakes. By 1971, there were only 134. In 2000, there were 127 — 42 "straight-deck bulkers" and 85 "self-unloaders."

➤ **Super ships:** At least 1,000 feet long and 100 feet wide. There are 13; the first was the Stewart J. Cort, built in 1972. The largest is the 1,013-foot Paul R. Tregurtha, with a capacity of 61,000 tons. That's enough space to carry 40,000 automobiles. The super ships mostly carry iron ore.

➤ **Cargo:** Iron ore, stones and coal. Transporting iron ore from Lake Superior ports to the heavy industrial regions along the lower Great Lakes is one of the main reasons lake freighters came into being. Freighters based in the United States carry an average of nearly 58 million tons of iron ore each season, twice that of stone or coal, according to the Lake Carriers' Association.

Limestone moves in more than one form. The steel industry uses fluxstone. The construction industry uses aggregate in highways and parking lots. Chemical and paper industries also use limestone. Freighters based in the United States carry an average of about 23 million tons a year. The world's largest quarry is in Rogers City.

U.S. freighters carry an average of about 20 million tons a year, and it comes in two types: metallurgical coal for steel making, and steam coal for power plants. Eastern coal is mined in Pennsylvania, West Virginia, Kentucky and Illinois and shipped from Lake Erie and Lake Ontario ports. Western coal is mined in Montana and Wyoming and is shipped by train to Superior, Wis., where it is loaded onto freighters.

SCOW SONG

The Julie Plante, immortalized in a French dialect folk song, was one of hundreds of family-run sailing scows with such shallow drafts that they were said to be able to sail on nothing more than a heavy dew. They carried building materials and firewood down the many rivers feeding into the Detroit River and Lake St. Clair in the latter half of the 1800s.

Dossin Great Lakes Museum
The steamer Michigan in 1833.

Free Press file photo
This postcard in 1927 shows D&C Line docks in Detroit.

Dossin Great Lakes Museum

The South American made excursion trips between Detroit and Chicago.

Burton Historical Collection

The steamer City of Detroit took passengers from Detroit to Cleveland.

Free Press file photo

A Harper's Weekly drawings shows a mailboat visiting a Great Lakes vessel in Detroit.

Burton Historical Collection

Workers at Great Lakes Engineering Works in Wyandotte build the Brittania, a Detroit-Windsor ferry, in 1905.

Classic ships of Detroit

The following are just a few of the hundreds of craft built along "the strait."

➤ **The canoe:** For much of the first few decades of Detroit's existence, the canoe was the chief means of transportation. Twenty-five long canoes brought Cadillac and his men to the Detroit River in 1701. The principal canoe was made of birch bark, and was invented by Indians. It was light, meaning that it drafted little water and allowed the French to explore small tributaries, and it could be easily carried over portages. French fur trappers built canoes that were 35 feet long, 5 feet wide and 4 feet deep that could cary 3 tons of furs and eight men.

➤ **Pirogue:** A boat dug out of a tree trunk that could carry up to eight people.

➤ **Bateau:** Means boat in French; also called a Mackinac boat, it was a 17th-Century flat-bottomed barge.

➤ **First ship:** The first known ship built in Detroit was the Enterprise, in 1769.

➤ **Built by the British:** The first sustained shipbuilding in Detroit took place during the American Revolution, when the British ruled Detroit. Between 1774 and 1782, nine ships, ranging in size from 18 tons to 136 tons, were built in Detroit. After 1776, only military vessels were allowed on the lakes.

➤ **Private stock:** The schooner Nancy, constructed at the Kings Shipyard of Detroit in 1789, was one of the first private vessels on the Great Lakes.

➤ **Go east, young man:** The schooner St. Clair was built at Marine City in 1824 with removable masts and a contrarian view about the Erie Canal, which opened the interior to a flood of settlers and a new market for eastern goods. With a cargo of potash, gun stocks and furs, the St. Clair became the first vessel to sail though the canal from the Great Lakes seaward in search of eastern markets.

➤ **Upper deck:** The Michigan, launched at Detroit in 1833, was one of the first steamers to have upper-deck passenger cabins.

➤ **Here come the brides:** The steamer May Flower, a side-wheel showpiece complete with 12 bridal chambers, was built in 1849 for the Michigan Central Railroad as a connector between Buffalo and Detroit.

➤ **Tough tug:** The Sport, a 57-foot tug built at Wyandotte in 1873, was the first commercial vessel on the Great Lakes to have an all-steel hull. The vessel sank in Lake Huron in

1920, about 3 miles from Lexington, Mich., and remained undiscovered until 1987.

▶ **Double-decker:** Another Michigan, built at the Detroit Drydock Co. in 1873, was the first schooner constructed with a second deck in the hold.

▶ **The Glass Hack:** The excursion steamer Tashmoo, launched in 1900, was the longest passenger vessel on the Detroit River. It was turned out with deck carpeting, mahogany furniture and twin grand pianos. A schedule as frantic as a busy taxi driver's and more than 600 windows gave "the Tash" another nickname: the Glass Hack.

▶ **Boblo bound:** The steamer Columbia, finished in 1902 in Wyandotte, was a much-loved day boat that ran excursionists to the Boblo Island recreation park.

▶ **Biggest side-wheeler:** The City of Detroit III, the largest sidewheel steamer in the world at 470 feet, paddled between Detroit and Cleveland from 1912-1950. It was launched at Wyandotte, but went to Detroit for finishing school before it went into service.

▶ **Sweetheart of the Lakes:** The steamer South American, built in 1914, was called "the sweetheart of the Lakes" and made excursion runs between Detroit and Chicago. The dining room seated 276 of the vessel's 540 passengers at a time. It was built at Ecorse.

▶ **The Gray Fox:** Gar Wood, whose gray hair earned him the nickname "The Gray Fox of Grayhaven," also was known as the "Speed-boat King" after he began putting airplane engines in his boats. This did not kill him, but made him the first man to travel at 100 mph on water — and then the first to top 120 mph. One of his speedboats, Miss America I, won the Harmsworth Trophy — the 1920s equivalent of the America's Cup.

▶ **Chris-Craft:** Chris Smith of Algonac was whittling wooden duck decoys one day around the turn of the century when he wondered how a boat hull would work if it were shaped like that of a duck — short, broad and flat. He went on to incorporate that idea in race, sail- and powerboats, and the company that he formed in 1922, Chris-Craft, became one of the world's most famous builders of pleasure craft. Smith, who died in 1939, was the Henry Ford of boatbuilding. He used an assembly line, and he sought to put a boat at everybody's dock. Well-preserved Chris-Craft 19-foot Runabouts from post-World War II, done in a varnished mahogany-like wood called luan, cost up to $50,000 today. The

Burton Historical Collection

Mariners' Church makes its way east in 1955. The City of Detroit paid $261,000 to move the 6-million-pound church.

Mariners' Museum in Newport News, Va., can determine the age of a Chris-Craft from its hull number, which is found on a brass tag on the engine. Call 757-596-2222 during business hours.

▶ **Big Fitz:** The Edmund Fitzgerald's legacy is that it sank in Lake Superior on Nov. 10, 1975, but let's not forget that, when launched at River Rouge in 1958, it was the longest vessel on the Great Lakes at 729 feet. This has since been surpassed by vessels of more than 1,000 feet.

▶ **Factory of firsts:** The Great Lakes Engineering Works at Detroit had several other notables in its dossier before it built the Fitz. They include the world's first self-unloading vessel (Wyandotte, 1908); the first "stemwinder," a freighter with the cabins over the stern (Edison Light, 1912); the first diesel-powered Great Lakes freighter (Benson Ford, 1924) and the labor-saving first Great Lakes bulk freighter with single-piece hatch covers and a traveling deck crane (William C. Atwater, 1925).

▶ **Detroit Drydock Co:** The other shipbuilder. Located at Orleans and Atwater and operating under different names since the 1850s, Detroit Drydock by the 1880s was making wooden ships at its Detroit complex and iron ships in Wyandotte. The Detroit dock covered 700 feet on Atwater, and employed 700 people.

SOURCES: JOHN POLASZEK, DOSSIN GREAT LAKES MUSEUM; JAMES CLARY'S "LADY OF THE LAKES"; THE MICHIGAN PIONEER AND HISTORICAL COLLECTIONS; TELESCOPE MAGAZINE, PUBLISHED BY THE GREAT LAKES MARITIME INSTITUTE.

MARINERS' CHURCH

Detroit has its own house of worship devoted to sailors and ships. Mariners' Church opened in 1849 at the corner of Woodward and Woodbridge and moved 800 feet east in 1955 to the corner of Randolph and Jefferson. Julia Anderson donated the original land so that Great Lakes sailors could have a church of their own. Architectural historian W. Hawkins Ferry wrote that Mariners' Church was the first of numerous gray limestone houses of worship in Detroit. The stone was floated upriver from Trenton; Malden, Ontario, and other Lake Erie quarries. At a Sunday service each November, the church bell tolls 29 times in memory of the crew members of the Edmund Fitzgerald, which sank in Lake Superior on Nov. 10, 1975.

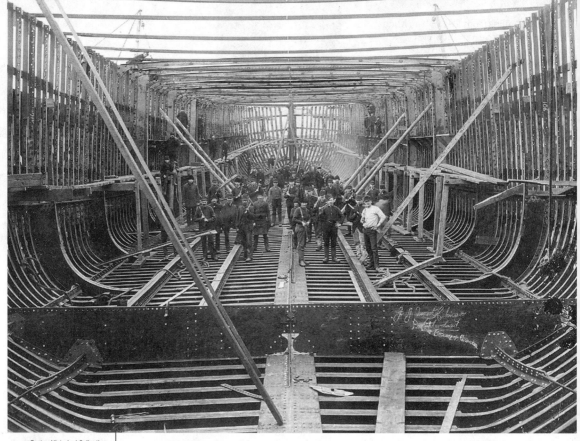

Workers stand in the skeleton of a ship under construction at Detroit Drydock Co. The firm employed 700 people in the late 19th Century.

Facts to float your boat

During the heyday of Great Lakes shipping, Detroit was considered a Lake Erie port.

➤ In **1842**, a newfangled steamer began appearing on the lakes: it was called a propeller. Until then, all the steamers had been side-wheelers. By 1857, most of the ships were propeller-driven.

➤ In **1849**, 43 steamers were registered in Detroit, which owned 30 percent of the vessels on the lakes.

➤ In **1857**, three of the largest steamers on the lakes ran daily between Detroit and Buffalo. The one-way trip took 15 hours.

➤ In **1859**, 3,065 commercial vessels passed Detroit headed upbound (with many of them stopping). Greatest number passing in one day: 85.

➤ In **1998**, 5,409 vessels passed Detroit headed upbound.

➤ In **1870**, there were still 1,545 sailing vessels on the lakes. They outnumbered steamships until the late 1880s, when 1,864 steamships were launched.

➤ In **1870**, there were eight lines of steamers out of Detroit. More than 70 steamers used Detroit as a terminus, or stopped at the city.

➤ In **1906**, Detroit processed 45 percent of Great Lakes passengers.

➤ **Last schooner:** A three-masted schooner named the J. T. Wing was built in 1919 and sailed the Great Lakes for several decades. When her sailing days were over in 1946 she was given to the Detroit Historical Museum and opened to the public on Belle Isle until 1956, when she was burned because of dry rot in a well-attended public ceremony.

➤ **Neither snow nor sleet nor waves:** Detroit is the only place in the country where ships can mail documents and receive deliveries — all while sailing through. Passing freighters on the Detroit River lower pails to collect their mail from the J. W. Wescott II, the small vessel that provides the service. It docks near the foot of West Grand Boulevard. The Wescott has its own ZIP code — 48222.

➤ **Web waves:** A comprehensive Web site devoted to Great Lakes shipping, including links to a number of other informative sites, is at **www.oakland.edu/boatnerd/.**

SOURCES: GREAT LAKES COMMISSION; FREE PRESS; "A PICTORIAL HISTORY OF THE GREAT LAKES."

Boat whistles

➤ **One short:** I am proceeding to starboard (right).

➤ **Two short:** I am proceeding to port (left).

➤ **Five or more short blasts sounded rapidly:** Danger.

➤ **One prolonged:** Vessel leaving dock.

➤ **One short, one prolonged, one short, sounded once per minute:** Vessel at anchor in fog.

Lighthouses

Michigan has more lighthouses than any other state — 124. Like little else on the Great Lakes, the lonely sentinels remain a touchstone to the era of sail, because a number of them remain from before the invention of electricity.

Although they were once crucial maritime landmarks, they are no longer as essential for boaters with modern electronic equipment. They remain part of the emotional landscape of maritime communities, though, and play a part in Michigan's tourist trade. But the Coast Guard, which owns more than half of the lighthouses in Michigan, says it can't afford nostalgia anymore, and is disposing of them. Some lighthouses are passing to local governments, private individuals are buying others and the fate of the remaining stations is uncertain. Here are the notable lighthouses in the waters off metro Detroit:

➤ **Oldest in Michigan:** Ft. Gratiot in Port Huron, at the entrance to the St. Clair River near the Blue Water Bridge. Opened in 1829, last rebuilt in 1861. It's open 1 p.m. -4:30 p.m. Wednesday-Sunday, as is the adjacent museum and the nearby Lightship Huron. 810-982-0891, 9-4:30 weekdays.

➤ **Best sister act:** The St. Clair Flats Old Range Lights, also known as the Old Twin Sisters, are floating brick towers that can be seen from Mt. Clemens and Harsens Island.

➤ **Most urban:** Windmill Point, near Alter Road and Jefferson Avenue in Detroit's Mariners Park.

➤ **Marble lighthouse:** The William Livingstone Memorial on Belle Isle is the only marble lighthouse on the continent.

➤ **Grosse Ile:** North Channel Front Range Light Station sits offshore.

➤ **St. Clair Shores:** Built in 1941, it's 3

Dossin Great Lakes Museum
Windmill Point lighthouse about 1900.

Free Press file photo
A leaning South Channel light built in 1859 near Harsens Island.

MARY SCHROEDER/Detroit Free Press
The Detroit River light is the most hit by vessels.

ERIC SEALS/Detroit Free Press
The Ft. Gratiot lighthouse first beamed in 1829.

miles off of St. Clair Shores.

➤ **St. Clair Flats:** There are two lights on the South Channel; one is on the front range, the other is on the rear range. Both were built in 1859.

➤ **More light:** For information about Michigan lighthouses and state assistance for their restoration, call 517-373-1630 from 7:30 a.m. to 4:30 weekdays or check out the Michigan Lighthouse Project Web site at **www.sos.state.mi.us/history/preserve/lights/milight2.html.**

MOST FREQUENT CRASH VICTIM

Detroit River light, where the river meets Lake Erie. It has been hit by freighters and pleasure craft. Constructed in 1884, the 49-foot-tall tower became automated in 1975.

Light House, Belle Isle, Detroit, Mich.

Dossin Great Lakes Museum

A literal lighthouse on the eastern end of Belle Isle, built in 1883, has long been demolished.

The William Livingstone Memorial on Belle Isle is the only marble lighthouse on the continent.

The Great Lakes

The five Great Lakes cover 94,000 square miles, drain more than twice that amount of land and hold an estimated 6 quadrillion gallons of water.

More than 10 percent of the U.S. population and 25 percent of the Canadian population live within the Great Lakes watershed. Half of Canada's manufacturing and 20 percent of U.S. manufacturing are located on the lakes. But the region also includes pristine forests, and millions of people use the lakes for recreation.

Some 3.7 million boats in eight Great Lakes states are registered for recreational use, including more than 800,000 in Michigan. Many more people use the lakes for their drinking water.

Lake Michigan

Third-largest Great Lake by surface area and the sixth-largest freshwater lake in the world. Hydrologists, however, consider lakes Michigan and Huron, connected by the Straits of Mackinac, to be one lake.
- ➤ **Name:** Originally called Grand Lac, Lac des Puants (Lake of the Stinking People, after nearby Indian tribes), Lac des Illinois (after the nearby Indian tribe), Lac St. Joseph and Lac Dauphin.

- ➤ **Length:** 307 miles.
- ➤ **Breadth:** 118 miles.
- ➤ **Depth:** 279 feet, average; 925, maximum.
- ➤ **Volume:** 1,180 cubic miles.
- ➤ **Water surface:** 22,300 square miles.
- ➤ **Shoreline:** Including islands, 1,638 miles.
- ➤ **Elevation:** 577 feet.
- ➤ **Outlet:** Straits of Mackinac to Lake Huron.
- ➤ **Retention/replacement time:** 99 years.

Lake Superior

Largest of the Great Lakes and largest body of freshwater in the world. It could contain all the other Great Lakes plus three more lakes the size of Lake Erie.
- ➤ **Name:** The French called it le lac superior, which means "upper lake."
- ➤ **Length:** 350 miles
- ➤ **Breadth:** 160 miles
- ➤ **Depth:** 483 feet, average; 1,332 feet, maximum
- ➤ **Volume:** 2,900 cubic miles
- ➤ **Water surface:** 31,700 square miles
- ➤ **Shoreline:** Including islands, 2,726 miles
- ➤ **Elevation:** 600 feet
- ➤ **Outlet:** St. Marys River to Lake Huron
- ➤ **Retention/replacement time:** 191 years

Lake Huron

Second-largest Great Lake by surface area and the fifth-largest freshwater lake in the world. Manatoulin Island is the largest freshwater island in the world. Georgian Bay itself is large enough to be listed among the 20 largest lakes in the world.
- ➤ **Name:** After the nearby Indian tribe. A 1656 map called it Karegnondi.
- ➤ **Length:** 206 miles.
- ➤ **Breadth:** 183 miles.
- ➤ **Depth:** 195 feet, average; 750 feet, maximum.
- ➤ **Volume:** 850 cubic miles.
- ➤ **Water surface:** 23,000 square miles.
- ➤ **Shoreline:** Including islands, 3,827 miles.
- ➤ **Elevation:** 577 feet.
- ➤ **Outlet:** St. Clair River to Lake Erie.
- ➤ **Retention/replacement time:** 22 years.

Lake Erie

The 11th-largest lake in the world and fourth-largest of the Great Lakes in surface area, but smallest by volume. About 95 percent of its inflow comes via the Detroit River from the upper lakes. It is the warmest and most biologically productive of the Great Lakes.

➤ **Name:** After a nearby Indian tribe.
➤ **Length:** 241 miles.
➤ **Breadth:** 57 miles.
➤ **Depth:** 62 feet, average; 210 feet maximum.
➤ **Volume:** 116 cubic miles.
➤ **Water surface:** 9,190 square miles.
➤ **Shoreline:** Including islands, 871 miles.
➤ **Elevation:** 569 feet.
➤ **Outlet:** Niagara River and Welland Canal.
➤ **Retention/replacement time:** 2.6 years.

Lake Ontario

The 14th-largest lake in the world but the smallest of the Great Lakes in surface area. It lies 325 feet below adjacent Lake Erie, at the base of Niagara Falls.

➤ **Name:** French explorer Champlain called it Lac St. Louis; later it was known as Lac Frontenac. "Ontara" in Iroquois means "lake;" "ontario" means "beautiful lake."
➤ **Length:** 193 miles.
➤ **Breadth:** 53 miles.
➤ **Depth:** 283 feet, average; 802 feet, maximum.
➤ **Volume:** 393 cubic miles.
➤ **Water surface:** 7,340 square miles.
➤ **Shoreline:** Including islands, 712 miles.
➤ **Elevation:** 243 feet.
➤ **Outlet:** St. Lawrence River to Atlantic Ocean.
➤ **Retention/replacement time:** 6 years.

Water levels

The Great Lakes fluctuate based on several variables. Long periods of less-than-average precipitation combined with warmer temperatures mean gradually lower water levels. Water levels rise during periods of wet and cold winters.

➤ **Water enters:** As rain, snow, hail, sleet, snowmelt, groundwater, inflow from upstream lakes add to levels.
➤ **Water leaves:** Evaporation is the major factor along with the transpiration of water released into the atmosphere from plants, groundwater outflow, consumption, diversions and outflow to downstream lakes and rivers. Water ultimately flows to the Atlantic Ocean through the St. Lawrence River.
➤ **The fluctuations:** Seasonal water-level fluctuations average from 12 inches to 18 inches from winter lows to summer highs.

Levels have fluctuated greatly over the centuries. In modern times, levels were low in the 1920s, mid-1930s and mid-1960s. Levels were extremely high in the 1870s, early 1950s, early 1970s, mid-1980s and mid-1990s. Water levels were low in 2000.

➤ **Lose an inch:** Here are the amounts of water in gallons each lake loses when it drops an inch: Superior: 551 billion; St. Clair 6.9 billion.

➤ **Water online:** These Web sites will flood you with Great Lake information:
   www.great-lakes.net
   www.glc.org
   www.lre.usace.army.mil/hmpghh.html
   www.crh.noaa.gov

SOURCE: GREAT LAKES COMMISSION.

Great Lakes time line

➤ **1 billion years ago:** Volcanic activity between present-day Oklahoma and Lake Superior spewed lava for 20 million years, creating mountains in today's northern Wisconsin and Minnesota. The Laurentian Mountains were formed in eastern Canada. Molten magma formed the rock basin that eventually would hold Lake Superior.

➤ **5 million years ago:** Glaciers began advancing and retreating; they did this several times, covering the land with sheets of ice sometimes 1,000 feet thick, carving out valleys and leveling mountains. As the glaciers retreated, their edges left behind lofty ridges, such as in Door County, Wis., or along Ontario's Bruce Peninsula. The departing ice left huge lakes among these ridges, and the bodies of water changed as the ice moved northward.

➤ **10,000 years ago:** People begin arriving in the Great Lakes region. By 1500, before the arrival of Europeans, an estimated 60,000 to 120,000 Indians live in the area.

➤ **7,000 to 9,000 years ago:** The last glacier had left the region. Drainage from the massive ice surfaces traveled through the Illinois Valley toward the Mississippi, through the Trent River Valley between today's lakes Huron and Erie and through the Lake Nipissing-Ottawa River Valley from Georgian Bay toward Montreal. With the heavy ice gone, land literally began to rebound. The northeastern corner of the Lake Superior basin bounced back more than 21 inches per century.

➤ **1534 AD:** Europeans began arriving. Jacques Cartier sailed into the St. Lawrence River.

➤ **1855:** Ship canal and locks opened in Sault Ste. Marie.

➤ **1959:** Opening of the 2,342-mile St. Lawrence Seaway.

Seasonal water-level fluctuations average from 12 inches to 18 inches from winter lows to summer highs. Levels were low in the 1920s, mid-1930s and mid-1960s.

ANDREW JOHNSTON/Free Press
A father and son fish at Cass Lake.

CASS LAKE

Cass Lake is the deepest and biggest lake in southeast Michigan. The lake also has the most speeding tickets because it is also the busiest lake for watercraft.

The lakes of Oakland County

Oakland County has more lakes than any Michigan county except Iron County.

Why?

The county is part of the Defiance Moraine, a region in southeastern Michigan where a glacier deposited hundreds of feet of sand and gravel as it melted between 7,000 and 10,000 years ago. Water passes more easily through sand and gravel than through heavier soils. The level of water in the soil is called the water table. When the land is lower than the water table, we call the place a lake.

Top 10 Michigan counties ranked by number of lakes and ponds:

County	Lakes/Ponds	Acres
1. Iron	2,175	29,456
2. Oakland	1,857	25,504
3. Marquette	1,824	30,062
4. Houghton	1,379	20,324
5. Gogebic	1,158	29,199
6. Baraga	1,147	10,152
7. Schoolcraft	1,095	28,801
8. Kent	854	9,974
9. Alger	821	14,235
10. Barry	816	13,949

Top 10 Michigan counties ranked by total lake and pond acreage

County	Lakes/Ponds	Acres
1. Cheboygan	344	51,358
2. Roscommon	126	39,132
3. Antrim	150	30,277
4. Marquette	1,824	30,062
5. Iron	2,175	29,456
6. Gogebic	1,158	29,199
7. Schoolcraft	1,095	28,801
8. Mackinac	454	28,547
9. Oakland	1,857	25,504
10. Charlevoix	97	23,415

SOURCES: "MICHIGAN LAKES AND PONDS," CLIFFORD HUMPHRYS AND JANET COLBY, 1965; STUDY DOCUMENTED LAKES AND PONDS AS SMALL AS 1/10 ACRE.

The inland lakes

➤ **Deepest lake in southeast Michigan:** Cass Lake, 123 feet, in West Bloomfield and Waterford townships.

➤ **Biggest lake in southeast Michigan:** Cass Lake, 1,280 acres.

➤ **Noisiest lake in Oakland County:** Lake Oakland, Waterford and Independence townships.

➤ **Busiest lake by watercraft in Oakland County:** Cass.

➤ **Clearest lake:** Elizabeth Lake, Waterford Township.

> **Fastest lake (most speeding tickets):** Cass.

> **Coldest lake:** Forest, in Bloomfield Township, with constant 3 degree Centigrade temperature at the bottom. Forest is a meromictic lake, meaning the water never turns over. Saltwater runoff from Telegraph settles in a layer at the bottom. Because saltwater is denser than freshwater, it tends not to rise.

Household water

With five treatment plants, the Detroit Water and Sewerage Department pumps more than 230 billion gallons of water each year to 4.2 million people in 126 communities across 1,005 square miles of southeast Michigan.

The intake stations are in Lake Huron, and in the Detroit River off Belle Isle and off southwest Detroit. On an average day, the DWSD pumps more than 636 million gallons through its 12,524 miles of mains. The department also operates wastewater collection for 78 communities, and its wastewater plant on the Detroit River in southwest Detroit is the largest in the United States, and most likely in the world. The plant, which has been under court order because it has dumped raw sewage into the river, handles the outflow from most of the toilets from Detroit to Flint. For Detroit's first 100 years, this is how residents obtained water for cooking, bathing and drinking: They walked out on a wooden plank from the shore of their farms and dipped a bucket into the Detroit River. It was that simple. Later, people carried two buckets hooked to a wooden yoke from the river to their homes.

By 1806, the city began digging wells and building pumps, but people and animals tumbled into them, and citizens complained. By the mid-1820s, a rudimentary pump house was built by a businessman on a river wharf that sent water to a reservoir on the bank, and then through tamarack logs to several downtown locations. Wells were never a good solution in Detroit because impervious clay is under most of the city, so the only water available is runoff.

The city was forced to take over water operations in 1836, when it built a waterworks at the foot of Orleans. Over the years, Detroit constructed bigger and bigger pumps and reservoirs. In 1838, the first iron pipes were laid on Jefferson Avenue. During this period, a 422,979-gallon reservoir was built along the riverfront. Drinking fountains first appeared in 1862.

By 1868, officials were planning Waterworks Park, a sophisticated complex on the present Water Works site on East Jefferson near Cadillac Boulevard. The original pump house opened in 1878. By 1886, it had a capacity of 78 million gallons a day. The leading water commissioner of the period was Chauncey Hurlbut, the namesake of the two-story stone gate at the foot of Cadillac. With 110 acres, gardens, a floral clock and recreation facilities, the waterworks became one of Detroit's premier parks by 1900.

The city began treating water with chlorine after the typhoid epidemic in 1912. The Springwells plant began operation in 1935; a plant in northeast Detroit opened in 1956 as the burgeoning suburbs decided it was more economical to tie into Detroit's pipes than to build their own. By allowing the new communities to join the system, Detroit officials did much to help the exodus from the city. The system expanded further when the Lake Huron intake plant opened in 1974.

Detroit's other rivers

The Rouge River

> **Name:** "Rouge" means red in French.

> **Length:** 126 miles through the most heavily urbanized area in Michigan.

> **Depth:** Shallow.

> **Watershed:** About 438 square miles of Wayne, Washtenaw and Oakland counties and includes more than 400 lakes, impoundments, ponds and some 2 million people. Only about 25 percent of the watershed area is undeveloped. More than 50 miles of the Rouge flow through parkland, making it one of the most accessible rivers in Michigan. The Rouge is actually four separate branches: the Main, Upper, Middle and Lower. It empties into the Detroit River at Zug Island.

> **Rouge River Pollution:** The Rouge is synonymous with pollution, though cleanup efforts have been under way since the 1940s and have gathered momentum in recent years. By the mid-1980s, the Lower Rouge River was so polluted that it smelled, fizzed and burped on the filth that lined its bottom.

When the Warren Valley golf course sucked water out of the Middle Branch to water its greens, the grass died.

It was so polluted that boaters using the Melvindale ramp saw large mats of floating sludge that smelled of human waste.

Human sewage poured into the river at some locations. In that oxygenless environment, the ooze was busily decomposing into methane and hydrogen sulfide gas, which rose to the surface in thousands of little pinprick bubbles. Such telltale bubbles were visible at many places along the Rouge, but at one espe-

WATER TREATMENT

The city began treating water with chlorine after the typhoid epidemic in 1912. The Springwells plant began operation in 1935; a plant in northeast Detroit opened in 1956 as the burgeoning suburbs decided it was more economical to tie into Detroit's pipes than to build their own. By allowing the new communities to join the system, Detroit officials did much to help the exodus from the city. The system expanded further when the Lake Huron intake plant opened in 1974.

Free Press file photo

A volunteer hauls debris from the Rouge River in 1989.

ROUGE RIVER

In 2000, the Rouge was the focus of what many believe to be the most comprehensive partnership of government and private interests ever assembled to restore life to a damaged river and its urban surroundings.

cially bad location the channel fizzed like ginger ale. Several times a minute, a really big bubble of gas formed on the bottom and rose —blurp! — to the surface, bringing with it another inky blob of sludge to float downstream, offending everyone in its path.

➤ **Cleanup:** In 2000, the Rouge was the focus of what many believe to be the most comprehensive partnership of government and private interests ever assembled to restore life to a damaged river and its urban surroundings.

On one hand, there is the Rouge River Project, which began in 1991. Managed by Wayne County, the project is a restoration effort that has targeted the entire watershed and its chief problem — so-called wet-weather pollution such as combined sewer overflows and polluted storm runoff. It is funded through grants from the U.S. Environmental Protection Agency. U.S. Rep. John Dingell, D-Dearborn, and others have steered more than $100 million into cleaning up the Rouge.

On the other hand, Ford Motor Co., the University of Michigan at Dearborn, the Hen-

ry Ford Museum & Greenfield Village, private companies along the river, federal and state environmental agencies, cities and governments have come together in the Rouge River Gateway Partnership.

The partnership wants to construct walkways and bikeways, greening what is now endless concrete. It wants boat tours along the river. It wants to create oxbow-shaped bends in the river, including one at Greenfield Village, to let fish get out of the fast-moving channel. Fish would swim upstream to a dam at Fair Lane, the Ford estate, where a proposed fish ladder would let them migrate further up the recovering river.

The annual Rouge River Clean-up each spring draws more than 1,000 volunteers to clean up the river.

The Rouge River Project's Web site is **www.waynecounty.com/rougeriver/.**

Clinton River

➤ **Name:** Like the township, named in honor of N.Y. Gov. DeWitt Clinton, prime mover on construction of the Erie Canal.

➤ **Length:** 80 miles from its headwaters to Lake St. Clair at Harrison Township.

➤ **Watershed:** Drains 760 square miles, including portions of Oakland and Macomb counties and small parts of St. Clair and Lapeer counties.

➤ **Wastewater:** About half of the river's flow is is treated wastewater from six municipal wastewater treatment plants.

➤ **Controversy:** The river's heavy pollution has become a major public issue in recent years. Oakland County's Twelve Towns sewage retention basin has been ordered by the state to undergo a costly upgrade. Macomb County officials pushed for the upgrade because storm overflows flow through Macomb County into the Clinton River and then to Lake St. Clair. Twelve Towns had been out of compliance with regulations for years. In 2000, though, it was shown that the Macomb County communities of Clinton Township and Fraser were major violators — dumping raw sewage directly into the Clinton. Other sources of pollution are seen as illegal sewer connections, septic tank maintenance and the paving over of remaining acreage that helps absorb rainfall and slows the gushing of water that leads to the overflows. Doug Martz, chairman of the Macomb County Water Quality Board, said: "Years ago they figured dilution was the solution to pollution. We know that doesn't work anymore. There's too much growth, too many toilets and too many people."

SOURCES: FREE PRESS AND THE U.S. ENVIRONMENTAL PROTECTION AGENCY AT **WWW.EPA.GOV/GLNPO/AOC/CLINTRIV/**.

St. Clair River

➤ **Name:** After the Roman Catholic saint.

➤ **Length:** At 39 miles it connects Lake Huron and Lake St. Clair, forming the boundary between Michigan and Ontario. The upper river is a deep channel; the lower 11 miles branch onto a broad delta of numerous channels that flow into the lake.

➤ **Depth:** The river channel is 27 feet deep.

➤ **Current:** At the city of St. Clair, 2.1 m.p.h. on average at high water flow.

➤ **Rapids:** For several hundred feet on either side of the Blue Water Bridge, where Lake Huron pours onto the narrow river, the St. Clair is marked by rapids.

➤ **Pollution:** Massive chemical plants and oil refineries squat densely along the Canadian bank near Sarnia. Contamination levels were high in the 1970s, but had diminished somewhat by the 1990s.

Huron River

➤ **Name:** After the Indian tribe.

➤ **Length:** About 125 miles.

➤ **Watershed:** About 908 square miles in seven counties west and south of Detroit. It flows through 53 cities, including Ypsilanti and Ann Arbor, and empties into Lake Erie

CLINTON RIVER
The watershed drains 760 square miles, including portions of Oakland and Macomb counties and small parts of St. Clair and Lapeer counties.

Left: Workers in 1988 use torches to burn crude oil from the surface of the Clinton River.

Free Press file photo

Bloody Run runs through a ravine in Elmwood Cemetery. Its long-obliterated mouth was the site of the famous 1763 battle between the British and Indians, which the Indians won. That violent encounter gave the creek its sanguine name.

south of Rockwood. About 500,000 people live in the watershed. In addition to the main river, 24 tributaries total about 370 miles and connect about 300 lakes. Most of the land along the river is privately owned.

➤ **Cleanup:** Volunteers in the Huron's Adopt-a-Stream program began collecting data in 1992, and are working to reduce runoff into the river from yards and parking lots.

The Huron River Watershed's Web site is **comnet.org/hrwc.**

Detroit's forgotten streams

When the French arrived, Detroit was crisscrossed with streams, but they fell victim to urbanization. Here's a recollection:

➤ **Conner's Creek:** Ran northward from the Detroit River, roughly parallel to Conner Avenue on the east side, but now travels underground for most of its length. The Ford Freeway rises out of the ditch next to the Chandler Park golf course to let the waterway flow underneath. French settlers boated up the Conner and settled near what is now French Road and City Airport. In the 19th Century, the village of Norris grew up along the Conner near today's Gratiot and Harper.

➤ **Fox Creek:** Runs out of the Detroit River along the Detroit-Grosse Pointe Park border near Alter Road. While it still exists in part as a visible body of water, it has long been a source of human sewage when the nearby storm drains overflow.

➤ **Bloody Run:** Also known as Parent's Creek, after an 18th-Century French gunsmith named Joseph Parent. The stream runs through a ravine in Elmwood Cemetery. Its long-obliterated mouth at the Detroit River near Mt. Elliott, was the site of the famous 1763 battle between the British and Indians, which the Indians won. That violent encounter gave the creek its sanguine name.

➤ **River Savoyard:** Named after an early French settler, this was the downtown river that passed behind the first fort. It flowed from a marsh on the old Gouin Farm on the near east side, ran parallel to Jefferson and entered the Detroit River at the foot of Third Street, near today's Joe Louis Arena. The city converted it into a drain in the 1830s. It's buried beneath the Civic Center today.

➤ **Cabacier's Creek:** The waterway used to run on the near west side, near today's Fort Street. The creek is memorialized by Cabacier Street west of Joe Louis Arena. Named after settler Joseph Cabacier, the creek also was called Campau's River and May's Creek.

Port of Detroit

➤ **Coming into Detroit from Canada:** Mainly crude material such as iron ore,

cement, nonmetallic minerals and coal.

➤ **Leaving Detroit for Canada:** Mainly fuel oil.

➤ **Coming into Detroit from overseas:** Almost all steel and iron products.

➤ **Coming into Detroit from the United States:** Iron ore makes up more than half of the total; also limestone, gypsum, sand, gravel and coal.

➤ **Leaving Detroit for the United States:** Petroleum products such as asphalt, tar and pitch.

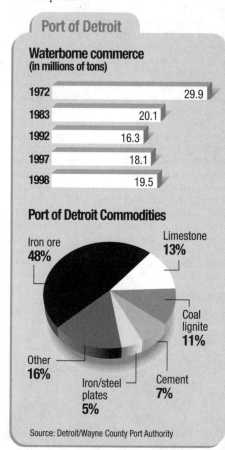

Port of Detroit

Waterborne commerce
(in millions of tons)

Year	Millions of tons
1972	29.9
1983	20.1
1992	16.3
1997	18.1
1998	19.5

Port of Detroit Commodities

- Iron ore **48%**
- Limestone **13%**
- Coal lignite **11%**
- Cement **7%**
- Iron/steel plates **5%**
- Other **16%**

Source: Detroit/Wayne County Port Authority

Port trading partners

Country	Total Tonnage, 1998
Canada	4,900,000
Lithuania	540,865
Germany	233,189
Latvia	133,548
China	114,213
Czechoslovakia	101,132
Australia	92,222
Netherlands	85,366
Belgium	71,914
Russia	67,446

SOURCE: DETROIT/WAYNE COUNTY PORT AUTHORITY.

Free Press file photo
**Flower Day at
Eastern Market, 1995.**

Flora & Fauna

Great dirt, green thumbs — how our gardens grow

Then: Three hundred years ago, tall swaying grasses grew along Detroit's riverfront. Up and down the shoreline of lakes St. Clair and Erie and the Detroit River, the land was lake plain prairie, a flat expanse that flooded in the spring and turned dry by midsummer.

Two hundred years ago, Michigan had 150,000 acres of lake plain prairie, mostly in Monroe, Oakland, Wayne and St. Clair counties. Today, only a tiny amount remains. Lake plain prairie remnants are still found around the St. Clair Flats and Algonac.

Lake plain prairies support lots of different plants, including big and little bluestem grasses and such wildflowers as blazing star and milkweeds.

Among the largest undisturbed remnants is the Ojibwa Prairie Complex, an Ontario provincial park near the Ambassador Bridge.

Visit there to see what Detroit may have looked like 300 years ago.

➤ **Ap*pear*ently fruitful:** Legend has it that French settlers brought seeds or cuttings of pear trees to plant along the Detroit River. Early farmers often grew several pear trees, which reached up to 100 feet tall.

The pears inspired at least two poems: "The Mission Pears" and "To the Old Pear Trees of Detroit."

A grove of a dozen known as the Twelve Apostles grew at what is now Waterworks Park. Gnarled descendants of the old French pears still can be found in the area, including the Grosse Pointes.

Now: A blooming tradition: Flower Day is a spring tradition held the third Sunday in May. As many as 100,000 people crowd Eastern Market for what is billed as the nation's

The timing of Flower Day puts the event right around the date of the last expected frost in Detroit. That way, purchasers can plant most of the tender annuals and vegetables as soon as they get home.

Free Press file photo

A shopper considers a pumpkin at Eastern Market in October 1932.

largest single-day flower display and sale.

Flower Day began growing in the 1960s. Southeast Michigan flower growers were shipping substantial quantities of bedding plants, such as marigolds and petunias, outside the area. They wanted to raise hometown awareness, so in 1966, they set up a one-day display of flowers at the Eastern Market. Although there were no plants for sale that year, about 20,000 people showed up.

For many families, Flower Day is a ritual that presents an annual dilemma — how to get those flats of plants back to the car? Baby strollers, red wagons and hospital carts get pressed into service.

The timing of Flower Day, which is sponsored by the Metropolitan Detroit Flower Growers Association, puts the event right around the date of the last expected frost in Detroit. That way, purchasers can plant most of the tender annuals and vegetable plants as soon as they get home.

➤ **Rich land:** Detroit's last frost is usually May 12 at City Airport, and the first frost is usually about mid-October. Compared with many areas of Michigan, Detroit's is a long growing season that allows a wide variety of plants to thrive.

Early settlers made good use of the rich land for farming — raising mushrooms, rhubarb and other crops, as well as fruit. Although relatively little crop land remains, farmers in Wayne, Oakland and Macomb counties and the surrounding counties grow corn, hay, soybeans, apples and pumpkins, among other produce. As the population reaches farther out into formerly rural areas, some farmers are turning over a new leaf,

engaging in a venture called agricultural tourism or agro-tainment. It allows them to supplement their farming income and also raises awareness of farming and agriculture.

They open their farms to people who want to pick apples or pumpkins, purchase cider and doughnuts, pet farm animals or watch demonstrations of old-fashioned crafts. Farm excursions are a family weekend destination, a way for city folk to experience a taste of the country.

Of trees we sing ...

Skyscrapers: There are some tall ones in southeastern Michigan marked as champions:

➤ **Black alder:** 66 feet tall, in Trenton.

➤ **Crab apple:** 52 feet tall, in Bloomfield Hills.

➤ **European weeping beech:** 86 feet tall, Pontiac.

➤ **River birch:** 58 feet tall, Ann Arbor.

➤ **American bladdernut:** 36 feet tall, Utica Recreation Area.

➤ **American hornbeam:** 41 feet tall, Bloomfield Hills.

➤ **American holly:** 25 feet tall, Mt. Clemens.

➤ **Tulip tree:** 105 feet tall, Lower Huron Metropark.

➤ **Honey locust:** 78 feet tall, Grosse Ile.

Michigan's Big Tree Register is compiled by the Michigan Botanical Club. In addition, the club and several other groups sponsor an annual Big Tree Hunt to locate trees with the widest girth by county. For information, contact Global ReLeaf of Michigan, 800-642-7353.

➤ **An enviable lawn:** Comerica Park's field is grown from three Kentucky bluegrasses: Blackburg, America and Midnight. Four acres of the sod were grown at a farm in Petone, Ill.

➤ **Tree isn't heavenly:** It comes up (and up and up) in yards, alleys, through sidewalk cracks, along fences and behind garages.

Tree of Heaven (Ailanthus altissima) is a fast-growing, malodorous tree that has become one of the most common trees in Detroit.

Native to China, it was brought to the United States in 1784 and was planted throughout southern Michigan.

Bad move.

Now it's mostly considered a weed tree with a noxious odor, a plant difficult to eradicate from a site once established.

It succeeds because it has an unusually large root system and large leaves, which give it an advantage at capturing water, nutrients and sunlight. If the tree is damaged, the roots send up a new stem. And its twisted, winged seeds are easily spread. Tree of Heaven tolerates drought, pollution and exposure to road salt.

The best way to get rid of it is to pull up

The pervasive Tree of Heaven on a street near Grand Circus Park in 1939.

Free Press file photo

Free Press file photo

Impatiens reign No. 1 as this area's fave bedding plant.

small young seedlings after a rain, when the soil is moist and it's easier to get the roots out. Larger saplings may have to be cut repeatedly to exhaust the plant's store of nutrients, and the stump painted with an herbicide.

Ailing elms

Their vase-like shapes lent an elegance to the landscape of Detroit and surrounding communities from the 1920s through the '60s. About 500,000 elm trees graced Detroit streets before 1954. That's when Detroit foresters discovered a fungus spread by bark beetles, causing Dutch elm disease. The fungus had entered the country through a shipment of logs from Europe to Cleveland during the 1930s. As the fungus became widespread in southeast Michigan and trees died, their skeletons turned into breeding grounds for the bark beetles and more disease. Communities tried a costly program of injecting trees with fungicide and mounting massive trimming programs. But dead trees kept piling up. Detroit, at one point, was removing 12,000 elms a year.

Now, you'll spot an occasional towering elm.

➤ **The lesson learned:** Foresters now rely on a variety of species, not just one, so if one kind of tree becomes diseased, other trees will be left.

Marty Hair's favorite area gardens

➤ **Ann Arbor:** Matthaei Botanical Gardens. The conservatory is a winter paradise for plant lovers, who will also enjoy the landscaped gardens and nature trails.

➤ **Bloomfield Hills:** Congregational Church of Birmingham. Tucked away just off Woodward, this is a mini-botanical garden of roses, peonies, perennials, hostas, daylilies, as well as trees and shrubs.

➤ **Bloomfield Hills:** Cranbrook Gardens. Serene landscapes surround Cranbrook House; don't miss the statues, reflecting pools, spring bulb display.

➤ **Dearborn:** Henry Ford Estate. Chicago landscape designer Jens Jensen turned a flat cow pasture into a fascinating sequence of vistas, meadows, ponds and paths.

➤ **Detroit:** Anna Scripps Whitcomb Conservatory. The Victorian conservatory on Belle Isle, designed by Albert Kahn, opened in 1904 and contains one of the country's largest collections of municipally owned orchids.

➤ **Grosse Pointe Shores:** Edsel & Eleanor Ford House. Jens Jensen used native plants and naturalistic design in a dramatic landscape at this estate along Lake St. Clair.

➤ **Novi:** Tollgate Education Center. A farm surrounded by suburbia, Tollgate is a haven with its display gardens, a pond and demonstration apple orchard.

➤ **Royal Oak:** Detroit Zoological Park. Originally famous for its plantings, the zoo grounds have been spiffed up over the last decade or so, thanks in part to a huge cadre of volunteers and the adopt-a-garden program.

➤ **Tipton:** Hidden Lake Gardens. It's worth the drive to visit this 700-plus acre preserve for its wildflowers, hostas, crab apples and superb collection of dwarf and unusual conifers, as well as its indoor conservatory.

TOP PLANTS

How does your garden grow? Michigan State's Department of Horticulture says these are currently the hottest bedding plants:

1. Impatiens
2. Geraniums (from cuttings)
3. Petunias
4. Geraniums (seed)
5. Begonias
6. Pansies
7. New Guinea impatiens
8. Marigolds
9. Tomatoes
10. Vinca

In the 1970s, petunias ranked first and impatiens, seventh.

J. KYLE KEENER/Detroit Free Press

A monarch rests atop a blazing star on Belle Isle.

MONARCH BUTTERFLY

This regal orange and black butterfly is known for the dramatic migration it makes each fall from northern latitudes to eucalyptus groves in California and piney mountaintops in the Mexican state of Michoacan. The butterflies mate in the spring, just before they head north again. On reaching their summer homes in Michigan, Canada and other points north, female monarchs lay their eggs on milkweed plants. After feeding on milkweed for about two weeks, monarch larvae form cocoons. Nine to 15 days later they emerge as butterflies. Adult monarchs feed on flower nectar and are a common summertime site in Michigan.

➤ **Short-tailed shrew:** Probably the most common mammal in southeast Michigan, the short-tailed shrew is often mistaken for a mouse. It's smaller than the average mouse: about 3 inches to 4 inches in length with a 1/2-inch to 1-inch tail, soft gray fur and eyes a tad smaller than a mouse's.

A short-tailed shrew eats about three times its weight daily. It prefers insects, nuts and larger animals such as frogs and birds. Shrews, like mice, may forage on table scraps. They seek shelter indoors in the fall. They are most common in damp woodlands and the brushy borders of fields.

Watch its bite. The short-tailed shrew releases a mild poison that can irritate humans and slow down prey. Shrews usually bite people only when handled.

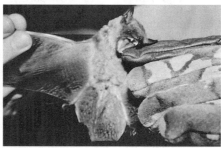

Free Press file photo

This big brown bat was caught in 1991.

➤ **Big brown bat:** Very common. Like many North American bats, the big brown bat has an intriguing way of reproducing. The bats mate in the fall, then the females store the males' sperm over the winter, ovulating and conceiving in the spring. The bats are insect eaters. They sometimes carry rabies.

➤ **American crow:** This hardy, black cawing creature is becoming a familiar sight in suburbs throughout the country. Scientists suggest crows are proliferating because of the shortage of predators, such as owls, in suburbs. In addition, crows often are hunted in rural or agricultural areas, where farmers want to rid their fields of the large, seed-snatching birds. Crows have big brains; their

Free Press file photo

Our venomous snake, the Massasauga rattler.

fans say that's the reason for the birds' complex social behavior, based on strong family relationships and lots of vocal communication. Some pet crows have learned to mimic speech, though not as well as parrots.

➤ **Eastern Massasauga rattlesnake:** The only venomous snake native to Michigan typically is 20 to 30 inches long with a row of dark blotches on its back and three rows of smaller blotches on each side of its body. Its background color is gray or brownish gray. Its belly is black, with a white or yellow pattern. This snake lives in marshes, preferring to hibernate in crayfish burrows. During the summer, the snake sometimes can slither into upland meadows and woods. Like other snakes, it usually avoids people. It will rattle and strike if threatened or surprised. Its venom can kill children and people in poor health and others who do not get treatment quickly. Dizziness and nausea can follow within minutes of being bitten. The snake prefers to hunt mice, which it tracks with heat-detection organs called pits that are located between its nostrils and eyes.

➤ **American cougar:** Although University of Michigan zoologists say that wolverine fossils have not been found in Michigan, bones of the American cougar have. Also known as the mountain lion, this animal used to have one of the biggest ranges of all American mammals. It roamed from Canada to Argentina. Today, the cougar lives only in mountainous, unpopulated regions. There are no cougars living wild in Michigan now. The large,

NATURE

slender cougar likes to eat moose and caribou, coyote, skunk, sheep and pigs. It hunts larger animals by leaping on their back and breaking their neck with a powerful bite below the base of the skull. The cougar is primarily nocturnal. It communicates with growls, low-pitched hisses and purrs. A loud, chirping whistle from a cub will draw its mother's attention. They can live for more than 20 years.

➤ **Golden garden spider:** Perhaps the most spectacular spider found in southeastern Michigan, the golden garden spider weaves webs of up to about 3 feet in diameter. They are common in meadows and gardens, particularly in the fall. Often, the center of the web is occupied by a yellow and black golden garden spider with a silvery head. This spider, like most others, is harmless.

➤ **Wolverine:** Despite its prominence as the University of Michigan's mascot and as the moniker for the state's informal nickname, the wolverine may never have lived wild in Michigan. Its range used to extend from northern Canada south to parts of the northern United States. Although fossil evidence of wolverines has been found in other border states, U-M zoologists say that no wolverine bones have been found in Michigan. Today, wolverines live mostly in northern Canada and in Scandinavia. The fierce mammals range in weight from 15 to 70 pounds and grow up to 41 inches in length, not including the tail. Wolverines look something like large martens. They eat food ranging from small eggs to deer.

Wolverines are territorial and generally solitary except during mating season. Females give birth once every two years. They breed several times with different mates between May and August. Ovulation is believed to be stimulated by copulation. Births occur from January through April in snow dens built by the mother. Wolverines have one to six kits in each litter. Each kit may have a different father. The young nurse for eight to 10 weeks, separate from their mothers in the autumn and reach adult size at one year of age. The wolverine was first identified with Michiganders during the 1830s border war between Ohio and Michigan. Ohioans attempted to insult their opponents by likening them to wolverines. University of Michigan officials weren't insulted and adopted the fierce animal as their mascot.

SOURCES: UNIVERSITY OF MICHIGAN MUSEUM OF ZOOLOGY'S ANIMAL DIVERSITY WEB SITE, **WWW.ANIMALDIVERSITY.UMMZ.UMICH.EDU**; CRANBROOK INSTITUTE OF SCIENCE.

Chirp! The birds of Detroit

Nearby water makes Detroit one of the best regions in the country for birds.

The seven-county region is home to about 300 of the almost 400 bird species that — during one season or another — frequent Michigan.

Lakeshores and river valleys throughout Wayne and Monroe counties funnel birds along north-south migration routes. Beach and rocky shores with pockets of deciduous forest provide habitat and foraging opportunities for many species. During autumn, thousands of hawks enter Michigan at the southern end of the Detroit River.

The most numerous migrant is the broad-winged hawk — and the best place to watch these annual migrations is Lake Erie Metropark. While you're there, check out Pte. Mouillee State Game Area, also on Lake Erie, just south of Lake Erie Metropark.

Other shorelines in Macomb County (Metropolitan Beach Metropark near St. Clair Shores) and St. Clair County shelter a wide variety of ducks, geese, terns and gulls. If you're lucky, maybe you'll spot a bald eagle or an osprey — fish-eating species well recovered after the elimination of the pesticide DDT that entered state waters in the 1960s.

Area parks and backyard feeders are bird magnets, attracting species that have adapted well to the urban setting — robins, house sparrows, cardinals, blue jays, house finches and starlings. Belle Isle is an excellent place for spotting migrating ducks such as the canvasback.

With the disappearance of southern Michigan's second-growth forests, state parks, game areas and other public land in the seven-county region play an important role in preserving biodiversity. These floodplains and beech and maple forests provide valuable habitat for many migrating songbirds in spring and fall. Fairlane Woods, alongside the Rouge River at University of Michigan-Dear-

Free Press file photo

This mastodon, found in Owosso, is at the University of Michigan's Exhibition Museum of Natural History.

AMERICAN MASTODON

These elephant-like creatures lived in southern Michigan until about 10,000 years ago. They stood about 10 feet tall and weighed more than 2,200 pounds. The remains of hundreds of mastodons have been found in central and southern Michigan. They lived in pen spruce woodlands, spruce forests and pine parklands. Their favorite foods included twigs and cones of spruce and pine as well as grasses and wetland plants. Both male and female mastodons had tusks, which they probably used to dig for water and food in the winter as well as for combat. Mastodons were hunted for food by humans who stored the meat in ponds to eat over the winter.

MICHIGAN SPECIES IN DANGER

Ninety species unique to Michigan are at-risk animals and plants, according to the Nature Conservancy in Washington, D.C. The species are at risk because of urban sprawl. Northwestern Oakland County is home to several rare species, including:

➤ Copperbelly water-snake
➤ Redside dace fish
➤ Three species of mussels
➤ American burying beetle
➤ Regal fritillary butterfly
➤ Red-shouldered hawk and common loon
➤ Five plants: gattinger's gerardia, white gentian, downy gentian, American chestnut and prairie fringed orchid

OTHER AT-RISK SPECIES IN MICHIGAN

➤ Smallmouth salamander
➤ Kirtland's snake
➤ Spotted turtle
➤ Short-eared owl
➤ Piping plover
➤ Prairie warbler
➤ Kirtland's warbler
➤ Peregrine falcon
➤ Barn owl
➤ Common loon
➤ Bald eagle
➤ Trumpeter swan
➤ Gray wolf
➤ Cougar
➤ Lynx
➤ Indiana bat

FOR THE COMPLETE LIST OF MICHIGAN'S AT-RISK SPECIES, GO TO **WWW.DNR.STATE.MI.US**. GO TO "DIVISIONS," THEN "WILDLIFE," THEN "NONGAME SPECIES" THEN SCROLL DOWN TO THE MICHIGAN NATURAL FEATURES INVENTORY.

SUSAN TUSA/Detroit Free Press

An adult plover with chicks (one peeking under a feather).

born, is an ideal spot to watch migrating songbirds.

Oakland, Washtenaw and Livingston counties have more varied terrain. They offer ponds and hills and the most extensive deciduous forests in the southern region of the state. If you want to see a black-capped chickadee, ruffed grouse or scarlet tanager, this is where you need to be. Highland Recreation Area, Stony Creek Metropark and Kensington Metropark are three top-notch spots for serious Oakland County bird-watchers.

Here are some of the most common and popular birds in the seven counties:

➤ **American robin:** Michigan's state bird doesn't spend winter here, making many birders clamor for the chickadee as a friendly replacement as Michigan's representative bird. Like it or not, the robin is still the truest harbinger of spring. North America's largest thrush (9-11 inches) is a common summer visitor of urban lawns, where it searches for earthworms.

➤ **House sparrow:** Sparrows, members of the weaverbird family, are probably Michigan's most widespread species — especially in urban areas. Sparrows chase one another from feeders, steal food from other species and compete for nesting sites with native species. They eat insects, bread and nearly any type of food at feeders.

➤ **House finch:** The eastern population, which includes a big Michigan presence, descended from tame birds released near New York in 1940s. They often are confused with purple finches, which lack striped flanks. House finches eat weed seeds such as thistle and dandelion. At feeders, they eat niger seeds and sunflower seeds.

bird calls and songs.

➤ **Chickadee:** The friendliest and most curious bird is many birders' choice to supplant the robin as the state bird. A year-round resident, the chickadee — member of the titmouse family — is attracted to feeders by suet and sunflower seeds.

➤ **Canada goose:** Numbers have rebounded dramatically — especially in southern Michigan. The populations along many inland lakes and golf courses in Oakland County are so vast that birds have been trapped and moved elsewhere. Recent mild winters in Michigan have spared Canadas a reason to migrate to warmer climates.

➤ **Red-tailed hawk:** Any highway cruising in southern Michigan provides a chance to see a red-tailed hawk. They perch on branches, wires and telephone poles, scanning the ground for rodents. They are Michigan's most widely distributed hawk, thanks in part to the DDT pesticide ban in the 1960s. Their wingspan can reach 46-58 inches.

➤ **Bald eagle:** Despite its national recognition, the bald eagle, like the red-tailed hawk and osprey, has recovered nicely along the Great Lakes and throughout the state since the DDT ban. They are primarily fish eaters. Their wingspan can grow to 7 feet. Eagles develop their brown body and white head in 4-5 years. Their nests measure 8 feet across. Much of the population is in the Upper Peninsula, but sightings no longer are rare in southern Michigan.

➤ **American crow:** Related to the raven, crows are large birds that gather in flocks after the nesting season. They eat dead fish, carrion, insects and eggs of other birds. Maybe the most intelligent of all birds, crows mimic other bird calls, the whine of a dog and sirens.

➤ **Cardinal:** Possibly Michigan's most popular bird. Males are nearly all red; females are olive gray. Pairs mate for life and are frequent feeder visitors for sunflower seeds and cracked corn. In summer, they eat berries, insects and fruits.

➤ **Blue jay:** A strikingly beautiful bird disliked by many birders because of its raucous behavior, which includes eating other birds' eggs and young. Much of its diet is grain. Not quite as proficiently as a mockingbird, the blue jay imitates many

Sex and the single Hexagenia limbata

Fish flies descend annually on the shores of Lake St. Clair and the Detroit River — single-minded sex machines.

This invasion might not be so bad if:

A. The fish flies didn't en masse smell like tons of rotten fish.

B. They didn't die en masse on streets and sidewalks, their little bodies piled around light poles, clinging to windshields and ATMs, crunching under foot and coating roads with a slick, gory goo.

For a few days each summer, many metro Detroiters have close encounters with these bugs, a.k.a may flies, a.k.a. Hexagenia limbata of the Ephemeroptera order.

Homo sapiens must hose smeared bugs off windshields and shovel great heaps of them off sidewalks, like some lingering biblical plague for a long-forgotten sin.

Fish flies are the price we pay for exceptionally clean and oxygenated lake water, and since the 1970s, the flies have done more than just gross out Detroit's east side, the Grosse Pointes, St. Clair Shores and other waterfront communities.

In 1995, fish flies caused a small power outage at Detroit Edison's Monroe plant when thousands of them piled around a transformer.

In 1974, the bugs wrecked a village fair in New Baltimore, horror-movie style. The flies darkened the sky, became caught in amusement-ride machinery and forced the fair to close. Townspeople recovered with good humor and renamed the event the Bay-Rama Fish Fly Festival. It's held each year well before fish fly season.

The fish fly phenomenon starts at the bottom of the cleanest lakes, up to 30 feet below surface and 8 miles off shore. They hatch on the lake bed in the heat of summer, then rise to the surface. There, they shed a layer of skin and use it as a tiny raft to sail miles to shore. The flotilla, numbering in the hundreds of millions, points itself landward.

Each year in late June or early July, the fish fly reaches dry land with a 2-day life span and a "Party-Like-It's-1999" attitude. For the males, the mating ends in immediate death. The females use the last of their strength to head back to the lakes and deposit eggs.

Dead fish flies are scooped away. They fly into town, they mate, they die.

J. KYLE KEENER/Detroit Free Press

LIGER, LIGER, BURNING BRIGHT:

Like the urban legend of the vanishing hitchhiker, big-cat sightings have occurred frequently in suburban Detroit since World War II. None of the animals listed were caught. Here's a look:

➤ 1947-1952, 1956: Panther sightings near Leonard in Oakland County.

➤ May 1984: Panther seen near Manchester in Washtenaw County.

➤ July 1984: Two large "jungle cats" seen between Manchester and Wixom.

➤ July 1986: Panther reported in Waterford.

➤ July 1986: A big cat is suspected in the death of a horse whose throat was gouged near Milford Township.

➤ April 1987: Another panther report in Wixom.

➤ March 1988: Two panthers seen in Wixom.

➤ May 1988: Warren police in a helicopter photograph a large black animal in Highland Township.

➤ February 1990: A panther is reported behind a Lake Orion home.

➤ March 1992: "Very large, black creature" seen in swampy area of West Bloomfield.

➤ September-November 1997: Reports of a so-called liger, a lion and tiger mix, in Macomb County.

➤ Autumn, recent years: Wixom sponsors a panther hunt in a city park that spoofs panther reports.

SOURCE: FREE PRESS.

Alexis Creevey of Oakland visits with Chelsea, a therapy dog. Alexis was undergoing chemotherapy treatments in 1998 at Children's Hospital in Detroit.

Pets

The pet pros say there are lots more cats than dogs in the country, but because Michigan law doesn't make you license your cat, there's no hard evidence cats rule here. Some communities do mandate cat licenses, however.

Another caveat: Pet pros also say despite dog licenses being a must, only half the dog owners in metro Detroit bother. The Pet Industry Joint Advisory Council has a formula for figuring out pet population. Applied to the following counties, here's the tally on pets by household:

COUNTY	DOGS	CATS	BOTH
LIVINGSTON	20,826	18,634	8,769
MACOMB	117,848	105,443	49,620
MONROE	21,043	18,828	8,860
OAKLAND	178,752	159,936	75,264
ST. CLAIR	23,971	21,448	10,093
WASHTENAW	47,635	42,621	20,057
WAYNE	295,059	264,000	124,235

Animal Tales

No reporters are worth their salt unless they've done the dog story. Usually the tale begins with a tip from a caller, a neighbor or a cop about a dog (or cat) that bowls or plays pool or knows how to dial the phone. Those yarns are usually written tongue in cheek. Then there are the animal stories that contain human drama. Here are some of our favorites:

➤ **Copy cat:** In 1929, when Detroiter Josephine St. John died, she made a will providing $5 a month to her cat, Billie.

Alas, a St. John survivor disputed the stipend and another potential heir challenged in court whether Billie was really Billie.

The judge ruled the gray cat in court was Billie and ordered the $5 a month retroactive to St. John's death.

➤ **Detroit's greatest canine hero:** The fire broke out at 2:30 a.m. on May 13, 1936, in the basement of an apartment building on Frontenac in Detroit. Adrienne Charette's Chow, Ming, began barking, waking up the 17-year-old and her family. Then Ming ran barking through the corridors of the three-story building to awaken the 120 occupants — all of whom escaped as thick, black smoke filled the building.

The three-alarm fire was extinguished, but when Adrienne searched for Ming, the dog was nowhere to be found. In the post-fire excitement, someone placed Ming's body in an alley where it was quickly removed by a public works crew called to the fire.

➤ **Cat scratch fever:** Michigan's first case of cat scratch fever was diagnosed at Henry Ford Hospital in May 1952.

Until then, only 50 cases had been reported in the United States.

When the word went out that cat fanciers could get sore throats, swollen glands and assorted aches from the bacteria beneath feline claws, there was fear among pet owners.

But Henry Ford's doctor of infectious diseases said the newly discovered disease — diagnosed first in France in 1949 — could be cured with an antibiotic.

➤ **Patient pup:** Medical science pawed forward in 1964 when researchers at the University of Michigan Medical Center successfully transplanted a lung into a mutt named Homer.

The playful, flop-eared dog made worldwide headlines when an anti-rejection drug called methotrexate perked him up after the surgery, sparking hopes that the drug could do the same for humans.

Doctors exchanged the 2-year-old black dog's left lung with that of another research dog.

➤ **King Boots, villain or victim?** In 1984, King Boots, a prize-winning Old English sheepdog from Birmingham, became a *cause celebre* when city officials ordered him killed for mauling 87-year-old Gertrude Monroe to death after she tripped over him.

King Boots made news around the world while he spent 40 days behind dog-pound bars as a court decided his fate.

The family of Bootsie, as they called him,

DETROIT ANIMAL FACTS

Number of horses, 1998
- ➤ Livingston 2,006
- ➤ Macomb 1,028
- ➤ Monroe 1,454
- ➤ Oakland 3,033
- ➤ St. Clair 1,505
- ➤ Washtenaw 2,448
- ➤ Wayne 805

SOURCE: MICHIGAN DEPARTMENT OF AGRICULTURE

Animal control and animal protection shelters, 1999
- ➤ Livingston 1
- ➤ Macomb 4
- ➤ Monroe 2
- ➤ Oakland 24
- ➤ St. Clair 2
- ➤ Washtenaw 1
- ➤ Wayne 49

SOURCE: MICHIGAN DEPARTMENT OF AGRICULTURE AND INDUSTRY SERVICES

Number of licensed veterinarians, 1999
- ➤ Livingston 66
- ➤ Macomb 105
- ➤ Monroe 20
- ➤ Oakland 346
- ➤ St. Clair 21
- ➤ Washtenaw 107
- ➤ Wayne..227

SOURCE: MICHIGAN DEPARTMENT OF CONSUMER AND INDUSTRY SERVICES

Number of pet shops, 1999
- ➤ Livingston 0
- ➤ Macomb 24
- ➤ Monroe 3
- ➤ Oakland 23
- ➤ St. Clair 2
- ➤ Washtenaw 6
- ➤ Wayne...35

SOURCE: MICHIGAN DEPARTMENT OF CONSUMER AND INDUSTRY SERVICES

FARM ANIMALS, 1998

	BEEF CATTLE	MILK COWS	HOGS	SHEEP
Livingston	1,139	3,042	3,061	1,229
Macomb	577	892	7,569	272
Monroe	484	751	36,858	1,229
Oakland	584	373	1,007	967
St. Clair	2,399	1,770	5,984	362
Washtenaw	1,317	4,985	21,881	11,315
Wayne	492	105	648	521

SOURCE: MICHIGAN DEPARTMENT OF AGRICULTURE

Michigan law doesn't require you to license your cat.

maintained that Monroe, a grandmother and the mother of King Boots' owner, had suffered a heart attack and fell over the sleeping, 100-pound dog. He merely defended himself instinctively, they said.

But those who preferred a death sentence said Boots was a danger to society.

In the end, the dog's life was spared, sort of. The judge gave the family the choice of killing the pet or having his fangs and testicles removed. Veterinarians castrated him and removed 16 of his front teeth.

King Boots died in August 1985. A television documentary of his travails keeps his memory alive.

➤ **Brandy: Legal precedent-setter:** Up until Brandy the dog died in 1995, Michigan courts viewed pets as property. That meant no court would hear a case requesting damages above the replacement value of the animal when it died because of someone's negligence.

Brandy — a nutmeg-colored Basenji dog — and Wayne County Circuit Judge Kaye Tertzag changed that.

For the first time in state court, the judge allowed Brandy's owner, Leah Murray of Belleville, to sue the kennel where Brandy was starved and deprived of insulin.

Murray argued that her dog was her closest companion. She was so distraught over the death that she slept with the 20-pound corpse for two days.

Brandy, 12, died in an emergency clinic shortly after Murray picked up the dog at the kennel. She said Brandy was covered in urine and feces and had blood oozing from her nose.

The jury decided the kennel operators were responsible for Brandy's death because they failed to get her medical attention.

Murray was awarded $5,000, and the case opened the way for other lawsuits over wrongful deaths of animals.

The Detroit Almanac

06.WO

"Come up to Detroit and see how we make things hum!"

— A character in "Dodsworth," by **Sinclair Lewis**

Our Lunch-Bucket Town

On the payroll

Metro Detroiters once had a menu of manufacturing jobs from which to choose. The auto industry changed that, but in recent years labor diversity has again become a feature of regional employment. In 1997, 22 percent of the region's workers made durable goods, compared with 9 percent in Atlanta and 3 percent in New York. Metro Detroit is the nation's largest metropolis with such a high proportion of workers in traditional manufacturing, according to "Divided Detroit," the 2000 book that analyzed local economic trends.

Before the oil crisis of 1974 impacted the manufacturing of automobiles, metro Detroit had 1.6 million jobs. That total remained the same until about 1983, when the economy began to expand, and there are about 2.1 million jobs today.

LABOR FORCE (2000)
➤ Workers, including the unemployed: 2,258,000 (Wayne, Oakland, Macomb, Livingston, Monroe and St. Clair counties)
➤ Jobs in region: 2,118,000

LARGEST EMPLOYERS (2000)
➤ Ford Motor Co., 80,000 workers
➤ General Motors Corp., 59,000
➤ DaimlerChrysler Corp., 48,000
➤ U.S. government, 29,000
➤ City of Detroit, 17,000

JOB BREAKDOWN
➤ **Goods-producing industries**
Motor vehicles, equipment: 187,000 jobs
Wholesale durable goods: 91,000
Construction: 73,000
Fabricated metal products: 65,000
Machinery, computers: 60,000
Rubber, plastics: 24,000
Printing, publishing: 17,000
Wholesale nondurable goods: 37,000

➤ **Service industries**
Wholesale trade: 128,000
Eateries, bars: 123,000
Transportation: 64,000
General retail: 61,000
Food stores: 42,000
Auto dealers and gasoline stations: 36,000
Electric, gas, sanitation services: 16,000
Communications: 14,000
➤ **Finance**
Insurance: 36,000
Real estate: 20,000
➤ **Private services**
Health: 178,000
Engineering, accounting, management: 74,000
Social services: 40,000
Auto repair, parking: 18,000
➤ **Federal government**
Post office: 16,000
Other: 13,000
➤ **State government**
Education: 13,000
Other: 13,000
➤ **Local governments**
Education: 110,000
Other: 66,000

SOURCE: MICHIGAN DEPARTMENT OF CAREER DEVELOPMENT.

The assembly line at Dodge Main around World War I.

Free Press file photo

Automation affected virtually every sector of Detroit's economy in the 1950s . . .

Ford Rouge plant jobs fell from 85,000 in 1945 to 54,000 in 1954 to 30,000 in 1960 to fewer than 10,000 in 2000.

SOURCE: "THE ORIGIN OF THE URBAN CRISIS: RACE AND INEQUALITY IN POSTWAR DETROIT," BY THOMAS SUGRUE.

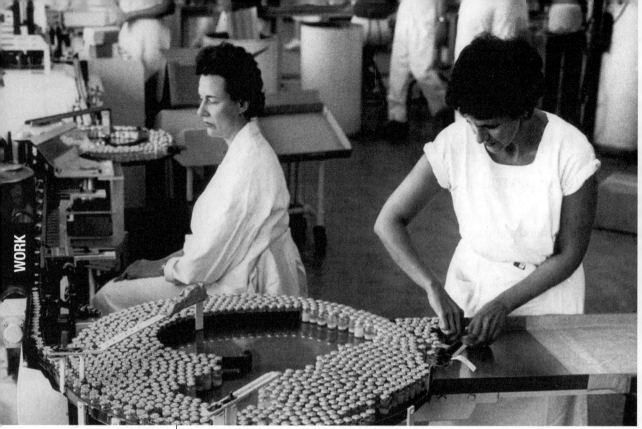

WORK

Free Press file photo

Workers at Parke-Davis & Co. with vials of antibiotics, 1966.

PER HOUR: Most recent wage increases have reflected low inflation nationally. Here are the most recent general figures for per-hour earnings in the Detroit-Ann Arbor-Flint region (1997)

All occupations	$16.92
Teachers (college and university)	36.28
Physicians	34.42
Teachers*	32.43

* (except college and university)

Administrators and managers	32.40
Engineers, architects, surveyors	28.26
Mathematical and computer scientists	27.45
Plumbers, pipefitters and steamfitters	22.36
Accountants and auditors	22.34
Electricians	21.77
Millwrights	21.76
Registered nurses	20.80
Police and detectives	18.76
Machinists	18.70
Supervisors, production occupations	18.44
Technical occupations	18.29
Truck drivers	15.56
Sales (supervisors)	15.44
Secretaries	13.25
Janitors and cleaners	11.28
Bookkeepers, accounting and auditing clerks	11.05
Stock handlers and baggers	8.82
Cooks	8.07
Cashiers	7.81
Nursing aides, orderlies and attendants	7.79

SOURCE: U.S. DEPARTMENT OF LABOR BUREAU OF LABOR STATISTICS

BY DAY (AND NIGHT) WE MAKE CARS: Automobile industry employment in metro Detroit by year

1904	2,034
1909	17,400
1914	60,000
1919	135,000
1929	205,000
1939	191,356 (a)
1978	242,842 (a)
1998	99,847 (a)

METRO DETROIT'S SHARE OF THE NATION'S AUTO EMPLOYMENT

1904	17 percent
1909	23 percent
1914	47 percent
1919	39 percent
1929	46 percent
1939	49 percent
1950	35 percent
1970	20 percent
1990	20 percent

SOURCES: "MOTOR CITY: THE IMPACT OF THE AUTOMOBILE INDUSTRY UPON DETROIT, 1900-1975," BY THOMAS TICKNOR; DETROIT ORIENTATION INSTITUTE; "DIVIDED DETROIT," BY REYNOLDS FARLEY, SHELDON DANZINGER AND HARRY HOLZER

(A) DOES NOT INCLUDE HEADQUARTERS STAFFS

Detroit at work

"Every manufacturer should be able to go into the shop and with his own hands make the thing that he wants to manufacture. If he cannot do this, he is no manufacturer at all ...

"His workingmen are the real manufacturers, and he is but a parasite that lives upon them."

— **Henry Ford**

MADE IN DETROIT: Here's a partial list of some of the region's chief exports — products and concepts — over the centuries.

Fur pelts, leather products, soap, flax and hemp goods, woolen goods, hats, candles, saddles and bridles, hardware, bags, billiard tables, baking powder, fish, cider, wood sashes, maple sugar, earthenware, cooper's products, flour, shingles, tinware, bricks, awnings, yeast, horse collars, edgers, sleds, maps, hoop rags, salt, skirts, artificial limbs, brooms, baskets, lumber products, staves, carriages, boxcars, train wheels, boilers, radiators, steam gauges, valves and traps, pipe fittings, carbon, organs, pins, coffee, combs, corsets, lubricating devices, adding machines, bolts, nuts, blinds, washboards, whips, windmills, wigs, wire.

Also: brackets, BB guns, iron, steel, meat, pipes, paper, rope, glasses, saws and sawing machines, sleighs, stoneware, bridges, barrels, coffins, combs, bread, boxes, boots, oil cups, ships, wagons, window shades, sails, tiles, varnish, pleasure craft, carpets, glue, gloves, glass, pottery, fishing tackle, carpets, chewing gum, doorknobs, flour, ink, jewelry, emery wheels, maps, electrical instruments, fences, monuments, matches, fertilizers, propellers, stoves, furnaces, injectors, brass castings, machinery, jigs, crackers, clothespins, fixtures, industrial films, chocolate sundaes, cold duck, ginger ale, red pop, potato chips, baking soda, coney islands.

Plus: automobiles, mass production, trucks, tractors, tires, diesel engines, airplane engines, airplanes, bombers, fighter planes, tanks, tank destroyers, fuses, mortar and artillery shells, cartridge cases, cannons, Jeeps, military trucks, navy boats, tank engines, gliders, amphibious vehicles, armored cars, jet engines, aircraft generators, bombsights, superchargers, B24 Liberator bombers.

And: radio and TV shows, blues, jazz, soul, rock 'n' roll, gospel, rap, classical music, plumbing supplies, toy trains, cigars, cigarettes, seeds, microfilm, industrial-strength software, pistachios, robots, Tomahawk cruise-missile engines, pizza, 30-minute pizza delivery, big bookstores, big malls, industrial cranes, axle assemblies.

Assembling auto bodies at Ford Motor Co.'s Highland Park plant around World War I.

Burton Historical Collection

METRO DETROIT'S HIGH WAGES: Median earnings for people ages 25 to 64 who reported earnings, metro Detroit and nationwide. (In 1997 dollars.)

	Men	Women	Metro	U.S.
1940	$17,284	$14,164	$9,280	$8,190
1970	$22,445	$20,435	$18,140	$16,829
1997	$40,000	$32,000	$21,000	$20,000

SOURCE: "DETROIT DIVIDED," BY REYNOLDS FARLEY, SHELDON DANZIGER AND HARRY HOLZER.

EMPLOYERS AND EMPLOYEES: These are the largest employers in the region (with number of employees) **in 2000:**

Ford Motor Co. 80,000
General Motors Corp. 59,000
DaimlerChrysler Corp. 48,000
U.S. government 29,000
City of Detroit 17,000

In 1900:
American Car and Foundry
  (railway cars) 4,875
Michigan Alkali (soda ash) 1,950
Parke, Davis & Co. 1,350
Detroit Shipbuilding 1,337
Detroit Stove Works 1,150

PERCENTAGE OF U.S. JOBS IN METRO DETROIT
1940   2.2 percent
1990   1.4 percent

SOURCES: GREATER DETROIT CHAMBER OF COMMERCE; FREE PRESS; CRAIN'S DETROIT BUSINESS; "DETROIT DIVIDED."

> The beaver was a chief reason that Detroit exists. The soft and shiny fur of **castor canadensis** became the rage in upper-class Europe in the 18th Century.

Free Press file photo

Detroit owes a lot to the Beav.

Detroit's jobs
The skills that made southeast Michigan famous

➤ **18th Century: The Trapper**

"Detroit was founded because an ancient king of France wore a beaver hat," Free Press editor Malcolm Bingay wrote in his 1946 book, "Detroit is My Hometown."

Detroit was one of North America's important depots for beaver fur in the 18th Century. Fur was a ruthless business, but it was the main economic activity while the French — and later the British — ruled Detroit.

The jobs: Voyageurs and coureurs de bois. Their legacy lasted for generations. They wore red flannel shirts, sashes and tassled caps and sang rowdy songs. Voyageurs paddled all day and carried their gear — plus 4 tons of cargo and canoes — over backbreaking portages between rivers. They also became known for their hardy cuisine: forest animals cooked in a pot with grease, pemmi-can (pounded venison with grease), pea soup and turtle eggs.

The voyageurs trapped mostly beaver, but also otter, mink, fox, raccoon and bear. They brought the pelts to the fort at Detroit, from where they would be transported to Montreal before being shipped to Europe. In 1784, exporters sent 5,000 packs of fur from Detroit; that output fell to 1,900 in 1796. The Indians, of course, also were key players in the fur trade, and the fur trade played a major role in their demise. The natives traded furs for trinkets or alcohol at Detroit and other posts, and became pawns in the battle among the Europeans for trade dominance. At times, the fur trade touched off wars among various Indian tribes.

➤ **The game:** The beaver was a chief reason that Detroit exists. The soft and shiny fur of *castor canadensis* became the rage in upper-class Europe in the 18th Century. Most beavers are 3 to 4 feet long and weigh between 50 and 100 pounds. Thousands of years ago, North America had a type of beaver that was 7½ feet long, but it died out. Beavers live in families and build dome-like lodges with underwater entrances. Beavers also construct dams out of trees, rocks and mud.

Beaver pelts were fashioned into hats; London hatmakers were the dominant manufacturers. "Beaver" came to mean both the animal and the hat.

➤ **19th Century: The Iron Molder**

Detroit in the 19th Century was one of America's leading producers of things made of iron, brass and other metals. By 1900, Detroit's six cast-iron stove companies accounted for 10.6 percent of the nation's stove and furnace production, according to historian Thomas Klug. In 1864, James and Jeremiah Dwyer and other investors organized the Detroit Stove Works, which soon grew into an 8-acre complex on the Detroit River near Belle Isle.

In the 1880s, the plant employed 800 work-

ers and produced 35,000 stoves a year.

Stove production, Klug wrote, involved nearly two dozen departments revolving around the foundry, whose chief employees were iron molders, the "skilled aristocrats" of the metal trades. In that era, the Iron Molders Union was one of the city's oldest, largest and strongest labor groups.

The molders' work, according to Klug, involved producing metal castings by using wood patterns to form hollow impressions or molds in sand. Molten iron was poured into the mold cavity. After cooling, the wood-framed flask that held the sand mold was dismantled and the casting shaken out from the sand. After cleaning and finishing, the completed casting was ready for further tooling.

➤ 20th Century: Assembler

Before Henry Ford adapted the assembly line to auto production, skilled and semiskilled workers made cars by standing in one spot. The chassis was placed on sawhorses, and outside suppliers delivered components. Ford began experimenting with an assembly line at his Piquette Avenue plant and made 10,607 Model T's there in 1909.

Ford was encouraged by efficiency studies coming out of the new scientific-management

movement led by Frederick Taylor, who advised owners to design jobs that did not require skilled, highly paid and independent craftsmen.

In 1910, Ford moved to the Highland Park plant, where he perfected the assembly line. At first, some parts were moved between work stations by gravity, conveyor belts or chains. Small components, such as magnetos, were assembled by individual lines. In late 1913, according to the Henry Ford Museum, Ford experimented with a line for the car's final assembly. Starting in 1914, complete cars were assembled on three lines. Each line was fed by components that also came off of assembly lines.

The creation of the assembly line meant that automakers needed far fewer skilled workers. Under the new arrangement, according to historian Steve Babson, engines were no longer made by one skilled worker and several helpers, but hundreds of workers on a line who performed elementary tasks every few seconds, such as filing bearings or putting bearings on camshafts. Workers could no longer move at their own pace; they moved at the speed of the line that was set by bosses.

The work was tough; some called it inhuman. Early workers on the line quit in droves.

Ford managers watch an assembler tweak a headlight on a 1947 truck.

"The Ford's Prayer"
From 1930s-era union organizers:

Our father, who art
in Dearborn,
Henry is thy name.
Let payday come,
Thy will be done,
At River Rouge as it is
at Highland Park.
Give us this day our
daily 5 bucks,
And forgive us
for taking it
As we forgive those
who take it from us.
And lead us not into
intelligent actions
(strikes)
For thine is the power
of production.

A worker rolls a stogie at La Dora Cigar Co. at Grand River and Rosa Parks in 1971.

slow down your assembly line.
No, I don't mind workin',
but I do mind dyin'.
— **Blues song by Joe L. Carter**

The $5 Day: Henry Ford announced in January 1914 that he would double the rate of pay for workers at his Highland Park plant from $2.50 to $5 a day. It was stunning news, but came with caveats:

➤ Workers had to apply for the raise.

➤ Women were ineligible.

➤ No one younger than 22 was eligible unless he was a breadwinner.

➤ Workers had to submit to a probe of their private lives. Ford rewarded thrift, sobriety and cleanliness. Ford investigators reviewed personal financial information and visited the workers' homes. They also interviewed neighbors and friends. In some cases, the investigators took photos of the workers' dwellings, inside and out.

➤ Requirements for the $5 wage included: Six months' residency in Detroit and six months' experience at Ford. The workers must not have been sending excessive amounts of salary abroad.

SOURCES: "INTERNAL COMBUSTION: THE RACES IN DETROIT," BY DAVID ALLAN LEVINE; "MUDDY BOOTS AND RAGGED APRONS: IMAGES OF WORKING CLASS DETROIT, 1900-1930," KEVIN BOYLE AND VICTORIA GETIS; "ROOTS OF THE OPEN SHOP," BY TOM KLUG (WAYNE STATE UNIVERSITY PHD DISSERTATION).

Other employers of note

➤ **Parke-Davis & Co.:** The company, one of the nation's premier pharmaceutical firms, was born in 1866 in a Woodward Avenue drugstore in which Dr. Samuel Duffield produced his own Ether, Sweet Spirit of Nitre, Oil of Wine, Hoffman's Anodyne and Blue Pill Mass. Duffield's business soon became the property of George Davis and Hervey Parke, who by 1873 had moved to the riverfront and began dispatching employees to far-flung locales to search for vegetale ingredients such as cocoa for new drugs. Inside the pill factory at the foot of McDougall, huge belts drove crushing machines, which pulverized raw materials into powders. In another department, the many women Parke-Davis employed assembled capsules by hand and earned about 80 cents a day during the 1890s. The workday lasted from 7 a.m. to 5:30 p.m. Everyone worked from 7 a.m to 1 p.m. on Saturdays. The company became a division of Warner-Lambert in 1970. In 2000, Parke-Davis Pharmaceutical Research employed 2,900 people and was Ann Arbor's biggest taxpayer. Pfizer purchased Warner-Lambert in June 2000 for $90 billion.

➤ **Cigar factories:** Detroit was one of the nation's most important cigar-making centers

Ford introduced the $5-a-day pay at Highland Park in 1914 in part because of high turnover. The speed of the line and working conditions are issues that never went away. In Highland Park in 1916, the Ford plant alone recorded 192 severed fingers, 68,000 lacerations, 5,400 burns and 2,600 puncture wounds, according to the Detroit Historical Museum.

Three decades later, French author Louis-Ferdinand Celine, who worked for Ford briefly at the Rouge plant, wrote: "One was turned by force into a machine oneself, the whole of one's carcass quivering in this vast frenzy of noise, which filled you within and all around the inside of your skull and lower down rattled your bowels, and climbed to your eyes in infinite, little quick unending strokes."

Line items

Foreman: In 1914, each foreman at Ford's Highland Park plant supervised an average of 53 workers. In 1917, the ratio was one foreman for each 15 workers.
"Please Mr. Foreman,
slow down your assembly line.
Please Mr. Foreman,

from the 1870s to World War II. At first, the employees were mostly German, but by the turn of the century, making cigars was the work primarily of young Polish women. By 1908, companies such as Mazer, Alexander Gordon, San Telmo and William Tegge operated factories in the near east side Polish neighborhood. Mostly, the women made the cigars by hand. Employers lured prospective employees with such perks as cafeterias and dressing rooms. One factory had a piano player entertain during lunch. In some factories, the workers would choose a colleague to read from a book while the others rolled; in turn, each worker would give the reader several cigars so she could meet her quota. In 1900, wages ranged from 77 to 90 cents a day, though men earned almost twice as much as women. Employees worked an average of nine to 11 hours a day.

➤ **D.M. Ferry's Seeds:** Detroit in the 19th Century was the seed capital of America, thanks largely to D.M. Ferry. By the turn of the century, Ferry's six-story headquarters downtown took up a block at Brush and Lafayette. He also ran seed farms that in one year grew 35,000 pounds of onion seeds and 93,000 pounds of beet seeds. Four hundred people worked at the main warehouse. They mailed seed packets to more than 80,000 merchants across North America. In 1883, according to historian Silas Farmer, Ferry mailed out 50 million packages of seeds and 325,000 catalogs.

➤ **R.L. Polk:** An information-age pioneer about a century before anyone used that term. In 1870, Polk, then 21, published a small directory of towns along the Detroit and Milwaukee Railroad. Then he issued a business directory for the state of Michigan, which led to the publishing of city directories. The directories are a treasury of details: house-by-house, street-by-street, business-by-business and resident-by-resident guides. Polk's books from the 19th and early 20th centuries are used today by historians and amateur genealogists. By 1922, Polk's company was into auto statistics such as registration reports, which became a source of marketing information. Direct marketing was next; then in 1958, the Polk company began using computers. Polk has expanded over the years by buying a number of firms in North America and Europe. Today, the Polk Co. concentrates on the automobile-related information business.

➤ **Compuware:** No metro Detroit company capitalized on the early digital era more than Compuware Corp. Its industrial-strength software and services are designed for the world's biggest companies. In 1999, Chairman Peter Karmanos announced that Compuware would move its headquarters from Northwestern Highway in Farmington

Mining salt deep below Detroit in 1962.

Free Press file photo

Rouge Plant
Ford Motor Company

A postcard of the Ford Rouge plant in the 1920s boasted of its 1,096 acres, 14 miles of roadways and 92 miles of railway track.

While the Rouge to many critics was hell on Earth, to others, the Rouge was an icon of the modern world.

Hills to a new building in downtown Detroit's Campus Martius. Compuware plans to bring a new way of working to the center of old Detroit. Compuware employees enjoy subsidized meals in a well-stocked cafeteria, on-site day care and a sparkling health club. Not to mention stock options.

➤ **Burroughs:** Founded by William Seward Burroughs as the American Arithmometer Co. in St. Louis in 1886, the company became Burroughs after it relocated to Detroit in 1904. From its headquarters on Second Avenue in the New Center, officials built a firm with 12,000 employees worldwide by 1920. Burroughs changed the lives of bankers, insurance brokers and merchants by making adding machines to "relieve the world of the drudgery of figures." Even after Henry Ford perfected mass production, skilled Burroughs employees — wearing dresses and ties — put together adding machines while seated at benches with the parts in front of them. The company introduced assembly lines in 1948. Burroughs turned to computer manufacturing after World War II and also designed systems for NASA missions. The old Burroughs facilities included an employee swimming pool, gym and tennis courts. Employees also could rent Livingston County cottages at low cost. In 1986, 100 years after its founding, Burroughs merged with Sperry Corp. to form Unisys.

➤ **Salt mines:** Deep below southwestern Detroit, Melvindale and Allen Park lies an abandoned city of salt with 50 miles of byways, some as wide as four-lane highways. Over the aeons, rich veins of salt formed after seawater washed into a basin and settled deep in the earth. For more than 100 years, hundreds of Detroiters made their living by mining the sparkling rock, which most recently was sold to Midwestern road crews under the name Sterling Halite. Other uses for the salt

over the years included ice cream and cattle licks. Operations began in 1896. Workers and equipment were lowered 1,200 feet through a 5-foot-by-6-foot shaft. People came up at the end of their shift; in the early days, mules went below and didn't resurface until they died.

The men toiled in a constant 58-degree temperature and 55-percent humidity. Giant trucks with 7-foot-tall tires hauled boulders of salt to crushers, which prepared it for removal by conveyor belts. By 1983, slow sales, plummeting profits and cut-rate competition from Canadian mines forced the closure of the mine. The mine twice reopened briefly for tours. In 1985, Crystal Mines bought the mine for $2.5 million and sought to turn it into a massive toxic-waste storage facility. Mining resumed in 1998.

➤ **Dodge Main, Hamtramck:** The Dodge brothers, Horace and John, supplied many of Ford's transmissions and engines in Ford's early years, and they built an engine plant in Hamtramck in 1910. The Dodges decided to manufacture their own car and produced the first one on Nov. 14, 1914. The Albert Kahn-designed complex, which included four- and eight-story buildings among its 60 structures, became a Hamtramck landmark and a magnet for immigrating Poles, as well as blacks, southern whites and people from eastern Europe. In the 1930s, after officials had boosted the line speed to 90 cars an hour, Dodge Main became a United Auto Workers citadel; it was the first major plant organized by the union, it was the site of a huge sit-down strike in 1937; UAW Local 3 grew to be the country's biggest union local at one plant. At one time, the Main included stamping, casting, transmissions and assembly, but after Chrysler Corp. acquired Dodge in 1928, it phased out many of those functions. The Dodge Revolutionary Union Movement took hold in the late 1960s. Peak employment was 40,000 during World War II. The plant closed in 1980.

➤ **The Rouge plant, Dearborn:** One of the world's most famous factory complexes, the Rouge came to symbolize capitalism, for better or for worse, and the growing power of the American economy in the 20th Century. Observers from around the world flocked to watch Ford Motor Co. workers bring in raw materials and send out fully built automobiles. While the Rouge to many critics was hell on Earth, to others, the Rouge was an icon of the modern world. Vanity Fair, in February 1928, called it "the most significant public monument in America." Its conveyor belts, smokestacks and anonymous employees made up the centerpieces of Diego Rivera's world-famous murals at the Detroit Institute of Arts and of Charles Sheeler's famous photos. The plant evolved slowly. Henry Ford bought the

Detroit was once home to hundreds of small machine shops and dozens of large factories. Countless parents grabbed a lunch pail and headed for "the shop." Here's a list of some famous plants and factories of the past along with current industrial sites.

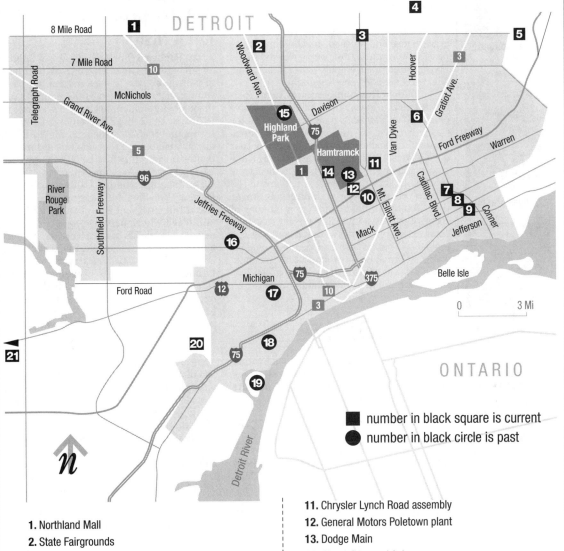

number in black square is current
number in black circle is past

1. Northland Mall
2. State Fairgrounds
3. Various Chrysler factories
4. To General Motors Tech Center, Warren
5. Eastland Mall
6. Detroit City airport
7. Dodge Viper plant
8. Budd Wheel
9. Chrysler Jeep assembly plant
10. Packard Motors

11. Chrysler Lynch Road assembly
12. General Motors Poletown plant
13. Dodge Main
14. Chevy Gear and Axle
15. Ford Highland Park plant
16. Dodge DeSoto plant
17. Cadillac Clark Street assembly
18. Fisher Body Fleetwood
19. Zug Island
20. Ford Rouge complex
21. Detroit Metropolitan Airport Romulus

Myra Wolfgang

Hodges Mason

Olga Madar

Nelson Jack Edwards

Mary Ellen Riordan

2,000-acre site a few miles from his boyhood home in Dearborn before World War I. His first business there was the manufacture of submarine chasers, called Eagle boats, for the U.S. Navy. With Albert Kahn as architect, Ford subsequently built about two dozen major structures along the Rouge River from 1917 to 1925, including a foundry, glass plant, tire plant, assembly building, cement plant, powerhouse and pressed steel building. At its peak, more than 75,000 people worked there. Today, the complex employs several thousand, who work for Ford and Rouge Steel.

➤ **Willow Run bomber plant, near Ypsilanti:** The U.S. government built this massive plant, Albert Kahn designed it and Ford Motor Co. ran it. It cost $65 million and existed for one reason: To produce B24 bombers. Its output during World War II was an astounding 8,685 planes. According to historian Charles Hyde, the factory was the largest war plant in the world. The single-story building was longer than 10 football fields and had a number of security features, including a solid roof with small exterior windows so that it could be easily blacked out. It also had two independent water systems, underground utility conduits and a system of pedestrian overpasses that served as employee checkpoints.

Solidarity

Belonging to a labor union is second nature to just more than 1 in 5 workers in Michigan in 1998; nationally that year, 1 in 8 workers was a union member.

LARGEST LOCALS (1998): Here's a list of the largest locals in the region by membership:

UAW Local 600	28,360
United Food and Commercial Workers Local 876	18,509
Service Employees International Local 79	14,944
Operating Engineers Local 324	11,994
UAW Local 900	10,110

SOURCE: CRAIN'S DETROIT BUSINESS

UNION MEMBERSHIP IN DETROIT, 1900: About 15 percent of workers, according to historian Thomas Klug. Among iron molders, machinists and printers, the rate would have been close to 90 percent or greater.

Big Three Hourly Employment

1979	752,000
1998	388,500

UAW membership

1979	1.51 million
1999	762,000

Working-class heroes
Notable people in Detroit labor history

➤ **Richard Trevellick:** With Thomas Dolan, started one of Detroit's earliest labor organizations, the Trades Assembly, in 1864. It eventually numbered 5,000 members in 14 unions before fading in the recession-racked 1870s. In the 1880s, Trevellick was instrumental in organizing the fight for the 8-hour day. British born, Trevellick was a ship's carpenter in Detroit before he quit to serve as a labor lobbyist in Washington.

➤ **Joseph Labadie:** Called "the dean of Detroit's Bohemia" by the Free Press when he was 72 in 1923, Labadie was a well-known organizer whose activism spanned several decades. While his politics were largely anarchistic, he was an iconoclast who participated in the Socialist Labor Party, the Knights of Labor, the Greenback Movement, trades councils, the typographical union, the 8-hour-day campaign and the American Federation of Labor. Labadie also was a prolific writer and poet. He grew up among the Potawatomi Indians in southwestern Michigan. He died in 1933.

➤ **Judson Grenell:** A printer who was the son of a radical Republican Baptist preacher who aided in the Underground Railroad, Grenell was a well-known Detroit socialist in the late 19th Century who later became a labor reporter and editor at the Detroit News. A native New Yorker, Grenell met Labadie in a Larned Street print shop, and together they launched the Socialist, the first of numerous Detroit labor publications in which Grenell would become involved. He once declared: "When there is a robber class and a robbed class, what else should be expected but revolution?" Grenell eventually abandoned his radicalism and became involved in mainstream politics.

➤ **Rosie the Riveter:** There was Rosie the poster woman for females joining the workforce during World War II, and there was the real Rosie, Rose Will Monroe. She was a riveter, building B24 bombers at the Willow Run plant near Ypsilanti, when officials asked her to star in a promotional film about the war effort. She became a patriotic icon, synonymous with thousands of women who took defense-industry jobs, working factory positions usually held by men. Monroe left Michigan after the war, drove a taxi, operated a beauty shop and started her own home construction firm in Indiana called Rose Builders. She died in 1997.

➤ **Myra Wolfgang:** For 40 years, Wolfgang championed Detroit's restaurant and hotel workers as the first female vice president of their 480,000-member international union and president of Detroit's Local 24. A fiery speaker and shrewd negotiator, Wolfgang bargained for better pay and conditions for workers ranging from Playboy bunnies to private-club waiters to hotel bartenders. A women's rights advocate, she called for day care centers and job training for women in the 1960s. In 1972, she barged through the front door of the Detroit Club when women were still barred. She died at age 61 in 1976.

➤ **Hodges Mason:** Fresh from Georgia, he began as an antiunion laborer at Bohn Aluminum and Brass Co. in the 1930s and saw the benefit of the labor movement when he experienced horrible working conditions. Mason rose to the UAW Local 208 presidency in 1944, the first black person in the Detroit area to become a UAW local chief. He went on to become a delegate to the Wayne County Congress of Industrial Organizations Council and led the fight to remove wage and job discrimination against black and female unionists.

➤ **Olga Madar:** In the depths of the Depression, Olga Madar got a job at Chrysler Corp.'s Kercheval Avenue plant because she could play softball. That the company would take her on just for athletic skills angered her so much that she spent the rest of her life fighting for unions. She rose through union ranks to become the first woman named international vice president of the United Auto Workers, in 1970. Madar used her position to fight for rights for women and minorities. She worked for 22 years in the UAW's recreation department, 19 years as director, before she was named to the international executive board. She died in 1996.

➤ **Nelson Jack Edwards:** The first African-American man to become an international UAW vice president, Edwards was the son of a sharecropper who moved from Alabama to Detroit as a teenager in the 1930s and began work at Dodge Main. Later, at Ford, Edwards became active in his union's local and was soon elected chairman of the overwhelmingly white group. In 1963, at the height of the civil rights movement, Walter Reuther named Edwards as the official UAW representative to Birmingham, Ala., to work with Dr. Martin Luther King Jr. Edwards was shot to death in 1974 while trying to break up a fight in a Detroit bar.

➤ **Mary Ellen Riordan:** A native Detroiter and teacher by trade, Riordan led the 10,000-member Detroit Federation of Teachers for 20 years until her retirement in 1980. Riordan received criticism from teachers in

Free Press file photo

Horace Sheffield in 1985

her later years as DFT chief, but few questioned her in the mid-1960s, when she led the union to its first collective-bargaining agreement. Under Riordan, the union raised the pay for starting teachers from $4,880 to $13,786, limited class size and won full life, health and dental insurance coverage.

➤ **Marc Stepp:** Like many Detroiters, his life has been intertwined with one auto company; in Stepp's case, it was Chrysler. Tipped that the company was hiring, Stepp signed on with Chrysler before World War II. After serving in the U.S. Army, Stepp returned to Detroit and took up arc welding at Chrysler, then machine operating, while becoming a force in Local 490. He rose from deputy chief steward in 1950 to local vice president in 1960. He was assistant Region 1B director when he was named an international vice president in 1974. In 1979, he sat down at the bargaining table for the first time as director of the UAW's Chrysler department.

➤ **Horace Sheffield:** In 1940, the National Association for the Advancement of Colored People was on Ford Motor Co.'s side as it squared off for a bitter test of strength with the UAW at the Rouge plant. Sheffield, president of the youth chapter of the NAACP, bucked his elders by renting a sound truck and boldly cruising Detroit streets, building support for the union. Sheffield, who died in 1995, worked for the UAW from 1940 until he retired in 1981. During the civil rights struggle of the 1960s, Sheffield represented the UAW in the South.

➤ **Bernie Firestone:** A longtime clothing union official and civic activist, Firestone was fatally shot in 1989 at his Detroit office by a former clothing store employee who said the union was treating him unfairly. Firestone was

Bernie Firestone

Mildred Jeffrey

Flora Walker

Free Press file photo

Walter Reuther during Senate testimony in late 1969, about 6 months before his death.

secretary-treasurer of the Amalgamated Clothing and Textile Workers Union, Chicago and Central States Joint Board, and vice president of the Metropolitan Detroit AFL-CIO. Labor organizers said Firestone could be counted on to show up in person to help out in any number of progressive causes.

➤ **Mildred (Millie) Jeffrey:** The UAW was her employer from the 1940s until 1978, but Jeffrey's activism for labor, women's issues and civil rights started in the 1930s and continued through Jeffrey's 89th year in 2000. She is a familiar face at rallies and meetings for progressive causes across southeast Michigan. Her first job: organizer for the Amalgamated Clothing Workers of America in Philadelphia in 1935. In 2000, she was awarded the Presidential Medal of Freedom.

➤ **Flora Walker:** Walker was a typist with the City of Detroit's Building and Safety Engineering Department when she organized clerical employees in 1968, because, she said, "I didn't like my supervisor." She discovered that she loved union work and later became friends with that supervisor. In 1971, Walker became an AFSCME staff representative working with other locals on negotiations and

grievances. In 1982, she was appointed to staff supervisor for Wayne, Oakland and Macomb counties and rose to be a vice president for Michigan's AFSCME Council 25.

Reuther and Hoffa
Tale of two giants

Out of the local labor movement of the 1930s emerged two Detroiters who would play major roles in American life for the next three decades: Walter Reuther, president of the United Auto Workers, and Jimmy Hoffa, president of the International Brotherhood of Teamsters. Reuther and Hoffa are strikingly alike — and different.

Walter Philip Reuther

Born: Sept. 1, 1907, in Wheeling, W.Va.

Came to Detroit: 1927.

Trade: Tool and die maker.

Education: Dearborn Fordson High; studied at Wayne State University.

Politics: Postwar America's definitive liberal Democrat. Was a Socialist as a young man; also was allied with Communists in the 1930s but later drove leftists from the UAW.

Formative years: Quit Ford Motor Co. and traveled around the world on boat and bicycle for nearly three years with brother Victor in the early 1930s. Worked at the Gorky Auto Works in the Soviet Union.

First strike: Led a sit-down in 1936 at Kelsey Hayes as president of fledgling UAW Local 174.

Relationship with the Kennedys: Close supporter who often counseled JFK.

Size: 5 feet 8, 170 pounds.

Feelings about Hoffa: Thinly veiled animosity.

Personal: Fiery, relentless, austere, aloof.

Marital: Met Mae Wolf at a Socialist Party meeting in Detroit. They married in 1936.

Lifestyle: A workaholic and devoted husband and father who did not drink or smoke and often had only a glass of milk for lunch.

Assassination attempt: Critically wounded on April 20, 1948, when an unknown gunman fired a 12-gauge shotgun through Reuther's kitchen window in Detroit.

Death: Died in a small-plane crash in 1970.

Legacy: Built one of the most sophisticated, powerful and corruption-free unions in modern America. While boosting the living standards of autoworkers, the UAW also helped to set the nation's progressive agenda and became a major source of funding for the civil rights movement.

Quote: "We are the vanguard in America of the great crusade to build a better world."

James Riddle Hoffa

Born: Feb. 14, 1913, in Brazil, Ind.

Came to Detroit: 1925.

Trade: Freight handler.

Education: Junior high dropout, but lectured at Harvard as Teamsters president.

Politics: Bragged he had no ideology; supported Republicans for president.

Formative years: Slugged it out in Detroit labor battles.

First strike: Led a work stoppage of 32-cents-an-hour Kroger workers in 1931 at age 17.

Relationship with the Kennedys: Mutual hatred. Bobby Kennedy led federal probes of Hoffa; eventually, Hoffa went to prison.

Size: 5 feet 5, 170 pounds.

Free Press file photos

Above: Jimmy Hoffa in the 1960s.

Left: Hoffa, left, regularly mixed with union workers during his Teamsters presidency.

Free Press file photo

The Labor Day parade in 1951 passes the old City Hall on Woodward. Gov. G. Mennen Williams, center in bow tie, leads dignitaries in a salute of the flag.

Feelings about Reuther: Thinly veiled animosity.

Personal: Pugnacious, street-smart, charismatic, mob-connected and accessible to the rank and file. Jack Nicholson played him in the movie "Hoffa."

Marital: Met Josephine Poszywak on a laundry workers picket line. They married in 1936.

Lifestyle: Workaholic and devoted husband and father who did not drink or smoke.

Assassination attempt: Left his suburban Detroit home for an afternoon meeting on July 30, 1975, and never returned. Last seen outside the Machus Red Fox restaurant in Bloomfield Township.

Death: Declared legally dead Dec. 9, 1982.

Legacy: Smart and effective bargainer who built the Teamsters into an influential union of more than 2 million members. Retained devotion of many Teamsters, but role in the union's well-chronicled corruption has sullied his reputation. His son, James P. Hoffa, became the union's president in 1999.

Quote: "We're not theorists, but practical people. . . . We've got the best contracts in the country."

Notable labor events

THE FIRST LABOR ORGANIZATION: In 1853, journeymen printers established Detroit's first permanent union, Local 18 of the National Typographers Union, according to historian Thomas Klug.

THE EIGHT-HOUR MOVEMENT: In the 1880s, Detroiters worked an average of 10 hours a day, five days a week — without overtime. And they worked a half-day on Saturday. Not surprisingly, they grew tired of it. Labor organizations set a deadline of May 1, 1886, for the implementation of an eight-hour workday. If owners refused, the workers threatened a general strike. But before the deadline, the Detroit Dry Dock Co. hiked its workday from nine to 10 hours, and the Knights of Labor Shipcarpenters Assembly 2124 walked out. After five weeks, the company gave in to all demands. Encouraged by that victory, Detroiters in other industries continued to agitate for a shorter workday. On May 3, workers struck the huge Michigan Car Works and marched en masse from factory to factory, swelling the number of strikers to 3,000. The strike spread to other industries. Organizers held mass rallies, and speakers urged workers in Polish, German and English to stay out. The results, according to historian Richard Oestreicher, were mixed: Less than 20 percent of the city's workers took part, but several thousand workers received a cut in daily hours or an increase in wages. The movement also turned thousands of previously unorganized workers into union members.

LABOR DAY: The workers' holiday caught on in Detroit in the 1880s, but employers refused to authorize time off, so workers held the parade at night. In 1886, the Knights of Labor and the Detroit Trades Council rallied an estimated 11,000 hooky-playing marchers for a midday parade in what basically was a general strike. In 1894, Labor Day became a legal holiday. Parades on the first Monday of September became a Detroit tradition for most of the 20th Century, and several Democratic presidential candidates used the occasion to launch their fall campaigns. By the late 1960s, though, participation dwindled and the parades were canceled. By 1981, unions has reinstituted the tradition, and the number of marchers sometimes hit more than 200,000, as vehicles and marchers tramped down Michigan Avenue (Teamsters) and Woodward (everyone else), meeting at Campus Martius for a giant rally.

THE BATTLE OF IDEAL MANUFACTURING: As the auto age began in the early 1900s, the city's brass, foundry and machine-shop owners tried to bust unions through the aggressive Employers' Association of Detroit, a powerful management group that served as both an employment agency and labor consultant. In late 1904, the Ideal Manufacturing Co., which made stoves and other metal products, unilaterally changed its contract with the metal polishers' union and laid off two-thirds of the polishers. A lockout ensued, followed by months of sometimes violent picketing, court battles and a public debate over the issue of the open shop. Finally, in August 1906, Ideal appeared to make concessions to the union, and the conflict abated.

CREATING THE OPEN SHOP: Unionized workers

Associated Press
Strikers in Flint in 1937 stay limber with exercise.

and employers fought a number of battles in 1907, especially in the metal trades. The Employers' Association of Detroit once again was in the middle of attempting to destroy unions. The metal polishers struck in April after the companies rejected their demands for a minimum wage of 33 cents an hour. According to historian Thomas Klug, the conflict turned violent when the companies began to hire strikebreakers. Union members attacked police and ambushed streetcars that carried replacement workers. In late June, the strike ended in confusion, with the union declaring victory and receiving a modest wage hike, but with the companies refusing the union demand that the plants be closed shops. Although the unions survived, Klug wrote that after 1907 "capitalists were able to transform Detroit into one of the most important industrial cities of the world — with minimal union interference." The near-absolute authority over workers — until the 1930s — did much to bring about the concentration of the auto industry in Detroit.

CIGAR MAKERS' STRIKE: On June 29, 1916, workers at the Lilies Factory No. 1 — led by women — walked out, and Detroit's 6,000 other mostly female cigar workers soon followed (though some were locked out before they could strike). Author Patricia Cooper wrote that the workers demanded $1 more per thousand cigars and a uniform wage scale for all cigar makers, since men made nearly twice as much as them. State and federal fact finders sided with the strikers, but the manufacturers refused to budge. Some women crossed the picket line. All efforts to arbitrate failed. In February 1917, the strikers declared a truce

With the sit-downs of 1937, the UAW mainly was seeking one thing: Recognition as the workers' bargaining agent.

WORK

and many of them went back to work. Owners raised the wage by 50 cents across the board.

Detroit's female workers, 1892: Age at which they began work

Ages 10 or younger	0.6 percent
Ages 11-13	15.3 percent
Ages 14-16	67.8 percent
Ages 17-19	13.0 percent
Ages 20-25	2.7 percent
Older than 25	0.7 percent

SOURCE: MICHIGAN STATE BUREAU OF LABOR STATISTICS, 1892, IN "SOLIDARITY AND FRAGMENTATION: WORKING PEOPLE AND CLASS CONSCIOUSNESS IN DETROIT, 1875-1900," BY RICHARD J. OESTREICHER

CHILD LABOR: In 1900, Detroit, with 285,704 residents, had 5,236 workers between the ages of 10 and 15, though historians say that figure is low because, as historian Tom Klug has written, parents, employers and children had reasons to disguise the true extent of child labor. Most children were male, and most worked as laborers. In 1900, state inspectors counted 2,042 children ages 14 through 16 working in 281 Detroit factories. Children comprised about 15 percent of the 2,309 tobacco workers. Most were girls.

FORD HUNGER MARCH: By the Depression's third year, many Ford employees were jobless, and Henry Ford was unsympathetic, insisting there was "plenty of work to do, if people would do it." On March 7, 1932, Detroit's Unemployed Councils led between 3,000 and 5,000 people in a protest on Ford's Rouge plant, the seat of Ford's empire and also the home of the many thugs and spies who enforced his strict rules. Starting at Fort and Oakwood on a frigid day, they walked peacefully down Miller Road toward Gate Three, where they met firefighters ready to soak them and police firing tear gas. The marchers responded by throwing rocks and coal. Dearborn police and Ford security workers, led by

CRAIG PORTER/Detroit Free Press
Detroit Federation of Teachers President Mary Ellen Riordan walking an informational picket line in August 1979.

security chief Harry Bennett, began firing into the unarmed crowd. Four marchers died on Miller; one died later in a hospital. A funeral five days later downtown drew 60,000. No official was charged.

➤ **Names of victims:** Joe Bussell, Curtis Williams, Joe York, Coleman Leny and Joe DiBlasio.

THE SIT-DOWNS OF 1937: On March 8, 1937, the message to strike surged through Dodge Main. More than 22,000 workers set down their tools, kicked out their bosses and began a sit-down strike. Across the city, in an extraordinary display of unity, about 35,000 other Chrysler employees at eight other facilities also sat down.

Just weeks after the UAW's General Motors Corp. sit-down in Flint successfully led to union recognition, the largest sit-down strike in U.S. history was under way. In all, during early 1937, Detroit workers occupied nearly 130 factories, offices, hotels and stores for periods ranging from a few hours to six weeks, Wayne State University historian Steve Babson wrote.

The UAW mainly was seeking one thing: Recognition as the workers' bargaining agent.

After considerable agitation, mass rallies and police raids on small sit-downs in Detroit, labor-friendly Gov. Frank Murphy succeeded in getting Walter Chrysler and national CIO President John L. Lewis, who represented the UAW, to agree on a truce that would end the sit-ins but keep the plants closed until negotiators worked out a final agreement. After 17 days inside, the sit-downers finally marched out, accompanied by a band and the UAW and American flags. Two weeks later, Chrysler and Lewis agreed that the union would make a no-strike pledge and the company would recognize the UAW and refrain from undermining it. The sit-down movement soon petered out. But by the end of April 1937, the UAW had signed its first agreements with Chrysler, GM, Hudson Motor, REO, Packard, Studebaker and assorted parts companies.

BATTLE OF THE OVERPASS: May 26, 1937: UAW organizers Walter Reuther, Robert Kantor, Richard Frankensteen and J.J. Kennedy traveled to the bridge over Miller Road next to the Rouge plant to pass out union literature. Ford Motor Co. security forces attacked them and beat them severely. At the time of the attack, the unionists were posing for photographers, so the beatings were well chronicled, and Ford suffered a major setback in public sentiment. The Ford enforcers also bloodied other UAW members; about 60 were treated for injuries that day. Kennedy died four months later. The UAW did not succeed in organizing Ford for four more years.

Walter Reuther joins Ford workers during a UAW strike in October 1967.

SOLIDARITY FOREVER, THE UAW ANTHEM:
"When the union's inspiration through the worker's blood
    shall run,
There can be no power greater anywhere beneath the sun.
Yet what force on earth is weaker than the feeble strength of one?
    But the union makes us strong.
    Solidarity forever!
    Solidarity forever!
    For the union makes us strong."

HATE STRIKES: During World War II, white workers in Detroit's auto plants would often walk off the job when black workers were promoted. During the first six months of 1943 alone, whites engaged in about a dozen such wildcat strikes. Just days before the 1943 race riot, more than 25,000 Packard workers walked off the job after management had upgraded three black workers.

GETTING MILITANT: Members of UAW Local 600 noticed that Ford Motor was moving numerous jobs out of the Rouge plant in the early 1950s and filed a lawsuit that charged the automaker was violating its contract with the union. The action asserted workers had a right to keep their jobs during the length of an agreement. The suit attacked sacrosanct rights of management such as layoffs and firings. The rebellion was too much for UAW leaders; they refused to support the suit and placed the local in trusteeship. A federal judge dismissed the suit. The job loss at Ford was just the beginning of the auto industry's massive post-war decentralization that would cost the region hundreds of thousands of jobs.

HOCKEY UNION: Red Wing star Ted Lindsay was one of the chief organizers of an attempt to form a players' association in the National Hockey League in 1957. The game's biggest star was Lindsay's teammate Gordie Howe, who did not support the effort. Partially because of Howe's refusal to lend his name to the drive, the attempt failed. Said Lindsay in 1999: "Gordie was a very naive young man....

He has to live with that for the rest of his life."

TEACHER SIT-DOWN STRIKE: About 60 Hamtramck teachers occupied Copernicus Junior High for four days in 1965 and ended up with the first teachers' union contract in Michigan history. The action by the members of the American Federation of Teachers, according to historian Steve Babson, was the first spark of an explosive movement for union recognition among public employees. Throughout the 1960s and 1970s, public-worker unions were the fastest-growing sector of Detroit's labor movement.

DODGE REVOLUTIONARY UNION MOVEMENT: DRUM didn't last very long, but it made history for the incendiary effort by black auto workers to attack racism in both the UAW and the auto industry, especially Chrysler Corp. Excluding "all honkies" from its membership, DRUM attempted to make wholesale changes at places like Dodge Main and the Eldon Avenue Axle Plant, where the group was known as ELRUM. Its demands included a general strike to end the war in Vietnam, recognition of DRUM as the official voice of black workers and immediate appointment of a black UAW president. While DRUM failed to launch a revolution, its militant rhetoric, wildcat strikes and M1 carbine symbols drew national attention to the plight of black workers in the white-run environment. DRUM died after the UAW and the company joined forces to crush it.

WILDCAT STRIKES: Detroit area auto plants and the UAW were racked by wildcat strikes in 1973 and '74 as young workers, both black and white, rebelled against the authority of the company and the union. Unauthorized work stoppages hit Dodge Truck, Mack Avenue Stamping, Detroit Forge and Jefferson Assembly. At Dodge Truck in Warren, workers upset over conditions shut the plant for four days in 1974, idling 6,000 workers who spurned pleas from UAW officials to return to work. After they defied a court order to stop picketing, Macomb County Circuit Judge Hunter Stair showed up in his judicial robe and held court on the back of a pickup. Stair banged his gavel on the roof of the truck cab. Workers returned to work after a series of arrests.

NEWSPAPER STRIKES: The Free Press lost one-third of its circulation in the 1880s because of a boycott called by the typographical union. There have been at least 17 work stoppages among Detroit newspaper workers since 1955. But the longest and most contentious strike in the turbulent Detroit newspaper industry began July 13, 1995, when almost 2,500 full- and part-time employees at the News, Free Press and Detroit Newspapers walked out after contract talks broke down and the Detroit News unilaterally changed the conditions of its contract with the Newspaper Guild. The papers continued to publish during the strike. About two months after the walkout began, the companies began hiring new workers who eventually numbered about 1,250. In addition, some strikers crossed picket lines and went back to work. In February 1997, the unions ended their strike with a formal "unconditional offer to return to work." They demanded that all strikers be taken back to their jobs immediately. But the companies said they would call back former strikers only as jobs became available and would not fire replacement workers. The gradual callback process has been moving forward since then. In July 2000, the U.S. Court of Appeals in Washington, D.C., ruled that the newspapers did not cause or prolong the strike by breaking federal labor laws. By Christmas 2000, all six unions involved in the dispute had ratified contracts.

SOURCES: "ONCE A CIGAR MAKER," BY PATRICIA COOPER; "WORKING DETROIT," BY STEVE BABSON; "THE ORIGINS OF THE URBAN CRISIS," BY THOMAS SUGRUE; "THE RISE OF THE 'REAGAN DEMOCRATS' IN WARREN, MICHIGAN: 1964-1984," BY DAVE RIDDLE (WAYNE STATE UNIVERSITY PHD DISSERTATION, 1998); "DETROIT: AN INDUSTRIAL HISTORY GUIDE," BY CHARLES HYDE; "SOLIDARITY AND FRAGMENTATION," BY RICHARD OESTREICHER; "ROOTS OF THE OPEN SHOP," BY TOM KLUG (WAYNE STATE UNIVERSITY PHD DISSERTATION).

Violence on the job

ELDON AVENUE GEAR AND AXLE PLANT, Chrysler Corp., Detroit, July 15, 1970
➤ **Assailant:** James Johnson
➤ **Victims:** Three killed. Johnson was a conveyor loader at Eldon Avenue in 1970 when he shot and killed a coworker and two supervisors with an M1 carbine. At his trial, Johnson's attorney, Kenneth Cockrel, accused Chrysler of forcing Johnson to violence through abusive conditions and racism in the plant. The jury agreed, finding Johnson not guilty on the grounds that he was temporarily insane. Chrysler later was forced to pay Johnson workers compensation.

ORION TOWNSHIP ASSEMBLY PLANT, General Motors, June 21, 1985.
➤ **Assailant:** William Carson.
➤ **Victims:** One dead. Carson found not guilty by reason of insanity.

The Dodge Revolutionary Union Movement didn't last very long, but it made history for the incendiary effort by black auto workers to attack racism in both the UAW and the auto industry.

ROYAL OAK POST OFFICE, Nov. 14, 1991.
➤ **Assailant:** Thomas McIlvane.
➤ **Victims:** Four dead, four wounded. McIlvane also committed suicide.

DEARBORN POST OFFICE, May 6, 1993.
➤ **Assailant:** Lawrence Jasion.
➤ **Victims:** One dead, two wounded. Jasion also committed suicide.

FORD ROUGE PLANT, Dearborn, Sept. 10, 1994.
➤ **Assailant:** Oliver French Jr.
➤ **Victims:** Two dead, two wounded. French was convicted of murder.

STERLING HEIGHTS STAMPING PLANT, Chrysler Corp., Dec. 9, 1994.
➤ **Assailant:** Clarence Woods.
➤ **Victims:** One dead, one wounded. Woods was convicted of murder.

FORD SHELDON ROAD PLANT, Plymouth Township, Jan. 7, 1995.
➤ **Assailant:** Michael Brattin.
➤ **Victims:** One dead, one wounded. Brattin also committed suicide.

STERLING HEIGHTS ASSEMBLY PLANT, Chrysler Corp., Dec. 19, 1995.
➤ **Assailant:** Gregory Christian.
➤ **Victims:** One dead. Christian also committed suicide.

FORD SHELDON ROAD PLANT, Plymouth Township, Aug. 18, 1996.
➤ **Assailant:** Stephen Cox.
➤ **Victims:** One dead. Cox also committed suicide.

OFFICE OF DR. REUVEN BAR-LEVAV, a Southfield psychiatrist, June 11, 1999.
➤ **Assailant:** Joseph Brooks, an ex-patient with schizophrenia.
➤ **Victims:** Bar-Levav and a patient were killed; four others were wounded. Brooks also committed suicide.

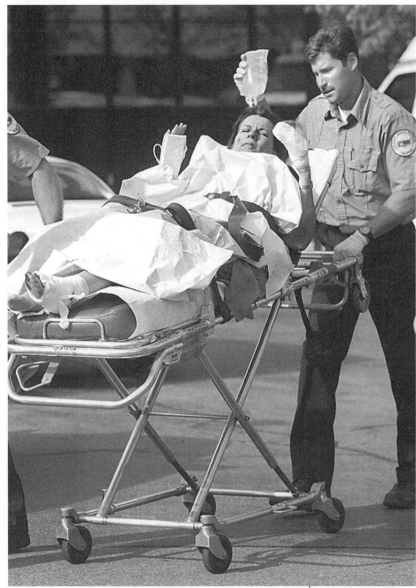

A woman injured when a gunman opened fire at the Town Center office building in Southfield in June 1999. The woman recovered, but the gunman killed two people before fatally shooting himself.

Dying on the job

In 1999, 87 workers died from injuries at work in Michigan because of safety problems, the highest number in 20 years. Explosions at the Ford Rouge plant in Dearborn and a fireworks factory in Osseo in Hillsdale County highlighted the deadly year.

Number of deaths on the job in southeastern Michigan:

Wayne	19
Oakland	11
Macomb	4
Washtenaw	2
Monroe	1
St. Clair	4

Metro Detroit's Top 20 Publicly Owned Companies By Revenue

Free Press file photo

Chrysler Corp. has been a major employer in metro Detroit. But after Daimler-Benz swallowed Chrysler in 1998, the company's world headquarters moved to Germany.

1. General Motors Corp.

Detroit
Revenue ....$176.5 billion
Earnings ....$6 billion
% return on equity 33.2
What it is: The Big Daddy of the auto industry. Major brands include Chevrolet, Buick, Cadillac, Oldsmobile, Pontiac, Saturn, GMC, Saab, Opel, Isuzu, Vauxhall and Holden. GM also runs the nation's largest satellite televi-

sion system, DirecTV, through its Hughes Electronics unit.

2. Ford Motor Co.

Dearborn
Revenue ....$162.5 billion
Earnings..$7.2 billion
% return on equity 28.5
What it is: The world's second-largest and most profitable automaker. Its brands are Ford, Lincoln, Mercury, Mazda, Jaguar, Volvo and Aston Martin. Soon to join the lineup: Land Rover.

3. Kmart Corp.

Troy
Revenue ....$35.9 billion
Earnings..$403 million
% return on equity 6.6
What it is: The nation's No. 3 retailer.

4. Delphi Automotive Systems Corp.

Troy
Revenue ....$29.1 billion
Earnings..$1.08 billion
% return on equity 33.8
What it is: World's largest auto parts supplier. It operates 168 factories worldwide. Delphi, once owned by GM, became a separate company in 1999.

5. Lear Corp.

Southfield
Revenue ....$12.4 billion
Earnings ....$257 million
% return on equity 18.6
What it is: In 1986, Wall Street buyout company Forstmann Little took over troubled conglomerate Lear Siegler, then sold the auto seat business to its managers. Led by Ken Way, the managers-turned-owners bought a chunk of Ford's auto interior business in 1993, Fiat's in 1994, GM's in 1998 and Hyundai's in 1999. The acquisitions paved the way for Lear to become the nation's largest supplier of auto seats and interior parts.

6. Federal-Mogul Corp.

Southfield
Revenue..$6.5 billion
Earnings...$243 million
% return on equity 12.7
What it is: Has been turning out engine bearings since 1899. Makes hundreds of other engine parts.

7. Masco Corp.

Taylor
Revenue..$6.3 billion
Earnings...$570 million
% return on equity 19.3
What it is: One of world's largest makers of faucets, cabinets, locks and other home-improvement and building products. One of the largest suppliers of products to two of the largest U.S. home-improvement outlets: Home Depot and Lowe's.

8. CMS Energy Corp.

Dearborn
Revenue..$6.1 billion
Earnings...$339 million
% return on equity 10.4
What it is: The energy company has pipelines and electricity plants in 22 countries throughout the world but makes almost 70 percent of its money from its utility company, Consumers Energy.

9. DTE Energy Corp.

Detroit
Revenue..$4.7 billion
Earnings...$483 million
% return on equity 12.7
What it is: The company owns Detroit Edison, the biggest electric utility in the state. It is diversifying into unregulated energy businesses. The most promising is fuel cell development. DTE owns about 32 percent of Plug Power, a fuel cell company based in Latham, N.Y.

10. Meritor Automotive Corp.

Troy
Revenue..$4.4 billion
Earnings ....$194 million
% return on equity 63.2
What it is: World's largest maker of heavy-truck axles and the No. 2 maker of sunroofs. Since its 1997 spin-off from Rockwell Inter-

national Inc., Meritor has been a supplier of components and systems for use in commercial, specialty and light vehicles. The automotive business serves its customers worldwide through heavy and light vehicle systems.

11. Kelly Services Inc.

Troy
Revenue..$4.3 billion
Earnings...$85 million
% return on equity 15.2
What it is: Creator of the famous Kelly Girls secretarial workers, Kelly Services provides temporary support staff personnel for its customers. The business, which once supplied only female clerical help, has expanded to include light-industrial, technical and professional employees of both genders, including information technology specialists and engineers. One of the top U.S. temporary help companies.

12. Comerica Inc.

Detroit
Revenue..$3.4 billion
Earnings...$673 million
% return on equity 21.8
What it is: The holding company for Comerica Bank, the largest bank in terms of assets in Michigan. With $38.6 billion in assets at the end of 1999, Comerica was the 25th-largest bank in the nation.

13. Pulte Corp.

Bloomfield Hills
Revenue..$3.7 billion
Earnings...$178 million
% return on equity 17.7
What it is: When it comes to home building, Pulte is the biggest house on the block. It's the No. 1 U.S. home builder, having erected 19,848 homes in 1999. Founder and chairman Bill Pulte built his first house in Detroit in 1950. It's still there. But Pulte's company now develops subdivisions in 40 major markets, including Florida, Minnesota, New Jersey and California.

14. Borders Group Inc.

Ann Arbor
Revenue..$3 billion
Earnings...$90 million
% return on equity 12.6
What it is: Nation's No. 2 bookseller. Shoppers can find all types of books and music at stores and at its Web site.

Comerica Inc. is the holding company for Comerica Bank, the largest bank in terms of assets in Michigan. With $38.6 billion in assets at the end of 1999, Comerica was the 25th-largest bank in the nation.

WORK

Compuware Corp. is one of the world's largest providers of business software and professionals who help corporations keep that software operating. Employs more than 15,000 people. Compuware maintains more than 100 offices in 45 countries. It is building an $800-million headquarters in downtown Detroit.

15. American Axle & Manufacturing Holdings Inc.

Detroit
Revenue..$3 billion
Earnings...$116 million
% return on equity 76
What it is: Something quintessentially Detroit is in the name American Axle. It speaks of heavy, old-line industry. This outfit's forges and machine shops produced axles under General Motors Corp.'s Saginaw division for much of the 20th Century. In 1994, GM sought cheaper parts and spun off the old axle plants to investors who modernized the factories and created American Axle. If you drive a Chevrolet Blazer or Suburban, you're rolling on its product.

16. Champion Enterprises Inc.

Auburn Hills
Revenue...$2.5 billion
Earnings...$50 million
% return on equity 12.3
What it is: Manufactured-housing company.

17. MCN Energy Group Inc.

Detroit
Revenue...$2.5 billion
Earnings.............................$30.8 million loss
% return on equity ....-7.6
What it is: Owns Michigan Consolidated Gas Co., a utility with 1.2 million gas customers in Michigan. Also operates some non-regulated businesses such as a heating and cooling installation and repair division. Being purchased by DTE Energy Co.

18. Detroit Diesel Corp.

Detroit
Revenue...$2.4 billion
Earnings...$49 million
% return on equity 13.2
What it is: General Motors' Detroit Diesel, founded in 1938, produced thousands of landing craft and tank engines for World War II, then cranked out big-truck and marine diesels for four decades. Roger Penske, race-car driver turned millionaire businessman, took control in a 1987 joint venture with GM, and in 1993 took Detroit Diesel public. In 2000, the company was sold to DaimlerChrysler for $423 million.

19. Hayes Lemmerz International Inc.

Northville
Revenue..$2.3 billion
Earnings...$65 million
% return on equity 29.5
What it is: World's largest supplier of wheels to the auto industry. Makes steel and aluminum wheels for consumer vehicles, plus tractor-trailer wheels, brake parts, steering and suspension components. It sells to just about all the major automakers, with about 60 percent of its market in North America and the rest overseas.

20. Compuware Corp.

Farmington Hills
Revenue ....$2.1 billion
Earnings...$429 million
% return on equity 39.8
What it is: One of the world's largest providers of business software and professionals who help corporations keep that software operating. Employs more than 15,000 people. Founded in 1973, Compuware maintains more than 100 offices in 45 countries. It is building an $800-million headquarters in downtown Detroit.

A rendering by Rossetti Associates of the proposed Compuware Corp. headquarters on Campus Martius in downtown Detroit. Phase one will cost $350 million.

Top private businesses
Southeast Michigan, 1999

1) PENSKE CORP., Detroit. Transportation services, truck leasing, diesel engine manufacturing, auto sales and service.
Revenue ....$6.4 billion
Chairman ....Roger Penske

2) GUARDIAN INDUSTRIES, Auburn Hills. Manufactures glass for construction; supplier of automotive trim components.
Revenue ....$2.5 billion
President
and CEO ....William Davidson

3) QUESTOR MANAGEMENT CO., Southfield. Investment group.
Revenue ....$1.437 billion
Managing principal ....Jay Alix

4) VENTURE HOLDINGS CO. LLC, Fraser. Auto supplier.
Revenue ....$1.366 billion
Owner and CEO.............Larry Winget

5) DOMINO'S PIZZA INC., Ann Arbor. Pizza carryout and delivery.
Revenue ....$1.156 billion
Chairman
and CEO....................David Brandon

6) FLINT INK CO., Ann Arbor. Manufactures printing inks.
Revenue ....$1.076 billion
Chairman
and CEO ....H. Howard Flint II

7) DON MASSEY CADILLAC, Plymouth. Auto dealership group.
Revenue ....$985 million
CEO ....Don Massey

8) BARTON MALOW CO., Southfield. Program management, construction management, design and building, general contracting.
Revenue ....$970 million
President ....Ben Maibach III

9) ASC INC., Southgate. Specialty vehicles.
Revenue ....$950 million
President
and CEO ....Lawrence Doyle

10) SOAVE ENTERPRISES LLC, Detroit. Diversified management holding company.
Revenue ....$801 million
Chairman and
president ....Anthony Soave

11) ILITCH HOLDINGS INC., Detroit. Holding company for Little Caesars Inc., Detroit Red Wings and Olympia Entertainment.
Revenue ....$800 million
Chairman ....Michael Ilitch

SOURCE: CRAIN'S DETROIT BUSINESS.

George Jerome & Co., a land survey and civil engineering firm in Roseville, is the state's oldest business, according to the Historical Society of Michigan. It was founded in 1828.

The 20 oldest companies
Southeast Michigan

1. George Jerome & Co.: Roseville, 1828.

George Jerome & Co. is the great-great-granddaddy among Michigan companies. The land survey and civil engineering firm is the state's oldest business, according to the Historical Society of Michigan.

Today's president, George Jerome, is a great-great-grandson of the founder, Edwin Jerome, who started the business in Detroit.

George Jerome & Co. counts laying out Detroit's Grand Boulevard in 1884 among its achievements. Its longtime clients include the City of Grosse Pointe, Redford Township and Great Lakes Steel.

During the last decade, the company's scientific tools have advanced spectacularly and now include lasers to help surveyors to more accurately measure altitude and distance and prepare computer-generated maps.

2. Detroit Free Press: Detroit, 1831.

3. Children's Home of Detroit: Grosse Pointe Woods, 1836.

4. Elmwood Cemetery: Detroit, 1846.

5. Michigan Consolidated Gas Co.: Detroit, 1849.

6. Comerica Inc.: Detroit, 1849.

7. The Stroh Brewery Co.: Detroit, 1850.

8. YMCA of Metropolitan Detroit: Detroit, 1852.

9. Miller, Canfield, Paddock and Stone, PLC: Detroit, 1852.

10. Butzel Long: Detroit, 1854.

11. Peninsular Machinery Co.: Farmington Hills, 1854.

12. William R. Hamilton Co.: Birmingham, 1855.

13. SHG Inc.: Detroit, 1855.

14. H.D. Edwards & Company Inc.: Detroit, 1855.

15. Schober Printing Co.: Detroit, 1862.

16. First America Title Insurance Co.: Troy, 1866.

17. Koenig Co.: Detroit, 1870.

18. R.L. Polk & Co.: Southfield, 1870.

19. The Detroit News: Detroit, 1873.

20. Kerr, Russell and Weber, PLC: Detroit, 1874.

FOREIGN INVESTMENT IN METRO DETROIT, 1999
Number of facilities by county:

County	Facilities
Oakland	342
Wayne	183
Washtenaw	44
Macomb	42
St. Clair	20
Livingston	9
Monroe	5

INVESTMENT BY COUNTRY

Country	Percent
Japan	41%
Canada	16%
Germany	13%
France	7%
United Kingdom	9%
Others	14%

S.S. Kresge

J. L. Hudson

Scott McNealy

Peter Karmanos

Steve Ballmer

Captains of industry

➤ **John Askin:** A fur trader, merchant, politician and militia member, the Irish immigrant became Detroit's best-known businessman of the 18th Century. He arrived in Detroit in the 1780s after having lived and traded at Ft. Michilimackinac (Mackinaw City). He dabbled in various businesses as a supplier for American Indians and fur-trading companies, then became a land speculator, obtaining a large tract in northern Ohio from the Indians. He also unsuccessfully attempted to secure title to the entire lower peninsula of Michigan. Askin remained a British citizen after the Americans seized control of Detroit and eventually moved to the British-controlled (Canadian) side of the Detroit River. He owned slaves.

➤ **Joseph Campau:** He was part of the third generation of a family that arrived in Detroit in 1708. Educated in Montreal, Campau returned to Detroit and opened a general store on Rue Ste. Anne in the 1790s. He also became a fur trader and a land speculator. Campau served as a trustee of Detroit, among other political posts. He learned several Indian dialects, according to historian Donald Voelker, and was known as *Chemokamun* (Big Shot). Campau also owned slaves and was somewhat of a slumlord, buying property and renting it to poor people on long-term leases. He and wife Adelaide Dequindre had 12 children. Campau, who lived on West Jefferson in a famous home with a yellow facade, died in 1863 at 95.

➤ **Jeremiah Dwyer:** Born in Brooklyn, N.Y., in 1837, Dwyer moved to Detroit as a child. He learned iron molding and bought into a small stove factory at Mt. Elliott near the Detroit River around the time of the Civil War. With brother James and other partners, Dwyer built the Michigan Stove Co. into one of the nation's largest stove manufacturers, which helped make Detroit the stove city of the 19th Century.

➤ **S.S. Kresge:** A mass-marketing genius, Sebastian Spering Kresge moved to Detroit in 1898, bought out retail partner John McCrory and, from his store on Woodward Avenue downtown, built a chain that by 1930 had grown to nearly 600 dime stores, second largest after F.W. Woolworth. In 1962, the S.S. Kresge Co. conceived the first Kmart discount store, which opened in Garden City. A pioneer of such benefits as sick leaves and profit-shar-

ing, Kresge was a well-known philanthropist. He also was a penny-pinching moralist who nonetheless married three times, twice to much younger women. He served as company chairman until 1962, the year he died, at age 99. His 1953 speech at Harvard University lasted several seconds: "I never made a dime talking," is all Kresge said.

➤ **J.L. Hudson:** Joseph Lowthian Hudson was born in England in 1846 and moved with his family to Canada, then Grand Rapids. Hudson followed his father into the clothing store business and opened the J.L. Hudson store inside the old Detroit Opera House in 1881. In 1891, he opened an eight-story building at Gratiot and Farmer. Eventually the company built the 25-story building on Woodward Avenue that dominated Detroit retailing for much of the 20th Century. Hudson died in 1912.

➤ **Steve Ballmer:** In 2000, at age 43, Ballmer took over as chief executive of Microsoft Corp. from founder Bill Gates. Ballmer grew up in Farmington Hills and graduated from Detroit Country Day School, returning to serve on its board of trustees in the mid-1990s. While Microsoft has made Gates the wealthiest individual in the world, with a net worth in 2000 of $85 billion, Ballmer is not far behind. After attending Harvard with Gates, Ballmer joined Microsoft in 1980. In 2000, he owned about 5 percent of its stock and ranked fourth on Forbes magazine's list of wealthiest people, with a personal fortune of $23 billion. Ballmer's father, an executive for Ford Motor Co., instilled in him the corporate loyalty that Ballmer proselytizes to others. Ballmer is known around Microsoft for refusing to drive cars not built by Detroit's automakers.

➤ **Scott McNealy:** He grew up in Birmingham, attended Cranbrook and in 1982 cofounded Sun Microsystems Inc., a Silicon Valley success story that is one of the world's leading suppliers of network computing systems. The television show "60 Minutes" called McNealy "one of the most influential businessmen in America." McNealy is a widely quoted speaker on information technology. Sun is known for its 1995 introduction of Java, the versatile computer programming language. McNealy plays hockey in his spare time.

➤ **Bill Joy:** Like fellow metro Detroiter McNealy, Joy is a cofounder of Sun Microsystems and serves as the company's chief scientist. Born in 1954, he attended North Farmington High School and the University of Michigan and grew into one of the most accomplished innovators of the high-tech era.

Mel Farr, the self-described Super Star auto dealer, ran the nation's largest black-owned business in 1998, according to Black Enterprise magazine.

Joy was among the first to see the potential for millions of people around the world exchanging information and ideas through networked computers, and as the Internet became a pervasive force, his stature in the industry grew. A cover story in Fortune magazine called him "the Edison of the Internet" and proclaimed that "the tousle-haired software wizard runs a close No. 2 to Microsoft's Bill Gates as the most influential person in the computer industry."

➤ **Peter Karmanos:** He's the cofounder, chairman and CEO of Compuware Corp., which became the biggest Michigan-based high-tech company by selling industrial-strength programs and expertise to the world's largest companies. Karmanos founded the firm at his dining room table in 1973 with Thomas Thewes and the late Allen Cutting. In 2000, Compuware had sales of more than $2.2 billion and 16,000 employees around the world. It plans to build a $600-million headquarters on Woodward Avenue downtown and a second office tower east of the Renaissance Center off the Detroit River. In Farmington Hills, employees enjoy subsidized meals in a well-stocked cafeteria, on-site day care and a sparkling health club. Karmanos, born in Detroit in 1943, was a rebellious teenager who was almost kicked out of Henry Ford High School, and he never graduated

from Wayne State University. Despite his high-tech savvy, Karmanos refuses to use a computer in his office. He feels it can be a waste of time for an executive.

➤ **Mel Farr:** The Oak Park-based Mel Farr Automotive Group was the nation's largest black-owned business in 1999, according to Black Enterprise Magazine, with $596.6 million in 1998 revenues. Farr, who owns nine dealerships in Michigan and Ohio, came to town as a Detroit Lion in 1967, the same year he began working in the off-season at Ford Motor Co. in dealer development. He retired from football in 1974 and purchased his first franchise, the company's Oak Park dealership, in 1975. The self-proclaimed "Super Star" dealer in a red cape, Farr propelled sales by appearing in television commercials with singing stars and promising to finance anyone who had a job and a down payment, through his Triple M Finance Co. But even though Farr envisions thousands of poor people flocking to used-car superstores he dreams of opening in Detroit and other large U.S. cities, nearly 250 customers filed lawsuits or regulatory complaints against him between January 1996 and January 2000, saying Farr sold them unreliable cars that drove them deeper into debt and ruined their credit. State regulators said they don't think Farr is a problem car dealer, but they said most of the complaints probably would go away if he tried hard-

Note: *Some of Michigan's best-known businessmen in the 19th Century were also politicians.*

A. Alfred Taubman

Dave Bing

Mike Ilitch

Don Barden

er to satisfy customers.

➤ **Max Fisher:** His parents were Russian Jews beset by pogroms who immigrated to Salem, Ohio, after the turn of the 20th Century. Fisher played football at Ohio State, then moved to Detroit, where his father settled after getting involved in the oil business. Max, too, got into oil, forming the Aurora Gasoline Co., which exploited black gold in Michigan. The firm merged with Speedway, then Marathon, and before long Fisher was one of the richest men in the United States. His investments included real estate, and in the 1960s he bought Detroit's Fisher Building, which had been built in the 1920s by the auto-body Fisher family (no relation to Max). Fisher has been an adviser to U.S. presidents and to Israel since its founding, and he has been a prolific fund-raiser for charities, the Detroit Symphony and the Republican Party. Though he lived much of his life in Oakland County, Detroit mayors counted on him as one of the city's greatest friends and benefactors. In addition, he was an advocate for civil rights before corporate America considered it politically correct. At his 90th birthday party in 1998, the guest list included former Secretary of State Henry Kissinger and former Presidents Gerald Ford and George Bush.

➤ **A. Alfred Taubman:** A college drop-out who became a global player in real estate and art, Taubman went from small-time suburban builder to brash billionaire who rescued Sotheby's, the venerable New York-based auction house. The son of immigrants from Germany (the A. stands for Adolph), Taubman grew up in Pontiac. In 1950, he borrowed $5,000 and began building. He built shopping malls from coast to coast, including Lakeside, Fairlane Town Center and Twelve Oaks, developments that greatly stretched the boundaries of metro Detroit. In the late 1970s, Taubman quarterbacked one of the biggest real estate deals of the 20th Century: the purchase of the Irvine Ranch in southern California, which later brought Taubman and pals Max Fisher and Henry Ford II a profit of more than $400 million. Taubman also bought the Washington, D.C., department store chain Woodward & Lothrop, but it cost him hundreds of millions of dollars, wound up bankrupt in 1994 and later closed. As a worldwide art dealer, Taubman served Mayors Coleman Young and Dennis Archer as head of the arts commission and has donated tens of millions of dollars to the Detroit Institute of Arts and the University of Michigan. In 2000, Taubman, 75, stepped down as director of Sotheby's while federal prosecutors were investigating whether Sotheby's had conspired with its chief rival, Christie's, to split business and fix commis-

sions. According to the New York Times, Taubman partly inspired a major character in author Dominick Dunne's novel "People Like Us." In the book, about the clash of old and new society in New York, the Taubman-like character is a rich trader who ends up in jail.

➤ **Dave Bing:** He's the chairman of the Bing Group that employs 1,080 people at auto-parts plants in Detroit, Melvindale and Dearborn. In 1999, sales were close to $300 million. Bing was born in 1943 in Washington, D.C., but has lived or worked in Detroit since the Detroit Pistons selected him No. 2 in the 1966 NBA draft. He played 12 years in the NBA, was inducted into the Hall of Fame in 1990 and named one of the top 50 basketball players of all time. He founded Bing Steel in 1980, Superb Manufacturing in 1985, Bing Manufacturing in 1994, Detroit Automotive Interiors in 1996 and Trim Tech in 1996. As he achieved increasing success, Bing became active in civic affairs, especially in the training of minority workers and entrepreneurs. His empire faced a setback in 1999 when arsonists caused millions of dollars of damage in fires at two of his facilities. Bing promised to forge on.

➤ **Tom Monaghan:** After 38 years of hustling pizzas, Tom Monaghan, one of the nation's most successful entrepreneurs, sold his Domino's Pizza chain in 1998 for $1.1 billion and retired to devote virtually all his time and money to Catholic education. "I plan to die broke," he said then, when he was 61. Monaghan grew up in an orphanage and founded Domino's with brother Jim in 1960 in Ypsilanti. By the 1980s, Monaghan had become so well-known that many Michiganders knew his three favorite people were Jesus, Mary and Frank Lloyd Wright. He had amassed such trappings of wealth as Wright homes, the Detroit Tigers baseball team, a helicopter, vintage automobiles, a buffalo herd at his Ann Arbor headquarters, a resort on Drummond Island in Lake Huron and $42 black socks made in Scotland of cashmere fibers. In 1992, Monaghan sold the Tigers to Mike Ilitch, chairman of rival Little Caesars, and forswore ostentation, promising to rededicate himself to the company. The results were phenomenal: Domino's revenue and profit growth rebounded from a long slump. After selling the nation's No. 2 pizza-maker, Monaghan made good on his vow to refocus on his religion. Among other things, he founded Ave Maria University, which in 2000 joined 115-year-old St. Mary's College in Orchard Lake.

➤ **Mike Ilitch:** With wife Marian, Mike Ilitch built Little Caesars into the nation's No. 3 pizza firm and became one of Detroit's most important sports and entertainment impresarios. Ilitch grew up around Fenkell and Livernois, was a jock at Cooley High School, and did stints in the U.S. Marines and the Detroit Tigers minor leagues. A top-selling door-to-door awning peddler known as the Hammer for his ability to nail a deal, he and Marian opened their first pizza joint in Garden City in 1959. Over the years, Ilitch, who turned 71 in 2000, bought the Red Wings, took over management of city-owned Joe Louis and Cobo arenas plus the concessions for Detroit's aquarium and two zoos, financed much of the renovation of the Fox Theatre and moved his corporate headquarters there. He also purchased the Tigers and, with some financial help from the public, built Comerica Park. In 2000, when Mike was 70 and Little Caesars was caught in a slump, Mike and Marian Ilitch handed the reins of the empire to daughter Denise and son Christopher, though the parents promised to stay involved.

➤ **Don Barden:** He's one of the most successful black businessmen in the United States. Born in 1943, Barden grew up a natural entrepreneur in Inkster in a family of 13 children. About age 9, he built a vegetable stand out of wood, stocked it from the garden and summoned passing cars. Later, Barden wired Detroit for cable, cashed out and made millions. He owns a riverboat casino in Indiana, though Mayor Dennis Archer said his proposal to run a Detroit casino failed to "measure up" to the three winning plans, a rejection that touched off months of controversy. Barden owns a real estate development company and, since 1996, an automobile manufacturing and conversion plant in Namibia, Africa. He also has negotiated to buy the Michigan Chronicle. In his spare time he is a Democratic Party bankroller.

Casinos by the numbers

Big-time, legal gambling came to Detroit on July 29, 1999, after an effort that lasted more than two decades. Detroit is the largest city in the United States with land-based casino gambling.

➤ **1970s:** Mayor Coleman Young suggests legalized gambling as a way to bring jobs and tax revenue.

➤ **1976, 1981, 1988 and 1993:** Detroiters vote down casino proposals.

➤ **1994:** Casino opens in Windsor, drawing 80 percent of its gamblers from the United States.

➤ **1994:** Detroit voters back plans for two

GABRIEL B. TAIT/Detroit Free Press
A blackjack deal at the MGM Grand Casino in Detroit.

casinos. Mayor Dennis Archer, who had been anti-casino, switches sides.

➤ **1995:** Gov. John Engler vetoes casinos for Detroit, saying voters statewide need to decide.

➤ **1996:** Voters statewide approve three casinos for Detroit.

➤ **1997:** Archer chooses three operators: the original Greektown partners, the original Atwater group, which was pursuing a riverboat casino, and Las Vegas-based MGM Grand, which has local partners.

➤ **1999:** MGM Grand Detroit opens a $212-million temporary casino in the remodeled former IRS office building off the Lodge Freeway. Current owners are MGM Grand of Las Vegas, which owns 97 percent of the shares, and seven local minority members who make up Partners Detroit: Joe Davis, the estate of the

JOHN COLLIER/Detroit Free Press
Fairlane Town Center.

CASINO TOTALS, 2000
Total revenues
(millions)

MGM Grand	$396.8
Motor City	$315.7
Greektown	$30.6
(opened Nov. 10)	
Total	**$743**

Tax revenues
(millions)

Detroit	$73.6
Michigan	$60.2

late radio personality Martha Jean Steinberg, Jane Garcia, Arthur Johnson, Ed Littlejohn, Dr. Lorna Thomas and Myzell Sowell. The partners will split a guaranteed minimum of $4 million.

➤ **1999:** On Dec. 14, the $160-million MotorCity Casino, another temporary facility, opens in the neighboring Wonder Bread factory and Continental Bakery buildings at the Lodge Freeway and Grand River. The principal owner is Mandalay Resort Group of Las Vegas, formerly Circus Circus, which owns 53.5 percent. Marian Ilitch and Tom Celani own 35 percent and Atwater Entertainment, a group of several dozen local minority investors, owns the other 11.5 percent. Two of Atwater's founding partners, Herb Strather and Nellie Varner, sold their shares because of

problems in their background investigations.

➤ **2000:** The Greektown Casino opened Nov. 10. The Sault Ste. Marie Tribe of Chippewa Indians, originally 50-percent partners, negotiated a deal to buy 90 percent of the estimated $200-million casino after longtime partners Ted and Maria Gatzaros and Jim and Viola Papas dropped out after state investigators found problems in their backgrounds. The remaining 10 percent is owned by local minority investors Victoria Suane Loomis, Arthur Blackwell, Christopher Jackson, the Rev. Robert Smith Jr., Marvin Beatty, Dr. Anthony Harris, David Akins and Dr. Hills Howard Jr. The tribe is expected to sell 10 percent to Detroit residents two years after the casino opens.

Malling

Ah, yes, where would we be without our malls? Probably traipsing through Hudson's downtown, eh? Here's a look at our malls:

➤ **Northland**
Location: Northwestern Highway between 8 Mile and 9 Mile, Southfield. Opened in 1954.
Owner: Equitable Life Assurance Society of the United States.
Stores: 136.

➤ **Eastland**
Location: Vernier near Kelly, Harper Woods. Opened in 1957.
Owner: Equitable Life Assurance Society of the United States.
Stores: 120.

➤ **Wonderland**
Location: 29859 Plymouth Road, Livonia. Opened in 1959.
Owner: Schostak Bros. & Co. Inc.
Stores: 100.

➤ **Summit Place**
Location: 319 Telegraph, Waterford Township. Opened in 1962.
Owner: Ramco-Gershenson Inc.
Stores: 160.

➤ **Macomb**
Location: Gratiot at Masonic, Roseville. Opened in 1964.
Owners: Schostak Bros. & Co. Inc.
Stores: 100.

➤ **Universal**
Location: 28582 Dequindre, Warren. Open: 1964.
Owner: Schostak Bros. & Co. Inc.
Stores: 100.

➤ **Livonia**
Location: 29514 Seven Mile, Livonia. Opened in 1964.
Owner: Jack Shenkman.
Stores: 86.

➤ **Westland**
Location: 35000 Warren Road, Westland. Opened in 1965.
Owner: Equitable Life Assurance Society of the United States.
Stores: 86.

➤ **Tel-Twelve**
Location: 28690 Telegraph, Southfield. Opened in 1968.
Owners: Ramco-Gershenson Inc.
Stores: 71.

➤ **Oakland**
Location: 14 Mile at John R, Troy. Opened in 1968.
Owners: Oakland Mall Ltd.
Stores: 140.

➤ **Somerset Collection**
Location: 2800 W. Big Beaver, Troy. South opened in 1969, north in 1996.
Owner: Forbes-Cohen Properties.
Stores: 173.

➤ **Southland**
Location: 23000 Eureka Road, Taylor. Opened in 1970.
Owner: Southland Center Joint Venture.
Stores: 100.

➤ **Briarwood**
Location: 100 Briarwood Circle, Ann Arbor. Opened in 1973.
Owners: Taubman Centers.
Stores: 150.

➤ **Fairlane Town Center**
Location: Michigan Avenue at Southfield, Dearborn. Opened in 1976.
Owners: Taubman Centers.
Stores: 172.

➤ **Lakeside**
Location: 14000 Lakeside Circle, Sterling Heights. Opened in 1976.
Owner: Taubman Centers.
Stores: 180.

➤ **Twelve Oaks**
Location: 27500 Novi Road, Novi. Opened in 1977.
Owner: Taubman Centers.
Stores: 190.

➤ **Horizon Outlet Center**
Location: 14500 LaPlaisance Road, Monroe. Opened in 1987.
Owner: Horizon Group.
Stores: 35.

➤ **Laurel Park Place**
Location: 37700 W. Six Mile, Livonia. Opened in 1989.
Owner: Newburgh/6 Mile Ltd. Partnership.
Stores: 72.

➤ **Birchwood**
Location: 4350 Twenty-fourth Ave., Ft. Gratiot. Opened in 1990.
Owner: General Growth Properties Inc.
Stores: 100.

➤ **Kensington Valley Factory Shops**
Location: 1475 N. Burkhart, Howell. Opened in 1996.
Owners: Fru-Con Development Corp. and Howard & Rice.
Stores: 90.

➤ **Great Lakes Crossing**
Location: 4000 Baldwin Road, Auburn Hills. Opened in 1998.
Owner: Taubman Centers.
Stores: 200.

ROWS TO HOE

In 1900, there were 203,000 farms in the United States. By the end of the century, the number was about 52,000 nationwide.

You might think there are fewer farmers around metro Detroit because farmland has morphed into subdivisions and shopping malls. You'd be right.

But Oakland and Wayne county farmers are defying national trends by running "micro farms," or "ranchettes" that specialize in niche markets.

THE FARM COUNT
Oakland County
1992 503
1997 544
Change .... Up 8%

Wayne County
1992 303
1997 303
Unchanged.

Washtenaw County
1992 1,057
1997 1,030
Change .... Down 3%

Macomb County
1992 558
1997 523
Change .... Down 6%

Livingston County
1992 683
1997 637
Change .... Down 7%

Monroe County
1992 1,135
1997 1,058
Change .... Down 7%

SOURCE: MICHIGAN DEPARTMENT OF AGRICULTURE.

WORK

Elijah McCoy

The late Alex Manoogian, left, in 1990 with his washerless faucet. Jerome Horwitz, right, in his lab at the Michigan Cancer Foundation in Detroit in 1989.

Inventive Detroit

A major reason Detroit became the Motor City: inventive minds. The region was loaded with people who tinkered with small engines or wondered "what if . . . "

That's been true for generations as people brought forth such inventions as refrigerated boxcars and one-armed faucets from workbenches in garages, kitchen labs, small shops and college classrooms.

A few of Detroit's inventions and inventors:

THE REAL MCCOY: Elijah McCoy (1843-1923) invented the first practical automatic lubricating cup for steam engines. During his career, he had more than 80 inventions and registered 57 patents. There were many automatic lubrication systems for trains, but McCoy's was considered the best. Thus, railroad engineers made a point of asking for "the real McCoy."

McCoy grew up in Ypsilanti, the son of escaped slaves. He studied mechanical engineering in Scotland, then returned to Ypsilanti in 1870 where he opened a machine shop.

FAUCET BY MANOOGIAN: In 1952, a California man asked Alex Manoogian's Masco Corp. to make some parts for a novel, single-handled faucet. The parts were sent, but months later, the engineer told Manoogian the faucet did not work. Manoogian acquired rights to the design and spent 1½ years perfecting it. The finished product led to the start of Masco's boom. The company has sold hundreds of millions of the devices.

The son of a grain merchant from Smyrna (now Izmir), Turkey, Manoogian (1901-1996) came to the United States in 1920 with two suitcases and $50. In 1924, Manoogian arrived in Detroit to get a job as a machinist in a screw factory. In late 1928, Manoogian and two partners took the first initials of their last names and $5,000 and set up Masco Screw Products in a loft near Greektown. Manoogian became a well-known philanthropist and donated his riverfront mansion to the city as the mayor's residence.

OVONICS BY OVSHINSKYS: Stan Ovshinsky is a self-educated physicist. Iris Ovshinsky earned a doctorate in biochemistry at Boston University. They formed Energy Conversion Devices on McNichols and Schaefer in 1960. Over the years, the company has obtained more than 150 patents for devices from batteries to digital switches. One of their most publicized inventions is a battery for powering pollution-free electric cars. The Ovonic battery will fuel a car for up to 250 miles on one charge, and recharge in 15 minutes on less than $3 worth of electricity. It'll last for the life of the car, and the chemicals inside will be as harmless as rainwater.

The Ovshinskys, now based in Troy, have won international renown for their work using amorphous materials, rather than silicon, in making electronic components. Companies around the world use their materials for video displays, copiers, solar power cells and computer memories.

TAKING ON HIV: Jerome Horwitz's main love has been "tinkering with molecules," a colleague once said of the Wayne State professor emeritus. Horwitz is a chemist who developed AZT, a drug proven effective in fighting HIV, the virus that leads to AIDS.

Horwitz never filed for a patent, so he has not reaped the financial windfall from AZT. At 81 in 2000, Horwitz continues to work. He designed AZT in 1964 as a cancer-fighting drug. It proved ineffective in trials on animals and was shelved in the early 1970s. In the 1980s, the drug company Glaxco Wellcome tested AZT on the AIDS virus and found that it delayed the development of HIV. That firm patented AZT.

Horwitz graduated from Central High School and holds degrees from the University of Detroit, the University of Michigan and Northwestern University.

A WILDER IDEA: Born in Attica, N.Y., in 1809, A.A. Wilder moved to Detroit in 1840. His inventions include an improved planing mill for processing wood, a ventilation pipe for stoves, a steamship propeller, a washing machine, an improved horseshoe, a process for tanning animal hides and a "dummy streetcar" that propelled the cars without scaring horses.

REFRIGERATED RAILROAD CAR: J.B. Sutherland of Detroit received a patent on an insulated car lined with ice bunkers on Nov. 26, 1867. Air entered through the top and was circulated through the ice chambers and dispersed through the car by gravity. William Davis, who owned a small Detroit fish store, received a patent for a refrigerated car in 1868 but failed to obtain financing until George Hammond, a successful Detroit meat packer, bought the patent and by 1886 had a fleet of more than 800 cars. Hammond, Ind., is named for him.

REFRIGERATORS: The fridge was invented in Detroit in 1914. Three men founded what became the Kelvinator Co. in a building on East Jefferson near Chene. Edmund Copeland, Nathaniel Wales and Arnold Goss named their company after Lord Kelvin, the British inventor who first worked with refrigeration. Until the late 1960s, Kelvinator made refrigerators in a plant on Plymouth Road.

Frigidaire also was born in Detroit in 1914, as the Guardian Frigerator Co. General Motors Corp. purchased it in 1919 and moved it to Dayton, Ohio.

THE SIPPY CUP: Edward Olsen, who worked in tool and die shops in Detroit for 25 years, invented the spill-proof container when his infant son had trouble learning how to drink from a cup. A baby must put a wedge-shaped spout in his mouth and tip the cup to get the liquid. His Toddler Tumbler was a huge hit in the early 1950s and remains a staple today.

HARVARD MADE: Claude Harvard (1911-1999) was accepted in 1926 to the Henry Ford Trade School, where the principal told him blacks seldom graduated because of a school rule against fighting.

"Anybody who got in a fight was kicked out. He figured that since I was black there was no way I was going to make it through without getting in a fight with the white kids," Harvard recalled in 1982.

There were no fights. Harvard graduated in 1932 near the top of the class. He was hired by Ford Motor Co. and in response to complaints about engine noise he invented a machine to find and reject faulty piston pins.

Ford sent him to the 1934 World's Fair in Chicago to exhibit his device. Ford went on to patent 29 of Harvard's inventions.

In 1937, Harvard appeared in a full-page Ford ad in Popular Science Monthly and on a calendar of "Celebrated Negro Inventors." Henry Ford sent Harvard to exhibit his invention at Tuskegee Institute, where he became friends with botanist and educator George Washington Carver and acted as a liaison between Carver and Ford. Harvard helped found the Machinist Training Institute at Focus: HOPE.

GELATIN CAPSULES: Detroit led the nation in developing medicinal capsules. Pharmacist F.A. Hubel, working with Parke, Davis & Co., created an early version of a machine-made gelatin capsule in 1874. In the 1930s, Detroit inventor Robert Scherer perfected a machine that fills the capsules during manufacturing.

BOATLOAD: Gar Wood (1880-1971) was a world-famous boat racer and a world-class inventor who lived in Detroit for decades. His hydraulic boat hoist made him a fortune. In 1917, he shocked the boat racing world by installing an airplane engine in a boat, changing the sport forever. Wood also produced ultra-strong boat hulls, and his design for a boat with a V-shaped bottom was adopted by the Navy for its World War II PT fleet.

BALL-O-MATIC MACHINE: George Gazan (1918-1999), an electrical engineer, invented the machine that sizes and finishes internal diameters of parts. A native Detroiter, Gazan also invented a license plate holder and a plastic credit-card case.

MEASURING ATOMIC HEFT: Willard Benett received a PhD from the University of Michigan in 1928 and became a pioneer in plasma physics — the study of gases ionized by high-voltage electricity. He developed the radio fre-

Patents

An inventor is issued a patent from the federal government that gives the inventor exclusive rights for a set number of years to make, use or sell the invention.

PATENTS BY METRO AREAS, 1990-98

Los Angeles	25,963
Boston	22,612
Chicago	21,356
San Jose, Calif.	19,022
Detroit/Ann Arbor	16,729
Minneapolis/St.Paul	13,027
Philadelphia	12,644
Rochester, N.Y.	11,761
New York	11,041
Houston	10,553

PATENTS BY COUNTY ISSUED TO INDIVIDUALS AND ORGANIZATIONS, 1998

Oakland	958
Wayne	568
Washtenaw	289
Macomb	274
Livingston	75
Monroe	47
St. Clair	35

PATENTS BY UNIVERSITIES, 1969-1997

University of Michigan	305
Michigan State	208
Wayne State	120
Eastern Michigan	5

PATENTS BY METRO DETROIT FIRMS, 1994-98

Individuals	1,555
Ford Motor Co.	1,103
Chrysler Corp.	545
General Motors	523
Ford Global Technologies	282
TRW Vehicle Safety Systems	220
BASF Corp.	215
Eaton Corp.	124
United Technologies	93

SOURCE: U.S. PATENT AND TRADEMARK OFFICE AT **WWW.USPTO.GOV.**

quency mass spectrometer in 1950, which was carried into space to measure the masses of atoms. He held 67 patents.

THE PILL: Carl Djerassi, a professor at Wayne State University from 1952 to 1959, helped develop oral contraceptives through his breakthroughs in chemistry.

STARTING YOUR ENGINE: Charles Kettering's auto-related inventions included the electrical ignition, the self-starter and a practical engine-driven generator. The longtime Detroiter held 140 patents. In 1909, with Edward Deeds, he established the Dayton Engineering Laboratories Co., or Delco, where he made many of his inventions. He sold his firm to General Motors Corp. in 1916, and worked for GM for 31 years as a director of research. Among his lab's inventions: a lightweight diesel engine that made the diesel locomotive possible, the refrigerant Freon, four-wheel brakes and safety glass. Kettering died in 1958 at age 82.

Charles Kettering in his workshop.

WORK

Free Press file photo

BLAST-OFF: Detroit-born inventor John Parsons (b. 1914) started as a tool-room apprentice, but by 1947, at age 34, he had mated a milling machine to a punch-card system conceived by Frank Stulen to solve design engineering problems. Parsons' invention gives numerical commands to machine tools, enabling them to repeatedly produce the same part with a precision far beyond the capabilities of a human operator.

Parsons also pioneered adhesive bonding in metal aircraft, and he helped to revolutionize the technology of ship propellers. He produced the massive fuel lines needed for the Saturn booster, brought computers to aircraft design and helped to improve the production of auto body dies.

SHEAROGRAPHY: Michael Hung of Rochester Hills, a professor of engineering at Oakland University, invented in the 1980s a technique to sense defects in aircraft tires using laser optics.

The rubber industry also uses shearography for evaluating tire quality.

WINDLESS CHIMES: Edd and Sandi Tury of Brighton in the late 1980s created Sunchimes — soothing wind chime music without the

wind. When sunlight or artificial light strikes the solar cell in the Sunchimes, they ring with the randomness of wind chimes. Then the Turys came up with a companion invention, the "Candle in the Wind ...Oh!" The decorative, electronic candle seems to flicker in a gentle breeze, with no messy wax to clean up.

POTTY TRAINER: Detroiter Laurita Bledsoe invented a potty training chair that talks to children, encouraging them to wipe themselves and put down the toilet seat.

ROAST SAVER: Detroiter Nellie Moncrief (b. 1937) devised a collapsible wire frame in 1986 to lift turkey and other roasted meat out of the oven.

SMASHMASTER: Homer H. Smith (1900-1989) worked several jobs around Detroit before his first patent in 1951 for a bottle breaker, used to dispose of bottles. He also invented a can crusher and, in 1958, an orthopedic pillow. He held 13 patents. In the mid-1950s, he owned three hotels: George Washington Carver, George Washington and Booker T. Washington, all near Canfield on Detroit's east side. He also owned a barbershop, gas station, restaurants and a factory used to make his inventions.

AUTOMATIC COFFEE: Detroit jeweler George Schuler invented the first automatic coffee maker in the 1850s.

SOURCES: FREE PRESS, DETROIT PUBLIC LIBRARY, NATIONAL INVENTORS HALL OF FAME AT **WWW.INVENT.ORG.**

Space aces

They had the right stuff and Michigan connections close to home

J.M. (Jerry) Linenger, M.D., born Jan. 16, 1955, reared in Eastpointe. He graduated from East Detroit High School in 1973 and the U.S. Naval Academy in 1977. He received his medical degree from Wayne State University in 1981, a master's in systems management from the University of Southern California in 1988, and a master's in health policy and a doctorate in epidemiology from the University of North Carolina, both in 1989.

Linenger's first mission took place Sept. 9-20, 1994, on shuttle Discovery, where he served as a mission specialist. He logged 10 days, 22 hours and 51 minutes during 177 orbits, or more than 4.5 million miles.

His second mission was aboard the Russian station, Mir. He was chief scientist on the mission, which began Jan. 12, 1997, when shuttle Atlantis blasted off to link with Mir. Linenger was on Mir with two cosmonauts until he

NASA

Jerry Linenger of Eastpointe works on an Earth-based treadmill preparing for a 1994 shuttle mission.

returned to Atlantis May 24, 1997. While on the station, the crew faced a fire, the failures of numerous systems — including urine collection and communications — a near collision with a resupply ship, loss of electrical power and loss of altitude control that resulted in a slow, uncontrolled tumble through space. But Linenger still conducted all of the science experiments, including a five-hour space walk. He logged 132 days, 4 hours and 1 minute, made more than 2,000 orbits and traveled about 50 million miles, averaging 18,000 m.p.h. Afterward, he talked of seeing I-75 from space, and peering through a 250mm camera to see Gratiot and Woodward.

Michigan raised

Jack Lousma, colonel, retired from the U.S. Marine Corps., born Feb. 29, 1936, in Grand Rapids. Lousma received an undergraduate degree in aeronautical engineering from the University of Michigan. He flew on Skylab 3 and the third space shuttle mission, logging more than 1,619 hours of space time. A Republican, he lost a U.S. Senate bid in 1984 to Democrat Carl Levin.

James McDivitt, brigadier general, retired from the U.S. Air Force, born June 10, 1929, in Chicago. McDivitt grew up in Jackson, and received a degree in aeronautical engineering from the University of Michigan. He flew on Gemini 4 and Apollo 9, and served as the Apollo spacecraft program manager.

Alfred Worden, colonel, retired from the U.S. Air Force, born Feb. 7, 1932, in Jackson. Worden graduated from the U.S. Military Academy and received a master's degree in astronautical and aeronautical engineering and instrumentation engineering from the University of Michigan.

He flew on Apollo 15 but stayed in lunar orbit while David Scott and James Irwin visited the surface.

The U-M connection

Theodore Freeman, captain, U.S. Air Force, born Feb. 18, 1930, in Haverford, Pa. After graduating from the U.S. Naval Academy, Freeman received his master's degree in aeronautical engineering from the University of Michigan. He died Oct. 31, 1964, at Ellington Air Force Base in Texas, in the crash of a T38 jet.

Karl Henize, civilian, born Oct. 17, 1926, in Cincinnati. After receiving undergraduate degrees in mathematics and astronomy at the University of Virginia, Henize obtained his PhD in astronomy from the University of Michigan. He spent more than 190 hours in space. He died Oct. 5, 1993, of respiratory and heart failure during a climb of Mt. Everest.

James B. Irwin, colonel, U.S. Air Force, born March 17, 1930, in Pittsburgh. Irwin, who landed on the moon during the Apollo 15 mission, received a master's degree in aeronautical engineering and instrumentation engineering from the University of Michigan. He died Aug. 8, 1991, of a heart attack.

James B. Irwin

Edward White II, lieutenant colonel, U.S. Air Force, born Nov. 14, 1930, in San Antonio. After graduating from the U.S. Military Academy, White received a master's degree in aeronautical engineering from the University of Michigan. He flew on Gemini 4 and died Jan. 27, 1967, in the Apollo spacecraft fire at the John F. Kennedy Space Center.

University of Michigan graduate Edward White walks in space during a Gemini IV mission in 1965.

NASA

The Detroit Almanac

07.W

Detroiters are "the most prosperous slice of average humanity that now exists or ever has existed."

— **New York Times**, *April 1927*

ALTH

On June 19, 1961, Henry's daughter Anne celebrated her debut. Henry Ford II, left, Anne, Henry's first wife Anne, daughter Charlotte and son Edsel.

The Edsel Ford family at its Grosse Pointe Shores mansion in 1937. Edsel was the only child of Henry and Clara Ford. Edsel, left, wife Eleanor, Henry II, Benson, Josephine and William Clay.

TONY SPINA/Detroit Free Press; Free Press file photo

The Bucks Stopped Here

By 1863, Detroit had become a fairly prosperous town with a diverse economy and a healthy number of rich folk. Lumber, real estate, railroads and sales were the routes to riches 15 decades ago. Here's a look at who had the wealth (you might note many names later became familiar streets):

Joseph Campau, about 1850

Wealthiest Detroiters, 1863

Name	Occupation	Property Valuation/1863	Income (if available)
Joseph Campau	landowner	$3.4 million	N/A
Lewis Cass	landowner/ politician	$1.2 million	$22,700
E.B. Ward	shipping/ transportation magnate	$1 million	$91,037
William Woodridge	landowner	$599,916	N/A
Albert Crane	landowner	$474,704	N/A
Charles Merrill	lumber merchant	$409,923	$11,026
Zachariah Chandler	merchant/politician	$433,288	$56,236
E.A. Brush	landowner	$392,646	N/A
William Hale	landowner	$354,228	N/A
James Joy	railroad magnate	$365,584	$19,918

SOURCE: POLITICAL AFFILIATIONS OF AMERICAN ECONOMIC ELITES, A. U. MCCOY, UNPUBLISHED PHD DISSERTATION, WAYNE STATE UNIVERSITY, 1965

By the early 20th Century, the millionaire list had grown, reflecting a vibrant city coming out of a depression in the 1890s ready to finance a new industry: motor vehicles. Here are the monied of a century ago:

Wealthiest Detroiters, 1902

R.A. Alger .... Lumber, manufacturing, railroads, banking, politics.
Luther Beecher .... Railroads, mines, real estate.
E. Alfred Brush .... Inheritance from land-baron father.
Clothilde Book .... Inheritance from father, Francis Palms; minerals and lumber.
C.C. Bowen .... D.M. Ferry & Co., the seed company.
Christian Buhl .... Hardware, tinware, iron; president of Detroit National Bank.
William Butler .... President, Mechanics' Bank; real estate.
Theodore Eaton .... Wholesale drugs, chemicals.
D.M. Ferry .... Seeds, banking, real estate.
F.J. Hecker .... Railroad car building.

PETE AND MIKE: That would be Karmanos, above, and Ilitch, below. Both have lots of money. Both own NHL teams. Both are the sons of immigrants. Both grew up in Detroit and were big fans of the Tigers and Red Wings. Both became world-class entrepreneurs. Both have undergone heart bypass surgery. A decade after Ilitch moved his Little Caesars headquarters from Oakland County to downtown, Karmanos is preparing to do the same with his Compuware Corp.

Monaghan says, "I plan to die broke" by donating his fortune to charities.

George Hendrie	City trolleys, banking.
Peter Henkel	Wholesale liquor, groceries.
Bela Hubbard	Real estate.
James Joy	Railroads, politics.
Edward Kanter	President, German American Bank; real estate.
G.V.N. Lothrop	Lawyer, real estate.
Hugh McMillan	President, Commercial National Bank; railroads and manufacturing. (Brother of James.)
James McMillan	Railroads, railroad car building, manufacturing.
William Moran	Partially inherited; real estate.
W.K. Muir	City trolleys, real estate.
S.J. Murphy	Lumber, saw mills.
T.W. Palmer	Lumber, real estate, banking, politics.
Lizzie Merrill Palmer	Inheritance from father, Charles Merrill, a lumber merchant. (Wife of T.W. Palmer.)
Francis Palms	Inheritance from father who made his fortune in land, banking, railroads and manufacturing.
Traugott Schmidt	Tanning, leather, furs.
Daniel Scotten	Tobacco manufacturing.
Allan Sheldon	Wholesale dry goods.
Alanson Sheley	Wholesale drugs, paints, real estate, banking.
M.S. Smith	Jewelry, lumber.
William Stevens	President, Third National Bank; stock farming.
E.W. Voight	Brewing, real estate.
Hiram Walker	Distilling.
David Ward	Lumber, minerals.
David Whitney	Lumber, shipping, real estate, banking.
W.C. Yawkey	Lumber.

SOURCE: SIDNEY RATNER, ED., "NEW LIGHT ON THE HISTORY OF GREAT AMERICAN FORTUNES," FREE PRESS.

So who are the high rollers entering the 21st Century? The estimated worths are from Forbes Magazine:

Wealthiest Detroiters, 2000

Name	Residence	Occupation	Value
Terence Adderly	Bloomfield Hills	Son of the late William Russell Kelly, founder of Kelly Services. Adderly is Kelly's president and CEO.	$570 million
Max Fisher	Franklin	Built a fortune in oil.	$700 million
Thomas Monaghan	Ann Arbor	Founder of Domino's Pizza, which he sold in 1998 for $1 billion.	$1 billion
Peter Karmanos	Orchard Lake	Detroit-born Karmanos started software and services giant Compuware Corp. with two friends in 1973.	$600 million to $1 billion
William Clay Ford	Grosse Pointe Shores	Grandson of Henry Ford. Retired chairman of Ford Motor Co.'s finance committee. His son, William Clay Ford Jr., took over as company chairman in January 1999.	$1.1 billion
Josephine Ford	Grosse Pointe Farms	Granddaughter of Henry Ford.	$760 million
Richard Manoogian	Grosse Pointe Farms	Chairman of Masco Corp.	$570 million
The Ilitches	Oakland County	Mike and Marian Ilitch founded pizza company Little Caesars in 1959. They own the Red Wings, Tigers and Fox Theatre and control city-owned Joe Louis and Cobo arenas. Marian Ilitch owns 17 percent of the MotorCity Casino. $600 million.	
William Davidson	Bloomfield Hills	Owns Guardian Industries, one of the world's top glass makers. Owner of the Detroit Pistons and part owner of the Palace of Auburn Hills.	Nearly $2 billion
Ernest J. Olde		Owns investment company.	$650 million
A. Alfred Taubman	Bloomfield Hills	Shopping mall developer, owns Sotheby's art auction house.	$840 million

Name	Title	Company	Salary	Bonus	Other annual compensation	Long-term compensation	Options exercised
Richard Dauch	chairman/president/CEO	American Axle	$750,000	$1,700,000	0	0	$96,417,891
Peter Karmanos	chairman/CEO	Compuware Corp.	$600,000	$1,600,000	0	0	$85,321,246
Richard Manoogian	chairman/CEO	Masco Corp.	$2	$2,000,000	0	$2,176,000	$26,073,000
Stephen Fagan	senior VP	Compuware Corp.	$330,000	$927,169	0	0	$23,479,044
Joseph Nathan	president/COO	Compuware Corp.	$500,000	$1,333,335	0	0	$21,760,003
John Smith	chairman/CEO	General Motors Corp.	$1,950,000	$4,840,000	$105,330	$5,250,000	$6,041,002
Henry Jallos	executive VP	Compuware Corp.	$350,000	$933,335	0	0	$12,805,182
Jacques Nasser	president/CEO	Ford Motor Co.	$1,500,000	$6,722,000	$1,842,269	$2,893,975	$802,740
J.T. Battenberg	chairman/CEO/president	Delphi Automotive Systems Corp.	$1,208,333	$2,200,000	0	$6,215,000	$2,280,837
William Stavropoulos	president/CEO	Dow Chemical Co.	$986,664	$1,560,000	0	$62,379	$7,842,814
John Shevillo	senior VP	Compuware Corp.	$320,000	$908,735	0	0	$9,344,454
G. Richard Wagoner	president/COO	General Motors Corp.	$1,350,000	$2,597,000	0	$2,250,000	$3,475,746
J. Michael Losh	executive VP	General Motors Corp.	$835,000	$1,593,000	0	$1,800,000	$3,741,982
Alfred Glancy	chairman/CEO	MCN Energy Group Inc.	$675,000	$994,781	0	$2,339,578	0
Robert Rewey	group VP	Ford Motor Co.	$702,500	$1,531,000	$227,588	$1,966,500	$3,116,452
Harry J. Pearce	vice chairman	General Motors Corp.	$1,350,000	$2,597,000	0	$2,250,000	$683,071
W. Wayne Booker	vice chairman	Ford Motor Co.	$763,333	$2,297,000	$405,871	$2,480,550	$735,964
Ronald L. Zarrella	executive VP	General Motors Corp.	$900,000	$1,180,000	$58,897	$1,505,000	$2,429,785
John M. Devine	former VP/CFO	Ford Motor Co.	$600,000	$1,720,000	$685,144	$2,604,750	0
Peter Pestillo	vice chairman	Ford Motor Co.	$763,333	$2,297,000	$225,426	$1,966,500	$155,687

WEALTH

Dossin Great Lakes Museum

A ship in E.B. Ward's fleet steams through the Soo Locks in 1855, soon after the passage opened.

Detroit's first millionaire: E.B Ward

Steel, spiritualism and strong women

Detroit's first millionaire, Eber Brock Ward, might also have been its most colorful. He owed most of the flash, and some of his brilliance, to the women in his life.

Born on Christmas Day 1811, E.B. lost his mother to illness in 1818. The eldest sister, Emily, who was just 10 at the time, took responsibility for raising E.B. and two sisters. Emily soon became known as Aunt Emily and, though she never married, she spent the rest of her life caring for children and, especially, E.B.

E.B. apprenticed in his father and uncle's shipbuilding business at Marine City and soon took the family business far beyond their vision.

Aunt Emily was at his side. While she had a soft heart for children, she was a hardheaded businesswoman. As E.B. built the largest fleet on the Great Lakes, she supervised the furnishing of cabins, saving as much as $5,000 on the larger vessels. The savings became her share, and she became E.B.'s trusted business adviser. When he suffered a reversal of fortunes, she bailed him out with the money she had earned. Capt. E.B. Ward, seeing as many opportunities on land as he did on water, began stretching, sometimes straining against Aunt Emily's better judgment.

He once remarked, "It was against Emily's advice I went into that land speculation. I wish I had not put my money into it. I have lost $20,000."

SUITS WIN: Executives made 419 times more than factory workers in 1998, compared with 42 times more in 1980, according to the private Institute for Policy Studies.

LOSING IT ALL: George Davis, a founder of Parke-Davis, had a thing for Napoleon. As his company prospered in the late 19th Century, Davis purchased rare Napoleonic relics, a lavish home on East Jefferson in Detroit, a farm in Macomb County and a yacht. He owned the autograph of every president from Washington to Cleveland. But after the Depression of 1893, when his California real estate investments tanked, Davis lost it all. By 1896, he was forced to sell his stock in the company to pay off his debts.

NUGGETS

300 years of history breeds lots of wealth, some of it by luck, much of it by skill, all of it bankable.

Metro Detroit median family income (in 1997 dollars):

	Detroit	suburbs
1950	$25,125	$25,795
1990	$24,262	$52,201
	blacks	**whites**
1950	$19,095	$26,456
1990	$26,456	$54,180

The poor: In 1950, the poverty rate was slightly higher in the suburbs than in Detroit. Median family incomes were about identical. Since 1950, the poverty rate for Detroit has doubled, while the rate for the suburbs has been cut in half.

During the past 50 years, whites in metro Detroit have fared much better than blacks in all economic indicators. One example: In 1950, the poverty rate for metro Detroit blacks was 35 percent. In 1990, it was 33 percent. In 1950, the poverty rate for whites was 16 percent. In 1990, it was 8 percent.

Working while black: Surveys and censuses since 1970 show that no more than about 65 percent of adult black men were employed at any one time. In the late 1990s, only two-thirds of Detroit's black men ages 25 to 64 were employed.

Black elite: Despite the persistence of poverty, a black economic elite developed in Detroit in the last half of the 20th Century. In 1990, about 12 percent of blacks

However, the Wards had always been risk-takers. When the Erie Canal opened the interior to New England, Sam was the first to sail eastward with a cargo of goods to sell. E.B. was first to put a ship on Lake Superior, having it hauled to the shore on rollers. When the locks to Lake Superior opened, another of his vessels was the first to lock through. He was an innovator of marine engineering, too, using some of the first iron mined in Michigan's Upper Peninsula in one of his boats, and putting the first steel-hulled vessel on the Great Lakes.

When railroads began to overtake Great Lakes shipping, many vessel owners went under. E.B. adapted. He built an iron works downriver that produced the first Bessemer steel made in the United States. At strategically important Chicago, E.B.'s rolling mills made the first railroad tracks produced in the United States. At Milwaukee, at Ludington, in the Upper Peninsula and all around the lakes, he had his hands in iron, copper and silver mining, lumber, steel, glass, banking, newspapers and politics. Aunt Emily remained his confidante in business and managed his Detroit mansion.

His prominent standing — and 1860s sensibilities — made his divorce from Polly, mother of his eight children, and remarriage within months to a young blonde, a tongue-wagging sensation.

By the time E.B. threw up his arms in an apoplectic fit and dropped dead on Griswold at 10:30 a.m. Saturday, Jan. 2, 1875, he was widely regarded as the richest man in Michigan. His fortune and two sets of children held the seeds for the wildest inheritance trial ever seen in Wayne County Circuit Court.

Spectators filled the courtroom, crowding even into areas in front of the bar. The doors were shut and the windows locked. Reporters noted an unusually large number of women and clerics in the crowd, and no wonder. In addition to the counsel of Aunt Emily, E.B. had communed with clairvoyants.

At the trial, critics attacked his will as demonic and called mystics to testify about their relationship with the millionaire. One spiritualist took the stand, fell into a trance and, her face contorted. identified herself as a

male and began speaking in German. Reporters crowded the witness stand for a closer look and the judge ordered the stenographer to continue taking down testimony, whether it be by human or spirit.

Although E.B.'s second wife, Kate, testified at the trial, she had fled the city soon after E.B.'s death, shivering under the icy regard of Detroit's polite society. She remarried and took her children, Eber Jr. and Clara, to the drawing rooms of Toronto. When her second husband also died, she fled to the salons of Paris, and married again.

E.B.'s youngest, Clara, a glamorous and strong-willed heiress by age 17, thrilled romantics on two continents with her marriage to Prince Joseph de Caraman-Chimay of the royal family of Belgium. Detroit society, which had found E.B.'s divorce so distasteful, now savored the city's association with royalty. Ah, but it was fleeting. Clara then fell in love with Rigo Jancsi, a gypsy violinist, and left the prince for a man considered far beneath her station.

She became known as "the madcap princess," and had only just begun. Clara dumped poor Rigo after falling violently in love with Giuseppe Ricciardi, a railway station master who, by some accounts, superintended the little railroad that ran sightseers up the volcano at Vesuvius. He divorced her after seven years, and she married a man named Cassolota, reported to be Ricciardi's driver, and was living with him when she died in 1916 in Padua, Italy.

One reporter wrote that madcap Clara, daughter of the city's first industrialist, was hot copy until a new industrialist announced the $5 workday in 1914. He was Henry Ford, of course, and it is strictly coincidental that his wife was also named Clara.

Burton Historical Collection

Polarization: The Kerner Commission in the late 1960s warned of impoverished central cities surrounded by affluent, white suburbs. They were wrong about such areas as New York, Washington and Los Angeles, where immigrants have changed central cities and significant numbers of blacks have moved into the suburbs. In Detroit, though, relatively few immigrants have moved into the central city and few blacks have migrated to the suburbs. More than most metropolitan areas, Detroit has become the polarized region the Kerner Commission forecast.

Detroit's Dodges

Auto pioneer Horace Dodge's only son, Horace Jr., a heavy drinker and boating enthusiast, acquired castles (one in France, another in England) and wife after wife. In honor of his engagement to fifth wife Gregg Sherwood, Horace Jr. threw a party in Cannes where he presented his fiancee with a $100,000 diamond while guests munched on 60 pounds of caviar. When he died in 1964, he left $2 million in his estate and $16 million in debt.

Free Press file photo

Mignon Fontaigne on the witness stand as prosecutors confer during an inquest into the death of John Duval Dodge.

THE ULTIMATE DODGE: John Dodge's family life was considerably more complicated than brother Horace. He had six children from two marriages, to Ivy Hawkins, who died in her early 30s, and then to the stern but industrious Matilda. (The secret marriage to his housekeeper produced no children.)

His two sons died young. Daniel Dodge died on his honeymoon in 1938, when he drowned under bizarre circumstances. Injured by an explosion of dynamite, he fell off a boat speeding to take him from an Ontario island to the mainland for help. His wife of 13 days relinquished claims to his estate in exchange for a cash settlement that, according to the Dodge biography, totaled $2.5 million.

The older son, John Duval Dodge, who had been jailed occasionally for various infractions involving alcohol and women, was disinherited by his father, except for a $150-a-month stipend. He spent most of his life seeking to wrest back some of his father's fortune.

A case contesting the will was pending in the Supreme Court when John Duval was arrested in 1942 outside an Indian Village home where his wife, Dora, found him with another woman. The other woman, Mignon Fontaigne, was "an attractive, unemployed interior decorator" who had been staying with neighbors of the Dodges. When John Duval forced his way into her room, Fontaigne told him, "I don't go in for love," she explained to police.

The scandal erupted into public view when Dodge died, under mysterious circumstances, at police headquarters. Police said he suffered a skull fracture when, drunk and argumentative, he fell to the floor. After his death, the Michigan Supreme Court ruled against his latest claim to his father's trust fund.

But John Duval Dodge's lifelong efforts to break his father's will were somewhat vindicated in 1980, when a judge ruled that John Duval's daughter Mary Ann Dodge Danaher, who lives in Grosse Pointe Farms, was entitled to 8.33 percent of her grandfather's trust.

DODGING DUTY? Auto pioneer John F. Dodge's oldest daughter, Winifred Dodge Seyburn, was a Grosse Pointe socialite famous for her Sunday night suppers and for her British butler who made a fortune in the stock market. "We'll have dinner if we can get this rich man to serve us," she would tell guests.

A GOOD DEAL: The Dodge brothers accepted $10,000 in Ford Motor stock as partial payment for work they did for Henry Ford. When Henry Ford bought back the stock about a decade later, in 1919, it brought them an estimated $32 million.

Brothers Horace, left, and John Dodge in 1914 are chauffeured in one of the first Dodges produced that year.

lived in households whose incomes were at least $87,500. In 1950, only 1 percent of families made that much money.

BIG EARNERS
Percentage of metro Detroit earners ages 25 to 64 who reported earnings of more than $60,000 (in 1997 dollars)

	White	Black
1950	2.80	0.00
1970	16.2	2.4
1990	17.6	7.1

Characteristics of those high earners:

	White	Black
Total by number:	220,368	20,473

Professionals by occupation:
24%   20%

Post-B.A. degree holders:
22%   19%

Employed in blue-collar manufacturing jobs:
18%   33%

Employed by government agencies:
6%   17%

Women:
10%   23%

Residents of Detroit:
2%   65%

SOURCE: "DETROIT DIVIDED," BY REYNOLDS FARLEY, SHELDON DANZINGER AND HARRY HOLZER.

Free Press file photo

GREAT PAYOFF: James Couzens, above in 1933, Henry Ford's accountant, borrowed about $2,000 to buy stock in the company. That was 1903. In 1919, Ford bought Couzens' stock, which was then valued at $29 million.

A TIGERS FIRST: Detroit Tigers legend Al Kaline turned down a contract for $100,000 in 1970. He said he didn't deserve it and he thought the Tigers were just rewarding him for longevity. The club convinced him to accept a $100,000 contract in December 1971, making him the first six-figure player in Tigers history. The 2000 season right-fielder, Juan Gonzalez, earned $7.5 million.

DIVVYING UP: Here's what Buffalo Bills owner and Grosse Pointe resident Ralph Wilson got in his 1971 divorce settlement: Some paintings, bedroom furniture, a piano, a portable sauna and a few other items. Here's what his wife, Janet, got: $2 million, a house in Grosse Pointe Shores and two Detroit Lions season tickets. The two married in 1944 when Wilson was a naval officer earning $350 a week. He inherited an insurance and trucking company from his father.

The wealth factor

RISE TO THE TOP: Oakland County's wealth increased much in the last decade, propelling it to No. 4 on a national ranking of 1999 median household income estimates of large U.S. counties. It trails Santa Clara County, Calif., Nassau County, N.Y., and Suffolk County, N.Y. Despite a booming economy, 14,045 households in Oakland — about 3 percent — still receive food stamps.

THE LIST: Counties with more than 1 million people (33 qualified) by median household income:

1. Santa Clara County, Calif.	$73,362
2. Nassau County, N.Y.	$70,505
3. Suffolk County, N.Y.	$65,410
4. Oakland County	**$64,710**
5. Middlesex County, Mass.	$59,945
25. Wayne County	**$35,891**

THE LIST II: The median household income for regional counties with fewer than a million people:

Livingston County	$65,343
Washtenaw County	$57,904
Monroe County	$49,068
Macomb County	$47,723
St. Clair County	$39,067

SOURCE: CLARITAS INC. OF ARLINGTON, VA.

BREAKING THE CODE

Add some zip to your life — move to 48301 and you'll be among neighbors with median household incomes of $110,287 a year. You'll also be in Bloomfield Hills. And you'll need lots of bucks to move in. That ZIP code is the region's top in terms of annual household income. The rest of the zippiest:

48302	$104,524
48304	$104,043
48323	$97,333
48331	$86,187
48306	$84,510
48322	$82,810
48098	$79,752
48025	$79,724
48138	$74,427
48309	$73,148
48324	$70,640
48009	$70,368
48230	$67,472
48084	$67,456
48316	$66,867

Free Press file photo

The $2-million Fisher mansion on Detroit's east side is now owned by the International Society of Krishna Consciousness.

THE FISHER ESTATE: Fisher Brother Lawrence was general manager of GM's Cadillac Division during the 1920s. In 1927, he spent the enormous sum of $2 million to build a home on a canal off Lenox on the city's far east side. The estate had a bowling alley and boat wells for Fisher's 106-foot Margaret IV and a smaller 64-foot boat that became John F. Kennedy's presidential yacht, the Honey-Fitz. But Fisher's love of two cocker spaniels, Lucky and Frisky, became legend. When the pooches died, he had them buried in baby caskets on the miniature golf course in his backyard. The estate is now owned by the International Krishna Consciousness Movement. The huge boat well has been filled and converted into a temple.

DEBUTANTES: "Coming out" had a special meaning in upper-class Detroit for the first six decades of the 20th Century. The daughters of the rich were introduced to society in elaborate debutante balls when they reached their late teens. Two of the grandest parties were thrown by Henry Ford II for his two daughters, Charlotte and Anne. Charlotte, the oldest, made her debut Dec. 21, 1959, before 1,000 guests who swizzled Dom Perignon 1949 and danced at the Country Club of Detroit in Grosse Pointe. The halls were papered with 2 million magnolia leaves.

Daughter Anne, left, debutante Charlotte, son Edsel, Henry and Anne Ford.

TONY SPINA/Detroit Free Press

The Ford Family

They are our Rockefellers, Vanderbilts and Kennedys.

We dote on their doings, follow their travails, keep abreast of their marriages and peek into their lives.

Locally, when it comes to power and wealth, no other clan comes close to the Fords. Starting with patriarch Henry Ford a scant century ago, the Fords have brought jobs through the company, wealth through company stock, art and music through their beneficence, leadership when the region needed it, and plenty of controversy.

KIRTHMON F. DOZIER/Free Press

THE CLUB: That would be the Yondotega. Since 1891, the Yon, as members call it, has survived as perhaps the most exclusive club in metro Detroit. Members are barred from discussing what happens in the modest-looking clubhouse behind the seven-foot walls at 1405 E. Jefferson. The cone of silence has helped to build a certain mystique about the Yon.

The club listed 171 members in the 1998 "Social Secretary of Detroit and Michigan," mostly old-money names — Fords, Fishers, Hudsons, Fruehaufs, Booths, McMillans, a Thurber and a Stroh. Testimony in a 1938 tax case revealed the club, then at 518 E. Jefferson, was mainly for eating, and that drawings of framed poker hands decorated the walls. A game called "pedro" was said to be the club favorite, and members used a deck of cards for only one hand; after that the deck was donated to charity. No women were allowed to join at least until the 1980s; it is unclear if that rule has changed. The name comes from an Algonquin word for village. Teddy Roosevelt, once a guest, pronounced it "the best club in America."

Four Contemporary Fords

William Clay Ford Jr. (b. 1957)

Relationship to Henry: Great-grandson.
Role: Chairman, Ford Motor Co.
Company shares (spring 2000): 3.3 million.
Education: Bachelor's degree, Princeton University; master's degree in management, Massachusetts Institute of Technology.
Career: When he became chairman in January 1999, it was the first time in 18 years that a family member was running the company, since his uncle Henry II.

Ford is a non-executive chairman. He confines himself to leading the board of directors in its support of the management running the business. The automaker's day-to-day operations are run by President and Chief Executive Officer Jacques Nasser.

Ford began his career in the family business in 1979, holding several positions. Named head of commercial vehicle marketing for Europe in 1986, he then became chairman of Ford Switzerland in 1987. He was elected to the board in 1988. Returning to the United States in 1989 as manager of Heavy Truck Engineering and Manufacturing, he subsequently was named head of Automotive Group business strategy in 1990, then executive director of the Business Group in 1991. In 1994, he was elected vice president and head of the Ford Automotive Commercial Truck Vehicle Center. The company made him chairman of the finance committee in 1995.

Personal: Wife, Lisa Bryant Vanderzee; four children. After living in Grosse Pointe like most of his family, bought a home in Ann Arbor in 1999.

Hobbies: Vice chairman of the Detroit Lions; fly-fishing, hockey, tae kwon do.

Clubs: Country Club of Detroit; Dearborn Country Club; Detroit Athletic Club; Detroit Club; Detroit Racquet Club; Detroit Zoological Society; Grosse Pointe Club; Grosse Pointe Hunt Club, Otsego Ski Club and the Yondotega Club.

Edsel Ford (b. 1948)

Relationship to Henry: Great-grandson.
Role: Board member and consultant.
Company shares: 5.6 million.
Education: Bachelor's in business administration, Babson College.
Career: Serves as a $500,000-a-year consultant on company projects, including dealer relations. Ford also serves as chairman of

WEALTH

TONY SPINA/Detroit Free Press

Detroit 300, the organizing committee for Detroit's tricentennial. He began his Ford career in 1974 as a product-planning analyst. He was assistant managing director of Ford of Australia from 1978 to 1980 and ran marketing and advertising in the Ford division starting in 1981. He moved to the Lincoln-Mercury division as general marketing manager in 1985. He became executive director of the corporate marketing staff in 1989 and served as president of Ford Motor Credit Co. from 1991 to 1998. Along with cousin William Clay Ford Jr., he was elected to the Ford Motor Co. board of directors in 1988, shortly after his father, Henry II, died. He was designated a vice president of the overall corporation in 1993, while remaining head of Ford Credit.

Personal: Married to Cynthia Neskow; four children. Lives in Grosse Pointe Farms.

Hobbies: Active in metro Detroit charities, including the Salvation Army, CATCH (Caring Athletes Team for Children's and Henry Ford Hospitals), and Detroit's Center for Creative Studies.

Clubs: Country Club of Detroit; Dearborn Country Club; Detroit Institute of Arts Founders Society; Detroit Zoological Society; Friends of the Public Library; Grosse Pointe Club; Otsego Club; Yondotega Club, and the Hundred Club.

William Clay Ford Sr. (b. 1925)

Relationship to Henry: Grandson.

Role: Owner, Detroit Lions; board member, Ford Motor.

Company shares: 15.1 million.

Education: Bachelor's in economics at Yale.

Career: His career was overshadowed by brother Henry Ford II. William Clay joined Ford after college and worked in sales and advertising. He later served on the industrial relations staff and as executive in charge of design, development and introduction of the Continental Mark II, the successor to the car that his father, Edsel, had developed. Ford resigned as vice chairman in 1989 but remains a member of the board and serves on the finance committee. He purchased the Detroit Lions in November 1963 for $4.5 million.

Personal: Married to Martha Firestone, granddaughter of tire magnate Harvey Firestone; four children. Captained the tennis and soccer teams at Yale. Underwent heart surgery in 1998. Served in the U.S. Naval Air Corps in World War II.

Hobbies: Active in charities including the Michigan Heart Association, Boys Club of America, Eisenhower Medical Center, United Way of Southeastern Michigan, Henry Ford Hospital.

Clubs: Country Club of Detroit; Detroit Athletic Club; Detroit Racquet Club; Friends of the Public Library, Grosse Pointe Club and the Yondotega Club.

Josephine F. Ford (b. 1923)

Relationship to Henry: Granddaughter.

Role: Arts patron.

Company shares: 14.4 million.

Career: She is best-known for donating tens of millions of dollars to the Detroit Institute of Arts and the Center for Creative Studies.

Personal: Lives in Grosse Pointe Farms. Was married to the late Walter Buhl Ford II, an architect who was not part of the automotive Ford family.

Hobbies: Antique collecting and horseback riding.

Controlling interest

A Ford family member likely could always be involved with running the family business. That's because the family holds all 71 million shares of the company's Class B stock, along with a small number of the company's 1.1 billion Class A common shares. Under rules designed to preserve family control and drafted when the company went public in 1956, the family holds 40 percent of the voting power at the company as long as it continues to own at least 60.7 million shares of the Class B stock — even though the Class B shares make up only 6 percent of the company's overall equity.

If the family sells too many shares of its Class B stock, the family's influence shrinks. If the family's holdings fall below 33.7 million shares, then all special voting privileges are lost.

When Class B shares are sold outside the family, they revert to common stock.

The way of the wills

Henry Ford: He willed his voting stock to his daughter-in-law (son Edsel died before him) and four grandchildren. He left his non-voting stock to the Ford Foundation. The federal government valued Ford Motor at $466 million when Ford died in 1947, and his estate was valued at $80 million. His estate included $26.5 million in a personal bank account and $20 "due from the sale of hay" from a Ford farm.

Free Press file photo

Henry Ford and son Edsel with a Model A at the 1928 Ford Industrial Exposition in New York.

Henry Ford II: Hank the Deuce as he was known locally left control of his estimated $250 million estate to his wife, Kathy DuRoss Ford, son Edsel Ford II and a longtime personal friend, Martin Citrin, according to documents filed in a court in Florida, where Ford maintained a residence when he died in 1987.

In the will, which was filed in Palm Beach Probate Court, Ford bequeathed his clothing, jewelry, club memberships, cars and insurance policies to Kathy DuRoss Ford, but left the bulk of his estate in a trust that will be supervised by her, Citrin and Edsel Ford II.

> "I haven't anything to say. Never complain. Never explain."
>
> — **Henry Ford II** in 1975, when asked by a Free Press reporter why he was arrested on suspicion of drunken driving in California with Grosse Pointe model Kathy DuRoss while his then-wife, Cristina, was in Nepal.

By leaving most of his estate in trust, Ford avoided listing his holdings publicly. In 1986, Forbes magazine estimated in its listing of the 400 wealthiest Americans that Ford had $250 million in net worth, but offered little substantiating information.

The assets included houses on Provencal Road in Grosse Pointe Farms, Palm Beach and England, as well as an art collection and a yacht.

SOURCES: FREE PRESS AND "FORD COUNTRY," DAVID LEWIS.

Not only a car guy

Henry Ford didn't limit his influence to crankshafts and Model Ts. Some of Ford's other interests:

Music: In the 1920s, Ford had a number of bands, including a 60-piece concert band that was based at the Highland Park plant.

THE NAME
The Ford Environmental & Conservation Education Center at the Detroit Zoo
Ford Field, Dearborn
Ford Field, Detroit (stadium for the Lions)
Ford Woods Park, Dearborn
The Henry Ford II (out-of-service freighter)
The Benson Ford (out-of-service freighter)
The William Clay Ford (out-of-service freighter)
Ford Community and Performing Arts Center, Dearborn
Walter B. Ford Building, Center for Creative Studies, Detroit

Family Tree

William Ford — m. — Mary Litogot
(1826-1905)   (1839-1876)

FIRST GENERATION

Henry Ford 1863-1947
m. Clara Jane Bryant

SECOND GENERATION

Edsel Bryant Ford 1893-1943
m. Eleanor Clay

THIRD GENERATION

Benson Ford 1919-78
m. Edith McNaughton
who died in 1980

Josephine 1923-
m. Walter Buhl Ford II
who died in 1991

Henry Ford II 1917-87
m.Anne McDonell div.
m. Maria Cristina Austin
div.
m. Kathleen King DuRoss

William Clay Ford 1925-
m. Martha Parke Firestone

FOURTH GENERATION

Charlotte 1941-
m. Stavos Niarchos div.
m. Anthony Forstmann div.
m. Edward Downe Jr. div.

Anne 1943-
m. Giancarlo Uzielli div.
m. Charles Scarborough
div.

Edsel Bryant Ford II
m. Cynthia Layne Neskow

Benson Ford Jr. 1949-
m. Lisa Adams div.
m. Melissa Lynn Flores
div.
m. Francee Beth Simmons

Lynn 1951-
m. Paul Alandt

Walter Buhl Ford III
1943-
m. Barbara Posselius div.
m. Charlene Decraene div.

Eleanor 1946-
m. Frederic Bourke Jr.

Josephine 1949-
m. John Ingle Jr.

Alfred Brush Ford 1950-
m. Sharmilla Bhattacharya

Martha 1948-
m. Peter Morse

Sheila 1951-
m. Steven Hamp

William Clay Ford Jr.
1957-
m. Lisa Vanderzee

Elizabeth 1961-
m. Charles P. Kontulis II

HENRY FORD'S HOMES

Ford's homes on Bagley downtown, at 4420 John R and in the 400 block of Harper have been demolished. Another home, where the Fords lived from 1908 to 1915, remains standing at 140 Edison in the Boston-Edison Historic District. Fair Lane, above, the mansion Ford occupied from 1915 until his death in 1947, is located on the Dearborn campus of the University of Michigan and is open to the public (313-593-5590). His son's residence, the Edsel and Eleanor Ford House at 1100 Lake Shore Road in Grosse Pointe Shores, is also open for tours (313-884-4222).

Many other Ford plants sponsored smaller bands. In Detroit alone, there were the Ford Hawaiian Quintette and the Ford Eagle Builders' Saxophone Band.

Movies: Ford started a film department before World War I. His highly acclaimed film operation produced newsreels and historical and educational films shown in theaters worldwide.

Politics: Ford filed for U.S. senator in both the Republican and Democratic primaries in 1918, lost the Republican, won the Democratic and then lost the general election to Republican Truman Newberry.

Housing: Ford constructed homes for workers worldwide but especially in Dearborn, where the Ford homes he built for executives in the World War I era form a stately historic district, Ford Foundation.

Farming: Ford was a farm boy who never lost interest in agriculture. He eventually purchased 26,000 acres of farmland in southern Michigan; 75,000 acres near Richmond Hill, Ga.; 400,000 acres of timber and mining land in the Upper Peninsula, and 2.5 million acres of tropical forest in Brazil. He also had farms in Florida, New England and Great Britain. In southern Michigan alone, Ford operated dozens of farms and hydroelectric plants. He had a grain elevator and flour mill on Oakwood Boulevard in Dearborn. Ford farms grew dozens of crops, but he always showed a special interest in soybeans.

Tractors: Ford experimented with tractors and produced them all of his life. His auto collaborators objected to his interest in tractors. So Ford founded Henry Ford & Son Inc., and manufactured Fordson tractors through that firm. Production eventually shifted to the Rouge plant and then to factories in England and Ireland. Today, the nickname of Dearborn Fordson High School is the Tractors.

Hydroelectric power: Ford built more than 30 hydroelectric plants, ranging from small mills to huge dams. In southeast Michigan, Ford's best-known water projects were at Northville, Nankin Mills, Saline, Ypsilanti and Dundee. In 1921, Ford unsuccessfully bid on the partially completed Muscle Shoals project on the Tennessee River in Alabama.

Airplanes: Ford did not fly in a plane until Charles Lindbergh took him up in 1927. Ford and his son, Edsel, participated in the design and production of a metal-skinned dirigible, a trimotor airplane, a midget plane called a Flivver, World War II combat gliders and, of course, 8,685 of the B24 Liberator bomber, which Ford produced at the Willow Run plant during World War II. Aviation pioneers who worked with Ford included the Loughead brothers, whose firm eventually became Lockheed, and James McDonnell, who was part of the McDonnell-Douglas Corp.

Free Press file photo

Henry Ford greets Thomas Edison on Edison's 80th birthday in 1927. They were close friends.

Trains: In 1920, Ford purchased controlling interest in the Detroit, Toledo and Ironton (Ohio) Railroad. He also experimented with the gasoline railcar.

Education: Ford founded several trade schools and spent tens of millions of dollars refurbishing schools in the farming communities where he owned property in Michigan and other states. In addition, he made large donations to educational institutions in Georgia, Tennessee and Alabama. And he founded the learning labs known as the Edison Institute at Greenfield Village, which instructed students ages 6 through 20. At the Highland Park plant, Ford opened an English language school for immigrant workers. Ford also had thousands of reprints made of the classic 19th-Century textbook, the McGuffey Reader. During World War II, Ford sponsored the U.S. Navy Service School for machinist mates at the Rouge plant. The Henry Ford Museum & Greenfield Village also were part of Ford's educational spirit.

Boats: Ford's first manufacturing products at the Rouge complex were 60 Eagle submarine chasers for the U.S. Navy in World War I. They were 204-foot vessels that cost $275,000 each. Though few engaged in battle, they saw plenty of peacetime action.

SOURCES: FREE PRESS; "THE PUBLIC LIFE OF HENRY FORD," BY DAVID LEWIS; "BEYOND THE MODEL T," BY FORD R. BRYAN.

"History is more or less bunk. It's tradition. We don't want tradition. We want to live in the present and the only history that is worth a tinker's damn is the history we make today."

— **Henry Ford**, Chicago Tribune, May 25, 1916

Free Press file photo

Edsel Ford waves as he drives the first Army Jeep off a Ford assembly line in February 1941.

ATTACHED: At their 1978 divorce trial, Christina Ford, soon-to-be ex-wife of Henry Ford II, testified that she was emotionally attached to every piece of property owned by the chairman of Ford Motor Co.

THE FORD FOUNDATION

Henry Ford and his son, Edsel Ford, founded the Ford Foundation in 1936. By 1950, as the foundation grew, its assets consisted almost entirely of non-voting Ford Motor Co. stock bequeathed from the estates of Henry and Edsel Ford. But between 1950 and 1974, the foundation diversified and disposed of all of its Ford stock. The foundation no longer owns Ford stock. Today, the only connection between the Ford company and foundation is historic.

Ford and Hitler

Henry Ford was arguably the most powerful anti-Semite in U.S. history. David Lewis, a respected Ford biographer, wrote in 1976 that attacks by Ford's newspaper on Jews "have cost the Ford Co. untold millions of dollars worth of sales, and have been a source of embarrassment to the firm and one of its leading public relations problems for decades."

Ron Rosenbaum, author of the widely praised 1998 book "Explaining Hitler," called Ford "one of the most vile and repulsive figures in American history . . . the spiritual godfather of mass murder."

Ford's nationally circulated paper, the Dearborn Independent, carried out an anti-Jewish campaign in virtually every issue from May 1920 to January 1922, and occasionally afterward, then started the attacks again in 1924. Articles attacked "the International Jew" as a cunning conspirator who started World War I. The Independent resurrected an infamously anti-Semitic tract, "The Protocols of the Elders of Zion," which accused Jews of scheming to dominate the world.

Ford later collected the anti-Jewish attacks in brochures and a book that were translated and widely distributed in Europe. "The booklets undoubtedly influenced many readers," wrote Lewis, "all the more because they carried the imprint, not of a crackpot publisher in an alleyway, but of one of the most famous and successful men in the world."

Hitler Youth Movement leader Baldur von Shirach testified at the Nuremburg war crimes trial that Ford's literature helped to make him an anti-Semite.

Ford is the only American mentioned in the U.S. edition of Hitler's biography, "Mein Kampf." Lewis wrote: "Hitler's ravings and public speeches against Jews frequently were based on Ford's anti-Semitic literature."

Ford issued a public retraction in 1927, but his booklets began to appear again in the 1930s in the United States and Europe. In 1938 Ford received the Third Reich's highest honor for a foreigner, an award created by Hitler, who had a photo of Ford on his office wall.

Although Ford never called for mass murder, Rosenbaum argues Ford was instrumental in shaping Hitler's views of Jews, recalling that Hitler was quoted in 1931 as saying: "I regard Henry Ford as my inspiration." Rosenbaum suggests Hitler also received from Ford's factory innovations the idea for the "the industrialization of killing perfected in the death camps, the mass production of death by assembly line . . . "

Lewis told the Free Press in 1999: "If I were Jewish, I don't know that I would admire him, and I would not forget what he did, and I'm not sure whether I would forgive him. But on balance, I think the world is a better place because of Henry Ford. And in terms of his anti-Semitism, he was not an Adolf Hitler."

Ford-Werke and slave labor

Ford Motor Co., through its German subsidiary, Ford-Werke AG, announced in 2000 that it would contribute about $13 million to a German fund to compensate thousands of Nazi-era slaves and forced laborers. The automaker said it wanted to make "a humanitarian contribution to help former forced laborers who are still alive and others who suffered particular hardship" under the Nazi regime.

Ford Motor has long maintained it was not responsible for what happened at its confiscated German manufacturing facilities at Cologne, where thousands of forced laborers — mainly non-Jews from eastern Europe — worked during the war. The company at first resisted participating in the German compensation fund, objecting to what it said were attached legal implications of guilt and responsibility. Ford talked of setting up a separate fund.

Ford-Dearborn owned 52 percent of Ford-Germany by the late 1930s. In December 1941, when the United States entered World War II after Pearl Harbor, Ford officials say Ford-Dearborn lost contact with Ford-Werke and did not regain it until the war's end in 1945. By the spring of 1942, the Nazi regime seized the Cologne plant, Ford officials say. The Nazis dismissed the board and appointed a verwalter, or custodian, who would report to the Reich.

The custodian was Robert Hans Schmidt, who had served as the Ford plant's co-chief executive leading up to the war and was well known to Ford executives in Dearborn. The Nazis did not impose Schmidt on Ford-Werke; his appointment had been negotiated in advance by the Ford-Werke board and the government, according to Ford Motor documents. After the war, Ford rehired Schmidt and other Nazi-era Ford managers.

The Fords as nouveau riche

Detroit's elite in 1900 sneered at Henry Ford, who was basically a working-class mechanic and farm boy before he became one of the richest men in the United States after 1912. Ford didn't care. He disdained the wealthy.

Author Donald Finlay Davis points out that Ford Motor's key entrepreneurs — Ford and James Couzens — were anti-establishment types who went against Detroit's conventional wisdom and kept their prices low so ordinary people could buy their cars. Other sources of conflict between Ford and Detroit's old money:

Banking practices: Ford refused to use elite-controlled banks in Detroit.

The $5 day: Detroit's industrialists considered Ford a class traitor for suddenly hiking workers' pay.

World War I: The elite supported national preparedness and even called for war; Ford was a steadfast pacifist.

Grosse Pointe: Ford despised the bastion of old money, and his feelings became more intense when his only child, Edsel, moved there. "Ford was so jealous of these people, and their real or imagined influence on Edsel, that he carried on a bitter feud with Grosse Pointers for 30 years," wrote Harry Bennett, Ford's right-hand man. Ford made repeated — and fruitless — efforts to persuade Edsel to move to Dearborn. Charles Sorenson, another of Henry Ford's top lieutenants, said in his autobiography that Henry Ford, a teetotaler, lamented the "evil influence" of Edsel's Grosse Pointe friends, especially when Henry heard Edsel drank an occasional cocktail at Grosse Pointe parties.

Politics: In 1918, Ford, running as a Democrat, opposed Truman Newberry for U.S. Senate. Newberry of Grosse Pointe was part of one of the oldest fortunes in the state. "Ford," wrote biographer Keith Sward, "had nothing but scorn for the 'Grosse Pointe crowd,' " whom he regarded as "mere wastrels and speculators." Newberry won but was later indicted and left office.

SOURCES: "CONSPICUOUS PRODUCTION: AUTOMOBILES AND ELITES IN DETROIT," BY DONALD FINLAY DAVIS; "THE PUBLIC IMAGE OF HENRY FORD," BY DAVID LEWIS; "MY FORTY YEARS WITH FORD," BY CHARLES SORENSON WITH SAMUEL WILLIAMSON; "WE NEVER CALLED HIM HENRY," HARRY BENNETT, AS TOLD TO PAUL MARCUS.

WEALTH

Free Press file photo

Henry and Clara Ford attend a social function in Detroit in July 1941.

The Detroit Almanac

08. TRA
PORT

"Paris dictates a season's silhouette, but Detroit manufactures a pattern of life."

— **Anne O'Hare McCormick**, *New York Times, 1934*

ANS-
ATION

Charles King, right, the first man to drive an automobile in Detroit, is shown in his homemade vehicle in 1896.

Free Press file photo

Planes, Trains and Automobiles

One hundred years of horseless carriages

"A motor carriage has made its appearance on the streets and it created quite a sensation as it ran up Woodward Avenue yesterday. It was in perfect control of its driver and ran very rapidly. There was no sound except a quiet clicking, and as it went up the avenue, dodging pedestrians and winding in and out of the crowds that were on that street at noon, there was considerable amount of comment as to the construction of the wagon."

— A Free Press description Aug. 15, 1896, of one of the first automobiles on Detroit streets.

With all due respect to the World Wide Web — and partly because of it — automobiles are likely to reign supreme as *the* most potent social, economic and political force influencing the lives of earthlings into the next century and beyond.

A hundred years ago, with help from men like Henry Ford and Karl Benz, the car replaced the horse (and one's own legs) as the mode of choice for moving from Point A to Point B. Who could foresee the broad impact cars and trucks would have on global society, culture, trade regulations, housing, privacy, morals and art?

Having witnessed the evolution of cars and drivers for the past century, it's safe to deduce that the impact of personal transportation on humanity isn't soon likely to abate. Vehicles will offer new features and unexpected benefits. The automotive companies, as they consolidate into one another, will grow more formidable. Countries such as China, where roads today are scarce, already have begun to build highways that will enable more and more people to buy vehicles.

Environmental activists decry vehicular proliferation, citing the burden on nonrenewable resources, such as fuel, oxygen and land. However, automotive engineers always seem to step forward with answers. For example: Energy-efficient and low-polluting automotive technology is about to enter the mainstream. Honda Motor Co. promises to put its first fuel-cell car on the road in 2003. Fuel cells convert hydrogen, or fossil fuel broken down to yield hydrogen, into electric power, while emitting water vapor.

With new energy technology at hand, developing nations will be more eager than ever to taste the fruits of industrial progress and personal comfort, as have their brethren from richer nations like the United States. Internal-combustion engines running on gasoline will prevail for awhile; however, their future isn't as bright as their past.

Wireless technology and the versatility of the Internet not only facilitate remote communication from behind the wheel but permit a vehicle to become, in effect, a rolling Internet plat-

Automobiles are likely to reign supreme as the most influential force on man.

Opening the Ford: Eleanor Clay Ford cuts the ribbon at Lonyo and the Edsel Ford Freeway, July 10, 1957.

Free Press file photo

MILES DRIVEN CUMULATIVELY BY COUNTY ON AN AVERAGE DAY
Wayne.........52.4 million
Oakland ......37.0 million
Macomb .....17.2 million
Washtenaw.....10.1 million
Livingston .....5.2 million
Monroe ....5.1 million
St. Clair.........5.0 million
TOTAL.........132 million

PASSENGER VEHICLES
There are nearly 5.8 million registered in Michigan, 2,868,085 in southeastern Michigan. Here's the breakdown by county:
Wayne 1,122,309
Oakland............803,741
Macomb...........499,465
Washtenaw 179,140
St. Clair..............92,696
Livingston 88,028
Monroe 82,706

COMMERCIAL VEHICLES
There are nearly 1.7 million registered in Michigan, 632,706 in southeastern Michigan. Here's the breakdown by county:
Wayne 220,011
Oakland............159,433
Macomb...........117,100
Washtenaw 38,710
St. Clair..............34,012
Monroe 32,729
Livingston 30,711

VEHICLES PER HOUSEHOLD

On average in metro Detroit by county:

Livingston 2.3
Monroe 2.1
St. Clair 2.0
Macomb 1.9
Oakland 1.9
Washtenaw 1.8
Wayne outside Detroit 1.8
Detroit 1.1

TRIPS

How we get from here to there daily:

Cars, minivans ....78 percent of trips
Van, light truck 9
On foot 6
Bus 4
Bicycle 1
Taxi, motorcycle 1
Car/van pool 1

COMMUTING

How we get from home to work:

Cars, minivans ....83 percent
Van, light truck 11
On foot 2
Bus 2
Bicycle, taxi, motorcycle 1
Car/van pool 1

ROAD TIME

How much time we spend commuting to work:

0-10 minutes ....18 percent
11-19 18
20-29 15
30-39 27
40-49 10
50 plus 12

The Ford Highland Park plant around 1920.

form. General Motors' OnStar service, which lets the driver or passenger speak to an "adviser" who can give street directions or make dinner reservations, is the first of many services that expand a vehicle's utility.

As deaths and injuries due to road accidents decline, the regulatory push for even greater safety increases. More than 60 years elapsed in the development of vehicles before seat belts finally were acknowledged as an essential safety device. Another 30 years went by before airbags became widespread. But now airbags are undergoing continuous and sophisticated upgrading, which should make them even more effective in protecting against injuries.

During the past few years, the world has watched while Ford Motor Co. gobbled up Volvo, Jaguar and others; General Motors Corp. gobbled up Saab, a piece of Fiat and others; Daimler gobbled up Chrysler, Renault gobbled up Nissan and everyone wondered which Korean automaker would become someone's next meal.

Automotive companies are consolidating as a necessary response to the realities, and expense, of worldwide operations. To succeed in the future, companies will have to sell in many countries to all kinds of people, employing complex skills and adhering to a myriad of regulations. Only the biggest and strongest automakers have a chance to prosper; most of the rest have decided they're not up to the contest.

Detroit's Big Two plus One

Burton Historical Collection

Ford Motor Co.

Ford is the No. 4 company on the Fortune 500 list of the largest U.S. corporations, based on sales. It employs 340,000 people and has operations in more than 30 countries. In addition to cars and trucks, Ford also produces industrial engines, glass, plastics and a wide range of automotive components. Ford also is involved in financial services and electronics.

The company's time line:
1896: Henry Ford drives the two-cylinder car he built on the streets of Detroit.
1903: After a couple of false starts, Henry Ford founds the Ford Motor Co. on June 17 in a converted wagon shop on Mack Avenue.
1907: Ford Motor Co. makes more than $1 million in profit.
1908: Ford introduces the Model T. It's available in black, red, green, pearl or gray.
1910: Ford begins making cars at his new Highland Park plant.

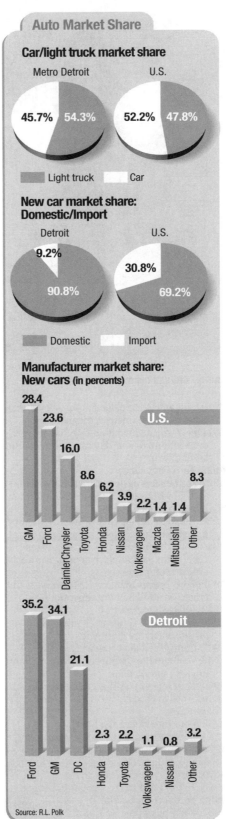

Auto Market Share

Car/light truck market share

Metro Detroit
45.7% | 54.3%

U.S.
52.2% | 47.8%

Light truck — Car

New car market share: Domestic/Import

Detroit
9.2%
90.8%

U.S.
30.8%
69.2%

Domestic — Import

Manufacturer market share:
New cars (in percents)

U.S.
- GM: 28.4
- Ford: 23.6
- DaimlerChrysler: 16.0
- Toyota: 8.6
- Honda: 6.2
- Nissan: 3.9
- Volkswagen: 2.2
- Mazda: 1.4
- Mitsubishi: 1.4
- Other: 8.3

Detroit
- Ford: 35.2
- GM: 34.1
- DC: 21.1
- Honda: 2.3
- Toyota: 2.2
- Volkswagen: 1.1
- Nissan: 0.8
- Other: 3.2

Source: R.L. Polk

Oops!

Traffic accident facts
Michigan: In 1998, the state had 1,367 traffic fatalities, down 5.5 percent from the 1997 figure of 1,446. Michigan also had 131,578 injuries and 403,766 total crashes in 1998.
Death rate: One person died in a traffic accident for every 67.5 million miles of travel, down slightly from 1997.
Historical death rate: It's declined dramatically.
Deaths per 100 million miles of travel
1948 ....8.2
1958 ....4.7
1968 ....5.0
1978 ....3.1
1988 ....2.2
1998 ....1.5

Driving while drunk
In 1998, 4.8 percent of all crashes involved drinking; 22.9 percent of all crashes resulted in injury or death. Of alcohol-related crashes, 46.9 percent resulted in injury or death, and 38.5 percent of total fatal crashes in 1998 involved drinking. The breakdown by county:

	Crashes	Deaths
Injuries	Had been drinking crashes	fatal crashes
Wayne		
	85,378	255
31,782	3,150	91
Oakland		
	47,445	92
16,921	1,962	32
Macomb		
	26,669	55
9,958	1,516	26
Washtenaw		
	12,227	34
3,914	514	5
St. Clair		
	5,372	22
2,017	360	10
Livingston		
	5,301	17
1,780	343	4
Monroe		
	4,301	23
1,762	308	10

TRANSPORTATION

MAKING CARS I

Sales in U.S. of cars and light trucks

Year	Sales
1900	2,288
1910	1.8 million
1920	1.6 million
1930	3.0 million
1940	3.8 million
1950	7.1 million
1960	7.2 million
1970	9.8 million
1980	11.2 million
1990	13.9 million
2000	17.4 million

SOURCE: JACK TEAHEN, AUTOMOTIVE NEWS.

MAKING CARS II

The share of U.S. automobiles made in Michigan declined from 35 percent in the early 1980s to 25 percent in the late 1990s.

SOURCE: AUTODATA CORP.

DEER MEETS CAR

The crashes between deer and car by county for 1999:

Oakland	1,759
Washtenaw	1,319
Livingston	1,116
St. Clair	979
Macomb	641
Wayne	352
Monroe	299

SOURCE: SOUTHEAST MICHIGAN COUNCIL OF GOVERNMENTS.

Burton Historical Collection

Henry Ford and his quadricycle, 1896.

1911: Ford wins the Selden patent lawsuit that threatened to constrict the industry.

1914: Ford rocks the nation by offering workers $5 for an 8-hour day as he perfects the assembly line.

1922: Ford buys Lincoln.

1927: Ford makes the last of its 15 million Model T's in May, and introduces its all-new Model A in December.

1932: Ford security forces and Dearborn police kill five unarmed hunger marchers.

1941: Ford finally relents and recognizes the UAW after violent clashes between workers and company guards.

1942: Ford begins building B24 bombers and other World War II armaments.

1943: Edsel Ford dies.

1945: Henry Ford II becomes president after an internal power struggle.

1947: Henry Ford dies at age 83.

1949: Ford and the UAW establish a company-funded pension plan.

1954: Ford introduces the Thunderbird.

1956: Stock in Ford is sold to the public for the first time.

1958: Ford introduces the Edsel.

1964: Ford introduces the Mustang.

1978: Ford Chairman Henry Ford II fires President Lee Iacocca.

1979: Ford buys an interest in Mazda.

1980: Henry Ford steps down as chairman.

1986: Ford introduces the Taurus.

1987: Ford buys part of Aston Martin, and completes the purchase in 1994.

1990: The Ford Explorer debuts; Ford buys Jaguar.

1999: Ford buys Volvo.

1999: William Clay Ford Jr. becomes chairman of the board.

2000: Ford spins off Visteon.

General Motors Corp.

GM is the No. 3 company on the Fortune 500 list of the largest U.S. corporations, based on sales. The company employs 388,000 people worldwide, has manufacturing plants in 50 countries and a corporate presence in more than 200 countries, and does business with more than 30,000 suppliers. GM also has interests in digital communications, financial and insurance services and locomotives. It has more than 260 major subsidiaries, joint ventures and affiliations around the world.

General Motors

General Motors Tech Center, the sprawling facility the automaker opened in Warren in 1956.

The company's time line:

1908: William Crapo Durant starts General Motors Co. by buying Buick, Olds, Cadillac, Oakland (which became Pontiac) and a collection of suppliers.

1909-1910: Banks that have loaned Durant $15 million force him out so they can reorganize GM.

1911: GM becomes the first automaker listed on the New York Stock Exchange. First shares are sold for $50.50 each. Durant buys Chevrolet and launches a scheme to regain control of GM.

1912: GM truck operations consolidated in Pontiac.

1915: Durant acquires 54.5 percent of GM stock and returns as president.

1916: GM expands into businesses such as refrigerators and auto financing.

1918: Chevrolet becomes part of GM.

1919: GM buys an interest in Fisher Body, laying the groundwork for taking it over in 1926. The GM Institute opens in Flint.

1920: With GM stock dropping to $14 a share, banks save the company from collapse and force Durant out again. Pierre DuPont takes over as president.

1921: New Center headquarters opens.

1929: Despite stock market crash, GM continues expansion into new businesses such as radios, aircraft and diesel engines.

1933: After 450 Michigan banks collapse, GM leads in creating National Bank of Detroit to pick up the pieces. GM sells its interest in the bank by 1945.

1937: Sit-down strike at Flint Fisher Body plant begins. When it ends 44 days later, the UAW has won the right to organize GM workers.

1940: GM goes to war, building $12.3 billion worth of military supplies in five years.

1945: UAW demands a 30-percent wage increase, and 113-day strike ends only with government intervention.

1951: Engine Charlie Wilson steps down as GM chairman to become secretary of defense.

1953: GM introduces Corvette.

1954: GM buys Willow Run plant from Ford.

1954-61: Series of antitrust campaigns fail to break up GM.

1956: GM opens Tech Center in Warren.

1970: UAW strike ends with first "30 and out" provisions.

1978: GM earns record $3.5 billion.

1979: Sales hit a record $66.3 billion.

1980: Company loses $762.5 million, only its second loss in 72 years.

1983: GM and Toyota announce a joint venture and GM launches Saturn.

1984: Company buys Electronic Data Systems Inc.

1986: Feuding between Chairman Roger Smith and EDS founder H. Ross Perot explodes, and GM agrees to buy Perot's stock for about $700 million to get him to go away.

1996: GM buys Renaissance Center for world headquarters.

Free Press file photo

A handshake in London between Daimler-Benz's Juergen Schrempp, left, and Chrysler's Robert Eaton announces DaimlerChrysler.

DC

DaimlerChrysler

DaimlerChrysler is based in Stuttgart, Germany; U.S. headquarters are in Auburn Hills. In November 1998, Daimler-Benz and Chrysler merged in what officials then described as a partnership. However, it is now clear that the deal was a Daimler-Benz takeover. While not ranked on the Fortune 500 because of its foreign base, the company is huge: It has 466,938 employees, sells products in more than 200 countries and has manufacturing facilities in 34 countries.

The company's time line:

1883: Gustave Daimler takes out patents on his internal-combustion engine and Karl Benz founds Benz & Co. Rheinische GasmotorenFabrik.

1923: Walter P. Chrysler becomes chairman of shaky Maxwell Motor Co. in Highland Park.

WHO DRIVES WHAT IN THE MOTOR CITY
Vehicles in operation, 2000

Oakland County
1) Ford Taurus
2) Pontiac Grand Am
3) Ford Escort
4) Ford Explorer
5) Chevrolet Cavalier
6) Pontiac Grand Prix
7) Honda Accord
8) Pontiac Bonneville
9) GMC S15 Jimmy
10) Dodge Neon

Wayne County
1) Ford Escort
2) Ford Taurus
3) Ford Explorer
4) Chevrolet Cavalier
5) Ford Tempo
6) Pontiac Grand Am
7) Mercury Grand Marquis
8) Mercury Sable
9) Mercury Cougar
10) Ford F150

Macomb County
1) Pontiac Grand Am
2) Ford Escort
3) Ford Taurus
4) Chevrolet Cavalier
5) Pontiac Grand Prix
6) Ford Explorer
7) Dodge Neon
8) Chevrolet Lumina
9) Pontiac Bonneville
10) Ford F150

Detroit
1) Ford Escort
2) Ford Taurus
3) Pontiac Grand Am
4) Chevrolet Cavalier
5) Ford Explorer
6) Pontiac Grand Prix
7) Ford F150
8) Ford Tempo
9) Mercury Grand Marquis
10) Ford F150 Super Cab

SOURCE: THE POLK CO.

1925: Maxwell Motor Co. ceases production, and Chrysler Corp. takes its place.

1928: Chrysler grows from newcomer to major player in one summer with the introduction of the DeSoto and Plymouth lines and the acquisition of Dodge Brothers.

1930s: Chrysler shifts its emphasis to the low-cost Plymouth brand.

1932: Plymouth climbs to No. 3 in production, trailing only Ford Motor Co. and Chevrolet.

1937: Chrysler recognizes the UAW after a multiplant sit-down strike.

1938: Illness forces Walter Chrysler to withdraw from active company management.

1942-45: Factories turn to military production, assembling M4 Sherman tanks, among other products.

1946: The wood-sided Town & Country convertible becomes Chrysler's showpiece.

1954: 4,000-acre proving ground opens near Chelsea as Chrysler posts its worst sales record since World War II.

1960: Chrysler adopts unibody construction on all models.

1961: DeSoto disappears as '61 model year begins. It's the final year for fins.

1962: Dodge and Plymouth launch downsized models. They flop.

1970: Chrysler launches Dodge Challenger.

1971: Chrysler buys a share of Mitsubishi Motors. Subcompact Dodge Colt debuts.

1976: Midsize Dodge Aspen and Plymouth Volare debut and quickly establish themselves as quality-control disasters.

1978: Dodge Omni and Plymouth Horizon become first U.S.-built subcompacts and Chrysler hires Lee Iacocca as president. He becomes chairman in 1979.

1979: Billion-dollar losses and second OPEC oil crisis push Chrysler to brink of bankruptcy.

1980: Iacocca gets federal loan-guarantee package totaling $1.5 billion. UAW supports rescue program with $475 million in wage concessions.

1981: Plain, brick-like K-cars — the Dodge Aries and Plymouth Reliant — propel Chrysler turnaround.

1983: Chrysler pays off federally guaranteed loans seven years ahead of schedule.

1984: First minivans hit the road.

1985: Chrysler and Mitsubishi announce joint-venture factory in Illinois.

1986: Iacocca becomes highest-paid automotive executive of all time, earning more than $20.5 million.

1987: Chrysler acquires American Motors Corp. and Jeep from Renault and buys Lamborghini.

Making cars

U.S. Market Share, July 2000

GM	28.5%
Ford	24.0%
Chrysler	4.8%
Total	**67.3%**

Note: Ford excludes Jaguar and Volvo; GM excludes Saab and Chrysler excludes Mercedes-Benz.

Japanese

Toyota	8.9%
Honda	6.3%
Nissan	4.1%
Mazda	1.4%
Mitsubishi	1.7%
Other	1.8%
Total	**24.2%**

Korean

Hyundai	1.4%
Daewoo	0.4%
Kia	0.8%
Total	**2.6%**

European

VW/Audi	2.4&
Mercedes-Benz	.1%
BMW	1.0%
Volvo	0.2%
Jaguar	0.2%
Other	0.5%
Total	**5.9%**

Source: Autodata Corp.

1992: The 400-horsepower Dodge Viper debuts. Iacocca reluctantly retires, replaced by Bob Eaton on Jan. 1, 1993.

1993: Chrysler launches landmark cab-forward design theme with new LH sedans — Chrysler Concorde, Dodge Intrepid, Eagle Vision. Jeep Grand Cherokee also debuts.

1994: Dodge/Plymouth Neon twins shake up the compact market. Rough-tough Dodge Ram does the same for full-size pickups.

1995: Chrysler staves off takeover effort led by Las Vegas financier Kirk Kerkorian and ex-chairman Iacocca.

1998: Chrysler and Daimler-Benz AG become DaimlerChrysler.

2001: Chrysler announces plans to eliminate 26,000 jobs as part of a 3-year, $3.9-billion restructuring effort.

Detroit = Motor City

Detroit? Why not St. Louis or Texarkana or Toledo? Here's why:

➤ Access to raw materials and semifinished materials, such as wood, iron, brass and coke.
➤ Availability of capital. Detroit had lots of rich people with money to invest, such as James McMillan and Henry Joy. The New York bankers didn't think much of the industry and figured if cars rolled, they'd be toys of the East Coast swells and therefore, factories to build 'em should be financed back East.
➤ The city was well served by railroads and lake transportation.
➤ Detroit had a history of being a capital of metal bending; it was a national leader in making boxcars and stoves, and the city had numerous machinists.
➤ There was little unionization in the early 1900s in Detroit.

You'd be correct in musing that those five reasons could apply to other cities then, too: Cleveland, Buffalo and Chicago among others. So, reason number 6:
➤ Serendipity. Michigan residents at the turn of the 20th Century included innovators, tinkerers and dreamers like Henry Ford and Ransom Olds and Charles King.

Notable auto people

HENRY FORD: The farm boy from Dearborn was the businessman of the 20th Century, according to Fortune magazine. Ford did not invent the auto or the assembly line, but he changed the world by making simple cars on assembly lines designed to enable the Ford Motor Co. to sell its product cheaply. Despite his genius, Ford nearly ruined his company before grandson Henry Ford II took control in 1945. Ford, who was born in 1863, died in 1947.

RANSOM E. OLDS: Born in Ohio in 1864, Olds moved with his parents to Lansing, where he began experimenting in his father's tool machine shop. He built his first gasoline-powered car in 1896, and founded the Olds Motor Works in Detroit in 1899. His plant, at East Jefferson and Concord near the Belle Isle Bridge, was the nation's first factory devoted to making automobiles. Olds' major innovation was his curved-dash car (see below). By 1904, Olds Motor Works was the leading auto company in the world. After a power struggle, Olds left the firm and founded the Reo (his initials) Motor Car Co. He died in 1950.

DODGE BROTHERS: John, left, and Horace Dodge were ambitious, risk-taking, hard-drinking mechanics. ("Cripple Beaten by Dodge Asks Damages," read one 1912 headline.) Together, they quickly soldered a reputation for precision machine work, which won them a contract to produce transmissions for early Oldsmobiles. They abandoned Ransom Olds for Henry Ford a few years later, gambling they could make money faster. It was the Dodges who built the chassis and most of the moving parts for the first Model T's. To raise cash for the enterprise, Ford sold stock, making the Dodges major shareholders and ensuring their fortune. By 1916, John and Horace Dodge had created Dodge Brothers Inc., with their own Hamtramck assembly line; soon after, it became the fourth-largest automobile company in the nation. The Dodge brothers died young (both in 1920) and, unlike Ford, left no descendants to run the auto company.

LOUIS CHEVROLET: Born in 1878 in Switzerland, Chevrolet was raised in France and became a bicycle racer before the auto age. He designed

Ransom Olds was Detroit's most successful automaker at the turn of the century. But his plant on East Jefferson burned on March 9, 1901, in a spectacular blaze highlighted by a series of interior explosions. Saved from the fire was one model of Olds' runabout, which he drove to Lansing, where it became the starting point of Olds' renewed venture.

his first Chevy in 1910. He came to Michigan, met GM founder William Durant, and with brother Arthur became part of a team that raced and designed cars for Durant and David Buick.

WILLIAM DURANT: Few had his daring or flamboyance. Starting with a small carriage-making company in Flint, Durant in 1908 launched a holding company that soon became General Motors, basing its success on products developed by individualists such as Louis Chevrolet, David Buick and Ransom Olds. Yet after the company was up and running, his energetic entrepreneurship and wildcatting financial methods were no longer considered useful by the bankers and managers who ran the company in its adolescence. He was booted out twice — finally for good in 1920 — and died nearly penniless in 1947. In "My Years at General Motors," former GM Chairman Alfred Sloan says of Durant: "I admired his automotive genius, his imagination, his generous human qualities, and his integrity . . . I recognized that he had created and inspired the dynamic growth of General Motors. But I thought he was too casual in his ways for an administrator, and he overloaded himself. Important decisions had to wait until he was free, and were often made impulsively."

ALFRED P. SLOAN: He had no hobbies. He rarely vacationed. He just worked. He was the purposeful professional manager who shaped GM into the highly structured organization that it is today, and virtually invented modern business management. He spent 38 years at GM, 14 as president and 19 as chairman, becoming the model for all future GM leaders. Indeed, he became the role model for all American businessmen and author of a book regarded as a management classic — "My Years at General Motors." By the time Sloan retired in 1956, he had established a careful system for detecting those young and ambitious employees who could be molded into future leaders on the GM pattern. The system is a GM trademark; even today, it is rare for the company to recruit a top executive from outside. However, the Sloan system left little room for people who didn't quite fit GM's mold.

WALTER CHRYSLER: Born in 1875, the son of a locomotive engineer, Chrysler got his hands dirty in railroad maintenance and manufacturing before being hired in 1910 as works manager at Buick. He transformed it into GM's biggest moneymaker but left in 1919 after colliding with GM founder Durant in a jurisdictional dispute, not long before Durant himself was ousted. Chrysler engaged in a couple of auto company rescue missions, and ended up heading Maxwell Motors. Sales doubled by 1923. Maxwell introduced "the Chrysler" in 1924; it sold so well Maxwell was reorganized as the Chrysler Corp. in 1925. Chrysler, mostly working out of New York, served as chairman and bought Dodge in 1928, and the company became part of the Big Three with models in all price ranges. He retired in 1935 but served as chairman until his death in 1940.

HENRY LELAND: Few figures cast a longer shadow over the early U.S. automotive landscape than Henry Martyn Leland, the man who created Cadillac and Lincoln. A master machinist from Vermont, Leland was 58 at the turn of the century, and his flowing white beard made him look like a character out of the Old Testament. What Leland brought to the fledgling auto industry was a near-fanatical dedication to precision, which helped the young Cadillac Motor Co. become "the standard of the world," according to the Royal Automobile Club in Britain. Leland took control of the failed Detroit Automobile Co. and renamed it in honor of Antoine de la Mothe Cadillac, Detroit's founder. Later, the Leland-inspired V8 engine was the first to achieve lasting success. Leland would employ the same technique in the first Lincoln engines, when he founded that company in 1920, choosing the name for the great president he'd voted for in 1864.

HARLEY J. EARL: He was one of the great shake-'em-up romantics of the car industry. His design work is legend: the famous fins on 1949 Cadillacs; maybe the most beloved car in hot-rodder Americana, the 1957 Chevrolet Bel Air; two-tone paint jobs, wrap-around windshields and the four-door hardtop. But Earl's history-making achievement is widely said to be his melding of automotive design with engineering. From Los Angeles, Earl joined General

Motors to create the 1927 LaSalle, at a time when Detroit was building cars as it did in horse-and-buggy days: a dark painted box dropped onto a chassis. A colorful dresser with a day-brightening smile, Earl favored two-tone shoes along with powder blue suits and white suits, and loved shoveling his 6-foot-4 frame into the low-slung prototypes he drove. He was born in 1893 and died in 1969.

HARLOW CURTICE: The GM president from 1953-58 was not a rebel but rather a man who reveled in GM's size and power and threw aside Alfred Sloan's policy of restraint. An uncanny judge of public taste and a lover of big cars when they were king, Curtice pushed GM into an orgy of tail fins and chrome. He was also a super salesman, driving the company to exceed its 45-percent market share, despite cautions against greed that might set off government antitrust action. His personal style was atypically flamboyant for GM. He often worked an entire week without leaving the GM Building, departing late on Friday night for his Flint home. Even as president, Red Curtice continued to play poker with his old friends on Saturdays in a back room at the Hotel Durant in Flint.

The grandsons of Henry Ford: William Clay, left, Benson and Henry Ford II in a Lincoln convertible, 1953.

HENRY FORD II: The last tycoon. Henry Ford II was the most powerful industrialist of his time and a man whose vision changed the face of Detroit. He ranked as royalty, both in the annals of American capitalism and on Detroit's social registry. Friend and foe called him the Deuce. He wrested control of Ford Motor Co. during World War II from his famous, reluctant and failing grandfather and saved it from chaos with a single-minded fervor. He ran the company during the postwar years when America fell in love with the automobile. In the last years of his life, he flouted social convention by his third marriage, to the daughter of a blue-collar worker. No businessman in modern history exercised so much personal authority over so large a corporation for so many years. He spearheaded the building of the Renaissance Center, Detroit's symbol of change for the better. In his last years, he withdrew from Detroit and from the company that bears his name, saying he wanted to spend more time enjoying life. One of his favorite possessions was a needlepoint pillow with the words, "Don't postpone pleasure." He was born in 1917 and died in 1987.

TONY SPINA/Detroit Free Press

Lee Iacocca, the guy Henry Ford II canned in the late 1970s, during his tenure as Chrysler chairman, in 1987.

LEE IACOCCA: By the mid-1980s, Iacocca was one of the best-known and most-admired businesspeople in the world after he had orchestrated the federal bailout that rescued troubled Chrysler Corp. from bankruptcy. He had become an industrial icon, pushing Chrysler cars in advertisements, spearheading the $300-million restoration of the Statue of Liberty, writing a best-selling autobiography, bashing Japan, hinting he might run for president. But he nearly put Chrysler back in bankruptcy in the late 1980s by growing distracted with nonautomotive acquisitions. Iacocca retired in 1992 but resurfaced two years later when he aided billionaire investor Kirk Kerkorian's ill-fated hostile bid to buy Chrysler. Born in Pennsylvania in 1924, Iacocca started in the auto industry in 1946, fresh out of Princeton. By 1956, he was an assistant sales manager in Philadelphia, where he showed the marketing prowess that attracted the attention of customers and Ford brass. Four years later, he was running the Ford division. In 1964, the Mustang captured the fancy of young Americans and brought Iacocca — its "father" —

MOTOR TREND MAGAZINE IMPORT OF THE YEAR

1970: Porsche 914
1971-75: no award
1976: Toyota Celica Liftback
1977: Mercedes-Benz 280E
1978: Toyota Celica
1979: Datsun 280ZX
1980: Honda Civic
1981: Mercedes-Benz 300SD
1982: Toyota Celica Supra
1983: Mazda 626
1984: Honda Civic CRX
1985: Toyota MR2
1986: Mazda RX7
1987: Acura Legend Coupe
1988: Honda CRX Si
1989: Mitsubishi Galant GS
1990: Nissan 300ZX Turbo
1991: Mitsubishi 3000GT R4
1992: Lexus SC 400
1993: Mazda RX7
1994: Honda Accord
1995: Nissan Maxima
1996: Mercedes-Benz E-Class
1997: BMW 5-Series
1998: Lexus GS series
1999: Volkswagen New Beetle
Award was discontinued because "import" has become less relevant in the global auto industry.

MOTOR TREND MAGAZINE TRUCK OF THE YEAR

1978: Ford Econoline Van
1979: Chevrolet 4X4 LUV Pickup
1980: Volkswagen Vanagon
1981-1988 no award
1989: Toyota SR5 V6 Pickup
1990: Ford Aerostar 4WD
1991: Mazda Navajo
1992: Ford Chateau Club Wagon
1993: Jeep Grand Cherokee Laredo V8
1994: Dodge Ram Pickup
1995: Chevrolet Blazer
1996: Chevrolet Tahoe
1997: Ford F150
1998: Mercedes-Benz M-Class
1999: Chevrolet Silverado
2000: Toyota Tundra

Carroll Shelby with his handmade Shelby Cobra in 1963.

Associated Press

BEST-ENGINEERED CARS IN AUTO HISTORY

As voted by members of the Society of Automotive Engineers, 2000

1908: Ford Model T
1910: Rolls-Royce Silver Ghost
1924: Chrysler Six
1930: Cadillac V16
1949: Volkswagen Beetle
1955: Mercedes-Benz 300 SL
1964: Porsche 911
1974: Honda Civic
1984: Plymouth Voyager
1999: Chevrolet Corvette Convertible and 1999 Mercedes-Benz S500

Overall winners:
1999 Chevrolet Corvette Convertible and 1999 Mercedes-Benz S500

national recognition and cover stories in Time and Newsweek. In 1970, he was named president of Ford Motor Co. But the strong-willed executive repeatedly butted heads with Henry Ford II and was fired on July 13, 1978. He joined Chrysler three weeks later, at the same time it reported a $160-million loss.

CARROLL SHELBY: The wild-haired buckaroo and former Texas chicken farmer loved to take inexpensive cars off the assembly line and, in the parlance of the industry, tweak them up. Shelby added equipment that made cars accelerate sharper, corner tighter and stop faster. He tossed in his own styling touches and sold the vehicles as affordable performance cars for the street or racetrack. In 1965, he developed for Ford the explosive, street-legal Cobra 427/SC that would go from 0 to 60 in 4.6 seconds. He said: "I like to try to build cars for those people so they can throw the two kids in the backseat on Saturday night . . . but when a Porsche comes along and challenges them on the way home from work once in a while, they don't have to feel like they have to tuck their head in shame and back off."

ROGER PENSKE: Most of the public recognizes Penske as a former race driver and sportsman whose car-racing teams won the Indy 500 ten times. But he is one of the major players in the worldwide transportation business. The Ohio-born Penske almost became CEO at Chrysler Corp. in 1991. In addition to owning tracks and racing teams, Penske has owned auto dealerships, racetracks, auto service centers, a maker of fuel injectors and a

truck-leasing firm. In the late 1980s, Penske bought a majority stake in Detroit Diesel from General Motors. He made investments and refurbished operations that GM had neglected. In mid-2000, Penske announced the sale of Detroit Diesel to DaimlerChrysler. He also addressed workers' complaints, spending a great deal of time on the factory floor. In May 2000, Penske and his son Greg said they were investing $17 million in **CarsDirect.com** to sell cars and trucks online from their United Auto Group Inc. and Penske Automotive Group.

CONNIE KALITTA: The Big K. A 22-time National Hot Rod Association national event finalist, Kalitta was the first man to do the quarter-mile at 290 m.p.h. (in 1989). Kalitta, of Washtenaw County, was made more famous when actor Beau Bridges played him as a charmingly thoughtless rogue in "Heart Like a Wheel." Kalitta stepped away from the sport in April 1997 to pay closer attention to his booming business: American International Airways, a worldwide cargo company he founded.

SHIRLEY (CHA CHA) MULDOWNEY: The drag racer from Mt. Clemens was the first woman licensed by National Hot Rod Association. Her trademark: A hot-pink car. She was the first driver, male or female, to win two world championships and won a third in 1982. She won the U.S. Nationals in '82 and the Winston world championship in '80. She's the only woman to have won the NHRA top-fuel title ('77, '80, '82). After she crashed in Montreal in '84, Muldowney spent 18 months in rehabilitation before returning in '86. She was the subject of the critically acclaimed film "Heart Like a Wheel."

RALPH NADER: In 1965, he published "Unsafe at Any Speed," an indictment of the compact Chevrolet Corvair. The book killed the car, which had been GM's response to rising import sales. The next year, the company was embarrassed before the nation when it was revealed it had hired an investigator to spy on Nader. He went on to become the well-known consumer advocate who would exert a profound impact

Free Press file photo
Ralph Nader at his leisure in the 1970s.

on auto safety. In 2000, Nader ran for president as the Green Party candidate.

A 1960 Chevy Corvair: Not to Nader's liking.

WALTER REUTHER: Before dying in a plane crash in 1970, Reuther built one of the most sophisticated, powerful and corruption-free unions in postwar America. The UAW played a major role in the auto industry as it boosted the living standards of

auto workers. The union also helped to set the nation's progressive agenda and became a major source of funding for the civil rights movement. Today, in many ways, it's a partner of the domestic automakers.

JUERGEN SCHREMPP: The chairman of Daimler-Benz AG engineered the takeover of Chrysler Corp. in 1997. He is a hard-charging corporate avenger the Germans have sardonically dubbed Neutron Juergen and Rambo, but he shares his headquarters suite in

Stuttgart with stuffed animals. In high school, Schrempp was an apprentice mechanic at a Mercedes-Benz shop in Freiburg. He wanted to study mechanical engineering, or possibly become a trial attorney, but his parents couldn't afford it. So Schrempp picked up his trumpet, which now sits on a glass shelf in his office, and started playing in a jazz band. He eventually earned enough for engineering school, and went to work for Daimler-Benz after graduation, spending time in South Africa and Ohio on his way up the corporate ladder.

Tony Swan's top cars

The Free Press auto critic picks the cars that captivated:

1) The Curved Dash Oldsmobile: 1900

The Curved Dash auto was built by Olds and engineer Horace Loomis. It was distinguished by a curved dashboard that looked like the front of a horse-drawn sleigh.

Like most early American cars, the Oldsmobile was essentially a self-propelled buggy with

buggy suspension. Transmissions had two speeds, with a bicycle-style chain delivering power to the rear axle.

Roy Chapin, later the head of Hudson, drove the little Oldsmobile from Detroit to New York for the auto show of November 1901 in 7½ days. The Curved Dash Oldsmobile helped touch off the love affair between Americans and the

Free Press file photo

The Curved Dash Oldsmobile, a cross-country traveler, promoted our love of the automobile.

Cars that stalled

Hundreds of brands failed. Here are 10, and their last year on the market.

RCH 1915
The Miller 1914
Pungs-Finch
Touring Car............1910
Lozier 1918
The Marvel 1908
Chalmers...............1922
Flanders 1912
Studebaker...........1954
Hupp Motors 1941
S & M....................1913

SOURCE: "HOW DETROIT BECAME THE AUTOMOTIVE CAPITAL," BY ROBERT SZUDAREK.

horseless carriage; the first car song — "In My Merry Oldsmobile" — became a nation-wide hit.

2) The Tin Lizzie: 1908

Free Press file photo

Within two decades, this vehicle would put practical private transportation within financial reach of almost anyone and would help make Henry Ford America's best-known businessman.

Five models were offered — Touring, Runabout, a Coupe tall enough to accommodate Abraham Lincoln in top hat, a fancy Town Car and a peculiar Laundelet, essentially a coupe with an open space up front for a chauffeur.

Contrary to Model T mythology, they came in colors at first. The all-black era didn't begin until 1914.

After the first 800 cars, all Model T's were equipped with three foot pedals, one for low speed, one for the brake and one for reverse, plus a lever for the parking brake. Hand controls included levers for the throttle and igni-

tion timing.

The last Model T was number 15,007,033, by most accounts, which left the line on May 26, 1927.

➤ **Model T prices:**
1908 A stripped-down Touring Car (no lights no top, no side curtains) .... about $850.
1914: Basic Touring Car .... $500.
1916: Basic Touring Car .... $440.
1922: Touring Car .... $298.
1925: Runabout Started at $260 (lowest price ever recorded for a full-size American car.)

3) The 1915 Cadillac Type 51 V8

Free Press file photo

Master machinist Henry Leland's V8 engine was the first to be produced in serious numbers and the first to achieve lasting success. The engine had its two banks of four cylinders separated by 90 degrees with a common crankcase. The cylinder heads were nondetachable, which made for awkward repairs and overhauls. But the new 5.2-liter V8 was smooth and powerful by that day's standards, developing 70 horsepower.

The so-called Type 51 cars that surrounded the new V8 — nine different models ranging from a $1,975 Touring model to a $3,600 limousine — were posh and big. The wheelbase of a 1916 Cadillac was 122 inches — 8 inches longer than that of the 1996 Cadillac DeVille.

➤ **Advertising for 1915 Cadillac:**
"In every field of human endeavor, he that is first must perpetually live in the white light of publicity. Whether the leadership be vested in man or manufactured product, emulation and envy are ever at work.

"Failing to equal or excel, the follower seeks to depreciate and to destroy, but only confirms once more the superiority of that which he strives to supplant.

THE NEW 1915

Eight Cylinder Cadillac

FOR SALE BY

GEO. W. McCASLIN
60 E. Central Ave.

"There is nothing new in this. It is as old as the world and as old as the human passions: envy, fear, greed, ambition and the desire to surpass. And it all avails to nothing. If the leader truly leads he remains — the leader … That which deserve to live — Lives."

4) Packard's Twin Six: 1915

Free Press file photo

By World War I, Packard was well on its way to becoming one of America's premier automobiles. Part of the credit goes to General Manager Alvan Macauley and engineer Jesse Vincent. The V12 — officially called the Twin Six — was their first great collaboration. The engine was a 60-degree design with two separate 6-cylinder blocks sharing a common crankcase. It produced 88 horsepower, more than the Cadillac V8, and in high gear, it could pull any of the many Packard models from 4 m.p.h. to a top speed of about 70 m.p.h. without a lurch or a shudder. They cost from $2,600 to $4,600.

5) 1934 Chrysler Airflow

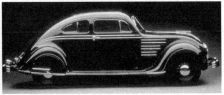

Reuters

It was the first mass-produced car to emphasize aerodynamics, but it flopped. Engineers Fred Zeder, Carl Breer and Owen Skelton created a shape that resembled an elongated football. Oliver Clark, in charge of the exterior styling, gave the car a sloping waterfall grille, voluptuously curved fenders, curved windshield and rounded roof line. The Airflow also featured a new approach to body structure with a beam and truss cage that surrounded the passenger compartment and extended down to the frame rails. People weren't ready for such a radical design, particularly one that ranged in price from $1,345 to more than $5,000. The Airflow ushered in the era of streamlining, pioneered the use of the wind tunnel for automotive applications and it embodied significant structural innovations.

6) 1932 Ford Model 18

Automobile History Collection

The Beach Boys' "Little Deuce Coupe" was a two-door 1932 Ford Model 18. The Deuce symbolized the last digit in the model year. The band's "flathead mill" was Ford's low-cost V8 engine that put high performance within reach of most car buyers — as little as $460. Ford engineers devised an engine that could be mass-produced in an era when crankcases for engines like the Cadillac V8 entailed lots of expensive hand labor by skilled craftsmen. Aside from the number of cylinders and low cost, the Ford V8 wasn't an exceptionally advanced engine. The 3.6-liter flathead Ford was potent for its day, producing 65 horsepower. The flathead V8 was Ford Motor Co.'s last big achievement under Henry Ford's direct command.

➤ **Fords were a steal:**

Besides the folks who were interested in low-cost performance, the Ford V8 also became popular with cops and robbers. The police loved them because they made excellent pursuit vehicles. The bad guys loved them because they were good for hasty getaways. John Dillinger, then Public Enemy No. 1, wrote Henry Ford in 1934 to say, "You have a wonderful car. It's a treat to drive one." Clyde Barrow, another man who found himself in need of speed, told Ford, "I have drove Fords exclusively when I could get away with one."

THAT GM QUOTE:

"What's good for General Motors is good for the U.S.A."

Actually that's NOT what **Engine Charlie Wilson**, above, GM president from 1941-1953, said. Wilson left GM to accept President Dwight Eisenhower's appointment as secretary of defense. At his Senate confirmation hearings, Wilson said: "For years, I thought what was good for our country was good for General Motors — and vice versa."

A 1931 Ford paddy wagon.
Automobile History Collection

7) The 1940 Lincoln Continental

File photo

1940 Lincoln Continental.

Edsel Ford was 3 when his father finished his first car, in 1896. Growing up, Edsel tinkered in a home workshop, and accompanied his father to his plants. He was driving by the age of 10 and had his own car at 15. He skipped college and went to work full-time at Ford Motor Co. in 1912. Henry and Edsel had rather different personalities, and Henry was widely seen as bullying his son throughout his life. Edsel's crowning achievement came as chief of the Lincoln Division. It was considered the most handsome American car of the prewar era. One much-copied design element: the covered spare-tire container. The car made its official debut as the Zephyr Continental on Oct. 2, 1939. The price was $2,916 for the convertible and $2,783 for the coupe.

8) The Jeep

Jeep! Jeep! Eugene drives his namesake.

Free Press file photo

No single vehicle, American or otherwise, has a more glorious heritage. Born at Willys-Overland in Toledo, Ford built more than one of every three Jeeps during World War II. DaimlerChrysler makes today's Jeep. Gen. George Marshall called the Jeep "America's greatest contribution to modern warfare." The original Willys Quad featured muscle — 63 horsepower and 105 foot-pounds of torque from the 2.2-liter, 4-cylinder Willys "Go-Devil" engine. About 600,000 were produced during the war and they served with distinction in every theater. Besides being almost unbreakable, World War II Jeeps were astoundingly versatile, serving as ambulances, command cars, pickup trucks, barbed wire layers, scout cars, light-artillery haulers and, when equipped with a .50-caliber machine gun, even fighting vehicles. Thousands of GIs readily acknowledged that they owed their lives to the Jeep.

➤ **Jeep: The name game**

Historians disagree on how the Jeep became the Jeep. Some suggest the name was borrowed from Eugene the Jeep, one of the supporting characters in E.C. Segar's "Popeye" comics who was a dog-like imp, capable of extra-dimensional travel and adept at resolving impossible problems — just like the Jeep.

Another theory: The name came from a specialized truck used in the Oklahoma oil fields in the '30s.

The most widely accepted theory: The name was distilled from the Army's ponderous nomenclature system that classified the vehicle as a "truck, one-quarter ton, general purpose," or GP. In GI lingo, it's not much of a stretch from GP to Jeep.

9) 1955 Chevrolet Bel Air

Free Press file photo

The V8-powered '55 Chevy Bel Air allowed drivers to see the U.S.A. in their Chevrolets at high speed. The small-block V8 became the most important power plant in American automotive history. The standard version produced 162 horsepower. With the Power Pack — a $59 option that included a bigger carburetor, different air cleaner, revised intake manifold and dual exhausts — the horsepower rating climbed to 180. Under master styler Harley Earl, GM that year introduced two-tone color schemes. Bel Air hardtop coupes were snazzy with their pillarless roof lines, color panel and trademark chrome accent on the rear fenders. The '57 Bel Airs eventually became the most desirable of all late-'50s Chevys. But many collectors say they prefer the clean, aggressive looks of the '55 edition.

10) 1959 Cadillac Eldorado Biarritz Convertible

The ultimate American car. It had acres of shiny trim, tail fins worthy of the Batmobile and those famous twin-bullet taillights. Cadillac was first to try tail fins, adding them to new cars in 1948. Chrysler became an imitator. Fins on the '59 Caddy were one of the last GM designs under Harley Earl. Fins were almost as high as the roof line. The twin-bullet taillights spliced on about halfway up. Illu-

Free Press file photo

About one week after D-Day, Army MPs in a Jeep patrol soldiers bivouacked on Belle Isle.

minated, the taillights suggested jet-assisted takeoff. The Eldorado Biarritz ragtop rode on a 130-inch wheelbase, weighed almost 5,000 pounds and sold for about $7,500. Like almost all carmakers in the '50s and '60s, Cadillac addressed the problem of excess weight by adding power. It got 345 horsepower from its 6.4-liter V8 engine.

PATRICIA BECK/Detroit Free Press

➤ Advertising for the 1959 Cadillac:

"The 1959 Cadillac speaks so eloquently — in so many ways — of the man who sits at its wheel ... This magnificent 1959 Cadillac will tell this wonderful story about you."

11) 1964 Ford Mustang

Mustang, a response to Chevrolet's youth-oriented Corvair Monza, inspired a new class of cars and became one of the most celebrated vehicles in history. Ford people involved in the project included Gene Bordinat, Don DeLaRossa and Donald Petersen. Ford division General Manager Lee Iacocca made two key contributions: He added a rear seat and sold the car to top management. Henry Ford II suggested a little more rear-seat legroom. They chose Mustang to conjure up the spirit of the famous World War II fighter plane. But the car appeared wearing the famous pony emblem in the middle of its grille. A fastback coupe was added to the Mustang lineup in 1965. Buyers could choose from three variations of Ford's new 4.7-liter V8 that produced 200, 225 and 271 horsepower, as well as a new 3.3-liter six-cylinder engine rated at 120 horsepower.

Horse power

In 1894, just two years before the first auto drove on city streets, Detroit had 95 black-smiths, 64 horseshoers, 82 livery stables, five stores that sold horse clothing, three stores that sold horse bedding and three manufacturers of horse collars. A horse hospital was located at Brush and Fort. Horses still pulled streetcars on some lines. As late as 1920, the horse population of Detroit was 35,000. A horse auction was held near Eastern Market each Saturday, at which 500 horses changed hands. Even in 1951, when junk dealers and others still drove wagons pulled by horses, the city had eight horse drinking fountains. Convicted horse thieves in Michigan could get three to 15 years in prison.

Free Press file photo

12) 1984 Chrysler minivan

JOHN COLLIER/Detroit Free Press

Lee Iacocca and a Plymouth Voyager launch the minivan revolution.

What was it? It looked like a conventional van, but on a smaller scale and with considerably less ground clearance. It had front-wheel drive, which was unique for vans at the time. It behaved on the road like a tall station wagon rather than a truck. It could hold a lot of cargo, but it would fit in your garage like a car. In 1983, Chrysler called it a minivan. An immediate success, it sent General Motors and Ford scrambling to the drawing boards. The minivan became an increasingly familiar part of our roads, largely displacing the old American family station wagon. As with the Ford Mustang, ultimate responsibility for the minivan project rested with Lee Iacocca, who took over the nearly bankrupt Chrysler after he left Ford.

Sex and the merry Oldsmobile

Detroit's premier export of the 20th Century exerted a profound effect on everything from art to agriculture to architecture.

The automobile also fueled the century's sexual revolution. Long before someone dubbed drive-in movies "passion pits" and the bumper sticker that said "If this van's a-rockin,' don't come a-knockin' " debuted, Americans discovered how the auto could enhance their love lives.

Cars, especially after Detroit started enclosing them in the 1920s, gave lovers far more privacy and mobility than a horse and buggy. The blending of cars and sex became a fixture of popular culture. Eventually, automakers started building cars that many people — psychologists, anyway — saw as possessing sexualized headlamps, hood ornaments and radiator grilles. Sleek hot rods were said to become an extension of male virility. And automobile advertising has long featured a heavy sexual flavor.

In a special edition of Michigan Quarterly Review in 1983, auto historian David Lewis traced the links between sex and the automobile and concluded:

"Autos have done more than enable couples to meet and make love and to inspire songwriters, Valentine and card designers, cartoonists and adsmiths. They also have influenced American culture by abetting prostitution, creating the "hot pillow" trade in tourist courts and motels, providing an impetus for drive-in restaurants and movies, and inducing many motorists to wear their hearts on license plates and bumpers."

Detroit designers built front seats of automobiles in the Roaring '20s that folded into the backseats to form beds. Cozy rumble seats fostered physical contact. Couples used cars' detachable seats as mattresses.

In My Merry Oldsmobile

WALTZ SONG

WORDS BY VINCENT BRYAN

MUSIC BY GUS EDWARDS

M. Witmark & Sons, New York, London, Chicago.

Lewis recounted popular postcards and cartoons of the 1930s that underscored the connection between lovemaking and cars. One, from the New Yorker in 1931, showed a bedraggled couple carrying a rear seat cushion and reporting a stolen car to police.

Songwriters mixed cars and love in such songs as "Take a Little Ride with Me Baby, In Our Little Love Mobile" and "On the Back Seat of the Henry Ford."

According to Lewis, the best-known song ever written about an automobile was "In My Merry Oldsmobile:"

"Come away with me Lucille,
In My Merry Oldsmobile
Over the road of life we'll fly
Autobubbling you and I,
To the church we'll swiftly steal,
And our wedding bells will peal,
You can go as far as you like with me, In our merry Oldsmobile."

Flying

Our biggie is the 13th-busiest airport on Earth — ahead of New York's JFK and major airports in London, Paris and Hong Kong.

Metro Airport

It was called Wayne County Airport when the first craft landed there Feb. 22, 1930. By 1958, it had been renamed Detroit Metropolitan Wayne County Airport, and in 1966 a second terminal opened and six airlines moved from Willow Run Airport to the facility. In December 2001, a 74-gate midfield terminal is expected to open at Detroit Metropolitan Airport.

The $2-billion expansion includes the mid-field terminal, an 11,500-space parking garage, the airport's fourth principal runway and a road that will connect the new terminal and the rest of the airport to Eureka Road.

➤ **Metro in its national context**: These are the busiest U.S. airports, ranked by the number of passengers in 1999:
1) Atlanta .... 77.9 million
2) Chicago .... 72.5 million
3) Los Angeles............................... 63.8 million
4) Dallas/Ft. Worth......................... 60 million
5) San Francisco............................ 40.3 million
6) Denver .... 38 million
7) Minneapolis/St. Paul................ 34.2 million
8) Detroit .... 34 million
9) Miami... 33.9 million
10) Newark, N.J.............................. 33.8 million

SOURCE: AIRPORTS COUNCIL INTERNATIONAL-NORTH AMERICA.

➤ **Metro's passenger growth:**
1990 .... 20.5 million
1995 .... 27.5 million
1998 .... 31.5 million
1999... 34 million

➤ **Metro Airport report card**: Conde Nast Traveler's 1999 Readers' Choice Awards

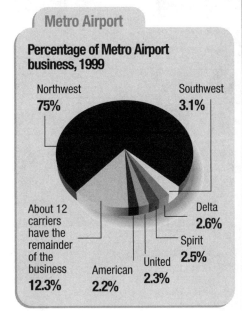

Metro Airport

Percentage of Metro Airport business, 1999

Northwest **75%**
Southwest **3.1%**
About 12 carriers have the remainder of the business **12.3%**
American **2.2%**
United **2.3%**
Spirit **2.5%**
Delta **2.6%**

dubbed Metro worse than Mexico City/Juarez, which it said was Latin America's worst airport. In a 1997 quality survey by Plog Research of Reseda, Calif., travelers rated Metro the worst of 36 major airports.

Detroit City Airport

Gratiot and Conner in Detroit.

Dedicated in 1930 as a base for a burgeoning airmail business, the 270-acre airport was laid out between two cemeteries on a swampy riverbed once used as a dump. City Airport was often criticized as being too small or sur-

Up and away

Takeoffs and landings, 1998:

Detroit Metro.............. 538,155
Oakland County Internat'l. 332,017
Willow Run..... 185,651
Ann Arbor Municipal 126,513
Detroit City..... 123,146
Mettetal-Canton.............. 82,800
Grosse Ile Municipal 60,000
Livingston County-Howell 59,000
St. Clair County Internat'l. 48,300
Berz-Macomb .. 43,900
New Hudson..... 40,000
Oakland-Troy ... 39,600
Brighton Field .. 31,060
Romeo 20,900
Monroe-Custer.............. 20,218
Marine City 17,800
Macomb-New Haven 3,220

SOURCE: MICHIGAN DEPARTMENT OF TRANSPORTATION, BUREAU OF AERONAUTICS.

Luggage lined up at Metro Airport, 1973. Passengers all ready for travel. Times change.

JOHN COLLIER/Detroit Free Press

rounded by too many hazardous gas tanks, buildings and homes. By the mid-1940s, the city-owned airport was home to Northwest Airlines, United, TWA, Pennsylvania Central and American Airlines. For $58.35, Eastern Airlines flew from Detroit to Miami in nine hours. The airport was handling 166 scheduled flight operations daily. But by 1949, many airlines had transferred to Willow Run Airport and later to Metro Airport. Detroit officials have tried over the years to rejuvenate City Airport, upgrading the terminal and expanding the runway. Discount airline Pro-Air is City Airport's only commercial service.

Oakland International

M-59 west of Crescent Lake Road in Waterford.

Pontiac officials purchased the first 160 acres for the airport in 1927, and the facility has gradually grown. Projections have airport business growing 30 percent more by 2020, largely from business travel. The growth is expected to include a doubling of the number of corporate jet takeoffs and landings before 2020. The airport's main runway length is 6,200 feet, long enough to handle a Boeing 727. There are no plans to lengthen the runway.

Willow Run Airport

Van Buren Township.

The federal government built the airport in 1941. During World War II, Willow Run was part of the largest bomber plant in the world. It employed 42,000 workers. In 1947, the University of Michigan purchased the airport from the government for $1 and used it for aeronautical research. Since 1966, when the last passenger airline moved to Metro Airport, Willow Run's business has been mostly cargo and corporate. U-M decided to get out of the airport business in 1977 and transferred ownership to Wayne County.

Catching a ride

DETROIT
Department of Transportation, 1990/1998:
Buses 477/442
Riders .... 83.6 million/55.2 million.
People Mover cars .... 10 (1991)/8
Riders .... 3.2 million/2.1 million
SUBURBS
SMART (Suburban Mobility Authority for Regional Transportation) 1990/1998:
Buses 203/237
Riders .... 8.7 million/10.9 million
ANN ARBOR
Transportation Authority (1990/1998):
Buses 53/58
Riders .... 3.7 million/4.1 million

SOURCE: SEMCOG.

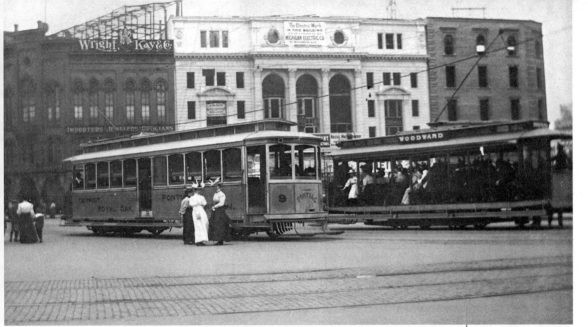

A Pontiac and Detroit Railway interurban downtown in 1897 next to a Detroit streetcar.

The railroad

Interurban lines after WWI

Michigan

Bay City

Saginaw

Grand Rapids

Owosso

Port Huron

Lansing

Kalamazoo

Jackson

Detroit

Toledo

Indiana

Ohio

1916: Passengers could travel every hour, and sometimes every half-hour, on interurban streetcars from downtown to Port Huron, Saginaw, Ann Arbor, Jackson and points in between.

➤ **MILEAGE:** There are 3,964 miles of railroad in Michigan that are owned by 34 companies, including 78 miles owned by Amtrak Here's a look back at rail mileage in Michigan:

1840	35 miles
1850	342 miles
1860	779 miles
1870	1,638 miles
1910	9,100 miles (high point)

➤ **AMTRAK:** The passenger count for:.
1990/1998 ....382,100/359,402
(Chicago-Detroit-Pontiac)

➤ **RAILROADS SERVING METRO DETROIT:**
Amtrak
Ann Arbor
Canadian National
Canadian Pacific
Coe Rail
Conrail
CSX Transportation
Delray Connecting Railroad
Indiana & Ohio Railroad
Norfolk Southern
Tuscola & Saginaw Bay Railroad

➤ **STREETCARS:** Detroit's extensive mass transit system was considered one of the best in North America about 80 years ago. All that remains are rails that sometimes poke through crumbling street surfaces.

Rail tonnage

Terminated within state:

Coal	33% of total
Metallic ores	32%
Chemicals	7%
Primary metal products	5%
Petroleum/coal products	4%

Originated within state:

Metallic ores	42%
Transportation equipment	18%
Waste and scrap	8%
Farm products	6%
Nonmetallic minerals	5%

Burton Historical Collection

A crew poses in front of a Detroit-bound interurban.

The People Mover in 1987. A circuit of the 2.9-mile loop through downtown takes 15 minutes.

A look back

➤ **1874**: People living out in what was then the country around Third and Holden could rumble 3 miles downtown on cars pulled by horses.

➤ **1890s**: An electric funeral car with an upholstered interior took caskets and mourners to Woodmere Cemetery.

➤ **1914**: A passenger on the meandering Sherman line would pass through successive neighborhoods peopled by Irish, Greeks, blacks, Italians, Germans and Belgians.

➤ **1916**: Passengers could travel every hour, and sometimes every half-hour, on interurban streetcars from downtown to Mt. Clemens, Port Huron, Pontiac, Flint, Saginaw, Ann Arbor, Jackson and points in between.

➤ **1930**: Within Detroit, the rail system peaked when about 30 lines stretched over 534 miles of track.

➤ **1941**: Streetcars ran on Woodward Avenue every 60 seconds at peak times.

➤ **1956**: Service was discontinued.

➤ **STAGECOACHES:** The first stage left Detroit in June 1822. Destination: Mt. Clemens.

By 1832, stages were departing almost daily for Monroe, Toledo, Plymouth, Ann Arbor and Pontiac. By 1837, stages linked Detroit with Chicago and Buffalo. A trip to Chicago took nearly five days. The last stage ran in 1873.

'The horse that never tires'
— Free Press headline, 1854

Free Press file photo

Free Press file photo

The travails of freeway travel. This jam happened in May 1978 on the northbound Lodge when a garbage truck overturned, spilling its goods over three lanes.

A primer on:
The streets
of Motor City

Streets

There are 22,576 miles of streets in metro Detroit, almost enough pavement to circle Earth at the equator (a distance of 24,902 miles). Detroit has 2,789 miles of streets. By county:

Wayne	6,977
Oakland	5,474
Macomb	2,965
Washtenaw	2,124
St. Clair	1,958
Monroe	1,593
Livingston	1,485

SOURCES: MICHIGAN DEPARTMENT OF TRANSPORTATION AND THE CITY OF DETROIT.

Stop-and-Go

In 2000, about 9 percent of Detroit area roads were considered congested, meaning traffic is often stop and go. By 2025, experts say 11 percent of the region's roads will be congested. Here's the breakdown by percent of roads congested:

City	2000	2025
Detroit	10.7%	9.2%
Livingston	2.7	6.8
Macomb	17.3	21.2
Monroe	1	2.3
Oakland	18.9	26.4
St. Clair	0.6	1.3.
Washtenaw	6.2	9.8.
Wayne (outside Detroit)	7.9	9.3.

SOURCE: SOUTHEAST MICHIGAN COUNCIL OF GOVERNMENTS ESTIMATE.

The dangerous intersections

Check your brakes before you cross these paths:
1. Van Dyke/East I-696 Service Drive in Center Line .... averaged 102 crashes over a 5-

Time to take your road test

PAY ATTENTION!
Take John R 4 miles down to the Reuther, over to the Chrysler, down to the Ford, then to the Lodge, to the Fisher and get off at the Boulevard. Go left a couple blocks.

WHERE WERE YOU AND WHERE ARE YOU?

(Need some help? The answer is on page 245.)

Surveying

Outside of the old French road system, the dominant features of metro Detroit's landscape are the mile roads and townships. Government surveyors began dividing southeastern Michigan after the War of 1812, based on requirements in the Northwest Ordinance of 1785.

The surveyors marked off one-mile-square sections — hence, mile roads. Thirty-six sections made up a township, which remains an important political division outside of heavily populated areas. In the 19th Century, large sections of Detroit were part of such townships as Greenfield, Hamtramck and Grosse Pointe.

Today's 8 Mile Road was the important baseline from which the surveying began.

year period
2. Greenfield/7 Mile in Detroit 90
3. McNichols/Schaefer in Detroit 82
4. Van Dyke/7 Mile in Detroit 81
5. 7 Mile/Outer Drive West in Detroit 79
6. Van Dyke/Hall Road in Utica 78
7. Big Beaver/Rochester in Troy 76
8. Orchard Lake/12 Mile in
   Farmington Hills 75
9. Southfield/West I-696
   Service Drive (WB 11 Mile)
   in Lathrup Village 73
10. McNichols/Livernois in Detroit 72

SOURCES: SEMCOG, BASED ON CRASH DATA PROVIDED BY THE MICHIGAN DEPARTMENT OF STATE POLICE; OFFICE OF HIGHWAY SAFETY PLANNING.

➤ **ADDENDUM:** State Farm Insurance in 1999 ranked Gratiot and 23 Mile Road in fast-growing Chesterfield Township the 10th most dangerous intersection in the nation.

The flow

Feeling a tad scrunched as you tool along I-75 between 9 Mile and I-696? That's the busiest stretch of roadway in the region, with a daily volume of 247,000 vehicles. Other busy stretches by freeway:

➤ **I-75:**
— between I-94 and I-696
   .... 200,000-plus vehicles
— between I-94 and I-375 123,000
— at the River Rouge Bridge 88,300
➤ **I-696:**
— between Woodward and I-75 .. 207,000
— between Telegraph and
   Southfield 149,000
— at Van Dyke 120,000
➤ **I-275:**
— between 6 Mile and I-96 200,000
— at Ford Road 97,000
— at I-94 54,000
➤ **I-96:**
— between Southfield and
   Telegraph 180,000
— south of I-94 98,700
— in Plymouth 65,200
➤ **M-39 (Southfield):**
— between Grand River and
   6 Mile 167,000
— at I-96 152,000
— at Michigan................................... 96,300
➤ **I-94:**
— between Woodward and
   Lodge Freeway 170,000
— between I-696 and 12 Mile 150,000
— between Wayne Road and
   I-275.. 118,000
➤ **Lodge Freeway (M-10):**
— between Davison and Linwood 150,000
— at Joe Louis Arena 94,000
— at 8 Mile 98,700

Surface streets

➤ **8 Mile:**
— at I-75 75,500
— at Grand River 38,000
➤ **Woodward:**
— at 14 Mile 78,300
— at 7 Mile 23,000
➤ **Telegraph:**
— at Long Lake................................. 73,300
— at Michigan 62,700
➤ **Northwestern:**
— at Southfield................................ 119,700
— at 12 Mile 52,100
➤ **Van Dyke:**
— at 15 Mile...................................... 69,100
— at 8 Mile 23,700
➤ **Michigan:**
— at Southfield 55,600
— at Trumbull.................................... 13,900
➤ **Gratiot:**
— at I-696 63,900
— at Conner 31,600
➤ **Fort:**
— at Eureka 46,300
— at Sibley 35,100
➤ **Ford Road:**
— at Telegraph 54,900
— at Canton Center 26,200

SOURCES: SEMCOG AND THE MICHIGAN DEPARTMENT OF TRANSPORTATION.

Freeway origins

They were called expressways and became part of the interstate highway system spawned by the Eisenhower Administration in the 1950s, although some of Detroit's e-ways were built in the 1940s. Police and transportation officials began an education program as more freeways opened in the 1950s to teach motorists the finer points of driving on the new, sunken highways. They issued instructions on how to merge and exit and how not to change lanes. It is impossible to calculate the total cost of building metro Detroit's freeways during more than 50 years. But the Michigan Department of Transportation says it costs an average of $39 million (in 2000 dollars) to build a mile of freeway.

➤ **Davison (M-8):** Many historians say it was the nation's first freeway, a fact disputed by California. The Davison was built in 1941-1942 to relieve heavy traffic in the Highland Park area. The Davison closed in 1996 and reopened 16 months later after a $45-million renovation.

➤ **Edsel Ford (I-94):** Called the Willow Run Expressway, it first linked Detroit and the Wil-

Construction of the Chrysler Freeway is under way in Detroit in April 1960.

low Run bomber plant. It was completed in 1942. The freeway opened as far as Vernier Road in Harper Woods in late 1959.

➤ **John C. Lodge (M-10):** Opened in stages starting downtown and extending to 8 Mile between 1953 and 1964. Motorists marveled that they could travel from the New Center neighborhood to downtown — less than 3 miles — in 3½ minutes. But traffic jams became a problem virtually from the first day of operation.

➤ **Walter P. Chrysler (I-75):** The first 2.7 miles from downtown northward — through what had been Detroit's main black neighborhood — opened in June 1964 and cost $50 million. I-75 already was open from 11 Mile to Sault Ste. Marie. The Chrysler link between I-94 and 8 Mile opened in January 1969 and cost $100 million.

➤ **Southfield (M-39):** Southfield Road was a four-lane divided highway in the early 1950s when officials began planning a high-speed expressway. The first 2.7 miles, from Ford Road to West Chicago, opened in December 1961, and small sections opened over the next three years. The 13-mile freeway, from I-94 to 9 Mile, was operating by mid-1964. The freeway cost $40 million.

➤ **Walter Reuther (I-696):** When this route opened on Dec. 14, 1989, it ended freeway construction in metropolitan Detroit. The final stretch completing the 28.2-mile freeway linked I-75 to Lahser Road in south Oakland County. The entire freeway took 30 years to build and cost $675 million.

➤ **I-275:** The north-south link on the western edge of metro Detroit stretches a little more than 30 miles from I-75 to the intersection of I696, I-96 and M-5 in Farmington Hills. The first 2 miles, near I-75, opened in Decem-

ber 1970. The last section — about 5 miles — opened between Ford Road and M-14 in November 1976.

➤ **Fisher (I-75):** Running from Downriver into downtown, the 14-mile link opened between 1967 and 1970 in stages. It's named after the Detroit banking and auto family.

Streetwise

The French set the pattern for metro Detroit's street system. And the French have a word describing it: bizarre.

In the 1700s, French settlers laid claim to narrow ribbon farms that ran perpendicular to the Detroit River — but never due north. Some of the first streets — including Beaubien, St. Antoine and Chene — were named for the farmers and ran parallel to their property boundaries. Thus, today the main roads within a couple of miles of the water from Monroe to St. Clair Shores travel in the same skewed direction as those 18th-Century farms.

Americans imposed a survey in which the roads run north-south and east-west. Central Detroit and much of the east side are laid out in the French pattern. Main streets in northwest Detroit and Oakland County are done American style: straight as compass points. The biggest mess is where the two systems converge:

➤ East of City Airport.
➤ Grand River and Livernois. Livernois, named after a French family, goes both ways: From the river to Tireman, its alignment is French. Above Tireman, it travels due north and south.

CONCRETE RIBBONS, BY THE NUMBERS:

309.5

Total freeway mileage in metro Wayne, Oakland, Macomb and St. Clair counties.

3,543

Bridges in metro Detroit. 3,068 of them cross highways.

THE NAME: Judge Augustus Woodward, above, named the street after himself when he drew up the plan for the city's new street system following the fire of 1805. Woodward was designed as a 120-foot-wide thoroughfare from the river to Grand Circus Park. The judge claimed he used "Woodward" because the street headed "toward the woods."

Metro Detroit's main street

Detroit's main drag within the original fort was Rue Ste. Anne. By the early 1800s, Atwater had evolved into the city's main street. After 1830, according to historian JoEllen Vinyard, it was Jefferson. But by 1850, Woodward had taken over as the main artery, a distinction it retains 150 years later.

Woodward Avenue

The axis of metro Detroit. State highway M1.

It begins at Jefferson by Hart Plaza, anchored in a way by a huge bronze fist that is a tribute to boxer Joe Louis. Woodward travels north by northwest for 28 miles, bisecting some of the region's richest, poorest, oldest, newest, ugliest and most beautiful territory.

Along Woodward are more than 350 historic and cultural sites, ranging from the Detroit Institute of Arts to the State Fairgrounds to the Detroit Zoo.

Here's the evolution of our main drag:

➤ **Indian trail:** Parts of Woodward follow a centuries-old route Indians used. The Woodward route led to a village near Saginaw.

➤ **Homes:** In the period after 1830, Woodward was a residential street north of Campus Martius in today's downtown. The mostly frame homes sat behind lawns and often were painted with yellow ocher and had green shutters. As the 19th Century progressed and Detroit grew, the homes became stores, and then were demolished to make way for buildings.

➤ **The rich:** In the late 19th Century, some of Detroit's wealthiest citizens lived on Woodward south of today's Cultural Center, includ-

Burton Historical Collection

The west side of Woodward near Clifford in 1907. Woodward has been Detroit's main drag for 150 years.

ing shoe magnate and politician Hazen Pingree; seed merchant D.M. Ferry; attorney Levi Barbour, department store owners J.L. Hudson and C.R. Mabley and U.S. Sen. Thomas Palmer. Most mansions are long gone, but two relics are the David Whitney home at Canfield, now the Whitney restaurant, and the chateau-like Hecker-Smiley Mansion near Ferry Street, which is a block of elegant 19th-Century homes. Today, Detroit's richest neighborhoods are just west of Woodward and south of 8 Mile, and Woodward runs through two of the wealthiest communities in Oakland County — and the nation: Birmingham and Bloomfield Hills.

➤ **Churches:** In the 1830s, First Presbyterian, St. Paul's Episcopal and First Methodist Episcopal were built on the east side of Woodward, north of Larned. Later in the 19th Century, the area north of Grand Circus Park had so many churches that it became known as Piety Hill. Temple Beth El was on Woodward and Eliot

from 1903 to 1922 before moving north to Woodward and Gladstone. Today, dozens of many old and new places of worship sit astride the avenue in both Detroit and Oakland counties, including Blessed Sacrament Cathedral, the seat of the Roman Catholic Archdiocese, the Episcopal Cathedral Church of St. Paul, Little Rock Baptist Church, Metropolitan United Methodist Church, Shrine of the Little Flower and the first temple in Michigan for the Church of Jesus Christ of Latter Day Saints.

➤ **Planks:** Starting in the mid-19th Century, Woodward — and all thoroughfares leading out of Detroit — were toll roads made of wood planks. By 1817, Woodward was planked with large logs placed closely together and covered with small timber, brush, clay and sand from Grand Circus Park to 6 Mile. In 1848, the state Legislature authorized private companies to operate toll roads. In 1849, Woodward was extended to Pontiac with oak planks 16 feet long and 3 inches thick. The toll on the Detroit and Pontiac Plank Road was 1 cent a mile for one- and two-horse vehicles. For each herd of cattle the toll was 2 cents a mile. The first toll gate outside of what was then the city was at present-day Adams at Grand Circus Park. Running a toll gate without paying was punishable by a $25 fine. Tolls were collected on some parts of Woodward near 8 Mile until 1908.

➤ **Pavement:** In 1909, the nation's first stretch of paved highway was built on Woodward between 6 Mile and 7 Mile. It was 18 feet wide, and cost $13,000. That portion was broken up in 1924 when Woodward was widened to 204 feet.

Dream cruisers tool along Woodward in 1999.

THE DREAM CRUISE

In 1995, business leaders along Woodward inaugurated the Dream Cruise, a summer weekend recalling those Woodwarding days of 30 and 40 years ago. It became a hugely successful run of muscle cars, street rods and custom collector cars. The event, held in late August, draws more than one million spectators.

Dream Cruise revelers head north on Woodward through Royal Oak in 2000.

Pedal carefully!

Metro Detroit's top bicycle crash locations (yearly average per 100,000 people, 1994-1998):

Michigan and Venoy, Wayne 2.2

12 Mile and Gratiot, Roseville...................1.4

Frazho and Gratiot, Roseville...................1.4

Garfield and 15 Mile, Clinton Township 1.2

Beech Daly and 7 Mile, Redford 1.2

Greenfield and Joy, Detroit.......................1.2

Ryan and 12 Mile, Warren 1.2

SOURCE: SEMCOG.

Eight Mile looking east in 1998. That's Oak Park on the left, Detroit on the right and power lines up the center.

ANDREW JOHNSTON/Free Press

Burton Historical Collection

A mother and daughter pedaling on a Detroit street in 1901.

➤ **Widening:** In 1933, work began to widen Woodward from Adams to Grand Boulevard. It took two years to widen from 66 feet in some spots to 90 feet, with 15-foot sidewalks. In 1932, after seven years of construction and moving everything from cemeteries to railroad tracks, a 204-foot superhighway opened to replace a road between the Detroit city limits that in places was as narrow as 16 feet. Construction for the project, dubbed Wider Woodward, cost $7.5 million.

➤ **Woodwarding:** Teenagers in the 1950s and 1960s turned Woodward in Oakland County into a nationally known strip for hot-rodding, cruising, motorized flirting and drag racing. The kids called it Woodwarding. Car and Driver Magazine proclaimed Woodward "the street-racing capital of the world." Young people, some in modified Corvettes, GTOs and Mustangs, flocked to such drive-in restaurants as Ted's, the Totem Pole, Big Boy's, Big Town, Susie Q's and Mavericks. On Friday and Saturday nights during summer, they made an 11-mile loop between 10 Mile and Square Lake Road, performing such rites of passage as Chinese fire drills, chicken, mooning and breasting (females bared their chests to passersby). So

renowned was the practice that car manufacturers would send engineers in prototypes to cruise Woodward, too, using the hot-rodding teens as a focus group for the concept cars.

Two other great streets

➤ **Jefferson:** For much of the 19th Century, Jefferson was Detroit's main street. Named for President Thomas Jefferson, it runs roughly parallel to the Detroit River. It was the first street to have streetcars, the first street on which great numbers of rich families built lavish homes, the site of the nation's first auto plant and the gateway to the wilds — and later resorts and mansions — of Grosse Pointe. By the 1920s, East Jefferson was home to churches, hotels, grand apartments, an amusement park and numerous factories. And that was just the east side. West Jefferson was the route to Ft. Wayne and the Delray neighborhood. Today, Jefferson hugs the water, extending from the northeast to the southwest edge of metro Detroit.

➤ **8 Mile Road:** The old surveying line forms the boundaries between southern Michigan counties and Illinois and Wisconsin. It is a muscle road, split by a fat median that for much of it carries huge electric power lines, the address of numerous factories, tool and die shops, bars, used car lots, factory closeout stores, salvage companies, resale shops and strip clubs. But 8 Mile's modern significance developed when Detroit's majority white population began moving north from the city in the 1950s to suburbs in Macomb and Oakland counties. The result: Eight Mile became a metaphor for polarization between the white suburbs and the now-majority black city. Mayor Coleman Young ordered bad guys to "hit 8 Mile" in his 1974 inaugural speech, and some people north of 8 Mile took that as a provocation. In 1998, Macomb Board of Commissioners chairman John Hertel floated the idea of changing 8 Mile's name. "Eight Mile Road has so many psychological, negative connotations to it," Hertel said. "This can be given as a signal that things can get better."

Street names

We'll take care of the most
pondered first:

Burton Historical Collection

John R. Williams, 1782-1854. He was Detroit's first elected mayor.

➤ **John R.** It's named for John R. Williams, Detroit's first elected mayor (1825). He is also the namesake of Williams Street in Detroit. Some others:

➤ **Gratiot:** Col. Charles Gratiot. He served in Gen. William Henry Harrison's army, which drove the British out of Michigan in the War of 1812. Gratiot also was commander of the U.S. garrison at Detroit in 1815. Work began on the Gratiot Turnpike in 1828, designed as a military road to connect forts in Detroit and Port Huron. By the 1850s, wooden planks connected Detroit and Mt. Clemens.

➤ **Grand River:** On Aug. 29, 1821, Lewis Cass and Solomon Sibley met the chiefs of the Ottawa, Chippewa and Potawatomi to negotiate a treaty in which the Indians relinquished land south of the north bank of the Grand River in western Michigan. The treaty permitted a military road running to the river, and that road became Grand River.

➤ **Fort:** Ft. Shelby once stood along what is Fort Street in downtown Detroit.

➤ **Mt. Elliott:** It passes a cemetery of that name on Detroit's east side. The cemetery and street are named after Robert T. Elliott, a Detroit businessman who in 1841 became the first person buried in the cemetery.

➤ **Big Beaver:** Sixteen Mile Road is named for the settlement of Big Beaver, which developed in the mid-19th Century at Big Beaver and Rochester Road.

➤ **Livernois:** Named for Francis Livernois, a French farmer in the 18th Century.

➤ **Schoolcraft:** Henry Schoolcraft was an explorer, pioneer and expert on Indian tribes. His six-volume "Archives of Aboriginal Knowledge" was one of nearly a dozen works he wrote on Indians in Michigan and surrounding areas.

➤ **Coolidge:** Named after President Calvin Coolidge.

➤ **Schaefer:** John Schaefer, a Dearborn real estate developer.

➤ **Dequindre**: Maj. Antoine Dequindre was a landowner and prominent participant in the War of 1812.

➤ **Stephenson Highway:** Burnette Stephenson was a land developer in the early 20th Century who purchased a 13-mile strip from Nevada Street in Detroit to Square Lake Road in Troy and donated the land (which ran along his subdivisions) to the Oakland County Road Commission for a highway. Part of it became a section of I-75.

➤ **Crooks:** Possibly named after Riley Crooks, an early Troy town clerk who was killed by a falling tree in 1830. The road might also be named for its serpentine shape.

➤ **Jos. Campau:** Joseph Campau was one of Detroit's richest residents in the 19th Century.

➤ **Charlevoix:** Pierre F.X. Charlevoix was an 18th-Century French priest.

➤ **Mack:** Landowner John M. Mack was the street's namesake, according to historian Silas Farmer. Others contend the street was named for Andrew Mack, a Connecticut native who sailed around the world three times as a ship's captain and arrived in Detroit in 1830.

➤ **Van Dyke:** James Van Dyke was a prominent attorney who saved Detroit from financial ruin when he was elected mayor in 1847, thanks to his tight supervision of city affairs. He was best known for organizing the city's fire department.

➤ **Oakman Boulevard:** Robert W. Oakman was a labor newspaper editor hired as a financial adviser by Mayor Hazen Pingree in the 1890s. Oakman, a socialist, ended tax breaks for businesses and railroads to bring rampant land speculation under control. Ironically, he later made a lucrative living in real estate. Oakman was the agent who sold Henry Ford the 62-acre tract in Highland Park where Ford built the world's first assembly line. The land cost $55,800. Twisting, stately Oakman Boulevard in Detroit, Highland Park and Dearborn connects Ford's Rouge and Highland Park plants.

➤ **Trumbull:** John Trumbull was an early American poet who moved to Detroit in 1825 to live with his daughter, who married William Woodbridge, an early governor of Michigan Territory.

➤ **Allen Road:** Lewis Allen was a pioneering

HENRY SCHOOLCRAFT

He's remembered with a county in the Upper Peninsula.

EDWARD N. HINES

You can thank him for all those center lines

JOHN C. LODGE

An ex-mayor and Free Press city editor.

TRANSPORTATION

TELEGRAPH: THEN AND NOW

Burton Historical Collection

Telegraph in Wayne County looked more like a northern Michigan trail about 90 years ago. At right, the road through Oakland County in 1998 is more familiar.

Free Press file photo

Namesakes

ZACHARIAH CHANDLER

Several hats: Detroit mayor, U.S. senator, secretary of Interior.

LEWIS CASS

This picture was taken in 1855, 11 years before the territorial governor's death.

lumberman and attorney who established a sawmill on the Rouge River and during winter months hauled logs to the mill from his woods. That route became known as Allen's Road, then Allen Road.

➤ **Eureka**: Eureka Iron Co. used this route to bring in supplies to its Wyandotte plant.

➤ **Hines Drive**: Edward N. Hines, chairman of the Wayne County Road Commission, authorized the first white center lines to separate lanes of traffic in 1911.

The French influence

Many were farmers or landowners, including: Antoine **Rivard**; Francis **St. Aubin**; Gabriel **Chene**; Louis **Beaufait**; Dominique **LaBrosse**; Dominic **Riopelle**, James **Dubois** and Charles **Guoin**. Maj. Antoine **Dequindre** and Lambert **Beaubien** served in the War of 1812. Beaubien also named a street after his patron saint, **St. Antoine.**

The Rev. Jacques **Marquette** and Gabriel **Richard** were French priests. Robert **La Salle** built the first Great Lakes sailing vessel in 1679. Marquis de **Montcalm** was the French general killed in the Battle of Quebec in 1759. Antoine de la Mothe **Cadillac** founded Detroit.

Count **Pontchartrain**, the French Colonial Minister of Marine, left his name to an appropriately classy west side drive. Count **Frontenac** was governor-general of New France.

All in the family

If you were an early Detroit citizen who aspired to be memorialized on a street sign, it helped to be a relative or friend of a prominent citizen or landowner.

Brush Street is named for Col. Elijah Brush, who went to the aid of prisoners held by Indians in Monroe County. His son, E.A. Brush, had streets named for his mother — **Adelaide**; his son — **Edmund**; his brothers **Alfred** and **Eliot**, and Alfred's wife, **Rowena**. Some say Alfred is actually named for E.A. Brush.

Lewis **Cass**, a landowner and 19th-Century Michigan territorial governor, took care of in-laws as well as immediate family. **Spencer** was the maiden name of his wife, **Elizabeth**. **Brainard** is named after his wife's grandmother, Martha Brainard Spencer. **Selden** is named after Deborah Selden Spencer, his mother-in-law. His son-in-law, Col. Canfield, also got a street. And **Belle Isle** honors his daughter, Isabelle. A good thing, too, since its name under the French was **Ile aux Cochons**, or **Hog Island.**

William B. **Wesson** was a real estate developer. With partner Albert **Crane**, Wesson developed huge sections of Detroit in the mid-

POLICING: THEN AND NOW

WILLIAM ARCHIE/Detroit Free Press

**Above: One of Detroit's finest urges drivers through an intersection in June 2000.
Right: An officer directs traffic on Woodward at Grand Circus Park around 1930.**

Burton Historical Collection

1800s. He also exercised his prerogative to name a score of streets after relatives and friends.

Baldwin was his father-in-law; **Cutler** and **Lysander** were brothers, and **Celia** was a sister-in-law.

Among streets named after friends, most of them from the East (he was born in Massachusetts), are **Aurelia, Bryant, Jane, Louisa, Marcy, Mark, Merrick, Morton, Oakley, Otis, Pelouze and Perkins.**

Crane, who left Detroit for Chicago, left a somewhat smaller street-name legacy. Aside from his own last name, he christened **Waterman, Brewster, Marion** and **Whitney** after friends and relatives.

Leaders and heroes

It would seem logical that mayors ought to have streets named after them.

Edward **Jeffries** and John C. **Lodge** have freeways named after them. James **Couzens** rated only a service drive.

Some past mayors are as well-known as the streets that bear their names, such as Hazen **Pingree**. But others have faded from memory. So here's to a few of the forgotten: Henry Jackson **Hunt** was Detroit's second mayor (1826); Dr. Zina **Pitcher** (1840, '41 and '43), Col. Henry **Ledyard** (1855); Charles **Trowbridge** (1834); John **LaDue** (1856-57),

and Asher **Bates** (1838).

Lesser city officials have streets named after them, too. **Ellery** is after Ellery Garfield, city controller in the 1870s. Chauncey **Hurlbut** was a water commissioner whose name also adorns the ornate gate to Waterworks Park, as well it might. He left his entire $250,000 estate for the improvement of the park, once one of the city's premier recreation spots.

Presidents have lent their names to plenty of Detroit streets. A partial list: George **Washington**, John **Adams**, Thomas **Jefferson**, James **Madison**, James **Monroe**, Andrew **Jackson**, William Henry **Harrison**, Franklin **Pierce**, James **Buchanan**, Abraham **Lincoln**, Ulysses S. **Grant** (who as a soldier was stationed briefly in Detroit in 1851), James **Garfield**, Grover **Cleveland**, Theodore **Roosevelt** — and **Woodrow Wilson.**

John P. **Hale** may have hoped getting a street named after him would further his political ambitions. Hale ran for president as an abolitionist candidate at the same time the street was named in the 1850s, but the east side road traveled farther than his political career.

Among streets named for other American heroes: John **Hancock** put his John Hancock on a street in what is now Detroit's Cultural Center. **Columbus** was named after the explorer.

Other notable citizens who left their

> "A Detroiter behind the wheel seemed changed into a Frankenstein."
>
> — **Arthur Hailey**, "Wheels"

Free Press file photo

Shock demolishers: Potholes on Cass Avenue in 1985.

AREA ROADS RATED POOR

Extra annual cost per car

	%	$
New Orleans	35	208
Detroit	35	186
Los Angeles	33	188
Indianapolis	31	171
San Jose	30	179

businesses. Ferry's warehouse was one of pre-automotive Detroit's largest employers. As a member of the Board of Park Commissioners in 1885, he prohibited beer from being brought to Belle Isle.

Clifford was originally Cliff's Ford, a crossing on the old St. Mary's Creek, which once flowed through downtown Detroit. The ford was west of Woodward, just south of Thomas Cliff's tavern.

Samuel **Zug** was a penniless Pennsylvania bookkeeper who came to Michigan in 1836 and got rich in the furniture business. He bought a chunk of land on the Rouge River for his estate. Someone later cut a canal that made his estate an island. Zug, who was Wayne County auditor in 1873, sold the land as an industrial dumping ground. It has been home to huge blast furnaces for more than 100 years.

Former Detroit streets

Apple Pie, A, Swain Avenue, Lover's Lane, Dred, Joe, 17½.

Detroit Street

One of the city's shortest streets, it runs for a block, starting at Cadieux between East Warren and Mack, and deadending before reaching Guilford to the east.

Roadwork
A brief history
(before the orange barrels)

➤ **1851:** Residents spread lime on streets as a disinfectant.

➤ **1858:** Detroiters complained about cattle, horses and pigs in the street.

➤ **1861:** Garbage in the streets was a major issue.

➤ **1919:** First asphalt paving was used on Gratiot.

➤ **1972:** Franklin, Detroit's last remaining cobblestone street, was unearthed for construction of the Renaissance Center. The street dated to the 1850s.

➤ **Potholes:** In 2000, the Road Information Project, a nonprofit group mostly financed by road-construction interests, identified the worst roads in the nation's big cities. Roads in each area were rated poor, mediocre, fair or good. Costs were partially figured on Transportation Department estimates on vehicle operating costs.

Signs of summer: This lane ends. Lane closed. Construction ahead. Detours posted.

J. KYLE KEENER/Detroit Free Press

names on Detroit streets:

Palmer Park and **Palmer** Avenue are named for U.S. Sen. Thomas W. Palmer, who was born in 1830. As a state senator, Palmer coauthored legislation to build **Grand Boulevard.** He became a U.S. senator in 1883.

Witherell Street was named for territorial judge James Witherell.

Chandler Park Drive is the namesake of Zachariah Chandler, a Republican senator in 1857-75 when he was appointed U.S. Secretary of the Interior. He was elected mayor of Detroit in 1851, after playing a leading role in the construction of plank roads around the city.

The Rev. John **Monteith** was the first Protestant missionary in Detroit in 1815.

Dexter Mason **Ferry** took a small seed store on Monroe Avenue and built it into one of the world's largest and most successful seed

A war worker assembles parts for bombs in 1944.

Free Press file photo

Detroit at war

Workers stopped making cars in 1942 and production shifted to war equipment, earning the city the title Arsenal of Democracy. "Detroit is winning the war," Soviet dictator Josef Stalin reportedly told President Franklin D. Roosevelt in 1945. And Gen. Dwight D. Eisenhower , the Allied commander of 3 million soldiers in Europe, said the weapons he valued most were the Detroit-made jeep, 2½-ton truck, bulldozer and transport planes.

Free Press file photo

Bombers are assembled at the Willow Run plant during World War II.

Free Press file photo

M4 and M5 tanks are parked in front of the General Motors Building in May 1943.

Answer to quiz

START

13 Mile
12 Mile
11 Mile
10 Mile
9 Mile
8 Mile

John R

75

696

Reuther Fwy.

Chrysler Fwy.

DETROIT

McNichols

Davison Fwy.

10

Woodward

Ford Fwy.

Lodge Fwy.

96

75

94

Grand Blvd

375

75   FINISH   Detroit River   Canada

N

Answer: You went from Oakland Mall to the Detroit River at West Grand Boulevard.

Missed the quiz?
Return to **Page 233**

Suburban street-finding trick

Looking for an address on the large north-south roads such as Woodward and Van Dyke? Take the first two numbers of the address — for example 35 for a business at 35000 Woodward — and subtract five. That gives you 30. Then divide by two — 15 — and that's your nearby mile road — 15 Mile. And remember: Even numbers are on the east side and odd numbers on the west.

The Detroit Almanac

09, PO

"Reward your friends and punish your enemies. I think that's a pretty good political rule."

— *Mayor* **Coleman Young**

LITICS

yes

VOTE YES
FOR DETROIT

Power Brokers, Past and Present

Southeastern Michigan had two local governments in the early 1800s: Wayne County and Detroit.

Today, metro Detroit is seven counties. In Wayne, Oakland and Macomb counties alone there are 76 cities, 42 townships, 13 villages, 83 school districts, 17 special districts, three circuit courts, 40 district courts and five municipal courts.

And lots of politicians.

Here's a list of the main political players in metro Detroit.

DENNIS ARCHER: The mayor of Detroit is the region's best-known public official. While the mayor is supreme inside the city and can be *tres* influential across the region and state, Archer has proven to be less aggressive than the late Mayor Coleman Young. Archer appears to be grooming his top lieutenant, Deputy Mayor Freman Hendrix, to succeed him.

BAPTIST PASTORS: Candidates for office in Detroit, Wayne County and even statewide must seek support from the members of the Council of Baptist Pastors of Detroit and Vicinity. The president for 2001 is the Rev. E. L. Branch, pastor of Third New Hope Baptist Church in Detroit. Some pastors have run for office.

JOHN COLLIER/Detroit Free Press

Mayor Dennis Archer is influential in the region and the state.

Left: Civil rights pioneer Rosa Parks and Mayor Coleman Young stump for a ballot proposal in the early 1980s.

Free Press file photo

DAVID BONIOR: Democratic whip in the U.S. House, the party's No. 2 job. Should the Democrats regain the house, Bonior of Mt. Clemens would likely become majority leader as U.S. Rep. Dick Gephardt of Missouri elevates to House speaker.

JOHN CONYERS: A founding member of the Congressional Black Caucus and ranking Democrat on the House Judiciary Committee, the Detroiter was elected to Congress in 1964. He continues to serve as sentinel with a national platform on important issues to many minorities, such as racial profiling and allegations of racism in the national guard.

THE DINGELLS: John Dingell is dean not only of the Michigan congressional delegation, but of Congress (he was elected in late 1955). Dingell of Dearborn wields tremendous influence as ranking Democrat on the House Commerce Committee, as a longtime friend of labor and also as a longtime ally of

David Bonior

John Conyers

POLITICS

John Dingell

Debbie Dingell

General Motors Corp.

Dingell's wife, Debbie, is not only a GM heiress (she's the granddaughter of one of the Fisher brothers) but also is president of the General Motors Foundation and a Democratic National Committee member.

MIKE DUGGAN: The deputy Wayne County executive ran the county on a daily basis and helped put together the big deals for the new baseball and football stadiums. He becomes Wayne County prosecutor in 2001.

BETH DUNCOMBE: As head of the City of Detroit's deal-making agencies, she would be a player even if her sister wasn't married to Mayor Dennis Archer.

JOHN ENGLER: His birthplace of Beal City is a long way from metro Detroit, but with the Legislature in GOP control, the Republican governor has been a major force in Detroit politics.

MARK GAFFNEY: President of the Michigan AFL-CIO, which, next to the UAW (its largest member union), is the most important segment in Democratic Party politics.

JOHN HERTEL: The chairman of the Macomb County Board of Commissioners is also a gubernatorial appointee who runs the Michigan State Fairgrounds in Detroit. Thus, he's one of the rare metro pols who operates in multiple jurisdictions.

JENNIFER GRANHOLM: The state attorney general, Granholm is a Harvard-educated lawyer. She was Wayne County government's top lawyer when she began an underdog bid to succeed the retiring Frank Kelley in 1998 as attorney general. There's much talk of her as a future governor.

THE LEVINS: Carl Levin is the senior U.S. senator from Michigan, first elected in 1978. He previously served as president of the Detroit City Council. Known as a stickler for such ethics issues as lobbying activities, he is one of the Senate's dependable liberals. The ranking Democrat on the important Armed Services Committee, he has, in general, maintained a low profile nationally while working quietly for local projects such as federal help for Metro Airport.

Sander Levin, Carl Levin's older brother, is the Democratic U.S. representative from Royal Oak, Troy, Warren and Sterling Heights. He was first elected in 1982. Sander Levin previously had been a state senator and unsuccessful gubernatorial candidate. A member of the House Ways and Means Committee, he concentrates on trade issues, and sparked controversy from labor allies in 2000 when he coauthored compromise language in the China trade bill that was credited with helping to win over many reluctant votes.

CANDICE MILLER: The Republican secretary of state, Miller upset long-serving incumbent Richard Austin in 1994. From Harrison Township, she's the daughter of marina owners and an avid sailor. Miller began her political career when she was elected Harrison Township trustee in 1979, and later township supervisor, the youngest person and first female to hold that post. When she was elected Macomb County treasurer in 1992, it was the first time a Republican had won a major Macomb County office in 40 years.

ED MCNAMARA: The executive of Michigan's most populous county seems low on energy, but his fat campaign treasure chest and networking ability can help a pol in need. Just ask Jennifer Granholm or Mike Duggan.

L. BROOKS PATTERSON: Less of a public persona than he was as the Oakland County prosecutor, the executive of the state's wealthiest county (Oakland) continues to influence local and state Republican politics.

STEVE YOKICH: Head of the UAW, which, for years in Michigan, has been the single most important player in Democratic Party politics.

**Mike
Duggan**

**John
Hertel**

**Jennifer
Granholm**

**Carl
Levin**

**Sander
Levin**

**Candice
Miller**

**Ed
McNamara**

**Steve
Yokich**

Politicians and plutocrats of the past

In the old days, some of Detroit's richest people also held public office.

Michigan Prisoner No. 284797.

HONORARY POLITICIAN: Jack Kevorkian is a pathologist by trade, but few politicians have succeeded in raising a political issue like he did in the 1990s. Kevorkian of Oakland County became world-famous for his advocacy of assisted suicide and for the help he gave to more than 120 people in ending their lives.

It was never a dull campaign. Kevorkian dropped off corpses at hospitals and left them in vans and motels. He showed up at Oakland County Circuit Court one day dressed in a rented colonial powdered wig, colonial knickers and shoes with large buckles to protest his prosecution under what he called an ancient legal concept.

Kevorkian is serving a 10- to 25-year sentence in state prison after an Oakland County jury in 1999 convicted him of second-degree murder for lethally injecting Thomas Youk, 52, a Lou Gehrig's disease patient from Waterford. In Michigan, legislators outlawed assistance in suicide and voters buried a ballot proposal to legalize it.

If appeals fail, Kevorkian will be eligible for parole on May 26, 2007 — two days before his 79th birthday.

LEWIS CASS (Oct. 9, 1782-June 17, 1866): Probably the most accomplished Detroit politician in terms of offices held, Cass is the only Detroiter to run for president on a major ticket. He also served as one of the main architects of U.S. policy toward Indians in the 1830s, and he was one of the city's wealthiest residents before the Civil War.

Born in New Hampshire, Cass was the youngest member of the Ohio legislature before he moved to Detroit in 1813 as governor of Michigan Territory. In that post, he made deals for Indian land in what is now metro Detroit and, coincidentally became a large property holder himself, just as land-hungry American settlers began arriving in Michigan.

President Andrew Jackson appointed Cass secretary of war, and he began to oversee Indian affairs at a national level. Cass orchestrated Jackson's now-notorious policy of Indian removal, and his writings about Indians appear racist when read today.

Fluent in French, Cass became the U.S. minister to France in 1836. He returned to Detroit in 1842 and became active in Democratic politics. Before popular election of senators, the Legislature elected him to the U.S. Senate, and Cass was the Democratic nominee for president in 1848. After losing his presidential bid, Cass returned to the Senate, but lost his seat in 1857, partially because of the rise of the Republican Party and antislavery sentiment in Michigan. He served as secretary of state under President James Buchanan, and died at his home in Detroit.

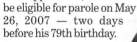

Lewis Cass is the only Detroiter to run for president on a major ticket.

> Kevorkian dropped off corpses at hospitals and left them in vans and motels.

POLITICS

HENRY ROWE SCHOOLCRAFT (March 28, 1793-Dec. 10, 1864): A public official in Michigan before it became a state, Schoolcraft lived in Detroit in the 1830s. He was best known as an author, historian, ethnologist, lecturer and Indian agent who helped negotiate treaties for considerable native land in Michigan. He served as a mineralogist in 1820 on the first American expedition to the upper Great Lakes, which was headed by Territorial Gov. Lewis Cass. Aided by his Ojibwa-Irish wife, Jane, Schoolcraft studied Indian language and traditions and published numerous books on the topics. Schoolcraft also founded the Michigan Historical Society. In an 1843 trial in Detroit, Schoolcraft was ordered to pay nearly $10,000 to the U.S. Treasury for misappropriating government funds. He is the namesake of Schoolcraft Avenue and Schoolcraft County.

RUSSELL ALGER (Feb. 27, 1836-Jan. 24, 1907): Born in Ohio, Alger moved to Grand Rapids, then settled in Detroit after fighting for the Union during the Civil War. He made a fortune in the lumber business, eventually owning property in several states and one Canadian province. He was elected governor as a Republican in 1885 and was talked about for president, although he never campaigned for the office. He became secretary of war under President William McKinley in 1897, and oversaw the U.S. military during the Spanish-American War, for which he received criticism for American blunders, although historians say he also achieved a numbers of successes. Alger served in the U.S. Senate from 1902 to 1907.

DOUGLASS HOUGHTON (Sept. 21, 1809-Oct. 13, 1845): Born in Troy, N.Y., Houghton was a physician and geologist who came to Detroit in 1830 to give science lectures. He explored mineral deposits and collected plants during a Henry Schoolcraft-led journey to Lake Superior and the Mississippi in 1831 and 1832. He practiced medicine in Detroit, became a real estate speculator, and was elected Detroit mayor as a Democrat in 1842. He also served as state geologist, University of Michigan professor and surveyor of Michigan's natural resources. He drowned in Lake Superior at age 36. Houghton County and the city of Houghton in the Upper Peninsula and Houghton Lake are named for him.

ZACHARIAH CHANDLER (Dec. 10, 1813-Nov. 1, 1879): A New Hampshire native, Chandler took the Erie Canal to Michigan like thousands of other easterners and opened a dry goods store in Detroit. Elected Detroit's first "dry" mayor as a Whig in 1851, Chandler fought in vain against the city's powerful saloon owners. He failed to win a second term, but became an early abolitionist and participated in helping people escape slavery along the Underground Railroad. One of the founders of the antislavery Republican Party in 1854, Chandler was elected to the U.S. Senate in 1857. He was a radical Republican who fought the spread of slavery and advocated war, if necessary, to save the union. Chandler served as a well-regarded secretary of the interior under President Ulysses S. Grant. He died one of the Detroit's richest residents, with holdings in banks, lumber and land.

JAMES MCMILLAN (May 12, 1838-Aug. 10, 1902): Rich, powerful and conservative, McMillan personified the establishment in late 19th-Century Detroit. McMillan got into the railroad business and then founded the Michigan Car Co., which made boxcars. Within a few years, his interests included the Detroit Car Wheel Co., Baugh Steam Forge and Detroit Iron Furnace. He was behind much of the rail expansion into the Upper Peninsula, and he also was involved in banks, shipping and private streetcar companies. By 1878, he was a member of the Republican State Committee, and he was running the Michigan Republican Party by 1886. McMillan went to Washington as a U.S. senator in 1889, becoming a successful and respected deal maker. As a wealthy Gilded-Age machine boss who became an advocate of urban planning, McMillan "stood at the juncture of the old and the new," wrote historian Jon Teaford.

ROBERT PELHAM JR.: Detroit's most prominent black politician of the 19th Century, the Republican activist was appointed to a number of state and national posts. He invented a tabulating machine while working for the Census Bureau. Pelham worked for the Detroit Post and was involved in the creation of the Detroit Plain Dealer, the city's black newspaper.

D. AUGUSTUS STRAKER: Born in Barbados,

Douglass Houghton

Zachariah Chandler

Robert Pelham Jr.

Augustus Straker

Straker was a lawyer who came to Detroit in 1887. He became involved in the state Republican Party and served as an organizer of several black organizations. Author David Katzman described Straker's politics as a mixture of W.E.B. Dubois' militance and Booker T. Washington's accommodation. In 1892 and 1894, Straker was elected a Wayne County Circuit Court commissioner, the equivalent of a judge. It was the highest elective office held by a black Detroiter before World War II.

TRUMAN NEWBERRY (Nov. 5, 1864-Oct. 3, 1945): Born wealthy in Detroit, Newberry was the son of John S. Newberry, the founder of the Michigan Car Co., congressman and business partner of James McMillan. Truman Newberry owned parts of utilities, shipping companies and banks, and was an investor in the Packard Motor Car Co. A Republican, Newberry served as secretary of the Navy under President Theodore Roosevelt. In 1918, Newberry ran against Henry Ford for U.S. Senate. Ford spent virtually no money and hardly campaigned, but lost by only 4,334 votes. Newberry's blue-blooded friends donated more than $200,000 to his effort, far above the legal limit, and for that, Newberry was indicted by a federal grand jury in Detroit. He was later convicted, sentenced to two years in prison and fined $10,000. In 1921, the U.S. Supreme Court reversed Newberry's conviction, arguing that Congress had no authority under the Constitution to regulate primary elections. Newberry served as senator for 10 months, but resigned when it appeared authorities might reopen the criminal case against him. He was ruined politically, but he continued to be a successful businessman.

Postwar pols

MARY BECK: The first woman to be elected to the Detroit City Council, and the first to be council president. When she took her seat in

Mary Beck

1949, spittoons still decorated the council chambers. Viewed as a liberal during her early terms, Beck was labeled a law-and-order conservative by the end of her council career. Most Detroiters remember Beck for wearing a new hat every day, and for having almost as many criticisms of the late Mayor Jerome Cavanagh. She ran for mayor in 1969 but failed to make the runoff election. She lives in Sterling Heights.

KEN COCKREL: An audacious radical who taunted, beat and later joined the system, Cockrel was one of the city's most charismatic leaders during the turbulent period in the 1970s and '80s when blacks gained political power in Detroit. Cockrel was a socialist, a successful attorney and a city councilman who was considering a run for mayor in 1989 when he died of a heart attack at age 50. He was never shy about picking fights. His most dangerous target was the white-dominated police department and its notorious undercover STRESS (Stop the Robberies, Enjoy Safe Streets) decoy unit. Cockrel led the fight to disband STRESS, and over the years, he also took on such local powers as Detroit Recorder's Court judges, businessmen Max Fisher and Al Taubman, General Motors Corp. and Chrysler Corp. The lanky Cockrel

POLITICS

COCKREL IN THE EARLY 1980S, ADDRESSING A PUBLIC MEETING OF RESIDENTS, CITY OFFICIALS AND GENERAL MOTORS' OFFICIALS ON GM'S POLETOWN PLANT PROJECT. HE SPOKE EXTEMPORANEOUSLY — NEVER MISSING A BEAT.

When firebrand Ken Cockrel joined the sometimes lethargic Detroit city council in 1977, one observer compared it to putting Mick Jagger on "The Lawrence Welk Show."

Free Press file photo

Erma Henderson

Martha Griffiths

Charles Diggs Jr.

Robert Millender

Thomas Poindexter led Detroit white home owners' last-ditch fight against integration.

always cut a distinctive figure, with his loping street walk, his black beret over a luxurious Afro (during the 1960s) and his smart suits and European-style man's purse (during the 1980s). He was known for a superior intelligence, a needling wit, a huge store of nervous energy and an incomparable command of language. Cockrel was married to Sheila Murphy Cockrel, a community activist who later was elected to the Detroit City Council. His son, by a first marriage, is Ken Cockrel Jr., also a member of the Detroit City Council.

ERMA HENDERSON: In 1972, Henderson became the first black woman to be elected to the City Council. She served as council president for 12 years, leaving her seat in 1989 after losing a mayoral primary to Coleman Young. Henderson battled the mayor over control of the city budget and helped pass a nuisance abatement ordinance which allows people to rehabilitate vacant, tax-delinquent property.

MARTHA W. GRIFFITHS: A Detroiter, she was a political pioneer: First woman elected Michigan lieutenant governor, first woman in the U.S. House appointed to its powerful Ways and Means Committee, and first female judge in Detroit's Recorder's Court. As a five-term congresswoman, she was the chief sponsor of the Equal Rights Amendment to the U.S. Constitution and succeeded in adding the word "sex" to the 1964 Civil Rights Act, which has enabled women along with minorities to benefit from the act's equal-employment provisions. To an airline executive who tried to defend a "singles only" policy for female flight attendants, Griffiths raged: "What are you running, an airline or a whorehouse?" And in 1982, with James Blanchard heading the Democratic ticket, she became the first woman elected to the state's No. 2 office. As lieutenant governor presiding over the state Senate, Griffiths on many occasions told lawmakers half her age to "sit down and be quiet." They did. She served for two terms until

Blanchard decided he didn't want Griffiths, then 78, on the ticket for a third run in 1990. Griffiths didn't go quietly, blaming her dismissal on age discrimination. Blanchard lost.

THOMAS POINDEXTER: The reactionary leader of Detroit's white home owners fought against neighborhood integration in the 1950s and '60s. A Democratic lawyer, Poindexter began his public career as a harsh critic of big business but switched his targets to crime and civil rights, becoming a sympathizer of both the John Birch Society and Alabama Gov. George Wallace. He was elected to the Detroit City Council in 1964, at the time he was championing the Homeowners' Rights Ordinance, which would have preserved the right of whites to discriminate against blacks in selling homes. Voters passed the measure, but courts ruled it unconstitutional.

CHARLES C. DIGGS JR.: In the mid-1970s, when he was at the peak of his political power, the Democratic congressman from Detroit was the dean of Michigan's congressional delegation, the senior black member of Congress, a founder of the Congressional Black Caucus and a leader in African foreign policy. Deliberate and dignified, Diggs was known as a quiet power broker and the heir to one of Michigan's largest funeral homes. But while he was steadily acquiring power in the nation's capitol, he had piled up bills at home. So to stave off his growing debt, Diggs concocted a scheme to raise his congressional employees' income and had them kick back $66,000. He left Congress in 1980 and served seven months in a federal prison camp for fraud. His downfall was, in some ways, an eerie repeat of the political misfortunes of his father, Charles Diggs Sr., who was found guilty of taking a bribe while a state senator and committed suicide in 1967. The younger Diggs died in 1998 at 75.

**Maryann
Mahaffey**

MARYANN MAHAF-FEY: A liberal's liberal who once chaired Detroit's "Free Angela Davis" Committee, the former Wayne State University professor was elected to the council in 1974, the year Coleman Young became mayor. Depending on your viewpoint, she is either an obstructionist or a tenacious leader of the opposition. But she is one of Detroit's best-known politicians, showing up everywhere, whether it be hugging the relatives of crime victims or joining protesters trying to block the state from closing a Detroit health clinic. In 1992, at age 67, she broke her right leg while dancing with elephants in Thailand.

ROBERT MILLENDER: Before his death in 1978 at age 61, Millender specialized in labor law as a partner in one of the nation's first racially integrated law firms — Goodman, Eden, Millender & Bedrosian in Detroit. But perhaps more importantly, Millender was a political strategist who played key roles in the election of many of Detroit's first generation of black leaders — Mayor Coleman Young, Congressmen John Conyers Jr. and George Crockett, Secretary of State Richard Austin and former Congressman Charles Diggs Jr., among many others. Quiet, modest, conservatively tailored, a smoker of slender imported cigars, Millender appeared the antithesis of the stereotypical political kingmaker. Yet he was credited with uniting disparate elements of the city — organized labor, church groups, and professional and corporate interests — into a powerful electoral coalition, often on the strength of his personality.

HUGH GRANNUM/Detroit Free Press

Geoffrey Fieger: Gov. John Engler kicked his gluteus maximus across the state. Fieger vowed to do just that in his attempt to oust Engler from his gubernatorial post.

Politics NOT as usual

FIEGER TIME: Geoffrey Fieger, the Oakland County attorney who represented Dr. Jack Kevorkian for much of Kevorkian's assisted-suicide crusade, also ran for governor in 1998. Fieger won the Democratic primary and faced incumbent Gov. John Engler in the general election. The campaign was enlivened by Fieger's bombast. Consider these Fieger characterizations of Engler:

Left: Police interrupted Cindy Darrah's nakedly ambitious 1977 campaign stunt. Darrah, above, was running for Detroit City Council.

Free Press file photo

**Dennis
Dutko**

**Henry
Stallings II**

**Basil
Brown**

**Daniel
West**

"Nincompoop," "simpleton," "the product of miscegenation between a human being and a barnyard animal," "semi-retarded" "having the policies of Adolf Hitler and Josef Stalin," "a racial bigot," "a liar," "a religious bigot," "much more of a danger to our freedoms than Saddam Hussein," "a draft dodger . . . a coward on the war," "a thief," "fat," "ugly," "dumb," "brutal."

Fieger repeatedly accused Engler of "hate-mongering," "religious polarization," "pandering to bigotry," "demonization," and "McCarthyism." Fieger also said he would kick Engler's "gluteus maximus across the state."

Engler won by 739,431 votes.

NAKED AMBITION: In her 1977 campaign for the Detroit City Council, Cindy Darrah attempted to float across the Detroit River — nude — on a door from a demolished house. A police boat plucked her from the door as she shivered, wearing only what was left of her handprinted campaign signs. Darrah, 33, was a city lifeguard.

Police sent her for a psychiatric evaluation. "If I did everything normal, I would have no chance to get elected," Darrah said. She lost.

Term limits

Do not pass go, or collect that public trough paycheck. These elected officials ran afoul of the law:

SEN. ANTHONY WILKOWSKI, a state legislator in the 1930s, is said to be the first Michigan lawmaker to hold office while in jail. The Detroit Democrat entered the prison at Jackson in the late 1930s after being convicted of fraud during a ballot recount. Republicans made no effort to oust him because his inability to vote while incarcerated thwarted a Democratic majority.

Wilkowski was re-elected but was denied

seat he won in 1950 and 1954 when senators refused to seat him, citing his previous conviction.

DENNIS DUTKO, a Democratic state representative from Warren, served 7½ months in the Ingham County Jail for drunken driving before resigning his seat Oct. 2, 1989.

He was paid while jailed but donated his salary to alcohol-rehabilitation programs.

Less than two weeks after his release, Dutko committed suicide on Jan. 17, 1990.

SEN. HENRY STALLINGS II, D-Detroit, resigned Feb. 25, 1998, after pleading guilty to a felony charge of using a state employee to work in his art gallery.

SEN. BASIL BROWN, D-Highland Park, was arrested in November 1985 and charged with delivering and possessing cocaine and marijuana. Facing up to 20 years in prison, the state legislator pleaded guilty, but reserved the right to appeal on grounds that police had entrapped him. He resigned in 1987. In 1992, after a 7-year legal battle, a judge tossed out the drug charges.

REP. DAISY ELLIOTT, D-Detroit, was charged in 1982 with possessing and driving a stolen 1977 Cadillac. She lost her re-election bid and was convicted that same year.

REP. CASMER OGONOWSKI, D-Detroit, pleaded guilty in February 1982 to federal extortion charges and resigned the next month.

REP. MONTE GERALDS, D-Madison Heights, the only state lawmaker ousted by the Legislature, was convicted in March 1978 in Oakland County Circuit Court of embezzling $24,000 from a client of his private law practice. The House voted to expel him after he refused to resign.

SEN. CHARLES YOUNGBLOOD JR., D-Detroit, resigned in 1974 after being convicted in

**Daisy
Elliott**

the

**Casmer
Ogonowski**

**Monte
Geralds**

**Charles
Youngblood Jr.**

Wayne County Circuit Court of bribing the chairman of the state Liquor Control Commission. The state Court of Appeals overturned the conviction in 1975.

JUDGE CRATER SYNDROME: And then there was Daniel West, the quiet, laid-back, distinguished-looking, 56-year-old Detroit Democrat who got bounced from the Michigan House of Representatives in 1965 after his colleagues discovered he'd fabricated key parts of his personal history, covered up a criminal past, adopted the background and lofty academic record of a deceased New York lawyer (also named Daniel West) and bilked the government and others by filing all sorts of phony income-tax refund claims.

A federal grand jury indicted him on 117 tax-related counts, and a Detroit Recorder's Court judge bound him over on bad-check charges. In July 1965, on the day before his federal jury trial was to begin, he vanished.

And he's still missing — if alive he'd be 91.

The 107 guys who've run Detroit

Sure, you've heard of Coleman Young, who put in 20 years — making him the longest-serving mayor of Detroit. But how about the 106 others who've run the city, or hamlet or fort since 1701?

Antoine de la Mothe Cadillac, 1701-1710: In 1696, with the North American fur market depressed by over-trapping, Jerome Phelypeaux, the Count de Pontchartrain and King Louis XIV's minister in charge of New France, ordered the closing of many French wilderness forts.

Enter Cadillac — new-world savvy and ambitious, with a solid record of good service to the crown. His plan in the face of the retrenchment: build a fort along *le detroit*, the stretch of water north of Lake Erie. The attraction: a fort, he convinced Pontchartrain, that would quickly become a regional center for the Frenchification of Indians — and would keep the English from moving into the void of the northwest that would be created if all the French posts closed.

So the native of St. Nicholas-de-la-Grave in southern French was given permission to build the fort, which he began on July 24, 1701.

Cadillac was born Antoine Laumet on March 5, 1658. He assumed the aristocratic name of de la Mothe Cadillac upon arriving in North America, where he married Marie-Therese Guion. The couple had 13 children.

Detroit — named Ft. Pontchartrain by Cadillac — was a continual crisis for him. He reported to Quebec for extended visits to fight a variety of charges. In 1703, fire destroyed several buildings in the fort, and officials accused him of mismanagement, but he was acquitted.

He also argued with the Jesuits over his penchant for supplying liquor to the Indians. The Jesuits strongly opposed booze-for-pelts. Cadillac's plan to Frenchify the Indians fell apart when the Indians began fighting among themselves. In 1707, Pontchartrain appointed Francois Clairambault D'Aigremont to travel to the French forts to assess the situation.

D'Aigremont ripped Cadillac, calling him a profiteer and a danger to France's goals in the West. "M. de la Mothe . . . was generally hated by French and Indians alike," D'Aigremont reported. Pontchartrain was forced to remove Cadillac from Detroit, but he appointed him governor of Louisiana in 1710. Cadillac took office in 1713, returned to France in 1719, and died in 1730.

Detroit historians often have given Cadillac strong marks for leadership and have treated him with the solemn respect accorded a founder.

Clarence Burton, Detroit's homegrown historian, said he believed Cadillac was a hero who was betrayed by numerous foes. "Men of positive natures invariably make enemies," Burton wrote.

Less provincial historians scoff:

Jean Delanglez, a Belgian-American Jesuit historian, questioned Cadillac's sanity, called him an "impudent liar" and concluded that Cadillac schemed to gain personal wealth at the expense of everyone around him.

W.J. Eccles, an expert in Canadian history, said Cadillac deserves to be ranked with the "worst scoundrels ever to set foot in New France."

Pierre Alphonse de Tonty, 1717-1727: Cadillac's deputy at the founding; filled in for Cadillac and ran the fort for a decade until his death in Detroit in 1727. Historian C.J. Russ said Tonty was "a talented officer" with a "streak of greediness."

Francois, Dauphin de la Forest, 1705 and 1710: Another fill-in for Cadillac, Forest was a wheeler-dealer whose life and business affairs were complicated and contentious. Although he received an order to command Detroit, it is unclear if he ever came to the fort, because of illness.

Antoine de la Mothe Cadillac, founder of Detroit, is often given high marks by historians for his leadership skills. However, others question his sanity and say he was a scoundrel and a liar.

In 1774, parliament passed a law placing English colonies in the northwest under the administration of London. On paper, Detroit became part of Quebec, and power was vested in a governor and lieutenant governor.

Etienne Venyard, Sieur de Bourgmont, 1705: Another temporary commander.

Jacques-Charles Renaud, Sieur Dubuisson, 1710-1715: A well-regarded soldier, Dubuisson led French troops against the Fox Indians in 1712. Casualties: 1,000 Fox and other Indians, and one French person were killed. He was technically an acting commander.

Jacques-Charles Sabrevois, Sieur de Bleury, 1715-1717: A good soldier who later ran afoul of his Quebec superiors.

Louis de la Porte, Sieur de Louvigny, and **Francois Marie Picote de Belestre**: Both commanded the fort between 1717 and 1728 when Tonty was absent.

Jean Baptist de St. Ours, Sieur Deschaillons, 1728-1730: Rose from cadet to king's lieutenant of Quebec and was a successful businessman.

Louis Henry Deschamps, Sieur de Boishebert, 1730-1734: An able officer whose reforms cleaned up corruption at the fort.

Jacques Hughes Pean, Sieur de Livandiere, 1734-1736: Successful businessman and soldier.

Nicolas Joseph Desnoyelles de Fleurimont, 1736-1740: Tenure troubled by problems with Indians. He also served as acting commander in 1720.

Pierre Jacques Payan de Noyan, Sieur de Charvis, 1740-1742: Officials in Paris and Quebec liked Charvis, who was considered an expert on the West. But he failed to control the brandy traffic and improve relations with the Indians.

Pierre Joseph Celoron, Sieur de Blainville, 1742-1744 and 1750-1754: Popular with Ottawa while commander at Michilimackinac, he encountered opposition from fur merchants during his first stint at Detroit. During his second stint, he angered superiors by refusing an order to attack the Miami Indians. Though spelled differently, Celeron Island at the mouth of the Detroit River is named for him.

Paul Joseph Le Moyne, Chevalier de Longueil, 1744-1749: Member of a well-known military family, he was considered a blood brother by Iroquois Indians. He dashed a planned Indian attack on Detroit in 1747. In 1748, Ottawa, Potawatomi, Huron and Ojibwa Indians returned as French allies.

Jacques-Charles de Sabrevois, fils, 1749-1750: Son of the Detroit commander in 1715-1717.

Jacques-Pierre Daneau, Sieur de Muy, 1754-1758: An able diplomat and sophisticated officer, he died in Detroit after a long military career.

Jean Baptiste Henri Beranger, 1758: Moved up temporarily after the death of de Muy.

Francois Marie Picote, Sieur de Belestre, 1758-1760: Last French commander; son of a former temporary commander. France lost North American to the British during the French and Indian War. Although the peace treaty was not signed until 1763, he lowered the French flag in Detroit on Nov. 29, 1760, after 59 years, 998 baptisms, 147 marriages and 475 deaths.

Maj. Robert Rogers, 1760: Led the troupe that took Detroit from the French and returned to fight during Pontiac's conspiracy in 1763. He later served at Michilimackinac. Rogers' life included leading his famous rangers against the French and Indians in the wilds of upstate New York. He's also acclaimed as an author of books about North America. In 1767, he was acquitted of treason with the French. He died in poverty after serving terms in debtors' prison in England.

Maj. Donald Campbell, 1760-1762: Hosted regular parties for the town's gentlemen and ladies. Campbell remained as second-in-command after Major Henry Gladwin became commander. Indians despised the British because they were less generous as traders than the French. During Pontiac's uprising in May 1763, Indians captured Campbell and Lt. George McDougall. In early July, McDougall escaped. Days later, the nephew of an Ojibwa chief was killed near the fort. The chief took vengeance on Campbell, who was tomahawked to death, scalped and cut to pieces. The chief tore out Campbell's heart and ate it. Body parts were thrown into the river and floated toward the fort, where the British retrieved them for burial.

Maj. Henry Gladwin, 1762-1764: Orchestrated the defense of Detroit in 1763 during the siege led by Pontiac.

Col. John Bradstreet, 1764: Had a reputation for tricking Indians in treaties. One of his first acts during his month-long command of Detroit was concluding a deal with the Indians that allowed the British to use a strip of land along the Detroit River toward Lake St. Clair.

Lt. Col. John Campbell, 1764-1766: Civilians continued to protest British tax policies under him. After leaving Detroit, he served as British superintendent of Indian affairs.

Maj. Robert Bayard, 1766.

Capt. George Turnbull, 1766-1769: Appointed Philippe Dejean to hold court and settle disputes like a justice of the peace and sheriff; Dejean overstepped his authority, however, and was later punished by Canadian courts.

Maj. Thomas Bruce, 1770.

Capt. James Stephenson, 1770-1772.

Maj. Henry Bassett, 1772-74: Settled land disputes by appointing a royal surveyor.

The Quebec Act:

In 1774, parliament passed a law placing English colonies in the northwest under the administration of London. On paper, Detroit became part of Quebec, and power was vested in a governor and lieutenant governor.

But in practice, the military retained control over the settlement at Detroit.

Capt. Richard Lernoult, 1774-1776 and 1777-1779: Britain declared martial law in the region in 1775 as the Revolutionary War was beginning. In November, **Capt. Henry Hamilton** (1775-1778) came to Detroit as lieutenant governor, a civil position. Lernoult retained the title of commander.

Under Lernoult and Hamilton, Detroit became Britain's main supply base for its Western military campaigns during the Revolutionary War. Detroit was never the scene of a battle, but it became well-known to American colonists as the originating point of numerous attacks on frontier settlements in Pennsylvania, Ohio, Virginia and Kentucky by redcoats and Indian allies. The brutality of the killing and scalping during the raids shocked Americans, who derided Hamilton as the "hair buyer." The Americans later captured Hamilton in Vincennes, Ind.

Under Lernoult, a new fort was constructed here that became known as Ft. Lernoult.

Capt. John Mompesson, 1776-1777: Interim commander during absence of Lernoult.

Col. Arnt Schuler De Peyster, 1779-1784: Known for his ability to handle the very different demands of the French and Indians. Encouraged further settlement of the area outside the fort, including Belle Isle. A longtime friend of poet Robert Burns, De Peyster often communicated with him in verse. Burns' last poem was a response to a letter from De Peyster inquiring about his fatal condition:

> "My honour'd colonel, deep I feel
> Your interest in the poet's weel;
> Ah! now sma' heart hae I to speel
> The steep Parnassus,
> Surrounded thus by bolus pill
> And potion glasses."

Detroit becomes American ... in theory

Detroit became part of the United States after the treaty ending the Revolutionary War in 1783, but Americans were unable to take control until 1796. Meanwhile, Detroit became part of upper Canada and was under the authority of a lieutenant governor, an executive council, a legislative council and an elected assembly. By 1792, Detroiters were electing representatives to the parliament. The military commander in Detroit continued to be the local official in charge.

Capt. Henry Bird, 1784-1785.

Lt. Gov. Jehu Hay, 1784-1785: Stationed at Detroit during Pontiac's siege, his diary has provided historians with many details of the conflict. He died in 1785: his walnut coffin was believed unearthed during downtown Detroit sewer construction in 1911.

Maj. William Ancrum, 1785: Tried to retain ties between the British and Indians. Once picked a fight with a French Detroiter, who gave him a thorough thrashing.

Capt. James Wiseman, 1787 and 1787-1788.

Capt. Robert Mathews, 1787.

Maj. Farman Close, 1788-1789.

Maj. Patrick Murray, 1789-1790: Led a court and land district created by the British to administer its shrinking empire.

Maj. John Smith, 1788-1792: Served as chairman of the local land board.

Col. Richard England, 1792-1796: The Irish-born England was 6-foot-6 and corpulent. He was known as a bon vivant and as a humane officer who once helped 50 Americans gain their freedom from Indians. He helped settle Amherstburg, Ontario.

The Americans arrive

A contingent of 65 U.S. soldiers led by Capt. Moses Porter took control of Detroit on July 11, 1796.

Authority in Detroit for several years was dispersed among a number of military and civilian leaders.

In 1787, Congress passed the Northwest Ordinance, which included Michigan, Ohio, Indiana, Illinois and part of Minnesota. Arthur St. Clair served as Northwest Territory governor, even as the territory was subsequently subdivided.

Free Press file photo

Capt. Moses Porter, 1796: Ran Detroit for one day until Hamtramck arrived.

Capt. John Hamtramck, 1796: Served a month until Wayne arrived, then returned in 1802.

Born in Quebec on Aug. 16, 1757, Hamtramck joined the U.S. Army in 1775 and changed his name from Jean Francois to John Francis. He fought with George Washington during the Revolution and with Anthony Wayne at Fallen Timbers (see below). He died in Detroit at age 46.

Maj. Gen. Anthony Wayne, 1796: The famous general died late in 1796 at age 51. While in Detroit, he served as commander of the U.S. Army.

Wayne spent the winter with George Washington at Valley Forge. In 1779, he commanded the daring assault on a British stronghold at Stony Point, N.Y., and became known as Mad Anthony for his audacious tactics. He was born in Chester County, Pa., and was a surveyor before joining the Continental Army. After the Revolution, Wayne retired and represented a Georgia district in Congress, but returned to the army after allegations of election irregularities. In 1794, Wayne defeated the Indians at the Battle of Fallen Timbers (Ohio), then signed a treaty with them that gave the United States a huge tract of land. In addition to Wayne County, counties in Georgia, Illinois, Indiana, Iowa, Kentucky, Mississippi, Missouri and Nebraska are named after him. Wayne is buried at St. David's Episcopal Church in Radnor, Pa., near where he died on Dec. 15, 1796.

Maj. Gen. James Wilkinson, 1797.

Col. David Strong, 1797-1799.

Maj. Henry Burbeck, 1799-1800, 1803.

Col. Moses Porter, 1800.

Maj. Thomas Hunt, 1800-1802, 1803-1805: The city turned 100 with little fanfare.

Col. John Hamtramck, 1802-1803.

Maj. John Whistler, 1803.

Maj. General Anthony Wayne's audacious tactics led him to be known as Mad Anthony. There are counties named after him in eight states besides Michigan.

Between town and city

In 1802, the Northwest Territory legislative assembly passed an act that incorporated the town of Detroit. Its boundaries: Brush and Cass streets to 2 miles north of the river. Detroit would be governed by five trustees, a secretary, an assessor, a collector and a town marshal.

The first appointees: Trustees John Askin (he never served), John Dodemead, James Henry, Charles Francois Girardin and Joseph Campau. Peter Audrain was secretary; Robert Abbott was assessor; Jacob Clemens was collector, and Elias Wallen was marshal.

In 1803, Ohio became a state, and half of Michigan — including Detroit — became part of Indiana Territory.

In 1805, Congress created Michigan Territory, with Detroit as the capital. President Thomas Jefferson appointed **William Hull** of Massachusetts as governor; Stanley Griswold of New Hampshire as secretary, and Augustus Woodward and Frederick Bates, both of Virginia, and John Griffin of Indiana as judges. Bates resigned and was replaced with James Witherell of Vermont.

These territorial officers had no direct authority over Detroit. But several arrived the day after the 1805 fire destroyed Detroit and they assumed control over rebuilding efforts. Woodward was appointed to lay out a plan for the new town.

During the War of 1812, William Hull surrendered Detroit to the British.

In 1815, Territorial Gov. **Lewis Cass**

Wards of Detroit 1890

approved a measure passed by the Legislature that granted a new charter for Detroit. It called for the annual election of five trustees. Solomon Sibley was the first chairman of the board. In 1816, these men were elected: Peter Desnoyers, Abraham Edwards, George McDougall, Stephen Mack and Oliver Miller.

The last trustees were elected in 1823: James Abbott, Calvin Baker, Louis Dequindre, Henry Hunt and John Sheldon.

POLITICS

> During the War of 1812, William Hull surrendered Detroit to the British.

The mayors

In 1824, the law changed again, establishing a mayor, recorder and City Council.

John R. Williams, 1824-25, 1829-1830, 1844-47: Born in Detroit in 1782, Williams was an agent for fur traders and spoke only French until he was in his 20s. He served as a colonel in the militia during the War of 1812, justice of the county court, trustee of the University of Michigan and the Detroit Board of Education, and delegate to Michigan's first constitutional convention in 1835. He died in 1854.

Henry J. Hunt, 1826: A merchant and former county judge, he died in office.

Jonathan Kearsley, 1826, 1829: Was serving as recorder of the city when tapped to serve out Hunt's term.

John Biddle, 1827-28: Registrar of the land office for Detroit before serving as mayor.

Marshall Chapin, 1831 and 1833: A doctor, he established Detroit's first drugstore in 1819.

Levi Cook, 1832 and 1835-36: Faced a deadly cholera epidemic, spread by contaminated water and poor sanitation. Other city officials were convinced that the cause was a deadly "miasma" in the air, and ordered barrels of pitch to be burned at every street corner. Clouds of thick, black smoke made for a macabre scene, as volunteers pushed carts through the narrow streets, calling for citizens to "bring out your dead."

Charles Trowbridge, 1834: Assistant to Gov. Lewis Cass, he cleaned up the city's finances and also arranged for the construction of a city hall. Built near Woodward at Cadillac Square, the building stood until the 1870s, when another city hall was constructed across the street in 1877.

James Van Dyke helped organize the Detroit Fire Department and was also a former Wayne County prosecutor.

Andrew Mack, 1834: Mack owned the riverfront Mansion House, Detroit's finest hotel. With former Mayor Williams and businessman Campau, he bought the presses, equipment and name of the Oakland Chronicle newspaper and moved it to Detroit in 1829. It later merged into the Detroit Gazette and then into the Detroit Democratic Free Press, the direct antecedent of today's Free Press.

Henry Howard, 1837: A dry-goods merchant and lumberman.

Augustus Porter, 1838: Lawyer and co-owner of the Daily Advertiser newspaper; served as a U.S. senator in 1840-45.

Asher B. Bates, 1838: Finished Porter's term. Bates was a former Detroit justice of the peace and city attorney.

De Garmo Jones, 1839: A farmer, railroad owner and first stockholder of the Bank of Michigan.

Zina Pitcher, 1840-41 and 1843: Doctor and explorer who was appointed assistant surgeon in the U.S. Army by President James Monroe in 1822. Historians say he robbed Indian graves for research material. A founder of the U-M medical school, a street in Ann Arbor is named for him.

Douglass Houghton, 1842: Doctor and geologist who was commissioned in 1831 by the U.S. government to find the sources of the Missouri River. He explored the Upper Penin-

sula and drowned in Lake Superior during a violent storm in 1845. Houghton County, Houghton Lake and Houghton are named for him.

James Van Dyke, 1847: Attorney and former Wayne County prosecutor, he helped organize the Detroit Fire Department and served as its president in 1847-51.

Frederick Buhl, 1848: A furrier and milliner, he became one of the country's largest fur shippers. His brother, Christian, was elected mayor in 1860. The Buhl brothers owned lots of downtown property.

Charles Howard, 1849-50: Railroad contractor and bank president.

John Ladue, 1850-51: A leather and wool dealer, he was elected mayor three years after coming from New York to Detroit.

Zachariah Chandler, 1851-52: A dry-goods merchant, he succeeded Lewis Cass as U.S. senator.

John Harmon, 1852-53: Publisher of the Free Press.

Oliver Hyde, 1854-55, 1856-57: A hardware merchant who owned a foundry and machine shop. He urged construction of the Detroit House of Correction.

Henry Ledyard, 1855-56: Former Detroit alderman and water commissioner.

John Patton, 1858-59: A carriage smith who later served as county auditor and sher-

Burton Historical Collection

Judges and county officials of the late 1870s.

iff and justice of the peace.

Christian Buhl, 1860-61: Fur merchant, hardware wholesaler, mining magnate and milliner.

William Duncan, 1862-63: A brewer who become a state senator.

Kirkland Barker, 1864-65: A tobacco salesman.

Merrill Mills, 1866-67: A gunpowder manufacturer, fur trader and tobacconist.

William Wheaton, 1868-71: A wholesale druggist and grocer.

Hugh Moffat, 1872-75: A lumberman.

Alexander Lewis, 1876-77: A flour and grain merchant, he was elected mayor because of his law-and-order platform.

George Langdon, 1878-79: A bookkeeper and brewer.

William Thompson, 1880-83: An attorney.

S.B. Grummond, 1884-85: Worked in shipping and real estate.

M.H. Chamberlain, 1886-87: A tobacconist.

John Pridgeon Jr., 1888-89: A Great Lakes shipper.

Hazen S. Pingree, 1890 to March 22, 1897: Named one of the 10 best mayors in U.S. history by a poll of scholars in a 1999 book, "The American Mayor."

"His role as an advanced social reformer was unmatched by any big-city mayor in the last half of the 19th Century," said Melvin Holli, who wrote the book and a biography on Pingree.

Pingree was a successful shoe manufacturer before being elected. His brand of social reform was the forerunner for reforms of the Progressive Era. He battled the phone, gas and light utilities, stood up to the privately owned streetcar companies and cut taxes. Under Pingree, Detroit formed the Public Lighting Commission to put streetlights under public control. Pingree also reached out to poor people during the 1893 Depression by initiating work-relief programs and establishing "potato patches" where residents could grow vegetables. He was elected governor while serving as mayor and tried to keep both posts. When courts ruled he couldn't, he went to Lansing.

William Rickert, March 22 to April 5, 1897: Served the remainder of Pingree's term.

William Maybury, 1897-1904: The son of Irish immigrants whose conservative, pro-business agenda became so popular that he was memorialized in the bronze statute in Grand Circus Park across from the statue of Pingree.

George Codd, 1905-06: His career was sidetracked by his failure to get a handle on the issue of regulating Detroit's streetcars.

William B. Thompson, 1907-08 and 1911-12: Son of an Irish-born Detroit policeman who became a successful businessman, his political career also was sabotaged by the streetcar issue.

Philip Breitmeyer, 1909-10: A florist and a parks commissioner who helped design Belle Isle's lagoons and canals. The streetcar issue proved to be his political undoing, too.

Oscar Marx, 1913-18: He was known as a builder who succeeded in meeting the city's needs during years of massive growth.

James Couzens, 1919-22: When Henry Ford secured financial backing for his third effort to start an automobile company (the first two had been failures), Couzens worked as his bookkeeper.

Couzens' political career included serving as Detroit's police commissioner, street railways commissioner, mayor and U.S. senator. Under Couzens, the city brought all the streetcar lines under municipal ownership, ending

Hazen Pingree is considered to be one of the best mayors in U.S history, according to a 1999 poll of scholars. He is known for his social reforms.

John C. Lodge had an illustrious career as both mayor and long-time city councilman.

Louis Miriani's law-and-order policy and bad relations between Detroit police and the black community helped end his mayoral career.

three decades of controversy. Couzens gave huge sums of money to charity. During his tenure, Detroit expanded to its present 138-square-mile boundaries.

John C. Lodge, 1922-23, 1924, 1927-29: A blue-blood in Detroit's political history, Lodge was son of an antislavery activist, traveled in privileged classes, helped organize the Detroit Athletic Club and had a distinguished career as both mayor and longtime city councilman.

One of Lodge's earliest ventures into public life involved religion. In 1914, he was local chairman for the national "Go to church on Sunday" campaign. The Free Press' city editor in the 1890s, Lodge entered politics and served in various capacities for 50 years.

Frank Doremus, 1923-24: His term was hindered by illness.

Joseph Martin, 1924: Served out Doremus' term.

John Smith, 1924-28: Known as Johnny. He was raised by a widowed mother, sold newspapers on the street as a youngster, boxed, played football and was a plumber's apprentice and a steamfitter. A pro-labor Republican, Smith used his job as U.S. postmaster in Detroit as a springboard to politics, ultimately becoming mayor in a special election in 1924.

That was one of the most tumultuous contests in Detroit history. Smith ran against Joseph Martin and Charles Bowles, with Bowles running as a write-in candidate supported by the Ku Klux Klan and rising anti-Catholic sentiment. Smith and Martin were Catholics. Bowles might have been elected, except that the city Election Commission threw out 15,000 ballots supporting him, effectively erasing his 14,000 vote plurality over Smith.

Charles Bowles, 1930: Bowles defeated Lodge, who had been ineffective at changing Detroit's bad image during Prohibition. The city's newspapers — especially the Detroit News — began a campaign against Bowles.

When Bowles removed a popular police commissioner, the recall pot boiled, and Bowles was removed by nearly 31,000 votes just seven months after taking office. It was the first recall of a big-city mayor in American history.

Frank Murphy, 1930-33: Murphy's political career was meteoric: Recorder's Court judge in the 1920s, mayor in the early 1930s, then governor-general of the Philippines and governor of Michigan, U.S. attorney general in 1940-41 and U.S. Supreme Court justice until his death in 1949.

As mayor during the Depression, Murphy beefed up welfare agencies, sponsored vegetable gardens and organized the U.S. Conference of Mayors to lobby Washington. The 1999 book, "The American Mayor," named him one of the nation's 10 best city leaders.

Frank Couzens, 1933-38: Son of James Couzens, he restored the city's financial health during the Depression, when it was paying employees with scrips.

Richard Reading, 1938-40: Reading's first act as mayor was purchasing a $6,000 LaSalle limousine. Two years later, he was defeated, and his political ambitions were dashed by grand jury indictments charging him with conspiring with 80 policemen in an elaborate protection system for Detroit's numbers racket.

As Reading was led out of the courtroom after receiving his sentence of 4½ to 5 years,

Frank Murphy before his stellar political career.

Free Press file photo

Above: Albert Cobo. Right: Future mayor Cobo in his candy store at 24th and Michigan in 1912.

he exclaimed: "This is the greatest injustice since the crucifixion of Christ!"

Edward Jeffries, 1940-48: When Jeffries died in 1950, a day short of his 50th birthday, one reporter wrote: "He broke some precedents, lambasted more people, started more arguments and caused more activity while playing a better game of gin rummy and holding a lower golf score than any mayor the town ever saw."

Jeffries was first elected as a pro-labor liberal, but grew more conservative as many white Detroiters became aroused about the growth of the city's black population.

Eugene Van Antwerp, 1948-50: The longtime city councilman was widely regarded as an ineffective mayor.

Albert Cobo, 1950-57: Building on the wartime master plan, Cobo oversaw a reconstruction of downtown, including the civic center and the expressway system. He was mayor at Detroit's peak of population (1.825 million), but auto company closings — and the expressways — helped contribute to the beginning of the long exodus of people and jobs. In gaining office, he played the race card, playing on white voters' fear of increasingly restive black Detroiters.

Louis Miriani, 1957-62: When Cobo died in office in 1957, Miriani, a Common Council president,

rose to the mayoralty. He was elected for a full term in 1958. Miriani would later complain that the city was in a depression for 36 of his final 48 months in office.

Miriani's law-and-order policy and bad relations between police and Detroit's growing black community helped contribute to his upset by Jerome Cavanagh in 1961. In April 1966, after Miriani was re-elected to the City Council, the federal government charged him with failure to report income of nearly $260,000 and failing to pay about $160,000 in taxes. In 1968, he was convicted and served a 1-year sentence.

Jerome Cavanagh, 1962-70: Cavanagh was 33 when he became mayor in an election considered one of the first major demonstrations of black political power in Detroit. The charismatic Cavanagh was white, but his liberal policies attracted 85 percent of the black vote, and 56 percent of the overall vote. He presided over a city that was considered a laboratory for urban-renewal concepts under President Lyndon B. Johnson's Great Society program. Look Magazine named Detroit an "All-American" city in 1966. But the 1967 riot shattered its reputation as well as Cavanagh's political ambitions. Cavanagh lost primaries for the U.S. Senate in 1966 and governor in 1974. He died of a heart attack in 1979.

A plaque honoring Jerome Cavanagh hangs in the City-County Building, now the Coleman A. Young Municipal Center.

Free Press file photo

Roman Gribbs struggled with the exodus of businesses and residents to the suburbs. Economic ills that began during his tenure would plague the city throughout the 1970s and 1980s.

Mayor Coleman Young atop the Riverfront Apartments in 1989.

Young holds Joel Loving, soon after the boy's birth in 1982. His mother, former city official Annivory Calvert, later sued Young for paternity. Young settled after tests showed chances were 1 in 270 billion he wasn't the father. Joel later changed his name to Coleman A. Young Jr.

POLITICS

Roman Gribbs, 1970-74: Detroit's first mayor of Polish Catholic descent, Gribbs had changed his name from Grzyb as a young adult. A former Wayne County sheriff and assistant prosecutor, Gribbs as mayor struggled with the exodus of businesses and residents to the suburbs and the onset of the economic ills that were to beset his successor and the city in the 1970s and 1980s. He launched an attack on crime that included the controversial STRESS undercover decoy squad. STRESS was an acronym for Stop the Robberies, Enjoy Safe Streets. Police dressed in civilian clothes posed as targets for street thugs in crime zones. But arrests sometimes involved violently subduing purse snatchers or petty thieves, angering many community leaders who feared the police unit was too aggressive. During his term, construction started on the Renaissance Center. He has served as a state appeals court judge since 1983.

Coleman Young, 1974-1993: Colorful, combative, controversial, witty and profane, Young's 20 years in office far surpassed the stay of any previous mayor. As the city's first black mayor, Young was seen as a liberator and symbol of hope by many black Detroiters

Detroit politicians march from the old city hall to its successor on Woodward Avenue in 1871.

Burton Historical Collection

after decades of neglect and mistreatment from city officials and police.

But many white residents and suburbanites resented Young's salty language, his liberal policies and what they perceived as his racism. But no one could deny that as mayor, Young dominated southeast Michigan for two decades.

Young came to power after a career as an auto worker, union activist and state senator. He experienced discrimination frequently as a child and adult, and he never forgot it. "When I see racism, I talk about it," he once said. "I've been doing that all my life and I hope I can stop talking about it. You know when that will happen? When I don't see any more racism."

Young never stopped trying to resuscitate Detroit, even when economic conditions were harsh, as they were in the early 1980s. He fought hard to institute affirmative-action plans, especially in the police and fire departments. He also made sure black contractors got a piece of city business. Before he took office, minority vendors received less than $20,000 of the city's business. By 1990, that figure had soared to $121 million annually.

Young died from complications from emphysema at age 79 on Nov. 30, 1997.

Dennis Archer, 1993-2001: The gentlemanly, judicious Archer won praise from

Detroiters and suburbanites during his first term for his bridge-building and temperament. But as Archer moved into his second term, he encountered problems over some of the same city services that troubled Young. And a snowstorm in early 1999 led to widespread criticism for the city's slow response and his whiny excuses.

Newsweek rated Archer one of the country's top 25 mayors in 1999, and he was instrumental in getting three casinos, two stadiums and Compuware and the General Motors Corp. headquarters to move downtown.

Kwame Kilpatrick, 2002-: At 31, Kilpatrick became Detroit's youngest elected mayor when he defeated City Council President Gil Hill in November 2001. Kilpatrick has politics in his blood: His mother is U.S. Rep. Carolyn Cheeks Kilpatrick, the Detroit Democrat, and his father is Bernard Kilpatrick, once the chief of staff for former Wayne County Executive Ed McNamara. Mayor Kilpatrick graduated from Cass Tech, Florida A&M and Detroit College of Law. He won election in 1996 to his mother's old seat in the Michigan House of Representatives, and became leader of the House Democratic caucus.

SOURCES: DETROIT FREE PRESS; "DICTIONARY OF CANADIAN BIOGRAPHY"; "BIOGRAPHICAL DICTIONARY OF AMERICAN MAYORS, 1820-1980," EDITED BY MELVIN HOLLI AND PETER D'ACQ JONES; "THE CITY OF DETROIT, MICHIGAN, 1701-1922," BY CLARENCE BURTON; "ORIGINS OF THE URBAN CRISIS: RACE AND INEQUALITY IN POSTWAR DETROIT," BY THOMAS SUGRUE; BRIAN DUNNIGAN, CLEMENTS LIBRARY, UNIVERSITY OF MICHIGAN.

The Governors

Governors of Michigan, 1835-2000: Biographical sketches of governors from metro Detroit:

Stevens Thomson Mason, 1835-1840, Democrat
Michigan's first governor was also the youngest elected leader in Michigan history. Mason was inaugurated four days after his 24th birthday on Nov. 2, 1835 — two years before Michigan was voted into the union. During his two terms, the Virginia-born Mason requested a state geological survey, proposed that the University of Michigan be established in Ann Arbor, endorsed a plan for a free school system, and encouraged building a state prison in Jackson.

William Woodbridge, 1840-1841, Whig:
Michigan's second governor participated in the state's 1835 Constitutional Convention and served as state senator before he was elected to the top post in 1840. But Woodbridge, a Whig, resigned halfway through his term to become a U.S. senator.

James Wright Gordon, 1841-1842, Whig.

John S. Barry, 1842-1846, Democrat.

Alpheus Felch, 1846-1847, Democrat:
This Democrat and Ann Arbor lawyer was elected in 1845 and had previously served as a state representative, auditor general and supreme court justice. He resigned in 1847 after he was elected to the U.S. Senate.

William L. Greenly, 1847-1848, Democrat.

Epaphroditus Ransom, 1848-1850, Democrat.

John S. Barry, 1850-1851, Democrat.

Robert McClelland, 1852-1853 Democrat:
A lawyer from Monroe, McClelland served a 1-year term, then resigned a year into his second term to become U.S. secretary of interior. He also served as a state representative, congressman and University of Michigan regent.

Andrew Parsons, 1853-1854, Democrat.

Kinsley S. Bingham, 1855-1858, Republican:
Bingham was Michigan's first Republican governor. A New York native, he moved to Livingston County and became known for founding the agricultural college that became Michigan State University.

Moses Wisner, 1859-1860, Republican:
Wisner was an Oakland County farmer and abolitionist who commanded troops during the Civil War, dying of illness in 1863. His Pontiac house is now headquarters for the Oakland County Historical Society.

Austin Blair, 1861-1864, Republican.

Henry H. Crapo, 1865-1868, Republican.

Henry P. Baldwin, 1869-1872, Republican:
This Detroit businessman helped with efforts to build a new state capitol and improved the state's charitable, penal and reform institutions.

John J. Bagley, 1873-1876, Republican:
A native of New York, Bagley moved to Detroit to work in a tobacco factory and eventually became one of the state's largest tobacco manufacturers. Bagley was a member of the Detroit Common Council and state board of education before being elected governor in 1872. He reorganized the state militia into the National Guard.

Charles M. Croswell, 1877-1880, Republican.

An expert square dancer known for his polka-dot bow ties, G. Mennen Williams ran a folksy campaign, crisscrossing the state in a beat-up DeSoto, stopping to call dances while forgoing stilted speeches.

David H. Jerome, 1881-1882, Republican:
The first Michigan native to become governor. Born in Detroit, he was a hardware and lumber merchant who moved to Saginaw. Jerome organized the 23rd Michigan Infantry during the Civil War and served as a state senator.

Josiah W. Begole, 1883-1884, Democrat.

Russell A. Alger, 1885-1886, Republican:
Born in Ohio, Alger moved to Grand Rapids, then settled in Detroit after fighting for the North during the Civil War. He made a fortune in the lumber business, eventually owning property in several states and one Canadian province. He was elected governor in 1885 and was mentioned as a possible presidential candidate, though he never campaigned for the office. He became secretary of war under President William McKinley in 1897, and he oversaw the U.S. military during the Spanish-American War, for which he received criticism for American blunders, though historians say he also had a number of successes. Alger served in the U.S. Senate from 1902 to 1907.

Cyrus G. Luce, 1887-1890, Republican.

Edwin B. Winans, 1891-1892, Democrat:
The Livingston County farmer benefited from the growing populist movement to defeat a Republican railroad baron in 1890. He served one term and also served in Congress, the state house, and as a county judge.

John T. Rich, 1893-1896, Republican.

Hazen S. Pingree, 1897-1900, Republican:
The Detroit shoe manufacturer and legendary progressive mayor served two terms as governor. Pingree's goal was to establish equal taxation in the state. His scientific appraisal of railroad and corporate property for tax purposes became a model for the country. His administration also brought mining companies under tougher control of the State Tax Commission.

Aaron T. Bliss, 1901-1904, Republican.

Fred M. Warner, 1905-1910, Republican.

Chase S. Osborn, 1911-1912, Republican.

Woodbridge N. Ferris, 1913-1916, Democrat.

Albert E. Sleeper, 1917-1920, Republican.

Alexander J. Groesbeck, 1921-1926, Republican:
Groesbeck, a Macomb County lawyer, built his reputation on two things: streamlining government and starting a state-coordinated system of building paved roads. He took road planning away from local communities and centralized it at the state level. He also instituted the state's first gasoline tax — 2 cents per gallon — to help pay for them, and used concrete instead of asphalt, macadam or gravel. Groesbeck merged 33 state agencies into five departments, created an Administrative Board to supervise all state business and centralized purchasing for all state agencies.

Fred W. Green, 1927-1930, Republican

Wilber M. Brucker, 1931-1932, Republican

William A. Comstock, 1933-1934, Democrat
Comstock grew up in Alpena and served as that city's mayor before moving to Detroit. The banker/businessman initiated a 3-percent sales tax to help the state out of debt. He served one term.

Frank D. Fitzgerald, 1935-1936, Republican.

Frank Murphy, 1937-1938, Democrat:
This famous Detroit mayor and Recorder's Court judge was elected governor in 1936. A Democrat and ardent supporter of President Franklin D. Roosevelt, Murphy is remembered as a friend of organized labor and for his commitment to good government. When the Flint sit-down strike was under way at General Motors in 1937, Murphy sent in the National Guard but refused to use it against strikers. He went on to resolve many labor disputes as governor. His administration implemented a New Deal program that strengthened the state's Department of Labor and Industry. Murphy also launched a hospital building program, focused on medical needs of poor people and established the nation's first Consumer's Bureau. His administration also enacted a civil-service law, eliminated favoritism in state purchasing and introduced effective budgeting and accounting systems.

Frank D. Fitzgerald, 1939, Republican.

Luren D. Dickinson, 1939-1940, Republican.

Murray D. Van Wagoner, 1941-1942, Democrat:
Van Wagoner, an engineer, grew up in Oakland County and served as state highway commissioner before being elected governor in 1940. During his tenure, Michigan conducted one of the nation's first highway needs studies, laying the groundwork for Detroit's extensive freeway system, and improved highway financing. He set up the Civil Service Commission, and construction began on the Blue Water International Bridge from Port Huron to Sarnia, Canada.

Harry F. Kelly, 1943-1946, Republican:
A Detroit lawyer and former secretary of state who helped the state mobilize for war. He later set up a trust fund for veterans and expanded a building program for state uni-

versities and colleges. He also was elected a state supreme court justice.

Kim Sigler, 1947-1948, Republican.

G. Mennen Williams, 1949-1960, Democrat:

One of the most popular political figures in Michigan history, Williams is credited with almost single-handedly turning Michigan into a two-party state. Born in midtown Detroit, Williams would be vilified by Republicans as a "traitor to his class," because of his patrician roots. But Williams, steeped in the New Deal politics of President Franklin D. Roosevelt, would become an archetypal new Democrat committed to working-class advancement and racial harmony. After the war, the Democratic Party in Michigan was an unresponsive machine largely run by corrupt allies of Teamster strongman Jimmy Hoffa. An expert square dancer known for his polka-dot bow ties, Williams ran a folksy campaign, crisscrossing the state in a beat-up DeSoto, stopping to call dances while forgoing stilted speeches. He received the support of the non-Hoffa segment of organized labor and defeated Republican incumbent Kim Sigler. As governor, Williams pushed through a voter-approved gas tax that led to the building of the state's modern freeway system. He improved mental health and other social programs. He pushed for human rights, appointing the first black judge in Michigan — Charles Jones to Detroit Recorder's Court — and named the first black people to state government posts. He led the push in the early 1950s to build the Mackinac Bridge — then called Soapy's Folly — and became part of the bridge's legend by starting the governor's annual Labor Day walk across the 5-mile span. After leaving office, Williams was appointed assistant secretary of state for African affairs by President John F. Kennedy. One day in Kenya he boldly declared "Africa for the Africans," in support of black rule. He brought back numerous pieces of African art, donating them to the Detroit Institute of Arts. Williams ran for the U.S. Senate in 1966 against Republican Robert Griffin. He lost; it was his only electoral defeat. In 1968, President Lyndon B. Johnson named Williams ambassador to the Philippines. He was elected to the state Supreme Court in 1971 and became its chief justice in 1983. He had a cerebral hemorrhage and died in 1988.

John B. Swainson, 1961-1962, Democrat:

Swainson, from Plymouth, lost both legs during World War II. He later received a law degree and returned to Michigan to launch his political

Free Press file photo

Gov. John Swainson lost both legs below the knee during World War II. A German anti-vehicle mine exploded under an ammo-laden Jeep, killing the two occupants and badly wounding 19-year-old Army Pvt. Swainson, who was nearby.

George Romney called himself "a citizen first" in campaign literature and during this tenure pushed for the first state income tax in 1967 to help solidify state finances.

Despite his wealth, G. Mennen Williams made his name as a New Deal Democrat.

Free Press filie photo, 1934

career as a war hero. He served in the state Senate and as lieutenant governor before he was elected in 1960. He also was a circuit court judge and a justice on the state Supreme Court. In 1975, a federal grand jury indicted Swainson on bribery and perjury charges. Swainson was convicted of perjury, acquitted of bribery. He resigned from the Supreme Court and spent 60 days in a halfway house.

George Romney, 1963-1969, Republican

Romney became well-known when he was chairman and president of Detroit's American Motors Corp., where he pushed for smaller, cheaper cars. In 1959, he formed Citizens for Michigan and pushed for the convention that drafted the state constitution that remains in effect today. He left his Republican identification off campaign material, calling himself "a citizen first." During his tenure, Romney pushed for the first state income tax in 1967 to help solidify state finances. He also called for more federal aid to cities after the Detroit riot. He made an unsuccessful presidential bid and later became Housing and Urban Development secretary under President Richard Nixon. Later, he became an advocate of volunteer programs.

William G. Milliken, 1969-1983, Republican:

William Grawn Milliken, Michigan's longest-serving governor, was and is an out-state Republican from Traverse City, but he is well-known in the Detroit area for having forged a working relationship with then-Mayor Coleman Young, a Democrat whose behind-the-scenes support allowed Milliken in 1978 to become the first Republican governor to carry Wayne County since Kim Sigler in 1946. Milliken, prior to becoming governor, was a third-generation state senator and was lieutenant governor from 1965 until succeeding Romney, who resigned in 1969 to join the Nixon cabinet. Milliken's resume also includes service in World War II where he flew 50 combat missions in B24s over Italy, received the Purple Heart (wounded by flak) and was forced to bail out when his crippled plane ran out of fuel short of its home base.

James J. Blanchard, 1983-1991, Democrat:

Blanchard, from Pleasant Ridge, served in the U.S. Congress before becoming governor. Perhaps the single most important decision Blanchard made in Lansing was among his first: Confronted by a massive budget deficit and a deep economic recession, the new governor guided the enactment of a 38-percent income-tax increase, along with appropriate budget reductions, to restore Michigan's fiscal stability and credit rating and to avoid more crippling spending cuts. Blanchard also remained a dependable advocate of abortion rights throughout his tenure. He fostered economic diversification — and "jobs, jobs, and jobs" — by bringing new, high-technology industries to Michigan. He also inaugurated the Michigan Education Trust prepaid college tuition plan. He sought, with some success, to implement welfare reforms and to improve the job training and skills of Michigan workers. After John Engler defeated him in 1990, Blanchard served as U.S. ambassador to Canada.

Free Press file photo

Gov. William Milliken visits with Detroiters, including Minnie Cooper, in an impoverished neighborhood on the north side in 1969.

James Blanchard brought economic diversification to Michigan and debuted the Michigan Education Trust prepaid college tuition plan.

A career politician, term limits kept John Engler from a fourth term as governor.

Michigan's first female governor, Jennifer Granholm, was an obscure Wayne County official before entering state politics as attorney general in 1998.

WILLIAM ARCHIE/Detroit Free Press

John M. Engler, 1991-2002, Republican:

Engler staged an election shocker in 1990, defeating two-term incumbent Blanchard by a hair-thin 17,000 votes and launching one of the most provocative ideological changes in state government in the 20th Century. Engler, who grew up on a cattle farm in Beal City, was first elected to the state House at age 22 while a senior at Michigan State University and rose to Senate majority leader. As governor he took a surprisingly hard turn to the conservative right, forcing deep budget cuts to offset what he said was a $1-billion state deficit. He angered Detroiters by eliminating general assistance welfare and the Lafayette Clinic psychiatric center and cutting much state funding to the Detroit Institute of Arts. He won re-election twice and has presided over Michigan's historic economic growth while becoming a national leader in welfare reform and charter schools. But to many Detroiters he remained a symbol of outstate antagonism to the city. The antipathy swelled in 1999 when Engler pushed two major actions: state takeover of Detroit's troubled school system, and the elimination of a requirement that city workers live in the city.

Jennifer M. Granholm, 2003-present, Democrat

Combining charisma, gender appeal, Republican fatigue and a $7 million war chest, Granholm was elected the state's first female governor in 2002. Her defeat of Lt. Gov. Dick Posthumus, a 20-year veteran of the Legislature and executive office, put an end to 12 years of GOP control of the governor's mansion (Engler was barred from running because of term limits). Granholm, 43 on election day, was born in British Columbia and moved to northern California when she was 4. Educated at the University of California and Harvard Law School, she moved to Michigan after marrying Dan Mulhern, a fellow Harvard student from Detroit. Granholm served as Wayne County's corporation counsel before being elected state attorney general in 1998.

Hail to the Chief

They've come here to look for votes, to review troops, to marvel at assembly lines, to help celebrate our history and to declare a Peace Corps and a Great Society.

In recent decades, U.S. presidents have visited Detroit bringing hundreds of support people and turning our freeways into empty canyons while they motor from one appointment to the next in un-jammed security.

Here's a look at Detroit and the presidency:

FIRST RUFFLES AND FLOURISHES: The first president to visit arrived via sailboat Aug. 13, 1817. Citizens met President **James Monroe** where he came ashore at the Ecorse River. They escorted him to the home of Gov. Lewis Cass. Monroe stayed 5 days, reviewed troops, paraded along Jefferson and received gifts of a sword, a carriage and horses. He attended a ball in his honor at Woodworth's Steamboat Hotel, where Charles Larned gave the banquet toast.

RUN, LEW, RUN: The only Detroiter to run for president on a major party ticket was Lewis Cass, a U.S. senator and Jacksonian Democrat who headed the ticket in 1848. He hated Britain and advocated U.S. expansion. He got support from the Midwest and the South. Cass tolerated slavery and favored allowing territories to vote on permitting slavery in their area. Cass narrowly lost to Whig **Zachary Taylor,** partly because of the split among Democrats over slavery and the third-party candidacy of Free-Soiler **Martin Van Buren.**

ASSASSIN FROM DETROIT: Leon Czolgosz shot President **William McKinley** on Sept. 6, 1901, in Buffalo, N.Y. McKinley died 8 days later. Czolgosz was executed Oct. 29, proclaiming he shot the president "because he was the enemy of the good people — the working people." Czolgosz (ZOL-gus) was an anarchist who hated rich people. The Free Press quoted a former Detroit neighbor who said Leon, as a child, "was a terror to manage and gave evidence of a perverted nature." The Czolgosz family had a home on Benton. They also were said to have lived in Alpena and Posen.

LABOR DAY TRADITION: It was short-lived, but

Detroiter Leon Czolgosz said he assassinated President William McKinley because "he was the enemy of the working people."

Democrats running for president would kick off their campaigns in Detroit on Labor Day, showing solidarity with local and national labor groups. Harry Truman began the tradition in 1948. **John F. Kennedy's** 1960 appearance was most memorable — more than 100,000 people jammed the Campus Martius/Cadillac Square area to hear him speak. By the 1970s, the campaign kickoff tradition had ended.

MORE KENNEDY: Kennedy, the candidate, first mentioned the Peace Corps on Oct. 14, 1960, during a 1:30 a.m. appearance at the University of Michigan Union. He hadn't planned a speech. But a crowd of 10,000 awaited his arrival. He asked them how many would volunteer their services in a foreign land, helping the poor. Sociology graduate Al Guskin led a rally around the idea, drawing petitions and keeping pressure on Kennedy. Days before the 1960 election, during a San Francisco speech, Kennedy credited the response of Michigan students when he formally announced his plan for a Peace Corps. Kennedy carried Detroit by a larger margin than any industrial city in the nation. In Hamtramck, he

HUSH-HUSH VISIT
Franklin D. Roosevelt also visited, on Sept. 18, 1942. But it wasn't publicized until early October. Roosevelt, on his second trip to Detroit as president, came to review war production. The trip was strictly top secret to assure his security. He visited the now-defunct tank plant in Warren, the Willow Run bomber plant and other spots.

President Lyndon B. Johnson announced his plans for the Great Society at a University of Michigan commencement in 1964.

POLITICS

Ike Eisenhower

Jimmy Carter

Ronald Reagan

George Bush

SAY CHEESE!
Free Press photographer Tony Spina got Ike Eisenhower, shown at left, to mug for the camera on a campaign stop in Detroit in 1952.

Photos by TONY SPINA/Free Press

John Kennedy, above left, addresses a crowd at Campus Martius in 1960. Robert Kennedy, above right, addresses supporters in Kennedy Square in 1968. The photos were merged.

The 250th birthday

President Harry S. Truman helped Detroit celebrate its 250th birthday in July 1951 as he led a huge parade along Woodward.

received 92 percent of the vote.

IKE'S ADIEU: Three weeks before Kennedy beat **Richard Nixon, Dwight Eisenhower** made his only visit to Detroit as president. He attended the National Auto Show at the then-new Cobo Hall on Oct. 17, 1960. That evening, Ike spoke to industrial leaders in Detroit at a stag dinner. He admonished them and their labor counterparts to stop behaving like adolescents and settle labor disputes quickly.

LBJ GOES BLUE: Lyndon Baines Johnson visited Detroit several times, but it was a commencement address to U-M grads May 22, 1964, in Ann Arbor that became his most famous sojourn to Michigan. LBJ chose the event to announce his Great Society. He exhorted 85,000 people in Michigan Stadium to "join in the Great Society," his domestic program that included Medicare, Medicaid, the Civil Rights Act of 1964 and the Voting Rights Act of 1965. There was also aid to poor and disadvantaged schoolchildren, the student loan bill for college students, plus the war on poverty, Head Start, the Job Corps, highway beautification, mass-transit aid, new housing money and creation of national foundations for the arts and humanities.

REAGAN DEMOCRATS: In the 1970s and 1980s, poly-sci types flocked to Macomb County — at least to the election stats — trying to figure out how such a working-class, middle-age, white-male, big-time Democratic Party enclave could do an about-face and go Republican. They were voting for conservative icons George Wallace, Nixon and **Ronald Reagan.** Wayne State University historian David Riddle noted Warren residents gave 69 percent of their votes to Kennedy in 1960, 77 percent to Johnson in 1964 and 58 percent to Hubert Humphrey in 1968. But in 1972, only 35 percent of Warren voters cast their ballots for Democrat George McGovern, and Reagan defeated **Jimmy Carter** in Warren, 49 percent to 44 percent in 1980. The rebellion, Rid-

Associated Press

President Bill Clinton and Detroit's No. 1 FOB (Friend of Bill), Mayor Dennis Archer.

dle and others say, was sparked by the Department of Housing and Urban Development's low-income housing controversy of the early 1970s, disgust with the anti-Vietnam War crowd and cross-district busing.

BROCCOLI ATTACK: President **George Bush** stumped Hamtramck for votes on Labor Day 1992. But the traditionally Democratic city responded with a shower of broccoli, Bush's detested veggie. The Secret Service took the hits for Bush.

ARCHER SLEPT HERE: The only Detroit mayor to sleep in the Lincoln Bedroom in the White House: Dennis Archer, Jan. 26, 1994. "I slept real good, but I had to pinch myself every now and then," Archer said the day after his special slumber. He watched a little basketball on TV with good buddy **Bill Clinton** and was there when first daughter Chelsea wandered into the family quarters to give the president a nite-nite kiss. Archer's quarters actually wasn't President **Abraham Lincoln**'s *real* bedroom. It was Lincoln's office and cabinet room, and was converted into a bedroom about 1902. And the bed, with a headboard of carved birds and vines, wasn't Lincoln's bed, either. Mary Todd Lincoln bought the bed in 1861 and used it in a guest room. Lincoln never slept in the bed, although Teddy Roosevelt and **Woodrow Wilson** did.

SOMETHING ABOUT SEPTEMBER
These presidents visited Detroit in September (when travel here was rare):
Andrew Johnson, Sept. 4, 1866.
Rutherford B. Hayes, Sept. 18, 1879.
Theodore Roosevelt, Sept. 21, 1902.
William Howard Taft, Sept. 18, 1911.
Millard Fillmore visited Detroit on Sept. 20, 1849. He became president in 1850.

Called to the Cabinet

Presidents from Andrew Jackson to Jimmy Carter have selected area leaders to serve in their cabinets. Here's a list:

SECRETARY OF WAR (DEFENSE AFTER 1947)
➤ **Lewis Cass**, former territorial governor, under Jackson, 1831-1835.
➤ **Russell Alger**, former governor, under William McKinley, 1897-1899.
➤ **Charles E. Wilson**, former General Motors president, under Dwight D. Eisenhower, 1953-1957.
➤ **Robert McNamara**, former Ford president, under John F. Kennedy and Lyndon B. Johnson, 1961-1968.

SECRETARY OF STATE
➤ **Lewis Cass**, under James Buchanan, 1858-1860.

SECRETARY OF INTERIOR
➤ **Robert McClelland**, former governor, under Franklin Pierce, 1853-1857.
➤ **Zachariah Chandler**, former senator, under Ulysses S. Grant, 1875-1877, and Rutherford B. Hayes, 1877.

POSTMASTER GENERAL
➤ **Don Dickinson**, under Grover Cleveland, 1888-1889.
➤ **Arthur Summerfield**, a former Flint Chevrolet dealer, under Eisenhower, 1953-1960.

SECRETARY OF COMMERCE
➤ **Roy. D. Chapin**, Hudson Motor founder, under Herbert Hoover, 1932-1933.

SECRETARY OF TREASURY
➤ **W. Michael Blumenthal**, former Unisys chairman, under Jimmy Carter, 1977-79.

ATTORNEY GENERAL
➤ **Frank Murphy**, former governor, under Franklin D. Roosevelt, 1939-1940. He later became a U.S. Supreme Court justice.

SECRETARY OF HEALTH, EDUCATION AND WELFARE
➤ **Wilbur Cohen**, former University of Michigan dean, under Johnson, 1968-1969

SECRETARY OF HOUSING AND URBAN DEVELOPMENT
➤ **George Romney**, former governor, under Richard Nixon, 1969-1973.

SECRETARY OF THE NAVY
➤ **Truman Newberry**, former senator, under Theodore Roosevelt, 1908-1909.
➤ **Edwin Denby**, former congressman, under Warren Harding, 1921-1923, and Calvin Coolidge, 1923-1924.

SECRETARY OF ENERGY
➤ **Spencer Abraham**, the defeated senator, under President George W. Bush, 2001-.

Roy. D. Chapin, founder of Hudson Motor, served as President Herbert Hoover's commerce secretary.

The Wings of Detroit (Left and Right)

From Commies to Klansmen, a look at radical life

POLITICS

WHITE PANTHER 10-POINT PROGRAM, 1968

1) Full endorsement of the Black Panthers' 10-point program.

2) Rock 'n' roll, dope and (sex) in the streets.

3) The end of money and free exchange of goods.

4) Free food, free clothes, free housing, free dope.

5) Free access to information.

6) Free time and space for all humans; no unnatural boundaries.

7) Free schools — turn buildings over to the people at once!

8) Free all prisoners.

9) Free all soldiers.

10) Free all people from leaders. Leaders suck! All power to the people!

Left wing

Palmer raids: On Jan. 2, 1920, U.S. Attorney Mitchell Palmer ordered the arrest in Detroit of about 800 people suspected of radical activity. Authorities questioned the suspects at length, but little evidence was found that any of them had any involvement in radical organizations. Similar raids were carried out in other cities.

Communist Party: More than 50,000 people jammed downtown on March 5, 1930, in response to a party-organized protest against unemployment. Communists were highly visible in Detroit during the Depression and union-organizing eras, often leading the fight against joblessness, evictions, workplace harassment and racial segregation. Many who joined the party paid a price: Punishments could range from being blacklisted to being clubbed on the head. At this demonstration, mounted police charged the peaceful crowd and attacked with clubs. About two dozen protesters were hospitalized.

Coleman Young and HUAC: Two decades before Coleman Young became Detroit's mayor, he made a name for himself on Feb. 28, 1952, by defying members of the House Committee on Un-American Activities when they came to Detroit to investigate communists during the McCarthy era. While the committee almost always intimidated its compliant witnesses, the 34-year-old Young took control of his interview from the outset, scolding a HUAC lawyer for "slurring" the word

Coleman Young's defiant testimony in 1952 before Communist hunters helped make him a household name in Detroit.

"Negro" as "nigra" and telling the committee he would refuse to inform on colleagues on the National Negro Labor Council. "You have me mixed up with a stool pigeon," Young said. He also lectured the committee's Southern chairman that what was really unconstitutional was his failure to investigate the South's denial of voting and other civil rights to blacks.

SDS and the Port Huron Statement: University of Michigan students were among the organizers and theorists of Students for a Democratic Society, one of the most important New Left political organizations of the 1960s. One SDS star was Tom Hayden, a graduate of Royal Oak Dondero High School who became editor of the U-M Daily. In June 1962, SDS leaders gathered at a union camp on Lake Huron to finalize what came to be known as the Port Huron Statement. It began: "We are the people of this generation, bred in at least modest comfort, housed now in the universities, looking uncomfortably to the world

Free Press file photo

Bringing the war home: Students for a Democratic Society protest the United States' involvement in Vietnam.

POLITICS

we inherit." Hayden went on to become a leading figure in the antiwar movement and one of the defendants in the famous Chicago Seven trial of protest leaders at the 1968 Democratic National Convention. He was married for a time to actress Jane Fonda, and has served as a state legislator in California.

Black Panther Party: Founded in 1966 by Huey Newton and Bobby Seale in California, the Black Panthers were active in Detroit in the late 1960s and early 1970s. Working out of houses and storefronts, they sold newspapers, performed community work and agitated for black power. On Oct. 24, 1970, Detroit police officer Glenn E. Smith, a black plainclothes officer, was shot and killed outside the 16th Street home of the National Committee to Combat Fascism, a Panther recruiting wing. Twelve men and women, ages 17 to 22, eventually were charged with first-degree murder and conspiracy to commit murder. In a trial that attracted national attention, a defense team led by Ernie Goodman won acquittals on all conspiracy and murder charges. Three defendants were convicted of felonious assault, but those sentences were overturned on appeal.

White Panther Party: With their fondness for loud music and marijuana, these Panthers influenced a generation of youthful Detroiters. The group, which included coun-

Free Press file photo

The Detroit Black Panthers' headquarters on 16th Street.

White Panthers fly their flags at a protest that was part of their "total assault on the culture" of Amerika (their spelling).

OPENING PARAGRAPH OF BLACK MANIFESTO:

"We the black people assembled in Detroit, Michigan, for the national Black Economic Development Conference are fully aware that we have been forced to come together because racist white America has exploited our resources, our minds, our bodies, our labor. For centuries we have been forced to live as colonized people inside the United States, victimized by the most vicious, racist system in the world. We have helped to build the most industrial country in the world. We are therefore demanding of the white Christian churches and Jewish synagogues which are part and parcel of the system of capitalism, that it begin to pay reparations to Black people in this country.'"

terculture leader John Sinclair and the MC5 band, formed after moving to Ann Arbor from Detroit in May 1968. Detroit police had been hassling them in their stronghold in the Forest-Warren area around Wayne State University. Ann Arbor offered sympathetic people and fewer cops. The White Panthers advocated "a total assault on the culture" of middle-class America.

Ernie Goodman: For half a century, Ernie Goodman was one of the most controversial lawyers in Detroit, maybe even in the country. He came out of a tradition of local legal activists that included Maurice Sugar, George Crockett and Ken Cockrel. Goodman, who died in 1997,

Ernie Goodman

defended blacks, unionists, illegal aliens and communists. He also was a partner in the country's first integrated law firm. He took on the auto companies and the American Automobile Association and helped integrate public parks in Dearborn. He argued five cases before the U.S. Supreme Court. Goodman once said: "You only change power in one way: by the struggle of different types of people together."

Black manifesto: A Detroit convention of militants called the Black Economic Development Conference in 1969 composed the manifesto, which called for $500 million in reparations for the historical suppression of

blacks. The document's authors named denominations from which to receive the money. That ploy, in turn, set up numerous confrontations: Manifesto backers sought to read their demands in front of white congregations. Sometimes they received invitations to do so; sometimes they took over services by intimidation. The demands touched off sometimes-heated debates among church members. In June 1969, worshipers at Christ Episcopal Church Cranbrook in Bloomfield Hills heard the manifesto by prearrangement, but the congregation rejected a call for a $100,000 donation.

Republic of New Afrika: Detroiters Richard and Milton Henry were instrumental in forming the Republic of New Afrika movement, which called for blacks to assume control of a new sovereign nation in the South. The RNA, based in Detroit, propelled Milton Henry into national prominence in the black liberation movement. A veteran defense lawyer, Henry later became a minister and pastor of St. John's Presbyterian Church in Detroit. He once said RNA members believed there was no reasonable way they could reason with people toward black liberation, and therefore advocated accomplishing it through force, violence and etc.

The Fifth Estate, the South End and Night Call: The Fifth Estate was founded in 1965 by Harvey Ovshinsky, now an award-winning TV producer. It is the oldest survivor from the hundreds of American "underground papers" published in the 1960s. And not only has it survived, the paper has become significantly more radical, though it still possesses its longtime sense of humor. Published quarterly by a group of friends in the basement of a Second

Harvey Ovshinsky

Avenue apartment building, the paper features long articles analyzing social issues from a point of view that is basically against modern civilization.

The Wayne State University student daily, the South End, drew national attention for its creative (and not-so-creative) radicalism during the era of student protest. The paper, named as a counterpoint to the presence of General Motors Corp. north of the campus, celebrated drugs, sex, rock music and anything that attacked authority. Its staff frequently ran afoul of the WSU administration. During one school year, the South End carried silhouettes of black panthers next to its masthead with the slogan: "One class-conscious worker is worth 100 students." The paper was mainly distributed at factory gates that year.

"Nightcall," the Sunday night call-in show

The office of the Fifth Estate in the 1960s.

Free Press file photo

on WRIF-FM (101.1), which began in 1970, is the longest-running talk show on Detroit radio, and it is also the most radical. Peter Werbe, the show's sole host throughout its existence, tackles issues such as work, technology, the environment, drugs and politics with a point of view rarely heard in mainstream media.

James and Grace Boggs: They were just two of the tens of thousands of sophisticated activists in metro Detroit during the past 50 years. Active in labor, black power, environmental, Marxist and youth movements, James and Grace Boggs could be seen frequently at a range of community activities in Detroit. The late James Boggs, a longtime Chrysler Corp. worker, was the author of several books. With Grace Boggs, he wrote "Revolution and Evolution in the Twentieth Century."

George Crockett Jr.: Congress was only the last stop for Crockett during an extraordinary life. He served as the first black lawyer in the U.S. Department of Labor in President Franklin D. Roosevelt's administration and made a name in Detroit during the 1940s as head of the UAW's Fair Practices Committee, which attempted to root out racism on factory floors and in union locals. In 1950, a judge sentenced Crockett to four months in federal prison for contempt of court committed while defending a man accused of being a communist. Crockett, who died in 1997, also was a judge and one of Detroit's best-known advocates for constitutional rights. He attracted criticism in the 1960s as white Detroiters fought attempts by the city's growing black population to gain a larger voice in such institutions as the Police Department and Recorder's Court.

George Crockett Jr.

Right wing

American Protective Association: The APA was the nationwide anti-Catholic, anti-immigrant and especially anti-Irish organization of the 1890s that railed against the "foreign ecclesiastical potentate," i.e., the pope. Many of the APA's top officers came from Michigan. Its president during the APA's heyday was William J.H. Traynor, who lived on East Jefferson in Detroit. Traynor published the APA's newspaper, the Patriotic American, which called for taxation of church-owned land and restriction of immigration. It also ran trumped-up stories about the sexual

THE OATH THAT APA LEADERS FALSELY CLAIMED AMERICAN CATHOLICS WERE FORCED TO TAKE:

"I, (name), do declare from my heart, without mental reservation that the pope is Christ's vicar-general and is the true and only head of the universal church throughout the Earth, and that, by virtue of the keys of binding and loosing given to his holiness by Jesus Christ, he has power to depose heretical kings, princesses, states, commonwealths and governments, all being legal without his sacred confirmation, and that they be safely destroyed . . ."

Free Press file photo

The Ku Klux Klan was a force in Detroit during the 1920s.

BLACK LEGION OATH:
"In the name of God and the devil, one to reward and the other to punish and by the powers of light and darkness, goodness and evil, here under the black arch of heaven's avenging symbol, I pledge and consecrate my heart, my brain, my body and limbs; and swear by all the powers of heaven and hell, to devote my life to the obedience of my superiors that I will exert every possible means in my power for the extermination of the antichrist, Communist, the Roman hierarchy and their abettors."

adventures of Catholic priests and nuns.

Ku Klux Klan, 1920s: Detroit's rapid growth brought with it elements that despised the city's emerging ethnic, religious and racial mix. Historian Kenneth Jackson estimated that about half of the state's 70,000 Klan members lived in Detroit. With and without hoods, the Klan gathered by the thousands at times in Detroit and suburbs. Members sold their newspaper, the Fiery Cross, on downtown streets. They became involved in city politics. On Christmas Eve 1923, the Klan burned a cross on the steps of City Hall while a masked Santa led a rally of several thousand in Cadillac Square. The Klan's mayoral candidate was Charles Bowles. In 1924, 6,000 Klan supporters marched down Woodward chanting "Bowles," and he nearly won the primary that year as a write-in candidate. The Klan was mostly out of business by 1934, but it resurfaced as a much weaker force in the 1960s, '70s and '80s, mainly because a white supremacist, Robert Miles, lived northwest of Howell in Livingston County. Miles was a grand dragon in the Michigan Klan, and he hosted Klan gatherings at his farm. In 1971, Miles and four associates were convicted of planning the bombing of school buses to be used for court-ordered desegregation in Pontiac. Two years later, he was convicted on a con-

spiracy charge related to the tarring and feathering of a Willow Run High School principal. He spent six years in federal prison for the crimes. Miles and his followers were featured in the 1992 film "Blood in the Face," a chilling documentary on the white supremacist movement in the United States. The title refers to their belief that only Aryans are capable of blushing.

Black Legion, 1936: Police probing the death of a young, unemployed auto worker stumbled onto a right-wing paramilitary organization that attacked blacks, union activists, Catholics, Jews and progressive politicians across metro Detroit during the Depression. The Legion was a Ku Klux Klan offshoot whose members wore black robes, trimmed in red, with skull and crossbones emblazoned on

Free Press file photo

Detroit detectives pose in the costumes of the Black Legion, a violent offshoot of the Ku Klux Klan. The Legion drew national attention to Detroit in 1936 when police tied members to murders, bombings and arsons against blacks, Catholics, Jews and labor organizers.

Harry Bennett was Henry Ford's enforcer in the 1930s and '40s.

Free Press file photo

their hoods. They signed an oath in blood and promised to support "100-percent American-ism." Legion members were convicted of several murders, inciting to riot and other crimes. Numerous bombings and arsons were attributed to the group. Many members were Detroit city employees, including police. In Oakland County, 86 state employees were discovered to be Legion members, including the chief of police in Royal Oak. The Legion disbanded quickly because of the prosecutions and publicity.

Harry Bennett: Ford Motor Co. muscle man Harry Bennett headed company security for Henry Ford in the 1930s and 1940s. He was a pug-faced former boxer who is best remembered for leading violent clashes with labor organizers and for his almost total influence over Ford. Henry Ford II referred to Bennett in a 1982 speech as a "henchman." The New York Times called the Ford security department the largest private police force in the world. Its undercover operatives spied on workers and used violence to carry out Bennett's orders. Bennett hired mobsters, ex-cons and washed-up boxers to staff the force. Bennett was fired from Ford in 1945 after backing down from a pistol-point confrontation with another company executive.

Orville Hubbard: His 36-year tenure as Dearborn mayor was one of the longest mayoral reigns in the nation. He made his city known for excellent services, extensive recreation facilities and exclusion of blacks, a reputation that has stuck with Dearborn to this day, even as it has become one of metro Detroit's most ethnically diverse suburbs. A bull of a man weighing 300 pounds, Hubbard was known across the nation. "I favor segregation," Hubbard told the New York Times in 1968. "Because, if you have integration, first you have kids going to school together, then next thing you know, they're grab-assing around, then they're getting married and having half-breed kids. Then you wind up with a mongrel race. And from what I know of history, that's the end of civilization." He practiced what he preached, killing plans for housing projects that would have attracted blacks. Hubbard, who would die at 79 in 1982, said in the 1950s: ". . . If whites don't want to live with niggers, they sure as hell don't have to. Dammit, this is a free country. This is America."

Orville Hubbard was known for much more than his excellent city services and segregationist views. Here are some examples.

➤ Following his 1950 conviction for libeling

political opponent John Fish, Hubbard refused to pay a court-ordered fine and the court barred him from leaving Wayne County. Hubbard set up a temporary government-in-exile in Windsor.

➤ In 1952, while the same travel ban was in effect, Hubbard announced he would go to the Republican National Convention in Chicago. Court officers went to the train station to stop him, but when they got there, they found Hubbard and two like-sized cohorts dressed in whiteface clown masks. Before officials could decide which clown to arrest, the three were on the train, bound for Chicago.

➤ New hires at city hall had to pen an essay on "A Message to Garcia," a classic discourse on loyalty and perseverance.

➤ He once gave the key to the city to transsexual Christine Jorgensen, saying: "What the hell. Some of the boys and I wanted to see what the hell she looked like."

➤ He once greeted Emperor Hirohito's horse on the steps of City Hall.

➤ In 1972, he became the state's first mayor since the 1920s to perform mass marriages, conducting the ceremonies on the front steps of City Hall. State auditors later censured him

> Orville Hubbard reigned in Dearborn for 36 years. The city became known for its excellent services and exclusion of black people.

Free Press file photo

Dearborn Mayor Orville Hubbard has a laugh while violating a court order in 1952.

POLITICS

RED SQUADS

In a scenario, ironically, out of Eastern Europe during communism, undercover officers working for the Detroit police and state police gathered files on people suspected of being dangerous to the system. Often those people were suspected of being Communists. The police used informants and spies, and compiled dossiers on 1.5 million people and organizations. Both units were disbanded in 1974 by a Wayne County circuit judge who declared their work illegal. In 1981, state police notified people who had files; Detroit notified people several years later. In another irony, several of the victims of illegal surveillance in Detroit were put in charge of distributing the files. In 1992, more than 500,000 of the Detroit police red squad files were put in storage at the Detroit Public Library, but access was closed until 2017.

for collecting more than $30,000 in personal fees from the participants.

➤ In 1966, he made Dearborn the first U.S. city to hold an advisory referendum on ending the Vietnam War. When voters rejected immediate withdrawal of U.S. troops, Hubbard put the question back on the ballot two years later, when it carried.

➤ He covered the walls of City Hall with adages; signed his name in inch-high letters in green ink; gave away autographed thimbles, sewing kits, and cans of beer as city souvenirs; sent cards to thousands of his constituents on their birthdays and anniversaries; and organized a flotilla to patrol the Rouge and Detroit rivers for Nazi submarines in the early 1940s.

Breakthrough: In the 1960s and 1970s, the rabidly anticommunist Breakthrough was a constant irritant to Detroit's liberal causes, staging catcalling counterdemonstrations that often led to fisticuffs. Led by Donald Lobsinger, Breakthrough members attacked everything from the liberalization of the Catholic Church to the anti-Vietnam war effort. Lobsinger and comrades picketed Dr. Martin Luther King Jr.'s 1968 appearance in Grosse Pointe and dressed in clown outfits and marched outside

Donald Lobsinger, with microphone, and fellow Breakthrough members keep Detroit safe from Communists during the Cold War.

Catholic churches to protest English-language guitar masses. Lobsinger was convicted of shoving a Catholic priest to the ground at a rally against the Vietnam War, and he greeted Coleman Young's 1973 election as first black mayor by putting a sign on his desk at his city job that read: "This white ain't running or bowing to black racism."

White Home Owners' Groups: As far back as the 1920s, white Detroiters used violence and the threat of violence to prevent blacks from moving into white neighborhoods. The violence grew after World War II. From the late 1940s to the 1960s, whites participated in more than 200 attacks on blacks trying to move into all-white neighborhoods, according to historian Thomas Sugrue. The attacks involved harassment, mass demonstrations, picketing, effigy burning, window breaking, arson, vandalism and physical harm. Much of the organization for the attacks came from white home owners' associations formed almost solely to combat neighborhood integration. Sugrue called the banding together of white home owners one of the largest grassroots movements in Detroit history.

SOURCES: FREE PRESS; "THE KU KLUX KLAN IN THE CITY," KENNETH JACKSON; "ALL-AMERICAN ANARCHIST: JOSEPH LABADIE AND THE LABOR MOVEMENT," CARLOTTA ANDERSON; "THE ORIGINS OF THE URBAN CRISIS: RACE AND INEQUALITY IN POSTWAR DETROIT," THOMAS SUGRUE.

Free Press file photo

Southeastern Michigan presidential votes

1836-2000

	1836		1840		1844		1848	
	William H. Harrison (W)	Martin Van Buren (D)	William H. Harrison (W)	Martin Van Buren (D)	Henry Clay (W)	James K. Polk (D)	Zachary Taylor (W)	Lewis Cass (D)
Livingston	73	142	700	844	587	1,087	764	1,127
Macomb	43	400	982	1,124	963	1,359	855	1,339
Monroe	1,147	2	939	1,023	870	1,282	791	1,155
Oakland	952	817	2,372	2,365	2,225	2,833	1,942	2,781
St. Clair	517	446	569	617	665	814		
Washtenaw	1,031	1,636	2,527	2,057	2,349	2,550	2,029	2,080
Wayne	1,527	1,578	2,246	2,237	2,346	2,736	2,540	3,305
State totals	**5,545**	**7,122**	**22,933**	**21,096**	**24,285**	**27,737**	**23,947**	**30,742**

1848: Freesoil candidate Van Buren received 10,393 votes statewide.

	1852		1856		1860		1864	
	Winfield Scott (W)	Franklin Pierce (D)	John Fremont (R)	James Buchanan (D)	Abraham Lincoln (R)	Stephen Douglas (D)	Abraham Lincoln (R)	George McClellan(D)
Livingston	931	1,419	1,765	1,711	2,075	2,003	1,604	1,983
Macomb	1,060	1,634	2,210	1,846	2,533	2,166	2,041	2,177
Monroe	1,112	1,582	1,777	1,703	2,282	2,165	1,659	2,331
Oakland	2,376	3,178	4,105	3,276	4,411	3,768	3,709	3,816
St. Clair	852	1,110	1,807	1,521	2,589	1,955	1,808	2,063
Washtenaw	2,274	2,604	3,570	2,833	4,286	3,630	3,632	3,836
Wayne	3,402	4,680	5,250	5,777	7,325	6,701	5,946	7,670
State totals	**33,800**	**41,842**	**71,762**	**52,139**	**88,450**	**64,889**	**79,149**	**68,513**

1852: Freesoil candidate Hale received 7,237 votes statewide.

	1868		1872		1876		1880	
	Ulysses S. Grant (R)	Horatio Seymour (D)	Ulysses S. Grant (R)	Horace Greeley (DL)	Rutherford B. Hayes (R)	Samuel Tilden (D)	James A. Garfield (R)	Winfield Hancock (D)
Livingston	2,238	2,409	2,335	1,912	2,735	2,929	2,879	2,819
Macomb	2,791	2,668	2,446	2,160	3,012	3,453	3,137	3,218
Monroe	2,529	2,914	2,645	2,192	3,032	3,893	3,178	3,701
Oakland	4,738	4,442	4,490	3,326	5,053	5,313	5,370	5,150
St. Clair	3,060	2,706	3,332	2,234	4,067	3,710	1,219	3,439
Washtenaw	4,463	4,496	4,106	3,029	4,565	5,117	4,629	4,957
Wayne	9,207	10,274	12,186	9,289	12,580	15,076	16,157	15,064
State totals	**128,560**	**97,060**	**138,758**	**78,551**	**166,901**	**141,685**	**185,335**	**131,597**

1872: Democrat candidate O'Conner received 2,875 votes statewide; Prohibition candidate Block received 1,271. **1876:** Greenback candidate Tilden received 9,023 votes statewide; Prohibition candidate Smith received 766 votes. **1880:** Greenback candidate Weaver received 34,895 votes statewide; Prohibition candidate Dow received 940.

	1884		1888		1892		1896	
	James Blaine (R)	Grover Cleveland (D)	Benjamin Harrison (R)	Grover Cleveland (D)	Benjamin Harrison (R)	Grover Cleveland (D)	William McKinley (R)	William J. Bryan (D)
Livingston	2,597	2,938	2,706	2,842	2,447	2,385	2,893	2,994
Macomb	2,782	3,464	3,245	3,708	2,788	3,584	4,153	3,400
Monroe	3,025	3,920	3,430	3,940	2,914	3,769	4,053	4,208
Oakland	4,842	5,386	5,389	5,410	4,763	4,925	5,846	5,271
St. Clair	4,017	4,668	5,419	5,286	5,371	5,248	7,160	5,130
Washtenaw	4,049	5,315	4,549	5,482	4,362	5,508	5,671	5,348
Wayne	17,315	29,930	21,326	25,986	26,361	27,580	36,400	26,231
State totals	**192,669**	**189,361**	**236,387**	**213,469**	**222,708**	**202,296**	**293,336**	**237,166**

1888: Prohibition candidate Fisk received 20,945 votes statewide; U.S. Labor candidate Streeter received 4,555 votes. **1892:** Prohibition candidate Bidwell received 20,857 votes statewide; Peoples' candidate Weaver received 19,931. **1896:** Four other candidates received 14,010 statewide.

	1900		1904		1908		1912	
	William McKinley (R)	William J. Bryan (D)	T. Roosevelt (R)	Alton B. Parker (D)	William H. Taft (R)	William J. Bryan (D)	T. Roosevelt (NP)	William H. Taft (R)
Livingston	2,860	2,727	3,288	1,988	2,740	2,418	1,455	1,408
Macomb	4,239	3,491	4,818	2,989	4,472	3,138	1,800	2,508
Monroe	3,876	3,859	4,407	3,127	4,206	3,451	1,881	2,253
Oakland	6,173	4,966	6,986	3,956	6,267	3,950	3,296	4,083
St. Clair	7,432	4,403	8,305	3,248	7,287	3,756	4,423	2,958
Washtenaw	5,369	5,072	6,566	3,779	5,845	4,441	3,642	2,495
Wayne	36,671	28,337	48,393	19,548	49,580	24,128	34,680	26,599
State totals	**316,014**	**211,432**	**361,863**	**134,163**	**333,313**	**174,619**	**213,243**	**151,434**

1900: Four other candidates received 16,343 votes statewide. **1904:** Four other candidates received 24,417 votes statewide. **1908:** Five other candidates received 30,142 votes statewide. **1912:** Democrat Woodrow Wilson received 150,201 votes statewide. Three other candidates received 33,093 votes statewide.

	1916		1920		1924		1928	
	Charles E. Hughes (R)	Woodrow Wilson (D)	Warren G. Harding (R)	James M. Cox (D)	Calvin Coolidge (R)	John W. Davis (D)	Herbert Hoover (R)	Alfred E. Smith (D)
Livingston	2,460	2,297	4,639	2,437	4,886	2,037	5,642	2,075
Macomb	4,552	3,108	9,735	3,023	11,147	3,191	12,845	7,363
Monroe	3,787	4,202	8,646	5,224	8,940	4,981	10,202	7,242
Oakland	7,730	6,659	19,321	6,421	28,603	4,105	45,343	10,011
St. Clair	6,538	4,617	14,938	4,566	17,435	3,600	18,177	7,151
Washtenaw	6,505	5,279	14,082	4,468	14,326	3,603	19,676	5,308
Wayne	70,056	60,935	220,482	51,773	268,653	23,817	265,852	157,047
State totals	**337,952**	**283,993**	**755,941**	**231,046**	**874,631**	**152,359**	**965,396**	**396,762**

1916: Three other candidates received 24,928 votes statewide. **1920:** Five other candidates received 50,994 votes statewide. **1924:** Robert LaFollete, the Independent Progressive candidate, received 122,014 votes statewide, including 39,773 in Wayne County, where he outpolled Davis. **1928:** Four other candidates received 9,924 votes.

COUNTIES	1932		1936		1940		1944	
	Herbert Hoover (R)	Franklin D. Roosevelt (D)	Alfred M. Landon (R)	Franklin D. Roosevelt (D)	Wendell L. Willkie (R)	Franklin D. Roosevelt (D)	Thomas E. Dewey (R)	Franklin D. Roosevelt (D)
Livingston	4,534	4,684	5,117	4,117	7,068	3,254	7,417	2,910
Macomb	8,649	16,539	9,383	17,593	17,848	21,003	21,305	23,506
Monroe	7,255	12,417	8,330	11,075	13,517	10,368	13,478	10,275
Oakland	32,462	33,135	30,071	40,329	49,002	47,022	59,627	55,272
St. Clair	14,883	12,776	12,760	12,663	18,635	12,259	19,175	11,813
Washtenaw	15,368	12,552	14,986	13,589	21,664	11,802	24,740	14,922
Wayne	212,678	310,686	190,732	404,055	275,974	451,003	316,270	554,670
State totals	**739,894**	**871,700**	**699,733**	**1,016,794**	**1,039,917**	**1,032,991**	**1,084,423**	**1,106,899**

1932: Six other candidates received 53,171 votes statewide. **1936:** Five other candidates received 88,560 votes statewide. **1940:** Four other candidates received 13,017 votes statewide. **1944:** Four other candidates received 13,895 votes statewide.

COUNTIES	1948		1952		1956		1960	
	Thomas E. Dewey (R)	Harry S. Truman (D)	Dwight D. Eisenhower (R)	Adlai E. Stevenson (D)	Adlai E. Stevenson (D)	Dwight D. Eisenhower (R)	John F. Kennedy & Lyndon B. Johnson (D)	Richard M. Nixon & Henry Cabot Lodge (R)
Livingston	7,368	2,813	9,790	3,086	3,845	10,315	5,608	10,340
Macomb	21,205	25,265	37,474	36,544	62,816	58,337	105,681	61,989
Monroe	11,070	10,434	17,159	12,758	14,414	18,782	19,684	18,607
Oakland	62,516	51,491	115,503	73,871	99,901	152,990	135,531	162,026
St. Clair	17,883	10,647	27,894	12,268	12,753	29,116	18,332	27,366
Washtenaw	24,588	12,721	35,826	17,671	19,124	38,911	25,129	39,632
Wayne	321,773	489,654	456,371	622,236	664,618	481,783	773,327	394,485
State totals	**1,038,595**	**1,003,448**	**1,551,529**	**1,230,657**	**1,359,898**	**1,713,647**	**1,687,269**	**1,620,428**

1948: Progressive Party Candidate Henry Wallace received 46,515 votes statewide including 29,615 in Wayne County. **1952:** Four other candidates received 16,403 votes statewide. **1960:** Five other candidates received 10,400 votes statewide.

COUNTIES	1964		1968		1972		1976	
	Lyndon B. Johnson & Hubert Humphrey (D)	Barry Goldwater & William E. Miller(R)	Hubert H. Humphrey & Edmund S. Muskie (D)	Richard M. Nixon & Spiro T. Agnew (R)	George McGovern & R. Sargent Shriver (D)	Richard M. Nixon & Spiro T. Agnew (R)	Jimmy Carter & Walter Mondale (D)	Gerald R. Ford & Robert Dole (R)
Livingston	9,698	6,723	7,052	10,034	7,634	16,856	12,415	19,437
Macomb	131,450	44,684	114,552	63,139	82,346	147,777	121,176	132,499
Monroe	26,528	11,499	18,921	15,685	17,726	23,263	23,290	20,676
Oakland	182,797	114,025	154,630	156,538	129,400	241,613	164,266	244,271
St. Clair	24,662	17,011	16,251	21,084	15,712	28,471	22,734	26,311
Washtenaw	42,089	25,595	33,073	36,432	55,350	50,535	50,917	56,807
Wayne	831,674	260,901	654,157	270,566	514,913	435,877	548,767	348,588
State totals	**2,136,615**	**1,060,152**	**1,593,082**	**1,370,665**	**1,459,435**	**1,961,721**	**1,696,714**	**1,893,742**

1964: Four other candidates received 6,335 votes statewide. **1968:** George Wallace received 331,968 votes statewide, including 105,606 in Wayne County; 29,239 in Macomb County; 33,024 in Oakland; 7,456 in Washtenaw; 5,261 in St. Clair; 2,543 in Livingston, and 4,873 in Monroe. **1972:** Four other candidates received 69,169 votes statewide. **1976:** Six candidates received 61,133 votes statewide.

COUNTIES	1980		1984		1988		1992	
	Jimmy Carter & Walter Mondale (D)	Ronald Reagan & George Bush (R)	Walter Mondale & Geraldine Ferraro (D)	Ronald Reagan & George Bush (R)	Michael Dukakis & Lloyd Bentsen (D)	George Bush & Dan Quayle (R)	Bill Clinton & Al Gore (D)	George Bush & Dan Quayle (R)
Livingston	12,626	25,012	10,720	31,846	13,749	31,331	17,851	27,539
Macomb	120,125	154,155	97,816	194,300	112,856	175,632	130,732	147,795
Monroe	20,578	25,612	19,617	29,419	21,847	26,189	24,957	20,250
Oakland	164,869	253,211	150,286	306,050	174,745	283,359	214,733	242,160
St. Clair	20,410	31,021	16,998	36,114	20,909	32,336	23,385	24,508
Washtenaw	51,013	48,699	55,084	58,736	61,799	55,029	73,325	41,386
Wayne	522,024	315,532	496,632	367,391	450,222	291,996	508,464	227,002
State totals	**1,661,532**	**1,915,225**	**1,529,638**	**2,251,571**	**1,675,783**	**1,965,486**	**1,871,182**	**1,554,940**

1980: John Anderson received 275,223 votes statewide, including 43,608 in Wayne; 38,273 in Oakland. **1992:** H. Ross Perot received 824,813 votes statewide, including 15,971 in Livingston; 7,954 in Macomb; 94,911 in Oakland; 13,551 in Monroe; 18,523 in St. Clair; 21,889 in Washtenaw and 102,074 in Wayne.

COUNTIES	1996		2000		
	Bill Clinton & Al Gore (D)	Bob Dole & Jack Kemp (R)	Al Gore & Joe Lieberman (D)	G.W. Bush & Dick Cheney (R)	Ralph Nader & Winona LaDuke
Livingston	22,517	30,598	28,780	44,637	1,498
Macomb	151,430	120,616	172,625	164,265	6,145
Monroe	26,072	19,678	31,555	28,940	996
Oakland	241,884	219,855	281,201	274,319	10,382
St. Clair	28,881	22,495	33,002	33,571	1,341
Washtenaw	73,106	40,097	86,647	52,459	4,843
Wayne	504,446	175,886	530,414	223,021	11,287
State totals	**1,989,653**	**1,481,212**	**2,170,418**	**1,953,139**	**84,165**

1996: H. Ross Perot received 336,670 votes statewide including 6,337 in Livingston; 29,859 in Macomb; 6,315 in Monroe; 36,709 in Oakland; 8,314 in St. Clair; 8,020 in Washtenaw and 43,554 in Wayne.

(W)=Whig; (D)=Democrat; (R)=Republican; (DL)= Democrat and Labor; (NP) = National Progressive Party

POLITICS

The Detroit Almanac

10. GEO GRA

"It's difficult to explain what makes Detroit Detroit..."

— Hollywood director and Detroiter **Vondie Curtis Hall**, *1990s*

FRANKLIN ROAD

F THIRTEEN MILE RD

FRANKLIN 1 | REDFORD 9

PONTIAC 9 | DETROIT 21

FARMINGTON 7 | ROYAL OAK 9

WALLED LAKE 11 | DETROIT 20

On the road

An old mile marker
in Franklin in
Oakland County.

East Side. West Side.

Choosing sides

For decades, Detroiters — even suburbanites — identified themselves by the side of town on which they lived. Woodward was the great divide. There are loads of east siders today who are flat-out lost west of Woodward, and vice versa. Simple reason: They did not care much for the other side of town. Few people moved to the other side of town. If you left Detroit proper, you kept going in the same direction — east siders moved to east-side suburbs and west siders moved to Livonia and other points west.

And side-chauvinists insisted there was merit in the distinctions. "The east-side kids were just hipper, sharper and funnier," Motown founder Berry Gordy Jr. wrote in his autobiography, recalling his family's unusual move from west to east.

The east side has the skewed streets with funny names like St. Jean, Kercheval and Cadieux. East siders have better access to the river and the lake, and groaning freighter horns haunt neighborhoods on foggy nights. If you live close enough to the water, you can lie in bed at night and hear the hum of engines turning those giant propellers.

The west side has the rigid, north-south streets and most of the city's fancy neighborhoods. Palmer Park, Sherwood Forest, Rosedale Park and the University District are some of the areas that are filled with huge, exquisite homes. The west side has a lot of smart people, too. Maybe it's because Wayne State, University of Detroit Mercy and Marygrove College are all on the west side of town.

Alas, times change. Metro Detroit has evolved. Choosing up sides by east and west in the new millennium is an anachronism.

After 300 years, Detroit needs — dare we say it? — a new paradigm.

In short, we need a new side of town.

The north side.

Using three sides of town will make comparisons more precise. It will give credit where credit is due.

Happily, today's geographic divisions permit an easy definition of which side of town is which.

The definitions: Oakland County, natch, is the north side. Everything to the east of Woodward in Detroit and Macomb County is the east side. Everything to the west of Woodward in Detroit, Wayne and Washtenaw counties is west side.

It's that simple.

May the best side win.

Here's a list of what's what where and what wears where. Why? Well, most folks here should understand. New to town? Ask a homey.

WEST SIDE	NORTH SIDE	EAST SIDE
Fisher Building	Max Fisher	Fisher Manse
Tom Monaghan	Mike Ilitch	Tony Buscemi
Iggy Pop	Glenn Frey	Kid Rock
Ford	DaimlerChrysler	General Motors
Maple Theatre	Main Art	Star Gratiot

DETROIT'S NICKNAMES
1890s:
City of Progress
19th Century:
City of the Strait
City of Churches
City of Trees
20th Century:
Motor City
Dynamic Detroit
1930s:
City of Champions
1940s:
Arsenal of Democracy
1950s:
Big D
1960s:
Motown
1970s:
Murder City
Snuff City
Renaissance City
1990s:
Hockeytown

SLOGANS

(1990s)
"It's a Great Time in Detroit"

(1990s)
"Detroit: Making It Better for You"

(1890s)
"The City Where Life is Worth Living"

OFFICIAL MOTTO
"Speramus meliora; resurget cineribus."
That is: "We hope for better days; It shall rise from the ashes."
(Written by the Rev. Gabriel Richard after fire destroyed Detroit in 1805.)

THE REGION

Wayne, Oakland, Macomb, Washtenaw, Livingston, Monroe and St. Clair counties. Seven-county population:

2000 U.S. Census . . . .
. 4,833,493
1990 4,590,468
1840 103,064
1880 383,528
1900 582,236
1920 1,467,964
1950 3,344,793
1970 4,731,655

In 1840, Wayne County had only 602 more people than Washtenaw; by 1990, the gap had grown to 1.8 million.

Tri-county population (Wayne, Oakland and Macomb counties):
2000: 4,043,467
Consolidated Metropolitan Statistical Area, 1997
Metro Detroit-Ann Arbor-Flint: 5,293,000
Rank: 8th in the United States

10 largest cities in United States
According to 2000 U.S. Census results:
New York 8,008,278
Los Angeles . . .3,694,820
Chicago 2,896,016
Houston 1,953,631
Philadelphia . . .1,517,550
San Diego 1,223,400
Phoenix 1,321,045
Dallas 1,888,580
San Antonio . . .1,144,646
DETROIT 951,270

Detroit is within 500 miles of 45 percent of the U.S. population; 46 percent of U.S. income; 44 percent of Canada's population and 45 percent of Canada's personal income.
SOURCE: DETROIT/WAYNE COUNTY PORT AUTHORITY.

WEST SIDE	NORTH SIDE	EAST SIDE
Fair Lane	Meadow Brook	Ford Mansion
H. Ford Museum	Detroit Zoo	Dossin Museum
Lily Tomlin	Robin Williams	Dave Coulier
Kronk Gym	Franklin Racquet Club	Brewster Center
Belleville Lake	Cass Lake	Lake St. Clair
The Big Tire	The Zoo Tower	The Hill
Charles Baxter	Elmore Leonard	Jeff Eugenides
Grosse Ile	Apple Island	Peche Island
Palmer Woods	Birmingham	Grosse Pointe
Metro Airport	Oakland County International	Selfridge ANG Base
Michigan Stadium	The Silverdome	Manz Field
Fairway Drive	Lone Pine Road	Lake Shore Drive
Ann Arbor	Royal Oak	Hamtramck
U of M	Cranbrook	Macomb C.C.
The Chop House	Tribute	Rattlesnake Club
Daly Burgers	Ted's Drive In	Dunkenburgers
Taurus	Mercedes	Grand Am
The Kids	Lawn service	Yourself
Fairlane	Somerset	Lakeside

Neal Shine on the east side/west side divide

"On that frigid morning in 1954, I was standing guard, in deep snow, over a battalion of sleeping American soldiers in a beautiful Alpine valley near the Austrian village of Lofer.

We were there on military maneuvers, exercises which were scheduled whenever the weather got bad enough. Across the road, standing guard at what I think now was a signal battalion, was a soldier who looked as cold as I felt.

We met in the middle of the narrow road and began to talk. Priority conversation. How cold it was. How much we hated being there. How much longer to go in the Army. Hometowns.

"Detroit," he said.

"Me, too."

We took off the heavy woolen gloves and shook hands.

"What part of Detroit?" I asked.

"West side," he said.

He did not misunderstand my hesitation in responding.

"You from the east side?"

I nodded.

He looked at me for a few seconds from beneath the hood of his parka and said finally: "Well, stay warm and take it easy. Maybe see you back in Detroit." He walked off into the darkness of that Austrian valley knowing as I did that further conversation about Detroit would have been a waste of time.

His Detroit world — schools, playgrounds, neighborhoods, hangouts — was on one side of Woodward, mine on the other. It was a difference we both understood."

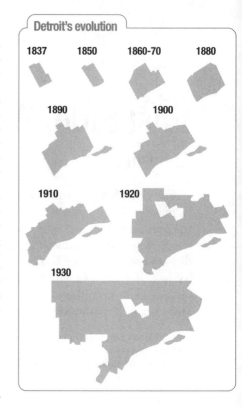

Detroit's evolution

1837　　1850　　1860-70　　1880

1890　　　　1900

1910　　　　1920

1930

Detroit: The lowdown

Name: Means "the strait" in French, as in a narrow body of water connecting two larger bodies. The French considered "le detroit" to be the Detroit River, Lake St. Clair and the St. Clair River connecting lakes Erie and Huron.

Population .951,270 (2000 U.S. Census), down from 1,027,974 in the 1990 Census.
Rank . . . . .10th-largest U.S. city
Area . . . . .137.9 square miles
Elevation . . . . .581 feet
Shoreline . . . . .10.66 miles
Streetlights 86,932
Fire hydrants 30,426
Parks . . . . .391, covering 5,863 acres
Recreation centers, playgrounds 127
Golf courses 6
Libraries 26
Streets . . . . .2,789 miles
Sidewalks . . . . .4,258 miles
Traffic tickets issued (including parking tickets, 1998) 681,166
City employees 17,416

SOURCE: CITY OF DETROIT ANNUAL FINANCIAL REPORT, 1999.

Trading places

While just 8 percent of metropolitan-area white people lived in Detroit in 1990, 14 percent worked there. Only 17 percent of metropolitan-area blacks lived in the suburbs, but 50 percent worked there. Suburban white women were much more likely than suburban white men to work in Detroit.

Transportation: In 1990, 35 percent of black households in Detroit reported they owned no car or van.

Making cars: The percentage of U.S. automobiles made in Michigan declined from 35 percent in the early 1980s to 25 percent in the late 1990s.

Detroit Census

July 23, 1701	0
July 24, 1701	100
1773	1,357
1778	2,144
1780	2,207
1783	2,291
1796	500
1810	1,650
1820	1,442
Black	67 (4.9%)
1830	2,222
U.S. rank	35
Black	126 (.56%)
1840	9,102
U.S. rank	25
Black	193 (2.1%)
1850	21,019
U.S. rank	23
Black	587 (2.8%)
Foreign born	10,019 (47.7%)

Of the 11,000-plus natives, 6,323 were born in Michigan. Of the 4,732 remaining, 4,173 were born in Ohio, New York, Pennsylvania, New Jersey or New England.

Of the foreign born, 3,289 (15.6%) were from Ireland; this was the year the Irish peaked in percentage of the city's population. The next leading foreign groups: Germans, Britons and French.

1860	45,619
U.S. rank	18
Black	1,402 (3%)
1870	79,577
U.S. rank	17
Black	2,235 (2.8%)
1880	116,340
U.S. rank	17
Black	2,821 (2.4%)
Foreign born	51,709 (44.4%)

Leading foreign-born groups: Germans, 23,769 (20.4%); Canadians, 10,754 (9.2%); Irish, 6,775 (5.8 percent). Michigan born: 46% of native born.

1890	205,876
U.S. rank	14
Black	3,431 (1.7%)
1900	285,704
U.S. rank	13
Black	4,111 (1.4%)
Foreign born	96,166 (33.7%)

Leading foreign-born groups: Germans, 32,000 (11.2%); Canadians, 28,900, (10.1%); Poles, 14,000 (4.9%); Irish, 6,400 (2.2%).

1910	465,766
U.S. rank	9
Black	5,741 (1.2%)

Blacks fell to their smallest percentage of Detroit's population since 1830, but the first great influx from the south would begin in the next decade.

Foreign born: 156,000 (33.5%). Germans (9.4%) and Canadians (8.8%) continue to be the leading foreign-born groups, but Russians — many of them Jews — were in third place (3.9%). Michigan born: only 9%.

1920	993,678
U.S. rank	4
Black	40,838 (4.1%)
Foreign born	289,000 (29.1%)

With the auto age in full bloom, immigrants were flocking to Detroit. In rank, they included: Canadians, 58,500 (5.9%); Poles, 56,600 (5.7%); Germans, 30,000 (3%); Russians, 27,200 (2.7%); British, 17,100 (1.7%); Italians, 16,000 (1.6%) and Hungarians, 13,500 (1.4%). The black population had begun to grow.

1930	1,568,662
U.S. rank	4
Black	120,066 (7.6%)
Foreign born	407,736 (26%)
1940	1,623,452
U.S. rank	4
Black	149,119 (9.1%)
Foreign born	320,833 (19.8%)

Detroit's already sizable black population was on its way to doubling during the next 10 years. The next four decades will see unrelenting conflict between white and black Detroiters, starting with the Sojourner Truth housing battle of 1942 and the 1943 race riot.

1950	1,849,568
U.S. rank	5
Black	300,506 (16.1%)
Foreign born	276,470 (14.9%)

Demographers believe Detroit's population peaked at close to 2 million in about 1953 before it began dropping. The white population of more than 1.5 million would dwindle to 222,000 by 1990.

1960	1,670,144
U.S. rank	5
Black	482,229 (28.9%)
Foreign born	201,713 (12.1%)
1970	1,511,482
U.S. rank	5
Black	660,428 (44.5%)
Foreign born	119,347 (7.9%)
1980	1,203,339
U.S. rank	6
Black	758,939 (63%)
Foreign born	68,303 (5.7%)

Detroit lost 20.4 percent of its population between 1970 and 1980, and blacks become the majority.

1990	1,027,974
U.S. rank	9
Black	777,916 (76%)
Foreign born	34,490 (3.4%)
2000	951,270
U.S. rank	10
Black	81.6%
White	12.3%
Hispanic	5.0%
Asian	1.0%

Detroit suffered white flight and, to a lesser degree, black flight between 1990 and 2000, U.S. Census figures showed. There are only 99,921 non-Hispanic whites left in Detroit, 10.5 percent. In 1950, the city had 1.5 million white residents. The 2000 Census recorded about 6,000 fewer black residents than in 1990, but the proportion of blacks in the city increased about 5 percent. Detroit's 7.5-percent population drop between 1990 and 2000 was the smallest such decrease since 1960. Only 2.3 percent of Detroiters identified themselves as multiracial.

The following statistics come from the 2000 book, "Detroit Divided," by Reynolds Farley, Sheldon Danzinger and Harry Holzer.

Percentage of tri-county population living in Detroit

1900	68 percent
1950	65 percent
1990	25 percent

Percentage of tri-county white population living in Detroit

1900	68 percent
1950	58 percent
1990	8 percent

Percentage of tri-county black population living in Detroit

1900	86 percent
1950	84 percent
1990	83 percent

Total jobs in

	1960	1990
Detroit	700,000	350,000
In tri-county suburbs	350,000	1.4 million

Jobs overall declined by half in Detroit in 30 years but quadrupled in the suburbs.

Manufacturing jobs in

	1947	1972	1992
Detroit	338*	239	62
In tri-county suburbs	219	356	339
Total	557	595	401

* In thousands

Good blue-collar jobs declined after 1970 across metro Detroit, but especially in Detroit.

GEOGRAPHY

NEIGHBORHOODS FROM THE 19TH CENTURY

Piety Hill: Woodward above and below Grand Circus Park; named for the many churches.

Kentucky: A predominately black neighborhood north of the Fisher Freeway and east of the Chrysler Freeway.

Dutchtown: The east-side German area along Gratiot.

Peddler's Point: Grand River near 12th Street, a favorite location for itinerant salesmen.

Swill Point: Larned Street near Second, because of the number of breweries.

Potomac: The area along the Detroit River on the east side, for forgotten reasons.

The Heights: East Fort Street, a poor area.

Notable Detroit neighborhoods

The city's most cohesive neighborhoods tend to have a few things in common: They are closely knit through active resident associations. They are filled with fine old homes. And they have pride — some of them hold tours or festivals at various times of the year. Here are sketches of some of Detroit's most interesting places to live.

Thomas W. Palmer.

Free Press file photo

Detroit's largest house, built by the Fisher brothers for Detroit's archbishops. It is in Palmer Woods.

Palmer Woods

Location: 7 Mile and Woodward, north of the Palmer Park Golf Course.

Selling points: The city's richest neighborhood.

History: Part of a farm owned by Sen. Thomas W. Palmer whose son sold the property to a developer with the stipulation that the area remain a credit to the Palmer name. The project was begun in 1915 and resulted in 300 exquisite homes that range in size from about 2,000 square feet to the 62-room, 35,000-square-foot estate the automotive Fisher family built for the Catholic Archdiocese of Detroit in 1926. Catholic bishops and cardinals lived in it for the next several decades, then a Detroit Pistons basketball player, John Salley, bought it in 1989 and converted the chapel into a big-screen TV room. "I'm not Catholic," he explained. Another Fisher mansion had 48 rooms, Baccarat crystal chandeliers and floor-to-ceiling inlaid marble. It burned in 1994.

Highlights: S-shaped drives and Tudor Revival mansions guarded by snarling stone lions. No curbs, just stones painted white. Highly personal styles and painstaking detail. Marble foyers and carved paneling. Pewabic tile and grand ballrooms. A 1950s house with five levels, a jukebox and an indoor pool right next to the breakfast room. A plaster satyr in a bathroom.

North Rosedale Park

Location: Northwest Detroit, bounded by Southfield, McNichols, Evergreen and Grand River.

Selling points: A handsome, planned, pre-Depression community. Wet plaster, leaded glass.

History: Developer Henry Shelden created

GEOGRAPHY

Corktown in the 1960s. *1950's ?*

a subdivision with a difference. He platted the three-quarters of a square mile, in what was then Redford Township, according to an innovative concept for the day — the garden suburb. He envisioned large, handsome homes on winding, tree-lined boulevards. Houses originally were to be built only on every other lot. Strict building codes were formulated to protect the architectural integrity. A park and a community house were essential to the plan. In the boom years of 1924-1926, Detroiters were leaving the inner city; Shelden capitalized on that boom and decided to lure the managerial and professional classes to his little Shangri-la.

Highlights: A number of stately trees, approximately 1,700 homes, many with hand-carved doors and intricate brick work. The North Rosedale Park's civic association, headquartered in the community house at 18445 Scarsdale Road, has served as the community glue for several decades.

Boston-Edison Historic District

Location: West of Woodward, about 1 mile north of Grand Boulevard.

Selling points: With 930 houses, it's one of the largest single-family historic districts in the country.

History: Starting in the 1890s, Henry Ford, Stanley S. Kresge, James Couzens, Walter Briggs, Horace Rackham, the Grinnell brothers, the Fisher brothers and the Siegel brothers all built mansions here when Detroit was a hot, young city and they were the people to watch. In more recent years, an integrated group of mostly professional people have purchased the homes and lovingly cared for them.

Highlights: To outsiders, the Boston-Edison District is the least visible of Detroit's large historic neighborhoods. But it's a gem. Henry Ford lived at 140 Edison for seven years before he moved to Dearborn in 1915; famed architect Albert Kahn designed homes at 150 Boston, 610 Longfellow, 52 Chicago and 100 Longfellow. One of the most elaborate homes, 1918 Boston, was bought in 1967 by Motown founder Berry Gordy Jr.

Hubbard-Richard

Location: Fort Street to the south, 16th to the east, West Grand Boulevard to the west, Toledo and railroad right-of-way to the north.

Selling points: Ethnically diverse but Latino-accented community near the Detroit River in the shadows of the Ambassador Bridge. Minutes from downtown.

History: Named after Bela Hubbard, an early farmer in what was then Springwells Township. He was also a meteorologist and developer. Ste. Anne's moved from the heart of downtown to its present site in the neighborhood in 1886.

Highlights: The area is undergoing a resurgence with new housing and commerce. It has Ste. Anne's Catholic Church and a variety of ethnic restaurants, retailers, bakeries and tortilla factories. The neighborhood is located near the heart of Mexican Town.

Corktown

Location: South of Tiger Stadium and west of the temporary MGM Grand casino.

Selling points: It's metro Detroit's oldest neighborhood. A walk through its streets recalls the 19th Century like no other part of town.

History: Irish immigrants began settling here and building cottages two decades before the Civil War, when they were Detroit's dominant ethnic group. The Irish are long gone

Location: About 2 miles north of downtown Detroit.

Selling points: Old but bustling.

History: Detroiters moving north settled in the area as early as the 1870s, and the pre-auto elite built churches and homes along Woodward. Detroit's Central High opened in the mid-1890s at Cass and Warren; it's now Wayne State's stately Old Main. The university's growth — it's now 203 acres — has been both blessing and curse. Expansion has mowed down blocks of old homes, especially those occupied by poor people west of the Lodge Freeway, but it also has brought residential safety and economic health.

Highlights: Residents are black, white, young, old, Asian, hippies — among others — and live in old apartments, some of them renovated, residences and student housing. The cultural center, including the Detroit Institute of Arts, is nearby. It's centrally located. Each September the neighbors put on "Dally in the Alley," perhaps metro Detroit's hippest block party. Below, WSU's Old Main in 1943.

INDIAN VILLAGE

Location: Iroquois, Seminole and Burns between Mack and Jefferson on the east side.

Selling points: Many of the homes were designed by some of the region's premier architects for the area's well-heeled in the early 20th Century. Some homes are 3,000 square feet a floor and have carved limestone, spiral staircases, ballrooms and carriage houses.

History: Platted as a subdivision in 1895, the area was organized largely by Detroit and Cleveland shipping heir John Owen. He organized the Cook Farm Co. Ltd. with the heirs of Abraham Cook, who had owned the land since 1811. Many of the homes were built by families that came from old Detroit money, including some heirs to J. L. Hudson. Major architects of the time, including Albert Kahn, Louis Kamper, John Scott and William Stratton, designed the homes. The area won historic designation in 1970. Property values have skyrocketed during the last decade, with home prices ranging from $300,000 to $1.2 million. A moderate home sold for about $35,000 in 1971.

Highlights: Still home to many of the area's lawyers, judges, elected officials and corporate types, the area also has working-class residents. Close to the river and downtown.

Free Press file photo

A 1933 view of what was then the Elks Lodge in Indian Village.

from there. Urban renewal almost killed the place. Of Corktown's 1,000 houses, bulldozers took down about 700 — some for land that's still vacant — leaving just 280. Values sank to a few thousand dollars per home, then fires and vandalism destroyed more houses. But starting in the 1990s, renovated homes began selling for big bucks. Before bank loans were available, architects and professional carpenters kicked Corktown restoration into gear. Then Mexican and Maltese families among others gave it a new character.

Highlights: Large Victorian houses are common in Michigan, but small Victorian workers' cottages like Corktown's are rare. The cottages are in the "shotgun" style of America's working-class housing in the late 19th Century — three little rooms lined up behind each other. Theoretically, you could fire a shotgun in the front door, and the blast would go out the back. Most Holy Trinity, the mother church of Detroit's Irish, anchors the eastern end of Corktown.

Brush Park

Location: East of Woodward, north of the Fisher Freeway and Comerica Park and west of I-75.

Selling points: One of the city's oldest neighborhoods features mammoth Victorian-style mansions, many with former storefronts. Among the more notable former owners were lumber baron David Whitney Jr., realtor Joseph Weber, retailer J. L. Hudson, philanthropist Grace Whitney Huff, and Charles Freer, a major art collector who rented rooms

in Brush Park and then built a home on East Ferry that's now the location of the Merrill-Palmer Institute, a childhood and family development research institution.

History: Established in the 1860s when Edmund A. Brush divided the family farm into subdivisions, this is one of the city's oldest neighborhoods. A typical lot sold for $5,000 in the 1880s, and up until about 1910, the homes with multiple chimneys housed much of the city's elite, who were largely Anglo and German Americans. Then a long decline set in. During the next 30 years, homes were downgraded into boarding houses. The site also felt the impact of the city's large, post-1950 population drop, and the Chrysler and Fisher freeways sliced through the neighborhood. Lofty restoration promises came as part of the city's East Woodward Project in the 1970s, but resulted in little more than landscaping upgrades.

Highlights: The grand houses continued to decay in the 1980s, though about a dozen ambitious people dumped substantial money into preservation attempts. That includes University of Windsor art professor Michael Farrell, who helped restore a 20-room Victorian mansion and turned it into the home of a nonprofit organization. Ground was broken in 1999 for the Woodward Place at Brush Park, a $75-million development of condominiums selling for up to $200,000.

The Riverfront

Location: From downtown to the far east side along the Detroit River.

Selling points: Water. View. Freighter whistles. Tranquillity — except during hydroplane races.

History: For more than 170 years, Detroiters lived near the river, traveled on the river and even — at first, anyway — drank from the river. But the industrial expansion beginning in the late 19th Century brought in factories and pushed out homes. Some high-end apartments were built east of the Belle Isle Bridge after World War I and have gone condo; Harbor Island, near Grosse Pointe, has long been one of Detroit's little-known gems; and the Jeffersonian apartment tower made a splash when it opened in 1964. But it wasn't until Coleman Young became mayor in 1974 that developers and the city got serious about replacing the shabby warehouses, rotting buildings and abandoned factories with housing, parks and commercial complexes.

Highlights: Max Fisher and Al Taubman built the Riverfront Apartments west of Joe Louis Arena; some tenants dock their boats in the downstairs marina. Harbortown, on East Jefferson near Mt. Elliott, is a 48-acre residential, retail and commercial project with condominiums and two apartment towers. Stroh River Place and surrounding streets feature housing, offices, restaurants and bars. Grayhaven Marina, near the foot of Lenox, opened in 1928, only to fail during the Depression, but apartments, townhouses and single homes flourish there now.

Conant Gardens

Location: East side, south of 7 Mile and north of Nevada, between Conant and Ryan.

Selling points: The Conant Gardens Homeowners Association, which is active in preserving the community history.

History: The land was originally owned by Shubael Conant, an early 19th Century merchant and president of the Detroit Board of Water Commissioners. Conant was an abolitionist who stipulated in his will that no deed restrictions be placed on his land to forbid blacks from owning parcels. As a result, Conant Gardens was one of the first places in the United States where African Americans could buy property. Many residents had gardens that gave rise to the neighborhood name.

Highlights: A small neighborhood comprised mainly of single-family homes. Pershing High School is located there.

Victoria Park

Location: An irregularly shaped east-side neighborhood south of Jefferson and bordered by Piper, Freud, Newport, Averhill Court, Lenox and Dickerson.

Selling points: 1990s homes that offer value over suburban counterparts. Nearby stores and services make it a convenient residential neighborhood.

History: The development was initiated through a public-private collaboration, with city subsidized construction. Lots here were sold to builders for $1 each to promote the area's renewal. In June 1992, it was the first urban Homearama in the U.S. and a showcase for urban residential development. It proved there was a demand for new housing in the city and sparked continued construction in the area and throughout Detroit.

Highlights: Offers a suburban feel, newer upscale housing and proximity to downtown and the riverfront.

The twin towers of Lafayette Park.

Free Press file photo

LAFAYETTE PARK

Location: East of the Chrysler Freeway and south of Gratiot.

Selling points: Integrated, upscale and located next to downtown.

History: A crowning achievement of four visionaries — architect Ludwig Mies van der Rohe, developer Herbert Greenwald, urban planner Ludwig Hilberseimer and landscaper Alfred Caldwel, Lafayette Park is one of Detroit's great post-World War II success stories. It was part of a controversial urban renewal plan of the 1950s that included the destruction of the city's largest black-populated neighborhood.

Highlights: Glassy low-rise and high-rise housing blend with lush trees and bushes. A long park runs down the center that residents can reach without crossing a street. Children can walk to school through that park without going on a thoroughfare. All parking is depressed 3 to 4 feet so people look over the cars, not at them. Nature is the dominant vision, not machines. Included in the van der Rohe section are two high-rise buildings that are all rental, plus two cooperative-housing high-rises in which each resident-owner is a shareholder in the corporation. There are 110 townhouses (two-story row houses) and 48 court houses (one-story attached homes that have a large walled courtyard). As appropriate for 1950s modernism, the main building materials are steel and glass. In fact, most exterior walls are a sheet of glass — van der Rohe's famous "glass curtains."

Much has been written and opined on what happened after 1955. Here are the main reasons Detroit began to empty:

Job loss. Starting about 1950, auto manufacturers and suppliers began moving to facilities in the suburbs. Historian Thomas Sugrue says between 1947 and 1963, Detroit lost 134,000 manufacturing jobs.

Freeways: First the Lodge, then the Ford, Chrysler, Fisher and Jeffries acted like pneumatic tubes hurtling workers from central city venues to myriad suburbs. Once commuting from downtown became a snap, more people moved to greener spaces beyond Detroit.

Cheaper housing: Detroit was growing; postwar families longed for three- or four-bedroom homes — which were relatively expensive on the rim of the city. Mortgage lenders often required a 30-percent down payment for a $24,000 brick house. Then the Eisenhower Administration, anxious to jump-start the housing industry, offered veterans super new-home deals. For as little as $800 down, a veteran could move to a newly built and inexpensive house in the "sticks" — like West Bloomfield or St. Clair Shores. Taxes were much lower, too.

Race: The growing African-American population in Detroit unsettled many whites who opted to move to communities where blacks were rare or unwelcomed.

The 1967 riot: It was a

Abandoned Detroit

Detroit was fat in 1955 — the Census Bureau estimated 2 million people crowded the nearly 140 square miles. But the decline already had begun.

The most severe decline in population occurred between 1955 and 1960 when the number dropped by nearly 25 percent. From 1960 to 1980, the drop was about 25 percent. And from 1955 to 2000, the drop has been about 50 percent.

When a city of 140 square miles loses half of its population, and a considerable portion of its tax dollars, blight and abandonment rapidly rise.

In 1989, Free Press reporters traveled the more than 2,000 miles of city streets and counted 15,215 vacant structures, including 9,017 single-family homes, 225 apartment buildings and 3,414 vacant businesses. The city estimated then that up to 200 structures a month were being abandoned in Detroit.

In 2000, city officials said there were more than 40,000 lots owned by the city, including 8,000 structures of which 5,000 were vacant or abandoned.

Vacant buildings became the most visible evidence of the city's social and economic problems in the last three decades of the 20th Century. Beyond giving parts of Detroit a war-ravaged appearance, abandoned buildings

The 2200 block of Montclair on the east side.

A lonely home on Hillger, near Charlevoix, 1989.

robbed the city and its schools of property taxes and created targets for arson. The buildings also became havens for criminals.

Vacant structures also spawned subcultures of scavengers who stripped copper wiring and leaded glass from discarded homes, young people who danced to throbbing electronic music at illegal raves in emp-

ty warehouses, and even artists who received inspiration in the epic abandonment. Fashion shoots became common at vacant buildings; a team from Amsterdam flew in to use the Michigan Central Depot in the late 1990s.

The city's ravaged neighborhoods were well chronicled. Camilo Jose Vergara told an international audience of the beauty he found in Detroit's abandoned buildings. His favorite is the train depot at Michigan and 14th.

Vergara is a sociologist and photographer known nationally for documenting the transformations of some of America's most devastated inner cities. He has made Detroit one of his chief exhibits in books such as "The New American Ghetto" (1996) and "American Ruins" (1999). His photographs have been displayed widely and he has received grants from the National Endowment for the Arts and the New York Council on the Arts.

He once proposed that 12 square blocks south and west of Grand Circus Park be preserved as an American Acropolis, a skyscraper graveyard. He also said the Michigan Central Depot should become an abbey or monastery.

Another artist who surveyed the evolution of the city's buildings was Detroiter Lowell Boileau, whose elaborate Web site of what he calls "my beloved Detroit" is at **bhere.com**

REASONS

factor, but by 1967, the exodus from Detroit had been in high gear for a decade.

Busing: The plan to bus Detroit schoolchildren between neighborhood schools to achieve integration caused many families to pull stakes saying they wanted to send their children down the street to school, not miles away.

Vacant land in February 2000

Detroit .... 40,000 lots
New York .... 9,800 lots
Chicago .... 4,000 to 5,000 lots
Philadelphia. 8,500 lots

When a city of 140 square miles loses half of its population, and a considerable portion of its tax dollars, blight and abandonment rapidly rise.

The Border/La

Border cities, motor cities, sister cities — Detroit and Windsor have been linked for 300 years. For nearly a century, in fact, the two sides of the river belonged to the same country — France, and then Britain. The border was open from 1796, when Americans took control of Detroit, to the 1880s. People crossed at will, and no one asked: "Citizen of what country?" Today, the two cities fly different flags, use different measurements and spend different money. But Detroit and Windsor continue to share all the important things: air, water, hockey, beer and history. What follows is an account of a beautiful friendship that has lasted for 200 years.

The Ambassador Bridge. Canada is south of the United States at this point. Windsor is on the left; southwest Detroit on the right.

frontière

Windsor

Name: Residents chose Windsor, a familiar British moniker, in 1836. It had been called, at various times: Richmond, the Ferry, Sandwich Ferry, South Detroit, Straits of Detroit, L'Assomption Settlement, the Ferry Opposite Detroit, the South Side.

Nickname: The City of Roses

Population: City: 197,694; metro: 300,000. It's Canada's 15th-biggest metro area.

Pioneers: Windsor became a city on May 24,

1892 — Queen Victoria's birthday. Its roots reach to 1742, when the Rev. Armand de la Richardie established a mission on Bois Blanc (Boblo)Island. In 1747, he moved the Assumption mission to the Windsor shore, on land occupied by Huron Indians. The current church, built in 1846, stands by the Ambassador Bridge. By 1749, the Gervais, St. Louis, Drouillard, Pilette and Lafleur families were staking claims on the south shore, which was then part of New France, just like the Detroit side. Windsor, the last stop on the Under-

GEOGRAPHY

FAMOUS DETROITERS FROM CANADA

James Couzens, above: Detroit mayor, police commissioner, aide to Henry Ford.

James McMillan: U.S. senator, industrialist.

Malcolm Bingay: Free Press editor and columnist.

Robert Bradby: Pastor of Second Baptist Church.

Rev. Charles Coughlin: Detroit's controversial radio priest.

John Hamtramck: Military commander.

John Swainson: Michigan governor and Supreme Court justice.

Byron MacGregor: CKLW-AM tabloid newsman whose rousing "Americans" was a national hit in 1974. He became a U.S. citizen and was living in West Bloomfield when he died in 1995.

Gordie Howe: Right winger.

HUGH GRANNUM/Detroit Free Press

Common customs: Waiting in line behind myriad big rigs, getting nervous at border control even though you have nothing to hide and breathing a little sigh of relief when you aren't searched.

ground Railroad, received numerous escaped slaves who fled across the Detroit River after harrowing journeys from the American south; some stayed, others moved inland. Windsor in 1854 was also the terminus of a real railroad, the Great Western, which connected Detroit to the east across southwestern Ontario.

Today: Windsor is Canada's Motor City and, at the size of Grand Rapids, it's the largest city in the Detroit area next to Detroit. It's a lunch-bucket town and the nation's southernmost metropolis, featuring manicured gardens, a lovely riverfront, a very diverse population and sophisticated nightlife. In fact, Windsor's naughtiness attracts large numbers of Americans, including lots of 19- and 20-year-old college students who can't legally drink in Michigan. A decade ago, Windsor was so uptight you couldn't shop on Sunday. Now, downtown is a flourishing entertainment district with crowded bars, European-style outdoor cafes, busy restaurants, a huge casino, nude dance clubs that cater to men and women and municipally licensed escorts. Nearby Point Pelee has nature, migrating birds and good vineyards.

SOURCE: "BIRTH OF A CITY," BY CARL MORGAN.

Border crossings

THE NUMBERS: Two routes are available from Detroit, which is the busiest northern border crossing in the United States. The nearest crossing from Detroit is Port Huron-Sarnia via the Blue Water Bridge. The 1999 figures for vehicles in both directions:

Ambassador Bridge: 12.4 million
Detroit-Windsor Tunnel: 9.6 million
Blue Water Bridge: 5.5 million

BRIDGE OR TUNNEL?: Until 1910, the only way to cross the river was by ferry. After the Civil War, Detroiters began making plans for a bridge or tunnel to Windsor.

➤ **Rail tunnel:** The $8.5-million Michigan Central Railroad tunnel under the Detroit River opened on July 1, 1910. Workers, according to author Almon Parkins, dredged a trough in the river bottom and sunk a prefabricated steel cylinder into the trough, covering it with cement and stone. Pride in the rail tunnel was great. Detroiters could buy postcards showing the tunnel entrance to send friends. In later years, the rail tunnel was used by illegal aliens to sneak into the United States.

➤ **Ambassador Bridge:** It extends like a

graceful handshake across the river. Construction of the $11.4-million bridge began in May 1927, after a nasty tussle between builder Joseph A. Bower and Detroit Mayor John W. Smith. The bridge also encountered financing obstacles, a construction deadline and a defect that led builders to remove cables from the main towers and begin again. The bridge was dedicated on Nov. 15, 1929, 2 weeks after the 1929 stock market crash, when R.L. Manning of Detroit drove his wife and daughters across the bridge in a four-speed Graham-Paige. The bridge's span of 1,850 feet made it the longest in the world for two years, until eclipsed by the George Washington Bridge in New York City. The Ambassador Bridge is about 1¾ miles long from entrance to exit. At center span, it's 152 feet above the river. The bridge's roadway is 152 feet above the river at midpoint.

➤ **Detroit-Windsor Tunnel:** Completed in 1930, the $25-million structure is the only motor vehicle tunnel between two countries (the Chunnel is a train ride). The project began in 1928 as workers dredged a 2,454-foot trench across the river bottom and sunk specially built steel tubes into it. The tunnel opened on Nov. 1, 1930. President Herbert Hoover pushed a button at the White House that touched off bells at the Detroit and Windsor sides. The first driver was Joseph Zuccatto, a construction worker on the site. The tunnel is 22 feet wide and nearly 1 mile long from entrance to exit. Machines pump more than 1.5 million cubic feet of air through the tunnel each minute.

➤ **Blue Water Bridges**: The original Blue Water Bridge connecting Port Huron and Sarnia, Ontario, opened Oct. 10, 1938. The second bridge opened July 13, 1997, with a daylong bridge walk for pedestrians. The bridges span 1.2 miles over the St. Clair River.

SOURCES: FREE PRESS; "A MONUMENT TO PROGRESS," PHILIP P. MASON'S BOOK ABOUT THE BUILDING OF THE BRIDGE; MICHIGAN DEPARTMENT OF TRANSPORTATION.

Windsor Laid Bare: Vive la difference. Things that are different in Windsor
1) Almost no resident owns a handgun.
2) You can't deduct interest on mortgage payments.
3) Everyone has free health insurance.
4) Capital-gains tax is almost double the U.S. rate.
5) French is an official language.
6) Only 10 percent of Canadians describe themselves as born-again Christians (compared with 30 percent of Americans).
7) The mail is slower.
8) You can drink beer at age 19, but it's harder to buy: Michigan has 9.8 million residents and 13,799 retail beer outlets. Ontario has 11.5 million residents and 1,027 retail beer outlets.
9) The city licenses female escorts.
10) The United States is to the north.
11) You can set your cruise control at 100 — kilometers an hour. (That's 62 m.p.h.)

Trade

➤ **Country to country:** In 1998, U.S. transactions with Canada reached $396 billion, almost 50 percent more than with the second-largest U.S. trading partner, Japan.

➤ **Exports to Canada:** In 1998, the United States sold $157 billion worth of goods to Canada, a 3-percent increase over 1997. Canada bought more American goods than did all 15 countries of the European Union. Ontario alone purchased more U.S. goods than did Mexico.

➤ **Auto exports:** In 1998, motor vehicles and parts accounted for 27 percent of U.S. merchandise exports to Canada, and 29 percent of Canada's exports to the United States.

➤ **Michigan and Canada:** Michigan is Canada's leading trading partner from the United States and Canada is Michigan's leading trading partner. Canada purchases more than half of Michigan's exports. The two-way exchange totaled to $57 billion in 1998 and supports thousands of jobs on both sides of the border.

➤ **It's the auto industry, naturally:** The auto industries of both countries are highly integrated. In 1998, they exchanged $28 billion in autos and trucks and $14 billion in parts. More than half of Michigan's exports and imports to Canada are auto-related.

➤ **Friendly, familiar, foreign and near:** In 1998, 1.2 million Canadians visited Michigan for one night or more, adding $216 million to the state's economy. Some 1.8 million Michiganders spent one night or more in Ontario, spending $351 million.

CUSTOMS: We're not talking *aboot* Dominion Day. There's a drill many Detroiters know about going to Canada: Don't joke. The customs officials at both sides don't take lightly to snarky remarks when they ask where you're from or whether you have anything to declare. Some more rules about crossing the international border:

➤ **The questions:** Be prepared to answer lots on both sides of the boundary. Officials on the Canadian side of the tunnel or bridge usually ask for citizenship, residence and destination. They may search anyone.

U.S. agents are likely to ask

Hiram Walker: Distiller who lived in Windsor from 1859 to 1864 and conducted business there for years.

Joyce Carol Oates, above: Famous author who moved from Detroit to Windsor, taught at the University of Windsor and cofounded the Ontario Review literary journal.

Michael Budman and Don Green: Grew up on the west side and cofounded Roots shoes.

Jim Blanchard: Former Michigan governor from Pleasant Ridge who became U.S. ambassador to Canada under President Bill Clinton.

Isiah Thomas: Longtime Pistons' star who became vice president of the Toronto Raptors.

Robin Seymour: Detroit deejay who hosted teen shows on CKLW-TV (Channel 9).

Jo-Jo Shutty: A metro Detroiter whose traffic reports on CKLW-AM were among the first broadcast from a chopper.

Pat LaFontaine: Waterford hockey star who set records as a teenager in Quebec.

SMUGGLING

Most common things smuggled into the United States:

1. Cigarettes
2. Alcohol
2. Over the last year, the drug ecstasy
3. Money over the $10,000 that must be reported
4. Marijuana (personal use)
5. Vehicles
6. People

He's got diamonds in the soles of his shoes: In 1899, Louis Bush smuggled 581 diamonds in his shoes as he entered Detroit from Canada. He was convicted of smuggling and had to forfeit the stones.

residence, citizenship, length of stay in Canada and purpose of the trip.

➤ **Your papers:** You may be required to show documents proving your citizenship or legal alien status. Immigration experts say you should carry proof such as a passport or birth certificate, although U.S. Customs officials usually recognize a driver's license as valid for U.S. residents.

➤ **Search me:** U.S. law allows Customs searches of travelers and baggage entering the country — including vehicles. They don't need a reason.

Customs officers are trained to spot people who may be trafficking in illegal items. However, they're also directed to treat people courteously and professionally. They may not use race, gender, religion or ethnic background as a reason to search someone.

➤ **Complaints:** If you have been stopped and feel you weren't treated in a professional manner, ask to talk to the supervisor. Some Customs offices have employees called Passenger Service Representative to handle complaints and questions.

Or write to: Director, Passenger Operations, U.S. Customs Service, 1300 Pennsylvania Ave., N.W., Room 5.4D, Washington, D.C. 20029. Include your means of travel; the location, date and time of the examination and the badge numbers of the U.S. Customs employees involved.

➤ **Ahoy!:** When traveling from Detroit to Canada by pleasure boat, you must call Canadian Customs as soon as you dock; the phone number is posted at harbors and marinas. Be ready to give your boat registration number, your destination, names of fellow passengers and how long you will be staying in Canada.

According to U.S. Customs regulations, U.S. pleasure boaters returning to the Detroit area should call the tunnel office at 313-226-3140 anytime.

➤ **Your due duty:** Duty is a fee on goods and services being imported from another country. You must declare everything you are bringing back that you didn't have when you left. This includes things you bought, inherited or got as a gift, as well as many repairs or alterations to goods you already owned. Returning to the United States after spending at least 48 hours in Canada frees a person from duty on permissible purchases up to $400 if the items are for personal use and they are with you as you cross the border.

Each person is eligible for a personal exemption every 30 days. The exemption can include up to 100 cigars (Cuban cigars are prohibited) and 200 cigarettes, and 33.8 fluid ounces of alcoholic beverages. You will be assessed duty on goods purchased at a duty-free shop if they total more than your personal exemption.

If you go to Canada for less than 48 hours, you receive a $200 exemption to bring back goods free of duty and tax, as long as they are for your personal use. This can include 50 cigarettes and 10 cigars, and 5 fluid ounces of alcohol or alcohol-based perfume. If you buy more than $200 worth, or if your purchases are less than $200 but include tobacco or alcohol, they are subject to duty.

➤ **Duty-free stores:** Anyone leaving the country can shop at duty-free stores, where tobacco and alcohol products are the most popular purchases. The goods are cheaper at duty-free shops because items there aren't subject to duty; officially, they are never considered to have entered the country. People may only buy them on the way out.

But just because you buy something in a duty-free shop doesn't mean you'll never have to pay duty on it. Purchases may be subject to duty when you enter Canada, or when you re-enter the United States Duty can be charged if the items total more than your personal exemption.

DIPLOMACY ASIDE:

➤ **Hockey night in Motown:** The cross-border rivalry gave Detroit hockey a rowdy reputation in its infancy. During the early years of Olympia Stadium in the late 1920s and 1930s, many of the fans came from Windsor. Their booing of the Red Wings and cheering for the Canadian teams touched off constant fights.

➤ **Those controversial Canadians:** In the 1880 and 1890s, Canadians working in Detroit became a hot political issue. Union members believed Canadians would work for less than Detroiters, and Detroit employers on several occasions used Canadians as strikebreakers.

➤ **Cruel Canadians:** Although Canadians have the deserved reputation as of being kinder and gentler than Americans, in the early 19th Century, they hanged criminals and let their bodies twist slowly in the wind for weeks while fastened to metal frames called gibbets.

➤ **Reason for Ft. Wayne:** The fort in Detroit opened in 1849 — as a defense against attack from Canada. It has worked.

➤ **The invasion of Windsor:** In 1837, Canada's Patriot War drew the interest of Americans, some of whom crossed the border uninvited to help liberate Canadians from what the Americans saw as British tyranny. In 1838, 25 American Patriots died in an attack on Windsor. Earlier, Detroiters had seized a schooner and exchanged fire with Amherstburg's Ft. Malden, then ran aground after the Canadian militia had opened fire on the ship. Twenty-one Americans surrendered. Michigan officials, who opposed the "invasions," subsequently dispersed the remaining Patriots.

JOHN COLLIER/Detroit Free Press

Suburbia: This is Southfield, one of Detroit's most diverse suburbs.

Beyond 8 Mile
(Telegraph, too)

Suburban Detroit, like suburban America, is vastly different from the notion of the bedroom community that defined metropolitan life 40 years ago.

Today, much of suburbia revolves around the automobile, three-car families, sport-utility vehicles and soccer moms. Suburbanites — urbanites, too — drive to boxy stores in myriad malls, and corporations transact business in towers surrounded by acres of parking for topline sedans.

Many cliches about suburbs being boring and sterile have faded. Suburban Detroit is home to the area's newest immigrants, hip destinations, sports palaces, golf domes, ice time and spas. The United States' current hit culture plays at our suburban venues from Freedom Hill to the Palace and Pine Knob.

At least 3 in 4 people in metro Detroit live in a suburb, an enormous turnaround from 50 years ago, when the suburbs were called the sticks and a daylong ride from Detroit's east side to Cass Lake featured farms and fields.

Since then, people and businesses have left the central city in huge numbers. The result of two generations of migration: a tremendous gulf between Detroit and its suburbs over race, wealth, education and employment.

In other metro areas such as Atlanta, Los Angeles, Washington and St. Louis, most black residents live in the suburbs. In Detroit, 82 percent of the region's black residents lived in the city in 1990. Only Chicago approaches that kind of segregation.

Notions of wholesome American living that attracted many to suburbia soon gave way to reality: Urban ills are suburban maladies, too. Illegal drugs, carjackings, random shootings, kidnappings and murders happen in the suburbs. A confessed serial killer lived in Dearborn Heights; a man in Lincoln Park shot to kill in a seniors complex; a Hazel Park attorney sleeping with a Warren judge killed his pregnant wife to keep his affair alive; a teen leader in Grosse Pointe was accused of raping classmates.

Metro Detroit's largest communities, 2000:

	Population
Detroit	951,270
Warren	138,247
Sterling Hts.	124,471
Ann Arbor	114,024
Livonia	100,545
Dearborn	97,775
Clinton Twp	95,648
Westland	86,602
Farmington Hills	82,111
Troy	80,959
Southfield	78,296
Rochester Hills	68,825
Pontiac	66,337

SOURCES: U.S. CENSUS BUREAU

Seven reasons Detroit's suburbs flourished

1) Home loans in the late 1950s from the Federal Housing Authority (FHA) and Veterans Administration (VA) available for suburban houses were often far cheaper than loans and housing in many areas of Detroit.

2) Metro Detroit's extensive freeway system.

3) The opening in 1954 of Northland Center in Southfield, which was followed by other regional malls in the suburbs.

4) The relocation of businesses, and workers who followed. Historian Thomas Sugrue says auto companies built 25 factories in metro Detroit between 1947 and 1958 — all in the suburbs.

5) Racial conflict, including the 1967 riot, the negative reaction of some whites to the 1973 election of Coleman Young as Detroit's first black mayor and busing plans to integrate schools in Detroit during the 1970s.

6) Fear. Crime, growing levels of poverty and neglect, abandoned buildings. Ironically, some of the first five reasons led to the sixth reason.

7) The desire of home owners for more personal space.

Oakland County

1200 N. Telegraph, Pontiac 48341
888-350-0900
www.co.oakland.mi.us.

Name: Lots of oak trees in early 19th Century.
Area: 867 square miles.
Population:

1910	49,576	1960	690,259
1940	254,068	1970	907,871
1950	396,001	1980	1,011,793
		1990	1,083,592

Population Breakdown, 2000 census results:

Total	1,194,156
White	988,194 (82.8%)
Black	120,720 (10.1%)
American Indian	3,270 (0.3%)
Asian and Pacific Islander	49,402 (4.1%)
Hispanic	28,999 (2.4%)
Some other race ("other")	10,064 (0.8%)
Two or more races	22,211 (1.9%)

History: Created by Territorial Gov. Lewis Cass in 1819, sparsely settled Oakland was twice its current size at first, but shrank as Michigan's population grew and new counties were established. A railroad from Detroit to Pontiac helped draw settlers in the 1840s, and officials eventually built a dirt road north from Detroit that became Woodward Avenue. By 1840, Oakland had more than 50 mills. Pontiac, located on the Clinton River, was Oakland's first town and became the county seat. After the Civil War, Oakland was mainly an agricultural county with numerous isolated villages. By the end of the 19th Century, three rail lines served Pontiac and the city attracted carriage and wagon factories. Streetcars began moving people in the late 1890s.

Developers turned southern Oakland County into a suburb of Detroit in the 1890s, when a Cincinnati firm platted a section of Royal Oak called Urbanrest. Migration worked both ways. Several thousand people moved from Oakland County farms to Detroit as the city attracted factories. By 1910, a number of rich Detroiters had summer homes and

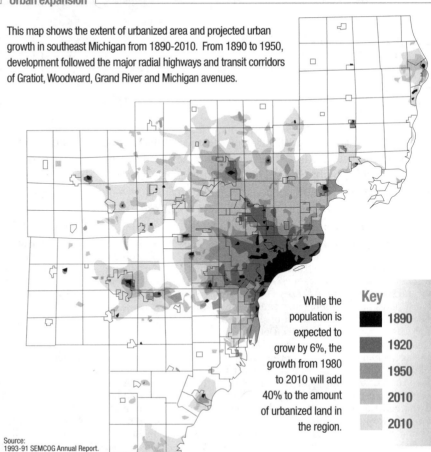

Urban expansion

This map shows the extent of urbanized area and projected urban growth in southeast Michigan from 1890-2010. From 1890 to 1950, development followed the major radial highways and transit corridors of Gratiot, Woodward, Grand River and Michigan avenues.

While the population is expected to grow by 6%, the growth from 1980 to 2010 will add 40% to the amount of urbanized land in the region.

Key
- 1890
- 1920
- 1950
- 2010
- 2010

Source:
1993-91 SEMCOG Annual Report.

The Palace of Auburn Hills.

some year-round residences in what became Bloomfield Hills. The auto age enveloped Pontiac in the early 1900s. The Oakland Motor Car Co. was born in 1907 and became a part of General Motors Corp., which was soon Pontiac's dominant firm.

In the 1950s, jobs and people began leaving Detroit. Northland Center opened in 1954. Oakland County passed Wayne County in effective buying power by 1961, when it ranked 28th in the nation in household income. By 2000, Oakland was one of the nation's most dynamic counties.

Nearly 24,000 jobs were created in 1999, and it ranked second-highest nationally in per capita income for counties of more than a million people, behind New York County, N.Y. (Manhattan).

The median price of a home in Oakland County had skyrocketed to $164,697, more than $30,000 above the national median.

Oakland meant business, too: It was world headquarters to Kmart Corp., DaimlerChrysler Corp., Compuware Corp., Kelly Services Inc. and auto suppliers Delphi Automotive Systems Corp., Lear Corp. and Federal-Mogul Corp.

The communities

Note: Population ranks are based on Michigan's 1,309 communities above 1,000 population.

Auburn Hills

Name: From Auburn, N.Y. Name changed to Amy in 1880 because there was another Auburn. The Legislature named it Auburn Heights in 1919. Incorporated as Auburn Hills in 1983.
Population: 19,837.
State rank (by population): 92.
Pioneers: Elijah Thornton of Canada arrived in 1821. Later in the decade, Aaron Webster named it Auburn and was the first pioneer to stay. Johnson Green was Auburn's first postmaster, in 1825.
Today: Auburn Hills is an inverted-L-shaped city wrapped around the northeast corner of Pontiac. Making a wide arc through town, I-75 is essentially the main street. The city is a strange brew: corporate headquarters, such as those of Daimler-Chrysler and a host of companies that service the auto industry; the Palace sports and entertainment venue; spanking new subdivisions, and older homes with barns and horses from Auburn Hills' rural past.

Beverly Hills

Name: Originally part of Southfield Township. During the 1920s, the Knight-Menard Co. of Detroit developed a subdivision and called it Beverly Hills. In 1958, became Westwood (west of Woodward), but took its current name in 1959.
Population: 10,437.
State rank: 177.
Slogan: "Beautiful Beverly."
Pioneers: Mainly farmland until World War I. During the 1960s, the village began to expand into subdivisions called Huntley, Westwood Estates, Georgetown, Metamora and Nottingham.
Today: Beverly Hills 48025 is mostly residential, an upscale suburb of Birmingham. Residents use the schools and library of its bigger neighbor.

Bingham Farms

Name: For Carson Bingham, an early settler.
Population: 1,030.
State rank: 1,294.
Pioneers: This affluent 780-acre community, formerly a part of Southfield Township, is situated among large tracts of rolling land and mature trees. Although early settlers worked to remain separate from Southfield, Beverly Hills and Franklin, the village charter was not approved until 1955.
Today: The village is entirely residential but allows commercial business on a small corner at Telegraph and 13 Mile.

Berkley

Name: First known as West Twelve Mile Road Community. Berkley evolved from an early street that was named after the California city, with one less "e."
Population: 15,531.
State rank: 118.
Slogan: "We Care."
Pioneers: Farmers Lyman Blackmon, Robert Brown, Robert Cromie and Henry Stephens came from New York and New Jersey in 1829. They drained the swamps and established farms. In the late 1920s, Berkley was one of the fastest-growing communities in the United States.
Today: A mature suburb with lots of homes and little commerce. Porch Light Drives, created in the 1940s, help raise money for special charities.

Clawson

Name: Once known as Pumachug, or the Corners. In 1880, area citizens were told to name the village to obtain their own post office. The story says residents, on a whim, adopted the name from an old woman in the village who stuttered and often referred to a local family named Lawson as "C . . . C . . . Clawson." Another version: An early clerk misread the name of the postmaster, C. Lawson, and wrote it "Clawson."

Population: 12,732.

State rank: 145.

Pioneers: Settled in the early 1820s by a farmer from Ohio, Calvin Marvin. Though the first settlement was in the northern area, which was still a part of Troy Township, it was in the southern area, then Royal Oak Township, that the first major industry, a sawmill by James B. Johnson, was developed.

Today: The population is shrinking slightly. Since the 1970s, four local elementary schools have closed, leaving the city with two.

Birmingham

Name: The first name for the area was Hamilton after settler John Hamilton, who in the 1820s built the first hotel for travelers along the railroad from Detroit to Pontiac. Eventually the settlement adopted the name Piety Hill. The name became Birmingham in 1832 after one of England's larger cities.

Population: 19,291.

State rank: 95.

Pioneers: Elijah Willits bought land there in 1818, but the first settler was John Hunter, who arrived in 1819. Birmingham was a stagecoach stop in the 19th Century between Detroit and Pontiac. Oakland County incorporated Birmingham into Bloomfield Township in 1864. Birmingham became a city in 1933.

Today: Wealthy Birmingham has a real downtown, attracting shoppers to its swank stores. Also widely admired are its lush neighborhoods, high-quality housing and top-notch schools.

Bloomfield Hills and Bloomfield Township

Name: Uncertain, but likely had to do with the blooming flowers that filled its fields each summer. Bloomfield Hills' former names were Bagley's Corners, after early settler Amasa Bagley, and Circle City.

Population: City, 3,940; township, 43,023.

State rank: City, 443; township, 37.

Pioneers: On June 28, 1820, Oakland County was divided into two townships — Pontiac and Bloomfield. Bloomfield then covered the southern part of the county and included West Bloomfield, Royal Oak and Southfield. Bloomfield Township shrunk from 36 square miles as those communities became cities. It remained a farming area until rich Detroiters bought spreads at the turn of the 20th Century. Bloomfield Hills became a village in 1927. Residents hurriedly voted to become a city in 1932 to avoid being incorporated into growing Birmingham.

Today: Both venues feature fine homes, classy shopping, renowned schools, lakes and rolling topography. Bloomfield Hills is one of the richest communities in the world, home to power brokers, pro athletes and celebrities. The rules are strict: Home construction and commercial lawn-mowing must cease at 5 p.m. Saturdays. Such work is forbidden on Sundays. Bloomfield Township offers sophisticated neighborhoods with tree-lined streets and manicured lawns, while remaining a center for expanding retail.

Hazel Park

Name: In 1884, a population swell brought about the formation of a new school district, originally called District No. 8. The school inspector changed the name to Hazel Park School District because of the many hazelnut bushes growing wild.

Population: 18,963.

State rank: 99.

Nicknames, slogans: Official slogan, "The Gateway to Oakland County"; unofficial nickname, "Hazeltucky," a reference to many residents' roots in Kentucky and Tennessee.

Pioneers: Settlers began moving into Hazel Park in the 1840s because the rich soil and flatness of the terrain were ideal for farming. The first person to clear, drain and farm a parcel was Anthony Neusius. His 80-acre farm was in an area south of 9 Mile and west of John R.

Today: The city has two commercial and two industrial corridors that provide direct access to I-75 and I-696. The city is trying to create an entertainment district with the Hazel Park Raceway and a new ice arena as its centerpiece. Other projects, such as a 1,000-seat dinner theater, are in the works. The city is the rare suburb with its own song — "Welcome Back to Hazel Park" — by Ron Sylvester, who grew up there.

The Hazel Park Raceway.

Clarkston

Name: Named after brothers Jeremiah, Nelson and Milton Clark in 1842.

Population: 962.

State rank: n/a.

Pioneers: First settler was Linus Jacox in 1830. He built the first house, a cedar pole shanty. Butler Holcomb built the second house and a sawmill in 1832. The Clark brothers platted and named the town in 1840. The Clarks planted apple trees, built a fish hatchery, ran a general store and served as postmasters.

Today: Clarkston is a half-mile square and is mainly residential, with a small business district.

Commerce Township

Name: From its earlier rate of business and industry.

Population: 34,764.

State rank: 48.

Pioneers: Abram Walrod arrived from New York in 1825 and built a log cabin at the site of Commerce Village. Cornelius Austin, a New Jersey migrant in this peri-

Huntington Woods

Name: Modeled after Huntingdon, England, with curving streets, numerous small parks and a variety of trees, the city was named when an early land investor visited Huntingdon. "Woods" was added because, long after surrounding cities were built, swampy Huntington Woods remained wooded. Before 1900, the area even had a cranberry bog, near Woodward and 11 Mile.
Population: 6,151.
State rank: 293.
Slogan: "City of Homes."
Pioneers: Early settlers were dairy farmers, including two who set up a neighborhood horse-racing course in the 1890s. When developers began selling land, they encouraged upper middle-class buyers by banning multiple-family dwellings except on boundary roads. In September 1926, six subdivisions plus 50 acres of small-farm area became the Village of Huntington Woods by a large majority vote of the 400 residents.
Today: Huntington Woods is the leafy home to many academic and health professionals of diverse religious backgrounds. Exotic sounds from the Detroit Zoo serenade nearby residents.

od, lived for more than 50 years on Walled Lake. By 1840, Commerce had a tavern, gristmills and roads.

Today: An abundance of parkland, lakes and golf courses — along with quick highway access via the M-5 connector — attracted suburbanization in the 1990s, and today about 90 percent of the land is developed. Modest lake cottages are giving way to large, modern homes, with commerce and industry centered along the busy Haggerty Road corridor.

Farmington and Farmington Hills

Name: After the New York hometown of settlers.
Population: Farmington, 10,423; Farmington Hills, 82,111.
State rank: City, 178; Hills, 12.
Slogans: City, "The Crossroads Where Dreams Come to Life"; Hills, "Faith in our Future, Pride in our Past."
Pioneers: Settled by Arthur Power and David Smith, Quakers from Farmington, N.Y.,

who arrived via sleigh across the Detroit River in 1824. First homes were established near today's 11 Mile and Power Road. Later, a settlement formed at the intersection of two American-Indian trails at today's Shiawassee and Farmington. Farmington became a village in 1867; the village became a city in 1926. Early families include the Warners, Botsfords, Garfields, Aldriches and Drakes. The area was a well-known stop on the Underground Railroad for blacks fleeing slavery.

Today: Farmington Hills is a fast-growing area that combines quiet subdivisions, roaring thoroughfares, placid nature parks and big business. Residents of both cities use Farmington's old-fashioned downtown as a gathering point for parades and festivals.

Ferndale

Name: Said to be named by an early electric lineman who didn't know what to call the countryside; seeing ferns in abundance, he penned Ferndale on his report and it stuck.
Population: 22,105.
State rank: 82.

Lathrup Village

Name: For founders Annie and Louise Lathrup, whose family name designates a group of country homes or a hamlet in old English.
Population: 4,236.
State rank: 413.
Slogan: "A Heritage of Good Living."
Pioneers: Early settlers include John Daniels, Galeb Hodge, Joseph Pearsall and Marvin Henry. The area became a part of Southfield Township in 1830 and was a farming community. Annie Lathrup and her daughter Louise began buying land in the mid-1920s to develop Lathrup Townsite, a quaint, suburban residential community. The 1,000 acres purchased by the Lathrups constitutes the city. Louise Lathrup came to be known as an innovative planner. She chose homes built of brick and stone, all bungalow style, with attached garages — a new concept in the 1920s. Lathrup Townsite, incorporated as a city in May 1953, was given the name City of Lathrup Village.
Today: Lathrup's 1 1/2 square miles is predominantly residential, with small businesses located along Southfield Road, the city's busy main artery.

Slogan: "The Friendly City."
Pioneers: First settled after the War of 1812, when people from Detroit moved inland in search of farmland. First permanent settler was Jabez White, who in 1821 built a log tavern on what is now 8 Mile. From 2,000 residents in 1918, the population swelled in six years to 13,000 as the auto industry took hold in the area. Ferndale became incorporated in 1927.
Today: Ferndale is a mature city of older homes, blue-collar retirees and light industry. Its shopping district has replaced closed retailers with restaurants and nightclubs.

Franklin

Name: Dr. Ebenezer Raynale, the community's first doctor, named the village in the late 1820s, but historians are uncertain which of the two following stories is true. The community may have been named after Benjamin Franklin, a friend of the Raynale family. It may also have been named after a young patient Raynale was unable to save. Franklin was formerly known as the Stoughton and Bullock Settlement, after the village's first European settlers.
Population: 2,937.
State rank: 610.
Slogan: "The Town that Time Forgot."
Pioneers: Dillucena Stoughton and Elijah Bullock settled in the 1820s.
Today: Incorporated in 1954, Franklin is a sleepy but affluent village. It was the first community to be registered as a Historic District in the State of Michigan, in February 1969. Once a community dotted with mills and light industry, the area is now predominantly residential, with small pockets of office and commercial businesses, plus one cider mill.

Keego Harbor

Name: Early in the 20th Century, real estate developer Joseph Sawyer dredged a canal linking tiny Dollar Lake and Cass Lake, calling the former pond Keego Harbor. "Keego" is an Ojibwa word meaning "fish."
Population: 2,769.
State rank: 640.

Northville's Mill Race Historical Village in 1977.

Slogan: "Heart of the Lakes."

Pioneers: Joseph Sawyer bought land in 1902 and began selling small lots to Detroiters. Sawyer said he wanted a place where people could spit on the street without getting a ticket. In accord with this hang-loose attitude, tradition says Detroit's notorious Purple Gang spent summers in Keego Harbor in the 1920s.

Today: Once mainly a resort town, Keego Harbor's residents now mostly stay all year. The resort flavor persists — a few home owners are lucky enough to own shoreline on Cass Lake — but all residents have access to city beaches.

Lake Orion, Orion Township

Name: Named Canandaigua in the 1820s after the town in New York because early settlers came from there. Orion Township was established in 1835 after the constel-lation Orion. In 1854, the post office was renamed Orion because it was easy to write. The post office was renamed Lake Orion in 1926 and the town took that name in 1929. Lake Orion sits beside a big lake of the same name, within Orion Township.

Population: Town, 2,715; township, 33,463.

State rank: Town, 654; township, 51.

Slogan: "Where Living is a Vacation."

Pioneers: Town: John Wetmore and Judah Church claimed the first land in 1819. James Stillson platted the town in 1836. Township: Samuel Munson arrived in 1825 and built a sawmill. In 1831, Elijah B. Clark of Pennsylvania, a veteran of the War of 1812, purchased 320 acres. The area was good for farming and lumber and later became a resort area. At the turn of the 19th century, religious revivals were held on Bellevue Island in Lake Orion. Park Island, also part of the lake, was the site of an amusement park.

Today: Lake Orion's 1.31 square miles includes most of the water called Lake Orion. Once known as a resort community, some houses had their mail delivered by boat. It is still mainly residential, with a business district on M-24. The resorts are all gone, but there are plans to promote bed-and-breakfasts. Orion Township is known for its lakes — there are 27 — and 4,000 acres of parkland. It is also the location of a General Motors plant. Since 1990, the population has grown by 40 percent.

Madison Heights

Name: A high school was built in the easternmost section of Royal Oak Township in 1924 and named after President James Madison, and the name stuck when the area was incorporated as a city. "Heights" was added simply because it sounded good.

Population: 31,101

State rank: 54.

Slogan: "City of Progress."

Pioneers: The city's first subdivision was created in 1920, bounded by 10 Mile and 11 Mile roads, John R and Campbell. It became a city Jan. 17, 1955.

Today: A combination of homes and industry, Madison Heights is probably best known for the Red Oaks Water Park, which features the state's largest water slide and wave-action pool.

Northville and Northville Township

Name: In the 19th Century, Northville was the northernmost village of the original township that included Northville and Ply-

Milford and Milford Township

Name: Founders came from New Milford, N.Y.

Population: City, 6,272; township, 15,271.

State rank: City, 289; township, 120.

Slogan: Milford has boasted of being "10 minutes ahead of the rest of the world," after the town telephone operator and noon-time whistle blower, Carrie Prior, was once tricked by pranksters who turned her clock 10 minutes ahead.

Pioneers: Levi Pettibone bought land about 1827. Brothers Elizur and Stanley Ruggles built a sawmill. They walked across southern Michigan in 1831 and stopped in Milford because of Pettibone Creek and its water-power potential. The village, originally part of Novi, by 1834 became a separate township called Milford, which bustled in the 19th Century with a railroad, general stores, mills and factories.

Today: Milford retains its Victorian look downtown and is booming at the edges. Kensington Metropark and Camp Dearborn, a private park owned by Dearborn, are in Milford Township.

Oak Park

Name: Very little development happened until 1914, when large portions of the land were sold to the Majestic Land Co. to divide and develop. The company named the subdivision Oak Park because oak trees dotted the land.
Population: 29,793.
State rank: 62.
Slogans: "The Family City" and "The City with a Future."
Pioneers: In 1817, surveyors reported to territorial Gov. Lewis Cass that the area was uninhabitable and must remain "in the possession of wild beasts." In 1836, several thousand acres were deeded by the government to Douglas Houghton and Henry and Thomas Hubbard. By 1840, a few pioneers settled in the corner of the township, which was swampy. They drained the swamps, cleared the land and began to build houses.
Today: Oak Park boomed in the 1950s with people leaving adjacent Detroit. Today, the Jewish, African-American, Chaldean and Arab populations provide a mix of races, cultures and religions in a relatively small area. With synagogues, schools and kosher markets, the city remains a stronghold for Orthodox Jews, some of whom have moved from the Bloomfields back to Oak Park in recent years. Oak Park lacks an identifiable nucleus, but city officials are working to create a town center near 9 Mile and Coolidge roads.

mouth townships.
Population: City, 6,459; township, 21,036.
State rank: City, 279; township, 88.
Nicknames, slogans: "The Switzerland of Wayne County," "Hamlet of the Hills" and "Beautiful Past, Promising Future."
Pioneers: Settlers from Otsego, N.Y., arrived in 1823, attracted by cheap land. The village of Northville was formed in 1867; it became a township in 1898 and a city in 1955. In 1919, Henry Ford opened a factory, creating jobs and attracting residents.
Today: The City of Northville is split between Oakland and Wayne counties; the township is contained in Wayne. The area features pleasant countryside with parks and cider mills, rapid urbanization and a downtown with turn-of-the-century charm. There's a state park, Maybury, and Wayne County's only natural lake, Silver Springs. The old buildings of Mill Race Historical Village are a short walk from downtown.

Novi

Name: One theory: Area was No. VI stop on the Detroit-to-Lansing toll road. Another theory: Was sixth township in southwest Oakland County. Originally known as West Farmington.
Population: 47,386.
State rank: 33.
Pioneers: The first settler was a member of the American Home Missionary Society, Deacon Erastus Ingersoll, of Ontario County, N.Y., who came in early 1825 to convert the Indians. He lived there for 11 years and is said to have invented, constructed and used the first farm mowing machine in the United States. Ingersoll also reportedly constructed the first plank road in the township. Cousins William Yerkes and Thomas Pinkerton were also among the first in the area. Walled Lake, which is

partly in Novi, became an entertainment center in the 1920s, eventually featuring cottages, dance halls and an amusement park. The building in the 1950s of the I-96 freeway to Lansing brought development to Novi. It became a city in 1969, and it boomed in the 1970s with Twelve Oaks Mall, the Novi Expo Center, other businesses and a new civic center on the old Fuerst farm on 10 Mile Road.
Today: Still booming, Novi is 45 percent more populous than it was in 1990 and has the traffic problems to prove it. Former farms on the city's south and west sides were bought up during the 1990s for upscale subdivisions. Residential growth came easily because of convenient freeways, quality schools and access to the Detroit water and sewer systems. Small and mid-size businesses have gobbled up the few industrial areas but are overshadowed by the huge and expanding retail, hotel, dining and entertainment district along Novi Road between Grand River and 12 Mile. With so many new people, the city has struggled to develop an identity for something besides shopping. The 1980s Town Centre project and the Main Street development a decade later are efforts to create a downtown, but Novi residents can find the real thing in neighboring Northville, or Plymouth.

Orchard Lake

Name: After the apple orchard on Apple Island in the middle of Orchard Lake.
Population: 2,215.
State rank: 788.
Slogan: "At Your Service."
Pioneers: The Ward and Strong families. In 1918, the village broke away from West Bloomfield and became a city in 1964. Orchard Lake Country Club was founded

The Pontiac Silverdome.

in the early 1920s as a tennis and sailing club.

Today: An affluent suburb in which residents can boat, sail and swim. Orchard Lake also is the home of St. Mary's Campus — a prep school, college, and seminary, plus the Polish-American Hall of Fame.

Oxford and Oxford Township

Name: Uncertain origin.
Population: Town, 3,540; township, 16,025.
State rank: Town, 800; township, 112.
Pioneers: In 1832, John and Fite Rossman, Samuel Axford, Alanson Decker, Jeremiah Hunt and the Wagoners bought the land from the U.S. government. As people arrived from the east, the township was organized in 1837. The village was organized in 1876. Brace Beemer, radio's original Lone Ranger, was from Oxford.
Today: Old homes and leafy streets in the center; development at the edges.

Pleasant Ridge

Name: In 1912, resident Leila Kennedy proposed naming the community after her childhood hometown of Pleasant Valley, Ky. Other residents lived along Ridge Road. The compromise: Pleasant Ridge.
Population: 2,594.
State rank: 684.
Pioneers: As Oakland County communities go, Pleasant Ridge is a youngster — it wasn't settled until the early 1900s. Though it was a location for vacation homes in the late 19th Century, Pleasant Ridge didn't become a village until 1919 and a city until 1927.
Today: Pleasant Ridge is distinctive because of its size. At only 0.58 square miles, it is the smallest incorporated city in Michigan.

Pontiac

Name: Pontiac, an Ottawa, was one of the greatest American-Indian leaders in the Great Lakes.
Population: 66,337.
State rank: 20.
Slogan: "The City with a Proud Past and a Bright Future."
Pioneers: Col. Stephen Mack, a soldier in the Revolutionary War, is considered Pontiac's founder. He bought the first land in 1818 for a group of 14 people called the Pontiac Company that attempted to develop the area. The settlers built Pontiac's first settlement — a small log cabin — during November 1818 to house themselves. Pon-

Free Press file photo

Royal Oak

Name: During an 1818 expedition to the future Oakland County, territorial Gov. Lewis Cass rested under a large oak tree that reminded him of the royal oak of Scotland beneath which Prince Charles II hid from enemies. Cass named the tree "Royal Oak," and it stuck.
Population: 60,062
State rank: 26.
Pioneers: William Thurber purchased the first land in the area, which would become the township of Royal Oak on Jan. 23, 1819, in an area south of Birmingham. Royal Oak remained a part of Bloomfield Township until the township divided in 1827, and Royal Oak became part of Troy. Charles Allen, "the father of Royal Oak," led a drive to make Royal Oak a village, which it became in 1891. Royal Oak became a city in 1921. George Dondero was the first mayor.
Today: During the last decade, Royal Oak has become one of metro Detroit's hippest destinations for shopping, dining, entertainment and coffee. Main Street is crowded day and night. The city also is home to the Detroit Zoo, whose water tower is shown above.

Southfield

Name: Coined the "south fields" by early settlers in northern Birmingham, Bloomfield Township and Royal Oak, the territory was known as Township 1 North Range 10 East, but was officially named Ossewa in July 1830 when it became an independent township. A citizen protest changed the name 17 days later to Southfield.

Population: 78,296.

State rank: 14.

Slogans: "The Center of It All" and "The International City."

Pioneers: John Daniels arrived in 1823. Most early settlers farmed the land while some used the Rouge River to power their gristmills, sawmills and flour mills. Farming remained dominant in Southfield until 1950, when J.L. Hudson announced plans to build Northland Center, which opened in 1954. Incorporation came in August 1957, and people and business followed.

Today: Southfield is surrounded by several major freeways, enabling the city to support commerce. More than 8,000 businesses, including 140 Fortune 500 companies, operate there. Half of its residents live in apartments and others live in wooded neighborhoods or modern subdivisions and condominiums. Southfield has a growing black population, and one recent challenge has been dealing with diversity issues in schools and city government.

---

tiac Township was formed in 1820, and the smaller settlement was later designated as Oakland County's official seat of government. In 1837, Pontiac became Oakland County's first village. Seven years later, a massive fire destroyed 25 buildings. Residents rebuilt, and Pontiac became the county's first city in 1861, the same year the county's first black residents formed the African Methodist Episcopal Church. Pontiac grew quickly in the early years of the auto industry. Pontiac developed a sizable black community; Dr. Howard McNeill was a pre-World War II leader who was the first African-American member of the county board of supervisors and city commission.

Today: Pontiac lost residents and businesses after 1950. The Detroit Lions football team moved to the Pontiac Silverdome in 1975, but will soon return to Detroit. In recent years, a number of clubs and restaurants have opened in downtown Pontiac.

Rochester and Rochester Hills

Name: Named after Rochester, N.Y., the hometown of settler James Graham's daughter-in-law.

Population: Rochester Hills, 68,825; Rochester, 10,467.

State rank: Hills, 19; town, 176.

Slogan: Hills, "We Live in Peace and Goodwill."

Pioneers: The area was settled by James Graham in 1817. Graham came from Detroit, drawn by the abundance of timber. In the spring of 1817, Graham's son, Alexander, is credited with building the first home in Oakland County — a log cabin on the plot just south of today's East Alley on Third Street. In 1869, Rochester became a village, and in 1967 it was incorporated into a city. On May 22, 1984, Avon Charter Township residents voted to become a home-rule city, the city of Rochester Hills.

Today: With bustling downtown Rochester at its core, both cities are home to a mix of city life and subdivision housing. In fact, a boom of suburbanites in Rochester Hills has led the city to make some major changes, such as expanding the volunteer fire department to a round-the-clock service that employs paid firefighters.

Royal Oak Township

Name: Named after Royal Oak.

Population: 5,446.

State rank: 323.

Curiosity: The township is situated in two locations about 2½ miles apart. One is near 8

Mile and Wyoming; the other is at 10 Mile and Greenfield.

Pioneers: Originally settled by black people who fled slavery via the Underground Railroad. There were two other migrations: The auto age and World War II, when many black people came north for jobs. The federal government built temporary barracks-type housing in the southwestern portion of the township, which was torn down after the war.

Today: The northern portion consists largely of apartment buildings, occupied mostly by whites. The southern portion is mostly black.

South Lyon

Name: After state legislator and surveyor Lucius Lyon.

Population: 10,036.

State rank: 184.

Slogan: "Best Little City."

Pioneers: In 1832, Thomas Dunlap, William Thompson, and Obed Letts settled the area. It was known as Thompson's Corners because William Thompson and his wife owned land at the corners of the city. The family built the first steam-operated sawmill. The city became South Lyon in 1847.

Today: It's one of the fastest-growing cities in Michigan.

Troy

Name: After Troy, N.Y.

Population: 80,959.

State rank: 13.

Slogan: "The City of Tomorrow, Today."

Pioneers: Johnson Niles built a log cabin in 1821 on the southwest corner of what is now Square Lake and Livernois. The township of Troy once included Royal Oak, which seceded in 1832. The tables turned when Troy was forced to adopt city status in 1955 to dodge Royal Oak's threat of annexation. In 1968, Troy adopted its city seal: It shows the goddess Athena — the protector of civilized life.

Today: With skyscrapers, corporate headquarters, upscale shopping and more than 100,000 jobs and swank restaurants, it's a sophisticated metropolis, even if its main street is called Big Beaver Road.

Walled Lake

Name: Named after the lake that lies on its southern boundary with Novi. The lake was so named more than a century ago because of the wall of stone that lined the west bank.

Population: 6,713.

Slogan: "Pride in our Past, Faith in our Future."
Pioneers: Settled in June 1825 by Walter Hewitt of New York. Two of Walled Lake's earliest settlers were American soldiers from the War of 1812 — Bela Armstrong in 1826 and Cornelius Austin in 1829. It became a city in 1954.
Today: The once seasonal homes that sprang up around the lake in the 1930s have changed into year-round neighborhoods. Walled Lake is a commercial center in southwestern Oakland County.

West Bloomfield

Name: West Bloomfield Township got its name from Bloomfield Township, which gave up 36 square miles to form the new municipality on April 22, 1833.
Population: 64,860.
State rank: 23.
Pioneers: The first settlers in West Bloomfield found a bonus — besides the rich oak, maple and beech forests, there were apple trees growing on an island in a big lake, apparently cultivated by Indians. The pioneers named the places Apple Island and Orchard Lake. They also found the biggest lake in southeastern Michigan at 1,280 acres and named it after the territorial governor, Lewis Cass. The first man to build a home in West Bloomfield was John Huff, who came from Orleans County, N.Y. In 1821, Huff built his cabin on Pine Lake. There are 26 lakes in West Bloomfield, which claims to have the second-highest number of lakes in the nation, behind a Minnesota township. Huff delayed registering his land claim until 1824, so two others — James Herrington and Benjamin Irish — were the first to record their property, in 1823. Township voters elected Terrel Benjamin supervisor in 1834. It was Benjamin's duty to inform his constituents that the township was being assessed $40,971 and that the bounty on wolves had been reduced. In the previous seven years, settlers had killed 370 wolves.
Today: The wolves are gone, but coyotes have moved into West Bloomfield and other areas of southeastern Michigan. Beaver were long absent but have recently resumed engineering operations in the township. Meanwhile, the human population has grown, and most buildable land has been developed. The lakes were for years the domain of small cottagers who spent weekends away from their permanent homes in Detroit. Now, most cottages are permanent homes and many have been

knocked down so that very large lakeside dwellings could be built. The juxtaposition of old inhabitants and newcomers has brought about a clash of values, and some tension. The old permissive attitudes that allowed a relaxed approach to home maintenance are giving way to the view that tidiness improves property values. Lakes are nearly 15 percent of the township's surface area, and how they and nearby areas are treated is a big concern to residents. The word "swamp" is politically incorrect here. The township has tough wetlands and woodlands laws and boards that try to prevent improper use of fragile land.

White Lake Township

Name: Its namesake body of water is, of course, White Lake. Other postal names that didn't stick include Plainville, Mayville and Oxbow (for Oxbow Lake).
Population: 28,219.
State rank: 67.
Nickname: "Four Seasons Playground."
Pioneers: Most, including Harvey Olmstead and Erastus Hopkins, were farmers from such places as New York and Ireland who came in the early 1830s. McKeachie and Brendel roads are named for early settler families.
Today: It is home to lakefront living, Alpine Valley Ski Resort and parts of two state recreation areas: Pontiac Lake and Highland Lake. Its population has nearly doubled since 1970.

Wixom

Name: First called Sibley's Corners, it was later renamed for one of the town settlers, Ahijah Wixom.
Population: 13,263.
State rank: 138.
Slogan: "A Community with Character."
Pioneers: Lewis Norton, Alonzo Sibley and Wixom came in the early 1830s and settled different parts. The downtown eventually was located near railroad tracks by what are now Wixom Road and Pontiac Trail.
Today: The area remained mostly agricultural until the 1950s, when Ford Motor Co. built its factory that makes the Lincoln Continental and Town Car. City officials occasionally resurrect plans to build a new downtown to replace the small one that burned in the 1920s.

POPULATION FIGURES FOR CITIES ARE FROM THE U.S. CENSUS BUREAU'S 1998 ESTIMATES. POPULATION FOR TOWNSHIPS ARE FROM SOUTHEAST MICHIGAN COUNCIL OF GOVERNMENTS 1999 ESTIMATES.

Waterford Township

Name: Some say the city received its name because the local Indians had to ford the water where the Clinton River crossed a trail. Others say the name was proposed by a settler, Shubael Atherton, who named it in 1825 because of the many lakes in the area.
Population: 73,150.
State rank: 17.
Pioneers: Maj. Oliver Williams, his brother-in-law Alpheus Williams and Capt. Archibald Phillips traveled to the area on the Indian road once known as the Saginaw Trail, now Dixie Highway, and settled in 1818. Waterford became a township in 1834 but remained secluded until the Saginaw turnpike linked it with the outside world the following year. Waterford became a major resort area in the early 1900s.
Today: One of the area's fastest-growing communities, Waterford is located at the center of Oakland County and is home to 34 lakes. It is also home to the Oakland-Pontiac airport, Summit Place Mall, golf courses and parks.

Belleville

Name: Two theories: After belle ville, French for "beautiful city." Or after early landowner James Bell.
Population: 3,997.
State rank: 437.
Slogan: "Quality Living."
Pioneers: In 1826, Caleb Marsh put a dam across the Huron River to provide power for a sawmill. Marsh sold his land to John Graham, who sold it to Bell. Belleville began as a tiny community within Van Buren Township and eventually became the township's hub because its water power ran mills and it provided access to the railroad. Belleville was incorporated as a city in 1946.
Today: A little more than 1 square mile in area, Belleville's location in western Wayne County's gently rolling hills along the southern shore of Belleville Lake offers a country-like residential retreat near Metro Airport. It's the hometown of the "Belleville Three" — world-famous techno music pioneers Juan Atkins, Derrick May and Kevin Saunderson.

Wayne County

County Clerk
201 Coleman A. Young
Municipal Center
Detroit 48226
313-224-5509
www.waynecounty.com

Name: Michigan's first county was named after Gen. Anthony (Mad Anthony) Wayne, a Revolutionary War hero who led troops against Indians in the 1790s.
Area: 622 square miles.

Population:

Year	Population	Year	Population
1910	531,591	1950	2,435,235
1920	1,177,645	1970	2,669,604
		1990	2,111,687

Population breakdown, 2000 census results:

Total	2,061,162
Total white	1,065,607 (51.7%)
Total black	868,992 (42.2%)
Total American Indian	7,627 (0.4%)
Total Asian and Pacific Islander	35,141 (1.7%)
Hispanic	77,207 (3.7%)
Some other race ("other")	32,020 (1.6%)
Two or more races	51,269 (2.5%)

History: The county was established in 1796 as part of the Northwest Territories. At first, its boundaries were immense: From Detroit, they covered virtually all of Michigan, northern Indiana, eastern Illinois, and a small part of Wisconsin. The borders shrank as settlement grew in those other places. By 1796, Wayne County was well settled: Europeans and Americans already had lived in the Detroit area for nearly 100 years, and by then were branching out to carve farms out of the wilderness along the river and lake.

The communities
Allen Park

Name: After lumber merchant and attorney Lewis Allen, an early settler.
Population: 29,376.
State rank: 64.
Pioneers: Allen, Hubert Champagne and Edward Pepper were among the first American settlers in what is now Allen Park. The area, part of Ecorse Township in the 19th Century, evolved from a lumbering and trapping area to farms by the 1830s. With the auto boom, developers began to subdivide it. The village was incorporated in 1927, when the population was 644. In 1930, the Borberly family opened the first significant modern business, a market on Allen Road. By the 1950s, the population had reached 12,000; it jumped to 36,000 by 1957, when the city was incorporated.
Today: Home to the distinctive red-brick Veterans Administration Hospital, Allen Park is a quiet town that combines homes, factories and commercial establishments.

Brownstown Township

Name: The origin is a mystery. Old reports indicate it might have been named after Adam Brown, an 8-year-old boy kidnapped in 1764 by Wyandot Indians — in Virginia. The problem: It's not certain that Brown lived in the township.
Population: 22,989.
State rank: 75.
Slogan: "Where the future looks brighter."
Pioneers: Brownstown was one of the nine orig-

A 1939 view of the Veterans Administration Hospital in Allen Park.

Free Press file photo

inal townships in Wayne County. It was organized in 1827, a decade before Michigan became a state.

Today: It's one of the fastest-growing Downriver communities and stretches from Taylor, on the north, to Lake Erie, on the south — skipping several incorporated towns in between.

Dearborn

Name: After Gen. Henry Dearborn, a physician, military leader in the War of 1812 and secretary of state in the early 19th Century.
Population: 97,775.
State rank: 9.
Slogan: "Hometown of Henry Ford."
Pioneers: One of Detroit's oldest, biggest, best-known, most diverse and most controversial suburbs, Dearborn has had an eventful history, due to its strategic setting on the old military road connecting Detroit and Chicago and its status as Henry Ford's birthplace and headquarters. Dearborn was settled by the Dumais and Cissne families in the 1780s. An early resident was Conrad Ten Eyck, who opened a tavern in 1826.

Incorporated as Dearbornville in 1838, it became home during this period to the 11-building U.S. Arsenal, parts of which remain standing on Michigan Avenue. A farming community in the 19th Century, Dearborn's most-famous family, the Fords, owned a spread near Greenfield and Ford Road. In January 1929, the cities of Fordson, Dearborn and part of Dearborn Township merged into present-day Dearborn. During this period, Ford built his world-famous Rouge complex and located much of

his company in the city, which put Dearborn at the forefront of some of the 20th Century's greatest dramas, such as industrialization and the labor movement. Dearborn police and Ford Motor Co. security guards shot and killed five unarmed workers during a 1932 protest on Miller Road. Orville Hubbard delivered excellent services during his 36 years as mayor, but he also was a segregationist who has tarnished Dearborn's reputation to this day.

Today: Dearborn is the opposite of a bedroom community. In addition to being Ford country, it has a wide range of housing, an extensive park system, colleges, factories, shopping and one of the nation's top tourist attractions in Greenfield Village & Henry Ford Museum. The large Mideastern population has rejuvenated the city's east side with restaurants, bakeries, sweet shops and markets. The city is building an expanded civic center that will include a water park, gym and theater. There are four business districts: one each on the east and west sides of Michigan Avenue and largely Mideastern districts at Vernor and Dix and along Schaefer and West Warren.

Ecorse

Name: From "*Riviere aux Ecorces,*" or Bark River. Previously called Grandport.
Population: 11,229.
State rank: 161.
Pioneers: Ecorse is one of the oldest Downriver communities. Indians frequented the area for years, and the French established ribbon farms like those upriver from the fort at Detroit to Grosse Pointe. In 1776, the

Canton Township

Name: After the city in China.
Population: 76,366.
State rank: 16.
Nickname: Used to be called the "Sweet Corn Capital."
Pioneers: Originally part of Plymouth Township, Canton became independent in 1834, when its population was about 150 families. It was a rural community for much of its history, and was made up of smaller communities named Sheldon Corners, Cherry Hill and Denton, in which one-room schoolhouses were built. Three of the schoolhouses have been restored. In the 20th Century, Canton became known for its sweet corn and dairy farms. Canton became a charter township in 1961. From 1970 to 1980, the population climbed from 17,000 to 48,000.
Today: Canton's eastern half is the heavily commercialized I-275 corridor; on the west is the remaining farmland. Canton continues to be one of metro Detroit's fastest-growing communities. Its population grew by more than 25 percent during the 1990s. Like many suburbs, Canton has been trying — in vain — to construct a downtown.

Dearborn Heights

Name: The wife of Walter Williams, one of the city's nine charter commissioners, suggested the name. The city was previously called Dearborn Township.
Population: 58,264.
State rank: 27.
Nickname: "City with a future."
Pioneers: When the City of Dearborn was established in 1929, a section north and south of the city was not included. Those portions remained Dearborn Township until 1963, when they became the City of Dearborn Heights. State law required that cities must be contiguous, so Dearborn Township had to acquire a small portion of Inkster to connect the north and sound ends of Dearborn Heights. That narrow sliver gave Dearborn Heights its odd shape. Historians say the city incorporated partly to keep white neighborhoods separate from black areas in Inkster. Inkster officials attempted through the courts to prevent the incorporation, but the Michigan Supreme Court found in favor of Dearborn Heights.
Today: Dearborn Heights is largely a bedroom community, with busy commercial strips along Telegraph, Warren and Ford Road.

Potowatami Indians deeded land in what is now Ecorse and other nearby communities to Pierre St. Dosse for "love and affection." Other early settlers were families named Riopelle, Campau, Salliotte, Cicotte, Bourassa and Champaign. Ecorse took its current name in 1903, when it was a swinging resort area. The steel industry arrived in the 1920s, and during Prohibition, Ecorse's claim to fame was rum-running and gang warfare. It became a city in 1942.
Today: Humongous Great Lakes Steel continues to produce on the riverfront, but the worldwide steel market is treacherous. Ecorse has battled severe money problems for years, partly because of plant retrenchment.

Garden City

Name: From its farming culture.
Population: 30,047.
State rank: 60.
Nicknames: "The Sun Parlor of Detroit." Once known as New Ireland or Irish Town.
Pioneers: New York farmers Marcus Swift and Luther Reeves settled in the area in 1825. Immigrants from Ireland followed in the 1830s. The original plan called for lots up to an acre that would be ample for small-scale farming, patterned after the "Garden City" concept in Great Britain. Farming remained the area's chief occupation until the auto age. Garden City was incorporated as a village in 1927. It became a city in 1933.
Today: Garden City is mainly a residential community with some light industry.

Gibraltar

Name: Once called *Grosse Roche, or Big Rock,* and *La Roche Debout,* or Standing Rock, by the French. English settlers changed the name to their favorite rock in Europe. The name was first spelled Gibralt*er* but was corrected to its current spelling in 1900.
Population: 4,264.
State rank: 409.
Nickname: "Venice of Michigan."
Pioneers: In the late 1700s, one of the first land owners was supposedly Adam Brown, who was captured in Virginia by Wyandot Indians when he was 8 and raised by them. But whether Brown, who might be the namesake of Brownstown Township, ever lived in the area is debated by historians. Other early settlers were Alexander Henry, John Askin Sr., John Askin Jr. and William Walker. In 1836, the Gibraltar-Flat Rock Land and Canal Co. was formed with plans to build a waterway from Detroit to Flat Rock to Ypsilanti and finally across the state to Muskegon and Lake Michigan. Two backers of the plan were Lewis Cass and orator Daniel Webster. Although the canal was never built, its potential drew many settlers who hoped the town would become a major city. Because of the many stands of oak and elm trees, three shipyards and a sawmill operated nearby. The town had 500 residents in 1877. In 1953, Gibraltar was incorporated as a village. In 1961, with a population of 2,187, Gibraltar became a city.
Today: Situated on the Detroit River and Lake Erie, Gibraltar is home to people who work at area factories and businesses during the week and enjoy water sports on the weekends.

Grosse Ile Township

Name: The French words for "Big Island."
Population: 10,894.
State rank: 167.
Pioneers: Grosse Ile Township is actually 14 islands in the Detroit River; the biggest one is by far the best-known. The Potawatomi Indians called the island *Kitche-minishen,* meaning large island. Early French explorers on Lake Erie and the Detroit River identified this island as *la grosse ile* because of its grandeur — 10 miles long and 2 miles wide. After the French departed in 1763, the *"la"* was dropped due to British influence. Alexander and William Macomb bought the island from the Indians in 1776 but development was delayed because of the Revolutionary War. The township was created in 1915. A $200,000 toll bridge was completed in 1913, linking the island and its 2,000 residents to the mainland. In 1972, Grosse Ile Municipal Airport opened.
Today: Filled with expensive homes and nice views, Grosse Ile is a quiet community that includes several prominent business and community leaders in the Downriver area. The northern tip of the island contains salt wells and alkali deposits, and is owned by BASF Corp.

Grosse Pointe

Name: French for "big pointe," a piece of land jutting into Lake St. Clair.
Collective population: 47,780.
Grosse Pointe Park: 12,443.
Grosse Pointe: 5,670.
Grosse Pointe Farms: 9,764.
Grosse Pointe Woods: 17,080.
Grosse Pointe Shores: 2,823 (partially in Macomb County).
State rankings:
Grosse Pointe Park: 149.
Grosse Pointe: 314.
Grosse Pointe Farms: 193.
Grosse Pointe Woods: 106.

The last home of Henry Ford II, on Provencal Road in Grosse Pointe Farms.

Grosse Pointe Shores: 629.
Nickname: "The Pointes."
Pioneers: Grosse Pointe's history is virtually as old as that of adjacent Detroit. Though swampy in parts, the area had a number of French farms in the 18th Century. In 1712, the Fox Indians and French fought a battle on what is now Windmill Pointe Drive in Grosse Pointe Park. A relic from the old days is the Provencal-Weir House, dating from 1823, which is preserved at 376 Kercheval. Detroit's upper crust began building elaborate summer homes in the late 1800s until Grosse Pointe was the midwestern Newport, R.I. With the dawn of the automobile industry, executives began moving into permanent homes in the Pointes. Some, like the Edsel and Eleanor Ford House (open for public tours), were magnificent estates for the auto barons; others, like the brick mini-manses that line the cozy, leafy streets in Grosse Pointe Park, were shelter for middle management. Though they're little-known, the Pointes even have sections of working-class residents. The community's reputation for snobbery was reinforced after World War II when it was discovered that real estate brokers were using a point system to screen people considered undesirable. Despite its genteel reputation, Grosse Pointe Park was home to a gaggle of Mafia families before and after World War II.
Today: The Grosse Pointes are much more diverse — in ethnicity, race and income — than most outsiders believe. But this emerald swath of metro Detroit remains one of the state's most affluent, exclusive and insular communities. The five "Pointes" are dotted with clubs, lakefront parks and some of the nation's best schools. The eastern half of the Grosse Pointes has an urban feel, with close-together homes, but even Grosse Pointe's boosters complain about a lack of choice in such cosmopolitan pursuits as eating, grocery shopping and cinema.

Harper Woods

Name: Formerly part of Gratiot Township and once known as Manchester Park, the name comes from Walter Harper, a Detroiter who is also the namesake of Harper Hospital and Harper Avenue.
Population: 14,254.
State rank: 125.
Pioneers: The first person to live in what is now Harper Woods was Casper Salter. He built a log cabin in 1850 amid dense woods along Pumpkin Hook Road — now known as Kelly — between Woodland and Woodcrest. By 1875, there were 11 families in the area. The U.S. Census from 1940 listed the Gratiot Township population as 836. The population began to grow after World War II; by 1950, it was 9,148, and it would grow by another 10,000 in the next 10 years as the Ford Freeway — which the city fought unsuccessfully — bisected Harper Woods, and Eastland Center opened. Harper Woods, the last portion of Gratiot Township, became a city in 1951.
Today: Mostly residential, small Harper Woods is home to five high schools: Regina, Lutheran East, Notre Dame, Bishop Gallagher and Harper Woods High.

Highland Park

Population: 16,746.
State rank: 108.
Pioneers: Early settlers named it Highland Park

Flat Rock

Name: From the smooth stones in the Huron River. Originally called Vreelandtville, after early settler Henry Vreelandt, and Smooth Rock.
Population: 8,488.
State rank: 212.
Pioneers: Located where the Huron River crosses Telegraph, Flat Rock was settled as early as 1817. By 1837, entrepreneurs formed a company and attempted to construct a canal across southern Michigan to Lake Michigan. They didn't make it. One early settler was Freeland Garretson, who arrived as a teenager from New Jersey in the 1830s. The Huron's water power attracted business people who built flour and saw mills. An reservation housing Wyandot, Huron and Seneca Indians was located nearby, but the U.S. government moved its residents to the west. Incorporated as a village in 1923, Flat Rock became the home of a Ford Motor Co. headlight plant in 1925.
Today: Flat Rock combines a rural ambience, industry — including a Mazda plant — and residential neighborhoods. It is planning an extensive civic center near its historical village.

**The statue
of Pope John
Paul II in
Hamtramck.**

Free Press file photo

Hamtramck

Name: John Francis Hamtramck was a Quebec-born soldier who fought for the Americans in the Revolutionary War and later served in the military command of Detroit. He died in Detroit in 1803.

Population: 22,976.

State rank: 77.

Slogan: "A Touch of Europe in America."

Pioneers: For much of the 19th Century, Hamtramck was the sparsely settled township north and east of the Detroit city limits, a place with a reputation for flourishing vice and rowdy politics. It became a village in 1901 and was incorporated as a city in 1922. By that time, with the auto age in full throttle, dynamic Hamtramck had become one of the centers of both Polish America and car production. The 6- and 8-story Dodge Main plant opened on Hamtramck's south side in 1914. By 1930, Hamtramck had a population of 56,268, many of Polish descent. It was a young city: In 1920, 1 in 5 Hamtramck residents was younger than 5 years old, the highest proportion in America.

Today: Hamtramck has long been one of Michigan's most distinctive cities. While the town has lost people, factories and Poles, what remains are tightly packed, two-story flats; neatly manicured; postage-stamp lawns; shot-and-a-beer corner bars; imposing churches and a multiethnic population. And it's one of metro Detroit hippest cities. How hip? So hip that Utne Reader, the Reader's Digest of the alternative press, called Hamtramck one of the 15 hippest neighborhoods in the United States and Canada in its December 1997 issue. Why? Nightlife, artists, entertainment venues and bohemian ambience. (Mayor Gary Zych is a painter.) And Hamtramck remains a magnet for the world. Two-thirds of the school district's students come from homes where English is not the primary language. While they represent 28 different languages, the vast majority of newcomers now are from Bosnia, Bangladesh and Yemen. Oh, and Hamtramck has money problems and big-city political intrigue.

because a hill on Woodward and the present Glendale was the only high, dry spot amid the swampiness between Detroit and Royal Oak. The area was mostly farmland until 1886, when Capt. William H. Stevens, a silver baron, decided to promote it as a rival to Detroit. He built a school, a waterworks, a fancy hotel and a racetrack. A city of 2.96 square miles, Highland Park is surrounded by Detroit except for a small stretch of border it shares with Hamtramck. In its heyday before the Depression, prosperous Highland Park's population was 65,000. The city was home to the third Ford Motor Co. factory, built in 1909, which made the Model T and pioneered the revolutionary concepts of the assembly line and $5 workday. The Chrysler Corp. once had its headquarters in the city, as did many auto suppliers.

Today: Chrysler is gone. The large upper-middle-class is gone. The premier shopping area? Gone. One of the state's best public school systems? Gone. Ford? Long gone. Highland Park has lost a greater percentage of its population and business than even Detroit, and it struggles with high crime and blight. A large number of residents receive some kind of public assistance. In recent years, the city has built new apartment developments and strip malls along Woodward. The former Chrysler headquarters is now occupied by a number of small businesses.

Huron Township

Name: After the Huron River, which flows diagonally through the township, and the Indian tribe that once inhabited the area.

Population: 13,737.

State rank: 131.

Pioneers: Undertakers George Burcott Uht and the Uht family; Ludqig Krzyske, who opened a retail lumberyard in 1890, and Rudolph Krause, whose general store opened in 1899.

Today: Three small residential settlements — Willow, Waltz and New Boston — are the principal commercial centers. Sod production, nursery and greenhouse stock are the principal industries. The Huron-Clinton Metropolitan Authority owns and operates three recreation facilities on 3,500 acres in the township. I-275 crosses the township, providing good access to the region.

Lincoln Park

Name: In honor of President Abraham Lincoln.

Population: 40,008.

State rank: 41.

Pioneers: What is now called Ecorse Creek in

Lincoln Park was the site of the important council called by the Ottawa chief, Pontiac, in 1763 to plan his siege of the fort at Detroit. Later in the 18th Century, Pierre St. Cosme and family settled on a large tract of land in what is now Lincoln Park and other nearby suburbs. The Goodells were the first English-speaking settlers in the area. The first homes were built along Goddard Road. Lincoln Park became part of Ecorse Township in 1827 and retained a rural character until the post-World War I era. That's when an influx of workers from the Ford Rouge plant in Dearborn began building houses. Lincoln Park became a city in 1925.

Today: Lincoln Park combines residential neighborhoods, industry and commerce.

Livonia

Name: Early settlers from the east named it after Livonia, N.Y., which was named by immigrants after a region in Latvia and Estonia.

Population: 100,545.

State rank: 8.

Slogan: "People come first in Livonia."

Pioneers: In 1818, Dennison Palmer purchased land in what became Livonia, which was created in 1835 out of Nankin and Pekin townships. Livonia grew slowly. Its population in 1840 was 1,169; eight decades later, it was only 1,608. Between 1950 and 1970, though, the number of residents soared from 7,534 to 110,109. Livonia retained its township size of 36 square miles and evolved into one of Detroit's megasuburbs. Developers created its first subdivision, Rosedale Gardens, in 1925, fashioned after Detroit's Rosedale Park. In addition to the exodus from Detroit, two developments of the 1940s spurred Livonia's growth: the construction of General Motors Corp.'s Hydramatic Plant on Plymouth Road and the opening of the Detroit Race Course.

Today: National surveys say Livonia is among the safest communities in the country and one of the best places to rear children. One of the city landmarks — Detroit Race Course — closed in 1998. Its 200-acre site is becoming a commercial and industrial development that will include a 752,000-square-foot warehouse. Livonia is the hometown of Wayne County Executive Ed McNamara and his top aide, Mike Duggan, who won the Democratic primary for county prosecutor in August 2000.

Melvindale

Name: After an early resident, Melvin Wilkin-son; formerly known as Oakwood Heights.

Population: 10,735.

State rank: 172.

Pioneers: Settlers began arriving in the 1830s, and what became Melvindale was farmland for the rest of the 19th Century. Early families included the Dashers, McKittricks, Dubkies, Longs and Fieldhauers. In the 1920s, when Ford built the nearby Rouge plant, a real estate company, Palmer and Flint, started buying up and subdividing the farms. Melvindale became a village in 1924 and a city in 1933, the depth of the Depression, and it immediately went broke. Residents were paying off debt until 1959. For years, all natural gas used in Detroit was piped from Texas to Melvindale.

Today: Melvindale is a combination of industry and homes.

Northville and Northville Township

Name: In the 19th Century, Northville was the northernmost village of the original township that included Northville and Plymouth townships.

Population: City, 6,459; township, 21,036.

State rank: City, 279; township, 88.

Nicknames, slogans: "The Switzerland of Wayne County"; "Hamlet of the Hills"; "Beautiful Past, Promising Future."

Pioneers: Settlers from Otsego, N.Y., arrived in 1823, attracted by $1.25-per-acre land. Northville Township was created in 1898; the village was formed in 1955. In 1919, Henry Ford opened a factory, creating jobs and attracting residents.

Today: The City of Northville is split between Oakland and Wayne counties; the township is contained in Wayne. The area features pleasant countrysides with parks and cider mills that are rapidly urbanizing and a downtown with turn-of-the-century charm. There's a state park, Maybury, and Wayne County's only natural lake, Silver Springs. The old buildings of Mill Race Historical Village is a short walk from downtown.

Redford Township

Name: From the Rouge (Red) River's shallow section (a ford).

Population: 51,622.

State rank: 29.

Pioneers: Americans began reaching the Upper Rouge River by barge and scows from the Detroit River in the 1820s. Among the first: Israel Bell, 19, and his 14-year-old wife, Laura. They homesteaded in the area of 5 mile and Telegraph. The township was established in 1833 from such settlements as

Inkster

Name: After founder Robert Inkster.

Population: 30,115.

State rank: 59.

Nickname, Slogan: "A Congenial Community," "Inktown."

Pioneers: Robert Inkster founded Inkster in 1863. It was largely a quiet, all-white hamlet on Chicago Road until the 1920s, when it became a haven for black people who just arrived from the South, looking for work in the Ford Rouge plant in adjacent Dearborn. At the time, Inkster was one of the few areas in southeastern Michigan where blacks could own property. Incorporated as a village in 1927, Inkster was 90-percent black by 1930, as white residents departed. When Inkster children started to enter Dearborn schools, white parents complained. So Henry Ford, who employed many of Inkster's men, helped pay for separate schools in Inkster. In 1944, white residents pushed to divide Inkster along racial lines into separate cities. But their efforts failed, and Inkster was incorporated as a city in 1964.

Today: Inkster is about 62 percent black and 35 percent white, and mostly residential.

Plymouth, Plymouth Township

Name: Adopted because some of early settlers came from Plymouth, Mass.

Population: City: 9,022; township: 27,798.

State rank: City, 202; township, 69.

Nickname: The downtown used to be called Podunk; the north was known as Joppa.

Pioneers: Plymouth was settled in 1825 and became incorporated in 1867. In 1871, George Starkweather — the first child born to Plymouth settlers — made North Village, around the corner of Liberty and Starkweather, the center of the emerging community. It's known today as Old Village, or lower town. That year, the Plymouth railroad station was built. At the time, it was the only place in Michigan where railroad tracks went in all four directions.

Today: Plymouth became a city in 1932, and is now bordered on the north, west and east by fast-growing Plymouth Township, whose $350,000 new homes and busy industrial parks line M-14. The city is known for its old-fashioned downtown of small shops. Its annual ice-carving show is one of the biggest in the world and draws hundreds of thousands of visitors.

Sand Hill, Duboisville and Fisher's Station. The Grand River plank road in north Redford and a railroad in south Redford spurred 19th-Century development, including mills, blacksmiths and a glue factory. In 1925, residents voted to annex the eastern two-thirds of Redford to Detroit. The township boomed after World Wars I and II; General Motors Corp. built the Detroit Diesel Allison factory in Redford.

Today: Mainly residential with industry on the outskirts. Redford has lost nearly one-third of its population since 1970.

Riverview

Name: Origin uncertain. The theory: City leaders chose it because of the area's riverside location. At one time, says Gerald Perry, the city's director of public works and unofficial historian, residents probably had a good view of the river, but heavy industry changed that.

Population: 13,272.

State rank: 137.

Slogan: "Building today for the use of tomorrow."

Pioneers: In 1875, the developer Frederick Baker Sibley purchased a huge portion of land, part of which now makes up the city of Riverview, and began operating a limestone quarry. In the course of the next several decades, many quarry workers began to build homes and settle nearby. Riverview was incorporated as a village in 1922 and as a city in 1959. For much of the early 20th Century, Riverview attracted heavy industry, such as the Pennsylvania Salt Manufacturing Co., a Firestone tire plant and steel factory.

Today: Riverview is becoming more of a bedroom community as the smokestacks come down and new homes are built.

River Rouge

Name: After the river on which it is located.

Population: 9,917.

State rank: 187.

Pioneers: French people from Detroit were the first settlers. The early residents — Visgers, Navarres, Cicottes, Riopelles, Campaus, Fergusons, Labadies and Godfreys — set up ribbon farms on the banks of the Rouge River. The growth of the community in the early 1800s can be traced to the sawmills on the Rouge and Detroit rivers. Other early industries were cedar blocks for street paving and a barrel company. The town was incorporated as a village in 1899; Henry Visger was the first president. River Rouge was incorporated as a city in 1921 as the population surged with auto workers toiling

at the Ford Motor Co. plant in Dearborn.

Today: After struggling with budget deficits in the 1980s and 1990s, the working-class city that is home to the Great Lakes Division of National Steel has rebounded from its financial difficulties.

Rockwood

Name: The village, established in 1861, was originally called Huron Station. In 1872, the name was changed to Rockwood, for unknown reasons.

Population: 3,442.

State rank: 516.

Pioneers: The first settlers were Huron Indians, who located their encampment a few miles west of Rockwood in Huron Township. The first white settlers were French, who made their livelihood by fur trapping and trading. The Huron River forms the city's southern boundary.

Today: Industrial development consists of Rockwood Commerce Park, a 100-acre industrial par which contains Penstone Inc., a major automotive supplier, and Benckiser Products. Residential development is fairly light but has been growing, due to highway access. I-75 enters Wayne County in Rockwood, paralleling Fort Street and Conrail's rail facilities.

Romulus

Name: In its early days, Romulus was heavily populated by wolves. It got its name from the ancient fable of Romulus and Remus, the twins who were raised by wolves and

founded Rome. It was once known as Pullen's Corners, after early settlers.

Population: 22,979.

State rank: 76

Slogan: "Gateway to the World."

Pioneers: Samuel Tobyne, a French Canadian, was the first European settler in Romulus, arriving in 1826 to a swampy land. Originally a part of Huron Township, Romulus Township was established in 1835. By 1840, two dozen more settlers had arrived, including John F. Smith, the only doctor for many years. Officials drained the swamps before the Civil War, and much of Romulus soon became farmland.

Today: In 1970, Romulus became a city and is now home to Metro Airport. Bisected by two major highways, I-94 and I-275, it has more hotels and motels than any other city in Wayne County.

Southgate

Name: Adopted because the community was the southern gateway to the Detroit metropolitan area.

Population: 30,136.

State rank: 58.

Slogan: "Symbol of Progress Downriver."

Pioneers: Early records are not clear as to who bought land from the Potawatomi Indians in the area now known as Southgate. By 1776, Pierre St. Cosme was recorded as a land purchaser. But family histories of the Labadie and Campau families indicate they settled in the area earlier. By the early 1800s the Salliottes, Cicottes, Champaigns, LeBlancs, LeDucs, Riopelles and Rousseaus also owned property. In 1827 the township of Ecorse, as Southgate was known then, was established. In the 1800s, Southgate residents — like others in many parts of Downriver — were farmers, but many worked in industries such as shipbuilding. In 1958, the remaining citizens of Ecorse Township decided to incorporate as a city and named the area Southgate.

Today: After a long lull in housing construction, Southgate is experiencing a boom. The city is known for its good schools and parks and a fine library.

Sumpter Township

Name: From Revolutionary War Gen. Thomas Sumter.

Population: 11,856.

State rank: 157.

Pioneers: The township was incorporated April 6, 1840. The spelling of the name is different because of a clerk's error. At one time, the mostly rural township had two small settlements: Martinsville and West Sumpter. The towns faded when the railroad came through and made Belleville the regional center of commerce.

Today: Sumpter Township is the most rural and sparsely settled municipality in Wayne County and has relatively few paved roads. Farms are still a part of the landscape, with agriculture output that includes sod, soybeans, corn, and small fruits. Although there are businesses in the township, most of the residents earn their primary income from employment outside the community.

Wayne

Name: After U.S. Gen. Anthony (Mad Anthony) Wayne. The city was first called Derby's Corners, after an early settler.

Population: 19,051.

State rank: 98.

Slogan: "A great place to live and work."

Pioneers: The early settlement was on the former Territorial Road between Detroit and Chicago. In 1834, one of the first settlers built a log house on the site of what would become the Village of Wayne.

Today: It's one of the largest manufacturing sites for Ford Motor Co. in the nation, but Wayne also features unique antique shops and other specialty stores.

Taylor

Name: In honor of Mexican War hero and President Zachary Taylor, above.

Population: 65,868.

State rank: 21.

Slogans: "Taylor made for you," "A Downriver Community."

Pioneers: Taylor was originally part of Ecorse Township, but became its own community in 1847. One of the first landowners was Peter Coan, in 1830. Taylor remained a farming area until Henry Ford built the Rouge plant in Dearborn, and people began building houses. Taylor, which became a city in 1968, is home to large retail and industrial outlets. Metro Airport is 1 mile to the west, and the city is framed on the north by I-94 and on the south by I-75.

Today: Taylor in recent years has built or refurbished its city buildings, including a Department of Public Works dedicated by President Bill Clinton in 1996. The city contains the Downriver campus of Wayne County Community College, Southland Mall and Masco Corp. headquarters. Each year, it hosts the Junior League World Series for teen ballplayers.

Van Buren Township

Name: From U.S. President Martin Van Buren, left, who never visited the community but did pass through on a train and later commented, like a good politician, that he liked what he saw.

Population: 23,559.

State rank: #####

Pioneers: The earliest settlers entered the township on flatbed boats via the Huron River. In 1825, the federal government surveyed an old Indian trail winding through a forest; it was later incorporated into U.S.-12, also known as Michigan Avenue. Lumber and grain mills were an important part of commerce. Millers Henry Snow and Caleb Marsh were among the earliest settlers.

Two important events shaped the development of the area:

➤ In the 1920s, Belleville Lake was created when Detroit Edison built a dam on the Huron River near Haggerty Road. The lake became a major tourist attraction.

➤ During World II, Henry Ford built a road linking Willow Run to River Rouge. That road was named the Willow Run Expressway, and later became I-94.

Today: The still largely rural township is home to Willow Run Airport, which is one of the main freight-handling facilities in the country. Also, it boasts great recreational areas: 101-acre Van Buren Park, a well-regarded public golf course; 1,200-acre Lower Huron Metropark, and Belleville Lake, the largest inland lake in Wayne County.

Trenton

Name: Detroit business-man Abraham Truax founded the village of Truaxton, which was later named Truago. Trenton, which came into use in the mid-19th Century, was a type of limestone similar to the limestone quarried in the area.
Population: 19,584.
State rank: 94.
Pioneers: Trenton became a busy cross-roads in the 19th Century because it was one day's journey south of Detroit and the last high ground before Monroe. In addition to the limestone quarry, a shipbuilding business took hold in Trenton, with the Alvin Clark being launched in 1847. The area also became home to the Church family's Arm & Hammer Baking Soda. Trenton became a city in 1957.
Today: Trenton features a mix of residential and industrial property. Business development is mostly along the Detroit River or Jefferson Avenue. County-owned Elizabeth Park is located on the south end.

Westland

Name: Originally Nankin Township, Westland became a city in 1966. Former state Sen. William Faust suggested the name Westland while he was Nankin Township supervisor — partly because of the community's location in the western Wayne County. A petition effort to keep the Nankin Township name failed in the mid-1960s.
Population: 86,602.
State rank: 11.
Slogans: "Progress and Promise," "The Place to Be."
Pioneers: The city rests on a former glacial lake bed along the Rouge River. The early settlers were three Algonquin Indian tribes — Potawatomi, Ojibwa and Ottawa — which met every season at the fork of the river.
Today: Located between Detroit and Ann Arbor, Westland has six industrial parks, a major retail shopping mall, more than 1,500 acres of parks and two golf courses.

Woodhaven

Name: After a village in the New York borough of Queens with the same name. One of the local leaders, the general manager of the Mobil Oil refinery, was from that area.
Population: 12,530.
State rank: 148.
Pioneers: Woodhaven did not become a village until December 1961, but it has a history that is almost as old as the nation itself. During the War of 1812, American troops clashed with British troops in the Downriver area, particularly in the section of the county that evolved into Brownstown. The original Brownstown comprised the cities of Flat Rock, Rockwood, Gibraltar and Woodhaven. Over the years, Woodhaven has managed to attract considerable industry. Mobil Oil built a refinery in 1929. Ford Motor Co. opened a major stamping plant in 1965. Woodhaven is also the home to the Woodhaven Commerce Park, which seeks to attract light industrial and light manufacturing companies.
Today: A city with growing residential, retail and industrial development. Woodhaven shopping consists primarily of three large shopping centers. A fourth is on the way.

Wyandotte

Name: After the Indian tribe that settled in the city.
Population: 28,006.
State rank: 68.
Pioneers: Wyandotte Indians, also called Hurons, built a village on land from what is now Elm Street to Eureka Avenue, calling it *Maquaqua*. John Biddle, a Princeton graduate and former U.S. Army major who was the third mayor of Detroit, settled in the area in the 1830s and named his house Wyandotte. The riverfront location made it a bustling 19th Century port town with Eureka Iron Co., shipbuilding, chemicals and metal-makers. Later, the All Metal Products Co. became a huge manufacturer of toy guns and sent famous Wyandotte Toys around the world. Wyandotte became a city in 1867; its street plan was copied from that of Philadelphia.
Today: Industry, especially chemical production, coexists with trendy downtown coffeehouses and historic homes.

Macomb County

40 N. Gratiot
Mt. Clemens, Mich. 48043
810-469-5100
www.macomb.lib.mi.us/macomb/
Name: The county was named in honor of Gen. Alexander Macomb, a highly decorated veteran of the War of 1812.
Area: 482 square miles.
Population:

1910	32,606	1960	405,804
1940	107,428	1970	625,309
		1990	717,400

Population breakdown, 2000 census results:

Total	788,149
Total white	730,270 (92.7%)
Total black	21,326 (2.7%)

Gen. Anthony (Mad Anthony) Wayne, namesake of the suburb, county and university.

Total American Indian	2,478 (0.3%)
Total Asian and Pacific Islander	16,843 (2.1%)
Hispanic	12,435 (1.6%)
Some other race ("other")	3,106 (0.4%)
Two or more races	13,948 (1.8%)

History: The county was organized by Territorial Gov. Lewis Cass in 1818 as Michigan's third county, after Wayne and Monroe. At the time, the county boundaries extended through much of southern Michigan and the Thumb, taking in what had been Indian-owned land in the present-day counties of St. Clair, Oakland, Livingston, Genesee, Lapeer and portions of Shiawassee, Ingham, Sanilac, Tuscola, Huron and Saginaw.

Largely rural throughout the 19th Century beyond the baths, shops and brothels of lively Mt. Clemens, Macomb doubled in population between 1920 and 1930 to 77,146. Industry and people — mostly from Detroit — increased the population by 440,000 between 1950 and 1970. By 2001, Macomb was an overwhelmingly white county of mostly working- and middle-class people with roots in Germany, Poland, Italy and Ireland.

Spurred by the bullish economy, Macomb expanded greatly during the 1990s. The county created thousands of jobs and boasted an unemployment rate of less than 3 percent. For 32 years, Macomb has boasted Michigan's lowest county-tax rate. County officials also say one of every four homes built in Michigan in 1999 was located in Macomb County, where rampant residential and commercial development is devouring farmland by the acre. As in the rest of metro Detroit, the leading employers are General Motors Corp., Ford Motor Co. and DaimlerChrysler AG.

Socially, Macomb County is chided by some observers as a country bumpkin to its more sophisticated Oakland and Wayne neighbors, and Macomb's frontier reputation was reinforced in recent years by a number of scandals, including a bribe-seeking city councilwoman; a judge accused of bartering leniency for sex; a school administrator suspected of embezzling $438,000; an adulterous judge accused of steering legal work to a lover later convicted of killing his pregnant wife, and a no-nonsense sheriff who was convicted of rape and sentenced to prison.

The communities

Armada Village/Township

Name: The area was originally named Burke's Corners, then Honeoye, after Honeoye Falls, N.Y. In 1867, a meeting to organize and name the village dragged on until Hosea Northrup rose and declared, "It will be Armada (ar-MAY-dah)." Yearning to go home, the group quickly agreed. Today, no one knows why Northrup picked the name or pronounced it that way.

Population: Village, 1,573; township, 5,246.

State rank: Village, 1,036; township, 330.

Pioneers: Founded by settlers from New York and Canada.

Today: Although still largely a farming area, development is pressing upon Armada, and the village and township are struggling to control it. An industrial district in the township has drawn about a dozen firms.

Chesterfield Township

Name: After the British defeated the French in North America in 1760, it was named Chesterfield in honor of England's fourth earl of Chesterfield.

Population: 37,405.

State rank: 44.

Pioneers: Settlers were drawn by its rich farmland. It began as part of Macomb Township, but in 1842, Macomb split, making Chesterfield a township in its own right.

Today: Farmland has given way to manufacturing plants, businesses and homes. Chesterfield boasts the world headquarters for Lionel, the 100-year-old model train company. The township borders Anchor Bay, and its shoreline is dotted with marinas. Because of its easy access to I-94, it serves as a bedroom community for a large part of southeastern Michigan.

Clinton Township

Named: In honor of New York Gov. DeWitt Clinton, a prime mover on construction of the Erie Canal, in 1824.

Population: 95,648.

State rank: 10.

Pioneers: On July 22, 1782, Moravian missionary David Zeisberger and the religion's followers founded the first settlement in Clinton Township. They named it New Gnadenhutten, or Tents of Grace, and built Moravian Drive, which remains a busy thoroughfare. The mission closed in 1786. Other villages that were originally part of Clinton Township include Mt. Clemens, Frederick, Warsaw, Marcellus and Cady's Corner.

Today: Michigan's most-populated township is a working-class community crisscrossed by the Clinton River and major arteries, including Metropolitan Parkway and Gratiot. It is home to at least three golf courses and Macomb County Community College. The community boasts of being the largest rose producer in Michigan since the 1920s. Clinton roses graced state dinners and other White House functions during President Gerald Ford's administration.

Center Line

Name: After the line that marked the middle point of Warren Township.

Population: 8,531.

State rank: 211.

Pioneers: Some early families were Belgian. When the Archdiocese of Detroit authorized the building of St. Clements Church, some of the priests who came spoke Flemish.

Today: A tidy middle-class suburb with a large population of retirees. Geographically, it is to Warren what Hamtramck and Highland Park are to Detroit, independent but hemmed in on all sides by its much bigger neighbor. Center Line is fighting age and the northward movement of younger generations. The busy commercial stretch of Van Dyke is the heart of the city.

Eastpointe

Name: After being part of Huron, Clinton, Orange and Erin townships, all of which contained several present-day Macomb County cities, it was called Halfway. That's because the town was halfway between Detroit and Mt. Clemens. In 1929, the city was named East Detroit because of its proximity to the booming city next door. In 1992, with Detroit shrinking in people and stature, East Detroit residents voted to change the name to Eastpointe, as in Grosse Pointe.
Population: 34,077.
State rank: 49.
Slogan: "A Family Town."
Pioneers: French, Irish and Germans were early settlers in the 1830s and 1840s. Early residents were Christian Gerlach, George Hund and Nicholas Ameis.
Today: Formerly a leading supplier of rhubarb, or pie plant, the city is now mostly a bedroom community that was once losing property values and population due to the flight of younger generations. It is now seen as a good place for young families looking for first homes. Winter Sausage and East Detroit Public Schools are the city's largest employers.

Fraser

Name: After businessman Alexander Frazer in 1857. The city has used both spellings, calling itself Frazer from 1895 to 1921, and Fraser starting in 1928 after a public vote. For a time, the city's name was McPhersonville after pioneer William McPherson.
Population: 15,297.
State rank: 119.
Pioneers: McPherson and Leonard Scott, both early postmasters. The railroad came through in 1865, spurring development. Fraser became a city in 1957.
Today: Fraser has been widely known for years across metro Detroit for its large complex of hockey rinks. Like much of Macomb County, development is stripping its rural roots.

Harrison Township

Name: Best guess by local historians is that the namesake was President William Henry Harrison.
Population: 24,461.
State rank: 71.
Nickname: "Boat Town."
Pioneers: At the turn of the 18th Century, a youngster named William Tucker was kidnapped by Indians — probably Ojibwas — from his home in Virginia and brought to the shores of Lake St. Clair, where he was raised as an Indian. He learned French and English and served as a tribal interpreter. For his services, he was given as much land as he could walk around in a day, and that became the core of today's township.
Today: As the doorstep to Lake St. Clair and the Clinton River, the township boasts a huge marina business. An industrial corridor with about 120 other businesses lies along the township's border with Selfridge Air National Guard Base. Easy access to I-94 makes Harrison a popular bedroom community.

Memphis

Name: Named for Memphis, Egypt, "the City on the Nile."
Population: 1,129.
State rank: 1,234.
Pioneers: Memphis, Mich., is "the city on the Belle River." Its virgin forests and abundant game drew migrants, who called it Wells Settlement, then Memphis. The city, which straddles the Macomb County-St. Clair County line, was established in 1835 and boasts that the first car with an internal combustion engine was built there about that time.
Today: Memphis is a bedroom community with a small-town atmosphere. On summer nights, families stroll the streets, chatting and stopping for ice cream. The town has some light industry ("But no pollution!" says clerk Liz Brusca) and is building a new school for sixth- through 12th-graders.

Mt. Clemens

Name: After Christian Clemens, an early settler. Prior name was High Banks.
Population: 17,312.
State rank: 105.
Nickname: "Bath City."
Pioneers: First settled in the late 18th Century, it was accessible via the Clinton River from Lake St. Clair and the road to Detroit that was cleared along present-day Gratiot. After the Indians, early settlers included Clemens, Oliver Wiswell, Nathan Williams, Jared Brooks and the Conner family, in addition to a group of Moravian missionaries who lived nearby. Mt. Clemens became a village in 1851 and a city in 1879. A booming town in the 19th Century, Mt. Clemens' businesses included rose cultivation, shipbuilding, lumber, carriage manufacturing and ice production. But it was especially known for bathing. The mineral water was smelly, but Dr. Abner Hayward noted in 1872 that the town's liquid possessed "restorative qualities." One man said bathing cured his eczema. Another story told of the waters serving as a fountain of youth for an old horse. Mt. Clemens was soon famous across America, and it attracted such VIPs as Babe Ruth and Clark Gable. Dr. Henry Taylor opened the Original Bath House in 1873. A dozen bathing establishments soon followed, including such famous ones as the Avery House, Medea, Colonial, Plaza, Olympia, Egnew, Park, Eureka and Arethusa. An order of nuns ran a bath house, as did a black family headed by George Hutchinson, who was once barred from taking a bath because of his race. Some of the houses were elegant; others were dives. The tourist trade brought along saloons, brothels and gambling joints, so Mt. Clemens also developed a naughty reputation, sort of a 19th-Century Windsor.
Today: The baths are gone and Mt. Clemens' population is about where it was in the 1920s. The St. Joseph Sanitorium and Bath House is now occupied by offices of the St. Joseph's Mercy Hospitals. Fire water has replaced mineral water. A lively, blue-collar town that still has many stately homes, the Macomb County seat is seemingly full of bars — from the Voodoo Lounge on Main Street to John Barleycorn's on Macomb. Residents fill downtown every New Year's Eve for fireworks. Clusters of

Macomb Township

Named: For Gen. Alexander Macomb, right, the long-time 19th-Century military leader in Detroit and namesake of Macomb County

Population: 50,478.

State rank: 30.

Slogan: "Center of the County-Heart of the World."

Pioneers: Immigrants from Belgium and German towns such as Frankfurt and Waldenburg formed two distinct communities and began farming Macomb Township not long after it was created in 1834.

Today: With a population of 22,714 in 1990, Macomb Township was the fastest-growing community in southeast Michigan over the next decade. Along dusty 23 Mile Road, farmland has disappeared beneath condominiums, subdivisions, strip malls and technological and industrial parks. But township planners hope to preserve the area's character by establishing a one mile planned town center with a $7.8-million municipal office building, shops and homes, all built in a turn-of-the-century motif.

motorcycles regularly rumble through town and, on warm Wednesday nights, dozens of folks line their classic cars along Main Street in front of the imposing county courthouse, built in 1967. The courthouse is one of three major county buildings that loom over the Clinton River, giving what would otherwise be a well-kept but typical small town a modest skyline. Across Cass Avenue from the 1931 Art Deco tower — notable for the giant, glowering heads of square-jawed American Indians and laborers set in it upper floor — is the gleaming new administrative office building. It features mirrored windows and a soaring flag pole that reaches dozens of feet above its roof.

New Baltimore

Name: Originally called Ashley, but was renamed New Baltimore for unknown reasons.

Population: 7,405.

State rank: 245.

Pioneers: Settlers began moving into the area in 1796, and in 1845, Alfred Ashley moved out from Mt. Clemens and built a sawmill and a dock. It was incorporated as a village in 1867 and was a thriving port in Victorian times. It became a city in 1931.

Today: "Still thriving, still growing," City Clerk Ann Billock says. Its easy access to freeways has made it a bedroom community, and the city has drawn young families looking for a good quality of life for their children. The town has more than 225 businesses, and its beach on Lake St. Clair draws visitors from across southeastern Michigan.

Romeo and Bruce Township

Names: Pioneer Laura Taylor gave the village its name, saying Romeo was "short, musical, classical and uncommon." Bruce Township — originally called Fourth Town — was established in 1833. Some of its founders were Scots, so they changed the township name to honor the Scottish national hero Robert the Bruce. The village was known as Indian Village, then Hoxie's Settlement until it was incorporated in 1838 as Romeo.

Population: Romeo, 3,421; Bruce, 8,158.

State rank: City, 473; Bruce, 226.

Pioneers: The area was settled by farmers in the 1820s and 1830s.

Today: The village is partly in Bruce Township, partly in Washington Township (see Washington, below), and its commercial district serves as a hub for those two townships, as well as for some in Armada and Ray townships. It is known for its lovingly restored Victorian houses, which mingle with newer homes. Bruce, which at one time had more than 200 farms, has only half a dozen today as development has pushed into the township. But Bruce still struggles to hang on to the rural character that drew its residents in the first place.

New Haven and Lenox Township

Name: Named after New Haven, Conn.

Name: In 1837, it was proposed that the three oldest men in what became Lenox Township select the name for the community, so Benjamin Haight, Mason Harris and Israel Dryer each suggested a name. Haight's and Harris' choices duplicated the names of other townships in the state, so Dryer's choice — Lenox — was adopted. But why Dryer picked that name is lost in the mists of history.

Population: Village, 3,071; township, 8,433.

State rank: Village, 579; township: 215.

Pioneers: Farmers were buying land in the area as early as the 1820s. The village — originally called New Baltimore Station — was settled in 1838 and incorporated as New Haven in 1869. The township was founded in 1837 with 29 farms on 2,600 acres. The earliest settlers were Irish — the Donleys, the Sullivans and the Fitzgeralds — and the old Sullivan one-room schoolhouse still stands at 28 Mile and Gratiot. One of the first electric stations was built on Omo Road, then later sold to Detroit Edison.

Today: "We're on the threshold of the population boom," Township Supervisor John Gardner says. "Macomb and Chesterfield are getting filled, so we're the next step." Sixty-five percent of township land is zoned for agriculture, while commerce is confined to strips along Gratiot and 26 Mile. The rest is residential, with a 2-acre minimum per house, an attempt to preserve the township's rural ambiance. The village economy is supported primarily by a foundry and small businesses. Despite growth, it has retained its small-town atmosphere.

Ray Township

Name: Originally known as Rhea, its origin is uncertain.

Population: 3,740.

State rank: 470.

Slogan: "The Jewel of Macomb County."

Pioneers: The first farmers moved into the area in 1825, and the township was founded in 1827. Originally, it also included Armada, Bruce and Washington townships.

Today: The township remains largely rural — by design. In the late 1980s, a survey showed residents wanted to keep their bucolic atmosphere, so the master plan bars water and sewer lines. "Over the last 10 years, we've averaged 30 new homes a year," clerk Robert Devers says. But the township has some small businesses and even small industries, such as a cabinet-making operation. Amateur astronomers like to set their telescopes up in Ray Township, because the relative lack of night light makes it easier to view the heavens.

Roseville

Name: After the town's first postmaster, William Rose. It was once part of the larger townships of Orange and Erin. The Village of Roseville was established in 1926, and the city was incorporated in 1958.

Population: 48,129.

State rank: 32.

Pioneers: After the Potawatomi Indians came Henry Savage, Thomas Bloss, Levi Frazos, John Martin and later the Common Brothers, Thomas and John. Early families include the Fischers, Templetons, Kaisers, Wards, Corbys, Blums, Redmonds, Nolans and Salters.

Today: Roseville is mostly a bedroom community with four shopping centers and many smaller shopping areas. The east side is home to many small industrial plants. The majority of Roseville is made up of modest homes, for a mix of retirees and families.

Shelby Township

Named: For Isaac Shelby, a hero of the American Revolution who became Kentucky's first governor and, at age 63, led troops from Kentucky into Detroit during the War of 1812.

Population: 65,159.

State rank: 22.

Slogan: "A Township and More . . . "

Pioneers: Nathaniel Burgess built the first house in the township during the winter of 1816-17, and on May 24, 1819, Blake Curtis became the first buyer of government land. The rest of the township was snatched up in the 1820s by folks such as Ezra Burgess, whose timber frame house still stands on Dequindre south of 25 Mile. In 1827, Perez Swift hosted the first township meeting at his log home, with Calvin Davis presiding, Abijah Owen as clerk and Joseph Lester as supervisor. Asa Price built the first saw mill in 1828, the same year Adam Price put up a grist mill.

Today: After spells as a stop on the Underground Railroad, home to a Mennonite community, whiskey runners, Packard Motors' testing grounds and Joe Louis' training camp, Shelby Township has shed its rural character and grown steadily since the 1960s. The community has a diverse character, ranging from parkland to miles of strip malls along busy Van Dyke and the sprawling Lakeside shopping center on M-59. In addition its residential growth, an industrial corridor has also flourished along 23 Mile. Ford Motor Co. also has a major presence, with a 3,400-employee plant in the township.

Sterling Heights

Named: Incorporated as Jefferson Township in 1835, it became Sterling Township in 1838 after Sterling, N.Y., the home of many early settlers. Renamed Sterling Heights in 1968 after it was incorporated as a city.
Population: 124,471.
State rank: 5.
Slogan: "To Strive On Behalf of All."
Pioneers: Some Detroiters came to Sterling Township after the War of 1812, building large homesteads and planting wheat and corn on 100-acre farms. Apple and peach orchards were also common and, by 1832, more than 2,500 sheep, 1,200 cows and 500 horses chewed and plowed the rich fields.
Today: After trying for most of the 1960s to incorporate, Sterling Township officially became the city of Sterling Heights on July 1, 1968. Home to many industries, including Ford Motor Co., the city is populated by a variety of people ranging from blue-collar workers to skilled tradesmen to young professionals. Most of the farmland has become housing, some of it subdivisions of modest homes and neighborhoods of mega-homes packed side-by-side on small residential lots. Amenities include golf courses, parks and busy Freedom Hill County Park. City officials often boast of Sterling Heights' recognition as one of the nation's wealthiest communities of its size, its excellence as a place to raise children, its low crime and fire rates and low tax rate. An image-conscious city actively hyping its accomplishments to residents and potential residents and business owners alike, Sterling Heights spends about $1 million a year on community relations.

St. Clair Shores

Name: From the lake.
Population: 63,096.
State rank: 24.
Pioneers: Several French families settled before 1790 along the Milk River, which now divides St. Clair Shores and Grosse Pointe Shores. Late 19th- and early 20th-Century pioneer families include the Trombleys, the Masons and the Verniers. Cottages dotted the shoreline for years. During Prohibition, St. Clair Shores' canals were on the receiving end of lots of illegal booze from Canada. Blossom Heath, now a banquet hall on Jefferson, was one of metro Detroit's most

notorious speakeasies. Jefferson Beach, a popular amusement park, is now a marina. The city did most of its growing after World War II. After being a village and part of Lake and Erin townships, St. Clair Shores became a city in 1951.
Today: It's a boating capital of Michigan, a city of mainly middle-class ranch houses known mainly for its lengthy shoreline, which is home to more than 3,500 boat wells and seven marinas, most of them off Jefferson. Part of Jefferson is known as the Nautical Mile, and officials have spruced it up with landscaping and a motorized trolley. New restaurants and bars that cater to the boating trade have sprouted in recent years.

Utica

Named: After Utica, N.Y., home of the original settlers.
Population: 4,577.
State rank: 385.
Nickname: "The Pioneer City."
Pioneers: Nathaniel Squires built the first house in what is now Utica during the winter of 1816-17. John Stead laid out the village's streets around 1820.
Today: Utica is a small town nestled among the large suburban communities that has retained its small-town flavor. Utica's historic downtown, which includes two buildings dating to the 1840s, is within walking distance of most homes in town. The community also features modern conveniences and shopping along M-59.

Warren

Name: There are two theories: 1) In honor of Dr. Joseph Warren, a casualty of the Battle of Bunker Hill. 2) After an itinerant preacher named Abel Warren. Once part of Orange Township and Hickory Township, the community's name was changed to Aba in 1838, then to Warren Township in 1839. In 1893, one crossroads on the west side of Warren Township, Beebe's Corners, became the village of Warren. Warren was incorporated as a city in 1956.
Population: 128,247.
State rank: 3.
Slogan: "City of Progress."
Pioneers: Snooty Detroiters once scorned Warren as "Mudville" for its unpaved roads and tar-paper homes. The preindustrial landscape featured beet, cranberry and rhubarb farms and tiny villages, and the township board paid bounties on wolves, bears and cows. But factories began opening on the cheap land in the 1930s, and people followed. Before World War II, Warren already had given birth to the Rotary Elec-

Richmond, Richmond Township

Name: Farmers from Richmond, N.Y., settled the area.
Population: City, 4,897; township, 3,416.
State rank: City, 352; township, 519.
Pioneers: Settlers began showing up in 1835, and the township was named Richmond in 1838. In the southeast corner, settler Erastus Beebe bought some land and named it Beebe's Corners. Nearby, communities named Ridgeway and Cooper Town formed, and in 1879, they were combined and incorporated as the village of Richmond. It became a city in 1966.
Today: The township remains an agricultural community and is working hard to preserve its farmland. But the city has blossomed as the hub between Mt. Clemens and Port Huron. It is home to a State Police post, an industrial park and three business districts — two traditional small downtowns and a commercial strip. In between the commercial districts lie historic homes and tree-lined streets, giving Richmond the charm of a Victorian-era small town.

Washington Township

Named: After George Washington.
Population: 19,080.
State rank: 97.
Pioneers: First surveyed in 1816, it became a township in 1827 and was settled primarily by families from New York state, along with one or two Detroiters, who began farming near the village of Romeo. The township's agricultural history includes a strong emphasis on orchards.
Today: You can still buy fruit from Washington Township's three remaining family-owned orchards, but the predominantly agricultural past has given way to rapid development. Farmland began disappearing at a breakneck pace about a decade before the turn the 20th Century. In one particularly striking scene, a deteriorating barn sits a few hundred feet north of a new subdivision and east of a new Meijer store and strip mall. Nearby is the landmark Octagon House, nationally recognized as a historic place, built around 1860. Although there is little retail or industrial presence in the township, its largest employer is automotive and aerospace supplier TRW, which has the world headquarters of its vehicle safety systems there.

RICHARD LEE/Detroit Free Press

The famous Octagon House in Washington Township.

tric Steel Plant (1933); Dodge Truck (1938); General Electric Carboloy (1940) and the Detroit Tank Arsenal (1940). President Franklin D. Roosevelt visited the tank plant in 1942. Many migrants crossed 8 Mile to escape housing-scarce Detroit, and Warren boomed with the post-war auto business. General Motors Corp. built the sprawling Tech Center in 1956, and the city had nearly 1,000 plants by 1966. Between 1960 and 1970, Warren was one of the fast-growing cities in America, doubling in population from 89,000 to 180,000. In 1970, one in five Warren residents had foreign-born parents (largely from Poland and Italy), and more than 13,000 residents had been born in the South. Warren made national news in 1970 when controversy arose over a federal plan to require open housing in return for urban-renewal funds. Voters rejected the federal money. Home to many Democrats and union members after the war, Warren became a sociological petri dish in the 1980s, when its blue-collar "Reagan Democrats" became a source of fascination for national media and political scientists.

Today: While still offering many of the best things of suburbia, Warren is facing the problems of many older cities. Warren remains the second-largest city in southeast Michigan (after Detroit) and is known for its size, industry and hardball politics.

City Council meetings drag on for hours, a jury in 1997 acquitted Mayor Mark Steenbergh on charges of assault and ethnic intimidation and the FBI was examining some city officials in 1999 and 2000.

Washtenaw County

County Clerk, 101 E. Huron St. or P.O. Box 8645, Ann Arbor 48107
734-994-2506
www.co.washtenaw.mi.us

Name: Uncertain. Among the theories: The name is a variant of Washtenong, the Chippewa name for Grand River, which seems a long way from Washtenaw, but in the early 19th Century all the unsettled land west of Detroit was considered part of the same region. Also: The name of an Indian, or a derivation from the Potawatomi word for large stream or river, or from the Algonquin word for far country, as in far from Detroit.
Area: 711 square miles.

Population:
1970 234,103   1990 282,937

Population breakdown, 2000 census results:

Total 322,895
Total white 249,916 (77.4%)
Total black 39,697 (12.3%)
Total American Indian 1,161 (0.4%)
Total Asian and Pacific Islander 20,338 (6.3%)
Hispanic 8,839 (2.7%)
Some other race ("other") 3,364 (1.0%)
Two or more races 8,293 (2.6%)

History: Territorial Gov. Lewis Cass organized the county in 1822. At first, Wayne County officials administered the county. Washtenaw was formally established in 1827 and divided into 20 townships. Population was nearly 1,000. The first session of county court was held in the home of Erastus Priest by Judge Samuel Dexter.

The communities
Ann Arbor

Name: There are several theories, most revolving around the fact that the names of the two founders' wives were Ann Allen and Mary Ann Rumsey. Another variation is the name comes from Ann d'Arbeur, an early resident.
Population: 114,024.
State rank: 7.
Nicknames: "The Athens of the Midwest," "The Dope Capital of the Midwest" (1970s), "Tree Town."

Pioneers: John Allen of Virginia and Elisha Rumsey of New York built a cabin in Ann Arbor in 1824, the year the city was made the seat of Washtenaw County. Allen became postmaster in 1825. The biggest event in Ann Arbor's history occurred in 1841, when the state Legislature voted to move the University of Michigan from Detroit. The city was incorporated in 1851. Starting about 1900, Ann Arbor became the nexus of big-time sports and high-power academia; most college towns are lucky to have one or the other. During the last 40 years, as Michigan teams piled up national championships, Ann Arbor also has been a breeding ground for such national movements as antiwar activism, environmentalism, feminism, gay rights, affirmative action and anti-domestic violence activism.

Today: Anchored by one of the nation's leading universities, Ann Arbor is a vibrant, growing community that consistently rates high on standard-of-living indexes. In addition to plenty of auto industry-related firms, the city has numerous high-tech, research and medical facilities. Ann Arbor is filled with parks, museums, sports venues and libraries, and the hipness quotient is very high. There are coffee bars of every mutation, bookstores galore, enough snazzy

University of Michigan students reading outside of University Hall in the 19th Century.

Free Press file photo

Ypsilanti

Name: After Demetrius Ypsilanti, a general in the Greek revolution. Pronounced IPS-a-lanty.
Population: 22,362.
State rank: 81.
Nicknames: Ypsitucky, for the significant number of southerners, and just plain Ypsi.
Pioneers: The city grew up where an old Indian trail crossed the Huron River. One of the earliest permanent white settlers was Benjamin Woodruff, who established his home about a mile south of Ypsilanti in 1823. A number of migrants from the east bypassed Detroit and staked claims in Ypsilanti after the opening of the Erie Canal; by the late 1830s, three stage lines, a railroad and the Chicago Road (Michigan Avenue) served the town, which became a commercial center and service depot for the many travelers heading into Detroit or westward into the wilderness. Eastern Michigan University, a former teachers' college, was founded in 1852; Cleary College opened in 1883.
Today: The auto industry's fluctuating fortunes have taken their toll on Ypsilanti, but the city still possesses considerable charm. Depot Town, several blocks of well-preserved 19th-Century buildings, includes Cady's Grill on East Cross Street, where President Bill Clinton ate n spring 2000, after delivering the EMU commencement address. The 250,000-gallon water tower, erected in 1890, remains the town's chief landmark. The annual Frog Island Jazz Festival attracts music lovers.

restaurants to satisfy the most demanding gourmand and a lively street life that over the years has included protests, free concerts, post-game riots and aggressive skateboarders, who have now been restricted. Since the 1970s, Ann Arbor has spawned the radical White Panther Party, the liberal Human Rights Party and one of the nation's least punitive marijuana laws. Each April, a few thousand people hold a dope-smoking Hash Bash in the center of campus. If that isn't enough, it's a pretty town, especially the old sections around the "U."

Livingston County

County Clerk, 200 E. Grand River, Howell 48843
517-546-0500
Name: In honor of Edward Livingston, a lawyer who lived in New York and New Orleans and who served as secretary of state and minister to France.
Area: 572 square miles.

Population:

| 1910 | 17,736 | 1980 | 100,289 |
| 1970 | 58,967 | 1990 | 115,645 |

Population breakdown, 2000 census results:

Total	156,951
Total white	152,439 (97.1%)
Total black	722 (0.5%)
Total American Indian	682 (0.4%)
Total Asian and Pacific Islander	896 (0.6%)
Hispanic	1,953 (1.2 %)
Some other race ("other")	503 (0.3%)
Two or more races	1,663 (1.1%)

History: What is now Livingston Township was part of Shiawassee and Washtenaw counties until Gov. George Porter and the state Legislature approved the establishment of Livingston in 1833. County officers were elected in 1836. Settlers, many from the east, already were moving into the county, whose land had been farmed for years by the Chippewa and Potawatomi. The first white person was Solomon Peterson, who built a home on Portage Creek, in what is now Putnam Township. Livingston County's most celebrated reminder of its early history is a magnificent 1889 courthouse in Howell. Livingston was mainly an agricultural community and recreation center for Detroiters until creeping urbanization reached the county's southeast corner in the past 30 years, during which Livingston has been one of Michigan's fastest-growing counties. The forecast: More growth. Its central location, near highways leading to Detroit, Lansing and Ann Arbor, make it a commuter's dream. Many Liv-

ingston residents have worked to overcome the county's reputation for hostility toward black people and other minorities that developed in part because the late Robert Miles was a nationally famous white supremacist who held cross-burnings on his farm in Cohoctah Township outside Howell.

The communities
Brighton, Brighton Twp.

Name: Originally called Ore Creek, the settlement became Brighton in 1840 because some settlers came from Brighton, N.Y.
Population: Town, 6,701; township, 17,673.
State rank: Town, 268; township, 102.
Pioneers: In 1832, brothers Maynard and Almon Maltby settled at Ore Creek and built a dam and sawmill. A church, school, post office, foundry and blacksmith soon followed. Brighton prospered from its location on the plank road (Grand River) between Lansing and Detroit, and became a village in 1867.
Today: Brighton has become increasingly upscale as executive-level employees move from older Detroit suburbs to Livingston. The county's new houses average well above $200,000. Meanwhile, the Brighton area copes with growth issues such as crowded schools and heavy traffic. Affordable housing is scarce, as are entry-level jobs. But Brighton retains its original recreational appeal with its proximity to several parks, including Kensington Metropark, Island Lake Recreation Area, Brighton Recreation Area and many other local lakes, where one-time vacation cabins have been converted into full-time homes. Mt. Brighton, the area's longtime ski resort, is adding an 18-hole golf course. Brighton's Main Street shops reflect trends, offering gourmet bakeries, new restaurants, antique shops, a farmer's market and a new playground and walkways at the city's old Mill Pond.

St. Clair County

County Clerk, 201 McMorran, Port Huron 48080
810-985-2200.
Name: After Lake St. Clair and the St. Clair River.
Area: 734 square miles.

Population:

| 1970 | 120,175 | 1990 | 145,607 |

Population breakdown, 2000 census results:

Total	164,235
Total white	155,962 (95.0%)
Total black	3,451 (2.1%)
Total American Indian	829 (0.5%)

Total Asian and Pacific Islander 650 (0.4%)
Hispanic . . . . 3,593 (2.2 %)
Some other race ("other") 1,052 (0.6%)
Two or more races 2,259 (1.4%)
  History: Established in 1820, the county is named after the lake and river.

The communities
Port Huron

Name: After either the huge body of water nearby or the Indian tribe. Early villages at the site were called Peru, Desmond, Gratiot and Huron.

Population: 32,338.

State rank: 53.

History: The French built Ft. St. Joseph here in 1688, 13 years before Cadillac built Ft. Pontchartrain in Detroit. But Port Huron's fort lasted only two years, and the area remained without a settlement for about a century. In 1788, Frenchman Anselm Petit built a home at the mouth of the Black River. By 1814, the Americans had established a military base, Ft. Gratiot, at the southern reaches of Lake Huron. Nine years later, the Ft. Gratiot lighthouse, Michigan's first coastal beacon, began guiding the growing ship traffic in Lake Huron and the St. Clair River. By 1836, a road — Gratiot — had opened between Port Huron and Detroit, and Port Huron became incorporated as a city in 1857, three years after the family of its most famous resident — Thomas Edison — moved to town. The population grew in the pre-Civil War era, fueled by the lumber, fishing, railroad and shipbuilding industries. Port Huron was the last stop on a branch of the Underground Railroad before Canada. It was also an early producer of oil and natural gas, and in 1844 it became home to one of Michigan's first electric utilities. In the 20th Century, Port Huron became a small industrial cen-

ter, with auto parts, salt and metal production. Today its downtown is filled with revitalized 19th-Century buildings, and the water makes it a huge center for pleasure boating. Since 1925 it has been the annual launching pad for the Port Huron-Mackinac Race.

Monroe County

County Clerk, 125 E. 2nd St.,
Monroe 48161
734-241-6574.

Name: The area was called Frenchtown but was renamed in honor of President James Monroe.

Area: 557 square miles.

Population:

1970	118,479	1990	133,600
1980	134,659		

Population breakdown, 2000 census results:

Total 145,945
Total white 139,264 (95.4%)
Total black 2,766 (1.9%)
Total American Indian 405 (0.3%)
Total Asian and Pacific Islander 679 (0.5%)
Hispanic . . . . 3,110 (2.1 %)
Some other race ("other") 907 (0.6%)
Two or more races 1,911 (1.3%)

  History: Long the home of Potawatomi and other Indian tribes, Monroe was settled by French people who traveled downriver from Detroit in the late 1700s and built homes along the River Raisin. As in Detroit, the settlers established narrow ribbon farms that stretched into the woods from the river, whose name means "grapes" in French. One of the first settlers was Francis Navarre, who built a log cabin in 1780. Other early families included the Latours, Labadies and LaSalles. Monroe County was the scene of bloody action during the War of 1812, when Indians killed a

The boyhood home of Thomas Edison in Port Huron in the early 1900s, long after he lived there.

Gen. George Custer once lived in Monroe.

Michigan by the numbers

TEN MOST POPULOUS CITIES
Detroit
Grand Rapids
Warren
Flint
Lansing
Sterling Heights
Ann Arbor
Livonia
Dearborn
Westland

Gross state product (1997): $272.6 billion

Media household income (1996): $39,225

Personal income per capita (1998): $25,857

Percent of people in poverty (1998): 11.2%

Motto:
Si Quaeris Peninsulam Amoenam, Circumspice (If you seek a pleasant peninsula, look about you).

large number of captive Americans in what has come to be known as the River Raisin Massacre. The county was established in 1817, and Americans began moving in. A land office opened in 1823. By 1847, I.E. Ilgenfritz emigrated from Pennsylvania and began planting trees in the rich, loamy soil, and that marked the beginnings of Monroe County's nursery industry. The county's most famous resident is Gen. George Custer, an Ohio native who attended the Stebbins Academy in Monroe and married a Monroe woman, Elizabeth Bacon, in 1864. A classic statue of Custer on horseback stands in downtown Monroe. The city is the home of the order of nuns known as Sisters, Servants of the Immaculate Heart of Mary, who have taught several generations of Catholic Detroiters. The county is also the home of the Fermi nuclear power plant and La-Z-Boy Inc., the furniture maker known for its recliners.

ALAN R. KAMUDA/Detroit Free Press

The cooling towers of the Fermi plant near Monroe.

Michigan

Metro Detroit's population is about half of Michigan's. The state is second-largest by land east of the Mississippi (Georgia is first). Michigan became a state in 1837.

Name: From the Indian word *Michigama*, meaning great or large lake.
Area: 56,809 square miles of land.
Water: 10,083 inland lakes of more than 5 acres; 1,305 square miles of inland water; 38,575 square miles of Great Lakes water area; 3,288 miles of Great Lakes shoreline.
Rank: Combined water and land area makes Michigan the 10th-largest state.
Population (2000): 9,938,444.
Elevation: Highest: Mt. Arvon in Baraga County, 1,981 feet above sea level; lowest: along Lake Erie shoreline, 572 feet above sea level.

Nicknames: The Wolverine State; the Great Lake State.
Flower: Apple blossom.
Bird: Robin.
Tree: White Pine.
Stone: Petoskey stone.
Gem: Chlorastrolite.
Fish: Brook trout.
Reptile: Painted turtle.
Game mammal: White-tailed deer.
Wildflower: Dwarf lake Iris.

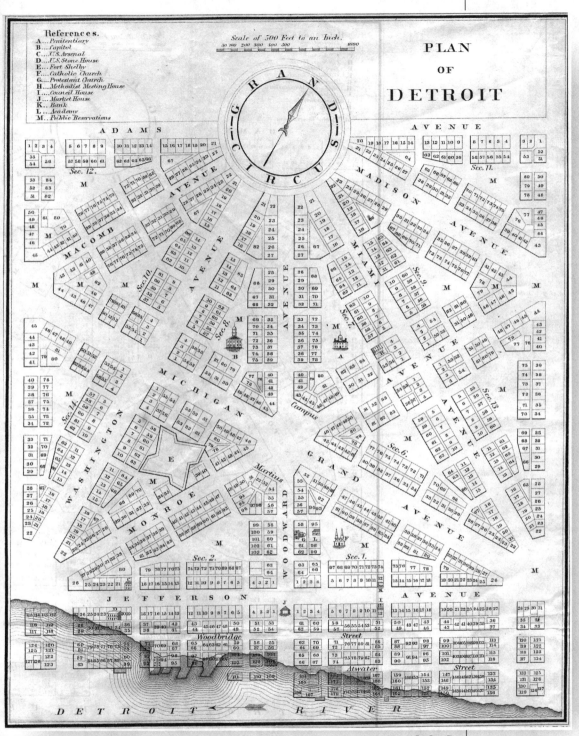

Judge Augustus Woodward's plan for Detroit from about 1820. He wanted to model the city after the new national capital, Washington, D.C.

The Detroit Almanac

11. CUL

"Got the rock from Detroit, the soul from Motown!"

— **Kid Rock**, *from his song "American Bad Ass"*

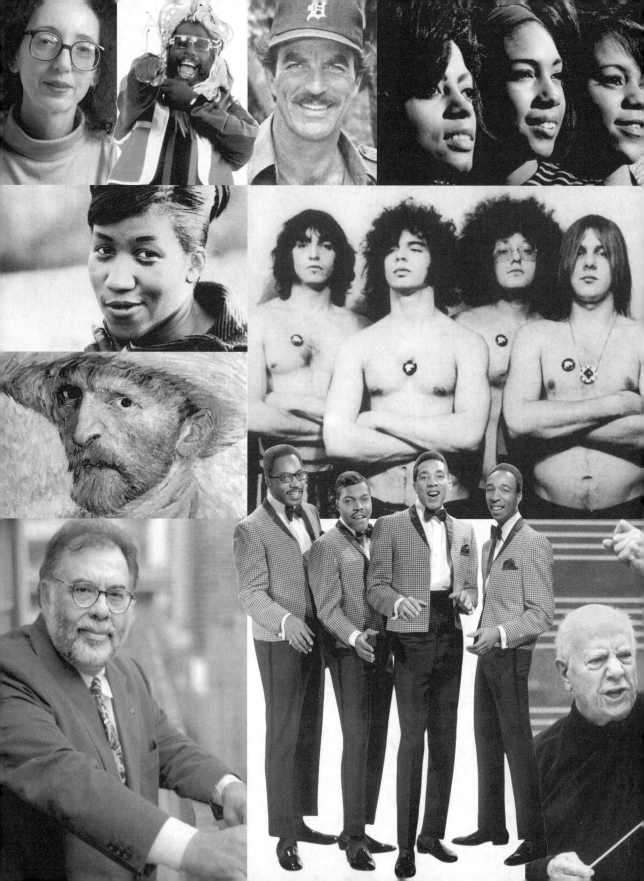

We got yer Kul-cher!

Nurtured by dynamic museums, libraries, clubs and churches, Detroiters have become some of America's most celebrated musicians, performers and writers. The city itself has served as the subject of countless films, books and songs.

Find out what all these entertainers and personalities added to the mix in the following hundred pages or so...

Literary
Detroit

Few American cities offer authors the diverse subject matter of Detroit. The dynamics of the automobile industry, the lives of laborers, the victims of bigotry, the dreams and drifters of society — we've got 'em in real life and writers have them in poetry, plays and prose.

Notable Detroit fiction writers

Free Press file photo

The prolific Joyce Carol Oates.

Joyce Carol Oates

Oates is perhaps the most prestigious writer to come out of Detroit; she won the National Book Award at age 31 with the novel "them" (1969), a story of generations of a Detroit family trapped in poverty. Born June 16, 1938, in Lockport, N.Y., Oates married and moved to Detroit in 1962.

She lived in the area until 1978, teaching English at the University of Detroit (1962-67) and at the University of Windsor (1968-78). Oates produced up to three books a year during this time, becoming one of the most respected writers in the United States. She joined the faculty of Princeton University in 1978. She has been a Pulitzer Prize finalist and won dozens of other awards.

Among her most praised work are "Black Water" (1992) and "Because It Is Bitter, and Because It Is My Heart" (1990). She has writ-

ten multiple novels, plays, short stories, poems and nonfiction. She also is the editor of the literary magazine Ontario Review.

She once wrote: "Detroit, my 'great' subject made me the person I am, consequently the writer I am — for better or worse."

Donald Goines

Born Dec. 15, 1937, in Detroit, Goines was an unlikely literary figure. While in the Air Force during the Korean War, he became addicted to heroin. For more than a decade he supported his drug habit as a criminal. He served seven prison terms for robbery, pimping and other crimes. While incarcerated at the state prison at Jackson, he wrote a harrowing novel about life on the street, "Whoreson," which a publisher bought. Released from jail in 1970, he wrote up to eight books a year, most of them while on heroin. Goines and his longtime companion were murdered, execution style, in their Highland Park home on Oct. 21, 1974, a gruesome case of life imitating art. He was at his typewriter, writing his 17th novel.

Goines' books were graphic, desolate and detailed. He told grim stories of pimps, prostitutes and criminals, all with tragic and bloody endings. His books include "Dopefiend" (1971), "Daddy Cool" (1974) and "Black Gangster" (1972.) Ironically, his death cemented his popularity with fans of his genre, even into the 1990s.

Harriette Simpson Arnow

Born July 7, 1908, in Wayne County, Ky., she moved to Detroit as an adult, then lived the rest of her life in Ann Arbor. Arnow wrote what she witnessed around her — the loss of rural life in industrial America, and the crush-

SUSAN TUSA/Detroit Free Press

Elmore Leonard in 1997.

Loren D. Estleman

He created hard-boiled Detroit private-eye Amos Walker, star of more than a dozen mysteries. Born Sept. 15, 1952, in Ann Arbor, Estleman began his career as a newspaper reporter. He covered the crime beat for various suburban newspapers. Yet he is known for setting his crime novels in Detroit's inner city, which he writes about with gritty authenticity. Praised for his poetic, clear style and tough, engaging characters, Estleman's books also include historical westerns and other novels: "Downriver" (1988), "City of Widows" (1994), "Edsel" (1995), "Billy Gashade: An American Epic" (1997), "Jitterbug" (1998) and "Journey of the Dead" (1998). He lives in Whitmore Lake, north of Ann Arbor.

ing of southern migrants' dreams in the cold-hearted big city.

Although Arnow wrote five novels, including "Hunter's Horn" (1949), her most notable was "The Dollmaker" (1954), a runner-up for the National Book Award that year. It is a wrenching portrayal of a Kentucky family's migration to Detroit during World War II, as seen through the eyes of Gertie Nevels, a doll-maker who must sacrifice her art to help her family survive. Critics called the novel so significant that Arnow earned a permanent place among American literary figures. Arnow died in Michigan on March 21, 1986.

Elmore Leonard

Born Oct. 11, 1925, in New Orleans, La., Leonard grew up in Detroit. The former advertising copywriter began writing fiction in 1951. He also wrote industrial films and educational films for Encyclopaedia Britannica. His first novel, a western, was "The Bounty Hunters" (1953). The Birmingham author has since written dozens of novels and screenplays, switching gears to write crime novels in the mid-1960s, including "Fifty Two Pickup" (1974) "Glitz" (1985), "Freaky Deaky" (1988) and "Get Shorty" (1990). In 1992, Leonard won the Grand Master Award from the Mystery Writers of America. Several of his books have been made into films, most notably "Pulp Fiction" from the novel "Rum Punch" (1992).

Yet Leonard wrote his first two dozen novels with only moderate success; it was in 1983 that critics began heaping praise on him.

Known for his wise-cracking, low-life protagonists, pitch-perfect dialogue and taut climaxes, Leonard's books also are noted for their casual violence. Many of his novels are set in Detroit or feature the city's seamy side.

Marge Piercy

Born March 31, 1936, this white feminist poet and novelist grew up poor in a mostly black section of Detroit and was the first member of her family to go to college. This early experience influenced her view of the world and led her to despise racism and sexism. Born at Livernois and Grand River, Piercy attended Sherill grade school, Mackenzie High and the University of Michigan on a scholarship, graduating in 1957. Piercy, a writing teacher and professor, was an activist in the radical Students for a Democratic Society (1965-69). Although her first six novels were rejected, Piercy's "Going Down Fast" was published in 1969. Other notable writings include the novel "Small Changes" (1973) and "Three Women" (1999) and many books of poetry. Piercy has had a controversial career; some have criticized her shrill form and abrasive substance. Others defend her powerful writing, which leaps off the page in defense of the oppressed. Piercy has also delved into science fiction, writing of a utopian society in "Woman on the Edge of Time" (1976). She lives in Massachusetts.

Lilian Jackson Braun

This best-selling author of more than 20 mysteries has deep Detroit roots. Born in 1916

> William X. Kienzle has written more than 17 mysteries, all with a rich background of Detroit and its religious inner workings.

in Massachusetts, Braun spent most of her adult life in Detroit. She was a features editor at the Detroit Free Press for 30 years (1948-78). During that time she wrote her first novel, "The Cat Who Could Read Backwards" (1966), which featured the most unlikely sleuths — two Siamese cats. She wrote three sequels, but then stopped writing to focus on her career. After retirement, Braun moved to Caseville and Bad Axe in Michigan's Thumb, where she continued the "Cat Who" series, including well-known titles, "The Cat Who Saw Red" (1986), "The Cat Who Played Brahms" (1987) and "The Cat Who Blew the Whistle" (1995). Braun later moved to North Carolina.

All the "Cat Who" books feature reporter and amateur detective Jim Qwilleran and his two cats, Koko and Yum Yum.

William X. Kienzle

Born Sept. 11, 1928, in Detroit, Kienzle was a Roman Catholic priest for 20 years (1954-74) and editor of the Michigan Catholic newspaper before he left the priesthood and began a second career as a novelist. His first book, "The Rosary Murders" (1979), introduced Father Robert Koesler, a priest who has to solve a murder in his Detroit parish. The book was made into a 1987 movie starring Donald Sutherland.

Kienzle has written more than 17 mysteries since then, all with a rich background of Detroit and its quirky religious inner workings. Among Kienzle's other novels are "Death Wears a Red Hat (1980), "Body Count" (1992) and "Call No Man Father" (1995).

Thomas Lynch

Born Oct. 16, 1948, in Detroit, Lynch is both a writer and a funeral director in Milford. His

first book, "Skating With Heather Grace" (1986), passed mostly unnoticed, but his third book, "The Undertaking: Life Studies from the Dismal Trade" (1997), garnered Lynch national attention. The book was runner-up for the National Book Award and propelled him into the company of other top American poets. He followed it with "Still Life in Milford" (1998), which was also well-received. Lynch uses his experience as an undertaker as inspiration for his poetry; it elegantly transforms both small moments and death into life-affirming events. Lynch also writes about Ireland, where he lives part-time after inheriting a family cottage. His work has been called eloquent and lovely.

Free Press file photo
Charles Baxter at his Ann Arbor home.

Charles Baxter

Baxter is director of the creative writing program at the University of Michigan in Ann Arbor. He is known for his novels, criticism and poetry, but mostly for his spectacular short stories. Born May 13, 1947, in Minneapolis, he started his career as a high school teacher in Pinconning, then taught at Wayne State University before joining the faculty at U-M. His first collection of short stories, "Harmony of the World" (1984), drew praise; his second, "Through the Safety Net" (1985), brought him more. His first novel challenged convention — "First Light" (1987) was constructed in reverse chronological order, following an adult brother and sister back into childhood. In 2000, he published "The Feast of Love" to acclaim. He weaves a Midwestern sensibility into all his writing. His characters are "middle-class in the middle of the nation," wrote one critic. He has won many literary prizes, including the O. Henry Prize in 1995.

Judith Guest

This former teacher and newspaper reporter hit it big with her first novel, "Ordinary People," in 1976. Born March 29, 1936, in Detroit, Guest lived and worked for many

Thomas Lynch at his northern Michigan home in 2000.
SUSAN TUSA/Detroit Free Press

years as a teacher in Birmingham, Troy and Royal Oak before moving to Minnesota. She began writing novels at age 35 and sent the manuscript of "Ordinary People" without an agent to a New York publisher. Amazingly, it was purchased, the first unsolicited manuscript the publisher had accepted in 26 years. "Ordinary People," about the disintegration of a family and a teen boy after the death of his brother, was a best-seller and made into an Oscar-winning film in 1980. Guest set the book in Illinois. She told an interviewer later that her Bloomfield Hills hometown was so familiar "I was scared to write about it." Other novels include "Seventh Heaven" (1982) and "Errands" (1997).

Christopher Paul Curtis

A Flint native, Windsor resident and former autoworker, Curtis won the John Newberry Medal and the Coretta Scott King Award in 2000 for his children's book, "Bud, Not Buddy." The Newberry Medal, awarded since 1922, goes to the most distinguished U.S. children's book. The King honor, given since 1970, recognizes authors and illustrators of African-American descent whose books promote an understanding of "the American dream." He was the first author to win both prizes for one book. Curtis, who was 43 when he won the prizes, did not start writing until about 1993. "Bud, Not Buddy" tells the story of a boy who sets off for Grand Rapids to look for his father, using clues left by his dead mother.

Terry McMillan

Her third novel, "Waiting to Exhale" (1992) was a phenomenal success that ushered in a new genre of contemporary black fiction and opened the door for several other black writers. In "Exhale," the Port Huron native wrote about the social lives of four girlfriends.

Terry McMillan in 1996.

The book alerted publishers to a greatly untapped audience made up mostly of black women. McMillan's work and that of other authors who followed in her footsteps also spawned a boom in black reading clubs throughout America. "Exhale" was eventually made into a hit movie, as was her fourth book, "How Stella Got Her Groove Back" (1995).

SUSAN TUSA/Detroit Free Press
Rosalyn McMillan in 1996.

Critics say McMillan's best work so far is her second novel, "Disappearing Acts" (1989), a drama centered around the love lives of a professional woman and her working-class, alcoholic and abusive boyfriend. Her first book, "Mama" (1987), was also highly praised, though McMillan had to do all the promotional work for the book.

McMillan, born Oct. 18, 1951, grew up in Port Huron. As a teen, she got her first job — which she believes was an omen — shelving books at the downtown St. Clair County Library, where she developed a love of reading.

She earned a bachelor's in journalism from the University of California at Berkley, where she began writing. She further developed her talent when she became part of a writers guild in Harlem. She now lives in California.

Rosalyn McMillan

She's the younger sister of Terry McMillan, but took great pains to launch her writing career on her own because she didn't want to be accused of gaining fame off her sister's name. Her first novel, "Knowing" (1996), is about a frustrated female autoworker who quits her good-paying, but boring job to pursue her dreams. The story resembles McMillan's own life except that auto accident-injuries forced her to retire from her job as a sewing machine operator at Ford Motor Co. That's when she began writing. She attended workshops and seminars and learned about how to get a book published by doing research at the public library in Southfield, where she lived until recently. Her second novel, "One Better" (1997), is based on the lives of two girlfriends and their struggles to raise their daughters. In "Blue Collar Blues" (1998), she returned to the auto factory for a story about the struggle for power and quest for love. "The Flip Side of Sin" was released in July 2000.

Jeffrey Eugenides

Eugenides has used Detroit and Grosse Pointe for the settings of novels "Middlesex" (2002) and "Virgin Suicides" (1993). Eugenides grew up on Middlesex in Grosse Pointe Park. He studied Latin at University Liggett School in Grosse Pointe Woods starting in seventh grade, and Brown University, where he acted in a play with John F. Kennedy Jr. Eugenides and his family have lived in Berlin for several years, but planned to move back to the U.S. in 2003.

Notable poets

Philip Levine

Though Levine left his native Detroit 40 years ago, his economical yet emotional poetry continues to pulsate with Motor City blood. His themes and subjects have been wide-ranging, but he is most known as a voice for the voiceless: the assembly line work-

ers, the beer-and-a-shot drinkers, the mid-century American dreamers. It almost goes without saying that Levine's character-driven portraits bestow warm dignity on their working-class protagonists; some believe he pulls the trick as well as anyone writing. A grad of what's now Wayne State University and a professor for many years following in Fresno, Calif., Levine is the author of 16 books of poetry, including the Pulitzer Prize-winning "The Simple Truth" and 1991 National Book Award-winning "What Work Is."

Alice Fulton

This poet is a professor of English at the University of Michigan. Born Jan. 25, 1952, in Troy, N.Y., Fulton's first book, "Dance Script with Electric Ballerina" (1983), garnered national attention for its stylish and energetic poetry. In 1991, Fulton won a MacArthur Foundation "genius" grant; she used the money to support herself while she wrote uninterrupted.

Fulton's book "Feeling as a Foreign Language: The Good Strangeness of Poetry" (1999) revealed her approach to poetry. She called most of modern poetry lightweight "Karaoke poetics." Critics called her book of essays "intriguing" despite "a tendency to trendy subversiveness." Fulton also gained notice for her poetry in "Sensual Math" (1995) and "Powers of Congress" (1990.) Fulton lives in Ypsilanti.

Edgar Guest

Perhaps the most prolific published poet of the century, Guest wrote at least a verse a day for more than 50 years in a Free Press column. At the height of his popularity he was syndicated in more than 300 newspapers. Guest's best-known poems celebrated home and family; among his most famous lines are "It takes a heap o' livin'/ In a house t' make it home." Literary critics never thought much of Guest's work, but the public adored it. "A Heap o' Livin'," one of his 25 published books, sold more than 500,000 copies. He was regularly featured on network radio and had an NBC-TV program in 1951. He died in 1959.

Dudley Randall

Detroit's poet laureate until his death at 86 in 2000, Randall also operated the Detroit-based Broadside Press, which published 90 titles of poetry from 1965 to 1977 and had 500,000 books in print. Broadside Press published poetry by a wide range of African-American poets including Nikki Giovanni, Haki Mahabuti and Amiri Baraka (formerly Leroi Jones).

After his poem "Detroit Renaissance" appeared in a magazine, Mayor Coleman Young named him poet laureate in 1981. The career crescendo marked 54 years of publishing poetry: His first poem was published in the Detroit Free Press when he was 13.

Said Giovanni about Randall: "He was the literary godfather to the black arts movement. He changed the literary landscape."

Excerpts from "Detroit Renaissance":
"Cities have died, have burned,
Yet phoenix-like returned
To soar up livelier, lovelier than before.
Detroit has felt the fire
Yet each time left the pyre
As if the flames had power to restore.
First, burn away the myths
Of what it was, and is —
A lovely, tree-laned town of peace and
     trade.
Hatred has festered here,
And bigotry and fear
Filled streets with strife and raised the
     barricade.
Wealth of a city lies,
Not in its factories,
Its marts and towers crowding to the sky,
But in its people who
Possess grace to imbue
Their lives with beauty, wisdom, charity.
The Indian, with his soul
Attuned to nature's role;
The sons and daughters of Cervantes'
     smile;

Poet Dudley Randall in his Detroit study in 1982.

Pan Tadeysz's children too
Entrust their fate to you;
Souls forged by Homer's, Dante's
Shakespeare's, Goethe's, Yeats's style.
Together we will build
A city that will yield
To all their hopes and dreams so long
    deferred.
New faces will appear
Too long neglected here;
New minds, new means will build a brave
    new world.

Theodore Roethke

"I learn by going where I have to go" is the climactic line of one of Roethke's most admired poems, "The Waking" (1953). His was a poetry of deceptively simple language but profound observation, a poetry that enchants the beginning student yet rewards the most sophisticated academic. The Saginaw-born Roethke was the son of a gardener; a clear love for nature is among his work's most cherished qualities. Roethke received bachelor's and master's degrees from the University of Michigan and later taught at Michigan State University, which he left after suffering the first of several mental breakdowns. He was a much-loved and influential teacher. Roethke had the good and rare fortune to have his genius recognized during his life, winning a Pulitzer Prize in 1954 and a National Book Award in 1959, among many other prizes. A second NBA was awarded to him posthumously in 1965. He continues to have many fans, who have migrated to the Web, setting up dozens of pages in his honor.

Robert Hayden

Born Asa Bundy Sheffey, Hayden wrote spare, incantatory poetry whose genius was not widely recognized until late in his life. He grew up in a poor and turbulent foster home in Detroit and began to write poetry at 16. The quiet power of his mature poetry spoke of the African-American experience and was imbued with his Baha'i faith, but he was obscured

through the 1960s by more militant and less gifted poets. In 1976, he was appointed to the post that became the United States' poet laureate — the first black American so honored.

Playwrights
Ron Milner

Milner, a Detroiter, is one of the nation's leading writers of plays reflecting African-American life. In addition to writing and directing, he also leads workshops on playwriting, and he has taught theater courses at both Michigan State University and Wayne State University.

Milner was born May 29, 1938, and grew up on Hastings, the main street of black Detroit.

He became interested in writing after receiving "The Adventures of Tom Sawyer" and "The Adventures of Huckleberry Finn" in a charity gift box one Christmas.

Author Langston Hughes, who was living in Detroit in the 1960s, was an early fan of Milner's. Hughes helped Milner get a Rockefeller grant that helped take one of his first plays "Whose Got His Own" (1965), to New York. It was first produced at the Unstable Coffeehouse, a small cabaret-style club in Detroit that fostered such talents as Mary Lou Tomlin (later to be known as Lily).

Several other plays of Milner's plays have since been performed on Broadway.

His other plays include "M(ego) and the Green Ball of Freedom" (1971), "What the Wine Sellers Buy" (1973), the musical "Jazzset" (1980), the musical "Crack Steppin" (1981), "Roads of the Mountaintop" (1986) and "Checkmates" (1987). The Broadway production of "Checkmates" starred Denzel Washington, Ruby Dee and Paul Winfield. He also wrote the musical "Don't Get God Started" (1987). In 1980, theater critics declared it one of the year's 10 best new plays.

Milner's work appears in various anthologies, including "Best Short Stories by Negro Writers," edited by the renowned Langston Hughes (Little, Brown, 1967); "Black Short Story Anthology," edited by Woodie King Jr. (Columbia University Press, 1972); and "Black Poets and Prophets," edited by King and Earl Anthony, (New American Library, 1972).

Arthur Miller

His reputation would be secure if he had written only "Death of a Salesman," for which he won the Pulitzer Prize in 1949. The Brooklyn, N.Y., native graduated from the University of Michigan in 1938. He later helped his alma mater — which has offered a course in his work — by establishing the $1,000 Arthur Miller Award to aid student writers. He has won a Tony, an Emmy and been a Kennedy Center honoree.

Literary quotes

Detroit people — Polish mothers, Polish children, old men out of work, middle-aged men out of work, welfare slobs, the sick, the dying, the prematurely gray and the prematurely wasted, all of them sitting staring at one another with gaunt, suspicious eyes.

— **Joyce Carol Oates**, "them"

Suddenly Tank changed his style. Furious at himself for letting the young boy last so long, Tank took two more blows to the head as he waited for his opportunity. Finally he caught Samson's arm, and holding it by the wrist, whirled around until his back was against Samson's chest. He held the arm out straight and turned it over so that the palm faced him. Using his forearm as a block, Tank broke Samson's arm quickly and expertly.

The scream that burst from Samson was terrifying. In anguish, the horrified man glanced down and saw the white bone protruding through the skin.

— **Donald Goines**, "Eldorado Red."

Mrs. Anderson, listening, nodded as over a page in a book. "That interests Homer a lot. He's working on his Ph.D. thesis in sociology, you know: The Patterns of Racial and Religious Prejudice and Persecution in Industrial Detroit." Gertie blinked, and Mrs. Anderson went on more rapidly. "That," and she nodded toward Mrs. Daly coming out the door, "interests him a lot. Almost nothing has been written about the hatred of the foreigner for many of our native-born Americans whose religion and social customs are different from his own. He's always finding evidence of it; it's interesting."

"*Bein*' th' evidence ain't so interesten'," Gertie said . . .

— **Harriette Arnow**, "The Dollmaker"

He had to get up and say how he was glad to get out there and be back in the great open spaces and the real manufacturing center of this country, and when you said manufacturing center of this country what you meant was manufacturing center of the whole bloody world.

— **John Dos Passos**, "The Big Money," on Charley Anderson's arrival in Detroit

He had a wonderful job taking care of the Mayflower, the actual carved-in-stone name of the apartment building on Selden, in the heart of the Cass Corridor, where he could sit in his window and watch muggings in broad daylight and the whores go by and the people from Harlan County and East Tennessee on their way to the grocery store for some greens and collards.

— **Elmore (Dutch) Leonard**, "Unknown Man 89"

And Dean and I, ragged and dirty as if we had lived off locust, stumbled out of the bus in Detroit. We decided to stay up in all-night movies on Skid Row. It was too cold for parks. Hassel had been there on Detroit Skid Row, he had dug every shooting gallery and all-night movie and every brawling bar with his dark eyes many a time. His ghost haunted us. We'd never find him on Times Square again. We thought maybe by accident old Dean Moriarty was here too — but he was not. For thirty-five cents each, we went into the beat-up old movie and sat down in the balcony till morning, when we were shooed downstairs. The people who were in that all-night movie were the end. Beat Negroes who'd come up from Alabama to work in car factories on a rumor; old white bums; young long-haired hipsters who'd reached the end of the road and were drinking wine; whores, ordinary couples and housewives with nothing to do, nowhere to go, nobody to believe in. If you sifted all Detroit in a wire basket the beaten soild core of dregs couldn't be better gathered.

— **Jack Kerouac**, "On the Road"

"Come up to Detroit and see how we make things hum! Come sit with us and hear us tell Congress where it gets off. Work! That's the caper! I tell you," with a grotesque, evangelical sonorousness, "I tell you, Dodsworth, to me, work is religion. 'Turn not thy hand from the plow.' Do big things! Think of it; by making autos we're enabling half the civilized world to run into town from their pigstys and see the movies, and the other half to get out of town and give Nature the once-over. Twenty million cars in America! And in twenty more years we'll have the bloomin' Tibetans and Abyssinians riding on cement roads in U.A.C. cars! Talk about Napoleon! Talk about Shakespeare! Why, we're pulling off the greatest miracle since the Lord created the world!"

— **Sinclair Lewis**, "Dodsworth"
(The head of a Detroit car company visits Sam Dodsworth in Zenith, Minnesota, to buy his Revelation Automobile Company.)

I thought Detroit was dry said my mother shyly. Did you said my father with a rye smile.

— **Ring Lardner**, "The Young Immigrants"

"Well, he's no use to us if Detroit is his idea of a small town … ''
— **F. Scott Fitzgerald**, "The Great Gatsby"

Perhaps it was because the city lived by automobiles, which became symbols of power, but for whatever reason, a Detroiter behind the wheel seemed changed into a Frankestein.
— **Arthur Hailey**, "Wheels"

Henry Ford had ideas about other things than production.

He was the largest automobile manufacturer in the world; he paid high wages; maybe if the steady workers thought they were getting a cut (a very small cut) in the profits, it would give trained men an inducement to stick to their jobs, well-paid workers might save enough money to buy a tin lizzie; the first day Ford's announced that clean properly married American workers who wanted jobs had a chance to make five bucks a day of course it turned out that there were strings to it; (always there were strings to it) . . .
— **John Dos Passos**, "U.S.A."

Great nonfiction books about Detroit

A dozen books we found most helpful in compiling this almanac.

➤ **"The City of Detroit, Michigan, 1701-1922,"** by Clarence Burton, editor (S.J. Clarke Publishing Co., 1922). Five volumes. This is the masterwork by the self-made historian and namesake of the Detroit Public Library's excellent local history collection.

➤ **"History of Detroit and Wayne County and Early Michigan: A Chronological Cyclopedia of the Past and Present,"** by Silas Farmer (Republished by Gale Research Co., 1969). Farmer, who was born in Detroit in 1839, was a map maker and historian who published this 1,028-page "cyclopedia" three times from 1884 to 1890.

➤ **"The Origins of the Urban Crisis: Race and Inequality in Postwar Detroit,"** by Thomas Sugrue (Princeton University Press, 1996). Sugrue, a Detroit-born history professor at the University of Pennsylvania, won numerous awards and sold lots of books nationally for his multilevel explanation of Detroit's industrial decline since World War II.

➤ **"The Changing Face of Inequality: Urbanization, Industrial Development, and Immigrants in Detroit, 1880-1920,"** by Olivier Zunz (The University of Chicago Press, 1982). A geographical and historical tour de force packed with data, charts and ideas about Detroit's era of hyper growth.

➤ **"Working Detroit: The Making of a Union Town,"** by Steve Babson (Adama Books, 1984). Combines excellent photos, graphics and text to tell the long and colorful story of Detroit's unionization struggle. It's from a Wayne State University professor who has written extensively on labor issues.

➤ **"Before the Ghetto: Black Detroit in the 19th Century,"** by David Katzman (University of Illinois Press, 1973). The percentage of Detroit's black population shrunk in the latter years of the pre-auto age, but those roots, which Katzman explores in lively detail, are even more important as the city enters the 21st Century as a black metropolis.

➤ **"Detroit Divided,"** by Reynolds Farley, Sheldon Danzinger and Harry Holzer (Russell Sage Foundation, New York, 2000). Following in the tradition of Sugrue's "Urban Crisis" and "Race, Class and Uneven Development," "Detroit Divided" greatly helps to answer the question of what happened to Detroit during the last 50 years.

➤ **"Detroit Perspectives: Crossroads and Turning Points,"** edited by Wilma Wood Henrickson (Wayne State University Press, 1991). This collection of essays and articles from scholars, journalists, participants in the building of Detroit and others offers historical analysis and insight into the city from its founding through the 1980s.

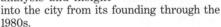

➤ **"The Public Image of Henry Ford,"** by David Lewis (Wayne State University Press, 1976). One of the most readable books on the first Ford, focusing on his treatment by and manipulation of the media.

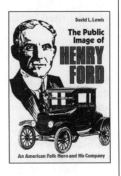

If you sifted all Detroit in a wire basket the beaten soild core of dregs couldn't be better gathered.

— **Jack Kerouac**, "On the Road"

➤ **"Life for Us is What We Make It: Building Black Community in Detroit, 1915-1945,"** by Richard W. Thomas (Indiana University Press, 1992). A history of black Detroiters when they were a distinct minority. It picks up about where "Before the Ghetto" leaves off.

➤ **"Michigan, a History of the Wolverine State"** by Willis F. Dunbar and George S. May (W.B. Eerdmans Publishing, Grand Rapids, 1995). An examination of Michigan from pre-Columbian days to the present.

➤ **"All Our Yesterdays, a Brief History of Detroit,"** by Frank B. Woodford and Arthur M. Woodford (Wayne State University Press, 1969). Very readable local history by a father and son team. The younger Woodford is now head of the St. Clair Shores library.

Other notable books

Epic

➤ **"American Odyssey: A History of a Great City,"** by Robert Conot (Wayne State University Press, 1986). The story of Detroit's industrialization told through people and events such as immigrants, Henry Ford, the Depression, the 1967 riot and Mayor Jerome Cavanagh.

The '67 riot

➤ **"The Algiers Motel Incident,"** by John Hersey (Republished by Johns Hopkins University Press, 1998). Originally published in 1968, "Algiers" is a circuitous but riveting account of the execution-style slaying of three young black men by white authorities at the height of the 1967 riot. Three Detroit police officers stood trial in the deaths but were not convicted. Hersey, also the author of the acclaimed "Hiroshima," wrote about the victims: "They were executed for being considered punks, for making out with white girls . . . for running riot — for being, after all and all, young black men and part of the black rage of the time."

➤ **"Violence in the Model City: The Cavanagh Administration, Race Relations, and the Detroit Riot of 1967,"** by Sidney Fine (University of Michigan Press, 1989). Fine, a popular U-M history professor, has written the most comprehensive look at the most cataclysmic week in Detroit's history, focusing on the sad irony of how then-Mayor Jerome Cavanagh was a true progressive when it came to civil rights and had tried to build a model city despite Detroit's bitter legacy of racial conflict. Fine, who was born in 1920, has written extensively on Detroit-area issues and figures, and his other books are highly recommended, too.

Other Fine stuff

➤ **"Frank Murphy,"** by Sidney Fine (University of Michigan Press, 1975-84). A three-volume biography of the man who was a Recorder's Court judge, Detroit mayor, Michigan governor, United States attorney general and U.S. Supreme Court justice. Of greatest interest for local history buffs is Volume I, "The Detroit Years."

➤ **"Sit-down: The General Motors Strike of 1936-37,"** by Sidney Fine (University of Michigan Press, 1969). The definitive history of the Flint sit-down, which launched the UAW and touched off Detroit's turbulent spring of 1937, when workers took over auto plants, hotels and dime stores in a wave of mass union organizing.

Architecture

➤ **"The Buildings of Detroit, A History,"** by W. Hawkins Ferry (Wayne State University Press, 1968). This 479-page tome takes the reader on a tour — in words and hundreds of photos — of local structures from Indian mounds to glass-and-steel homes. "Buildings" offers a way to get a feel for how Detroiters lived and worked from the 1850s through 1950s.

➤ **"The Ambassador Bridge: A Monument to Progress,"** by Philip P. Mason (Wayne State University Press, 1987). Spanning the Detroit River took decades to accomplish; engineers finally did it in 1929. Mason, a Wayne State University history professor and archivist, tells the tale of the builders, the workers and the cities.

Counterculture

➤ **"Detroit: I Do Mind Dying: A Study in Urban Revolution,"** by Dan Georgakas and Marvin Surkin (St. Martin's Press, 1975). A brief history of radical Detroit after the 1967 riot, including the battle against STRESS, the rise of the League of Revolutionary Black Workers and the tale of Justin Ravitz, a Marxist on the Recorder's Court bench.

➤ **"Class, Race and Worker Insurgency: The League of Revolutionary Black Workers,"** by James Geschwender (Cambridge Uni-

"GUITAR ARMY," by John Sinclair (Douglas Book Corp., 1972). Hippie seer of Detroit and Ann Arbor in the 1960s and '70s, Sinclair and his collection of writings perfectly capture that era. The book is filled with photos, plus designs by graphic artist Gary Grimshaw.

versity Press, 1977). A sociologist's take on black radicals in Detroit's factories.

Labor

➤ **"Muddy Boots and Ragged Aprons: Images of Working-Class Detroit, 1900-1930,"** by Kevin Boyle and Victoria Getis (Wayne State University Press, 1997). The Detroit-born Boyle and his University of Michigan-educated wife assembled dozens of rare photographs and a compact text that tell an almost tangible story about the people who put the world on wheels during Detroit's go-go years. Boyle also is the author of **"The UAW and the Heyday of American Liberalism, 1945-1968"** (Cornell University Press, 1995), which dissects the postwar period, when the union's progressive policies came up against the country's growing obsession with satisfying the demands of the marketplace, no matter the cost.

➤ **"Maurice Sugar: Law, Labor and the Left in Detroit, 1912-1950,"** by Christopher Johnson (Wayne State University Press, 1988). A chronicle of the eventful life of Sugar, a lawyer born in the Upper Peninsula who became a leader on the left flank of Detroit's labor movement — the flank that lost out to Walter Reuther's faction after World War II. The author is a longtime Wayne State history professor.

➤ **"All-American Anarchist: Joseph A. Labadie and the Labor Movement,"** by Carlotta R. Anderson (Wayne State University Press, 1998). Labadie was one of the best-known members of Detroit's pre-UAW union movement, and this biography, by Labadie's granddaughter, provides a window into working-class Detroit before and after the turn of the last century. The book drew on material in the University of Michigan's excellent Labadie Collection, which is named for the subject.

➤ **"The Most Dangerous Man in Detroit: Walter Reuther and the Fate of American Labor,"** by Nelson Lichtenstein (BasicBooks, 1995). A professor of history at the University of Virginia, Lichtenstein puts Reuther in the big picture of American labor, society and politics, and he casts a critical eye on the man, his policies and actions.

Black Detroit

➤ **"Dancing in the Street: Motown and the Cultural Politics of Detroit,"** by Suzanne E. Smith (Harvard University Press, 1999). Smith, a native Detroiter who teaches at

George Mason University in Virginia, received critical raves from Los Angeles to London for her examination of why one of America's most celebrated examples of black success rose out of Detroit neighborhoods at the precise moment that the civil rights revolution was breaking out across the country.

➤ **"Untold Tales, Unsung Heroes: An Oral History of Detroit's African American Community, 1918-1967"** by Elaine Latzman Moon (Wayne State University Press, 1994). Stories about living in Detroit before and after World War II, as told by dozens of Detroiters, most of whom are not public figures.

➤ **"Internal Combustion: The Races in Detroit, 1915-1926,"** by David Allan Levine (Greenwood Press, Westport, Conn., 1976). This book makes clear that the famous Ossian Sweet racial violence case is only the most famous incident of that turbulent time.

➤ **"Detroit: City of Race and Class Violence,"** by B.J. Widick (Wayne State University Press, 1989). An updated version of Widick's 1972 book, "Detroit" is unsparing in its examination of why the city produced so much mayhem over the decades. Widick's conclusions raise questions about the metro area's corporate establishment.

➤ **"Black Detroit and the Rise of the UAW,"** by August Meier and Elliott Rudwick (Oxford University Press, 1979). In general, the UAW has been a progressive force in civil rights. But in the beginning, many prominent black Detroiters supported Henry Ford in his epic battle with the union, and once inside the UAW, black members had to fight racism, just like they did in the outside world. This book tells that complicated tale in a concise fashion.

➤ **"Paradise Valley Days: A Photo Album Poetry Book: Detroit's 1930s to 1950s,"** by the Detroit Black Writers Guild (published by the guild with a grant from the Michigan Council for Arts and Cultural Affairs, 1998). The photos alone are a treasure, but sprinkled among the photographs are poems, essays and articles about Paradise Valley, a section of Detroit's east side that literarily danced and rocked with music and excitement.

Q. Who is Detroit's most successful author?

A. Mitch Albom.

Albom's former teacher, Morrie Schwartz, inspired "Tuesdays with Morrie."

The Free Press sports columnist's book "Tuesdays with Morrie" has outsold every hardback novel and work of nonfiction except Margaret Mitchell's "Gone with the Wind," which sold 6 million copies through 1987.

The ABC adaptation of "Morrie" won a trio of Emmys in 2000, including outstanding TV movie.

The book is about weekly visits Albom made with terminally ill Morrie Schwartz, Albom's former college professor and mentor.

Mitch

"THIS IS DETROIT, 1701-2001," by Arthur M. Woodford (Wayne State University Press, 2001). An illustrated history of the city as it celebrated its 300th birthday. It covers everything from Antoine Cadillac to Coleman Young.

"DETROIT IN ITS WORLD SETTING," edited by David Lee Poremba (Wayne State University Press, 2001). A 399-page time line of Detroit's history that also provides a national and international context for local events. Assembled by the person who runs the Burton Historical Collection at the Detroit Public Library.

➤ **"Remembering Detroit's Old Westside: 1920 to 1950,"** by the Westsiders (Westsiders, Detroit, 1997). A pictorial history of black people's move to the city's west side from those who lived it. In addition to numerous photographs of the people, the churches, the schools and the clubs, the book contains several essays about life on the west side.

➤ **"Blacks in Detroit, 1736 to 1833: The Search for Freedom and Community and Its Implications for Educators,"** by Norman McRae (University of Michigan dissertation, 1982). McRae is retired director of social studies and fine arts for the Detroit Public Schools and the leading authority on black history in this region. He's also written textbooks on Michigan history at the elementary-school level.

Contemporary Detroit

➤ **"Devil's Night and Other True Tales of Detroit,"** by Ze'ev Chafets (Random House, 1990). Probably the most controversial book about Detroit in the last 20 years, "Devil's Night" wasn't so much about Devil's Night as it was an impressionistic account of an expatriate's extended visit to metro Detroit. Chafets, a successful Israeli author who grew up in Pontiac, displayed affection for his hometown but wrote honestly about the tribal rivalries he saw that reminded him of the warring factions of the Mideast.

➤ **"Detroit Lives,"** edited by Robert Mast (Temple University Press, 1994). More stories from Detroiters, though Mast's subjects are mostly activists.

➤ **"Detroit: Race, Class and Uneven Development,"** by Joe T. Darden, Richard Child Hill, June Thomas and Richard Thomas (Temple University Press, 1987). The authors, then associated with the Urban Affairs program at Michigan State University, use demographic data to flesh out developments such as the rise of black power in Detroit, the flight to the suburbs and the building of the Renaissance Center.

➤ **"Detroit Images: Photographs of the Renaissance City,"** edited by John J. Bukowczyk and Douglas Aikenhead with Peter Slavcheff (Wayne State University Press, 1989). An excellent photo book, "Images" documents the lives of Detroit people, places and things during the early 1980s, when the city's Rust Belt atmosphere stood in contrast to the Reagan-era prosperity supposedly breaking out across the country. Interesting commentary is provided by the two principal authors and poet Philip Levine.

Old Detroit

➤ **"Legends of Le Detroit,"** by Marie Caroline Watson Hamlin (Thorndike Nourse, 1884). In the 1870s and 1880s, Hamlin collected folk tales that had been told by Detroit's French by listening to the elderly descendants of those habitants. The result is authentic local fairy tales about *loup garoups* (werewolves); *nains rouges* (red dwarfs) and *feux follets* (wills-o'-the wisp).

➤ **"Reform in Detroit: Hazen Pingree and Urban Politics,"** by Melvin Holli (Oxford University Press, 1969). A biography of one of Detroit's most successful and colorful politicians that paints a vivid picture of the pre-auto city when Irish, Germans and Anglo-Saxons competed for power.

➤ **"Rumrunning and the Roaring Twenties: Prohibition on the Michigan-Ontario Waterway"** by Philip Mason (Wayne State University Press, 1995). A local historian's entertaining and authoritative look at what seems — from 70 years away — to be a ludicrous period in local history.

➤ **"Detroit's First American Decade,"** by F. Clever Bald (University of Michigan Press, 1948). A compelling look at the chaotic era when Detroit was under its third flag in 100 years.

➤ **"Pontiac and the Indian Uprising,"** by Howard Peckham (a 1947 book republished by Wayne State University Press in 1994). Considered the most authoritative account of the great pan-Indian uprising.

➤ **"The British Regime in Michigan and the Old Northwest,"** by Nelson Russell (Carleton College Press, 1939). Everything you need to know about the years Detroit was part of the British Empire.

➤ **"Gabriel Richard,"** by Frank Woodford and Albert Hyma (Wayne State University Press, 1958). Biography of the famous priest who served Detroit from 1798 to 1832.

➤ **"Out of Small Beginnings,"** by Richard Lee Waddell (Oakland County Bicentennial Commission). This is a tome on Oakland County's origins that begins in 1815 and ends in 1976.

➤ **"The Purple Gang: Organized Crime in Detroit, 1910-1945,"** by Paul R. Kavieff (Barricade Books, 2000). An engineer and historian, Kavieff devoted a decade to this informative labor of love about Detroit's rock-'em, sock-'em gangster era. It includes excellent crime scene photos.

Sports

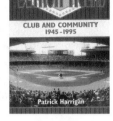

➤ **"The Detroit Tigers: Club and Community, 1945-1995,"** by Patrick Harrigan (University of Toronto Press, 1997). Named book of the year by the Society for American Baseball Research, "Club and Community" goes far beyond the usual sports fare, investigating the Tigers' modern owners, front office, quest for a new stadium and their relationship to the city around them. The author is a Detroit-born history professor at the University of Waterloo (Ontario, Canada).

➤ **"The Tigers of '68: Baseball's Last Real Champions,"** by George Cantor (Taylor, 1997). The 1968 Tigers were the last team to win the World Series the old-fashioned way, before the American and National leagues split into divisions. Cantor, a Detroit News writer who covered the '68 team for the Free Press, tells the story of the club, the players and the city.

➤ **"Paper Lion,"** by George Plimpton (Harper & Row, 1966). The skinny author from New York showed up at the Lions' camp during the team's "Fearsome Foursome" years and told them he wanted to play quarterback so he could write a book about it. The Lions agreed, and the result is a funny book.

➤ **"Century of Champions,"** by Nicholas J. Cotsonika, Gene Myers and the Free Press sports staff (Detroit Free Press, 1999). The definitive compilation of the 20th Century in sports, by the staff of the newspaper that covered each World Series and extra point.

➤ **"Turkey Stearnes and the Detroit Stars,"** by Richard Bak (Wayne State University Press, 1994). A detailed history of Detroit's Negro League team by one of the metro area's most prolific local authors.

Bak talk

Bak, of Dearborn, also has published these books of local interest:
"Michigan in the Civil War" (Arcadia, 2000).
"The Corner" (Triumph/Free Press, 1999).
"A Place for Summer" (Wayne State University Press, 1998).
"Detroit Red Wings" (Taylor, 1997).
"Joe Louis: The Great Black Hope" (Taylor, 1996).

"Ty Cobb: His Tumultuous Life and Times" (Taylor, 1994).
"Cobb Would Have Caught It" (Wayne State University Press, 1991).

The Ford family

➤ **"My Life and Work,"** by Henry Ford and Samuel Crowther (Doubleday, Page & Co., 1925). Ford's autobiography.

➤ **"The Legend of Henry Ford,"** Keith Sward (Atheneum, 1968). An attempt to demystify Henry I.

➤ **"The Fords of Dearborn, An Illustrated History,"** Ford D. Bryan (Harlo, 1989). Photos and anecdotes about several generations.

➤ **"Henry Ford: The Wayward Capitalist,"** Carol Gelderman (St. Martin's Press, 1981). Well-researched bio by a college professor.

➤ **"Ford: The Men and the Machine,"** Robert Lacey (Ballantyne Books, 1986). Titillating tales by the British author.

➤ **"The Fords: An American Epic,"** Peter Collier and David Horowitz (Summit, 1987). A sexy best-seller from the authors of "The Rockefellers" and "The Kennedys."

➤ **"Ford: The Times, the Man, the Company,"** Allan Nevins (Charles Scribners Sons, 1954). A three-volume look at Ford that stands the test of time.

➤ **"Henry Ford vs. Truman H. Newberry,"** Spencer Ervin, Richard D. Smith (1935). A focus on Ford's 1918 U.S. senate campaign.

➤ **"Henry: A Life of Henry Ford II,"** Walter Hayes (Grove Weidenfeld, 1990). Close-up view of Hank the Deuce from a former colleague.

The auto industry

➤ **"Taken for a Ride: How Daimler-Benz Drove off with Chrysler,"** by Bill Vlasic and Brad Stertz (W. Morrow, 2000). Hot off the press: How the Germans took over the United States' No. 3 automaker, by two Detroit News staffers.

➤ **"Chrysler: The Life and Times of an Automotive Genius,"** by Vincent Curcio (Oxford University Press, 2000). Biography of the auto pioneer.

➤ **"Irreconcilable Differences: Ross Perot versus General Motors,"** by Doron Levin (Little, Brown, 1989). The ex-Free Press colum-

"FRONTIER METROPOLIS: PICTURING EARLY DETROIT, 1701-1838," by Brian Leigh Dunnigan (Wayne State University Press, 2001). Dunnigan collected hundreds of maps, drawings and other images from archives in Europe and North America to tell a vivid story of Detroit before the age of photography. "Frontier" is one of the most distinctive, artistic and painstakingly researched books dealing with Detroit. At $125, it's also one of the most expensive.

nist's look into the ill-fated marriage of two opposite corporate cultures, GM and EDS.

➤ **"Behind the Wheel at Chrysler: The Iacocca Legacy,"** by Doron Levin (Harcourt Brace, 1995). Lido, the Japanese and Chrysler in the 1980s, by the Free Press columnist.

➤ **"A Most Unique Machine: The Michigan Origins of the American Automobile Industry,"** by George S. May (Eerdmans Publishing, 1975). A highly regarded view of the early years.

➤ **"My Years with General Motors,"** by Alfred Sloan (Doubleday, 1964). Wisdom from the man who reinvented big business.

➤ **"The Reckoning,"** by David Halberstam (Morrow, 1986). The bitter saga of Detroit and Japan.

➤ **"Taurus: The Making of the Car that Saved Ford,"** by Eric Taub (Dutton, 1991). Behind the scenes at Ford.

➤ **"The Whiz Kids: The Founding Fathers of American Business and the Legacy They Left Us,"** by John Byrne (Currency/Doubleday, 1993). The story of the best and the brightest and how they helped rescue Ford.

➤ **"Car: A Drama of the American Workplace,"** by Mary Walton (W.W. Norton, 1997). Crisply written, insightful and dirt-dishing on the Taurus launch.

➤ **"Chrome Colossus,"** by Ed Cray (McGraw-Hill, 1980). A history of General Motors.

➤ **"Boss Kettering,"** by Stuart Leslie (Columbia University Press, 1983). A biography of GM's famous research director.

➤ **"On A Clear Day You Can See General Motors,"** by J. Patrick Wright (Wright Enterprises, 1979). Maverick auto executive John DeLorean's scathing account of life at GM.

➤ **"Iacocca: An Autobiography,"** by Lee Iacocca (Bantam Books, 1984). Lido lets it all hang out (ego included) in one of the best-selling books of all time.

➤ **"Rude Awakening: The Rise, Fall and Struggle for the Recovery of General Motors,"** by Maryann Keller (Morrow, 1989). An ex-auto industry analyst questions GM's course.

➤ **"Collision Course: Inside the Battle for General Motors,"** by Micheline Maynard (Birch Lane Press, 1995). A veteran auto writer's examination of the Roger Smith-Jack Smith years at GM.

➤ **"The Dream Maker: William C. Durant, Founder of General Motors,"** by Bernard Weisberger (Little, Brown, 1979). The biography of the entrepreneur named Billy.

➤ **Two special references: These editions of the Michigan Quarterly Review, published at the University of Michigan, contain much information on Detroit.** Spring 1986 Issue. "Detroit: An American City." Combined Fall 1979 and Winter 1981 issue. "The Automobile and American Culture."

MICHIGAN HISTORICAL REVIEW

The MRH published a special issue on Detroit in spring 2001 that is a must for any serious student of Detroit history. The review carried seven long articles by scholars that discuss the books that have been written (and, in some cases, that should be written) about such topics as early Detroit and the city's founding, religion, industry, women, African-American culture and the urban crisis of the past 50 years. The issue also carries a huge bibliography. The MRH is available for $10 from Clarke Historical Library, Central Michigan University, Mt. Pleasant, MI 48859. It is also carried by libraries at local colleges and the main Detroit Public Library.

Novels set in Detroit

➤ **"Appointed: An American Novel,"** Walter Stowers and William Anderson, writing under the pseudonym Sanda, 1894, reprinted in 1977:

This story of the friendship between a rich young white man and a young black cabin attendant includes lynching and segregation, subject matter unusual for that time.

➤ **"Heart and Soul,"** Henrietta Dana Skinner, 1901:

French Detroiters, including Roderick Fremont, help a runaway slave flee to Canada in the 19th Century.

➤ **"The Homebuilders,"** Karl Edward Harriman, 1902:

Short stories that examine the lives of Poles in late 19th-Century Detroit.

➤ **"The Groper,"** Henry Aikman (Harold H. Armstrong), 1919:

A small-town man migrates to Detroit to find his fortune in the auto business, among other industries. University of Michigan-educated Armstrong, writing under the Aikman pseudonym, also published **"Zell"** (1921), another novel about a fortune-seeker that was praised by critics. Armstrong also wrote **"The Red Blood"** (1923), the story of an Ontario immigrant to Detroit who becomes mayor and fights streetcar moguls.

➤ **"Temper,"** Lawrence H. Conrad, 1924:

Conrad is a University of Michigan graduate who studied the auto industry. "Temper" is the story of an Italian American with big dreams who works in an auto plant and helps immigrants.

➤ **"Conveyor: A Novel,"** James Steele, 1935, reissued in 1976:

Steele is a pseudonym for Robert Cruden, a former auto factory mechanic who became a history professor. "Conveyor" takes place during the 1928 Al Smith-Herbert Hoover presidential campaign, when an autoworker protesting an assembly-line speedup is fired and blacklisted.

➤ **"The Flivver King: A Story of Ford-America,"** Upton Sinclair, 1937:

This attack on Henry Ford hardly received the praise that was accorded Sinclair's 1906 expose of the meat industry, "The Jungle." But the 155-page "Flivver" was widely read. The populist Sinclair follows Ford's life through a narrator named Abner, a Ford neighbor who watches as Ford ages from a tinkerer to industry titan to paranoid anti-Semite.

➤ **"F.O.B. Detroit,"** Wessel Smitter, 1938:

Holt Motor Co., where the motto is "Machinery — The New Messiah," speeds up production and a resulting accident costs a worker his legs. After recovering, the man goes to work in the factory's salvage department. Smitter, who attended Calvin College and the University of Michigan, received widespread praise for the book.

➤ **"The Underground Stream: A Historical Novel of a Moment in the American Winter,"** Albert Maltz, 1940:

Set during one weekend in 1936 during Detroit's great unionization movement, the critically praised "Stream" depicts organizer Princey Prince, who is murdered by a right-wing paramilitary organization. Maltz was an academic who spent time in Detroit during the 1930s.

➤ **"Willow Run,"** Glendon Swarthout, 1943:

Seven people working on one night shift in the mammoth bomber factory are the focus of the novel, which received mixed reviews.

➤ **"A Moth of Time,"** Nolan Miller, 1946:

Set along Trumbull Avenue before World War I, "Moth" received praise for the way it describes the downward spiral of a family and its neighborhood.

➤ **"Blue River,"** Mary Frances Doner, 1946:

The daughter of a showgirl marries a man who builds an auto empire and sleeps around on him. The title was a takeoff on the Rouge (Red) River.

➤ **"Uncle Bosko,"** Vern Sneider, 1951:

This short story is about a family reunion set in Hamtramck by the Pulitzer Prize-winning ("Teahouse of the August Moon") Monroe native. "Uncle Bosko" is included in a collection titled **"A Long Way Home."**

➤ **"The Dollmaker,"** Harriette Arnow, 1954:

Probably the most critically acclaimed novel set in Detroit, "The Dollmaker" finished second to William Faulkner's "The Fable" for the 1954 National Book Award, and it tied as the best novel of 1954 in the Saturday Review's nationwide poll of literary critics. The book went through 16 printings and was a best-seller for 31 weeks. Jane Fonda starred in a made-for-TV movie version in 1984.

A long and powerfully tragic portrayal of a Kentucky family's migration to Detroit during World War II, "The Dollmaker" portrays Detroit as an allegory for hell, with its fire-belching steel mills, roaring airplanes and stressed-out people.

Arnow lived for years in southeastern Michigan and died in a home near Ann Arbor at age 78 on March 21, 1986. She was buried near her birthplace in her beloved hills of Pulaski County, Ky. Her late husband, Harold Arnow, was a reporter for the Detroit Times.

➤ **"Black as Night,"** Daniel Nern, 1958:

A black family migrates from Atlanta to Detroit amid violence and desperation.

➤ **"The Detroiters,"** Harold Livingston, 1958:

A Detroit ad writer describes the Detroit advertising world.

➤ **"Where the Boys Are,"** Glendon Swarthout, 1960:

Yes, the song and movie that celebrate spring break on the beach were based on a novel about a University of Michigan student who travels to Florida and meets boys, becomes pregnant and quits school.

➤ **"Anna Teller,"** Ruth Seid, 1960:

A Jewish immigrant from Hungary survives World War II and arrives in Detroit with lots of cultural baggage.

➤ **"Fireball,"** Henry B. Hager, 1963:

Sex and corporate climbing inside Detroit's auto ad community are the subjects of this little-known work.

➤ **"The Hard Winners,"** John E. Quirk, 1965:

This novel chronicles the search for a new president of a Detroit auto firm.

> **"American Chrome,"** Edwin Gilbert, 1965:
The sometimes unethical relationship between auto companies and dealers is the unusual subject of Gilbert's novel.

> **"No Transfer,"** Stephen Walton, 1967:
A futuristic horror novel by a University of Michigan senior that expresses the alienation of the 1960s. The school, Modern University, has two facilities: a 50-story building and a football stadium. Sirens summon students to assemblies, at which they witness fellow students being guillotined. Received mixed reviews.

"The Betsy," Harold Robbins, 1971: Another look at the auto industry and the sex habits of its leaders that was turned into a movie filmed in Detroit.

Harold Robbins in 1982.

Associated Press

> **"them,"** Joyce Carol Oates, 1969:
The 508-page, critically acclaimed "them" depicts a nightmarish Detroit from the Great Depression to the 1967 riot, in which the Wendall family confronts violence, intolerance, poverty, racism and loneliness. Detroit, according to Oates, is "a kind of stretched-out hole with a horizon." She describes the "emptiness" of Grosse Pointe, its "lawns blemished by scraps of newspapers blown over from Detroit." Oates taught English at the University of Detroit from 1962 to 1967. During that time, she met the young woman whose story became that of Maureen Wendall of "them." Oates wrote that the stories of Maureen and her brother haunted her, "so I began to dream about them instead of about myself, dreaming and redreaming their lives."

> **"Waiting for the News,"** Leo Litwak, 1969:
A story of Detroit during the 1930s and 1940s that highlights labor violence and family revenge.

> **"The Weedkiller's Daughter,"** Harriette Arnow, 1970:
This tale of suburban angst is set in a fictional Detroit-area community called Eden Hills.

> **"Snakes: A Novel,"** Al Young, 1970:
His parents dead from a car wreck, a teenager named MC moves from Mississippi to live with his grandmother in Detroit, where he hopes to become a musician. Critics noted Young's use of lyrical street language.

> **"When the Fire Reaches Us,"** Barbara Wilson, 1970:
A story that describes a black Detroit neighborhood after the 1967 riot.

> **"Wheels,"** Arthur Hailey, 1971:
Readers nationwide loved this novel about Detroit and the auto industry, but critics were less enthusiastic. Hailey, the author of "Airport" and "Hotel," thrived on stereotypes: The black workers are angry; the bosses are better designers than lovers; the Polish assistant plant manager is a bigot. Helped by cooperative executives, Hailey spent months researching the industry. He reported how cars made on Mondays and Fridays can be shoddy because of absentee workers partying on their paychecks. Hailey portrays an Oakland County dealer as a chiseler who hustles customers, his bank and manufacturers with equal zeal. He calls Detroit drivers "near savage."

> **"Do With Me What You Will,"** Joyce Carol Oates, 1973:
Jack Morrissey is a radical lawyer in Detroit with a wife who was abused and a client who has the same type of marijuana trouble that got real-life John Sinclair a 9½- to 10-year sentence in 1969.

> **"Who is Angelina?"** Al Young, 1975:
A travelogue of Angelina's territorial and psychological journeys as she joins her father in Detroit. The New York Times said Young puts a new take on urban blues, race and the need for roots.

> **"The High Cost of Living,"** Marge Piercy, 1978:
Love among grad students at a Detroit college is depicted by the Detroit-born and U-M-educated Piercy.

> **"The Hard Rain,** Dimitia Smith, 1980:
A 1960s radical autoworker flees the law after he accidentally kills a plant guard in a bombing incident.

➤ **"Braided Lives,"** Marge Piercy, 1982:
This romantic drama centers on a lesbian studying at U-M.

➤ **"Second Heaven,"** Judith Guest, 1982:
Detroit-born and University of Michigan-educated Guest set her second novel, after "Ordinary People," in a rich Detroit suburb. The son of a religious fanatic runs away and ends up with a disturbed divorced woman.

➤ **"Knowing,"** Rosalyn McMillan, 1996:
This former factory worker writes a story that is partially her own true story. The heroine quits a good-paying auto-factory job to pursue her dreams, much to her husband's chagrin. He thinks she should be satisfied with the smartly decorated Palmer Woods home the factory has allowed them to have. Modern-day Detroit scenes are scattered throughout this drama, including dining at the Whitney and the Golden Mushroom and relatives who live in downtown Detroit lofts. Chapters are named after Motown songs. McMillan is a Port Huron native and Southfield resident who also is the sister of best-selling author Terry McMillan. She follows her Detroit factory connections with her book, **"Blue Collar Blues."**

➤ **"Virgin Suicides,"** Jeffrey Eugenides, 1993:
In "Suicides," Grosse Pointe's annual fish-fly deathfest is the leading metaphor in a poetic mystery without a solution. Its primary subject — the suicides of the five Lisbon sisters — hardly seems the stuff of megaplex entertainment. But the critically acclaimed book was made into a well-received movie, directed by Sophia Coppola, that was released in 2000.

➤ **"Middlesex,"** Jeffrey Eugenides, 2002:
Highly acclaimed "Middlesex" tells the story of three generations of the Stephanides family, from Mt. Olympus, Greece, to Detroit and then to Grosse Pointe. Central to the saga is Calliope, a pseudohermaphrodite (began life as a girl, at puberty, became a boy).

SOURCES: FREE PRESS; "THE IMAGE OF DETROIT IN TWENTIETH CENTURY LITERATURE," LAURENCE GOLDSTEIN, MICHIGAN QUARTERLY REVIEW, SPRING 1986; "MICHIGAN IN LITERATURE," CLARENCE ANDREWS; "LITERARY MICHIGAN," THE MICHIGAN COUNCIL FOR THE HUMANITIES.

Moving pictures

For a century, going to the movies has been a major Detroit pastime. Grab a seat up front:

First runs

➤ **First movie shown**: "The Eidoloscope," at the Wonderland Theater, 1895.
➤ **First extended run**: Summer of 1896, at the Detroit Opera House. The films were a bicycle parade, a wrestling match and a Mexico City bullfight.
➤ **First motion picture theater**: The 200-seat Casino, on Monroe, opened by John Kunsky.
➤ **Movie palaces:** By World War II, huge, opulent theaters drew large crowds downtown and in the New Center in such favorite theaters as the Michigan, Fox, State, Fisher and United Artists. First-run movies did not open outside of downtown until the 1960s.

Main attractions

➤ **Classics:** In 1950, Detroit, Hamtramck and Highland Park had 131 movie theaters. There were 21 theaters in the suburbs. The neighborhood theaters, now closed or demolished, carried catchy names: Admiral, Avalon, Mars, Punch and Judy, Ramona, Vogue, Booker T., Carver and Cinderella.
➤ **Now playing:** In 2001, there was one first-run theater remaining in Detroit with four screens. In the suburbs, there was a total of more than 400 screens.

Of the more than 40 movie theaters in metro Detroit, six are considered megaplexes with 16 or more screens, and that multi-screen venue is clearly the trend.

Michigan's first 30-screen cinema — the AMC Forum 30 at Mound Road and M-59 in Sterling Heights — opened in November 1999. With 6,026 seats — including two 700-seat

Making movies

From the 1930s to about the 1970s, Detroit was the nation's leading maker of commercial films and slides. Companies such as Jam Handy, Metropolitan Motion Picture Co. and Wilding Picture Productions made thousands of movies that were seen by millions of people around the globe.

auditoriums — in its 185,000-square-foot facility, the 20-screen Star Southfield is larger than the 130,000-square-foot AMC Forum 30, which has 5,800 seats and two auditoriums seating 558.

Serious cinema

Detroit Film Theatre

Since January 1974, the DFT has shown mostly internationally acclaimed films to nearly 3 million patrons inside the lavish theater at the Detroit Institute of Arts. In so doing, the DFT has a reputation that extends beyond Detroit.

With a mission to show films beyond mainstream commercial movies, the DFT started with a $10,000 grant from the National Endowment for the Arts. Elliot Wilhelm designed the program, and he remains in charge.

By 2000, the DFT had screened nearly 2,000 films. DFT films that had their first metro Detroit screenings include "The Piano," "Taxi Driver," "The Last Metro," "The Crying Game," "Shoah," and "The Life and Times of Hank Greenberg."

The DFT's best-attended single event was the 1980 festival of a dozen rare prints of 3-D films, all of which were shown in their original two-strip format, which required two projectors operating in frame-by-frame synchronization.

The 1,200-seat theater was built in 1927, a collaboration between museum architect Paul Cret and Detroit architect C. Howard Crane, who specialized in designing opulent theaters such as the Fox.

Ann Arbor Film Festival

The festival, in mid-March each year at the Michigan Theater, is a nonprofit arts organization that has a tradition of showing 16-millimeter independent and experimental films. Founded in 1963 by George Manupelli, it is the oldest festival of its kind in the country. Among the entrants: Brian DePalma, Andy Warhol, George Lucas, Yoko Ono and Gus Van Sant. More than 350 films are entered each year; about 100 are selected for the festival-week showings.

Passion pits

Remember your first time at the Jolly Roger? Or the Blue Sky, the East Side, the Bel-Air, the Miracle Mile, the Algiers? The circumstances were likely:

➤ Hot date; steamy windows.

➤ Comfy in pajamas, secure with mom and dad, you fell asleep after the 'toons.

➤ You sneaked in with five others in the trunk. In 1966, metro Detroit had 31 drive-in theaters. In 2000, only one remained — the Ford-Wyoming in Dearborn.

Experts say drive-ins closed because of cable television, video games, high-tech indoor theaters, changing sexual mores, the aging of the baby boomers and rising land costs.

The Detroit area's first drive-ins, the East Side on Harper, and the West Side, on 8 Mile and Schaefer, opened in the 1930s.

The Gratiot, at 13½ Mile in Roseville, was said to be the nation's largest drive-in. It was an art deco structure with a 60-foot illuminated waterfall that offered free pony rides and a restaurant that would warm baby bottles.

"The play's the thing"

Detroit's classic showplaces

Inside the 5,000-seat Fox Theatre on Woodward.

Free Press file photo

Fox Theater

2211 Woodward, Detroit

Designed by Charles Howard Crane and completed in 1928, the 5,000-seat Fox is the culmination of flamboyant movie-palace architectural design. It is one of the largest continually operating theaters in America and one of the few remaining movie palaces. Crane, a Detroiter who once worked for noted architect Albert Kahn, designed more than 250 theaters and considered the Fox his crowning achievement. It took 18 months to build and cost about $12 million. Designed for William Fox and the Fox Theatre chain, the theater's decor is a combination of Far Eastern, Indian and

The main entrance to the Masonic Temple. The huge ediface boasts more than 1,000 rooms and a 4,400-seat auditorium.

Egyptian styles. When it opened, it had the largest clear-span balcony and the finest projection room and equipment of any theater in the world. Various owners kept the Fox open during the 1940s with acts such as Benny Goodman, Sarah Vaughn, Louis Armstrong and Jack Benny. During the early 1960s, Berry Gordy's Motown Revue held annual Christmas shows featuring talent such as the Temptations, the Supremes and Smokey Robinson. The theater changed hands several times before Mike and Marian Ilitch of Little Caesar Enterprises closed a deal in 1987 to purchase it and a connecting office building. A multi-million-dollar restoration project, which included a new 10-story marquee, culminated in a gala reopening Nov. 19, 1988.

Masonic Temple

500 Temple, Detroit

The cavernous Masonic Auditorium inside Masonic Temple is an ornate performance hall that seats 4,400 people. Opened in 1926 by the Masonic fraternity, the temple is an architectural masterpiece that houses the auditorium and 1,036 other rooms, including three ballrooms, five dining rooms, a cathedral and a gymnasium.

For the interior, sculptor Corrado Parduc-

ci left his mark on every statue, tile and ornamental feature. Each lodge room is finished in one of the major classical architectural styles including Doric, Greek Ionic and Romanesque.

The Masonic Temple was opened to the public on Feb. 22, 1926, and cost $7 million to build.

A $5-million renovation in 1990 included restoration of the theater's seats and a redesign of the 17,000-square-foot Fountain Ballroom on the lower level of the auditorium. Today, the Masonic Temple hosts more than 125 performances each year.

Above the main auditorium is a ballroom known as the Drill Hall. This room has one of the few "floating floors" in the nation. The 17,500square-foot wood floor is set on felt-cushioned coils, which give it a spring-like quality. Originally designed to relieve the tired feet of Masonic groups that would practice marching, the Drill Hall is used today by opera stars to vocalize before a performance.

Music Hall

350 Madison Ave., Detroit

The Music Hall was built as a repertory playhouse in 1928 by Matilda Dodge Wilson, the widow of automobile pioneer John Dodge. In the early 1950s, Detroit steel executive

Mervyn Gaskin converted it to a movie theater featuring Cinerama, a movie gimmick with three screens to give the audience a sense of being involved in the action.

The facility struggled as a rental hall and movie house until 1973, when Michigan Opera Theatre impresario David DiChiera became its executive director. Stage productions, the beginning of a much-loved dance series, and DiChiera's operas occupied it.

Music Hall was renovated in 1995. The large side boxes to the right and left of the stage were restored (they were taken out in 1952 to accommodate Cinerama). The ceiling — Wilson's pride — was restored, radiant in medallions of lustrous red and grassy green. The six-story facade was blasted to its original earth tones of sandstone and brick. Look up near the roofline and you'll see the coral-and-green diamond motif.

Today, the 1,800-seat theater is part of a burgeoning entertainment district that includes the nearby Gem and Century theaters and the Detroit Opera House.

Gem and Century Theatres

333 Madison Ave., Detroit

The Gem is a 1927 Italian Gothic theater built by the Twentieth Century Club, an organization of socially prominent women whose headquarters in 1903 was next door.

The theater seats 400 and was known over the years as the Little Theatre, Rivoli, Drury Lane, Europa and Vanguard. From 1967 to 1978, it showed X-rated flicks as the Gem.

Developer Charles Forbes bought the building for $5,000 and began renovation in 1990. Workers restored the intricate red, gold and blue patterns of the proscenium panels and recreated the carpeting from historic photos. Lighting fixtures were salvaged from the Ambassador Theatre in St. Louis. The Gem reopened on New Year's Eve 1991 with the musical revue "The All Night Strut!"

The theater closed again during preparation for the construction of Comerica Park, and appeared to be doomed. But

Workers install the neon sign on the Gem Theatre in 1998.

Free Press file photo

Forbes reached an agreement with the city, and the 5.5-million-pound building was moved five blocks in 1997. The move was estimated to have cost $1.5 million; the Guinness Book of Records states the Gem is the heaviest building ever moved on rubber wheels.

After the relocation, Forbes began renovating the Century Building and its 200-seat theater to its original Arts and Crafts style. The Century now houses artifacts such as Pewabic tile and leaded-glass doors from the historic YWCA building, which the city condemned for Comerica Park. The Century opened in 1999 with "Forbidden Hollywood," a musical tribute to filmdom.

Detroit Opera House

1526 Broadway, Detroit

The Opera House, which opened in 1996, is the home of the Michigan Opera Theatre.

After performing at various locales, it became clear by the mid-1980s that the MOT needed its own home. Under David DiChiera, the MOT board approved the purchase of the Grand Circus Theatre, and after a a multimillion-dollar makeover, the Grand Circus became the Detroit Opera House, which seats 2,700. In 1990, the fund-raising campaign also helped raise money for other parcels of land nearby, including the Roberts Fur Building, which was demolished in 1993 to make way for a 75,000-square-foot stage house. On April 21, 1996, the Detroit Opera House held its inaugural gala concert, featuring Luciano Pavarotti. Future phases of the project include the construction of an educational resource center. Adjoining office towers are being converted into dressing rooms.

Orchestra Hall

3711 Woodward, Detroit

This elegant facility with exceptional acoustics opened in 1919 and is one of the city's greatest preservation success stories. The home of the Detroit Symphony Orchestra, the hall is the centerpiece of Orchestra Place, an ambitious remaking of its immediate midtown neighborhood. Designed by Fox Theatre architect Charles

Orchestra Hall shortly after it opened in 1919. More than classical music is performed there.

Howard Crane, Orchestra Hall debuted as a classical music venue, but the Depression forced the DSO to move to Masonic Temple in 1939, leaving Orchestra Hall empty for years. It was later reborn as the Paradise Theatre, one of the country's most famous stages for black jazz musicians. But by the late 1960s, the structure was abandoned and on the verge of being razed.

In the early 1970s, DSO assistant principal bassoonist Paul Ganson launched the campaign to "Save Orchestra Hall." It started a 19-year, restoration process that cost $6.8 million and culminated in the DSO's return in September 1989.

The DSO in the late 1990s embarked on the creation of the $125-million Orchestra Place, a sweeping renovation project along Woodward Avenue adjacent to Orchestra Hall. The project includes a five-story office and retail center and a future Detroit Public Schools performing-arts high school. In May 2000, the DSO announced that the final portion of the expansion — including a lavish atrium lobby, the already-named Jacob Bernard Pincus Music Education Center and a 550-seat performance hall — would be known as the Max M. Fisher Center for the Performing Arts. The name honors the Detroit businessman and philanthropist who donated $5 million to the project.

In addition to being the DSO's home, Orchestra Hall is used for chamber music, jazz, world music and other performances.

Fisher Theatre

3011 W. Grand Blvd., Detroit

The Fisher Theatre, originally built as a movie and vaudeville house within the Fisher Building, opened Nov. 11, 1928. Although the building was designed by noted architect Albert Kahn, the theater design was handled by the architectural firm of Graven and Mayger of Chicago. The firm designed the movie house as a Mayan temple and borrowed historic designs from such places as Chichen Itza on the Yucatan Peninsula. The theater originally seated 3,500.

The Fisher Theatre became an all-movie house after the debut of motion pictures with sound. It closed Dec. 31, 1960, because of declining attendance.

The theater reopened under the management of the Nederlander Theatrical Corp. in September 1961. The interior was redesigned by the architectural firm of Rapp and Rapp of Chicago. The interior is rich with marble, Indian rosewood and walnut paneling. The seating was also reduced to 2,089 to ensure good sound and sight lines throughout.

Today, it offers audiences live productions and musical concerts. Like Broadway, the Fisher tends to be heavy on musicals. The theater has other uses as well; in 1996, President Bill Clinton gave a major foreign policy speech there.

President Bill Clinton gave a major foreign policy speech at the Fisher in 1996.

CULTURE

SHOWPLACES

Lights!
Camera!
Motown!

Movies that have Detroit settings. Some were even filmed here.
Rated by Free Press Film Critic Terry Lawson:

"Black Legion," 1936: *Humphrey Bogart, Dick Foran, Erin O'Brien-Moore and Ann Sheridan. Director: Archie Mayo.*

Ripped from the headlines of contemporary Detroit newspapers, Warners Bros. cast Bogie to play a Detroit auto worker who becomes involved with the Legion, a Ku Klux Klan-like group that terrorized blacks, Catholics and labor organizers in southeast Michigan during the Depression. ★★★

"T-Men," 1947: *Dennis O'Keefe, Alfred Ryder and June Lockhart. Director: Anthony Mann.*

A U.S. Treasury agent goes undercover to nab counterfeiters in Detroit. The cinematographer, John Alton, employed long shadows and shot in confined spaces to suggest a city closing in on itself. But it wasn't Detroit; it was shot on back lots in LA. ★★★

"All My Sons," 1948: *Edward G. Robinson and Burt Lancaster. Director: Irving Reis.*
"All My Sons," 1986: (*TV version*) *James Whitmore, Aidan Quinn, Joan Allen. Director: John Power.*

Watered-down version of University of Michigan graduate Arthur Miller's play that seemed to indict the capitalist system in its story of a man who sells faulty war goods from his factory, which is supposedly set in Detroit.

Feature version: ★★★
Television adaptation: ★★
"Inside Detroit," 1955: *Dennis O'Keefe, Pat O'Brien, Tina Carver. Director: Fred Sears.*

An expose of a racketeer's efforts to take control of an auto union. The movie was produced by the legendary Sam Katzman, whose B-movie resume also includes "Rock Around the Clock" "Earth vs. the Flying Saucers." It was typical of Detroit's cinematic treatment in two ways:

The city was seen as a dark and oppressive haven for underworld manipulators.

The people who made the movie never came near Detroit. It was shot in Hollywood. ★★
"Paper Lion," 1968: *Alex Karras, Ann Turkel, Alan Alda, Lauren Hutton, Sugar Ray Robinson, Roy Scheider. Director: Alex March.*

A funny film based on George Plimpton's book about his "tryout" with the Detroit Lions, it featured real players from the '60s in supporting roles, including Karras, who parlayed his performance into an acting career. ★★★
"Blue Collar," 1978: *Richard Pryor, Harvey Keitel, Yaphet Kotto, Ed Begley Jr., Lucy Saroyan. Director: Paul Schrader.*

Partially filmed in Detroit, this is an intense drama about the downside of the American dream. The film won acclaim for its realistic portrayal of Detroit assembly-line workers who find evidence of union corruption when they rob the local's safe. Pryor jokes that "plant" is short for "plantation"; a line of graffiti says "UAW" stands for "U ain't white." ★★★
"Detroit 9000" 1973: *Alex Rocco, Scatman Crothers, Hari Rhodes.*

A pair of Detroit policemen investigate a robbery that occurred at a black congressman's fund-raising banquet. Music by Motown legends Holland-Dozier-Holland

Our Terry Lawson thumbs through Detroit-themed flicks.

and a role by then-Police Commissioner John Nichols, who plays himself. The movie was blaxploitation at its best, or worst, and it enraged city boosters when it came out. Its ads proclaimed: "It's the murder capital of the World — Motortown, where the honkies are the Minority Race!" The patronage of Quentin Tarantino, who used clips from the movie in his own film "Jackie Brown" earned it a brief rerelease in 1998. ★★★

"Scarecrow," 1973: *Al Pacino and Gene Hackman. Director: Jerry Schatzberg.*

Hackman is a drifter looking to start a car wash; where better than the automobile capitol of the world? He ends up here with traveling buddy Pacino, who is seen in the film's final scene wading in the greenish pool of Belle Isle's Scott Fountain. A Cannes Film Festival award winner, it makes great use of Detroit locations. ★★★

"The Betsy," 1978: *Laurence Olivier, Robert Duvall, Katharine Ross, Tommy Lee Jones, Jane Alexander, Lesley-Anne Downs, Edward Herrmann. Director: Daniel Petrie.*

A sexy soaper with an all-star cast topped by none other than Olivier, playing the randy patriarch of an automotive empire. Harold Robbins allegedly based the the trashy novel from which this was adapted on the Fords, but the film, made partially in Detroit, is less interested in boardroom maneuvers than the bedroom variety. ★★

"One in a Million: The Ron LeFlore Story," 1978: *LeVar Burton, Madge Sinclair, Billy Martin. Director: William Graham.*

Made-in-Detroit, made-for-television movie about the ex-con who became the Tigers centerfielder, its uplifting without being sappy, but could use an epilogue; LeFlore's post-baseball career was something less than inspirational. ★★★

"Tiger Town," 1983: *Roy Scheider, Justin Henry, with appearances by Sparky Anderson and Ernie Harwell. Director: Alan Shapiro.*

Another inspirational, if completely uninspired made-for-television movie about an aging Tiger and a young fan. Major league problem: Film shows the young fan racing by bicycle from his home to Tiger Stadium — via the Belle Isle Bridge. ★★

"Aspen Extreme," 1983: *Paul Gross, Peter Berg. Director: Patrick Hasburgh.*

Two Detroiters head for the Rockies and encounter sex, drugs and snow. The opening shot is Mt. Brighton's maintenance building with its colorful welcoming sign. And one of the stars wears a cap whose logo reads: "Mt. Brighton Maintenance." ★

"Mr. Mom," 1983: *Michael Keaton, Teri Garr, Christopher Lloyd, Martin Mull. Director:* *Stan Dragoti.*

Keaton is an auto exec who loses his job and becomes a househusband, to mildly amusing results. Set in metro Detroit, filmed in an interchangeable California suburb. ★★

"Beverly Hills Cop," 1984: *Eddie Murphy, Judge Reinhold, Bronson Pinchot. Director: Martin Brest.*

Detroit cop Murphy thinks Detroit is a tough town until he tracks a suspect to Beverly Hills, Calif., and has to deal with all

Gil Hill gets waxed in "BHC III."

the super-rich white people, often while wearing his Mumford High letter jacket. This megahit and its two sequels were filmed in Los Angeles, but Detroit was well represented by City Council President and former police inspector Gil Hill, cast as Murphy's exasperated police inspector boss. The movie begins with a shot of a sign proclaiming: "It's Nice to Have You in Detroit," then follows with scenes of Detroit at its worst — abandoned factories, burned-out buildings, general litter, street people and a car chase in which vehicles by the score are demolished. In "BHC III," Hill gets blown away. ★★★

"The Dollmaker," 1984: *Jane Fonda, Levon Helm, Geraldine Page, Amanda Plummer. Director: Daniel Petrie.*

This adaptation of Harriette Arnow's 1954 novel features Fonda's TV debut. Fonda, won an Emmy for her portrayal of a character all too familiar to Detroiters; she's a woman from the Kentucky hills who follows her husband to Detroit during World War II. Generally considered to be one of the all-time best made-for-television movies. ★★★★

"Crimewave," 1985: Also known as "XYZ Murders." *Louise Lasser, Paul Smith. Director: Sam Raimi.*

Crazed comedy about rat exterminators-turned-hit men which, had it not been so cartoon-like, could have contributed to Detroit's image as a bad place to be an innocent bystander. Script was written by Joel and Ethan Coen, who went on to win an Academy Award for 1996's "Fargo." ★★

"Mirrors," 1985: *Timothy Daly, Marguerite Hickey. Director: Harry Winer.*

A Detroit ballet dancer seeks fame in New York City in the made-for-television drama, which earned plaudits for his realistic portrait of backstage Broadway. ★★

Free Press file photo

Belinda Bauer plays Free Press reporter Pat Lennon in a scene along the Detroit River with Donald Sutherland from "The Rosary Murders."

"The Rosary Murders," 1987: *Donald Sutherland, Charles Durning, Belinda Bauer. Director: Fred Walton.*

Filmed in Detroit, with inside shots at Holy Redeemer Catholic Church, it was adapted from local author William X. Kienzle's whodunnit about a killer who targets nuns and priests; neither Kienzle, or Elmore Leonard, credited with cowriting the script, thought much of the final product. ★★

"RoboCop," 1987: *Peter Weller, Nancy Allen and Ronny Cox. Director: Paul Verhoeven.*

A future Detroit has been rebuilt by a corporation that protects its holdings with a metal-encased enforcer who reads no one their Mirandas and was created from the brain of a mostly dead Detroit cop. A great cartoon of an action thriller, director Paul Verhoeven, who went on to make "Basic Instinct" and "Showgirls," wanted to film it in Detroit, but said he couldn't find enough tall buildings without completely shutting down downtown. Two inferior sequels followed. ★★★★

"Action Jackson," 1988: *Carl Weathers, Vanity, Craig T. Nelson, Sharon Stone. Director: Craig Baxley. Music: Herbie Hancock.*

Detroit supercop battles a corrupt auto tycoon, his mistress and assassins. Only the opening credits and establishing shots were filmed in Detroit, but the spirit is pure Motor City. In the opening scene, the crooked auto boss's henchmen burst through the RenCen's windows, slinging knives, blasting away with a flamethrower and dispatching a union official, whose body promptly falls onto a dinner on a RenCen terrace. "Action" made a splash at the Cannes Film Festival, which featured a full-color blowup of the Detroit skyline. ★★

"Tucker, the Man and His Dream," 1988: *Jeff Bridges, Martin Landau, Dean Stockwell, Frederick Forest, Joan Allen, Christian Slater, Lloyd Bridges. Director: Francis Ford Coppola.*

Detroit-born Coppola's father fell in love with the prototype of the 1948 Tucker auto and invested $5,000 in the company. Coppola created a Capra-esque portrait of the dreamer who attempted to launch the new car. With slicked-back hair and spiffy wing tips, Bridges resembled a Tucker Torpedo, the car that challenged Detroit's Big Three from Tucker's Ypsilanti barn. ★★★

"Chameleon Street," 1989: *Wendell B. Harris Jr., Angela Leslie, King Vidor. Director: Wendell B. Harris Jr., an award-winning filmmaker from Flint.*

The story of William Douglas Street, a Detroit con man who impersonated a Time Magazine reporter and a surgeon before he was jailed. He escaped, and went on to hoodwink Yale and the city of Detroit. Coleman Young makes a cameo appearance. ★★★

"Collision Course," 1989: *Jay Leno and Pat Morita. Director: Lewis Teague.*

Filmed in Detroit, it starred talk-show-titan-to-be Leno as a Detroit cop and Morita as a Japanese detective who team to track a tough gangster. ★

"Roger and Me," 1989: *Michael Moore, Bob Eubanks, Anita Bryant, Pat Boone, Roger Smith. Director: Moore.*

Funny, controversial documentary of Moore's efforts to confront GM Chairman Smith about the automaker's treatment of Moore's native Flint. Moore's travels take him through the GM and Fisher Building and all over Genesee County. ★★★

Associated Press

Michael Moore: He took on General Motors in "Roger and Me."

"Presumed Innocent," 1990: *Harrison Ford, Brian Dennehy, Bonnie Bedelia, Greta Scacchi, Raul Julia, Paul Winfield. Director: Alan Pakula.*

In the best-selling novel, the city was unidentified but seemed like Chicago. Pakula set it in Detroit, but aside from a few establishing shots of the skyline, Pakula filmed in New York and simulated a Detroit courtroom by hanging a picture of Michigan Attorney General Frank Kelley on the wall. Biggest faux pas: prosecutor Ford takes the ferry to work, which means he lives in Windsor. ★★★

"Bird on a Wire," 1990: *Mel Gibson and Goldie Hawn. Director: John Badham.*

Set partly in Detroit but filmed in British Columbia. Former criminal Gibson and his moll, Hawn, escape Detroit to Wisconsin — by ferry. ★★

"Coupe de Ville," 1990: *Patrick Dempsey, Daniel Stern, Alan Arkin. Director: Joe Roth.*

Three battling brothers are ordered to deliver their father's beloved Caddy from Detroit to Florida. Binder's memory serves him well, even though the metro Detroit scenes were filmed in Ontario and South Carolina respectively. ★★

"Crossing the Bridge," 1991: *Josh Charles, Jason Gedrick, Stephen Baldwin, David Schwimmer. Director: Mike Binder.*

A barely released drama by writer-director Binder about some Detroit teenagers who try to smuggle hash from Canada in the 1960s. Binder, who grew up in the Detroit suburbs, manages to get most of the Detroit details right, even though the movie was filmed in Minnesota. One miscue: The night shot of downtown features the Renaissance Center — which didn't open until 1977. ★★★

"Hoffa," 1992: *Jack Nicholson, Danny DeVito, Armand Assante. Director: DeVito.*

DeVito said the Detroit sequences of his sympathetic Hoffa biography had to be shot in the Motor City. "Come on, what are you going to do? It's Jimmy Hoffa. His story is the Detroit story; you have to be there." Some of the

The real Jimmy Hoffa. The movie offers an opinion on his demise.

Detroit scenes ended up being filmed in Pittsburgh for scheduling reasons. The way Hoffa meets his end is long on conjecture, but then who really knows? ★★★

"Zebrahead," 1992: *Michael Rappaport, N'Bushe Wright, Ray Sharkey, DeShonn Castele, Ron Johnson. Director: Tony Drazan.*

A Motown love story for the '90s. A white guy and black girl fall in love at Cody High, where filming took place. Great music, real Detroit scenery, including a shootout at a roller-skating joint and real-

istic dialogue: "You'd kick it with an I-talian boy?" "I-talian's a white boy." "No, not really." "They don't look white but they act white." ★★★

"Let's Kill All the Lawyers," 1993: *Rick Frederick, James Vezina, Michelle DeVuono. Director: Ron Senkowski, of Farmington Hills.*

The satirical tale of a young man's inner struggle over whether to attend law school received its title from Shakespeare's "Henry VI, Part II." Shot in Detroit by Senkowski and his production company, Southfield-based Lighten Up Films, it features cameos by a number of local celebs. ★★★

"True Romance," 1993: *Christian Slater, Patricia Arquette, Gary Oldman, Brad Pitt, Val Kilmer, Dennis Hopper, Christopher Walken, Samuel L. Jackson, Bronson Pinchot. Director: Tony Scott. Written by Quentin Tarantino.*

Partially filmed in Detroit, the story tracks a street-smart young Detroit couple who marry on a whim and take off to California when they unwittingly anger a deadly Detroit crime boss. The Detroit scenes encouraged the notion that the city was indeed a rotting hulk full of people with bad tempers and long memories. ★★★

"Renaissance Man," 1994: *Danny DeVito, Gregory Hines, James Remar, Mark Wahlberg. Director: Penny Marshall.*

Opening scenes are a Detroit travelogue that includes the big tire and downtown. The movie depicts some borderline Army recruits ennobled by their exposure to William Shakespeare's "Hamlet." Based loosely on the real-life experiences of screenwriter Jim Burnstein, a Plymouth man who taught English at Selfridge Air National Guard Base. DeVito, who is shorter than Burnstein, plays a Detroit advertising executive who becomes a teacher. ★★

"The Last Word," 1995: *Timothy Hutton, Joe Pantoliano, Chazz Palminteri. Director: Tony Spiridakis.*

Hutton is a journalist whose columns about gangsters from his Detroit hometown are culled from info supplied by an old pal, who also hooks him with a Hollywood deal; stars like Jimmy Smits and Richard Dreyfuss appear as themselves. ★★

"Private Parts," 1996: *Howard Stern, Robin Quivers, Mary McCormack. Director: Betty Thomas.*

The life story of Stern, the self-proclaimed "king of all media," chronicles his passage through Detroit during his struggling years as "Country Howie." ★★

"Gridlock'd," 1996: *Tim Roth, Tupac Shakur. Director: Detroit native Vondie Curtis Hall.*

Hall says half the battle in making his underrated autobiographical urban come-

Exit Wounds

"Exit Wounds," 2001: Steven Seagal, DMX, Isaiah Washington, Anthony Anderson, Michael Jai White, Tom Arnold. Director: Andrzej Bartkowiak.

Steven Seagal, above, plays a Detroit Dirty Harry, assigned to the city's toughest precinct, out to nab a millionaire drug dealer (played by rapper DMX) with ties to the cops. Set in Detroit but filmed in Calgary, Alberta, "Wounds" opens with a vice presidential assassination attempt by the Michigan Militia that supposedly takes place on the Belle Isle Bridge. Perceptive viewers may wonder, during the countless car chases, when we got all those Tim Hortons downtown. ★

8 Mile

"8 Mile," 2002: Eminem, Kim Basinger, Britanny Murphy, Mekhi Phifer. Director: Curtis Hanson.

Hanson, producer Brian Grazer and, most impressively, Marshall Mathers III didn't drive down Easy Street. They chose to make "8 Mile," a movie that is for Eminem what "A Hard Day's Night" was for the Beatles: a film that codifies a myth while turning it inside out and holding it up so we can see our reflection. Their "8 Mile" is a formula movie that tweaks the formula in so many inventive, intelligent, insightful ways as to transcend it altogether. It is a movie that will satisfy hip-hop and Eminem fans in ways they never expected. Filmed entirely in and around Detroit. ★★★★

J. KYLE KEENER/Detroit Free Press

Tupac Shakur, left, and Tim Roth in a scene from "Gridlock'd."

dy "Gridlock'd" was capturing the distinctive "Detroitness" of his hometown while filming in Los Angeles. "I wanted more than anything to make it in Detroit. But it was my first movie, and the producers knew it would be easier and more efficient to shoot it in LA." ★★

"Grosse Pointe Blank," 1997: *John Cusack, Minnie Driver, Dan Aykroyd, Alan Arkin, Joan Cusack. Director: George Armitage.*

A dark comedy in which a hit man attends his 10th reunion at GPHS. Except for a few shots, the film was made in the Los Angeles area, but it does an adequate job of capturing the small-town

Director Theresa Connelly on location for "Polish Wedding."

Minnie Driver and John Cusack at the premiere of "Grosse Pointe Blank."

affluence of the Pointes. "It was the Midwestern upper class we were looking to lampoon," Cusack said. "And the name Grosse Pointe seemed to signify that." An attempt to shoot a scene at Grosse Pointe South high school was soundly rebuffed. "They just said, 'Thanks, but no thanks,' which was so Grosse Pointe." ★★

"Polish Wedding," 1998: *Gabriel Byrne, Lena Olin, Claire Danes. Director: Theresa Connelly.*

Connelly grew up in Hamtramck, where the film was shot. This is Hamtown Retro: No trendy clubs and cof-

fee shops, but lots of pierogi and ethnic angst. The story revolves around a Polish-American family and its rebellious daughter. Some Poles thought it stereotyped the Hamtramck experience. ★★

"Out of Sight," 1998: *George Clooney, Dennis Franz, Albert Brooks, Dennis Farina and Jennifer Lopez. Director: Steven Soderbergh.*

Filmed in Detroit, which is one of the stars in this adaptation of the comic crime novel/love story by Elmore Leonard. Bank robber Clooney looks to rip off a Bloomfield Hills embezzler, but is sidetracked by murderous misadventures on the scary looking east side and by some nasty local lowlifes who are littering up the legendary Kronk Gym. ★★★★

George Clooney encounters some unsavory characters at the Kronk Gym.

"Detroit Rock City," 1999: *Giuseppe Andrews, James De Bello, Edward Furlong, Sam Huntington, Natasha Lyonne. Director: Adam Rifkin.*

The authenticity of this teen comedy about four members of the Kiss army who will do anything to score tickets to a 1978 Cobo concert can be summed up like this: It was filmed in Toronto. ★★

Famous lines

What film characters said about Detroit. Remember — they were only acting:

"Detroit isn't a very exciting place. Big chimneys. Black smoke."
— **Tom Bradley to Madeleine de Beaupre in "Desire."**

"You come to Detroit and you rent a Beamer? That's like going to Germany and and eating Jimmy Dean sausages."
— **Rick Jarmin in "Bird on a Wire."**

"Hell, man. In Detroit, my hometown, they shoot *everybody* in the streets."
— **Sinclair in "Iron Eagle II."**

"That X-ray lady's back, she's out back right now by the van. She's got a man with her the size of Detroit."
— **Fool in "People Under the Stairs."**

"If you gave me a million years to ponder, I would've never guessed that true romance and Detroit would ever go together."
— **Alabama in "True Romance."**

"I especially want to apologize to the Trochman family in Detroit . . . I never delivered a baby before, and I just thought that ice tongs were the way to do it."
— **Leonard Zelig in "Zelig."**

"When I find myself in a position like this, I ask myself, 'What would General Motors do?' And then I do the opposite.
— **Johnny Case in "Holiday."**

"I've never been banished before. Except for that time in Abilene. Cowboys just didn't get Motown."
— **Rembrandt Lee (Crying Man) Brown in "Sliders."**

SOURCE: IMDB: INTERNET MOVIE DATABASE **WWW.IMDB.COM.**

Names & Faces

Lily Tomlin

1939-

Lily Tomlin wasn't the first person to put forth the idea that comedy comes from character, not jokes, but she is a wonder at putting that idea into action. Thirty years after her characters Edith Ann, the precocious little girl, and Ernestine, the passive-aggressive telephone operator, first appeared on television (on "Rowan and Martin's Laugh-In"), they remain American icons.

Her later, more complex work grows out of that concept, too, including her Tony-winning performance in the one-woman play "The Search for Signs of Intelligent Life in the Universe."

Born in Detroit, Tomlin attended Cass Technical High School and Wayne State University, but her education began long before that.

She grew up in an apartment house on the corner of Byron and Hazelwood on the west side of Detroit. "It was filled with all kinds of people, a little microcosm of humanity," she says. For little Mary Jean Tomlin (she later

altered her name), it was the closest thing to heaven. She found herself welcome in everyone's apartment and would often stick around until late into the night.

"I was one of those kids you can't beat me off with a stick. Even if they were an old couple, in their 80s, I would listen to them tell stories. Then I would sit in another apartment with somebody who was an old communist who would propagandize me."

Thus, Mary Jean learned to observe and appreciate. Lily has spent the rest of her life extolling what we have in common and what makes each of us special, a tribute to her talent and a view of humanity made in Detroit.

Gilda Radner

1946-89

Gilda Radner was the merry, multiple-personality prankster of cutting-edge comedy on "Saturday Night Live" in the '70s, the shining female standout in the legendary first generation of Not Ready for Prime Time Players. The Detroit native who graduated from the Liggett School in 1964 became an

"A BMW? In Detroit? That's sacrilege."

— **Martin** in "Grosse Pointe Blank."

inspired comedy chameleon with her oddball gallery of unforgettable "SNL" characters: Roseanne Roseannadanna, Lisa Loopner and Emily ("Nevermind!") Litella.

She died at age 42 after a long battle with ovarian cancer and her legacy — beyond the rare gift of her comic genius — resides in Gilda's Club, a growing network of cancer support group centers in Detroit, New York and other cities.

Tim Meadows

1961 —
Pershing High grad Tim Meadows is a veteran Saturday Night Live cast member who has performed scathing impressions of Johnny Cochran, O.J. Simpson, a crude but hilarious ladies' man, Colin Powell, Sammy Davis Jr., Ike Turner and Michael Jackson. He was born in Highland Park and attended Wayne State University and participated in Jonathan Round's Detroit Time Improvisational Theatre.

Meadows on childhood:
"I was actually kind of shy, but around my friends, I was the one who would eat paste."

Tim Allen
1953-

As Tim (Tool Man) Taylor on "Home Improvement" for seven years, longtime Michigan resident Tim Allen became the archetypal TV dad of the 1990s. Born Timothy Allen Dick in Denver, Allen moved to Birmingham at age 13, graduated from Western Michigan University and then left a job in advertising to pursue his dream of becoming a stand-up comic during the comedy club boom of the 1980s.

Allen's offbeat and unique schtick as a grunting macho man-child, obsessed with power tools and the aggravating, everyday misunderstandings between men and women, served as the foundation for the phenomenally popular "Home Improvement."

Robin Williams
1952-

Robin Williams was born in Chicago and educated at Juilliard, but spent his formative years in Bloomfield Hills. His father was a Ford executive, and Williams admits to being a "juvenile pain in the ass" at Detroit Country Day school.

His remarkable

talent for free association and wordplay, coupled with his admiration for Midwestern comic Jonathan Winters, led him to stand-up comedy and television. But in the '80s, he harnessed his talents in the service of serious movies like "Dead Poets Society." His dramatic turn in 1997's "Good Will Hunting" finally earned him an Oscar.

Jeff Daniels
1955-

Central Michigan University grad Jeff Daniels had to leave the state he loved to earn his acting stripes in acclaimed performances in off-Broadway productions of "Johnny Got His Gun" and "Fifth of July." But after establishing himself as a nice guy with lots of odd corners in films such as "Terms of Endearment" and Woody Allen's "The Purple Rose of Cairo" and as a nimble and affable leading man in family entertainment including "101 Dalmatians," he returned to Chelsea, his hometown, to raise his family and start the successful theater company he named Purple Rose.

Danny Thomas
1914-1991

If father knew best on 1950s television, Danny Thomas, the fifth of 10 children born to Lebanese immigrants in Deerfield, Mich., in 1914, proved that he was a TV father who really knew funny on "Make Room for Daddy." That broadly popular family comedy series debuted in 1953 and ran for nine seasons on ABC and then CBS, making the onetime nightclub entertainer and comic a beloved household name. Thomas was perhaps better known to later generations as the father of "That Girl" star Marlo Thomas.

George C. Scott
1927-99

With a confidence born of talent, George C. Scott played Gen. George Patton in the 1970 film "Patton" and won the Academy Award

J. KYLE KEENER/Detroit Free Press

Jeff Daniels in 1999.

for best actor. With a confidence born of conviction, he refused the Oscar, excoriating the competition for awards as "offensive, barbarous and innately corrupt." Scott was born in Virginia but grew up in Detroit, graduating from Redford High School in 1945. After military service and college, he embarked on an acting career which, for a time, led him back to Detroit, but ultimately took him to Broadway and Hollywood.

Associated Press

George C. Scott as George S. Patton. Scott died in 1999.

Soupy Sales

1926-

The birth certificate originally said Milton Supman. But it's been sublimely silly Soupy Sales since 1957, when the Motor City's groundbreaking, pie-in-the-face kiddie show host embraced his screwball stage name. Those were the days when the North Carolina-born funnyman was in the midst of a wild, seven-year run on Detroit's WXYZ-TV (Channel 7), creating manic live television magic on "Lunch with Soupy Sales," which eventually became "The Soupy Sales Show."

That dizzily imaginative, freewheeling children's series — a weekend network edition became ABC's first non-animated Saturday morning series — featured Sales in all his irreverent glory, wearing a crazy get-up of oversized polka-dot bowtie and crumpled top hat, trading hipster wisecracks with off-the-wall animal puppets with names like Black Tooth, White Fang and Pookie the Lion.

Though Soupy's growing national fame would take him to Los Angeles and then New York in the 1960s — where such celebrities as Frank Sinatra and Sammy Davis Jr. took pies in the face — his witty slapstick genius first reached critical chucklehead mass during that twisted Detroit heyday in the 1950s.

John Witherspoon

1942-

You don't even need to hear one of his jokes to laugh at this comedian. All it takes is one look. Witherspoon, who modeled for Hudson's ads in Detroit in the 1960s, is best known as an unknown whose characters all have one thing in common: their bad fashion sense. In character, the Detroit native consistently sports polyester with signature white shoes and belts. But Witherspoon is more than a non-savvy dresser. Among comics, he's known as an improv genius. In every film and TV show in which he has appeared — "Boomerang" and "Hollywood Shuffle" among them — he goes in without a script.

Della Reese

1931-

At age 13, she was touring with gospel great Mahalia Jackson. In 1957, she was voted "most promising singer" by several trade magazines. In 1989, she couldn't pay anyone to help her put

Julie Harris

1925-

Grosse Pointe Park native Julie Harris, winner of five Tony Awards (a record for actors), two Emmys and even a Grammy, developed a love of acting as a child when she went to plays in downtown Detroit. Known for one-woman shows like "The Belle of Amherst" (about poet Emily Dickinson), Harris has graced stages and screens since 1945 and had a busy 1999. "I'm as enthusiastic about the theater and films and television as I always was," she says. It shows.

David Alan Grier

1955-
A comedian and actor, Grier is a Detroit native whose most recent TV gig was as the lively host of Fox's "Random Acts of Comedy." He hit the big time in the early 1990s as a regular sketch artist on "In Living Color."

out a record. Then in 1999, record executives once again were pursuing her strong voice. Born Deloreese Patricia Early, Della Reese first learned to perform by imitating the movies that she saw with her father in Detroit theaters. She's perhaps best known now as the costar of CBS's hit "Touched By an Angel."

Ellen Burstyn
1932-
When Ellen Burstyn was acting and modeling as a teen in Detroit, she was still known by the name her Irish-American parents gave her: Edna Rae Gillooly. She had tried out a number of names and showbiz jobs — chorus lines, TV series, Broadway understudy — before she got Actor's Studio-serious in the '70s with her Oscar-nominated role in "The Last Picture Show." She went on to give decade-defining performances in "The Exorcist" and "Alice Doesn't Live Here Anymore."

Michael Moriarty
1941-
Born in Detroit and educated at the University of Detroit High School, Moriarty is a veteran TV character actor. He played assistant district attorney Ben Stone in "Law & Order" among dozens of TV appearances going back to 1972, including "Holocaust." He's a descendant of the Tigers' George Moriarty and sold tires in Detroit before he went Hollywood.

Courtney B. Vance
1960-
As a young man, Vance chose an acting career over a job at General Motors Corp. Good move. From a notable part among Hollywood heavyweights as the SONAR whiz who figures out how to track a supposedly untrackable ship in "The Hunt for Red October" in 1990, he went on to a busy career in TV and movies. Born in Wayne, Vance grew up in Detroit and graduated from Detroit Country Day school, Harvard and Yale Drama School.

David Patrick Kelly
1951-
While not a household name, the Detroit-raised Kelly has enjoyed a 25-year career in films, TV and the New York stage. He played a creepy character named Luther in two of

the best known of his nearly 30 films — "The Warriors" and "48 Hours." He also had leading roles in "Last Man Standing" and "Dreamscape." Other credits include "Twin Peaks," "Commando," "Mad About You" and "Moonlighting." Kelly grew up on Harvard Road and attended Bishop Gallagher High School. His politician brother, John, is a member of the Wayne State University Board of Governors.

S. Epatha Merkerson
1952-
Saginaw-born, Detroit-raised and Wayne State-educated, Merkerson has played Lt. Anita Van Buren on TV's long-running "Law & Order." Merkerson is an accomplished stage actress who earned a 1990 Tony Award nomination for

her Broadway performance in August Wilson's "The Piano Lesson." She also played Reba the Mail Lady on "Pee-wee's Playhouse," the late 1980s cult favorite.

Tom Sizemore
1964-
Sizemore was the relentlessly self-promoting detective in Oliver Stone's "Natural Born Killers." He staged heists with pal Robert De Niro and Val Kilmer in "Heat." He lured detective Denzel Washington into a dangerous game in "Devil in a Blue Dress." In "Strange Days," he hung out with hardware hustler Ralph Fiennes. He played Sgt. Horvath in "Saving Private Ryan."

Sizemore was a football and basketball star at Bishop Gallagher High School. After studying theater at Wayne State, he went to Temple for his master's degree. Then he was off to off-Broadway; he later turned small parts in a half-dozen good minor films into a major career in Hollywood.

Tom Sizemore, left, as Sgt. Horvath.

Curtis Armstrong

1953-

Armstrong, raised in Berkley, played Herbert Viola, the young aspiring private eye of the Blue Moon Detective Agency on television's "Moonlighting;" Tom Cruise's know-it-all friend, Miles, in the movie "Risky Business," and Booger in the movie "Revenge of the Nerds." Armstrong also has a cult fave role in the John Cusack teen flick, "Better Off Dead."

Dave Coulier

1959-

Coulier is the former costar of the family TV sitcom "Full House," former host of "America's Funniest People," stand-up comedian and master of cartoon voices. He was born in Detroit, reared in St. Clair Shores and graduated from Notre Dame High in Harper Woods, where he was Dave Couwlier.

Dann Florek

1950-

Florek grew up in Flat Rock and has played Capt. Donnie Cragen on "Law & Order" and "Law & Order: Special Victims Unit." He has a long list of TV and movie credits.

Mike Binder

1958-

Binder has written ("Coupe de Ville," "Crossing the Bridge") directed ("Blankman," "Bridge" and "Indian Summer") and acted in a career that started in Detroit-area comedy clubs. He grew up in Birmingham.

Chad Everett

1936-

Dearborn-raised Everett had dozens of film and television roles going back to 1958, when he appeared in TV's "77 Sunset Strip." He graduated from Fordson High.

Tom Hulce

1953-
The Plymouth native's big break was playing Wolfgang Amadeus Mozart in the 1984 film, "Amadeus." Other credits: "Animal House," "Murder in Mississippi" and the "Hunchback of Notre Dame."

THE VOICE BEHIND THE MASK:
James Earl Jones
1931-

The voice of Darth Vader and an admired presence on the stage and screen, this urbane actor grew up on his grandparents' farm near Manistee (he was born in Mississippi) and began acting at the University of Michigan. He credits a teacher at Dickson High School in Brethren, Mich., for helping him overcome a stutter.

Jones' films include "Field of Dreams," "Matewan" and "The Great White Hope."

Onstage, he won a Tony Award as best actor for "Fences" and was the first black actor to play Big Daddy in "Cat on a Hot Tin Roof" and probably the only one who could get away with it.

Jones, of course, has been the famous – and again faceless – voice of many years of CNN station identification ads.

The ominous Darth Vader.

Free Press file photo

Christine Lahti

1950-
Lahti, who grew up in Birmingham, has acted in dozens of TV shows and movies since the late 1970s. From 1994 until 1999, she played Dr. Kathryn Austin on "Chicago Hope." She also won an Academy Award in 1995 for her live-action short film "Lieberman in Love."

Ted Raimi

1965-
The brother of director Sam Raimi, and friend of the above-mentioned Bruce Campbell, has played numerous film and TV roles, including as Lt. Tom O'Neill on "SeaQuest DSV."

Dick Martin

1922 -
The comedian and costar of television's "Rowan and Martin's Laugh-In" was born in Battle Creek but grew up in Detroit. He remembers the day he left: "It was February 1943, and there I was with my lunch bucket waiting for the Vernor streetcar to go work at Ford's when a car drove by and splashed me with slush. I left for California the next day." On the West Coast, Martin acted, directed and produced.

Tom Skerritt

1933-
Born and raised in Detroit, the "Picket Fences" star fell into acting while attending Wayne State. He took part in student productions and appeared with the Dearborn Players before leaving school to do two seasons of touring stock shows. Later, at UCLA, he was spotted in a student production by filmmaker Terry Sanders, who cast him in the film "War Hunt" with another unknown young actor, Robert Redford. Skerritt has several dozen acting roles to his credit.

George Peppard

1928-1994
"The A Team" actor, below, graduated from Dearborn High. His 44 credits include "Pork Chop Hill," "Breakfast at Tiffany's" and "The Carpetbaggers." His mother, opera singer Vernelle Rohrer, taught at the Detroit Conservatory of Music.

Pam Dawber

1951-
Born in Detroit, Dawber, above, grew up in Farmington Hills and starred with fellow Detroiter Robin Williams in "Mork and Mindy," a big hit of the late 1970s.

Bruce Campbell

1958-
Longtime friend and partner of Michigan-born director Sam Raimi, Campbell is a Royal Oak native and Michigan State alum. He is perhaps best known to horror movie mavens for his over-the-top lead performances in director Raimi's hilarious gorefest classics "Evil Dead" and "Evil Dead II." He also starred in Raimi's "Army of Darkness," a 1993 swashbuckler-from-hell adventure comedy that was actually a sequel to the bloodier "Evil Dead" movies. Campbell also has worked as a producer, director, writer, editor and sound crew member.

Selma Blair, second from right, as Zoe Bean in "Zoe, Duncan, Jack and Jane."

Free Press f

Selma Blair

1972-
A down-to-earth Southfield native who starred in TV's "Zoe, Duncan, Jack and Jane" in early 1999, Blair displayed her screwball comic flair in "Cruel Intentions," a colorfully campy teenage adaption of "Dangerous Liaisons." Her supporting role included a funny, tongue-in-cheek (so to speak) French-kissing scene with "Buffy the Vampire Slayer" star Sarah Michelle Gellar. Then came a flurry of Selma-rific magazine covers, with Blair looking like everyone from the wholesome girl next door on Seventeen to every frat boy's dreamy sex bomb fantasy on Details. She also starred with Freddie Prinze Jr. in the romantic comedy "Down to You."

Behind the scenes:
Writers and directors

Ken Burns

Just call him Mr. History. The most influential and acclaimed American documentary filmmaker of the last two decades, Burns has been hailed for a succession of stirring, often multipart historical documentaries, including "The Civil War" (1990), "Baseball" (1994) and "Thomas Jefferson" (1997). Born in Brooklyn, N.Y., Burns moved to Ann Arbor with his family in the mid-1960s, where he attended Ann Arbor Pioneer High School. It was there that he first fell under the spell of filmmaking, making several student films during his high-school years. "The Civil War," a sweeping 11-hour documentary epic that became the highest-rated series in PBS history, turned Burns into a household name. In that project, Burns managed to weave a rich new view of our shared American heritage by focusing on human stories and everyday people. His impact? Immense. Says historian and author Stephen Ambrose: "More Americans get their history from Ken Burns than any other source."

Sam Raimi

The prolific filmmaker, writer and producer achieved major success in the 1990s with the hit television series "Hercules: The Legendary Journeys" and "Xena: Warrior Princess," as well as mainstream movie recognition as director of the critically acclaimed "A Simple Plan." But Raimi, who was born in Royal Oak in 1959 and raised in Detroit and Franklin, first rattled the cultural cage with "The Evil Dead" (1983), the wildly imaginative, low-budget horror movie that gurgled with his signature blend of dark humor, absurdist gore and visual flair. Teamed with longtime Detroit and Michigan State University pals Bruce Campbell and Rob Tapert, Raimi generated additional spooky vibrations with two "Evil Dead" sequels before making his first major Hollywood studio film, the fantasy suspense thriller "Darkman" (1990).

Kurt Luedtke

A screenwriter who lives in Birmingham, Luedtke won the Academy Award for his work on "Out of Africa," (1985). He also wrote "Random Hearts" (1999) and "Absence of Malice," (1981), a critically acclaimed film that explored a disturbing truth about the news business: It is possible to report a set of facts accurately that nevertheless fail to tell the whole story. Luedtke is the former executive editor of the Free Press and served as U-M's second James Gindin Visiting Artist.

Francis Ford Coppola in 1996. He left Detroit as a child.

Associated Press

Francis Ford Coppola

The film director's middle name was a tribute to his father's Dearborn-based employer. Carmine Coppola, who would later win an Oscar for writing the score for his son's "The Godfather, Part II," was the assistant conductor and arranger for the popular radio show "Ford Sunday Evening Hour," as well as first flutist with the Detroit Symphony Orchestra. The family left Detroit when Francis Coppola was a child, but Detroit never left him. After directing "The Godfather," its sequel and "Apocalypse Now," Coppola released "Tucker: The Man and His Dream" in 1988, an unapologetically optimistic biography about a would-be Detroit automaker starring Jeff Bridges. Coppola's father had been an ill-fated investor in the real Tucker Co.

Lawrence Kasdan

In the 1960s, West Virginia-born, U-M-educated Kasdan wrote copy and commercials for Detroit advertising agencies while honing the screenwriting skills that would  take him to Hollywood and, in time, earn him a place in its hall of fame. Three movies with Kasdan's name on them —"The Empire Strikes Back," "Return of the Jedi" and "Raiders of the Lost Ark" — are among the 20 most popular movies of all time, while "Raiders," taught in film schools as a model of the modern screenplay, was added to the Library of Congress's National Registry. Kasdan's most personal film, however, was "The Big Chill," in which he used a reunion of '60s-era U-M grads to examine how the dreams of his generation were altered by time and clouded by contradictions. Not only did it sum up an era, it turned Motown music into its unofficial soundtrack.

Paul Feig

Feig grew up as "a tall, skinny, geeky kid" in Mt. Clemens, where he graduated from Chippewa Valley High School in 1980. He is the creator of "Freaks and Geeks," a funny, poignant and sharply observant story of growing up absurd on the pimply Planet Adolescence. The TV show, praised by critics in 2000, was set at McKinley High in an unnamed Michigan town in 1980. In one 2000 episode, a girl read a grim account of the teenage life she wants put in the yearbook. The adult advisor demurs, calling her Sylvia Plath. "It's a little dark," he says. "We want to sell yearbooks, not tell the truth."

Lloyd Richards

In 1999, Richards offered some advice to theater students at Wayne State University, his alma mater: "Study your craft. Master your craft. Be realistic as to what you are." Richards, born in Canada in 1923 and raised in Detroit, has done just that. In 1959, he directed the original Broadway production of "A Raisin in the Sun" and went on to direct many other plays, including "Fences," for

 which he won a Tony Award. A noted educator as well, Richards spent 12 years as dean of the Yale School of Drama and three decades as artistic director of the National Playwrights Conference, where he nurtured the careers of such playwrights as Wendy Wasserstein, David Henry Hwang and "Fences" author August Wilson.

Pamela Conn, Sue Marx

Detroiters whose 1988 "Young at Heart" won the Academy Award for best short film, a light-hearted real story of the companionship of two octogenarian artists, Louis Gothelf, Marx's father, and the widowed Reva Shwayder.

Ted Talbert

A former truck driver, Talbert has produced more than 20 documentaries that explore the lives of Detroit's famous and not-so-famous African Americans. Talbert has  been connected with WDIV-TV (Channel 4) since 1989, and his work has won numerous awards. In 2000, he was inducted into the Michigan Journalism Hall of Fame. Talbert also established the Joe Louis Video Memorial in Cobo Hall that features the award-winning documentary, "And Still the Champ." Talbert was also a freelance writer; among his best pieces were an account of a night on the town with Detroit Mayor Coleman Young and a story about Detroit's junkyard guard dogs, though Talbert managed to find one junkyard that was guarded by a ferocious monkey.

Harvey Ovshinsky

Harvey O is Detroit's king of all media. As a young man in 1965 he started the Fifth Estate, the city's premier "underground" newspaper that 35 years later (but three decades after Ovshinsky's departure) continues to publish as an anarchist journal. In the late 1960s, he was one of the pioneering "Air Aces" on WABX-FM, Detroit's celebrated free-form radio station for

HUGH GRANNUM/Detroit Free Press
Harvey Ovshinsky, Detroit's multimedia guy.

which Ovshinsky set a distinct tone with his alternative news broadcasts. Then, as an adult, Ovshinsky got into TV, and before long was winning awards for his documentaries. His "Close to Home: The Tammy Boccomino Story," a documentary he did along with WKBD-TV (Channel 50) about a Warren homemaker infected with the AIDS virus, won two national awards: the 1993 Emmy Award for community service programming and the George Foster Peabody Award for distinguished achievement in broadcasting. A Mumford High School graduate who did not attend college, Ovshinsky runs a metro Detroit video and radio production company today.

John Nelson

The visual effects superhero behind such movies as "Gladiator," "Johnny Mnemonic," "City of Angels" and "Terminator 2: Judgment Day," Nelson grew up in Grosse Pointe and worked as a teen at the old Vogue Theater on Harper and Cadieux in Detroit. He won an Oscar in 2001 for his work on "Gladiator."

Others with show business links to metro Detroit

Mike Wallace　　　**Betty Hutton**

Lucille Ball

Tom Selleck

Mike Wallace ("60 Minutes") attended the University of Michigan and broke into radio at Detroit's WWJ-AM ... **Ed Bradley** ("60 Minutes") spent childhood summers in Detroit visiting his father ... **Hugh Downs** ("20/20") attended Wayne State University and worked in Detroit radio ... **Dick Enberg**, NBC sportscaster, was born in Armada, grew up in Mt. Clemens and graduated from Central Michigan ... **Max Gail** ("Barney Miller" and "D.C. Cab") grew up in a Detroit showbiz family. Dad ran the Gail & Rice booking agency, as well as an office supply company ... Detroit's **Suzy Garrett** ("Punky Brewster") got her acting break with her sister, **Marla Gibbs** ("The Jeffersons"), who got her acting start on Channel 7's "Juvenile Court" ... **Mitzi Gaynor** was Mitzi Gerber when she went to Detroit's Chandler and Tilden Elementary Schools ... **Betty Hutton**, film star of the 1940s and 1950s, sang in Detroit bars for pen-

nies as a youngster to add to the family income ... Game show host **Art James** was born Artur Efimchik and graduated from Fordson High in Dearborn and Wayne State. He got into radio in Saginaw and in TV at WWJ (now WDIV) ... **Harry Morgan** ("M*A*S*H") was Harry Bratsbrug when he left Detroit in the 1930s to study law at the University of Chicago ... **Tom Selleck** ("Magnum, P.I.") was 4 when he left his hometown of Detroit, but that didn't stop him from wearing a Tiger cap on his show ... Theater star **Elaine Stritch** graduated from Detroit's Convent of the Sacred Heart ... **Leigh Taylor-Young** ("Peyton Place") graduated from Birmingham's Groves High School ... **Robert Wagner** was 9 when the family moved from Detroit to Los Angeles ... **Lucille Ball** lived in Wyandotte as a baby ... **Piper Laurie** was born Rosetta Jacobs in Detroit in 1932. She left at age 6 ...

SOURCES: FREE PRESS FEATURES STAFF; FREE PRESS LIBRARY; THE INTERNET MOVIE DATABASE, **WWW.US.IMDB.COM**; VIDEOHOUND'S GOLDEN MOVIE RETRIEVER, 2000.

CULTURE

LIGHTS! CAMERA! MOTOWN!

Theater

All theaters great and small
Take your seat, please

From the 50-seat Planet Ant Theatre in Hamtramck to the 5,000-seat Fox Theatre in Detroit, the theatrical landscape in southeastern Michigan is something to behold.

At small theaters like Planet Ant you might see a new play or an old standard staged in a surprising way. In the 2000 season, for instance, Planet Ant produced Shakespeare's "The Comedy of Errors," with design elements of the computer age.

At large theaters like the Fox, which need big audiences, you see plays that have proven themselves elsewhere. In 2000, the Fox offered a touring production of the Broadway hit "Smokey Joe's Cafe."

The theatrical landscape is always evolving. A performance changes from one night to the next, or even from one minute to the next; that's part of the excitement of live theater.

The movers and shakers

➤ PLOWSHARES

In mid-2000, Plowshares Theatre was scheduled to move into its latest home, the 600-seat Anderson Theater at Henry Ford Museum, and present a new play, "Full Circle," by Jeff Chastang, a veteran Plowshares actor.

Plowshares, Detroit's professional African-American theater, has moved a half dozen times in its 9½-year history. Its goal is a home of its own. Founder Gary Anderson pulled off a small miracle in 2000 by having a season after Plowshares lost its theater at the Museum of African American History. Most of the 2000-2001 season is to take place at the Anderson Theater at the Henry Ford Museum in Dearborn. **For information, call 313-872-0279.**

➤ PERFORMANCE NETWORK

Performance Network is getting a home of its own. In September 2000, Performance Network began its first season at its brand-new theater, in the former Ann Arbor Inn, at Fourth Avenue and Huron.

Performance Network, which has been housed in a converted factory at 408 W. Washington in Ann Arbor, has a knack for grabbing the rights to hot off-Broadway plays and producing them well. Its 1999-2000 season began with two: Douglas Carter Beane's "As Bees in Honey Drown" and Richard Greenberg's "Three Days of Rain." Performance Network even beat Broadway to the punch with its 2000 production of Arthur Miller's "The Ride Down Mt. Morgan."

The move will take Performance Network from a venue where capacity is about 113 seats to a 165-seat space designed specifically for theater. **Call 734-663-0681.**

➤ PURPLE ROSE

Purple Rose Theatre in Chelsea has a home, but it needed remodeling. Purple Rose closed for the 1999-2000 season and construction was scheduled to be finished by January 2001.

The theater, at 137 Park Street, will grow from 119 seats to 160 seats, which is one extra row of seats on each of three sides. Public and work space will be expanded.

Founded by actor, playwright and Chelsea native Jeff Daniels, the Purple Rose champions new plays, especially those with a Midwestern sensibility. Scheduled to open the renovated theater is a new play the Purple Rose commissioned from Lanford Wilson who, in addition to being a Pulitzer Prize winner, is a native Midwesterner, from Missouri. **Call 734-475-7902.**

The standards

➤ FOX THEATRE

Glorious to behold, the lavishly restored Fox is too big for most traditional musicals (and way too big for straight plays), unless you nab seats in the first 12 rows. It puts on a few musicals every season. The year 2000 saw an elaborately costumed road show of "The King and I." Shows with huge casts or special effects — "Riverdance," for instance, or David Copperfield's magic extravaganzas — are right at home.

Ambience: The lobby and auditorium are breathtaking in the manner of those overdone vaudeville houses and movie palaces of yesteryear. Alcoholic beverages, soft drinks and snacks can be purchased.

Insider's tip: Allow an extra 30 minutes to park. Parking was a lengthy chore even before new baseball stadium Comerica Park opened. Management is aware of the problem, and the Fox has been known to hold its curtain for 20 minutes or more. The Fox Garage, on the north side of Montcalm, is reserved for theater patrons when a show and a ballgame are scheduled.

Address: 2211 Woodward, Detroit.

Seating: 5,000.

Tickets: $20-$45.

Parking: Many choices nearby, all in the $6-$7 range.

➤ DETROIT REPERTORY THEATRE

A beautifully tended oasis in a desolate patch of city, the Rep, as it's known to its friends, demonstrates a similarly fierce independence in choosing its productions, staging unknown plays and those by world-renowned playwrights with the same degree of loving care. During the 1999-2000 season, for example, the world premiere of "Revival at Possum Kingdom Community Church" by Michigan writer Linda LaRocque was followed by a production of "Valley Song" by acclaimed South African writer Athol Fugard, and it was followed by the virtually unknown "The Angels of Lemnos" by Jim Henry.

Ambience: Superb. A full bar offers alcoholic and nonalcoholic beverages, homemade soups and cookies. Cozy lobby with many places to sit. Walls serve as an art gallery.

Insider's tip: For a surprisingly unobstructed view try Row B, the second row. It's 12 inches higher than Row A, whereas the interval between other rows is only 6 inches.

Address: 13103 Woodrow Wilson, Detroit.

Seating: 194 seats.

Tickets: $15.

Parking: Free, in a fenced, well-lit lot.

➤ GEM AND CENTURY THEATRES

The beautifully restored Gem and Century Theatres, in the same building, are a piece of Detroit history. The Gem claims the longest-running musical ("The All Night Strut") and play ("Escanaba in Da Moonlight") in local history. Crowd-pleasing light comedies and musical revues, with about a half-dozen performers each, are the Gem and Century's stock-in-trade, and they tend to stay a while. Except for a few traditional theater seats in the Gem's balcony, the audience sits at small cabaret tables at both theaters.

Ambience: The best, with a bar in each theater lobby, an upscale restaurant in the building and commodious rest rooms.

Insider's tip: Nearly all seats are at tables for four. If you don't enjoy sitting with strangers (it can be fun), be sure to go as part of a foursome.

Address: 333 Madison Ave., Detroit.

Seating: 400 in the Gem, 200 in the Century.

Tickets: $24.50-$34.50.

Parking: $6 in the lot behind the building; $6-$7 in lots across Madison Avenue.

➤ FISHER THEATRE

Every city worth the name has a big theater where big Broadway shows on tour take up residence for a few weeks. In Detroit that theater is the Fisher. Like Broadway itself these days, the Fisher tends to be heavy on musicals. The 1999-2000 season featured traveling versions of three musicals — "Fosse," "Footloose" and "Cabaret" — and one straight play, "Art," starring Judd Hirsch.

Ambience: Pleasant. Thick carpeting. Candy and beverages in the lobby; coffee, other drinks and more elaborate snacks in the Fisher building hallway just beyond the lobby.

Insider's tip: For a shortcut to the parking garage and lot, leave through the doors on the left side (stage right to serious thespians) near the front of the theater. You'll emerge in the hallway of the Fisher Building, near the exit to the parking areas.

Address: Fisher Building, West Grand at Second, Detroit.

Seating: 2,200 seats.

Tickets: $33-$65.

Parking: $6 in a garage and lot on the west side of the theater.

➤ MUSIC HALL

An entertainment district has grown up around Music Hall. The Gem and Century Theaters literally moved in across the street, the Detroit Opera House was built down the block, new restaurants have sprung up in Harmonie Park, and there's that new baseball stadium. Now Music Hall is assessing its artistic position. In 2000, Youtheatre moves to Southfield, which makes Music Hall available for plays that can run longer than a week. Currently, the theater's offerings consist of weeklong or shorter runs of touring plays too small for bigger theaters but capable of drawing more patrons than a small theater can hold. This season has included Sandra Bernhard's solo show "I'm Still Here . . . Damn It" and the revue "The Irish . . . And How They Got That Way."

Ambience: Cheerfully crowded. Alcoholic beverages, soft drinks and snacks available in the lobby.

Insider's tip: If the Tigers have a game, competition for parking spaces could be fierce.

Address: 350 Madison Ave., Detroit.

Seating: 1,750.

Tickets: $20-$35.

Parking: Nearby lots, $6-$7.

➤ MASONIC TEMPLE THEATRE

Detroit's other home (besides the Fisher) for big Broadway musicals, Masonic Temple is a vast U-shaped hall. The U must stand for unique, or at least unusual, as it applies to the seating arrangements. Besides the typical array of orchestra seats, Masonic has chairs on risers along the sidelines, as well as similarly elevated sections behind the orchestra, but under the balcony. The views from the sides are unobstructed and surprisingly good. Masonic's big musicals tend to feature big stars. The 1999-2000 season saw Robert Urich in "Chicago" and Richard Chamberlain in "The Sound of Music."

Ambience: Big and cavernous, with beverages and snacks one flight down.

Insider's tip: The stage door is just to the left of the theater's rear entrance, in the parking lot. Well-wishers and autograph seekers usually find their wait rewarded.

Address: 500 Temple, Detroit.

Seating: 4,444.

Tickets: $25-$55.

Parking: A parking lot behind the building ($6), private lots nearby.

➤ MEADOW BROOK THEATRE

The area's biggest nonprofit theater generally permits itself one new play a season; the rest of the time it applies impressive stagecraft to the tried-and-true, which in the 1999-2000 season included the female version of Neil Simon's "The Odd Couple" and Arthur Miller's "All My Sons." Meadow Brook patrons appear to prefer familiar offerings; theater officials often cite the influence that audience feedback has on play selection.

Ambience: Comfortable. For chocoholics, a dandy candy stand sells chocolate-covered pretzels and other goodies. The art gallery across the hall is usually open during intermission.

Insider's tip: Don't bother parking near the long, gold canopy; you'll only have to walk down and then up. Park near the lobby's other door, at the right end of the hallway windows.

Address: Oakland University campus, Auburn Hills.

Seating: 608 seats.

Tickets: $24-$35.

Parking: Free, across the road.

➤ THE THEATRE COMPANY

Seasoned professionals share the stage with undergraduates at the University of Detroit-Mercy's Theatre Company. Correspondingly, the fare ranges from the venerably modern to the brand new.

Ambience: A basic, unadorned lobby. Snacks

and beverages sold during intermission.

Insider's tip: The campus entrance is on Outer Drive, west of Southfield. You don't have to stop at the guard station if you know where you're going. This is where you're going: Turn right just past the guard station, then left at the end of the road. The theater will be straight ahead, down the drive.

Address: McAuley Theatre, University of Detroit Mercy, Outer Drive at McNichols, Detroit.

Seating: 315 seats for auditorium productions; 80 on the stage for onstage productions.

Tickets: $10.

Parking: Free in adjacent lot.

➤ HILBERRY THEATRE

An actor who plays, say, Hamlet on Thursday night at the Hilberry Theatre might be doing a walk-on in a Neil Simon comedy on Friday night. As Wayne State University's graduate professional company — members receive a salary, free tuition, health insurance and, after three years, a master's degree — the Hilberry exists to train as well as to entertain.

Ambience: A spacious lobby with beverage, candy and souvenir sales counters (T-shirts, coffee mugs), staffed by company members who aren't performing that night.

Insider's tip: Thirsty? Be careful at the water fountains. They don't call them Old Faceful for nothing.

Address: Cass at Hancock, Detroit.

Seating: 534 seats.

Tickets: $11-$18.

Parking: $3 in a lot across Cass Avenue.

➤ JEWISH ENSEMBLE THEATRE

Plays at the Jewish Ensemble Theatre (JET) are by Jewish playwrights or have main characters who are Jewish, but audiences of any religion or ethnic background can relate to them. Indeed, Neil Simon and Arthur Miller — whose "The Prisoner of Second Avenue" and "Broken Glass," respectively, JET produced in the 1999-2000 season — have almost universal appeal, and JET's production values are top-notch.

Ambience: Comfortable; soft drinks and candy available.

Insider's tip: There are no Friday performances, in observance of the Sabbath.

Address: Aaron DeRoy Theatre, Jewish Community Center, 6600 W. Maple, West Bloomfield Township.

Seating: 185 seats.

Tickets: $21-$25.

Parking: Free in an adjacent lot.

Free Press file photo
The Planet Ant Theatre. Don't expect much elbow room.

➤ PLANET ANT THEATRE

With only 50 seats (they can haul out maybe 10 more for an overflow crowd), this storefront theater is very small but it thinks big. For two seasons in a row it inventively staged plays by Shakespeare — 1999 "The Tempest," 2000 "The Comedy of Errors." Planet Ant also embraces the modern and the hot-off-the-press, which helps explain why it attracts award-winning local actors and directors as well as theater artists with less experience. Geographically, Michigan is off-Broadway, but psychically, Planet Ant is very close to off-off-Broadway.

Ambience: Friendly and funky. Candy and soft drinks available in the tiny lobby.

Insider's tip: The rest room (there's only one, it's unisex) is backstage, behind the curtain.

Address: 2357 Caniff, Hamtramck.

Seating: 50 seats.

Tickets: $10.

Parking: Free, on neighboring streets.

➤ MACOMB CENTER

The Macomb Center, metro Detroit's most comfortable auditorium, has good sight lines and incredible legroom. Macomb Center likes to stretch, offering concerts, theater, comedy and dance. The theater ranges from touring Shakespeare productions to bus-and-truck companies of Broadway musicals that spend one to three nights before moving on.

Ambience: Airy. Spacious, nicely carpeted lobby with several beverage and snack stands. There's an art gallery at the end of the lefthand hallway.

Insider's tip: The rest room doors are almost undistinguishable from the wood-and-mirror walls around them. Don't waste time looking for handles. Just push.

Address: 44575 Garfield Road at M-59, Macomb County Community College, Clinton Township.

Seating: 1,264.

Tickets: $22-$42.

Parking: Free in adjacent lots.

Free Press file photo
Second City features comedy, some of it with strictly local flavor.

➤ SECOND CITY DETROIT

Laughter is the goal at Second City, but its quick-thinking performers consider themselves actors, not comedians. Nobody stands up and tells jokes; the humor arises from characters, situations and suggestions from the audience. Everything is fair game for these satirists — they usually write their own material — and some of their skits are strictly local. If you happen to be Mayor Dennis Archer, Gov. John Engler or even landlord Mike Ilitch, prepare to take your lumps.

Ambience: Nightclub lively, with patrons packed close together at tables. Alcohol is readily available, as well as snacks and soft drinks.

Insider's tip: The warmer it gets outside, the colder it gets inside. Bring a sweater, sweatshirt or jacket.

Address: Woodward at Montcalm, Detroit.

Seating: 350.

Tickets: $10-$19.50.

Parking: Nearby in lots and garages, in the $6-$7 range.

Detroit's theater royalty

As a Free Press writer and reviewer, Lawrence DeVine wrote about the theater for 30 years before he retired in 1998. He estimated he had seen 4,000 plays — all over the world — during that stint. What follows is his take on the metro Detroit theater scene.

Joe Nederlander relaxes in the back row at the Fisher Theatre in 1997.

Titans of seasons past

➤ **David T. Nederlander** (1886-1967): The earth father of Detroit theater was the patriarch of the theatrical family whose far-flung enterprises today include the Fisher and Masonic theaters in Detroit, a string of theaters in New York that includes the historic Palace, and others in a half-dozen major U.S. cities. The Detroit-born showman began a half-century career by taking over the old Detroit Opera House in 1914, operating the prominent Shubert-Lafayette Theatre downtown from 1940 to 1965 and opening the Fisher in 1961. He also ran the now-gone Riviera and Vest Pocket theaters on the west side. Active in the business

today are his five sons: Harry, James, Fred, Joseph and Robert (daughter Frances is not). D.T.'s theatrical line now extends to several grandchildren who are producers.

➤ **Leonard Leone** (1914-): High on anyone's fame list is the Highland Park-born son of immigrant Italian grocers who put Wayne State firmly on the theater map in the United States. In a 40-year career, he set up its theater training program, founded the Hilberry, Bonstelle and Studio theaters and the black theater program. His programs turned out more than 400 actors, designers, technicians and administrators. Among those he mentored were Lloyd Richards, former dean of the Yale University School of Drama and Tony Award-winning director, and actors Lily Tomlin, Jeffrey Tambor, David Regal, Chad Everett, Max Wright, Earl D.A. Smith, Arthur Beer and scores of others.

➤ **Lavina Moyer** (1947-): For nearly 20 years, she was cofounder, artistic director and mother to the Attic Theatre, when its off-Broadway brand of risk-taking often made it the most exciting show in town. She was the prime mover for such shows as "Streamers," "El Grande de Coca-Cola," "Steambath," "The Diviners," "Lydie Breeze," "Getting Out," "Spokesong" and "Back in the World" — an amazing list. She came east from Puyallup, Wash., in 1973 to study with a new generation of Michigan talent at the old Academy of Dramatic Art at Oakland University. With pals Divina Cook and Jim Moran, she opened the Attic in 1976 in a second-floor space above the Pegasus Restaurant in Greektown. The Attic moved many times and she was nearly broke when she resigned to take a job with employment benefits at St. Olaf's College in Minnesota. Now 51, she is back in Detroit, not directing, but teaching part time at Wayne State.

➤ **Earl D.A. Smith** (1940-1986): The powerfully built, intense actor, director and teacher was an early hero in Detroit's black theater scene. He was the first black Hamlet many people here had ever seen, cast in 1967 by Hilberry Theatre's Leonard Leone, who said Smith simply was the best actor he knew for the role. Along with colleagues like Council Cargle, Kent Martin and Maggie Porter, Smith created a new climate for black plays and players here. He worked all over Detroit — at Hilberry, in storefronts with his and David Regal's experimental company, at Martin's State Fair Theatre and alongside Regal as associate director of the University of Detroit's Theatre Company. His most memorable roles were the storytelling sharecropper Cephus Miles in "Home" and the Irish mountain man in "Devour the Snow."

➤ **Joseph Z. Nederlander** (1928-): The fourth of D.T. Nederlander's five sons, he made a mark on Detroit theater by opening the Fisher Theatre with his father in 1961, then shepherding it through growth years of pre-Broadway tryouts and healthy subscription series into the 1980s. In recent years, he has participated less in day-to-day operations of the Fisher and

Free Press file photo

Earl D.A. Smith, kneeling, with Marcus Neville in a 1983 production of "Kismet."

Masonic Temple theaters. He began by sweeping floors and taking tickets at the Shubert-Lafayette Theatre and worked his way up to national prominence as his family's theater holdings grew locally — the family launched Pine Knob Music Theater — and also became powerful nationally. He is one of the best-liked producers in a business not known for its kind hearts.

➤ **Alan Lichtenstein** (1950-): More people in Detroit this season will see stage shows presented by this man than by anyone else. The manager from Yale Drama School picks the seasons for the Nederlander Organization's Fisher and Masonic Temple theaters and for whatever it books into the Detroit Opera House. He recently estimated that his shows annually draw 700,000 people. That's more than the season total for the Detroit Lions. He does not book his own taste, but what he thinks will sell, based on the touring shows' track records on Broadway. He is a businessman who likes musicals. A producer does not need highly paid stars for a musical like "Chorus Line" or "Annie." Lichtenstein is well organized, a straight shooter who is liked by the press and respected by his peers. He has put down roots here with a wife, children and a home.

**Johanna Broughton in her
eclectic office in 1999.**

David Regal
has become
a theater elder
in an art form
and a city
where short
careers are
the rule.

➤ **Chuck Forbes** (1930-): Forbes could retire tomorrow to a Florida shuffleboard court and his place would be secure in Detroit theater history because he raised our morale. Fifteen years ago Forbes said there would be a theater district downtown. People said it wasn't possible, yet today there is a theater district, and he's still Mr. Nice Guy. He spurred Mike Ilitch to renovate the Fox, he rehabbed the State, and, most famously, he made a going concern of the gorgeous old Gem Theatre. Then when the sports stadium big shots said they'd tear down his Gem, he got $15 million for the land, picked up his theater and moved it! And every time we hear that story, we smile.

➤ **David L. Regal** (1943-): The iron man of Detroit theater, this actor-director-survivor's 31 years around greasepaint earn him a place on any and every list of people who have affected the way we look at art. Beginning with the Hilberry Theatre company, Regal has endured triumph and tragedy. His noisy, combative personal style has ripened, and he has become a theater elder in an art form and a city where short careers are the rule and polite speaking is the preference. He has won many awards, and he usually has two or three jobs going at once: actor, director, teacher, administrator. Regal also is the second most successful producer in America of the work of

the famous, mysterious and wonderful playwright Jane Martin, behind only Martin's Kentucky hometown alter ego, Jon Jory at Actors Theatre of Louisville.

Titans of tomorrow

➤ **Johanna Broughton** (1965-) and
➤ **Daniel C. Walker** (1962-): Broughton is executive director and Walker is artistic director of Ann Arbor's Performance Network. Under their collaborative leadership (they are also wife and husband), Performance Network has progressed from a sometimes professional theater to a full-fledged professional theater, while also nurturing community-based and experimental ventures in playmaking. Recently Performance Network has developed a knack for securing the local performing rights to the most significant new plays, becoming the first theater in Michigan to perform "How I Learned To Drive," "The Ride Down Mt. Morgan" and "Wit." After years in a converted factory, Performance Network begins its 2000-2001 season in a brand-new home, a few blocks away geographically but light years away in every other sense.

➤ **Guy Sanville** (1953-): Among all the zany comedies about gassy deer hunters and alien milkmen, there is this aesthete who looks like a nose tackle. Sanville, as artistic director of Jeff Daniels' Purple Rose Theatre, has pushed toward new levels of acting and production. With last season's world premiere of a new Lanford Wilson play, "Book of Days," and now with Daniels' own new drama, "Boom Town," Sanville is working on weightier evenings that make people talk to one another at intermission and in the bar after the show. The theater on a side street in Chelsea is already one of the most important in the Midwest, and Sanville could make it more so.

➤ **Gary Anderson** (1962-): In three or four years, Anderson hopes to begin a series of world premieres of plays for his Plowshares Theatre Co. and also be in his own building. High aspirations are nothing new for Anderson, who talks the talk but also walks the walk. He began in storefronts and church auditoriums and moved his company into the Anderson Theater at Henry Ford Museum in June 2000. He envisions Plowshares as the bridge to black theater that has lanes for blacks and whites alike. He expects to do more plays about women and more plays about the black middle class. But getting it done will take some financial help. "None of it's been easy so far," he said. "We need a clear understanding that if the citizens of Detroit want to sustain productive local cultural institutions, they're going to have to invest in those. And rather quickly, or else a number of them are going to go away."

➤ **Greg Young** (1964): If Greg Young has his way, Detroit is on its way to becoming a production center for everything from Broadway-bound theatrical productions to feature films. As executive producer concert/theatrical for Olympia Entertainment — a wing of the Ilitch family's far-flung entertainment empire — he's

MARY SCHROEDER/Detroit Free Press

Gary Anderson, founder and artistic director of Plowshares Theatre Co. in Detroit.

responsible for booking and creating productions for a slew of Detroit's most notable entertainment venues, including Cobo Hall, Joe Louis Arena and, on a limited basis, Music Hall, the Masonic Temple Theatre and the Detroit Opera House. Though still young, the Indianapolis native has spent more than a decade producing major theater productions, from touring shows — "A Chorus Line," "Cirque Ingenieux" and "The Sound of Music" with Marie Osmond — to the recent Broadway production of "Wait Until Dark," starring Quentin Tarantino and Marisa Tomei.

DeVine's picks
Ten best Detroit-area productions
1. "Orphans" — The Theatre Company, 1987
2. "Nicholas Nickleby" — Hilberry Theatre, 1988
3. "Much Ado About Nothing" — Hilberry, 1994
4. "The Diviners" — Attic Theatre, 1982
5. "Book of Days" — Purple Rose Theatre, 1998
6. "Home" — Theatre Company, 1982
7. "Talking With" — Theatre Company, 1985
8. "Ah, Wilderness!" — Meadow Brook Theatre, 1970
9. "El Grande de Coca-Cola" — Attic, 1977
10. "Time Steps" — BoarsHead Theatre, Lansing, 1979

MUSIC

The
Maestro

Detroit Symphony conductor Neeme Jarvi rehearses with the orchestra before a Hollywood Bowl performance in 1994.

CULTURE

Music

At the baton: classical music

Classical music in Detroit is largely the story of the Detroit Symphony Orchestra, founded in 1914, though civic symphony, choral and opera societies first began appearing in the 1850s. The DSO ranks as one of America's leading symphonies, just behind the traditional big five of New York, Chicago, Boston, Cleveland and Philadelphia.

The DSO was a pacesetter in its early years, giving the world's first radio broadcast of an entire symphony concert in 1922 and inaugurating the first regular series on the radio by a symphony in 1934. The orchestra disbanded twice during the '40s because of money troubles but enjoyed a golden age artistically from 1951-62 under conductor Paul Paray.

The '80s brought more financial woes and two debilitating strikes, but the '90s saw the DSO rebound. Under music director Neeme Jarvi, the orchestra began recording and touring again, while symphony management retired its debt, raised millions in endowment funds and spearheaded the Orchestra Place renovation project including an office building, a new performing arts high school and renovations to Orchestra Hall, an acoustic gem built in 1919.

Michigan Opera Theatre was founded in 1971 by general director David DiChiera. Now a top regional opera company, quality has steadily grown, especially after MOT opened the $40-million Detroit Opera House, a renovated theater, in 1996.

DSO conductors

The Detroit Symphony Orchestra has had 11 music directors since its founding in 1914. Here are capsule profiles:

WESTON GALES, 1914-17
Gales (1877-1939) was a 27-year-old Boston church organist who had conducted in Europe when Frances Sibley, of a prominent Detroit family, invited him to be the DSO's first conductor.

OSSIP GABRILOWITSCH, 1918-36
Gabrilowitsch (1878-1936), an internationally known Russian-born pianist, put the DSO on the map. The son-in-law of Mark Twain, Gabrilowitsch knew all the most important musicians of his era. He threatened to quit the DSO unless officials built the orchestra a home. Four months and 23 days later, Orches-

tra Hall was opened in 1919.

FRANCO GHIONE, 1936-1940
Ghione (1886-1964), an Italian with an operatic background, spoke no English. His short temper and inability to communicate with musicians led to a short tenure.

VICTOR KOLAR, 1940-42
Kolar (1888-1957) had joined the DSO as a violinist before becoming an associate conductor under Gabrilowitsch. Not flashy, he nonetheless deserves credit for implementing young people's concerts and summer concerts at Belle Isle and for some early DSO recordings.

KARL KRUEGER, 1944-49
Krueger (1894-1979), previously a staff conductor with Vienna State Opera, was handpicked for the DSO by millionaire Henry Reichhold, who, by himself, resurrected the orchestra after it had briefly disbanded. Under Krueger the DSO played at Music Hall (old Wilson Theater). The DSO disbanded again when both Krueger and Reichhold quit, unhappy with the internal bickering among "old" and "new" patrons.

PAUL PARAY, 1951-62

The French-born Paray (1886-1979) presided over what many call the DSO's golden age. His rapport with the orchestra proved uncanny, especially in French repertoire in which Paray cultivated a clarified sparkle, tonal elan and rhythmic suppleness. The DSO made 70 recordings with Paray for the Mercury label, many still prized for distinguished performances and sonic excellence. The DSO moved in 1956 from Masonic Auditorium to Ford Auditorium.

GUNTHER HERBIG, 1984-1990
Herbig (1931-), a Czech-born German conductor, came to the DSO with a long resume. He was best known for his meticulously rehearsed interpretations of the standard central European repertoire. He took the DSO on a 14-city tour of Europe in 1989.

HUGH GRANNUM/Detroit Free Press

Renown violinist Itzhak Perlman holds a baton given to him by Neeme Jarvi, the Detroit Symphony Orchestra's conductor. Perlman was named principal guest conductor in 2000.

SIXTEN EHRLING, 1963-73
The Swedish-born Ehrling (1918-) was a workhorse, conducting a DSO record of 722 concerts during his tenure. His repertoire was wide and his performances were well-considered and reliable. The depth of the string tone he drew from the orchestra was particularly admirable.

ALDO CECCATO, 1973-77
Ceccato (1934-) never meshed with the DSO, leaving some to wonder if the orchestra is cursed when it comes to Italian conductors — Ceccato's short tenure matched the brief stay of Franco Ghione in the 1930s.

ANTAL DORATI, 1977-81
Hungarian-born and demanding, Dorati (1906-1988) capped off his career in Detroit, coming to the DSO with a well-deserved reputation as a world-class conductor. Under Dorati, the DSO resumed recording, hosted festivals and in 1979 went on its first European tour, which garnered rave reviews but left the orchestra in debt. He resigned after a well-publicized tiff with management over budget cuts.

NEEME JARVI, 1990-
Jarvi (1937-) brought to the DSO enormous personal charisma, extraordinarily eclectic repertoire interests and a discography that marked him as one of the most recorded conductors in the world. Some speak of Jarvi's tenure as a second golden age for the orchestra. Under the Estonian-born Jarvi, the DSO recorded 28 CDs for the Chandos label, including a widely praised series by American composers such as Any Beach and Samuel Barber. Jarvi's interpretations emphasize spontaneity, excitement and emotionalism. In 1998, he led the DSO on a 3½-week European tour and a 10-day trip to Japan.

ITZHAK PERLMAN, 2001
Perlman (1945-), a violinist who is one of the biggest stars in classical music, was named principal guest conductor for three seasons beginning in the 2001-2002 season. His duties, in addition to conducting three weeks of concerts each season, were to include youth education and working with the DSO youth orchestras.

Under Dorati, the DSO resumed recording and hosted festivals and in 1979 went on its first European tour.

Jazz in Detroit

Detroit's jazz heritage ranks among the most illustrious of any city in the country. The jazz tradition here was built by a vibrant black middle-class — fueled by the auto industry — that supported a thriving entertainment business and demanded schools with excellent music programs. Big-city competitiveness sharpened local heroes while small-town warmth nurtured them.

In the late 1920s, Detroit was home base for one of the most important early jazz bands, McKinney's Cotton Pickers. But the city really came into its own in the '40s and '50s, when it was the country's most prolific feeder of talent to the national scene — the list of stars included Tommy Flanagan, Barry Harris, the Jones brothers (Hank, Thad, Elvin), Paul Chambers, Ron Carter, Donald Byrd, Curtis Fuller and dozens more. Among the most important clubs at the time were Baker's Keyboard Lounge, the Bluebird Inn, Klein's Showbar and the Minor Key.

Even as the club scene splintered in the 1970s and '80s, Detroit continued to produce important musicians such as Geri Allen and Kenny Garrett. Begun in 1979, the Montreux Detroit Jazz Festival — a four-day, outdoor festival at Hart Plaza billed as the largest free jazz festival in North America — became the city's signature jazz event, drawing hundreds of thousands of people downtown to hear a mix of top national and local talent. In 2000, the festival was renamed the Detroit International Jazz Festival.

Detroit's all-stars

Detroit has always been a prolific jazz incubator. Listed by instrument, here are many of the most famous jazz musicians associated with the city. Birthplaces are given for those not born in Detroit.

ALTO SAXOPHONE
Kenny Garrett..b. 1960
Sonny Red.............b. Junior Sylvester Kyner, 1932-1981
Charles McPherson..........b. 1939, Joplin, Mo.

TENOR SAXOPHONE
Yusef Lateefb. William Evans, 1921. Also flute, oboe.
Billy Mitchell...........b. 1926, Kansas City, Mo.
Joe Henderson...................b. 1937, Lima, Ohio
Teddy Edwards..........b. 1924, Jackson, Miss.
Wardell Gray...1921-55
Oklahoma City, Okla.
Lucky Thompson....................................b. 1924
James Carter..b. 1969

BARITONE SAXOPHONE
Pepper Adams..1930-86, Highland Park, Fla.

TRUMPET
Thad Jones...........................1923-1986, Pontiac
Donald Byrd...b. 1932
Marcus Belgrave.............b. 1936, Chester, Pa.
Charles Moore.............b. 1940, Sheffield, Ala.
Tom Saunders..b. 1938

TROMBONE
Curtis Fuller...b. 1934
Frank Rosolino...1926-78
George Bohanon...................................b. 1937

EUPHONIUM
Kiane Zawadi......b. Bernard McKinney, 1932

PIANO
Tommy Flanagan..................................b. 1930
Barry Harris...b. 1929
Hank Jones...............b. 1918, Vicksburg, Miss.
Hugh Lawson.....................................1935-1997
White Plains, NY
Sir Roland Hanna ....b. 1932
Kirk Lightsey..b. 1937
Geri Allen.................................b. 1957, Pontiac
Kenn Cox..b. 1940
Johnny O'Neal...b. 1956
Carlos McKinney ....b. 1973
Terry Pollard ....b. 1931. Also vibes

BASS
Major Holley.............................b. 1924-91
Paul Chambers.........1935-69, Pittsburgh, Pa.
Doug Watkins..1934-62
Ernie Farrow ....b. 1928
Bob Hurst...b. 1964
Ron Carter ....b. 1937, Ferndale
Rodney Whitaker ....b. 1968
Ralphe Armstrong ....b. 1956
Jaribu Sahid ....b. 1955

DRUMS
Louis Hayes..b. 1937
Elvin Jones............................b. 1927, Pontiac
Roy Brooks...b. 1938
Bobby Battle ....b. 1944
Ralph Penland
Tani Tabbal ....b. 1954, Chicago

VIBES
Milt Jackson......................................b. 1923-99
Jack Brokensha ....b. 1926, Nailsworth, Adelaide, Australia

FRENCH HORN
Julius Watkins..b. 1921

VIOLIN
Regina Carter..b. 1969

GUITAR
Slim Gaillard ....1916-91. Also vocals.
Kenny Burrell...b. 1931

VOCALS
Betty Carter ....1929-98, Flint
Herb Jeffries ....b. 1916

BIG BAND
McKinney's Cotton Pickers ....led by Don Redman, 1927-31

In the late 1920s, Detroit was home base for one of the most important early jazz bands, McKinney's Cotton Pickers.

MUSIC / CULTURE

Come and get these memories

The Motown sound

Only the automobile is more closely associated with Detroit than Motown Records, which stands as the city's most notable contribution to American arts.

The label's startlingly rich roster of Michigan stars continues to reverberate in popular culture: **Marvin Gaye**, **Smokey Robinson**, **Stevie Wonder**, **Diana Ross** and the Supremes, the Temptations, the Four Tops — all groomed for mainstream success by savvy, Detroit-born entrepreneur **Berry Gordy Jr.**

Gordy, left, was a budding songwriter when he started Motown in 1959, and with help from protege Robinson, he turned the label into one of the next decade's most prolific hit machines. The Motown sound was crafted in assembly-line fashion at a small home studio on West Grand Boulevard, brashly dubbed Hitsville USA. It was a catchy blend of sweet pop and earthy soul, and bridged black and white audiences like no previous American music. Future stars included the **Jackson 5**, **Lionel Richie and Gladys Knight**.

By the early 1970s, when Gordy moved his headquarters to Los Angeles, Motown was the biggest black-owned business in America; Gordy went on to sell the company in 1988 for $61 million. Today, Motown is owned by the international Seagrams conglomerate, but its fortunes are still dominated by the vintage song catalog created in Detroit. The Hitsville house is now the Motown Museum, and is open daily for tours. 2648 W. Grand Blvd. 313-875-2264.

A Smokin' 45

The Motown label became Detroit's calling card.

Dancing in the street: These 40 singles define Detroit's Motown era

Talk all you want about Motown — the stars, the personalities, the controversies, the drama. Just don't forget the music.

Motown was propelled by its singles, those fabulous 45s, glorious nuggets of sound tailored on West Grand Boulevard for your home turntable, transistor radio or car stereo. Indeed, full-length albums on Motown's various labels (Tamla, Gordy, Soul) were often pressed and released only to follow up on an artist's hit single. That's because at Hitsville USA, the

song — conceived, crafted and tested by a pack of sharp-eared staffers — always came first.

So here are our picks: the 40 definitive singles from Motown's Detroit era, 1958-1971. We've ranked them based on their commercial impact, artistic worth and endurance.

Chart figures represent each song's peak position on the Billboard Hot 100.

1. "I HEARD IT THROUGH THE GRAPEVINE,"
MARVIN GAYE
1968, No. 1 (seven weeks). Motown's Christmas present to the world in 1968: Gaye's aching falsetto, Norman Whitfield's haunt-

Marvin Gaye, far left, in the early 1960s, Gladys Knight, Michael Jackson and The Diva, Diana Ross, flanked by Motown founder Barry Gordy and Smokey Robinson at Motown's 40th anniversary in 1998.

Left: Stevie Wonder performs at the Inaugural Ball for President Bill Clinton in 1997.

ing arrangement and the biggest piece of recorded music ever to come out of Detroit.

2. "BABY LOVE," THE SUPREMES
1964, No. 1 (four weeks).
Been missin' ya, miss kissin' ya ... ahhh, yes ... Diana Ross coos her way into the world's arms.

3. "I CAN'T HELP MYSELF," FOUR TOPS
1965, No. 1 (two weeks).
Two studio takes were enough to capture what endures as one of pop's most blessed vocal performances: If Levi Stubbs' passionate pleading doesn't smolder in your chest, you might want to check for a heartbeat.

The Temptations in 1996: Sunshine on a cloudy day.

Free Press file photos

4. "MY GIRL," THE TEMPTATIONS
1965, No. 1 (one week).
Sunshine on a cloudy day? Indeed. David Ruffin's rough-hewn voice traipses through the flower patch of puppy love.

5. "DANCING IN THE STREET," MARTHA & THE VANDELLAS
1964, No. 2 (two weeks).
Hear that tambourine mixed high on the second and fourth beats? The horns, guitars and piano congested in the middle? The limber bass bouncing around below like a pinball? That's the Motown sound.

6. "SHOP AROUND," THE MIRACLES
1961, No. 2 (one week).
Patent it, fellas, this one's the prototype: Commercial R&B dance-pop, with Smokey's whimsical lyric and an infectious vocal hook. The coming-of-age for Detroit pop.

Smokey Robinson and the Miracles, about 30 years ago.

7. "I'LL BE THERE," JACKSON 5
1970, No. 1 (five weeks).
The biggest hit for one of the biggest groups of the decade. With its shiny melody, echoed background vocals, quirky harpsichord and slick production, it blended the best of the Detroit sound with the label's oncoming West Coast vibe.

8. "SIGNED, SEALED, DELIVERED I'M YOURS," STEVIE WONDER
1970, No. 3.
Motown on 425 degrees of groove, deep-fried and served with tangy sauce. As the song progresses, listen to Wonder — singing with a sweaty, magnetic urgency — gulping for breath between lines.

9. "WHERE DID OUR LOVE GO," THE SUPREMES
1964, No. 1 (two weeks).
The inaugural No. 1 for the girls from the Brewster-Douglass housing projects. And there were nine more to go before their run was over.

10. "WHAT'S GOING ON," MARVIN GAYE
1971, No. 2 (three weeks).
Considered by critics to be among the finest work not only from Motown, but from the last half-century of popular music. The rich, silky track was also one of the last significant songs cut at the Hitsville studio.

11. "THE WAY YOU DO THE THINGS YOU DO," THE TEMPTATIONS
1964, No. 11.
Miracles Bobby Rogers and Smokey Robinson penned this one driving back from a New

Free Press file photo

The Marvelettes: Deliver de letter, de sooner de better . . .

York gig to Detroit; producer Robinson turned it into the Tempts' warm 'n' smooth breakthrough hit.

12. "FINGERTIPS — PART 2," LITTLE STEVIE WONDER
1963, No. 1 (three weeks).
Live and deliciously sloppy, this record was far removed from Motown's compressed studio sound. But then, Wonder — little or big — never did quite fit the standard mold.

13. "PLEASE MR. POSTMAN," THE MARVELETTES
1961, No. 1 (one week).
Motown's first pop chart-topper — featuring young Marvin Gaye on drums — had as much in common with New York's girl-group sound as Detroit's burgeoning soul-pop.

14. "MY GUY," MARY WELLS
1964, No. 1 (two weeks).
Cosmopolitan vocals, big beats, a jaunty air — and one of the only American tunes able to bust the Beatles' lock on the top spot in the spring of '64.

15. "MONEY (THAT'S WHAT I WANT)," BARRETT STRONG
1960, No. 23.
Some might say this blustery song — Motown's first top 40 hit — set the tone for Berry Gordy Jr.'s musical empire: "Give me money/Lots of money . . . "

16. "REACH OUT I'LL BE THERE," FOUR TOPS
1966, No. 1 (two weeks).

Dark, dramatic, gritty balladry. There are few more tension-filled moments in popular music than the one-bar break that sits between this song's verse and chorus.

17. "ABC," JACKSON 5
1970, No. 1 (two weeks).
Sweet soul bubblegum.

18. "STOP! IN THE NAME OF LOVE," THE SUPREMES
1965, No. 1 (two weeks).
The little record that spurred teenage girls — black and white — to sing and strut in front of their bedroom mirrors.

19. "(LOVE IS LIKE A) HEAT WAVE," MARTHA & THE VANDELLAS
1963, No. 4.
The Holland-Dozier-Holland songwriting team found its legs on this ebullient summer smash. Note the repetitive swap of brief verse and chorus, rather than pop's standard verse-verse-chorus-verse layout — a brand of song construction that would become a Motown trademark.

20. "YOU'RE ALL I NEED TO GET BY," MARVIN GAYE & TAMMI TERRELL
1968, No. 7.
One of the all-time classic duets, as Gaye and Terrell match each other note for passionate note in this slow-build, long-burn slice of soul drama.

21. "UPTIGHT (EVERYTHING'S ALRIGHT)," STEVIE WONDER
1966, No. 3.
An ecstatic gush of overdriven sound, with a

> "You best be believing, I won't be deceiving my guy."
>
> – **My Guy**, by Mary Wells

rock beat so brisk it threatens to trip over itself.

22. "BABY I NEED YOUR LOVING," FOUR TOPS
1964, No. 11.
Recorded at 2 a.m., after a gig at Detroit's 20 Grand club, "Baby" made for one heck of a sleeper breakthrough.

23. "YOU CAN'T HURRY LOVE," THE SUPREMES
1966, No. 1 (two weeks).
Diana Ross may have been Motown's queen, but James Jamerson is boss here, driving the music with that familiar stuttering bass line.

24. "TOO BUSY THINKING ABOUT MY BABY," MARVIN GAYE
1969, No. 4.
To understand why Gaye was among the best vocalists of the last three decades, listen to his voice as he arrives at the last word of each verse. Most singers would emphasize the downbeat; Gaye eases up, letting his voice softly massage the note through the change, as if he's caressing a feather.

25. "DO YOU LOVE ME," THE CONTOURS
1962, No. 3 and 1988, No. 11.
Frat-party R&B, Motown style. Custom built for "Dirty Dancing."

26. "THE TEARS OF A CLOWN," SMOKEY ROBINSON & THE MIRACLES
1970, No. 1 (two weeks).
Stevie Wonder wrote the music for this calliope-touched track, recorded by the Miracles in 1967. It was released as a U.S. single three years later — only after the track had managed to sneak to No. 1 in England.

27. "IT TAKES TWO," MARVIN GAYE & KIM WESTON
1967, No. 14.
All the exhilaration of happy love, packed right into the cathartic chorus of this buoyant duet.

28. "JUST MY IMAGINATION (RUNNING AWAY WITH ME)," THE TEMPTATIONS
1971, No. 1 (two weeks).
Eddie Kendricks, singing lead after David Ruffin's departure, tucks a translucent vocal atop this soft-lit track — another dreamy Norman Whitfield soundscape.

29. "COME SEE ABOUT ME," THE SUPREMES
1964, No. 1 (two weeks).
Lamont Dozier hurriedly penned this mid-tempo classic, an exemplar of pop songwriting, under pressure to follow up the Supremes' first hit ("Where Did Our Love Go").

30. "YOU'VE REALLY GOT A HOLD ON ME," THE MIRACLES
1963, No. 8.
Adolescent ache for the ages.

31. "I HEARD IT THROUGH THE GRAPEVINE," GLADYS KNIGHT & THE PIPS
1967, No. 2 (three weeks).
Recorded after Marvin Gaye's version — but released first — this is the versatile song's righteous, stompin' rendition.

32. "BACK IN MY ARMS AGAIN," THE SUPREMES
1965, No. 1 (one week).
The Supremes scored five consecutive No. 1 hits in '64-'65. This warm track was the fifth.

33. "HOW SWEET IT IS TO BE LOVED BY YOU," MARVIN GAYE
1965, No. 6.
With its spare and simple instrumentation, this track leaves ample room for young Gaye to slip his supple vocals right into your ear.

34. "STANDING IN THE SHADOWS OF LOVE," FOUR TOPS
1967, No. 6.
A showcase track from Holland-Dozier-Holland's so-called classical period, drenched in strings, marked by theatrical shifts in dynamics and grounded in the same dark key — B-flat minor — as Chopin's "Funeral March."

The Supremes
Diana Ross, Mary Wilson and Flo Ballard in the mid-1960s. Soon after this photograph, the group was reorganized as Diana Ross and the Supremes.

TONY SPINA/Detroit Free Press

For further reading

"**The Story of Motown**," Peter Benjaminson (Grove Press).

"**To be Loved: the Music, the Magic, the Memories of Motown: an autobiography**," Berry Gordy, (Warner Books).

"**One Nation Under a Groove: Motown and American Culture**," Gerald Lyn Early (Ecco Press).

"**Berry, Me and Motown: the Untold Story**," Raynoma Gordy Singleton (Contemporary Books). Singleton is Berry Gordy's former wife and business associate.

"**Dancing in the Street: Motown and the Cultural Politics of Detroit**," Suzanne E. Smith (Harvard University Press).

"**Where Did Our Love Go? The Rise and Fall of the Motown Sound**," Nelson George (St. Martin's Press).

SOURCES: "HEAT WAVE: THE MOTOWN FACT BOOK"; "HITSVILLE USA: MOTOWN 1959-1971" COMPACT DISC SET; ABC-TV; FREE PRESS ARCHIVES; "ROLLING STONE ROCK ALMANAC: THE CHRONICLES OF ROCK & ROLL"; "ROCK MOVERS & SHAKERS."

35. "THE TRACKS OF MY TEARS," THE MIRACLES

1965, No. 16.

By this point, Smokey had learned how to steer that stratospheric voice, and he uses it to craft one of his top vocal performances.

36. "YOU KEEP ME HANGIN' ON," THE SUPREMES

1966, No. 1 (two weeks).

This Holland-Dozier-Holland opus is one of Motown's most prolific cover songs: Rockers Vanilla Fudge took it to the top 10 in 1968, and British pop star Kim Wilde carried it back to No. 1 in 1987.

37. "I WANT YOU BACK," JACKSON 5

1970, No. 1 (one week).

With the Jacksons' vocals tucked onto an instrumental track originally cut for Gladys Knight & the Pips, this debut single practically drips with exuberance.

38. "AIN'T TOO PROUD TO BEG," THE TEMPTATIONS

1966, No. 13.

Yeah, so what man wouldn't beg if he could do it with David Ruffin's raspy tenor? And what woman's heart wouldn't melt?

39. "SOMEDAY WE'LL BE TOGETHER," THE SUPREMES

1969, No. 1 (one week).

Someday, actually, they wouldn't. But this song did make for a poignant — if unintended — farewell just before Diana Ross split for a career as a full-time solo diva.

40. "AIN'T THAT PECULIAR," MARVIN GAYE

1965, No. 8.

Marv Tarplin's guitar and Smokey Robinson's clever lyric turn this one into a winner.

Motown time line

February 1958 — Gordy, acting as an independent producer and cowriter with Robinson and Tyrone Carlo, releases the first Miracles record, "Got a Job," to New York's End label.

January 1959 — Gordy forms Motown Records after borrowing $800 from the family loan fund.

1960 — A two-story house at 2648 W. Grand Blvd. becomes Motown's first headquarters. A prophetic sign is hung out front: "Hitsville USA."

January 1961 — The Primettes sign with Motown and opt for a more regal moniker: the Supremes. Gordy also will ink contracts with the Marvelettes and Marvin Gaye, among others, this year.

August 1961 — The Elgins, as they were known when they signed with Motown earlier in the year, become the Temptations.

June 1966 — Motown establishes an L.A. office.

March 1968 — Motown moves its Detroit offices from West Grand Boulevard to a building at Woodward and I-75.

October 1968 — Gordy and his three children move to Los Angeles. He soon rents a house on the same street for Diana Ross, with whom he had begun a romantic affair.

January 1970 — Diana Ross' final performance with the Supremes.

January 1972 — Robinson's farewell tour with the Miracles begins in Windsor and ends six months later at New York's Apollo Theater.

1972 — A Motown newsletter in March claims there are "no plans at present to phase out the Detroit operations, as many rumors suggest." In June, Motown announces the closing of its Detroit offices and its relocation to Los Angeles.

January 1973 — Gordy resigns as president of Motown Records to assume leadership of Motown Industries, which includes film, TV, record and publishing divisions.

April 1984 — Gaye dies from a gunshot wound inflicted by his father.

March 1988 — Motown Records fires 12 Detroit promotion staffers, marking the first time there are no such workers in the company's hometown.

JUNE 1988 — Motown Records is sold to MCA Inc. (the parent company of MCA Records and Universal Studios) and Boston Ventures, an investment banking firm, for $61 million. MCA gets the Motown record label. Gordy retains the company's songwriting licensing (Jobete Music Corp.) and its film business.

August 1993 — Dutch-owned PolyGram acquires Motown Records from Boston Ventures for $325 million. Gordy returns to Motown's board of directors as chairman emeritus.

January 1998 — The Denver Broncos win the Super Bowl and Motown's 40th anniversary is the focus of the game's halftime show.

The blues

" . . . I'm goin' to Detroit, get myself a good job
Tried to stay around here with the starvation mob.
I'm goin' to get me a job up there in Mr. Ford's place,
Stop these eatless days from starin' me in the face."

— **Blind Blake**

When African Americans began migrating north in the 1900s, they brought blues with them.

Detroit is far better known for the Motown sound and hard-driving rock music, the city was no slouch on the blues scene, thanks to the famous, such John Lee Hooker and Sippie Wallace, and the not-so-famous, such as One-String Sam, who performed on street corners.

A number of prominent singers and musicians emerged from Detroit and, though most never gained the fame of Hooker or Wallace, they were also superior talents.

Here is a sampling:

Eddie Burns

A harmonica and guitar player who still travels internationally playing the blues. He was most prominent in the 1940s and '50s.

Olive Brown

She was dubbed "princess of the blues" in the 1940s when she began singing at Detroit clubs with musicians including Todd Rhodes, T.J. Fowler and Sonny Stitt.

Famous Coachman

Yes, that's his real name. He isn't a blues artist, but he's probably the city's biggest and longest promoter of the music. Starting in 1976 and continuing for 21 years, he hosted a blues show on WDET-FM and was instrumental in organizing blues festivals in the city. He also owns a record store specializing in blues music, called Coachman's Records, on Detroit's east side.

Little Mack Collins

A guitarist and brother of Mr. Bo. Little Mack was prominent from 1950s on.

Free Press file photo

Louis Collins, a.k.a. Mr. Bo, playing his guitar at a Detroit concert in 1995.

Mr. Bo (Louis Collins)

He's a prominent guitarist whose career began in mid-1950s and continued into the early '90s.

Boogie Woogie Red (Vernon Harrison)

The Louisiana native became popular playing the blues on piano at clubs between Detroit and Chicago in the 1940s and 1950s. He was John Lee Hooker's pianist for 11 years. For a period, he was also known as Vernon Reid. He came to Detroit in 1927 at age 2 and died here in 1992.

Washboard Willie (William P. Hensley)

He got his stage name because he made music using metal thimbles attached to his fingers to strum a washboard. In the 1940s, he formed a band called Washboard Willie and the Super Suds of Rhythm. He toured Europe in the early '70s, retired in 1985 and died in 1991.

John (Bobo) Jenkins

From the 1950s through the early '80s, this blues guitarist and

Johnnie Bassett

A blues singer and guitarist who came to Detroit in the 1940s and started playing in clubs before he was old enough to be a patron. He recorded with several groups, the most well-known of which is the Blue Notes. Among the younger musicians he influenced, when he temporarily moved to Seattle, was Jimi Hendrix.

ROCK
AND
ROLL

Rock, Kid!

Detroit's own Kid Rock plays Woodstock '99.

CULTURE MUSIC

Big Maceo Merriweather

A blues recording artist who was most popular in the 1940s. Rocker Eric Clapton, among others, was inspired by his style.

singer was also a major promoter of the music. He organized blues festivals that eventually became a part of the summer ethnic festivals on Hart Plaza, and he recorded blues artists on his Big Star label. He also had a studio where artists could record, and he pushed for airtime for blues music on the radio. An Alabama native, he came to Detroit in the 1940s and began playing and recording in the '50s. He died in 1984.

King Porter

One of the city's leading musicians in the 1940s and '50s, this trumpeter was widely respected for his jazz and blues.

Todd Rhodes

One of the major band leaders of what's known as jump blues, which mixes swing, blues, bebop and jump music. A keyboardist, he worked with swing bands until he started his own bands in the 1940s. Although Rhodes played various kinds of music, his blues work was most popular.

Sippie Wallace (Beulah Thomas)

She came to Detroit in the late 1920s from Texas and continued to sing the blues well into her 80s. She was known as one of the last true blues shouters, but she was also known for her lyrics and singing. She was a prolific writer; most songs spoke of the pain and joy of women, but as survivors, not victims. One of her admirers, Bonnie Raitt, has recorded a couple of her songs.

Bob White

That was the stage name for the Detroit Count. Count, a Chattanooga native, came to Detroit in 1938, and performed at clubs in Detroit's Paradise Valley. Though initially known for his piano styling, he switched to Hammond organ in 1953. He wrote and recorded a song called "Hastings Street Opera" in 1948 that became his claim to fame.

SOURCES: THE ARTISTS AND "BEFORE MOTOWN: A HISTORY OF JAZZ IN DETROIT: 1920-1960," BY LARS BJORN WITH JIM GALLERT (UNIVERSITY OF MICHIGAN PRESS), TO BE PUBLISHED IN JUNE 2001.

Alberta Adams (Roberta Louise Osborn)

Began singing in Detroit clubs in the 1940s. She traveled nationwide and became known as Detroit's blues queen, although her repertoire included jazz.

Detroit's Queen of Blues, Alberta Adams, at a 1999 concert on the city's east side.

J. KYLE KEENER/Detroit Free Press

MUSIC CULTURE

Little Sonny
(Aaron Willis Sr.)

A legendary harmonica player, he began playing at age 7 and turned professional in the mid-1950s, playing in Detroit, and eventually at clubs worldwide. He has played with such greats as B.B. King and John Lee Hooker and has garnered state and national awards.

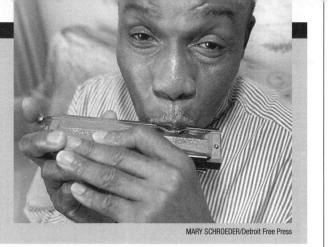

MARY SCHROEDER/Detroit Free Press

Play that funky music, white boys
Detroit rock

There's a reason the band Kiss wrote a rambunctious 1976 anthem called "Detroit Rock City." By that time, the Motor City had well established its reputation as a rock 'n' roll gold mine for both homegrown and touring acts.

Detroit's combination of blue-collar mettle and notoriously spirited fans ideally positioned the city as a rock capital. Motown Records, too, was a resounding influence on the area's white musicians; the city's rich R&B roots are reverently cited by rockers ranging from Bob Seger to Kid Rock.

Seger, who blended earnest proletarian sentiments with soaring guitar rock, is perhaps the quintessential Michigan rocker, having established an enduring national presence after toiling in local clubs during the late 1960s. His contemporaries included soul rocker Mitch Ryder, outdoorsy rocker Ted (Motor City Madman) Nugent and the Frost.

Punk and heavy metal — two of the most notable musical movements of the last 30 years — both have vital seeds in Detroit, with influential work produced in the late 1960s by high-throttle rockers the MC5, Alice Cooper and Iggy (Pop) and the Stooges.

As a concert stop, Detroit became a key player early in the budding tour business thanks largely to the Grande Ballroom (1967-72), which welcomed such big names as Jimi Hendrix and the Who. Today, touring rockers still cherish Detroit's enthusiastic concert crowds, and often pay homage to the city's musical legacy with snippets of familiar local fare. The Palace of Auburn Hills and Pine Knob amphitheater typically rank among the top-grossing U.S. venues.

Kick out the jams, brothers and sisters

For all of Bob Seger's earnestness and Motown's puppy love, Detroit's pop music history is loaded with a heaping helping of outrageous acts. Here are the most influential.

MC5 (1965-1971): These quintessential rock heathens made crashing, high-decibel rock that preached the religion of dope and cultural revolution.

IGGY POP (b. 1947): As leader of the Stooges and later as a solo artist, the Godfather of Punk was known for maiming himself and writhing naked onstage.

ALICE COOPER (b. 1948): Vincent Furnier perfected the craft of shock-rock, donning a feminine pseudonym, loading his shows with horror-film imagery, and generally scaring the heck out of parents.

TED NUGENT (b. 1948): The Nuge's unique status — a rock 'n' roll Natty Bumpo — lent him the enduring nickname Motor City Madman.

HALLOWEEN (1980-present): The group's heavy-metal horror fests were a longtime staple of Detroit's club scene, theatrical presentations that landed somewhere between sincerity and camp.

EMINEM (b. 1972): Marshall Mathers III earned himself ample controversy with 1999's pot-

Uncle Jessie White

A pianist, songwriter and singer. In the 1950s and '60s, his house was home to numerous blues artists looking for a place to play or practice. He had his own group called Uncle Jessie White and the 29th Street Band.

THE MACOMB SOUND
Kid Rock

(b. 1971): As one of Detroit's biggest breakout artists of the 1990s, Kid Rock went multi-platinum with his "Pimp of the Nation" persona, exemplified by trailer-park raps and an omnipresent middle finger. Robert Ritchie (Kid Rock) still lives in Macomb County.

(Even bigger was the multi-platinum, multi-persona Eminem, Marshall Mathers III, Slim Shady, who won three Grammys in 2001. He also still calls Macomb home. **See page 414.**)

ty-mouthed "Slim Shady LP" — edgy rap with a sick humor fetish.

GEORGE CLINTON (b. 1939): With his rotating crews of supporting players, Clinton took funk into outer space in the '70s, supplemented by a live show somewhere on the cosmic side of theater of the absurd.

Music sales by Detroit-area artists in the 1990s

SALES OF NEW SINGLES AND ALBUMS
(Figures in millions)

1. **Kid Rock** ....*rap-rock*.......4.6
2. **Eminem**.............................*rap* 2.8
3. **Anita Baker** ....*R&B* 2.7
4. **The Verve Pipe**.................*rock*..............2.0
5. **Bob Seger** ....*rock* 1.8
6. **BeBe & CeCe Winans**......*gospel-pop* ...1.6
7. **Aretha Franklin** ....*R&B-po*........1.6
8. **Insane Clown Posse** ....*rap-rock* 1.9
9. **Sponge** ....*rock* 1.0
10. **Fred Hammond** ....*gospel*..........0.5

SALES OF ALL SINGLES AND ALBUMS, INCLUDING BACK CATALOG
(Figures in millions)

1. **Bob Seger** ....*rock* 10.7
2. **Aretha Franklin** ....*R&B-pop* 5.2
3. **Kid Rock** ....*rap-rock*.......4.6
4. **Anita Baker** ....*R&B*.............4.2
5. **Eminem**.............................*rap* 2.8
6. **Ted Nugent**.........................*rock*.............2.2
7. **The Verve Pipe**.................*rock*..............2.0
8. **BeBe & CeCe Winans**......*gospel-pop* ...1.9
9. **Insane Clown Posse** ....*rap-rock* 1.9
10. **Sponge** ....*rock* 1.0

SOURCE: DATA SUPPLIED BY SOUNDSCAN.

Detroit techno

Initially overlooked in the United States but embraced in Europe, Detroit techno today stands as one of the most profound influences on contemporary music. While hip-hop blossomed in East Coast cities in the 1980s, techno bloomed in Detroit.

Three Detroit artists are primarily responsible for the introduction of techno: Derrick May, Juan Atkins and Kevin Saunderson, all with middle-class roots in Belleville. Working off the blueprint provided by the electronic German act Kraftwerk, the music was sparse, futuristic and tinged with melancholy. Mostly instrumental and created primarily with synthesizers and drum machines, the repetitive rhythms became a musical flavor of choice at European dances and raves.

Unlike house music, which developed simultaneously in Chicago as an updated

CHIP SOMODEVILLA/Detroit Free Press

Garage rock

What's that? Think sweaty bars, loud guitars, stripped-down but propulsive arrangements, a reverence for the blues and Detroit rock heroes. The city's garage music scene was muscular as the 21st Century began - especially in Britain, where the **White Stripes** were tremendously popular. The guitar-and-drum duo, comprised of formerly married couple Jack and Meg White, won international acclaim for their stripped-down blues-garage sound. Jack, above, is from southwest Detroit, Meg from the Grosse Pointes. Other Detroit garage rockers include the **Von Bondies, Sights, Paybacks, Dirtbombs** and **Detroit Cobras.**

Insane Clown Posse

(1993-present): Both scorned and adored, ICP was Alice-Cooper-meets-Kiss-meets-the-Beastie-Boys.

brand of disco, techno found only minimal success in U.S. dance clubs. But a decade later, techno and its offshoots echo in the electronic-oriented pop music dominating the mainstream charts.

Techno's greatest public moment came over Memorial Day weekend 2000, when the first Detroit Electronic Music Festival drew record crowds to Hart Plaza. City officials said the three-day festival, which featured 70 techno and dance acts, drew between 900,000 and

Juan Atkins, left, Kevin Saunderson and Derrick May at their Powerhouse Studios in 1989.

PATRICIA BECK/Detroit Free Press

1.5 million people, more than such Hart Plaza favorites as the Downtown Hoedown and the renamed Detroit International Jazz Festival.

Country/folk

Like most U.S. cities north of the Mason-Dixon line, Detroit has offered scant star power to Nashville's long legacy of artists. But as in most blue-collar spots, country music is a big deal in Detroit. The city's annual Downtown Hoedown in May is among the most notable country concerts in the United States, attracting more than 700,000 fans for a weekend of music on the riverfront.

Significant local artists include Eddie Jackson and the late Lonnie Barron, who starred at local honky-tonks in the 1950s, along with Randy Barlow, who scored a nominal string of country hits in the mid-1970s.

R&B/hip-hop

While Motown dominated Detroit's black music scene in the '60s, it wasn't alone in breeding prolific soul music.

From Cass Corridor clubs to street corners in the Black Bottom neighborhood, the city's R&B students had ample opportunities for musical education. Little Willie John, Hank Ballard and Jackie Wilson are names that led the 1950s, introducing a blend of cosmopolitan suave and gritty soul that would go on to define Detroit R&B.

Aretha Franklin ("Respect," "Natural Woman") was dubbed the Queen of Soul upon her astounding national success in the '60s and '70s, and she is certainly the exemplar of the Detroit sound. Her singular voice — which could handle Southern gospel, urban blues and even opera with effortless passion — has ranked her among the leading artists of the modern era.

Despite hip-hop's liberal use of George Clinton samples in its songs, Detroit itself struggled to produce hip-hop artists of note. As the '90s drew to a close, the area's only notable national rap acts were Eminem and Kid Rock, both white suburban artists with a penchant for shock.

BeBe and CeCe Winans were among the first gospel acts to successfully cross over into secular markets.

In praise of Detroit gospel

The collective sound Sunday morning across metro Detroit is mostly the sweet noise of gospel. And Detroit can claim a major role in the nourishment, development and popularity of gospel music.

Detroit bloomed as a city of gospel because a large population of African Americans from the South brought faith and music traditions honed in countless Southern churches.

In Detroit's churches, African Americans released their workday blues in glorious songs at Sunday morning and weeknight church services.

Many early Motown artists and other top R&B and pop artists first sang in church choirs or were inspired by the harmonizing they heard at gospel concerts. Perhaps the best known is Aretha Franklin.

Gospel music spread nationally through black radio stations and the concert circuit.

Some of Detroit's major gospel-promoting churches: New Bethel Baptist Church, the Church of Our Prayer, its offshoot Prayer Tabernacle, and King Solomon Baptist Church. The Goodwill Musical Union was founded in Detroit in 1943 by Sallie Jones. It is a branch of the National Convention of Gospel Choirs and Choruses, which was founded by the father of gospel music, Chicago native Thomas Dorsey, in 1932.

In 1968 in Detroit, the undisputed king of gospel, the late Rev. James Cleveland, founded the Gospel Music Workshop of America — the nation's leading association of gospel artists and lovers.

Among the many prominent gospel artists with Detroit ties:

Mattie Moss Clark

(1925-1994)

Affiliation: Church of God in Christ. Nationally revered choir director, writer and teacher of gospel music. Many of her songs became standard fare for choirs. Her students and those she influenced include Vanessa Bell Armstrong, Rance Allen, John P. Kee, the late Donald Vails and her daughters, the Clark Sisters — Elbernita (Twinkie), Jacky, Denise, Dorinda and Karen. Karen also has a solo career as Karen Clark Sheard.

The Rev. James Cleveland

(1931-1991)

Affiliation: Baptist and Prayer Tabernacle in Detroit. He was the king of gospel music who played keyboards and directed choirs in several Detroit churches. While at New Bethel Baptist, his musical mastery inspired the pastor's daughter, Aretha Franklin. As minister of music at Prayer Tabernacle, he recorded some of his biggest hits with the Voices of Tabernacle.

The Rev. Charles Ashley Craig II

(1929-1968)

Affiliation: Church of Our Prayer. Outstanding gospel singer and musician. He was head of music at the church from the late 1940s to the late 1950s. He was then pastor at Prayer Tabernacle until his death. Great gospel soloists such as Mahalia Jackson and Clara Ward called on him to play for them. His children and grandchildren are respected musicians and singers. His namesake, the Rev. Charles A. Craig III, pastors Craig Memorial Tabernacle on Detroit's west side.

SUSAN TUSA/Detroit Free Press

Fred Hammond at his Southfield recording studio in 1999.

Fred Hammond

(b. 1960)

The person behind the beat of a new wave of gospel music that is taking the secular world by storm. For years, Hammond has lived in the background, playing instrumental backup to the Winans and producing works for CeCe Winans and Kirk Franklin. Now he's one of the musical genre's leaders. His style shaped the gospel sound of the '90s — he's famous for dropping urban beats behind spiritual lyrics. In 1999, the native Detroiter won a record eight Stellar Awards (accolades that honor gospel music).

The Rev. Carol E. Hayes

(1918-1995)

Affiliation: Goodwill Community Chapel in Detroit. A Mississippi native who rescued troubled youth through music. Through her Goodwill Musical Youth Union, she brought together talented singers and musicians. They included Unity Baptist Church minister of music Dorgan Needom, the late Rev. Charles Nicks Jr., the late Harold Smith, Detroiter Della Reese, now an actress, and the keyboardist Herbert Pickard.

Lucylle Lemon

(1916-1982)

Affiliation: Baptist. Gospel lovers know the Winans got their start from gospel-singing parents, but where did David and Delores Winans start? With the Lucylle Lemon Gospel Chorus. An outstanding gospel music singer, writer, choir director and teacher, Lemon inspired many of today's gospel artists. She led choirs at New Bethel Baptist Church, Eastlake Baptist Church, Elyton Baptist Church and other places. She was known as the nation's "doll of gospel music." She started the Lemon Gospel Singers in Detroit in 1943.

Elma Lois Hendrix Parham

Affiliation: A longtime choir director at Greater New Mt. Moriah Baptist Church. In 1955 this businesswoman — she and her husband owned a record store — founded the Community Youth Ensemble, which attracted and encouraged young people ages 4 to 20 who were interested in gospel music.

The Rev. Charles Nicks Jr.

(1941-1988)

Affiliation: St. James Missionary Baptist Church. Probably Detroit's greatest gospel choir director, he established St. James as a powerhouse of great gospel singing. It remains so under the musical direction of Jimmy Dowell. In addition to playing keyboards, singing and producing, Nicks wrote songs that choirs still sing throughout America.

Herbert Pickard

(b. 1934)

Affiliation: Greater New Mt. Moriah Baptist Church and New Light Baptist Church. Although retired, Pickard remains one of the city's greatest gospel keyboardist. His talent

Free Press file photo

It all started for the Winans in 1949, when Delores (Mom) and David (Pop), seated in center, met while performing in the Lucylle Lemon Gospel Chorus, directed by the Rev. James Cleveland. Mom was 16 and played the piano. Pop, 18, was a singer and joined because his mother made him.

Delores Winans with her son, the Rev. Marvin Winans, who is pastor of Detroit's Perfecting Church in addition to being a core member of the multiple-Grammy-winning Winans gospel group.

The Winans dynasty

Vickie Winans
(b. 1953)
A Winans by marriage, with talent long before wedding the Rev. Marvin Winans, from whom she is now divorced. She hosts a gospel music television program, stars in gospel plays, continues to sing powerfully and is gaining a reputation for Christian-oriented comedy.

When Mom and Pop Winans (David and Delores) married in 1953, they became parents of a choir. Their million-record selling children include the Winans (Ronald, Carvin, Marvin and Michael), breakout duo BeBe and CeCe (who were among the first gospel acts to successfully cross over into secular markets), singer Daniel, guitarist David Jr. and the babies of the bunch, duo Angie and Debbie. Now their grandsons are in the business and Mom and Pop have discs, too. The whole family is known for contemporizing the gospel sound often mixing it with urban beats and R&B vocals.

The result: more Grammy, Dove and Stellar Awards than Mom knows what to do with.

Free Press file photo

on piano combined with the late Alfred Bolden's mastery on organ laid the early foundation some of the city's finest gospel music. He's also an outstanding gospel music writer, having penned classics such as "If You Just Hold Out Til Tomorrow" and "God Never Fails."

Edward M. Smith
(1935-1994)

Although he could sing — he was an original member of one of the city's great choirs, the Harold Smith Majestics — Smith's greatest contribution was managing artists such as his longtime friend, the Rev. James Cleveland, and promoting the music through concerts and programs sponsored by the Gospel Music Workshop of America. In addition, Smith was a gospel music disc jockey on several radio stations and from 1970 to 1975, he hosted a gospel music television show on WBJK-TV (Channel 2). He was the executive secretary of the Gospel Music Workshop of America and from 1992 until his death, he served as executive director of the organization.

Donald Vails
(1948-1997)

He came from Atlanta to Detroit in the mid-1960s to sing and play music with one of the choirs directed by Mattie Moss Clark. He eventually established his own award-winning group, the Donald Vails Choraleers in 1968. He left Detroit in 1985 to pursue music education in Washington, D.C. He was in charge of music for President Bill Clinton's 1993 inaugural parade.

Thomas Whitfield
(1954-1992)

Nicknamed Maestro of Gospel because of his polished, innovative style, he played keyboards and directed choirs, most notably the famed Thomas Whitfield Co. which he established in 1977. He also produced music for Aretha Franklin, the Rev. James Cleveland, Vanessa Bell-Armstrong and Yolanda Adams, among others. Contemporary artists such as Kirk Franklin and Fred Hammond credit Whitfield with influencing their musical style.

Etcetera

Pop music landmarks

The rich and lively sounds that filled many of these sites are now simply whispers across time: Buildings have been abandoned; some have been torn down. The melodies may be gone, but stand near these sites and you'll likely feel the vibes still there.

Motown: Hitsville, U.S.A.
2648 W. Grand Blvd. in Detroit.

The most important Detroit music landmark is the onetime homestead for Motown Records, which survives as a museum. Stevie Wonder, Marvin Gaye, Smokey Robinson and Diana Ross bumped elbows in the tight corridors. In its '60s heyday, Berry Gordy's label created a music mecca in this and seven other Grand Boulevard houses, with late after-

From the historical marker at Hitsville U.S.A.:

"The Motown Sound was created on this site from 1959-1972."

Free Press file photo

Where it all began: Motown's first headquarters. A basement room served as a recording studio.

noon street traffic clogged with gawkers.

The Motown Historical Museum offers daily tours: 313-875-2264 anytime.

Aretha's roots

**New Bethel Baptist Church,
8450 C.L. Franklin Blvd.
in Detroit.**

New Bethel is far from a relic: The choir at the late Rev. C.L. Franklin's church — where daughter Aretha cut her singing teeth — is one of the city's best. Aretha was 8 when she sang her first solo here; in 1956, she recorded hymns at New Bethel for the Checker label. Within four years, she was in New York and embarking on a red carpet promenade to the Queen of Soul throne.

1960s rock shrine

**Grande Ballroom, 8952 Grand River
(at Beverly) in Detroit.**

The city's most legendary rock locale. Built in the 1930s as a classic-style ballroom, it was a roller rink and mattress warehouse before debuting as a rock hall in 1967, just as the rock tour concept was gaining momentum. It became an important stop for the big rock acts — Led Zeppelin, the Who, Janis Joplin, the Doors — and a crucial stepping-stone for locals such as the MC5, the Stooges and Alice Cooper.

The reviews: "A definite gaudy Midwestern hippodrome look," Rolling Stone, 1969. "Dark, dirty, disorganized and drug-infested," remembers Ted Nugent. Says Iggy Pop: "A lot of it was an imitation of the San Francisco scene. But Detroit wasn't San Francisco. So you had these heavy-lidded, peace-and-love people on the edge of violence."

The Grande closed in 1972, and sits abandoned and graffiti-stained.

Into the groove

**Menjo's nightclub,
928 McNichols in Detroit.**

With a nudge from mentor and ballet teacher Christopher Flynn, Rochester Hills teenager Madonna Ciccone took her first steps into the trendy dance scene with visits to this longtime hot spot. It was the mid-'70s, the disco was typically packed late into the evening and the dance floor was dark, loud and jammed.

Smokin' in the noise room

**The Hideout, 20542 Harper
(at Beaufait) in Harper Woods.**

Michigan's first live rock club — one of the first in the country — debuted in this VFW Hall in 1963. It was open Friday and Saturday nights for loud music and mostly clean fun. Managed by young Dave Leone and Punch Andrews, it was the first of a string of Hide-

outs, featuring shows from local up-and-comers Bob Seger & the Last Heard, Ted Nugent & the Lourdes, Glenn Frey & the Mushrooms, and Terry Knight & the Pack (which became Grand Funk Railroad). Patrons paid $1 for admission to the small hall, which got so hot the dance floor soon became slippery with sweat. Still, even at its most raucous, the aura was more akin to a frat party. The Harper Woods Hideout shut down in 1966. The building has since been converted to office space.

ANDREW JOHNSTON/Free Press

The Harper Woods location of what once was The Hideout.

A walk on the wild side

**Eastown Theater, 8041 Harper
(at Van Dyke) in Detroit.**

The Eastown opened in 1969 as a hard-core blue-collar venue. A former movie palace built in 1930, the 1,500-capacity hall became the city's foremost rock palace, hosting shows from the Who, Cream and Steppenwolf. The dank, red-and-black Eastown was shut down in 1971 for violating city health and safety codes. A Free Press investigation also found the theater's mezzanine was a "veritable drug supermarket." The club opened again in 1973 for a short time.

Eastown regular Alice Cooper remembers it fondly: "It was the best audience in the world. And I'm not saying that just because you're writing it down. Any other city, people went home from work to put on their Levi's and black leather jackets for a concert. In Detroit, they came from work like that. The Eastown, those were pure rock 'n' roll times." The place is vacant today.

Funk foundations

**United Sound Systems, 5840 Second
(at Antoinette) in Detroit.**

The massive recording studio inside this tough brick building seems stuck in the '70s — yellow-and-green swirls on the walls, plastic swivel chairs — but United has been around since 1933, and it thrives today. It's been home to key sessions, notably the first records for the Miracles and John Lee Hooker, and groundbreaking funk work by George Clinton and Bootsy Collins.

Platinum records line the walls of Don and Will Davis' charmingly cluttered office: Johnnie Taylor's "Disco Lady," Aretha Franklin's "Freeway of Love," Anita Baker's "Rapture." Other clients have included the Rolling Stones, Red Hot Chili Peppers and Whitney Houston.

Setting the stage

Flame Show Bar, southeast corner of John R and Canfield in Detroit.

Berry Gordy saw his future during trips to the Flame Show Bar, where R&B was presented with cocktail glitter in performances by Sam Cooke, Dinah Washington, Johnnie Ray and LaVern Baker. It was among the swankiest spots on John R's "Uptown" district of clubs such as the Garfield Lounge, the Chesterfield Lounge and the Frolic Show Bar. Gordy's sister Gwen ran the Flame's photo concession, and sister Anna worked for her. The Flame was a "black-and-tan," which meant the clientele was integrated. The Flame closed in 1963 and was torn down a few years later. The corner is now occupied by a parking garage.

Moving on up

Motown offices, 2457 Woodward Ave. (at Fisher Freeway) in Detroit.

Albert Kahn's 10-story building was decked in blue and white in 1968 for the arrival of Motown headquarters, which, with 450 employees, had outgrown its houses on Grand Boulevard. Studios remained back at the Hitsville house, but this is where Michael Jackson and his brothers took care of business as they jumped into their Motown career. The label moved to L.A. in 1972, and the building has been vacant for several years. But it is still owned by the Gordys, and someday could house a Motown museum.

Inventing the future

Music Institute nightclub, 1315 Broadway (at Randolph) in Detroit.

Short life, big results: From its May 1988 opening to its closing 17 months later, the Music Institute served as a crucial breeding ground for Detroit techno — groundbreaking sounds that altered Europe's musical culture and starting making their way back to the

states as electronica. International visitors regularly stop to pay homage to the site, which is abandoned and boarded up. Many declare it to be techno's ground zero. Pioneering Motor City artists Derrick May, Kevin Saunderson and Juan Atkins perfected their craft at the institute, where the progressive music often throbbed until 8 on Saturday mornings, attracting a dance-minded blend of Detroiters, suburbanites, gays and straights.

Counterculture castle

MC5 house, 1510 Hill St. in Ann Arbor.

Detroit's hard-rocking MC5 held court in this pleasant house on Ann Arbor's frat row in the late '60s. It served as headquarters for manager John Sinclair's White Panther Party and Trans-Love Energies communal group, though time has revealed that band members were more interested in partying and jamming in the basement. Ted Nugent was among many musicians who frequented the house, and remembers it as a "revolutionary youth epicenter," though other guests suspected the straight-arrow Nugent of being an undercover narcotics officer.

MC5 drummer Dennis Thompson notes that the house next door — 1520 Hill — housed the band's roadies, friends and various hangers-on. University of Michigan students now live there as part of a housing co-op, and MC5 lore remains strong.

Birthplace of punk

The Stooges' farmhouse, corner of Eisenhower and Packard in Ann Arbor.

Iggy Pop and his band mates wrote the future of punk rock in the big house off Packard. They also maintained one of the premier party pads in late-'60s Michigan. "It was a beautiful house," says Iggy, whose unkempt bedroom was in the cedar attic of the 12-room white manor, a "pastoral" place that featured parquet floors. "A farmer had built it himself, but he moved to Ft. Lauderdale when they ran an expressway through the land. The police were always out there knocking on the door: 'Keep the noise down!' We came up with 2½ albums worth of innovative material there. Anybody who was anybody — George Clinton, Alice Cooper, Bob Seger — dropped by." New York's arty-trendy Nico lived in the house for a spell, frequently cooking brown rice and veggies for the five Stooges and their guests. The house was torn down in the 1970s, and a spiffy Standard Federal Bank sits on the site.

The Gordys still own the vacant Motown offices on Woodward. The building could someday house a Motown museum.

Memorable concert dates

Elvis!

CRAIG PORTER/Detroit Free Press

The King in his final Detroit appearance in April 1977. Four months later, he was dead.

MAY 25, 1956: Presley's first Detroit appearance. He does three sold-out shows at the Fox Theatre — 15,000 fans, mostly female. The Free Press calls Elvis a "hillbilly blues singer" and "rock 'n' roll dreamboat." Elvis said of his fans: "I'd like to take them for a ride in my new car." Twenty years later, the then-40-year-old Elvis plays the Pontiac Silverdome before 60,000 fans on New Year's Eve 1975. The Free Press describes him as "bulgy, blow-combed, dressed in rhinestone and looking like his old self — with the emphasis on old . . . with an extra 40 pounds on his pulsating pelvis." Elvis rips his pants, but the concert is considered a huge success — a then-record gross of more than $800,000 for a one-night stand by a single artist. Elvis would stage his final Detroit concert on April 22, 1977, at Olympia Stadium. He was doing his multidrug cocktails and would be dead by Aug.

16. The last concert lives in an infamous bootleg recording that finds him onstage laughing, inexplicably, for several minutes nonstop. In all, the King gave eight concerts in Detroit.

Little Stevie Wonder

JULY 23, 1963: Stevie Wonder performs "Fingertips, Pt. 2" in a concert that also features the Temptations and Supremes at the Graystone Ballroom, recently purchased by Motown Records founder Berry Gordy Jr.

Motown at the Fox

JULY 23, 1967: Uptown, the riot is about 12 hours old. Downtown, deejay Robin Seymour is hosting his "Swinging Time Revue" at the Fox Theatre. Martha Reeves and the Vandellas are headlining a show that includes the Dramatics and Parliaments. The music comes to an abrupt halt when a stage manager tells Reeves about the arson and looting.

Aretha Franklin Day

FEB. 10, 1968: Dr. Martin Luther King Jr. presents Franklin with an award from the Southern Christian Leadership Conference, one of 11 testimonials she receives that night at Cobo. After the speeches, Franklin performs "Natural Woman" and "Respect," among other hits. The ABC network films the evening for a TV special.

MC5

OCT. 30-31, 1968: The quintessential Detroit rock band — the MC5 — records its debut album for Elektra Records at the Grande Ballroom. That would also be the site of the final show for both the group and the venue, Dec. 31, 1972.

Free John

DEC. 10, 1971: The Free John concert is a major moment for the metro Detroit counterculture. John Lennon, Yoko Ono, poet Allen Ginsberg, Black Panther Bobby Seale and Yippie Jerry Rubin appear at a rally in Ann Arbor's Crisler Arena for John Sinclair, the Detroit-Ann Arbor poet/musician/provocateur who is in the second year of a 9½- to 10-year sentence for the possession of two marijuana joints. Four days later, the Michigan

CULTURE

ETCETERA

Kiss plays Tiger Stadium. About 40,000 fans attended the June 1996 show.

Seger

SEPT. 4-5, 1975: Hometown hero Bob Seger records at Cobo Arena. The recording, released the following April, is the "Live Bullet" concert album. Like the Kiss record from Cobo, it remains one of rock's best-selling live albums.

Led Zeppelin

APRIL 30, 1977: Led Zeppelin sets a world record for largest audience at a single concert: 76,229 at the Silverdome.

Hoedown

MAY 13, 1989: Garth Brooks plays a largely unnoticed set at the Downtown Hoedown, the opening date on his first national tour; by year's end, he's a star, selling out four nights at the Fox Theatre.

Madonna

MAY 31-JUNE 1, 1990: Madonna rolls out two shows at the Palace of Auburn Hills; her hometown angst backstage is recorded for the film "Truth or Dare."

SOURCES: FREE PRESS AND "DANCING IN THE STREET."

Supreme Court frees Sinclair after the Legislature passes a bill that lessened marijuana penalties.

Kiss

MAY 16, 1975: Kiss' sold-out Cobo Hall show is recorded and released in August as the band's seminal concert album, "Alive!"

Led Zeppelin set a world record for attendance with their show at the Silverdome.

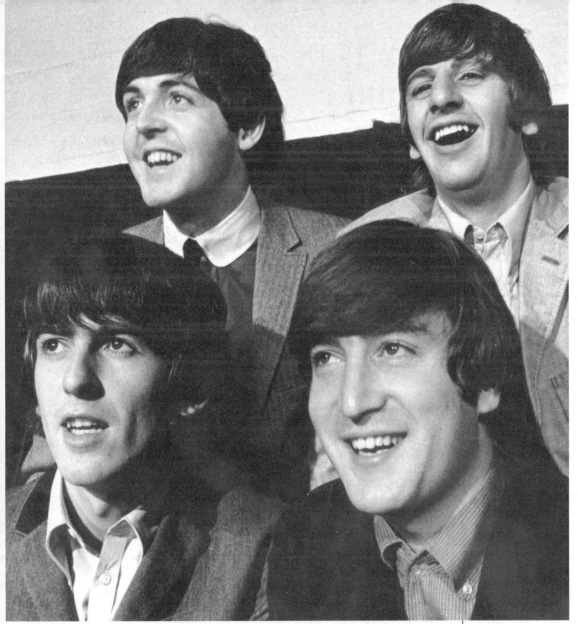

Long before Yoko and sitars, before the White Album and Abbey Road, the Beatles played Detroit. "I Wanna Hold Your Hand" was the highlight at Olympia in 1964. If you can't remember, the Beatles are, clockwise from left, George, Paul, Ringo and John.

The Beatles!

Sept. 6, 1964: The Fab Four's first Detroit appearance — two half-hour shows at Olympia Stadium that featured constant screaming and lightbulb flashes. A Chicago radio station bought 12 bedsheets the Beatles used from the Whittier Hotel, selling 72,000 1-inch squares for $1 each. The Beatles returned to Detroit in 1966.

A few bars to hum

Not only have Detroiters made a lot of music over the years, but singers have made a lot of music about Detroit.

Motown headliners

Excerpts of songs about Detroit:

➤ **"DETROIT CITY"** — Bobby Bare
"Home folks think I'm big in Detroit City
From the letters that I write, they think I'm fine
But by day I make the cars, by night I make the bars
If only they could read between the lines."

➤ **"PANIC IN DETROIT"** — David Bowie
"He looked a lot like Che Guevara, drove a diesel van
Kept his gun in quiet seclusion, such a humble man
The only survivor of the National People's Gang
Panic in Detroit, I asked for an autograph
He wanted to stay home, I wish someone would phone
Panic in Detroit."

➤ **"BLACK DAY IN JULY"** — Gordon Lightfoot.
A ballad about the 1967 riot.
"Black day in July. Black day in July.
Motor City madness has touched the country-side.
And the people rise in anger, and the streets begin to fill
And there's gunfire from the rooftops and the blood begins to spill.
Black day in July."

➤ **"MOTOR CITY IS BURNING"** — MC5; John Lee Hooker. Two slightly different versions of the 1967 riot, one by the hard-rocking radicals; the other by the famous bluesman.

Hooker's version:
"It started on 12th and Clairmount one morning,
I just don't know what it's all about.
It started on 12th and Clairmount that morning,
I don't know what it's all about.
Fire wagons kept coming,
Snipers just wouldn't let them put it out."

MC5's version:
"It started on 12th and Clairmount that morning.
It made the big cops all jump and shout.
I said it started on 12th and Clairmount that morning,
It made the pigs in the street freak out."

> # "Stand up and tell 'em you're from Detroit"
> *— Rousing cheer for Motown from WXYZ-TV (Channel 7).*

➤ **"HELLO DETROIT"** — Sammy Davis Jr.
Written by Motown founder Berry Gordy Jr.
"Hello, Detroit
You've won my heart
Your Renaissance and waterfront give you a flare
You're irresistible
hug and kissable . . . "

➤ **"DETROIT ROCK CITY"** — Kiss

"I feel uptight on a Saturday night
Nine o'clock, the radio's the only light
I hear my song and it pulls me through
Comes on strong, tells me what I got to do.
I got to / Get up / Everybody's gonna move their feet
Get down / Everybody's gonna leave their seat
You gotta lose your mind in Detroit Rock City."

> "It started on 12th and Clairmount that morning, I don't know what it's all about."

What was Detroit's contribution to the King of Rock and Roll?

Elvis was a big fan of Detroiter Jackie Wilson. The two met for the first time in Las Vegas in 1966. The King asked Wilson about his profuse sweating. Wilson told him he produced the perspiration by swallowing salt pills and drinking large quantities of water before taking the stage. "The chicks really dig that," Wilson said, according to Elvis biographer Peter Guarlnick. Presley began using the trick to lose weight. Don't try this at home.

Tributes to Motown

Songs with "Detroit" in their names:

"Around the Motor City" ....Andantes
"Back to Detroit" ....Wayne Kramer
"Be a Part of the Heart of Detroit"
....Four Tops
"The Biggest Thing in Detroit" ....Del 5
"Bloated in Detroit".............................Latimer
"Blowing Up Detroit" ....Charlie Sexton
"City of Motors" ....Soul Coughing
"Death in Detroit (Frontline Assembly mix)"
.................................Christian Death
"Detroit".................................Marcella Detroit
"Detroit After Dark"............Terrence Parker
"Detroit Blood Box" ....Frantic Flintstones
"Detroit Blues" ....Swamp Mama Johnson
"Detroit Bound Blues"..................Blind Blake
"Detroit Breakdown" ....J. Geils Band
"Detroit Bridge" ....Revelers
"Detroit City No. 2"
.................Sheb Wooley (aka Ben Colder)
"Detroit Cobras".....................Multiple artists
"Detroit December" ....Si Kahn
"Detroit, Detroit" ....Carol Dunitz
"Detroit Diesel" ....Alvin Lee
"Detroit Dirt Box" ....Frantic Flintstones
"Detroit for All" ....Multiple artists
"Detroit 442"..............................Blondie
"Detroit 4 Life" ....Gangsta Chronicles
"Detroit Hardcore Mix"............Lords of Acid
"Detroit Has a Skyline, Too" ....Superchunk
"Detroit Iron"..............................Darts
"Detroit Jewel" ....Jimmy Rip
"Detroit Jump" ....Big Maceo
"Detroit Love Animals"
....Muddy Frankenstein
"Detroit MI" ....Dork
"Detroit Michigan"
.............................Billy Branch/The S.O.B.s
"Detroit Moan"
..............Ann Arbor Blues & Jazz Festival
"Detroit Night" ....Multiple artists
"Detroit 9000"....Jackie Brown (soundtrack)
"Detroit or Buffalo".....Melanie"Detroit Rock
Island" ....Eddie Kirkland

"Detroit Rocks" ....Montana Taylor
"Detroit 1763" ....Mustard's Retreat
"Detroit Shuffle" ....Steve Nardella
"Detroit Skies" ....Juicy
"Detroit Snackbar Dreamer"....Edgar Froese
"Detroit Special" ....Big Bill Broonzy
"Detroit Stomp"................................Big Maceo
"Detroit Swing City" ....Ultra Swing Nouveau
"Detroit Valentine" ....Red Aunts
"Detroit Walkabout".......Drug Free America
"Detroit Winter"
........................Kanabis The Edit Assassin
"Don't Stop Believin' " ....Journey
"Duet in Detroit" ....Roy Brooks
"Get Up Offa That Thing/Dr. Detroit"
.................................James Brown.
"Goin' on to Detroit"..........Wes Montgomery
"Going Back to Detroit" ....The Platters
"Henry Ford Invents Detroit"...Stan Freberg
"Hey Now, Motor City" ....Vandalias
"I Care About Detroit"
..........Smokey Robinson and the Miracles
"I'm Going to Detroit"...........Multiple artists
"I'm Leaving Detroit" ....Third Tyme Out
"If You Can't Stay in Detroit, Then Come Back
When You Can" ....Willie Johnson
"Jungle Bass from the Planet Detroit"
.................................Maggotron
"Little Detroit" ....Tenderloin
"Making It Better" ....Rena Scott
"Motor City" ....Counts
"Motor City Boy"..............................Lee Aaron
"Motor City Concerto" ....101 Strings
"Motor City Dragway"
.................................Demolition Doll Rods
"Motor City Madhouse"...............Ted Nugent
"Motor City Man" ....Uncle Walt's Band
"Motor City Magic"........................Motor City
"Motor City Mix (Motown)" ...Multiple artists
"Motor City Rock 'n' Roll"........Streetwalkin'
Cheetas
"Once Upon a Time in Detroit"
.................................Orquestra Was
"One for Detroit"...................Randy Johnston
"We Almost Lost Detroit" ....Ron Holloway
"When Detroit Was Burning".....Cathie Ryan
"Worse Than Detroit" ....Robert Plant

ALL-S

CULTURE

STARS

"Church was never more beautiful than during candlelight services. In darkness the choir entered from the rear, each member holding a flickering candle while singing 'Jesus Is the Light of the World.'"

Aretha Franklin first sang in public at Detroit's New Bethel Baptist Church, whose famous pastor was her father, the Rev. C. L. Franklin. That's Aretha in 1961.

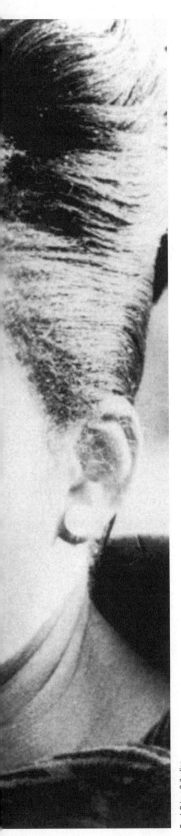

Frank Driggs Collection

Metro Detroit's musical all-stars

Aretha Franklin

1942 –

Truth be told, there isn't much royal about it.

Call Aretha Franklin the Queen of Soul and you acknowledge her status as the most vaunted artist in the rich history of R&B. But leave it at that and you betray the true depth of the music. Righteous, raw, seductive, cathartic . . . now those are the adjectives that tell the story. "Royal" just doesn't quite do it.

Listen to her at age 16, belting out "Precious Lord" at her father's New Bethel Church in west Detroit. Listen as she turns the word "Jesus" into an epiphany all its own, not so much twisting the syllables as massaging them, kneading them, venerating them.

Listen to her at age 25, transforming "Respect" from an assertive appeal for household equality into a national anthem for black America. Listen as her brassy delivery drives the song straight to the heart of the enduring American consciousness.

And listen to her at age 55, swooning breathlessly through "The Woman," stamping her name firmly onto trendy '90s R&B — as if it were ever missing. Others have tried to out-Aretha Aretha. Countless singers, both famous and forgotten, have toiled to capture the style, the sound, the effect. None have nailed it. Typically, they overbake it where Franklin employs nuanced restraint, or substitute blatant emoting where Aretha wields genuine passion.

She's had the gift all her life. Even she knew it, at an early age, growing up in Detroit and tinkering at the piano as notable house guests — gospel greats like Clara Ward and the Rev. James Cleveland — paid visits to her eminent preacher father.

Many artists paved the way for Franklin's marriage of gospel and secular soul, but only she brought it to this level. She's been miscast at times — first, in her early days at Columbia, where she was groomed as a torch singer; later, when she signed with Arista, which burdened her with a glossy pop image. But regardless of the material she's been saddled with — even a Verdi aria, when she abruptly filled in for Pavarotti at the 1998 Grammys — Franklin has always found transcendence.

In person, Franklin is something of a mystery — an impetuous, impulsive diva who often seems haunted by fathomless sorrow. It's when her voice takes over that it's all converted into unbridled fire.

So, sure, go ahead. Call her Queen. Just know that it's by divine right.

Aretha at the 1998 Grammys.

Stevie Wonder jams with Marvin Gaye.

Hank Jones: The family pianist.

Thad Jones worked with Count Basie.

Stevie Wonder
1950 –

Give him this much: Stevie Wonder was the first person to coax a supremely lucrative contract — and complete artistic control — from Motown chief Berry Gordy Jr.

By 1971, eight years after bursting onto the charts with his rollicking "Fingertips (Part 2)," Stevie Wonder was on the cusp of superstardom. The Saginaw native born (in 1942) Steveland Morris, blind since birth, had already decorated the nation's airwaves with a stream of infectious, upbeat singles: "Uptight (Everything's Alright)," "Signed, Sealed, Delivered I'm Yours," "For Once In My Life." He'd grown from a Motown novelty project — albeit a talented one — into a writer, singer, performer and producer to be reckoned with.

Now it was time to truly blossom. Stymied by Gordy's weighty hand, Wonder cut two full-length records on his own, confident they would be uncontestable bargaining chips in his contract negotiation. Gordy gave in, and the era of Stevie Wonder as legendary artist began.

Those LPs — "Where I'm Coming From" and "Music of My Mind" — were the beginning of a decade of extraordinary creative output. Ambitious, seemingly effortless and increasingly complex, Wonder's albums were cogent declarations, in both theme and sound.

In 1999, he remains on the Motown roster, less prolific than in the past, but his potent reputation intact.

Hank Jones
1918-

Thad Jones
1923-86

Elvin Jones
1927 –

By mid-century, Detroit was nurturing some of the most imposing jazz talent in America. The Jones brothers of Pontiac — Hank, Thad and Elvin — head the list, partly because of their innovations and partly because they epitomize Detroit jazz: craftsmanship at the highest level, where the assembly line produces one brilliant stylist after another.

Hank, born in Vicksburg, Miss., is the eldest brother and the only one not born in

Pontiac-born drummer Elvin Jones at the 1999 Montreux Detroit Jazz Festival.

Pontiac. He assimilated every major jazz piano style through bebop into an integrated voice of liquid single-note lines, luxurious chords and deft interplay between hands — all realized with impeccable taste and a touch as luminous as satin.

Thad became a hugely influential big band composer-arranger by grafting sophisticated post-bop harmony and rhythm on top of a Count Basie-inspired pulse. He played trumpet with Basie, but it is as a composer and coleader of the Thad Jones-Mel Lewis Orchestra in the '60s that he made his largest impact.

Elvin forever altered the rhythmic foundation of jazz in the '60s as the drummer with the John Coltrane Quartet. His style — an intense storm of polyrhythms, shifting accents and multilayered triplets — echoes the complexities of African drumming and blurs the distinction between solo and accompaniment in a jazz band.

Ossip Gabrilowitsch

1878-1936

The Detroit Symphony Orchestra was founded in 1914, but it wasn't until Ossip Gabrilowitsch, a brilliant Russian pianist of international standing, became conductor in 1918 that it began to thrive. Gabrilowitsch gave the fledgling DSO instant credibility, built the orchestra into one of the country's finest and at his death in 1936 left a legacy that continues to resonate through the cultural life of Michigan.

Born in St. Petersburg, he toured widely as a pianist before turning to conducting. A man of great personal charisma — he was Mark Twain's son-in-law, having married Twain's daughter, soprano Clara Clemons, in 1909 — Gabrilowitsch had appeared with the DSO as a soloist before being lured to Detroit as conductor.

His first act proved historic: Gabrilowitsch threatened to quit in 1919 unless DSO leaders built a home worthy of his orchestra. Less than five months later, Orchestra Hall opened and Detroit had a world-class concert venue.

Under Gabrilowitsch, the DSO was a pacesetter. He conducted the first complete symphony concert on radio (WWJ) in 1922. He inaugurated the first regular radio series by a symphony in 1934, the "Ford Sunday Evening Hour," which went national on CBS in 1936. More than anyone, Gabrilow-

TOM SAWYER VISITS BOSTON-EDISON
Ossip Gabrilowitsch, married Clara Clemens, a concert contralto who was the daughter of Samuel Clemens, also known as Mark Twain. The couple lived at 611 W. Boston Blvd. One day, someone found the original manuscript for Twain's "Tom Sawyer" in the house. It's uncertain what happened to the papers.

itsch is the true godfather of classical music in Michigan.

Madonna

1958-

It's hard to be sure just who the real Madonna is.

During her 16 years in the glaring spotlight of this era's media culture, she has been coy and explicit, loose and sophisticated, a sexy vamp and a doting mother. She's a dancer, a singer, an actress, a fashion statement, a celebrity for the sake of celebrity.

As a teen, Bay City native Madonna Louise Ciccone got her first taste of the high life at Menjo's, a gay dance club in Detroit, where mentor Christopher Flynn introduced her to the flashy, hardcore disco scene. She'd already dabbled in theater and dance as a student at Adams High School in Rochester, and studied ballet at the University of Michigan for a year. Soon she was in New York, where she worked her way into the pop scene.

While it's easy to say Madonna was destined for fame, it's more accurate to say she was driven to it — rabidly so. Even in 1983, during promotional appearances for her self-titled Sire Records debut, Madonna came off as brazenly self-assured. Chomping gum, baring her midriff, flirting with TV hosts, she was the bad girl who wanted to take over the world. For a while there, it seemed as if she did. Her relentless string of hits — "Like a Virgin," "Express Yourself," "Justify My Love" — were merely background music to her omnipresent media profile. Her sexually explicit videos spawned evening-news controversy, her rocky trysts with Sean Penn and Warren Beatty endless tabloid fodder. As the century winds down, Madonna — now a mom — maintains a lower profile than in years past. But in this age of disposable modern culture, her impact is, conversely, an enduring one.

Kevork Djansozian
Madonna expresses herself during the 1990 Blond Ambition tour.

Milt Jackson

1923-99

Milt Jackson, the first vibes player to translate bebop to the instrument in the '40s, was best known as a member of the Modern Jazz Quartet, but the roots of his influential style were forged in his native Detroit. Jackson, one of the most naturally swinging jazz musicians, reinvented the sound of the vibes by slowing the speed of his vibrato for more human warmth and playing ebullient solos of blues-drenched melody, drama and sly grace notes.

William (Smokey) Robinson

1940-

There would have been a Stevie and a Marvin without Motown, but would there have been a Motown without Smokey? The singer and songwriter whom author Gerri Hirshey once called "the steadfast keeper of the eternal flame of pop romance" had filled his first Big Chief writing tablet with song lyrics by the time he was 12. And by the time he was 18, he and the singing group he formed in high school, which would become the Miracles, had made their first record, "Get a Job," cowritten by Smokey and Berry Gordy Jr.

Robinson developed into a songwriter whose craftsmanship was matched only by his shimmering faith in ideal love. In the sublime "Ooo Baby Baby" and the heartbreaking "The Tracks of My Tears," Smokey served up his emotions raw and real, sans the smoke and mirrors of chart pop. Bob Dylan jokingly retracted his famous claim that Robinson was his favorite poet, claiming he must have meant Arthur Rimbaud. But for a generation, Robinson was a backseat laureate: We second that emotion.

Holland-Dozier-Holland

Formed 1962

If Motown Records was an assembly line, as the conventional metaphor goes, then songwriters-producers Brian Holland, Eddie Holland and Lamont Dozier were among the most vital cogs in the machine. Churning out hits for the Supremes, the Four Tops and Marvin Gaye, the prolific trio notched 16 No. 1 songs on Billboard's Hot 100 — second only in pop history to Lennon-McCartney.

Self-taught and influenced by the cosmopolitan pop-soul of New York's Brill Building songwriters, H-D-H crafted a distinctive style, with honey-sweet melodies atop a tightly compacted bed of sound. Their compositions were molded to fit their artists — the spirited "Heat Wave" for Martha & the Vandellas, the lollipop love of "Back in My Arms Again" for the Supremes, the yearning "Reach Out I'll Be There" for the Four Tops. After a sour split from Motown in '68, the trio sustained some success with other R&B acts (Honeycone, Freda Payne) and was inducted into the Rock and Roll Hall of Fame in 1990.

Rev. James Cleveland

1931-1991

Without him, there would be no Aretha Franklin as we know her. There would probably be no Motown sound. And certainly, without this man, the King of Gospel, there would be no upbeat church sound, much like what we hear in the rafters of African-American churches today.

The Rev. James Cleveland came to Detroit in 1949 as choir director at New Bethel Baptist Church, which was pastored by the Rev. C.L. Franklin, Aretha's father. Aretha Franklin has said that as a young girl, she would listen and learn as she watched Cleveland play the piano in her Detroit home. "I think he was probably the single greatest influence on gospel music. ...He was a trendsetter and... a leader," Franklin said after Cleveland's death in 1991.

Before he died, Cleveland wrote more than 400 songs and brought home three Grammy Awards. His two all-time classics are "Peace Be Still" and "I Stood On the Banks."

In the 1960s, Cleveland took a handful of Detroit artists and formed the Gospel Music Workshop of America, which today has hundreds of chapters and tens of thousands of members across the nation. It's a group that brings together anyone with an interest in gospel music, from Detroit to England to Japan.

Marvin Gaye

1939-1984

Marvin Gaye was an artist of many stripes: sensual soul man, enlightened social delegate, elegant nightclub romantic. But first and foremost, he was a singer. With a voice that could evoke chills at the same time it raised temperatures, Gaye stands as one of the most gifted vocalists of the last 50 years.

Born in Washington, D.C., the son of an apostolic minister, Gaye moved to Detroit in 1960 and worked his way into the burgeoning Motown family. He toiled as a session drummer and backup vocalist before getting his break with 1962's "Stubborn Kind of Fellow." From there, the shy, enigmatic young singer emerged as one of Motown's A-list artists, racking up a solid bank of hits, including 1968's "I Heard It Through the Grapevine," the biggest chart smash Detroit has produced.

It was 1971's epic album, "What's Going On," however, that established Gaye as a legend. Today, 15 years after being shot and killed by his father during an argument, his legacy endures as one of the most hallowed in popular music.

CHUCK PULIN/Star File

"I Want to Be Your Dog": Iggy symbolizes the savage side of Detroit rock.

Iggy Pop

1947-

In the rock annals, he's the godfather of punk, the misfit behind one of the most important movements in modern culture. But the real measure of Iggy Pop can't be calculated in dusty books. With the Stooges in the late '60s and later as a solo artist, his onstage performances were the definition of primal energy, the very essence of rock 'n' roll's fiery immediacy. "It's about totally losing yourself," he once said, "and understanding that what you're doing right here, right now, is the most important thing in the world."

Writhing in broken glass, leering lustfully, belly flopping into the audience, Iggy was all about extremes. Born James Osterberg near Ann Arbor, he was baptized by rock 'n' roll at a local Jerry Lee Lewis concert in 1961. His eventual plunge into drug-induced depravity is well-chronicled. Today, clean and sober, his wiry, gnarled body stands as testament to a life of brutal rapture.

Bob Seger

1945-

Few artists have captured the spirit of the Midwest working class as has Bob Seger. More sentimental than Mellencamp, less preachy than Springsteen, Seger has endured for more than two decades as a classic-rock icon. He got his start on the same Detroit garage circuit that bred Mitch Ryder and Ted Nugent. By the late '60s, he had turned his writing pen to more reflective works, and with his Silver Bullet Band, he became one of the most prominent rockers of the '70s and '80s. Seger's deeply devoted audience has matured with him, maintaining faith in the opening verse of "Beautiful Loser": "He wants to dream like a young man/ With the wisdom of an old man."

Paul Paray

1886-1979

French-born conductor Paul Paray presided over what many recall as the golden age of the Detroit Symphony Orchestra: 1951-62. He led the DSO back to prominence after a troubled decade in which it was forced to disband twice. Paray's rapport with the DSO was uncanny, especially in French repertoire. The DSO made 70 records with Paray for the Mercury label. Many are still prized for their artistic vitality and superb sonics.

The Temptations

Formed 1961

Here's the way they did the things they did: with polish, poise and flair. The Tempts were Motown's signature guy group, blending the feel of a gospel quintet with the urbane delivery of a superstar R&B act. Much of their success can be attributed to songwriters Smokey Robinson and Norman Whitfield, who provided them with such classic fare as "My Girl," "Ain't Too Proud to Beg" and "Cloud Nine." But it was the Tempts' stylized presentation, led initially by mercurial vocalist David Ruffin, that sketched the blueprint still followed by male groups, from Boyz II Men to the Backstreet Boys.

George Clinton

1939-

"The sky was not the limit," recalls P-Funk bassist Bootsy Collins. "With George, there were no walls behind the sky." Musical mastermind George Clinton, a native of North Carolina, called Michigan home from the late '60s on. It was here that he and his chameleonic collaborators crafted their colorful sci-fi funk, a blend of free-form soul, art rock and absurdist theater. At 60, Clinton maintains a relentless concert schedule, and his vast musical catalog is among the most sampled bodies of work in hip-hop.

Motown Records

The tempting Temptations Walk.

Paul Chambers
1935-69
Ron Carter
1937-

Detroit bred the definitive jazz bassists of the 1950s and 1960s. Paul Chambers, born in Pittsburgh and raised in Detroit, played with a purring tone, deep groove and melodic imagination that outpaced his hard bop rivals. Ferndale-born Ron Carter, above, who succeeded Chambers in the Miles Davis Quintet, developed an elastic approach to rhythm and harmony, balancing timekeeping duties with the group interaction demanded by '60s postbop.

Eminem
1972-
Kid Rock
1971-

White rappers Eminem and Kid Rock (born Marshall Mathers III and Bob Ritchie, respectively) are the biggest stars to emerge from Detroit's music scene in a decade. In 1999, they were two of the best-selling acts in popular music, and in 2000, they seemed to be everywhere. In storied Motor City tradition, their vibrant but off-color music — distinctly Detroit in its gritty, devil-may-care delivery — bred controversy from coast to coast. Rock made the cover of Rolling Stone, and he and his band, Twisted Brown Trucker, created a sensation on the Grammy Awards before appearing on "Saturday Night Live." And that was just in the spring. Within a similarly short time span, Eminem, shown above, released the hugely successful "Marshall Mathers LP," was charged with gun-related felonies in Warren and Royal Oak and encountered trouble with city officials over a provocative video that was to be shown during rap shows at Joe Louis Arena and the Palace.

The Winans family
Mom and Pop married in 1953

Mom and Pop Winans thought they wanted only two kids. Instead, they birthed an entire choir. Their million-record selling children include The Winans (Ronald, Carvin, Marvin and Michael), breakout duo BeBe and CeCe (who were among the first gospel acts to successfully cross over into secular markets), singer Daniel, guitarist David Jr. and the babies of the bunch, duo Angie and Debbie. Now their grandsons are in the business with a new CD, and Mom and Pop have discs, too. The whole family is known for contemporizing the gospel sound, often mixing it with urban beats and R&B vocals. The result: more Grammy, Dove and Stellar Awards than Mom knows what to do with.

The Four Tops
Formed 1953

Growing up in Detroit's north end, Levi Stubbs, Abdul (Duke) Fakir, Lawrence Payton and Renaldo (Obie) Benson were working on their harmonies — and toiling for a handful of record labels — long before 1963, when they hooked up with Berry Gordy Jr. About a year later, the group was paired with crack songwriting team Holland-Dozier-Holland, and the magic really started bubbling: Two No. 1 hits considered definitive Motown followed: "I Can't Help Myself (Sugar Pie, Honey Bunch)" (1965) and "Reach Out I'll Be There" (1966). In all, there would be 13 Top Tens from 1964 to 1971. But the group's impact can't be limited to chart tallies: It was that just slightly ragged yearn-and-burn — particularly the holy smoking of frontman Stubbs — that cements the Tops' place in the pop pantheon.

Free Press file photo

The Four Tops: Abdul (Duke) Fakir, clockwise from top, Lawrence Payton, Levi Stubbs and Renaldo (Obie) Benson.

ETCETERA / CULTURE

John Lee Hooker

1917-

In fall of 1948, John Lee Hooker, who had come to Detroit to work in the auto plants after being discharged from the Army in the early '40s, felt comfortable enough to audition for a local record label. He'd show off the thumping, guttural blues style he had practiced in a shack at the corner of Monroe and Orleans and perfected in Black Bottom clubs such as the Apex and Lee's Sensation. When the record producer demanded some boogie-woogie, Hooker improvised his autobiography into an electrifying riff and chant that would be known as Boogie Chillen. In months, the sound that came to be known as low-down

John Lee Hooker, in his 80s, boogies on.

blues had swept the nation, and Hooker held the broom. At 82, he boogies on.

Diana Ross

1944-

Diana Ross, born into poverty in the Brewster Projects, is one of those celebrities who maintains a strange love-hate relationship with the public. For all the acclaim she has received — as leader of the Supremes, as a solo artist and as an actress — she has taken potshots, too: Her voice is too thin. Her hair is too big. Her personality is off-putting. But such are the travails of a bona fide diva, a status that Ross has enjoyed since doing more than anyone else to help Motown's music cross over to the international mainstream.

McKinney's Cotton Pickers

Formed 1922

Originally formed as the Synco Jazz Band in Ohio, this pioneering black jazz band became known as McKinney's Cotton Pickers in 1926 after relocating in Detroit. Innovative composer-arranger Don Redman assumed leadership from 1927 to 1931, which coincided with a legendary tenure at the Graystone Ballroom. Recordings established the band's national reputation as one of the top big bands in jazz along with those of Duke Ellington and Fletcher Henderson.

Diana Ross with the songwriters Lamont Dozier, left, Brian Holland and Eddie Holland in 1990.

Betty Carter

1929-98

Born in Flint, Betty Carter came of age in Detroit during the flowering of bebop in the 1940s. She taught musicians, critics and fans that a jazz singer, employing the scat singer's vocabulary of sounds and syllables, could improvise with as much sophistication and surprise as any horn player. Later in life, she morphed from jazz singer to jazz griot, founding her own record label and training young rhythm sections like a hip drill sergeant.

CULTURE

ETCETERA

Allan Barnes

Kevin Saunderson works his techno magic at the Shelter club in Detroit in 1998.

Derrick May

Juan Atkins

Robert Ashly
1930-

Roger Reynolds
1934-

Composers Robert Ashly (born in Ann Arbor) and Roger Reynolds (born in Detroit) were associated with the University of Michigan in the 1960s and were part of a group of experimental artists who founded the influential ONCE festival in Ann Arbor. Ashly is known for provocative and theatrical multimedia works that use electro-acoustic sounds, voice, text and video. Reynolds' music is abstract, often computer-generated, full of serial techniques and literary ideas.

Juan Atkins
1962 -

Derrick May
1963 -

Kevin Saunderson
1964 -

Unheralded in their native land, the Belleville Three quietly became one of the biggest influences on '90s music worldwide. As progenitors in the mid-'80s of techno music — a futuristic, rhythmically based electronic sound — the three made their biggest headway in Europe, where, along with Chicago house music, they transformed the musical culture. Collectively dubbed electronica, techno and its subsequent offshoots have remained primarily underground in the States, but their stealthy influence can be heard all over mainstream radio today.

Albert von Tilzer
1878-1956

Harry von Tilzer
1872-1946

Their real last name was Gumm, and songwriting brothers Albert and Harry gave America plenty to chew on, including Albert's "Take Me Out to the Ball Game" (1908) and "I'll Be with You in Apple Blossom Time" (1920) and Harry's "A Bird in a Gilded Cage" (1900) and "I

Want a Girl Just Like the Girl That Married Dear Old Dad" (1911). Harry was born in Detroit, and both brothers grew up in Detroit.

Hank Ballard and the Midnighters

Formed as the Royals about 1951

Though Chubby Checker is known as the king of "The Twist," Hank Ballard wrote the quintessential dance craze song in 1959 and first recorded it with the Midnighters. This incendiary R&B group, originally known as the Royals and formed at Detroit's Dunbar High School in the early 1950s, became the first group to have three singles in the Billboard top 50 at the same time when "The Twist," "Finger Poppin' Time" and "Let's Go, Let's Go, Let's Go" simultaneously hit the charts in the spring and summer of 1960. By then, Ballard and the Midnighters were already well known for a string of smoldering hits that included "Work with Me Annie," "Sexy Ways" and "Annie Had a Baby."

Hank Ballard, the R&B wizard.

Yusef Lateef

1920-

As a stalwart on the Detroit scene in the 1950s, reedman Yusef Lateef, born in Chattanooga, Tenn., was the first to bring the colors and rhythms of Asian and Middle Eastern instruments to jazz. Even before he moved to New York in 1959, Lateef's records with his Detroit band had secured his reputation. An experimentalism rooted in tradition has fueled his career, from swinging tenor sax work to pioneering jazz on the oboe to his current multiethnic music.

Jackie Wilson

1934-84

Detroit native Jackie Wilson, a walking, talking, shouting and soaring R&B legend, carved out a majestic career as a soul-singing dynamo and hit maker during the 1950s, '60s and early '70s. Acclaimed for his phenomenal live performances and cosmic vocal dexterity on such signature hits as "Lonely Teardrops," "Baby Workout" and "Higher and Higher," Wilson first rose to prominence after replacing Clyde McPhatter as a member of Billy Ward's Dominoes 1953. Wilson suffered a massive heart attack onstage at the Latin Casino in Camden, N.J., in 1975, and languished in a coma for nine years before dying.

Del Shannon

1934-90

Often overlooked on the state's extensive roster of rock 'n' rollers, Del Shannon was most certifiably a Michigander when he hatched one of the genre's quintessential works. "Runaway," written in 1960 while the Coopersville native toiled in the house band at Battle Creek's Hi-Lo club, became the biggest hit in the United States the next year. Though he never recaptured the success of that infectious hit, Shannon continued record-ing until his death by a self-inflicted gunshot wound in southern California.

Johnnie Ray

1927-90

Just before the dawn of the rock era in the early '50s, there were popular singers who hinted at what was to come. With a searing voice and an emotional stage shtick perfect for the new medium of television, Johnnie Ray was the cat's meow before the King, as in

Proudly sporting their White Panther buttons, the MC5 were the essence of Detroit high energy in the late 1960s.

Free Press file photo

MC5

1965-72

Svengali John Sinclair's vision for the Motor City Five, compressed to MC5 before the group raised sonic street hell at the head-busting 1968 Democratic National Convention, was Chuck Berry hooks up with Sun Ra to play tunes inspired by Chairman Mao's Red Book. No one could really hear the sloganeer-ing on the group's sludgy, much-hyped debut album, "Kick Out the Jams," which is recalled for obscenity and general nastiness, and its records never captured the raw rudeness of the live shows. Nevertheless, the MC5 can claim paternity for punk provocation from the Sex Pistols to Henry Rollins.

CULTURE

Tommy Flanagan

1930-
By the time Detroit native Tommy Flanagan left Ella Fitzgerald's band in 1978 to form his own trio, he had established himself as a leading jazz pianist. But in recent decades, his musicianship has deepened further. Nobody plays with more finesse, marrying grace and guts, swing and sagacity, wit and warmth. His touch is like satin, and his book is legendary. Flanagan doesn't know every tune, just the best ones.

Elvis. He was born in Oregon but was a pal of Detroit blues singer LaVern Baker and was discovered here by disc jockey Robin Seymour. "Cry/The Little White Cloud That Cried" was his quintessential jukebox hit. In all, he scored 25 charted hits from '51 to '57 and was the link between Big Band crooners and the first platoon of rock stars.

Fred Hammond

1960-
Call him the Prince of Gospel. Hammond is the man behind the beat of a new wave of gospel music that has wowed the secular world. For years, Hammond lived in the background, playing instrumental backup to the Winans and producing works for CeCe Winans and Kirk Franklin. Now his style is shaping the gospel sound of the '90s. He's famous for dropping urban beats behind spiritual lyrics. The native Detroiter, who still calls metro Detroit home, this year grabbed a record-setting eight Stellar Awards, which honor gospel music.

William Revelli

1902-94
Born in Spring Gulch, Colo., William Revelli served as band director and chairman of the wind instrument department at the University of Michigan from 1935 to 1971. Revelli's effect on American band music was profound; his bands played with clear and sharp perfection that raised standards everywhere. A widely covered tour of the Soviet Union, Eastern Europe and Middle East in 1961 brought U-M bands international acclaim.

William Revelli was the University of Michigan's Music Man for 36 years.
Free Press file photo

Barry Harris

1929-
Even before leaving his native Detroit in 1960, pianist Barry Harris had become an influence, first as part of the house band at the legendary Blue Bird Inn and second as a mentor to young musicians on the city's jazz scene. Today, with a resume and discography a mile long, Harris is arguably our greatest living bebop muse, channeling the music of Charlie Parker, Bud Powell and Thelonious Monk through his own unique touch and rhythmic rumble.

Motow

The Motown house band with James Jamerson behind drummer Benny Benjamin.

James Jamerson

1938-83
Listen to virtually any hit from Motown's heyday, and it jumps out of your speakers: that fat, fluid, dancing bass line. As bassist for Hitsville's studio group, the Funk Brothers, James Jamerson was the cornerstone of the Motown Sound — and one of the most influential instrumentalists in popular music. For Jamerson, it wasn't just about complementing drummer Benny Benjamin. It was all about feel. "He defined the ultimate in bass — what the bass was all about and what it was supposed to do," says Bootsy Collins, a formida-

ETCETERA   CULTURE

ble four-string player in his own right. "It was so progressive compared to everything else that was going on."

Alice Cooper
1948-

Whether it's the water or social climate, Detroit has a knack for producing rockers with a grand sense of theater. Insane Clown Posse and Eminem are merely the latest peddlers of a brand of schlocky shock rock molded by Alice Cooper in the '70s. His gore-laden stage shows — featuring guillotines, fake blood and mutilated dolls — were delivered with a wink, but controversy dogged him nonetheless. Now a reformed Christian and golfer, Cooper (born Vincent Furnier) tours occasionally to revisit his archive of glam-tinged hard rock.

Kenny Burrell
1931-

Of all the jazz greats to have either originated or begun their careers in the Motor City, Detroit-born guitarist Kenny Burrell may be the most versatile and most recorded. Since being plucked from the Wayne State University jazz band in 1951 to record a solo on Dizzy Gillespie's bebop classic "Birks' Works," Burrell has made more than 80 albums as a leader and played hundreds of sessions as a sideman, adding his relaxed, horn-like lines to brilliant recordings by John Coltrane, Coleman Hawkins, Jimmy Smith, Herbie Hancock and Duke Ellington, who hailed him as the greatest jazz guitarist of all. Burrell has repaid the compliment by devoting much of his later career to the Ellington songbook and by teaching Ellington courses at UCLA.

Martha Reeves
1941-

In every graduating class, there is someone who stays home and keeps it real. At Berry Gordy Jr.'s unofficial University of Motown, it was Martha Reeves who lingered in her hometown to fan the distinctly Detroit musical flame that started at that converted studio on West Grand Boulevard. Long after the torch was carried to Los Angeles by others (such as Gordy fave Diana Ross), Reeves was Motown's home girl. As the lead singer for the Vandellas, her voice made hits like "Come and Get These Memories," "Heat Wave" and "Dancing in the Street."

Anita Baker
1958-

With a voice that evokes the softness of Sarah Vaughan and the brassiness of Ella, Baker deserves credit for paving the road for many black female contemporary pop singers. She began her career singing in Detroit nightclubs and joined the group Chapter 8 in the 1970s, but it was when she signed as a solo artist with Elektra Records that she attained icon status with the release of "Rapture" in 1986. Hit after radio-ready hit in the 1980s and early '90s kept Baker on the charts.

William Bolcom
1938-

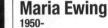

Seattle-born William Bolcom has risen to the front rank of American composers. Bolcom, a University of Michigan faculty member since 1973 and Pulitzer Prize winner in 1988, is a pioneering postmodernist. He breaches the previously puritanical separation between classical music and vernacular styles such as jazz, ragtime, parlor music, pop and rock. His scores range from solo piano and orchestral pieces to song cycles and opera.

? and the Mysterians
Formed 1964

Led by singer Rudy (Question Mark) Martinez, this Flint band created the legendary rock 'n' roll anthem "96 Tears," a perpetual party classic

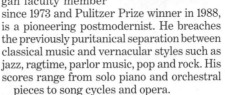

Martha Reeves stayed in Detroit to keep the hometown sound alive.

Maria Ewing
1950-

A star on the international opera scene, Detroit-born mezzo-soprano Maria Ewing has made an intriguing career of sidestepping the path of least resistance. She began by conquering soubrette and ingenue roles like Rosina and Cherubino, characters tailored for her light and agile voice. Then, surprisingly, she sang the heavier diva roles of Carmen, Tosca and Salome, employing her extraordinary acting skills and intensity to cover any vocal shortcomings.

Gonzo guitarist, great white hunter, champion of nature, gifter of venison and New Year's Eve party host Ted Nugent.

Ted Nugent
1948-

It wasn't a gimmick: The Motor City Madman's feral, loincloth persona onstage was very much adapted from the real-life Ted Nugent, an avid outdoorsman and hunter. Staunchly conservative in an age of rock debauchery, the Nuge got his break in the late '60s with the Amboy Dukes. He emerged in the next decade as a top-selling solo artist. As a guitarist, his playing was workman-like but thunderous, and his riffs on songs like "Cat Scratch Fever" and "Stranglehold" are now hard-rock staples.

Nugent in 1996 on bow hunting:

"Get your kid a bow and arrow and you won't have to worry about nuthin' — except maybe a few dead squirrels. ... And they're yummy!"

Don Was

Glenn Frey

Mitch Ryder

with a cheesily brilliant organ riff that has influenced several generations of garage and punk rockers since it first soared to No. 1 in 1966. Born in Mexico in 1945, Martinez was raised in Saginaw, where he and his Mysterians band mates, Bobby Balderrama, Frank Rodriguez, Frank Lugo and Eddie Serrato, unleashed a song that has unquestionably become a beloved piece of pop culture mythology.

Don Was

Longtime rock-funker earned further fame as a record producer for such acts as Bonnie Raitt and the Rolling Stones. Grew up in Oak Park as Don Fagenson.

Glenn Frey

Detroit-born Frey grew up in Royal Oak and cofounded the Eagles, whose "Greatest Hits, 1971-1975" has sold more than 26 million copies, the top-selling album in American history.

Mitch Ryder

With his band, the Detroit Wheels, the revved-up Ryder charted with such party hits as "Jenny Takes a Ride."

Old stuff to see, lots of it, too, and statues galore — we're cultured

Art
Eye Feasts

BIG!: Largest piece is "Gracehoper" (1961) by Tony Smith, on the front lawn.

You gotta have art

William H. Brearley, an advertising executive who helped found the Detroit News in 1873, is chiefly responsible for the founding of the Detroit Institute of Arts.

The culture bug was biting in the late 19th Century. The library opened in 1865. In 1868, the Detroit Opera House was built. In 1882, Brearley, 36, decided it was high time Detroit got art. To generate interest in funding a museum, Brearley decided to stage an art exhibition. Within months, he convinced 57 prominent Detroiters to fund it.

Even Pope Leo XIII contributed a work: "Spiritual Betrothal of St. Catherine of Alexandria with the Infant Jesus," on condition that the painting become part of a permanent collection.

Brearley raised $100,000, and on Sept. 1, 1888, the Detroit Museum of Art opened in a blockhouse of a building on the southwest corner of Jefferson and Hastings — where I-375 now runs under the street.

The renamed DIA opened in 1927 in the city's newly named Cultural Center.

More than 1 million people annually stroll through the corridors of the museum. Let's go:

DIA superlatives

Bricks, mortar and marble: At 596,000 square feet, the DIA is the fifth-largest museum in the country. The biggest: the Metropolitan Museum of Art in New York. The DIA has three floors and more than 100 galleries.

Stuff: The collection totals more than 62,000 objects; more than 20,000 are works on paper. Most are in storage; only 10 percent to 15 percent are displayed at one time. By 2002, all will be cataloged on-line.

Small: Among the tiniest are Egyptian faience beads shaped like scarabs, ancient Celtic gold pieces, and tiny paintings on ivory.

Borrowed much: Emil Nolde's "Sunflowers" and Ernst Kirschner's "Winter Landscape in the Moonlight" from the German Expressionism collection; "Cubi I," a large sculpture by Tony Smith.

Most-attended shows: "Van Gogh: Face to Face" (March 12-June 4, 2000), with an estimated 315,500 visitors; "The Splendors of Ancient Egypt" (July 16, 1997-Jan. 4, 1998),

290,000 visitors.

Ranking: The DIA's American painting collection is ranked third behind New York's Metropolitan Museum of Art and the Museum of Fine Arts in Boston.

Ranking II: The DIA is considered one of the top

WILLIAM ARCHIE/Detroit Free Press
Woodward entrance to the Detroit Institute of Arts.

Poster

It's a toss-up on the best-selling museum poster. "The Nut Gatherers" or the north wall of the Rivera mural.

DIA favorites

"The Nut Gatherers," by William Bougereau, French, 1882. Championing traditional values, Bougereau recalls the vulnerability and innocence of youth in this painting of two young girlfriends.

Time for Howdy Doody

Howdy Doody came home to the DIA in 2001. The freckled-faced puppet was liberated from a Rhode Island bank vault after a U.S. District Court in Connecticut ruled against the estate of Howdy's last caretaker, Rufus Rose. The judge ruled Rose had intended to give the puppet to the DIA for its renowned puppet collection. Rose's family tried to sell Howdy. Experts figure H.D. would fetch more than $100,000.

The 2000 show on Van Gogh set a record.

Coups

In 1922, Vincent van Gogh's "Self-Portrait" was the first painting by the artist to enter a U.S. museum collection. Henri Matisse's "The Window" (1916) was the first work by this important French painter to enter an American public collection.

DIA Favorites

"Self-Portrait," by Vincent Van Gogh, Dutch, 1887. Van Gogh often used himself as a model. This relatively upbeat portrait of the artist was done in Paris in 1922.

six large civic museums in the country; it is noted for its broad, well-rounded collections, especially in American Indian and African art, French decorative art, American painting and German Expressionism.

Ranking III: The DIA's defining work is "Detroit Industry," considered the finest mural created in the United States by Mexican artist Diego Rivera.

Studying: The Research Library, founded in 1905, contains more than 167,000 volumes and more than 250 current periodical subscriptions.

Donating: The largest cash gift was offered in 1999 — $50 million from Josephine Ford, A. Alfred Taubman and Richard A. Manoogian.

Our favorites

DIA associate educator Linda Margolin says these rank as visitors' favorites.

"The Wedding Dance," by Pieter Bruegel the Elder, Flemish, ca. 1566. Fascinated by the peasant life around him, Bruegel specialized in capturing joyous events that showed people in somewhat exaggerated detail.

Mummy, Egypt, Roman period, 300 BC-395 AD. The mummy is wrapped in linen and has a gold mask.

Rivera LIVE!

Diego Rivera's "Detroit Industry" frescoes might have been whitewashed or reduced to plaster dust if some outraged citizens had had their way back in the 1930s.

Rivera was outsized in everything from his

"The Wedding Dance": This popular piece gives insight into 16th Century peasant life.

ART CULTURE

genius to his girth — he weighed 300 pounds when he arrived in Detroit in the spring of 1932 — and rambunctious in both his politics and his busy romantic life.

Diego Rivera's murals brought acclaim and controversy.

Rivera believed murals could be used to educate people about politics, history and democracy. For a time he was a member of the Communist Party, but he quit over Stalin's repression of artists.

Then DIA director William Valentiner's only stipulation was that the paintings reflect Detroit's role as an industrial powerhouse. The artist's $20,899 fee was paid by Edsel Ford, president of the Arts Commission.

Rivera spent weeks touring Detroit's factories and ethnic working-class neighborhoods before starting to paint.

Fresco is the technique of applying paint to wet plaster so the pigment is absorbed and becomes a permanent part of the wall. Rivera spent up to 20 hours a day on the scaffold. Once the day's quota of wet plaster had been laid on by assistants, the artist could not stop until the area was covered. Between a diet and the 120-degree sauna-like temperatures under the Garden Court skylight, the artist shed 100 pounds during eight months of painting.

The finished murals tell the story of raw materials wrested from the earth to create steel and autos. Four heroic nudes at the top of the north and south walls celebrate the contribution that each race — American Indian, Asian, white and black — made to the building of a continent. Other panels celebrate the fertility of the earth and the power of technology to be used for good or evil.

Within hours of being put on public view in March 1933, the murals generated an uproar that delighted Rivera, who said the controversy proved his art was alive.

Some members of the media, clergy and city council attacked Rivera's politics and assailed his work as pornographic, sacrilegious and un-American. Critics were especially incensed at the vaccination panel, showing a child with a halo-like hairdo, attended by a doctor, a nurse and a group of animals (from whose blood vaccines were manufactured); they claimed it was a blasphemous parody of the Christian Holy Family.

In the monstrous machines that seem to overwhelm the workers beneath them, the protesters saw a dangerous attack on the capitalist system. They said Rivera had foisted the "philosophy of Moscow" on Detroit and

had perpetrated "a heartless hoax" on his benefactor, Edsel Ford, and demanded that the murals be whitewashed or destroyed.

Defenders countered that it honestly portrayed the city's raw vitality and rugged industrial power.

Rivera called the frescoes his most important work.

In 1952, at the height of the Cold War, there was a renewed outcry for the removal of the murals. But they endure today, a monument to the city, the artist and the people who rallied to defend them. Look in the lower right-hand corner of the south wall. The second figure from the right is Edsel Ford, the capitalist who had the wealth to commission Detroit's unique murals — and the wisdom to leave them in place for future generations to judge and admire.

CULTURE

Free Press file photo

Grown-up mini tour

This stroll should take an hour and includes **"Detroit Industry"** and **"The Wedding Dance"** mentioned above.

Chapel from Chateau de Lannoy, French, ca. 1522-24. This limestone late-Gothic chapel, constructed in the 16th Century by a noble family for private devotion, is an example of French flamboyant architecture because of its flame-like window tracery.

"Noah's Ark: Genesis," by Charles McGee, American, 1984. This 10-foot-by-15-foot mural in mixed media is a familiar piece in the Modern and Contemporary galleries.

"Detroit Industry"

Diego Rivera, Mexican, 1932. Considered the finest mural by Mexican artist Rivera in the United States, its theme relates to Detroit's role in the development of industry. The work took eight months to complete.

© Detroit Institute of Arts
Chapel from Chateau de Lannoy.

© Detroit Institute of Arts
"Noah's Ark: Genesis": The mural was completed in 1984.

© Detroit Institute of Arts
"Madonna and Child": ca. 1500.

"Nail Figure"

Central Africa, 1875-1900. Studded with nails and with a cowrie shell protruding from his abdomen, this figure was carved to capture the spirit powers necessary for healing and making judgments.

© Detroit Institute of Arts

"Madonna and Child," by Pietro Perugino, Italian, ca. 1500. Italian Renaissance painters lessened the division between worshipers and the divine by humanizing their figures. Here the mother and child wear only discreet halos and no finery.

"Sakyamuni Emerging from the Mountains," China, late-13th to mid-14th Century. The founder of Buddhism is shown after renouncing his life as a prince and spending six years in the mountains fasting and meditating in search of enlightenment.

Children's mini tour

Another one-hour stroll that includes the **Mummy** and the **"African Nail Figure"** mentioned above.

"Watson and the Shark," by John Singleton Copley, American, 1782. This dramatic painting depicts the rescue of Brook Watson, who decided to swim in shark-infested waters while his ship was docked in Havana Harbor. He was saved, but he lost his left leg and was fitted with a peg leg.

Shield, Southern Cheyenne, 1860-68. This shield made of buffalo rawhide, tanned buckskin, bells, feathers, corn husks and natural pigment, probably belonged to Little Rock, a Cheyenne man killed in battle in 1868.

"Video Flag," by Nam June Paik, American, 1985. Red, white and blue images move rapidly on video monitors to form the stars and bars of a U.S. flag. The piece speaks to pop culture as well as the dominance of technology in the 20th Century.

Boy's Corselet armor, Italian, ca. 1605. Made for Duke Cosimo II (1590-1621), this corselet protected his torso during foot tournaments but left him unprotected below the waist.

"Quilting Time," by Romare Bearden, American, 1986. This mosaic by the well-known African-American artist is of a typical quilting scene. It was commissioned in 1983.

Other great local stuff

American painting

The highlights according to James Tottis, acting curator.

"Cotopaxi," Frederic Edwin Church, 1862. Church is considered the leading American landscape painter of his generation and the only pupil of the father of the Hudson River School, Thomas Cole. "Cotopaxi" is the quintessential example of principles embraced by the Hudson River painters as well as Church's own ideas on atmospheric effects. Painted as the Civil War was raging, many Americans viewed the canvas as a parable of the war.

Duke Cosimo II's corselet — the sports gear of his day.

© Detroit Institute of Arts

"Sakyamuni Emerging from the Mountains": The search for enlightenment.

Man overboard: Watson is rescued from the shark.

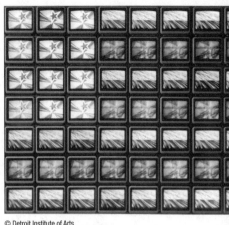

"Video Flag": The work gives new meaning to big-screen TV.

"Nocturne in Black and Gold: The Falling Rocket," James McNeill Whistler, 1874. Whistler was an innovator of his generation and developed complex ideas of abstraction. He experimented with a style known as Tonalism, which explores the variations achieved from a specific color. "Nocturne" is one of his most famous paintings.

"McSorley's Bar," John Sloan, 1912. Sloan was a leading figure among the Ash Can painters, so titled because of their choice of subject matter drawn from New York City streets. Although not open to women until the mid-1970s, McSorley's provided the average New Yorker with a venue for socializing. The DIA's version is the most recognizable and famous Sloan painted of this popular watering hole. Ironically, the DIA acquired "McSorley's Bar," which still operates today, in 1924 during the height of Prohibition.

Ancient art
The highlights according to DIA senior curator William Peck.

Islamic: "Ardashir Battling Bahman," a page from the Demotte Shah-nameh (Book of Kings), 1325-1350 AD. One of the earliest and most significant Persian miniatures, not only in the DIA collection but in the world.

Egyptian: "Peasants Driving Cattle and Fishing," Old Kingdom, Early Dynasty 6, circa 2200 BC. Vivid scene of daily life from a tomb, recently featured in the major Old Kingdom exhibition in Paris and at the Metropolitan Museum of Art in New York.

Mesopotamian: "Dragon of Marduk: Tile Relief from the Ishtar Gate," Babylonian, circa 604-562 BC. The only image of the mythical beast from the Ishtar Gate in North America, purchased directly from the German excavators of Babylon when the gate was reconstructed in Berlin.

Greek: "Aphrodite: the Venus Genetrix Type," Roman copy of the lost Greek original, 1st Century AD. An elegant example of the type of ideal Greek art admired by the Romans and the inspiration of later Western art.

Asian art
The highlights according to associate curator Laurie Barnes.

Japanese: Document Box (Ryoshibako), Momoyama period, 1568-1615. This box belongs to a large and varied group of 16th- and early 17th-Century lacquers called "Kodai-ji style." In 1606, the wife of the powerful warlord Toyotomi Hideyoshi built a family mausoleum on the grounds of the Buddhist temple, Kodai-ji. This daring new style of lacquer was created for the temple's furnishings. The drawing and the variety of color combinations on this box combine with its unusual shape to mark it as one of the finest Kodai-ji style lacquerwares in a Western collection.

Korean: Pillow, Koryo dynasty, late 12th Century. The ceramics of the Koryo dynasty are the best-known to the outside world. The Chinese first made celadon wares in an attempt to recreate sacred jade. Korean potters went one step further and made the outstanding achievement of inlaying their celadon wares. In Asia, ceramic pillows were placed under the neck, comfortably support-

"Aphrodite: the Venus Genetrix Type": This hands-down favorite inspired later Western art.

© Detroit Institute of Arts

Indian

"Parvati, Consort of Shiva," Tamil Nadu, 1200-1300.

Parvati is modeled in the round so her back is as carefully detailed as her front. This particular bronze figure was part of a temple set of great size and importance in its time. This figure is one of the finest late Chola bronzes in existence.

ing the head while cooling the skin. There are only a few Korean celadon pillows supported by pairs of lions remaining in the world.

Chinese: "Early Autumn," scroll, ink and color on paper, signed Qian Xuan (1235-c. 1305), Yuan dynasty, 1279-1368. Depiction of the most delicate forms of plant and animal life developed into a specialized form of painting in the 900s known as "bird and flower," which also includes paintings of "insects and grass." "Early Autumn" is among the most well-known paintings of this tradition.

European paintings

The highlights according to associate curator Iva Lisikewycz.

"The Wedding Dance," Pieter Bruegel the Elder, about 1566. One of the rare oil paintings in this country by the foremost Northern European Renaissance artist. This painting appeals to viewers on many levels: the humor in the caricatured participants, the swinging rhythms of the dance, the moralizing overtones implied by the shadowy viewer at the right edge of the painting. It also sends many people to their dictionaries to look up "codpiece."

"View of Le Crotoy, Upstream," Georges Seurat, French, 1889. Seurat brilliantly applies the science of optics to the art of painting. This luminous landscape is made up of tiny dots of color "mixed" in the brain instead of on the palette. Remarkably, the painting retains its original frame, which was painted by the artist to compliment the canvas.

© Detroit Institute of Arts

A ceramic pillow from the late 12th Century.

"The Nightmare," Henry Fuseli, Swiss, 1781. Fuseli's striking image of a recumbent woman oppressed by a demon gives visual form to the often unnamed terrors associated with bad dreams. The artist adds a touch of macabre humor by including the "night mare," who seems to peer into the bedroom.

European sculpture and decorative arts

The highlights according to associate curator Tracey Albainy.

Tureen with Lid and Stand, Thomas Germain (French, 1733-1734). This 30-pound tureen is part of the Penthivre-Orlans Service, the only complete 18th-Century French silver service formerly in royal use. It is supported by wild boars at either end, with a naturalistic still life on the lid composed of a dead hare, crawfish, oysters, mushrooms and other luxuries of the French table.

Boni Coat of Arms, design attributed to Donatello, execution attributed to Desiderio

© Detroit Institute of Arts

"View from Le Crotoy, Upstream."

© Detroit Institute of Arts

"The Nightmare" visualizes the unnamed terrors that often inhabit bad dreams.

© Detroit Institute of Arts

The Boni Coat of Arms.

da Settignano and workshop, Florence, ca. 14551459.

This large coat of arms, carved of gray Florentine sandstone, is one of the finest of all surviving Florentine stemmi, or coats of arms, of the Renaissance. It was originally installed on the facade of the palace constructed in the 1450s by the Boni family, a prominent Florentine family engaged in the silk industry. It was a collaboration between two leading Italian sculptors.

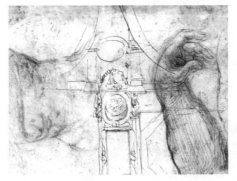
© Detroit Institute of Arts

"Scheme for the Decoration of the Sistine Ceiling" by Michelangelo.

Modern and contemporary art

The highlights according to curator MaryAnne Wilkinson.

"Detroit Industry," Diego Rivera, 1931-33. The only complete mural cycle by Rivera in the United States, and arguably his most important work outside of the Mexico City murals. Plus, it chronicles not only the industries upon which this city is founded but also some of the changing politics.

"The Window," Henri Matisse, French, 1916. The first work by this important French painter to enter an American public collection was purchased with funds from the City of Detroit. It's a textbook example of Matisse's mastery of color as well as the influence of Cubism on his interiors.

"Winter Landscape in Moonlight," Ernst Kirchner, 1916. A signature work of the expressionist movement in modern German painting, this work is the lynchpin of the DIA's superb collection of early German painting.

"Be I (second version)," Barnett Newman, 1970. A perfect expression of the balance between spirituality and minimalism in Abstract Expressionist painting. One of the last works completed before Newman died.

Graphic arts

The highlights according to curator Ellen Sharp.
"Scheme for the Decoration of the Sistine Ceiling," Michelangelo Buonarroti, Italian, 1508. This drawing in pen, brown ink and black chalk is one of a few in U.S. collections related to the Sistine Chapel.

"Portrait of Sir John Herschel," Julia Margart Cameron, English, 1867. The first great female photographer offers a compelling study of the well-known scientist.

"The Thinker"

Auguste Rodin French, designed ca. 1880, cast in Paris in 1904. Perhaps Rodin's best-known monumental work. Rodin designed the figure for the tympanum of "The Gates of Hell," commissioned in 1880 by the French government as the doors of a new museum of decorative arts in Paris. It is one of 20 cast by Rodin.

© Detroit Institute of Arts
"The Window" shows Cubism's influence on Matisse's interiors.

© Detroit Institute of Arts
"Be I (second version)," an Abstract Expressionist work.

© Detroit Institute of Arts
"Winter Landscape in Moonlight" is the lynchpin of the DIA's early German paintings.

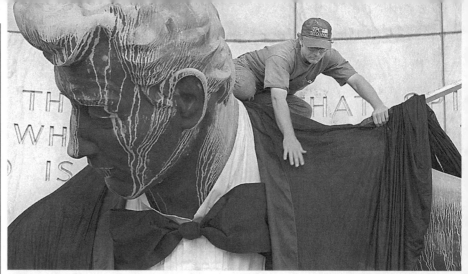

TOM PIDGEON/Special to the Detroit Free Press

"The Spirit of Detroit" is dressed in honor of the Three Tenors concert in 1999.

Detroit-area art notables

Cass Corridor art movement

Capitalizing on the tough industrial nature of Detroit in the late 1960s and early 1970s, artists living around Cass Avenue near Wayne State University evolved with a scrappy, assemblage style of art that gained national attention. The artists had the support of local collectors and the Detroit Institute of Arts, where they showed their wares in a memorable exhibition called "Kick Out the Jams" in the late '70s. Some noted artists: Jim Chatelain, Robert Sestock, Michael Luchs, Gordon Newton, Brenda Goodman.

Marshall Fredericks
(1908-1998)

Michigan's best-known sculptor is recognized worldwide for his monumental bronze public sculptures. Detroiters know him best for downtown's "The Spirit of Detroit," a 26-foot figure holding a globe. At 89, he installed the 40-foot "Star Dream Fountain" in Royal Oak. His sculptures also appear in the State Department courtyard in Washington, the U.S. Embassy in London and parks and castles throughout Scandinavia. He had studios in Bloomfield Hills and Royal Oak. The Marshall M. Fredericks Sculpture Museum is housed in the Arbury Fine Arts Center on the campus of Saginaw Valley State University.

Tyree Guyton

This active native Detroit painter, sculptor and mixed media artist is best-known for his "Heidelberg Project" that transformed a blighted east side neighborhood into a "living canvas" filled with polka-dotted houses, painted car hoods, dangling shoes and lots of heart. Though internationally known, the project was partly dismantled in 1999, when city government responded to residents' requests to remove it because it attracted animals.

Center for Creative Studies

Located behind the DIA, the Center for Creative Studies-College of Art and Design is a private, four-year college offering bachelor of fine arts degrees in animation and digital media, communication design, crafts, fine arts, industrial design, interior design and photography. Founded in 1926 as an independent art and design program, the center was created by the Detroit Society for Arts and Crafts. The program expanded at such a rate that, by 1975, the society changed its name to the Center for Creative Studies.

ART CULTURE

Cranbrook Academy of Art Educational Community

Established in 1927 in Bloomfield Hills, this sprawling campus was conceived by Detroit newspaper magnates George and Ellen Booth as a utopian educational community stressing personal growth, spiritual development and commitment to community service. The Academy of Art began formal art classes in 1932, with Finnish architect Eliel Saarinen, who designed much of Cranbrook, serving as president. Sculptor Carl Milles, who created many of the remarkable sculptures on campus, headed the first sculpture department. The private graduate art school has a strong national reputation, and its Museum of Art presents outstanding contemporary art exhibitions as well as graduate student shows.

Public art

The Calder

Actually, "Jeune Feill et Sa Suite (Young Lady and Her Suite)," Alexander Calder, 1970, painted steel.

The bright red-orange sculpture fills a triangular space in front of the Ameritech Building at Cass and Michigan avenues. An important piece of art by the American sculptor famous for his mobiles, this work is a stabile, an abstract sculpture similar to a mobile, but stationary. The whimsical, fluid forms suggest a titled young lady and her attendants.

"Deliquenscence"

John Chamberlain, 1979-1981, painted steel and chrome-plated steel.

Made of salvaged auto parts — twisted bumpers, fenders, doors and hoods — this red, white and blue sculpture at the McNamara Federal Building at 477 Michigan Ave. at Cass recalls the automotive history of Detroit.

"Untitled"

W. Robert Youngman, 1970, concrete.

Art and architecture come together at the Comerica Building at 411 W. Lafayette with Youngman's 26 cast-concrete relief panels depicting machine shapes used in the automotive industry wrapping around the black granite and steel building.

"The Hand of God, Memorial to Frank Murphy"

Carl Milles, 1953 (installed 1970), bronze and granite.

Well-known Detroit politician Frank Murphy — Detroit mayor, Michigan governor, U.S. attorney general, U.S. Supreme Court justice — is memorialized as an awestruck newly created man perched on the hand of God atop a 26-foot granite shaft. The work is fittingly at the Frank Murphy Hall of Justice at Beaubien and Gratiot. Milles, resident sculptor at Cranbrook Academy of Art from 1931-1950, also created a wonderful body of highly stylized, elegant, decorative work incorporated into the grounds of Cranbrook in Bloomfield Hills.

Pewabic Pottery

This working pottery east of downtown Detroit was started by Mary Chase Perry Stratton in 1903, at the height of the American Arts and Crafts movement. The pottery now is a nonprofit organization dedicated to the preservation of Arts and Crafts ideals while advancing contemporary ceramics through exhibitions and educational programs. An arm of the pottery operates for profit by fabricating commercial tiles that still use the special glazes Stratton developed. Comerica Park is the latest landmark to sport Pewabic products.

This polka-dotted house, one of Tyree Guyton's remaining works, is on Heidelberg Street, near Mt. Elliott and Mack Avenue on Detroit's east side.

CARLOS OSORIO/Associated Press

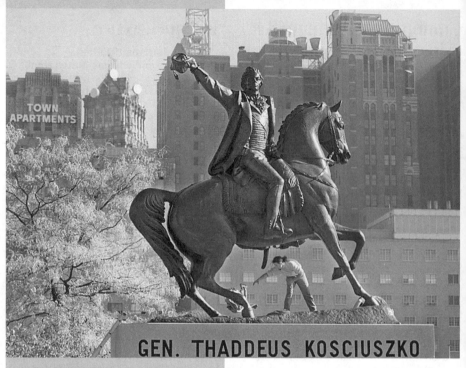

GEN. THADDEUS KOSCIUSZKO

"Detroit is no stranger to the ills that plague the human condition, which may be precisely why artists find it to be such a valuable resource for their images."

— Dolores S. Slowinski

The general is immortalized at Michigan Avenue and Third Street.

"General Thaddeus Kosciuszko"

Leonard Marconi, 1978, bronze and granite.

As if welcoming people to Detroit, the jaunty figure of Gen. Kosciuszko, a Polish native who fought for this country during the Revolutionary War, sits astride his mount and waves his hat from his lofty vantage point at Michigan Avenue and Third Street.

People Mover stations

Fifteen artists were commissioned to create art for 13 People Mover stations downtown. The diverse pieces enliven the functional stations. Materials include mosaics, neon lights, ceramic tiles, bronze and baked enamel.

"Trilogy"

Louise Nevelson, 1979, painted steel and aluminum.

This work in the Orchestra Place Courtyard, Woodward at Parsons Street, consists of three elements — two towering constructions of curved and sharp geometric planes and one low-lying circular piece of rounded forms. Though suggesting a family, the "child" (the circular piece) is curiously placed on the side of the building away from the other forms.

"The Freedom of the Human Spirit"

Marshall Fredericks, 1964, bronze.

Known as Michigan's greatest sculptor, Fredericks created many public pieces including the well-known "Spirit of Detroit" downtown. This work is at the center of a fountain in Shain Park, Bates and Merrill streets, in Birmingham. A man, woman and three geese seem to soar effortlessly into the sky in celebration of the human spirit.

"Untitled"

John Egner, 1974, wall painting.

Located at the Park Shelton Apartments (north wall) on Woodward Avenue at Kirby Street, this was conceived as an entrance to the city's Cultural Center. Up close, the 96-foot wall painting looks like a mosaic quilt pattern, but from a mile away it looks more like broad Woodward Avenue flanked by tall buildings. A recent repainting restored the vibrancy of the painting, but the addition of the building's name at the top compromised its original integrity.

SOURCES: "ART IN DETROIT PUBLIC PLACES" BY DENNIS ALAN NAWROCKI AND DAVID CLEMENTS (WAYNE STATE UNIVERSITY PRESS, 1999).

The
Museums

Henry Ford Museum & Greenfield Village

Oakwood Boulevard south of Michigan, Dearborn 48124; 313-271-1620; www.hfmgv.org

A world-class, world-famous complex that celebrates American ingenuity and where seldom is heard a discouraging word about this great nation. The museum is a 12-acre repository of artifacts from a gigantic coal-hauling locomotive to tiny kitchen implements. Listing the categories in the collection would require a chapter. Highlights include tractors, airplanes, plows, buggies and, of course, cars. Lots of cars. There's also the chair in which Lincoln was shot; the limo in which Kennedy was shot; a room from a postwar Holiday Inn; a 1950s soda fountain, and a massive generator. An IMAX theater was added in late 1999.

Greenfield Village, equally a world tourist destination, tells the story of industrial change in the United States from the nostalgic point of view of founder Henry Ford, who played such a large role in the transformation. From the Firestone Farm to the Wright Brothers bike shop to Noah Webster's home to Thomas Edison's Menlo Park laboratory, visitors can walk through and touch history in buildings that are either painstakingly restored or artfully reproduced.

Graystone Jazz Museum

Book Building, Suite 201, 1249 Washington, Detroit 48226; 313-963-3813

A small museum with a big vision, and perhaps the only museum in the United States founded by a transit worker. From its latest home, in a downtown skyscraper, the Graystone seeks to preserve one of Detroit's great art forms in videos, photos and other displays. Its name conjures up visions of the Graystone Ballroom on Woodward between Willis and Canfield, once one of the greatest dance and concert halls in the country. The ballroom opened in 1922 with a huge dance floor, over which hung a glittering glass ball; a fountain with colored lights; an outdoor garden with a stage, and a spiral staircase to the mezzanine.

Top jazz groups such as the Woody Her-

Barbara King of Livonia dresses like a pioneer to sift coal dust on the Firestone Farm at Greenfield Village in 2000.

RICHARD LEE/Detroit Free Press

man, Paul Whiteman, Jimmie Lunceford and Cab Calloway orchestras entertained. It was also home base for Detroit's McKinney Cotton Pickers, the first black band to play there.

The ballroom closed in 1957 and in 1962, Rayber Corp., a local enterprise headed by Berry Gordy Jr., bought it for $125,000. News reports at the time said Gordy would open the largest nightclub in the Midwest. Private parties were held at the Graystone, but it never reopened full-time to the public. Museum founder James Jenkins, a retired Detroit bus driver, got the idea in 1974 after the death of Duke Ellington. Jenkins' memory of the bandleader was strong: Three months earlier he had booked the Ellington Orchestra for a concert at the Light Guard Armory. So Jenkins gathered support from other enthusiasts. He credits former musicians union local official Jim Lewis, an early participant, for coming up with the name.

On Aug. 19, 1980, the ballroom, in a state of disrepair, was destroyed. The site is now a vacant lot.

Some of the attractions at Henry Ford Museum are a big generator, a locomotive and the chair in which Lincoln was shot.

Automotive Hall of Fame

21400 Oakwood Blvd., Dearborn 48124
313-240-4000; www.theautochannel.com

The cross-section of inventors, accountants, tinkerers and bicycle racers who kickstarted the world into the horseless-carriage age are enshrined in a museum next to Greenfield Village that combines hands-on displays, graphics and real cars. After 58 years of quiet existence in Midland, the modest, friendly hall opened in 1997 in the middle of Dearborn's Ford country.

Walter P. Chrysler Museum

One Chrysler Drive,
Auburn Hills 48326; 888-456-1924

The museum features more than 70 vintage vehicles, a 125-seat amphitheater, archives and a replica 1932 Plymouth dealership. The cars trumpet the glory of Chrysler's history.

J. KYLE KEENER/Detroit Free Press

A testament to Chrysler: The Walter P. Chrysler Museum in Auburn Hills.

Motor Sports Museum and Hall of Fame

Novi Expo Center, 43700 Expo Center Drive, Novi 48375; 248-349-7223
www.mshf.com

The museum has more than 100 items on display, many of them cars or craft that broke speed records on land or sea. The "Heroes of Horsepower" exhibit honors speed merchants in airplanes, sports cars, stock cars, motorcycles, drag racing and powerboats.

HUGH GRANNUM/Detroit Free Press

From left, Lions tackle Alex Karras; George Wilson Jr. and his mother Claire, son and wife of the late Lions coach George Wilson; college boxing great Chuck Davey and bowler Joe Joseph at Cobo Hall in 1980.

Michigan Sports Hall of Fame

Cobo Hall, Washington Boulevard and Jefferson, Detroit.

The hall is actually a Cobo hallway lined with plaques honoring Michigan athletes and sports supporters. It is accessible whenever Cobo is open, which is virtually every day.

WILLIAM ARCHIE/Detroit Free Press

Four 1993 inductees: Golf pro Dave Jackson, MSU football star Bubba Smith; basketball legend Spencer Haywood and the late Tigers player Harvey Kuenn, represented by his widow, Audrey Kuenn.

Dossin Great Lakes Museum

Belle Isle, 313-852-4051

A boat-watchers' paradise, the museum is located just off the Detroit River freighter channel. It contains a working pilot house from the William Clay Ford, from which visitors can watch passing ships as they listen to chatter on the ship's radio. There's also a working submarine periscope, a gallery of model ships, a collection of model yachts of the auto barons, numerous paintings and other memorabilia of centuries of lake commerce, travel and recreation.

Ashton James, who was 3½ in 1995, takes the helm at the Dossin Museum.

ALAN R. KAMUDA/Detroit Free Press

Cranbrook

Bloomfield Hills
www.cranbrook.edu

The 315-acre complex has an international reputation for artistic excellence. From the dramatic swooping roof of the Woodward Avenue entrance to the distinctive doorknobs, Cranbrook's buildings and grounds resonate with cutting-edge industrial design and modern art. Cranbrook includes elementary, middle and high schools; an art museum; science institute; a graduate school of art, design and architecture, plus exquisitely designed buildings, gardens and works of art. The site, begun in 1908, was the work of Detroit News publisher and art aficionado George Booth and Finnish artist Eliel Saarinen, whose son, Eero, continued the family's artistic tradition as a well-known architect. Cranbrook's grounds are renown for walking, and four buildings are open to the public:

➤ **Cranbrook House and Garden**: 380 Lone Pine Road, Bloomfield Hills 48303; 877-462-7262

Albert Kahn designed this mansion in 1908. It's now an administration building with a lovely, sculpture-studded garden that's open spring, summer and fall.

➤ **Institute of Science**: 1221 N. Woodward Ave., Bloomfield Hills 48303; 877-462-7262

A $31-million renovation, completed in late 1999, brought new interactive exhibits and added 33,000 square feet of space, an updated planetarium, modernized exhibits and a new message: Everything in nature is connected. There's a large mineral hall, ant colony, exhibits on animals past and present and plenty of other displays to appeal to both children and adults.

➤ **Cranbrook Art Museum**: 1221 N. Woodward Ave., Bloomfield Hills 48303;

877-462-7262

The collection emphasizes work by Cranbrook's faculty and students, including Eero Saarinen, Marshall Fredericks, Bill Viola, Bruce Nauman and Lynda Benglis. The focus is on Cranbrook's impact on modern art, architecture and design.

University of Michigan Museum of Art

525 S. State St., Ann Arbor 48109
734-764-0395; www.umich.edu

One of the top university art museums in the country, it houses the second-largest art collection in Michigan next to the Detroit Institute of Arts. It has a permanent collection of 14,000 objects, including works by Monet, Cezanne, Picasso and Rembrandt. There are also galleries dedicated to the displays of African, Chinese and Japanese artists.

The Kelsey Museum of Archaeology

University of Michigan,
434 S. State St., Ann Arbor 48109
734-764-9304; www.umich.edu

The Kelsey has two exhibit halls: one for Greek and Roman material, the other for Near Eastern artifacts. The turreted building, finished in 1891, is somewhat of an art object itself, containing two Tiffany windows and carefully selected stones.

Protruding from the Detroit River side of the Dossin Museum on Belle Isle is the pilot house of the William Clay Ford, which gives visitors a sense of cruising the lakes on a big freighter.

CULTURE

MUSEUMS

Exhibit Museum of Natural History

University of Michigan, 1109 Geddes at Washtenaw, Ann Arbor 48109
734-763-6085; www.umma.lsu.umich.edu

The museum features exhibits related to paleontology, anthropology, zoology, geology and botany and includes a Hall of Evolution, Hall of Natural Sciences, Hall of Anthropology and a planetarium that offers weekend shows.

The Dr. Charles H. Wright Museum of African American History

315 E. Warren at Brush, Detroit 48201
313-494-5800; www.maah-detroit.org

This museum is dedicated to the preservation and presentation of African and African-American history and culture. Started by Dr. Charles Wright in 1965, the museum has been housed since 1997 in a 120,000-square-foot facility that cost $38.4 million. The structure is a solid block of gray rock, its dual entryways topped by gleaming, masklike sculptures created by Detroiter Richard Bennett, who also designed the burnished 1,000-pound doors that lead into the building. The heart of the museum is its central rotunda. Dominated by a soaring 100-foot-diameter glass dome 55 feet above the floor, the rotunda provides a great sunwashed axis for the

building, with walkways leading to the museum's various working centers: the core exhibit, the educational department and library, the special exhibits, a 317-seat theater and the museum store. The rotunda itself is a showpiece, ringed with dozens of flags from the African diaspora and sprinkled with tiny sculptural panels depicting lizards, sunbursts and frantically jagged graphic designs. At the center of the room is "Genealogy," a sweeping, boldly colored terrazzo depicting the arc of African-American history.

Holocaust Memorial Center
6602 W. Maple Road
West Bloomfield 48322; 248-661-0840
www.centerholocaust.org

The killing of 6 million Jews by Hitler's Nazis during World War II is documented in a chilling, low-key manner. Displays use historical artifacts, photos and film footage to illustrate the Holocaust's horror. Also in the complex are the Maas Garden of the Righteous and the Schaver Library Archive.

Note: Because of the graphic nature of this display, children younger than 12 are not advised to visit this museum.

Motown Historical Museum
2648 W. Grand Blvd., Detroit 48208
313-875-2264

This Detroit music landmark is the onetime homestead for Motown Records, which survives as a living music museum. The museum traces the history of the world-famous record

The second floor of the Detroit Historical Museum contains an exhibit on the Underground Railroad.

Dr. Charles Wright outside the old Museum of African American History, which he founded.

MARY SCHROEDER/Detroit Free Press

Michael Jackson, Stevie Wonder and Esther Gordy Edwards inside the Motown Museum in 1998. Gordy directs the museum.

company created by Berry Gordy Jr. and is filled with publicity photos, album jackets and newspaper clippings of Motown stars such as Smokey Robinson, the Four Tops, Diana Ross, Stevie Wonder and the Jackson 5. Visitors also can visit the old recording studio. One of metro Detroit's most popular stops for Eurotourists.

Detroit Historical Museum

**5401 Woodward Ave. at Kirby,
Detroit 48202; 313-833-1805
www.detroithistorical.org**

The museum presents a vivid collection of more than 300 years of local history including a 10-part exhibit, "Frontiers to Factories: Detroiters at Work, 1701-1901," which covers pre-Cadillac American Indians to the auto age. In the basement, an old favorite, "Streets of Old Detroit," depicts 19th-Century nighttime scenes with cobblestone streets and working stores. The "Glancy Trains" are an extensive display of toy choo-choos. The second floor contains an exhibit on the Underground Railroad.

Algonquin Club

Another local society whose members take history seriously and enjoy themselves while exploring it. 248-399-0114.

Detroit Public Schools Children's Museum

**67 E. Kirby, Detroit 48202;
313-873-8100**

An old mansion with displays of things kids like: planets, the Earth and art.

Historic Fort Wayne

**6325 W. Jefferson at Livernois
Detroit 49209; 313-833-1805
www.detroithistorical.org**

Built during the 1840s and 1850s to defend Detroit from Canada, the fort dramatizes the city's military history. Visitors can explore tunnels and casemates (chambers for guns) within its outer walls. Today, the fort's residents include the National Museum of the Tuskegee Airmen, the Medicine Bear Indian Academy and Mosaic Youth Theatre.

Note: The fort and Tuskegee Museum are open to the public on special occasions only.

Detroit Science Center

**502 John R, Detroit 48202
313-577-8400; www.sciencedetroit.org**

The goal of the Detroit Science Center is to inspire young and old alike to discover and appreciate science, technology and engineering. The center features an IMAX Dome Theater and more than 25 hands-on exhibits. A $25-million renovation, expected to be finished in 2001, will double the size. New attractions will include a Digital Dome Theater, a walk-through rain forest, indoor lightning storm, cable-suspended bicycle ride, science camp labs, and large spaces for traveling exhibits and programs for children younger than 10.

Margaret Dow Towsley Sports Museum

**University of Michigan,
Schembechler Hall, 1200 S. State St.,
Ann Arbor, 48109
734-7634422; www.mgoblue.com**

Ground zero of maize-and-blue madness. The museum deals only with Michigan sports — all 23 of them — in display cases and video displays.

Yankee Air Force Museum

**Willow Run Airport, Ecorse and Beck,
Belleville; 734-483-4030;
www.yankeeairmuseum.org**

Dedicated to World War I, female aviators, World War II, the B24, which was built nearby, and aircraft from Korea and Vietnam. More than two dozen aircraft are on display, and the museum has a library specializing in aviation.

Detroit Historical Society

An organization of local history buffs.
5401 Woodward Ave.
Detroit 48202;
313-833-1805;
**www.detroithistorical.
org**

CULTURE

MUSEUMS

The Zoo!

MENAGERIE SUPREME: The Detroit Zoo, Woodward and I-696, Royal Oak 48067; 248-398-0900; **www.detroitzoo.org**

Zoo factoids

Heaviest animal: A 9,300-pound elephant named Wanda.

Lightest animal: Reticulated poison dart frog at one gram.

Oldest animal: Aldabran tortoise, somewhere between 75 and 100 years old.

Animals at the zoo: 9,116.

Species represented: 573.

Food consumed by one elephant each day: 111 pounds of hay and produce.

Crickets fed weekly to creatures in the reptile house: 35,000.

Temperature of snow monkeys' hot tub: 103 degrees Fahrenheit.

Frequency of pedicures given to elephants: All four feet, every 4 to 6 weeks.

Visitor record: The one-day attendance record was set Aug. 14, 1992, when 25,677 visitors came through.

➤ **A gem, bar none:** The world-class Detroit Zoo had inauspicious beginnings in the 1880s, when a small traveling circus went bankrupt and its owners fled Detroit in the middle of the night. Detroiters cared for the abandoned animals, took up a collection and in 1883 opened the Detroit Zoological Gardens at the corner: Michigan and Trumbull, where Tiger Stadium stands. Admission then was steep: a dime for kids, a quarter for adults.

➤ **Too much adoration:** The tiny zoo failed a year later as its animals disappeared one by one — carried off, some believe, by adoring members of the public. The remaining animals went to Belle Isle, where the Belle Isle Zoo was established a few years later.

➤ **From vacant farmland:** A group of community leaders formed the Detroit Zoological Society in 1911, but it took many years before the group built the Detroit Zoo's main facility on farmland. It opened in 1928. The Detroit Zoo, on 125 acres in Royal Oak, was North America's first virtually barless zoo. Its moated enclosures marked it as one of the most progressive zoos in the country.

➤ **Jo Mendi:** Arguably the most loved animal at the zoo was Jo Mendi, a cigar-smoking, brandy-drinking roughneck of a chimpanzee who performed up to a dozen shows a day after his acquisition in 1932. Mendi once upstaged Franklin Delano Roosevelt during a campaign swing in Detroit, outdrawing the president, 40,000 to 20,000, on the chimp's first day back performing after an illness. Jo Mendi died in 1934.

➤ **Paulina the Pachyderm:** Also much-loved was Paulina, the zoo's first elephant, who gave rides to an estimated 500,000 children during her 22-year career that began in 1928 until her death in 1950.

➤ **Maximo:** The celebrity gorilla survived surgery for an umbilical hernia shortly after his birth at the zoo in 1955. The massive primate was a visitor favorite until he was loaned to the National Zoo in Washington in 1987. He died there April 13, 2000.

➤ **Security:** Following the theft of the zoo's funds — all $1,600 — one night in 1936, the director declared the zoo safe would be kept for awhile in the lions' den.

➤ **War hero:** GI Joe, a homing pigeon, retired to the zoo after serving in World War II. Joe was credited with flying 20 miles in 20 minutes on Oct. 18, 1943. His mission: to deliver a message canceling a flight of bombers about to target an Italian town that had just been captured by the Allies. Without Joe's speed, 1,000 British soldiers would have been bombed by friendlies.

➤ **The great escape:** The most legendary zoo escape occurred in 1950, when 11 baboons raced out an open cage door into the surrounding streets. It took several days for keepers to round them all up — the last one, ironically, was found in the chief zookeeper's yard.

➤ **Controversy:** A zoo policy of euthanatizing surplus animals broke out during the 1980s. The controversy ended with the departure in 1991 of Director Steve Graham.

➤ **A human hero:** In 1990, Jackson County trucker Rick Swope scaled a fence to rescue a chimpanzee that was drowning in a moat. A home videotape of the rescue played on national newscasts.

➤ **Staying on top:** A number of additions and improvements have helped maintain the zoo's international reputation, among them: a reptile and amphibian house (1960); the penguinarium (1968); a free-flight aviary (1977); the world's largest chimpanzee exhibit (1989) and butterfly-hummingbird garden in the Wildlife Interpretive Gallery (1995). An amphibian conservation center with two acres of wetlands is scheduled to open in the fall of 2000, and a polar bear exhibit is expected to be open in 2001.

SOURCES: FREE PRESS AND THE DETROIT ZOOLOGICAL SOCIETY.

CULTURE

Libraries
(Check 'em out)

Detroit Public Library

5201 Woodward,
Detroit 48202
313-833-1000; www.detroit.lib.mi.us/

Detroiters dedicated their first public library on March 25, 1865, inside the Capitol High School at State and Griswold. In its first 100 years, the DPL grew to a sprawling downtown library and 26 branches, though budget cuts in recent years have trimmed the branches to 24. The Main Library is a superb institution in a lovely building.

In addition to its estimated 6.6 million books, the DPL has eight special collections, most of which are located at the Main Library. It also will try to answer any question through its TIP information and referral service (313-833-4000).

Burton Historical Collection

Main Library, 313-833-1480

Widely known to scholars and amateur genealogists, the Burton is a large repository of materials about the history of Detroit, Michigan, the Great Lakes, New England and New France. The original collection was donated to the city by Clarence Monroe Burton, an attorney and founder of the Burton Abstract and Title Co., who was also an amateur historian.

The collection contains books, journals and manuscript materials. There is also a large map collection, pamphlets, newspapers, newspapers clippings, broadsides, photographs and scrapbooks. The archives include papers of individuals, groups, businesses, churches and city of Detroit records.

The genealogical collection is one of the finest in the country, with census information, family charts, vital records, military records, biographical encyclopedias and local histories.

The Burton also contains the Ernie Harwell Collection of historical baseball materials; the Edgar DeWitt Jones Collection of books and manuscripts on Abraham Lincoln and the Rare Book Collection.

E. Azalia Hackley Collection of Negro Music, Dance and Drama

Main Library, 313-833-1460

The Hackley Collection was the first of its kind in the world, and dates to 1943, when the Detroit Musicians Association presented material to the DPL.

Named after a Detroit music educator and performer, the collection includes rare books, photos, recordings, manuscripts and archives for serious researchers. The recorded sound section includes music either composed or performed by black musicians, and it documents the evolution of spirituals,

Free Press file photo

The Detroit Public Library on Woodward Avenue was designed by Cass Gilbert and opened in 1921.

gospel, ragtime, jazz, blues, opera and orchestral music. In addition to the Hackley Collection, the library's Music and Performing Arts Department contains a general reference collection of books, periodicals and music scores available to the public. The department also has a vertical file of more than 250,000 items.

National Automotive History Collection

Main Library, 313-833-1456

The NAHC dates to 1944 and documents the history and development of the auto industry. It's the world's largest public automotive archive. The collection contains literature, books, manuals, photos and advertisements — more than 440,000 items in all.

The Walter P. Reuther LIbrary contains 1,600 collections of personal papers and documents from people and organizations that include the United Farm Workers, virtually every UAW local, Mayor Jerome Cavanagh and, of course, Walter Reuther.

Great Lakes Patent and Trademark Center

Main Library, 313-833-3379

Established in November 1995 as a partnership between the DPL and the U.S. Patent and Trademark Office, the center provides specialized services for a fee for inventors, researchers and attorneys. The DPL has been a repository for patents and trademarks since 1871. The center offers a searchable database of African-American inventors at:
www.detroit.lib.mi.us/glptc/aaid/

International Language Collection

313-852-4027

Established in 1866, the ILC is the oldest of the DPL's collections. It contains more than 70,000 volumes in more than 50 languages. Newspapers are in the Browsing Department at the Main Library; books and magazines are at the Parkman Branch, 1766 Oakman Blvd.

Map Collection

Main Library, 313-833-1445

The DPL has more than 150,000 sheet maps and thousands of atlases, making it the nation's second-largest map collection at a public library. The emphasis is on Detroit and Michigan, but there are maps of virtually every place on Earth, plus satellite-imagery maps, navigation charts, national forest maps, CIA maps and U.S. Geological Survey maps. The Map Room is in the History and Travel Department.

Municipal Reference Library

Room 1004, Coleman A. Young
Municipal Center at Woodward and
Jefferson, 313-224-3885

Located in the former City-County Building, the library is open to the public but operates to help government employees in their jobs. The library has shelves filled with reports and documents from every city department, plus a wide range of books and reports from other U.S. cities. The library also contains a grants and proposals center, census data and budgets and financial reports for the country's 10 largest cities.

Wayne State University

313-577-2424; www.lib.wayne.edu

The Web address provides access to information about hundreds of electronic indexes, abstracts, databases and full text collections, ranging from American history to criminal justice abstracts to liquid crystals.

The Web address also will provide access to DAL-NET, the Detroit Area Library Network, a consortium of academic, public and special libraries in southeast Michigan.

Walter P. Reuther Library

5401 Cass, Detroit 48202; 313-577-4024
www.reuther.wayne.edu

The library is the home to the Archives of Labor and Urban Affairs, the Wayne State University Archives and the Douglas Fraser Center for Workplace Issues. The internationally renowned Archives of Labor and Urban Affairs was established in 1960 to preserve records of the U.S. labor movement, with special emphasis on industrial unionism and related social, political and economic institutions. It also collects historical records related to urban affairs, with special focus on Detroit. The library's holdings comprise 70,000 linear feet of records in 1,600 individual collections of the papers, documents, letters, clippings and other archival material from individuals and organizations.

The library also has more than 2 million audiovisual items, such as photos, including the archives of the late Tony Spina, the well-known Free Press chief photographer.

Also available: a collection of WSU students' papers on folklore topics.

Purdy/Kresge Library

Main Campus; 313-577-6424

Contains books and other materials on business, education, fine arts, humanities, library science and social sciences. The Kresge wing houses more than 8,000 journals, newspaper collections, general reference material and U.S. government documents.

Purdy/Kresge Media Library

Located on the first floor of the Purdy wing of the Purdy/Kresge Library, the media library contains films, videotapes, faculty lecture tapes, audio recordings and microfilm collections.

Science and Engineering Library

5048 Gullen Mall; 313-577-4066

Contains more than 500,000 volumes, along with 3,000 current journals, in physical and natural sciences, math, engineering, nursing, nutrition and food science. The library has one of the largest collections of technical journals in southeast Michigan.

David Adamany Undergraduate Library

5155 Gullen Mall

Contains 700 computer workstations offering undergraduates access to electronic resources, books and magazines.

Detroit Institute of Arts Research Library

Michigan's largest art library is nearly 100 years old and has a collection of more than 160,000 books, many of them rare. The library has regular hours for students from WSU and the Center for Creative Studies; the public can call 313-833-3460 for an appointment. The library is located at the Detroit Institute of Arts.

University of Michigan

Ann Arbor; 734-764-1817
www.lib.umich.edu

What began in 1839 as the General Library of the University of Michigan with 3,400 volumes has grown into one of the major research libraries in the world, with 7 million items. With 20 separate libraries, the University Library is the nation's eighth-largest academic library system. The biggest of U-M's libraries is the Harlan Hatcher Graduate Library, with more than 3 million volumes in several hundred languages. Its on-line catalog, MIRLYN, which can be accessed from the home page (above), contains more than 31.5 million citations, 40 indexes, catalogs of 19 libraries and access to hundreds of journals.

Bentley Historical Library

North Campus, Ann Arbor
734-764-3482

The Bentley specializes in manuscript collections — letters and other personal documents — related to Michigan history. Among its strengths are African-American organizations, architecture, city directories, Civil War documents, the conservation movement, gay organizations, genealogy, newspapers and newspaper history, politics, religious history and women's history. Non-Michigan features include U.S. involvement in the Philippines, the national temperance and prohibition movement and the "Polar Bear Expedition" to northern Russia, 1918-1919.

The Labadie Collection of Social Protest Literature

711 Harlan Hatcher Library
734-764-9377

Established in 1911 when prominent Detroit anarchist Joseph Labadie donated his library, the collection has gone far beyond the cataloging of anarchist materials. Material is now collected from around the world from both the extreme left and extreme right. The collection has 35,000 books, 8,000 periodicals and 6,000 subject vertical files of ephemera such as brochures, leaflets and clippings.

Clements Library

909 S. University, Ann Arbor 48109
734-764-2347

The Clements houses original sources for the study of American history and culture from the 15th Century to the early 20th Century. Opened in 1923, the library has assembled a large collection for research of British colonial and military policy in North America from 1755 to 1783. Other highlights: 19th-Century reform movements, especially anti-slavery; the Civil War; the War of 1812; American Indian-white relations; naval history; travel; religious intellectual history; women's history; the social impact of war, and social and cultural history of the late 18th Century through early 20th Century. The Clements also has a large collection of crime literature.

Gerald R. Ford Library

1000 Beal Ave., Ann Arbor 48109
734-741-2218

The library, not to be confused with the Ford Museum in Grand Rapids, is part of the U.S. presidential library system. It houses Ford's papers and promotes the study of U.S. history during the Cold War era. Other library collections at U-M:
➤ Papyrus Collection: About 10,000 items from the 3rd Century BC to the 8th Century AD.
➤ Transportation History.
➤ History of Science and Mathematics.
➤ Theater and Drama Collection.
➤ American Music Collection.
➤ Literary Manuscripts of Hopwood Award Winners.
➤ Fantastic Voyages Collection.
➤ Shakespeare Collection.
➤ Herbarium Collection.

➤ First editions of Darwin, Newton, Galileo and others.
➤ Extensive collections of Milton, Dryden, Dickens, James, Faulkner and Yeats.

University of Detroit Mercy

313-993-1071
ids.udmercy.edu

In addition to historical material pertaining to the individual histories of U-D and Mercy before their 1990 merger, the U-D library on the McNichols campus contains the **Lawrence DeVine Playbill Collection**, which includes playbills, books and other media from DeVine's 30 years as Free Press drama critic.
The Bunge/Fitzgerald Neighborhood Collection: Documents from author William Bunge's 1970 book about the area west of the university, "Fitzgerald: Geography of a Revolution."
Football Collection: Records, photos and memorabilia on the U-D football team from 1894 to 1964.
Marie Morelli Collection: Letters of a British novelist from 1906 to 1923.
The Father Edward J. Dowling Marine Historical Collection: Documents, publications and photos amassed by the Jesuit professor during 70 years. The collection includes 55,000 photos and 10,000 information sheets on specific ships.

Oakland University

248-370-2100
www.kl.oakland.edu

The library's Web site contains links to a number of databases.

Henry Ford Centennial Library

16301 Michigan, Dearborn
313-943-2330
www.dearborn.lib.mi.us

This is Ford country, and the library's Ford Collection contains about 500 books about the man, the family, the car and the company. Many books circulate.

Macomb County Library

16480 Hall Road, Clinton Township
810-286-6660; www.libcoop.net/mcl/

The MCL has an extensive electronic index of magazines and reference works.

Baldwin Public LIbrary

300 W. Merrill, Birmingham; 248-647-1700
www.baldwinlib.org/index.html

The Baldwin is one of Oakland County's most complete libraries, and its Web site contains a number of links to electronic databases.

The Michigan Electronic Library

mel.org

A huge electronic database on subjects that includes a list of magazines held in Michigan libraries and a list of Michigan libraries.

Metro Net Library Consortium

www.metronet.lib.mi.us/index.html

The unusual Labadie Collection began when Joseph Labadie, a Detroit activist from the late 19th and early 20th centuries, donated his papers and books to the University of Michigan.

Trying to 'Return'

Music legend Diana Ross reunited with most recent Supremes, Lynda Laurence, left, and Scherrie Payne, right, for the 'Return to Love' tour during the summer of 2000.

The Detroit Almanac

12. COM
UNICA

"No cue cards, no idiot boards, no reruns; just plain ad-lib conversation."

— *TV talk show host* **Lou Gordon**

JAMES · J · BRADY
FOUNDER
OLD NEWSBOYS GOODFELLOW

Expressing Ourselves

Talking the Talk, Detroit-style

The way Detroiters talk fascinates linguists.

For one thing, we're a metro area packed with dozens of ethnic groups, speaking English with all sorts of accents that change with new generations.

Native Detroiters belong to what linguists call the Northern Inland Region. That means we tend to share certain ways of pronouncing words. Most of us, for example, pronounce "marry," "merry" and "Mary" to sound exactly the same, unlike people in other parts of the country. We say "creek," not "crick," "fawg" not "fahg" for fog and "greesy" not "greezy" for greasy.

Because of our proximity to Canada, we also engage in what's called "Canadian raising," meaning we pronounce some words in a different, higher part of our mouths. "Wife" doesn't sound like why with an "f" at the end, but more like "woif." "House" doesn't sound like "how" with an "s" at the end, but more like "howoos."

At the turn of the 21st Century, though, Detroit is best known among linguists for being at the epicenter of what they call "the Northern Cities Shift."

> **Our way of pronouncing vowels puts us at the epicenter of a lingual shift.**

It's a new way of pronouncing vowels that is sweeping a vast area of the northern United States, from Rochester and Buffalo, N.Y., to Minneapolis.

What's shifting?

The shape of our mouths as we pronounce vowels. "Better" ends up sounding more, but not quite, like "butter." "Link" sounds more like "lenk." "Uncomfortable" becomes "oncomfortable," and "slang" becomes "sleng."

It's subtle, but linguists hear it loud and clear and say it's the most significant change in U.S. pronunciation in many decades.

Linguists say it's most prominent among young, white, middle-class women. Lesley Milroy, a University of Michigan linguist, says it's always women who lead linguistic change because "men are more anxious to conform to the behavior of their peers and not put themselves out on a limb."

Nobody knows why people change the way they pronounce words, but everyone agrees it's subconscious: You pronounce a word differently because those you hang out with do. What's most interesting, says Milroy, is that many African Americans in Detroit are not participating in this vowel shift. Instead, she says, "African Americans are getting progressively *less* like Anglo speakers in Detroit." Especially young African Americans, born in Detroit. They are taking on more Southern ways of speaking.

An older black Detroiter might say "nice white rice," while his grandson might say "nahss whaht rahss" — as if he grew up white in the South.

Linguists hope to study other Detroit populations — Chinese and Latino, for example — to see whether they are pick-

WORDS DETROITERS THINK ARE UNIQUE TO THE REGION, BUT AREN'T

- Party store
- Pop

WORDS AND EXPRESSIONS THAT ARE UNIQUE

- "Help the poor!" as a Halloween chant
- Brush cut, for crew cut
- Hot dish, for a potluck casserole

DETROIT TEENAGE SLANG FROM 1950s

George = cool
Shafty = especially cool
Nerd = nerd (duh!)
Scurve = lesser nerd
Rambling = On a roll
Cut the gas = shut up

COMMUNICATIONS

Newsboys who sold the Free Press in the late 19th Century. Inset: The statue of James Brady, founder of the Old Newsboys Goodfellows Fund, sits on Belle Isle.

Burton Historical Collection photos

... . - . -- . . -- . . -. -- / - . . . . . -. . - . -. . . - . .

TOWN CRIER

In the late 1700s, a town crier rang a bell or beat a drum to attract a crowd, after which he would announce important happenings. Theophilus Mettez, a printer, "cried" the news after Sunday mass at Ste. Anne's Catholic Church.

Neither snow nor sleet . . . Mail carriers in Detroit in the late 1800s.

Burton Historical Collection

ing up the vowel shift.

Because of its large black population, Detroit has also been an epicenter for Ebonics, or African-American English, which has a distinct vocabulary and pronunciation.

Geneva Smitherman of Michigan State University says "black talk" is a very deliberate dialect that many black speakers can use or drop at will.

Among its pronunciation principles:

➤ The final "R" in words is dropped, so "torn up" sounds like "toe up," and "your" sounds like "yo."

➤ The first syllable of words is stressed. "For example," Smitherman writes, "speakers say "PO-leece," not "po-LEECE," and "DE-troit," not "De-TROIT." And Arab is pronounced "AY-rab" not as a slur, but to be phonetically consistent.

➤ "Be" and "Bees" indicate continuous

action, or infrequently recurring activity. For example, "Every time we see him, he be dress like that." And "It bees dat way."

It's also rich in slang that many white people use daily without realizing their words were coined by urban blacks in Detroit and other northern cities. Among such crossover terms: badmouth, big time, brew (for beer), flaky (for weird), catch you later, check it out, lighten up, uptight, dude, busted and what's up?

Black Detroiters also originated the terms "Motor City," "Motown" and "Big D" as slang for Detroit, and "Inktown" as slang for Inkster, which was populated in the 1920s by many Southern blacks who came north to work in the Ford Rouge plant.

All Detroiters sometimes think certain words we use are exclusive to us. We like to think we're the only ones who buy "pop" from "party stores," for example, but linguists say

COMMUNICATIONS

Answer, next page >>

Burton Historical Collection

U.S. mail trucks in Detroit in 1913 looked a bit different from today's delivery trucks.

TELEGRAPH
About 3½ years after it was first used by Samuel F.B. Morse between Baltimore and Washington, telegraph service came to Detroit on Nov. 29, 1847. The first message was sent between Detroit and Ypsilanti. In 1848, Detroit was connected to Chicago and Buffalo. In 1857, Detroit was wired to Windsor via a cable across the Detroit River.

Communications

Please, Monsieur Postman: Deliver de letter, de sooner, de better.

Back in 1701: If founder Cadillac sent a letter to Paris, it took several months to get there, depending on weather, courier reliability, ship schedules, environment, wars and robbers.

By 1761: A letter from British officers in Niagara to colleagues in Detroit took 16 days to arrive.

Around 1814: Mail from Washington took about two months to reach Detroit. It was carried partly by horseback and partly by foot.

Postal route: One opened between Detroit and Mt. Clemens in 1820 — via Pontiac.

After 1831: The Erie Canal was operational and mail from the East arrived daily. But mail from Detroit took 14 days to reach New York.

The 1870s: Detroiters deposited mail in street boxes. Deliveries were made within certain neighborhoods up to five times a day.

Today: The U.S. Postal Service moves about 1 million pieces of mail daily in the 481 and 482 ZIP codes each.

those words are common across the Midwest.

As easy travel and the Internet erase geography and blend people and their ways of talking, very few words remain exclusive to Detroit or Michigan, although surveys have found some among old-timers.

"Help the poor!," a Halloween night chant known to Detroiters who grew up before the 1960s, is a very Detroit thing. That's according to the revered Dictionary of American Regional English. It asked for word choices from 2,777 native Americans in 1,000 communities throughout the country. Of those, 123 lived in Michigan, all born between 1890 and 1970.

Among the words it found only or chiefly in Michigan:

➤ Baga — for rutabaga.
➤ Brush cut — for crew cut.
➤ Booya — a hunter's stew.
➤ Cathole — a small pond or deep place in a river.
➤ Cry-eye — used in the expression "For cry-eye," as in "for crying out loud."
➤ Fish tug — a fishing boat.
➤ Hamburg — for hamburger.
➤ Hot dish and covered dish — for casseroles brought to potluck dinners.

SOURCES: "BLACK TALK: WORDS AND PHRASES FROM THE HOOD TO THE AMEN CORNER," GENEVA SMITHERMAN, HOUGHTON MIFFLIN, 1994, REVISED EDITION 2000, INCLUDES A DICTIONARY OF MORE THAN 2,000 WORDS AND PHRASES; "DICTIONARY OF AMERICAN REGIONAL ENGLISH," VOLS. I (1985), II (1991) AND III (1996), FREDERIC G. CASSIDY, ED., BELKNAP PRESS OF HARVARD UNIVERSITY.

Post office employees sort mail in 1942.

Free Press file photo

COMMUNICATIONS

Free Press file photo

**"May I have your number please?"
Detroit operators in the 1950s.**

Telephone

The telephone soon appeared in several Detroit locations in 1877, a year after Alexander Graham Bell introduced the gadget. By 1887, Detroit had 2,600 phones in use.

The exchanges: For some 50 years until the early 1970s, Detroiters knew phone numbers by prefixes, such as VA 1-8107. The VA stood for the Valley exchange, located on the city's far east side. Here are more — out of sight, but not out of memory:

TUxedo ....Grosse Pointe, Detroit
MIdwest...Birmingham
MAyfair ....Birmingham
LOrain...........................Detroit, near Belle Isle
LOgan ....Dearborn
TOwnesend ....Detroit, near 8 Mile
 and Woodward
UNiversity ....Northwest Detroit
WOodward......................Downtown Detroit
TEmple...............................Midtown Detroit
ADams...Indian Village
SUperior ....North side of Detroit
TRenton ....Downriver
LIncoln.................................Northern suburbs
VErmont ....Northwest Detroit
TYler..................................Northwest Detroit
LAkeview ....East side of Detroit
WAlnut ....East side of Detroit
AVenue ....Wyandotte
KEnwood ....Northwest Detroit
PRescott ....St. Clair Shores
EDgewater......................East side of Detroit,
 along the water
TRinity...................................Northeast Detroit
DRexel...................................Northeast Detroit
VInewood...........................Southwest Detroit
TWinbrook.....................North side of Detroit

Free Press file photo

**A rotary pay phone
from the 1970s.**

The morgue:
Dead newspapers

Detroiters of the 18th Century received their news in printed notices delivered to their doors. But the "news" was actually weeks or even months old. During the 19th Century, Detroit residents published dozens, if not hundreds, of newspapers, magazines and journals — many highly partisan.

➤ **The Michigan Essay, or Impartial Observer, 1809:** The first paper, it was 9¼ by 16 inches and published by James Miller on the press that the Rev. Gabriel Richard imported to Detroit. Only one issue has been located. The paper included articles in French and English on such subjects as politeness, early rising and devotion by Catholics to the Sacred Heart of Jesus.

➤ **The Detroit Gazette, 1817-1830:** A weekly published by Ebenezer Reed and John Sheldon at the behest of Democratic Party power broker Lewis Cass. It was mainly in English, with some articles in French. By 1820, the Gazette had 152 subscribers, 90 of whom had paid. It published articles in 1829 by Sheldon while he was jailed for nine days for having criticized the Michigan Supreme Court in an early freedom-of-the-press cause celebre.

➤ **The Michigan Herald, 1825-1829:** A Whig paper.

➤ **The Detroit Times, 1842:** An antislavery paper.

➤ **The Detroit Daily Gazette, 1842-1845:** A daily and weekly.

➤ **The American Vinyard, 1843-1848:** Pro-prohibition and anti-Catholic.

➤ **The Detroit Daily News, 1845-?:** Considered Detroit's best paper of the period.

➤ **The Western Excelsior, 1848-?:** Perhaps Detroit's first paper oriented toward African Americans.

➤ **The People's Press, 1860-61:** A working person's paper.

➤ **Froth, 1864:** An illustrated weekly comic published by people who worked for the railroad.

- **Detroit Journal of Commerce, 1865-1876:** Merged in 1871 with **the Daily Sun.**

- **The Odd Fellow's Wreath, 1868-1869:** Moved to Chicago and became **the Western Odd Fellow.**

- **The Detroit Daily Hotel Reporter and Railway Guide, 1877-1885:** News for travelers.

- **The Popular Era, 1879:** A paper geared to African Americans.

- **Chaff, 1881-1885:** A paper for the rich.

- **The Detroit Times, 1883-1885:** A fire stunted its growth.

- **The Detroit Post Tribune, 1829-1891:** One of the most important papers in 19th-Century Detroit, the Post Tribune's ancestors go back to the 1829 weekly **Northwestern Journal**, a paper partial to John Quincy Adams. In 1830, the paper became the **Detroit Journal and Michigan Advertiser,** which evolved into the

Detroit Journal in 1833. In 1836, the first edition of the **Detroit Daily Advertiser** appeared. The paper merged with several smaller papers and became a Republican antislavery paper in the pre-Civil War era. In 1862, the Advertiser joined with the **Detroit Daily Tribune**, which subsequently absorbed other papers, changed its name to the **Advertiser and Tribune** and acquired new management, including James Scripps, future founder of the Detroit News. The Advertiser and Tribune merged in 1877 with the 11-year-old **Detroit Daily Post**, a paper associated with U.S. senator and abolitionist Zachariah Chandler. The new paper was called the **Post and Tribune.** In 1884, after more ownership changes, the name was shortened to the **Daily Post**, then changed to the **Tribune** in 1885. In 1891, Scripps, by now running the Detroit News, bought the Tribune, and Scripps' paper became known for a while as the **Detroit News Tribune.**

- **Detroit Journal, 1883-1922:** Published at first by Lloyd Brezee, the Journal struggled financially, and in 1901 was sold to a

Newsstands used to dot downtown Detroit. This one at Woodward and Michigan was across from old City Hall.

Burton Historical Collection

WIRE SERVICE FORMED

Early in the Civil War, a group of newspaper people gathered at the Free Press and formed the forerunner of the Associated Press, which is now the world's largest news-gathering agency.

FIRST WOMEN'S SECTION

In 1878, the Free Press began the Household, the first American newspaper supplement aimed at women.

syndicate that included future Free Press owner E.D. Stair. The Detroit News bought it in 1922.

➤ **Detroit Saturday Night, 1907-1938:** A business-oriented weekly started by two newspapermen, H.M. Nimmo and William Orr, Saturday Night was a unique and influential publication often cited by historians writing about Detroit's golden age. Commenting on the review's tart but conservative slant, an observer once said Saturday Night "did Grosse Pointe's swearing for it."

➤ **Detroit Mirror, 1931-1932:** Backed by Chicago Tribune owner Robert McCormick and New York Daily News chief J.M. Paterson and published by Max Annenberg, the Mirror tried to take on the Free Press in the morning market, but failed.

➤ **Detroit Times, 1900-1960:** Brought to life by James Schermerhorn as **Detroit Today,** William Randolph Hearst bought the paper in 1921 and dispatched famed editor Arthur Brisbane to Detroit to kickstart the Times. The paper was brash and unpredictable. It championed the liberal Frank Murphy for mayor but angered unionists because of its pro-management coverage of the 1937 sit-down strikes. It specialized in rock 'em, sock 'em crime coverage, and ran headlines such as: "Sordid Vice Ring Barred" and "She Sold Her Baby For a Drink." The Times, which operated out of a building downtown at Times Square, was popular in Detroit's black community after World War II. The Detroit News bought it in 1960, after circulation had slipped from a 1951 daily high of 438,757 toward 400,000.

Extra! Extra!

DETROIT FREE PRESS: A short history.

The first Free Press hit the stoop during President Andrew Jackson's first term in 1831. The paper is the oldest business in Detroit, the second-oldest in the metro area, and one of the oldest newspapers in the United States. It will be 170 years old in 2001. Highlights:

➤ Sheldon McKnight first published a 4-page weekly May 5, 1831, on a crude handpress. Its name: The Democratic Free Press and Michigan Intelligencer. McKnight began publishing daily in 1835. He sold the paper in 1836, nine days after being acquitted of manslaughter after a fight in a saloon.

➤ In 1853, Wilbur Storey became owner and editor and introduced numerous innovations such as beat reporting. The first beat: the busy waterfront. He began publishing court testimony and expanded use of the telegraph.

Free Press file photo

Edgar Guest, the poet laureate of the Free Press, with Bismarck. His popular poetry ran in more than 300 papers nationwide.

Storey also opposed the freeing of the slaves and regularly used racial slurs in writing about the turbulent events leading to the Civil War.

➤ In 1881, editor William Quinby began publishing an edition of the Free Press in London, England, that sold more than 90,000 copies a week. Quinby formed a "writers' paper" of talented stylists whose star was Charles Lewis, a humorist who wrote under the nom de plume of M. Quad. Lewis, who was white, created the Lime Kiln Club, a fictional group of black Detroiters whose stereotypical language and actions appear condescending at best a century later.

➤ The paper hired one of its most unusual staffers, Edgar Guest, in 1895. Guest remained for more than 60 years. His popular poetry ran in the Free Press every day for more than 30 years, and more than 300 papers across the nation published his verse.

➤ The Free Press became part of a chain in May 1940, when E.D. Stair sold the paper to John S. Knight, who owned newspapers in Ohio and eventually joined with another chain to form the Knight Ridder Corp., the current Free Press owner. Under Knight, the paper's staff and coverage expanded, and the editorial page took on a more liberal orientation. After more than a century of incurring the wrath of black readers, the National Association for the Advancement of Colored People praised the Free Press for its even-handed coverage of the 1943 riot.

➤ Starting in 1960, when the Detroit News purchased the Detroit Times, the Free Press and News began a nearly 30-year duel for Detroit readers. The Free Press won a

Pulitzer Prize for its coverage of the 1967 riot, and over the next decade, developed a national reputation as a lively, irreverent and hard-hitting paper. But the News continued to lead the all-important circulation war.

➤ By 1986, after the Gannett Corp. had purchased the News, the two papers applied for federal permission to form a joint operating agreement, an exemption from antitrust law designed to preserve independent editorial voices. The JOA began in November 1989. Today, the Free and News share business operations and profits but maintain independent newsrooms.

THE DETROIT NEWS: A *very* short history.

➤ **Aug. 23, 1873:** James Scripps publishes the first Evening News. It changed its name to the Detroit News in 1905.

➤ **1906:** Scripps dies; he is succeeded by son-in-law George Booth. The paper would be run by the family company until the 1980s.

➤ **1920:** The paper's radio station, WWJ-AM, hit the air.

➤ **1986:** Gannett Corp. acquired the News by paying $717 million for the Evening News Association, whose president, Peter B. Clark, was the great-grandson of News founder James Scripps.

Airwaves

From its start in 1920 with WWJ-AM, Detroit radio has flourished.

The region had about 10 stations by World War II; the number grew to 40 in the mid-1960s and reached 60 by 2000. Metro Detroit also spawned innovative formats and personalities who not only brought music from around the world to Detroiters, but also helped disseminate the groundbreaking music Detroiters produced.

Today the radio dial offers a smorgasbord. There's sophisticated French programming from Canada, CBEF-AM (540); sports talk, WDFN-AM (1130); classic soul, WGRV-AM (105.1); public radio outlets — WDET-FM (101.9), WUOM-FM (91.7) and WEMU-FM (89.1) — and much more.

The powerhouses at the start of the 21st Century are adult contemporary WNIC-FM (100.3); all-news WWJ-AM (950); oldies WOMC-FM (104.3), black youth-oriented WJLB (97.9), the rocker WRIF-FM (101.1) and WJR-AM (760).

Landmarks of Detroit radio

WWJ-AM (950)

Noteworthy alone for allowing Sonny Eliot to read his wacky weathercasts for more than 40 years. But in 1920, predecessor station 8MK, owned by the Detroit News, was among the first U.S. installations to transmit words and music across the ether. (Pittsburgh's KDKA is usually recognized as the first *regular* broadcaster.) Besides Sonny, the station had Bob Allison's "Ask Your Neighbor" (one of radio's first regular call-in shows), broadcasts of U-M football and most recently, "all-news-all-the-time-with-traffic-and-weather-on-the-eights." Can't get to work without it.

Sonny Eliot: Must be rainy and windy – "Rindy kind of weather."

Free Press file photo

Channel 4, WDIV, introduced weathercaster Sonny Eliot to metro Detroit television audiences.

COMMUNICATIONS

WXYZ radio creative types Brace Beemer, left, and Frank Striker.

Free Press file photos

George Trendle, left, a creator of "The Lone Ranger," celebrates the show's 25th anniversary in 1958 with Clayton Moore, who played the Masked Man on TV and in the movies.

Mike Wallace was the announcer for "The Hornet."

"The Lone Ranger," "The Green Hornet" and "Challenge of the Yukon"

Back before radio played rock music and allowed callers to rant and rave endlessly about their sports teams, there was ... melodrama!

Like "The Lone Ranger," first broadcast from WXYZ-AM (1270) — "the last word in radio" — on Jan. 31, 1933, and lasting until the Rock Era dawned in 1956, though the show was not always broadcast from Detroit.

The real men behind the mask were station co-owner George Trendle, radio repertory titan James Jewell, writer Fran Striker and Brace Beemer, who played TLR for 13 years. Uh, and oh yes, that "William Tell Overture" theme music.

"The Hornet" spun off "The Lone Ranger" with most of the same creative types in control. "60 Minutes" scourge Mike Wallace, left, was once the show's announcer. It ran from Jan. 31, 1936, to 1952. The Hornet was news-

paper publisher Britt Reid, who fought crime by night behind a mask.

In February 1938, the Ranger-Hornet creatives launched the tales of Sgt. William Preston of the Royal Canadian Mounted Police and his faithful dog, Yukon King. It lasted through June 1955, brought to you by "Quaker Puffed Wheat and Puffed Rice — the only cereal shot from guns!"

WJR-AM (760)

In a bit of questionable future-think, the Free Press decided radio wouldn't amount to much and sold what was then WCX-AM in 1925. Thus WJR was born. It has had nicknames galore — "The Goodwill Station," "The Great Voice of the Great Lakes," "Superstation 760." It has a powerful 50,000-watt clear-channel signal that makes it listenable during the day across Michigan, Ontario, Ohio and Indiana and even farther at night.

It had featured voices that grabbed you by the ears and by the heart: Bud Guest, J.P. McCarthy, Jimmy Launce, Jay Roberts, Karl Haas, Bob Reynolds and many others. And it had the civic image — the complex voice of a complex place. It was the station your mom and dad listened to when the weather acted up. The station you listened to coming home after a long drive east, west, north or south. The station you tuned to the morning after the big Tiger win to hear J.P. and Sparky Anderson say absolutely nothing comprehensible. But it sounded good. The station where you took make-believe all-night journeys with Roberts when he commanded "Night Flight 760." It was, well, sublime.

CKLW-AM (800)

When the Big 8 was big, it was very, very big. When RKO General owned the 50,000-watt station in Windsor, it found a winning formula by mixing a steady diet of top 40 hits with minimal disk jockey banter and the bloodiest newscasts on the air. Starting in the late 1960s, CK was such a power that at times, it was the most listened-to radio station in

Cleveland and Toledo — let alone Detroit. Between the shouts of "Much more music" there was the incessant ID-jingle "See-Kay-El-Double-You, The Motor City." And when Twenty-Twenty News guys Byron MacGregor, Joe Donovan, Don Patrick, Grant Hudson or Randall Carlisle would tell you "THERE IS FRESH BLOOD ON THE STREETS OF DETROIT," get out the mop, compadre!

WJLB and WCHB

The WC and HB in WCHB: Founders Wendell Cox, left, and Haley Bell.

Radio somehow gets away with something the law usually frowns upon — separate-but-equal audience targeting. Hence, WJLB (first an AM station at 1400, then in the '70s an FM powerhouse at 97.9) and WCHB — its call letters are the initials of its founders, black dentists Wendell Cox and Haley Bell — aimed at black listeners and gathered almost all of them during the tension-soaked '60s, the disco-freak '70s, the chilled-out '80s and '90s. Playing the hits of Motown, blues and the imported Sound of Philadelphia, the names Donnie Simpson, Wade (Butterball Jr.) Briggs and Frantic Ernie Durham were as popular among Detroit's black community as J.P. McCarthy and Dick Purtan were to the white suburban audience.

WABX-FM (99.5)

For old times' sake, light up your bong and put on your old Hendrix LP. WABX was one of the nation's first free-form stations. All of the things CKLW was, ABX in the late '60s and early '70s, was not. It was album cuts from bands like Quicksilver Messenger Service. Dude! It was not "Sugar, Sugar" from the Archies. It was free-form sets where the deejays played what they wanted. It was news, by Harvey Ovshinsky, with a counterculture bent. It was kite-flying promotional events on Belle Isle. You got the impression the program hosts — self-described Air Aces Dave Dixon, Jerry Lubin, Dan Carlysle and others — were toking while the discs went round and round. All power to the megahertz! Mellow!

Martha Jean (the Queen) Steinberg: Her voice carries on.

Martha Jean (The Queen) Steinberg

Up from the South with thousands of other blacks looking for postwar work in Detroit in the '50s and '60s, Steinberg became one of the first female — let alone black — broadcasters that mattered on WJLB-AM and FM and later her own station, WQBH-AM. Motown stars dropped by *her* show when Hitsville was cranking out the Gordy gold. The Queen issued the call to chill when the '67 riot got out of hand. And in her later career, she turned into the city's genuine certified Holy Ghost-preaching machine. Baptizing the faithful in the Belle Isle lagoon? You betcha. Steinberg died Jan. 29, 2000, but she continued to fill QBH's noon-2 p.m. time slot, thanks to the station's voluminous library of her old broadcasts, some going back 45 years.

Good morning, Detroit

J.P. McCarthy as a new WJR staffer in 1964 and as Detroit's top morning man in 1991.

Most everyone agreed that in August 1995 an epoch ended when Joseph Priestly McCarthy died at 62 from complications of a blood disorder. The top-rated morning voice and favorite son on WJR-AM for more than 30 years, McCarthy was the city's conscience, prodder, scourge, do-gooder, next-door neighbor and muse. A Sinatra or Bennett tune, weather banter with John McMurray, an impromptu aria from Fat Bob Taylor, a revelation from the chairman of GM, Chrysler or Ford, a report from Grosse Pointe Charles or the Lady in Blue. Only in Detroit, only from J.P. McCarthy.

Public radio

Back in the late 1940s, the United Auto Workers got a federal license for a radio station. But it was on the then-little appreciated FM side of the dial, and none of the labor titans could quite figure out what to do with it.

Deeded to Wayne State University, WDET-FM (101.9) was a lot of nothing through the 1950s and '60s.

But in the ultra-democratic '70s, it was local radio's version of the later Balkan Wars, with ethnic and other special interest groups vying for air time and control of the growing-in-importance FM outlet. Sit-ins, protests and some four-letter-word shouting abounded.

Finally in the 1980s, Wayne State leaders pulled in the reins. WDET emerged as part-National Public Radio feeder, part oasis for musical hipsters (thanks to Anne DeLisi and Judy Adams). General manager Caryn Mathis stayed the course.

Never a power in numbers of listeners, WDET's muscle is as the perceived best preserver of Detroit's varied musical, political and social legacy.

Mystery deejay

Does the name Charles Johnson strike a familiar note?

In the early to mid-1980s, Johnson, evening disc jockey on the little-listened-to R&B sta-

Free Press file photo

Dick Purtan, left, clowns with longtime sidekick Tom Ryan in 1981.

tion WGPR-FM (107.3), started mixing the hit music of the day with little regard to the artist's race or music inspiration — soul, funk, rock, hard rock, whatever. And he created his own spaced-out broadcast world, its swirling sound effects grounded only by his own deep voice.

Breaking down the segregated radio dial, Johnson attracted hoards of hip white teens to dial his way, accounting for the highest ratings in the station's history. They have never been equaled.

Of course, it's a mercenary society, and competitors WJLB-FM (97.9) and WHYT (96.3) lured him from his mothership with filthy lucre. He went, but the magic didn't as the demands of radio formatting stifled such a free spirit. (Promotions that went awry — like Boblo boat cruises that didn't embark — helped too.)

Still perplexed about Charles? Perpetually camera shy, maybe you remember his nom-de-megacycle — the Electrifying Mojo.

Dick Purtan

All of what J.P. McCarthy was, Purtan wasn't. Funny. Sarcastic. Full of piss and vinegar. Irreverent. No GM chairman called him up. The broadcast pepper to McCarthy's salt, Purtan toiled at WKNR-AM, WXYZ-AM, CKLW-AM, WKQI-FM and WOMC-FM over three decades of waking up Detroiters who preferred burnt toast rather than McCarthy's white bread and butter. Satire was his metier. He started out poking fun at councilwoman

Legendary deejay the Electrifying Mojo, a.k.a. Charles Johnson. He got his nickname from the song, "Got my Mojo Working," by Jimmy Smith.

Free Press file photo

Mary Beck's hats in the '60s and succeeded in getting Coleman Young to chortle in the '90s. There was a big heart behind the mask of comedy, too. Ask anyone who ever was helped by his pet charities.

Ernie Harwell

Baltimore has been extraordinarily generous to Detroit, when it comes to baseball. In 1953, the Maryland city shipped Al Kaline here. In 1960, it exported Ernie Harwell.

Through riots and recessions and boom times, basebrawls and disco riots, the kindly, Christian Harwell was the voice of summer in Detroit for several generations. With a style honed in Atlanta, Brooklyn and New York, Harwell delivered Tiger radio play-by-play is an easygoing, molasses-tinged Southern dialect. It was succinct — never bombastic — with trademarked phrasing like the called-third strike where the batter "stood there like the house by the side of the road." He gave voice to baseball's true soul.

In a city with plenty of historic maelstroms, none was quite as intense as the one in 1991 when grid-Luddite-turned-Tiger-president Bo Schembechler and WJR-AM (760) decided Harwell was too old to continue. When his replacements fanned, Harwell was re-installed and calls six innings of every game at age 82 in the new century. Inducted into the Baseball Hall of Fame's broadcast wing, his absence then gave an unfortunate glimpse at what life after Ernie might be like. Ponder things far more pleasant.

WXYT-AM (1270)

The house Chuck Fritz built. Start your broadcast day with a defrocked baseball star whose love of the scam meant he had to be kept on a short leash at all times (Denny McLain). Follow him up with an ex-Marine, kung-fu fightin', former fundamentalist preacher (Mark Scott) who styled himself as the cure for White House "commun-Nazis!" Pick up the syndicated national Republican of the year every year (Rush Limbaugh). Next up, a 25-year talk vet who is smarter than you are and tries to prove it every day (David Newman). End the day with a down-turned hat-brimmed refugee from the '30s (Tommy McIntyre) and the doyenne of suburban conservatism (Ronna Romney), and you had the talk station of the '90s that the right loved and the left loved to hate. It all started in the '70s with Dr. Sonya Friedman and Jacqui the Astrologer.

WNIC-FM (100.3)

Owner Ed Christian and Paul Christy took WABX-wanna-be WKNR-FM in the 1970s,

GABRIEL B. TAIT / Detroit Free Press

Hall of Fame Tiger broadcaster Ernie Harwell in the booth as the Tigers and Kansas City Royals play the final game at Tiger Stadium in Detroit on Monday, Sept. 27, 1999.

changed the call letters and created an aural ambience based on soft rock music and a long line of comfy broadcast voices. (Among the noteworthys: Jerry St. James, Jim Harper, Alan Almond.) A quarter century later, it's still, er, pretty NICe. And one extra for good measure — the Radio Pied Pipers of the '50s and '60s: Ed (Jack the Bellboy) McKenzie, Robin Seymour, Lee (The Horn) Alan, Frantic Ernie Durham, Dave Prince, Tom Clay, Tom Shannon and Mickey Shorr. Where they led, the teens of Detroit followed.

WRIF-FM (101.1)

In the spring of 1970, Dick Kernen, now a renowned broadcast educator but then the fledgling program director of WXYZ-FM (soon to become WRIF), hired Arthur Penhallow for an off-the-air job. On July 9, 1970, Penhallow debuted in a regular deejay shift. Three decades later, Arthur P is still rocking, and so is the 'RIF. It's an amazing feat for both, given the capricious world of Detroit radio. A free-form station like

No stunt was too weird for deejays in the 1950s. Robin (Rockin' Robin) Seymour interviewed a Detroit lion in 1957.

Free Press file photo

"This is the Frantic One!"

− **Ernie Durham**, WJLB-AM.

'Get outta bed!'

− **Fred Wolf**, from his "Wacky Wigloo" on WXYZ-AM.

WXYZ-AM's broadcast booth on East Jefferson in 1955. The deejay was Fred Wolf.

Free Press file photo

WABX-FM at first, WRIF bought into consultant Lee Abrams' tightly formatted "album-oriented rock" in 1971. The playlist remains tight, and the station remains a ratings leader, thanks in part to its ear-grabbing personalities, from Penhallow's gruff trademark "Baby!" to popular morning men Drew and Mike's raucous humor.

Soundchecks
1950s deejays and their mantras

"Get outta bed," Fred Wolf, from his "Wacky Wigloo" on WXYZ-AM.

"Make it or break it," Mickey Shorr, WJBK-AM.

"This is R.K., your swing and sway deejay on CK," Ron Knowles, CKLW-AM.

"This is the Frantic One," Ernie Durham, WJLB-AM.

"Good night, Detroit Baby," Paul Winter, WXYZ-AM.

"Be sure and save your Confederate bread, your Dixie cups, and, of course, always walk tall. Till tomorrow, long about 2:05, this is your boy, Robert E. Lee, the rebel with a cause, saying farewell, cool world," Robert E. Lee, WJBK-AM.

"Who you expectin,' the Lone Ranger?" Joltin Joe Howard, WJLB-AM.

"It's a very ordinary world, and you're a most extraordinary audience," Joel Sebastian, WXYZ-AM.

SOURCE: "ROCKIN' DOWN THE DIAL," BY DAVID CARSON.

Tidbits

➤ The first Top 40-format first aired on WJBK in 1956. Detroit radio historian David Carson credits Robin Seymour as the first deejay to host sock hops, in 1952. Seymour's personal jingle, as recorded by the Four Lads: "Bobbin' with Robin/ No more time for sobbin,'/Go and let the mob in/ Everybody flies sky high."

➤ Carson identifies Mickey Shorr as Detroit's first all-out rock and roll

Free Press file photo
Deejay Mickey Shorr in 1959.

deejay, on WJBK in the mid-1950s. Shorr also was the first to play an Elvis Presley record, "Mystery Train," in 1955.

➤ Several Detroit radio personalities played roles in the payola scandal of the 1950s. In November 1959, veteran announcer Ed McKenzie wrote an article for Life Maga-

All the hits, all the time!

Top 10 songs in Detroit on Sept. 22, 1958, WJBK-AM

1) "It's All in the Game," Tommy Edwards
2) "Rockin' Robin," Bobby Day
3) "Poor Boy," the Royal Tones
4) "Bird Dog," the Everly Brothers
5) "Nel Blu Dipinto Di Blu," Modugno/Martin
6) "Summertime Blues," Eddie Cochran
7) "You Cheated," the Shields
8) "Tea for Two Cha Cha," Tommy Dorsey Orchestra
9) "Tears on My Pillow," the Imperials
10) "Susie Darlin'," Robin Luke

Top 10 songs in Detroit on Nov. 7, 1963, from WKNR

1) "Louie, Louie," Kingsmen
2) "Since I Fell for You," Lenie Welsh
3) "Can I Get a Witness," Marvin Gaye
4) "Misery," Dynamics
5) "Everybody," Tommy Roe
6) "She's a Fool," Leslie Gore
7) "Dominique," Singing Nun
8) "Baby I Love You," Galens
9) "Nitty Gritty," Shirley Ellis
10) "24 Hours from Tulsa," Gene Pitney

Top 10 songs in Detroit on April 14, 1964, on CKLW

1) "My Guy," Mary Wells
2) "Hello Dolly," Louis Armstrong
3) "Do You Want to Know a Secret?" the Beatles
4) "Bits and Pieces," Dave Clark 5
5) "Ronnie," 4 Seasons
6) "Across the Street," Lenny O'Henry
7) "Can't Buy Me Love," Beatles
8) "(The Best Part of) Breaking Up," Ronettes
9) "Dead Man's Curve," Jan and Dean
10) "Money," Kingsmen

Top 10 songs in Detroit on Nov. 14, 1966, on WJLB

1) "Whispers," Jackie Wilson
2) "Standing on Guard," the Falcons
3) "I'm Your Puppet," James and Bobu Purify
4) "Look at What I Almost Missed," Pat Lewis
5) "But It's Alright," J.J. Jackson
6) "Don't Answer the Door," B.B. King

Free Press file photo

White toughs chase a black man during the 1943 riot.

CBS radio carried a groundbreaking documentary across the nation after the 1943 Detroit riot. One critic described it as a "blistering condemnation of racism in American society." The show — "An Open Letter on Race Hatred" — linked brown-shirt fascists in Europe with the white gangs in Detroit that attacked blacks. Time Magazine called "An Open Letter" one of the "most elegant programs in radio history."

zine that described how promoters often paid disc jockeys to play records. He didn't name names, but said the practice was common in Detroit. Several deejays resigned or were fired in the ensuing controversy, including the popular Tom Clay, who said he accepted some payola, and Shorr, who denied he had accepted payments.

SOURCES: FREE PRESS; "ROCKIN' DOWN THE DIAL," BY DAVID CARSON.

Free Press file photo

Casey Kasem receives Wayne State University's Distinguished Alumni Award in 1987. His actress wife, Jean Kasem, and WSU President David Adamany look on.

CASEY'S COUNTDOWN
One of the best-known deejays to emerge from Detroit is **Kemal Amin (Casey) Kasem**, the "American Top 40" impresario who got his start in 1950 at WDTR, the Detroit Public Schools station. At Wayne State University, Kasem starred as "Scoop Ryan, Cub Reporter" in a children's show on WJR.

7) "Somebody Needs You," Darrell Banks
8) "Don't Be a Drop Out," James Brown
9) "Secret Love," Billy Stewart
10) "Tell It Like It Is," Aaron Neville

Top 10 songs in Detroit on Feb. 13, 1969, on WKNR

1) "Build Me Up Buttercup," Foundations
2) "Dizzy," Tommy Roe
3) "Indian Giver," 1910 Fruitgum Co.
4) "Twenty-Five Miles," Edwin Starr
5) "Kick Out the Jams," MC 5
6) "Proud Mary," Creedence Clearwater
7) "Hot Smoke & Sasafrass," the Bubble Puppy
8) "You Gave Me a Mountain," Frankie Laine

9) "My Whole World Ended," David Ruffin
10) "Traces," Classics IV

Top 10 songs in Detroit on March 8, 1971, on WKNR

1) "What's Going On," Marvin Gaye
2) "Me and Bobby McGee," Janis Joplin
3) "Love Story," H. Mancini/A. Williams
4) "She's a Lady," Tom Jones
5) "Stay Awhile," the Bells
6) "Just My Imagination," the Temptations
7) "Woodstock," Matthews' Southern Comfort
8) "Another Day," Paul McCartney
9) "Eighteen," Alice Cooper
10) "Proud Mary," Ike and Tina Turner

Free Press file photo

Saint Ernie reveals the public relations blunder of the decade: His 1991 firing. He returned to the booth and continues to call Tigers games.

Excerpt of Ernie Harwell's first farewell Sunday, Oct. 6, 1991:

"Well, as a lover of baseball, a man who has been in the game for almost 50 years, I know for certain that nobody can last in a job forever. Everybody can be replaced; all of us must move along.

"I've had a gratifying career as your Tiger announcer, and now I say good-bye. I'll never be able to repay all the warmth and affection you fans have shown me. It has been a tremendous 32 years, but I don't want to look back. I agree with Satchel Paige and with William Shakespeare.

"Ol' Satch said: 'Don't look back; something may be gaining on you.' And Mr. Shakespeare once wrote: 'To have done is to hang quite out of fashion.'

"So I press forward and look to the future. God has a new adventure waiting for me. It might be a rocking chair; it might be a microphone. But either way, I welcome a new challenge and a new opportunity . . .'"

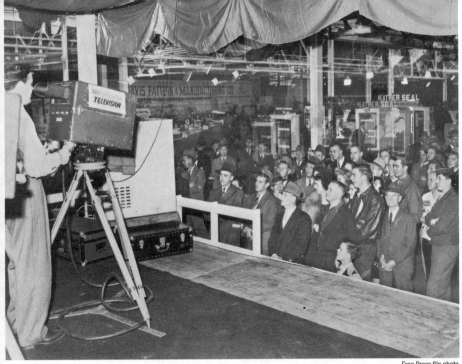

Free Press file photo

WWJ-TV, now WDIV-TV (Channel 4), gave the first demonstration of TV in March 1946 in Detroit's old Convention Hall.

Local TV

Channel 2

WJBK-TV, FOX 2
First broadcast, Oct. 24, 1948.

➤ **Then: Bwana Don and Lucy.** In the 1950s, Channel 2 originated cowboy cartoon host Sagebrush Shorty and animal show host Bwana Don, played by Don Hunt with his chimpanzee sidekick, Bongo Bailey. In the 1960s, Morgus, the creepy host of a sci-fi movie show, also did weather reports. Dale Young hosted a dance show, "Detroit Bandstand."

Channel 2 carried huge national hits, too: "The Ed Sullivan Show," "The Jackie Gleason Show," "The Life of Riley" starring William Bendix, "Gunsmoke," "I Love Lucy" and the quiz show "What's My Line."

➤ **Now:** A CBS affiliate in its first 45 years, Channel 2 has been reborn as an anything-goes Fox station. The youthful attitude adjustment goes beyond edgy Fox network series such as "The Simpsons" or "Malcolm in the Middle." It's also evident in WJBK's revved-up, populist approach to local news, including reporter Scott Lewis' tabloid-sharp, hidden-camera "Busted on the Job" reports.

Channel 4

WDIV-TV, NBC AFFILIATE
First broadcast Oct. 23, 1946. It was the first in Michigan and sixth TV station in the nation.

➤ **Then: Milky, Sonny, lots of firsts.** It was WWJ and owned by the Detroit News until 1978, when Washington-based Post-Newsweek Stations bought the station and changed the call letters. Channel 4 broadcast the first televised Tigers game and later the first Red Wings, Lions and Michigan-Michigan State games. In November 1947 it was first to broadcast the Thanksgiving Parade. Other firsts: Color broadcast in Michigan

Kid Rock and the rapping little guy, Joe C., appeared with homer Simpson on "The Simpsons" in April 2000.

Fox

The talent that made Channel 7 great in the 1970s: Doris Biscoe, left, Jim Herrington, general manager Jim Osborn, Bill Bonds, Al Ackerman, Marilyn Turner, John Kelly and news director Phil Nye.

WXYZ-TV

Soupy Sales during his popular Channel 7 lunchtime show in 1955.

Free Press file photo

(Jan. 1, 1954); stereo broadcast (1985) and Doppler radar (1988).

In the 1950s, kids watched magician Milky the Clown who let studio audience kids dip their hands into his penny bowl. The station also introduced weathercaster Sonny Eliot, a local fixture still.

It refused in the 1970s to carry the risque "Saturday Night Live," but relented when the program became a huge national hit.

➤ **Now:** The "Go 4 It" station introduced "ME TV" videocam kiosks in area shopping malls allowing people to "Go 4 It" by recording their gripes, thoughts and songs for airing on WDIV newscasts.

Channel 7

WXYZ-TV, ABC AFFILIATE
First broadcast Oct. 9, 1948.

➤ **Then: Wixie and Soupy.** Network affiliate ABC was weak in TV's early days, so WXYZ-TV produced a schedule of local programs that became legends. Shows included local bowling and wrestling programs with Fred Wolf, and the "Pat and Johnny Show," with Johnny Slagle and Pat Tobin, which Channel 7 says was the first morning television show in the country. Gravelly voiced George Pierrot hosted a travel show. Adults-only comic Marv Welch was hired to play Wixie Wonderland, a kids' favorite who wore a gyrocopter-topped beanie and Edith Fern Melrose held court daily as "The Lady of Charm."

But the Channel 7 program most likely remembered by today's grown-ups was "Lunch with Soupy," starring the zany Soupy Sales, various puppets and dogs White Fang and Black Tooth, seen only as paws grabbing Soupy for a kiss... "DON'T KISS!" Sales' staples included his Words of Wisdom, the Soupy Shuffle and pies in the kisser.

Channel 7 built Detroit's top television newsroom in the late-1960s when it hired reporters Jim Herrington and Bill Bonds (see below). By the late 1970s, WXYZ was the dominant station in Detroit.

➤ **Now:** The golden age of WXYZ dominance is gone, along with once prominent local programs like "Kelly & Company." Once unchallenged as No. 1 in the afternoons, "The Oprah Winfrey Show" also has faded as a syndicated afternoon powerhouse. And since Bonds' personal and professional meltdown in the mid-1990s, Channel 7 news has been in search of a signature personality.

Channel 9

CBET-TV
First broadcast Sept. 17, 1954.

➤ **Then: Hockey and "Swingin' Time."** Windsor station CBET began as CKLW-TV, financed by Canadian and American investors. CKLW became Canada's 15th TV station, and made Detroit one of only eight U.S. cities to have four or more stations. Its transmitter tower looms over the Windsor skyline near the Ambassador Bridge and is physically closer to the heart of Detroit than the towers of channels 2, 4 and 7. Early CKLW-TV programs included "Captain Video," talks by Bishop Fulton J. Sheen, wrestling, "Swingin' Time" with popular deejay Robin Seymour, and "Roller Derby." Toby David started with the station reading the Sunday funnies on the air. But he's best known for spending 1957 to 1967 as Captain Jolly, the host of "Popeye and His Pals" cartoons in the afternoon. From 1957-63, CKLW-TV carried the outspoken views of Guy Nunn, the voice of the UAW, after Detroit stations refused to carry his pro-worker views. CBC took over the station on July 15, 1975.

➤ **Now:** A pale echo of its former self, Channel 9 offers only minimal amounts of local programming and news today. Today's CBET-TV is almost exclusively an outlet for CBC programming. But that includes everything from "Hockey Night in Canada" to the sophisticated nightly newscast, "The National."

Channel 20

WDWB-TV
First broadcast Sept. 15, 1968, as WXON (Channel 62).

➤ **Then: Wrestling and the Ghoul:** In the beginning, there was wrestling, Robin Seymour's teen dance parties that had been on Channel 9, religion shows and horror flicks hosted by the Ghoul. In the mid-1970s, Channel 20 became ON-TV, a subscription service for movies and sports. By the mid-1980s, Channel 20 returned to free TV — a mishmash of infomercials and poorly edited old movies. It lucked out occasionally with a syndicated hit like "Baywatch."

➤ **Now:** Upbeat. The harmonic convergence of owner Granite Broadcasting Corp. and affiliation with the fledgling WB network has brought younger viewers to Channel 20. The WB hits that account for the attraction: "Buffy, the Vampire Slayer," "Dawson's Creek" and "Felicity," as well as popular syndicated programs like "Xena: Warrior Princess" and reruns of "The Drew Carey Show."

Channel 50

WKBD-TV
First broadcast, Jan. 10, 1965.

➤ **Then: Lou Gordon and Sgt. Sacto.** Channel 50 introduced Detroit to UHF — if you had a set then that could receive the ultra-high frequency signal. As more viewers got those sets, WKBD's programming of sports, personalities and talk made it one of the nation's top independent stations. Channel 50, owned then by Kaiser Broadcasting, was far ahead of its time in figuring out that the American public has a huge appetite for televised sports.

WKBD also wasn't afraid to let original characters on the air, including talk/interview host Lou Gordon ("no cue cards, no idiot boards, just plain ad-lib conversation") and Tom Ryan as Sgt. Sacto. Sportscaster Ray Lane and newsman Woody Willis were also 50 staples. In 1979, WKBD was the highest-rated UHF station in the country. In the mid-80s, 50 became a founding affiliate of the fledgling Fox network — and brought Detroit "The Simpsons."

➤ **Now:** Detroit teams — including telecasts of the Tigers, Pistons and Red Wings — still give Channel 50 the major portion of its local broadcast personality. Fox left 50 in the mid-1990s and took its high-rated shows, too.

LOU GORDON

A colorful and bombastic magazine publisher and TV talk-show host, Gordon was a populist who specialized in raising hell with public officials. Gordon, below left, whose popular show ran on Channel 50 from 1965 to 1977, called Detroit Edison Chairman Walker Cisler "Walking Chisler," and in 1967 got presidential candidate George Romney to admit U.S. officials had brainwashed him during a fact-finding trip to southeast Asia. Result: Romney quickly became an ex-candidate. Gordon also liked to have fun on the air. His wife, Jackie, asked him questions supposedly sent in by viewers, and Gordon often aired shows whose subject matter was the kind of kinky personal behavior seen on tabloid TV shows today.

Free Press file photo

That left 50 with the newer, less successful UPN network.

Channel 56

WTVS-TV First broadcast, Oct. 3, 1955.

➤ **Then: Educational TV.**

Channel 56 is Detroit's viewer-supported, noncommercial station, one of 242 channels set aside nationally for educational use after World War II. The station grew slowly. Congress created the Corporation for Public Broadcasting in 1967, which would provide public funding for education-based television and radio. In 1968, with cameras borrowed from WXYZ-TV (Channel 7), it opened its first studio. In 1971, the station bought the former headquarters of WJBK-TV (Channel 2) in Detroit's New Center area.

Early programs were strictly educational. In 1966, WTVS produced its first program for use by others, the 13-part "People in Jazz." Other notable programs have included "Who Killed Vincent Chin?" "Lionel Hampton,"

"Maya Angelou," "A Wedding in Basra," "Club Connect," "LateNight America;" "Country Express," the 13-part Beethoven Festival, "Detroit Black Journal" (now "American Black Journal"), "Detroit Week in Review" and "Backstage Pass."

Channel 56 is governed by a 56-member board of trustees composed of Detroit-area residents. The station also receives advice from Community Advisory Panel of volunteers from metro Detroit and Windsor. The public is invited to the meetings, and can receive more information by calling 313-876-9510.

➤ **Now:** Same as it ever was, Channel 56 is an invaluable alternative to the commercial networks thanks to such classy, high-quality PBS series and documentaries as "Masterpiece Theatre," "Nova," "The Civil War," "Antiques Roadshow," "American Experience," "Sesame Street" and "Frontline." Even in a competitive television environment that offers somewhat similar programming on such cable channels as Bravo and A&E, the WTVS schedule frequently qualifies as the real "Must See TV." The station boasted record viewership in 1999, with more than 1 million households in southeast Michigan and another million households watching via satellite and cable across Canada.

Channel 62

WWJ-TV

➤ **Now: CBS on UHF**. CBS was bounced into the UHF boondocks in the mid-1990s, after being exiled from Channel 2 when Fox took over that station. To maintain a CBS outlet in Detroit, the Tiffany Network purchased WGPR-TV (Channel 62), the nation's first black-owned TV station. WGPR had limped along on low-budget programming since going on the air in the 1970s. CBS quickly changed the call letters to WWJ, matching the network's popular Detroit radio station. Initially burdened with the weak signal of the old WGPR transmitter, CBS's local ratings tumbled and bruised such popular attractions as "60 Minutes" and "Late Show with David Letterman." Those numbers are slowly climbing. CBS has long delayed the launch of a Channel 62 news operation, further diminishing the station's local profile.

Fringe benefits

➤ **WLPC-TV (Channel 26):** A low-power outlet for Christian programming, including "Deliverance" and "Faith Clinic."

➤ **PAX-TV (Channel 31):** Family-friendly programming, which includes reruns of "Touched by an Angel" and original series like "Hope Island" and "Little Men."

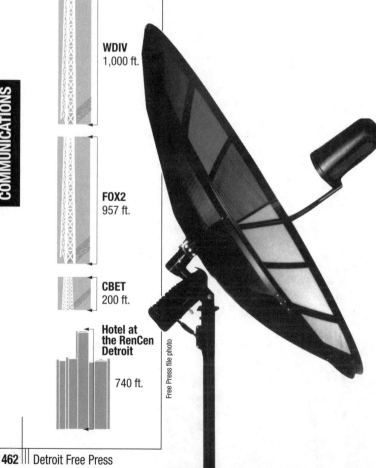

Free Press file photo

COMMUNICATIONS

The Detroit Almanac

13. BUIL

"Nonwithstanding so large an industrial population, Detroit may fairly be described as a slumless city."

— **National Geographic**, *1928*

DINGS

The Penobscot in 1935. For 50 years, Detroit's tallest building. Now at 557 feet, it's the third tallest.

Metro Detroit features many architectural landmarks, from the Fisher, Guardian and Penobscot towers downtown to the campus of Cranbrook Educational Community in Bloomfield Hills. Hidden among the great and famous are a lot of other gems that often get overlooked or underrated.

Detroit's Masterpieces

FISHER BUILDING, Grand Boulevard at Second (1928). Architect: Albert Kahn. One of Kahn's acknowledged masterpieces, the Fisher would have stood as one of three such towers had the Great Depression not truncated plans. Even in this downsized version, the Fisher remains as rich and inviting as any building in Detroit.

McGREGOR MEMORIAL CONFERENCE CENTER, Wayne State University campus (1958). Architect: Minoru Yamasaki. A reflecting pool, skylights, white marble and other rich materials give this elegant building a delicate yet lasting appeal.

GUARDIAN BUILDING, 500 Griswold (1929). Architect: Smith, Hinchman & Grylls. Justly famed for the gaily colored patterns of Pewabic Pottery tiles and its elaborate brickwork drawn from the Arts and Crafts movement, the Guardian holds its place as one of Detroit's greatest landmarks.

THE FOX THEATRE, 2211 Woodward (1928). Architect: C. Howard Crane. Gold-painted plaster, marble on the floors and grand stairway, fierce lions and elephants standing guard — all made the Fox Detroit's grandest (if architecturally over-the-top) movie palace, rescued from oblivion in the '80s for a second life.

CRANBROOK EDUCATIONAL COMMUNITY, Bloomfield Hills (1907). Architects: Eliel Saarinen and others. Newspaper publisher George Booth started Cranbrook in 1907. Nineteen years later, he hired Finnish architect Eliel Saarinen to plan and design the Cranbrook campus. He finished Cranbrook's main buildings by 1943. Thankfully, modern designers have taken care not to overwhelm his masterpieces when designing their modern additions.

Free Press file photo

The Fisher Building at Second and West Grand Boulevard.

Other buildings

TROWBRIDGE HOUSE, 1380 E. Jefferson Ave. (1826) Architect: unknown. Many of Detroit's pre-1900 buildings have been demolished. Those that remain are often squeezed into oblivion by new development. This home, built by wealthy banker Charles Trowbridge, was a landmark when he built it in a much younger Detroit. Even altered and reduced in size over the years, it's Detroit's oldest-known building and one of our few remaining relics of the city's early history.

BAGLEY MEMORIAL FOUNTAIN, Woodward and Monroe. (1887) Architect: H.H. Richardson. Detroit's only example of work by the man many consider to be America's best architect. Sadly, the city doesn't seem to know what to do with

BUILDINGS

ARCHITECTS

The first building in Detroit was a church, thrown up in late July 1701 in the style of the day: whatever works quickly. Today, buildings and houses representing a multitude of styles are found in metro Detroit. And some of the world's premier architects have designed the marvels.

Albert Kahn
(1869-1942):

If Henry Ford accelerated the modern age with mass production, Albert Kahn was the technocrat who enabled him. A German-born art student, Kahn's color-blindness led him from painting to architecture. As Ford's chosen designer, Kahn replaced the cramped workhouses of the 19th Century with well-lit, efficient factories that ideally suited Ford's vision of 20th-Century mass production.

Kahn was equally adept at creating business organizations; his architectural firm, still a powerhouse, turned out factories, hospitals and government buildings almost as fast as Model T's came off Ford's assembly lines. Amid the flow of more routine projects, his Fisher Building skyscraper in the New Center (1927-1929) remains a masterpiece.

Ironically, most of Kahn's early factories >>

his fountain. It was moved in 1925 from its original location near what is now the Banc One headquarters, and, as this is written, there are plans to move it again because of the Campus Martius development plans.

TRINITY EPISCOPAL CHURCH, Myrtle and Trumbull. (1892) Architect: Mason & Rice. Detroit has a rich store of church buildings from a century ago, a tribute to both the faith and the generosity of its citizens. Newspaper publisher James Scripps built this church in the then-unknown style of Gothic Revival or Neo-Gothic. It's one of the first and best examples in the nation of a church built on historical plans yet with clean and efficient lines.

DUMOUCHELLE BUILDING, 409 E. Jefferson. (circa 1902) Architect unknown. Detroit has demolished much of its early automotive history. Albert Kahn's historic Packard building is due to fall soon, and Paul's Car Wash on West Fort Street, the nation's first automated car wash, came down a few years ago for a parking lot. One piece of hidden history that survives is the DuMouchelle Building, now an auction house but originally the site of the nation's first independent automobile showroom. Remnants of this history can be seen in the overhead alley door, the large freight elevator, and the interior turntable that allowed cars to be driven in and lifted up to the second-floor showroom.

FORD BUILDING, 615 Griswold. (1909) Architect: Daniel Burnham. When structural steel and elevators first made skyscrapers possible, this is what one looked like. The clean, sharp lines express the inner steel frame, and the strong vertical lines emphasize height. This is one of Detroit's handful of buildings by Burnham, an immortal in architectural circles for his sweeping plan for Chicago's riverfront.

AFFLECK HOUSE, 1925 N. Woodward, Bloomfield Hills. (1942) Architect: Frank Lloyd Wright. Michigan features a surprisingly large number of Wright homes, many of them in the western part of the state. The Affleck House, now owned by Lawrence Technological University, presents the most approachable example in metro Detroit of Wright's trademarks: the jutting overhangs, the marriage with the landscape, the sense of a home rooted to its site as if by God.

JEFFERSONIAN APARTMENTS, 9000 E. Jefferson Ave. (1965) Architect: Giffels & Rossetti. Almost no building in Detroit so expresses the Corbusian ideal of efficient residential architecture. The clean lines, the elevation of the

The Renaissance Center, East Jefferson Avenue. (renovations, 1999-2000 and beyond) Architect: Skidmore, Owings & Merrill. Architect John Portman's original RenCen reflected the best and worst of '70s design: the soaring use of atria space and spiraling glass towers, and the brutish overkill of its size and its rude hulking stance on the riverfront. When General Motors bought the RenCen in 1996, it asked SOM to rationalize its labyrinthian byways. The results, especially the glowing elevated glass circulation ring and the soon-to-open winter garden, take a flawed but important landmark and give it a classy new persona.

main structure on slender first-floor columns, and the great expanses of glass look as modern today as when built in the '60s.

FEDERAL-MOGUL CORP., Northwestern and Lahser, Southfield. (1966) Architects: Giffels & Rossetti. As a type, the suburban office building may present one of the more dreary faces of modern suburbia. One exception is this design, which elevated the main body of the building above an all-glass lobby and enclosed it in a web of delicate pre-cast concrete tracery. Simple yet elegant, it demonstrates that suburban architecture doesn't have to be boring.

STROH RIVER PLACE, Jos. Campau and the river. (Mid-1980s) Architect: James Stuart Polshek and others. This is one of Detroit's few waterfront projects that respects the riverfront and allows the public to enjoy it. The buildings themselves, carved out of the former ParkeDavis Pharmaceutical Co. offices and labs, present a thoughtful example of historic preservation. But it's the delightful waterfront promenade, open to all, that shows what's possible if owners, architects and city planners have vision.

FOR FURTHER STUDY: "THE BUILDINGS OF DETROIT," W. HAWKINS FERRY, WAYNE STATE UNIVERSITY PRESS, 1968; "THE LEGACY OF ALBERT KAHN," THE DETROIT INSTITUTE OF ARTS, 1970; "SMITH, HINCHMAN AND GRYLLS," THOMAS J. HOLLEMAN AND JAMES P. GALLAGHER, WAYNE STATE UNIVERSITY PRESS, 1978; "BUILDINGS OF MICHIGAN," KATHRYN BISHOP ECKERT, OXFORD UNIVERSITY PRESS, 1993; "DETROIT ARCHITECTURE AIA GUIDE," REVISED EDITION, WAYNE STATE UNIVERSITY PRESS, 1980.

Free Press file photo

Our landmarks

OK, so the Thinker in front of the DIA isn't the only Thinker. And you can find the Westin Hotel in Atlanta and Los Angeles, too, but there are some landmarks that make Detroit Detroit:

THE BIG FIST: Depending on how you look at it, the 8,000-pound fist of bronze and painted steel at Woodward and Jefferson is either a stunning artistic statement, or the statuary equivalent of an ugly necktie from your grandma at Christmas. The fist and forearm, 24 feet long and suspended from a pyramid 24 feet high, was bestowed upon the city in 1986 by Sports Illustrated as a $350,000 tribute to boxer Joe Louis. Some see California artist Robert Graham's piece as a symbol of human potential. Others look at $350,000 that could have been used to cast a statue of Louis.

THE BIG TIRE: The Big Tire along I-94 in Allen Park began as a whitewalled Ferris wheel at the 1964-65 New York World's Fair. It held 24 four-passenger gondolas where the treads are today. Nearly 2 million people rode it. Built of steel, Fiberglass and flame-resistant polyester resin, the 80-foot-tall tire was set in place in 1966. It's been updated since with blackwalls, fancier white lettering, a modern hubcap and the slightly squatty look of a radial, accented by a huge protruding nail. In 1971, the tire broke loose, rolled across I-94, crushing a semi loaded with olive oil and two trucks hauling cucumbers and tomatoes, thus making the largest cuke and tomato salad in history. OK, so that really didn't happen. The tire weighs 12 tons and was built to handle hurricane-force winds. It's not going anywhere.

THE BIG STOVE: Stotown Records. The Stove City. Mitch Ryder & the Detroit Grills. Long before Detroit was the Motor City, it was the stove capital of the United States. The Garland Stove was built in 1893 and displayed at the 1893 World's Columbian Exposition in Chicago in honor of Detroit's stove industry. A bruising 25 feet tall, 30 feet long and 20 feet wide, the 15-ton oaken replica sat at Jefferson and East Grand Boulevard for years, then was moved to the State Fairgrounds. Rotting away in a warehouse at Historic Ft. Wayne, it was rescued in 1995, rebuilt over the next three years and returned to the fairgrounds.

ARCHITECTS
(Kahn, con't.)

The first building in Detroit was a church, thrown up in late July 1701 in the style of the day: whatever works quickly. Today, buildings and houses representing a multitude of styles are found in metro Detroit. And some of the world's premier architects have designed the marvels.

Albert Kahn
(1869-1942):

If Henry Ford accelerated the modern age with mass production, Albert Kahn was the technocrat who enabled him. A German-born art student, Kahn's color-blindness led him from painting to architecture. As Ford's chosen designer, Kahn replaced the cramped workhouses of the 19th Century with well-lit, efficient factories that ideally suited Ford's vision of 20th-Century mass production.

Kahn was equally adept at creating business organizations; his architectural firm, still a powerhouse, turned out factories, hospitals and government buildings almost as fast as Model T's came off Ford's assembly lines. Amid the flow of more routine projects, his Fisher Building skyscraper in the New Center (1927-1929) remains a masterpiece.

Ironically, most of Kahn's early factories
>>

ARCHITECTS
have long since been replaced by newer facilities, and today Detroiters know Kahn chiefly for his meticulous copies of English Cotswold manor homes that he built for Edsel and Eleanor Ford

RICHARD LEE/Detroit Free Press

Love it or hate it, the fist depicting Joe Louis' right knuckle sandwich is uniquely Detroit.

Free Press file photo

Before the giant tire was parked on I-94, it served as a Ferris wheel at the 1964 New York World's Fair.

ARCHITECTS
Louis Kamper
(1861-1953):

In a decade of creativity, Kamper created Washington Boulevard by designing monumental buildings for the Book brothers — J. Burgess, Herbert and Frank. Trained by the legendary Stanford White in New York, Kamper created the 13-story Book Building in 1917, followed by the Book-Cadillac Hotel in 1924, and the 36-story Book Tower in 1926. (Plans for an even greater 70-story Book Tower were shelved by the Depression.) Kamper also designed the stately Italianate mansion at Jefferson and Burns in Indian Village, as well as his own home at 2150 Iroquois, one of Indian Village's grandest houses. Somewhat stuck in the 19th Century of his youth, Kamper drew on Old World classicism for his designs. It's clear he didn't quite get what the skyscraper was all about. He failed to see that a skyscraper's power lies in its elemental lines and massing, not in the doodads drawn from antiquity with which he adorned his buildings. Hence the various Book properties look older than they need to and even slightly absurd. Compare, for example, the Book Tower to the still powerful Penobscot Building, designed at the same time by Smith, Hinchman & Grylls. Nonetheless, Kamper's influence on the look of downtown ranks second only to Albert Kahn's. >>

THE BIG POPE: Hamtramck couldn't wait to honor Polish Cardinal Karol Wojtyla after he became Pope John Paul II. Nearly half the city boasts Polish ancestry. But patience would have been a virtue. America's first public park honoring John Paul II was dedicated in 1982, with its centerpiece a 10-foot-tall, 6,000-pound bronze sculpture by Floridian Ferenc Varga atop an 18-foot pedestal. Alas, fund-raising for the $225,000 mini-park and statue at Belmont and Jos. Campau ran well behind construction. The first lawsuit by an irate contractor was filed in 1984, and various parties were still squabbling publicly into the late 1990s.

THE BIG WATER TOWER: How much water would a water tower hold if a water tower did hold water? Oh, about 1.5 million gallons. But the 165-foot-tall tower at the Detroit Zoo has been empty since 1983. Now the relic from the Roaring '20s is just an exotic billboard. The current mural, depicting various animals, the name of the zoo and the name of Detroit Mayor Dennis Archer, is made of 318 adhesive panels laid atop a coating of 1,000 gallons of white primer.

THE SEVEN SISTERS: The Seven Sisters were the most distinctive feature on the Detroit River for 75 years, a landmark for sailors and aviators alike. Built between 1914 and 1921, they stood 352 feet tall at the foot of Lycaste Street at the Connors Creek Power Plant. Their part of the plant had been idle for 13 years before Detroit Edison imploded them in August 1996, sending 9 million tons of bricks, steel and cement thundering to the ground. Despite their absence, no Great Lakes freighters have reported getting lost.

ROBERT BURNS STATUE: 18th-Century poet Robert Burns gave the world "Comin' Thro' the Rye" and "Auld Lang Syne." In 1921, commemorating his genius and his Scottish heritage, the Jean Amour Women's Auxiliary and the Burns Club placed a 9-foot-tall statue of Burns in Cass Park, at the corner of Second Avenue and Temple. The sponsors were able to obtain a casting of a statue of Burns already standing in Ayr, Scotland, and thus did not have to resort to their second choice, an enormous bronze haggis.

LOS GALANES MURAL: One of the city's most vibrant artworks commemorates teamwork, diversity and a pretty darned good buffet. Arturo Cruz was 18 in 1996 when he designed the 50-foot-wide mural on the back wall of the Los Galanes Mexican restaurant, facing West Vernor at 23rd Street. More than 70 people helped paint the piece, which shows people from a smorgasbord of ethnicities joining hands across the Ambassador Bridge. Cruz was a refugee from Nicaragua passing through Detroit en route to Canada.

KOSCIUSZKO STATUE: First, Poland gave America Gen. Thaddeus Kosciuszko, who helped save our *dupas* during the Revolutionary War. Then, in 1976, the citizens of Krakow, Poland, gave us the spirited statue of the general that stands 12 feet tall at Michigan Avenue and Third. A familiar sight to those visiting the corner of Michigan and Trumbull, Kosciuszko extends his feathered hat high in the air, waving good-bye to the Detroit Tigers.

SCOTT FOUNTAIN: Landowner James Scott left $500,000 to the City of Detroit to build a lavish fountain on Belle Isle featuring a life-sized statue of himself. This was in 1910, when $500,000 would buy more than a utility infielder. But it would be awhile until the fountain spit water. Scott was so reviled that many prominent citizens campaigned against taking the money. A boor, a bore and a bully, Scott was known for telling long, loud and profane tales of his days as a roving gambler. The ever-so-distinguished J.L. Hudson growled that the fountain "would be a monument to nastiness and filthy stories. Mr. Scott never did anything for Detroit in his lifetime." The debate raged for years before the fountain was finally dedicated on May 30, 1925.

THE BARRY SANDERS AD (RIP): That faintly familiar figure hovering 15 stories above Detroit on the Cadillac Tower was Barry Sanders. Remember him? Little guy from Oklahoma State? Used to play for the Lions? Nike — the shoe company, not the goddess — painted him in Cadillac Square in 1994. The image was 170 feet high and 100 feet wide and was based on a photo from the 1991-92 season, which explains the football-shaped patch on his jersey bearing the initials JRT: It was a memorial to Detroit Lions general manager John Russell (Russ) Thomas, who died in 1991. The ad was removed in January 2000, after Sanders' abrupt retirement made him so unpopular in Detroit that Nike painted over his image.

SOLDIERS AND SAILORS MONUMENT: That helmeted, sword-wielding figure overlooking the warriors on the Michigan Soldiers and Sailors Monument is a woman. (Men weren't willing to give women the vote in those days, but a little symbolism was fine, as long as it didn't go to their heads.) Commissioned in 1867, the soaring monument at Campus Martius and Woodward was one of the country's first Civil War memorials. Sculptor Randolph Rogers,

SPIRIT OF DETROIT
The Spirit of Detroit, also known as the Big Green Guy, is one of many metro Detroit artworks by the late Michigander Marshall Fredericks. Seated gracefully in front of the Coleman A. Young Municipal Center, the 16-foot-tall figure holds a sphere in his left hand (representing God) and a bunch of little people in his right (representing a bunch of little people). The Spirit was dedicated in 1958 and clothed in 1997, when an east-side sporting goods company outfitted him in a size 360 Detroit Red Wings sweater during the Stanley Cup playoffs.

who grew up in Ann Arbor, grouped his many figures symmetrically on four levels. The relief portraits are Farragut, Grant, Lincoln and Sherman. The 7-foot-tall fighting men stand for Artillery, Cavalry, Infantry and Navy. The four seated women stand for Emancipation, History, Union and Victory. The four eagles stand for eagles.

PASSO DI DANZA: Passo di Danza, or Dance Step, joined the Spirit of Detroit near Woodward and Jefferson in 1963. The 11-foot-tall dancing nude, modeled after the wife of sculptor Giacomo Manzu, won the heart of the Spirit shortly after her arrival. In a particularly stylish prank, fraternity brothers from what is now the University of Detroit Mercy painted big green footprints leading across Woodward from the Spirit to his bronzed babe.

ORVILLE HUBBARD: Dearborn's statue of its longtime mayor was featured in the 1999 book, "Lies Across America: What Our Historic Sites Get Wrong" (The New Press), a compendium of tributes to supposedly great people who, in reality, weren't. Author James Loewen noted that Hubbard's plaque makes no mention of his ultra-segregationist views.

SILVERBOLT THE STALLION: Silverbolt is composed of chrome car bumpers. It has stood in front of the Detroit Public School Children's Museum at 67 E. Kirby since 1972.

NEWSBOY AND HIS DOG: A. T. Dunbar sculpted the drinking fountain of these bronze, life-sized figures in 1897 to honor the city's newsboys. It's on Central Avenue on Belle Isle.

MAJ. GEN. ALPHEUS STARKEY WILLIAMS: A classic equestrian statue. An oversized General Williams is depicted astride his horse on Central Avenue at Inselruhe on Belle Isle.

Williams lived from 1810 to 1878. The sculpture, by Henry Merwin Shrady of New York, was completed in 1912. Williams was a soldier, judge, editor, postmaster, diplomat and member of Congress. "An untiring servant of the People, an honor to the City of Detroit," reads words chiseled in the base. The horse — at least the horse Williams rode and named — was Plug Ugly.

KENNETH TOWNSEND: Townsend stamped his mark on Detroit's landscape as indelibly as Augustus Woodward or Albert Kahn. For 33 years, he ran the Townsend Sign Co., which built instant landmarks along city streets and freeways. Townsend imported the giant tire from the New York's World Fair (see page 603) and he erected the original Goodyear car production-count sign, the General Tire logo and, his favorite, the old AC spark plug at 8 Mile and Woodward. That was an ad for the AC Spark Plug Division of General Motors Corp. The 60-foot display showed a white plastic spark plug, illuminated from inside, ringed by orange, yellow and blue flames. It was supported by 47 tons of steel, 40 feet off the ground.

Bastion Detroit

Long before that standoffish berm went up around the RenCen, soldiers built forts to protect themselves and settlers. Here's a look at our military installations, from stockades to Selfridge Air National Guard Base. Remember: No enemy has attacked since the Brits took the city in 1812.

FT. PONTCHARTRAIN: Almost immediately after Cadillac landed on July 24, 1701, his men cleared an area and began erecting a square fort with walls of oak logs about 10 feet high, sharp points honed on their ends, placed

Minoru Yamasaki
(1912-1986):
Although his buildings are not numerous, they lend an air of fantasy to Detroit's workaday urban landscape. A native of Seattle, Yamasaki was a second-generation Japanese-American who struggled in his youth against poverty and racism. As a young architect, he studied in a period of minimalist modernism, but his tours of Japan and Europe persuaded him to soften and humanize the glass-box style. He tried to create an atmosphere of serenity in his buildings, using skylights, reflecting pools, pearl-white exteriors and triangular motifs repeated throughout the structure. His buildings in Detroit — the McGregor Conference Center on the Wayne State University campus and the ANR office tower at Woodward and Jefferson — are unmistakably modernist. But their shimmering white facades, clad in geometric patterns that evoke an otherworldly symmetry, are like nothing else in Detroit. >>

Eliel Saarinen
(1873-1950) and
Eero Saarinen
(1910-1961):
  Finnish-born Eliel Saarinen, above, arrived in Detroit in the 1920s and spent the next quarter-century creating the campus of the Cranbrook Educational Community. Inspired by the Arts and Crafts movement, Saarinen labored under a self-imposed discipline to make every building, every light fixture and every doorknob contribute to a campus marked by serenity and beauty. His son, Eero, leaped ahead to mainstream modernism by creating the General Motors Tech Center in Warren, a monument to steel-and-glass efficiency heightened by the use of glazed ceramic brick on the exterior and its suspended staircases. The younger Saarinen went on to create the St. Louis Arch, Dulles Airport in suburban Washington, D.C., and the TWA terminal at Kennedy Airport in New York. >>

After 1777, there were two fortresses in Detroit: Ft. Lernoult, top, and the original fortress, bottom. Both are shown superimposed on a map of today's downtown streets.

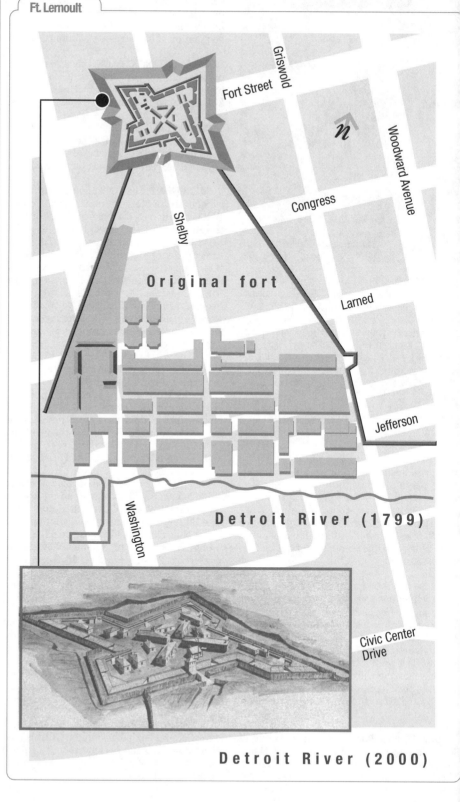

Ft. Lernoult

Griswold

Fort Street

Woodward Avenue

Congress

Shelby

Original fort

Larned

Jefferson

Washington

Detroit River (1799)

Civic Center Drive

Detroit River (2000)

upright in a 3-foot-deep trench. There were fortified bastions at the corners. It took up an area as big as a quarter of a city block just south of today's Jefferson and Griswold. Cadillac named the stockade for Count Pontchartrain, the minister in charge of New France. The fort was rebuilt and modified in 1718 with oak logs 15 feet high and further expanded in 1749 and in the 1750s.

When the British took control of Detroit on Nov. 29, 1760, they increased the number of buildings to 80, most of them one-story log structures. The fort's perimeter was now four blocks square. Blockhouses were built over gates on the east and west side. Each wooden gate had a passage for one person.

By 1775, the fort contained an Indian Council House, about 20 stores and a complex of military buildings and parade grounds known as the Citadel. The fort's dimensions: about 300 feet long and 1,500 feet wide. It had four gates on each side and blockhouses on the east, west and north sides. Two batteries of six guns faced the river. The fort included the land between present-day Griswold and Cass streets, Larned and the river. The streets were at least 10 feet wide.

At the foot of Woodward was a dock for five British warships: two armed schooners and three sloops.

FT. LERNOULT: In 1777, Capt. Richard Lernoult feared the fort was too weak to withstand an assault and grew concerned about American cannons on high ground to the north. So he built a new fort.

It was named Ft. Lernoult and was centered on present-day Fort Street (hence the name), between Washington Boulevard and Griswold. Capt. Henry Bird designed the structure, which was completed in April 1779. Historian Phil Mason describes the fort's earthen ramparts as 11 feet high, 26 feet thick at the base and 12 feet wide at the top of the parapet. On the exterior wall of each earthen rampart was a horizontal row of sharpened pickets called a fraise. There was a ramp for gunners along the inside of the parapet called a banquette. Outside the ramparts was a ditch 12 feet wide and 4 to 5 feet deep in which was placed a row of cedar pickets 12 feet high. Beyond this line of defense was a low rampart of earth called a glacis. And projecting from the glacis was a row of trees with their sharpened branches facing outward. That was called an abatis.

The fort's entrance faced south, toward the village. A drawbridge passed over the ditch. On each side of the entrance was a cannon. Each bastion held four cannons and each wall had another cannon.

A stone-walled powder magazine was several hundred feet south and connected to the fort by a tunnel. The old stockade surrounding the village was connected to the new fort. American troops took command of the fort in 1796.

When fire consumed the village in 1805, the separate Ft. Lernoult was spared.

FT. SHELBY: During the War of 1812, the British occupied Detroit from Aug. 16, 1812, to Sept., 28, 1813, when they evacuated the fort. Detroiters soon renamed it Ft. Shelby after Kentucky Gov. Isaac Shelby, who led reinforcements to Detroit during the War of 1812.

By 1826, Detroit's remaining troops were transferred to Green Bay, leaving the city without military protection for the first time in its 125-year history.

Ft. Shelby was leveled in 1827, but remnants have surfaced up until 1962 during excavation for new buildings.

FT. CROGHAN: In 1806, U.S. troops erected a small fort north of today's downtown. It was used to harass American Indians. The fort was a circular earthen embankment about 40 feet in diameter and surrounded by a ditch. It was later used by children as a play fort and nicknamed Ft. Nonsense.

DETROIT BARRACKS: From about 1830 to 1855, the U.S. Army occupied barracks near the intersection of Gratiot and Russell, near today's Eastern Market. Among the officers in charge: Lt. Ulysses S. Grant.

THE ARSENAL: In 1833, the federal government opened an arsenal of several buildings in what was then called Dearbornville. The arsenal was used as a training camp for Civil War soldiers and a storage facility for muskets, cannons and ammunition. It started the first big development boom in western Wayne County. After the arsenal closed in 1875, the commandant's house was preserved as a cour-

An artist's rendering of Ft. Pontchartrain. If accurate, those two beached canoes are about where the Veterans Memorial Building is today.

BUILDINGS

ARCHITECTS
Smith, Hinchman & Grylls:

Not all good architecture comes from the hand of a lone genius. Smith, Hinchman & Grylls, now known as SHG and tracing its history to the mid-19th Century, has created dozens of important designs, even as it grew to be Michigan's largest architectural firm. With a score or more talented designers sharing the credit, the firm's designs include the Penobscot, Guardian and Buhl towers of the 1920s, Hart Plaza and Joe Louis Arena in the late '70s, and the Veterans Administration Hospital of the '90s. The firm's success shows it is possible to renew a company's creative spirit decade after decade, even as the architectural world undergoes substantial changes.

William Kessler
(born 1924):

Trained at Harvard in the heyday of modernism, Kessler has graced Detroit and its suburbs with many sleek glass-and-steel creations. His buildings include the silvery Detroit Receiving Hospital, the playful Detroit Science Center, and the thought-provoking Center for Creative Studies. Not a routine glass-box architect, Kessler has given modernism a clean, brisk, and sun-dappled style, emphasizing atria and other public spaces within his buildings.

Free Press file photo

Planes with the 3d Attack Group, U.S. Army Air Corps, soar over the administration building during an air show at Selfridge Field in 1935.

thouse, school, church, library, police station and fire department until 1949, when the Dearborn Historical Commission turned it into a museum, which is still open. It's at Michigan and Monroe.

FT. WAYNE: About 1,250 years ago, American Indians built a burial mound of earth now located inside Ft. Wayne, the structure the federal government built for $150,000 from 1843 to 1849 to protect Detroit from Canadian attack.

It's worked.

Located at West Jefferson and Livernois, the 82-acre fort was named after Gen. Anthony Wayne, the Revolutionary War hero.

During the Civil War, Ft. Wayne served as a mustering post for Michigan's volunteer regiments. During World War I, Ft. Wayne housed troops, including construction battalions and an aero-squadron.

During World War II, the fort became the Motor Supply Depot, serving as the parts warehouse for the armed forces. The fort also was a temporary internment center for Italian prisoners of war. More buildings went up on the 83-acre site.

In the 1950s and 1960s, Ft. Wayne was one of the largest induction centers in the Midwest during the Korean and Vietnam wars.

After the 1967 riot in Detroit, many families whose homes were burned lived in Ft. Wayne. Some lived there until 1971.

The fort includes a large parade ground that fronts on the river, several streets of handsome brick dwelling for officers and senior enlisted men and their families and a restored frame house once occupied by the post commander.

The barracks, a four-story building that's the focal point of the fort, has walls nearly 2 feet thick.

But for generations of Detroiters who've toured the place, the real attraction is walking through the tunnels and fortifications and peering through gunslits, imagining irate Canadians charging over a nearby hill.

The oldest part of the fort became a museum in 1950. During the 1970s and 1980s, the fort hosted Civil War and World War I reenactments and other summertime events. When state funding for Detroit's historical museums was cut in 1991, the fort closed to the public.

One of the remodeled officer's homes has become the national museum of the Tuskegee Airmen.

SOURCES: DETROIT HISTORICAL MUSEUM; FARMER'S "HISTORY OF DETROIT AND MICHIGAN"; "DETROIT, FORT LERNOULT AND THE AMERICAN REVOLUTION," BY PHILIP MASON; FREE PRESS.

Macomb County's Fortress

SELFRIDGE: It spreads from the shores of Lake St. Clair for 3,600 acres — nearly four times the size of Belle Isle. Selfridge Air National Guard Base began as Selfridge Field in 1917, just after the United States entered World War I. It was named for Army Lt. Thomas E. Selfridge, considered the military's first pilot, who also became the military's first air crash casualty. That flight on Sept. 17, 1908, was piloted by Orville Wright with Selfridge his passenger, demonstrating a new aircraft for army brass outside Washington, D.C. Wright was hospitalized for several months.

The original 640 acres of land was bought for $190,000 from Detroit financier Henry Joy. Famous fliers, including Eddie Rickenbacker, Charles Lindbergh, Jimmy Doolittle, Billy Mitchell and Curtis LeMay served at Selfridge in Harrison Township.

The army expanded the base to its present size in 1942 as thousands of air corp troops trained for World War II duty.

The 332nd fighter squadron, also known as the Tuskegee Airmen, trained at the base. The all-black unit was commanded by Benjamin Davis, the first black general in the Air Force.

But the training, like the times, was unequal. On May 18, 1944, black aviators protested segregated quarters and officers' clubs. The general in charge of the training

BUILDINGS

command ordered the black officers to the base auditorium where he announced: "Gentlemen, this is my airfield. As long as I'm in command, there will be no socializing between white and colored officers."

Days later, the black aviators were transferred under guard to a South Carolina air base.

In 1947, Selfridge became an air force base; in 1971, an Air National Guard Base. It hosts an annual air show and houses hundreds of military families. Active duty military at the base number about 1,000. The National Guard and Air Force Reserve members who serve there total about 5,400 troops.

Oakland County's Bastion

FROM SWORDS TO PLOWSHARES: When state Supreme Court Judge Joseph Tarr Copeland retired in 1858, he built a 10-room mansion on Orchard Lake that locals soon dubbed the Castle because it looked it. In 1872, the manse was converted into a hotel — short-lived, however, when the economy took a dive in 1873.

In 1874, Detroit High School teacher Capt. Joseph Rogers bivouacked his drill students for two weeks of summer camp at Orchard Lake. Rogers imagined the castle would make a dandy military academy. In 1877, with money borrowed from Gov. John Bagley and prominent Detroiters, Rogers opened the Michigan Military Academy at Orchard Lake. The academy soon gained an outstanding reputation as a finishing school for West Point hopefuls — called at times the West Point of the West.

A sentinel guards the West Jefferson entrance to Ft. Wayne in April 1939.

Free Press file photo

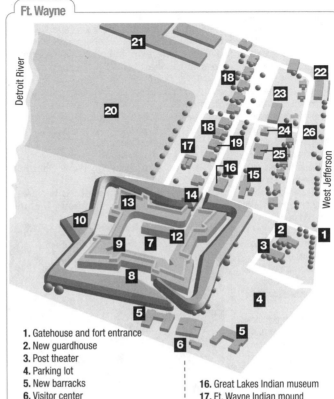

Ft. Wayne

Detroit River

West Jefferson

1. Gatehouse and fort entrance
2. New guardhouse
3. Post theater
4. Parking lot
5. New barracks
6. Visitor center
7. Old Ft.Wayne
8. Sally Port (entrance to fort)
9. Postern (exit from fort)
10. Demilune
11. Army Corps of Engineers Boat Yard
12. Old barracks
13. Powder magazine
14. West wall entrance
15. Post hospital
16. Great Lakes Indian museum
17. Ft. Wayne Indian mound
18. Officers' row
19. Commanding officer's house
20. Parade ground
21. Warehouse
22. Stables
23. Post Quartermasters
24. Old guardhouse
25. Post headquarters
26. NCO row

SOME TOUCHSTONES

Elmwood Cemetery: The graveyard opened in 1846 on Detroit's east side and retains some of the topography from 300 years ago, too. There is the same gently rolling land and the same jumble of hillock and stream cutting a jagged path through the land.

Sheds: Detroit's older neighborhoods have frame houses with what appear to be afterthought sheds on the back. Those houses date to the late 1800s and those sheds were in many cases kitchens — set off of the house because wood-burning stoves created a fire hazard.

No parking: You can date some Detroit and suburban neighborhoods to pre-1910. The clue: no driveways.

Warming up: Houses with chimneys sprouting from the center of the roof most likely are 100-plus years old. The heat then was radiated, and a furnace in the center helped disperse it more economically.

Grand Circus: Visit the downtown park and you'll be standing on the oldest thing in Detroit. The street design promoted by Judge Augustus Woodward after the fire of 1805 can best be understood at the park. Grand Circus was to be a circle — the hub of a wheel from which spokes began a ¾-mile run to another hub. These spokes still exist: Broadway and Washington Boulevard. But Woodward's plan of linked equilateral triangles died before 1820. Detroiters called the idea dumb.

On June 19, 1879, Civil War hero Gen. William Tecumseh Sherman gave the commencement address. As he ended his lengthy remarks, Sherman looked at his eager audience and spoke off-the-cuff:

"Boys, I've been where you are now and I know just how you feel. It's entirely natural . . . Suppress it!

"I've seen cities and homes in ashes. I've seen thousands of men lying on the ground, their dead faces looking up to the skies.

"I tell you, war is hell!"

The quote, of course, became Sherman's epitaph.

In 1906, the Academy closed because of declining enrollment. Students included Edgar Rice Burroughs, who wrote the Tarzan novels, and John C. Lodge, who became Detroit's mayor.

The grounds and buildings were bought by that year by Polish Catholic priests who ran Detroit's St. Cyril and Methodius Seminary.

SOURCES: DETROIT HISTORICAL MUSEUM; FARMER'S "HISTORY OF DETROIT AND MICHIGAN"; "DETROIT, FORT LERNOULT, AND THE AMERICAN REVOLUTION," BY PHILIP MASON; FREE PRESS.

Below: Grand Circus Park in February 1964. The building in the upper left is gone; a Comerica Park entrance is now there.

Free Press file photo

The ways we've lived

Cadillac and his men saw the heavily timbered islands we know today as Belle Isle, Fighting Island and Grosse Ile. The narrowest part of the strait, where he chose to build his fort in 1701, was framed by a 40-foot-tall bluff on both sides of the river. Marshy land stretched off to the east, where the Renaissance Center now rises. Beyond the bluff, virgin forest grew to the Straits of Mackinac.

Much has changed in 300 years.

But there are places to go and sites to see to get a feel for what life must have been like 100, 200, even 300 years ago.

Jobs and economic cycles play a big role in the kinds of houses we build.

The region continues to have one of the highest single-family home ownership levels in the country.

Here are five boom periods that spurred major residential construction in southeastern Michigan:

LATE 1800s: Detroit had a population pushing 300,000 in 1900, but most of the homes were torn down during the auto boom.

Victorian homes were the hallmark of that era and featured turrets on elaborate rooflines, leaded glass windows and ornate details.

A few of the mansions still exist, such as the house that's now the Whitney restaurant at Woodward and Canfield. It was built in 1894 by lumber baron David Whitney Jr.

Other Victorian homes may be seen on Detroit's near west side as well as on Canfield Street west of Second. Older communities such as Mt. Clemens, Wyandotte, Ypsilanti, Armada, Richmond and Pontiac also have a few of the Victorian homes from that early industrial era.

Small Victorian workers' cottages still dot old neighborhoods such as Detroit's Corktown.

1910-1930: As auto plants opened, workers began to earn enough money for new houses, often built near their employers. These working people wanted the 1½-story bungalows with wide, low porches.

Michigan has more of these Craftsman-style houses than any other state except California, where the style began. The Craftsman style was promoted as home of the "intelligent working man." In 1920, the average new home in Detroit cost about $5,600.

New construction widened the residential band to about 5 miles from downtown. Craftsman-style homes also went up in communities

Free Press file photo
Lumber baron David Whitney's manse on Woodward is now a restaurant.

on the interurban trolley line to River Rouge, Lincoln Park, Melvindale and Wyandotte, as well as to Ferndale, Royal Oak, Pleasant Ridge and Birmingham. In northwest Highland Park, a neighborhood of Craftsman-style homes is a National Historic District.

Also in this period, many two-family flats, often of wood-frame construction, were built. The owner lived downstairs and rented the upstairs to tenants. Many of these flats survive on Detroit's east and west sides as well as in Hamtramck. Brick flats were built in some areas, such as along 12th Street, now Rosa Parks Boulevard.

The Depression stalled housing construction until after World War II.

1945-1956: The end of the war brought young people eager to work and start families. That released a huge demand for new homes and they were built at a rate never matched again in the metro area.

New houses filled remaining land in the city and went up in suburbs such as Oak Park, East Detroit, Roseville and Livonia.

In 1950, more than 33,000 houses — typically, tidy brick bungalows — were built in Wayne, Oakland and Macomb counties. The typical new house had two bedrooms, one bath and an unfinished attic and measured 800 to 1,000 square feet. Building permits in the City of Detroit showed an average cost of $9,750 per home.

As the brick ranch became popular, the average size grew, like the number of children being born as the postwar baby boom continued. By 1956, a typical new house was 1,300 square feet with three bedrooms and a bath and a half. Forced air heat allowed for more

Manoogian Mansion:
The Detroit mayor's official residence at 9240 Dwight on the east side was built in 1928 for $300,000, but the owner lost the home during the Depression. It stood vacant until auctioned off in 1939 to entrepreneur Alex Manoogian for $25,000. By 1965, with his family grown, Manoogian gave the mansion to the City of Detroit. It was the Armenian immigrant's way of thanking his adopted hometown. The home is said to have 4,004 square feet, but looks bigger. The style has been described as both Italian and Spanish. It has a terra-cotta tile roof. The physical layout is dominated by walls of windows — bowed windows, arched windows, leaded windows — that let light stream in and open onto a spectacular view of the grounds and the Detroit River. The downstairs has three sunrooms facing south and the river. There are 15 rooms in all, including a large living room, library, kitchen and two dining rooms — a formal room and a more casual one that looks toward the river. It has four bedrooms, plus two small bedrooms for servants. There are three full baths, a servants' bath and two half-baths.

Free Press file photo

compact furnaces and more basement space for recreation rooms. Living rooms had picture windows.

Exhaust fans and garbage disposals — options in kitchens in 1950 — became standard as the decade progressed. The average cost of a new home in the City of Detroit in 1956 was about $13,000. Land costs alone in the Detroit area doubled from 1946 to 1956.

During this housing boom, brick homes by the thousands went up in Pontiac, Royal Oak, Birmingham, Lincoln Park, Clawson, Madison Heights, Allen Park and Taylor. Then the home construction stalled, although it was revived somewhat during the 1960s.

1970s-1980s: As the first baby boomers reached their mid-20s, they started buying new homes, spurring construction booms in 1971-73 and 1976-79. In the years in between, the oil crisis hit, followed by a recession and rising interest rates that depressed the new-home market.

But before and after that, there were bursts of construction in Detroit suburbs such as Troy, northern Southfield, northern Farmington and Sterling Heights. Many homes were two-story colonials, about 1,650 square feet, with brick-and-aluminum exteriors and attached garages.

A recession in the late 1970s and rising inflation in the early 1980s stalled the housing market. Aging northern industrial areas like southeast Michigan were being denigrated as the Rust Belt, places past their prime with little to offer for the future. Many people moved away, in search of jobs and better times. By 1982, the number of houses built in the seven counties of southeast Michigan had fallen to 1,742.

As the 1980s continued, new-home starts inched up to 12,000 for the seven-county area. Square footage sizes reached 2,000 in 1987 and began to increase.

1990s TO THE PRESENT: Times have been good as unemployment, inflation and interest rates stay low. Prices of houses in metropolitan Detroit, long a bargain compared with many other cities, have climbed at one of the fastest paces in the nation.

Jobs and good income produced a demand for bigger and better homes, but not for first-time home buyers. People looking for new homes now are move-up buyers, in the market for their second or third house.

The kind of house they want is a far cry from the typical house built in the Detroit area in the late 1940s or the 1970s. Today's new-home buyers want size and amenities like two-story entries, gourmet kitchens and expansive marble baths. There were 18,411 new homes built in the seven-county region in 1999.

They are going up about 30 or more miles from downtown Detroit in places such as Macomb Township, western Canton, Independence Township and Chesterfield Township, as well as in Washtenaw and Livingston counties.

It is no longer unusual to see ads for new homes with 3,000 square feet and prices of $400,000 or more. In early 2000, 73 homes valued at $1 million or more were on the market in Oakland County.

The big houses

EDSEL AND ELEANOR FORD HOUSE: The impressive stone structure at 1100 Lake Shore Drive in Grosse Pointe Shores is not the Edsel & Eleanor Ford mansion.

It's the gatehouse.

The 60-room home sits on a lovely 90-acre estate beyond the stone wall. Now a conference center and open for tours, the house on Gaukler Point on Lake St. Clair is among the last of Grosse Pointe's great mansions. Designed by Albert Kahn, it was the Fords' dream house. But in 1943, only 13 years after the $3-million house was built, Edsel died at the age of 49. Eleanor Ford, who died at age 80 in 1976, established a $15-million endowment to preserve the home, which is rambling and reminiscent (in facade, not size) of the Cotswold cottages of England. The public tour explores most of the first floor, including the gallery where Henry Ford I and his wife, Clara, celebrated their 50th wedding anniversary. Much of the original furniture survives. Visitors can see the main stairway of weathered oak, brought over from Lyveden Manor in Northants, England.

Kahn and the Fords traveled together to England, taking photographs and collecting parts of old British estates. Another treat is the children's playhouse. Tour information: 313-884-4222 anytime. While most of the mansions are long gone, the length of Lake Shore remains an interesting architectural showcase.

MEADOW BROOK HALL: The 100-room Meadow Brook Hall on the Oakland University campus in Rochester was the home of Matilda Dodge Wilson, the auto baroness who built the $4-million estate. She was the multimillionaire widow of auto magnate John Dodge,

who gave Michigan State University the 1,600-acre estate and a building fund — worth a total of $10 million — to begin the Oakland University campus in 1957. The mansion is now a museum and conference center. What visitors see on the public tour is magnificent. Heroic 10-foot paintings of Matilda and her second husband, Alfred Wilson, grace the dining room, with its elaborately carved ceiling. In Alfred's paneled study, a secret door opens to a spiral staircase that leads down to a basement games room and up to the third and fourth floors. All work, including the magnificent wood carvings in many of the rooms, was done by American craftsmen with American materials.

The mansion, with 39 chimneys and tile roof, was finished in 1929. Tour information: 248-370-3140, 9 a.m. to 5 p.m. weekdays.

FISHER MANSION: It was 1927 and Lawrence P. Fisher, Cadillac general manager and one of the seven founding brothers of the Fisher Body Co., wanted a dandy place to live.

Fisher, an impeccably groomed but beefy bachelor, built a $2.5-million, cream-colored stucco mansion with a red tile roof at 383 Lenox in Detroit. The Fisher Mansion was Detroit's answer to William Randolph Hearst's San Simeon in California. What Fisher got was a 50-room mansion in a Hollywoodish blend of Italian, Moorish and Spanish styles, set on the Grayhaven Canal at the mouth of the Detroit River. It is glitzy bordering on garish. Pounds of pure gold and silver leaf adorn the ceilings and tile floors. An orange Neptune (later discovered to have been made from slightly radioactive material) grins from a fountain in the entryway, and naked Cupids frolic on carved wooden doors in the music room.

The estate is now the Detroit home for the Hare Krishna movement. The mansion houses the Bhaktivedanta Cultural Center of the International Society for Krishna Consciousness and a vegetarian restaurant called Govinda's. The estate was bought in 1975 for $295,000 by Krishna devotees Alfred Brush Ford — great-grandson of Henry Ford, a competitor of Fisher and GM — and Elisabeth Reuther Dickmeyer, daughter of the late UAW President Walter Reuther. Tour information: 313-331-6740 anytime.

HENRY FORD'S FAIR LANE: The $2.5-million Fair Lane mansion at 4901 Evergreen on the University of Michigan-Dearborn campus was Henry Ford's 15th and final residence. Built in 1914, the home was donated to U-M by the

Ford Motor Co. in 1957, along with 210 acres and more than $6 million. U-M built its Dearborn campus there. Fair Lane is now used by the university as a museum and conference center. A restaurant sits atop the old indoor swimming pool. The house remains a curiosity, with its adjacent four-story powerhouse that Ford designed himself and used as a combination laboratory, hobby shop and dance hall, and the 1,300-acre estate that is lush with exquisite landscaping. The side of the mansion facing the Rouge River looks like a brooding feudal manor. The other side is more contemporary, but hardly stylish. Ford wanted Frank Lloyd Wright to design the estate, but when the architect ran off to Europe with the wife of a client, Ford settled on Marion Mahoney Griffin, one of Wright's students.

Ford died in the house on April 7, 1947. Ironically, the powerhouse engines, which were driven by a 14-foot waterfall created by damming the Rouge, failed due to a massive flood. Ford died with wife Clara and maid Rosa Buhler at his side. Light came from two candles and a flashlight. Tour information: 313-593-5590, 9 a.m. to 5 p.m. weekdays.

Top: The sprawling, 100-room Meadow Brook Hall in 1976.

Left: A corridor at Meadow Brook. The mansion was completed in 1929 for $4 million.

HOUSING STARTS
Number of single-family homes built in southeastern Michigan

2000	17,253
1999	18,641
1998	18,831
1997	17,634
1990	10,710

BUILDINGS

Detroit Almanac

"There are too many armed citizens in Detroit now."

— *Police Commissioner* **John Gillespie**, *January 1914*

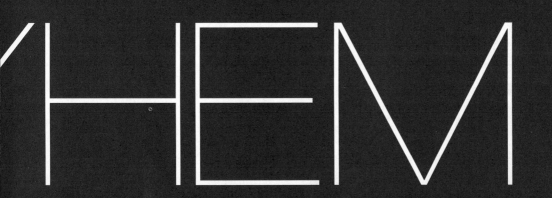

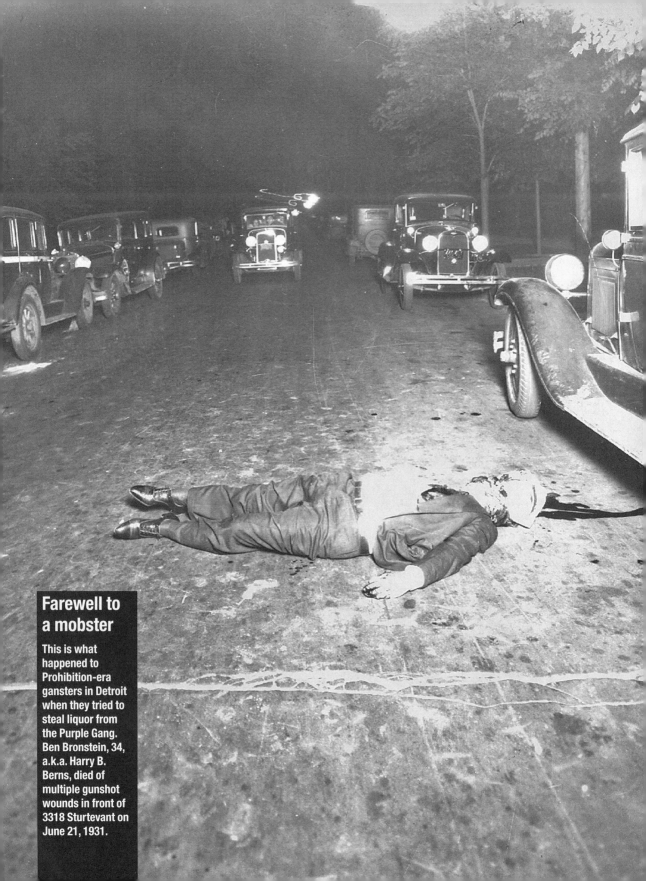

Farewell to a mobster

This is what happened to Prohibition-era gansters in Detroit when they tried to steal liquor from the Purple Gang. Ben Bronstein, 34, a.k.a. Harry B. Berns, died of multiple gunshot wounds in front of 3318 Sturtevant on June 21, 1931.

Free Press file photo

'Slain man in lingerie eaten by dog' – *1982 Free Press headline*

CRIME IN DETROIT

Like most big cities, Detroit has battled a crime problem for nearly 40 years, though in 1999 it enjoyed an overall crime drop. It still led the nation in auto thefts for the third straight year and inched up the rankings in homicides, according a Free Press analysis of FBI crime statistics.

The overall drop in Detroit is part of a trend in Michigan and the nation. Serious crimes have declined nationwide for eight consecutive years, dropping 7 percent in 1999, according to the FBI numbers.

Six of Michigan's eight largest cities recorded decreases in crime in 1999 — Ann Arbor, Detroit, Flint, Lansing, Livonia and Sterling Heights. No comparisons could be made for Warren's crime rates because the FBI has not had access to the city's statistics for the last three years. Grand Rapids sent incomplete data to the FBI and was left out of the comparison.

Detroit, which saw a nearly 12-percent reduction in the overall crime rate, as measured per resident, now ranks No. 13, behind such cities as Kansas City, Mo.; Chattanooga, Tenn.; Macon, Ga., and Jackson, Miss. Detroit went from fifth to third nationally in homicides, though. During much of the 1990s, Detroit had one of the highest crime rates in the country; in the 1970s it became known as the Murder City for its nation-leading homicide rate.

"Dude, Where's my car?"

Detroit led the nation in auto thefts during the late 1990s; nearly 26,770 cars were stolen in 1999 alone. By 2000, Phoenix and Miami had overtaken Detroit in the hot-car department. The cars most often stolen in Michigan:
1) 1995 Plymouth Neon
2) 1995 Dodge Neon
3) 1989 Chevrolet Caprice
4) 1998 Dodge Neon Highline
5) 1993 Dodge Shadow
6) 1988 Chevrolet Caprice
7) 1990 Chevrolet Caprice
8) 1997 Ford Escort
9) 1993 Plymouth Sundance
10) 1994 Ford Thunderbird LX

SOURCE: CCC INFORMATION SERVICES.

MAYHEM

GABRIEL B. TAIT/Detroit Free Press

Detroit Police Officer Charles Wilson inspects a stolen Camaro in 2000.

Detroiters considered stolen cars a serious problem in 1912. Thieves helped themselves to 546 cars that year. That's fewer than two a day, but there weren't as many cars in existence. By 1925, driving away cars made up 53 percent of all felonies in 1925.

DETROIT HOMICIDES 1920-2000

International attention has focused on Northern Ireland for more than 30 years because an estimated 3,600 people have been killed in sectarian fighting. In Detroit, more than 3,600 people were slain during the 1990s alone, which was a relatively quiet time in the homicide department compared with earlier decades. The following is a year-by-year accounting of homicides in Detroit for 80 years of the 20th Century.

Year	Homicides
2000	396
1999	415
1998	430
1997	469
1996	407
1995	461
1994	554
1993	559
1992	593
1991	587
1990	557
1989	586
1988	586
1987	686
1986	648
1985	636
1984	514
1983	581
1982	515
1981	502
1980	549
1979	451
1978	498
1977	478
1976	662
1975	607
1974	714
1973	672
1972	601
1971	577
1970	495
1969	439

CONTINUED >>

* Preliminary total.

Detroit Police Department

A Detroit police bicycle squad from 1901.

Detroit Police

Employees	4,011
Vehicles	1,387
Stations	51

(includes 38 mini-stations)

Traffic tickets issued (including parking)
1999 681,166
Arrests, 1999 78,300

Detroit has never been completely peaceful. In fact, as the city grew in the 19th Century, so did the opportunity for crime. Much of it was pegged to the idle hours of young men living in boarding houses who got liquored up and brazen as they roamed streets, mostly near the waterfront.

For its first century, Detroit was a garrison town controlled by the military. In the early 19th Century, before a police force was formed, the county sheriff upheld the law and often soldiers acted as cops with army commanders appointing militias to protect the public.

But militias and a volunteer force would keep the peace until after the Civil War when the need for a full-time police department was recognized.

A four-member Police Commission appointed by the governor hired 40 uniformed officers, who began patrolling May 15, 1865.

At first, patrolmen were not issued revolvers. They could carry their own pistols. That first year, police made 3,056 arrests, mainly for assault, larceny and drunkenness. Police also rounded up 200 loose animals and 1,700 stray geese.

In recent years, the department has been a flash point of race relations between police and taxpayers who provide their wages. As Detroit approached a majority black population, the department remained rigidly white, and some street cops gained a notoriety for the brutal treatment of black people they arrested.

In the early 1970s, civil rights leaders charged that the department's decoy unit, STRESS (for Stop the Robberies, Enjoy Safe Streets) targeted African Americans.

That unit was disbanded after Coleman Young became the city's first African-American mayor in 1974. In 1976, he appointed William Hart, a veteran cop who made his reputation as an undercover officer, the city's first black chief. Here are some other historic moments for the cops:

William Hart, the city's first black police chief

➤ **1807:** Governor William Hull forms a militia and appoints Peter Denison, a black man, to lead it.

➤ **1870:** Police begin to use patrol wagons.

➤ **1877:** One officer is given authority over juvenile offenders.

➤ **1877:** Police Commissioner Andrew Rogers becomes the first Detroiter to have a telephone installed at home.

➤ **1893:** L.T. Toliver becomes city's first black police officer. Three years before, Joseph Stowers, a black man, was appointed to the force on probationary period, but was dropped from the force after two months.

➤ **1893:** Marie Owen is hired by police superintendent Morgan Collins. She is likely the first female police officer in the United States.

➤ **1897:** Police begin patrolling on bicycles, becoming known as "scorcher cops" who pursue speeding bike riders. After the auto age began, Detroit police were among the first to use traffic lights and stop signs.

➤ **1901:** Daniel O. Smith, an African American, joins the department. He made detective in 1914, sergeant in 1918 and lieutenant in 1927. He retired in 1932 and died Jan. 5, 1939.

➤ **1922:** Detroit police become first in the nation to be radio dispatched.

➤ **1998:** About 61 percent of force is African American.

Deadly cops

In 2000, Detroit led the nation's largest cities in the rate of fatal shootings by police, according to a Free Press analysis of FBI statistics. Detroit's rate is nearly 2 1/2 times higher than New York's rate and more than 1 1/2 times that of Los Angeles.

Notorious serial killers (Seven painful reminders)

Bigfoot: Name given to man who raped, beat and killed seven prostitutes and assaulted other women in the Cass Corridor in 1975. Survivors said their assailant had enormous feet. The killings remain unsolved.

Benjamin Atkins: He raped and strangled 11 women in Detroit and Highland Park during a nine-month period in 1991 and 1992. Said by the FBI to have killed the greatest number of victims in the shortest period of time in the United States.

Oakland County Child Killer: Two boys and two girls were kidnapped and killed — the boys sexually molested — in a two-year period in southern Oakland County, beginning in 1976. No one has been charged.

Leslie Allen Williams: Abducted, raped and killed four teenage girls between Sept. 14, 1991, and Jan. 4, 1992. Williams, right, was free on parole and living in Detroit when he confessed in 1992.

Victor Malone: Found guilty of the first-degree murder of a prostitute in Southfield in 1986 after he had been convicted of murdering two prostitutes in Detroit.

Donald Murphy: In 1980, 11 prostitutes were among 18 young women killed in similar circumstances. Murphy was convicted of two of the killings and confessed to four others. But Murphy's confessions came only after David

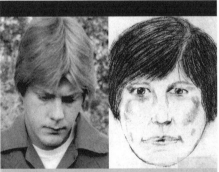

According to testimony, coworkers teased Ronald Bailey when they saw this artist's sketch on a wanted poster.

Ronald Bailey: Convicted in 1986 in the kidnap-slayings of 13-year-old Shawn Moore of Green Oak Township in August 1985 and 14-year-old Kenny Myers of Ferndale in July 1984.

At Bailey's sentencing for Shawn's murder, Livingston County Circuit Judge Stanley Latreille ordered him to prison for 65 to 100 years. Bailey, the judge said in court, "cultivated evil as a habit, until indeed you could rape and kill almost as a reflexive action — without much thought or concern. You have become a cold, calculating predator."

Payton, the former girls basketball coach at Highland Park High School, had told police he committed some of the same killings. Payton quickly recanted, claiming coercion by police. The murder charges against Payton were dismissed, and he also was acquitted of robbing and raping two other prostitutes. Payton won $8 million from Detroit in 1991 after a jury found that police had coerced the murder confessions.

DETROIT HOMICIDES 1920-2000 (con't.)	
1968	389
1967	281
1966	214
1965	188
1964	125
1963	125
1962	131
1961	136
1960	150
1959	106
1958	110
1957	119
1956	105
1955	140
1954	108
1953	130
1952	109
1951	129
1950	113
1949	103
1948	105
1947	112
1946	109
1945	101
1944	102
1943	97
1942	89
1941	78
1940	80
1939	79
1938	67
1937	74
1936	66
1935	60
1934	60
1933	78
1932	96
1931	107
1930	114
1929	158
1928	128
1927	134
1926	225
1925	153
1924	138
1923	123
1922	55
1921	76
1920	94
TOTAL	**23,394**

Amazing tales of death

Murder on the river

But which side of the border?

Luke Phipps shot and killed his wife, Effie, on the Detroit-Windsor ferry on Aug. 19, 1883.

Phipps' guilt was not an issue: He did it. But where he pulled the trigger was a life-or-death issue for Phipps: Canada then had capital punishment; Michigan did not. The ferry crossing was from Detroit, at the foot of Woodward. His attorneys lost their argument that the shooting occurred on the U.S. side of the river. Phipps, 40, was tried in Windsor, convicted and sentenced to hang. On June 17, 1884, Phipps walked to the scaffold and led witnesses in singing hymns until a hood was slipped over his head. The hanging took place. Phipps seemed dead when taken down from the scaffold. But in a special test, physicians attempted to resuscitate him, using a galvanic battery. It worked. Phipps started breathing. But authorities halted the medical work and let the prisoner die on the jailhouse floor.

Don't touch that biscuit!

A scrubwoman's revenge?

Forty families who lived at the Alhambra Apartments at Cass and Temple were poisoned Jan. 20, 1905. Two people died. The Alhambra wasn't comparable to today's Cass Corridor apartment buildings. It was a swank address along one of the city's silk-stocking streets.

Police arrested scrubwoman Rose Barron, who had doled out her arsenic-laced homemade biscuits to tenants. Barron was dying of cancer, but her motive was revenge: She had been demoted from cook to scrubwoman. And she had a history: Police said her father-in-law had died of arsenic poisoning.

The trial lasted 19 weeks and Barron's attorneys argued plumbing poisoned the tenants. At one point, a juror clutched his stomach and screamed: "My God, I've been poisoned!" and fell to the floor. He had merely fainted. Barron was acquitted.

Who killed Grace Loomis?

Her husband fit pre-scription

Grace Loomis was found bludgeoned to death at her home by her husband, Dr. Frank Loomis, on Feb. 22, 1927.

The doctor, bloodstains on his disheveled

Arrows point to bloody footprints in the home of cult leader Benny Evangelista.

Free Press file photos

Benny and Santina Evangelista

clothing, walked into the police station to report the discovery at the couple's Marlowe Avenue home. When police arrived, they found a 2-by-4 wooden stake burning in the furnace. Police sought to charge Loomis, but a judge refused to sign the arrest warrant. But after police discovered Loomis had a girlfriend named Gertrude, he was arrested. After a three-week trial, the jury took 35 minutes to acquit him. On May 23, 1928, one year to the day after his trial had begun, Loomis turned on the gas in his house and killed himself. He left two suicide notes. One proclaimed his innocence. The other said: "G." — the initial of both women in his life — "drives me crazy."

MAYHEM

Six caskets carrying members of the Evangelista family arrive at the Church of San Francisco at Rivard and Brewster.

A family is massacred

Was it a cult killing?

Police arrived July 23, 1929, at the Evangelista house at 3587 St. Aubin near Mack and found the family slaughtered.

Benny Evangelista, 43, was found sitting at his desk, his clothes neat, his arms across his chest, his severed head resting at his feet. His wife, Santina, and their children, 18-month-old Mario, Eugenia, 4, Margaret, 5, and Angelina, 7, were found slashed to death in upstairs bedrooms.

Evangelista, a former carpenter, was a self-styled mystic and faith healer. He wrote his own bible, proclaimed himself a prophet and conducted candlelight services for a small group of followers in the green-draped base-ment of the house. More than 500 people were questioned about the killings but no one was charged.

When kidnapping was king

The Jackie Thompson abduction

On Sept. 30, 1929, weeks before the great stock market crash, petty hoods snatched 5-year-old Jackie from in front of his west side home. They demanded $35,000 for his release. Twenty-four days later, after $17,000 in ransom was paid, Jackie was freed, physically unharmed.

Abducting children had become too common in the late 1920s. It was a way criminals could secure quick money by holding children for ransom. Jackie's kidnapping seemed the

Detroit Free Press

Warrior's Farewell: Bands

99 Bill Wars

Fire Kills Mom, 6 Children; Neighbor Rescues Father

Exile Chief Captured, Cubans Say

Herman Follows A Bouncing Mom

Man torches his family

HE WANTED OUT OF MARRIAGE

On Jan. 25, 1964, Ferndale resident Harry Belcher doused his sleeping wife with gasoline and set her on fire. The blaze spread, killing their six children. The motive, according to police: Belcher wanted out of his marriage for another woman. At the funeral, five small caskets were in a half-circle around a larger one. That casket had two people in it — Catherine Belcher, cradling her baby. Harry Belcher was sentenced to life in prison.

last straw. The Thompsons were well-off, owners of a real estate company and former Ford dealers. Among the people angered by the abduction was Henry Ford, who ordered his infamous security chief Harry Bennett to help find Jackie.

Police squeezed underworld bosses — and their businesses — in an attempt to put so much heat on crime, the hoods would find Jackie just so they could get back to business.

After three weeks, Hamtramck gang czar Chester LaMare and Downriver mob boss Joe Tocco put out the word for the kidnappers to take their money and return the kid. It worked. Jackie was found in a home on Chene. Marked ransom money led to three two-bit hoods. They were jailed for 20 years. Jackie Thompson served as a B29 gunner in World War II and later moved to California.

A little girl's murder

Kidnapped walking to school

Barbara Gaca, 7, disappeared as she walked home from school on March 24, 1955. A week later, she was found dead.

Barbara's abduction brought hundreds of people together to search for her. But her strangled and stabbed body was found in a grimy Army blanket in a dump in West Bloomfield. She had been raped. Barbara was grabbed somewhere between Assumption Grotto School near Gratiot and McNichols and her home six blocks away as she walked home for lunch. Suspects included a Roman

Catholic priest, but police were unable to solve the crime.

The case has haunted detectives, some of whom continued searching for leads even after they retired. A West Bloomfield police detective has identified a retired carnival worker as a suspect, but that man died in 1992.

A Sabbath killing service

Rabbi Morris Adler murdered

A disturbed member of Congregation Shaarey Zedek in Southfield grabbed the microphone during the service, began a tirade, then shot Rabbi Morris Adler, right, before turning the weapon on himself.

The shooting of Adler, 59, was sudden and brazen, done before 900 congregants at the Southfield synagogue on Feb. 12, 1966.

Adler had just finished a sermon about the life of Abraham Lincoln when congregant Richard Wishnetsky, 23, grabbed the microphone.

"This congregation is a travesty. It has made a mockery by its phoniness and

Goldie Adler follows the casket of her husband, Rabbi Morris Adler.

MAYHEM

Free Press file photo

hypocrisy of the beauty and the spirit of Judaism . . . " Wishnetsky said.

Another congregant tried to intervene.

"Get back. He has a gun," Adler told that man.

Wishnetsky fired twice into the ceiling, shot Adler in the left arm and then shot him in the head before firing a final time into his own head.

Adler, in a coma, died nearly one month later. Wishnetsky died three days after the shooting. A Phi Beta Kappa graduate of the University of Michigan, Wishnetsky was described as a troubled man. He was taking graduate courses at the University of Detroit. His professor: Joyce Carol Oates.

Years later the famous author wrote a fictional reconstruction of the shooting as a short story. It's found in "Last Days" (Dutton, 241 pages).

Death in a dope house

8 die in worst mass killing

It is Detroit's worst mass killing: Eight people executed June 14, 1971, in a west-side dope house.

Four men and four women were shot in the head at close range in the house in the 1900 block of Hazelwood. All were found in the living room. The hands of three victims were bound in front of them with surgical rubber tubing. One woman's hands were wrapped around another woman's waist. Police recovered heroin and syringes from the house. No arrests were made.

Murder capital accolade

Detroit gets a rep in '74

In 1974, 714 people were murdered in Detroit. The figure screamed across the country and soon Detroit was tagged Murder Capital. Murder City. Ironically, the rate of murders for every 100,000 residents — a more accurate assessment of homicides — put Atlanta on top of Detroit. Alas, the murder rate in 1975 and 1976 *did* put Detroit in first place. So did the rate in 1983.

But it was the killings of '74 that grabbed headlines. About 80 percent of the victims were black. The killings include one man slain because the killer, who escaped, was bothered by his smelly feet. Friends of the dead man said he was known only as "Looney."

Stonehead killings

Father's love turns to rage

Angry father Arville Garland burst into the off-campus apartment at 2:30 a.m., pumped slugs into his 17-year-old sleeping daughter, her boyfriend and two others, killing them all.

Sandra Garland had left home several days before the May 8, 1970, shooting after a disagreement over issues typical between parents and kids: clothes and lifestyle. She wound up in Stonehead Manor, a counterculture commune near Wayne State University's campus.

Garland, a 45-year-old railroad engineer, carried a .38 in one hand and a Luger in the other when he fired repeatedly into Sandra's sleeping body.

"Sandra was our princess," her mother, Martha, said later. "If we wouldn't have loved her so much, it never would have happened." Garland was convicted of second-degree murder.

Arville Garland:
He killed his "princess"
because she was a hippie.

Free Press file photo

Killing spree grips campus

Six cases remain unsolved

Seven young women were found murdered in the Ann-Arbor-Ypsilanti area over a two-year period in the late 1960s. The murders ended in 1969 after police arrested 21-year-old John Norman Collins.

The last woman killed was Karen Sue Beineman, an 18-year-old Eastern Michigan University freshman from Grand Rapids. Collins was charged and convicted in her death, but was not charged with the six other killings. Those cases have never been solved.

Collins was sent to prison for life without parole. He changed his name to Chapman and in the mid-1980s, petitioned to be sent to a Canadian prison, a request that was denied. Chapman, a Canadian, could have been freed on parole had he been successful in his petition.

The wanted poster for John Norman Collins. Collins, left, was a suspect in a string of killings in Washtenaw County. He was convicted of one.

Free Press file photos

ALAN R. KAMUDA/Detroit Free Press

Drowning the family
The Delisle's last outing

Lawrence Delisle drove into the Detroit River in Wyandotte on Aug. 3, 1989. He and his wife, Suzanne, escaped, but their children — Bryan, 8; Melissa, 4; Kathryn, 2, and Emily, 8 months — drowned. Delisle, convicted of first degree murder, maintained he had suffered a leg cramp and the car accelerator stuck. " A father's job is to protect his children and I failed," DeLisle said at his sentencing. "I panicked. I froze. That is my guilt, not murder... I was paralyzed with shock and unable to react. That is my crime." Prosecutors and police believed the troubled DeLisle was probably trying to kill himself, along with his family.

Fast-working killer
Atkins blamed his upbringing

Benjamin (Tony) Atkins, below, grew from a tortured childhood into a fast-working serial killer. During a nine-month period in 1991 and 1992, Atkins raped and strangled 11 women in Detroit and Highland Park. Many of the victims had histories of prostitution and drug abuse.

Atkins amassed the greatest number of victims in the shortest period of time in the United States, according to FBI investigators. Atkins said he was driven by hatred of prostitutes. He grew up in boys' homes when not living with his mother, a prostitute.

Atkins died in September 1997, four years into the 11 life terms to which he was sentenced.

Top: The body of Kristine Mihelich is removed from a snowbank in Franklin. She was one of four victims of the Oakland County Child Killer, who struck in 1976-77. The above sketch is a police rendering of the suspect, who was never caught. Local TV stations often report the case is close to being solved; the reports come mainly during ratings periods.

The worst kind of crime
Oakland County child killer

Two boys and two girls were kidnapped and killed — the boys sexually molested — in a two-year period in southern Oakland County, beginning in 1976. No one has been charged.

A 300-member task force, unprecedented in size in the United States and equipped with then-new computers, pored over hundreds of leads and discounted dozens of suspects. The conventional wisdom was to search for someone who likely wore a uniform that wouldn't alarm a kid. Maybe a minister, maybe a cop. There was one major clue: The killer was believed to own a blue AMC Gremlin, like 7,000 other people in Michigan. For months, motorists kept their eyes peeled for blue Gremlins.

The first victim was Mark Stebbins, 12, of Ferndale, missing four days before his body was discovered in a Southfield shopping plaza in February 1976. In December, 12-year-old Jill Robinson left her Royal Oak home and never returned. Her body was found near I-75 in Troy four days later. One month later, 10-year-old Kristine Mihelich of Berkley was missing 19 days before her body was found in a roadside ditch in Franklin.

Timmy King, 11, of Birmingham was the last known victim. He was missing for six days before his body was found in a ditch off 8 Mile Road in Livonia in March 1977. Mark, Kristine and Timmy were smothered. Jill died from a shotgun blast that, police say, the killer may have fired in panic.

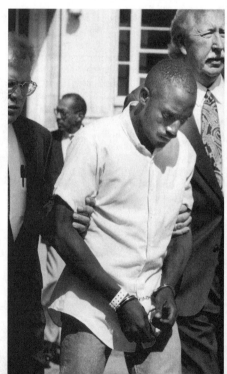

Police lead Benjamin Atkins to his arraignment in 1992.

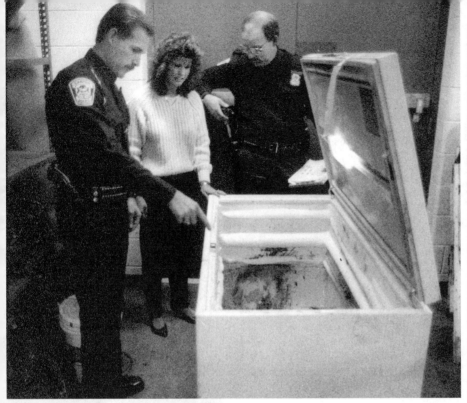

Free Press file photos

Canton police examine the freezer in which Leonard Tyburski stored his wife's body for more than three years.,

Leonard and Dorothy Tyburski, left, at a 1966 Christmas party; Leonard, right at a court appearance in 1989.

Death did them part
Wife found in freezer

Leonard and Dorothy Tyburski confronted each other in their Canton basement Sept. 28, 1985. Only he would leave, and walk free until his arrest in 1989 for killing his wife and hiding her body in the basement freezer.

Dorothy Tyburski taunted Leonard, during the basement confrontation, about her affair with their daughter's 17-year-old boyfriend. Then she attacked Leonard Tyburski with a knife. He slammed her head into a post 11 times and flung her into a freezer.

Later, he found her not breathing and never opened the freezer again. He told daughters Kelly and Kim that their mother left him for another man. Kelly pried open the freezer on Jan. 2, 1989, and found her mother's frozen body. Tyburski, former dean of students at Mackenzie High School in Detroit, originally was sentenced to 20 to 40 years in prison. In 1994, Tyburski agreed to a plea bargain after the state Supreme Court ordered a retrial because of possible prejudicial publicity. He was resentenced to nine to 20 years.

Deadly liaisons
Psychologist butchered after affair

Dr. W. Alan Canty, 51, a prominent psychologist, went to the Cass Corridor apartment to end two years of noontime trysts with Dawn Spens, 20, a suburban woman turned junkie/hooker. Spens' pimp hit Canty with a baseball bat, killing him. Then John (Lucky Johnny) Fry, 38, dismembered Canty's body, dumping parts across Michigan. The head, hands and feet were buried in the woods in Emmet County.

The liaisons had cost Canty about $140,000 in one year alone.

At trial, Fry admitted the killing. Canty had wanted out of the costly relationship, prosecutors said. Fry and Spens planned a scam: If

Malice Green
CASE DIVIDED DETROITERS

The emotional and racially charged case polarized metro Detroit.

Veteran Detroit cops Larry Nevers, above, and Walter Budzyn, both white, encountered the 35-year-old Green, an unarmed black man, outside a West Warren Avenue crack cocaine house on Nov. 5, 1992. Within a few minutes, Green was dead. He had been beaten with heavy police flashlights. The officers said that Green — who had been using cocaine — refused to obey orders. They feared for their lives in the struggle, they said.

Juries convicted Budzyn and Nevers of second-degree murder in 1993. Budzyn, who testified he didn't hit Green, was sentenced to 8-18 years in prison. Nevers, who admitted hitting Green, was sentenced to 12-25 years in prison. Both served part of their sentences before being released in separate appeals cases.

Budzyn was convicted of involuntary manslaughter in his 1998 retrial and given a 4- to 15-year sentence.

Nevers was convicted of the same charge two years later and ordered to serve 7 to 15 years in prison. Both cases were being appealed in 2000.

Inkster motel firefight

WARRANT TRIP TURNS DEADLY FOR POLICE

They drifted from one fly-by-night scam to another and were living in an Inkster motel when Inkster police arrived July 9, 1987, to serve Alberta Easter, above, and her sons with a warrant for a $286 bad check.

Easter, 69, protested, insisting the warrant was improper. Officers Clay Hoover, 24, and Daniel Dubiel, 36, called their supervisor, Sgt. Ira Parker. He drove to the Bungalow Motel on Michigan Avenue. Seconds after Parker, 41, entered the motel room, gunfire began. The cops didn't have a chance. Twenty-nine slugs were pumped into the three officers, including rounds from their own weapons.

Then Easter and sons George, 45, Roy, 47, and William Lemons, 43, fired at random out the motel door at Michigan Avenue. A 10-hour standoff ended when the family surrendered. All were convicted of first-degree murder and are serving life terms.

Canty gave Fry $30,000, Fry would leave town — leaving Spens to Canty. Had Canty come through, Fry and Spens together would have left town.

But Canty wasn't biting. He wanted out, period.

Fry testified that Canty manipulated them, fostered their heroin addictions and then introduced them to cocaine. He killed Canty in a burst of anger because Canty took Spens to get more drugs.

Fry was sentenced to life without parole. Spens served 10 months in prison and was ordered to a drug-counseling program.

Six men were shot at this house on St. Aubin.

An 'angel of death'

Six gunned down in robbery

Six people in a dope house on St. Aubin near Nevada were shot dead in the head at close range during a robbery. Four others escaped the April 4, 1990, massacre.

A jury convicted Tamara Marie Marshall, an 18-year-old former girlfriend of one of the victims, as the ringleader. Wayne County Assistant Prosecutor Augustus Hutting labeled her an "angel of death." Three others also received long prison terms.

The slayings happened about two blocks south of then-Police Chief William Hart's house.

Free Press file photo

Above: Tamara Marshall, ringleader of the 1990 killing of six people during a robbery at a dope house.
Below: Mark Bell, left, Marc Caison, Jamal Bigs and Tamara Marshall at trial.

PATRICIA BECK/Detroit Free Press

MAYHEM

VINCENT CHIN: A Chinese-American beaten to death because of his Asian appearance.

RONALD EBENS: The autoworker received probation for his role in Chin's death.

MICHAEL NITZ: He pleaded no contest to manslaughter.

Vincent Chin

DEATH BY BASEBALL BAT

Vincent Chin, a Chinese-American engineer from Oak Park, was beaten to death by a Louisville Slugger-wielding autoworker on June 19, 1982 — a time of deep recession and lagging auto sales. The autoworker, Ronald Ebens, and his unemployed stepson, Michael Nitz, apparently believed Chin was Japanese, whose cars were outselling many American models at the time. The three met at the Fancy Pants Lounge on Woodward in Highland Park, where Chin was celebrating his upcoming wedding. Ebens and Nitz received three years' probation and $3,780 fines for their roles in the death. Ebens pleaded guilty and Nitz pleaded no contest to manslaughter charges. The sentences by Wayne County Circuit Judge Charles Kaufman touched off waves of protest from Asian Americans across the United States. Federal charges followed. Nitz was acquitted of them in 1984; Ebens' conviction was overturned, and he was eventually acquitted.

Tonya and Nancy

The whack heard 'round the world

"No . . . Why me? Why now?" Those were the anguished words of Olympic figure skater Nancy Kerrigan after a large man in a black leather coat ran toward her from behind and whacked her right knee with a metal baton. The assault, which took place in a Cobo Arena hallway on Jan. 6, 1994, was one of the most dramatic sports stories of the century, and it made headlines around the world for weeks. Kerrigan was considered a gold-medal favorite in the upcoming Olympics. And before long, Detroit police turned up information that a gang of associates of one of Kerrigan's chief rivals, Tonya Harding, had plotted the crime. Before long, Harding's on-again, off-again husband, Jeff Gillooly, was charged with planning and bankrolling the attack, and three of his friends confessed to being involved. At the Olympics, the rehabilitated Kerrigan skated, as did the out-of-shape Harding. Kerrigan won a silver medal. Harding failed to place. After the Olympics, Harding pleaded guilty to hindering prosecution and was fined $100,000, sentenced to 500 hours of community service and banned for life by the U.S. Figure Skating Association. Kerrigan went onto become a millionaire skater.

Tonya failed to place...

...but Nancy won a silver.

Fought law — law won

EMINEM GETS PROBABTION ON WEAPONS CHARGE

Eminem, the world-famous rapper who sang about brutalizing his mother and wife, got a real rap sheet in 2000. Macomb County prosecutors charged him after a confrontation outside a Warren nightclub. Police said Eminem struck a man he says he saw kissing his estranged wife, Kim. Eminem, whose real name is Marshall Bruce Mathers III, went to court meekly and pleaded guilty to carrying a concealed weapon. In April 2001, a Macomb County Circuit judge sentenced him to two years probabtion and ordered him to undergo counseling and submit to drug testing. Eminem also faced charges in Oakland County that he illegally possessed and brandished a concealed weapon during an earlier confrontation with Douglas Dail, an associate of Insane Clown Posse, a Detroit-based rap group.

Goodfellas

Detroit mobsters
of the 1930s:
Joe Bommarito,
left, Jimmy Licavoli
and Nick Desmond.

Self-made men

Big city....Prohibition....large ethnic communities....lots of money....

Detroit for much of the last 100 years possessed the ingredients for a bumper crop of hoods. Gangsters have been part of daily life in the city and suburbs. Some of their stories:

The Black Hand

Extortionists who became so prolific that Detroit police in the 1920s created the Black Hand Squad to combat the group. The police division's previous name was the Italian Squad.

The Purple Gang

Detroit's best-known bad guys, the Purples, had a short but sensational reign. They began as a dozen tough west side kids who cut their teeth on stealing and selling protection to merchants. The Purples' home turf was the near northwest side between Pingree and Clairmount, from Woodward to Grand River — though its reach was extensive. From the mid-1920s to the early 1930s, the gang's 50 members made national headlines as toughs who preyed upon other hoods through such tactics as kidnappings, contract hits and the hijacking of illegal liquor. Chicago police suspected Purples made up the hit squad that killed seven members of the Bugs Moran gang in the St. Valentine's Massacre, but that was never proved. The Purples' climactic moment was the Collingwood Massacre (see below), after which the leadership ended up in prison. The Purples' demise ended the era of the Jewish gangster in Detroit.

Free Press file photo

Detroit detectives question mafia don Peter Licavoli, right.

Collingwood Massacre

The Little Navy Gang — so named because of its fleet of rum-running boats on the Detroit River — thought a truce was at hand with its rivals, the Purples. In September 1931, the Purples coaxed three Navy members to Apartment 211 at 1740 Collingwood. One of four Purple Gang members left the apartment. When he revved a car on the street, the remaining Purples pulled revolvers and shot and killed the Navy men. The Purples convicted of murder and sent to prison were Harry Keywell, Irving Milberg and Ray Bernstein.

The Roaring '20s

During Prohibition, the mob operated in an atmosphere of lawlessness. In 1924, there were 21 gangland murders. In 1925, police recovered 53 bodies from the Detroit River. In 1926, eight cops were killed on duty and 10 were wounded; police killed 44 citizens and wounded 89; citizens killed 56 people who allegedly were committing crimes.

Free Press file photo

MAYHEM

Mourners at
Joseph Zerilli's
funeral included
his wife,
Josephine.

Milaflores massacre

On March 27, 1927, Frankie Wright, Joseph Bloom and George Cohen were cut down by more than 100 bullets in the hallway of the Milaflores Apartments, 106 E. Alexandrine. It was the first time a machine gun was used in a Detroit gangland slaying. Police blamed the Purple Gang.

The Cleaners and Dyers War

This battle was touched off by a group of wholesale cleaners in the 1920s who wanted to boost the price of cleaning and pressing a suit from about 50 cents to $1.50 across Detroit. In what turned out to be a grave mistake, the wholesalers hired Purples to persuade cleaners who balked at the new prices, and the campaign quickly got out of hand. The Purples dynamited buildings, kidnapped some cleaners, executed others, even inserted incendiary chemicals into clothes that would explode when touched by water.

The unmasking

In 1963, Detroit Police Commissioner George Edwards told the U.S. Senate that organized crime had infiltrated at least 98 legitimate businesses in Detroit. And Edwards named names. One business that he identified as mob-run was Home Juice, a Detroit-based firm whose 65 trucks delivered fruit drink throughout the city. Edwards said the firm was partly run by Vito (Billy Jack) Giacalone and his brother, Anthony Giacalone. Both men would surface frequently in law enforcement investigations for the rest of the century.

Edwards gave Senate investigators a now-famous chart that he said detailed the structure of organized crime in Detroit. Of the five "dons" listed, Joseph Zerilli was often listed as

Vito (Billy Jack) Giacalone and Anthony (Tony Jack) Giacalone spent much of the last half of the 20th Century fighting criminal charges.

don No. 1 by local and federal law enforcement officials. Zerilli said he was in the bakery business. Zerilli was only convicted once — for carrying a concealed weapon in 1919.

Edwards also named 35 lieutenants and section leaders.

Capo di tutti capi

Joseph Zerilli, right, rose from the gangs of the 1920s to become Detroit's reputed Mafia boss for nearly half of the 20th Century. Zerilli, above, who died in 1977, was also considered a power in national organized crime. Zerilli emigrated from Favarotta (sometimes called Terrasini), Sicily, to Detroit in 1914. By the time he was 20, he had joined an east side bootlegging gang with William (Black Bill) Tocco and Angelo Meli. Mr. Z got respect. It was not unknown to see grown men

scurry to dust his chair with their handkerchiefs. Zerilli's legitimate businesses were produce and baking and the long-defunct Lake Shore Coach Lines. Local and federal officials said Zerilli received cuts from such illegal businesses as loan-sharking, numbers, sports betting and other forms of gambling, such as a popular dice game known as barbut.

All in the family

Two of Zerilli's sisters were married to Detroit Mafia bosses. They and other mobbed-up clans in the 1950s and 1960s lived in what was then a well-known Mafioso colony on Middlesex and Westchester streets in Grosse Pointe Park. Pete Corrado was one of Zerilli's brothers-in-law. When he died in 1957 of natural causes, a funeral procession of 400 cars followed him to the grave.

Dying with the fishes

On May 31, 1930, two emissaries of Zerilli went for a meeting with representatives of gang boss Chester LaMare at a fish market on East Vernor at Jos. Campau. Gunmen killed both the Zerilli gang members.

A don done in by his own

LaMare, public enemy No. 1 in Detroit for years, a Zerilli rival and the crime czar of wide-open Hamtramck, was killed in the kitchen of his fortified home at 15505 Grandville on Feb. 6, 1931. Police said he was shot through the head by at least one of his own bodyguards. At the time of his death, a grand jury — called as a result of the killing of radio broadcaster Jerry Buckley — was seeking LaMare for questioning.

New don, same as the old don

In 1998, a federal jury in Detroit affirmed what the U.S. government had been saying for decades: Jack Tocco is the modern boss of the Detroit Mafia. The jury found Tocco, then 71, of Grosse Pointe Park and three other men guilty of violating the Racketeer Influenced and Corrupt Organizations law. Tocco and Anthony Corrado also were found guilty of a second racketeering count and an extortion conspiracy. During a subsequent sentencing hearing, the feds showed Tocco no respect: For two days in a Detroit courtroom, the intensely private and proud Tocco grimly sat as intimate details of his failing body were laid out in an effort to minimize the time he would have to spend in prison. Not only did medical testimony and affidavits strip Tocco down to

Jack Tocco leaves U.S. District Court with two unidentified women in 1998.

his ingrown toenails and daily teaspoon dose of Metamucil, the fears and ills of his wife, Maria Tocco, were laid bare from the witness stand. His sentence: 34 months, less the 366 days he had served.

Stool pigeon

In March 2000, mobster Nove Tocco became the first Detroit Mafia member to rat out the feared underworld organization when he testified for an hour in U.S. District Court about the hoodlum empire run by his cousin, Jack Tocco. The organization authorized murders, beatings and extortions while demanding fealty, Nove Tocco said. Exposing the organization once run by his grandfather, Joseph Zerilli, Nove Tocco testified that he and partner Paul Corrado were maneuvered by other gangsters into planning a preemptive killing aimed at Harry (Taco) Bowman, international president of the Outlaws motorcycle gang and Detroit area gambling figure. (See Ten Most Wanted.) Tocco said they didn't carry out the killing because they learned they were "being pushed into a conflict" by other mobsters struggling with Bowman to control a gambling spot. Tocco said his work as a mob member included "street-taxing" — or shaking down — illegal gamblers. There were strict rules for Nove Tocco and Paul Corrado when working the streets:

➤ They couldn't "grab people that were

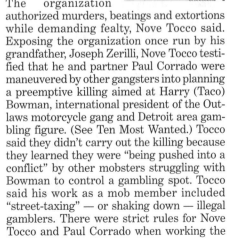

Nove Tocco, left, was the first Detroit Mafia member to rat out his organization.

MAYHEM

already affiliated with the old-timers," and new street-tax targets had to be approved.
➤ Word to and from Jack Tocco would be through their uncles.
➤ A little rough stuff was OK, but "anything that got more serious than minor physical endeavors had to be checked through them."

Mafia? What Mafia?

Also in 1998, after years of assertions that the Mafia was confined to Hollywood back lots and overheated federal imaginations, a top Detroit mob boss admitted that the fraternity is for real and that he is a member. Vito (Billy Jack) Giacalone pleaded guilty before U.S. District Judge John Corbett O'Meara to a single conspiracy count of collecting unlawful debts from sports gambling and racketeering. The admission was part of Giacalone's plea agreement.

Name game

Names for the mob over the years have ranged from the Mafia to La Cosa Nostra, but mobster Nove Tocco, in his testimony about local organized crime in March 2000, said to Detroit insiders its name was the Combination, the Partnership or the Partners. Tocco said street people used terms such as Outfit.

The Marzette Method

In Detroit dope circles of the 1960s, the method was a way of torture devised by a former Detroit cop-turned heroin chieftain named Henry Marzette, a tough west sider who had received a total of 200 stitches in his face from knife fights, auto accidents and shrapnel from his Army days in Korea. His method: cutting off the fingers joint by joint. Marzette, who died of kidney failure in 1972, was an undercover cop who once made more than 100 dope arrests in a year and broke up a prison drug ring. Kicked off the force in 1956 and sent to prison for a year for heroin dealing (his only jail time), Marzette returned to Detroit and became king of one of the city's largest heroin distribution systems, raking in $5 million a year and supplying 100 dope houses. In 1971, Marzette helped set off a dope war in which more than 50 people died. He lived in a modest home in Highland Park but owned a plantation in the Bahamas and a fleet of Cadillac Fleetwoods. His funeral procession included 41 Cadillacs and Lincolns. Said one former cop: "Old Zette has real class, you dig? He's not out there busting his butt off for the Man. Hell no, he's got the Man working for him."

Earl Flynns, Black Killers (BKs) and Coneyoneys

These gangs of teenagers weren't very organized, and they died out after just a few years, but they terrorized parts of Detroit in the mid-1970s.

The Chambers Brothers

Federal officials in Detroit described the Chambers Brothers drug ring as the biggest crack-cocaine organization to be smashed in U.S. history. They said the brothers — Billy Joe, Willie, Larry and Otis — operated up to 300 crack-cocaine houses in Detroit in 1983-88 at a profit of almost $1 million a week. The brothers, who were convicted of narcotics trafficking-related offenses in 1988, recruited many of their 500 employees from Detroit high schools and their impoverished hometown of Marianna, Ark. They kept their troops in line with brutality and intimidation.

Young Boys Inc.

YBI was a Horatio Alger story run amok. In the late 1970s, Milton (Butch) Jones did for narcotics trafficking what Henry Ford did for the auto industry: He revolutionized the way business was done. On the Birney Elementary School playground on the west side, Jones called a meeting of friends from the Monterey-Dexter neighborhood and told them they could be millionaires. His plan: Use juveniles as cogs in a highly organized machine and have each person perform a specific task. YBI's dealership network moved specific drug mixtures under imaginative brand names such as Atomic Dog, Whipcracker, Rolls Royce and Freak of the Week. A hard-working youngster could quickly rise through the ranks — provided he lived. Violence was a work hazard. In 1984, the gang's A-Team enforcement arm was blamed by police for at least nine slayings in Detroit, Highland Park and Troy in little over a month. Beginning in December 1982, the gang's hierarchy was rocked with a series of federal indictments. Eventually, Jones, cofounder Raymond Peoples and their supplier, Sylvester (Seal) Murray, and many underlings went to prison.

Best Friends

East side drug lord Richard (Maserati Rick) Carter formed the gang because he wanted a front-line force to fight turf wars while he handled the crack-cocaine-dealing side of the operation, investigators say. Best Friends was also thought to have been the brawn for teenage drug figure Richard (White Boy Rick) Wershe

Jr. At its peak in 1986, Best Friends had 25 to 50 members, all of whom used automatic and semiautomatic weapons such as Uzis and AK47s and protected themselves with body armor suits and bulletproof vests, officials said. Many of them drove Volvos

and some even flaunted their reputation by wearing jackets with Best Friends embroidered on the back. They also turned on each other: Best Friends hit man Reginald (Rockin' Reggie) Brown was sentenced May 20, 1988, to life in prison for the shooting death of a Wershe associate, Steve Roussell.

Gunfire in the surgery ward

In 1988, Best Friends boss Richard Carter, shown at left, lay on his bed in Room 307 at Mt. Carmel Mercy Hospital in Detroit, recovering from a gunshot wound, when a gunman walked in and shot him in the face. The gunman fled. Carter, 29, died immediately. He had been shot in the stomach several days earlier in a gunfight with a man at a car wash on West 7 Mile Road. A gold crucifix and a loaded 9mm Smith & Wesson automatic pistol were found in Carter's bedside table. He was buried in a $16,000 casket customized to look like a Mercedes-Benz automobile.

Other notable mob passings

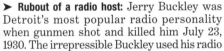

➤ **The Giannola-Vitale feud:** A war between these two factions around World War I claimed dozens of lives. Then the real battle started. On Feb. 26, 1919, three mobsters entered an office at the Wayne County Jail. They were there to visit a colleague accused of a gangland murder. As the three stood waiting for their friend, a car roared up and four rivals marched into the jail, firing their guns, killing the trio. One victim, riddled with 21 bullets, managed to whisper the name "Sam Giannola" as one of the killers before he died. Giannola was arrested but later acquitted in the killings. But on Oct. 3 of that year, gangsters fired on Giannola as he entered a bank at Monroe and Russell. Giannola staggered inside, made it to a teller's cage and collapsed, dead with 28 bullets in him.

➤ **Rubout of a radio host:** Jerry Buckley was Detroit's most popular radio personality when gunmen shot and killed him July 23, 1930. The irrepressible Buckley used his radio

reach to stump for the recall of Mayor Charles Bowles, a pillar of corruption and an ally of the Ku Klux Klan. Buckley, 39, had just finished his broadcast at the LaSalle Hotel studio of WMBC-AM (1400). Bowles had lost the recall election, and Buckley, shown at left, could crow as victor. After the broadcast, he lounged in the LaSalle lobby. It was about 1 a.m. when a gunman approached Buckley, firing four shots into him. He died at Detroit Receiving Hospital. More than 20,000 people attended Buckley's funeral; 100,000 filed past his coffin. His killer was never caught; speculation suggests a mob rubout because Buckley was about to broadcast incriminating information concerning Detroit mob bosses.

Jerry Buckley's information about Detroit's mob bosses may have led to his unsolved murder.

In Loving Memory
Anthony J. Giacalone

JANUARY 9, 1919
FEBRUARY

Prayer cards from the funeral of Anthony Giacalone, who died of natural causes in 2001.

MAYHEM

"The Little Guy never came home last night," said Louis Linteau. "Maybe he took a little trip," responded Anthony (Tony Jack) Giacalone.

➤ **Death in a clothing store:** The odds finally caught up with Demetrius Holloway, right, in 1990. Holloway, 32, had dodged indictments and rivals for five years before dying a gangster's death, gunned down in the Broadway clothing store in downtown Detroit

with $14,000 and a .32 caliber pistol in his pocket. A reputed drug lord who federal agents once said ran 80 percent of Detroit's cocaine trade, Holloway had described himself as a newspaper carrier, a postal clerk, a landlord, sports shop entrepreneur and a pool hall manager.

Hoffa was seen waiting in the parking lot of the Machus Red Fox restaurant in Bloomfield Township. Hoffa was due home at 4 p.m., but he never arrived. "The Little Guy never came home last night," longtime friend Louis Linteau told Giacalone. "Any idea where he could be?" Linteau asked. "Maybe he took a little trip," Giacalone said, according to law enforcement files. Authorities say they believe Hoffa was lured into a car and killed. His body was never found. Despite reports that he was dumped in Lake Michigan or buried in the end zone of the Meadowlands stadium in New Jersey, internal FBI reports indicate Hoffa's remains may have been disposed of through a Detroit-area industrial scrap and refuse company.

➤ **Requiem for a ladies' man:** Reputed mobster Peter Cavataio was slain execution-style in a garage near the Ambassador Bridge in 1985. Cavataio was a convicted gambler whom authorities said had a reputation as a ladies' man involved in many illegal activities. The body of Cavataio, 55, was found behind a garage in the 5800 block of Harvey in southwest Detroit. His hands were tied in front of his body and he had been shot several times in the head. In 1997, the U.S. Attorney's Office said John Pree, a convicted criminal in the witness protection program, and others admitted sticking a heated knife into Cavataio in 1985 to get Cavataio to reveal the location of a large amount of money. Pree pleaded guilty to racketeering in connection with the murder of Cavataio.

➤ **Gone for a ride:** Peter Lucido and Sam Scroy were small-time hoods who worked for Maxie Stern, whom police in the 1940s described as a Detroit gambling boss. The three men had a spat; two months later, in June 1948, Lucido and Scroy vanished. That angered Scroy's brother, Chris, who got even by pumping Stern with eight bullets in 1950. Chris Scroy confessed and went to prison for five years. After his release in April 1959, he also disappeared. Chris Scroy eventually turned up. Or at least his body did. It was contained in seven bags found in a farmer's field in northern Macomb County in 1960. The medical examiner determined that Scroy had been garroted.

TONY SPINA/Detroit Free Press

Jimmy Hoffa was last seen in the parking lot of the Machus Red Fox restaurant in 1975.

➤ **The disappearance of Jimmy Hoffa:** The ultimate hit. Paroled from federal prison 3½ years earlier, former Teamsters President Jimmy Hoffa had announced his plans in 1975 to again seek the union leadership. On July 30, 1975, Hoffa left home for an afternoon meeting. He told people the participants would include reputed Mafia boss Anthony (Tony Jack) Giacalone.

MAYHEM

Drugs

Drug abuse has been a major public issue in Detroit for more than 100 years. In the early 1900s, officials recognized that a number of Detroiters were addicted to opium, heroin and cocaine and estimated there were 10,000 drug users in the city. Since the flower-power days of the 1960s, the metro area has been awash in illegal drugs. The use of most drugs reflects larger trends, but the level of consumption in metro Detroit is significantly above national averages. In Detroit alone, costs associated with substance abuse total more than $925 million a year for such things as health care, accidents and criminal justice. The statistics below come from the Michigan Department of Community Health and Drug Strategies, a nonprofit policy-research institute in Washington, D.C. Many experts say the figures underrepresent actual drug use.

Cocaine

Cost: About $20 for a rock of crack.
Metro Detroit's use vs. America's: The rate of cocaine mentions in emergency rooms per 100,000 population was 192 in 1997 in the Detroit area. Nationally, it was 68.

➤ Deaths from cocaine increased by 10 percent in Wayne County in 1998 over 1997 after remaining stable for three years. Cocaine is the leading drug involved in emergency-room admissions. Cocaine treatment admissions totaled 6,230 statewide in 1998, with 34 percent (2,111 cases) coming from Wayne County. Crack is predominantly smoked. Cocaine was present in 384 autopsied bodies in 1998, compared with 262 in 1991.
➤ Cocaine (including crack) has been the foremost illicit drug of abuse among admissions to state-funded treatment programs in Wayne County and statewide since 1986.
➤ Cocaine users admitted for treatment are getting older: In Wayne County, those ages 36-44 accounted for 42 percent of admissions. Those younger than 21 make up less than 1 percent of Wayne County admissions.
➤ The proportion of arrestees in Detroit jails testing positive for cocaine was 53 percent in 1987 and 31 percent in 1998. Among men in 1998, the figure was 28 percent. Among women, it was 46 percent.
Local history: Cocaine was used in many medicines in the 19th Century, and by 1912, the Free Press reported a large number of addicts — or "dope fiends" — in Detroit ... By the 1980s, cocaine had evolved into the most notorious recreational drug in America ... Some people with money snorted coke through rolled-up $20 bills. Other people smoked crack cocaine, and Detroit in 1986 was said to have registered the nation's fastest accelera-

tion of crack abuse — police estimated that at least 50,000 metro Detroiters were hooked on the little rocks. Crack was a $1-billion-a-year business in the area ... Neighbors on Sharon Street banded together to close down a crack house. Mothers gave birth to addicted babies. Addicted parents abused and neglected kids. A mother sold her 13-year-old daughter for sex to pay a drug debt. Police caught a 10-year-old selling crack. Turf wars among gangs cost numerous lives.

Heroin

Cost: $10-15 per packet.
Purity: Average of 46.7 percent in 1998. In 1990, it averaged 21.6 percent.
Metro Detroit's use vs. America's: Emergency room heroin mentions in the Detroit area in 1997 per 100,000 population were 72. Nationally, the rate was 30.

➤ Fatal heroin overdoses, which had increased by 19 percent during the past two years, rose again in 1998, but at a slower pace. Heroin purity is at the highest level ever, and prices are declining. Heroin is increasingly being used by suburban youth.
➤ Heroin or morphine was found in 118 cases in 1992 by the Wayne County Medical Examiner's Office. In 1998, it was found in 308 cases.
➤ In Wayne County, the largest group among heroin admissions was ages 45-54 (43 percent) for the first half of fiscal 1999.
➤ In Oakland County, though, admission for heroin use have been increasing sharply. Cases involving those younger than 21 have more than doubled during a one-year period.
Local history: Heroin was considered a problem in Detroit from at least the early 1900s, but abuse surged in the late 1960s, and

MAYHEM

police said stealing goods to exchange for heroin accounted for much of the large increase in crime at the time . . . By 1970, the city had opened four clinics where addicts could receive methadone, a heroin substitute. . . . In the 1980s, local heroin dealers marketed their wares in small coin envelopes stamped with such names as P-Funk, Raw Dog, Pony Down, Reaganomics, Hootchie-Khan and Bill Bonds, after the flamboyant former Detroit anchorman.

Marijuana

Cost: $150-$300 an ounce; twice that for hydroponically grown indoor marijuana.

Types: Mexican marijuana continues to be increasingly available in Michigan, more so than indoor-grown or outdoor-grown domestic varieties.

Metro Detroit's use vs. America's: Emergency room admission rate for marijuana per 100,000 population in 1997 was 89, nearly three times the national rate.

➤ Users are young. In the first half of fiscal year 1999, 39 percent of marijuana admissions both statewide and in Wayne County were under 21. Among Detroit jail arrestees, 47 percent of males and 22 percent of females tested positive for marijuana in 1998. At the Wayne County Juvenile Detention Facility, 54 percent of youths tested positive for marijuana between October 1997 and December 1998. As in most cities, marijuana is the most commonly used illicit drug among adults in Detroit. In 1995, 31 percent of adults surveyed in Detroit reported having used marijuana at some time; 6 percent said they had used it within the previous 30 days.

Local history: Detroit made marijuana possession illegal on Feb. 24, 1928 . . . A decade later, the national "reefer-madness" scare about the supposed dangers of smoking marijuana made a large impact in the city, as police stepped up enforcement against the "laughing weed" or "loco weed" and the media reported horror stories of students losing their minds after smoking "muggles," as powerful marijuana was then called . . . In 1969, Recorder's Court Judge Robert Colombo Sr. sentenced counterculture leader John Sinclair (see LSD) to 9½-10 years in prison for possessing two joints. He was freed in 1971 . . . Ann Arbor became known as the "dope capital of the Midwest" after students and others on April 1, 1972, held the first "hash bash" smoke-in — a tradition that continues. In 1973, Ann Arbor voters approved a charter amendment making marijuana possession a civil infraction punishable by a $5 fine. In 1990, voters increased the penalty to $25 for a first offense, $50 for a second offense and $100 for subsequent offenses.

FACTOID: The three drugs most often found in bodies autopsied at the Wayne County morgue:
1) alcohol
2) nicotine
3) cocaine

FACTOID: Among teenagers, the rates for smoking, drinking, using inhalants and taking cocaine, LSD or heroin are less inside Detroit than outstate. Binge drinking — consuming five or more drinks at one time — is less than half the rate in Detroit than among youths statewide.

GHB

Numerous reports of GHB — the date-rape drug — have surfaced during the past two years, especially among young people. Four men who played roles in the GHB poisoning death of a 15-year-old Rockwood girl on Grosse Ile in 1999 were sentenced to prison in 2000 — three of them for up to 15 years. They were convicted of involuntary manslaughter. The fourth man received 3 to 5 years for being an accessory to manslaughter after the fact.

Name: Gamma-hydroxybutyrate.

Nicknames: Scoop, Liquid Sex, Liquid Ecstasy and Great Bodily Harm.

Penalties: Convictions for selling or manufacturing can bring up to 7 years in prison. Possessing the drug can bring a 2-year prison term. Use can result in up to a year in jail. New federal laws call for up to 20 years in prison upon conviction of manufacturing or selling it.

Symptoms: Feeling intoxicated when drinking nonalcoholic beverage or after only one alcoholic drink.

Hallucinogens

LSD is mainly found among suburban and rural youth, but state health officials said they saw no indications of rising use. **PCP** is rarely reported. **Ecstasy** (MDMA) was responsible for one death in Wayne County in 1998; Detroit Police reported 10 to 15 contacts with the drug since 1998.

Local history: LSD — or acid — arrived in Detroit in the mid-1960s. "The Whole World Was WOW" proclaimed the headline on a 1966 front-page story written by a Free Press reporter who attended a party by LSD "cultists" near Wayne State. Said one participant: "The first time I got high, I walked down the street, and there was this stoplight, and it was . . . like all the red there ever was . . ." Canadian officials in 1967 barred LSD high priest Timothy Leary from entering Windsor. While officials warned that taking LSD would destroy chromosomes and damage future children, which proved to be untrue, Detroit counterculture leader John Sinclair praised LSD, writing in 1971 that "acid blasted all the negativism and fear out of our bodies and minds and gave us the vision we needed . . ." In 1990, students at Troy Athens High School put LSD in the coffee of a teacher, causing him to hallucinate. After two trials, an 18-year-old student was convicted of having dropped the drug into the coffee. She was sentenced to 6 months in a jail work-release program.

Stimulants

No Wayne County emergency rooms have

reported the once heavily used **methamphetamine** since 1995. However, mentions of **amphetamines** went from 27 in 1992 to 357 in 1997, and experts say that may represent some metamphetamine use. **Methcathinone** (Cat) use appears small.

Nicotine

In 1997, more than two-thirds of Detroit high school students said they had tried cigarettes. One in 5 reported having smoked during the last month, which is lower than last-month rates for Michigan teens, but identical to the rates for African-American teens nationally. In Michigan, 26 percent of adults smoke; in Detroit, 29 percent of adults smoke.

Alcohol

In 1995, 41 percent of Detroit adults reported drinking within 30 days of the survey. Officials and community groups in Detroit have made alcohol and tobacco advertising on billboards a public issue.

Inhalants

The chemical vapors produce mind-altering effects. Young people in Michigan use inhalants about twice as often as the national average, officials say. A 1993-1994 survey of 24,000 Michigan eighth-graders found that 31.4 percent said they had tried inhalants. Surveys in 1991-1992 and 1992-1993 showed that 26.6 percent and 27 percent of eighth-graders had tried them.

SOURCES: FREE PRESS; DRUG STRATEGIES; MICHIGAN DEPARTMENT OF COMMUNITY HEALTH'S DRUG UPDATE BY RICHARD F. CALKINS. FOR MORE, VISIT **WWW.MDCH.STATE.MI.US/BH/DRUGTRENDS/**.

OTHER DRUGS

Officials see increasing reports of **Ketamine**, a veterinarian anesthetic that can cause hallucinations in humans; steroids, especially those being smuggled via Canada; and **khat**, the mild plant narcotic from the Middle East.

Poster Boys

Local criminals who made the FBI's 10 Most Wanted list

The FBI began its 10 Most Wanted list in 1950. Of the 458 people who made the list in those 50 years, 429 were caught, with several choosing to shoot it out with authorities. Cases against 15 individuals never caught were eventually dropped, and four more fugitives were removed from the list because others were considered more deserving. Here's a list of local connections to the 10 Most Wanted list:

Giachino Baccolia

A New Jersey mobster and reputed gangland muscle with illegal interests spreading into the Midwest, Baccolia made the Top 10 in August 1951 when he was charged with the Detroit slaying of jeweler Albert Swarz, who was scheduled to testify in Chicago against hoodlums involved in a $25,000 film heist. Baccolia was arrested in New York in December 1951. A Detroit jury acquitted him of murder, but a federal jury convicted him of smuggling narcotics.

Kenneth Maurer

Eighteen-year-old Maurer of Detroit was a shy, assistant Boy Scout leader with a love for gardening and stray animals. But the placid exterior masked an explosive temper that often raged unexpectedly at his mother.

In November 1951, Kenneth's father, Lawrence, came home to an eerily quiet home. A quick check revealed the horrifying reason: His wife was dead in the master bedroom, stabbed and hacked to death with a knife and hatchet; his daughter, also stabbed and hacked, crouched dead in her closet. A doll was tucked in the child's bloody bed.

At first, Kenneth Maurer was thought to have been abducted, but suspicion soon turned to him. The autopsy suggested the blows came from a Boy Scout knife and hatchet.

Authorities launched a nationwide manhunt, and Maurer was reported sighted in California, Mexico and New Jersey. His trial led investigators through Ohio, Tennessee and Florida before growing cold. The FBI put Maurer on the list in February 1952. They nabbed him in January 1953 after tipsters had led agents to Miami, where he lived in a trailer park and worked in a cabinet shop under the name John Arthur Blotz.

Afraid to fly, Maurer was returned by train to Detroit, where he was judged insane and committed to the Ionia State Hospital. He turned up missing in May 1964; a search found his body floating in a hospital reservoir. The cause of death was not established.

Isaie Aldy Beausoleil

When Canadian visitor Rose Tabram was found facedown in a Monroe County culvert in 1949, attention turned to her last-known companion, a bootlegger, armed robber and prison escapee from Ontario.

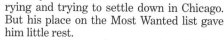

Beausoleil dodged police across the country before marrying and trying to settle down in Chicago. But his place on the Most Wanted list gave him little rest.

Beausoleil was desperate, but by June 1953, he thought he had a plan to avoid the cops. It proved to be his undoing.

Police responded to reports of a pervert in the women's dressing room of a Chicago beach and found a strapping woman. In a squeaky falsetto, the person identified herself as Rita Bennett.

A quick search showed Rita to be the elusive Canadian. Beausoleil's plan was to disguise himself as Rita whenever he left his home.

Returned to Michigan, he was convicted and sentenced to life in prison.

Isaie Beausoleil, above, as Rita Bennett and, right, as himself.

Lloyd Reed Russell

Ohio badman Russell escaped from prison with his brother and fled to Michigan in 1950. He was captured after a series of shoot-outs, including one in which he wounded a police officer.

He drew a 10-year sentence at Marquette, but soon started planning another escape. Russell and six other inmates overpowered guards and sawed their way to freedom through the barred windows.

Russell took off for the West Coast and took part in a series of stickups and safe-crackings in Washington.

His career ended with a police bullet through the head after he and a partner were spotted staking out a Spokane, Wash., supermarket in 1954. He fled on foot, and died trying to outshoot pursuing officers.

Willie Hughes

A three-time loser with a bad temper, Hughes was on the run from Detroit police for a parole violation in June 1960 when he shot and killed his closest friend and fled the state.

He joined the list in March 1961. Hughes led the FBI on a wild chase through seven western states over six months. Dressed as cowboys, agents finally nabbed him in August 1961 as he left a motel in Pocatello, Idaho.

Raymond Lawrence Wyngaard

In 1961, Wyngaard already had an extensive criminal record when he bolted from police while being taken for arraignment on an armed robbery charge.

With an accomplice, Wyngaard roared through Detroit in a three-day crime wave. After looting a gun store for weapons, he robbed a supermarket, shot a police officer, robbed 10 people in a downtown office building, stole three cars and abducted two motorists.

It was not until 1964 that the FBI tracked him down in Madison, Wis., and arrested him outside a pizzeria.

Life on the run was confining. He told G-men: "I felt hemmed in."

Charles and Gordon Ervin

These Michigan twins were authorities' double-trouble nightmare.

In 1954, the twins were facing sentencing for robbing a supermarket when they made a break for freedom. Charles was injured in a 40-foot fall and Gordon was shot.

Bundled off to prison with 40- to 60-year sentences, they worked their way to trusty status by 1965 with permission to work outside the walls of Jackson prison. One day they failed to return. In April 1967, they made the Top Ten.

Charles was arrested in Canada in July 1967, but Gordon remained on the loose until 1969. A squad of Mounties got their man in a Winnipeg rooming house.

Back in Michigan, officials sent one Ervin to Jackson, the other to Marquette.

Lawrence (Pun) Plamondon

Opposition to the Vietnam War and general social upheaval spawned a new type of target for the FBI. Disaffected and radicalized middle-class young people often proved to be more elusive than the numbskull thugs who formerly made their way onto the Top Ten.

Plamondon, a Traverse City native and the Minister of Defense for the Ann Arbor-based White Panther Party, was among more than a dozen activists charged in a series of bombings of government offices and facilities in Michigan in 1968.

Avoiding the initial sweep, Plamondon

remained at large. In 1970, he was put on the Most Wanted list. Six months later, a police officer in the Upper Peninsula pulled over a van for littering after a beer can was tossed from a window. Inside were Plamondon and fellow Panthers Skip Taube and Jack Forrest.

A chagrined Plamondon, above, explained his littering on a lack of "revolutionary discipline."

Plamondon was acquitted in federal court, but was convicted in state court in 1973 of extortion for threatening a marijuana dealer. After serving a probation sentence, Plamondon moved to western Michigan and dropped out of the public limelight.

Larry Smith

Smith was a convicted robber who was serving a life term in Texas when officials brought him to Michigan to face a charge of murdering a Detroit man. He complained of an injured finger and was taken to the jail ward of a local hospital, from which he escaped in May 1977. He made the FBI list in July, and was caught in Toronto a month later during a routine stop for a traffic violation. He was convicted of murder.

Harry (Taco) Bowman

A tidy, tree-shaded brick house in upscale Grosse Pointe Farms was the unlikely roost for the international president of the Outlaws, a rogue motorcycle club branded by authorities as a massive criminal enterprise. Bowman, whose appearance ranged from raffish bearded biker to neatly barbered suburbanite, dropped from sight when federal agents raided the group's Detroit clubhouse in 1997. He was named in a federal indictment alleging murders, bombings, drug dealing, racketeering and conspiracy.

He was placed on the Most Wanted list in 1998, but managed to avoid arrest for another year. In 1999, tipsters alerted authorities that he was hiding out in Sterling Heights. FBI agents, a SWAT team and local police surrounded the house. Bowman surrendered after a brief standoff.

Out-of-town Most-Wanted fugitives captured in southeast Michigan

John Thomas Hill

Hill, right, was a foul-tempered alcoholic who participated in the 1951 robbery of a Maryland store and the ax murder of the owner. He turned up in Hamtramck, where a resident saw his mug on a wanted flyer. Agents crashed through the door of his hideout while he slept.

Edwin Sanford Garrison

A math whiz, career criminal and mob guy, Garrison was an accomplice of notorious New York numbers boss Dutch Schultz. In 1952, Garrison was serving a life term in Alabama when he and 11 inmates broke out. He ended up in Detroit, where FBI agents and cops collared him uneventfully in 1953.

Thomas Viola

A hit man for the Ohio mob, Viola was in prison for the rubout of a Youngstown numbers chieftain. Fourteen years later, he was considered a model prisoner until he escaped from the prison's honors area. With dyed hair and new mustache, he settled down in Detroit with a manicurist girlfriend, but authorities got him in 1961 after a Detroiter recognized his photo in a magazine three months after he joined the list.

Jimmy Lewis Parker

Sentenced to life in North Carolina in 1961 for the murders of his in-laws and the kidnapping of a family of four, Parker busted out of prison in 1964. The FBI found him in a Detroit apartment, where they arrested him without resistance.

Levi Washington

A drug dealer and bank robber, Washington also was charged with robbing a church. He escaped from jail in Chicago in 1968, and fled to Jackson, where he got in more trouble for another bank robbery, plus the bombing of Jackson City Hall, which turned out to be a planned diversion for the robbery that went awry. In July 1969, Washington and his accomplices were headed to trial in the Detroit federal building when they attempted to escape. With U.S. Marshal's guns blazing, one prisoner and three bystanders were wounded. Washington was caught in the building's basement.

Motor City is burning

An 1805 fire destroyed almost everything in Detroit, but no one was killed.

Detroit's first 100 years weren't without calamity, considering the main resource used for structures: Build with wood, have a bucket nearby. The first church in the fledgling fort burned soon after it opened. And fire was a weapon various Indian groups used to assault the stockade.

Here are the most famous blasts and fires since 1800:

MAYHEM

Burton Historical Collection

The whole town

June 11, 1805 — Sparks from a tobacco pipe lit hay in a small stable. The resulting inferno consumed more than 150 buildings. "In the course of three hours . . . nothing was to be seen of the city except a mass of burning coals and chimney tops stretching like pyramids in the air," wrote the Rev. John Dilhet. None of the city's 1,500 people were killed.

The riverfront

May 9, 1848 — A blaze from the river up Woodward to Jefferson destroyed more buildings than the fire of 1805. But this time, the rest of the town was spared — and, again, no one was killed.

Detroit and Milwaukee Depot

April 26, 1866 — At 10 p.m., leaking naphtha barrels exploded at a rail terminal. The terminal, a parked train loaded with sleeping passengers, 73 freight cars, piles of grain and potatoes and 210,000 staves were consumed. The fire struck the steamer Windsor and severed its lines, causing it to float eerily down the river as it burned. Reported the Free Press, "Huge, lurid flames forking and branching out in all directions shot upward, wrapping the surrounding buildings in their terrible embrace, then roiling and roaring like some giant Cyclopean forge." The death toll: 21.

The Edson-Moore fire

Nov. 23, 1893 — The Edson-Moore Wholesale Drygoods Store was one of the biggest in Michigan, a five-story structure at E. Jefferson and Bates. The fire broke out at 1 p.m. Most employees and customers escaped, but seven workers were trapped on the top floor. A brave elevator boy ascended through the smoke, calling for the men, but he returned to the first floor alone. Five of the men died in the flames. Two died when they fell to the street from smoke-filled windows as hundreds of people watched. City inspectors had ruled the building did not need fire escapes.

A firefighters' nightmare

Oct. 5, 1894 — The Keenan & Jahn furniture store on Woodward Avenue downtown collapsed shortly after fire companies arrived with their horse-drawn rigs to fight a blaze that began in its basement. About 20 men were trapped. Their horrified colleagues rushed into the ruins and began digging before the dust had settled. Five firefighters and one spectator died.

The deadliest story

Nov. 6, 1895 — The Detroit Journal was preparing to go to press with the story of the previous day's re-election of Mayor Hazen Pingree. Newsboys lined up outside the five-story Journal at Larned and Shelby, waiting for papers. About 9 a.m., a boiler explosion ripped through the building, showering the street with bricks and timber, and igniting it. The death toll: 37. Most were carried by the falling floors into the basement, where an electric wire ignited the ruins.

Police arrested building engineer Thomas Thompson, who according to the Free Press, was "in the habit of leaving his engine and boilers and visiting the saloons in the neighborhood."

The Journal moved into an unoccupied church at Fort and Wayne and was absorbed by the Detroit News in 1922.

D.M. Ferry Seed Co.

Jan. 1, 1901 — A spectacular New Year's Day fire destroyed the five-story seed company that was one of Detroit's best-known businesses. Ferry Seed occupied the entire block at Brush and Lafayette. It collapsed after burning for hours. One firefighter, Lt. Richard Filban, died after he fell from a 90-foot ladder. The origin was never established. Damage was put at $1.5 million.

Penberthy Injector Plant

Nov. 26, 1901 — A boiler explosion at this sprawling industrial site at Brooklyn and Abbott left 30 people dead and dozens injured. The plant burned after the explosion, and hundreds of rescuers combed the ruins for victims. From his bed at Grace Hospital, chief plant engineer Samuel Riley — his body scalded from head to foot by steam — said: "It seems like a terrible dream."

Fields and Fyfe building

March 5, 1917 — Five firefighters died when the five-story structure on Woodward in the central business district collapsed during a fire. "There wasn't the slightest warning," said Chief Timothy Callahan. "The floors slid down with a rush, like a snowslide from a steep roof."

Briggs plant

April 23, 1927 — The ruins were searched for days. Eventually, 21 people were found dead. The paint shop of the auto body plant, at Harper and Russell, sustained $3 million in property loss. Authorities said 200,000 people gathered to watch the blaze and salvage efforts. Officials credited firefighters from preventing the flames from spreading throughout the congested industrial district. The cause was a spark that ignited flammable chemicals.

Study Club

Sept. 20, 1929 — Panic swept a second-floor dining room as flames engulfed this speakeasy/dance hall named the Study Club at 65 E. Vernor — a spot where the Fisher Freeway now runs. About 200 patrons were inside. The death toll: 22.

Afterward, the city passed stricter fire-safety laws. The owner was acquitted of manslaughter. Investigators believed the cause was a discarded cigarette.

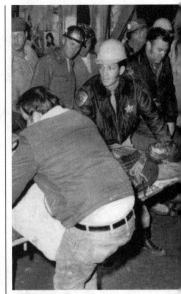

Free Press file photo
Rescue efforts at the tunnel.

Port Huron Tunnel

Dec. 11, 1971 —
A gas explosion killed 22 workers in a water intake tunnel under construction by the Detroit Water Department. The tunnel stretched 220 feet under Lake Huron. Lack of proper ventilation was blamed in the $120-million project, which was nearly complete when the explosion took place. The blast, at 3:11 p.m., blew debris out both ends of the tunnel. Survivors said the blast sounded like a sonic boom. Victims were mangled beyond recognition.

MAYHEM

A homeless man was sentenced to life in prison for the arson fire at an abandoned factory that killed three firefighters in 1987.

MAYHEM

Export Box and Sealer Co.

Aug. 13, 1945 — A fast-moving fire caused employees to jump from the windows, their clothes aflame. Some were trampled; others smashed through a large plate-glass window on the ground floor of the building at Grand River and Hancock. Death toll: 15.

GM Transmission plant

Aug. 12, 1953 — Four died in the Livonia fire that caused $50 million in damage, more than five times the total fire loss in the previous year. The fire in the massive facility at Plymouth and Middlebelt raged for hours, attracting 25,000 onlookers. Black smoke was seen in Warren, 20 miles away. The fire was caused when a spark from a welder's torch ignited a pool of oil. The flames raced along the trail of oil and ignited a vat of cleaning chemicals, which exploded.

Ford Rotunda

Nov. 9, 1962 — Built for the 1934 Chicago World's Fair and reassembled in 1936, Ford Motor Co.'s round-shaped exhibition hall on Schaefer Road in Dearborn was one of the nation's top tourist attractions. From 1953 to 1961, the Rotunda mounted an extravagant Christmas display that thrilled Detroiters. Designed to look like a stack of automotive gears from above, the Rotunda was 212 feet in diameter and nearly 12 stories tall. It also had an interior courtyard that held one of the first geodesic domes engineered by architect R. Buckminister Fuller. Workers repairing the roof started a fire that left the Rotunda in ruins. No one was injured.

Buhl Building

June 11, 1982 — Robert Harrington, armed with a shotgun, .22 pistol and a jar of gasoline went to an eighth-floor law office looking for an insurance settlement check. When he was turned away, he started shooting, then poured the gasoline on the floor and ignited it. The blaze forced some people to jump from windows several floors above the roof of a lower portion of the building. Firefighters stacked ladders to reach some trapped workers. Law student Eve August, 24, died; a man was left paralyzed; 30 others were wounded. Harrington was convicted of murder.

House in Canton Township

Dec. 22, 1990 — A Christmas tree in a Proctor Road home burst into flames, igniting the house. Martin Dell'Orco, 38, died trying to save his children. Bonnie, 12; Sara, 9; Katie, 8; twins Megan and Michael, 5, and Robert, 4, also died.

Warehouse fire

March 12, 1987 — Three firefighters were killed and six were injured fighting a five-alarm arson blaze at an abandoned factory along the Jeffries Freeway, south of Warren. Flames spread to an adjacent structure, Continental Paper & Supply Co. The victims were Lt. Paul Schimeck, a 26-year veteran; Lt. David Lau, a 31-year veteran, and Trial Firefighter Larry McDonald Jr., 24, who was to receive his badge in less than two weeks. A homeless man was sentenced to life in prison for starting the fire.

Free Press file photo

A firefighter mops up after the Pingree Street blaze that killed 10 people in 1992.

Pingree Street Group Home

June 2, 1992 — Ten mentally impaired people died. The operators of what authorities called an unlicensed adult group home had a history of safety violations.

2258 Mack

Feb. 17, 1993 — Leroy Lyons had crawled underneath his 130-year-old home and applied a lighted torch to exposed pipes, believing they were frozen. He didn't know the city had turned off his water that morning because of unpaid bills. Smoldering embers from his thawing attempt led to a fire that ignited while Lyons and Shereese Williams, both unemployed, were scavenging abandoned buildings for scrap they could sell to support their children. Their seven children died in the fire; bars to protect the house from thieves prevented them from fleeing. Lyons and Williams were acquitted of involuntary manslaughter by a jury whose members shook their hands after the trial. They had suffered enough, jurors said. "We loved our kids. We did the best we could," said Williams.

CARLOS OSORIO/Associated Press

Rouge plant

Feb. 1, 1999 — A boiler explosion in the sprawling Ford plant killed six workers and injured 14. Estimates said the insurance loss could reach $1 billion, one of the costliest blasts in U.S. history.

State investigators later said Ford officials had been warned for years about safety problems, but did nothing to solve them. The state fined Ford $1.5 million for violations, the largest state fine ever for violations of worker-safety laws. Ford also agreed to pay up to $5.5 million to promote worker safety, fund medical burn research and establish scholarships. Under the agreement, though, Ford admitted no fault. Dearborn Fire Marshal Richard Polcyn said miscommunication among workers led to the blast. Polcyn said a valve on a natural gas line that led to boiler No. 6 was left open, allowing gas to build up for two minutes before exploding.

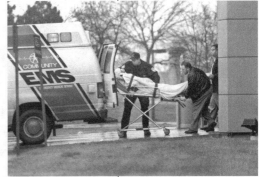

GABRIEL B. TAIT/Detroit Free Press

EMS technicians rush a victim of the Rouge plant explosion into an ambulance. Below: Smoke billows from the generating plant at the Rouge complex.

MAYHEM

Devil's Night: A history

Detroit youngsters have been pulling pranks on the night before Halloween since the 1890s, and that eve was known as Devil's Night for most of the 20th Century.

For decades, though, the worst you could expect on Oct. 30 was a broken window or a false alarm. In 1963, police reported nearly 400 incidents of malicious destruction of property, including one case of what was called "major vandalism" — five broken windows in Courville School on St. Aubin.

In 1970, vandals forced several city buses out of service by smashing their windows with rocks. And the fire department reported nearly 300 false alarms in 1970, about 200 of them turned in at street-corner fire boxes, which subsequently were phased out.

The flare-up

In the early 1980s, a wave of arson fires began sweeping Detroit during the 3-day period of Halloween. So many fires were set in abandoned homes and factories and in garbage bins — especially on Devil's Night — that television news crews from around the world would descend each year on Detroit to record the madness. Buildings were set ablaze by juvenile pranksters, pyromaniacs, neighbors settling disputes or slumlords trying to collect insurance.

City officials denied a significant problem until 1984, the year of the worst Devil's Night, with 297 officially recorded fires. About 65 fires of all sizes break out in an average 24-hour period in Detroit.

Beginning in 1986, the city set a dusk-to-dawn curfew for juveniles and, in later years, instituted a juvenile night court to process violators. Mayor Coleman Young also mobilized 5,000 city employees and 5,500 volunteers in 1986 to patrol the city. It wasn't enough. Fires

Devil's Night 1987: Fire engulfs an abandoned house on Iroquois near Harper.

Devil's Night 1990: Neighbors, above, watch a house burn on Gray Avenue. Right: Devil's Night 1991: James Stokes, 50, uses a garden hose when overwhelmed firefighters are late arriving at a garage fire next to his house on Seneca.

MAYHEM

Detroit fires

Fires during the Halloween period in Detroit, by year.

Year	Fires
1984	810
1985	479
1986	386
1987	290
1988	229
1989	223
1990	281
1991	156
1992	167
1993	155
1994	354
1995	158
1996	142 (including 11 storm-related fires)
1997	168
1998	155
1999	167

SOURCE: DETROIT FIRE DEPARTMENT.

blazed across the city.

Detroit drew hundreds of "fire bugs" from around the world who wanted to see a city set itself on fire. Off-duty firefighters from other cities arrived with their gear to help out. Each year, the city stepped up its anti-arson campaign, enlisting more volunteers.

In 1989, Young ordered the fire department to stop including trash fires during the Halloween period in the final tally, which reduced the official totals. By 1992, the city began making headway, enlisting up to 45,000 citizen volunteers to augment the city workforce. They renamed the night before Halloween Angel's Night.

Apparently believing the worst was over when he took office, Mayor Dennis Archer dropped his guard for his first Devil's Night, in 1994. He failed to organize a strong community effort, and the arsons surged again. But in 1995, a cooperative effort of state and local agencies, including Wayne County Juvenile Court and the Michigan Family Independence Agency, helped bring a measure of control.

By 1999, fewer fires were recorded during the 3-day Halloween period than on a normal night in Detroit.

Detroit Fire Department

Firefighters... 1,221
Engine houses... 46
Vehicles.. 297
Runs in 1999 26,328
(including 12,087 false alarms)
Special runs and EMS runs............. 69,636
Hydrants 30,426
Estimated loss of property
to fires in 1998............................ $294 million

History

From 1701 to the Civil War, fire protection in Detroit was left to citizens. Volunteers fought fires — and sometimes each other — in the years before the city organized its paid fire department.

In 1778, the British brought to Detroit the first firefighting machine, a hand-operated tub that had to be filled by buckets carried from the river. After the Americans took over and Detroit grew during the early 1800s, ordinances required residents and storekeepers to keep leather buckets and ladders on hand to help extinguish fires. Chimneys had to be swept on a regular basis, and all men had to turn out upon the cry of "FIRE!"

Volunteer companies began to form around fire halls, where members held balls, organized parades and skill contests. To be a volunteer firefighter in Detroit in the 1830s and 1840s was to be part of one of the city's elite clubs. The firefighters wore red shirts, black pantaloons and silver helmets and were considered the city's dashing young men. The companies also became a force in local politics.

Companies gave themselves such names as "Protection No. 1" and "Lafayette No. 4" and often sabotaged competitors in their frenzied attempts to be first at a fire. By the 1830s, wooden pipes from Jefferson Avenue reservoirs began to provide water to city neighborhoods. In the winter, manure was packed around the wooden hydrants to keep the water flowing.

The Legislature established a fire commission and a paid fire department in 1867. Horses hauled firefighters and engines through the streets during the late 19th Century and early 20th Century. Horses were used until 1922; some engine houses in Detroit still have haylofts and barns.

As its population has dropped, the city has taken 18 rigs out of service since 1974 and trimmed the force by 470 employees.

In 1988, **Harold Watkins** became Detroit's first black fire chief, and later Mayor Dennis Archer appointed him fire commissioner, the department's top civilian job.

SOURCES: FREE PRESS; "DETROIT FIRE HISTORICAL RECORD," BY CLARENCE WOODARD.

MAYHEM

> # "I wasn't allowed to eat with the other firemen."
> — Marcena Taylor

Civil Defense volunteers pose with then-Sgt. Marcena Taylor in front of Engine Co. 34's quarters in the early 1950s.

Free Press file photo

Free Press file photo
Marcena Taylor, one of the first black firefighters in Detroit and the first to make battalion chief, in front of Engine Co. 34 after his retirement.

Diversity

Integrating the Detroit Fire Department was hard work. When Marcena Taylor reported for his first day of work, a small riot broke out. Taylor was one of the first black men hired by the department. The arrival of Taylor and anther black rookie one morning in 1938 brought out about 200 angry neighbors who blocked the entrance to the engine house on Livernois near Warren. The standoff lasted for hours until police dispersed the mob and allowed Taylor to start a career that lasted 33 years, culminating in his being named the department's first black battalion chief in 1969.

"I wasn't allowed to eat with the other firemen," Taylor recalled in a 1988 interview. "I wasn't allowed to use the bathroom facilities. I wasn't allowed to sleep in the same room."

It took 10 years for the fire union to make him a member. Taylor retired in 1971 and died in 1994.

The Detroit Fire Department is unusual among big-city departments in that members rise through the ranks by seniority only. In other words, firefighters' promotions to sergeant, lieutenant, captain and chief are governed by the retirements or deaths of members who joined the department before them. In other large departments, seniority is not the only factor. Promotions are based on test scores, other measurements of merit, politics — and how long a firefighter has been on the job.

Aircraft disasters

▶ **Nov. 11, 1918:** On the same day World War I ended, one of four stunt planes swooping low over celebrating crowds downtown ripped into the flagpole atop the Fife Building at Grand Circus Park. The plane crashed, killing the pilot.

▶ **June 23, 1948:** Two Navy pilots died and two Detroiters were injured when two Navy planes collided over Benson Street near McDougall and Gratiot during Aviation Week. The planes were part of a formation of seven aircraft performing a flyover of Briggs (later, Tiger) Stadium in a "W" to honor Tiger outfielder Dick Wakefield, who had served as a naval air cadet during the war. The falling debris destroyed three homes and part of a small factory.

▶ **Nov. 19, 1949:** A DC3 cargo plane crashed into a home at 12140 Flanders in Detroit while attempting to land at City Airport. Two crew members were killed, as was one man on the ground.

▶ **Oct. 24, 1958:** A British Royal Air Force bomber jet — trailing smoke and flame and its pilot calling out "mayday" — crashed on Ashland Avenue near the Detroit River on the city's far east side. All six crew members were killed. Three homes were destroyed and about 40 others were damaged. Wreckage was scattered into nearby Grosse Pointe. No one on the ground was killed; two women were treated for burns.

The four-engine delta-winged plane was on a training mission, flying from Lincolnshire, England, to Lincoln, Neb. Crippled, it dived from 45,000 feet, passing over hospitals and schools on its path to the ground. The impact was so hard that searchers dug 70 feet in an unsuccessful effort to find the plane's cockpit. The largest piece of wreckage found was a six-foot section of wing that landed on a porch.

▶ **May 8, 1959:** An Air National Guard F84 fighter crashed in the middle of Northville, narrowly missing two schools and seriously burning two of the police chief's children. The pilot parachuted to safety.

▶ **Jan. 19, 1979:** The first fatal accident at Metro Airport. A private Lear jet crashed on landing, killing six people.

▶ **March 4, 1987:** A Spanish-built CASA 212 Series 200 Aviocar, operated by Fischer Bros. Aviation of Galion, Ohio, for Northwest Airlines crashed as it approached its runway. Nine people died. The twin turbine-powered propeller plane bounced onto a taxiway. Witnesses said the plane then flipped and exploded as it slid into food-service trucks and baggage equipment and stopped just 15 yards from a passenger terminal.

▶ **Jan. 1, 1983:** A United Airlines DC8 cargo plane crashed and burned on take-off from Metro Airport, killing the three crew members. The plane, carrying mail, auto parts and a small amount of radioactive material, crashed in a field near Wayne and North Line roads in Romulus. An improperly set stabilizer was blamed, and investigators said an unqualified crew member was flying the plane.

▶ **June 13, 1984:** A USAir DC9 carrying 50 passengers and a crew of five crash-landed on a Metro Airport runway after trying to abort a landing because of an approaching storm. Five people were injured, one seriously, as the plane skidded on its belly into a grassy area.

▶ **Aug. 16, 1987:** As the McDonnell Douglas MD80 left Metro Airport en route to Phoenix, its left wing dipped and clipped a light pole. The jet struck another light pole and slashed the roof edge of an Avis car-rental building before breaking in a huge fireball as it slammed into Middlebelt near I-94. The crash killed 154 people on board and two on the ground. Passenger Cecelia Cichan, a 4-year-old reportedly saved by the body of her 33-year-old mother, Paula Ciamaichela Cichan, survived. Cecelia suffered broken bones and burns on 30 percent of her body. An aunt and

Associated Press

Cecelia Cichan, 4, is the only survivor of Northwest Flight 255. Her parents were among the 156 people killed when the plane crashed on Middlebelt near I-94 in 1987. Relatives in Alabama raised her.

MAYHEM

A portion of Flight 255 sits on Middlebelt Road near the I-94 overpass.

RICHARD LEE/Detroit Free Press

➤ **March 10, 1988:** A twin-engine cargo plane plunged into a two-story home on Toepfer in Warren, about three miles northwest of Detroit City Airport, exploding and killing a young couple and the pilot. The couple's three young daughters were rescued.

➤ **Jan. 9, 1997:** Comair's Detroit-bound flight 3272 from Cincinnati nose-dived into the ground in Monroe County, killing all 29 people aboard. The National Transportation Safety Board said that the Federal Aviation Administration should have adopted more stringent rules for flying in icy conditions. The NTSB faulted Comair's pilots for flying too slowly and for not deicing the wings.

uncle in Alabama have raised her and kept her shielded from most publicity.

The National Transportation Safety Board attributed the crash to the crew's failure to ensure that the jet's wing flaps and slats were properly extended for takeoff. It noted that the pilots were preoccupied with meeting their schedule, possible wind shear, responding to an airport order to use a different runway, and chatting with a flight attendant when they should have been performing the safety checklist. Once airborne, the report said, the crew had time to recover but apparently did not recognize the cause of the problem. The Air Line Pilots Association, defending the crew, suggested that the flaps may have malfunctioned.

The crash was the worst air disaster in Michigan, and the third-worst in U.S. aviation history.

➤ **July 31, 1999:** A Beech King Air 65A90 twin-engine plane crashed after takeoff from Marine City Airport and killed nine skydivers and their pilot. The plane took off about 8:20 a.m. from the airport in Cottrellville Township. It climbed 200 feet before tilting 60 degrees to the left and crashing into a field. Investigators said all the skydivers were thrown from the plane on impact. The pilot was found in the cockpit.

The resting place of Comair Flight 3272 in a field near Monroe in 1997.

KIRTHMON F. DOZIER/Detroit Free Press

MAYHEM

Mobocracy

No single incident in Detroit's past defines the region for contemporary metro Detroiters like the 1967 riot. That's because it is still fresh in many minds and because it was the most deadly riot in U.S. history until the Los Angeles insurrection of 1992.

But '67 was just one of many riots in Detroit. From 1849 to 1863, there were 12 major riots in Detroit. Over the decades, Detroiters rioted over brothels, runaway slaves, streetcars and ditch-diggers' pay, among other issues. The following is a summary of the most significant melees.

1833

On June 17, a crowd of black Detroiters gathered at Wayne County Sheriff John Wilson's jail protesting a court verdict that would return a fugitive slave couple to Kentucky. Black people accounted for 138 of 5,000 Detroiters in 1833. Runaway-slave hunters came to Detroit looking for Thornton and Ruth Blackburn, who had fled their Kentucky owner. A court ruled the slave hunters could seize the Blackburns, citing the 1793 Fugitive Slave Act. The crowd brought weapons determined to keep the Blackburns from being returned. A day earlier, however, a black woman visited Ruth Blackburn in jail and swapped clothing with her, allowing Ruth Blackburn to escape. She quickly fled to Windsor, Canada.

As Wilson brought Thornton Blackburn out to transport him to a waiting steamer, he was attacked and Blackburn escaped, eventually reaching Windsor, too. Wilson suffered a fractured skull during the melee and died within a year. Thirty blacks were arrested for conspiring to free the Blackburns. White Detroiters demanded controls on black residents. Soon, a 9 p.m. curfew for black people was issued and blacks were prohibited from docking their boats. A volunteer police patrol also was organized. The Blackburns lived out their lives in relative peace and prosperity in Canada.

Dec. 13, 1849

More than 60 middle-class Detroiters, some armed with crowbars, ripped up railroad tracks belonging to the Detroit and Pontiac Railroad that ran along Gratiot. The rioters were shop owners who had been frustrated in their attempts to have the city do away with the noisy and dirty trains from the fronts of their stores. When the track was re-laid, a mob tore it up again. Finally, the tracks were rerouted in 1852.

1850s

Using violence to fight vice was common in pre-Civil War America, and so-called whore-house riots broke out frequently in Detroit after 1834. Stone-throwing mobs attacked brothels, especially those in predominately German neighborhoods that catered to black men. Between 1855 and 1859, though, the mob violence in Detroit escalated. Historian John Schneider counted 12 major incidents in which at least 17 brothels were either seriously damaged or destroyed. All of the attacks took place on the east side, near today's intersection of the Chrysler Freeway and Gratiot, and next to the old railroad tracks along Dequindre. Usually from 50 to 300 rioters would order out the prostitutes and their customers and then smash the furnishings and sometimes torch the buildings.

1863

Stirred into a racist frenzy by what critics called the Negrophobic Free Press, crowds of white people gathered in front of city hall on March 6 to await the verdict in the trial of William Faulkner, a black man accused of molesting two girls, one white and one black. He was convicted and sentenced to 10 years in prison. Soldiers escorted Faulkner to the jail at Beaubien near Gratiot. But as a crowd of thousands surged toward them, the soldiers fired, killing one person.

The mob then attacked the nearby black neighborhood, assaulting black residents along Beaubien, St. Antoine, Fort and Lafayette. One man died. Rioters burned some 30 buildings, and the crowd urged firefighters not to put water on the homes of blacks.

Years later, the girls admitted they had lied; Faulkner was freed after serving five years.

1891

The operation of Detroit's privately owned trolley system was one of the most contentious public issues in the late 19th Century. A strike on April 23 by rail workers led to three days of rioting "of crowds of workers and citizens, in a vengeful mood, who wreaked havoc on the City Railway," wrote historian Melvin Holli. Throngs on Michigan, Gratiot, Woodward and other main streets stoned trolley cars, unhitched horses, ripped up rails and fought police with paving stones and fists. By Day 3, barricades on tracks paralyzed

> Ruth Blackburn, a captured runaway slave, escaped when a visitor to her jail cell swapped clothes with her. Freedom for Ruth, and her husband Thornton Blackburn, brought hardships for black residents in Detroit.

MAYHEM

1934

On Oct. 10, Game 7 of the World Series, the Tigers vs. St. Louis Cardinals at Navin Field, sixth inning: Joe Medwick tripled, slid into third, where the Tigers' third baseman Marv Owen stepped on him. Intentional? It appeared that way when Medwick, still on the ground, kicked at Owen's legs with his spikes. The umpire, players and coaches prevented a fight. But when Medwick returned to left field at the bottom of the sixth, Tigers fans pelted him with fruit, bottles and garbage. After 17 minutes of hurling, order was restored when Baseball Commissioner Kenesaw Mountain Landis ordered Medwick out of the game. "Bleacher fans stage most tumultuous riot ever seen in a World Series game," proclaimed the Free Press. The Tigers lost the game, 11-0, and the series.

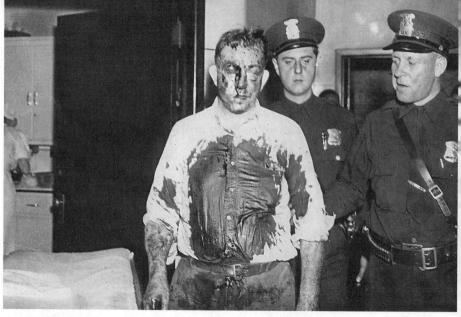

A victim of the 1943 riot. Hundreds were injured. Thirty-four people died: 25 blacks and 9 whites.

Detroit's transit. Among the rioters: future mayor and U.S. Sen. James Couzens. Clothier J. L. Hudson collected contributions for the strikers and their families. Another citywide trolley riot broke out in 1918.

1894

An economic depression in the 1890s strained relations between the city's growing ethnic communities and Detroit's leaders and the wealthy. So workers on an excavation project for the Water Board were quickly angered April 18, 1894, when the board changed its pay plan from a wage system to piece work. About 500 men at the work site on East Jefferson near Conner, mostly Polish immigrants, charged Sheriff C.P. Collins, his deputies and anybody who appeared well dressed. Deputies opened fire. Three people were killed and more than a dozen were injured, including Collins, who was badly beaten about the head.

1942

More than 1,000 people gathered at Ryan and Nevada on Feb. 28 to protest a black family moving into the newly built Sojourner Truth housing project. The project had been built for black people working in war plants, but the buildings had been erected in a predominately white neighborhood. Police battled rioters for several hours; there were no deaths, but dozens of injuries. Family members delayed their moves for several days. When they finally entered their new homes, it was without incident.

Cars are overturned on Woodward Avenue, near Mack Avenue, during the 1943 riot.

1943

Detroit was considered a tinderbox ready to explode in racial strife. It was a city with little room; war workers migrating from Southern states brought the city's occupancy rate to nearly 100 percent. Those new workers numbered about 255,000, both black and white, mostly from the South. Incidents between races had been common for months. On June 20, a hot, humid Sunday, more than 100,000 people jammed Belle Isle. Interracial brawls broke out across the island and on the bridge. A rumor rapidly spread to black clubs and bars, by Paradise Valley and Hastings Street just east of downtown, that white sailors had thrown a black woman and her baby off the bridge. By midnight, blacks smashed the windows of white-owned stores along Hastings. The riot continued two more days.

Whites pulled blacks off buses and out of cars along Woodward near Orchestra Hall and beat them senseless. Federal troops and police finally brought order. The toll: 34 dead — 25 blacks, nine whites. Seventeen of the 25 blacks were killed by police. No whites were killed by police. Hundreds were injured and more than 1,800 arrested. Of those arrested facing formal charges, 970 were black and 212 were white, which experts say suggests police concentrated on taking blacks into custody. It was one of the worst civil disturbances in the United States since New York's Civil War draft riots in which about 1,000 people were killed. A commission led by an army general investigated the rioting and concluded police in many cases overreacted.

1975

The white owner of Bob Bolton's Lounge on Livernois near Fenkell shot and killed a black 18-year-old he said was about to steal a car. Crowds of protesters gathered for two nights beginning July 28. There was looting and rock throwing, and demonstrators at one point rammed the bar's front door with a car. Mayor Coleman Young, who walked the streets for hours, was credited with helping to calm the crowds.

1984

The Tigers beat the San Diego Padres on Oct. 14 to take the World Series in five games. But the victory celebration left one man dead,

The widely seen symbol of the 1984 World Series rioting: Bubba Helms and the burning police car.

scores injured, three women reportedly raped, stores looted, one police car torched and four others severely damaged. Police spokesman Lt. Fred Williams blamed the violence on "young suburbanites coming into Detroit and wreaking havoc." Others said many injuries were caused by free-swinging police officers who allegedly struck out indiscriminately while trying to control the estimated 100,000 people who clogged downtown streets. Police said 34 people were arrested for charges that included assault, robbery and disorderly conduct. At one point, about 50 riot-equipped police chased a crowd estimated at 6,000 to 10,000 up Woodward Avenue from Hart Plaza. The riot was widely reported around the world, accompanied by the Associated Press photo of Kenneth (Bubba) Helms, 17, of Lincoln Park, who leaped in front of the burning police car at Michigan and Trumbull, holding a Tiger pennant. "I was jumping in front of every camera I could," said Helms, who, with his friends, had drunk "a fifth of Jim Beam, smoked a few bad ones" and gone downtown to join what began as a mass party.

SOURCES: FREE PRESS; "WHO IS THE CHURCH? CONFLICT IN A POLISH IMMIGRANT PARISH IN LATE NINETEENTH-CENTURY DETROIT," BY LESLIE WOODCOCK-TENTLER, IN COMPARATIVE STUDIES IN SOCIETY AND HISTORY, APRIL 1983; "VIOLENCE IN THE MOTOR CITY: THE CAVANAGH ADMINISTRATION, RACE RELATIONS, AND THE DETROIT RIOT OF 1967" BY SIDNEY FINE; "LAYERED VIOLENCE, THE DETROIT RIOTERS OF 1943" BY DOMINIC CAPECI JR. AND MARTHA WILKERSON; "THE DETROIT RIOT OF 1943," BY HARVEY SITKOFF, IN MICHIGAN HISTORY, FALL 1969; "REFORM IN DETROIT: HAZEN PINGREE AND URBAN POLITICS," BY MELVIN HOLLI; "DETROIT AND THE PROBLEM OF DISORDER: THE RIOT OF 1863," BY JOHN SCHNEIDER IN MICHIGAN HISTORY, SPRING 1974; "BEFORE THE GHETTO: BLACK DETROIT IN THE 19TH CENTURY," BY DAVID KATZMAN; "URBANIZATION AND THE MAINTENANCE OF ORDER IN DETROIT, 18241847," BY JOHN SCHNEIDER, IN MICHIGAN HISTORY, FALL 1976; "DETROIT AND THE PROBLEM OF ORDER, 1830-1880," BY JOHN SCHNEIDER.

MAYHEM

Free Press file photo

Police surround Bob Bolton's, the Livernois Avenue bar whose owner sparked two nights of disturbances in 1975.

1967: Detroit's worst week

July 23, a Sunday morning

Police raided a private club above a print shop on the east side of 12th Street south of Clairmount, about an hour before daylight. The club called itself the United Civic League for Community Action. But its action was dispensing booze after 2 a.m. In Detroit parlance, it was a blind pig.

A crowd formed as police brought the 82 arrested out of the second-story speakeasy. Someone hurled a brick that smashed the rear window of a police cruiser. Soon, rioters began overwhelming cops at the scene. Reinforcements were few because so many officers were on vacation. There were 193 police officers patrolling the entire city when the riot began.

Rioting and looting spread along 12th Street, then to 14th, Linwood, Dexter and Grand River. By evening, rioting broke out on the east side near Van Dyke and Mack. Gov. George Romney activated the National Guard to help Detroit police and state police, but the guardsmen were poorly trained for quelling urban disturbances. They often overreacted, leading to needless deaths and injuries. Finally, President Lyndon B. Johnson ordered U.S. Army paratroopers from the 82nd and 101st Airborne Divisions to Detroit. By Friday, there were 4,400 Detroit police, 8,000 national guardsmen, 4,700 federal troops and 360 state police patrolling Detroit. Order was restored.

A deep polarization between races grew out of that riot, even though it was not a race riot. In fact, the first person killed was a white looter, Walter Grzanka, 45. He was shot by the owner of a market on Fourth Street. Police found nine pairs of shoelaces, four packages of tobacco and had seen cigars in Grzanka's pockets.

The aftermath of the 1967 riot on a west side block

Some social commentators said the race factor was at play, however, because nearly all the rioters were black and nearly all the police and guardsmen were white. Army paratroops were integrated.

The police officer who made the buy in the blind pig that led to the arrests that led to the riot was Charles Henry. He retired a commander in charge of central narcotics.

The 43 who died

The final death toll from the riots was 33 blacks and 10 whites.

A Free Press investigation found that 30 of the 43 victims had been killed by the police or military. Detroit police shot 18 people; 14 of them were looters. The other four were a sniper, an unconfirmed arsonist and two of three men killed at the Algiers Motel on Woodward Avenue.

At least six victims were killed by the National Guard. In five more cases, the police and National Guard were involved. Four of those five victims were innocent of wrongdoing. Store owners shot and killed two looters.

Private citizens killed three people. Two looters died in a fire. A firefighter and civilian were killed by downed power lines. An Army paratrooper accidentally killed a 19-year-old man; an unknown gunman killed a 23-year-old visitor in the window of a midtown motel; a firefighter was struck by the bullet of either a sniper or a Guardsman; a policeman was shot as a fellow officer struggled with a prisoner, and a third man died in the Algiers Motel.

A cop

Isaiah McKinnon worked from 6 a.m. that Sunday until 2 a.m. the next morning. A two-year veteran cop, he patrolled sections of Detroit with other police and National Guardsmen.

"You could hear the bullets skipping off the tank" he was riding in, he said, "especially at night."

McKinnon was driving home in uniform after riot duty one night in his Mustang convertible, the top down. Suddenly, police shot at his car. He got out with his hands up. The officer who shot said, "Hey, I'm sorry. I didn't know who you were."

All the other cops knew was that McKinnon was young, black and cruising in a riot-torn city.

"I saw things that were ugly and it con-

TONY SPINA/Detroit Free Press

A National Guardsman searches for snipers along Linwood Avenue during the 1967 riot.

"I saw things that were ugly and it convinced me that, to remedy things, it would be better to do it at another level."

— Isaiah McKinnon, former Detroit chief of police

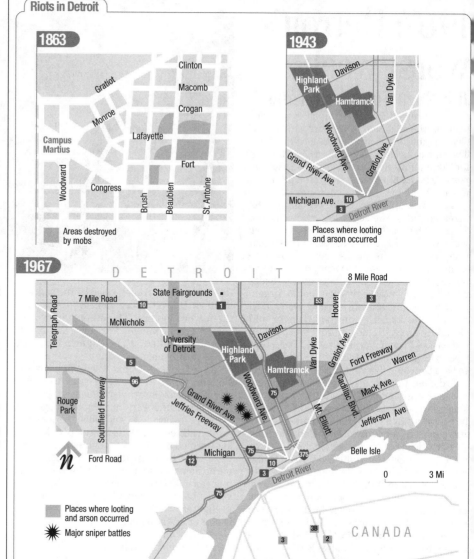

Riots in Detroit

1863

Clinton
Macomb
Crogan
Gratiot
Monroe
Lafayette
Campus Martius
Fort
Woodward
Congress
Brush
Beaubien
St. Antoine

Areas destroyed by mobs

1943

Highland Park
Davison
Hamtramck
Van Dyke
Woodward Ave.
Gratiot Ave.
Grand River Ave.
Michigan Ave. 10
3
Detroit River

Places where looting and arson occurred

1967

D E T R O I T
8 Mile Road
7 Mile Road 10
State Fairgrounds 1
53
Hoover 3
Telegraph Road
McNichols
University of Detroit
Davison
Highland Park
Van Dyke
Gratiot Ave.
Ford Freeway
Warren
5
Southfield Freeway
96
Hamtramck
Cadillac Blvd
Mack Ave.
Woodward Ave.
75
Rouge Park
Grand River Ave.
Jeffries Freeway
Mt. Elliott
Jefferson Ave.
Michigan
75
Belle Isle
Ford Road
12
10
375
N
3
Detroit River
0   3 Mi
75
3B
3   2
CANADA

Places where looting and arson occurred

Major sniper battles

Riot in song

Two songs about the riot have been recorded by at least three different groups. Canadian singer Gordon Lightfoot did "Black Day in July," and John Lee Hooker and the MC5 did slightly different versions of "Motor City is Burning."

➤ **Check out the lyrics in Culture, Chapter 11, page 404**

vinced me that, to remedy things, it would be better to do it at another level."

McKinnon went to college, earning a doctorate in philosophy from Michigan State University in 1981. He was Detroit's chief of police from 1993 to 1997.

A victim

Her name was Tonia Blanding; she was only 4. She lived in a second-floor apartment in a frame dwelling at Euclid and 12th Street. Michigan Guard members said sniper fire from the building was directed at them. They returned fire with a .50-caliber machine gun, an indiscriminate weapon with bullets that easily rip through wooden frame dwellings. Tonia

was shot dead. Her family said the firing began after a family member lit a cigarette and the flash of the match triggered the Guard's response. Police found a spent shell and a box of .38-caliber bullets in the apartment where Tonia was shot. Normal police response to reports of sniper fire would not include blasting the dwelling with a machine gun.

The Algiers Motel incident

Carl Cooper, 17, Fred Temple, 18, and Aubrey Pollard, 19, had minor police records, but there was no hard evidence they were breaking the law nor threatening law enforcement officials on the night of July 26 when police responded to a report of sniping at the motel. Several black men and two white women, with records as prostitutes, were at the motel on Woodward at Virginia Park that night.

Police "just could not stomach the idea of these Negro men in the motel with white girls," said Roy Wilkins of the National Association for the Advancement of Colored People. Police used racial and sexual taunts and brutalized all the people in the motel during a nightmarish and chaotic siege in which officers fired their guns into the floor to pretend some people had been shot to get the others to talk. Two autopsies concluded the three were shot at close range with 12-gauge shotguns. Detroit police officers Ronald August, Robert Paille and David Senak faced a variety of charges related to the killings. Some of the charges were thrown out in a ferocious legal battle that went to the Michigan Supreme Court. August and Paille admitted shooting two of the victims, but called it self-defense. In two trials, no one was convicted.

The numbers

467 injured: 181 civilians, 167 Detroit police, 83 Detroit firefighters, 17 National Guard, 16 State Police, 3 U.S. Army.

7,231 arrested: 6,528 adults, 703 juveniles; 6,407 blacks, 824 whites. The youngest, 10; the oldest, an 82-year-old white man. Half of those arrested had no criminal records. Three percent of the arrested went to trial; half of them were acquitted.

2,509 stores looted or burned: One month after the riot, a city tally showed 388 families homeless or displaced and 412 buildings burned or damaged enough to be demolished. Dollar losses from arson and looting were difficult to pin down, but the revised figures ranged from $40 million to $80 million, a fraction of the original estimate of $500 million. About 27 percent of the stores destroyed in the riot were black-owned. About 1,700 firefighters with 153 pieces of equipment fought the fires. Firefighting help came from 44 communities, including Lansing, Flint and Windsor.

An eyewitness

A 14-year-old Free Press carrier left his Boston Boulevard home at about 5 a.m. to pick up his Sunday papers. He pulled a wagon and was joined by his Airedale, Hamlet. When he reached 12th Street, he saw about 500 people milling in the street, which glittered with broken glass. The carrier's station manager had just been robbed and the father of another paperboy told the carrier he'd better get home fast.

The carrier and Hamlet ran home, burst into the bedroom of his sleeping father: "Dad, I think the riot has begun."

The carrier was former state Supreme Court Justice **Conrad Mallett Jr.** His dad, Conrad Mallett Sr., was an aide to Mayor Jerome Cavanagh the day the riot began.

Mayday!

Disasters on the waters of Detroit

You likely have heard of the Edmund Fitzgerald, the largest freighter ever to sink on the Great Lakes, going down in Lake Superior during a November storm in 1975, with its crew of 29.

The worst storm toll on the Lakes was also in November — a fierce month for navigation because of the seasonal, powerful northwesterly winds. That storm on Nov. 10, 1913, sank 12 vessels, killing 248 people. Waters around Detroit, including the 31-mile Detroit River and Lake St. Clair, haven't been as vulnerable to maritime disasters mostly because of the lake's shallow depth — 27 feet — and the river's closeness to shore. But there have been some:

Guerriere

May 29, 1832: This 75-foot schooner sank in a storm at the mouth of the Detroit River. A woman and her four children died.

Atlantic

Aug. 20, 1852: Built at Detroit, the side-wheel steamer was considered one of the lakes' most majestic and fastest ships. The steamer, jammed with immigrants, collided with the freighter Ogdensburg and sank off of Long Pointe, Ontario, in Lake Erie, while en route to Detroit. At least 150 passengers out of 600 died. The Canadian government has successfully fought attempts to salvage the wreckage.

E.K. Collins

Oct. 8, 1854: This side-wheeler caught fire at the mouth of the Detroit River near Amherstburg, Ontario. At least 23 passengers died.

Fame

Aug. 17, 1858: The Detroit-built, three-masted schooner experienced a star-crossed career. It was struck by lightning twice, stranded twice and sustained two collisions. In 1858, it capsized in a squall in Lake Erie, 6 miles from Monroe. The crew was rescued. The owner's 9-year-old son clung to a plank for 70 hours before he was rescued.

Nile

May 21, 1864: A boiler explosion ripped through the ship as it was docked at Detroit, killing eight crew members. It sank on the spot.

B.B. Jones

May 25, 1871: Sitting at a dock in Port Huron, the Jones' boiler exploded, sending pieces through buildings hundreds of yards away. Seven crew members died.

The captain of the British freighter Montrose, Ralph Eyre-Walker, stands atop his ill-fated ship for a final inspection

Montrose

JULY 30, 1962: A barge, pushed by the tug B.H. Becker, rammed the 444-foot British freighter in the Detroit River under the Ambassador Bridge. The 41 Montrose crew members were saved. The ship rested on its side in about 40 feet of water, drawing huge crowds to the riverfront for weeks. By November 1962, workers succeeded in righting the slime-ridden ship and pumping water from its hull. It was towed to be refitted.

The Mamie and the Garland

July 22, 1880: Returning from an outing in Monroe, the yacht Mamie was smacked by the much larger excursion steamer Garland in the Detroit River near Wyandotte. "That boat is coming unpleasantly near to us," the Rev. Aloysius Bleyenbergh, a priest at Holy Trinity Catholic Church, remarked before the accident. The Garland crushed the yacht. The priest and other parishioners including 14 altar boys were on the Mamie when it was struck.

Seventeen people were killed, including all the acolytes, sexton Thomas Kelly, rectory housekeeper Lizzie Murphy and convent servant Mary Hahn.

The much larger Garland was carrying 1,000 people.

Omar D. Conger

March 26, 1922: The passenger ferry blew up at dock on the Black River and scattered debris over Port Huron. Four people died. The cause was variously reported as a boiler blast or a cargo explosion.

Yantic

Oct. 22, 1929: The three-masted Yantic was built in 1864 to be Abraham Lincoln's presidential yacht. After he was assassinated, the vessel went into Navy service. It survived wars and an excursion to the Arctic, was decommissioned and became part of the now-disbanded Michigan Naval Militia, which used it for training. The Yantic sank, mostly because of age, at dock at the foot of Townsend Avenue. Today the ship's remains rest under Gabriel Richard Park east of the Belle Isle Bridge.

Tashmoo

June 18, 1936: A luxurious, triple-deck side-wheeler, the Tashmoo ferried passengers from Detroit to Tashmoo Park on Harsens Island from 1908 to 1936.

On a moonlight cruise with 1,400 passengers from a Hamtramck social club, the vessel struck a submerged rock, opening a hole in its hull. The captain beached the ship at a Canadian dock near Grosse Ile. As the band played on, the Tashmoo partly sank in 18 feet of water. All passengers were led off safely.

America

Oct. 21, 1941: A tugboat, the America capsized while pulling the B.F. Jones off a sandbar near Belle Isle. Six crew members died.

Noronic

Sept. 17, 1949: The 362-foot passenger ship caught fire while tied up at Toronto's pier No. 9. Of the 119 casualties, at least 25 were Detroiters who had boarded four days earlier when the Noronic stopped in Windsor.

Hydroplane deaths

The 3-mile oval course west of the Belle Isle Bridge and north of the island has claimed three lives during hydroplane races:

Warner Gardner died in the 1968 Gold Cup race when his Miss Eagle Electric crashed at 160 miles per hour.

Chuck Thompson was killed in the 1966 Gold Cup when his Miss Smirnoff hit a wave, went airborne and disintegrated.

Bob Hayward died in 1962 driving Miss Supertest.

Special note: Detroit-born Bill Muncey became hydroplane racing's most successful driver — 62 wins — before he was killed in a race in Acapulco in October 1981 while driving his Atlas Van Lines boat. He was 52. Among his boats that raced in Detroit: Miss Thriftway, Notre Dame and Miss U.S.

Survival on the lake

Sept. 22, 1989: About 8 p.m., Gary Fuson, Mark Ciraulo and Richard Van Hevel were swamped in their 14-foot fishing boat as gale winds surged over Lake St. Clair. Four miles east of the Grosse Pointe Yacht Club, and aided by life vests, the trio began their struggle. Ciraulo, 19, of Sterling Heights and Van Hevel, 20, of Mt. Clemens opted to let winds carry them to the Detroit River. Fuson, 20, of Detroit shot flares into the stormy sky seconds before the boat sank. He opted to swim toward shore. They kept calling to one another, but after 10 minutes, Fuson no longer heard his friends.

Waves reached 6 feet. The water was 66 degrees, chilly enough to cause hypothermia. Fuson kept swimming toward shore, guided by car lights along Jefferson and focused, too, on three gulls that hovered above.

He swam to within 25 feet of the Yacht Club, but current pulled him back into the lake. At 7:42 a.m. — nearly 12 hours after his ordeal began — a boat approached. Fuson raised an arm. Coincidentally, the boaters were two friends and Van Hevel's uncle, searching for the trio. Fuson was pulled on board. He survived.

Ciraulo and Van Hevel drowned, their bodies found near the mouth of the Detroit River.

Death in Vietnam

The following list shows the population of various metro Detroit cities in 1970 during the Vietnam War. The next number shows the U.S. military personnel from that city who died, are missing or are classified as "captured declared dead." The final number is the proportion of deaths by population. The information comes from the National Archives and Record Administration.

Not all cities, and no townships, were listed in the records. During the war, there was considerable public debate over whether poor and working-class youths were shouldering too much of the burden of fighting the war. Wealthier youth often evaded the draft legally by obtaining college deferments.

RICHARD LEE/Detroit Free Press

Vietnam vet Dick Rucker of Waterford finds the name of his cousin on a traveling replica of the Vietnam Veterans Memorial that stopped in Rochester Hills in 1999.

City	1970 pop.	DIA/MIA
Belleville	2,406	7
	1 death per 344 residents	
Utica	3,504	7
	1 death per 501 residents	
Bloomfield Hills	3,672	5
	1 death per 734 residents	
Rockwood	3,225	4
	1 death per 806 residents	
Flat Rock	5,643	7
	1 death per 806 residents	
Mt. Clemens	20,467	23
	1 death per 890 residents	

City	1970 pop.	DIA/MIA
Walled Lake	3,759	4
	1 death per 940 residents	
Wayne	21,054	15
	1 death per 1,404 residents	
Melvindale	13,862	8
	1 death per 1,733 residents	
Hazel Park	23,764	13
	1 death per 1,828 residents	
Pontiac	85,279	45
	1 death per 1,895 residents	
Birmingham	26,170	13
	1 death per 2,013 residents	

AVID F HEISER · DOUGLAS E HOFFMAN · HOMER W HOL
JACKSON · RANDALL L JENKINS · CARL R KECK · ASA MA
ARRY W NEILL · ARTHUR A CALLISTER · RAYMOND NITO R
OMERO · PAUL C RUDY · THEODORE M RUSH · RONALD
OHN J SENOR · KENNETH H SHELLEMAN · LEONARD D SM
TRESSLER Jr · JAMES B WHITE · RAY M WILLIAMS · JERRY R
ISIAH BARNES Jr · RONALD G BAUGHMAN · DONALD C
CASSIDY · THOMAS CLARK · OTIS J DARDEN · ALVIN J DE
T · GORDON D GARDNER · GARY LEE GLEAR · DENNIS J
EN · LESLIE A JERSTAD · LESTER JOHNSON Jr · WILLIAM R L
MICHAEL S MASSONE · WILLIAM H MILLER · RICKEY C C M
USSEN · JOHN R REBITS · ROBERT E SHERLOCK · JAMES E SK
PLE · JOHN T WALLS · DENNIS R WHICKER · DAVID R AUGU
AEL A BARNES · ROBERT E BEAUMONT · BENJAMIN H BINE
H BRUBAKER Jr · LEE E BURNOR · JIMMY O CALL · JAMES D
ANTHONY A BARBARINO · JOHN A DURHAM · ROBERT L E
GILDOW · OTIS GREEN · ANDREW M HAGLAGE · ROBERT K
· DAVID HOWZE Jr · GREGORY J NICCOLI · ANTHONY A K
ANTHONY L QUINN · HAROLD R RICHARDSON · JUAN R
GERALD L THOMAS · HOUSTON F THOMAS · JAMES W T
ALKER · FRANKIE R WILLIAMS · RAY L GOOD · WILLIAM E B
URKHART · JAMES L CLARK · LOUIS J CLEVER · JAMES V DOR
BRUCE B BERNSTEIN · ALVIN GORDON Jr · GERALD J JOH
GARY R HALEY · ROBERT W HAMLIN · TIMOTHY M HARRIN
· WILLIAM C ... ... ACKSON · GARY M JOH
J KMIT · HOME ... DONADO-AG
EY · CLARENCE L ... NEUB
Jr · JOHN E NORDE ...
R · RUSSELL E REINE ...
OHN W SPA ...
DANA L Z ...
RIS · MICH ...
TA · RAFA ...
ER · DON ...
DY N ... · CHA
ROBER ...
ARRETT ...
ARVIS · G ...

Associated Press
An unidentified man at the Vietnam Veterans Memorial in Washington, D.C., in 1997.

City	1970 pop.	DIA/MIA
Dearborn	104,199	48
	1 death per 2,171 residents	
River Rouge	15,947	7
	1 death per 2,278 residents	
Roseville	60,529	25
	1 death per 2,421 residents	
Ecorse	17,515	7
	1 death per 2,502 residents	
Center Line	10,379	4
	1 death per 2,595 residents	
Hamtramck	26,763	10
	1 death per 2,676 residents	
Royal Oak	86,238	32
	1 death per 2,695 residents	
Allen Park	40,747	15
	1 death per 2,716 residents	
Lincoln Park	52,984	19
	1 death per 2,789 residents	
Detroit	1,514,063	521
	1 death per 2,906 residents	
Fraser	11,868	4
	1 death per 2,967 residents	
Trenton	24,127	8
	1 death per 3,016 residents	
Southgate	33,909	11
	1 death per 3,083	
Highland Park	35,444	11
	1 death per 3,222 residents	
Ferndale	30,850	9
	1 death per 3,428 residents	
Ann Arbor	100,035	28
	1 death per 3,573 residents	
Troy	39,419	11
	1 death per 3,583 residents	
Inkster	38,595	10
	1 death per 3,859 residents	
Harper Woods	20,186	5
	1 death per 4,037 residents	
Wyandotte	41,061	10
	1 death per 4,106 residents	
Madison Heights	38,599	8
	1 death per 4,824 residents	
Warren	179,260	41
	1 death per 4,372 residents	
Taylor	70,020	14
	1 death per 5,001 residents	
Livonia	110,109	22
	1 death per 5,005 residents	
Southfield	69,285	12
	1 death per 5,773 residents	
Grosse Pointes	55,857	9
	1 death per 6,206 residents	
Dearborn Heights	80,069	12
	1 death per 6,672 residents	
St. Clair Shores	88,093	12
	1 death per 7,341 residents	
Westland	86,749	6
	1 death per 14,458 residents	
Oak Park	36,762	2
	1 death per 18,381 residents	

In memorium

Police officers who have died in the line of duty

Detroit: Glen E. Clark, Edward J. Barney, Peter J.L. Sprott, Raymond Mundy, Wilfred Golla, Douglas Minton, William F. Konkel, Reed Howard, Paul Pawlowski, Barney Fox, Edward Sampson, Wayne W. Nelson, Fred W. Behrend, James C. Harrelson, Louis M. Levine, Edward F. Bayer, Andrew H. Edeen, Frank J. Winarski, Howard A. Booth, John R. Sheridan, Stephen E. Villaire, John J. Heffron, William M. Gratton, Albert J. Fink, William G. Ashworth, Frank E. Hage, Fred V. Breslin, Phelim McDonough, Elmer Cox, Casimir B. Kaliszewski, Wm. F. Hackebruch, Frank Marcinkowski, Sim D. Martin, William E. Wagner, Herman M. Jolly, Andrew Rusinko, Raymond Vollertsen, Boyd Badour, Walter L. Darsee, Earl J. Kobinsky, George Kimball, Alonzo E. Bullard, Albert W. Thayer, Edward Shoemaker, Charles J. Stewart, Clarence R. Cummings, John F. Daley, George H. Wilson, Franklin M. Smith, Lloyd N. Robinson, James M. Griffin, Charles W. Schoof, Fred Holwedel, Warren K. Snow, Thomas F. Madden, John Gordon, Leland Alexander, Edward M. McLaughlin, Emil R. Schmidt, Charles W. Sieger, Samuel C. Marquardt, Emmanuel Roggers, Richard H. Diamond, Norman F. Towler, Henry G. Angell, Elmer M. Powers, Louis Bomka, Gordon R. Davis, Harold G. Roughley, William S. Wollborg, Peter F. McGuigan, Arthur R. Huhnke, Philip Ellenstein, David Morris, Herbert J. Bischoff, Otto A. Balk, Daniel J. Coughlin, Isaac Kruka, Allan O. Linsday, Thomas J. Collins, Frank W. Reynolds, Valentine M. Lukowiak, Edward D. Perrin, Stacey C. Mizner, David G. Snell, William F. Frahm, Henry G. Puffer, Glenn R. Hunter, Fred A. Brumm, George Barstad, Peter Helko, Clarence J. Hans, Ulric A. Johnston, Clarence L. Stadler, Benjamin F. Smith, William W. Spencer, David E. Coy, Lloyd

O. Schultz, Dayton A. Winegar, Charles C. McMillan, Conrad W. Sippel, Hiram Reno, Seymour Lawler, Warren K. Raby, John E. Vandenberg, VanBuren Quarles, Joseph P. Husken, Mitchell A. Lipinski, Lawrence A. Adam, John E. Zeh, Leo F. Hilenski, Alphonse H. Kemper, Joseph Salatowski, Henry J. Mach, John A. Barringer, David I. Bergum, Clarence W. Bracy, Joseph G. Meglinske, Andreas Mellert Jr., Stanley J. Jerlecki, Gilbert Stocker, Gerald J. Riley, Robert P. Bradford Jr., Harold E. Carlson, Robert T. Moore, Alvis Morris Jr., Leonard M. Todd, Edward Pakula, Gerald Morrison, Brendt L. Stephens, Jon Ryckman, Byron Soule Jr., Robert J.

Members of the Detroit Police honor guard pause at the casket of Officer Shawn Bandy, 23, who was shot by kidnapping suspects in November 1998 on the city's east side.

Hogue, James Watts, William Paris, Frank Siemion, William Green, Michael J. Bossuyt, Mark C. Radden, Giacomo Buffa, Russell Blanchard, Arthur E. Meyers, George E. Krueger, Sidney A. O'Connor, Donald W. Coulter, Harry A. Thom, John B. French, Ronald I. English, James E. Meeks Jr., Gordon G. Schneider, Stanley Sech, Selwyn C. Adams, John Calandro Jr., Thaddeus W. Szczesny, James E. Wolframe, Harold F. Tullke, Marlyn W. Bateson, William L. Bell, John J. Hartenstein, Jerome J. Olshove, Edward Wolski Jr., Ricktor A. Gutowsky, Stanley Rapaski, Michael J. Czapski, Carter L. Wells, Paul E. Begin, Richard P. Woyshner, William Slappey, Glen E. Smith, Joseph M. Soulliere, Danny Lee Watson, William Wortmann, Joseph K. Siepak, Daniel Ellis, Ulysses Brown, Marta Shanaman, Merlin Leo Ray, Frederick D. Hunter Jr., Alonzo Marshall Jr., William Schmedding, Anthony A. Williams, Everett Williams Jr., Freddie L. Jackson, Johnnie Shoates, Richard L. Fortin, John J. Fitzpatrick, Andre Barksdale, Linda C. Smith, James Schmit, Frank Walls, Charles Beasley, Vikki Hubbard, Sherdard R. Brison, Rodney Bennett, Richard Leskie, Norman Spruiel, Jerry Philpot II, Lindora Smith, Earl White, Patrick Prohm, Bruce Williams, Shawn Bandy, Richard Scalf, Shynelle Mason, Neil Wells, Scott Stewart, Michael Scanlon, Ronald Sheffield (Federal Protective Service).

Suburbs: Roy Lee Graham, Robert Pare, Leonard Anderson, Thomas Andrews, William Dickerson, Henry Henderson, Thomas Wojtowicz, Charles Brososky, Edmond Dull, Robert Hutchin-

son, Edward Kinsey, Lepo Borders, Frank Crampton, Harold Ewald, Jerry Russo, Leonard Alber, Headley Downey, Kenneth Payne, Clifford Stang, Douglas Downing, Andrew Cain, Robert Dowidait, Louis Hinkel, Norbert Szczygiel, Claude Lanstra, Erhart Meyer, Steven Molitor, Kenneth Pine, Frank Snay, Frank Boza, John Goralczyk, John Michley, Philip Genna, Robert Micheletti, Ernest Jones, John Tsolis, Daniel Dubiel, Clay Hoover, Ira Parker, Kenneth Woodmore, Sidney Dethloff, James Kelley, Cashel Furgerson, Donald Harding, James McMahon, Martin Chivas, Charles Smetana, Eugene King, Henry Wolf, Donny Ashley, Millard Blynn, Gerald Carpenter, George Corneail, Thomas Metcalf, Frank Powley, Allison Schultz, Lee Cole, Jesse Crowe, James Gatewood, James Riley, Omer Reygaert, Lawrence Cooney, Albert DeSmet, William Oliver, Leroy Imus, Norman Stolzenfeld, Roy Shambleau, Andrew Bastendorff, Christopher Wouters, Richard Vauris, Jessica Wilson.

State Police in metro area: Harold Anderson, Milan Pratt, Harvey Bolen, Richard Hammond, John Cain, Charles Wood, Robert Gonser, Vicki Moreau DeVries, Tony Thames, Paul Hutchins, Kermit Fitzpatrick, James DeLoach, Steven Niewiek, Byron Erickson, Byron Egelski, Frederick Hardy.

Firefighters who have died in the line of duty

Detroit: John Miller, James H. O'Grady, Michael McQueen, Richard Filban, James J. Powers, Isaac M. Clark, Patrick J. Coughlin, Peter D. Schwartz, Hugh Garruty, David Boyd, Henry M. Turner, Octavace G. Robinson, Eugene M. McCarthy, Joseph R. Dely, John W. Pagel, Thomas E. Hogan, Julius J. Cummings, Michael H. Donaghue, Anthony Korte, Moses Fortune, Timothy Keohane, August W. Regentine, George S. Hough, Michael J. Sheahan, James F. Briggs, Davis Murduff, James R. Downey, Louis A. Staub, John J. Wallace, James W. Connors, Charles J.

Free Press file photo

Detroit firefighters stand in formation before the symbolic empty gear at the funeral of three colleagues in 1987.

Hawk, Cornelius Vaughn, Richard Murphy, Frank Gallagher, Michael J. Neville, George M. Aylsworth, Milton J. Emhoff, Davis A. Brown, Levi T. Fletcher, Arthur A. Fitch, Louis Rosen, Timothy F. O'Shea, Otto Habermas, William Huffman, William J. Moran, William J. Shill, Otto Mattick, Oscar Locke, Alexander Cockburn, Alonzo F. Raymond, Richard Beard, Stanley Doptis, William O'Brien, James Condry, Louis Purol, Maurice Kelly, Oscar Reidel, Joseph Lewandowski, Frederick Stolp, Edward L. Vernier, Clarence W. Belleau, George McPhee, Louis Digue, James F. Thornton, Aubrey Chamberlin, Andrew Nolan, Anthony J. Doemer, Frank Domagalski, Malcolm Baxter, Patrick Black, Thomas J. Sullivan, Wendell P. Laderoot, Lief J. Christiansen, Walter Sweeney, Harvey Peterman, George Hawkins, Edward E. Stephens, Edward B. Whalen, Robert J. Hummel, Alfred Huether, David Mitchel, Joseph E. Jones, William M. Burgess, George F. Pokriefke, Frank J. Riopelle, James J. Templeton, Stanley T. Hanley, George A. Merrill, Anthony Brosowski, Luther Adams, Louis A. Pape, Chester G. Simcox, Russell M. Kelly, Shirley R. Colburne, Joseph P. Hallman, George D. Wilson, William M. Mroscake, Louis A. Stoecklin, Robert C. Cody, Edward N. Mitten, Stanley Jankowski, Joseph R. Schaening, Ernest Fox, Stanley Haush, Joseph M. Donnelly, Harry Scholotzhauer, Oliver J. Strong, Albert A. Austin, Charles B. Parish, Paul J. Reiner, Raymond A. Benedict, Fred J. Bergman, John Gibbons, Clay Carpenter, Charles Regnier, Chauncey Wilmot, Elmer Morrell, Joseph Bergin, Charles Phillips, Clifford Bannon, James Daggett, Harry Steinhebel, Stanley Thornton, Werner Blaess, Ellsworth Carroll, Dwight Higinbotham, Nicholas Konen, Bruno Koluch, Stephen Szpunar, Albert Booth, Jack L. Campell, Chester R. Beals, Jack Trim, Lyle W. Ingram, Alex Ori, Frederick Davis, Frederick Taylor, Paul Mack, Carl Smith, John Charles Ashby, Frank Roeback, Joseph Falkiewicz, Leonard Grice, Donald Barr, Stanley Lada, Frank Vuichard, Elwyn Girodat, Robert Lee, Thomas Killion, Edward Dugelar, Bruno Vanderski, Leo Yeanoplos, Joseph Makie, Ross J. Klemet, Terrence M. McHugh, Edward G. Gargol, Steve Mirka, Chester Pierce, William P. Ponton, Earl Dunlap, Thaddeus M. Potocki, James W. Blastow, Gerald Walsh, Charles Grabman, Curtis Randolph, Michael Johnson, Charles Gates, Robert Franquist, Gerald Baggot, Edward A. Zablocki, Alphonse Green, George Bartley Jr., Coleman Tate, Clyde Sanders, David Lau, Paul Schimeck, Larry McDonald, Karl Ryan, Roland D. Waters, Robert English, John Weingart, Wayne Fogel.

Suburbs: Walter Elmy, Edwin Harris, Allen Fairall, Thomas Brown, Raymond Susko, Joseph Riesterer, Richard Tucker, Donald Graham, James Nelson, Gary Kreski, Leonard Gierak, Marsha Baczynski, Robert Gregory Sr., Thomas Phelps, Tracy Williamson, Michael Vancalbergh, Donald Daughenbaugh, Henry Moran, Dennis Dearing, Thomas Chappelle, David Sutton.

MAYHEM

Detroit firefighter Stephen Babicz rushes a victim to an ambulance. The child was one of seven siblings who died in a 1993 blaze on Mack Avenue. In 1997, Babicz died of a heart attack at age 47 while off-duty.

The Detroit Almanac

15. FUN

"I thought Detroit was dry, said my mother shyly. Did you, said my father with a rye smile."

— **Ring Lardner**, *"The Young Immigrants"*

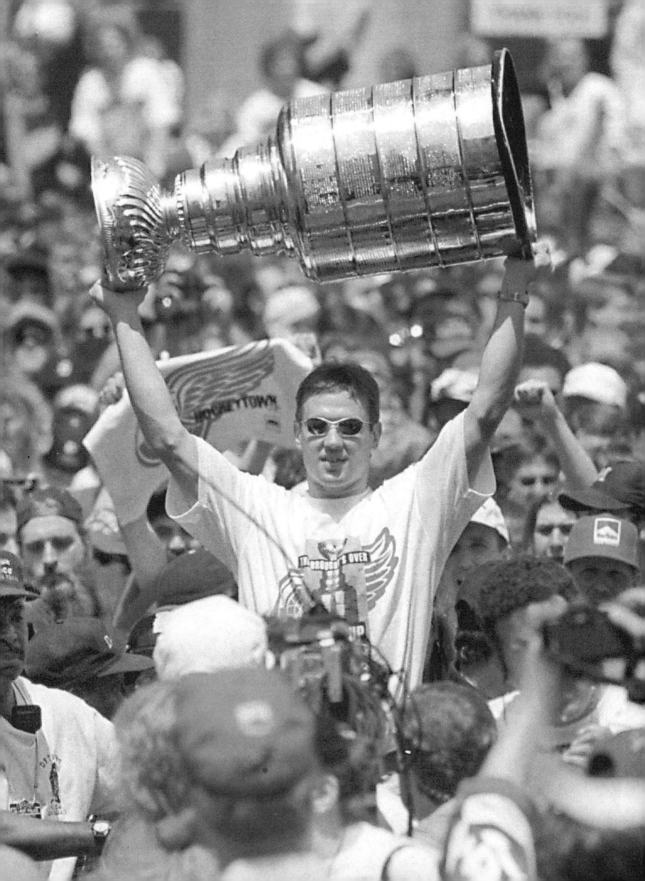

The Good Life

Great celebrations

▶ **Detroit celebrates statehood, Feb. 9, 1837:** Detroiters awakened to the firing of a 26-gun salute to symbolize Michigan's new status as the 26th state. An afternoon dinner was held in Woodworth's Hotel with speeches and numerous toasts. Residents lit bonfires, and Jefferson Avenue appeared to be ablaze.

▶ **Train service links Detroit with the East, Jan. 17, 1854:** Immense crowds gathered at the foot of Woodward to watch as the Great Western Railroad arrived in Windsor from Niagara. Soldiers and firefighters, their engines decorated, paraded along Jefferson. The steamer Dart ferried passengers across the river, where they landed to the firing of a salute, speeches and an elaborate banquet. For the first time, Detroit was connected to the East, as well as to Chicago and the West.

▶ **Ratification of the 15th Amendment, celebrated April 7, 1870:** Virtually all of the 2,235 black residents of Detroit and many whites turned out to celebrate black Americans receiving the right to vote. A parade began with the firing of a cannon; the marchers included black masons, schoolboys, club members, a white band, residents in carriages and members of the 102nd United States Colored Infantry. At the Opera House, speakers included George DeBaptiste, William Lambert, Michigan Gov. Henry Baldwin and white abolition leaders.

▶ **Grand Army of the Republic, first week in August 1891:** The organization of Union Army veterans from the Civil War came to Detroit for its silver anniversary. An estimated 100,000 visitors jammed the city, which was decorated with flags, bunting and four massive arches at main intersections. The Aug. 4 parade included 138 bands, and a picnic the next day on Belle Isle is said to have drawn 150,000 people — more than half of Detroit's population. In 1899, city funds and private donations were used to build the castle-like building at Grand River and Cass for GAR veterans.

▶ **The 20th Century, Jan. 1, 1901:** Detroiters waited until 1901 to celebrate the new century, which they greeted the way their descendants would greet new years — by shooting guns into the air. They also used bells, whistles, fireworks, gongs and other noisemakers. Thousands of people gathered on the Campus Martius Dec. 31 to celebrate as the city hall clock struck 12.

▶ **Detroit's bicentennial, July 24, 1901:** Leading citizens re-created the arrival of Cadillac 200 years earlier amid high-octane boosterism over Detroit's industrial growth. The cele-

Library of Congress
Detroit's 200th birthday is celebrated July 24, 1901, with a parade south on Woodward. The photographer is facing Campus Martius from just south of today's Kennedy Square.

Red Wings Captain Steve Yzerman hoists the Stanley Cup at Woodward and Jefferson at the 1997 victory parade.

CRAIG PORTER/Detroit Free Press

FUN!

bration began at dawn with a salute from three U.S. Navy vessels in the river. The City Hall bell tolled 200 times at 6 a.m. In the afternoon, as church bells pealed and whistles blew, the flotilla of *voyageurs* started downriver from Belle Isle, coming ashore at the foot of Randolph. Tens of thousands of spectators watched two parades: One was composed of flower-covered floats; the other was a procession of brightly lit trailers, running along streetcar tracks that showed allegorical scenes of Detroit's history. The city had planned to build a memorial to Cadillac, but it ran out of money.

► **Cadillaqua, July 1912:** Detroit was really on a roll, with its population ballooning to an estimated 541,213, thanks largely to the booming auto industry. To celebrate the city's growth and its maritime facilities, public officials and business leaders staged the Cadillaqua — a combination of Cadillac and the Latin word for water. They wanted it to become an annual event. (It didn't.) Among the events: A parade said to number 5,000 autos; a parade of floats evoking Detroit's history; a giant Venetian night off Belle Isle. Each event drew hundreds of thousands of people, some of the biggest crowds in city history. The week of unbridled boosterism ended with a huge municipal corruption story — several council members were arrested for accepting bribes.

► **Armistice Day, Nov. 11, 1918.** Peace in the Great War as first signaled in Detroit at 3 a.m. when a factory whistle shrieked. Hundreds of other whistles joined in. Within a couple of hours, joyfully screaming residents,

joined by factory workers leaving their night shifts, were pouring downtown in streetcars and autos. Street bonfires burned in neighborhoods. Firefighters decorated their rigs with flags and sped down streets with their sirens wailing. Women wore red, white and blue sashes. Morning masses at Catholic churches were jammed across the city. The mayor proclaimed a holiday. Effigies of the German Kaiser were strung from light poles and trees. Factory bands led spontaneous parades, and a huge procession started at Woodward and Grand Boulevard at 3 p.m. A plane, performing aerial stunts as part of the celebration, struck the flagpole atop the Fyfe Building on Woodward and crashed, killing the pilot.

► **The last horse-drawn fire rig, April 10, 1922.** More than 50,000 people lined Woodward Avenue to watch the last truly horse-powered fire engine roar down a Detroit street. As the fire department band played "Auld Lang Syne," Engine Co. 37, from Central and Dix, raced down the street to a pretend alarm in a bank. The engine was pulled by department veterans Pete, Jim and Tom. Behind them, Babe and Rusty yoked the hose cart. The five white horses' last real run had taken place several days earlier.

► **Electric light's golden jubilee, Oct. 21, 1929.** Led by Henry Ford, Detroit pulled out all the stops to pay tribute to 82-year-old Thomas Edison on the 50th anniversary of his invention of the electric light. An estimated million people jammed streets in Detroit and Dearborn during a freezing rainstorm to greet President Herbert Hoover, one of hundreds of out-of-town VIPs. At a candlelight dinner at Henry Ford Museum, such world-class celebrities as Madame Marie Curie, John Rockefeller, Adolph Ochs, Walter Chrysler and Will Rogers joined in toasting Edison. An international radio audience listened, and Albert Einstein joined in via a special hookup. (The banquet is memorialized today at the Ford museum with a large painting, which identifies the guests.) After dinner, Edison, Ford, Hoover and others traveled by carriage to the Menlo Park laboratory, where Edison re-enacted the lighting of the bulb as announcers narrated the scene over NBC radio. When the light appeared, Detroit erupted in sirens and whistles.

Armistice Day, Nov. 11, 1918, at Campus Martius in Detroit. The replica of the Statue of Liberty was used to urge people to buy war bonds.

Free Press file photo

FUN!

Joe Louis decks Max Schmeling in the first round of their title fight. The knockout and Louis' win set off a celebration in Detroit, the Champ's hometown.

➤ **Opening of the Ambassador Bridge, Nov. 11, 1929.** An estimated 100,000 people jammed the U.S. side of the $22.5-million bridge after an Armistice Day parade. A smaller crowd gathered on the Canadian approach. After dignitaries opened the span by snipping two white ribbons, both sides surged across the bridge and met in the middle in a spontaneous display of international friendship.

➤ **The Big Parade, Sept. 22, 1931.** "The Legion marched." That was the first sentence of a Free Press story on a parade of at least 85,000 American Legion veterans of World War I that a million people watched. The procession, along East Jefferson and Woodward, lasted nine hours; nearly 2,000 spectators were treated at first-aid stations and 341 seriously injured people were taken to Detroit Receiving Hospital to be treated for heat prostration and other ailments. The Free Press won a Pulitzer, journalism's biggest prize, for its coverage.

➤ **Joe Louis KOs Max Schmeling, June 22, 1938.** When hometown hero Louis avenged his 1936 knockout by the German heavyweight, a predominantly black crowd in Paradise Valley erupted in dancing and song that went on for hours. Loudspeakers carried the fight broadcast from Yankee Stadium to an estimated 10,000 listeners gathered in St. Antoine and Beacon streets. They didn't wait long. Louis scored his knockout at 2:04 of Round 1, and the party was on. A swing rhythm band headed by Cecil Lee played on a truck in front of the B. and C. Club, and at one point did a 20-minute version of a song titled "Flatfoot Flootie with a Floy Floy."

➤ **Detroit turns 250, 1951.** Fresh from victory in World War II, Detroit — the Arsenal of Democracy — and the United States appeared to be peaking in power and influence. The city reached what would be the official apex of its population, 1.85 million. Its cheerleaders were bursting at the seams, bragging about Detroit's industrial might, though it is clear now that jobs were starting to be lost in significant numbers. The city scheduled more than 100 programs throughout the year, culminating in July, when Secretary of State Dean Acheson and President Harry S. Truman came to talk and take part

FUN!

MANDELA'S SPEECH

Excerpt from Nelson Mandela's speech at Tiger Stadium:

"How do I even begin to thank you, the wonderful people of Detroit and the Midwest, and through you, the lovely people of this country, who have received us with such warmth and affection?

. . .

It is the working people of the industrial heartland of America who have helped to make this country a great industrial power

. . .

When we were in prison, we appreciated and always we listened to the sound of Detroit "Motortown." It is Motortown that gave the world a great singer, Steve Wonder. On reaching Detroit, I recalled some of the words of a song sung by Marvin Gaye, another famous Motortown product. The words go, 'Brother, brother, there's far too many of you dying. Mother, mother, there's far too many of you crying.'

These words are a reflection of the South African condition. For how long must our brothers and sisters go on dying? For how long must our children be deprived. . . . For how long must our color and dignity be trampled upon? We declare: Not for long . . .

Thank you for your solidarity and support. Thank you for your warm embrace. And thank you for being with us when we need you most. From this rostrum, let me say I respect you, I admire you, and above all, I love you."

in a parade with 20,000 others. The celebration's organizing committee alone had 35 subcommittees and 1,000 members. The city opened neighborhood libraries, the International Institute and the Historical Museum. In Grand Circus Park, workers erected a giant stage built to resemble a birthday cake. At the University of Detroit, the Rev. Daniel Lord celebrated a musical spectacular with 1,200 actors, singers and dancers on a five-level stage. In keeping with the new Cold War, the extravaganza's theme was "City of Freedom."

➤ **Greeting Pope John Paul II, Sept. 18 and 19, 1987.** Heavily Catholic and Polish metro Detroit prepared for months for the first and only visit of a leader of the Roman Catholic Church. But turnout was small for most events during the visit of John Paul II, the church's first Polish leader. The Hart Plaza crowd was about one-tenth of the half-million predicted and the throng in Hamtramck about one-fourth of the expected 200,000. People complained that the Popemobile traveled too fast as it whisked the pontiff down Jos. Campau. The faithful did jam one event, though: The pope's mass at the Silverdome. About 90,000 people packed the sports arena for the well-rehearsed combination of showmanship and worship. In his homily, the pontiff spoke of the dignity and rights of workers. Before bidding the United States farewell at

Metro Airport, the pope issued an especially strong condemnation of abortion.

➤ **Greeting Nelson Mandela, June 28, 1990.** Just months after his release from a South African prison, where he had served 27 years, the then-deputy president of the African National Congress created a huge stir during a brief visit to Detroit. Black, green and gold ANC flags hung in the windows of police cars. At Tiger Stadium, souvenir hawkers wore dashikis. Parents brought children to see Mandela, teaching them a new word, *amandla* or power. At the Ford Rouge plant, Mandela's presence brought the Mustang production line to a halt as he pledged his fidelity to exuberant autoworkers. At Tiger Stadium, some of the nearly 50,000-person crowd danced in the aisles, shouting "Mandela! Mandela!," swaying together to the sounds of a huge choir. "Oh happy day!" the choir sang. "Freedom's gonna come some day," shouted Detroiter Ortheia Barnes. Mandela told the crowd: "Right now, I wish I could climb down the stage and join you in the stands and embrace you one and all."

➤ **Hockeytown cheers the Red Wings, June 18, 1998.** Detroit's love affair with its hockey team busted out all over on an 85-degree day as an estimated 1.2 million people toasted the back-to-back Stanley Cup champion Red Wings. Fans turned downtown

Free Press file photo

Detroit Mayor Coleman Young gives a long-awaited greeting to Nelson Mandela at Metro Airport in 1990 as Gov. James Blanchard, far left, and UAW President Owen Bieber applaud. Young had once worried that he or Mandela might die before they could ever meet.

FUN!

Free Press file photo

A Thanksgiving parade favorite, the Doodlebug, worms its way down Woodward. The old Hudson's store is on the far right.

Detroit into a gleeful village of jersey-wearing, flag-waving, broom-wielding, hand-pumping fanatics. "Let's party," suggested a gap-toothed, grinning Tomas Holmstrom, the Swedish Red Wing who captured the spirit of the sizzling celebration during the post-Wood-ward-Avenue-parade rally at Hart Plaza. "There ain't no party like a Dee-troit party 'cuz a Dee-troit party never stops," pro-claimed backup goalie Kevin Hodson as thou-sands of partyers cheered. Bodies painted with players' names took the place of three-piece suits for the day. People danced, sang and chanted "Let's go, Red Wings" back and forth across Woodward. Traffic gridlocked on normally smooth-flowing streets. The crowd was one of the largest gatherings in Detroit history, and by far the biggest of any of the many sports celebrations over the years. Its size surpassed estimates of the previous year's Red Wings' victory parade by at least 200,000. Police made 24 arrests for minor infractions, but reported no major incidents or injuries and called the crowd well-behaved.

Metro area fun

➤ **The J.L. Hudson downtown store:** For decades, when Detroiters said "Let's go down-town," what they meant was "Let's go to Hud-son's."

The flagship store of the J. L. Hudson Co. once reigned over Woodward Avenue and the city like a grand and gracious lady, the arbiter of taste, the purveyor of fashion and the epit-ome of service. Downtown Hudson's was big-ger than Marshall Field and more elegant than Macy's, and it dominated Detroit retail-ing, its hold on its customers as much a senti-mental phenomenon as a commercial one.

TONY SPINA/Detroit Free Press

Santa Claus arrives in Detroit at the end of the Thanksgiving Day parade in 1987.

The store probably reached its apogee between the 1920s and the 1950s, a time when a visit to Hudson's was a social occasion as well as a shopping trip.

Those were the days when women wore hats and pearls to shop and little girls put on their patent leather Mary Janes and white string gloves to accompany them. The Hud-son's they entered, debarking from streetcars on Woodward and Gratiot and Grand River, was a spacious, high-ceilinged place laid out in the days before sales were calculated by square foot of selling space.

It was a store for all seasons. For years, Christmas in Detroit did not start until the moment the most awesome Santa in the world alit from his sleigh onto Hudson's marquee and the double doors swung open to receive him. The next day, hundreds of youngsters would be stretched in a line before the eleva-tors, waiting to ride up to a fairyland of car-nival rides, hot dogs and cotton candy, miles of spun angel floss and twinkling lights.

Year in and year out, Hudson's downtown supplied everything a family needed. You could buy a dictionary or a doll dresser, a bolt of *peau de soie* or a half-dozen chocolaty

HUDSON'S HISTORY

J. L. Hudson opened his first store in 1881. Detroiters shopped at a J. L. Hudson store at Gratiot and Farmer beginning in 1891, but the 25-story building imploded in 1998 was a patchwork of structures built between 1911 and 1946.

In the 1920s, the company demolished its original 1891 building, along with a 1907 addi-tion. By 1946, Hudson's contained 2.2 million square feet and 49 acres of floor space.

The last day of busi-ness was Jan. 17, 1983.

The building was imploded with 2,728 pounds of plastic explo-sives on Oct. 24, 1998.

For an Internet view of Hudson's last sec-onds, check out the Fabulous Ruins of Detroit. It's an interac-tive Web site that con-tains an interesting and comprehensive tour of Detroit's great old build-ings: **www.bhere.com/ ruins/ home.htm**

FUN!

Burton Historical Collection

Opening Day, 1904. These Tigers fans are not doing the wave.

brownies baked on the premises, a penny stamp from Bechuanaland or a grand piano from Steinway. Hudson's would cut your hair, store your furs, shine your shoes and install your new storm windows.

Young women whose christening dresses were bought at Hudson's returned to choose their bridal gowns and wedding cake, to outfit their children and furnish their homes from the washing machine in the basement to the carriage light on the front porch. In the music shop there were booths for listening to classical records before you bought them and a piano for trying out sheet music. In the fourth-floor lounge, stationery and pens were always in the desks, should you be struck with a sudden need to write to Aunt Emma while shopping.

The downtown store seemed cool, unhurried and spacious. Its glass cases of silver and crystal and bone china were a guidebook and finishing school for thousands of Detroiters who were not born to wealth and gracious living. If you bought it at Hudson's, it had to be in good taste.

➤ **Old-time horse racing:** One of the biggest amusements of the 19th Century was horse racing. The French started it, racing sleds, buggy-like sulkies and horses throughout the year. In winter, they raced on the frozen Detroit and Rouge rivers. In summer, they raced down Jefferson. Even as late as the 1850s, Ulysses S. Grant, then an Army officer stationed in Detroit, raced horses on West Jefferson.

➤ **Storytelling:** Tales told by Detroit's French settlers on cold winter nights during the 1700s were passed among families into the 19th Century and were collected in the 1890s by Marie Hamlin in "Legends of Le Detroit." The French told of "red dwarfs," will-o'-the-wisps and *loup garoups,* which were werewolfs,

especially one *loup garoup* that kidnapped and ate brides on the day of their wedding then escaped pursuers by diving into the mouth of a catfish in Lake St. Clair.

➤ **Public baths:** In 1827, Maj. David McKinstry opened the city's first amusement park. It was actually a garden, located in an old orchard at Randolph and Lafayette. Attractions included a landscaped walk, band pavilion, restaurant and bathhouse. Bathers could choose a wooden tub inside a plain stall and, while soaking, listen to the band play such riffs as "Captain Kidd's Lament" and "Hail Columbia." McKinstry's baths became so popular that others sprang up at Monroe and Randolph and Jefferson near Shelby.
SOURCE: "FUN AND FROLIC IN EARLY DETROIT," BY KENNETH METCALF.

➤ **North American International Auto Show:** The show began in 1907 at a beer garden near the Belle Isle Bridge with 17 exhibitors displaying 33 vehicles. Today it's a glitzy global event at which more than 40 manufacturers exhibit about 700 cars and trucks and make news by introducing new concept and production vehicles. More than 6,000 media members from more than 60 countries cover the event; several hundred thousand visitors attend the public showing. The show moved to Cobo in 1965 and became the North American International show in 1989, when Toyota and Nissan introduced their luxury divisions. Since the show went international, automakers have premiered more than 560 vehicles. The show's annual charity preview has raised more than $20 million for children's charities since it began in 1976. The 1999 charity preview, attended by 17,500 people, raised $4.4 million. The show is owned and operated by the Detroit Auto Dealers Association.

➤ **Opening Day:** Over the years, the opening of the Tigers season became an unofficial civic holiday. In earlier seasons, Detroit's wealthiest residents turned up in the box seats — as they turn up in the luxury boxes today — and thousands of other fans would skip work and school to crowd into the cheaper seats. No matter how good the team or how bad the weather, an air of celebration prevailed. Sometimes things got out of hand: Dozens of fans ran onto the field during a couple of openers at Tiger Stadium. From dawn on Opening Day, the streets around the stadium would transform into a huge, open-air party, and radio stations and companies would throw private receptions on vacant lots. Even Detroiters who didn't have a ticket would take part: In many schools across the city, teachers would let students listen to radio accounts of the game, or watch the televised account. The Tigers' first Opening Day was April 25, 1901, at Bennett Park, a forerunner to Tiger Stadium at Michigan and Trumbull. A crowd of

MARY SCHROEDER/Detroit Free Press

The annual International Freedom Festival fireworks draw about a million people along both sides of the Detroit River.

10,023 people saw the Tigers score 10 runs in the bottom of the ninth to defeat Milwaukee, 14-13.

➤ **Freedom Festival and fireworks:** The first International Freedom Festival, a celebration of the friendly U.S.-Canadian border, took place in 1959. The festival is held each year around July 1 (Canada Day) and July 4 (Independence Day), and events range from a cross-river tug-of-war between Detroit and Windsor police to a rubber ducky race between the cities' mayors. But the signature event is the huge annual fireworks show. In 1959, an estimated 1 million people watched from downtown Detroit, Windsor, Belle Isle and boats anchored on the Detroit River. Sponsored by J. L. Hudson, the 2.5 tons of explosives were produced by a Japanese firm. Queen Elizabeth and Prince Philip, touring Canada, departed for Sarnia on board the Britannia before the pyrotechnics began.

➤ **Port Huron-to-Mackinac Race:** Since 1924, the big weekend for metro Detroit sailors comes in mid-July. In 2000, more than 260 sailboats filled with 2,500 people of varying degrees of skill departed Port Huron, after a night of partying, for Mackinac Island, where there is more partying at which every-

DAVID P. GILKEY/Detroit Free Press

Sailboats at the start of the annual Port Huron-to-Mackinac Race.

one spins tales of their adventures on the high seas of Lake Huron. The race is organized by Bayview Yacht Club in Detroit.

➤ **Michigan State Fair:** The grand melding of corn dogs, elephant ears, horse shows, carnies, sideshows, lemonade, the Ferris wheel and milk-them-yourself cows. Held during the two weeks before Labor Day, the Michigan State Fair is the oldest in the nation, being first staged in 1849 in Detroit. Between 1850 and 1905, the fair moved to Ann Arbor, Jackson, Grand Rapids, Kalamazoo, Saginaw, Pontiac and Lansing, but resettled in Detroit, where merchant king J. L. Hudson donated the fairgrounds at Woodward and 8 Mile. The fair got schlocky in the 1980s; attendance plummeted to an all-time low of 163,000 in 1993. At that point, former state Sen. John Hertel took over the management and cleaned up the fair's act. And the public responded: Despite three days and one night of rain, attendance at the 1999 fair was 458,000.

➤ **The Detroit International Jazz Festival** (formerly the Montreux Detroit Jazz Festival): Under the watch of Jim Dulzo, who resigned in early 2000 after six years as festival director, Montreux grew from the brink of extinction into North America's largest free

---

FUN!

The Ford Rotunda, built in the shape of a gear with rectangular wings on two sides and sculptured gardens around it, is most often remembered for elaborate Christmas displays.

jazz festival, encompassing four days and 125 national and local acts over Labor Day weekend.

Montreux, which began in 1979, is known nationally for its uncompromising artistic excellence and thriving attendance — 770,000 in 1999 — which ranks among the country's best. When Detroit Renaissance Inc. ceded Montreux to Music Hall at the end of 1993, a steady stream of red ink, declining attendance and artistic stasis left the festival's future in doubt.

The numbers speak for themselves. Attendance has more than doubled from the 350,000 when Dulzo took over. The festival's budget has swelled from $400,000 to $1 million. Sponsorship dollars have increased from $135,000 to $500,000. The festival now breaks even. In February 2000, Ed Love was named to replace Dulzo, and then in July 2000, he was replaced by Frank Malfitano.

► **UM-MSU game:** The ultimate state of Michigan football experience. The air is cool, the leaves are blazing red, the stands are jammed and the bands are jamming. The Wolverines and Spartans played for the first time in 1898 and have missed only a few years since. Michigan leads the series, 61 to 26. Five games were tied.

► **Thanksgiving Day Parade:** Since 1924,

Santa Claus has arrived in Detroit in only one way — at the end of a spectacular parade down Woodward Avenue. Horses pulled floats in the first parade, which was headed by Mother Goose. The J. L. Hudson Co. started the tradition, and for decades the parade terminated outside of its now-demolished flagship store, where Christmas Carol and Santa would accept the key to Detroit. Charles Wendel, a Hudson's employee, is credited with the inspiration for the parade. While the parade has grown and shrunk and grown again over the years, it almost always has consisted of floats, marching bands, clowns and giant handmade heads that are worn by marchers. For nearly 50 years, officials have chosen the design of an elementary-school student to be made into a float. In 1990, Chilly Willy, the penguin balloon, escaped from his handlers and landed 25 miles away in Lake St. Clair. Since Hudson's ceded sponsorship of the parade in 1978, a variety of businesses have contributed funds. The Parade Co. and numerous volunteers now organize the gala march.

► **Ford Rotunda:** The Rotunda was a 130-foot-high building in the shape of a gear, with rectangular wings on two sides and sculptured gardens around it. An array of lights bathed the building in a palette of colors that could be seen for miles. Henry Ford spent $2.6

million at the height of the Great Depression to build the Rotunda at the Chicago World's Fair. Few people remember that. Many middle-aged Detroiters, though, recall the funny-shaped building as an amazingly elaborate Christmas fantasyland, with holiday cartoons in the theater, animated displays, waltzing skaters, Christmas carols by Alvin and the Chipmunks, and an enormous ramp that led children to the lap of Santa Claus. Ford moved the Rotunda from Chicago to Schaefer and Rotunda in Dearborn and used it as a company hospitality center. Closed during World War II, it opened again in 1953. Nearly 6 million people flocked to see the Christmas show in the nine years it was held. A fire destroyed the Rotunda on Nov. 9, 1962. Ford decided not to rebuild. The Rotunda was a throwback to an earlier time, when showmanship had a place in corporate economics.

➤ **Downtown Hoedown:** Since 1972, country music fans have kicked off summer with their own festival in late May that attracts several hundred thousand people during its three-day run at Hart Plaza. The 2000 festival was broadcast by WCYD-FM (99.5) and featured its own Web site — www.wycd.com

Detroit's amusement parks

➤ **Boblo:** The grandaddy of Detroit's amusement parks, Boblo is the source of vivid memories for four generations of Detroiters: Their first kiss on a moonlight cruise. Their first ride on the Wild Mouse. The romance of dancing their way home from the island late at night as the lights from Detroit twinkled from the shore. The sight of midget Captain Boblo, in his official hat, waving good-bye to boats departing from the foot of Woodward. For 100 years, boat trips to Boblo were such a part of Detroit that one radio station used a recording of the blustery Boblo boat whistle as its promotional ditty. The 2,500-passenger Columbia and Ste. Claire began service to the island, 18 miles southwest of downtown in Canadian waters, in the early 1900s. At first, there was nothing more

Motown can hoedown — and has every spring since 1983. The country music fest draws several hundred thousand people each year.

WILLIAM ARCHIE/Free Press

than picnics, dancing and a merry-go-round. The Ferris wheel, rides, funhouse and skating pavilion came later. Boblo was not a happy recollection for all: Park officials denied Coleman Young entrance as a child when they discovered he was black. The park and boats shut down in the early 1990s.

➤ **Walled Lake Amusement Park and Casino:** Walled Lake was a tremendously popular destination for young Detroiters before and after World War II. There were rides in the amusement park, boats on the lake, steaks in the restaurant and big bands (but no gambling) in the casino. Under sparkling spangled stars dangling from the ceiling, hundreds of couples did the Charleston on the 120-by-140-foot polished maple floor while listening to Glenn Miller a generation before their children grooved to Stevie Wonder and deejay Lee (The Horn) Alan. The Flying Dragon roller coaster is often remembered as the best ride. The park, at Novi and 13 Mile, opened in 1926 and closed in 1968. Fire destroyed the casino in 1965.

➤ **Eastwood Park:** With its roller coaster, swimming pool and roller rink, Eastwood served as a recreation mecca from 1928 to 1949. The park, at 8 Mile and Gratiot in what is now Eastpointe, made news for other reasons, too. A 1936 fire in a walk-through attraction called the Jungle killed three people. In 1943, a mob of white youths attacked young blacks, an incident that helped fuel the devastating race riot one week later in Detroit. In the late 1940s, a bitter controversy erupted over attempts by local officials to close the park. They succeeded, but not until the dispute ended up in federal court.

➤ **Jefferson Beach:** Starting in the 1930s, many east siders spent much of their sum-

Free Press file photo

Riders enjoy a mechanical race on wooden horses at Jefferson Beach amusement park in 1939. The park in St. Clair Shores closed in 1959.

FUN!

➤ **Celebrity samplers:** Pope John Paul II — the first Polish pope — has sampled locally made kielbasa. Former Wayne County Probate Judge Frank Szymanski once conducted a three-hour "Kielbasa College" course at his home, teaching neophytes how to make the food.

➤ **The sausage cheer:** In the 1960s, Detroit high school students screamed a sausage cheer:
"Ooo-sa-sa-sa, ooo-sa-sa-sa!
Hit 'em in the head with a big kielbasa."

➤ **Size does matter:** In 1986, Hamtramck's Kowalski Sausage Co. and a firm in Massachusetts got into a squabble in the wurst way. At issue: whose sausage was biggest. Chicopee Provision Co., which since 1974 has been making a huge kielbasa every year, unveiled a 412-pounder for that year's World Kielbasa Festival in Chicopee, Mass. But Kowalski already had produced a one tonner for the Hamtramck Festival. Chicopee's "is a midget compared to what we did," said a Kowalski spokesman. "Ours was 2,208 pounds, 32 feet long. We've definitely qualified for the world's largest kielbasa." Rules for world's largest: It must be made in a ring and must have a natural (intestine) casing.

FUN!

mers at Jefferson Beach in St. Clair Shores. But the roller coasters stopped rolling at Jefferson Beach in 1959, when pressure from public officials closed the park, and the land was turned into Jefferson Beach Marina.

➤ **Electric Park:** From 1906 to 1928, the years of Detroit's most frenetic growth, Electric Park sat next to the Belle Isle Bridge at East Grand Boulevard and East Jefferson, a 7-acre oasis of frivolity among the nearby auto factories, office buildings and schools. Insurance man Arthur Gaukler built the park on the ruins of an older amusement resort. For 10 cents, Detroiters could take in the most modern rides, including one of the nation's largest roller coasters, vaudeville shows, soda foun-

tains and a large pier.

➤ **Edgewater Park:** Opened in 1927 in what was then the rural area of 7 Mile and Telegraph, Edgewater closed in September 1982. It was a modest, somewhat seedy facility of 25 acres and 20 rides, but it served as a nearby place for a fling with your Friday-night date on the giant octopus or dodge'em cars. In the early 1960s, Barbra Streisand was the screaming voice on Edgewater radio commercials ranting about the "pay-one-price plan." Then a fledgling entertainer, Babs did the commercial while in town for a Caucus Club gig. The park, at the edge of the Rouge River, was operated by the Wagner family, which at one time also ran Electric, Eastwood and Jefferson Beach parks.

We are what we eat

Metro Detroit is a gourmet's paradise . . . for a gourmand into spicy sausage, ribs, chili dogs, doughnuts oozing jelly, and, yes, muskrat. Yum. Here's a menu of Detroit-generated food — and some appetizers about how we get what we eat.

➤ **CHIPS**
"Bet ya can't eat just one"

Twenty companies made potato chips in Detroit in the late 1940s. By the mid-1980s, only Better Made was chipping away. Its familiar yellow panel trucks rolled out of a sprawling east side plant on Gratiot near French Road, carrying chips to metro Detroiters who per capita led the nation in chip eating.

Better Made began in 1931 when boyhood friends Cross Moceri and Peter Cipriano formed Cross & Peters Co., making chips on East Forest between Baldwin and Seyburn. They later moved to McDougall and Ferry. In the mid-1940s, they churned 'em out at Woodward and Sproat. People gathered at the windows to watch the chips being made.

Better Made's years as the only chip maker here ended in the late 1990s. Ray Jenkins started making chips at a factory at I-96 and Wyoming. "Uncle Ray's" pushed the chip envelope with such quirky flavors as coney, ketchup, jalapeno and kosher dill, in addition to the traditional ones.

➤ **MUSTARD**
Hot stuff

Belgian immigrant Henry U. Sabbe wanted to journey to the United States on the maiden voyage of the Titanic in 1912. Alas, the ship booked quickly, so Sabbe landed safely in New York about a week before the liner sank. He came to Detroit, where he opened a grocery on Gratiot near Harper, stocking it with many items that appealed to the east side's Belgian population. In 1923, he developed a hot mustard like the ones from his homeland. It was a hit. He called it Red Pelican and started making it in the basement of his home on Bewick Avenue near Harper. Later, he erected a small building behind the house and, in 1941, a building on St. Jean between Shoemaker and Harper. That's where Red Pelican has been made ever since, along with a salad-style mustard and vinegar. Sabbe died in 1968. His son-in-law and grandson carried on the business.

➤ PICKLES
Funny business

Robert J. Vlasic captured a big wedge of America's pickle market by making people laugh. What else could he do with pickles?

When Vlasic, fresh from the University of Michigan, took over the family's modest food distribution business in 1949, he figured he'd have some fun. "There's nothing very serious about a pickle," he said later. "So I took a funny tack." Ads featured pregnant women and their cravings. His pickle joke book with 101 "favorite dillies" was published in 1973.

Q: What's a pickle's favorite TV show? A: What's my brine?

By the mid-1970s, Vlasic was puckering all the way to the bank. Before selling the company to the Campbell Soup Co. in 1978, he was making 115 varieties of pickles, peppers, relishes and sauerkrauts and had cornered 17 percent of the national market.

➤ HAM
A honey of a slicer

Harry Hoenselaar kept going to the wooden garage at his home on Gruebner Avenue in northeast Detroit in the late 1940s trying to make a machine that would carve ham off the bone in one perfect, unending slice. A tinker-

er, he was sure he could turn a kitchen knife, scrap wood, a metal pie tin and a washing machine motor into a machine the restaurant industry would love. But no one cared. So Hoenselaar created a whole new product category: the spiral-sliced ham. He launched a family business, Honey Baked Ham, that eventually numbered more than 300 stores nationwide. In 1957, Hoenselaar (pronounced HUNS-ler) opened his first store on Fenkell in Detroit. His smoky hams with their sweet, crunchy glazes grew into a local holiday staple. Detroiters began standing in long lines to pick them up at Christmas and Easter. By 1980, his spiral-slicer patents had expired and scores of imitators jumped into the market.

➤ HOT DOG, PART I
The coney island

Rare is the Detroiter who hasn't heard the accented order yelled from a waiter to a cook 5 feet away: "Two-to-go-no-onions."

The coney/Detroit relationship began with Gust Keros, who came to Detroit from Greece in 1910. He swept floors at Kelsey-Hayes Co., pushed a popcorn concession wagon around Belle Isle and ran a hat cleaning and shoe shine shop at the corner of Lafayette and Griswold before opening the American Coney Island there in 1929.

Nickel coneys proved popular and prof-

Ummm. Coneys. With. Without. To go. But don't ask for a 65-cent draught. This is a picture from 1977.

FACTOID

In Quebec, coney islands are called Hot Dogs Michigans, or simply Michigans.

FUN!

Farmer Keith Cronovich bags tomatoes for an Eastern Market customer in 1998.

itable, so Keros brought brother William over from Greece.

William Keros learned the business at the American and, when the storefront next door became free, started the Lafayette Coney Island.

What followed was enough coney begetting to rival the Bible, and Keros coneys eventually were served in shopping malls and eateries all over southeastern Michigan, outstate and even out of state.

The families remained friendly rivals, but at least once the competition turned a bit too intense. In 1969, there was a lawsuit over a secret chili recipe reportedly stolen by a disgruntled employee who jumped ship from the Lafayette to the American. The dispute was resolved out of court and bruised feelings were healed at a family picnic.

➤ HOT DOG, PART II

They plump when you cook 'em

Hygrade Food Products started in Brooklyn, N.Y., but moved in 1947 to a plant on Michigan Avenue in Detroit. In 1957, Detroit Tigers owner John Fetzer was hunting for a better dog to serve to fans. Hygrade won a competition among local sausage-makers, and Hygrade's Ball Park Franks became a part of Tigers lore. The company moved its headquarters to Southfield in 1969 and was acquired by a British conglomerate in 1976 and by the Sara Lee Corp. in 1989. And even though the baseball team was under new management and playing in a new stadium by

opening day 2000, Fetzer's choice franks were still on the menu at Comerica Park.

➤ SAUSAGE

Health? Eh. Tasty? You bet!

Wolfing down helpings of fatty, spicy, smoky sausages is a Detroit tradition, thanks to the large Central and Eastern European population. Kielbasa in Polish, *kolbasz* in Hungarian, *wurst* in German — whatever, they're ultra-caloric, often highly seasoned chunks of pork, sometimes other meats, mixed with fat and spices, and usually squeezed into 2-inch-diameter casings. The Center for Science in the Public Interest says to think of sausage as "heart attacks in a tube." But they're delicious. Many families make their own, guarding recipes with near-religious fervor. Those who buy them generally swear by their favorite brand. In Hamtramck, butchers work double time to meet holiday demand.

➤ MUSK-WHAT?:

Muskrat love

This tradition traces to the French settlers of the 1700s. People dined on muskrat along the lower Detroit River and Monroe County. It's usually reserved for special occasions, but in the late 1980s, state health officials cracked down on a restaurant that was serving muskrat regularly.

It is now illegal to sell muskrat in restaurants or private clubs unless the rodents came from an approved source. During the protests, muskrat lovers sang "Rally 'Round the Rat" to the tune of "Rally 'Round the Flag."

"Rally 'round the rat, boys
Rally 'round the rat
Nuts to the state boys
Let's give 'em chicken fat."
Muskrat tastes like, well, depends on whom you ask: Some say rabbit; others, squirrel or duck.

➤ EASTERN MARKET

Face-to-face with farmers

Farmers arrive early — some by 1 a.m. Many come six days a week — one day to sell to you, five days to sell to supermarkets and restaurants, hospitals and hotels.

The market actually is busiest between midnight and 6 a.m. on weekdays. Saturday, for many farmers, is a lark — a way to make extra money.

Eastern Market is the largest open-air wholesale-retail market in the United States., according to Lois Johnson and Margaret

FUN!

Thomas, who published a 166-page examination of the place titled "Detroit's Eastern Market."

On an average summer Saturday, about 325 farmers and about 100 vendors and 150 shopkeepers market their goods on the grounds along Russell just north of Gratiot. At least 15,000 people shop at Eastern Market on Saturdays.

Numerous languages representing myriad ethnic groups can be heard among the shoppers as they stroll the stalls of fresh vegetables, fruit, eggs, plants, condiments . . . you name it.

The city has run markets since 1802. Earlier venues: inside city hall in the 1840s and in Cadillac Square.

Eastern Market has been there since 1887. Before then? It was a city graveyard; 6,500 bodies were exhumed and moved by 1891. Most of those dead bodies were moved east to a spot that seemed remote back then: Conner, just south of I-94. A hay market stood on the site, too; so did the Detroit House of Correction, before the facility moved to western Wayne County.

➤ **VERNORS**

Yeah, it's an acquired taste

James Vernor was a druggist with a shop at Clifford and Woodward, experimenting on the side with ginger drinks, something of a rage in 1861. The Civil War began; Vernor joined the Union Army, serving with the Michigan unit that captured Confederate President Jefferson Davis. He returned to Detroit at the end of the war to find a ginger drink he stored in an oak cask tasted downright dandy.

The aged-four-years-in-wood formula remained a family secret years after Vernor left his downtown pharmacy and went into the soft-drink business full-time.

The drink has been enjoyed many ways since then: served with vanilla ice cream, called the Boston cooler; served piping hot, or served as a medicinal prescribed by countless doctors and moms for kids with upset tummies.

Until 1985, Vernors was made and bottled in Detroit, for many years at a riverfront plant, and after 1951 at a green-and-yellow, glass-fronted plant on Woodward near Wayne State. The building was famous for its sign: Hundreds of flickering lights showed Vernors being poured into a glass by a gnome.

In 1966, the family-owned company was sold to a group of investors, sold several times again and is now part of . . .

➤ **FAYGO**

Which way did he go?

Brothers Perry and Ben Feigenson founded Faygo Beverages in Detroit in 1907. Their soft-drink company became one of the nation's top independent bottlers, though it always lived in the shadows of Coca-Cola and Pepsi. But Faygo was a market leader in what the Two Big Guys couldn't bottle: red pop.

From cola to red pop, Faygo has quenched Detroit's thirst since 1907.

For a time in the '50s and '60s, though, Faygo's television commercials that were the talk of the land. One spot, now in the Advertising Hall of Fame, featured the villain Black Bart, who tried to rob the Wells Faygo Express and was foiled by the Faygo Kid.

It featured the memorable line, "Which way did he go? Which way did he go? He went for FAAAYYY-GOOOO!"

Another favorite was the Uptown Bottle Blower, who was "too pooped to participate" until he guzzled a slug of Faygo's Uptown lemon-lime. In 1986, Faygo was bought by the TreeSweet Cos. of Houston.

➤ **SANDERS**

From fountain to hot fudge

Frederick Sanders opened his first candy and ice cream store on Woodward in 1875. He invented the ice cream soda after the sweet cream he usually mixed with carbonated water and chocolate syrup turned sour. A customer suggested he substitute ice cream. The rest is soda fountain history.

Generations of Detroiters remember the treat of going to a neighborhood Sanders for a sundae or soda. The business leveled off at 145 outlets regionally in 1965. But in the mid-1970s increased competition led to Sanders' slide. In the 1980s, Sanders twice filed for bankruptcy protection. It remained family-owned until Country Home Bakers of Bridgeport, Conn., bought its assets in 1988. Today, the Sanders name continues on candy and hot fudge produced by Country Home's Sanders Sales Inc. And Detroiters can still satisfy their hot fudge cream puff cravings at scores of local restaurants.

➤ **The proper soda:** Fred Sanders' great-grandson, Jack Sanders, once gave this recipe for the family's original ice cream soda:

"First you spoon in a ladle full of chocolate syrup. You add a few squirts of carbonated

The Woodward Avenue building where Vernors was made and bottled was famous for its sign: Hundreds of flickering lights showed Vernors being poured into a glass by a gnome.

FUN!

A very young Jimmy Schmidt prepares oysters at the now-closed London Chop House in 1979.

The highest flier of all was Jimmy Schmidt. Like other local culinary notables, he earned his toque at the legendary London Chop House, succeeding the above mentioned Poncho in 1977 at the tender age of 22. By age 30, the Illinois native had teamed up with a flashy California restaurateur to create a huge, trendy restaurant called the Rattlesnake Club in Denver. It earned raves nationally, but as the partners expanded the concept to Detroit and Washington, D.C., the marriage broke up. Schmidt walked away with the Detroit Rattlesnake, which opened in 1988. He later operated at least seven other restaurants in and around the city. But by early 2000, he was down to one — the Rattlesnake — and a catering business. "Things were getting stretched too thin," he said.

➤ **PIZZA! PIZZA!**

Our slices of the pie

In the late 20th Century, Detroit was literally (and figuratively) rolling in pizza dough. We had huge competitors such as Ann Arbor-based Domino's, the world's largest pizza chain, and Little Caesars of Detroit and regional chains such as Hungry Howie's, Papa Romano's, Cottage Inn, Buddy's and Shield's tossing their fortunes into the ring. Many Detroiters remembered a simpler time — when the debate was over who made the best square deep-dish pizza in town, Buddy's or Shield's. The two had their beginnings in 1946 as watering holes on Detroit's east side — Buddy's at 6 Mile and Conant, where it still operates, and Shield's at 6 Mile and Davison. According to published accounts, their rivalry developed after the 1970 defection of the pizza chef from Buddy's to Shield's, where he began making deep-dish pizzas. The parody punk band the Polish Muslims later immortalized the stuff in the song "My Pizza's Shield's," sung to the tune of "My Lips Are Sealed."

water. You drop in two scoops of ice cream. You add two more squirts of carbonated water. Mix it with a spoon. And you have a wonderful, frothy drink." The trick: Don't hit the ice cream with the carbonated water, or the ice cream will turn to ice.

➤ **WHITE CAPS**

The great chefs of Detroit

A lot of fine chefs have made Detroit restaurants famous. (Remember Poncho at the London Chop House?) But until the 1970s and '80s, not many stirred the pot like Duglass Duglass and Jimmy Schmidt.

Duglass, a Detroiter whose real name was Douglas Grech, burst onto the local scene in the early '70s as executive chef of the Pontchartrain Hotel and maestro of his own locally televised cooking show, "Duglass Duglass" (pronounced doo-GLAHSS doo-GLAHSS). He studied in France and picked up the moniker from the French pronunciation of his name.

Later, he opened Restaurant Duglass in Southfield, morphing it into Brasserie Duglass before closing it in 1989. Duglass drifted from the food scene and later worked as an interior designer.

FUN!

Fat Tuesday treat

Polish pastries known as paczki (POONCH-key), oozing jelly or custard and dusted with confectioners' sugar, became the pre-Lenten piece de resistance in Detroit in the 1980s and '90s. No one knows exactly why these hefty, deep-fried orbs, containing as much as 25 grams of fat and far more grams of guilt, suddenly became THE thing to eat on Fat Tuesday, the day before Lent begins. Some Free Press staffers blamed the newspaper for writing so much about them. Purists say the commercial ones bear no resemblance to traditional paczki, which are more like beignets than the oversized jelly doughnuts the Polish bakeries in Hamtramck began churning out by the box load. Lines formed outside the shops before dawn on Fat Tuesday. Soon every pastry shop and supermarket in town was making them, and before long, paczki fever swept the nation.

➤ **Say it correctly:** One pastry is a paczek (POON-check). Two or more are "paczki."

Free Press file photo

Paczki. They are sinfully fattening and have no redeeming nutritional value, but every Lenten season finds metro Detroiters wolfing 'em down big time.

Detroit's gift to gourmands

Gael Greene was New York City's (and, ergo, the nation's) most influential restaurant critic for much of the 1970s and 1980s. She grew up in northwest Detroit and attended the University of Michigan. Greene gained attention for being one of the first critics who took her eyes off the plate and began to write about the experience, instead of the art, of dining.

Greene's lifestyle matches her writing in walking the thin line between the flamboyant and the outrageous — she has written several erotic novels and had a much publicized relationship with a leading porn film star. "What I am and do reflects lust, greed, and curiosity," Greene said in a 1985 interview. What contribution did Detroit make to Greene's gastronomic development? In her first book, "Bite," Greene calls Detroit "the frozen steppes of a vast culinary wasteland." Meeow.

Our history with booze

Some American cities were founded by groups like the Puritans who disdained alcohol. Not Detroit. It was settled by the French, who brought 15 barrels of brandy when they landed on July 24, 1701.

The next two ethnic groups to dominate the city were the Irish and Germans, for whom drinking was social tradition. For 300 years, alcohol has played a major role in Detroit's business, culture and politics.

Try this bracer:
The value of all alcoholic beverage sales in Michigan 1999: $4.6 billion.

This natty 1920s fellow reveals his illegal stash strapped to his argyled calf.

Free Press file photo

FUN!

> "The leading chiefs complain that the English are killing their young men with spirits . . . They say they lose more men by rum than they lose by war . . . "

➤ **Detroit's first controversy:** Two Catholic missionaries who came with Cadillac to Detroit immediately fought the French practice of supplying alcohol to the Indians. Cadillac got into several rows with Jesuits, complaining that the priests were getting in his way with their anti-booze policy.

➤ **Enter the Brits:** When the British ran Detroit later in the 18th Century, an officer wrote to the governor about a complaint from the Indians: "The leading chiefs complain that the English are killing their young men with spirits . . . They say they lose more men by rum than they lose by war . . . "

➤ **Lewis Cass and the Indians:** Cass, the territorial governor, negotiated several treaties with the Indians in the early 19th Century. He denounced supplying the tribes with alcohol but at the same time used alcohol to bend them his way. Between 1813 and 1836, Cass was the governor of the Michigan Territory, superintendent of Indian Affairs for the upper Great Lakes and U.S. secretary of War, the department which then supervised Indian business. Geographer Bernard Peters wrote that Cass used copious amounts of whiskey to persuade Michigan Indians to give up their land. The Saginaw Chippewa, for example, turned over 6 million acres in 1819 after negotiations that Cass lubricated with 662 gallons of whiskey.

➤ **Whiskey democracy:** In 1798, an election was held in a Detroit bar for the Wayne County representative to the legislature of the Northwest Territory. Opponents charged the winner provided liquor to voters. One of Michigan's first seats of government was in another drinking establishment, Richard Smythe's Tavern, starting in August 1805.

➤ **A new concept in drinking:** By the Civil War, German immigrants had introduced beer gardens to Detroit. They came to dot the east side — outdoor taverns decorated with trees, shrubs and vines, where patrons often were serenaded by bands. One beer garden in 1865 was 4 acres in size and highlighted by gravel walks, statues and carnival-like shooting galleries.

➤ **Hiring the inebriated:** In the 19th Century, Detroit saloons served as informal hiring halls as well as union halls, especially during strikes. In 1906, Cadillac Motor chief Henry Leland and the Board of Commerce wrote that saloons in factory neighborhoods "lessen the efficiency of workmen . . . "

➤ **Saloon ambience:** Most Detroit saloons before World War I served free food during lunch, from elaborate spreads in the tonier places to hearty stews and soups in the working person's establishments.

➤ **Females forbidden:** For many years, a 19th-Century Detroit law forbade women to work in bars. It was often ignored.

➤ **Buy signal:** Anglim's bar on Gratiot had an electrified chair: The bartender would switch it on to jolt an unsuspecting customer after it was announced that the next patron to stand would buy a round for the house.

➤ **Beer and brats:** In Corktown and Detroit's German neighborhoods, owners often combined saloons and grocery stores, in which the aroma of malt would mix with the smell of potatoes, cheese and onions.

➤ **Beat goes on:** A description of a typical Detroit saloon piano player from the 1900 era: "Pallid young men, addicted to strong drink or dope, who could play with one hand, roll a cigarette with the other, carry on a conversation with a waiter and every few minutes toss off a drink, without ever missing a note."

➤ **Brewski — the craft:** Beer making was an important industry that employed tens of thousands of Detroiters, many of them immigrants, for 150 years. The British, Irish, Scottish, Germans and Poles were the principal brewers.

➤ **How wet I am:** Between 1875 and 1925, saloons were a major political force in Detroit. In some years, more than one-third of the city council members were saloon owners or bartenders, and saloon interests controlled many voting districts. The saloon operatives stuffed ballot boxes, corrupted voting rolls and used alcohol in an attempt to sway voters. Even Detroit's great reform mayor, Hazen Pingree, kicked off his 1889 campaign in Baltimore Red's bar to quell potentially damaging rumors that he was dry.

➤ **Nomenclature:** "Big Fives" were 5-cent glasses of beer; "boombas" were big mugs of beer; "shells" were small, thin glasses of beer.

➤ **Prohibition I:** Detroiters ignored state laws that banned the sale of alcohol between 1853 and 1867. During that time, the number of Detroit saloons tripled, the number of breweries doubled and the number of distilleries quintupled.

➤ **Prohibition II:** In 1916, Michigan voters approved a statewide prohibition on alcohol that went into effect at midnight April 30, 1918. Two years later, the nation went dry.

➤ **What prohibition?:** Before Prohibition, Detroit had 1,500 bars. By 1925, the number of blind pigs was estimated at 5,000 to 25,000. The New York Times called rum running Detroit's second-biggest industry, after cars. In 1932, thousands of Detroiters — led by Mayor Frank Murphy and a 200-piece band — paraded against Prohibition. The Free Press' Malcolm Bingay wrote: "It was absolutely impossible to get a drink in Detroit unless you walked at least 10 feet and told a busy bartender what you wanted in a voice loud enough for him to hear you above the uproar." In 1933, Michigan became the first state to ratify the 21st Amendment, and Prohibition ended after Utah became the 36th state to ratify the amendment, on Dec. 5, 1933.

Detroiters celebrate the end of prohibition in December 1933. During prohibition, Detroit was far from dry. One estimate suggested Detroit had 25,000 illegal drinking joints in 1925.

FUN!

Free Press file photo

Detroit's most famous beer, Stroh's, bragged about being fire-brewed. The beer was a staple here for more than 100 years until the brewery closed in 1985.

HEAD OF THEIR GLASS: In the 1870s, Detroit had 105,000 residents and 29 breweries. By 1986, the metro area had 4.5 million residents and no major beer maker. For 150 years, brewing beer was a dog-eat-dog business in Detroit. Here is a look at bygone brewers:

➤ **William Moloney**: Brewed 1877-1891. Moloney, from Ireland, appealed to two sizable ethnic groups by naming his Corktown firm the Vienna Brewing Co. and making Dublin Stout.

➤ **The Grieser Family**: Brewed 1871-1900. German-American Eliza Grieser inherited the Grieser Brewery on Detroit's east side from her late husband and became one of the few female brewery owners in Detroit.

➤ **Wolverine**: Brewed 1933-1942. This post-Prohibition brewery in Pontiac was a hit among Oakland County drinkers, who quaffed its Dark Horse Ale, Rhein-Brau and Chief Pontiac brands until wartime restrictions killed it.

➤ **Goebel**: Brewed 1873-1964. For decades, Goebel provided stout competition to next-door neighbor Stroh's. In the 1880s, Goebel was Detroit's third-largest brewer after Voigt and Kling. During its death throes in the 1960s, the company tried a new marketing angle — by strangling its well-known cartoon rooster in a TV ad. Customers jokingly referred to low-cost Goebel as *Zhoe-bell*, "the fine French import."

➤ **Pfieffer:** Brewed 1889-1972. The patriarch was German immigrant Conrad Pfieffer. Alfred Epstein, a rare Jewish brewer in Detroit, turned Pfieffer into one of the hottest regional brands after World War II. Unable to compete nationally, Pfieffer went pfft in 1972.

➤ **Zynda:** Brewed 1886-1948. One of Detroit's leading Polish brewers, John Zynda came to Detroit in 1880. His White Eagle beer was made near Eastern Market, and the family home on Bellevue had geese on the grounds and a chapel with pews on the second floor. Many a guest at Detroit's Polish weddings in the early 20th Century toasted the bride and groom with Zyndapride lager.

➤ **Stroh:** Brewed 1850-1985. Bernhard Stroh arrived from Germany in 1850. By the 1880s, the Stroh family had temporarily renamed the Stroh Brewery the Lion Brewing Co. and built a beer factory with two sculpted 12-foot lions crouching on the roof. Stroh flourished, outlasting all Detroit brewers, but it failed to make it as a national brand in a time of beer-industry consolidation.

➤ **19th-Century brew pubs:** Most of Detroit's breweries before the turn of the century offered a pub where the samples were free. The pubs were open each day, and "important" residents — meaning cops, judges, politicians or journalists — would be served to their hearts' content. The Strohaus in the old Stroh brewery continued a version of that tradition into the 1980s.

➤ **Microbreweries:** The beer business has come full circle. After Stroh's became the last beer maker to brew in Detroit — in 1985 — about two dozen microbreweries have opened in southeastern Michigan. That puts the local beer industry at about the size it was during the Civil War era, according to beer expert Peter Blum. The Traffic Jam in Detroit in 1993 became Michigan's first brew pub — a bar making its own beer.

SOURCE: "BREWED IN DETROIT: BREWERIES AND BEERS SINCE 1830," BY PETER H. BLUM.

Four famous bars

➤ **Old Hotel Pontchartrain:** The Tiffany-styled bar in the old hotel, which opened in 1907 on Woodward Avenue, was a gathering place for car people in the early days of the industry. Whiskey was 15 cents a glass; beer was 10 cents. As General Motors' Alfred Sloan wrote: "The Pontchartrain was where motor-car gossip was heard first. New models customarily had debuts there ... Even on ordinary days ... the tablecloths would be covered with sketches: crankshafts, chassis, details of motors . . . and all sorts of mechanism. Partnerships were made and ended there."

➤ **Billy Boushaw's:** Known affectionately as Billy da Bum, Boushaw for many years operated a saloon at Atwater and Beaubien. From its opening in 1888, Boushaw's place became a hangout for politicians, seafarers and various Detroit characters. His beef stew became famous across the city. About nine sailors bunked there, but on election days, up to 300 voters would give their address as 459 E. Atwater. He called his establishment "da foist of da foist" because it was in the First Ward's first precinct. Boushaw died in 1937.

➤ **The Bucket of Blood:** The Bucket, at Hastings and Clinton, was widely regarded as a tough town's toughest joint at the turn of the century. An all-night saloon with an integrated clientele, the often-crowded Bucket was the scene of card games, crap games, dice games, open prostitution, so-called "wild music" and considerable knife and gun play. The bouncer was known as Big Boy. He was heavily muscled, 6-foot-4, 260 pounds, and he carried a blackjack and a .44 revolver.

➤ **The Flame Show Bar:** At Canfield and John R, the Flame in the 1950s featured such hot acts as Dinah Washington, Billie Holiday and Sarah Vaughan. Gwen and Anna Gordy, sisters of Motown founder Berry Gordy, ran the photo concession, snapping shots of customers that were developed on the premises by their brothers, Robert and George. Berry Gordy, then a young songwriter, got a break at the Flame when owner Al Green, who was also Jackie Wilson's manager, started using Gordy's songs.

Detroit models

Detroiters are credited with inventing at least four drinks: The Hummer, the Bullshot, Cold Duck and the Angel Kiss. Oh, and the Freaky Deaky.

➤ **The Hummer, version I:** Jerome Adams, tending bar at Detroit's Bayview Yacht Club in 1968, whipped up the concoction of ice cream, rum and Kahlua and passed out samples to people at the bar. One patron remarked that a couple of them "would make you want to hum," Adams said in 1998.
His recipe: ½ cup white Bacardi rum, ½ cup Kahlua, 1⅓ cups vanilla ice cream and 1 cup crushed ice, blended until smooth in an electric blender and served in a cocktail glass.

Free Press file photo

A driver loads cases of Goebel into a delivery truck in the 1950s. Aging east siders will tell you Stroh's fire-brewed beer outclassed Goebel's extra-dry.

➤ **The Hummer, version II:** Some credit the Hummer to experiments in the early 1970s by London Chop House bartender Farouk Elhaje and owner Lester Gruber.

➤ **The Bullshot:** Gruber also was present at the creation of the Bullshot, invented in 1952 at Detroit's Caucus Club by John Hurley, a local advertising man. Hurley had Campbell's Soup Co. as a client and was trying to invent a drink that would boost sales of its beef bouillon. The drink that Hurley and Gruber concocted contains 1½ ounces of vodka, 3½ ounces of bouillon, 3 ice cubes and a wedge of lemon, flavored with a generous dash of a special concoction made up of Worcestershire sauce, Tabasco, Angostura bitters and celery salt.

➤ **Cold duck:** The sparkling wine known as Cold Duck was invented in 1937 by Harold Borgman, then owner of Detroit's Pontchartrain Wine Cellers, who picked up on an old German custom. According to Joe Beyer, who later owned the Wine Cellars, it was customary at the end of an evening of revelry to combine the dregs of all of the opened bottles and mix them with champagne. The result was known as Kalte Ende — Cold End — until some Teutonic punster changed the name to Kalte Ente, which means Cold Duck. Borgman's version combines 1 part dry California burgundy with two parts New York State champagne. Bottled Cold Duck became so popular that, for a time, it was the best-selling sparkling wine in America.

➤ **Angel Kiss:** Brandy, whipped cream and half a maraschino cherry. From the 1890s.

➤ **Freaky Deaky:** A bartender came up with a cocktail to celebrate Detroit's sexually explicit dance of the 1970s that made headlines nationwide: Equal parts of Southern Comfort, curacao, pineapple juice and cranberry juice. Add a splash of soda; serve over ice.

The Detroit Almanac

16. SPO

"The entire town went gaga. Everybody was downtown, whoopin' and hollering."

— *Second baseman* **Charlie Gehringer** *on Detroit after the Tigers' 1935 World Series victory. "I tried to take a friend downtown, but golly, everything was blocked up. You couldn't cross the streets, the city was such a mess."*

It was the free world vs. Nazi Germany when Joe Louis fough[t] Max Schmeling in 1938.

Joe, Gordie, Isiah & Ty...

Few places in the world offer metro Detroit's range of big-time sports. And few groups of people take their sports more seriously than metro Detroiters. Major-league sports. Minor-league sports. College sports. Prep sports. Good sports. Bad sports. You name it; we've got it, at the highest level of competition.

Boxing

Joe Louis: No. 1

"When Joe's in the room," Muhammad Ali once said, "I am not the greatest."

Boxer Joe Louis was Detroit's greatest athlete. He held the heavyweight championship longer than any man — from 1937 to 1949. He fought 71 professional bouts and won 68 — 54 by knockout.

> A Joe Louis jab was "like someone jammed an electric bulb in your face and busted it."

But his most memorable victory came in knocking down racial barriers that had withstood every other opponent. At the beginning of his career, Detroit stopped what it was doing to listen to Joe's bouts on the radio. By his prime, when Louis knocked out Max Schmeling in a bout that pitted the free world against Nazi Germany, the nation stopped to listen.

He was born Joseph Louis Barrow, the grandson of slaves, on May 13, 1914, in a small Alabama town.

In his early teens, he moved with his family to Detroit. Soon, he had dropped out of school to deliver coal and ice, trying to help his family survive tough economic times.

His mother scratched together enough money to give the young Louis violin lessons. But he secretly used it to pay for boxing lessons at the Brewster Recreational Center on the near east side. He fought 58 times as an amateur and won 54, including a national Golden Gloves championship. He used sneakers instead of boxing shoes and reused the wrapping that bandaged his knuckles.

Then he met Detroiter John Roxborough, bail bondsman, numbers runner, politician and philanthropist. That meeting changed the young boxer's life.

"Name's Joe Louis Barrow," he told Roxborough after sparring one day in the Brewster ring.

"That's too long," Roxborough replied. "We'll just call you Joe Louis."

Louis went 27-0 with 23 knockouts when, on June 13, 1936, he met a 31-year-old German underdog named Max Schmeling. Twelve rounds later, Louis was 27-1 and Adolf Hitler had a new hero.

Barely a year later, June 22, 1937, the 6-foot-1, 197-pound Louis won the heavyweight championship, knocking out James J. Braddock — who said being hit by a Joe Louis jab was "like someone jammed an electric bulb in your face and busted it."

Winning the championship served to set up the rematch with Schmeling, exactly one year later, June 22, 1938, as Hitler prepared for war.

Perhaps no athlete before or since carried the mantle that Louis carried going into that match.

President Franklin D. Roosevelt, feeling the champ's biceps weeks before the fight, told him, "Joe, we need muscles like yours to beat Germany."

SPORTS

Joe Louis: Tale of the tape

1934

Date	Opponent	City	Decision
July 4	Jack Kracken	Chicago	Won on KO in first round.
July 11	Willie Davis	Chicago	Won on KO in third round.
July 29	Larry Udell	Chicago	Won on KO in second round.
Aug. 13	Jack Kranz	Chicago	Won on decision in sixth round.
Aug. 27	Buck Everett	Chicago	Won on KO in second round.
Sept. 11	Alex Borchuck	Detroit	Won on KO in fourth round.
Sept. 24	Adolph Wiater	Chicago	Won on decision in 10th round.
Oct. 24	Art Sykes	Chicago	Won on KO in eighth round.
Oct. 30	Jack O'Dowd	Detroit	Won on KO in second round.
Nov. 14	Stanley Poreda	Chicago	Won on KO in first round.
Nov. 30	Charley Massera	Chicago	Won on KO in third round.
Dec. 14	Lee Ramage	Chicago	Won on KO in third round.

1935

Date	Opponent	City	Decision
Jan.4	Patsy Perroni	Detroit	Won on decision on 10th round.
Jan.11	Hans Birkie	Pittsburgh	Won on KO in 10th round.
Feb. 21	Lee Ramage	Los Angeles	Won on KO in second round.
Mar. 8	Donald (Reds) Barry	San Francisco	Won on KO in third round.
Mar.28	Natie Brown	Detroit	Won on decision in 10th round.
Apr. 12	Ray Lazer	Chicago	Won on KO in third round.
Apr.22	Biff Benton	Dayton	Won on KO in second round.
Apr. 27	Roscoe Toles	Flint	Won on KO in sixth round.
May 3	Willie Davis	Peoria	Won on KO in second round.
May 7	Gene Stanton	Kalamazoo	Won on KO in third round.
June 25	Primo Carnera	New York	Won on KO in sixth round.
Aug. 7	King Levinksy	Chicago	Won on KO in first round.
Sept. 24	Max Baer	New York	Won on KO in fourth round.
Dec. 13	Paolino Uzcudun	New York	Won on KO in fourth round.

1936

Date	Opponent	City	Decision
Jan. 17	Charley Retzlaff	Chicago	Won on KO in first round.
June 19	Max Schmeling	New York	Loss: KO in 12th.
Aug. 17	Jack Sharkey	New York	Won on KO in third round.
Sept. 22	Al Ettore	Philadelphia	Won on KO in fifth round.
Oct. 9	Jorge Brescia	New York	Won on KO in third round.
Dec. 14	Eddie Simms	Cleveland	Won on KO in first round.

Max Schmeling is knocked to the canvas by Joe Louis during their rematch in 1938, the bout that made Louis an American hero.

1937

Date	Opponent	City	Decision
Jan. 11	Steve Ketchell	Buffalo	Won on KO in second round.
Jan. 27	Bob Pastor	New York	Won on decision in 10 rounds.
Feb. 17	Natie Brown	Kansas City	Won on KO in fourth round.
June 22	James J. Braddock	Chicago	Won on KO in eighth round. Louis wins heavyweight title. Total gate receipts: $715,470. Louis' purse: $103,684.
Aug. 30	Tommy Farr	New York	Won on decision in 15th round. Total gate receipts: $325,707. Louis'purse: $102,578.

1938

Date	Opponent	City	Decision
Feb. 22	Nathan Mann	New York	Won on KO in third round. Total gate receipts: $111,718. Louis' purse: $40,522.
Apr. 1	Harry Thomas	Chicago	Won on KO in fifth round. Total gate receipts; $48,192. Louis' purse: $16,659.
June 22	Max Schmeling	New York	Won on KO in first round. Total gate receipts: $1,015,012. Louis' purse: $349,228.

1939

Date	Opponent	City	Decision
Jan. 25	John Henry Lewis	New York	Won on KO in first round. Total gate receipts: $102,015. Louis' purse: $34,413.
Apr. 17	Jack Roper	Los Angeles	Won on KO in first round. Total gate receipts: $87,679. Louis' purse: $34,850.
June 28	Tony Galento	New York	Won on KO in fourth round. Total gate receipts: $333,308. Louis' purse: $114,332.
Sept. 20	Bob Pastor	Detroit	Won on KO in 11th round. Total gate receipts: $247,870. Louis' purse: $118,400.

1940

Date	Opponent	City	Decision
Feb. 9	Arturo Godoy	New York	Won decision in 15 rounds. Total gate receipts: $88,491. Louis' purse: $23,620.
Mar. 29	Johnny Paycheck	New York	Won decision in fourth round. Total gate receipts: $62,481. Louis' purse: $19,908.
June 20	Arturo Godoy	New York	Won on KO in eighth round. Total gate receipts: $164,120. Louis' purse: 55,989.
Dec. 16	Al McCoy	Boston	Won on Ko in sixth round. Total gate receipts: $51,014. Louis' purse: $17,938.

1941

Date	Opponent	City	Decision
Jan. 31	Red Burman	New York	Won on KO in fifth round. Total gate receipts: $62,899. Louis' purse: $21,023.
Feb. 17	Gus Dorazio	Philadelphia	Won on KO in second round. Total gate receipts: $57,199. Louis' purse: $18,731.
Mar. 21	Abe Simon	Detroit	Won on KO in 13th round. Total gate receipts $54,736. Louis' purse: $19,400.
Apr. 8	Tony Musto	St. Louis	Won on KO in ninth round. Total gate receipts $52,993. Louis' purse: $17,468.
May 23	Buddy Baer	Washington D.C.	Won on disqualification in seventh. Total gate receipts: $105,183. Louis' purse: $36,886.
June 18	Billy Conn	New York	Won on KO in 13th round. Total gate receipts: $456,743. Louis' purse: $152,905.
Sept. 29	Lou Nova	New York	Won on KO in sixth round. Total gate receipts: $583,711. Louis' purse: $199,500.

1942

Date	Opponent	City	Decision
Jan. 9 to	Buddy Baer	New York	Won by KO in first round. Total gate receipts: $189,700. Louis' purse: $65,200. Donated Naval Relief Fund.
Mar. 27	Abe Simon	New York	Won on KO in sixth round. Total gate receipts: $139,136. Louis' purse: $45,882.
			Donated to Army Relief Fund.

1946

Date	Opponent	City	Decision
June 19	Billy Con	New York	Won on KO in eighth round. Total gate receipts: $1,925,564. Louis' purse: $625,916.
Sept. 16	Tami Mauriello	New York	Won on KO in first round. Total gate receipts: $335,063. Louis' purse: $103,611.

1947

Date	Opponent	City	Decision
Dec. 5	Jersey Joe Walcott	New York	Won on decision in 15 rounds. Total gate receipts: $216,497. Louis purse: $75,968.

1948

Date	Opponent	City	Decision
June 25	Jersey Joe Walcott	New York	Won on KO in 11th round. Total gate receipts: $841,739. Louis' purse: $252,522.

1950

Date	Opponent	City	Decision
Sept. 27	Ezzard Charles	New York	Loss: Decision in 15 rounds. Total gate receipts: $205,370. Louis' purse: $53,908.
Nov. 29	Cesar Brion	New York	Won on decision in 10 rounds.

1951

Date	Opponent	City	Decision
Jan. 3	Freddie Beshore	Detroit	Won on KO in four rounds.
Feb. 7	Omelio Agramonte	Miami	Won on decisions in 10 rounds.
Feb. 23	Andy Walker	San Francisco	Won on KO in 10th round.
May 2	Omello Agramonte	Detroit	Won on decision in 10 rounds.
June 15	Lee Savoid	New York	Won on KO in sixth round.
Aug. 1	Cesar Brion	San Francisco	Won on decisions in 10 rounds.
Aug.15	Jimmy Bivins	Baltimore	Won on decision in 10 rounds.
Oct. 26	Rocky Marciano	New York	Loss: KO in eighth round.

SPORTS

Hitler replied with a prefight cable to Schmeling: "To the coming World's Champion, Max Schmeling. Wishing you every success."

It was over in the first round, after 2 minutes and 4 seconds and 40 vicious Louis punches. Boxing had the same heavyweight champion. Americans had a new hero — and white Americans found themselves looking up to a black man.

Louis continued to fight often and well, retiring as heavyweight champion on March 1, 1949.

Life outside the ring, however, wasn't nearly as simple. Money woes prompted comebacks and losses, the saddest in 1951 when an aging Louis was knocked out by the young, strong Rocky Marciano.

Purses from Louis' fights added up to $4.7 million, but tax woes and health problems dogged him for the rest of his life. He lived off of his fame, serving as a greeter at Caesar's Palace in Las Vegas. He died April 12, 1981, at age 66 — the morning after he'd sat in a wheelchair watching Larry Holmes successfully defend his heavyweight championship.

Other Detroiters subsequently made their names in the boxing ring — notably longtime champion Thomas (Hit Man) Hearns and trainer Emanuel Steward.

But no boxer — and no Detroit athlete — would ever again approach the pinnacle Joe Louis ascended the night he knocked out Schmeling.

Thomas Hearns: Sports Illustrated called him "one of the greatest fighters ever" after Hearns, then 41, hurt an ankle and failed to come out for the third round of a scheduled 12-round bout against Uriah Grant in April 2000. It was supposed to be Hearns' last fight, but he never got around to actually declaring his retirement. His 23-year career began at the now-famous Kronk Gym on Detroit's west side.

He was a tall, skinny kid who quickly won the nickname Hit Man because of his tough hometown and his quick fists. In early bouts at the now-demolished Olympia Stadium, the red-robed Hearns would enter the ring to the pounding beat of the "Rocky" theme song. Many of Hearns' fights were the most dramatic of his time. He knocked out Roberto Duran, one of boxing's great champions, with an awesome right-handed punch that frightened all who saw the Panamanian collapse and fall on his face, then dragged, still unconscious, to his corner. Hearns won seven titles in six divisions at weights from 145 to 190, unprecedented in boxing.

Even his defeats by Marvin Hagler and Sugar Ray Leonard in the early 1980s are counted as among the best fights of the 20th Century. (After a ferocious 8 minutes, Hagler refused to fight a rematch.) Hearns won 32 fights in a row to open his career, then lost to Leonard in a sudden 14th-round KO after being ahead on the judges' scoring cards. In 60-plus bouts, Hearns earned purses totaling more than $60 million.

ALAN R. KAMUDA/Detroit Free Press

SPORTS

Our Favorite Teams

1. 1901 Michigan Wolverines

Record: 11-0. **Coach:** Fielding H. Yost.

A new era started at Michigan: Fielding H. Yost became coach; he unleashed his "Point-a-Minute" attack; the Wolverines outscored their opponents, 550-0; and U-M captured its first national championship. Michigan won the title the next three years, too. The season ended with a 49-0 victory over Stanford in the first Rose Bowl, which was so disappointing to the Tournament of Roses committee that a second Rose Bowl wasn't held until 1916. The committee unsuccessfully switched to polo, chariot races and ostrich races.

2. 1979 Michigan State Spartans

Record: 26-6. **Coach:** Jud Heathcote.

It was the Magic season and it was Magic's game. Sophomore Earvin (Magic) Johnson scored 24 points and grabbed seven rebounds as the Spartans beat Larry Bird and unbeaten Indiana State, 75-64, for their first NCAA basketball championship. More key Spartans: Greg Kelser, Jay Vincent, Terry Donnelly, Mike Brkovich and Ron Charles.

3. 1997 Detroit Red Wings

Record: 38-26-18. **Coach:** Scotty Bowman.

The Red Wings ended Detroit's 42-year wait for its eighth Stanley Cup. After a so-so regular season, the Wings stormed through the playoffs, beating St. Louis in six, Anaheim in four, Colorado in six and Philadelphia in four. Goalie Mike Vernon won the Conn Smythe. More key Wings: Captain Steve Yzerman, Nick Lidstrom, Brendan Shanahan and Igor Larionov.

4. 1968 Detroit Tigers

Record: 103-59. **Manager:** Mayo Smith.

In the Year of the Pitcher, Denny McLain won the AL Cy Young and MVP awards by winning 31 games. But Mickey Lolich's heroics brought Detroit its first World Series title since 1945. He beat St. Louis three times, including the decisive Game 7 against Bob Gibson, 4-1. Other key Tigers: Al Kaline, Willie Horton, Mickey Stanley and Jim Northrup.

5. 1989 Detroit Pistons

Record: 63-19. **Coach:** Chuck Daly.

The Pistons won their first NBA championship when the best of their Bad Boys-era teams swept Magic Johnson's Los Angeles Lakers. The Pistons lost only two of 16 playoff games, both to Chicago. Joe Dumars, who averaged 27.3 points against LA, was the playoffs' MVP. Other key Pistons: Captain Isiah Thomas, Bill Laimbeer and Vinnie Johnson.

6. 1935 Detroit Tigers

Record: 93-58. **Manager:** Mickey Cochrane.

After failing in four World Series, the Tigers finally won the title, despite Hank Greenberg's broken wrist in Game 2. The decisive run came in the bottom of the ninth in Game 6 against the Chicago Cubs, when Goose Goslin singled in Mickey Cochrane with two out. Other key Tigers: Charlie Gehringer, Schoolboy Rowe, Tommy Bridges and Billy Rogell.

7. 1966 Michigan State Spartans

Record: 9-0-1, 7-0 Big Ten. **Coach:** Duffy Daugherty.

The '65 Spartans won a national championship but the '66 team played the "Game of the Century," a controversial 10-10 tie with Notre Dame. Irish coach Ara Parseghian ran out the clock instead of trying to win. MSU finished No. 2 in the polls behind the Irish. Key Spartans: George Webster, Bubba Smith, Gene Washington and Jimmy Raye.

8. 1959 Hamtramck Little League

Record: 13-0. **Manager:** Gene Piontkowski.

The Hamtramck Nationals won the state's only Little League World Series championship, at Williamsport, Pa. Art (Pinky) Deras won seven of the 13 tournament games and was selected player of the year. In the 7-1 semi-

Associated Press

Earvin (Magic) Johnson and the Spartans were No. 1 after beating Indiana State in the 1979 NCAA championship.

final victory over Kailua, Hawaii, Deras struck out 17 and came within an out of a no-hitter. In the 12-0 final victory over Auburn, Calif., Deras struck out 14 and hit a three-run homer. That gave him a streak of 75 scoreless innings. For the summer, he had 10 no-hitters and 296 strikeouts in 108 innings. The team was flown to California to appear on "The Lawrence Welk Show." Two years later, as a 14-year-old, Deras led virtually the same team to the national Pony League championship.

9. 1952 Detroit Red Wings

Record: 44-14-12. **Coach:** Tommy Ivan.

Perhaps the strongest of the Gordie Howe-led teams, the Wings won their fourth straight regular-season title with 100 points and then won all eight playoff games. Goalie Terry Sawchuk had two shutouts against Toronto in the semifinals and two against Montreal in the finals. He gave up only five goals for an unbelievable 0.63 goals-against average.

10. 1957 Detroit Lions

Record: 8-4. **Coach:** George Wilson.

To win their third NFL championship of the '50s, the Lions overcame: the resignation of coach Buddy Parker right before the season; Bobby Layne's broken ankle in the final home game; and a 27-7 deficit at San Francisco in a divisional playoff. George Wilson coached, Tobin Rote quarterbacked, and the Lions beat Cleveland, 59-14, in the championship game.

11. 1984 Detroit Tigers

Record: 104-58. **Manager:** Sparky Anderson.

The Tigers sprinted to a 35-5 start, led wire-to-wire, and beat the San Diego Padres in five games for their first World Series title since 1968. Bless You Boys! Jack Morris threw a no-hitter in April. Kirk Gibson belted a classic home run against Goose Gossage in Game 5. Larry Herndon caught the final out. Alan Trammell was MVP of the Series.

MARY SCHROEDER/Detroit Free Press

Sparky Anderson and the '84 Tigers lit up Detroit, bringing home the first World Series title since '68.

12. 1968-75 Hudson High Tigers

Record: 72 consecutive victories. **Coach:** Tom Saylor.

Hudson High won 72 straight football games in 1968-75, breaking the national record set by Jefferson City, Mo., in 1958-66, with a 24-14 victory over Kalamazoo Hackett on Nov. 15, 1975. The streak ended in the first Class C state title game, 38-22 to Ishpeming. The Michigan Sports Hall of Fame has inducted one team: the Hudson Tigers, in 1976.

13. 1983 Michigan Panthers

Record: 12-6. **Coach:** Jim Stanley.

Although the team existed only two years — and the USFL three — the Panthers captured the hearts of fans. Why? Detroit's teams had been basically awful since the '68 Tigers. In the playoffs, 60,237 saw the Panthers beat the Oakland Invaders, 37-21, and thousands ripped down the Silverdome goalposts and ripped up the turf. In the title game, at Denver's Mile High Stadium, the Panthers beat the Philadelphia Stars, 24-22. Bobby Hebert, MVP of the title game, connected with Anthony Carter on a 48-yard, game-clinching touchdown late in the fourth quarter.

14. 1992 Michigan Wolverines

Record: 25-9. **Coach:** Steve Fisher.

The Fab Five. Chris Webber, Juwan Howard, Jalen Rose, Jimmy King and Ray Jackson, who started a fashion trend by wearing baggy shorts, had the nation buzzing when they led Michigan to the NCAA championship game as freshmen. Jackson was the last to join the starting lineup, against Notre Dame in February. Duke, though, won the title, 71-51.

15. 1934 Stroh's Bohemian Beer

Stroh's was the first of the great beer teams that dominated bowling for two decades. In 1934, one year after it was formed by captain Joe Norris, Stroh's became the first team from Detroit to win the ABC national tournament and won the first of five World Match Game titles. The original team was Norris, Phil Bauman, John Crimmins, Cass Grygier and Walter Reppenhagen. Fred Gardella sometimes replaced Crimmins.

Baseball in Detroit

Detroit Tigers history: The moniker "Tigers" comes from the imagination of an anonymous headline writer at the Free Press, who wrote in the paper of April 16, 1895, "Strouther's Tigers Showed Up Very Nicely," and it stuck. The club owner was James Burns, a hotelier and Wayne County sheriff. In 1902, Burns sold the team to Samuel Angus, who sold it to William Hoover Yawkey in 1904 for $50,000. In 1907, a team executive, Frank Navin, purchased half interest from Yawkey for $40,000 and became president. Yawkey died in 1919. His heirs sold his half-ownership to industrialists Walter O. Briggs and John Kelsey for $500,000. In 1927, Briggs bought out Kelsey, and bought Navin's half-ownership from his estate after Navin died Nov. 13, 1935. Briggs died Jan. 17, 1952. Walter O. Briggs Jr. became president. The Briggs heirs sold the stock on Oct. 1, 1956, to a group of 11 broadcasters led by John Fetzer, Fred Knorr and Kenyon Brown for $5.5 million. Fetzer bought out Brown in 1960, and purchased Knorr's portion on Nov. 14, 1961, making him full owner. Domino's Pizza founder Tom Monaghan bought the team on Oct. 10, 1983, and sold it on Aug. 26, 1992, to rival and Little Caesars founder Mike Ilitch for about $83 million.

2000 value: $200 million, according to Forbes magazine.

Memorable fan moments at Tiger Stadium, 1912-1999

Bleacher Riot I, Oct. 9, 1934: Baseball officials yanked St. Louis outfielder Ducky Medwick from the seventh game of the World Series after bleacher fans pelt him with fruit, garbage and bottles for 18 minutes. Reason: Medwick had spiked the Tigers' Marv Owen. The Tigers lost the game and the series.

Biggest crowd, July 20, 1947: A standing-room-only throng of 58,369 watched the Tigers whip the Yankees in both games of a doubleheader.

First night game, June 15, 1948: The 182-million candlepower lights flashed on at sundown, and the crowd of 54,480 was "momentarily speechless" as the Tigers became the last American League team to play under the lights.

Tigers blow pennant, Oct. 1, 1967: The Tigers lost the pennant by blowing the second game of a doubleheader on the final day of a thrilling season. One fan jumped to the field and knelt in prayer outside the dugout. After-

First recorded game: Aug. 15, 1857. Members of the Franklin Baseball Club played at the corner of Beaubien and Adams, the Free Press reported.

First game between two teams: Aug. 8, 1859. The Detroits, composed of rich men, defeated the Early Risers, a team of working stiffs, 59-21, at a field near Grand River and Cass.

First pro game: May 12, 1879. Detroit's Hollinger's Nine lost to the Troy, N.Y., Haymakers, 7-1, before 1,500 fans at Recreation Park in today's Medical Center.

First major-league game: May 2, 1881. The Detroit Wolverines of the National League lost to Buffalo, 6-4, before 1,265 fans at Recreation Park. They played in the National League through 1888.

Tigers' first game: May 2, 1894. They actually didn't get the name until the 1895 season, but the team played in the Western League in this era, and lost its opener to Toledo, 4-3, at Boulevard Park near Belle Isle.

Tigers' first major-league game: April 25, 1901. They beat Milwaukee at Bennett Park (shown above), 14-13.

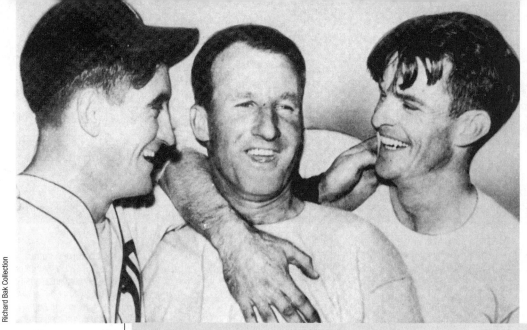

Mickey Cochrane, left, Goose Goslin and Tommy Bridges celebrate after the World Series victory in 1935. Bottom right: Al Kaline hit his way into the Hall of Fame.

WORLD SERIES VICTORIES

1984: The Roar of '84 began with a 35-5 start and didn't end until Kirk Gibson homered twice and the Tigers beat the San Diego Padres, 8-4, in the fifth and final game at Tiger Stadium.

1968: Denny McLain won 31 games in the regular season, but roly-poly left-hander Mickey Lolich was the World Series hero, winning three games as the Tigers beat St. Louis. He beat the Cardinals in Game 7, 4-1, in St. Louis.

1945: The Tigers clinched the American League pennant on Hank Greenberg's grand slam on the final day, then beat the Chicago Cubs, four games to three, in the World Series as Hal Newhouser fanned 22 and won twice. He beat the Cubs, 9-3, in Game 7 in Chicago.

All-time Tigers

MANAGER
Sparky Anderson
Tiger: 1979-95
Legacy: Won World Series in 1984. Twice American League manager of year. Holds club record for games (2,579), victories (1,331) and losses (1,248).

EXECUTIVE
Bill Lajoie
Tiger: 1968-91
Legacy: Best known as GM in 1983-91. Built '84 and '87 teams through draft and trades. Quit over low pay, tight budgets and Sparky's veto power.

OWNER
Frank Navin
Tiger: 1902-35
Legacy: Turned ragtag franchise into AL power. Started as bookkeeper in 1902. Built Navin Field in 1912. Died five weeks after first World Series title in '35.

FIRST TEAM
1B Hank Greenberg
Tiger: 1930, '33-41,
'45-46
Batting average: .319
Games: 1,269
Homers: 306
Runs batted in: 1,202
2B Charlie Gehringer
Tiger: 1924-42
Average: .320
Games: 2,323
Homers: 184
RBIs: 1,427
SS Alan Trammell
Tiger: 1977-96
Average: .285
Games: 2,293
Homers: 185
RBIs: 1,003
3B George Kell
Tiger: 1946-52
Average: .326
Games: 826
Homers: 25
RBIs: 414
C Mickey Cochrane
Tiger: 1934-37
Average: .313
Games: 315
Homers: 11
RBIs: 152
LF Harry Heilmann
Tiger: 1914, '16-29
Average: .343
Games: 1,989
Homers: 164
RBIs: 1,442

CF Ty Cobb
Tiger: 1905-26
Average: .368
Games: 2,805
Homers: 112
RBIs: 1,804
RF Al Kaline
Tiger: 1953-74
Average: .297
Games: 2,834
Homers: 399
RBIs: 1,583
PH Gates Brown
Tiger: 1963-75
Average: .257
Games: 1,051
Homers: 84
RBIs: 322
RHP Denny McLain
Tiger: 1963-70
Record: 117-62
Earned run average: 3.13
Strikeouts: 1,150
Shutouts: 26

Free Press file photo

Ty Cobb

LHP Hal Newhouser
Tiger: 1939-53
Record: 200-148
ERA: 3.07
Strikeouts: 1,770
Shutouts: 33
RP John Hiller
Tiger: 1965-70, '72-80
Record: 87-76
ERA: 2.83
Games: 545
Saves: 125

SECOND TEAM
1B Norm Cash 1960-74
2B Lou Whitaker 1977-95
SS Billy Rogell 1930-39
3B Aurelio Rodriguez 1971-79
C Bill Freehan 1961, '63-76
LF Willie Horton 1963-77
CF Sam Crawford 1903-17
RF Kirk Gibson 1979-87, '93-95
PH Bob Fothergill 1922-30
RHP Jack Morris 1977-90
LHP Mickey Lolich 1963-75
RP Guillermo Hernandez 1984-89

ward, several thousand frustrated fans stormed the field, tore up the turf and dug up home plate.

Tigers clinch pennant, Sept. 17, 1968: Don Wert singled in the ninth, and the Tigers won their first pennant since 1945. Fans rushed the field, dancing, hugging, kissing, climbing the protective screen and digging up turf.

Naked fans, April 9, 1974: At the height of the streaking craze, dozens of fans celebrated opening day by taking off their clothes and running around the stadium, mostly in the bleachers. The temperature was 38 degrees.

Mark (The Bird) Fidrych, 1976 season: Perhaps no Tiger electrified the crowd like the exuberant Bird, the AL rookie of the year who talked to the ball, groomed the mound with his hands and attracted thousands of delighted fans every time he pitched. An injury cut short his career.

The Wave, May 1984: Taking a cue from college football fans, Tiger Stadium crowds begin to celebrate the team's 35-5 start by standing and sitting in an undulating fashion around the stadium that continued throughout the championship summer.

Kirk Gibson's World Series homer, Oct. 14, 1984: Gibby ignited the crowd by dancing around the bases and thrusting his fists in the air after hitting his second four-bagger of the day. It put the game on ice for the Tigers and gave them their most recent title.

Bleacher Riot II, May 1985: After the longtime practices of chanting obscenities, throwing beach balls and staging food fights spiraled out of control, the Tigers closed the bleachers for seven games.

The Hug, April 20, 1988: Hundreds join the Tiger Stadium Fan Club in joining hands and embracing the stadium to publicize efforts to save it.

VICTORIES (CONT'D)
1935: The Tigers won 93 games in the regular season and beat the Cubs, four games to two, in the World Series under manager-catcher Mickey Cochrane. He scored the winning run on Goose Goslin's single as the Tigers beat the Cubs, 4-3, in Game 6 in Detroit.

Associated Press

State Archives of Michigan

Walter O. Briggs puffs on a cigar at the stadium he named for himself. He owned the Tigers for 17 years.

Year	Pos	W-L	Pct.	GA/GB	Manager	Attendance
1901	3	74-61	.548	8.5	George Stallings	259,430
1902	7	52-83	.385	30.5	Frank Dwyer	189,469
1903	5	65-71	.478	25	Ed Barrow	224,523
1904	7	62-90	.408	32	Ed Barrow-Bobby Lowe	177,796
1905	3	79-74	.516	15.5	Bill Armour	193,384
1906	6	71-78	.477	21	Bill Armour	174,043
1907	1	92-58	.613	1.5	Hughie Jennings	297,079
1908	1	90-63	.588	0.5	Hughie Jennings	436,199
1909	1	98-54	.645	3.5	Hughie Jennings	490,490
1910	3	86-68	.558	18	Hughie Jennings	391,288
1911	2	89-65	.578	13.5	Hughie Jennings	484,988
1912	6	69-84	.451	36.5	Hughie Jennings	402,870
1913	6	66-87	.431	30	Hughie Jennings	398,502
1914	4	80-73	.523	19.5	Hughie Jennings	416,225
1915	2	100-54	.649	2.5	Hughie Jennings	476,105
1916	3	87-67	.565	4	Hughie Jennings	616,772
1917	4	78-75	.510	21.5	Hughie Jennings	457,289
1918	7	55-71	.437	20	Hughie Jennings	203,719
1919	4	80-60	.571	8	Hughie Jennings	643,805
1920	7	61-93	.396	37	Hughie Jennings	579,650
1921	6	71-82	.464	27	Ty Cobb	661,527
1922	3	79-75	.513	15	Ty Cobb	861,206
1923	2	83-71	.539	16	Ty Cobb	911,377
1924	3	86-68	.558	6	Ty Cobb	1,015,136
1925	4	81-73	.526	16.5	Ty Cobb	820,766
1926	6	79-75	.513	12	Ty Cobb	711,914
1927	4	82-71	.536	27.5	George Moriarty	773,716
1928	6	68-86	.442	33	George Moriarty	474,323
1929	6	70-84	.455	36	Bucky Harris	869,318
1930	5	75-79	.487	27	Bucky Harris	649,450
1931	7	61-93	.396	47	Bucky Harris	453,056
1932	5	76-75	.503	29.5	Bucky Harris	397,157
1933	5	75-79	.487	25	Bucky Harris-Del Baker	320,972
1934	1	101-53	.656	7	Mickey Cochrane	919,161
1935	1	93-58	.616	3	Mickey Cochrane	1,034,929
1936	2	83-71	.539	19.5	Mickey Cochrane	875,948
1937	2	89-65	.578	13	Mickey Cochrane	1,072,276
1938	4	84-70	.545	16	Mickey Cochrane-Del Baker	799,557
1939	5	81-73	.526	26.5	Del Baker	836,279
1940	1	90-64	.584	1	Del Baker	1,112,693
1941	T4	75-79	.487	26	Del Baker	684,915
1942	5	73-81	.474	30	Del Baker	580,087
1943	5	78-76	.506	20	Steve O'Neill	606,287
1944	2	88-66	.571	1	Steve O'Neill	923,176
1945	1	88-65	.575	1.5	Steve O'Neill	1,280,341
1946	2	92-62	.597	12	Steve O'Neill	1,722,590
1947	2	85-69	.552	12	Steve O'Neill	1,398,093
1948	5	78-76	.506	18.5	Steve O'Neill	1,743,035
1949	4	87-67	.565	10	Red Rolfe	1,821,204
1950	2	95-59	.617	3	Red Rolfe	1,951,474
1951	5	73-81	.474	25	Red Rolfe	1,132,641
1952	8	50-104	.325	45	Red Rolfe-Fred Hutchinson	1,026,846
1953	6	60-94	.390	40.5	Fred Hutchinson	884,658
1954	5	68-86	.442	43	Fred Hutchinson	1,079,847
1955	5	79-75	.513	17	Bucky Harris	1,181,838
1956	5	82-72	.532	15	Bucky Harris	1,051,182
1957	4	78-76	.506	20	Jack Tighe	1,272,346
1958	5	77-77	.500	15	Jack Tighe-Bill Norman	1,098,924
1959	4	76-78	.494	18	Bill Norman-Jimmy Dykes	1,221,221
1960	6	71-83	.461	26	Jimmy Dykes-Joe Gordon	1,167,669
1961	2	101-61	.623	8	Bob Scheffing	1,600,710
1962	4	85-76	.528	10.5	Bob Scheffing	1,207,881
1963	T5	79-83	.488	25.5	Bob Scheffing-Chuck Dressen	821,952
1964	4	85-77	.525	14	Chuck Dressen	816,139
1965	4	89-73	.549	12	Chuck Dressen-Bob Swift	1,029,645
1966	3	88-74	.543	10	Dressen-Swift*-Frank Skaff	1,124,293
1967	T2	91-71	.562	1	Mayo Smith	1,447,143
1968	1	103-59	.636	12	Mayo Smith	2,031,847

In the American League East

Year	Pos	W-L	Pct.	GA/GB	Manager	Attendance
1969	2	90-72	.556	19	Mayo Smith	1,577,481
1970	4	79-83	.488	29	Mayo Smith	1,501,293
1971	2	91-71	.562	12	Billy Martin	1,591,073
1972	1	86-70	.551	0.5	Billy Martin	1,892,386
1973	3	85-77	.525	12	Billy Martin-Joe Schultz	1,724,146
1974	6	72-90	.444	19	Ralph Houk	1,243,080
1975	6	57-102	.358	37.5	Ralph Houk	1,058,836
1976	5	74-87	.460	24	Ralph Houk	1,467,020
1977	4	74-88	.457	26	Ralph Houk	1,359,856
1978	5	86-76	.531	13.5	Ralph Houk	1,714,893
1979	5	85-76	.528	18	Les Moss-Sparky Anderson	1,630,929
1980	5	84-78	.519	19	Sparky Anderson	1,785,293
1981	4	60-49	.550	2	Sparky Anderson	1,149,144
	T2	29-23	.558	1.5	(2nd Half)	
	4	31-26	.544	3.5	(1st Half)	
1982	4	83-79	.512	12	Sparky Anderson	1,636,058
1983	2	92-70	.568	6	Sparky Anderson	1,829,636
1984	1	104-58	.642	15	Sparky Anderson	2,704,794
1985	3	84-77	.522	15	Sparky Anderson	2,286,609
1986	3	87-75	.537	8.5	Sparky Anderson	1,899,437
1987	1	98-64	.605	2	Sparky Anderson	2,061,830
1988	2	88-74	.543	1	Sparky Anderson	2,081,162
1989	7	59-103	.364	30	Sparky Anderson	1,543,656
1990	3	79-83	.488	9	Sparky Anderson	1,495,785
1991	T2	84-78	.519	7	Sparky Anderson	1,641,661
1992	6	75-87	.463	21	Sparky Anderson	1,423,963
1993	T3	85-77	.525	10	Sparky Anderson	1,971,421
1994	5	53-62	.461	18	Sparky Anderson	1,184,783
1995	4	60-84	.417	26	Sparky Anderson	1,180,979
1996	5	53-109	.327	39	Buddy Bell	1,168,610
1997	3	79-83	.488	19	Buddy Bell	1,365,157

In the American League Central

Year	Pos	W-L	Pct.	GA/GB	Manager	Attendance
1998	5	65-97	.401	24	Buddy Bell-Larry Parrish	1,409,391
1999	3	69-92	.429	27.5	Larry Parrish	2,026,441
2000	3	79-83	.488	16	Phil Garner	2,533,752
Totals		7,914-7,548	.512		100 Seasons	110,113,900

In the National League

Year	Pos	W-L	Pct.	GA/GB	Manager
1881	4	41-43	.488	15	Frank Bancroft
1882	6	42-41	.506	12.5	Frank Bancroft
1883	7	40-58	.408	23	Jack Chapman
1884	8	28-84	.250	56	Jack Chapman
1885	6	41-67	.380	44	Charlie Morton-Bill Watkins
1886	2	87-36	.707	2.5	Bill Watkins
1887	1	79-45	.637	3.5	Bill Watkins
1888	5	68-63	.519	16	Bill Watkins-Bob Leadly

Teammates congratulate Hal Newhouser after the Game 7 victory over the Cubs in 1945.

Richard Bak Collection

SPORTS

Charter members of the National Negro Baseball League, the Detroit Stars showcased black talent while the major leagues were segregated.

Negro Baseball Leagues

In 1920, Andrew (Rube) Foster of Chicago gathered other black businessmen and formed the National Negro Baseball League. Each team owner paid $500 for a charter. The first eight teams: Detroit Stars, Chicago American Giants, Chicago Giants, Indianapolis ABCs, Kansas City Monarchs, St. Louis Giants, Dayton Marcos and Cincinnati Cuban Stars.

In 1923, the Eastern Colored League was formed and the first Negro World Series was played a year later — the Monarchs beat a team from Hilldale, Pa., five games to four.

By the mid-1930s, league games were drawing at least 20,000 fans for weekend games. In 1943, the East-West Negro All-Star game at Chicago's old Comiskey Park drew 51,723.

Several players belatedly entered the Baseball Hall of Fame, including Satchel Paige, James (Cool Papa) Bell and 15 others. Detroit's Norman (Turkey) Stearnes was voted into the hall in 2000.

Detroit roots

➤ **Turkey Stearnes:** Top Negro League player in Detroit. Norman Stearnes got his nickname for the way he flapped his arms as he ran the bases. Stearnes was a left-handed batter and centerfielder from Nashville, Tenn. He played with the Stars from 1923 to 1931 and holds virtually all of the team's offensive

The Detroit Stars played independent black and white teams in 1919. From 1920 to 1933, the Stars played in the National Negro Baseball League. Their games were played at Mack Park on the east side. Game days meant picnics, music and fellowship. The Stars never won a championship.

records, including winning or sharing six home run titles.

After Detroit, he played with the American Giants in Chicago, winning a seventh home run crown and a batting championship. Stearnes was notoriously quiet, but entertained fans by having conversations with himself in centerfield or the on-deck circle.

In nine seasons with the Stars, Stearnes led in most offensive categories. He had 783 hits and batted .353, the best in club history. His slugging percentage was .678, with 143 doubles, 79 triples and 140 homers, the most of any Star. He also stole 67 bases in his career, a team record.

➤ **Other stars:** First baseman **Edgar Wesley,** who usually batted fourth, behind Stearnes, gave the Stars one of the most devastating 1-2 punches in organized ball. Wesley won the home-run title in 1920 and shared it with Stearnes in 1923 and 1925. Wesley also added a batting title in 1925, hitting .424.

Orville (Mule) Riggins was a rangy, spray-hitting shortstop, and catcher **Bruce Petway** earned a bit of fame while on a Cuban team for throwing out Ty Cobb when he tried to steal in a 1910 exhibition series.

➤ **Stars vs. Tigers:** In 1930, the Stars approached Tigers owner Frank Navin about arranging an exhibition series. Navin declined.

In 1922, the Tigers played a three-game series in Chicago against the powerful American Giants. Without Ty Cobb, a blatant racist who refused to play, and a few other regulars, the Tigers went 1-1-1.

➤ **Stars vs. major leaguers:** In 1923, the Stars played a three-game series against the St. Louis Browns. The Stars won the series, overcoming five-run deficits to pull out ninth-inning victories in two of the games.

Major League Commissioner Kenesaw Mountain Landis needed a face-saving measure and ruled that only All-Star squads, not whole teams, could barnstorm against Negro Leaguers. Until Landis' edict, city series

between black and white teams had taken place in Philadelphia, St. Louis and Chicago.

➤ **The lifestyle:** It wasn't glamourous. Often players took the field for two or three games a day to earn enough money to eat, sleep and buy gas to travel to the next town for more of the same. In Detroit, players stayed at black hotels such as the Gotham and Mark Twain.

Their fans enjoyed the games, which became major weekly social events for black Detroiters.

➤ **Negro Leagues' demise:** After the integration of the majors in 1947, when Jackie Robinson played for the Brooklyn Dodgers, the Negro teams began to struggle. Weeks after Robinson began playing, Larry Doby became the first black player in the American League when he took the field for the Cleveland Indians.

The Tigers did not integrate until 1958, when they put Ozzie Virgil on their roster. The Negro Leagues died by 1950.

After baseball: Many black players who did not make it to the majors, typically because they had passed their athletic primes, moved to the Detroit area in the late 1940s. They found jobs in the auto industry and continued their baseball careers in local industrial leagues and other Wayne County sandlots.

Stearnes settled in Detroit in that era and went to work at the Ford Rouge plant. He married a schoolteacher and lived on Detroit's east side until his death in 1979.

SOURCES: "TURKEY STEARNES AND THE DETROIT STARS: THE NEGRO LEAGUES IN DETROIT, 1919-1933," BY RICHARD BAK; FREE PRESS; "ONLY THE BALL WAS WHITE," BY ROBERT PETERSON.

FOR MORE INFORMATION ON THE NEGRO LEAGUES, GO TO THE SITE OF THE NATIONAL BASEBALL HALL OF FAME IN COOPERSTOWN, N.Y. WWW.BASEBALLHALLOFFAME.ORG; THE SITE OF THE NEGRO LEAGUES BASEBALL MUSEUM IN KANSAS CITY, MO., AT WWW.NLBM.COM; OR TRY WWW.BLACKBASEBALL.COM AND WWW.NEGROLEAGUEBASEBALL.COM.

Norman (Turkey) Stearnes entered the Baseball Hall of Fame in 2000.

Free Press file photo

Hockey

TEN REASONS WHY DETROIT IS HOCKEYTOWN

1) Sid Abel, Gordie Howe, Ted Lindsay, Steve Yzerman.
2) Lots of big-time hockey at every level: NHL, minor pro, college, junior and amateur.
3) Most people understand icing.
4) Two NHL owners live here — Mike Ilitch (Wings) and Peter Karmanos (Carolina Hurricanes).
5) The Ontario Hockey League has teams in Plymouth and Windsor.
6) The Zamboni driver is a celebrity.
7) Beer leagues.
8) Octopus.
9) The Russian Five.
10) Former NHL President John Ziegler grew up in St. Clair Shores; Bob Goodenow, the president of the NHL players union, is from Dearborn.

Detroit Red Wings history: A group of Detroit businessmen bought the Victoria (British Columbia) Cougars of the Western Hockey League on Sept. 25, 1926, and moved them to Detroit. The team played the 1926-27 season in Windsor, but moved into Olympia Stadium on Grand River Avenue for the next season. In the summer of 1932, industrialist and fight promoter James Norris purchased the franchise and renamed it the Red Wings. The name comes from a team Norris had played for in Montreal, the Winged Wheelers. Norris thought the wheel insignia was a natural for Detroit. The Norris family owned the team for 50 years. After James Norris died in 1952, his daughter, Marguerite, served as president until her brother, Bruce Norris, took over in 1955. He sold the club to Mike Ilitch in 1982. The Wings played their first game at Joe Louis Arena on Dec. 27, 1979.

2000 Value: $194 million, according to Forbes magazine.

Bringing home Stanley

2002: The Wings won their 10th Stanley Cup by beating the Carolina Hurricanes, owned by Detroiter Peter Karmanos Jr. Playoff highlights included a 7-0 defeat of Colorado in game 7 of Round 3 and a triple overtime victory in Game 3 of the finals.

1998: The Wings defeated Washington after a season dedicated to Vladimir Konstantinov, the star defenseman, and team masseur Sergei Mnatsakanov who was injured in the previous year's limousine crash.

1997: The Wings swept Philadelphia. Dar-

All-time Red Wings

COACH
Scotty Bowman
Red Wing: 1993-2002
Legacy: Won three Stanley Cups. Posted NHL-record 62 victories in 1995-96; only coach with nine career Stanley Cups.

GENERAL MANAGER
Jack Adams
Red Wing: 1927-62
Legacy: Built the foundation. Won seven Cups, 12 regular-season titles (seven straight).

OWNER
Mike Ilitch
Red Wing: 1982-present
Legacy: Paid Norris family around $10 million in 1982; the team is now worth $194 million.

FIRST TEAM
LW Ted Lindsay
Red Wing: 1944-57, '64-65
Goals: 335
Assists: 393
Legacy: Terrible Ted retired as NHL's highest-scoring left wing and leader in penalty minutes. First-team All-Star eight times. Won four Stanley Cups.

C Steve Yzerman
Red Wing: 1983-present
Goals: 658 (through 2001-2002 season)
Assists: 1,004
Legacy: At 21, youngest captain in team history. Longest-serving captain in NHL history. Scored 50 goals five times. Won two Cups. Conn Smythe in 1998 as playoffs MVP.

RW Gordie Howe
Red Wing: 1946-71
Goals: 786
Assists: 1,023
Legacy: Mr. Hockey. League MVP six times. Leading scorer six times. Retired as NHL's all-time scoring leader. Won four Stanley Cups.

D Red Kelly
Red Wing: 1947-60
Goals: 154
Assists: 297
Legacy: Won very first Norris Trophy as the NHL's top defenseman in 1954. First-team All-Star six times. Won four Cups with Detroit, plus four more with Toronto.

D Marcel Pronovost
Red Wing: 1949-65
Goals: 80
Assists: 217
Legacy: Twice a first-team All-Star, twice on second team. Made debut during '50 playoffs, helping injury-depleted team win Stanley Cup. Won three more in Detroit.

G Terry Sawchuk
Red Wing: 1949-55, '57-64, '68-69
Record: 352-244-130
Goals-against average: 2.46
Shutouts: 85
Legacy: More games, more victories, more shutouts than any other NHL goalie. Won three Cups in Detroit.

SECOND TEAM
RW Larry Aurie
1927-39
C Alex Delvecchio
1950-74
LW Sid Abel 1938-43, '45-52
D Jack Stewart
1938-43, '45-50
D Ebbie Goodfellow
1929-43
G Harry Lumley
1943-50

Mr. Hockey

Gordie Howe starred for the Red Wings for 25 years, and scored 15 goals in his last season in the National Hockey League, when he was 51.

SPORTS

KIRTHMON F. DOZIER/Detroit Free Press

After 42 years, the Wings once again hoisted the Stanley Cup banner in 1997.

games to one. In the first-round series, goalie Normie Smith beat the Montreal Maroons, 1-0, in a record six-overtime game.

Great moments in Red Wings' history

Ten moments were selected in 1999 by a panel of Detroit hockey experts; fans voted on the top three (and just happened to pick the three most recent moments as the top happenings).

1) June 7, 1997: Steve Yzerman hoists the Cup after the Wings sweep the Philadelphia Flyers to end Detroit's 42-year hockey championship drought.

2) June 16, 1998: The Wings capture the cup again by defeating the Washington Capitals, and Yzerman hands the trophy to Vladimir Konstantinov, the star defenseman who was injured in the previous year's limousine crash.

3) March 26, 1997: Darren McCarty's overtime goal caps off one of the team's most memorable games. The 6-5 victory over archrival Colorado at Joe Louis featured a first-period fight between McCarty and Claude Lemieux, the Avalanche player whose check from behind had injured Kris Draper. Both goalies, Patrick Roy and Mike Vernon, also tangled.

Runners-up:

March 24, 1936: Mud Bruneteau scores at 16:30 of the sixth — yes, sixth — overtime period, ending the longest game in NHL history. The Wings defeated the Montreal Maroons, 1-0.

April 11, 1936: The Wings defeat the Toronto Maple Leafs, 3-2, and win their first Stnaley Cup.

April 23, 1950: Pete Babando scores at 8:31 of the second overtime, the first time a Stanley Cup final was decided in the overtime of a seventh game. The Wings defeated the New York Rangers, 4-3.

1952 playoffs: Talk about a sweep! The 1951-52 Wings eliminate the Toronto Maple Leafs in four straight games and then swept the Canadiens in four en route to winning the Cup. Neither Toronto or Montreal scored in the four games at Olympia.

Nov. 10, 1963: Gordie Howe scores his 545th goal to surpass Maurice (Rocket) Richard for No. 1 on the all-time list.

April 14, 1996: The Wings defeat Dallas, 5-1, and establish the NHL regular-season record for wins (62) and points (130) in one season.

May 16, 1996: At Joe Louis Arena, Steve Yzerman scores on a nearly 60-foot slap shot at 1:15 of the second overtime as the Wings eliminate the St. Louis Blues in Game 7 to advance to the conference finals.

ren McCarty scored the winning goal in Game 4 and there were Stanley sightings across metro Detroit all summer. But the tragic limo crash put things in perspective.

1955: The Wings defeated Montreal, four games to three. The home team won each contest, the Wings taking Game 7, 3-1.

1954: The Wings defeated Montreal, four games to three, winning Game 7 on Tony Leswick's overtime goal at Detroit.

1952: The Wings swept Toronto and Montreal to become the first NHL team to go through a postseason without losing. Terry Sawchuk had four shutouts in eight games.

1950: The Wings defeated the New York Rangers, four games to three. Defenseman Leo Reise's overtime goal knocked out the Maple Leafs in Game 7 in the first round, and Pete Babando's 15-foot backhander did in the Rangers in OT in Game 7 as the Wings won without Gordie Howe, who was recovering from a severe head injury.

1943: The Wings defeated Boston, four games to none, getting two shutouts from Johnny Mowers.

1937: The Wings defeated the Rangers, three games to two. Marty Barry scored two goals in the final game, a 3-0 shutout for goalie Earl Robertson.

1936: The Wings defeated Toronto, three

SPORTS

Season	W	L	T	OT/Loss	PTS	Position	Coach
926-27	12	28	4		28	5th x	Art Duncan/Duke Keats
927-28	19	19	6		44	4th x	Jack Adams
928-29	19	16	9		47	3rd	Adams
929-30	14	24	6		34	4th x	Adams
930-31	16	21	7		39	4th x	Adams
931-32	18	20	10		46	3rd	Adams
932-33	25	15	8		58	2nd	Adams
933-34	24	14	10		58	1st	Adams
934-35	19	22	7		45	4th x	Adams
935-36	24	16	8		56	1st SC	Adams
936-37	25	14	9		59	1st SC	Adams
937-38	12	25	11		35	4th x	Adams
938-39	18	24	6		42	5th	Adams
939-40	16	26	6		38	5th	Adams
940-41	21	16	11		53	3rd	Adams
941-42	19	25	4		42	5th	Adams
942-43	25	14	11		61	1st SC	Adams
943-44	26	18	6		58	2nd	Adams
944-45	31	14	5		67	2nd	Adams
945-46	20	20	10		50	4th	Adams
946-47	22	27	11		55	4th	Adams
947-48	30	18	12		72	2nd	Tom Ivan
948-49	34	19	7		75	1st	Ivan
949-50	37	19	14		88	1st SC	Ivan
950-51	44	13	13		101	1st	Ivan
951-52	44	14	12		100	1st SC	Ivan
952-53	36	16	18		90	1st	Ivan
953-54	37	19	14		88	1st SC	Ivan
954-55	42	17	11		95	1st SC	Jimmy Skinner
955-56	30	24	16		76	2nd	Skinner
956-57	38	20	12		88	1st	Skinner
957-58	29	29	12		70	3rd	Skinner/Sid Abel
958-59	25	37	8		58	6th x	Abel
959-60	26	29	15		67	4th	Abel
960-61	25	29	16		66	4th	Abel
961-62	23	33	14		60	5th x	Abel
962-63	32	25	13		77	4th	Abel
963-64	30	29	11		71	4th	Abel
964-65	40	23	7		87	1st	Abel
965-66	31	27	12		74	4th	Abel
966-67	27	39	4		58	5th x	Abel
967-68	27	35	12		66	6th x	Abel
968-69	33	31	12		78	5th x	Bill Gadsby
969-70	40	21	15		95	3rd	Gadsby/Abel
970-71	22	45	11		55	7th x	Ned Harkness/Doug Barkley
971-72	33	35	10		76	5th x	Barkely/Johnny Wilson
972-73	37	29	12		86	5th x	Wilson
973-74	29	39	10		68	6th x	Ted Garvin/Alex Delvecchio
974-75	23	45	12		58	4th x	Delvecchio
975-76	26	44	10		62	4th x	D.Barkley/Delvecchio/ Dea
976-77	16	55	9		41	5th x	Dea/Larry Wilson
977-78	32	34	14		78	2nd	Bobby Kromm
978-79	23	41	16		62	5th x	Kromm
979-80	26	43	11		63	5th x	Kromm/Marcel Pronovost
980-81	19	43	18		56	5th x	Ted Lindsay/Wyne Maxner
981-82	21	47	12		54	6th x	Maxner/Dea
982-83	21	44	15		57	5th x	Nick Polano
983-84	31	42	7		69	3rd	Polano
984-85	27	41	12		66	3rd	Polano
985-86	17	57	6		40	5th x	Harry Neale/Brad Park
986-87	34	36	10		78	2nd	Jacques Demers
987-88	41	28	11		93	1st	Demers
988-89	34	34	12		80	1st	Demers
989-90	28	38	14		70	5th x	Demers
990-91	34	38	8		76	3rd	Bryan Murray
991-92	43	25	12		98	1st	Murray
992-93	47	28	9		103	2nd	Murray
993-94	46	30	8		100	1st	Scotty Bowman
1995	33	11	4		70		Bowman
995-96	62	13	7		131	1st	Bowman
996-97	38	26	18		94	3rd SC	Bowman
997-98	44	23	15		103	3rd SC	Bowman
998-99	43	32	7		93	3rd	Bowman
999-00	48	24	10		108	2nd	Bowman
2000-01	49	20	9	4*	111	2nd	Bowman

JULIAN H. GONZALEZ/Detroit Free Press

Wings goalie Chris Osgood comes to blows with Colorado's Patrick Roy near center ice, the second time Roy took on a Detroit goalie. This battle took place in 1998.

* The NHL started giving points for regulation ties and overtime wins during the 2000-01 season.

THOSE CHAMPIONSHIP SEASONS

1990: Detroit beat Portland in five games, clinching the title, 92-90, on the road.
1989: Detroit swept the Lakers in the Finals, winning Game 4, 105-97, at Los Angeles.

DUANE BURLESON/Associated Press
Chuck Daly coached the Pistons to two straight championships.

Detroit Pistons history: The Pistons were born in Ft. Wayne, Ind., for the 1941-42 season, and moved to Detroit for the 1957-58 season by owner Fred Zollner, who sold the club July 29, 1974, to a 12-person group headed by Bill Davidson. The price was $8.1 million. The Pistons originally played at the old Olympia Stadium but moved to Cobo Arena in 1961.

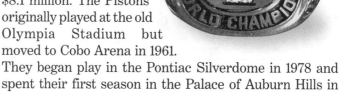

They began play in the Pontiac Silverdome in 1978 and spent their first season in the Palace of Auburn Hills in 1988-89.

2000 value: $226 million, according to Forbes magazine.

All-time Pistons

COACH
Chuck Daly
Piston: 1983-92.
Legacy: Back-to-back NBA titles.

GENERAL MANAGER
Jack McCloskey
Piston: 1979-92.
Legacy: Hired Daly. Drafted Dennis Rodman.

OWNER
Bill Davidson
Piston: 1974-
Legacy: Built Palace, bought plane.

FIRST TEAM
F Grant Hill
Piston: 1994-2000.
Games: 361.
Points: 20.7.
Rebounds: 8.1.
Legacy: Co-rookie of year in 1995. One of only three NBA players to lead his team in scoring, rebounding and assists at least two seasons. First-team All-NBA once.

F Dave DeBusschere
Piston: 1962-68.
Games: 440.
Points: 16.1.
Rebounds: 11.2.
Legacy: Hall of Fame in 1982. Named to NBA 50th anniversary team. At 24, became youngest-ever coach in NBA after second season. Pistons' player-coach for three seasons. Overall record, 79-143.

C Bob Lanier
Piston: 1970-80.
Games: 681.
Points: 22.7.
Rebounds: 11.8.
Legacy: Hall of Fame in 1991. No. 16 retired in '93. All-Star Game MVP in '74. Led team in scoring eight times, rebounding seven.

First overall pick in '70 draft out of St. Bonaventure.

G Isiah Thomas
Piston: 1981-94.
Games: 979.
Points: 19.2.
Assists: 9.3.
Legacy: Guaranteed a championship as a rookie and made good on promise in 1989 and '90. Finals MVP in '90. All-Star Game MVP twice. Named to NBA 50th anniversary team.

G Dave Bing
Piston: 1966-75.
Games: 675.
Points: 22.6.
Assists: 6.4.
Legacy: First Piston to have his number (21) retired. Rookie of year in 1967. Named to NBA 50th anniversary team. First-team All-NBA twice, second-team once. Hall of

Fame in 1989.
6TH Dennis Rodman
Piston: 1986-93.
Games: 549.
Points: 8.8.
Rebounds: 11.5.
Legacy: Defensive player of year in 1990, '91. All-Defensive team 1989-93. Rebounding champ in '92, '93. On two Bad Boys title teams. Single-game team rebounding record (34).

SECOND TEAM
F Bailey Howell 1959-64
F Kelly Tripucka 1981-86
C Bill Laimbeer 1981-94
G Joe Dumars 1985-99
G John Long 1978-86, '88-89, '90-91
6th Vinnie Johnson 1981-91

Year	W	L	Pct.	Coach
1957-58	33	39	.458	C. Eckman/Red Rocha
1958-59	28	44	.389	Red Rocha
1959-60	13	21	.382	Red Rocha
	17	24	.414	Dick McGuire
1960-61	34	45	.430	Dick McGuire
1961-62	37	43	.463	Dick McGuire
1962-63	34	46	.425	Dick McGuire
1963-64	23	57	.288	Charles Wolf
1964-65	2	9	.182	Charles Wolf
	29	40	.420	Dave DeBusschere
1965-66	22	58	.275	Dave DeBusschere
1966-67	28	45	.384	Dave DeBusschere
	2	6	.250	Donnis Butcher
1967-68	40	42	.488	Donnis Butcher
1968-69	10	12	.455	Donnis Butcher
	22	38	.367	Paul Seymour
1969-70	31	51	.378	Bill van Breda Kolff
1970-71	45	37	.549	Bill van Breda Kolff
1971-72	6	4	.600	Bill van Breda Kolff
	0	2	.000	Terry Dischinger
	20	50	.286	Earl Lloyd
1972-73	2	5	.286	Earl Lloyd
	38	37	.507	Ray Scott
1973-74	52	30	.634	Ray Scott
1974-75	40	42	.488	Ray Scott
1975-76	17	25	.405	Ray Scott
	19	21	.475	Herb Brown
1976-77	44	38	.537	Herb Brown
1977-78	9	15	.375	Herb Brown
	29	29	.500	Bob Kauffman
1978-79	30	52	.366	Dick Vitale
1979-80	4	8	.333	Dick Vitale
	12	58	.171	Richie Adubato
1980-81	21	61	.256	Scotty Robertson
1981-82	39	43	.476	Scotty Robertson
1982-83	37	45	.451	Scotty Robertson
1983-84	49	33	.598	Chuck Daly
1984-85	46	36	.561	Chuck Daly
1985-86	46	36	.561	Chuck Daly
1986-87	52	30	.634	Chuck Daly
1987-88	54	28	.659	Chuck Daly
1988-89	63	19	.768	Chuck Daly
1989-90	59	23	.720	Chuck Daly
1990-91	50	32	.610	Chuck Daly
1991-92	48	34	.585	Chuck Daly
1992-93	40	42	.488	Ron Rothstein
1993-94	20	62	.244	Don Chaney
1994-95	28	54	.341	Don Chaney
1995-96	46	36	.561	Doug Collins
1996-97	54	28	.659	Doug Collins
1997-98	37	45	.451	Alvin Gentry
1998-99	29	21	.580	Alvin Gentry
1999-2000	42	40	.512	A. Gentry/George Irvine
2000-01	32	50	.390	George Irvine

When drafted by the Pistons, Isiah Thomas guaranteed a championship. The Bad Boys captain delivered in 1989 and '90.

MANNY CRISOSTOMO/Detroit Free Press

Coach Buddy Parker gets carried away after the Lions won the championship in 1953.

Football

Detroit Lions history: The Lions were Detroit's fourth professional football team, but they have certainly been the most successful, at least when it comes to longevity. The Detroit Heralds, in 1920, were a charter member of the American Professional Football Association, the NFL's original name. The Heralds folded after two years. The Detroit Panthers disbanded after the 1925 and 1926 seasons. The Detroit Wolverines went out of business after the 1928 season. The Lions emerged in 1934, when radio executive George Richards bought the Portsmouth, Ohio, franchise for $7,952.08 and moved it to Detroit. The Lions won the NFL championship in their second season. They played in the University of Detroit stadium before crowds averaging 16,000. Chicago businessman Fred Mandel purchased the team. In 1948, he sold it for $165,000 to a local group headed by Edwin Anderson, who sold it to William Clay Ford in 1964 for $4.5 million. The Lions played their first game at the Pontiac Silverdome on Aug. 23, 1974. The Lions are scheduled to leave the Silverdome upon completion of Ford Field in downtown Detroit by the 2002 season.

2000 value: $293 million, according to Forbes magazine.

Richard Bak Collection

In only their second season in Detroit, the Lions were crowned NFL champions in 1935.

CHAMPIONSHIP SEASONS:

1952, 1953 and 1957: Quarterback Bobby Layne led the Lions through their most dominating era. Detroit beat the Cleveland Browns three times for NFL championships: 17-7 in Cleveland in 1952, 17-16 in Detroit in 1953 and 59-14 in Detroit in 1957.

1935: George (Potsy) Clark was the coach and Hall of Famer Earl (Dutch) Clark one of the stars as the Lions won the NFL title in their second season in Detroit. They beat New York, 26-7, in Detroit in the championship game.

All-time Lions

COACH
Buddy Parker
Lion: 1951-56
Legacy: Coach for NFL titles in '52 and '53, runner-up in '54. His 0.671 winning percentage (50-24-2) is team's best.
EXECUTIVE
Edwin Anderson
Lion: 1948-73
Legacy: President, 1949-61; GM, 1962-73. Praised in '50s; ripped in '60s, when players hung him in effigy from goalposts.
FIRST-TEAM OFFENSE
QB Bobby Layne
Lion: 1950-58
RB Barry Sanders
Lion: 1989-98
RB Doak Walker
Lion: 1950-55
OG Harley Sewell
Lion: 1953-62
OT Lou Creekmur
Lion: 1950-59
C Alex Wojciechowicz
Lion: 1938-46
OG Dick Stanfel
Lion: 1952-55
OT Lomas Brown
Lion: 1985-95
TE Charlie Sanders
Lion: 1968-77
WR Cloyce Box
Lion: 1949-50, '52-54
WR Herman Moore
Lion: 1991-
PK Jason Hanson
Lion: 1992-
KR Mel Gray
Lion: 1989-94
FIRST-TEAM DEFENSE
DE Bubba Baker
Lion: 1978-82
DT Alex Karras
Lion: 1958-62, '64-70
NG Les Bingaman
Lion: 1948-54
DT Roger Brown
Lion: 1960-66
LB Wayne Walker
Lion: 1958-72
LB Joe Schmidt
Lion: 1953-65
LB Chris Spielman
Lion: 1988-95
CB Lem Barney
Lion: 1967-77
CB Dick (Night Train) Lane
Lion: 1960-65
S Yale Lary
Lion: 1952-53, '56-64
S Jack Christiansen
Lion: 1951-58
P Yale Lary
Lion: 1952-53, '56-64
PR Jack Christiansen
Lion: 1951-58
SECOND-TEAM OFFENSE
QB Dutch Clark 1934-38
RB Billy Sims 1980-84
RB Nick Pietrosante 1959-65
OT Rockne Freitas 1968-77
OG John Gordy 1957, '59-67
C Ed Flanagan 1965-74
OG Kevin Glover 1985-97
OT Keith Dorney 1979-87
WR Gail Cogdill 1960-68
WR Leon Hart 1950-57
TE David Hill 1976-82
PK Eddie Murray 1980-91
KR Pat Studstill 1961-67
SECOND-TEAM DEFENSE
DE Larry Hand 1964-77
DT Doug English 1975-79, '81-85
DT Jerry Ball 1987-92
DE Darris McCord 1955-67
LB Ox Emerson 1934-37
LB Mike Lucci 1965-73
LB Charlie Weaver 1971-81
CB Dick LeBeau 1959-72
CB Jim David 1952-59
S Don Doll 1949-52
S Bennie Blades 1988-96
P Jim Arnold 1986-93
PR Mel Gray 1989-94

Year-by-year results

Year	Coach	Regular Season	Pct.	Spartans Points	Opp. Points	Conf./Div. Finish
1930	Tubby Griffen	5-6-3	.455	176	161	T7th NFL
1931	Potsy Clark	11-3-0	.786	175	77	2nd NFL
1932	Potsy Clark	6-2-4	.750	116	71	3rd NFL
1933	Potsy Clark	6-5-0	.545	128	87	2nd NFL Western
Portsmouth totals		**28-16-7**	**.618**	**595**	**396**	

Year	Coach	Regular Season	Pct.	Lions Points	Opp. Points	Conf./Div. Finish
1934	Potsy Clark	10-3-0	.769	238	59	2nd Western Div.
1935	Potsy Clark	7-3-2	.700	191	111	NFL Champions
1936	Potsy Clark	8-4-0	.666	235	102	3rd NFL Western
1937	Dutch Clark	7-4-0	.636	180	105	3rd NFL Western
1938	Dutch Clark	7-4-0	.636	119	108	2nd NFL Western
1939	Gus Henderson	6-5-0	.545	145	150	3rd NFL Western
1940	Potsy Clark	5-5-1	.500	138	15	3rd NFL Western
1941	Bill Edwards	4-6-1	.400	121	195	3rd NFL Western
1942	Bill Edwards#	0-11-0	.000	38	263	5th NFL Western
1943	Gus Dorais	3-6-1	.333	178	238	3rd NFL Western
1944	Gus Dorais	6-3-1	.667	216	151	2nd NFL Western
1945	Gus Dorais	7-3-0	.700	195	194	2nd NFL Western
1946	Gus Dorais	1-10-0	.091	152	310	5th NFL Western
1947	Gus Dorais	3-9-0	.250	231	305	5th NFL Western
1948	Bo McMillin	2-10-0	.167	200	40	5th NFL Western
1949	Bo McMillin	4-8-0	.333	237	259	4th NFL Western
1950	Bo McMillin	6-6-0	.500	321	295	4th NFL Western
1951	Buddy Parker	7-4-1	.636	336	259	2nd NFL Western
1952	Buddy Parker	9-3-0	.750	344	192	NFL Champions
1953	Buddy Parker	10-2-0	.833	271	205	NFL Champions
1954	Buddy Parker	9-2-1	.818	337	189	NFL Runner-up
1955	Buddy Parker	3-9-0	.250	230	275	6th NFL Western
1956	Buddy Parker	9-3-0	.750	300	188	2nd NFL Western
1957	George Wilson	8-4-0	.667	251	231	NFL Champions
1958	George Wilson	4-7-1	.364	261	276	5th NFL Western
1959	George Wilson	3-8-1	.213	203	275	5th NFL Western
1960	George Wilson	7-5-0	.583	235	212	2nd NFL Western
1961	George Wilson	8-5-1	.615	270	258	2nd NFL Western
1962	George Wilson	11-3-0	.786	315	177	2nd NFL Western
1963	George Wilson	5-8-1	.385	326	265	4th NFL Western
1964	George Wilson	7-5-2	.583	280	260	4th NFL Western
1965	Harry Gilmer	6-7-1	.462	257	295	6th NFL Western
1966	Harry Gilmer	4-9-1	.308	206	317	6th NFL Western
1967	Joe Schmidt	5-7-2	.417	260	232	3rd NFL Central
1968	Joe Schmidt	4-8-2	.333	207	246	4th NFL Central
1969	Joe Schmidt	9-4-1	.692	259	193	2nd NFL Central
1970	Joe Schmidt	10-4-0	.714	347	202	2nd NFC Central
1971	Joe Schmidt	7-6-1	.583	341	286	2nd NFC Central
1972	Joe Schmidt	8-5-1	.607	339	290	2nd NFC Central
1973	Don McCafferty	6-7-1	.464	271	247	2nd NFC Central
1974	Rick Forzano	7-7-0	.500	256	270	2nd NFC Central
1975	Rick Forzano	7-7-0	.500	245	262	2nd NFC Central
1976	Rick Forzano*	6-8-0	.429	262	220	3rd NFC Central
1977	Tommy Hudspeth	6-8-0	.429	183	252	3rd NFC Central
1978	Monte Clark	7-9-0	.438	290	300	3rd NFC Central
1979	Monte Clark	2-14-0	.125	219	365	5th NFC Central
1980	Monte Clark	9-7-0	.563	334	272	2nd NFC Central
1981	Monte Clark	8-8-0	.500	397	322	2nd NFC Central
1982	Monte Clark	4-5-0	.444	181	176	4th NFC Central
1983	Monte Clark	9-7-0	.563	347	287	1st NFC Central
1984	Monte Clark	4-11-1	.281	283	408	4th NFC Central
1985	Darryl Rogers	7-9-0	.438	307	366	4th NFC Central
1986	Darryl Rogers	5-11-0	.313	277	326	3rd NFC Central
1987	Darryl Rogers	4-11-0	.267	269	384	5th NFC Central
1988	Darryl Rogers@	4-12-0	.333	220	313	4th NFC Central
1989	Wayne Fontes	7-9-0	.438	312	364	3rd NFC Central
1990	Wayne Fontes	6-10-0	.375	373	413	3rd NFC Central
1991	Wayne Fontes	12-4-0	.750	339	295	1st NFC Central
1992	Wayne Fontes	5-11-0	.313	273	332	5th NFC Central
1993	Wayne Fontes	10-6-0	.625	298	292	1st NFC Central
1994	Wayne Fontes	9-7-0	.563	357	342	3rd NFC Central
1995	Wayne Fontes	10-6-0	.625	436	336	2nd NFC Central
1996	Wayne Fontes	5-11-0	.455	302	369	5th NFC Central
1997	Bobby Ross	9-7-0	.563	379	306	3rd NFC Central
1998	Bobby Ross	5-11-0	.313	306	378	4th NFC Central
1999	Bobby Ross	8-8-0	.500	322	323	3rd NFC Central
2000	Bobby Ross/Gary Moeller	9-7-0	.563	307	307	3rd NFC Central
Detroit totals		**429-456-25**	**.485**	**17,655**	**17,555**	
FRANCHISE TOTALS		**457-472-32**	**.492**	**18,250**	**17,951**	

All-time club record (including post-season): 464-482-32   .491

Karcis (0-8) replaced Edwards who began 1942 season with a 0-3 record   * Hudspeth (5-5) replaced Forzano who began 1976 season with a 1-3 record   @ Fontes (2-3) replaced Rogers who began 1988 season with a 2-9 record

Free Press file photo

Lions running back Billy Sims was the NFL's Rookie of the Year in 1980, and ranks second all-time behind Barry Sanders in Lions rushing and career rushing touchdowns.

College Sports

University of Michigan

Basketball

National champs:
Michigan basketball teams have advanced to the NCAA final four six times; they have won the championship once.

1989: Assistant Steve Fisher took over as interim coach before the NCAA tournament and the Wolverines responded with six consecutive wins, culminating with an 80-79 overtime victory over Seton Hall in Seattle.

Football

National champs:
1997: Led by Heisman Trophy winner Charles Woodson, the Wolverines capped a 12-0 season with a 21-16 victory over Washington State in the Rose Bowl. They shared the national title with 13-0 Nebraska.

1948: A 13-3 victory over Ohio State at Columbus capped a 9-0 season in Bennie Oosterbaan's first season as coach.

1947: The Wolverines (10-0) routed Southern Cal, 49-0, in the Rose Bowl in Fritz Crisler's final season as coach.

1932-33: A scoreless tie with Minnesota in '33 was the only blemish on a 15-0-1 record under coach Harry Kipke.

1901-04: Fielding Yost's teams were 43-0-1 and outscored their opponents, 2,326-40, in these four seasons.

Rose Bowl Record
Games: 17 W: 8 L: 9
Overall bowl record, including Rose Bowl:
Games: 31 W: 16 L: 15

Cazzie Russell's dominant play had many calling Crisler Arena "The House that Cazzie Built."

Special to the Free Press

SPORTS

All-time U-M basketball

COACH
Johnny Orr
Wolverine: 1969-80.
Legacy: School-best 209 victories.
ASSISTANT
Bill Frieder
Wolverine: 1973-89.
Legacy: Coach of year in '85. Not allowed to coach in '89 NCAA tourney.
ASSISTANT
Steve Fisher
Wolverine: 1982-97.
Legacy: Recruited Fab Five. Fired after Ed Martin scandal.
FIRST TEAM
F Glen Rice
Wolverine: 1986-89.
Games: 134. Points: 18.2. Rebounds: 6.4.
Legacy: Top scorer in Michigan history. Scored NCAA-record 184 points in six games to help Michigan win 1989 title. All-America in '89.
F Chris Webber
Wolverine: 1992-93.
Games: 70. Points: 17.4. Rebounds: 10.
Legacy: Only player to make NCAA all-tourney team as freshman and sophomore. Led Fab Five to two NCAA finals appearances.
C Bill Buntin
Wolverine: 1963-65.
Games: 79. Points: 21.8. Rebounds: 13.1.
Legacy: Two-time All-America. Three-time All-Big Ten. School MVP award named in his honor. First Wolverine drafted by NBA.
G Cazzie Russell
Wolverine: 1964-66.
Games: 80. Points: 27.1. Rebounds: 8.5.
Legacy: Only U-M basketball player to have number (33) retired. Three-time All-America. Career scoring-average leader. Three Big Ten titles.
G Rickey Green
Wolverine: 1976-77.
Games: 60. Points: 19.7. Assists: 4.1.
Legacy: Speedy fast-break specialist from junior college ranks. All-Big Ten twice. All-America and runner-up to Marques Johnson as player of year in '77.
6TH Rudy Tomjanovich
Wolverine: 1968-70.
Games: 72. Points: 25.1. Rebounds: 14.4.
Legacy: Averaged 30.1 points, 15.7 rebounds as All-America in '70. U-M's all-time leading rebounder with 1,039. Twice led Big Ten in rebounding.

SECOND TEAM
F Bennie Oosterbaan 1926-28
F Henry Wilmore 1971-73
C Juwan Howard 1992-94
G Rumeal Robinson 1988-90
G Gary Grant 1985-88
6th Roy Tarpley 1983-86

Walter Camp, left, was known as the father of American football. Wolverines coach Fielding Yost, right, followed in his footsteps.

All-time U-M football

COACH
Fielding H. Yost
U-M: 1901-41
Legacy: National titles in '01-04, '18, '23. Went 56 straight without loss in '01-05.
ASSISTANT
Bo Schembechler
U-M: 1969-90
Legacy: Won or tied for 13 Big Ten championships. Ten Rose Bowls.
FIRST-TEAM OFFENSE
QB Rick Leach
Wolverine: 1975-78
RB Tom Harmon
Wolverine: 1938-40
RB Rob Lytle
Wolverine: 1974-76
OT Dan Dierdorf
Wolverine: 1968-70
OG Reggie McKenzie
Wolverine: 1969-71
C Ernie Vick
Wolverine: 1918-21
OG Julius Franks
Wolverine: 1941-42
OT Greg Skrepenak
Wolverine: 1988-91
E Ron Kramer
Wolverine: 1954-56
E Bennie Oosterbaan
Wolverine: 1925-27
WR Anthony Carter
Wolverine: 1979-82
PK Remy Hamilton
Wolverine: 1994-96
KR Desmond Howard
Wolverine: 1989-91
FIRST-TEAM DEFENSE
DL Bill Yearby
Wolverine: 1963-65
DL Francis Wistert
Wolverine: 1931-33
DL Albert Wistert
Wolverine: 1940-42
DL Mark Messner
Wolverine: 1985-88
LB Germany Schulz
Wolverine: 1904-05, '07-08
LB Erick Anderson
Wolverine: 1988-91
LB Ron Simpkins
Wolverine: 1976-79
CB Charles Woodson
Wolverine: 1995-97
CB Thom Darden
Wolverine: 1969-71
S Tripp Welborne
Wolverine: 1987-90
S Tom Curtis
Wolverine: 1967-69
P Harry Kipke
Wolverine: 1921-23
PR Gene Derricotte
Wolverine: 1944, '46-48
SECOND-TEAM OFFENSE
QB Benny Friedman 1924-26
RB Ron Johnson 1966-68
RB Willie Heston 1901-04
OT Jumbo Elliott 1984-87
OG Albert Benbrook 1908-10
C Charles Bernard 1931-33
OT Tom Mack 1964-65
OG Stefan Humphries 1980-83
TE Jim Mandich 1967-69
WR Desmond Howard 1989-91
WR Jim Smith 1973-76
PK J.D. Carlson 1989-91
KR Anthony Carter 1979-82
SECOND-TEAM DEFENSE
DL Curtis Greer 1976-79
DL Otto Pommerening 1927-28
DL Alvin Wistert 1947-49
DL Chris Hutchinson 1989-92
LB John Anderson 1974-77
LB Calvin O'Neal 1974-76
LB Maynard Morrison 1929-31
DB Pete Elliott 1945-48
DB Rick Volk 1964-66
DB Bump Elliott 1946-47
DB Dave Brown 1972-74
P Monte Robbins 1984-87
PR Derrick Alexander 1989-90, '92-93

SPORTS

Year	W	L	Big Ten Finish	Coach
1909	1	4	NA	G.D. Corneal
1918	6	12	10	Elmer Mitchell
1919	16	8	4	Elmer Mitchell
1920	10	13	Tie 7	E.J. Mather
1921	18	4	Tie 1	E.J. Mather
1922	15	4	Tie 2	E.J. Mather
1923	11	4	3	E.J. Mather
1924	10	7	7	E.J. Mather
1925	8	6	5	E.J. Mather
1926	12	5	Tie 1	E.J. Mather
1927	14	3	1	E.J. Mather
1928	10	7	5	E.J. Mather
1929	13	3	Tie 1	George Veenker
1930	9	5	3	George Veenker
1931	13	4	Tie 2	George Veenker
1932	11	6	4	Frank Cappon
1933	10	8	Tie 3	Frank Cappon
1934	6	14	Tie 8	Frank Cappon
1935	8	12	9	Frank Cappon
1936	15	5	Tie 3	Frank Cappon
1937	16	4	3	Frank Cappon
1938	12	8	Tie 5	Frank Cappon
1939	11	9	Tie 7	Bennie Oosterbaan
1940	13	7	6	Bennie Oosterbaan
1941	9	10	7	Bennie Oosterbaan
1942	6	14	Tie 7	Bennie Oosterbaan
1943	10	8	8	Bennie Oosterbaan
1944	8	10	Tie 6	Bennie Oosterbaan
1945	12	7	5	Bennie Oosterbaan
1946	12	7	7	Bennie Oosterbaan
1947	12	8	5	Osborne Cowles
1948	16	6	1	Osborne Cowles
1949	15	6	3	Ernest McCoy
1950	11	11	Tie 6	Ernest McCoy
1951	7	15	Tie 9	Ernest McCoy
1952	7	15	Tie 8	Ernest McCoy
1953	6	16	Tie 9	William Perigo
1954	9	13	Tie 9	William Perigo
1955	11	11	Tie 6	William Perigo
1956	9	13	Tie 8	William Perigo
1957	13	9	Tie 5	William Perigo
1958	11	11	7	William Perigo
1959	15	7	Tie 2	William Perigo
1960	4	20	10	William Perigo
1961	6	18	10	Dave Strack
1962	7	17	8	Dave Strack
1963	16	8	Tie 4	Dave Strack
1964	23	5	Tie 1	Dave Strack
1965	24	4	1	Dave Strack
1966	18	8	1	Dave Strack
1967	8	16	10	Dave Strack
1968	11	13	Tie 6	Dave Strack
1969	13	11	4	Johnny Orr
1970	10	14	Tie 6	Johnny Orr
1971	19	7	2	Johnny Orr
1972	14	10	Tie 3	Johnny Orr
1973	13	11	Tie 6	Johnny Orr
1974	22	5	Tie 1	Johnny Orr
1975	19	8	2	Johnny Orr
1976	25	7	2	Johnny Orr
1977	26	4	1	Johnny Orr
1978	16	11	Tie 4	Johnny Orr
1979	15	12	6	Johnny Orr
1980	17	13	Tie 6	Johnny Orr
1981	19	11	7	Bill Frieder
1982	8	19	Tie 7	Bill Frieder
1983	16	12	9	Bill Frieder
1984	24	9	4	Bill Frieder
1985	26	4	1	Bill Frieder
1986	28	5	1	Bill Frieder
1987	20	12	5	Bill Frieder
1988	26	8	2	Bill Frieder
1989	30	7	3	Frieder/Fisher
1990	23	8	3	Steve Fisher
1991	14	15	8	Steve Fisher
1992	25	9	Tie 3	Steve Fisher
1993	31	5	2	Steve Fisher
1994	24	8	2	Steve Fisher
1995	17	14	3	Steve Fisher
1996	20	12	Tie 5	Steve Fisher
1997	24	11	Tie 6	Steve Fisher
1998	25	9	4	Brian Ellerbe
1999	12	19	10	Brian Ellerbe
2000				Brian Ellerbe

Year	Coach	Overall W	L	T
1879		1	0	1
1880		1	0	0
1881		0	3	0
1882	No Games			
1883		2	3	0
1884		2	0	0
1885		3	0	0
1886		2	0	0
1887		3	0	0
1888		4	1	0
1889		1	2	0
1890		4	1	0
1891	Murphy & Crawford	4	5	0
1892	Frank Barbour	7	5	0
1893	Frank Barbour	7	3	0
1894	William McCauley	9	1	1
1895	William McCauley	8	1	0
1896	William Ward	9	1	0
1897	Gustave Ferbert	6	1	1
1898	Gustave Ferbert	10	0	0
1899	Gustave Ferbert	8	2	0
1900	Langdon Lee	7	2	1
1901	Fielding Yost	11	0	0
1902	Fielding Yost	11	0	0
1903	Fielding Yost	11	0	1
1904	Fielding Yost	10	0	0
1905	Fielding Yost	12	1	0
1906	Fielding Yost	4	1	0
1907	Fielding Yost	5	1	0
1908	Fielding Yost	5	2	1
1909	Fielding Yost	6	1	0
1910	Fielding Yost	3	0	3
1911	Fielding Yost	5	1	2
1912	Fielding Yost	5	2	0
1913	Fielding Yost	6	1	0
1914	Fielding Yost	6	3	0
1915	Fielding Yost	4	3	1
1916	Fielding Yost	7	2	0
1917	Fielding Yost	8	2	0
1918	Fielding Yost	5	0	0
1919	Fielding Yost	3	4	0
1920	Fielding Yost	5	2	0
1921	Fielding Yost	5	1	1
1922	Fielding Yost	6	0	1
1923	Fielding Yost	8	0	0
1924	George Little	6	2	0
1925	Fielding Yost	7	1	0
1926	Fielding Yost	7	1	0
1927	Elton Wieman	6	2	0
1928	Elton Wieman	3	4	1
1929	Harry Kipke	5	3	1
1930	Harry Kipke	8	0	1
1931	Harry Kipke	8	1	1
1932	Harry Kipke	8	0	0
1933	Harry Kipke	7	0	1
1934	Harry Kipke	1	7	0
1935	Harry Kipke	4	4	0
1936	Harry Kipke	1	7	0
1937	Harry Kipke	4	4	0
1938	Fritz Crisler	6	1	1
1939	Fritz Crisler	6	2	0
1940	Fritz Crisler	7	1	0
1941	Fritz Crisler	6	1	1
1942	Fritz Crisler	7	3	0
1943	Fritz Crisler	8	1	0
1944	Fritz Crisler	8	2	0
1945	Fritz Crisler	7	3	0
1946	Fritz Crisler	6	2	1
1947	Fritz Crisler	10	0	0
1948	Bennie Oosterbaan	9	0	0
1949	Bennie Oosterbaan	6	2	1
1950	Bennie Oosterbaan	6	3	1
1951	Bennie Oosterbaan	4	5	0
1952	Bennie Oosterbaan	5	4	0
1953	Bennie Oosterbaan	6	3	0
1954	Bennie Oosterbaan	6	3	0
1955	Bennie Oosterbaan	7	2	0
1956	Bennie Oosterbaan	7	2	0
1957	Bennie Oosterbaan	5	3	1
1958	Bennie Oosterbaan	2	6	1
1959	Bump Elliott	4	5	0
1960	Bump Elliott	5	4	0
1961	Bump Elliott	6	3	0
1962	Bump Elliott	2	7	0
1963	Bump Elliott	3	4	2
1964	Bump Elliott	9	1	0
1965	Bump Elliott	4	6	0
1966	Bump Elliott	6	4	0
1967	Bump Elliott	4	6	0
1968	Bump Elliott	8	2	0
1969	Bo Schembechler	8	3	0
1970	Bo Schembechler	9	1	0
1971	Bo Schembechler	11	1	0
1972	Bo Schembechler	10	1	0
1973	Bo Schembechler	10	0	1
1974	Bo Schembechler	10	1	0
1975	Bo Schembechler	8	2	2
1976	Bo Schembechler	10	2	0
1977	Bo Schembechler	10	2	0
1978	Bo Schembechler	10	2	0
1979	Bo Schembechler	8	4	0
1980	Bo Schembechler	10	2	0
1981	Bo Schembechler	9	3	0
1982	Bo Schembechler	8	4	0
1983	Bo Schembechler	9	3	0
1984	Bo Schembechler	6	6	0
1985	Bo Schembechler	10	1	1
1986	Bo Schembechler	11	2	0
1987	Bo Schembechler	8	4	0
1988	Bo Schembechler	9	2	1
1989	Bo Schembechler	10	2	0
1990	Gary Moeller	9	3	0
1991	Gary Moeller	10	2	0
1992	Gary Moeller	9	0	3
1993	Gary Moeller	8	4	0
1994	Gary Moeller	8	4	0
1995	Lloyd Carr	9	4	0
1996	Lloyd Carr	8	4	0
1997	Lloyd Carr	12	0	0
1998	Lloyd Carr	10	3	0
1999	Lloyd Carr	10	2	0
2000	Lloyd Carr	8	3	0
Totals		784	257	36

Mateen Cleaves planted a kiss on the Breslin Center floor after a victory over U-M during the 1999-2000 season.

Michigan State

Basketball

National champs

The Spartans have advanced to the NCAA Final Four four times, and have won the championship twice:

2000: Mateen Cleaves overcomes an injured ankle to score 18 points in Michigan State's 89-76 victory over Florida. Cleaves is named the tournament's most valuable player.

1979: Sophomore Earvin (Magic) Johnson's Spartans beat Larry Bird's Indiana State Sycamores, 75-64, in Salt Lake City, in a preview of their many showdowns as NBA professionals.

All-time MSU basketball

Coach
Jud Heathcote
Spartan: 1976-95
Legacy: NCAA title in '79. All-time leader in victories.
Assistant
Tom Izzo
Spartan: 1983-present
Legacy: Promoted to head coach in '95. Reached Final Four in '99. Won NCAA title in 2000.
Assistant
Forrest Anderson
Spartan: 1954-65
Legacy: Forddy. Coached MSU to first NCAA tourney in '57.
FIRST TEAM
F Greg Kelser
Spartan: 1975-79
Games: 115
Points: 17.5
Rebounds: 9.5

Legacy: Special K. Cocaptain (with Magic) of 1979 NCAA championship team. Career leader in rebounds. All-America in 1979.
F Terry Furlow
Spartan: 1972-76
Games: 100
Points: 17.8
Rebounds: 6.3
Legacy: In 1976 had school's best single-season scoring average (29.4) and scored most points in a game — 50 — against Iowa. All-America in '76.
C Johnny Green
Spartan: 1956-59
Games: 63
Points: 16.9
Rebounds: 16.4
Legacy: Jumpin' Johnny. Big Ten MVP and All-America in

1959. Had school-record 392 rebounds in 1957-58. Career leader in rebound average. MSU's first first-round NBA pick.
G Earvin Johnson
Spartan: 1977-79
Games: 62
Points: 17.1
Assists: 7.9
Legacy: Magic. Beat Larry Bird's Sycamores for 1979 NCAA title. Holds school record for single-game assists (14) in Big Ten game, season steals overall (75). All-America, Big Ten MVP in 1979.
G Steve Smith
Spartan: 1987-91
Games: 122
Points: 18.5
Rebounds: 6.1
Legacy: Big Ten MVP in 1990. Two-time All-America ('90,

'91). MSU's second all-time leading scorer. Big Ten scoring champ (23.2) in 1991. Led team to Big Ten title in '90.
6th man Scott Skiles
Spartan: 1982-86
Games: 118
Points: 18.2
Assists: 5.5
Legacy: All-time assists leader (645) and third all-time in scoring. Cocaptain and Big Ten MVP in 1986. Big Ten scoring champ (29.1) in '86, when he led Spartans to regional semifinals of NCAA tourney.
SECOND TEAM
F Julius McCoy 1954-56
F Ralph Simpson 1970
C Jay Vincent 1978-81
G Mateen Cleaves 1997-00
G Shawn Respert 1991-95
6th Sam Vincent 1982-85

All-time MSU football

COACH
Duffy Daugherty
Spartan: 1947-72.
Legacy: UPI national champion in '65. Coach of year in '55 and '65.
ASSISTANT
Biggie Munn
Spartan: 1947-71.
Legacy: National championship in '52. Coach of year in '52. Head coach, 1947-53.
FIRST-TEAM OFFENSE
QB Earl Morrall
Spartan: 1953-55
RB Lorenzo White
1984-87
RB Clinton Jones
Spartan: 1964-66
OG Dave Behrman
Spartan: 1960-62
OT Don Coleman
Spartan: 1949-51

C Dick Tamburo
Spartan: 1950-52
OG Joe DeLamielleure
Spartan: 1970-72
OT Tony Mandarich
Spartan: 1985-88
TE Billy Joe DuPree
Spartan: 1970-72
WR Gene Washington
Spartan: 1964-66
WR Kirk Gibson
Spartan: 1975-78
PK Morten Andersen
Spartan: 1978-81
KR Derrick Mason
Spartan: 1993-96
FIRST-TEAM DEFENSE
DE Sam Williams
Spartan: 1956-58
DE Bubba Smith
Spartan: 1964-66
DT Frank Kush
Spartan: 1950-52

DT Buck Nystrom
Spartan: 1953-55
LB Carl Banks
Spartan: 1980-83
R George Webster
Spartan: 1964-66
LB Percy Snow
Spartan: 1986-89
DB George Saimes
Spartan: 1960-62
CB Herb Adderley
Spartan: 1958-60
S Brad Van Pelt
Spartan: 1970-72
S Lynn Chandnois
Spartan: 1946-49
P Ray Stachowicz
Spartan: 1977-80
PR Derrick Mason
Spartan: 1993-96
SECOND-TEAM OFFENSE
QB Steve Juday 1963-65
RB John Pingel 1936-38
RB LeRoy Bolden 1951-54
OT Flozell Adams 1994-97

OG Don Mason 1948-49
C Dan Currie 1955-57
OG Ed Bagdon 1946-49
OT Jerry West 1964-66
TE Mark Brammer 1976-79
WR Andre Rison 1985-88
WR Bob Carey 1949-51
PK John Langeloh 1987-90
KR Eric Allen 1969-71
SECOND-TEAM DEFENSE
DL Dorne Dibble 1949-50
DL Don Dohoney 1951-53
DL Larry Bethea 1974-77
DL Sid Wagner 1933-35
LB Rich Saul 1967-69
LB Ron Goovert 1963-65
LB Dan Bass 1976-79
DB James Burroughs 1977-79, '81
DB Allen Brenner 1966-68
DB James Ellis 1951-53
DB Bill Simpson 1971-73
P Greg Montgomery 1985-87
PR Jesse Thomas 1948-50

Football

National champs
1965: UPI ranked the Spartans, who had a 10-0 regular season under coach Duffy Daugherty, No. 1; a 14-12 Rose Bowl loss to UCLA cost MSU an undisputed championship. The AP ranked Alabama No. 1.

1952: The Spartans, with a 9-0 record for the second consecutive season under coach Biggie Munn, won by an average of 25 points and were ranked No. 1 in both wire-service polls.

Bowl Record:
Games: 15 W: 6 L: 9

Michigan State Basketball

Year	G	W-L	Pct.	Place	Coach
1898-99	2	0-2	.000		No established coach
1899-00	4	2-2	.500		Charles O. Bemies
1900-01	3	3-0	1.000		Charles O. Bemies
1901-02	5	5-0	1.000		George E. Denman
1902-03	6	6-0	1.000		George E. Denman
1903-04	8	5-3	.625		Chester L. Brewer
1904-05	8	5-3	.625		Chester L. Brewer
1905-06	13	11-2	.846		Chester L. Brewer
1906-07	16	14-2	.875		Chester L. Brewer
1907-08	20	15-5	.750		Chester L. Brewer
1908-09	15	10-5	.667		Chester L. Brewer
1909-10	15	10-5	.667		Chester L. Brewer
1910-11	14	5-9	.357		John F. Macklin
1911-12	15	12-3	.800		John F. Macklin
1912-13	13	8-5	.615		John F. Macklin
1913-14	12	8-4	.667		John F. Macklin
1914-15	16	7-9	.438		John F. Macklin
1915-16	16	8-8	.500		John F. Macklin
1916-17	16	11-5	.688		George E. Gauthier
1917-18	16	6-10	.375		George E. Gauthier
1918-19	18	9-9	.500		George E. Gauthier
1919-20	23	12-11	.522		George E. Gauthier
1920-21	21	13-8	.619		Lyman L. Frimodig
1921-22	24	11-13	.458		Lyman L. Frimodig
1922-23	19	10-9	.526		Fred H. Walker
1923-24	20	10-10	.500		Fred H. Walker
1924-25	19	6-13	.316		John H. Kobs
1925-26	18	5-13	.278		John H. Kobs
1926-27	18	7-11	.389		Benjamin F. VanAlstyne
1927-28	15	11-4	.733		Benjamin F. VanAlstyne
1928-29	16	11-5	.688		Benjamin F. VanAlstyne
1929-30	16	12-4	.750		Benjamin F. VanAlstyne
1930-31	17	16-1	.941		Benjamin F. VanAlstyne
1931-32	17	12-5	.706		Benjamin F. VanAlstyne
1932-33	17	10-7	.588		Benjamin F. VanAlstyne
1933-34	17	12-5	.705		Benjamin F. VanAlstyne
1934-35	18	14-4	.778		Benjamin F. VanAlstyne
1935-36	17	8-9	.471		Benjamin F. VanAlstyne
1936-37	17	5-12	.294		Benjamin F. VanAlstyne
1937-38	17	9-8	.529		Benjamin F. VanAlstyne
1938-39	17	9-8	.529		Benjamin F. VanAlstyne
1939-40	20	14-6	.700		Benjamin F. VanAlstyne
1940-41	17	11-6	.647		Benjamin F. VanAlstyne
1941-42	21	15-6	.714		Benjamin F. VanAlstyne
1942-43	16	2-14	.125		Benjamin F. VanAlstyne
1943-44		No Schedule - World War II			
1944-45	16	9-7	.588		Benjamin F. VanAlstyne
1945-46	21	12-9	.571		Benjamin F. VanAlstyne
1946-47	21	11-10	.524		Benjamin F. VanAlstyne
1947-48	22	12-10	.545		Benjamin F. VanAlstyne
1948-49	21	9-12	.429		Benjamin F. VanAlstyne
1949-50	22	4-18	.182		Alton S. Kircher
1950-51	21	10-11	.476	T-7th	Peter F. Newell
1951-52	22	13-9	.591	T-5th	Peter F. Newell
1952-53	22	13-9	.591	T-3rd	Peter F. Newell
1953-54	22	9-13	.409	8th	Peter F. Newell
1954-55	22	13-9	.591	4th	Forrest A. Anderson
1955-56	22	13-9	.591	5th	Forrest A. Anderson
1956-57	26	16-10	.615	T-1st	Forrest A. Anderson
1957-58	22	16-6	.727	3rd	Forrest A. Anderson
1958-59	23	19-4	.826	1st	Forrest A. Anderson
1959-60	21	10-11	.476	8th	Forrest A. Anderson
1960-61	24	7-17	.292	9th	Forrest A. Anderson
1961-62	22	8-14	.381	T-9th	Forrest A. Anderson
1962-63	20	4-16	.200	9th	Forrest A. Anderson
1963-64	24	14-10	.583	T-4th	Forrest A. Anderson
1964-65	23	5-18	.217	10th	Forrest A. Anderson
1965-66	22	15-7	.682	2nd	John E. Benington
1966-67	23	16-7	.696	T-1st	John E. Benington
1967-68	24	12-12	.500	T-6th	John E. Benington
1968-69	23	11-12	.478	T-5th	John E. Benington
1969-70	24	9-15	.375	T-6th	Gus G. Ganakas
1970-71	24	10-14	.417	T-7th	Gus G. Ganakas
1971-72	24	13-11	.542	T-5th	Gus G. Ganakas
1972-73	24	13-11	.542	T-6th	Gus G. Ganakas
1973-74	24	13-11	.542	T-4th	Gus G. Ganakas
1974-75	26	17-9	.654	5th	Gus G. Ganakas
1975-76	27	14-13	.518	4th	Gus G. Ganakas
1976-77	27	12-15	.444	5th	Jud Heathcote
1977-78	30	25-5	.833	1st	Jud Heathcote
1978-79	32	26-6	.813	T-1st	Jud Heathcote
1979-80	27	12-15	.444	9th	Jud Heathcote
1980-81	27	13-14	.481	8th	Jud Heathcote
1981-82	28	12-16	.429	T-7th	Jud Heathcote
1982-83	30	17-13	.566	T-6th	Jud Heathcote
1983-84	28	16-12	.571	T-5th	Jud Heathcote
1984-85	29	19-10	.655	T-5th	Jud Heathcote
1985-86	31	23-8	.742	3rd	Jud Heathcote
1986-87	28	11-17	.393	7th	Jud Heathcote
1987-88	28	10-18	.357	8th	Jud Heathcote
1988-89	33	18-15	.545	T-8th	Jud Heathcote
1989-90	34	28-6	.824	1st	Jud Heathcote
1990-91	30	19-11	.633	T-3rd	Jud Heathcote
1991-92	30	22-8	.733	T-3rd	Jud Heathcote
1992-93	28	15-13	.536	T-8th	Jud Heathcote
1993-94	32	20-12	.625	T-4th	Jud Heathcote
1994-95	28	22-6	.785	2nd	Jud Heathcote
1995-96	32	16-16	.500	7th	Tom Izzo
1996-97	29	17-12	.586	T-6th	Tom Izzo
1997-98	30	22-8	.733	T-1st	Tom Izzo
1998-99	38	33-5	.868	1st	Tom Izzo
1999-00	39	32-7	.821	1st	Tom Izzo
Totals	2,141	1,236-905	.732		

NCAA photo

Sophomore Earvin Johnson, a star at Lansing Everett High, led the Spartans to their first national title in '79.

Michigan State University

Michigan State football

Year	W	L	T	Coach
1896	1	2	1	No Established Coach
1897	4	2	1	Henry Keep
1898	4	3	0	Henry Keep
1899	2	4	1	Charles O. Bemies
1900	1	3	0	Charles O. Bemies
1901	3	4	1	George Denman
1902	4	5	0	George Denman
1903	6	1	1	Chester L. Brewer
1904	8	1	0	Chester L. Brewer
1905	9	2	0	Chester L. Brewer
1906	7	2	2	Chester L. Brewer
1907	4	2	1	Chester L. Brewer
1908	6	0	2	Chester L. Brewer
1909	8	1	0	Chester L. Brewer
1910	6	1	0	Chester L. Brewer
1911	5	1	0	John F. Macklin
1912	7	1	0	John F. Macklin
1913	7	0	0	John F. Macklin
1914	5	2	0	John F. Macklin
1915	5	1	0	John F. Macklin
1916	4	2	1	Frank Sommers
1917	0	9	0	Chester L. Brewer
1918	4	3	0	George E. Gauthier
1919	4	4	1	Chester L. Brewer
1920	4	6	0	George "Potsy" Clark
1921	3	5	0	Albert M. Barron
1922	3	5	2	Albert M. Barron
1923	3	5	0	Ralph H. Young
1924	5	3	0	Ralph H. Young
1925	3	5	0	Ralph H. Young
1926	3	4	1	Ralph H. Young
1927	4	5	0	Ralph H. Young
1928	3	4	1	Harry J. Kipke
1929	5	3	0	James H. Crowley
1930	5	1	2	James H. Crowley
1931	5	3	1	James H. Crowley
1932	7	1	0	James H. Crowley
1933	4	2	2	Charles W. Bachman
1934	8	1	0	Charles W. Bachman
1935	6	2	0	Charles W. Bachman
1936	6	1	2	Charles W. Bachman
1937	8	2	0	Charles W. Bachman
1938	6	3	0	Charles W. Bachman
1939	4	4	1	Charles W. Bachman
1940	3	4	1	Charles W. Bachman
1941	5	3	1	Charles W. Bachman
1942	4	3	2	Charles W. Bachman
1943				
1944	6	1	0	Charles W. Bachman
1945	5	3	1	Charles W. Bachman
1946	5	5	0	Charles W. Bachman
1947	7	2	0	Clarence L. Munn
1948	6	2	2	Clarence L. Munn
1949	6	3	0	Clarence L. Munn
1950	8	1	0	Clarence L. Munn
1951	9	0	0	Clarence L. Munn
1952	9	0	0	Clarence L. Munn
1953	9	1	0	Clarence L. Munn
1954	3	6	0	Hugh (Duffy) Daugherty
1955	9	1	0	Duffy Daugherty
1956	7	2	0	Duffy Daugherty
1957	8	1	0	Duffy Daugherty
1958	3	5	1	Duffy Daugherty
1959	5	4	0	Duffy Daugherty
1960	6	2	1	Duffy Daugherty
1961	7	2	0	Duffy Daugherty
1962	5	4	0	Duffy Daugherty
1963	6	2	1	Duffy Daugherty
1964	4	5	0	Duffy Daugherty
1965	10	1	0	Duffy Daugherty
1966	9	0	1	Duffy Daugherty
1967	3	7	0	Duffy Daugherty
1968	5	5	0	Duffy Daugherty
1969	4	6	0	Duffy Daugherty
1970	4	6	0	Duffy Daugherty
1971	6	5	0	Duffy Daugherty
1972	5	5	1	Duffy Daugherty
1973	5	6	0	Dennis Stolz
1974	7	3	1	Dennis Stolz
1975	7	4	0	Dennis Stolz
1976	4	6	1	Darryl Rogers
1977	7	3	1	Darryl Rogers
1978	8	3	0	Darryl Rogers
1979	5	6	0	Darryl Rogers
1980	3	8	0	Frank (Muddy) Waters
1981	5	6	0	Muddy Waters
1982	2	9	0	Muddy Waters
1983	4	6	1	George Perles
1984	6	6	0	George Perles
1985	7	5	0	George Perles
1986	6	5	0	George Perles
1987	9	2	1	George Perles
1988	6	5	1	George Perles
1989	8	4	0	George Perles
1990	8	3	1	George Perles
1991	3	8	0	George Perles
1992	5	6	0	George Perles
1993	6	6	0	George Perles
1994	0	11	0	George Perles
1995	6	5	1	Nick Saban
1996	6	6	0	Nick Saban
1997	7	5	0	Nick Saban
1998	6	6	0	Nick Saban
1999	10	2	0	Nick Saban/Bobby Williams
2000	5	6	0	Bobby Williams
Totals	**561**	**369**	**44**	

Michigan State University

Biggie Munn, far left, in his playing days and Duffy Daugherty, above, were two of the Spartans' greatest football coaches.

HOCKEY
D - Mark Howe
D - Derian Hatcher
F - Pat LaFontaine
F - Mike Modano
F - Doug Weight
G - John Vanbiesbrouck

BASEBALL
2B — Charlie Gehringer
OF — Willie Horton
OF — Ron Leflore
OF — Kirk Gibson
OF — Alex Johnson
C — Bill Freehan
P — Hal Newhouser
P — Frank Tanana
P — Billy Pierce
P — John Smoltz
P — Bob Welch
C — Ted Simmons
1B — John Mayberry

Preps

Local boys and girls made good: Metro Detroit's best jocks

Criteria: To make the list, the athlete must have grown up in Wayne, Oakland, Macomb, Monroe, Livingston, St. Clair or Washtenaw counties. In other words, simply playing at U-M doesn't count.

BOYS BASKETBALL TEAM
Dave DeBusschere, Detroit Austin
Spencer Haywood, Detroit Pershing
Curtis Jones, Detroit Northwestern
Rudy Tomjanovich, Hamtramck
Chris Webber, Birmingham Detroit Country Day
Coach: Lofton Greene, River Rouge

GIRLS BASKETBALL TEAM
Franthea Price, River Rouge
Katie McNamara, Farmington Hills Mercy
Dena Head, Plymouth Salem
Nikita Lowry, Detroit Cass Tech
Melanie Megge, Detroit Dominican
Coach: Mary Lillie Cicerone, Birmingham Marian

Prep stars Franthea Price, Spencer Haywood and Jerome Bettis

Free Press file photo

Free Press file photo

Associated Press

FOOTBALL TEAM
Offense
E: Tom Beer, Detroit St. Ambrose
OL: Luis Sharpe, Detroit Southwestern
OL: Kevin Hart, Birmingham Brother Rice
OL: Ken Dallafoir, Madison Heights
OL: Dan Currie, Detroit St. Anthony
OL: Joe Henze, Detroit St. Catherine
E: Ron Kramer, East Detroit
QB: Mill Coleman, Farmington Hills Harrison
RB: Tom Tracy, Birmingham
RB: Jerome Bettis, Detroit Mackenzie
RB: Tyrone Wheatley, Dearborn Heights Robichaud
K: Dave Blackmer, Farmington Hills Harrison
Defense
DL: Harold Lucas, Detroit Southwestern
DL: Gilbert Brown, Detroit Mackenzie
DL: Mark Messner, Redford Catholic Central
DL: Ed Budde, Detroit Denby

DL: John Ghindia, Trenton
LB: Paul Rudzinski, Detroit Catholic Central
LB: Thomas Johnson, Detroit Mackenzie
LB: Jim Paciorek, Orchard Lake St. Mary's
DB: Gary Coakley, Harper Woods Notre Dame
DB: John Miller, Farmington Hills Harrison
DB: Greg Washington, Detroit Western
Coach: John Herrington, Farmington Hills Harrison

The Goodfellow Game
Super Bowl of Prep Sports

From 1938 to 1967, the football champions of the Detroit Catholic and Detroit Public Schools high school leagues met at Tiger Stadium in a championship game. Proceeds went to the Goodfellow Fund charity. The first points in the first game were registered by Catholic Central's John McHale, the father of Tiger President John McHale Jr., who intercepted a Hamtramck pass and ran it back for a touchdown. The chart below shows the Catholic University of Detroit playing against Catholic schools — that is because U-D for many years played in the Public School League.

The Denby Tars went to the championship game a record 9 times.

Year	Attendance
1938 Catholic Central 19, Hamtramck 13	20,857
1939 University of Detroit 20, Catholic Central 0	23,120
1940 Cooley 6, St. Theresa 6	14,861
1941 Cooley 47, St. Theresa 6	30,175
1942 Catholic Central 46, Hamtramck 0	26,495
1943 Catholic Central 8, Cooley 0	17,500
1944 Mackenzie 3, Holy Redeemer 0	30,054
1945 Catholic Central 19, Denby 19	22,140
1946 Cooley 21, St. Anthony 13	35,201
1947 Denby 14, Redford St. Mary 0	28,528
1948 Denby 28, Redford St. Mary 0	39,004
1949 St. Anthony 19, University of Detroit 13	34,038
1950 Redford 7, St. Gregory 6	30,119
1951 Redford St. Mary 23, Western 6	29,283
1952 Redford St. Mary 13, University of Detroit 6	25,776
1953 Pershing 21, Lourdes 7	29,454
1954 University of Detroit 23, Redford St. Mary 20	30,593
1955 Pershing 13, Redford St. Mary 7	29,830
1956 De La Salle 26, Denby 20	28,343
1957 Redford St. Mary 25, Southeastern 6	34,538
1958 Redford 27, Redford St. Mary 7	38,896
1959 St. Ambrose 13, Cooley 7	30,062
1960 Denby 21, Catholic Central 18	39,196
1961 St. Ambrose 20, Pershing 13	37,157
1962 St. Ambrose 19, Cooley 0	37,763
1963 Denby 7, Notre Dame 0	23,500
1964 St. Ambrose 20, Southeastern 0	15,000
1965 Notre Dame 14, Denby 14	25,435
1966 St. Ambrose 33, Denby 19	12,337
1967 Divine Child 14, Denby 7	15,186

SPORTS

WILLIAM ARCHIE/Detroit Free Press

Tree Service team members Earl Justice, left, Verlin Terry, Steve Bradley, David Boyd and Carleton Chambers

Bowling

Men's three-game series world record: 3,870, set by Just-Us Tree Service of Detroit in a tournament in Toledo, Ohio, on May 1, 1999. Earl Justice, captain and sponsor, shot 792. His teammates were Carleton Chambers (805), David Boyd (774), Steve Bradley (761) and Verlin Terry (738). It was the first time the five men had played as a team.

Women's world record: On March 20, 1998, Contour Power Grips of the Detroit All-Star Bowlerettes league broke its WIBC five-player team, three-game series world record and set a single-game world record. Contour shot 3,552 at the Detroit Women's Bowling Association city tournament at Sterling Lanes, 16 pins higher than its previous record, set in league play in 1994. In the final game of the new-record series, Contour shot 1,328, breaking the existing single-game mark of 1,284. Team members were captain Jeanne Gebbia, Kathy Haislip, Aleta Sill, Cyndi Black and Lisa Bishop. The same Bowlerettes franchise, under different sponsors and with different bowlers in and out of the lineup, has the top six team spots in the WIBC record book.

Bowling alleys peak: In 1984-85, 176 establishments were registered with the Greater Detroit Bowling Association.

Bowling membership peaks: In 1979-80, membership in the Greater Detroit Bowling Association reached 151,097.

An ABC tourney: Cobo Hall in 1971 drew 6,216 teams from 48 states for an ABC tournament, which runs 10 weeks. Detroit has not been a tournament host since.

That championship season: The National Bowling League completed its first and only season in 1962. The Detroit Thunderbirds from Thunderbowl Lanes of Allen Park won the championship. The team featured Ed Lubanski, Billy Golembiewski, George Howard, Bob Crawford, Tom Harnisch, Joe Fazio and Dale Seavoy. Bowling alley builder Don Rogers was the owner; George Prybyla was the general manager.

Bowling liberation: A women's team whose averages were considered too high for them to compete in the All-Star Bowlerettes League joined the South Macomb Men's League in 1962 at Harbor Lanes in St. Clair Shores. Although not a first for the country, it was the first time in Detroit that women competed in a previously all-male Detroit League. The groundbreakers were Elvira Toepfer, Anita Cantaline, Ann Setlock, Helen Weston and Connie Bayma.

Perfection on the tube: In 1959, Ed Lubanski, in a nationally televised program that was the finale of an AMF bowling school in Miami, rolled back-to-back 300 games, still the only time that has been done on television. Later in his career, he turned in another perfect game, this time on a local show.

Team of the '50s: The Pfeiffer Beer team

WHEN IT COMES TO BOWLING, METRO DETROIT IS NO. 1.

➤ The Greater Detroit Bowling Association has 68,838 individual members, tops in the United States, according to the American Bowling Congress. Chicago is second with 29,201.

➤ The Detroit Women's Bowling Association has 46,349 members, tops in the nation. Chicago is second with 19,122.

➤ The Young American Bowling Association, which oversees youth leagues, puts Detroit at the top with 13,640 youth members. Chicago is second with 1,760.

➤ Detroit also leads the nation in number of bowling centers with 104.

from the All-Star Classic in 1953 won the first of its three ABC regular team titles. Pfeiffer also won in 1955 and 1959. Pfeiffer also won the team all-events title each of those years. Lou Sielaff captained the 1953 and 1955 teams, which featured the same basic lineup as the ABC-champion 1952 E & B team, and Ed Lubanski captained the '59 team with a new lineup that won with a record score of 3,243. Lubanski cleaned house in 1959, winning the individual singles and all-events titles as well. He is one of only three bowlers ever to win four ABC "eagles" — as the championship titles are called — in one tournament.

Kegler media pioneer: Detroit broadcaster Fred Wolf produced a one-shot bowling show, "Make It and Take It," on WXYZ-TV in 1949, and then in 1950, started a weekly series called "Champions Bowling." In 1956, he replaced Chris Schenkel and started a 12-year network stint with "Championship Bowling." In 1961, Wolf did the commentary for the first televised PBA tournament (in Paramus, N.J.), which was used to sell the PBA to the ABC television network, which then carried the 1962 PBA winter tour, starting a 36-year relationship.

Post-war tourney: The 1948 ABC tournament at the State Fair Coliseum drew a record 7,348 teams from 42 states, almost 4,000 more than the previous year in Los Angeles. Wolf broadcasts from the Coliseum each of the 80 days of the tournament. The Grand Central Recreation team of Detroit won the booster team title.

Wolf, part II: Wolf, who became the leading morning radio-show host in Detroit with WXYZ-AM (1270), now WXYT, in 1945 started a 15minute weekly show called "The Tenpin Talker." Before a back injury ended his bowling career, Wolf was a star on the Stroh's team and led the All-Star Classic with a 201 average in 1941-42.

The perfect woman: During the 1943-44 season, Hattie Woosters became the first woman in metro Detroit to bowl a 300 game.

Bowltown: ABC figures in 1942 showed that Detroit, with more than 14,000 sanctioned teams and more than 70,000 bowlers, had more organized bowlers per capita than any other city.

Prewar stats: Detroit had 162 bowling alleys in 1940, only 14 fewer than the peak in 1984-85, when the region had 2 million more people than in 1940.

Birth of a bowling metropolis: In 1935, the foundation for Detroit's nationwide reputation was laid when Joe Norris, in association with industry leaders Herb Mertens and Harold Allen, started what became known as the Detroit All-Star Classic League. Norris formed the league because his Stroh's team

and other elite squads were discouraged from joining the city's strongest leagues because they were too good. The league started with 10 teams, and by 1937, it had been increased to 16 teams as ace bowlers nationwide — including the great Don Carter — moved to Detroit, clamoring for admittance. The original Classic League, which sometimes was exclusive to one house and sometimes traveled, has been stationary since the mid-'70s, bowling Tuesdays at Thunderbowl Lanes in Allen Park with 18 teams. In 1974-75, a companion traveling league was formed, bowling on Thursdays in a different center each week. The Tuesday league holds the national record for one-night pinfall for an 18-team league with 61,128 in 1988, an average of 226.4 per man. The traveling league holds the national 16-team record with 53,925 in 1998, an average of 224.7 per man.

Bowling and beer: Joe Norris in 1932 formed a team and talked Stroh's Brewery into sponsoring it. This set the stage for an era of brewery-sponsored teams battling nationwide for another 30 years. Brewmeister John Stroh, upset by bowling's sometimes ragtag image, insisted that his team be smartly clad, leading to the creation of its trademark white uniforms — sharp-creased flannel trousers and longsleeved shirts, red ties, white belts and white shoes.

The bowling Mecca: Detroit Recreation, then the world's biggest bowling center, opened in 1918 across from the federal building on West Lafayette. It has four floors dedicated to bowling, with 22 lanes each. At the time, the few women who dared to bowl had to enter through side doors and then bowl behind curtains. But Detroit Rec's Jim Shillady reserved one of the building's 22-lane floors exclusively for women. The floor even featured female pinsetters. Detroit Recreation closed in September 1960. Thunderbowl is now the third-largest in the country, with 94 lanes.

Rock and bowl: Garden Bowling Alleys became the 14th bowling center in Detroit in 1913. Now known as Garden Bowl, it is still operating at the same location on Woodward Avenue. It's the fifth-oldest bowling center in the United States, and now is patronized mainly by casually dressed college students cavorting in the strobe lights. Bowlers in 1913 wore ties and white shirts with sleeve garters.

A perfect game: Robert Waller bowled Detroit's first 300 game in 1911.

Turn-of-the-century: Detroit in 1900 had six bowling alleys, according to the R.L. Polk directory. The city's first bowling alley opened in 1861 on East Jefferson. The number of bowlers in the city was estimated at 1,000.

Free Press file photo

Meg Mallon, who grew up in Birmingham and attended Farmington Hills Mercy High School, has become a leading money winner on the LPGA tour.

Above: Mallon celebrates her Du Maurier victory in August, 2000.

Left: Mallon rejoices after sinking a putt on the 18th to win the 1991 LPGA Championship.

Golf

FORE!

For golfers, Michigan is the holey land. The state leads the nation with nearly 700 public courses, and it has led the nation in recent years in building new courses. Here are the number of public courses in metro Detroit by county:

➤ **Oakland** ....56 courses
➤ **Wayne**...37
➤ Macomb 29
➤ Washtenaw 24
➤ Monroe 18
➤ Livingston....................................15
➤ St. Clair 11

The Legends

Walter Hagen: Colorful, flamboyant and one of the greatest of early American players, Hagen became head pro at Oakland Hills Country Club in 1919, the year he won his second U.S. Open. Although "the Haig" represented the club for only one year, he lived at the Detroit Athletic Club and drew great attention to Michigan golf in the '20s by winning five PGA Championships (four of them in a row) and four British Opens and captaining

SENIOR PLAYERS CHAMPIONSHIP, 1990: The tournament was won by Jack Nicklaus in 1990 at the Dearborn Country Club while its permanent home down the street at the TPC of Michigan course, designed by Nicklaus with spectators in mind, was completed. Now the event provides an annual senior major, a long-awaited regular tournament, in the biggest metro area of a golf-happy state.

Jack Nicklaus won the 1991 U.S. Senior Open at Oakland Hills after a playoff with Chi Chi Rodriguez.

the first-ever U.S. Ryder Cup team in '27. Hagen began the golf equipment company bearing his name in Grand Rapids and for the latter part of his life, made his home at Long Lake near Traverse City.

James Standish: What Hagen did for the status of the club professional and tournament golf, Standish accomplished for amateur golf at both the private club and public links level. He won three Michigan Amateurs (1909, '12 and '24). He was also president of the United States Gold Association from 1952-57, and while amateur golf was dominated by private club players, he worked to upgrade public links golf. He conceived a national publinx championship and donated the trophy emblematic of that title. The tournament was twice held at the City of Detroit's Rackham municipal course.

Chuck Kocsis: Generally considered the finest amateur player in Michigan history, his legacy began when he hitchhiked to Grand Rapids as a 17-year-old Redford schoolboy and defeated PGA and British Open champion Tommy Armour in a playoff for the 1931 Michigan Open title. Kocsis' brilliant career, spanning more than seven decades, included NCAA and Big Ten championships, a record six Michigan Amateurs, a record five Michigan Medal Plays, three U.S. Walker Cup appearances, runner-up in the 1938 U.S. Amateur, nine Masters tournaments (low amateur twice) and 13 U.S. Open appearances (low amateur three times). He capped his career by winning four World Senior titles (1970, '73, '83 and '88), the last at St. Andrews at the age of 73.

Everett Kircher: A former Studebaker dealer in Detroit, Kircher pulled up stakes and bought a parcel of rolling land in northwestern Michigan, where his invention of the ski lift assured winter success for his burgeoning resort areas. But in 1964, when he brought in golf architect Robert Trent Jones to build a course to promote summer activity at the resort, Kircher touched off one of the biggest business booms in northern Michigan history. Other promoters and resort owners followed Kircher's lead. The original Boyne Highlands course opened in 1967 and the state's golf growth continues almost unabated.

Calvin Peete: Although he never played golf until age 23 and had a crooked arm as the souvenir of a childhood injury, Peete caught on quickly enough to turn pro five years later. The native Detroiter won 12 PGA Tour tournaments in the '80s and '90s, then added four more Senior Tour events. Peete won the Vardon Trophy for low scoring average in '84 and is considered one of the straightest hitters in history. He also was the foremost black player of the pre-Tiger Woods era. Peete is an inspiration to both minority and handicapped golfers and continues to promote golf and teach the game through big-city clinics.

Memorable Championships

PGA Championship, 1953: Held at the Birmingham Country Club, this extended the popularity of match play golf in the Detroit area and was a breakthrough victory for Detroiter Walter Burkemo, who had finished runner-up to Sam Snead in the 1951 PGA. Another of the state's foremost players, Chick Harbert, also excelled at match play and was twice a PGA runner-up (including 1947 at Southfield's Plum Hollow Country Club) before winning in '54 at St. Paul, Minn., where the runner-up again was Burkemo. The championship returned here one more time, with Doug Ford beating Cary Middlecoff in the '55 finals at the Meadowbrook Country Club in Northville, before the PGA changed its match play format to stroke play in '58.

Buick Open, 1953: The commercialization of the PGA Tour traces its roots to Grand Blanc, where Buick public relations majordomos, cognizant of the sport's drawing appeal from Detroit-area events, decided that golf, with its upscale image, would be a great advertising vehicle. With a top field lured by a then-record $50,000 purse and a common man's touch with $1 admission and free parking at Warwick Hills, the tourney was a hit as Billy Casper was the first champion. The tourney survived an eight-year hiatus in the '70s during a change in company management, then returned and remains one of the PGA Tour's mainstay events.

U.S. Amateur, 1954: The Country Club of Detroit in Grosse Pointe Farms hosted the championship, usually dominated by the nation's private club elite. But this time the muscular son of a Pennsylvania pro, stepping up after golf at Wake Forest and Navy service in Cleveland, marched to the title, then turned pro. Thus started the saga of perhaps the most popular golfer in history — Arnold Palmer.

U.S. Women's Open, 1989: The tournament had been staged in the Detroit suburbs before. In 1953, at Forest Lake Country Club, Mickey Wright won in relative privacy. Area interest in the LPGA continued to flounder (the Lady Stroh's at Dearborn failed to make it) until Stan Aldridge bought and refurbished the grand old Indianwood Golf and Country Club course at Lake Orion and held the '89 Open. Betsy King won before such responsive galleries that the USGA returned on short notice in '94 and a victory by Patty Sheehan proved Michigan fans appreciated big-time golf, be it men's or women's.

Senior Players Championship, 1991: The tournament was won by Jack Nicklaus in 1990 at the Dearborn Country Club while its permanent home down the street at the TPC of Michigan course, designed by Nicklaus with spectators in mind, was completed. Now the event provides an annual senior major, a long-awaited regular tournament, in the biggest metro area of a golf-happy state.

U.S. Open Senior Open, 1991: Michigan became the capital of senior golf in '91. The USGA coincidentally selected the same year as the TPC of Michigan debut with the Senior Players to return the Senior Open to Oakland Hills. It was a memorable event as Nicklaus shot a record 65 to defeat Chi Chi Rodriguez in a playoff, but it had even bigger ramifications. The seniors set the table for yet another U.S. Open at Oakland Hills in 1996 and the success

Associated Press

U.S. OPEN, 1951: Although two earlier Opens were staged at Oakland Hills, '51 was a benchmark as designer Robert Trent Jones was summoned to toughen up the classic old Donald Ross course to challenge "modern-era" players, setting a trend for future big tournaments. Ben Hogan won his second straight Open, shooting a final-round 67 to conquer Jones' "Monster" while the Detroit area became solidified as a strong golf tournament site.

of both events made it a no-brainer to extend golf history at Oakland Hills in the new millennium. The U.S. Amateur is scheduled there in 2001 and the Ryder Cup matches in 2003.

Gar Wood, left, was a pioneer in his sport and the dominant racer of his time.

HYDROPLANE DEATHS
The 3-mile oval course west of the Belle Isle Bridge and north of the island has claimed three lives during hydroplane races:

Warner Gardner died in the 1968 Gold Cup race when his Miss Eagle Electric crashed at 160 m.p.h.

Chuck Thompson was killed in the 1966 Gold Cup when his Miss Smirnoff hit a wave, went airborne and disintegrated.

Bob Hayward died in 1962 driving Miss Supertest.

Start your engines!

Powerboat racing

Powerboat racing on the Detroit River has been graced by a long list of luminaries, from an Italian count to a famed band leader to an automobile pioneer.

They and drivers such as Gar Wood and Bill Muncey — and let's not forget the anonymous genius who invented the portable beer cooler — have made Detroit the premier venue for speed freaks of the water variety since 1916.

In 1915, the year before the first race on the river, a boat named Miss Detroit won the Gold Cup on Manhasset Bay in New York. The boat was owned by a syndicate headed by automobile builder Horace Dodge and newspaper publisher William Scripps.

The following year, they brought the Gold Cup to Detroit, where the race has been run 26 times.

Calling the Detroit River the "Yankee Stadium of boat racing" actually understates the case. Even in the 1920s, Wood was drawing crowds of around 200,000 to the river with his combination of record-setting speed and a promotional knack that puts Donald Trump to shame.

Wood raced trains from Miami to New York — and beat them, on elapsed time — to prove how fast his boats were. An inventor, he was a charter member of Detroit's industrial aristocracy. He was the first of generations of

SPORTS

Detroit barons — such as the Dodge boys, Horace Sr. and Jr. — who went racing.

From his base on Grayhaven near the current Detroit course, Wood won five consecutive Gold Cups beginning in 1917, a string unmatched until Chip Hanauer won seven straight in the '80s.

Besides its unmatched waterfront access, Detroit got boosts in the early racing years from two social upheavals, the War to End All Wars and the Volstead Act. Detroit's Packard car company was the prime contractor for the World War I Liberty airplane engines, which were snapped up by powerboat racers after the war. Prohibition created a demand for fast boats, which had only to cross "le Detroit," the strait, to be in Canadian Club land.

In 1946, band leader Guy Lombardo won the Gold Cup in Detroit. He was one of the biggest names in music at the time, and fans flocked to see him.

Lombardo, from London, Ontario, grew up around boats and in his youth had seen Wood race in Detroit. Lombardo also won a 1948 race, one of three Detroit races that year.

The modern racing era began in 1950. Slo-Mo-Shun IV's 1950 victory was a mixed blessing for Detroit, signaling the beginning of glory years for competition and the beginning of the end of Detroit's unchallenged powerboat domination. Though built by Michigan's Les Staudacher, Slo-Mo-Shun was designed by Ted Jones, a supervisor at Boeing from Seattle.

Detroit owners and racers, including the Schoeniths (Joe, Lee and Jerry), the Dossins (Walt, Roy and Russ) and Jack Schafer, continued to be successful, but the momentum shifted west. Aluminum baron Edgar Kaiser and Nevada casino owner Bill Harrah raced winning boats on the river in the 1950s and '60s, but the ultimate indication of the change came when Muncey, the son of a Royal Oak auto dealer, started winning for Seattle owners. It was the heyday of the Detroit-Seattle rivalry, and Muncey was widely considered a traitor by Detroit fans.

A balding, compact man with an insatiable appetite for ice cream and hydroplane racing, Muncey won 62 races, more than double any other driver, and eight Gold Cups. He won 10 races in Detroit. His best years came under the sponsorship of O.H. Frisbee, founder of Atlas Van Lines, who caught the racing bug in his Detroit riverfront apartment when he heard the thunder of the racing boats.

Muncey died at age 52 with the throttle down in a 1981 Acapulco race that was essentially a promotional venture.

Hanauer took over for Muncey in 1982, and the changing of the guard was completed later that season when Dean Chenoweth, Muncey's nemesis and up to then, the second-leading winner for Bernie Little's Budweiser team, died in an equally meaningless qualifying session in Washington.

Though the recent racing in Detroit has been lackluster, the partying has been no less intense. The 1976 race attracted about 500,000 fans, the largest single event of that bicentennial year. Most of the crowds since then have been in the same ballpark.

The Detroit Grand Prix

Formula One racing roared into Detroit in 1982 with the Detroit Grand Prix. Drivers didn't care for the rough course that wound through downtown, though the city looked great on international television. The worldwide organization demanded changes after the 1988 race. Negotiations broke off, and the race was switched to CART's Indy-style cars.

Year	Boat	Owner	Driver	Speed
1916	Miss Minneapolis	Miss Minneapolis Power Boat Association	Bernard Smith	49.7 21
1917	Miss Detroit II	Gar Wood	Gar Wood	56.5 23
1918	Miss Detroit III	Gar Wood	Gar Wood	52.1 25
1919	Miss Detroit III	Gar Wood	Gar Wood	56.3 26
1920	Miss Detroit IV	Gar Wood	Gar Wood	70.0 27
1921	Miss America	Gar Wood	Gar Wood	56.5 28
1922	Packard ChrisCraft	Jesse G. Vincent	Jesse G. Vincent	40.6 29
1923	Packard ChrisCraft	Jesse G. Vincent	Caleb Bragg	44.4 30
1924	Baby Bootlegger	Caleb Bragg	Caleb Bragg	46.4 31
1933	El Lagarto	George C. Reis	George C. Reis	60.8 43
1937	Notre Dame	Herb Mendelson	Clell Perry	68.645 47
1938	Alagi	Theo Rossi	Theo Rossi	66.08 48
1939	My Sin	Zalmon Guy Simmons Jr.	Zalmon Guy Simmons Jr.	67.05 49
1946	Tempo VI	Guy Lombardo	Guy Lombardo	70.878 51
1948	Miss Great Lakes	Albin Fallon	Dan Foster	57.452 53
1949	04My Sweetie	Ed Gregory & Ed Schoenherr	Bill Cantrell	78.645 54
1950	Slo Mo Shun IV	Stannley S. Sayres	Ted Jones	78.216
1956	Miss Thriftway	Willard Rhodes	Bill Muncey	96.552 59
1963	Miss Bardahl	Ole Bardahl	Ron Musson	105.124
1964	Miss Bardahl	Ole Bardahl	Ron Musson	103.433
1966	Tahoe Miss	Bill Harrah	Mira Slovak	93.019
1968	Miss Bardahl	Ole Bardahl	Bill Shumacher	108.173
1972	Atlas Van Lines	Joe Schoenith	Bill Muncey	104.277
1976	Miss U.S.	George Simon	Tom D'Eath	100.412
1982	Atlas Van Lines	Fran Muncey	Chip Hanauer	120.05
1986	Miller American	Fran Muncey	Chip Hanauer	116.523
1990	Miss Budweiser	Bernie Little	Tom D'Eath	143.176
1991	Winston Eagle	Steve Woomer	Mark Tate	137.771
1992	Miss Budweiser	Bernie Little	Chip Hanauer	136.282
1993	Miss Budweiser	Bernie Little	Chip Hanauer	141.296
1994	Smokin' Joes	Steve Woomer	Mark Tate	145.26
1995	Miss Budweiser	Bernie Little	Chip Hanauer	149.16
1996	PICO American Dream	Fred Leland	Dave Villwock	149.328
1997	Miss Budweiser	Bernie Little	Dave Villwock	129.366
1998	Miss Budweiser	Bernie Little	Dave Villwock	140.309 68
1999	Miss PICO	Fred Leland	Chip Hanauer	152.591

DETROIT GRAND PRIX WINNERS

1982 John Watson, Britain
1983 Michele Alboreto, Italy
1984 Nelson Piquet, Brazil
1985 Keke Rosberg, Finland
1986 Ayrton Senna, Brazil
1987 Ayrton Senna, Brazil
1988 Ayrton Senna, Brazil
1989 Emerson Fittipaldi, Brazil (First CART race)
1990 Michael Andretti, USA
1991 Emerson Fittipaldi, Brazil
1992 Bobby Rahal, USA (First Belle Isle race)
1993 Danny Sullivan, USA
1994 Paul Tracy, Canada
1995 Robby Gordon, USA
1996 Michael Andretti, USA
1997 Greg Moore, Canada
1998 Alex Zanardi, Italy
1999 Dario Franchitti, Scotland
2000 Helio Castroneves, Brazil

SPORTS

Our rinks, courts, fields of dreams

Comerica Park

➤ **Cost:** At least $361 million.
➤ **First game:** April 11, 2000. Tigers defeated Seattle, 5-2, in miserable, 34-degree weather before 39,168 fans.
➤ **First hit:** The Mariners' John Olerud doubled off Brian Moehler in the first inning.
➤ **First home run:** The Tigers' Juan Gonzalez, in their fourth game.

With its artsy statues of Tigers greats, post-free construction, amusement-park rides, luxury boxes, food court, dining clubs and centerfield waterfall, Comerica Park could not be more different from Tiger Stadium. For fans, the change to the new stadium also produced a new effect on the pocketbook.

A national survey showed the average price of a baseball ticket in Detroit jumped 103 percent over the winter the team switched

J. KYLE KEENER/Detroit Free Press

Brian Moehler throws the first pitch on Opening Day at Comerica Park.

left-center (the park's signature dimension) and 380 to right-center (a distance made more daunting by an 11½-foot fence — 3 feet higher than anything on the leftfield side of center).

Many American League parks have power alleys of fewer than 380 feet. The only one that appears to have a power alley as large as Comerica's 398-footer is Yankee Stadium, which is 399 to left-center. (There's no league-wide standard spot between the foul pole and center for taking power-alley measurements.)

Tiger Stadium in its old age certainly didn't provide any advantage for the Tigers, given the frequent inability of their starting pitchers to keep them in games. In the 1990s, the Tigers hit more homers than any team except Seattle — but lost more games than any team. Tigers followers might not have known that statistic, but they have known its pain.

Remember that 440 sign in centerfield at Tiger Stadium? It was wrong.

The distance from home plate to centerfield at the old ballpark wasn't 440 feet — even though for decades the Tigers displayed that distinctively Detroit depth on the centerfield wall. The actual distance from the plate to the wall in dead center was about 425 feet, president John McHale said. That still made it the deepest dimension in the majors. The Tigers discovered the discrepancy while doing precise measurements in preparation for their move to Comerica Park. No one could say how or why the different distances came about.

Detroit's baseball parks

Woodward Avenue Grounds, 1850-1913: Five-acre parcel on west side of Woodward between Canfield and Forest near present-day Wayne State University hosted baseball and cricket. The site later became Convention Hall and a Vernors bottling plant. A gas station and parking lot are there today.

Recreation Park, 1879-1894: This multi-use facility was located at Brush and Brady in today's Detroit Medical Center. It hosted bicycle races, cricket and other amusements, plus it served as Detroit's first enclosed ball yard. The city's first professional baseball teams — Hollinger's Nine and the Detroit Wolverines of the National League — called the place home between 1879 and 1888. The park closed as the northward-growing city gobbled up the land for homes and businesses.

Boulevard Park, 1890s: The Tigers' first home — a wobbly, 3,500-seat structure at Helen and Champlain (now Lafayette) near the Belle Isle Bridge. The Western League Tigers played there in 1894 and 1895 until owner George Vanderbeck decided to build Bennett Park.

Final game at Tiger Stadium: Sept. 27, 1999. Tigers defeated Kansas City, 8-2. **Attendance:** 43,356.

Final highlight: Rob Fick's grand slam off the rightfield roof; moving postgame ceremony involving 63 former players.

Final out: Carlos Beltran struck out against Todd Jones.

Tigers' final record at the Corner: 3,764-3,090 (.549).

Burns Park: A wooden facility on Dix between Livernois and Waterman where the Tigers played 34 bootleg Sunday games between 1900 and 1902. It's now a weed-choked industrial site.

Mack Park, 1910-1960s: The 5,000-seat park at Mack and Fairview on the east side became best known as the home field for the Detroit Stars of the Negro National League from 1919 to 1929. The park hosted other events, including soccer. An apartment building sits on the site today.

parks. In 1999, the average price of a ticket to a Tigers game was the 20th most expensive in Major League Baseball. In 2000, Detroit was fourth most expensive, behind the Boston Red Sox, Seattle Mariners and New York Yankees.

Team Marketing Report, a Chicago Business trade publication, said the average price of a Tigers ticket went from $12.23 to $24.83 — not the kind of hike usually seen by teams that lost 92 games, as the Tigers did in 1999. On the other hand, pre-Comerica Park prices were considerably lower than those in most major markets. The cost for a family of four to attend a game and buy a modest amount of concessions was $108.41 at Tiger Stadium. That soared to $165.31 at Comerica.

The new park was vastly different from Tiger Stadium on the field, too. At Tiger Stadium, the fence in left-center measured a mere 365 feet from home plate, the one in right-center 370 feet. At Comerica Park, it's 398 feet to

SPORTS

MICHIGAN STADIUM

There was a lot of Michigan football before there was a Michigan Stadium. The U-M football team played its first game in Ann Arbor on May 12, 1883. For the next decade, the team used fields in Ann Arbor, on the present-day sites of the Waterman Gym and Burns Park, and in Detroit.

Regents Field, 1893-1905: First permanent field on campus opened on Oct. 7, 1893, on the site where Schembechler Hall is today on South State Street. Capacity: Listed as 400 to 800, though crowds reached 5,000 after 1900.

Ferry Field, 1906-1926: In 1902, Detroit seed merchant Dexter Ferry donated land for a new stadium, which became Ferry Field. That land is now the university's athletic complex off South State Street. Later, another Ferry Field was built, on the site of today's outdoor track. It opened on Oct. 6. Capacity: 18,000-46,000.

Michigan Stadium, 1927-present: The idea of building a new, huge stadium became a controversial public issue in Ann Arbor during the 1920s. But legendary coach Fielding Yost and others continued to pressure the U-M regents, and they approved the new $950,000 stadium in 1926. A large underground lake made construction difficult, and necessitated building three-quarters of the stadium below ground. The quicksand-like earth swallowed a crane, which remains

The Corner, 1896-1999
Bennett Park 1896-1911
Navin Field 1912-1938
Briggs Stadium 1938-1961
Tiger Stadium 1961-1999

Baseball moved to the corner of Michigan and Trumbull on April 28, 1896, when the Tigers were part of the Western League, a minor-league circuit of Midwestern clubs that in 1900 formed the nucleus of the American League. Bennett Park was demolished after the 1911 season to make room for Navin Field, a modern facility whose concrete-and-steel horseshoe frame, stretching from first to third base, provided the foundation for several stages of expansion in the 1920s and 1930s.

The Lions moved from the University of Detroit's stadium to Briggs Stadium in 1938 and played there for the next 36 seasons. Starting with the 1975 season, the team moved to the Pontiac Silverdome.

The Pontiac Silverdome: The Dome, at M-59 near I-75, opened in 1975 at a cost of $55.7 million, although with interest, the stadium will cost $107 million by the time it is paid for in 2004. Its main tenant over the years has been the Detroit Lions, and the Detroit Pistons played there from 1978 to 1988. But the Silverdome also hosted Super Bowl XVI in 1982, the 1979 National Basketball Association All-Star game, a 1993 U.S. soccer game between England and Germany and World Cup soccer games in 1994. Also playing the Dome were tractor pulls, rock concerts, religious rallies and other events. The Dome has a number of superlatives, including the 10-acre, Teflon-coated fiberglass roof that is 202 feet high and weighs 200 tons. The Lions are scheduled to leave the Silverdome upon completion of Ford Field in downtown Detroit by the 2002 season. Officials are studying how to redevelop the site. Pontiac taxpayers gave birth to the Silverdome in a 1972 election, passing by just 296 votes a bonding plan to finance it. The Dome was controversial because it received taxpayer subsidies from the State of Michigan, Pontiac property taxes and revenue from the city's general budget.

Ford Field: The Lions' new home next to Comerica Park downtown is scheduled to open by 2002. Its design is to incorporate the old Hudson's warehouse as luxury suites on one side of the field. Even the highest seats will be relatively close to the field. And a glass wall in one end zone will allow fans a view of downtown Detroit, a unique feature in a domed stadium.

The Palace of Auburn Hills, 1988-present: The Palace opened as the home of the Pistons, who left the Pontiac Silverdome and promptly won back-to-back championships in their new home. Financed privately, the Palace was built by Arena Associates, headed by Pistons' man-

JOE LOUIS ARENA, 1979-PRESENT: Mayor Coleman Young began building the Joe behind Cobo Hall in the late 1970s before he had a tenant. It cost $34 million. The Red Wings, under former owner Bruce Norris, already had announced their move to a new arena near the Pontiac Silverdome when Young lured them downtown with a sweetheart contract that minimized rent and property taxes. After a University of Detroit-University of Michigan basketball game on Dec. 12, 1979, the Wings opened the hockey era on Dec. 27, with a 3-2 loss to the St. Louis Blues before a crowd of 19,742. On Feb. 7, 1980, Gordie Howe's return during the NHL All-Star game drew an exuberant crowd of 21,002. The city-owned Joe is sterile as arenas go, and there have been plenty of complaints about the lack of rest rooms and poor access. But the arena has no view-obstructing pillars, and the Wings draw more than 19,000 fans for every game. Away from hockey, the Joe hosted the 1980 Republican National Convention, and it has been the scene of numerous concerts, though the Palace took away much of its music business after 1988. Rumors persist that Red Wings owner Mike Ilitch would like to build a new arena near his Foxtown entertainment complex, but the city has a lease with him through 2009, and the city owes more than $45 million on construction bonds. Capacity for hockey games is 19,275.

aging partner William Davidson, along with David Hermelin and Robert Sosnick. The Palace has been widely praised for its design, which among other things, took luxury boxes from their usual perch far above the action and placed them as close as 16 rows from the floor. Performance magazine has named the Palace "Arena of the Year" seven times. In addition to the Pistons, the Palace houses the Detroit Shock of the WNBA and the IHL's Detroit Vipers. Between sports events, it is the venue of choice for big-name concert stars — Barbra Streisand, Garth Brooks, Paul McCartney and Bob Seger are just a few of the many who have sold it out — and draws families with circuses, ice shows and other entertainment that keeps the lights on nearly 300 nights a year. The Palace also owns and operates the Pine Knob and Meadow Brook outdoor theaters in northern Oakland County, which have both become better venues with the Palace touch. Palace capacity is 22,076 (basketball), 20,804 (hockey), and 6,000 to 23,000 for concerts.

Olympia Stadium, 1927-79: The long-demolished Red Barn at Grand River and McGraw was made of red brick and featured a large, movielike marquee over its main entrance. Designed by famous theater architect C. Howard Crane, the Olympia was an intimate setting for hockey, Elvis Presley, the Beatles, boxing matches involving Joe Louis or Thomas Hearns, and religious revivals. Spec-

buried there today. Michigan defeated Wesleyan, 33-0, on Oct. 1, 1927, in the first game. Capacity: 72,000 (1927); 85,753 (1928); 101,001 (1956) 107,501 (1998)

Oct. 6, 1975, the Michigan-Michigan State game drew the first six-figure crowd — 101,001. On Nov. 8, 1975, 102,415 fans watched Michigan defeat Purdue, 28-0, starting a streak of six-figure crowds that has not stopped. By 1998, capacity was hiked to 107,501, and the Wolverines drew an NCAA single-game record of 111,575 against Ohio State in 1999.

Yost Ice Arena: Began life as Yost Fieldhouse in 1924, the original field-house in the United States. For the next four decades, Yost hosted basketball, track and field, even baseball practice. Roundball went to Crisler in 1967, and Yost became home of the Wolverine hockey team in 1973. Capacity is 6,343.

tators in the cozy balcony enjoyed the sensation of looming over the action. And one of the coolest things about Olympia was the corridor, which players had to cross to get from their locker room to the ice. Fans would line up behind wooden barriers, and some could reach out and touch their heroes as they walked by, looking like giants on their skates. In the 1940s and 1950s, a number of Red Wings lived in a neighborhood boarding house run by a woman named Ma Shaw. The last real game was Dec. 15, 1979, a 4-4 tie with Quebec, though the Red Wing Oldtimers played the final exhibition game Feb. 22, 1980. The site is now a National Guard armory. Capacity ranged over the years from 11,000 to 15,000.

Compuware Sports Arena: In a metro area studded with several dozen hockey rinks, Compuware stands out. Located on Beck Road in Plymouth, the complex is actually two ice surfaces: one is a 100-by-200-foot Olympic surface with 800 seats; the other is the 85-by-200-foot NHL-size surface with 3,800 seats. The latter is the home of the Plymouth Whalers of the top-notch Ontario Hockey League, one of the chief stepping-stones to the NHL. That surface also has a private suite and a press box. The complex includes the Ginopolis Parthenon restaurant, a pro shop and 14 locker rooms.

Crisler Arena: Named after U-M football coach and athletic director Herbert (Fritz)

Crisler. The area cost $7.2 million and opened on Dec. 2, 1967. The architect was Dan Dworsky, a U-M linebacker on Crisler's undefeated 1947 and 1948 teams. Informally known as the House that Cazzie Built after U-M basketball star Cazzie Russell, who never played there. Capacity is 13,562.

Cobo Arena: Opened in 1961 as part of the massive Cobo Hall convention complex. The city-owned arena is managed by Mike Ilitch's organization. The former longtime home of the Pistons, Cobo also has hosted hockey, wrestling, concerts, rallies and the speech by Dr. Martin Luther King Jr. after the huge civil rights march down Woodward in 1963. Capacity is 12,191.

Calihan Hall, University of Detroit Mercy: Dedicated as the Memorial Building May 25, 1952, the arena became Calihan Hall in 1977 in honor of star athlete, coach and athletic director Bob Calihan. The Titans played in Cobo Arena for five seasons starting in 1993, before returning to their ancestral home on the McNichols campus. Capacity is 8,837.

Olympia, at Grand River and McGraw, was an intimate setting for hockey.

SPORTS

The Detroit Almanac

17. RITU

"I believe the spiritual combat to be more desperate in the center of chaos, which is Detroit."

— **Theodore Roethke**, *"Straw for the Fire," 1940s*

The Spiritual Side of Detroit

The Believers

Faith is a force that cuts across civic and cultural boundaries in southeast Michigan and touches the lives of nearly every person.

Counting the members of each religious group in the Detroit area is virtually impossible. When asked for membership numbers, some denominations count only active adults, while others include inactive members and children; some religious traditions, such as Islam, do not require followers to become members — and a few groups, such as the Church of Christ, Scientist, decline to count their members.

But some information is clear: Over many years, 9 out of 10 Americans have told pollsters that they believe in God and heaven — and pray. In addition, more than 90 percent of people identify themselves as part of some religious group, even though only 40 percent of people say they attend religious services each week.

Here, based on Free Press reporting, is a breakdown of area faith-based groups:

LOCAL CONGREGATIONS

More than 3,300, representing 120 denominations, including groups from nearly every faith in the world.

➤ **Largest faith:** Christianity. It's the religious affiliation of nearly 90 percent of people in southeast Michigan, or about 4 million people.

➤ **Largest Christian denomination:** The Catholic church by far. Church officials estimate that there are 1.5 million Catholic adults and children in the Detroit area, including both active and inactive Catholics. That estimate is backed up by pollsters, who say that Catholics make up about one-third of the local population. That's a relatively high concentration of Catholics, who comprise about 27 percent of the U.S. population overall.

In Detroit, founded by French Catholics, there had been for years a larger proportion of Catholics than the national average. In the past 50 years, as the city became increasingly populated by African Americans, that proportion decreased. Today, there are many Catholic churches in the city, but about 9 out of 10 Catholics in southeast Michigan are white and live in the suburbs.

➤ **Protestants:** A little more than half of the people in southeast Michigan describe themselves as Protestant. Baptists are the largest Protestant group and make up about 18 percent of the local population, although Baptists are divided into more than a dozen denominations. Lutherans from at least four denominations represent about 9 percent of the population and probably are the second-largest group. Six denominations of Presbyterians and five denominations of Methodists are tied for third place at about 5 percent. Episcopal and Eastern Orthodox groups probably are significantly smaller than that. However, the margin of error in such polls is 3 to 4 percentage points, so the actual population of the smaller groups could vary. Detroit has

The altar at Holy Redeemer Catholic Church, 1980. Just after World War II, the church was the largest English-speaking parish in the world.

PATRICIA BECK/Detroit Free Press

The way we wed: Life's hitches

MARRIAGE

There is a plethora of customs in a community as diverse as ours, but some things remain standard. Here's a look.

WEDDINGS (1998)
Statewide 65,642
Wayne County.....10,146
Oakland County 7,870
Macomb County....5,494

THE COST

For 200 guests, $20,000-$25,000. The range: $17 to $60 a guest. A breakdown:

➤ **The reception:**
Usually accounts for at least 60 percent of the total cost. A $20,000 wedding, a $12,000 reception. The cost usually includes invitations, the hall, bar, food, cake, table centerpieces, photographer and videographer, DJ or band, and tips and taxes.

➤ **The ceremony:**
Most of the remaining $8,000 would pay for ceremony site, minister/rabbi/imam/judge/justice of the peace, flowers, music, decorations and programs.

➤ **The dress:**
The cost of the bridal gown, about $1,200 to $2,000, is usually separate from the total. Off-the-rack gowns cost $500-$700. Tuxes cost about $75-$100 a day to rent.

TOP RECEPTION VENUES

➤ Wayne County: Dearborn Inn, Ritz-Carlton Hotel, Atheneum Hotel, the Castle, Westin Hotel, Grosse Pointe Yacht Club, Henry Ford Mansion.

➤ Oakland County: Addison Oaks County Park, Townsend Hotel, Meadow Brook Hall, Butterfly House at the Detroit Zoo, Birmingham Community House, Shenandoah Country Club, King's Court Castle.

➤ Macomb County: Penna's, Villa Penna, Sterling Banquet Center, Andiamo, Barrister Gardens, St. Josaphat Banquet Center.

HONEYMOON
Most popular destination: Maui, Hawaii.
Second-most popular: a cruise in the Caribbean.

>>

Associated Press

Hare Krishna devotee Alfred Brush Ford, great-grandson of Henry Ford, at his 1984 wedding to Sharmilla Bhattacharya in Australia.

Free Press file photo

Ste. Anne's Catholic Church near the Ambassador Bridge in southwest Detroit.

become a largely Protestant city: 71 percent of Detroit residents are Protestant; at least 76 percent of Detroiters are black — and 84 percent of all blacks throughout southeast Michigan are Protestant.

➤ **Jews:** The Jewish population in southeast Michigan is about 100,000, based on an in-depth, scientific study sponsored by Jewish community leaders.

➤ **Muslims:** Less is known about the local Muslim population, partly because Muslim leaders have never conducted a community-wide census. The question of numbers is complicated, because most Muslims do not follow the Christian or Jewish tradition of becoming members of a congregation. They feel free to visit any mosque. Over the years, this situation has resulted in widely divergent claims about the size of the Muslim community. Among the few pieces of data available is a

1991 Free Press Gallup poll of Detroit-area residents that took an in-depth look at religious groups. In that poll, 1 percent of respondents said they were Muslim, which represents roughly 50,000 people. In addition, there are about 40 mosques spread across southeast Michigan and most of them are attended by fewer than 1,000 people. So, the population of Muslims who are active in local mosques probably is around 50,000. However, Muslim leaders describe their community as growing each year and often claim a higher population. They also point out that some Muslims do not visit any mosque and, because of language or cultural differences, some Muslims decline to participate in polls.

➤ **Arab Christians:** While the Muslim population remains a hotly debated question, it is clear that the majority of Arab-Americans in southeast Michigan are Christian. The largest group of Arab Christians are 80,000 Chaldeans: Iraqi Christians who are part of the Catholic church. Among the other local Arab-Christian groups are Maronites, who are Lebanese Catholics; Copts, who are Egyptian Orthodox; and Antiochian Orthodox, a group that includes many Palestinian Christians.

Houses of worship

More than 3,000 churches, mosques, synagogues and temples serve southeast Michigan, forming communities of faith within the larger secular community. Nine out of 10 people in the Detroit area tell pollsters that they have some religious affiliation — the vast majority of them Christian. There are hundreds of historically significant houses of worship, representing many faiths in southeast Michigan. Here are a handful that represent milestones in Detroit's religious history.

1701

Ste. Anne, 1000 Ste. Anne in Detroit

On July 26, 1701, two days after Antoine de la Mothe Cadillac arrived in Detroit, he had a chapel built to honor Ste. Anne, patron saint of New France. Although the current Gothic Revival building was finished in 1887, Ste. Anne is the oldest continuously attended parish in Michigan and claims to be the second oldest in the United States. The church contains the crypt of its most famous pastor, the Rev. Gabriel Richard, who arrived in 1798 and was a pioneer in many fields. Among his

achievements: He brought the first printing press to Michigan and helped found the University of Michigan.

1820

First Presbyterian Church/Ecumenical Theological Seminary, 2930 Woodward in Detroit

The First Protestant Society of Detroit was organized in 1820 by the Rev. John Monteith, a cofounder of the University of Michigan. Five years later, the church became specifically Presbyterian. The huge red Richardsonian Romanesque building on Woodward, dedicated in 1891, was the congregation's fourth home. The building currently houses the seminary, serving students from many denominations.

1821

Central United Methodist Church, 23 E. Adams in Detroit

Before the Civil War, the Methodist Church was the largest denomination in the United States. Central was Detroit's first Methodist congregation, which did not move into its present English Gothic church on Grand Circus Park until 1867. In the 20th Century, Central was known as a center of liberal

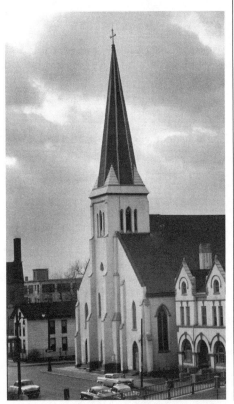

TONY SPINA/Detroit Free Press

MONTHS
Few vows are exchanged January, February and March. Most vows are exchanged May through November.

AGE
Average for brides 26
Grooms.....................27

Divorce

OK, so it didn't work. In 1998, 38,623 marriages ended in divorce in Michigan: 6,996 in Wayne County, 4,651 in Oakland and 2,893 in Macomb. That means, roughly, that there were two divorces for every three weddings in 1998.

THE COST
A petition for divorce in circuit court runs $100 without minor children, $130 with.

Attorney fees, on average, are about $3,500.

A rule of thumb, according to family law attorney Harriet Rotter of Franklin: **The divorce should cost no more than the wedding.**

Detroit's Most Holy Trinity parish, at 1050 Porter, was started in 1855 and dedicated in 1866. This photo was taken in 1962.

political activism. Its stained glass windows include a rare homage to the United Nations. It was one of the first predominantly white churches in Detroit to welcome black worshipers.

1824

Episcopal Cathedral Church of St. Paul, 4800 Woodward in Detroit

St. Paul was the first Episcopal parish in southeast Michigan and eventually became the headquarters for the Episcopal Diocese of Michigan. Since the 1960s, bishops at the cathedral have been outspoken on many public issues from support of civil rights to concern for the poor. The massive Neo-Gothic building is known nationally as a prime example of work by architect Ralph Adams Cram.

1832

Assumption Grotto Catholic Church, 13770 Gratiot in Detroit

A group of German Catholic immigrants, living in what was then farmland northeast of Detroit, built a log cabin for Sunday mass — to avoid the long journey to Ste. Anne's. In 1881, the parish began building what it says is the oldest outdoor shrine in Michigan devoted to Mary.

1834

Most Holy Trinity, 1050 Porter St. in Detroit

Irish migration to Detroit swelled in the early 1830s and Most Holy Trinity was established to serve the immigrants' needs. The current brick church was started in 1855 and dedicated in 1866. To this day, it remains the spiritual home for thousands of Irish Catholic families across southeast Michigan.

1841

Bethel African Methodist Episcopal Church, 5050 Richard Allen Blvd. in Detroit

A group of black Detroiters known as the Colored Methodist Society organized Bethel, which became the mother church for dozens

1836

Second Baptist Church, 441 Monroe St. in Detroit

Founded by 13 former slaves, Second Baptist says it is the oldest African-American congregation in the Midwest. In 1839, the church founded the city's first school for black children. Abolitionist Frederick Douglass preached there and the church served as a stop on the Underground Railroad. The photograph is from 1964.

of other African Methodist Episcopal congregations.

1849

Fort Street Presbyterian Church, 631 W. Fort St. in Detroit

Despite two major fires, Fort Street's towering steeple remains a landmark in downtown Detroit. Once a congregation dominated by the wealthy elite of Detroit society, in recent decades the congregation has pioneered in assisting poor and homeless people.

1850

Temple Beth El, 7400 Telegraph Road in Bloomfield Township

Michigan's oldest Jewish congregation began in Detroit and moved through a series of buildings, following the northwestern migration of the Jewish community, before constructing a spacious synagogue, library and school in Oakland County in 1973. Now a Reform congregation, Beth El maintains museum exhibits of the history of the Jewish community throughout the complex. Since World War II, Beth El has been a pioneer in improving interfaith relations.

1850

Historic Trinity Lutheran Church, 1345 Gratiot in Detroit

The first Missouri Synod Lutheran Church in Detroit established many other local Lutheran churches. The current Gothic church was built in 1931. Over the past two decades, Trinity has become a major center for promoting religious themes in the fine arts and for collecting historical information about Detroit houses of worship.

1877

Metropolitan United Methodist Church, 8000 Woodward Ave. in Detroit

The church says its history extends to an 1877 Methodist Sunday School in what is now the New Center area, but it really took off as a 1901 merger of two smaller Methodist churches. Its pastors have played an active role in Detroit politics, including campaigning against casinos. Since the mid-1970s, the congregation has been one of the most racially and ethnically diverse in metro Detroit.

1880

Holy Redeemer Catholic Church, 1721 Junction in Detroit

Redemptorist priests founded the parish and built it up into the largest English-speaking Catholic parish in the world. In its heyday just after World War II, 15,000 people packed 14 Sunday masses. Always devoted to serving immigrant families, the parish has evolved from serving Irish-Americans to celebrating masses in Spanish today. In 1999, the Redemptorists were facing dwindling numbers in their religious order and left the parish, turning over its care to the Archdiocese of Detroit.

1905

Catholic Cathedral of the Most Blessed Sacrament, 9844 Woodward in Detroit

The parish of the Blessed Sacrament was founded in 1905 and the soaring limestone Gothic church was built between 1913 and 1915, but it was not until 1938 that Archbishop Edward Mooney made it his cathedral church. Since then, Detroit's top Catholic leaders have lived adjacent to Blessed Sacrament, which is the central church for more than 300 parishes across the archdiocese.

Workers in 1986 repair the gleaming golden dome of St. John Armenian Church, a familiar landmark in Southfield.

1907

Saints Peter and Paul Russian Orthodox Church, 3810 Gilbert in Detroit

A Russian Orthodox priest from Cleveland began conducting services in 1907 and, soon, the church became the spiritual home for people from many Orthodox denominations: Russians, Ukrainians, Greeks, Syrians, Romanians, Bulgarians and Albanians. These groups eventually established their own congregations, and Saints Peter and Paul became known as Detroit's mother church of Orthodoxy.

1913

St. John Armenian Church, 22001 Northwestern Highway in Southfield

The roots of the famous gold-domed church near the intersection of the Lodge and Southfield freeways extend back to 1913, when Detroit received its first full-time Armenian pastor. The community later migrated northwest of Detroit. The church, which opened in 1961, is modeled after traditional churches in Armenia.

Beyond worship, St. John is a major center for preserving Armenian language, history and the arts.

1917

Hartford Memorial Baptist Church, 18700 James Couzens in Detroit

In 1917, the Rev. Edgar Wendell Edwards split away from Second Baptist Church in Detroit to found the first African-American church west of Woodward Avenue in Detroit. From 1920 until today, Hartford has had only two senior pastors: first, the Rev. Charles Hill and, since 1968, the Rev. Charles Adams. Both men were nationally known preachers who shaped their Detroit congregation into a powerhouse of political activism and concern for community development.

1928

Christ Church Cranbrook, 470 Church Road in Bloomfield Hills

This Gothic Episcopal church was a gift to the community from Detroit News publisher George Booth, who also played a major role in designing the building and obtaining its impressive collection of carved woodwork, frescoes and stained glass. The church was an essential part of Booth's vision for the innovative Cranbrook community, which includes schools and museums.

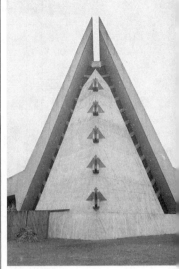

CRAIG PORTER/Detroit Free Press

1861

Congregation Shaarey-Zedek, 27375 Bell Road in Southfield

In 1861, some of the more traditional members of Beth El split to form Michigan's second Jewish congregation. In 1962, Shaarey-Zedek moved into its soaring, triangular, concrete-and-steel synagogue in Southfield. Shaarey-Zedek drew nationwide headlines in 1966 when Rabbi Morris Adler was shot and killed during sabbath services by a young member of his congregation who then took his own life. Under Rabbi Irwin Groner, Adler's successor, Shaarey-Zedek has been influential throughout Conservative Judaism.

Free Press file photo

1947

Kirk in the Hills, 1340 W. Long Lake Road in Bloomfield Hills

This may be the only major church in southeast Michigan that started out as a house. Industrialist Col. Edwin George, an early developer of the lawn mower, decided to build a monumental Presbyterian church as his legacy. The main part of the Gothic church is modeled after Melrose, a 13th-Century Scottish abbey, and displays a museum-quality collection of 16th- and 17th-Century religious art. Part of the building, the Kirk House, originally was George's home, Cedarholm.

1955

Islamic Center of America, 15571 Joy Road in Detroit

Muslim congregations were organized in southeast Michigan as early as 1910, when Muslim workers at the Ford Motor Co. in Highland Park started planning for a small mosque near their homes. But the local Muslim community rose to national prominence after the arrival in 1955 of Imam Mohammad Jawa Chirri, an author and scholar who helped build what was then called the Islamic Center of Detroit. For a while after its opening in 1964, the congregation claimed to have the largest Muslim center in North America.

1972

St. Mary's Antiochian Orthodox Church, 18100 Merriman in Livonia

Organized in 1972, the church has become a rallying point for hundreds of Palestinian families who maintain close ties to their homeland. To celebrate the year 2000, St. Mary's has built a massive Byzantine basilica.

1975

Bharatiya Temple, 6850 N. Adams Road in Troy

Founded in 1975, this Hindu temple has become a major center for Indian-Americans. Devotees practice a wide range of Hindu rituals and teach Hindu philosophy and culture.

1995

Islamic House of Wisdom, 7258 Chase Road in Dearborn

Imam Mohammad Ali Elahi founded his congregation in a former VFW hall in east Dearborn, but soon moved to a large former church in Dearborn's traditional Muslim community. Elahi has been an influential force in improving Muslim relations with Christians and Jews — and in building bridges between Shi'ite and Sunni Muslims.

Free Press file photo

1926

National Shrine of the Little Flower, 2123 Roseland in Royal Oak

The Rev. Charles Coughlin, the priest who became internationally famous for his politically charged radio broadcasts, built this massive church partly with a flood of donations from his listeners. Coughlin's anti-Semitism on the eve of World War II, before he was silenced in 1940, made him a highly controversial figure and left a lingering stain on his parish. Over the past decade, however, the Archdiocese of Detroit took several symbolic steps to welcome Detroit's interfaith community to the Shrine.

1998

Jain Temple, 29278 W. Twelve Mile Road in Farmington Hills

The Jain Society of Greater Detroit was organized in 1975 by a handful of Indian families who follow this ancient faith that stresses nonviolence. It's a sign of metro Detroit's growing religious diversity that the Jain congregation expanded and was able to dedicate this elaborate marble temple in 1998.

1999

Temple of the Church of Jesus Christ of Latter-day Saints, 425 N. Woodward in Bloomfield Hills

After decades of hoping for approval from Salt Lake City, local Mormons were able to dedicate their own temple in October 1999. It is Michigan's only Mormon temple, a place where members believe that holy rituals can be performed to bind families in heaven.

SOURCES: FREE PRESS RESEARCH; STATE OF MICHIGAN HISTORICAL CENTER AND HISTORIES WRITTEN BY MEMBERS OF THE CONGREGATIONS.

Of the cloth

Hundreds of nationally known religious leaders practiced their vocation in Detroit. Among the more renown:

The Rev. Gabriel Richard (1767-1832):

Born in France, he left his home in 1792 during the height of the French Revolution to avoid an oath of allegiance to the revolutionaries. His Detroit assignment as assistant pastor at Ste. Anne's came after several years ministering to American Indians along the Mississippi River.

He arrived in 1798; his duties required him to spend much time traveling to Catholic communities as far north as Mackinac Island. By 1832, when he died of cholera, Richard had become the most influential religious leader in Michigan history. Some of his contributions:

➤ During the fire of 1805 that destroyed most of Detroit, Richard coordinated efforts to help homeless people and save the community. He also gave the city its motto: *Speramus meliora; resurget cineribus.* (We hope for better things; It will rise from its ashes.)

The Rev. Gabriel Richard, who gave Detroit many firsts.

The Rev. Charles Hill, a champion of civil rights.

➤ In 1809, he brought the first printing press to Michigan and began producing a newspaper, books and pamphlets — including one urging trade with China.

➤ In 1817, Richard was among the three cofounders of the University of Michigan.

➤ In 1823, he was elected one of Michigan's first territorial delegates to the U.S. Congress.

➤ In 1827, a group of Vatican officials wanted Richard to be named the first Catholic bishop of Michigan to head a new diocese based in Detroit, but disputes among Vatican clergy delayed any appointment for six years. In 1833, a year after Richard's death, Bishop Frederic Rese was named the first bishop of Detroit.

Rabbi Leo Franklin (1870-1948):

From 1898-1942, Franklin led Detroit's oldest Jewish congregation, Temple Beth El — and became famous within the Jewish community and in the larger Christian community as a pioneer in improving interfaith relations. He was the first rabbi in Michigan who was invited to speak from a broad range of Christian pulpits. Later, he convinced many factory owners, for the first time, to allow their Jewish employees time off work for their major religious holidays. But one of Franklin's greatest accomplishments came shortly after he arrived in Detroit: In 1899, he was a cofounder of the United Jewish Charities to help poor members of the Jewish community and immigrants from Europe. That group was so important in branching off a myriad of other organizations that, in 1999, the founding of United Jewish Charities was celebrated in the Detroit area as the centennial of the organized Jewish community.

The Rev. Robert Bradby (1882-1948):

The pastor of Second Baptist Church in Detroit played a major role in helping the thousands of African-American families who came into Detroit during the Great Migration from the South that began around 1916 and continued for a decade. Bradby sent teams of his members to meet trains from the South and help new families settle in the city. By 1918, he also had forged a close relationship with the Ford Motor Co. and became virtually a recruiting manager for Ford. The company accepted any black workers recommended by Bradby and soon other prominent black pastors formed similar ties to Ford.

The Rev. John Monteith (1788-1868):

Monteith, a graduate of Princeton Theological Seminary, was 28 when he arrived in Detroit as a Presbyterian missionary in 1816. He quickly organized Detroit's first Protestant congregation, which eventually became First Presbyterian Church. He toured eastern states to raise $1,000 to build a meeting house for his congregation. In 1817, Monteith helped the Rev. Gabriel Richard cofound the University of Michigan.

Sisters, Servants of the Immaculate Heart of Mary:

In 1845, Sister Theresa Maxis Duchemin and Sister Ann Constance Schaaf founded this religious order in Monroe. Because Duchemin and Schaaf had both black and white ancestors, their order had a distinctive reputation for taking in sisters from many ethnic backgrounds. They wore blue habits and were nicknamed the Blue Nuns. During the next 150 years, the order produced the teachers who educated many generations of Detroit children. At its post-World War II peak, the Monroe order had 1,500 nuns, including many feminists. Among the sisters were renowned theologians, economists, and the professionals who staffed ministries in 23 states, Central America, Haiti and Africa. The order's nuns helped build many parishes and schools in Detroit, among them Marygrove College and Marian High School in Birmingham.

The Rev. Reinhold Niebuhr in 1963.

The Rev. Reinhold Niebuhr (1892-1971):

One of the 20th-Century's most influential theologians, Niebuhr's pragmatic sense of the struggle between good and evil was forged in Detroit, when he served Bethel Evangelical Church from 1915 to 1928. One of his most famous books, "Leaves from the Notebook of a Tamed Cynic," was based on his years in Detroit. While in Michigan, he campaigned against the Ku Klux Klan and was one of the first Protestant ministers to welcome interfaith relations with Jewish leaders. Later, he moved to New York to teach and write. He was influential in convincing Christian leaders to support World War II. After the war, his ties to the State Department helped shape Cold War policies in Europe. His entry in the Encyclopedia Britannica says that, before his death in 1971, he was "the greatest living political philosopher in America."

The Rev. Charles Hill (1893-1970):

In 1921, Hill broke with the Rev. Robert Bradby because Hill believed the paternal relationship between pastors and Ford should give way to black church support for labor unions. He became pastor of the small, struggling Hartford Avenue Baptist Church and, by the 1950s, had built it into one of the largest churches in Detroit with a national reputation for supporting civil rights and liberal political causes. Paul Robeson and Thurgood Marshall were close to Hill and spoke at Hartford. Hill was one of the first black Detroiters to run for a seat on what was then the city's Common Council. Although he never won, Hill served as a mentor to many young politicians, including Coleman Young.

The Rev. Charles Coughlin (1891-1979):

An infamous chapter in Michigan's religious history revolves around Coughlin's extremely popular radio broadcasts from his Shrine of the Little Flower Catholic church in Royal Oak. In the 1920s and 1930s, he used WJR radio to develop a huge nationwide audience for his populist messages that championed the rights of working-class Americans. He liked to boast that the Shrine was built with dimes and quarters mailed to him by his fans. However, Coughlin was an anti-Semite who attacked Jewish groups on the eve of World War II — and apologized for Nazi attacks on Jews in Europe. Among his many targets was President Franklin D. Roosevelt, whom Coughlin called a "liar" and "anti-God." The FBI and the Vatican both failed to silence the radio priest. Eventually, though, his audience abandoned him and his last national broadcast was in May 1940.

The Rev. Henry Hitt Crane (1890-):

Crane was the pastor of what is now Central United Methodist Church in Detroit from 1938-1958 and became nationally famous as a pacifist during World War II. He also was an influential — and sometimes controversial — advocate of integration. Central was one of the first predominantly white churches in the city to welcome black members. Crane led the American Civil Liberties Union in Detroit in the 1940s and was a cofounder of the Detroit Round Table of Christians and Jews.

The Rev. Solanus Casey (1870-1957):

The Capuchin priest, who greeted thousands of visitors at his order's Detroit mission and prayed with them, is now considered venerable by the Catholic church — and could become the first American-born male saint ever canonized by the church. He was the doorkeeper of the mission from 1924 until his departure for Brooklyn in 1945. Thousands of

Free Press file photo

The Rev. Solanus Casey: He could become the first American-born male saint in the Catholic Church. He is entombed on the east side.

Catholics credited his prayers with providing healing, help during pregnancies and other forms of spiritual assistance. After his death in 1957, people continued to pray for Casey's aid. Thousands have visited his tomb on Detroit's east side. Supporters of Casey's cause at the Vatican hope that the Vatican might soon declare him blessed, which is only one step away from canonization and would allow Catholics throughout the Detroit area to venerate Casey in their churches.

The Rev. James F. (Prophet) Jones (1908-1971):

One of Detroit's most flamboyant clergymen, Prophet Jones began preaching at age 11 in his native Alabama. At 21, he arrived in Detroit and founded the Church of Universal Triumph, the Dominion of God Inc. He renovated the former Oriole Theater on Linwood for his 5-day-a-week services and installed a red-and-gold throne on stage for himself. He named the building the Shrine of Lady Catherine, after his mother. Sometimes he preached for more than 5 hours and often claimed to dispense miraculous spiritual cures. He also claimed to offer divine insights into which numbers would win in the daily numbers racket, an illegal precursor to the lottery. Gifts from his admirers allowed Prophet Jones to lead a lavish lifestyle that included a $12,900 white mink coat and a fleet of luxury cars. As his popularity grew, he began wearing velvet-and-silk robes, a $12,000 ball gown covered with crystal beads, topaz earrings and a white headdress encrusted in jewels. He dubbed his lieutenants with royal titles, including prince and princess. Some of his followers regarded him as a god, although Jones died of heart failure in 1971.

Imam Mohammad Jawad Chirri (1913-1994):

When Chirri came to Detroit in 1949 from his native Lebanon, he was the first prominent Muslim theologian to leave the Middle East to head a Michigan congregation, the Islamic Center of America. His arrival helped to spur the development of the local Muslim community into an important part in the local religious landscape. Chirri was the author of 10 books, including a basic guide to Islam that was widely distributed in the Detroit area. A strong supporter of improving interfaith relations, Chirri helped to break down prejudice against Muslims.

The Rev. C.L. Franklin (1915-1984):

The man born Clarence LeVaughn Franklin is best remembered as the father of singer Aretha Franklin, who launched her career by taking her on his nationwide revival tours when she turned 14. But the pastor of New Bethel Baptist Church in Detroit, known throughout his life by his initials, also was an influential force in shaping modern preaching styles in many black churches. His trademark style involved building to an emotional crescendo in which he loudly chanted and sang the final lines of his sermons. Franklin developed a national audience through frequent cross-country tours, weekly radio broadcasts and the recording of 76 albums of his preaching and singing — one of which sold 1 million copies. Franklin helped to organize a

Elijah Muhammad (1897-1975):
The Nation of Islam was born in Detroit, after the 1931 meeting of Elijah Poole, the son of a Baptist preacher, and Wallace D. Fard, a mysterious confidence man who described himself as an "Asiatic black man." Poole was a Georgia native who had moved to Detroit in 1923. He was drawn to Fard's eccentric description of Islam and, when Fard left Detroit in 1934, Poole changed his name to Elijah Muhammad and took over as head of a group that eventually became the Nation of Islam. Muhammad recruited black members nationwide with a version of Islam that called for black separatism and regarded white Americans as tools of the devil. At the height of his movement, his followers regarded him as a prophet sent by God.

milestone in the civil rights movement: the June 1963 freedom march down Woodward Avenue with the Rev. Martin Luther King Jr. The march drew more than 100,000 people and served as a prototype for King's later march on Washington, D.C. He died tragically, shot during a burglary at his LaSalle Boulevard home.

The Rev. Albert Cleage Jr. (1911-2000):

By the late 1960s, the Rev. Albert Cleage Jr. was nationally known as a leading figure in trying to forge a bond between black churches and the Black Power movement. In the mid-1950s, Cleage founded the Central Congregational Church in Detroit and began preaching that liberal notions of integration were naive and that the black community must build its own political and economic power. On Easter 1966, he unveiled a huge painting that depicted Mary and the baby Jesus as black and, at the same time, he renamed his church the Shrine of the Black Madonna. He eventually changed his name to Jaramogi Abebe Agyeman. Black politicians such as Detroit Mayor Coleman Young and former U.S. Rep. Barbara-Rose Collins received influential support from Cleage.

The Rev. William Cunningham (1930-1997):

As an English professor at Sacred Heart Seminary in Detroit, Cunningham got a close-up view of the 1967 riot and vowed to combat racial injustice. In 1968, he, the Rev. Jerome Fraser and suburban homemaker Eleanor Josaitis formed Focus: HOPE, which grew into one of the nation's most unusual civil rights organizations. Part charity, part for-profit business and part job-training program, Focus: HOPE became one of modern Detroit's most important institutions, with sophisticated machinist and engineering training programs for women and minorities, as well as an automotive parts manufacturing complex occupying a 22-acre campus on Oakman Boulevard between Linwood and Rosa Parks Boulevard. At its height, the organization had an annual budget of more than $60 million and 700 employees.

Malcolm X (1925-1965):

Born Malcolm Little, his attitudes about race were shaped when he was 6 years old by the murder of his father in Lansing after threats by the Ku Klux Klan. He later moved to the East Coast, fell into a life of crime and discovered the Nation of Islam while serving a prison sentence in 1946-1952 for burglary. He returned to Michigan, joined a Nation of Islam mosque in Detroit and changed his name to Malcolm X. The next five years in Detroit, he proved himself to be such a successful recruiter of new members that he quickly caught the eye of the movement's leader Elijah Muhammad, and eventually became the group's national spokesman. However, his pilgrimage to Mecca in 1964 transformed his understanding of Islam and he returned to the United States, determined to break down barriers between the races. He adopted the name El-Hajj Malik El-Shabazz and was murdered in 1965 by men connected to the Nation of Islam.

Free Press file photo

between labor and big business. They also spent about $2 million restoring the mansion. In the 1970s, the Krishna movement still was a controversial offshoot of Hinduism but, by the late 1990s, the movement and the Detroit temple had been embraced by the rapidly growing Indian immigrant community.

Bishop Judith Craig:
In 1984, at age 47, Craig became the third woman ever elected as a bishop in any mainline Christian denomination. From 1984 to 1992, Craig served as the United Methodist bishop of Michigan. Because of her unusual status, Craig often was invited to appear at interfaith gatherings in the Detroit area and across the country, although her duties supervising nearly 1,000 Michigan churches consumed most of her time. She was a feminist pioneer, but Craig rarely spoke in public about feminism. Born in Missouri, Craig loved to tell folksy stories about country life as a way to persuade people about the church's teachings. She was scheduled to retire from the ministry in late 2000.

Cardinal Edmund Szoka (born 1927):
In 1987, Szoka became the first Detroit Catholic leader to welcome a pontiff, Pope John Paul II, to the city. Szoka also was a major force in the worldwide Catholic church in promoting more compassion toward divorced couples by speeding up the annulment process that is necessary before Catholics can remarry in the church. His tenure in Michigan ended with the closing of nearly 40 Detroit churches, which angered thousands of Catholics. Given Szoka's financial savvy, in 1990, the pope appointed him to manage the Vatican budget and, after decades of deep deficits, Szoka balanced the budget within a few years. Eventually, Szoka was promoted to manage the Vatican city-state.

Sister Agnes Mary Mansour (born 1931):
In 1983, Mansour was caught up in an international dispute over the Catholic church's opposition to abortion and to the involvement of priests and nuns in politics. On Dec. 29, 1982, Michigan Gov. James Blanchard appointed Mansour, a member of the Religious Sisters of Mercy, to head the Michigan Department of Social Services, an agency whose many responsibilities included Medicaid-funded abortions for poor women. Within weeks, Pope John Paul II sent orders to U.S. Catholic leaders, including Szoka, that Mansour must be forced to resign from her job — or from her religious order. Mansour refused to be forced

Msgr. Clement Kern (1907-1983):
This humble priest became a friend to the rich and powerful as well as the poor and homeless. In 1943, he was appointed pastor of Most Holy Trinity Catholic Church in Detroit. Until his retirement in 1977, he worked tirelessly to help poor people — and to lobby for the rights of minorities and labor unions. One union boss joked that Kern attended more labor gatherings than most elected union officials. For many years, adding Kern's name to a petition or a public protest added authenticity to the demonstration.

Auxiliary Bishop Thomas Gumbleton (born 1930):
Ironically, Gumbleton has become as famous internationally for his activism as any of the Catholic cardinals who have been his bosses in Detroit. In the 1960s, he was regarded as one of the brightest young men in the Catholic church. He had been valedictorian of his seminary class in Detroit, earned a doctorate in church law and, in 1968 at age 38, became one of the youngest men ever made a bishop in the modern era. A pacifist, Gumbleton has circled the globe in support of causes ranging from his opposition to the Vietnam War to his concern for poor people in Iraq after the Gulf War. The bishop often has touched off controversies for his outspoken political stands and his encouragement of equal rights for gay people and women. Some Catholic leaders wish he would stop speaking out — while others welcome him as a prophetic figure in the worldwide church.

Elisabeth Reuther (born 1947) and Alfred Brush Ford (born 1950):
In 1975, the daughter of the late UAW president Walter Reuther and the great-grandson of Henry Ford brought the Krishna movement to a new prominence in Michigan by jointly paying $295,000 for a mansion on Detroit's east side. It was built for $2 million in 1927 by Cadillac general manager Lawrence P. Fisher. Reuther and Ford said they wanted their partnership to symbolize a peaceful reconciliation

Sister Agnes Mary Mansour in 1985.

Free Press file photo

Martha Jean (the Queen) Steinberg in her Detroit office in 1984. The radio personality became a minister in 1972.

She began broadcasting in Detroit in 1963. During the 1967 riot, she pleaded with Detroiters to get off the streets. In the 1970s, she used her radio show to ease the anger between residents and the police. In 1982, she helped to found WQHB-AM. She worked as its general manager until she bought the station for $4.1 million in 1997. Steinberg helped to bring casinos to Detroit and became a partner in the MGM Grand Casino. She was inducted into the Rock and Roll Hall of Fame in 1998 as a distinguished radio personality.

Cardinal Adam Maida (born 1930):

After the demoralizing closure of nearly 40 Catholic churches in Detroit in the late 1980s, Maida was named head of the Archdiocese of Detroit in 1990 and soon earned a national reputation as an innovator and bridge builder. He launched the first ecumenical parochial school system in the United States to involve a broad cross-section of mainline churches. In an effort to shore up ailing Catholic schools, Maida raised more than $100 million. He also directed a nationwide campaign to build a multimillion-dollar papal visitors' center and Catholic think tank in Washington, D.C. He was elevated to the rank of cardinal in 1994.

out of her post and resigned from her religious order, instead. She served as head of the state's largest department for four years.

Martha Jean (the Queen) Steinberg (Died in 2000):

A Detroit radio personality for nearly four decades, Steinberg was so deeply concerned for the people of Detroit that she eventually entered the ministry in 1972 and founded a nondenominational church, the Home of Love.

Cardinal John Dearden (1907-1988):

Dearden led the Catholic Archdiocese of Detroit from 1958 to 1980, but his influence was felt around the world. Through his role in the Second Vatican Council in the early 1960s, he was one of the chief architects of the modern Catholic church. He helped to organize Catholic leaders across the United States and was the first president of the National Conference of Catholic Bishops, which speaks for American Catholic churches on many social and political issues.

The Rev. C.L. Franklin affectionately greeted by daughters Aretha, left, and the late Carolyn.

ED HAUN/Detroit Free Press

CEMETERIES There are 3,800 in Michigan. The metro breakdown by county:

Wayne 134
Oakland 119
Washtenaw.............109
Livingston 84
Monroe 80
Macomb 75
St. Clair....................71

WAYS TO GO

Disposal: About 77 percent of bodies in Michigan are buried; 23 percent are cremated.

Cost: Average funeral in Michigan, $4,700.

Undertakers: 864 funeral directors in the seven-county region.

Do-it-yourself: Nothing in Michigan law prohibits burying a family member on your property. But only as long as the property is not located within a city. Private family burials may require registration under Michigan's Cemetery Regulation Act.

Ground rules: Michigan law does not require a casket for burial. It does not require a burial vault, though most cemeteries require one.

Stand-up corpse: It is legal to bury a body vertically. However, experts caution that this would be difficult because the body would collapse.

SOURCE: MICHIGAN FUNERAL DIRECTORS ASSOCIATION.

Death be not proud

We're not sure of the identity of the first person interred in Ste. Anne's Cemetery, most likely in 1701, because the first two years' worth of records were destroyed in 1703 by a fire. But we can tell you where that cemetery was: just about where motorists enter the Lodge Freeway from Jefferson at Griswold.

And did you know Eastern Market sits on what once was the city's cemetery? About 4,000 bodies were dug up in the 1880s to make way for the market. They were reburied in one big grave — just east of where Conner crosses I-94. There's a marker.

Dead beat

THE EARLY YEARS: In the city's first 140 years, nine cemeteries were used — all gone now, paved over or built on. Some bodies were transferred to the city's oldest cemetery, Mt. Elliott, and its neighbor, Elmwood. Skeletons, coffins and tombstones have surfaced numerous times downtown during construction.

"It is a sad commentary on the spirit of the age that there is scarce a grave or gravestone left, or even a record of the present place of burial of those who died at Detroit a century ago," historian Silas Farmer wrote in 1890.

In early Detroit, Catholics were buried in a graveyard next to Ste. Anne's.

Protestants were buried in a cemetery at Woodward and Larned. Soldiers were buried near what is today's Veterans Memorial Building and later near what is now Lafayette and Washington Boulevard. Protestants later bought 2½ acres of Antoine Beaubien's farm near today's Frank Murphy Hall of Justice.

THE DEATH KNELL: In the late 1820s, the city hired its first sexton, E.W. Barnes, to supervise the cemeteries. To augment his income, he was paid 50 cents for ringing the town bell to announce a death. Three years later, he had to give up the bell-ringing gig because of the cholera outbreak that claimed scores of lives. He couldn't keep up. The office lasted until 1879.

OLDEST CEMETERY: In Detroit, that would be Mt. Elliott Cemetery, began with an 11-acre parcel bought by a group of Detroiters headed by Robert Elliott.

"This cemetery, we pray, will never be desecrated," Elliott said at the Aug. 31, 1841, opening. Less than 2 weeks later, Elliott would be the first person interred after he died of natural causes. The cemetery fronts on Mt. Elliott near Kercheval.

SECOND-OLDEST CEMETERY: That would be Elmwood Cemetery, which is just west of Mt. Elliott. It opened in 1846 to serve the city's Protestant population. A fenced corner in the southeast portion of the cemetery was used to bury Jewish dead.

Elmwood has been racially integrated since it opened. And among the more than 52,000 people buried there are some of the city's and nation's leading citizens. The list includes 29 Detroit mayors, at least six Michigan governors, 11 U.S. senators and 12 presidential cabinet members. Elmwood's ranks include:

John Autrobus — Designer of the Medal of Honor.

TONY SPINA/Detroit Free Press

The tomb of Lewis Cass at Elmwood Cemetery. Cass died in 1866.

RICHARD LEE/Free Press

William Austin Burt — Inventor of the solar compass, T-square and equatorial sextant.

George DeBaptiste — Leader of the Underground Railroad and organizer of the U.S. 102nd Colored Infantry.

James F. Joy — Attorney-scholar who financed and coordinated construction of the Soo Locks.

Robert Millender — Prominent black attorney.

Bernhard Stroh — Founder of Stroh Brewery in 1850.

Samuel Thompson — Hall of Fame baseball player with Detroit in 1881-1888, and 1907.

Hiram Walker — Established Hiram Walker and Sons Distillery in 1858.

Daniel T. Wells — Cofounder of Wells Fargo.

Emma Berry — Assistant treasurer of the Confederacy and an aide to Jefferson Davis; her signature appeared on some Confederate paper currency.

D. Augustus Straker — Michigan's first black judge.

Gen. Charles Larned — Aide-de-camp to Gen. George Washington during Revolutionary War.

Count Cyril Tolstoi — An officer in the Horse Guards of the Imperial Russian Army; grandson of Russian novelist Leo Tolstoi.

Coleman Young — Detroit's longest-serving mayor and the city's first black mayor.

Joyce Garrett — A city official and Young's longtime companion. (They are buried some distance apart.)

Gen. Alpheus Williams — Commanding officer of Michigan's Civil War volunteer regiments.

Civil War Soldiers Lot — Includes Michigan infantry and cavalry soldiers and members of the 102nd U.S. Colored Infantry.

West side burials

Woodmere Cemetery is the oldest cemetery on the west side. It opened in 1869 and is located between Fort Street and Dix on the southwest Detroit border with Dearborn. Famous people buried there include ginger ale inventor James Vernor; J. Bagley, governor from 1873 to 1876, and lumber baron David Whitney.

INTERRING THE BRITISH: In Flat Rock, 17 British airmen are buried at a tiny cemetery called Oakridge. Most were killed during World War II training at Grosse Ile. The others were killed in a plane crash on Detroit's far east side near the Detroit River in 1958.

Excavators at Michigan and Cass in 1984 found the remains of four War of 1812 soldiers. The bodies were reburied at Woodmere Cemetery in 1986.

DR. DEATH: In the 19th Century, the coroner investigated all sudden or unexplained deaths and could call an inquest of six members who would rule, like a jury, on cause of death. The county medical examiner investigates deaths today. In the 1890s, the county paid the coroner $3 for every body he saw, plus 10 cents for each mile traveled to see it. Detroit's first coroner, Herman Eberts, assumed his duties in 1796.

RITUALS

Mourners file past the coffin of Henry Ford on April 9, 1947, at Greenfield Village. His funeral was April 10 and some 100,000 people filed past before the service.

THE BAYING HOUND: For three sleepless weeks in the summer of 1939, residents living near Elmwood and Mt. Elliott cemeteries heard wolf-like howling at night. Some thought a restless spirit was loose. But police knew it as one of their own — a police dog that possibly followed a funeral procession into one of the cemeteries and stayed there. It eluded capture by running through a hole it had dug between the two cemeteries. It was finally caught but soon died.

ENDING BIGOTRY: In 1961, the state Legislature passed a bill that ended discrimination by private cemeteries for race or color. The bill resulted from the denial of burial of George Vincent Nash, a Winnebago Indian, in White Chapel Memorial Cemetery in Troy.

In 1966, the Michigan Supreme Court sided with an African-American Flint man who wanted to bury his mother in a cemetery in that city. The cemetery argued that the con-tract for its plots included a provision that only whites could be buried there. The court said J. Merrill Spencer had the right to bury his mother at the cemetery.

PAUSE THAT REFRESHES: In 1970, the state Attorney General's Office said it was OK for funeral homes in Michigan to serve coffee to mourners. In the early 1950s, funeral homes were barred from serving food and beverages because of the danger of infection.

THE LAST DRIVE: Detroiters carried coffins to the grave by hand or with the wooden box resting on their shoulders until someone invented the horse-drawn hearse around 1830. At rich people's funerals, the coffin bearers wore long, white linen scarves.

In the 1890s, an electric funeral streetcar with an upholstered interior took caskets and mourners to Woodmere Cemetery.

DRIVE-BY MOURNING: In 1971, funeral home operator Frank Givens introduced a drive-by window so mourners didn't have to get out of their cars to pay their respects. The funeral home, on Rosa Parks in Detroit, had two spotlighted coffins behind unbreakable glass along a horseshoe-shaped driveway. The drive-by window wasn't widely popular and soon was shuttered.

BIG FUNERALS: The biggest was for Henry Ford I, who died at 83 on April 7, 1947. He was buried April 10. In the first moments of that day, workers at Ford plants around the world halted production in their founder's honor. Over a 15-hour period on April 10, 100,000 mourners shuffled along in a line up to 2 miles long to pay their final respects to Ford, whose coffin lay in state in a marble-walled room at Greenfield Village.

Thirty-eight police officers directed traffic, which was backed up bumper-to-bumper for 5 miles along Michigan Avenue and Oakwood Boulevard. Flags flew at half-staff. Detroit City Hall was draped in black crepe, while a giant photograph of Ford hung on an outside wall. Detroit Mayor Edward Jeffries ordered all city operations suspended for the afternoon and asked Detroiters for a moment of silence at 2:30 p.m. — the time Ford's funeral began at St. Paul's Episcopal Cathedral. Buses and street cars were also halted across the city during that time.

Motorists stopped their cars. Gas stations across the state closed for 30 minutes. Thousands stood outside the cathedral. Of the 1,400 seats in the church, 250 were reserved for family, close friends and company executives. The rest were filled by people who'd waited outside for hours. After the 40-minute service, Ford's flower-decked casket was taken to the tiny Ford family cemetery at St. Martha's Episcopal Church, on Joy Road west of Greenfield, for private burial beside the graves of his parents. His son, Edsel Ford, is buried in Woodlawn Cemetery.

➤ **Henry Ford II:** He had two funerals — one private, one public — after he died from pneumonia Sept. 29, 1987, at age 70. His remains were cremated. William Clay Ford said his brother did not want a "slab of stone to say Henry Ford II is buried here."

➤ **Richard (Maserati Rick) Carter:** The reputed drug dealer was gunned down in his bed at Mt. Carmel Mercy Hospital in 1988 while recovering from an earlier attempt on his life. The body of the 29-year-old east sider was laid out in a $16,000 casket styled like a Mercedes-Benz, complete with grille and wheels.

➤ **Coleman Young:** Detroit's first black mayor died at 79 in 1997. His funeral at Greater Grace Temple lasted nearly four hours. More than 4,000 people attended and thousands more lined the 15½-mile route from the church in northwest Detroit to Elmwood Cemetery. The funeral and burial followed two days of viewing at the Dr. Charles H. Wright Museum of African American History, during which as many as 90,000 people passed by Young's body.

➤ **C.L. Franklin:** The preacher, civil rights leader, humanitarian and recording artist was laid to rest in August 1984 in a roaring four-hour display of oratory, music and hand-clapping. About 3,000 people packed into the 2,200-seat New Bethel Baptist Church where Franklin was pastor for 38 years. Another 6,000 to 7,000 people either viewed the body before the service or listened to the service as it was broadcast into the streets near Franklin's church at West Philadelphia and Linwood.

ALAN R. KAMUDA/Detroit Free Press

The Dodge family mausoleum at Woodlawn Cemetery in Detroit. Brothers Horace and John are entombed here.

➤ **Jerry Buckley:** In July 1930, more than 20,000 people crowded inside and outside of St. Gregory Church for the funeral of the popular radio host who had been gunned down in the lobby of the Lasalle Hotel. His wake was held in his Pasadena Avenue home; more than 100,000 people walked passed his bier.

➤ **Margaret Mather Finlayson:** About 5,000 people attended the Elmwood Cemetery burial of Finlayson, who died suddenly on April 7, 1898, at 38 during a performance at the height of her career as a leading Shakespearean actor. She was buried in the white gown she wore as Juliet.

Free Press file photo

Richard Carter lies in state in 1988 in the $16,000 casket styled like a Mercedes. The 29-year-old reputed drug dealer was buried in Elmwood Cemetery.

RITUALS

The Detroit Almanac

18. ENC

"Det
would
very h
on the l

Bishop **Desmon**
on where he might live if no

CORE

KIRTHMON F. DOZIER/Free Press

The J.L. Hudson Co.'s longtime flagship store is imploded on Oct. 24, 1998.

"It was awesome, awesome!"

— *Detroiter* **Paul Johnson**, *seconds after the landmark J.L. Hudson's department store was imploded, October 1998*

Some memorable finals

Remember the last time you sipped a Detroit-bottled fire-brewed Stroh's? Or shopped downtown Hudson's? Or called I-94 the E-way? Or caught a foul behind the dugout at the Corner? Some more lasts...

INDIAN ATTACK: Sept. 10, 1815. Indians killed Ananias McMillan at what is now the corner of Griswold and State. His son, Archie, 11, was taken captive and held for ransom until spring.

EXECUTION: Sept. 24, 1830, under local authority. Stephen Simmons, a huge, burly man found guilty of beating his wife to death, was sentenced to hang.

The hanging drew a large, boisterous crowd to the gallows, near the site of the future Compuware headquarters, just south of the downtown library. Simmons addressed the crowd with final words about the evils of drink. Then he sang a hymn that spoke of God's forgiveness. Then he was hanged. Simmons' contrition, the hymn and his dangling body swayed Detroiters against capital punishment.

In 1847, Michigan became the first state — most likely the first democratic government in world history — to ban the death penalty.

PARADE OF VOLUNTEER FIREFIGHTERS: June 14, 1861.

TREASON TRIAL: July 1942. The United States vs. Max Stephan. The prosecution won and Stephan, a German immigrant, was sentenced to hang. His crime: He sheltered an escaped Luftwaffe pilot who spent about two days in Detroit.

In April 1942, Lt. Hans Peter Krug fled a POW camp near Toronto, took a bus to Windsor, stole a rowboat, crossed to Belle Isle, walked across the bridge, then 5 miles to the house of a German-American pen pal. That astonished person contacted local German ethnic leader Stephan, who promptly took Krug on a whirlwind tour of the German community on Detroit's east side. Stephan, described as gregarious but, well, stupid,

Max Stephan, above with newspaper, after his arrest in April 1942. Stephan, sans newspaper at left, was tried and convicted of treason in federal court in Detroit for sheltering an escaped German pilot — in Detroit.

Free Press file photos

HORSE-DRAWN FIRE ENGINES

April 10, 1922. More than 50,000 people gathered to watch Pete, Jim and Tom pull an engine down Woodward as the Detroit Fire Department band played "Auld Lang Syne."

apparently didn't connect that he was aiding an enemy of the United States. He fed Krug beer and took him to a brothel, then put him on a bus for Chicago. Krug, 21, was captured in San Antonio. Stephan was turned in by several of the German-Americans.

His trial included Krug as a prosecution witness.

In August 1943, just 8 hours before the noose was to be placed around Stephan's neck, President Franklin D. Roosevelt commuted the sentence to life in prison. Stephan died in prison at age 59 in 1952.

Krug was repatriated in 1946 and worked as a steel salesman in Germany. He wrote the Free Press in 1992 that Detroit was an exciting city but Stephan was pretty foolish.

ENEMY BOMBING: May 1945. Detroit was shelled from Windsor during the War of 1812. But in May 1945, a balloon bomb launched from Japan dropped in a Livonia field and exploded. No one was injured. Authorities kept a lid on it until August when Japan surrendered. Balloon bombs were the last desperate moves Japan tried to inflict damage on the U.S. mainland. The high-altitude weapons were launched to fall whenever and wherever they ran out of air. In Oregon in May 1945, five people were killed while hiking in the wilderness when a balloon bomb fell nearby.

GIG AT WALLED LAKE CASINO: Dec. 26, 1965. Fire that day destroyed the famed hall where for decades people flocked to dance on the highly polished 120-by-140-foot maple dance floor. Big bands were the casino's hallmark, but by late 1965, it had become a teenage dance venue called Club A-Go-Go. The last group to play before the dance ended and the early-morning fire: the Barons.

A Japanese-launched balloon bomb like this one exploded in Livonia during World War II.

Toll booths, like this one on Woodward near Grand Boulevard, were used in the 19th Century.

TOLL GATE: Near 7600 E. Jefferson by Belle Isle. Torn down in 1895 after 44 years of collecting travelers' tolls.

NOTES FOR MOTOWN: June 1972, when Motown Records announced it was moving to Los Angeles.

BEER BREWED: May 1, 1985. Stroh stopped production in Detroit.

ELMS: A scant few remain; probably the last great stand of the trees that once gave Detroit the subtitle "City of Elms" now grow about 1,000 strong in Birmingham.

TITLES:
➤ **Tigers:** World Series, 1984
➤ **Red Wings:** Stanley Cup, 2002
➤ **Pistons:** NBA championship, 1990
➤ **Lions:** Forget it. Oh, OK: 1957

Free Press file photo

BOBLO EXCURSION: Labor Day 1991. The S.S. Columbia and S.S. Ste. Claire, both built to ferry patrons to the amusement park at the end of the Detroit River, stopped running because they cost too much to operate. Boblo opened in 1898. The Columbia went into service in 1902; the Ste. Claire, above, in 1911.

Elm trees, which once gave Detroit the subtitle of "City of Elms," number about 1,000 in Birmingham.

Page 1 heralds the last Lions' championship in 1957.

Free Press file photo

MARY SCHROEDER/Free Press

Kirk Gibson roars in '84 World Series win.

CRAIG PORTER/Free Press

Isiah Thomas epitomizes Pistons' glories.

DAVID P. GILKEY/Free Press

Bowman with Wings' tenth Stanley in 2002.

Happy Birthday, Detroit…

Mayor Dennis Archer, the 107th person to lead Detroit, frames the city celebrating its 300th anniversary in 2001.

Detroit's symbols

The official seal of the city of Detroit was created by artist J.O. Lewis, who was paid $5. It commemorates the great fire of 1805. The seal shows two women. The one on the left is crying; she represents Detroit at the time of the fire. The one on the right, who represents hope and the future, is comforting her. In the background, the burning city is shown on the left, and a new city is on the right. The Latin words *Speramus Meliora* and *Resurget Cineribus* accompany the drawing. They mean: "We hope for better things. It shall arise from the ashes."

Detroiter David Heineman designed the city flag. It first flew on June 12, 1908, at a celebration honoring the Detroit Tigers. The flag became official in 1948, when the City Council adopted it.

In the upper left section is a blue field with 13 white stars that represents the American occupation of the city from 1796 to 1812 and from 1813 to the present. The lower left section is a white field with five gold fleur-de-lis, representing the French period in Detroit from 1701 to 1760. The upper right section shows a red field with three gold lions, representing the British period of Detroit, from 1760 to 1796. The lower-right section consists of red and white stripes that represent the American reoccupation of Detroit. In the center of the flag is the city's seal, surrounded by a gold circle.

We are not alone!

Other Detroits

Detroit, Alabama ....Population 291
Detroit, Illinois 126
Detroit, Maine 751
Detroit Beach, Michigan........................... 2,113
Detroit Lakes, Minnesota........................ 6,635
Detroit Township, Minnesota 2,348
Detroit, Oregon 331
North Detroit Township, South Dakota 84
South Detroit Township, South Dakota.. 100
Detroit, Texas... 706
Detroit Division, Texas............................ 1,594

ENCORE!

Going to college

The first university in Michigan opened in Detroit near today's Coleman A. Young Municipal Center (the former City-County Building): The University of Michigan, in 1817. It was joined over the next century by:

Eastern Michigan University

Ypsilanti 48197; 734-487-1849; founded 1849.
Enrollment: 24,000.
The institution: Four-year public university; 113 bachelor's degrees, 64 graduate degrees. Strongest departments are education, technology, business, health and human services, and arts and sciences.
Nickname: Eagles.
➤ **Famous grads:** U.S. Secretary of Transportation Rodney Slater; former president of Chrysler Europe Timothy Adams; Discount Tire founder Bruce Halle; Academy Award winner Char DeWolf; Louis Williams, the U.S. Navy's first African-American admiral, and John DiBiaggio, former president of Michigan State University and now president of Tufts University;

Oakland University

204 Wilson Hall, Rochester Hills 48309; 248-370-2100; founded 1957.
Enrollment: 15,000.
The institution: Four-year public university; 74 bachelor's degrees and 54 master's and doctoral degrees. Strongest departments are schools of engineering and computer science.
Nickname: Golden Grizzlies.
Famous grads: Ameritech Michigan President and Chief Executive Officer Robert Cooper; ANR Pipeline Senior Vice President Stan Babiuk; St. John Health System President and CEO Anthony Tersigni; notable Detroit lawyer David Lewis.

University of Michigan

Three campuses — Ann Arbor (main), Flint and Dearborn. 503 Thompson St., Ann Arbor 48109; 734-764-1817; founded 1817
Enrollment: 37,800. One of the nation's premier public universities. Widely known for a number of departments, including the medical and business schools. Michigan also is one of the nation's top research institutions; the National Research Council ranked U-M second among public universities in 1999 in scholarly quality and doctoral program effectiveness. The U-M library system boasts more than 6,600,000 volumes, making it the sixth-largest collection in the country.
Nickname: Wolverines.

Famous grads: Former President Gerald Ford; actor James Earl Jones; assisted-suicide crusader Jack Kevorkian; Pulitzer Prize-winning playwright and "Death of a Salesman" author Arthur Miller; opera star Jessye Norman; Holocaust rescuer Raoul Wallenberg; "60 Minutes" journalist Mike Wallace; comedian David Allen Grier; the late comedian Gilda Radner, and famed trial attorney Clarence Darrow.

Michigan State University

450 Hannah Administration Building, East Lansing 48824; 517-355-1855; founded 1855.
Enrollment: 42,600.
The institution: A pioneering public, four-year, land-grant university that offers 146 bachelor's, 161 master's and 124 doctoral degrees. Some of its strongest programs include education, agriculture, business and political science.
Nickname: Spartans.
Famous grads: Gov. John Engler; former Gov. James Blanchard; screenwriter Jim Cash; novelist Richard Ford; Congressional Gold Medal recipient Ernest Green; author Jim Harrison; Nobel Prize winner for microbiology (DNA) Alfred Hershey; director Walter Hill; Teamster President James Hoffa Jr.; USA Network founder Kay Koplovitz, and actor Robert Urich.

Wayne State University

6050 Cass Ave., Detroit 48202; 313-577-2424; founded 1868.
Enrollment: 31,200.
The institution: Public, four-year university that offers 126 bachelor's degrees, 139 master's degrees, 60 doctoral degrees, three post-bachelor's programs, 18 graduate certificates, nine specialist programs and two professional programs. Strongest departments are elementary education, biology, psychology, pharmacy, social work, nursing and theater.
Nickname: Warriors.
Famous grads: Astronaut Dr. Jerry Lineger; deejay Casey Kasem; actress Lily Tomlin; actors Ernie Hudson, Tom Skerritt, Tom Sizemore, Jeffrey Tambor, Lloyd Richards and Garth Fagan; Pulitzer-Prize-winning journalist Mark Fritz; comedian Thom Sharpe; former UPI White House correspondent Helen Thomas; art critic Arthur Danto, and jurist Damon Keith.

Baker College

Three campuses — Mt. Clemens, Auburn Hills and Port Huron; 34950 Little Mack, Clinton Township 48035; 810-7916610; founded 1911.
Enrollment: 2,350 (Mt. Clemens); 1,560 (Auburn Hills); 1,104 (Port Huron).
The institution: A private, independent career college specializing in business, technical, and health and human services. It boasts one of the largest online enrollments in the country with more than 3,000 students. The school grants certificates and associate's, bachelor's and master's degrees.

Center for Creative Studies

201 E. Kirby, Detroit 48202; 313-664-7400; founded 1926.
Enrollment: 1,025.
The institution: Undergraduate college for fine and performing arts; awards bachelor's degrees in animation and digital media, crafts, communication design, fine arts, industrial design, interior design and photography. Best-known programs are transportation design, digital communication design, animation and digital media and interior design.
Nickname: CCS.
Famous graduates: Whale muralist Robert Wyland; Jerry Palmer, General Motors director of design and designer of the 1984 Corvette; Wendy Midener-Froud, doll and puppet maker who helped design Yoda while working for the Jim Henson Co.; and Dave Jordano, one of the best-known food photograpers in the country.

Cleary College

2170 Washtenaw, Ypsilanti 48197; 734-332-4477; founded 1883.
Enrollment: 900.
The institution: Private business college that offers associate's, bachelor's and master's degrees and certificate programs.
Famous grads: Harvey Kapnick, retired chairman of Arthur Andersen Consulting; Vern Buchanan, founder and CEO of American Speedy Printing; and Charles Knabusch, former chairman of the board and president of La-Z-Boy Inc.

Concordia College

4090 Geddes Road, Ann Arbor 48105; 734-995-7300; founded 1963.
Enrollment: 467.
The institution: Four-year Christian college affiliated with the Lutheran Church Missouri Synod. A member of the Concordia University system. It offers seven bachelor's degrees and one master's in organizational leadership.
Nickname: Cardinals.
Famous grads: James Geyer, meteorologist at WLNS-TV in Lansing; Rich Luker, founder of ESPN/Chilton sports poll; Martin Jean, professor at Yale University's Institute of Sacred Music; Dr. Gary Quick, chief of emergency medicine and surgery at the University of Oklahoma health sciences center.

Davenport University

(formerly Detroit College of Business) Campuses in Dearborn, Warren, Flint, Romeo and Lapeer, along with numerous off-campus locations. 4801 Oakman Blvd., Dearborn 48126; 313-581-4400; founded 1962.
Enrollment: 7,000.
The institution: Regional university that offers more than 45 associate's, bachelor's and master's degree programs in business, health and computers.

Lawrence Technological University

21000 W. Ten Mile, Southfield 48075; 800-225-5588; founded 1932.
Enrollment: 5,000.
The institution: Private liberal arts college that focuses on architecture, engineering, math, science and management. Two-year, four-year and master's programs.
Nickname: Blue Devils.
Famous grads: Lewis Veraldi, who launched the original Taurus and Sable as a vice president of car development for Ford Motor Co.; Ronald Knockert, inventor of the laser bar code scanner; Donald Date, chief architect of the United States' Panama Canal Co., and Bennie Benjamin, recently retired as director of the Detroit Water and Sewerage Department.

Lewis College of Business

17370 Meyers Road, Detroit 48235; 313-862-6300; founded 1928.
Enrollment: 300.
The institution: Michigan's only Historically Black College or University. Two-year college specializing in business-related subjects, particularly a hospitality management program.
Nickname: LCB.
Famous grads: Castell Vaughn-Bryant, chancellor of Miami-Dade Community College — North Campus; Marc Stepp, former vice president of the UAW; Thelma Vriend, former vice president Wayne County Community College.

Madonna University

36600 Schoolcraft, Livonia 48150; 734-432-5300; founded 1947.
Enrollment: 4,000.
The institution: Independent liberal arts university run by the Felician Sisters of Livonia. Nursing, business and teacher education are most popular programs. Bachelor's degrees are awarded in 55 areas of study; master's degrees in 17 areas; 30 associate degrees, and there are 22 certificate areas of study.
Nickname: Crusaders.
Famous grads: Sister Mary Cynthia Strzalkowski, minister general of the Felician Sisters, located in Rome; Sister Mary Francilene Van de Vyver, president of Madonna since 1976; Arthur Lenaghan, Novi fire chief; Dan King, dean of faculty of applied science and education at Buffalo (N.Y.) State College.

Marygrove College

8425 W. McNichols, Detroit 48221; 313-927-1200; founded 1905.
Enrollment: 4,906.
The institution: An independent, coeducational, Catholic college offering two-year and four-year degrees and programs. Noted for its social work, teacher education, visual and performing arts, and business programs.
Famous grads: Nettie Seabrooks, City of Detroit CEO; Maura Corrigan, Michigan Supreme Court justice; the Rev. Wendell Anthony, president of the Detroit chapter of the National Association for the Advancement of Colored People and pastor of Fellowship Chapel United Church of Christ; Monique Garrity, special representative to the United Nations, representing the World Bank; the Rev. Wilma Johnson, pastor of New Prospect Missionary Baptist Church and the first female pastor of a major black Baptist church in Detroit.

Rochester College

800 W. Avon Road, Rochester Hills 48307; 248-218-2000; founded 1959.
Enrollment: 600.
The institution: Four-year liberal arts Christian college, offering 12 majors and 11 concentrations for a bachelor's degree. Largest programs are business and psychology.
Nickname: Warriors.
Famous grads: Joyce Todd, assistant prosecutor for Oakland County, and Carl Randall, manager of Oakland International Airport.

St. Mary's College of Ave Maria University

3535 Indian Trail, Orchard Lake 48234; 248-683-0521; founded 2000.
Enrollment: 470.
The institution: St. Mary's College has a rich Polish history having been founded in 1885 by a Polish immigrant priest. Ave Maria College was founded in 1998 by Domino's Pizza founder Thomas Monaghan, who sold the pizza business to devote his energy to Catholic education. The two schools were officially merged on July 1, 2000. The new, coed liberal arts university will combine the best of both schools — St. Mary's strong science and premed programs, with Ave Maria's theology, literature and philosophy programs.
Nickname: Eagles.

University of Detroit Mercy

P.O. Box 19900, Detroit 48219; 313-993-1000; founded: 1990. The University of Detroit was founded in 1877 by the Jesuits. Mercy College of Detroit was founded in 1944 by the Religious Sisters of Mercy. In 1990, the schools merged.
Enrollment: 6,600.
The institution: Michigan's largest four-year Catholic university. Widely recognized for its programs in engineering, law, business, architecture and education.
Nickname: Titans.
Famous grads: Frank Kelley, former Michigan attorney general; Benny Napolean, Detroit police chief; Elmore (Dutch) Leonard, writer; Michael Cavanagh, Michigan Supreme Court justice, and Neal Shine, former Free Press publisher.

Walsh College of Accountancy

3838 Livernois. P.O. Box 7006, Troy 48006; 248-689-8282;founded 1922.
Enrollment: 3,000.
The institution: The college offers junior- and senior-level course work toward bachelor's degrees in accounting and business administration, as well as an MBA, master of arts in economics, and master of science degrees in finance, accounting, management, taxation and business information technology.

William Tyndale College

35700 W. Twelve Mile Road, Farmington Hills 48331; 248-553-7200 or 800-483-0707; founded 1945.
Enrollment: 650.
The institution: Christian, nonsectarian, liberal arts college with 22 academic majors, 26 minors and concentrations and six certificate programs in humanities and social sciences, math and natural sciences, professional studies, Christian studies and continuing education. Also offers certificate programs through the Tyndale Bible Institute.
Famous grads: Thomas Fleming, 1992 National Teacher of the Year.

Ships that have come in

An account of nearly a quarter-billion dollars in the biggest lottery drawings.

Prize	Game	Date	Name	Winner's City	Retailer	City
$36,540,213	Lotto 6/47 Bonus	8/28/93	Claimed anonymously	Rochester	Perry Drug Store #228	Rochester Hills
$29,994,387	Big Game	5/16/97	Joseph Yelds	Detroit	Arbor Drugs #52 (15080)	Harper Woods
$29,071,177	Lotto 6/47	8/15/90	Claimed anonymously	Dearborn Hts.	Mike's Party Store	Dearborn Heights
$25,805,336	Lotto 6/47	12/2/92	Claimed anonymously	n/a	Northville Wine Shoppe	Northville
$25,588,139	Lotto 6/47	4/10/91	The Primadonnas A Mich Co-Partnership	Wyandotte	Langley's Liquor/Lottery	Lincoln Park
$22,000,000	Big Game	6/9/98	Over Due Lotto Club	Pontiac	Joslyn Market	Pontiac
$20,000,000	Lotto 6/47 Bonus	10/23/93	Claimed anonymously	Ann Arbor area	7-eleven Southfield Corp. Store #13489	Southgate
$20,000,000	Lotto 6/47 Bonus	3/27/93	Claimed anonymously	Roseville	Tommy D's Party Store	Roseville
$18,716,113	Lotto 6/49	5/12/99	Claimed anonymously	Clinton Twp.	Garfield & Canal Shell Story #80647	Clinton Twp.
$16,628,666	Lotto 6/49	11/5/94	Claimed anonymously	Detroit	Superland Mkt.	Detroit

Detroit companies of the past

Some firms have merged or been absorbed by other businesses; some are history.

Year Founded	Foundry/Company	Product Line	Workers at capacity
1899	American Car & Foundry Co.	railway cars	4,875
1890	Michigan Alkali Co.	soda ash	1,950
1875	Parke, Davis & Co.	pharmaceuticals	1,350
1856	Detroit Shipbuilding Co.	ships, brass goods	1,337
1864	Detroit Stove Works	stoves	1,150
1885	Ideal Mfg. Co.	plumbing supplies, gas stoves	1,100
1871	Michigan Stove Co.	stoves	1,000
1896	Solvay Process Co.	soda	1,000
1892	American Radiaor Co.	radiators, boilers	912
1856	D.M. Ferry Co.	seeds	900
1881	Peninsular Stove Co.	stoves	800
1879	Detroit Steel & Spring Co.	springs, castings	700
1866	Pingree & Smith Co.	shoes	700
1882	Michigan Malleable Iron	castings	700
1899	Brown Bros.	cigars	675
1898	American Lady Corset Co.	corsets	555
1891	Hamilton, Carhartt Co.	clothing	535
1861	Detroit House of Correction	chairs, etc.	509
1863	Detroit Bridge & Iron Co.	bridges	500
1880	Detroit Copper & Brass Co.	brass goods	500
1896	Buhl Malleable Co.	castings	500
1889	Ireland & Matthews Co.	brass goods	500
1873	Michigan Central Railroad Car	railway cars, repairs	500

Destination Detroit

A look at the foreign-born population through the decades.

MACOMB COUNTY	1990	1980	1970	1960
Total population	717,400	694,600	625,309	405,804
Foreign born	49,109	53,394	42,581	32,286
Percent foreign born	6.8%	7.7%	6.8%	8.0%

OAKLAND COUNTY	1990	1980	1970	1960
Total population	1,083,592	1,011,793	907,871	690,259
Foreign born	76,157	72,078	54,904	47,238
Percent foreign born	7.0%	7.1%	6.0%	6.8%

WAYNE COUNTY	1990	1980	1970	1960
Total population	2,111,687	2,337,891	2,666,751	2,666,297
Foreign born	102,336	147,541	196,884	285,051
Percent foreign born	4.8%	6.3%	7.4%	10.7%

DETROIT	1990	1980	1970	1960
Total population	1,027,974	1,203,339	1,511,482	1,670,144
Foreign born	34,490	68,303	119,347	201,713
Percent foreign born	3.4%	5.7%	7.9%	12.1%

Really big car payments

National sales figures of top-of-the-line automobiles.

1999 Ranking	1998 Ranking	Luxury Brand	1999 Sales	1998 Sales
1	3	Mercedes-Benz	189,437	170,245
2	4	Lexus	185,890	156,260
3	2	Cadillac	178,507	182,570
4	1	Lincoln	176,493	187,121
5	5	BMW	153,658	131,559
6	6	Acura	118,006	110,392
7	7	Volvo	116,692	101,172
8	8	Infiniti	72,637	63,649
9	9	Audi	65,959	47,517
10	10	Saab	39,541	30,757
11	11	Jaguar	35,039	22,503
12	12	Land Rover	29,380	21,422
13	13	Porsche	20,875	17,243
14	14	Ferrari	1,000	820
15	15	Rolls-Royce	*642	*537

SALES FIGURES INCLUDE CARS AND LIGHT TRUCKS (SPORT-UTILITY VEHICLES).
*INCLUDES CANADA.

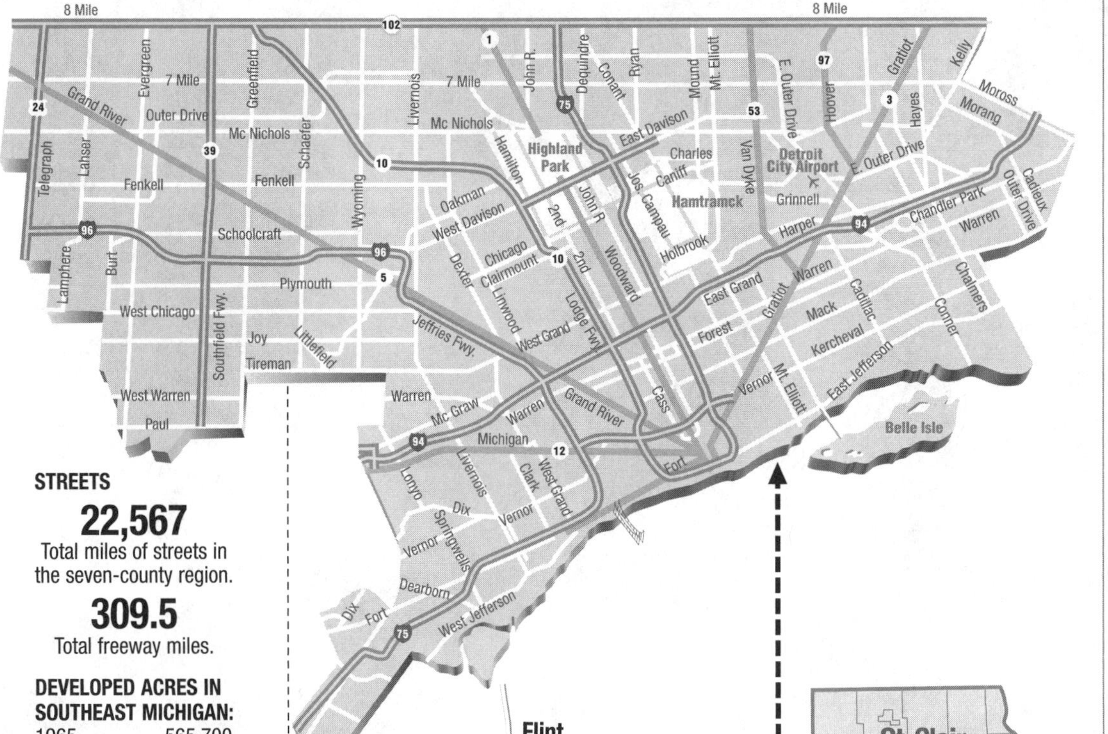

8 Mile

8 Mile

STREETS

22,567
Total miles of streets in
the seven-county region.

309.5
Total freeway miles.

**DEVELOPED ACRES IN
SOUTHEAST MICHIGAN:**
1965.................565,700
1995.................975,400
2020.............1,209,400
(projected)

PEOPLE
Percentage of metro
Detroit that is...
White.......................75%
Black......................22%
Foreign born..........5.5%

POPULATION
Seven-county region
.......................4,773,909
Tri-county region
.......................3,912,679
Wayne Co........2,118,129
Oakland Co. 1,176,488
Macomb Co. 787,698
Livingston Co. 146,165
Washtenaw Co...303,069
St. Clair Co.........159,769
Monroe Co. 143,499
Detroit...............970,196

Detail

Flint

St. Clair

Port Huron

Oakland

Macomb

Livingston

Howell

Pontiac

Mt. Clemens

Washtenaw

Detroit

Lake St. Clair

Wayne

Ann Arbor

Windsor

C A N A D A

Monroe

Adrian

Monroe

Regional map labels: Highland Park, Hamtramck, Detroit City Airport, Belle Isle

ENCORE!

The Corner, Sept. 27, 1999.
The last Tigers game
at Tiger Stadium.

J. KYLE KEENER/Detroit Free Press

ND.

The Detroit Almanac

INDEX

"When people talk about Detroit, what they really mean is anything east of Ann Arbor..."

SPIN Underground USA, *1997*

INDEX

513 – 514
Northwestern Journal, 449
Northwestern Women's
    Suffrage Association, 42
Norton, Lewis, 311
Notorious B.I.G., 66
Novak, Kim, 84
Novels set in Detroit, 348 – 351
Novi, 308
NOW International, 116
Nugent, Ted, 393, 420
Nunn, Guy, 461
"Nut Gatherers, The," 422
Nye, Phil, 460
Nystrom, Buck, 579

Oak Park, 308
Oakland County, 37 – 38, 144,
    302 – 311
Oakland County Child Killer,
    485
Oakland International Airports,
    230
Oakland shopping mall, 189
Oakland Township, 37 – 38, 38
Oakland University, 439, 620
Oakman, Robert, 63
Oakridge cemetery, 609
Oates, Joyce Carol, 299, 336,
    342, 350, 489
Ochs, Adolph, 532
Octagon House, 326
Octopus throwing, 63
Odd Fellow's Wreath, 449
Official mottoes, 287, 330
Official seal, 619
Ogonowski, Casmer, 256
O'Hare, Anne, 79
Ojibwa, 91
Ojibwa Prairie Complex, 149
Oldenburg, Claes, 428
Olds, Ransom, 43, 61, 219
Oldsmobile, 43, 223 – 224
Olerud, John, 590
Olmsted, Frederick Law, 128
Olmstead, Harvey, 311
Olsen, Edward, 191
Olympia Stadium, 45, 592 – 593
O'Meara, John Corbett, 498
*On a Clear Day You Can See
    General Motors*, 348
"One in a Million: The Ron
    LeFlore Story," 357
*One Nation Under a Groove:
    Motown and American
    Culture*, 388
O'Neal, Calvin, 576
O'Neal, Johnny, 382
One-String Sam, 389
Ono, Yoko, 352
Oosterbaan, Bennie, 575, 576
Open shops, 175
Open-air markets, 58

Opening Day, Detroit Tigers,
    536 – 537
Oral contraceptives, 192
Oram, John, 130
Orchard Lake, 308 – 309
Orchestra Hall, 45, 354 – 355
Organized crime
    See Gangs and gangsters
*Origins of the Urban Crisis: Race
    and Inequality in Postwar
    Detroit, The*, 343
Orion Township, 307
Orr, Johnny, 576
Orr, William, 450
Osborn, Chase S., 269
Osborn, Jim, 460
Osborn, Roberta Louise, 392
Osby, William, 108
Oscar winners, 80
Osgood, Chris, 569
Other Detroits, 619
Ottawa, 33 – 34, 91
Ottawas, 32
"Out of Africa," 80
"Out of Sight," 360
Out of Small Beginnings, 346
Over Due Lotto Club, 622
Ovonics, 190 – 191
Ovshinsky, Harvey, 278 – 279,
    368 – 369, 453
Ovshinsky, Stan, 190 – 191
Owen, Abijah, 324
Owen, John, 292
Owen, Marie, 484 – 485
Owen, Marv, 516
Oxford and Oxford Township,
    309

Packard building, 468
Packard Motor Co., 47
Packard's Twin Six, 225
Paczki, 545
Paige, Satchel, 564
Paik, Nam June, 424
Paille, Robert, 521
Paint-by-Numbers, 24
Paintings
    See Art
Palace of Auburn Hills, The, 592
Palestinians, 96
Palmer, Arnold, 587
Palmer, Dennison, 317
Palmer, Mitchell, 276
Palmer, Stephanie, 80
Palmer Woods, 290
"Panic in Detroit," 404
Panthers, Detroit, 573
Panthers, Michigan, 558
Papa Romano's pizza, 544
Papas, Jim and Viola, 188
"Paper Lion," 347, 356
Paradise Valley, 107, 108
*Paradise Valley Days: A Photo

    Album Poetry Book: Detroit's
    1930s to 1950s*, 345
Paray, Paul, 380, 413
Parham, Elma Lois Hendrix,
    396
Parke-Davis & Co., 162, 166, 191,
    622
Parker, Buddy, 572, 573
Parker, Edith Francis, 72
Parker, Ira, 492
Parker, Jimmy Lewis, 505
Parking garage, biggest, 58
Parking meters, 59
Parks, 288
Parks, Rosa, 79, 110, 111
Parsons, Andrew, 268
Parsons, John, 192
"Parvati, Consort of Shiva," 426
Passo di Danza, 471
Passos, John Dos, 342 – 343
Patent and Trademark Center,
    Great Lakes, 438
Paterson, J. M., 450
Patrick, Don, 453
Patrick, William, 49, 110
Patriot War, 300
Patriotic American, 279
Patriots, 39
Patterson, L. Brooks, 250
Patton, John, 262 – 263
Paulina the elephant, 436
PAX-TV, 462
Paybacks, 394
Payola scandal, 456 – 457
Payton, David, 485
PBS, 462
Pearl Harbor, 47
Pears, 149
"Peasants Driving Cattle and
    Fishing," 425
Peche Isle, 132 – 133
Peckham, Howard, 346
Peddler's Point, 290
Peeble-Meyers, Marjorie, 116,
    117
Peete, Calvin, 586
Pelham, Benjamin, 106
Pelham, Robert, Jr., 252
Penberthy Injector Plant explo-
    sion, 507
Penhallow, Arthur, 455 – 456
Peninsular Machinery Co., 183
Peninsular Stove Co., 622
Penland, Ralph, 382
Penobscot Building, 45, 466, 467
Penske Corp., 183
Penske, Roger, 222
People Mover, 85, 232, 430
"People Under the Stairs," 361
People's Press, The, 448
Peoples, Raymond, 498
Peppard, George, 366
Pepper, Edward, 312
Performance Network, 370
Perlman, Itzhak, 381
Perugino, Pietro, 424
Peters, Bernard, 546
Petit, Anselm, 329

Petok, Ted, 80
Pets, 156 – 157
Pettibone, Levi, 307
Petway, Bruce, 565
Pewabic Pottery, 429
Pfeiffer Beer bowling team, 583
    – 584
Pfeiffer brewery, 548
Pfeiffer, Conrad, 548
PGA Championship, 586
Phelan, Michael, 40
Phillips, Archibald, 311
Phipps, Effie, 486
Phipps, Luke, 486
Phone books, 62
Picasso, Pablo, 428
Pickard, Herbert, 396, 398
Pickles, 540
Piercy, Marge, 337, 350, 351
Pierrot, George, 460
Pietrosante, Nick, 573
Piety Hill, 290
Pingel, John, 579
Pingree & Smith Co., 622
Pingree, Hazen, 43, 263, 269,
    546
Pingree Street Group Home
    fire, 509
Pinkerton, Thomas, 308
Piontkowski, Gene, 557
Pirogues, 138
Pistons, Detroit, 557, 570 – 571
Pitcher, Zina, 262
Pittman, Don, 129
Pizza, 544
Place for Summer, A, 347
Plain Dealer, 105
Plamondon, Lawrence, 504 –
    505
Plan, city, 36, 331
Plane crashes, 513 – 514
Planet Ant Theatre, 370, 373
Plants and factories, 169
Playgrounds, 288
Playwrights, 341 – 342
Pleasant Ridge, 309
"Please Mr. Postman," 385
Plessy v. Ferguson, 69
Plimpton, George, 347
Plowshares Theatre, 370
Plymouth and Plymouth
    Township, 318
Poets, 340 – 341
Poindexter, Thomas, 254
Polcyn, Richard, 509
Poles, 101 – 102
Poles, firehouse, 66, 67
Polio vaccine, 49
Polio vaccines, 49
Polish community, 42, 44
Polish Muslims, 544
"Polish Wedding," 360
**Politicians and political play-
    ers**
    African American, 111, 114
    – 115
    current, 249 – 251
    past, 251 – 255

INDEX

Z

About the editors

ALAN R. KAMUDA/Detroit Free Press

PETER GAVRILOVICH and **BILL MCGRAW** together have more than 55 years of experience writing about metropolitan Detroit for the Free Press. Both are east siders, both attended Wayne State University, both covered the 1984 World Series and both share a passion for Detroit history.

McGraw, 50, is a graduate of Bishop Gallagher High School. Since 1977, he has written the "Tipoff" column and covered federal court, city hall, urban affairs, casinos, the Red Wings and Tigers. He has served as a general assignment reporter and the Toronto-based Canada correspondent. He was also the editor of "Great Pages of Michigan History" (Wayne State University Press) and "The Quotations of Mayor Coleman A. Young" (Droog Press).

Gavrilovich, 53, was president of his senior class at Denby High. He began at the Free Press in 1966 as a copy aide and has been a reporter, assistant city editor, Michigan correspondent, city life columnist, senior writer and, since 1993, deputy Nation/World editor.

– – 30 – –